# FDR
## Into the Storm
### 1937-1940

# FDR

## Into the Storm
## 1937-1940
## A History

*Kenneth S. Davis*

Random House  New York

Library of Congress Cataloging-in-Publication Data
Davis, Kenneth Sydney
FDR, into the storm 1937–1940: a history/Kenneth S. Davis.—
1st ed.
p. cm.
Includes bibliographical references and index.
ISBN 0-679-41541-6
1. Roosevelt, Franklin D. (Franklin Delano), 1882–1945.
2. Presidents—United States—Biography. 3. United States—Politics
and government—1933–1945. 4. United States—Foreign
relations—1933–1945. I. Title.
E807.D34 1993
973.917′092—dc20
[B]  92-21640

Manufactured in the United States of America on acid-free paper
24689753
First Edition

*In loving memory of*
*FLO, who died;*
*and*
*With love and thanks to*
*JEAN, who lives;*
*Each of whom contributed greatly*
*To the making of this book.*

# Contents

# BOOK ONE

-»><«-

# The End of the
New Deal

# 1

->->-X-<-<-

## The Pride That Goeth Before a Fall?

I

"THERE'S one issue in this campaign," he had said to one of his advisers in late May 1936. "It's myself. . . ."[1]

And having conceived the issue to be himself as personification of the New Deal, Franklin Delano Roosevelt had designed his presidential reelection campaign deliberately to make the manifest personal hatred of him by the American electorate's right wing an energy that drained strength from the left toward the vital center where he himself stood, or which he himself *was,* while at the same time enlarging, solidifying, and exciting on his behalf that large majority of the electorate which was not ideologized. He had welcomed, he had even invited, the attacks upon him of the so-called American Liberty League, which, organized by corporation lawyers and financed by such multimillionaire industrialists as the Du Ponts, automobile manufacturer Alfred Sloan, steelman E. T. Weir, and oilman J. Howard Pew, defined "liberty" as an absence of governmental restraints upon their pursuit of personal profit. "Economic royalists," Roosevelt had called them in his campaign oratory. They subverted the American democracy, they exploited the Common Man in their selfish interest; to the extent that they could do so, they would transform the Republic into a dictatorship of the wealthy. Roosevelt had proclaimed this, sometimes explicitly, more often by implication, as he sallied forth to do battle against the organized "forces of selfishness and lust for power," forces he was determined to "master" during his second term in the White House.[2]

Hence his 1936 election victory, unprecedented in its magnitude, was an overwhelmingly *personal* triumph such as no American had ever won before. It seemed designed by fate (it certainly was, to the extent that one's character is one's fate and that Roosevelt had personally shaped the campaign) to encourage in him, as he faced the most pressing of his immediate problems, an egotistical mood, a sense of omnipotence, that was far less conducive to sober thought than it was to a willful assertiveness, a reckless disregard of opposition.

And abundant further encouragement of such a mood had been provided by his experience of the weeks following election day. He had voyaged then to South America, on a battle cruiser, to open in person an international conference he himself had instigated, a conference of twenty-one Latin American nations which assembled in Buenos Aires on December 1, 1936, "to determine how the maintenance of peace among the American Republics may best be safeguarded. . . ."[3] Whether or not the conference accomplished much, he personally had scored a public-relations triumph of awesome proportions, especially so when measured against the enmity most Latin Americans had come to feel toward "Yankee imperalists" over the years. The huge crowds shouting "Democracy! Democracy!" when they sighted him along his parade routes through Rio de Janeiro, Buenos Aires, Montevideo; the kind of personal tribute paid him in public prints and public speech in each of the countries he visited; the reports he received aboard ship from his ambassadors all around the globe, telling of reactions abroad to his reelection triumph—these had increased or sharpened his realization that, while dark clouds of war thickened over Europe and the Far East, he personally was regarded by the great mass of people abroad, no less than by the great mass of people in the United States, as democracy's shining hero, the one major statesman in the world who stood tall and straight as the people's champion against Nazism, Fascism, Communism. On the evidence, he was widely deemed the only man in the world who might block or reverse the trend toward new world war.

This might well have increased the impatience with big-business men, an impatience tinged with anger and contempt, that had become an important part of Roosevelt's political attitude in the late summer of 1934 and had been growing ever since. Did not these businessmen, with their minions on the judicial bench, stand squarely in the way of what he wanted to do? And was not what he wanted to do what *had* to be done for the good of humankind? How dare they persist so stubbornly in their selfish aggressions against the public will and weal, forcing him to divert to the curbing of their greed an attention he should be focusing upon the rising threat to free-world survival!

Out of such impatience, in his present circumstances, could come dangerous mistakes. He and the country faced at that moment a constitutional crisis widely deemed the most serious since the Civil War—a crisis brought on by a series of pro-business, anti–New Deal Supreme Court decisions that, in sum and ultimate effect, insofar as they implied future decisions along the same line, could be as disastrous to the Republic as the Dred Scott decision of 1857 had been. There was urgent immediate need, it appeared, for a redefinition of the relationship, a redistribution of the effective powers, among the judicial branch, the legislative branch, and the executive branch of government, as regards their dealings with social and economic concerns. It was a redefinition and redistribution that must be either explicitly made, through legislative and constitution-amending processes, or practically achieved through a retreat by the Court (it must evidently be a forced retreat) from the ground it had so aggressively occupied since 1934. Coolness of temper, acuteness and precision of analysis, great rational self-control, and much delicacy of handling on the part of the executive were called for. If, instead, presidential anger and impatience were joined with hubris in the way Roosevelt's fated experience seemed designed to join them—if they became organically linked with an excessive self-confidence growing out of an exaggerated sense of personal power—if, in consequence, his decision-making became a process flawed by rashness, corrupted by megalomania, permeated with error, he as President, and the nation he headed, could suffer catastrophe. "Pride goeth before destruction," saith the Lord, "and an haughty spirit before a fall."

The brilliant lawyer Benjamin V. Cohen had become by this time a principal legal draftsman of the New Deal. With his close friend Thomas G. Corcoran he had devoted a great deal of thoughtful effort during the last year to the problem created by the Supreme Court's evident determination to destroy the New Deal. And Cohen would soon be convinced that the President's huge triumph at the polls had indeed had the psychological effect here indicated— that it had "gone to his head," giving him a heady sense of near-absolute power.[4]

How accurate was this conclusion as factual description?

How true was it as idea?

## II

A FACTOR to be considered in any calculation of Roosevelt's psychological state during these post-election weeks is the unwonted loneliness of his personal life. Two deaths within the last nine months had deprived him of easy familiarities, wholly relaxed and relaxing, from which he had derived not only emotional sustenance but also clearly defined outer checks and measurements of his attitudes, opinions, proposals for action.

The earlier and more consequential of the two had occurred in the last hour of Saturday, April 18, 1936. It was then that Louis McHenry Howe, whose life had been totally submerged in Roosevelt's for nearly two dozen of its sixty-five years, died after a long illness.[*] With him died out of the Roosevelt lives— out of Eleanor's (since 1920) as well as Franklin's (since 1912)—a vital force of great importance. Operating at the very center of the innermost circle of the Roosevelt menage, Howe had held things together there. Because he loved (narrowly, within the innermost circle almost exclusively, but with a proportionately intense focus), he was loved. Because he was loyal, he evoked loyalties. Because he was absolutely trustworthy in his personal relationships, he was absolutely personally trusted. And this enabled him to become a means of human communication of the kind that makes for community: He facilitated compassionate understandings between an estranged husband and wife, and among the core group of Eleanor's coterie of longtime friends. His death had been followed by a further widening of the rift between husband and wife,[†] and by a loosening of the bonds of affection that had held together those intimate friendships of Eleanor's which, all through the 1920s and early 1930s, had done most to inspire Eleanor's "liberation" and to nourish her growth into

---

[*]The origin of the remarkable relationship between Roosevelt and Howe is discussed in *FDR: The Beckoning of Destiny,* pp. 283–96. Its nature is assessed in *ibid.,* pp. 310–14. Of Howe's long dying, the story is told in *FDR: The New Deal Years,* pp. 599–603.

[†]"I realize more & more that F.D.R. is a great man, & he is nice to me but as a person, I'm a stranger & I don't want to be anything else!" wrote Eleanor Roosevelt to Lorena Hickok shortly before election day, 1936. See Joseph P. Lash, *Love, Eleanor* (New York, 1982), p. 242.

the remarkable woman, the unprecedentedly great First Lady, whom she now was. As for Roosevelt himself, Howe's passing meant a drastic weakening of that capacity for objective self-appraisal whence derive self-corrections and rational self-controls. In important respects, Howe had operated as Roosevelt's second self. His voiced commentary had been a species of Rooseveltian talking-to-himself, his often harsh strictures a species of Rooseveltian self-criticism. Howe could and did (he was perhaps the only man who ever dared) curse Roosevelt angrily to his face when convinced that Roosevelt had gone wrong or was about to do so. "You damned fool!" he had snarled on occasion. Or: "Goddammit, Franklin, you can't do that!" Or: "Mein Gott! [the German expletive was a favorite of his] That's the stupidest idea I ever heard of!"

The void created at the very center of Roosevelt's life by this death was achingly wide and destined never to be completely filled. Roosevelt attempted to fill it, as 1936 drew toward a close, by persuading his eldest son, James, to accompany him as aide on the South American voyage and then to abandon an insurance business in Boston in order to come onto the White House staff as Howe's replacement. The move had been furiously opposed by Eleanor, and strongly by the President's uncle Frederick A. Delano, on the ground that it would expose James to vicious personal attack by Roosevelt-haters; but it had been made. James and his remarkably attractive wife, Betsey (née Cushing), were moving into a house in Georgetown. They were virtually living, however, and would continue to live, both of them, in the White House, where their presence contributed greatly to Roosevelt's pleasure and spiritual ease. But the void, much of it, remained empty. James was incapable of the critical nay-saying role that Howe had performed so effectively. He was too much in awe of his father ever to challenge him strongly, and in any case he lacked the requisite experience, knowledge, wisdom.

The other death had occurred just a month ago.

For nearly eight years, ever since Roosevelt as governor of New York had moved into the Executive Mansion in Albany, his personal bodyguard and most constant companion had been a former New York City policeman who had won medals for bravery, was physically unusually strong, and was skilled in the use of his fists and firearms. His name was Augustus (Gus) Gennerich. It was upon Gus that Roosevelt had most often leaned as he stood or "walked" in public upon steel-braced legs. It was Gus who had most often wheeled him from one place to another in his wheelchair. It was Gus who had lifted him into and out of automobiles with such practiced ease that the extent to which Roosevelt needed such help was minimized in the eyes of beholders. And around this forced physical intimacy had grown up a deep and warm personal friendship between two very different men. The former cop had had but a minimum of formal education; his interests were the physical, practical interests of the archetypical Common Man; and his aspirations, his ambitions in life were proportionately humble, modest. Yet he was also a gentleman in the most literal sense, being of a quiet and gentle nature, instinctively courteous, warmly sympathetic. To most observers he seemed to have a single aim in life (he had never married), namely, the service of Franklin Roosevelt. Roosevelt had called him his "humanizer," his "ambassador to the man in the street"; had often asked his opinions of things said or done or proposed to be done by the White House; had sometimes tried out on him speech ideas and language. The end to all this had come abruptly, with no warning, during Roosevelt's South American trip. In the dark second hour of December 1, 1936, in a Buenos Aires café, Augustus Adolf Gennerich, aged fifty, having just danced and returned to his party's table, dropped dead, apparently of a heart attack, though James Roosevelt believed it to be a cerebral hemorrhage.

And this void, too, at the center of Roosevelt's life, though less great than that left by Howe's passing, was great enough, and destined never to be completely filled.

There had been losses, also, from Roosevelt's innermost circle of advisers —losses that reduced both the amount and the quality of truly disinterested advice he received, concerning official acts, on a regular basis.

Of the three key members of the original Brain Trust, recruited from the faculty of Columbia University, only Adolf A. Berle, Jr., who alone of the three had refused to accept office in the administration in 1933,* remained and would remain in fairly frequent contact with the President. Berle, however, was not in Washington but in New York City where, having greatly aided Fiorello La Guardia's campaign for the mayoralty of that city, he was now city chamberlain in Mayor La Guardia's government. With Raymond Moley, the Brain Trust's acknowledged head, upon whom Roosevelt had most heavily depended as idea man and executive assistant during the Hundred Days and as speechwriter thereafter, the break had been total and final. Early in the 1936 campaign, Moley's increasingly strong bias in favor of big business had come into head-on collision with Roosevelt's increasingly sharp recognition of big business's unalterable enmity toward the New Deal, and toward him personally. The clash had become acrimonious one warm June evening, during a dinner in the small family dining room of the White House, where Marguerite (Missy) LeHand, Roosevelt's confidential secretary, had presided as hostess in Eleanor Roosevelt's absence, as she often did.† Acrimony remained. Almost as total for the time being was the break with Rexford G. Tugwell, now returned to New York City, where he planned to resume at Columbia the academic career he had interrupted to become a Brain Truster in 1932. James A. Farley as manager of the national Democratic campaign had insisted that Tugwell be kept under wraps during the 1936 campaign. Roosevelt's acquies-

---

*"I am by no means clear that the intelligentsia who had a hand in the campaign will retain any position now the campaign is over," said Berle in a letter, November 16, 1932. "If they do, I shall choose merely that of being an intellectual jobber and contractor from time to time when jobs come forward." (See Beatrice Bishop Berle and Travis Beal Jacobs, *Navigating the Rapids, 1918–1971, From the Papers of Adolf A. Berle* [New York, 1973], p. 81.). This was the role Berle had played during Roosevelt's first term. Recognized as an authority on Latin American affairs, he had been a member of the U.S. delegation to the Buenos Aires conference.
†See *FDR: The New Deal Years,* p. 635.

cence in this had been personally hurtful to Tugwell. It meant that the President agreed with Farley that he, Tugwell, was a political liability to the administration, which in turn meant (so Tugwell concluded) that his usefulness in Washington was at an end. He had promptly submitted his resignation from the double post of under secretary of agriculture and head of the Resettlement Administration that he had occupied. At Roosevelt's request, however, he had made the resignation effective on December 31, 1936, rather than immediately—this to avoid the popular perception that his departure was a yielding to opposition pressures upon the President, he being sacrificed by the President's need for votes in the November election. There was no acrimony in all this. Tugwell felt none; certainly Roosevelt did not, being truly grateful for the very great service Tugwell had rendered. But this departure removed from the President's ear a voice of intelligence, knowledge, and much imaginative force.

III

ON the morning of Sunday, January 3, 1937, Franklin Roosevelt stayed somewhat later abed than usual, for he was not fully recovered from the head cold that had struck him down three days after Christmas, almost totally incapacitating him for a day or so. Rest in bed had been prescribed by his physician, navy captain Ross T. McIntire, who was worried by his eminent patient's chronic sinus trouble and susceptibility to respiratory infection— properly worried, if improperly equipped professionally to deal with the problem, as a majority of the medical profession would ultimately conclude. Yet as the President sat propped up against pillows piled high against the bed's backboard, his thick shoulders and torso clad in a worn gray woolen sweater, his polio-withered legs hidden under bedclothes, Roosevelt had not at all the aspect of a sick, crippled man. His complexion was clear, his skin still tanned by the tropic suns of his South American voyage. His mood was buoyant. His appetite was manifestly robust; he consumed with gusto his large breakfast of ham and eggs, orange juice, and coffee. And as he shook his first cigarette of the day from the pack that lay on the table beside his bed, fit it carefully into a long quill holder, then lit it and blew smoke toward the ceiling, his vital presence filled the room with good cheer and radiant zestful energy.

His perusal of the half-dozen newspapers deposited at his bedside this day was more leisurely than usual. It was as usual, however, that he read most carefully *The New York Times,* where, he knew, the news was more fully presented, carefully analyzed, and authoritatively interpreted than it was in other papers. He found in the *Times* this morning much that addressed directly his major concerns of the moment. He found nothing to challenge (all seemed on the contrary to confirm) the judgments of priority he had made for the ordering of his presidential acts during the months just ahead.[5]

For instance, he had based economic policy for his second term on the assumption that the Great Depression had virtually ended in America; and the validity of that assumption seemed abundantly confirmed by what he now read in the *Times*'s financial section. Nothing was said there about unemployment; this, admittedly, remained unacceptably high. But the reemployment of men laid off, the full employment whereby jobs for new entrants into the labor market would be provided, must inevitably lag behind business recovery, according to the theory of the profit system, whose tenets Roosevelt refused to question. And business recovery proceeded with gratifying rapidity. All market signs pointed upward. Domestic copper prices were the highest they had been since 1930. Utility bond financing, upon which the New Deal's attack on holding companies was supposed to have a devastating effect in 1936, was now reported to have been higher for that year than it had been in any other since 1927; a total of $1,894,713,000 in new issues had been offered, as compared with $1,085,029,000 in 1935. And the men of big business were "showing more optimism than they have at any time in recent years," as a *Times* news story said of the mood of railroad executives at the end of "the old year." Martin W. Clement, president of the Pennsylvania Railroad, had issued a statement saying that "if current uncertainties, legislative and regulative, could now be removed, the railroads of this country could be in a position through steadily increasing employment and purchases to give returning prosperity a continuing and greater impetus than could come from perhaps any other source"— a cautiously worded verbosity implying that the New Deal, while it might have had something to do with this "return of prosperity," should now stand aside, out of the businessman's way, and permit "natural" economic forces (that is, the acquisitive energies of businessmen) to do their work unhindered.[6]

And this was substantially the conclusion Roosevelt himself had reached.

The primary aim of his fiscal policy was to bring the federal budget into balance during fiscal 1938, which would begin on July 1, through a combination of reduced federal expenditures and increased federal receipts, the latter resulting, without increase of tax rates, from rising personal and business incomes. "Business conditions have shown each year since 1933 a marked improvement over the preceding year," he would say in his annual budget message to Congress, to be delivered four days hence. ". . . These gains make it possible to reduce for the fiscal year 1938 many expenditures of the Federal Government which the general depression made necessary. Although we must continue to spend substantial sums to provide work for those whom industry has not yet absorbed, the 1938 Budget is in balance; and except for debt reduction of $401,515,000, it will remain in balance even if later on there are included additional expenditures of as much as $1,537,123,000 for recovery and relief. We expect, moreover, if improvements in economic conditions continue at the present rate, to be able to obtain in 1939 a completely balanced budget, with full provision for meeting the statutory requirements for debt reduction." But this happy event could occur only if business did its part, cooperating "in employing men and women from the relief rolls in larger numbers than during the past year. . . . Without such cooperation on the part of employers, the question of a balanced budget for 1938 must of necessity remain an open one, for the very good reason that this Government does not propose next year, any more than during the last four years, to allow American families to starve."[7]

There was an element of threat in this, certainly. If businessmen refused to do what must be done and what was their plain duty to do—this on the businessman's own assumption that prosperity, with its full employment, was the creature of business (depression was not, of course; it was caused by impersonal outside forces)—then the federal government would do what must be done and charge them for it in taxes, perhaps punishing them also with more stringent regulation. Such was the message's implication. But on the whole this message, already drafted in final form, would seem to indicate, to most who read it, an attitude toward businessmen that was far more conciliatory, far less impatient and vindictive on Roosevelt's part, than myriads of observers, including most businessmen, had feared and expected it to be.

Certainly he could afford to be magnanimous, and fairly confident of the kind of business "cooperation" he stipulated as necessary for a balancing of the budget. The election returns had clearly had a chastening effect upon the big-business community with its Liberty League. Witness the phone call made by William Randolph Hearst from his palace in California to Hyde Park on the night of election day. All through the election campaign, Hearst and his national chain of newspapers had mounted the most vicious possible attack upon Roosevelt and the New Deal, an attack in which factual distortions and outright lies were abundantly used as ammunition; the great publisher now phoned to say, not that he regretted what he had done, but that he realized "we have been run over by a steam roller" and wanted the President to know "there are no hard feelings at this end." If this expressed willingness of the Lord of San Simeon to forgive the President of the United States for the latter's triumph was less gratefully received by the President than Hearst expected (Roosevelt, in fact, reported it to his Cabinet with a roar of contemptuous laughter), it *was* gratifying to Roosevelt as an admission by an enemy of a diminished power to frustrate and obstruct him.[8] Witness, too, the announced "decision" of the National Association of Manufacturers, at its annual dinner meeting just three weeks ago, to "drop its fight on the administration" and "cooperate to end unemployment throughout the nation"—an announcement reflecting the businessman's "wider appreciation and understanding of the social responsibilities of business," as the president of the Johns-Manville corporation, manufacturer of asbestos, said in a formal address to his NAM colleagues.[9]

Roosevelt knew, however, that this proclaimed change of heart by big-business men was no sudden, deep commitment to the general welfare. It expressed no realization that the businessman's immediate selfish interest and the long-term good of society are not necessarily identical and that, when they aren't, the former must be subordinate to the latter. The likelihood of the big-business man's cooperation in any enterprise that limited his acquisition of wealth and power was directly proportionate to the force that coerced him into doing so, as witness the fact that he continued to challenge in the courts every New Deal statute that imposed such a limitation, and that he continued to hope against hope that, despite the election returns, the U.S. Supreme Court would complete the work on the New Deal that it had begun—the series of declarations that the New Deal was unconstitutional.

It was with a special attention, therefore, if an attention insufficiently close and analytical, that Roosevelt read on an inside page of the *Times* that morning a news story about "five cases of great importance" that would face the Supreme Court when it opened its new session tomorrow. The Court was to rule on the constitutionality of a retroactive 50 percent tax on the profits made by dealers in silver while the Silver Purchase Act of 1934 was on its way through Congress; on the question of whether the joint congressional resolution of 1933, abrogating payments in gold, extended to rental contracts based on gold bullion; on the legality of the Ashurst-Sumners Act barring transportation of prison-made goods into states prohibiting their sale, and requiring the labeling of such products as convict-made; and on the constitutionality of an Oregon criminal-syndicalism law under which one Dirk De Jonge, a Communist, had been sentenced to seven years in prison for conducting a Communist meeting during the longshoremen's strike of 1934. But from Roosevelt's point of view, and history's, the most important by far of the five pending cases was the one to which the *Times* also gave top billing; namely, a case testing the constitutional right of the State of Washington to enact a minimum-wage law for women "similar" to the New York law struck down by the Court in a 5–4 decision just seven months ago.

When the latter decision, that of *Morehead* v. *Tipaldo,* was announced the previous June, it had shocked and outraged conservative as well as liberal public opinion all across the land—for different reasons, of course. In numerous earlier decisions, the Court majority, having asserted that the national government had no regulatory power over strictly "local" economic activity, had gone on to define as "local" virtually every economic activity that human beings can engage in, save only the physical transport of economic goods across state lines—this on the sophistical ground that every economic function (farming, mining, lumbering, construction, manufacture, and so on) must be performed someplace, in some "locality." The clear implication of this series of decisions seemed to be that regulatory authority over economic activity, an authority obviously needed to keep business from becoming the government itself, was reserved to the several states. Not so, said the Supreme Court majority in its *Tipaldo* decision. No more than the national government could a state government establish minimum wages for women—or, by implication, deal with most other elements or aspects of labor-management relations. There was thus created what Roosevelt in a press conference had called, with some bitterness, a "no-man's-land" where no government, state or national, could operate[10]—a land of large dimensions that was heavily populated with potentially violent conflicts of interest.

But since a Court majority had so ruled, and so recently, how did it happen that a Court majority had accepted for review and adjudication this Washing-

ton State case, designated *West Coast Hotel Co.* v. *Parrish* on the Supreme
Court docket? (Strange that no sharp-eyed New Deal lawyer—not the attorney
general, not the solicitor general, neither Corcoran nor Cohen, all of whom
were actively concerned with the Court as problem—had taken note of this
possibly highly significant docketing when it was announced last October!) For
the Washington law here challenged was not merely "similar" to the New
York law destroyed by the Court in June 1936; it was to all intents and purposes
identical with it, having been closely modeled upon it in response to a public
plea addressed to the state governors by a newly installed President Roosevelt
in the spring of 1933. Why, then, this review of it? In the furious aftermath of
the *Tipaldo* decision, had the Court undergone a change of heart and mind,
recognizing that it had made a bad mistake? Was it now about to reverse itself,
wiping out this mistake?

Alas, the indicated questions did not arise in the President's mind on this
Sunday morning. The *Times* story served only to remind him, who really
needed no reminder, that during the session that opened tomorrow the Supreme Court would have at its mercy New Deal legislation every bit as important as 1933's Agricultural Adjustment Act and National Industrial Recovery
Act, each a pillar of the New Deal's initial recovery program, each shattered
by Court edict. There would be brought before these same judges in coming
months cases challenging the constitutionality of both Social Security and
National Labor Relations, twin pillars, as many would say, of a second New
Deal, and there seemed to Roosevelt little likelihood that either enactment
would survive the hostile scrutiny of the Court as presently constituted. This
Court, then, of Nine Old Men (so they were labeled in Roosevelt's mind by
an about-to-be-published book descriptive of them and their doings, entitled
*The Nine Old Men,* written by newspaper columnists Drew Pearson and
Robert S. Allen, a copy of which had already come to the White House*)—
this Court, so constituted, was a major hazard to the campaign against poverty
in America, the consolidation of social and economic gains made since March
1933, and the initiation of other reforms, which were to be the central business
of Roosevelt's second term, as he conceived it. The hazard must be removed
—and would be! Roosevelt was confident of it, having already essentially
decided the way in which the removal would be accomplished. He had done
so during lengthy tête-à-têtes with politically adroit, manipulatively shrewd
Homer Cummings, the attorney general—meetings held under a thick cloak
of secrecy several times a week immediately before and after the South Ameri-

---

*According to Raymond Moley (*After Seven Years* [New York, 1939], p. 353), Thomas G.
Corcoran referred to *The Nine Old Men* during a conversation about the Supreme Court problem
that the two men had on November 13, 1936. It is, of course, possible that a copy of the book,
or galleys of it, had come to Corcoran thus far in advance of its publication date, though the
normal interval between the delivery of a book manuscript of this topical kind, and its publication
was only two months or so in 1936. Probably, however, Moley confused this conversation with
a later one.

can trip. Only procedural details remained to be worked out, in further secret meetings during the days just ahead.

There were, however, two major hazards to his program, and each of them was indicated by a long news story under a two-column headline on the front page of this morning's *Times.*

One was the threat of American involvement in world war—the tragedy that had overwhelmed Woodrow Wilson and the New Freedom in the opening months of Wilson's second term and that Franklin Roosevelt was determined would *not* overwhelm him and the New Deal. This determination constituted the main thrust of his foreign policy, and it was at that moment especially strong and specifically focused upon fires now raging in Spain. The *Times* reported that a Spanish vessel had been seized by Germany in reprisal for the Spanish government's seizure at Bilbao, a few days earlier, of a cargo of German arms landed from a German ship and intended for delivery to rebels who warred against this government. The *Times* also spoke of Madrid's worrisome belief that two full divisions of the Reich army were now, by Hitler's orders, on their way to Spain to fight for the rebel cause, side by side with "volunteers" from Fascist Italy. Thus did Spanish fires threaten to spread into a world-consuming conflagration.

Spain had long been a harsh land, its favorite sport the torturing to death of animals in ways dangerous to the torturers, its general population less well educated than any other in western Europe, more than half of it actually illiterate, Spanish popular education having been in the hands of the Catholic Church, almost exclusively, through all the centuries since the expulsion of the Moors and the Jews. Among this populace were myriad men and women who were at one with the Irish, the Poles, the Arabs, in their religious intransigencies—men and women who were trained to see differences of opinion and oppositions of interest as clashes of religious principle, as affairs of honor involving fundamental Good and fundamental Evil, men and women who therefore were bound to extract blood and agony in fullest measure from confrontations that in lands less religious and more reasonable might be negotiated or ameliorated. Few countries could have been less prepared for any swift growth of healthy democracy than Spain when the Industrial Revolution came belatedly upon her during and following the Great War. Spain remained neutral in the war; she was nevertheless transformed by it. The insatiable appetite of the warring nations for iron, munitions, manufactured goods of all kinds stimulated an abrupt expansion of Spain's theretofore meager industry, concentrated in Catalonia. This in turn provoked violent social protest against outmoded social forms and institutions of government—a protest that, if not quite a full-scale social revolution, was certainly revolutionary in nature. The reaction to it was a military coup that made a dictator, in 1923, of General Primo de Rivera who, unable to stifle the unrest, resigned his power in 1930. In the following year, the Bourbon king of Spain vacated his throne, without abdicating, and Spain declared herself wholly democratic, establishing a constitution that radically reordered every phase of national life. It instituted universal suffrage—a risky step for the liberal democrats who initiated it, since the women of Spain, being much more under the thumbs of the priests than were Spanish men, were virtually certain to vote for extreme conservatism on their first trip to the polls. The constitution also secularized education and proclaimed religious freedom along with a complete separation of church and state; nationalized much church property; made army officers and the clergy ineligible for parliamentary election and hence, the government being parliamentary, ineligible for ministerial office; and granted to the government power to expropriate private property, socialize large landed estates, and nationalize utilities.

Thus economic democracy was to march hand in hand with political democracy, as indeed it must if the whole truth of democracy is to be realized. And thus, too, inevitably, violent reaction was provoked from those in Spain, including most emphatically the Catholic Church, whose wealth, privileges, and power were to be reduced or altogether taken away. New turmoil ensued. Yet the democracy raised up on this constitutional base managed to survive its initial tests. Uprisings on the right and left were put down by the government in 1932. In 1933, when the first regular parliamentary elections under the new constitution were held, right-wing parties won 44 percent of the Cortes (Parliament) while leftist parties won only 21 percent, thanks in good part to the women's vote; the remaining 35 percent was split among moderates and centrists. There followed an abrupt ending of reforms under a succession of coalition ministries that were increasingly unpopular, increasingly helpless to govern. Great strikes marked by much bloodshed occurred in industrial areas. There were political assassinations, left and right. But there was no organized revolution from the left, no forcible seizure of power in Madrid. Instead, in the spring of 1936, there was a free election in which the leftist parties and the moderates joined in a "Popular Front" coalition to win a decisive majority at the polls, establishing then a government of the moderate left that included Communists but was very far from being dominated by them, the Communists having won barely 4 percent of the popular vote. Nevertheless, a newly formed Spanish Fascist party, the Falange, in which were joined the Catholic hierarchy, great landed aristocrats, big industrialists, big bankers and merchants, high officers of the army, all of whom together made up a decidedly small percentage of the whole population—this party promptly and loudly charged that Madrid was now Moscow-dominated, its ministers puppets on Stalin's string. The Falange proceeded to organize a "patriotic" conspiracy out of which soon flared, in the summer of 1936, armed insurrection. It was led by one Francisco Franco, a fanatically reactionary general who had been removed as head of the army General Staff and retired to Spanish Morocco. It was incontrovertibly a revolt against the principle as well as the practice of democracy; it was designed to destroy Spanish democracy root and branch, replacing it with a Catholic Fascist dictatorship (with Franco the dictator), as Franco frankly proclaimed. And this rebellion would have been crushed in a few days or weeks, given the meagerness of its popular support (such crushing was predicted in an August 1936 letter to Roosevelt from the U.S. ambassador to Spain, Claude G. Bowers[11]), had it not at once received massive aid from Mussolini's Italy and Hitler's Germany. Italian and German planes airlifted Moorish troops from Morocco to Spain; Franco's initial invasion would otherwise have failed. Moorish troops were and remained the backbone of his army.

This aid by the dictators was only weakly countered by Stalin's Russia, whose commitment to democracy, despite the current Popular Front strategy, was in any case no greater than that of the Nazi-Fascists; it was countered not at all by the major European democracies, Britain and France, whose overwhelming concern was, not the preservation of Spanish democracy, but the prevention at all costs of general war—a concern joined with a wishful hope on the part of powerful private interests in France and England that Hitler and Mussolini would become strong enough not only to prevent the spread of Communism into the West but also, eventually, to crush it in Russia. In implementation of this concern and conjoined hope, whereby tyranny gained enormous material advantage over freedom, a so-called International Non-Intervention Committee had been organized in London. Its members, among whom were official representatives of Germany and Italy, had pledged their governments to maintain absolute neutrality toward the Spanish conflict. But it was, of course, obvious to London and Paris—also to Washington—that such a pledge by Mussolini and Hitler was falsely made; it continued to be flagrantly violated by both dictators, neither of whom bothered to dissemble his determination that Franco conquer Spain. This meant that strict compliance with their pledge on the part of Britain and France, joined with their refusal to do anything effective to force compliance by Germany and Italy, was in effect an act of war against the Spanish Republic. It ensured that the Spanish Loyalists, as they were called, would continue to be denied desperately needed arms and war matériel in the face of an utterly ruthless enemy abundantly supplied by the Nazi-Fascists, not only with arms but also with actual units of the air forces and infantry of Italy and the Reich.

All this was clearly indicated on the front page of this morning's *Times.*

Yet Roosevelt's reading of the long story from Spain did not change his mind about American policy, a policy that in effect committed the United States to the one-sided Franco-British "nonintervention." Any slight tendency in that direction which this reading might have induced would in any case have been more than offset by other news he now read: the news from Berlin that twenty-seven cardinals, bishops, and other of the higher clergy of the Catholic Church in Germany had just signed a pastoral letter "pledging anew their support of Hitler in war on the Reds," as the *Times* correspondent put it. This suggested to Roosevelt what the American Catholic clergy would do if, or when, American popular opinion became sufficiently informed and concerned about events in Spain to make our Spanish policy a strongly felt, hotly debated issue. The Catholic clergy, whose political potency was considerable, especially within the Democratic party, would exert this influence overwhelmingly on the side of the policy Roosevelt now espoused; it would do so precisely because the policy favored Franco over the "godless" Loyalists.

Thus, by what he read this morning, Roosevelt was confirmed in the decision he had made with regard to a certain Robert Cuse, president of the Vimalert Company of New Jersey, dealer in used aircraft, who was boldly defying the "moral embargo" imposed by the administration upon arms and war-matériel shipments by American businessmen to strife-torn Spain. The embargo must be merely "moral," the product of individual voluntary choice rather than of enforced law, because 1935's Neutrality Act, while prohibiting shipments of matériel to either side of an international conflict, made no reference to civil wars. Moreover, the United States formally recognized the legitimacy of the duly elected government of Spain and continued uninterrupted its diplomatic ties with that government. There was nothing in long-established international law that would deny to a legitimate government, diplomatically recognized by other nations, the right to import from those nations whatever it needed to defend itself against rebellion. Hence, when Cuse on the day before Christmas made formal application to the State Department for licenses to export nearly $3 million worth of planes and used parts to the Spanish government, the department could not legally refuse him. It must and did issue the licenses. But it accompanied this issuance with a public statement blasting Cuse for sacrificing patriotism to greed in clear violation of announced government policy, a statement whose essence was repeated by Roosevelt in his press conference a few days later. Cuse, however, stubbornly persisted in his "perfectly legal but thoroughly unpatriotic act," as Roosevelt had called it. He was applying for licenses to export an additional $4.5 million of planes and parts to the Spanish government. This aroused in Roosevelt much the same kind of wrath he had felt toward Rabbi Stephen S. Wise and the Reverend Dr. John Haynes Holmes when they made him "look bad" as a New York governor dealing with Tammany corruption—the kind of wrath he had felt toward Bronson Cutting when Cutting challenged his government economy policy as it applied to war veterans during the Hundred Days, and challenged his siding effectively with management against labor later on—the kind of wrath he had felt toward Robert Moses when Moses challenged him in the matter of New York City's Triborough Bridge Authority.* There was vengeful animosity, a grim determination to frustrate Cuse's designs, in the motivation of Roosevelt's decision to ask Congress, when it convened next week, to revise at once the Neutrality Act in ways that widened his discretionary power with regard to foreign conflicts, enabling but not compelling him to impose an arms embargo in civil as well as international wars. If this request were refused, as it might well be, given the hostility of powerful isolationist congressmen toward any expansion of executive discretionary power over foreign relations,

---

*See pp. 234, 263–64 of *FDR: The New York Years*, and pp. 147–48 and 497–501 of *FDR: The New Deal Years*. For the roots of the quarrel between FDR and Moses, see *FDR: The Beckoning of Destiny*, pp. 791–92.

Roosevelt intended to call for mandatory embargo legislation applying specifically and exclusively to the civil war in Spain.

The second of the two-column headlines on the *Times*'s front page this Sunday morning, indicative of a developing major hazard for Roosevelt's second-term program, was over a long story about a strike against General Motors in Flint, Michigan, which had begun three days ago. Seven plants were shut down; 33,400 workers were idle; and it appeared that GM "faces a shutdown of all its plants" across the nation, placing "211,000 jobs in peril." At issue were workers' demands for increased wages, decreased hours, various improvements in working conditions, and, above all, management recognition of the United Auto Workers (an industrial union affiliated with John L. Lewis's CIO) as sole collective-bargaining agent for GM employees—this in accord with the Wagner Labor Relations Act. Roosevelt, to whose 1936 reelection campaign Lewis's United Mine Workers had contributed some $470,000, now acquiesced in the popular belief that the Wagner Act was a pillar of the New Deal. He fully realized that organized labor, and especially the industrial unions now joined together in the CIO, constituted a major element of the so-called Roosevelt coalition. But this development had come about almost, if not quite, against his personal wish and will. He had not personally favored the labor-relations bill when New York's senator Robert Wagner introduced it in Congress—had not lifted a finger on its behalf until he realized it would pass through Congress with a large majority whether he did so or not. Only then had he placed it on his list of 1935 "must" legislation.* He now recognized the need for a new balance of power between labor and management, whereby the former gained at the latter's expense; he further recognized that such new balance could be achieved in the auto industry only if the UAW were victorious in this GM strike; but he was nevertheless gravely concerned about the tactic that the striking auto workers employed, to the horror of the business community and the unease of much of the general public. This tactic was the literally revolutionary "stay-in" or "sit-down" strike, first employed in France and then in the United States (against rubber manufacturers in Akron, Ohio) a year earlier. In a sit-down strike, workers did not content themselves with picketing plants but actually occupied them, holding them against their legal owners by force or threat of force. The auto workers had so occupied two large plants in Flint, Fisher Body plants Number 1 and Number 2, in defiance of a court injunction just obtained by General Motors (the enjoining judge, as the public would soon learn, happened to be a large holder of General Motors stock[12]). The Genesee County sheriff had mobilized deputies, hundreds of them, to eject the strikers, but he had taken no action; he and his men were obviously extremely reluctant to act, and with good reason.

Here, surely, was incipient Red Revolution! It was rendered all the more ominous by the fact that dedicated Communists, as Roosevelt had been told, were among the most effective UAW organizers, and held high offices in the

*See *FDR: The New Deal Years,* pp. 322–26, 525–29.

union. For what if the workers, having seized plants, decided not only to occupy them but also to operate them, eliminating business and businessmen from the industrial process? This was an assault upon private property and the profit system that Roosevelt could not long tolerate—an assault not only ideologically repugnant to him but bound to provoke New Deal–threatening reaction by propertied interests. It was all too likely to initiate an action-reaction that would go completely out of control. Certainly, if General Motors now forced a full use of police power to eject the strikers and reclaim its corporate property, blood would flow copiously—and most of it would be the blood of strikers. The streets and walls of Flint would be stained and splashed with the very color of Red Revolution, and there would result to a considerable degree, over the country as a whole that "radicalization of the masses" at which the Communists constantly aimed. Roosevelt could only work and hope and pray for an avoidance of precipitate action on either side, and thank God that Frank Murphy, former mayor of Detroit, was now, as a result of the election of 1936, governor of Michigan.* Murphy was an enlightened as well as skilled politician, in Roosevelt's view; he had an acute sense of justice and an equally acute sense of when, how, and to what extent coercive power could be employed by government in service of the general welfare.

There was also on the front page of the *Times* this morning, sandwiched between the story from Spain and the story from Michigan, news of a kind rarely so prominently displayed and even more rarely noticed, much less attentively read, by Franklin Roosevelt. He may have read this particular story, however, because of its relevance to that quest for the cause, the cure, the prevention of poliomyelitis that was the prime object of the Warm Springs Foundation, of research financed by proceeds from the President's Birthday Balls, and of Roosevelt's efforts on his own behalf after he was struck down by crippling polio in 1921. It was science news, written by William L. Laurence, the *Times*'s science editor. He filed his story from Atlantic City, where the American Association for the Advancement of Science was holding its annual meeting. The assembled scientists had just honored a thirty-two-year-old bio-chemist named Wendell Meredith Stanley of the Rockefeller Institute for Medical Research, awarding him a thousand-dollar prize for his discovery that "viruses producing certain dread diseases (poliomyelitis, for one) are protein molecules existing on the borderline between the living and the non-living," possessing some of the definitive characteristics of each. These "extremely large" protein molecules, Laurence emphasized by repetition, "represent a new type of being; a creature neither alive nor dead, but one that dwells in the mysterious twilight zone between the living and the dead." And though Stanley's results came from research done on "plant viruses" only, they were confidently believed to apply to "animal viruses" as well, thus opening up the

---

*G. Hall Roosevelt, Eleanor Roosevelt's younger brother, not yet wholly incapacitated by chronic alcoholism, had been city comptroller during Murphy's term as mayor of Detroit.

possibility of developing new "vaccines and serums as defenses against" viral infection.[13]

IV

WHETHER or not Roosevelt read this story of scientific discovery, he certainly read with close attention a story on an inside page of the *Times*, telling of a public statement about governmental reorganization issued the day before in Washington by Senator Harry F. Byrd of Virginia.

Byrd was a conservative Democrat who, as the *Times* correspondent pointed out, represented a "substantial bloc in Congress"; he was chairman of a special Senate committee investigating the executive organization of the federal government, and his statement was to the effect that "wide economies in government" might be achieved through governmental reorganization. The implication was that the achievement of "economies" was, in Byrd's view, the chief purpose of reorganization, and this implication was at variance with the President's published view, as the *Times* reporter pointed out. Only a few days ago "sources close to the President" had stressed that "wholesale savings could not be made without curtailment of some of the essential services of government" and that increased efficiency of operation, not reduced cost, was the purpose of a proposed restructuring of the executive. Of course, an increase in efficiency would mean, in some degree, an increase in economy of operation, "but the latter is incidental to the former, in Mr. Roosevelt's view."[14] Would this difference between President and senator become an opposition, hence a debated issue, in the halls of Congress?

The possibility could not but arise in Roosevelt's mind as an immediate concern. For, as it happened, the subject uppermost in his mind on this third morning of the new year was not the state of the economy, not the threat of foreign war, not Robert Cuse's infuriating defiance of his authority, not even the Supreme Court as obstacle to progress; it was precisely this subject of governmental reorganization. He would be dealing with it in tactically decisive ways within the hour, seated at his desk in the Oval Room—would do so in the knowledge that his successful dealing with it was far more important to the overall success of his second term, and to the whole future of the federal government, than the general public would ever realize.

The need for a thorough overhaul of the federal bureaucracy in accordance with soundly conceived organizational principles had become evident to students of government well before the New Deal began. All through the 1920s, despite the commitment of three successive Republican administrations to big business and small government, the executive branch of government had increased in size, with no increase in efficiency. There was, as a matter of fact, a loss of efficiency. For the increase in size came about in piecemeal fashion, resulting in a bureaucracy that was far less an organization than an almost haphazard accumulation of separate agencies, each specifically implementing a congressional act or a loosely defined set of acts. Each agency had become a sovereign power to some considerable degree, possessed of its own staff "patriotism" or esprit de corps along with, in many cases, its own special constituency in Congress and among the public. Cooperation among agencies that reduced the sovereignty of any of them was always difficult, often impossible, to achieve. And a bureaucracy that had become cumbrous, unwieldy, by the spring of 1933 had since become much more so. The New Deal's abrupt and huge expansion of the federal government, coupled with Franklin Roosevelt's helter-skelter administrative techniques (his blithe disregard of consistency among his endless improvisations; his penchant for blurred and duplicative delegations of authority and responsibility among a multiplicity of new "alphabetical" agencies), had made of the federal executive a monstrous incoherence, not only deficient in sharp definitions of function or power but also clotted, here and there, with wasteful redundancies. It was shot through with imperialistic willfulness, destructive competitions for power, rancorous jealousies. No chief executive, certainly none with as meager a staff as the White House now had, could deal with it in rational ways, much less master it and use it as a tool of government.

It was therefore with a sense of urgency, if also with pleasurable anticipation, that Roosevelt prepared himself, body and mind, for a conference this morning with a nationally recognized authority on public administration, Louis Brownlow, who would bring with him the final product of a long process of study and planning.

V

THE process may be said to have begun only a few months after the New Deal itself began, in "a series of conversations" among, chiefly, four men, in Washington's Hay-Adams House across Lafayette Park from the White House. The conversations were about ways and means of achieving a now sadly lacking coordination "of the several programs being carried on to increase employment and relieve the victims of unemployment."[15] The four men were Charles E. Merriam, chairman of the department of political science at the University of Chicago; Beardsley Ruml, dean of that university's social-science division; Guy Moffet, who had succeeded Ruml as executive director of the Rockefeller Foundation's Spelman Fund; and Louis Brownlow, a former newspaperman who had become a District of Columbia commissioner during Woodrow Wilson's presidency, had since made his career in the field of public administration, and had become in 1933, as he still was, the director of the Public Administration Clearing House, an organization linked closely if informally with the University of Chicago. Soon these four were participating in meetings of the National Planning Board, whose chairman was Franklin Roosevelt's favorite uncle, Frederic A. Delano. They became actively involved, or two of them did, when in November 1933 the planning board received from the Public Works Adminstration (PWA), headed by Secretary of the Interior Harold L. Ickes, a grant of $35,000 to finance the making of "a plan for a plan" to improve the federal governmental structure. Heading this planning group, at Delano's request, was Charles Merriam. Brownlow became Merriam's principal assistant.

There was thus initiated an arduous search by professional experts for practical and politically feasible ways of creating order out of administrative chaos; and the President himself became a part of it, to a degree, when he presided over White House meetings of the National Resources Board (so the National Planning Board was renamed in 1934) wherein problems of "overall" or "top" management of government were discussed. Months passed. A year passed. New agencies were created and jammed willy-nilly into the executive structure. Then, in October 1935, Roosevelt asked Merriam for a memorandum on the "plan for a plan." The memorandum then prepared proposed assigning to the national Social Science Research Council's public administration committee, a committee chaired by Brownlow, the task of making "a thorough study . . . directed toward institutional arrangements, general understandings and practices which will most effectively aid the Executive in the double task of management plus political leadership and direction."[16] As things turned out, however, the proposed assignment was never made. Instead, in March 1936, soon after Senator Byrd's special Senate committee on reorganization of executive agencies was set up, and almost simultaneously with the setting up of a similar House committee, Roosevelt appointed a President's Committee on Administrative Management consisting of Brownlow, Charles Merriam, and Luther Gulick, who was director of the New York City–based Institute of Public Administration.* Brownlow was named chairman. These, with the aid of an expert staff whom they themselves selected, were to study "the relation" between the "existing regular organizations of the Executive Branch of the Government" and "the many new agencies which have been created during the emergency" (some of which "will doubtless . . . be dropped or curtailed, while many others will have to be fitted into the permanent organization"), and also "determine the best way of fitting new agencies into the regular organization." This last required that the study "cover the regular as well as the emergency agencies."[17]

It was a sweeping assignment, certainly, and with a severe time limit upon it, considering its scope and difficulty, for the President's stated "intention" was that the report be in his hands "in time for submission to the 75th Congress of such recommendations as may be based on the report."

It was also an assignment perceived by Brownlow and his associates to be of major importance, even of a finally decisive importance, to the survival of democracy as a political system in the face of totalitarian threats throughout the world.

As Barry Dean Karl has written,[18] there had been over the last half-century "a growing awareness throughout the western world of the need for the

---

*So far as the public was concerned, the committee was established in May 1936, for it was not until then that its appointment was announced by the White House.

application of rational, systematic processes to the complex bureaucracy which all governments had tended to develop in the wake of modern industrialism." Increasingly recognized, Karl goes on to say, were two needs: first, "the need for greater communication between knowledge or special skill and the actual, day to day operations of government"; second ("almost as a correlate," says Karl), "the need for the delimiting of arbitrary executive will in areas and circumstances where that will could be inefficient or incorrect."

Fundamentally involved in this concern were questions about the proper relations between freedom and organization—that is, between the individual person and the social organism of which he or she is necessarily an element —in a modern industrial state that wished to remain democratic. To what extent did or should the ever closer interdependencies bred by technological advance require the sacrifice of personal liberty to collective efficiency? Or, to look at the question from the other side, the human side (few Americans ever did), to what extent could or should technological "progress" be sacrificed to the liberty and happiness of the individual person, or subordinated to these in ways that shaped the technology? The question was, ultimately, one of choice between ends and means, or, rather, between alternative ends and means. Was the end pursued to be a maximization of machine (economic) efficiency? Or was it to be a maximization of the human values that add up to human freedom —an enhancement and enlargement of the human spirit, the individual personal self in its unique totality? That such questions should arise—that this antagonism between machine efficiency and human freedom should arise—was ironic in view of the fact that, in the beginning, Man created the Machine precisely for the purpose of enhancing his freedom, his self-realizing happiness, by releasing him from bondage to time- and energy-consuming labor. In its original conception, the Machine was but an extension of the human body and, as such, wholly an instrument or agent of Man's individual spirit, mind, conscious will. But as its power and complexity increased, so did the socioeconomic organization it necessarily implied, and after the Industrial Revolution was well under way the Machine may be said to have begun creating Man, molding his mind and spirit in ways that, from the humanist's point of view, were often direfully unfortunate. The fundamental historical question now was whether or not the original basic relationship between Man and Machine was to be restored. Would Man become again master of the machine, his technology again truly *his* in the sense of ownership and control, or was it to be the other way around?*

Brownlow, Merriam, and Gulick were, of course, concerned with only a narrow if highly important segment of this very broad and deep question. They were inclined by their assigned task to identify the Machine with the American federal bureaucracy—inclined to see this as a cumbrous clanking monster that operated increasingly out of control, as if possessed of a will of its own, though one that was erratic and self-frustrating since it was composed of a hundred

*See *FDR: The New Deal Years,* p. 673.

separate clashing wills and was undisciplined, or inadequately disciplined, by thoughtfulness or idea. Their assignment was to devise ways and means of making the Machine, so viewed, into an efficient instrument of Man, with the latter defined as the general executive mind and will operating within a pattern of purpose imposed through the legislative process. At the same time they must be extremely wary of mistaking the metaphor for a strictly accurate description of objective realities, else they would promote the very totalitarianism they were at pains to prevent. They must not for a moment forget that the Machine they proposed to remodel was not made up of inert inorganic materials; it was composed of living, breathing, willing, thinking human beings whose individual humanity must be respected.* And time was running out! In an increasingly troubled world, the need to restructure the American executive and reform its procedures for greater efficiency was little short of desperate.

As Brownlow would write in a later year, the democratic faith had been waning "in our country as in other democratic countries" ever since the end of the Great War, democracy being seen more and more as "an endless debating society, . . . a form of organization that was futile and futilitarian and that inevitably selected governments that would not, could not, act." The one "institution" in the world "around and behind which the democrats of the world might rally to repel the enemy" was, in Brownlow's conviction, the presidency of the United States. But if this were to happen, it was "absolutely necessary that the President be better equipped for his tremendous task."[19]

This was a view in which Franklin Roosevelt would publicly concur. "In these troubled years of world history," he would say in a special message to Congress nine days from now, using words supplied him by Luther Gulick, "a self-government cannot long survive unless that government is . . . effective and efficient. . . . A government without good management is a house builded on sand." And good management was sadly absent from the American government at the present time. ". . . It is humanly impossible for the President . . . to carry out his Constitutional duty as Chief Executive because he is overwhelmed with minor details and needless contacts arising from the bad organization and equipment of the government." Rectification of the situation was an immediate necessity. There must be, at once, reorganization of the executive branch along the lines laid down in a "five-point program" developed by the President's administrative management committee. "In placing this proposal before you I realize that it will be said that I am recommending the increase of the powers of the Presidency. This is not true. . . . What I am placing before you is the request not for more power, but for the tools of management and the authority to distribute work so that the President can effectively discharge those powers which the Constitution now places upon him."[20]

---

*"Reorganization is not a mechanical task, but a human task, because Government is not a machine, but a living organism," Luther Gulick would write, as words to be spoken by the President in a special message to Congress. See *The Public Papers and Addresses of Franklin D. Roosevelt 1937* (New York, 1938), p. 674.

Yet Roosevelt well knew on this first Sunday morning of 1937 that the reorganization he proposed would in fact change significantly the balance of power between executive and legislature, strengthening the former relative to the latter.

From the earliest days of the Republic, the organization and control of the departments, bureaus, and other elements of the executive branch had been deemed a congressional prerogative. Only grudgingly and under emergency pressures had Congress legislated any shifting of powers from its own hands into those of the President. Under the war powers given by Congress to the chief executive during Wilson's second term, the President was permitted to do some shifting and reorganization of bureaus and divisions. During the first half of Hoover's term, a Republican Congress had enacted a law allowing the President to make limited organizational changes by executive order, each order to become effective in sixty days if not specifically overruled by Congress within that time. But these were minor exceptions to the general rule. The traditional democratic fear of strong centralized government, joined with the businessman's hostility to federal regulation, remained potent indeed; Congress remained in control of the executive organization; and since what was now proposed would concentrate in the White House powers long dispersed among the elements of the two houses of Congress and exercised there in discrete, scattered, often clashing fragments by individual senators, individual representatives, individual congressional committees, it was bound to be opposed by powerful members of each house. Much of the energy of this opposition would derive from the desire of such congressional conservatives as Byrd to abolish or at least reduce the funding of New Deal agencies they disliked. "Economy" would be their watchword, their rallying cry, and the smokescreen for their effort to retain, to the maximum extent possible, the power balance that now prevailed.

Nor was there any enthusiasm for reorganization among those now staffing the agencies of the executive branch, including members of the White House staff. In April 1936, Appointments Secretary Marvin McIntyre had said flatly and sourly to the President that there "ought not to be" any such committee as the one the President had then just appointed, Brownlow its head, since it would mean a "stirring up of everybody about whether or not they are going to be shifted from one place to another." Press Secretary Stephen T. Early agreed with him.[21] There were similar nervous reactions elsewhere throughout the bureaucracy. Among them was a "stirring up" of a long-chronic quarrel between the Department of Agriculture, where the U.S. Forest Service now resided, and the Department of the Interior, where this service had first been placed and to which, said Interior Secretary Harold L. Ickes loudly (Roosevelt was inclined to agree), it ought now to be returned.

Clearly, if the President were to have his way, gathering unto himself the governing power he needed, he must use to the utmost his tactical and human-manipulative skills, and he must strike swiftly, before there was any reduction, as soon there must be, of the immense popular prestige and aura of invincibility that had come to him from his election triumph. But his realization that this was so did not dismay him. On the contrary—rising from his bed, shaving, dressing (with assistance), seating himself in his wheelchair (with assistance) ready for removal to the Oval Room next door—he was exhilarated. The felt challenge and risk added to his eager anticipation of the conference with Louis Brownlow that would begin in a few minutes, a conference of just the two of them alone, during which he would store up mental ammunition and make final tactical decisions for the battle that impended.

VI

AND as he conferred, on this Sunday morning, did he give signs of the hubris of which he was soon to be accused by Ben Cohen and myriad others?

He seemed perfectly self-confident, certainly, and with a rock-hard confidence, though in ways more amusingly boyish than repulsively smug and conceited, as he welcomed into the Oval Room a stocky, balding, bespectacled man of fifty-odd years, broad and pleasant of face, quick to smile, who carried with him a well-stuffed briefcase.

Louis Brownlow was of a type to which Roosevelt's loyal friend and immensely useful confidential servant, New York Supreme Court Justice Samuel I. Rosenman, also belonged. He had little ambition for personal glory but much devotion to what he perceived to be the public good, was little jealous of popular credit for his achievements (he happily settled for the esteem of his professional peers) but much concerned to do well what he was assigned or set himself to do.

Last summer he had been in England pursuing "researches in the general field of administrative management," this as part of the current job assigned him by the President. In London, he had conferred with one of his own kind, plain Tom Jones by name, who had served in the secretariat of the Cabinets of three British prime ministers in succession (David Lloyd George, Stanley Baldwin, Ramsay MacDonald) and who glowingly described to him the successes of the Committee of Imperial Defence which, established inside the British Cabinet in 1905, was converted into a Cabinet secretariat after the end of the Great War.* Jones gave most of the credit for the success of the Cabinet secretariat, however, not to it as an institution but to the man who headed it, Sir Maurice Hankey. "Tell the President," said Jones to Brownlow, "that the way to solve his problem is to find that one man who will turn out to be another Maurice Hankey, a man of high competence, great physical vigor, and a passion for anonymity." These last words would forever stick in Brownlow's mind; he had inserted them in the draft of his committee's report to the

---

*The Committee of Imperial Defence inspired the creation in the American government of a Council of National Defense, a development in which Franklin Roosevelt, as assistant secretary of the navy, had a leading part. Established by congressional act in 1916, this council was a first step toward what became notorious in the late 1950s as the military-industrial complex. See *FDR: The Beckoning of Destiny*, pp. 415, 421–22, and note 22 on p. 879.

President, using them to describe the kind of man who should be chosen for the six-man White House secretariat that the committee recommended; and when the President read them in the company of Brownlow and Luther Gulick in mid-November 1936, a few days before his departure for South America, "he burst out laughing, and read the phrase out loud a second time."[22]

It was a phrase descriptive, in a general way, of Brownlow himself; certainly it was so of Brownlow's self-conception and -perception. And precisely because he had no hankering for a starring role on history's stage and was actually averse to the spotlight, if not a bit afraid of it, he inclined toward a somewhat excessive admiration of those who, having boldly sought the spotlight, operated in its full and risky glare to "get things done" on a large scale. Yet Brownlow had not always been uncritical of Franklin Roosevelt. An old Wilsonian, he had been outraged in 1932 by the speech in which Roosevelt came out against U.S. membership in the League of Nations; he had also deplored Roosevelt's waffling on the tariff issue; he had gone so far as to write letters to influential friends, shortly before 1932's Democratic National Convention, suggesting "that we all switch to Newton D. Baker." During the 1932 campaign itself, he had tried through telegraphed protests (he addressed them to Brain Trust members) to prevent Roosevelt's delivery of the ultra-conservative Pittsburgh speech, Brownlow having been shown an advance copy of it by his longtime friend Daniel C. Roper, now secretary of commerce.[23] But all this now seemed very long ago. With the launching of the New Deal, Roosevelt became a hero in Brownlow's eyes. And to his heroic stature had been added a dimension of great personal affection on Brownlow's part, this in consequence of repeated direct exposure to Roosevelt's personal charm. It was a charm to which Brownlow, like Rosenman, was peculiarly vulnerable.

The remarkably empathic Roosevelt was perfectly aware of this last fact. He may have known, too, that the man before him had not always admired him greatly and had still in him a capacity for disapproval, even rejection, latent amid the general tendency to approve and admire. Brownlow was no mere human putty to be shaped without effort into another's designs; he had a resistant quality that required effort to handle. He was therefore a man *worth* impressing. And Roosevelt, as he plunged zestfully into his work for this morning, employed words and gestures he knew would delight his one-man audience and inspire admiration.

From his stuffed briefcase, Brownlow extracted the page proofs of the final report of the President's Committee on Administrative Management, proofs received only the day before from the Government Printing Office. He passed these into Roosevelt's eager hand, across the clutter of mementos on the presidential desktop—a widely various clutter, which, according to some observers, was a projection of the President's cluttered mind and might also be deemed symbolic, in this same regard, of the pluralistic, individualistic society whose government centered here. Roosevelt began at once to go over the printed pages.

Already he knew and approved his committee's recommendations, having reviewed the draft report of these last November. He read now, not for new information, but for mnemonic reasons. His purpose was to master the document so thoroughly that he could present the whole lengthy gist of it to the Cabinet and to Democratic congressional leaders during the next few days, and could also answer questions about its every important detail, with no reference to notes and little to such members of the committee and its expert staff as might then be at his side. He proposed to make the committee's work his own —so much so that those who witnessed his presentation of it, his actor's performance of it, would be as hesitant to criticize it sharply, challenge it harshly, as they would be to criticize or challenge him personally in this way, face to face. Concentratedly, then, he devoted himself to the task of memorizing. For nearly three hours he did so. He read and reread key passages aloud, clarifying their meanings for himself by asking questions of Brownlow now and then. He commented on what he read, and flatteringly asked Brownlow's opinion of the commentary. Only once was he interrupted, by a phone call. Ambassador William C. Bullitt phoned from Paris, where he was attempting busily and conspiratorially, as was his wont, to arrange a reconciliation of Hitler's Germany with Léon Blum's France—an attempt based on false premises and fueled by false information, as history would soon show. Ordinarily, the ebullient Bullitt had ready and full access to the eye and ear of the President, who thoroughly enjoyed his excitingly dramatic conception of world and self. Today, however, Roosevelt cut him off very shortly, and in a way that also flattered Brownlow. "Bill, I just can't discuss it now, I'm too busy with an important matter," said the President, and hung up.

But when at last his memory exercise was ended, during the noon hour, he leaned back in his chair to talk in relaxed fashion to his conferee. He talked about the importance of memory to his success as President of the United States. He told how once he had asked the White House executive clerk, an intimidatingly dignified and coldly reserved man named Rudolph Forster, to compare the number of decisions made by him, Roosevelt, in a given time span with the number made by those of his predecessors whom Forster had served —and Forster had served every one of them since Grover Cleveland's second administration. Forster told him, said Roosevelt, that he made dozens more decisions than any of his predecessors, and at least twenty-five times as many as Calvin Coolidge.

"You know, Louis, there is only one way I can do it," Roosevelt went on. "My memory. They can't fool me. I have a long memory, and an accurate memory, and when they talk to me or write to me and try to obfuscate past events, I simply know better."[24]

It was a boast whose objective truth was questioned by several who worked closely with the President. Brownlow himself would later say that "some persons" thought Roosevelt's pride of memory "inordinate." And the historical record shows that, though Roosevelt did indeed have a remarkably capacious memory, with a rare grasp of detail, it was also a highly selective memory on occasion, and sometimes a totally false one—unless, of course, what he said he remembered was a deliberate misstatement of what he actually did remember. The boast, however, was flattering to Louis Brownlow; it indicated a wish by the President of the United States to impress him favorably.

So it was in a glow of affection and admiration for the man he served, and a glow, too, of enhanced self-esteem, that Brownlow, having risen to take his departure, accepted from the President two culminating assignments. He was asked to write or have written (he would later ask Luther Gulick to draft) the special message with which the committee report would be sent by the President to Congress. He was also asked to have his committee's recommendations put into legislative language by some legal draftsman, as a bill to be introduced in Congress.

And Brownlow, as he left the White House, carried with him no impression of Roosevelt as a swellhead or megalomaniac. On the contrary, it seemed to him that the President, in his initial dealings with this intricate and tricky business of administrative reform, was measuring realistically the extent of the power and prestige that were his at the moment. Roosevelt was obviously aware of the risks in what he was prepared to do. He calculated them with utmost care.

As for the self-confidence and self-satisfaction Roosevelt had manifested, they seemed to Brownlow not foolishly excessive, or even excessive at all, in the circumstances. They seemed actually to have at their heart—strangely, incongruously, endearingly, as Brownlow may have sensed rather than explicitly recognized—a certain diffidence.

A kind of humility.[25]

## VII

MUCH the same impression of mood, of attitude, was made on others who were in personal contact with Roosevelt during the three days that intervened between his conference with Brownlow and his delivery, on January 6, of his State of the Union address to Congress. Generally speaking, it was also the impression he made on the nation as a whole by what he said in his address, and the way in which he said it.

He was given a tumultuous reception when, one hand grasping son James's strong arm, he entered the House chamber at two o'clock on that Wednesday afternoon and made his way slowly, but with a show of smiling ease, down the aisle to the podium. Thereafter, as he spoke, he was interrupted again and again by applause. "At two or three points there were actual cheers from the members of Congress and the people in the galleries," recorded Harold Ickes in his diary. "I found myself yelling on one occasion, and that is something I do not often do."[26] Roosevelt accepted this applause with modest mien, as if to say he realized it was not for him personally but for the great victory he shared with those who applauded. To most of his immediate audience—the hundreds who sat before him, the millions who heard him over the radio— it seemed that the election triumph, far from going to his head, had had a sobering effect, he feeling the full weight of the historic responsibility it placed upon him. The words he spoke were an appeal to reason, not emotion. He sought to persuade, not overcome, his opposition. He was the opposite of assertive in his making of proposals.

For instance, having encountered during the last few days the expected opposition from isolationist congressmen to his desire for a revision of the Neutrality Act that would give him expanded discretionary powers, enabling him to apply the act to civil wars, he made now no effort to overcome that opposition. He could probably have done so, with difficulty. Instead, he asked, in tones somewhat more urgent than he employed in the bulk of his address, for immediate consideration of a joint resolution introduced, at his behest, by Nevada senator Key Pittman that morning—legislation flatly prohibiting the export of arms and other war matériel to Spain. It applied to the Spanish conflict (that is, essentially, at that moment, to Robert Cuse) alone.

As *The New York Times* reported, "every remark" by the President in his speech "that appeared aimed at the Court was cheered" by the Democrats. But it was also noted that the "remarks" differed greatly in tone from the perceived harsh bitterness of the famous "horse-and-buggy" press conference, and even more from the bellicosity, the searing contempt, of the campaign attacks on "economic royalists" who hid "behind the Flag and the Constitution" in "vain" efforts to escape the "overthrow" of "their kind of power." The message was firm but sweetly reasonable and wholly "inoffensive" (Ickes's adjective) in its dealings with the constitutional crisis, if also somewhat displeasing, even dismaying, to those—a majority of the country's liberals—who were convinced that a constitutional amendment was required in order to make explicit and specific, in its application to social and economic concerns, the "general welfare" clause of Article I, Section 8. "During the past year there has been a growing belief that there is little fault to be found in the Constitution . . . as it stands today," the President said with quiet emphasis, clearly indicating that this belief had at least grown in his own mind. "The vital need is not an alteration of our fundamental law but an increasingly enlightened view with reference to it. . . . [R]ightly considered it can be used as an instrument of progress and not as a device for the prevention of action." (In the Cabinet meeting to which Roosevelt read his draft message on the day before he delivered it, Ickes and Secretary of Agriculture Henry Wallace both pounced on that portion of it. Did Roosevelt really want to close the door so emphatically upon the possibility of constitutional amendment? they asked. Roosevelt denied that the words really closed the door: the amendment option remained open, he asserted.[27]) He went on to speak of the cordial and effective cooperation that had been achieved by the legislative and executive branches as they attacked Depression problems; he invited and predicted a joining by the judiciary in this necessary working relationship. "With a better understanding of our purposes, and a more intelligent recognition of our needs as a nation, it is not to be assumed that there will be a prolonged failure to bring legislative and judicial action into closer harmony," he said. "Means must be found to adapt our legal forms and our judicial interpretations to the actual present needs of the largest progressive democracy in the modern world. . . . We do not ask the courts to call non-existent powers into being, but we have a right to expect that conceded powers or those legitimately implied shall be made effective instruments of the common good."

His closing words were expressive of his belief that the Depression was over. "Your task and mine is not ending with the end of the depression," he said. "The people of the United States have made it clear that they expect us to continue our active efforts in behalf of their peaceful advancement. In that spirit of endeavor and service I greet the 75th Congress at the beginning of this auspicious New Year."[28]

As tumultuous as the welcome he had received when he entered the chamber was the ovation given him as he turned from the lectern and, again on the arm of son James, made his way, arduously, but again with smiling seeming ease, from the chamber.

He returned to the White House elated by the reception Congress had given him; he was frankly, boyishly revelatory of that fact. He promptly acquiesced in the suggestion made by Marvin McIntyre that the event be celebrated with an impromptu poker party in the Oval Room as soon as he had concluded a conference with members of his administrative management committee—a conference he had arranged for the purpose of reviewing and approving in final form the reorganization bill, which Brownlow had had drafted by a Treasury Department lawyer, and the accompanying special message to Congress, which Brownlow had asked Gulick to draft. Seven men were seated at the poker table, after it had been brought into the room along with a platter of caviar and cheese and "liquid refreshments"; and of these seven only one, WPA administrator Harry Hopkins,* was a bigger winner than the President (he pocketed close to fifteen dollars) when the game ended at seven-thirty—surely a sign of Providence's continued blessing upon Franklin Roosevelt.[29]

By that time the joint resolution prohibiting matériel shipments to Spain was ready for Roosevelt's signature. Within an hour after the last word of the annual message was delivered, the Senate had unanimously consented to a consideration of this proposal without referring it to committee and had adopted it by voice vote, with none voting nay. The House had followed suit, approving the resolution 406–1.

The event, little noted in the press, was noted hardly at all by the public at large.

And we may well pause here to consider the significance of this popular inattention, this manifest unconcern.

Surely it implies that Roosevelt, who from the first personally favored the Loyalists over the rebels, had at that juncture, a very considerable freedom of

---

*The others were McIntyre; Early; Ickes; Colonel Edwin (Pa) Watson, the President's military aide; and James Roosevelt.

choice with regard to the Spanish war, as Robert Dallek, among others, has pointed out.[30] He had a proportionately large opportunity for educational leadership of the electorate. Socialist leader Norman Thomas and others said publicly at the time that Roosevelt would have done far better if, instead of calling for special legislation applying exclusively to Spain, he had taken advantage of existing neutrality law to dissociate America's Spanish policy from that of Britain and France. This would have been, of course, a policy reversal on his part, he having committed himself to the Franco-British policy when he declared his "moral embargo" on shipments to Spain; but since the reversal would have been made through a simple refraining from action, it would have been generally perceived as a submission to congressional will, an admission of necessity. Indeed, he could probably have gone much further than this with little political risk: He could have reversed himself openly, had he done so in ways carefully designed to inform and persuade. For it cannot be too strongly stressed that at that time Americans in general had little information about what was happening in Spain (what little they had was mostly wrong) and that, though most of them were sympathetic to the Loyalists while the Catholic hierarchy favored Franco, there had not yet developed any widespread emotional attachment to either side of the conflict. What the American people *were* aware of, and desperately feared, was the threat evidently posed by Spain of a new world war in which America might become involved. If they had been told by their President, at the height of his post-election prestige, that in the present instance the best insurance against world war was not to break off but to maintain normal trade relations with the legitimate Spanish government, if he had presented to them fully and frankly the reasoning that "obviously" led to this conclusion ("as you and I know"), they almost certainly would have believed and supported him in overwhelming majority. They would have done so, probably, if he had simultaneously prohibited shipments of arms and other war-stuff to the Fascist rebels (the United States had repeatedly taken such action against forces seeking to overthrow Latin American governments that U.S. business interests wished to keep in power).

Of course, leadership by the President would have been required to maintain this position against the protests of the Church and of Britain and France. The effort, however, need not have been especially strenuous. Neither London nor Paris was in a position to protest strongly, convincingly; their arguments could have been easily countered, in view of their refusals to act against Nazi-Fascist aid to the rebels; and Americans in general reacted with fear and angry resentment against whatever they perceived to be a "meddling" in American politics by the authoritarian Church of Rome. Hence, these combined protests, if loudly made, would have been more likely to gain than to lose isolationist support of the President's stand.

In following days, the conservative press bestowed upon the President's annual message a grudging praise, but praise nevertheless. Even the arch-Republican

New York *Herald Tribune* seemed willing to give him the benefit of the doubt: "It is possible to interpret [what Roosevelt had said about the Supreme Court] . . . as a warning to the Court. But . . . [the words'] good temper and restraint . . . seems to us such a vast improvement on the 'horse and buggy episode' . . . that we prefer to accept it as a promise of new wisdom rather than an exhibition of old wounds."[31] Other right-wing papers said similar things. They blamed Roosevelt, not the Court, for all the difficulty, of course; they laid heavy emphasis on his "bad temper" and "unreasonableness," and on the "sloppy draftsmanship" of New Deal legislation in the past; but they professed to be relieved and gratified by his evident change of attitude, his now expressed willingness to work with rather than against the institutional guardian of the Constitution as he entered his second term.

As for the liberal press, it, too, commented favorably, if somewhat more qualifiedly than the conservative press, upon the message's firm but conciliatory tone.

VIII

AT two o'clock on the afternoon of Sunday, January 10, while a cold and heavy rain splashed the White House windows and chilled the mansion's second floor as it had not been chilled earlier that winter,* Franklin Roosevelt, clad in a light gray suit, a burning cigarette in an extremely long paper holder slanting up from his smiling lips, launched the performance for which he had so arduously studied and carefully rehearsed during the long conference with Louis Brownlow just one week before. He sat on a leather couch placed against the study walls; the uselessness of his withered legs, the fact that he had to lift them in his hands when he wished to cross them or otherwise change their position, was not hidden behind a desk from others in the room as it usually was. Even so, because his hands made the needed arrangements of his limbs with such practiced swift efficiency, he continuing uninterrupted a flow of talk, his disability was barely noticeable. He gave no slightest sign of tension or embarrassment. Physically and mentally he seemed perfectly at ease, comfortable, secure, confident. Yet those in the room most intimately concerned with the matter he now dealt with (included in the company were all three members of his Committee on Administrative Management, plus four of the committee's expert staff) knew him to be acutely aware that he faced an audience that was highly critical, even hostile to the explicit meanings and wide implications of what he was about to say. He had a selling job to do that was as difficult as its success was important, and the importance was great indeed.

*All through the autumn and early winter of 1936–1937 the weather in Washington was unseasonably warm. In early January the grass was as green as in a Washington April, lilacs were actually budding, moths fluttered through open windows. In the late afternoon of Saturday, January 9, Harold Ickes placed a thermometer on the front porch of his home and found that, in the shade, it registered 77.5° Fahrenheit. The sudden drop in temperature on Sunday afternoon was therefore a surprise that made "the room in the White House where the meeting was held rather cool, in fact unpleasantly so to many of the persons present."[32]

For seated in a semicircle of chairs before him were the Democratic leaders of a Congress that, uniquely in history, was more than two-thirds Democratic in both houses—men upon whom the President had to depend for the legislation of his program—and every one of them was more strongly inclined to resent and resist the sweeping proposals they had all been summoned to the White House to hear than most other members of Congress would have been. Each was a Southerner, committed by regional political tradition to states' rights and congressional government.

It was, therefore, with a special warmth of smile and spoken word that Roosevelt had welcomed to this room John Nance Garner, vice president of the United States and presiding officer of the Senate, a native of Texas; William B. Bankhead of Alabama, newly elected speaker of the House (his actress daughter, Tallulah, was much better known to the general public than he was); Joseph T. Robinson of Arkansas, Senate majority leader; Pat Harrison of Mississippi, chairman of the Senate Finance Committee; James P. Buchanan of Texas, chairman of the House Appropriations Committee; and Robert L. Doughton of North Carolina, chairman of the House Ways and Means Committee. He, the President, called attention to a huge humidor of inlaid wood placed on a table in the center of the room. It was filled with Havana cigars, of which his guests were invited to partake. Not until several of them had done so and the room was redolent of tobacco did he begin his game of persuasion, with a move whose risks were great but carefully calculated. He led "with the worst he had to say [so it seemed to a watching, listening Louis Brownlow] in order to be able . . . to make tactical retreats" later on "without sacrificing his strategical position." He told the congressional leaders that on this coming Tuesday he would send the final report of the Committee on Administrative Management up the Hill, along with a special message. He very carefully did *not* say that the message was already prepared—he wanted his listeners to believe that their discussion this Sunday afternoon would largely determine the message's form and content—but he boldly announced that a bill incorporating the committee recommendations had been prepared (to do this, he had told Brownlow in advance, would be "very dangerous" insofar as it might be deemed a flouting of congressional prerogatives) and that the proposed bill, too, would go up the Hill on Tuesday. Mimeographed copies of it were available.* He asked his son and secretary, James, to give one to each of his guests. But he gave the senators and representatives no time to study the document, plunging at once into a presentation and explication of the committee's findings and recommendations.

He did so without regard for the order, the emphases or priorities, of the report as written, but with the closest regard for the sensitivities and proclivities of his listeners, and for the various and continuously varying psychological

---

*As a matter of fact, far too many copies were available, from Roosevelt's point of view. The staff of the Brownlow Committee (so, inevitably, it was dubbed by the press) had mimeographed, not the dozen or so copies now needed, but more than five hundred of them.[33]

pressures in that room. His blue-eyed gaze darted from one face to another as he made continuous empathic assessment of the shifting weights of opinion and interest (in both meanings of the word "interest") among the politicians before him, shaping and reshaping his performance accordingly.

For instance, the report started off with a statement of the importance of the American presidency to the preservation of democracy, and of the consequent urgent need to increase the efficient management of the office. To this, Roosevelt, deferring to recognized prejudices against strong, centralized national authority, made no reference whatever. He wanted no attention called to the fact that, since executive efficiency and executive power are causally linked, an increase of the former inevitably meant an increase of the latter. So he began by stressing that the committee had operated wholly independently of himself, of his personal guidance. When he had established it the previous spring, he said, he ordered its members not to communicate with him until after the election, because it was a presidential committee, not a Roosevelt committee, and its recommendations could not be implemented until after the next President, whoever he might be, was inaugurated. He had therefore had no inkling of what the final report would say until he reviewed a preliminary draft of it, in the company of committee members, in mid-November.

All the same (was it by sheer happy accident? a cynical listener might have asked), this committee had evidently operated as an extension of Roosevelt's mind; it had answered questions, solved problems, and reached conclusions precisely as Roosevelt would have done had he been able to perform these labors personally. Hence the mind Roosevelt spoke as he made his presentation was his own, and he knew it so perfectly that he could skip about in it with perfect ease. He could improvise freely on his central theme—he could shift and dodge, shock and soothe, emphatically affirm and categorically deny—he could wholly hide or attractively disguise what his hearers would have found repulsive had they seen it naked—and he could do these things in instantaneous response to audience reactions, without outright falsification or serious distortion of the report in toto or in detail. He referred to no notes. He referred to committee members only for confirmation or expansion of things already said. When he widely opened the door to hostile questionings and strong objections it was with regard to matters, relatively unimportant within the context of the whole, upon which his own opinion was tentative, uncertain, and which might therefore be painlessly used as bargaining chips.

He placed heavy emphasis upon the significance of the word "management" in the presidential committee's title, saying that "management is a most admirable trait," that "one of the highest encomiums that one American can give another . . . is to say 'He is a good manager,' " and that the "whole business of this report is to emphasize management." He also stressed the constitutionality of this "whole business," though without once mentioning the Supreme Court in this connection. He said, in effect, over and over again: "The President must have the authority to conduct his affairs commensurate with the responsibility imposed upon his office by the Constitution."

In sum, his was a virtuoso performance that aroused astonished admiration, and even awe, among the three committee members and four staff experts who witnessed it. One of the latter, Herbert Emmerich,* wrote into his diary that night: "The President . . . jumped around like a cat, three steps ahead of everyone. Among the numerous branches of this complicated tree, he barely touched the branches that seemed to give slightly under his weight and rested securely upon those which seemed to support him." By the time the meeting broke up, at six o'clock, Roosevelt seemed almost as much master of the senators and representatives who filed out "in respectful and troubled silence" (Brownlow's words) as he had proved himself to be of the committee's work.

As for Roosevelt himself, though obviously pleased with himself, he was by no means cocksure regarding the outcome of the battle that now began.

"You see, Louis, what I'm up against," he said to Brownlow as the committee and staff were leaving the room. "This was quite a little package to give them this afternoon. Every time they recovered from a blow, I socked them in the jaw with another. . . ."[34]

Next day, Monday, January 11, in another virtuoso performance, but one wholly different in form and tone from that of Sunday, Roosevelt, in the presence of all his Cabinet, his three secretaries, and three committee members, presented his "little package" to reporters in a more than normally crowded press conference. This time, as if he were a professor lecturing a class, he reviewed the report from first to last in precisely the order in which it was written, and in detail. He placed great emphasis upon the introductory remarks which, the day before, he had refrained from mentioning at all; he stressed several other things which, yesterday, he had played down.

On the following day, as promised, the committee report ("a great document of permanent importance," as Roosevelt called it) was delivered to Congress, along with a summary of it and the accompanying special message.

By Wednesday evening, January 13, all readers and hearers of the news were aware that Roosevelt had proposed what one reporter called a "breath-taking, almost revolutionary plan for modernization of the executive branch of the government."[35]

The "five-point program" would, in the words of the report summary:

Modernize the White House business and management organization by giving the President six high-grade executive assistants to aid him in dealing with the regular departments and agencies.

Strengthen the budget and efficiency research, the planning and the personnel services of the Government, so that these may be effective managerial arms of the President, with which he may better coordinate, direct and manage all the work of the Executive Branch for which he is responsible under the Constitution.

Place the whole governmental administrative service on a career basis and under

---

*The Brownlow Committee "borrowed" Emmerich from the Farm Credit Administration, of which he was, in 1936, deputy governor and chief executive officer.

the merit system by extending the civil service upward, outward and downward to include all non-policy-determining positions and jobs.

Overhaul the more than 100 [actually there were 105] separate departments, boards, commissions, administrations, authorities, corporations, committees, agencies . . . which are now part of the Executive Branch and theoretically under the President, and consolidate them within twelve regular departments, which would include the ten existing departments and two new departments, [namely] a Department of Social Welfare and a Department of Public Works. . . .*

Make the Executive Branch accountable to the Congress by creating a true post-audit of financial transactions by an independent Auditor General who would report illegal and wasteful expenditures to Congress without himself becoming involved in the management of departmental policy, and transfer the duties of the present Comptroller in part to the Auditor, to the Treasury, and to the Attorney General.[36]

In this program, there was much that did not merely tread upon tender congressional toes but actually stomped upon them. The grouping of all governmental agencies within twelve departments (the placing of them under a dozen "big tents," as Roosevelt put it) would effectively destroy many a congressman's and senator's special segment of sovereign executive power. Extending the merit system to virtually all governmental employment would wipe out congressional patronage. The breaking-up of the office of the Comptroller General was a proposal especially obnoxious to congressional conservatives, Democrats and Republicans alike, since Comptroller General J. R. McCarl, a Republican appointee, had used his powers, in what the conservatives deemed precedent-setting ways, to curb the liberal tendencies of the New Deal from 1933 through 1936. In its "ambition, not to say daring," the President's plan was "startling," wrote Turner Catledge in *The New York Times* for Sunday, January 17. Yet instead of emitting "howls of rage," reported Catledge, "Congress appears in a stupor." Why? "Because of the election."

Thus was reinforced a popular belief, widespread since Election Day, that Franklin Roosevelt, though there was now no such desperate national emergency as had faced him at his first inaugural, could still assume dictatorial powers if he chose to do so. And hence his calculated use of a public speech and a public demeanor indicating that he had no slightest desire for such powers, nor intent to assume them.

On the same Sunday, January 17, when Turner Catledge published his report, Anne O'Hare McCormick (she was the *Times*'s foreign-affairs columnist) told in *The New York Times Magazine* of a lengthy and far-reaching personal interview she had had with the President a week earlier. Roosevelt had talked of "peace and the vindication and strengthening of democracy," saying that the "crisis" with which he had had to deal during his first term was not merely "economic." It was "really a breakdown of the democratic system." But Roosevelt's own personal commitment to democracy remained absolute; he wholly lacked, wrote the columnist, a "dictator's temperament."

---

*The name of the Department of the Interior was to be changed to the Department of Conservation, as Secretary of the Interior Harold Ickes had long wished for it to be.

For instance, as regarded the Supreme Court, it was extremely doubtful that Roosevelt, "on sober second thought . . . would abridge, if he could," the Court's powers. "All he asks of that body, he says, is that it shall be reasonably contemporary," and this wish could be made reality "through his appointive power." He had no longing for, he was indeed temperamentally averse to, such "lonely grandeur" as Hitler sought in his mountaintop retreat at Berchtesgaden. He would be, instead, "friend to all the world," hospitable to widely varying points of view and concerned to learn from all kinds and conditions of human beings. He loved to converse with people. He had great faith or confidence in the efficacy of face-to-face meetings for the solution of momentous public problems, including international problems. In fact, at that very moment, he was "toying with" the idea of arranging soon a personal "get-together" of the heads of government of five major powers to talk over ways and means of easing international tensions that now threatened a new world war, the five being himself, the British prime minister, the French premier, Italy's Mussolini, and Germany's Hitler.

Mrs. McCormick, it was obvious from what she wrote, had left the White House heartened and reassured by the President's words and evident attitude. These were calmly confident and realistically optimistic, by her assessment.

And what she reported of Roosevelt's mind and mood on this eve of his second inaugural accorded perfectly with the general impression he had made upon the public mind with what *New York Times* reporter Delbert Clark called "the very moderate and good-tempered tone of his four messages to Congress since January 5."[37]*

There was encouraged in millions of Americans a hope and belief that, with the President in the mood he was in, and with his conservative opposition in forced but openly admitted acceptance of the basic tenets of the New Deal, there opened for the country a new and genuine Era of Good Feeling—this despite the as yet unsolved problem of the Supreme Court, the current troublesome rash of labor-management disputes, and the growing threat of "foreign war."

---

*One of these messages, unmentioned in the text, urged Congress on January 14 to extend for another three years executive authority to negotiate reciprocal trade treaties with other nations. The original grant of such authority, made by act of Congress in 1934, was due to expire on June 12.

# 2

## The Initiation and Anatomy of
## a Tragic Error

I

FOR the first time in history, the Twentieth Amendment having gone into effect in February 1933, a President of the United States was being inaugurated on January 20 instead of on March 4. All agreed that the change of date was salubrious insofar as it reduced the danger of grave injury to the Republic when next there was a transfer of power from one party to another in time of crisis: shortened by six weeks was the interregnum wherein troubles and anxieties had piled up to terrifying height four years before. Yet none could deny that the gained advantage had an unhappy offset: The shift of event from Washington's early spring to the depth of the Washington winter meant an increase in the risk of foul weather on the ceremonial day. And on this Wednesday morning, alas, the risk had become miserable actuality.

Franklin Roosevelt became aware that this was so as soon as he awoke from his usual eight hours or more of sound sleep. Looking out his bedroom window he saw that the physical heavens not only frowned upon his triumph (dark clouds were lowered almost to rooftop) but also wept copious tears upon it (intermingled with the abundant rain was sleet) while a raw high wind shrieked and sighed and moaned around the cornices and the Grecian columns of the White House and through the leafless tops of trees upon the White House lawn. Was this a fateful sign, portentous for his second presidential term?[1] He who was so addicted to "luck" objects and so averse to gestures and small happenings deemed unlucky by popular superstition may well have asked himself this question. But if he did, he could consult his memory of the first inaugural ceremony in which he had been a central figure, that of New York's governor eight years before, and be reassured. Then and there the weather had been as foul as it was here and now, yet had been for him no evil omen. For poor Al Smith it may have been: Out of the sadness of Al's farewell to public office on that black noon had grown the bitterness that would conspicuously absent him from the scene today. (The absence would be much commented upon in the public prints, Al having been so prominently present on March 4, 1933.) But for Roosevelt what followed had been, on the whole, glorious— an almost precise working-out of the long perceived pattern of his high destiny. Hence no metaphysical terror was stirred in him, nor did any other deep perturbation of spirit darkly color his vision, as he gazed upon the day's inclemency. He regretted what he saw, of course. He was evidently condemned to hours of exposure to raw, wet wind; he'd doubtless be chilled to the bone and had good reason to fear another nasty head cold. Certainly his physician,

Ross McIntire, did so, and said so during that morning's routine physical checkup.

But this fear, if admitted at all, was not so great as to permit Roosevelt's acquiescence in certain protective measure that had been taken on his behalf. As he breakfasted in bed he learned that contingency planners had prepared for him a glass cubicle in which to stand while delivering his inaugural address, and another, of bulletproof glass, heated by electric radiators, in which to stand while reviewing the inaugural parade. He at once ordered the glass walls and roofs removed. The parade was to be military, by his prior order. In a symbolic pageantry highly disturbing to pacifists and others who feared dictatorial tendencies in the executive's psychology, Franklin Roosevelt would stand at attention on steel-braced legs before a replica of the Hermitage, itself a reminder of martial and political glory cohered in the person of Andrew Jackson, while bands and flags, marching men and clanking tanks, motorized cannon and motorized cavalry passed before him. He was Commander in Chief. These men marched under his supreme command. And he flatly refused to be walled off from them in seeming privilege and ostentatious privilege, while drenched, chilled thousands looked on.

He made only one concession to the elements. He consented to ride, shortly after ten o'clock, in a closed limousine to the religious services, which, as on the morning of inaugural day 1933, were conducted by the Reverend Dr. Endicott Peabody in St. John's Episcopal Church, across Lafayette Park from the White House. The services were brief. (It was noted that the Reverend Peabody's prayer, which in 1933 had ended with "save us from violence, confusion and discord," ended today with a simple plea for Divine Providence's guidance of "its son, Franklin.") He was back in the White House by ten-forty. An hour later, with Senator Joseph Robinson beside him, he rode in the same closed car from White House to Capitol (he insisted that he would return to the White House and the reviewing stand in an open car, no matter what the weather), preceded by motorcycle police and, instead of the long-traditional horse escort, armored cars from the motorized cavalry. Behind him were two open cars bearing Secret Service protectors, followed by closed cars in which rode his mother, his wife and children, and others of the Roosevelt and Delano families.

By then the weather was at its worst. Rain fell in torrents. Pennsylvania Avenue's gutters and pavements were "running with water like trout streams," as *The New York Times* would report, yet were lined by thousands. And at the Capitol, instead of at once mounting the long ramp to the ceremonial platform, as he had expected to do, the President was escorted to the offices of the Senate's sergeant-at-arms where he waited nearly half an hour for the storm to let up. It didn't. The ramp carpet squashed like a saturated sponge underfoot and the lash of rain fell as hard as before when, at twelve-twenty-three P.M., Roosevelt, leaning upon the arm of son James, Eleanor beside him, appeared before the throng (it was remarkably large, in the circumstances) that was standing ankle-deep in mud, huddled under umbrellas, on the Capitol's east grounds. At that moment, according to those versed in and concerned with legal niceties (the Senate parliamentarian, Charles Watkins, for one), Franklin Roosevelt was no longer and not yet President of the United States, his first term having expired at precisely noon. For twenty-three minutes the nation had been without a chief executive: No one had had the power to act for the Republic as a whole. And this executive impotence continued for six more minutes, while John Nance Garner was sworn in as vice president. Not until twelve-twenty-nine did Roosevelt stand up in the downpour before Chief Justice Charles Evans Hughes and take the oath of office, his right hand upraised, his left hand upon the Claes Martenszen Van Rosenvelt Bible (a cover had been placed over it to protect it from the wet).

To the two principals, and to hundreds among the multitude who watched and listened through the rain, today's oath-taking had a special symbolic meaning —a historically echoing and anticipatory significance greater, perhaps, than any other since Abraham Lincoln was sworn into the presidency by Chief Justice Roger Taney, author of the Dred Scott decision, on March 4, 1861. Now as then, Court and Executive faced one another grimly.* Seemingly hard as granite stood each against the other. And the Executive, by general manner and particular emphases, did something to dramatize the adversarial nature of the proceeding while at the same time affirming the common traditional ground on which the adversaries stood. He did not say merely "I do," as Garner had done when the oath question was asked. Instead, he repeated the oath verbatim, stressing the word "Constitution" and singing out loudly the phrase "preserve, protect, and defend," throwing his head back in a leonine gesture as he did so. (Later, Roosevelt confessed to Samuel I. Rosenman that he had wanted to add, "Yes, but it is the Constitution as *I* understand it, flexible enough to meet any new problem of democracy—not the kind of Constitution your Court has raised up as a barrier to progress and recovery."[2])

Then his second inaugural address.

On no other speech since he became President had he worked as hard as on this one. With Sam Rosenman, Tom Corcoran, and Donald Richberg he had gone over draft after draft—excising, rewriting, simplifying, translating abstract generalities into concrete particulars—until the rain-splattered large-type reading copy now on the lectern before him bore but slight resemblance to the original complete draft that Richberg had prepared. Over and over again he had read the final draft aloud, marking in pencil the places where he wanted special emphasis and the places where he might go wrong. ("Hard-headedness will not easily excuse hard-heartedness" was one epigrammatic sentence he

---

*Many were reminded of a passage in Lincoln's first inaugural speech: "If the policy of the government on vital questions is to be irrevocably fixed by the decisions of the Supreme Court the instant they are made in ordinary litigation between parties in personal actions, the people will have ceased to be their own rulers, having to that extent practically resigned their government into the hands of that eminent tribunal." The passage had been quoted by Senator Alben Barkley of Kentucky in his keynote address to the 1936 Democratic National Convention.

might easily misread, with a disastrous reversal of meaning; he had placed a pencil-drawn head above "-headedness" and a pencil-drawn arrow-pierced heart above "-heartedness" to make sure this did not happen.)[3] And despite the rain, which continued relentlessly, he stood hatless and spoke his piece as he had practiced it.

He reminded his listeners of his first inaugural's promise "to drive from the temple of our ancient faith those who had profaned it," and asserted that his first administration had actually done so. "We did these first things first," he declared. This, however, was the merest beginning—a clearing-away of hampering rubbish. "Instinctively we [of the Republic] recognized a deeper need," that of making government "the instrument of our united purpose" to solve for "the individual" the problems arising out of an increasingly "complex civilization." Earlier attempts to solve these problems "without the aid of government" had ended in failure. "For without that aid, we had been unable to create those moral controls over the services of science which are necessary to make science a useful servant instead of a ruthless master of mankind." The achievement of such controls meant the establishment of "practical controls over blind economic forces and blindly selfish men"; which was to say that the "essential democracy of our nation and the safety of our people depend not upon the absence of power, but upon lodging it with those whom the people can change or continue at stated intervals through an honest and free system of elections." Certainly the Founding Fathers had purposed a centralized governing power great enough to formulate and implement a *national* will. Out of the chaos following the Revolution they had deliberately ordered "a strong government [he emphasized "strong"] with powers of united action sufficient then and now [he laid heavy stress on "now"] to solve problems utterly beyond individual or local solution. . . . They established the Federal Government in order to promote the general welfare and secure the blessings of liberty to the American people. Today we invoke these same powers of government to achieve the same objectives. . . . The Constitution of 1787 did not make our democracy impotent."

Then he spoke of the "progress out of . . . depression" that had been made during the last four years—of how far the Republic had "come . . . from the days of stagnation and despair"—and claimed that this progress, as presided over by his administration, was "beginning to wipe out the line that divides the practical from the ideal." He spelled out his meaning in the prudential terms of a Ben Franklin: "We have always known that heedless self-interest was bad morals; we now know that it is bad economics. Out of the collapse of a prosperity whose builders boasted their practicality has come the conviction that in the long run economic morality pays." But he spoke more emphatically of what yet needed to be done and of the paradoxical fact that the doing of it might be inhibited by the effects of the very progress thus far made. The "goad of fear and suffering" that had made "advance . . . imperative" in 1933 was now removed from those whom recovery had most benefited. These might now cry "Halt!" Indeed, they were doing so. And since they had, with their disproportionate share of the national wealth, a disproportionate share of the national power, their voices rang with an ominous authority across the land. There was again a fusing of the immoral with the impractical, and the consequences were greatly to be feared. "Dulled conscience, irresponsibility, and ruthless self-interest already appear," said the President of the United States. "Such symptoms of prosperity may become portents of disaster."

Then followed the portion of the speech that would be most remembered in history—a call for action to banish poverty from America:

> In this nation I see tens of millions of its citizens . . . who at this very moment are denied the greater part of what the very lowest standards of today call the necessities of life.
>
> I see millions of families trying to live on incomes so meager that the pall of family disaster hangs over them day by day.
>
> I see millions whose daily lives in city and on farm continue under conditions labelled indecent by so-called polite society a half-century ago.
>
> I see millions denied education, recreation, and the opportunity to better their lot and the lot of their children.
>
> I see millions lacking the means to buy the products of farm and factory and by their poverty denying work and productiveness to many other millions.
>
> I see one-third of a nation ill-housed, ill-clad, ill-nourished.

It was "not in despair that I paint you that picture," Roosevelt went on, after a tactical pause. "I paint it for you in hope—because the nation, seeing and understanding the injustice of it, proposes to paint it out. We are determined to make every American citizen the subject of his country's interest and concern. . . . The test of our progress is not whether we add more to the abundance of those who have much; it is whether we provide enough for those who have too little."

He paused again, to wipe dripping rain from his face—and Sam Rosenman, knowing what came next, turned to watch closely the impassive bearded countenance of the Chief Justice of the United States.

The President resumed. The people of the Republic, said he, speaking now with a special careful emphasis, "are overwhelmingly . . . men and women of good will; men and women who have more than warm hearts of dedication; men and women who have cool heads and willing hands of practical purpose as well. They will insist that *every* agency of popular government use effective instruments to carry out their will."

And Rosenman saw that the implicit threat of that heavily underscored "every" struck hard into the mind of Charles Evans Hughes. The Chief Justice stiffened visibly.[4]

II

ON the face of it there impended, as the greatest single domestic threat to the opening of a new Era of Good Feeling, the culmination of what leading opinion-makers had been describing for two years as the gravest constitutional crisis since the Civil War.

The inaugural's declaration of all-out war against poverty was perfectly consistent with the climactic phrase of the climactic speech of Roosevelt's reelection campaign, his cry that "we have only just begun to fight"—and everyone recognized (it was especially remarked in published commentary) that the waging of such war would require bolder, deeper, more massive legislative penetrations than any thus far pressed into a country that Congress had been forbidden to enter, and from which it had been forced again and again to withdraw, by the Supreme Court majority. The New Deal, overwhelmingly endorsed by the People, seemed grimly determined to advance willy-nilly; the Court majority, wedded with iron bonds to Property, seemed as grimly determined to stop it. And if this seeming were literal truth, an impasse had been reached of a kind the American political system, reflective of the American pragmatic temperament, is in general well designed to prevent—a rare moment of flat confrontation in a sharply defined quarrel from which one side or the other must emerge victorious, the outcome providing unequivocal answers to fundamental questions. Certainly the present questions *were* fundamental. They went to the very heart of the meaning of America as a national enterprise in this twentieth century. Where lay in actual fact, behind formal appearance, the preponderance of ruling power in our highly industrialized society? Where *ought* it lie in a time when unique individualities were increasingly and, as some said, necessarily absorbed into large organizations? Insofar as power was identified with private wealth, private income, how to correct its present obvious maldistribution, assuming that a just distribution was one giving equality of individual opportunity and a decent living for all, without violent social revolution, and in ways that enhanced instead of diminishing true (economic as well as political) democracy? What was the proper and just distribution of power between public and private sectors of the economy, between political and economic institutions, between state and national government, and among the three branches of the federal government itself? In sum, was American freedom now to be defined in terms of the human person, as the Declaration of Independence and the Gettysburg Address defined it, or in terms of that "corporate personality" to which a business-serving Supreme Court extended the guarantees and protections of the Fifth and Fourteenth amendments?

There was, however, yet another question, of different order and more immediate reference—the question of whether the *appearance* of impending final head-on collision was the *reality* of the situation. Evidently, many if not most informed people doubted it. For though the great quadrennial national ceremony certainly sharpened the Court issue in the public mind, there was no perceptible heightening of popular suspense over it during the days immediately following. If anything, tensions that had slackened during the relative calm of the immediate post-election period were now further reduced. A close study of the inaugural address in its current historical context, added to that

already given the annual message of two weeks before, yielded soothing interpretations of its import by professional commentators. Encouraged thereby,
among those who cared and kept themselves informed about public affairs, was
a widespread belief that in actual fact the issue was now in process of resolution
on, in general, the side of the New Deal—indeed, that the process was quite
far advanced. To sophisticated observers, certainly, the tone of weary, regretful
resignation that had characterized conservative editorial commentary upon
the annual message seemed clearly to indicate that the conservatives had
already tacitly conceded to Roosevelt a victory in the constitutional quarrel.
The conservatives saw the President offering the Court an opportunity to yield
gracefully to the necessity imposed by the election results and the obvious
temper of the new Congress; they regretfully and reluctantly approved, in the
circumstances, the Court's acceptance of this offer. For what, after all, was the
alternative, in the conservatives' evident view? If the Court stubbornly persisted along the way it had been following, its cloak of sanctity as priest and
agent of Higher Law, a cloak already torn and tattered by rising winds of
hostile opinion, would be wholly stripped away. The Court would then stand
nakedly exposed as but another agent of exploitive Property and might be
emasculated, its self-asserted powers of legislative review removed, by the
agents of an angry People.

As for the commentary in the liberal press, it too indicated the assumption
(or much of it did) that an accommodation was being reached between executive and judiciary whereby the former's interpretation of the constitutional
distribution of powers among the three branches would, perforce, become the
latter's as well. The liberals, of course, stressed openly, as they always did and
as conservatives seldom did, the *political* nature of the Court and its decisions.
They professed to find in this a firm basis for hopeful conclusion. They quoted
Finley Peter Dunne's hilarious commentary, in the voice of Mr. Dooley, upon
the Supreme Court's *Downes* v. *Bidwell* decision of 1901, concluding with Mr.
Dooley that "no matther whether th' constitution follows th' flag or not, the
supreme court follows th' iliction returns."[5] They reminded the public that it
was none other than Charles Evans Hughes who had said that "we are under
a Constitution, but the Constitution is what the judges say it is";[6] that he had
said it while governor of New York in 1908; and that he had won that office
and a subsequent Republican presidential nomination through shrewd exercise
of the political arts of compromise and ingratiation. For all his Jovian appearance and Olympian manner, he had proved in the past to possess rather more
than his fair share of worldly ambition and, in his pursuit of it, to be highly
mindful of what people said and thought about him. Even in his present august
post, purportedly so high above marketplace, political arena, and "social
whirl" as to render him wholly aloof from their considerations—and even
though the Court he presided over had placed itself squarely athwart the
manifest popular will—his way of handling his work had shown him not
insensitive to public opinion or undesirous of personal popularity. Quite the
contrary, or so some liberals alleged. They had noticed, they said, that when

Hughes and Associate Justice Owen Roberts sided with the Court's liberal wing, rendering thereby a liberal and popular decision, the Chief Justice assigned the writing of it to himself rather more often than an evenhanded distribution of workload would require; when he voted with the conservative wing, on the other hand, assuring a decision illiberal and unpopular, he nearly always assigned the drafting of it to one of his brethren.[7] Also, when he dissented from conservative majority opinion in a landmark case, he was at great pains to phrase his dissent in ways as conciliatory of conservatives as possible (*within* the Court he operated more as pacificator and compromiser than as forceful leader; he wanted to be liked) while leaving intact behind him bridges to the ground that the majority had never left. He personally recoiled from sweeping decisions: He clearly wished to be as free to retreat as to advance when the next landmark case came along. Such a man could be counted upon to read fateful handwritings-on-walls from as great a distance as any who dealt with public affairs, and to be influenced in his judicial acts by what he read whenever it presaged important effects upon his personal power, prestige, and historical reputation.

From all this, sophisticated minds, both liberal and conservative, concluded a probability that the Chief Justice, at some point in the historic proceedings, would closet himself in heart-to-heart with Associate Justice Roberts. On the scale between the extreme liberal (Justice Benjamin Cardozo) and the extreme reactionary (Justice James C. McReynolds) ends of the Court, Justice Roberts had placed himself just to the right of the Chief Justice, a pivotal position that enabled him to determine with his swing vote whether the complexion of the Court as a whole was to have the ruddiness of the left or the paleness of the right, and in what degree. To him, in earnest private tête-à-tête, the Chief Justice could certainly say that the Court had placed itself in the gravest danger by its long series of 5–4 New Deal decisions grounded in an excessively broad definition of "states' rights" and an excessively narrow one of "interstate commerce," a series climaxed by *Morehead* v. *Tipaldo,* in which even "states' rights" with respect to the regulation of economic and social concerns were virtually denied. The popular reaction to *Tipaldo,* which included major defections from the ranks of conservative Court support, must alarm any justice possessed of a sense of history and political realities. Surely it was practical wisdom if not a necessity of survival for the justices tacitly to admit "th' iliction returns" to their deliberations during the upcoming Court session! And it was inconceivable that the practical-minded and self-protective Hughes would not indicate as much in frank talk with a colleague who, occupying with him a middle ground, doubtless shared his anxiety. The upshot was likely to be a shift of Roberts's pivotal opinion from right to left in future 5–4 decisions on crucial legislation.

As for the President who symbolically confronted the Chief Justice at the moment of oath-taking, he could be expected to possess himself in patience, as regards the Court, for some weeks or months to come, meanwhile vigorously pressing the legislative program implied by his campaign, his message, his inaugural. The latter two, joined with his general public demeanor since the election, impressed upon popular consciousness the image of a man rendered selfless by the very immensity of his personal triumph in November— a man enlarged in generous feeling and personally immunized against carping criticism by that triumph—a man utterly confident of his mandated presidential authority to advance the New Deal, and determined to do so as expeditiously as possible, yet sensitive to the feelings of his defeated adversaries and eager to sugar-coat as thickly as possible the bitter pill (a flat reversal of earlier decisions) that the Supreme Court must now swallow.

He could afford to wait. Indeed, he would be highly unwise *not* to wait at least until the Court, in its new session, had had a chance tacitly but unmistakably to accept or reject (with the odds strongly favoring the former) his invitation to cooperate in the business of government. This would be soon— late spring at the latest. By then he might have in hand a single and popularly supported, or supportable, proposal for judicial reform. A national conference specifically to achieve this, shaping it out of the many proposals put forward in Congress and elsewhere, had been formally summoned by Senator George Norris of Nebraska and other leading liberals a day or so after the inaugural. It would meet in a few weeks. From it, with some published encouragement by the White House, could come a widely agreed-upon legislative proposal, generally recognized to be neither excessive nor deficient in the force needed to reduce whatever obstacle was yet maintained (by late spring) in the way of progress, by reactionary judicial intransigence—also to prevent such dangerous obstructionism in the future.

Then, finally, of course, there was the factor that could not be openly stressed by administration spokesmen but that was background and reinforcement of all that counseled executive patience: namely, the operation of the actuarial laws. It did sometimes seem, as jokesters said, that these had been declared unconstitutional by the Nine Old Men just to spite Franklin Roosevelt. He alone among twentieth-century Presidents had not been permitted a single Supreme Court appointment in four years (Harding had made four in two and a half years); during the first Cabinet meeting after the election, he himself had voiced the joyless expectation that Mr. Justice McReynolds would be on the bench at age 105.[8] All the same, these actuarial laws remained in full force as a description of probabilities—and the average age of the present members of the Court was seventy-one.* It was virtually beyond belief that the President would not be enabled by the "natural course of events" to appoint at least one new justice before the midterm elections, and the chances were that this appointee would replace one of the extreme conservatives, since there were

---

*Louis D. Brandeis was eighty; Willis Van Devanter seventy-seven; James C. McReynolds seventy-five; Charles Evans Hughes seventy-five; George Sutherland seventy-four; Pierce Butler seventy; Benjamin N. Cardozo sixty-six; Harlan F. Stone sixty-four; and Owen J. Roberts sixty-one.

four of these over seventy years of age now on the bench compared with but one solid liberal, and one "soft" one, of similar age.

### III

TEN days passed by. No whisper from the White House indicated to the public the imminence of any particularly dramatic development. Nor was there any hint of this to those whom Roosevelt most often and intimately consulted in the process of decision-making and whom he would certainly consult, it appeared, on any such matter as major court reform. Thus, Sam Rosenman, New York Supreme Court justice, and Thomas Corcoran, happiest of the potent "Happy Frankfurters," had been told by the President while they worked on his annual message to "leave the whole thing [any reference to the Court problem] very general for now"[9]; Richberg had had the same direction given him while working on the inaugural address. Felix Frankfurter himself was similarly uninformed, though on January 15 a letter on another subject had gone to him that closed with a couple of cryptic sentences. "Very confidentially," said the letter, and Frankfurter might envision the mischievous twinkle in the President's eye as he wrote, "I may give you an awful shock in about two weeks. Even if you do not agree, suspend final judgment and I will tell you the story." Frankfurter had not known what to make of this, but it is highly improbable that he connected it with the problem of the judiciary, being assured in his own mind that this was one problem in whose solution he himself would, by Roosevelt, be directly involved. "Are you trying to find out how well I can sit on top of a Vesuvius by giving me notice that an 'awful shock' is in store for me . . . ?" he had asked in his (typically) courtier's reply of January 18. "Well, I shall try to hold my patience . . . , but you certainly tease my curiosity when you threaten me with something with which I may not agree. That, certainly, would be a great surprise."[10]

Came Saturday, January 30, the fifty-fifth anniversary of the birth of Franklin Roosevelt.

The President was supposed to lunch that day downstairs in the White House with a number of motion-picture actors and actresses; they were assembled for participation that night in the President's Birthday Ball, in Washington. Instead, having sent his regrets (they were sincere: the occasion was an annual event, and Roosevelt always greatly enjoyed associating with people of the theater), he lunched upstairs at a table set for five in the Oval Room. With him were Attorney General Homer Cummings, Solicitor General Stanley Reed, Donald Richberg, and Sam Rosenman—and, of these, the last-named was greatly and increasingly puzzled as the luncheon proceeded.[11] His presence was in response to an urgent summons to "a very important conference" issued by the President's confidential secretary, Missy LeHand, to him over the phone, he being in New York City, the night before. Yet there was no sign of urgency in Roosevelt's demeanor (it seemed totally relaxed) nor in the table

talk he led (it was light, general) as food was served. At one point he remarked
that this luncheon, in its peace and quiet, reminded him of a certain "Q-boat,*
the *Santee*, employed by the British against German U-boats in the Great War,
a remark which seemed to Rosenman irrelevant if not inane but which provoked hearty laughter from the others around the table. Evidently he, Rosenman, was the only man in the room who had no inkling of the purpose of this
gathering; and he could hardly have failed to regard his host with some
impatience as the luncheon, the bantering talk, continued at leisurely pace. Not
until the dishes were cleared away, the doors carefully closed, the President
seated behind his desk with the others in easy chairs before him—not until then
did the Q-boat reference come clear to Rosenman, along with a sense of sharp
contrast between the public appearance (which Rosenman himself had not
seriously questioned) and the reality of Roosevelt's post-election mood and
consequent mental processes.

The President spoke calmly and quietly, in conversational tones. Nevertheless there was that in his voice and manner which betrayed, to such as Rosenman, an unwonted inner tension. He had, he said, two documents he wished
to read aloud. One was a letter from the attorney general, with an appended
draft bill for reorganization of the federal judiciary—and he nodded toward
Cummings, who tapped and twirled the pince-nez in his hand but gave no
other sign of excitement. The second document was a special draft message to
be sent to Congress; the Cummings letter and proposed bill would be attached
to it. He began to read. And as he did so the aptness of the *Santee*–luncheon
comparison, and of the *Santee* as a metaphor applying to the substance of the
documents themselves, was borne in upon Rosenman. For of the thousand
words in Cummings's letter, the three thousand in the draft message to Congress, not one directly addressed or even implicitly recognized, frankly, the
central problem that was their obvious concern.

"Delay in the administration of justice is the outstanding defect in our
judicial system" began the letter. ". . . It is a mockery of justice to say to a
person when he files a suit that he may have a decision years later. . . . The
course of litigation should be measured in months and not in years." Judges
were increasingly burdened with work. The average caseload per federal judge
had "grown nearly fifty percent since 1913, when the District Courts were first
organized on their present basis," despite the fact that a "small number of
judges have been added from time to time." Obviously there must be more
federal judges, many more; and the cost of adding them "would result in a
hardly perceptible percentage increase in the total annual budget." Also, the
Chief Justice of the Supreme Court should be authorized to appoint a "func-
tionary . . . charged with the duty of continuously keeping informed as to the

---

*Q-boats were combat vessels disguised as ordinary merchantmen. Their guns were hidden behind
false hull sidings; they remained so while hostile submarines, suspecting nothing, surfaced and
approached. When the submarine was within point-blank range, the false siding dropped down
and the exposed guns blazed away.

state of federal judicial business throughout the United States and of assisting the Chief Justice in assigning judges to pressure areas." The draft message to Congress, with whose final drafting Rosenman now knew he would be concerned (obviously this was why he had been urged to attend this meeting), continued with no deviation the line projected by the letter. "Since the earliest days of the Republic, the problem of the personnel of the courts has needed the attention of the Congress," the President read. ". . . In almost every decade since 1789, changes have been made by the Congress whereby the numbers of judges and the duties of judges in the federal courts have been altered in one way or another. The Supreme Court was established with six members in 1789; it was reduced to five in 1801; it was increased to seven in 1807; it was increased to nine in 1837; it was increased to ten in 1863; it was reduced to seven in 1866; it was increased to nine in 1869." The "new need for legislative action" today arose "because the personnel of the Federal Judiciary is insufficient to meet the business before them"—and the message went on to stress, as the Cummings letter had done, crowded dockets, postponed trials, and justice denied by its long delay. "I attach a carefully considered draft of a proposed bill, which, if enacted, would, I am confident, afford substantial relief." Its proposals "do not raise any issue of constitutional law."

The President then read aloud, with interpolated commentary, the fifteen-hundred-word "draft of a proposed bill." The bulk of it, composed in typically densely qualified lawyers' prose, dealt with the expeditious handling of cases in the lower courts through employment of a proctor, and with devices for shifting judges from areas sparsely inhabited by pending cases to areas that were "congested."

But the controversial gist of it, ostensibly designed solely to increase judicial efficiency, was stated in its initial section. This provided that, whenever "any judge of a Court of the United States" had "attained the age of seventy years" and had not "resigned or retired" by the end of six months thereafter,* the President should "appoint one additional judge to the court to which the former is commissioned." Limits were set. No more than fifty new judges altogether could be appointed. No more than two additional members could be appointed "to a circuit court of appeals, the Court of Claims, the United States Court of Customs and Patent Appeals, or the Customs Court." The number of judges for any district or, "in the case of judges appointed for more than one district, any group of districts" could not be more than doubled. And the members of the Supreme Court could not number more than fifteen.[12]

The latter stipulation, applying to the highest tribunal, was of course all-revealing—was, indeed, to the initiate, a veritable blaze of light cast upon the most important but unstated reason for this entire transaction. The President would be enabled to appoint at once six new Supreme Court Justices if, of the

---

*Already in effect was a law guaranteeing a resigned justice full salary for life. Proposed and being considered by Congress was a law protecting a resigned justice from salary cuts and exempting him, as active justices then were, from income tax.

present justices aged seventy or more, none retired or resigned immediately. He could "pack the Court" with justices whose view of constitutional law was akin to his own.

The transparency of the disguise for this intention, along with the dubious morality of any such attempt to bemuse and deceive the public about important public business, disturbed not only Roosevelt's chief speech draftsman but also Stanley Reed and Donald Richberg. These latter two, like Rosenman, realized that the President had made up his mind to act, and act now, on the Court issue, and to act toward court enlargement. There was no point in their counseling further patience, further waiting, or in their attempting to change the proposal itself, even had they been of a mind to—and there is no evidence that they were. But Reed and Richberg could and did join Rosenman in questioning, gently, deferentially, the wisdom of the approach taken by letter and message. Was it likely to be persuasive of public opinion? How *could* the public become persuaded that the President's primary concern with the judiciary, which he had publicly castigated in the past for its "horse-and-buggy" decisions, had now all at once become its "inefficiency"? Would it not be better to state frankly the real reason for the proposed legislation? Surely this real reason, forcefully presented, would be persuasive enough. The popular will toward progressive government, the obvious crying need for such government, was being denied, as a studied policy, by aged justices who grounded their judicial acts, not in the explicit or implicit meanings of the Constitution, but in their personal conservative predilections.

The President, however, had no ear for such advice. With a wave of hand and nod of head he referred all critical questionings to his attorney general— and the tall, lean, bald, elderly Homer Cummings was fully prepared to defend the course he had helped devise. He was a Connecticut Yankee, shrewd and dry and spare, seemingly imperturbable; a Yale man who, virtually alone among those in his class in college, had been converted to the Democratic party by Bryan's silver-tongued oratory; a political animal if ever there was one; and he had a Yankee horse-trading bias toward the smart trick, the ingenious diversionary tactic, when engaged in adversary proceedings. Consistent with this bias was his bland refusal now to admit that any indirection was being practiced. He insisted that the situation was as his letter said it was. Federal judges were overburdened, those of the Supreme Court especially so, being wholly unable to keep abreast of their work. Why, in the last fiscal year, 867 petitions for review were presented to the highest tribunal, and of these only 150 were accepted for hearing! If government cases were excluded, the statistics showed 803 applications and 108 acceptances, which is to say that the Supreme Court had declined, "without even an explanation, to hear 87 percent of the cases presented to it by private litigants."[13] Other statistics showed that, year by year, the time span between the initiation and the conclusion of litigation grew longer. This was the central problem—and the solution of it (Cummings and the President exchanged delighted glances) had been suggested more than a quarter-century ago by none other than James C. McReynolds! Back in 1913, when McReynolds was attorney general in Wilson's Cabinet, he had "recommended . . . that when any federal judge, except justices of the Supreme Court, failed to avail himself of the privilege of retiring at the age [seventy] provided by law, the President should appoint another judge to preside over the affairs of the Court" jointly with the older man. "This will insure . . . the presence of a judge sufficiently active to discharge promptly and adequately all the duties of the Court," McReynolds had said.[14] The proposed bill simply extended this general recommendation to include the Supreme Court, where the need for it was demonstrably as great as in the lower courts. If such extension, in the process of solving the "efficiency" problem at which it was directly aimed, happened also to provide the means of obtaining more enlightened Supreme Court decisions, why, well and good! One need not tempt fate by calling attention to such lucky accidents.

Cummings twinkled. The President beamed.

Clearly this sly turning against himself of the implacably reactionary McReynolds was for these two a delicious joke, to be relished for its own sake. They "loved" it, as Roosevelt would have said, and perhaps enough to make it, for them, a decisive factor.

Which is to say that what most appalled Sam Rosenman in this chosen strategy—"the cleverness, the too much cleverness," as he later put it,[15] whereby Court conservatives would be made acutely aware of the personal contempt in which they were held by the President—was precisely what most appealed to Franklin Roosevelt. Rosenman might well wonder if the streak of vindictiveness that flawed Roosevelt's moral character, contradicting a generally prevailing kindness and generosity, might not have led Roosevelt to prefer the crooked and covert in this particular instance even had he been convinced, as he evidently was not, that the direct and open would be more efficacious and less risky. At any rate, further argument against it was obviously futile. At least for the time being. Rosenman, Reed, and Richberg soon desisted.

But when these same five men were again assembled in the Oval Room on the afternoon of Tuesday, February 2, the argument was resumed with a sharper, more probing definition.

By then the original draft message, which all agreed lacked "pep" and "punch," had been completely rewritten. Rosenman had done the job at the President's request, working in intensely concentrated snatches through a long and crowded weekend during which he also attended his first annual "Cuff Links Club" dinner, with the traditional stag poker session afterward (he had received his gold cuff links from the President after the 1936 election), then traveled to and from Philadelphia where he made, on Monday, a long-scheduled speech of his own. In his redrafting, he had brought forward the "delicate question of aged and infirm judges," stressing far more emphatically than the original draft had done the "natural conservatism" of the elderly as a factor in the present unhappy Court situation. (Indeed, the original draft had scarcely hinted at this notion.) "A lowered mental or physical vigor leads men to avoid the examination of complicated or changed conditions," said the new draft, to which Roosevelt had added touches of his own. "Little by little, new facts become blurred through glasses fitted, as it were, for the needs of another generation; older men, assuming that the scene is the same as in the past, cease to explore or inquire into the present or future. . . . A constant and systematic infusion of younger blood will vitalize the courts and better equip them to recognize and apply the essential concepts of justice in the light of the needs and facts of an ever-changing world." These sentences remained and others along the same line had been added when that Tuesday's long discussion-and-drafting session ended.

The revision, however, worked no improvement on the final product—had actually a contrary effect, overall—because Rosenman and Reed and Richberg wholly failed in their now quite determined effort to shift the basic strategy from one of indirection to one of direct frontal attack. The President, Rosenman would remember in a later year, "insisted on his chosen course."[16] And in the context thus so stubbornly retained, the new emphasis upon the infirmities of the aged simply pointed up the trickiness, the intent to deceive (with its implicit contempt for the general intelligence), that was of the essence of the strategy, while simultaneously offending the popular sense of fair play and human decency. It added further personal insult to the injury which, if designed for the four conservative stalwarts of the Court, was equally inflicted upon the great liberal Brandeis and the intermittently liberal Hughes.

Nor was Roosevelt's deviousness limited in this case to the Court proposal per se, as Rosenman discovered when the afternoon session ended.

The chronic general enmity between Cummings and the liberal intellectuals of Roosevelt's inner circle had in the last weeks become specific and acute between Cummings and Tom Corcoran. Despite the President's strong hint in his annual message that the Constitution as it now stood was in his view wholly adequate to the national need, if only it were properly interpreted by the judiciary, Corcoran and Ben Cohen continued to believe that the President was inclined to favor, among proposed solutions to the Court problem, a constitutional amendment. They had, in fact, nearly completed by February 2 a lengthy memorandum recommending an amendment that would, first, permit Congress to override by a two-thirds majority any Supreme Court decision on federal legislation immediately after such decision was rendered, or to do so by simple majority after an intervening election; and second, enable Congress to validate state legislation that the Court had rejected. They planned to attach to the memorandum a draft presidential speech tacitly warning the Court that a drastic curtailment of its power was in the offing but might yet be avoided if it reversed the trend of its legislative decisions and refrained from further violations of territory properly belonging to the legislative branch.[17] At some point in these labors, Corcoran had come against Cummings in head-on collision. There had ensued a particularly angry quarrel. Roosevelt knew of it—knew that Cummings and Corcoran could not now work together on any matter, certainly not that of Court reform. And since he had made up his mind in early January to adopt the strategy Cummings proposed, and had good reason to believe Corcoran might strenuously oppose this strategy for objective reasons as well as for subjective (anti-Cummings feeling) ones, he had assured the attorney general, probably at the latter's behest, that Corcoran would be permitted no part whatever in the preparation of the special message—would, indeed, be denied all knowledge of its contents until it was delivered.

So when Rosenman on this Tuesday afternoon, after the others had left the Oval Room, asked if he might talk over the draft message with Corcoran (this of course meant that Cohen, too, would be involved), Roosevelt at first said no. Not until Rosenman had pressed quite hard for permission was it granted, and then in highly ambiguous and qualified form. *If* Tommy were consulted, said the President, Cummings must never learn of it. Whereupon, probably within the hour, the consultation took place—and it was then a felt necessity on Rosenman's part not only to impress upon Corcoran (and Cohen) the imperative importance of keeping the consultation secret from the attorney general but also to say frankly why the President insisted upon it. Corcoran was in no way shocked, or even surprised: ". . . Like me, he had grown used to this weakness of the President," explained Rosenman in a later year.[18]

IV

YET Corcoran and Cohen were shocked by the message's substance and, even more, by the way in which this whole business was being managed.

Cohen was especially shocked. He had no such passion for active, overt participation in great events as Corcoran had, no such love of interpersonal excitements. Quite the contrary. He also differed in basic intellectual attitude from his friend. To some indeterminate degree, Cohen was philosophically an idealist, concerned with general ideas and committed to the idealist's consistency test of truth, whereas Corcoran, despite a reverence for the great teacher of his Brown undergraduate days, idealist Alexander Meiklejohn, was wholly a pragmatist, an operator who, focusing on concrete particular facts, identified truth with immediate practicality. By every test of consistency, the Cummings-Roosevelt judicial-reform proposal seemed to Cohen false. It failed equally the pragmatic test. Which is to say it made no sense either as "practical idealism" or "idealistic practicality," to employ the fusion terminology of Roosevelt's second inaugural—though Cohen would, of course, do his best to make sense of it if Corcoran was enlisted as chief administration lobbyist on its behalf.[19]

He and his great friend, a year and more ago, had themselves pondered a court-packing scheme and tried it out as a tentative proposal on people whose judgment they valued. They discovered that court-packing was the one proposal, of all those that had been suggested, that virtually everyone found unacceptable.* Most of the opposition to it, moreover, was of a peculiarly profound and stubborn nature.

Millions had been dismayed by the Court's NRA decision, no doubt of that. Farmers and farm leaders were enraged by the AAA decision. Workers and labor leaders were infuriated by the Guffey Coal and Railroad Pension Act decisions. Almost everyone found the *Tipaldo* decision outrageous. But the general anger thus aroused was focused on individual decisions, along with the trend they indicated, and upon individual present members of the Court, not upon the Court as an institution. (Hamilton Fish, for instance, in the very statement in which he expressed "shock" at the *Tipaldo* decision, insisted: "I am not criticizing the Supreme Court.") Even among the most politically sophisticated and historically knowledgeable, the Supreme Court in its present institutional form and general role as independent arm of government, immune from direct coercive pressures exerted by other arms, continued to be regarded by many as absolutely essential to the peaceable and orderly ongoingness of the national enterprise. It was deemed part and parcel of the national permanence that is the substance of national change. Any proposal to weaken it in its relations with the other federal branches was adjudged literally subversive of the Republic, striking at the very foundations of American democracy and weakening its defenses against dictatorship. As for the multitude, though they were by no means as blindly worshipful of the Constitution as the Liberty League's founders had assumed them to be,† a large majority yet viewed the Court, for all the unpopularity of its individual decisions, as a sacred and patriotic symbol, akin to cross and flag, and as a national and "holy" patriarchical institution, to be venerated in somewhat the same way as the British people reverenced the monarchy. In the multitude's evident thought and feeling, Court-and-Constitution provided the ground and reference frame for all citizenship—the very means of their own self-identification as American citizens insofar as identity is a defined place, a specific location, in a generally recognized and permanent scheme of things. ("Attacks upon the dignity of the Court are secret threats of alienation, as they attack whatever insignia of 'reasonableness' our ailing economic structure is still felt to possess," Kenneth Burke would be writing in the spring of 1937.[21] "The Court is a 'vessel,' a 'psychological investment' in which even the victims of its decisions share, being 'stockholders' by identification with its insignia. And scrupulous people, prone to such naive but profound responses, can agree with the President's proposals [for Court reform] only insofar as their anguish or their impatience makes them willing to adopt somewhat the role of 'symbolic parricides.' ")

*In late 1935 or early 1936 they had gone so far as to draft a speech making this proposal and tried in vain to persuade Senator Burton K. Wheeler to deliver it. The vehemence of Wheeler's refusal had been a major factor in Corcoran's decision to abandon the court-packing approach, though Wheeler did not know such a decision had been made.[20]

†See *FDR: The New Deal Years,* p. 400.

All of which had led Corcoran and Cohen to conclude that, though the Supreme Court was assuredly not "beyond criticism," was not "to be regarded as too sacred to be disagreed with" (the quotes are from a rhetorical question asked by Senator Barkley during his 1936 Democratic National Convention keynote address), the administration must be very careful to avoid even the appearance of attempting to destroy the Court's dignity, or to strip it wholly of its self-assumed power to review legislation, or to alter in any important way the historic power balance among the judiciary, the legislature, the executive. Court-packing *would* alter this balance. Not only would it render the judiciary subordinate to the executive in the immediate situation, it would also establish a precedent—for none of the earlier enlargements or contractions of the Court had been obviously deliberately designed to influence Court decisions. Court-packing, therefore, after a few months of covert exploration and trial-ballooning, had been abandoned by Corcoran and Cohen as a scheme impractical, impolitic, and, in long-term effect (if Congress sanctioned it), possibly seriously injurious to the nation.[22]

How could the President have failed to do the same? Franklin Roosevelt was certainly himself a traditionalist, normally instinctively resistant to any proposal for truly radical change; one would have expected him not only to sense and measure the general mood but also to share it in considerable degree. More amazing still, having arrived at this contrary decision, how could he, the master politician of his age, now choose to implement it in the tricky, "smarty" manner Homer Cummings had devised? It would be hard to conceive a strategy more inimical to the achievement of its object, the circumstances being as they were.

Cohen could only conclude, as has been said, that Roosevelt's overwhelming election victory had "gone to his head" disastrously.

V

But if one accepts as true the charge that Roosevelt was now corrupted by a heady sense of limitless power, one must give to "corruption," in this context, a rather special and subtle definition. So it would appear, at any rate, to one later historian.

Certainly, on this evidence, what happened in the feeling and thought of Franklin Roosevelt in the autumn and early winter of 1936 was very different from the corruption-by-power that Woodrow Wilson manifested in the autumn and winter of 1918–1919; there was in Roosevelt virtually none of the messianic egotism that led Wilson into his disastrous error of the 1918 elections and the tragic wrongheadedness of his later operations at Versailles.* One finds more similarity between this Rooseveltian decision-making and that of Stephen A. Douglas in the late summer and autumn of 1853, when the Little

---

*See *FDR: The Beckoning of Destiny,* pp. 503–10, 533–45, 553–59, 562–67.

Giant, "corrupted" by a compound of power and ambition for power, made his catastrophic miscalculations about slavery in the territories and wrote repeal of the Missouri Compromise into the Kansas-Nebraska Bill. Yet between these two, also, the difference is great. It is a difference proportionate to that between Roosevelt's faith in God and Douglas's in natural law. The faith that Douglas reposed in the political efficacy of "isothermal lines"—his oft-expressed belief that climatic factors, not men's moral choices, would ultimately decide the territorial slavery question—was utterly devoid of awe and contained no sense whatever of personal responsibility for the consequences of the "decision" so rendered. Roosevelt's faith, on the other hand, was truly religious—it was very deeply felt, despite (or because of) its simplistic character—and it contained elements of free will that imposed upon him an acute if limited sense of individual moral responsibility: It was his fault, self-recognized and productive of guilt feelings, when he missed a cue or failed to read aright the lines written for him by the Cosmic Author. If in this case he disastrously failed to heed what he himself tacitly admitted in retrospect were clear signs and portents, it is instructive to review analytically, as the evidence enables us to do, the process of his error. Doing so may enable us to understand the nature and assess the magnitude of his "corruption."

By election day 1936 he had acquired from a wide variety of sources, including Corcoran's report on the Corcoran-Cohen explorations described above, an abundance of information warning him against the proposal and strategy he ultimately embraced. The voluminous file of speech material kept for him in his personal office, a file to which he himself made frequent contributions, and the relevant portions of which he reviewed whenever a major speech impended, contained several items that defined with clarity the nature of the dangers he now faced. For instance (particularly apropos, in agreement with the above parenthetically quoted statement by Kenneth Burke), there was an article by historian Charles A. Beard entitled "Corporations and Natural Rights," published in the summer 1936 issue of the *Virginia Quarterly Review*. It had come to Roosevelt in tear sheets from his mother, who, at her summer home on Campobello, had been sent it by her friend William Tobias Butler;[23] it began by saying that "in every age, in every society" were two opposing groups of people who, within their groups, were "more or less closely united" and had "a realistic view of affairs and politics." These people, a distinct minority of the whole, possessed wide knowledge derived in good part from wit-sharpening experience. "They know what they want. They are acquainted with ways and means calculated to attain their objectives." But between these two relatively small groups, said Beard, were "the great mass of people" whose energies were almost wholly absorbed by the tasks of daily life. "They have little knowledge of society. They have hazy ideas about the world and its work. They read little. Their experience is limited." Only in times of domestic or foreign crisis did they become agitated or "deeply stirred about anything outside the daily grind"; and in such times *"they are likely to be swept one way* *or another by signs, symbols, myths, and slogans.* "* Even in crisis times, there-fore, in any competition for mass popular support, conservatives defending the status quo were likely to hold a large initial advantage over those proposing new departures: They could appropriate, and manipulate as their own, sym-bolic materials in which the masses had, as Kenneth Burke would say, a large emotional (or spiritual) investment. The whole of the American Liberty League's propaganda campaign had been designed to capitalize on this fact—and Roosevelt knew well that this was so. It was to the Liberty League's psychological strategy that he had referred when, during the election cam-paign, he spoke contemptuously of the deceitful use "economic royalists" made of "the flag and the Constitution."

But the force of the warning given Roosevelt by such items as these was greatly diminished by the fact that the American Liberty League had failed of its objectives. Its massive propaganda campaign, aimed at whipping the public into a frenzy of "worshipful" defensive feeling for Court and Constitu-tion, had fallen flat. Indeed, the most (if not only) important effect of the entire effort would seem to have been the influence it exerted upon Roosevelt himself; for it had been one of the factors causing him to shy away from the Court as a major campaign issue, though many had urged this issue upon him, last summer and fall. He had then accepted as probably accurate campaign man-ager Farley's assessment of the current lack of interest in or understanding of the problem of Court-and-Constitution, a public indifference that Farley had used as an argument against campaign use of the question,[24] and that Roosevelt himself had tested with a trial-balloon article, based on an interview with him, by George Creel in *Collier's* magazine.† But would this manifest lack of popular interest have continued if he, accepting the Liberty League's chal-lenge, had campaigned on the Court issue? His doing so would have enabled the league to bring its massive propaganda resources into concentrated focus upon him as enemy of Flag, Court, Constitution. The result might have been a drastic narrowing of the wide victory margin he then anticipated, and this, he had decided, was a risk that outweighed the merely probable gain of a clear, definite mandate to move directly and forcefully against the Court's intransi-gence. His characteristic conclusion had been to "let sleeping dogs lie" while he took care of "first things first," the absolutely first and most necessary thing being his reelection by the largest possible majority.

The event seemed to him to justify his conclusion.

For if he now had no explicit, sharply defined mandate to act upon the Court problem, his election triumph had surely given him, implicitly, a mandate to move in *some* effective way upon it. After all, he reminded himself, and said to Arthur Krock of *The New York Times* in an interview published on Febru-ary 28, he had had no explicit popular mandate to do what he had done

---

*Italics added.
†See *FDR: The New Deal Years,* pp. 605, 632–33.

immediately after taking office in his first term. At that time he had (to quote
Krock) "found it necessary . . . to divert the course plotted by the party
platform on which he was elected because of a change in conditions between
June 1932 and March 1933. And this diversion had been stressed by the Republicans as an issue in the congressional elections of 1934." Responding to this,
"Democratic candidates for Congress offered the President himself as the only
issue," wrote Krock. " 'Shall Franklin D. Roosevelt's course thus far be approved and he be given a congressional majority to proceed with the New
Deal?' was the question as the people went to the polls in 1934. . . . The answer
was overwhelmingly in the affirmative. In 1936 the President's diversion was
again made an issue by the Republicans, who also pointed out that, if reelected,
he would probably have several new appointments to the Supreme Court.
. . . Whether or not the voters troubled themselves much on that point the
President does not know. But he does know that once again his course was
given high majority approval."

And the mandate was not only popular, it was also, in his own perception,
divine.

He was brought closer than ever before to an actual identification of himself
with the power he wielded as God's chosen instrument. For obviously God
approved almost unmitigatedly his past performance of his presidential role,
and now meant him to act even more boldly and *individualistically* than ever
before the great part that had been assigned him. The felt need to pay close
heed to outward signs and portents, to pray for guidance from on high including the "prayerfulness" of his teleological gambling, and to seek advice and
counsel before taking action—the felt need to do this was replaced to an
unprecedented degree (never wholly) by a belief that he need now consult, as
the internalization of God's will, only his own deepest desire, his own pro-
foundest wish and purpose and emotion. Encouraged thus was an inclination
to regard as, in essence, a divine wrath the anger aroused in him by the harsh
ingratitude, the insulting antagonism, the implacable selfishness of the business
community.

It was in this mood—it was with this unprecedented degree of self-identification with the power in his hands—that he, upon his return to Washington
from South America in mid-December, addressed himself directly, almost
exclusively, to the Court problem as, for the moment, his supreme concern.

The constitutional-amendment idea, which had in fact not been high on his
list of possible choices for a long time, was now once and for all rejected. "I
knew how long it would take to get the approval of thirty-six states," he later
explained. "I had seen the long year-after-year ordeal of the proposed child-
labor amendment, which involved opposition which was picayune in comparison with the entrenched antagonism to the new social program. No! It would
take years and years to get a constitutional amendment which would meet our
difficulties. Time was too pressing for that."[25] And this same pressure of time
militated against the option of waiting quietly for God and nature to operate
upon the Court while he himself did nothing at all save retain and, so far as

possible, increase the present mobilization of public opinion against the current trend of Court decisions. It might be "years and years" before aged reactionaries died or resigned; and Roosevelt, unlike many sophisticated observers, saw no likelihood that Roberts would shift to the liberal wing when voting on the crucial cases now pending. (Looming large in Roosevelt's mind were Roberts's Railroad Retirement Act vote, his majority opinion on AAA, his concurrence in Butler's incredible *Tipaldo* opinion. As has been said,* he had not noticed [neither had Cummings, who should certainly have done so] the appearance upon the Supreme Court docket, in October 1934, of *West Coast Hotel Co.* v. *Parrish.*)

Similarly swiftly discarded were bills proposing that Supreme Court decisions rendering unconstitutional acts of Congress or (in some cases) of state legislatures must be unanimous. Or must be 8–1. Or 7–2. What was to prevent the present Court from declaring this very legislation unconstitutional? And if it did, what could Congress or executive do about it? The problem, in Roosevelt's mind, always resolved itself into one of the present Court personnel. They it was whose tortured interpretations of the Constitution forced the organic law into the service of special interests while denying to government the possibility of progressive action. And always Roosevelt came back to the enlargement of the Court, enabling him to appoint new justices, as the problem's only true solution. The idea had been long in his mind. Back in November 1935, talking of the Court while lunching with Harold Ickes, he had "recalled that when Lloyd George came to power . . . under Edward VII, he went to the King and asked his consent to announce that if the [House of] Lords refused again to accept the bill for Irish autonomy, which had been pressed upon them several times since the days of Gladstone, he would create several hundred new peers, enough to out-vote the existing House of Lords."[26]†

Yet he still shied away from attempting Court enlargement "outright." His later published reason was that "outright" court-packing "would have been an expedient to correct the Court of 1937 only" whereas he was in quest of a permanent "correction."[27] Clearly he also had another reason: He continued to fear the popular outcry that, with abundant encouragement from the right, might ensue if he did frankly declare his intention to enlarge the Court in order to change the tenor of its decisions. At the same time, in seeming contradiction to this fear, he assumed a continuing lack of informed public interest in the problem—a popular ignorance and indifference probably sufficient, when conjoined with his own immense popular prestige, to make effective with the general public even a thin disguise of his purpose.

*See p. 12.

†Lloyd George never "came to power" as prime minister under Edward VII. He became prime minister in 1916, under George V. It was Prime Minister Asquith who, having obtained the king's consent, threatened to pack the House of Lords with new royal appointees (new titles) if the Lords continued to block, not "Irish autonomy," but a parliamentary-reform measure that would reduce their veto power over the House of Commons. In this, Asquith followed a precedent set during the great Reform Bill struggle in 1832, when the House of Lords was brought to passage of the bill only by the threat of a royal creation of new peers.

Thus the balance of factors presented to his judgment was very close at this point. He must carefully weigh his fear against his assumption. And elementary prudence required that he test the validity of the latter, by whatever means he could devise, before he made his absolutely final decision.

So it was that, a day or so after his return from South America, he arranged to launch another trial balloon via a *Collier's* article. He summoned George Creel to the Oval Office for an exclusive interview. He was abandoning the amendment approach, he said for publication. Instead he was concentrating upon the Supreme Court's own patent violation of the Constitution as it then stood, through usurpation of legislative powers assigned Congress by the organic document. He proposed that Congress reclaim its just powers in the coming session by attaching to every major piece of social legislation "a rider *charging* the Supreme Court to bear in mind that the law was enacted pursuant of the Constitutional provision vesting *all* legislative power in Congress, and explicitly authorizing it 'to provide for the general welfare of the United States.' " What if the Supreme Court ignored the charge? " 'Then,' said the President, his face like a fist, 'Congress can *enlarge* the Supreme Court, increasing the number of justices so as to permit the appointment of men in tune with the spirit of the age." This was a much more drastic proposal, of much greater immediate impact, than that of a proposed amendment, and Creel fully expected it to produce an explosion of controversy immediately upon its publication in the December 26 issue. It didn't. "Incredibly . . . ," Creel later wrote, "not a newspaper in the country" so much as commented on the crucial statement, "although dealing at length with other things in the article."[28]

Hence Roosevelt's final acceptance, a few days later, of Cummings's intricate plan to solve the Supreme Court problem, as if incidentally, within a general judicial-reform bill applying to the lower federal courts also—and solve it, moreover, not for "1937 only," but in a way that "provided for a continuous and recurrent addition of new blood, new vigor, new experience, and a new outlook."[29] As for the decision he now made regarding strategy, nothing else is so revealing of his basic mind-set, along with his calculation of the relative weights of opposing pressures.

Almost always he had sought the advice of a great number of people of widely varying views in the process of strategical as well as substantive decision-making about legislative proposals that were bound to provoke major controversy. He had consulted people outside government as well as in it, had carefully reconnoitered and prepared the ground across which legislative attacks must be made, and had involved in this preparation, to the greatest possible degree, those House and Senate leaders who must fight for his proposals in Congress.* This time, having directly consulted no one save Cummings while deciding the substance of his proposal, he asked none for advice as to the way in which the proposal should be presented or about the strategy to

---

*Perhaps the single most notable exception to this general rule had been his handling of the wealth-tax legislation of 1935. See *FDR: The New Deal Years,* pp. 542–48.

be employed in the legislative war for its enactment. Indeed, as we have seen, having been forced by the necessity of message preparation to enlarge by three the number of people who definitely knew what he planned to do, he not only rejected almost cavalierly the critical strategical advice offered by these three but also insisted upon a continuation of the most extreme secretiveness regarding the whole enterprise. He wanted to achieve the greatest possible surprise, the highest degree of dramatic impact, when he sprang his proposal upon Congress and public.

And this, considering how difficult and prolonged had been the process of decision, and how narrow had been his final choice among alternatives, indicates a confidence in the soundness of his judgment in this matter that is astounding. Normally, whenever he proposed a major new departure, one that made an important change in long-established institutions or ways of doing things, and of whose popular acceptance he was uncertain, his procedure was to minimize in his public presentation the amount of change to be made. He strove to reduce the shock of recognized novelty, or to prevent it altogether. He described his proposal as a perfectly simple and obvious extension or complement of the old ways, the old institutions—something Everyman was bound to see as necessary when it was pointed out to him, if he had not already done so. ("You and I know . . ." he would say, in cozy intimacy, in a fireside chat.) When, however, he proposed something of whose ultimate popular support he was absolutely sure, his habit was to present it with a flourish, as dramatically as he could, maximizing in imagery a change or novelty that might be, in sober fact, of relatively little consequence. Clearly, then, he was absolutely confident of the outcome of the presently impending battle. His chief enemies would, of course, see at once through the thin disguise of his intention—would rant and rave about it, their angry voices hugely amplified by the mass-communications facilities they controlled. But the people at large would discount such fulminations by considering them in terms of their discredited source. They would believe him, not them. And the net result of all the sound and fury would be to point up the heroism of his battle against entrenched greed, to enhance the glory of his ultimate triumph, and to strengthen his hand in future dealings with the conservative wing of his own party.

This last was an important consideration.

He well knew—his long experience of Georgia confirmed—that in no other region were the Constitution and the Supreme Court so revered as in the South; it was a traditional piety born of the fact that, for generations, Court-and-Constitution had been the bulwark of the South's Peculiar Institution, protecting it against the moral outrage, or any effective political implementation of the outrage, that it aroused in its opponents. (By that same token, one must add, the South's view of the Constitution as a sacred document was, in 1937, highly qualified; emphatically excluded from it were the Fifteenth Amendment and the whole of the Fourteenth save the "due process" clause of section 1 as applied to property.[30]) Roosevelt's chosen strategy would place such piety in jeopardy; his victory would greatly weaken it as a basis of conservative opposition to his programs. Those Southern Democrats whose natural inclination was to vote with the Republicans, negatively, whenever a piece of progressive legislation was presented to them would be cowed and forced into conformity with the New Deal.

Yes, he was sure of the outcome.

Yet *was* he, absolutely?

## VI

ON the night of Tuesday, February 2, 1937, there was a ceremony at the White House that would soon seem, in the eyes of some observers, akin to the Duchess of Richmond's famous ball on the night before Waterloo. (Actually it "topped the duchess' celebrated rout," according to Joseph Alsop and Turner Catledge,[31] "by being given on the eve of a great battle by the commander of one side for the members of the other.") The occasion was the annual Judiciary Dinner, presided over by President and First Lady in the East Room, honoring the justices of the Supreme Court. As always, it was a large affair, with a guest list of nearly ninety. As always, it was attended by several persons who, having nothing to do with current affairs, were themselves historical. (Mrs. Woodrow Wilson was there.) And, as it had been every year since Roosevelt's first inaugural, it was remarkably free of a stiff and stifling formality, being characterized instead by much spontaneous good talk and great good humor. Each of the seven justices who came,* save only the chronically morose, taciturn, suspicious McReynolds, seemed thoroughly to enjoy himself; and it was noted that the Jovian Chief Justice was in his most ostentatiously jovial mood. Nevertheless, there was tension, a tension that heightened significances. Everyone had a sense of submerged conflict, of dissembled hostility, when, following the retirement of the ladies after dinner, Van Devanter moved up to sit beside Roosevelt at the head of the dining table and there joined the President and Chief Justice in bantering exchanges.

Among four who observed this—Reed, Richberg, Cummings, Rosenman, all of whom had accepted invitations because they were to spend the morrow with the President, putting the special message into final shape—among these four the tension was acute. They cast upon one another, from time to time, glances heavily weighted by their shared secret. Upon the subject uppermost in their minds they occasionally communicated with one another in whispers. (Cummings, in one such interchange, confessed to Rosenman that he was decidedly "uncomfortable," feeling "too much like a conspirator.") Nor was Roosevelt himself, for all his show of relaxed affability, basically at ease. He had revealed as much, to Rosenman at least, while Eleanor greeted the other

---

*Louis Brandeis was absent; he seldom attended ceremonial functions of any kind, almost never at night; he had not attended the inaugural two weeks before. Harlan F. Stone was also absent, recuperating from a nearly fatal illness that had laid him low the previous mid-October.

arriving guests in the West Hall just prior to the dinner. He served cocktails in his study to a handful of intimates that included his fellow "conspirators." An almost unprecedented post-decision anxiety was indicated by his saying "several times," in almost precisely the same words, that he simply had to act now on the Court problem. Further postponement was impossible: "Unpleasant as it is, I think we have to face it."[32]

And this unease continued all through the next day. Having taken elaborate precautions against any last-moment leak (the maintenance of secrecy seems to have been, at that point, his chief concern), he labored with the others most of the day upon the message's final draft. By the evening of that Wednesday, February 3, the labor was done, with only a few "judicial statistics" remaining to be checked. Rosenman prepared to entrain for New York. But as he did so, Missy LeHand came to him with a personal plea that he not go. Not yet. The President, she said, was "terribly nervous about this message"; she was sure it would be "helpful and comforting to him" if Rosenman would stay over in the White House "until the thing [the message] is finally . . . put to bed" (that is, sent to the mimeographing room).[33]

So Rosenman was still at hand when the President, late in the following afternoon, ordered the White House staff to report for duty at the unheard-of hour of six-thirty next morning (hundreds of copies of message, letter, and bill must be duplicated within three hours or so); told Steve Early to set up a special late-morning press conference (ordinarily he met with the press on Tuesdays and Fridays); and instructed Marvin McIntyre to phone Vice President Garner and all Cabinet members who were in town,* requesting their presence in the Cabinet room promptly at ten o'clock next morning to deal with a "confidential matter." What the "matter" was he did not say to Mac even then, though from the presidential appointments secretary he normally kept no official secrets whose public exposure immediately impended. Rosenman could see that Mac's natural surprise and curiosity were increased when Roosevelt told him to invite also to this special Cabinet meeting the chairmen of the House and Senate judiciary committees, Representative Hatton Sumners of Texas and Senator Henry Ashurst of Arizona; the speaker of the House, Congressman William Bankhead of Alabama; and the House and Senate majority leaders, Congressman Sam Rayburn of Texas and Senator Joseph Robinson of Arkansas. "By that time the President seemed quite confident," Rosenman would remember.[34]

And certainly he made a great show of confidence—in the correctness of his procedure, in the certainty of its success—when he was wheeled into the Cabinet room at ten o'clock next morning, followed by a secretary who placed before each of those assembled there the three documents (message, letter, bill) that, barely two hours hence, were to be delivered to Congress. He was in a great hurry, he said; there'd be no time for questions or comments; he was to

---

*Both Secretary of State Cordell Hull and Secretary of the Treasury Henry Morgenthau, Jr., were away from Washington.

meet his press conference in just a few minutes. He therefore confined himself
to a brief explanation of what the documents were, read a few key sentences
from the message aloud, rather perfunctorily, asked that nothing be said of
what had been heard until it became public knowledge; asked, too, that all
documents be left on the table when his auditors departed; and then had
himself wheeled from Cabinet Room to Oval Office seemingly utterly incurious
as to the effect his carefully contrived "bombshell" was having upon responsible colleagues who must make personal and career decisions concerning it.[35]

Far different in tone and temper was his press conference, one of the longest
he had yet conducted. And he did conduct it, like a maestro who, reading a
score, strives for maximum dramatic impact invested with ironic humor. To
the assembled reporters he read virtually the whole of the attorney general's
letter and the message itself, with explanatory interpolations, stressing the
"simple fact," as Cummings had written, ". . . that . . . the personnel of the
Federal Judiciary is insufficient to meet the business before them." He cited
in evidence the "tremendously important fact" that, during "the last fiscal
year," the Supreme Court had "declined without an opinion even to hear" 717
of the 867 petitions for review that were presented to it. Hence the clear
necessity for increasing the number of judges, including the number on the
Supreme Court. He gave no other reason. Yet he permitted sly innuendo to
suggest, no doubt with some thrill of risk-taking, his real and deeper purpose.
For instance, when he read from the message how, during the first several
decades of the Republic, justices of the Supreme Court were required "to 'ride
Circuit' and . . . hold trials throughout the length and breadth of the land,"
he looked up from the paper to explain "that riding Circuit in those days meant
riding on horseback." "It might be called a pre–horse and buggy era," said he
to the reporters, who roared with laughter at this reminder of his exasperation
with the present Supreme Court personnel. "That is not in the message," he
added, with mock solemnity, provoking more laughter. He also placed dramatic emphasis upon the "fact" that the "solution to the problem" had been
originally suggested, in part, by James C. McReynolds—the suggestion that
the bill now embodied. He did this deadpan, in a seemingly offhand manner.
Yet he clearly wanted and expected the reporters to share with him the
deliciousness of this rare joke. Indeed, to at least two of the correspondents
present, he seemed throughout the conference "to be asking . . . the newspaper-
men to applaud the perfections of his scheme, to note its nicely calculated
indirections. . . ."[36] When his lengthy presentation was at last completed he,
in sharp contrast with his Cabinet Room behavior, invited and answered, or
adroitly parried, several questions.

By that time it was near noon of Friday, February 5, 1937. The President's
message with attachments had arrived, was actually physically present, on
Capitol Hill. Soon copies were on the desks of all senators, all representatives,
and the message was being read aloud, not only to Congress, but through radio
to millions across the land, for microphones had been hastily assembled upon

the rostrum in the last hour of the morning—a first hint to most members of Congress that an event of special import impended.

Thus was the "bombshell" exploded.

VII

THE immediate effects, in sum, justified Roosevelt's confidence in ultimate victory—though there were unpleasant surprises.

Judging from the reports of his Capitol henchmen and from what he read in the papers that evening and heard over the radio, things in general went pretty much as anticipated. There were the expected snarls and wails of doom from Republicans. There were the equally expected public expressions of opposition from conservative Democrats, including the two Virginia senators, Carter Glass and Harry F. Byrd. There was no surprise, if no pleasure either, in the strong opposition that Justice Brandeis privately expressed to Tommy Corcoran when Corcoran, as Roosevelt's personal emissary, told him of the message shortly before it was delivered.[37] The immediate public expression of disapproval by George Norris ("I am not in sympathy with the plan to enlarge the Supreme Court") was, however, unexpected; and so was the expression of disapproval, privately made, by Texas's Hatton Sumners, whose chairmanship of the House Judiciary Committee made him of special importance in the upcoming struggle. These responses were disturbing to Roosevelt, being viewed by him as disaffections. They were not, however, actually alarming. Their practical effects were mitigable. Brandeis's position on the Court made impossible any active open opposition on his part; Norris, immediately summoned to the White House for a private talk with the President, could surely be persuaded that "court enlargement" was the only feasible scheme (none other, save actual amendment, was clearly and uncontestably constitutional);* and Sumners had already promised White House representatives that he would make no public statement of opposition for the time being, which is to say he remained in a position, if he was not in fact prepared, to change his mind. Meanwhile, both Senate Majority Leader Robinson and House Speaker Bankhead had publicly approved the bill, predicting that it would pass easily after what might become a prolonged debate. Glass, too, was certain of the bill's passage, wrathfully so, his wrath increased by his doubt that there would even be much debate over it. "Of course . . . I shall oppose it with all the strength

---

*In the event, Norris, who in a March 1936 letter to Felix Frankfurter had hoped Roosevelt would make "the judicial question" a major campaign issue, remained unpersuaded that Court enlargement was the best possible, or even a viable, scheme; but he did agree that immediate action was called for and, since this was the way chosen (the executive commitment having been made), he "went along" with it or, at any rate, did nothing active against it. In late April, he was quoted in a United Press dispatch as saying that he "saw no merit" in the President's plan. In June he did vehemently defend the President personally against charges by opponents of the court bill that he, Roosevelt, "wants to be a dictator, that he is ruthless, hard-hearted, corrupt, ignorant, and sometimes insane."[38]

that remains to me," he said when a Washington correspondent interviewed him, by phone, in his Lynchburg home, "but I don't imagine for a minute that it will do any good. Why, if the President asked Congress to commit suicide tomorrow they'd do it."[39]

Glass's assumption that the bill must certainly pass was generally shared by news reports bearing the bylines of politically astute reporters in the papers Roosevelt read, over coffee and cereal upon his breakfast tray, in bed next morning. *The New York Times* for Saturday, February 6, had on its front page a five-column headline summarizing the conclusion reached, upon adduced evidence, by Arthur Krock, chief of the paper's Washington bureau. Krock was certainly no friend of the New Deal. He could be counted upon, in Roosevelt's view, to discredit and discomfit the President to the maximum possible extent in whatever he wrote. Yet he virtually took for granted the President's victory in this instance, as the banner headline indicated:

ROOSEVELT ASKS POWER TO REFORM COURTS,
INCREASING THE SUPREME BENCH TO 15 MEMBERS:
CONGRESS STARTLED, BUT EXPECTED TO APPROVE

Roosevelt could even read, on these same front pages, speculation as to whom he would appoint as "his" new justices, under the new law. Prominently mentioned were James M. Landis, soon to resign his chairmanship of the Securities and Exchange Commission to become dean of the Harvard Law School; Felix Frankfurter, "close friend and influential adviser of the President"; Lloyd Garrison, dean of the law school at the University of Wisconsin; senators Wagner and Ashurst; and Hatton Sumners, whose mention in this connection just *might* help change his mind. Joseph T. Robinson was not mentioned, though it was well known among his congressional colleagues that his highest ambition was to become a Supreme Court justice and that, in fact, he had received positive assurance from the White House two years ago, via Jim Farley, that he would be appointed to fill the first vacancy to occur. Most news commentators deemed Robinson an impossible appointment for a President who wished to "liberalize" court decisions, for Robinson, though he had served the New Deal well out of party loyalty, was notably conservative in his economics and actually reactionary with regard to civil rights.

In general, the initial response was highly satisfactory, even gratifying. But Roosevelt's pleasure in what he read that morning, and on those immediately following, was by no means unalloyed. There was increasing reason to believe, from what he read, that the premonitory "nervousness" he had revealed to Missy and Rosenman might prove to have been justified after all—some sense that he may have "made . . . a major mistake" when, rejecting all warnings, he persisted in the strategy Cummings had devised.

"Congress instantly recognized the outstanding feature and purpose" of the proposed legislation, said the Krock story, which went on to hint at resentments and fears aroused by the President's refusal to state his purpose frankly, openly. The *Times* and every other paper prominently displayed Herbert Hoover's statement, released within an hour or so after the message's delivery, that the President's "real aim" was "to pack the Court." The sinister nature of this aim, whose achievement would destroy the foundations of the Republic, was emphasized by the manner in which Roosevelt had sought to disguise it. The manner, said Hoover, evinced the President's contempt for free institutions, and for the popular intelligence upon which such institutions depend; evinced also his personal power-lust, his dictatorial tendencies in a time when totalitarianism rose in flood tide over Europe and the Far East. Similar views were expressed by other conservative leaders. They were echoed and re-echoed on most of the nation's editorial pages.

Normally, Roosevelt gave slight weight to newspaper editorials as policy-deciding factors. In general, they represented, to his mind, no considered, objective judgment of public issues: Their so-called ideas were simply the businessman-publisher's perceived (often falsely perceived) pocketbook interests traveling in verbal disguise; and certainly they had a negligible influence upon public opinion. In the present instance, however, he had to be impressed by the unanimity with which editorialists agreed that his was a very bad way, if not the worst possible way, to conduct this immensely important public business. It was deplored in those journals (relatively very few) which were friendly to the New Deal; it was damned root and branch, along with its author, in those journals (the vast majority) hostile to the New Deal. "Because he is adroit and not forthright, he arouses irritating suspicions, probably needlessly, about his ultimate intentions as the leader of his party and the head of Government," wrote the most widely quoted editorialist of the day, the moderately liberal, generally pro–New Deal Republican William Allen White, in his Emporia (Kansas) *Gazette* for February 6, 1937. "Too clever, too damned clever," proclaimed the pro–New Deal New York *World-Telegram* —a phrase that stuck in Rosenman's mind.* And these were among the sweetest notes in a generally harsh chorus of editorial condemnation focused on Roosevelt's "trickiness," his "dishonesty," and the callousness, even cruelty (Pearson and Allen's *The Nine Old Men* was referred to) of his implication that to be old was to be, inevitably, senile and contemptible. Liberal editorialists, especially, protested the injustice thereby done Hughes and Brandeis, particularly the latter, for whose judicial mind FDR had every reason to be profoundly grateful and whose continuing intellectual vigor certainly testified to the falsity of the proposal's general implication.

Accompanying this negative criticism was a vast puzzlement over Roosevelt's essential reason, his basic motive, for proceeding as he had. Was it a mingling of fear with guilt feeling, atop his exasperation? Was he uncertain or

*See p. 51.

ashamed of "court-packing" and therefore afraid nakedly to expose it? But, if so, why did he implement this choice of mendacity over candor in such a way as to make the latter an adjectival modifier of the former? For was not his a candid mendacity? His indirection was all too obviously calculated, his subterfuge all too transparent. One was virtually forced to conclude that his attempt to deceive had been intended to be perceived as an attempt to deceive.

# 3

->>X<<-

## Tragic Error Is Compounded by a
## Stubborn Persistence in It

I

ON Tuesday, February 9, the President received a letter from Harvard Law
School's Felix Frankfurter, written in Cambridge, Massachusetts, two days
before—a letter typical of the professor's correspondence with the President
insofar as it was unctuously deferential, ingratiating, uncritical. It opened with
a reference to "the top of Vesuvius where you set me some weeks ago" and
from which he, Frankfurter, was now "blown . . . off."* "Yes, you 'shocked'
me," the professor went on, "by the deftness of the general scheme. . . . You
'shocked' me no less by the dramatic untarnished secrecy with which you kept
your scheme until you took the whole country into your confidence [sic]. But
beyond that—well, . . . means had to be found to save the Constitution from
the Court, and the Court from itself. . . . There was no perfect easy way out.
Risks had to be taken." At which point the professor's prose went lame with
repetition. Clearly, "some major operation was necessary" and any such operation upon "the body politic" was bound to produce shock. "But [use of the
conjunction is revealing.] I have, as you know, deep faith in your instinct to
make the wise choice. . . ."[1] Notable, if not noted, was the fact that the
professor did not say, despite his courtier's urge to say, that Roosevelt had
actually made the wise choice.

Roosevelt's prompt reply, which was of unusual length, opened with an
expression of relief. "I am awfully glad to have your Sunday letter and to know
that . . . you have survived," he began; "but most important of all that you
understand the causes and motives." He then reviewed "the process of elimination" by which he had arrived at his decision, concentrating on his reasons for
rejecting the amendment approach. "The Nation cannot wait until 1941 or
1942" for "social and economic national legislation to bring it abreast of the
times. . . ." (He deplored the fact that the "return of prosperity, at this moment,
may blunt our senses" to the necessity for such action, adding that "it is the
same old story of the failure of those who have property to realize that I am
the best friend the profit system ever had. . . .") But the most significant portion
of the letter was its conclusion. "Probably, I shall in the course of a normal
fireside chat, in a few weeks, dwell on the reorganization of the judiciary, at
the same time I speak on the reorganization of the executive, flood relief, etc.,"
he said, as if the issue of his court plan were of the same order of emotional
magnitude as the others mentioned. "Do you want to send me a little elabora-

*See p. 47.

tion of what you mentioned in your letter and anything else you think I could use in a talk to the people themselves?"[2] Which suggests, to one who studies Roosevelt's psychology, that he was not now as absolutely certain of an overwhelming popular acceptance of his court plan as he had asserted himself to be the week before, and that he wished to revert, so far as yet remained possible, to the practice he normally followed when proposing a new, highly controversial departure—that of minimizing the shock, the degree of change involved.

At that moment an informal White House staff was being hurriedly improvised to direct, under the President's personal command, the executive's forces in the legislative war for the bill. Tommy Corcoran became in effect the chief of staff, but would also function as one of the two White House lobbyists in the Senate, the other being Joseph Keenan, an assistant to Cummings in the Justice Department who dealt largely with patronage matters and was, in appearance as in fact, a shrewd, hardheaded, practical politician, liked and trusted by rank-and-file senators as Corcoran could never be. Charles West, under secretary of the interior, had functioned as White House lobbyist with representatives since early 1936 and would continue in that role on this bill in the House. Also intimately involved would be the President's son and secretary, James. Others who would act and confer in the matter were Ben Cohen (of course), publicity man Charles Michelson of the Democratic National Committee, and the assistant attorney general, Robert H. Jackson, who often and profoundly disagreed with the policy line of his immediate superior.

The initial legislative strategy called for action on the bill first in the House, then in the Senate. This was the usual order of legislating an administration measure. In the House, with its tremendous New Deal Democratic majority, victory for a New Deal bill was generally by a margin sufficiently wide and productive of momentum (including a buildup of popular pressures) to ensure that the Senate would go along, despite the tendency of Senate Republicans and Southern Democrats to coalesce in formidable opposition. As for Roosevelt's role, it would be largely confined to a personal persuasion of doubtful legislators; these he would summon singly or in small groups to the Oval Room or Office for frank, private talk. In public he would say nothing until the opposition had had ample opportunity to "talk itself out," with (for the opponents) a disastrous revelation of real motives, and this might not be until sometime after his return from the Warm Springs vacation he would begin in the second week of March. Thus, the address he was to present to the hundred-dollar-a-plate Democratic victory dinner, thence by radio to the nation, in Washington's Mayflower Hotel on March 4, was to make no mention of court reform.

But this legislative and personal strategy was soon forcibly changed by a rising tide of untoward event.

For one thing, an unexpectedly huge volume of mail began to pour at once onto Capitol Hill from the electorate, and reportedly it ran nine or ten to one against the bill—a margin wide enough to more than offset the normal discount of negativism (the normal rate, that is, at which specifically expressed opposition exceeds specifically expressed support of any proposal of important institutional change). For another thing, Hatton Sumner's fervent opposition was impressed upon his colleagues on the House Judiciary Committee, and with devastating effect, even while he remained publicly quiet about it: Roosevelt was informed, within a week following his message, that if a vote were taken at that moment in this committee his proposal would be defeated by a majority of five. For a third thing, two senators upon whose support Roosevelt had absolutely counted—Joseph C. O'Mahoney of Wyoming and Tom Connally of Texas—let it be known that they opposed the measure, provoking in the deepest privacy of the White House a rare explosion of personal anger by the President. Presaged by this, clearly, were other defections from the ranks of senators whose support had been assumed.

The most dangerous of these was soon disclosed, that of Montana's Burton K. Wheeler.

Wheeler's credentials as a fighting liberal were far less peccable than Franklin Roosevelt's. He had been a key figure in the exposure of big-business thievery at Teapot Dome; had been the elder Bob La Follette's running mate on the Progressive ticket in 1924, when Roosevelt supported archconservative John W. Davis; had been in the forefront of every battle of People against Property throughout his stormy political career. He had practical and personal reasons for loathing Cummings. The attorney general was a close friend of Wheeler's most powerful political enemy in Montana, one J. Bruce Kremer, machine- and money-politician par excellence, who had been greatly rewarded for his lobbying services to Montana's remarkably powerful and predatory copper interests even (or especially) while serving as his state's Democratic national committeeman. Well-founded rumors of Kremer's Washington money-politicking, heard in Montana, had caused his resignation from the national committee. Nevertheless, Cummings (and Joe Keenan) had continued richly to endow the Kremer organization, implacably hostile to Wheeler's, with Justice Department patronage. Wheeler had reason, also, to dislike and distrust Franklin Roosevelt, who owed much to Wheeler's early support of his presidential candidacy and to Wheeler's fighting advocacy of the administration's 1935 utilities holding-company bill, yet had been repaid by repeated White House snubs. There can be no doubt that Wheeler's natural resentment of all this contributed to the rapidity and energy with which he sprang into opposition to a court plan having Cummings as principal author.

But he had another, deeper motive, rooted in a commitment to personal liberty and a genuinely free society—rooted also in a growing suspicion that Roosevelt did not, at heart, share this commitment but had, instead, as Hoover believed, dangerously authoritarian tendencies. His suspicion hardened to conviction as he listened to the court message and studied the accompanying bill. His own proposed solution to the Supreme Court problem had been a constitutional amendment whereby Congress by a two-thirds vote could, after an intervening election, override any Supreme Court veto of a congressional act—the very amendment that Corcoran and Cohen were preparing to recommend in a memorandum to the President when the latter delivered his court message. This solution, he felt, would preserve or restore a proper balance of power among the three arms of government. What Roosevelt proposed, in Wheeler's view, was a structured imbalance—a large measure of the power presently reposed in the Court would be transferred to the White House, with none transferred to Congress—and this at a time when the chief executive was a power-lustful man whose word could not be trusted and who believed that atrocious means could be justified by shining ends.

"A liberal cause," said Burton K. Wheeler, "was never won by stacking a deck of cards, by stuffing a ballot box, or by packing a court."[3]

And having forcefully announced his opposition, Wheeler resisted all White House blandishments, even refusing a personal dinner invitation to "dear Burt" from his "old friend" Franklin.* He also refused all pleas (they were couched in terms, alternatively, of advice and threat) that he at least confine his opposition to an expression of personal view. Instead, he proposed to organize and lead Democratic opponents of the bill, and this despite the fact that doing so meant allying himself, not just with disaffected liberals and moderates, but with die-hard Southern conservatives whose general political views he abhorred. With disaffected Western liberals he was immediately and, from Roosevelt's point of view, dangerously effective: Within a day or two he had recruited for the opposition senators Gerald P. Nye and Lynn Frazier of North Dakota, two independents whom Roosevelt had planned to recruit for his side by means of Wisconsin's "Young Bob" La Follette. Soon thereafter, at Wheeler's behest, Minnesota's Farmer-Labor senator, Henrik Shipstead, joined the opposition.

There was no blinking the fact that the party and the liberal coalition were badly split.

The probability that they would be had evidently been recognized by leading Republicans on the instant, even as these first read and heard the message. Within a few days thereafter, in a (for them) rare exercise of psycho-political intelligence, Republican congressional leaders had decided that they, whose opposition would be taken for granted in any case, should keep quiet about the court scheme, rigorously refraining from any word or deed that might make the issue a partisan one and thereby encourage a closing of breached Democratic ranks. Let the Democrats fight it out among themselves! They pressed this policy, persuasively argued, upon fellow Republicans, and it was reluctantly accepted, or at any rate complied with, by Herbert Hoover, Alf Landon, John D. M. Hamilton, and the state and national Republican organization. Landon was expected to make a vehement attack on the court plan

---

*According to Joseph Alsop and Turner Catledge, who had it from Wheeler, the senator was given to understand by Corcoran, evidently speaking for the President, that he, in return for his support, would be permitted to name two or three of the new justices, once the bill passed (*The 168 Days*, New York, 1937, p. 100).

when he addressed the Lincoln Day dinner of the National Republican Club in New York City on February 9. Instead he made but passing mention of it. Hoover, known to be preparing a national radio address denouncing court-packing in doomsday terms, neither gave that address nor issued further major public statements on the issue. As for the Liberty League, launched to "save the Constitution" as presently interpreted by the Court, surely it must spring to life again under the stimulus of this awful threat! It didn't. Moribund since the election, it continued so.

No other tactic available to the Republicans could have been as disconcerting to administration Democrats as this conspiracy of silence.

Nor did the storm that had been raised across the land show any sign of early abatement. On the contrary, it gave every sign of increasing in intensity. Nothing like it—in terms of universality of passionate citizen involvement, in terms of widespread depth perception of a single central issue of truly fundamental national importance, and in terms of disruptive effect upon long-established political alignments—had happened in America since Stephen Douglas proposed "popular sovereignty" as the answer to the territorial slavery question in 1854.

Hence the shift in administration strategy.

Roosevelt was informed by House Speaker Bankhead and Majority Leader Rayburn that, though the bill could doubtless be pushed through the House despite an unfavorable committee report, the forceful tactics required would do serious and probably permanent damage to New Deal support there. In the process, the chances for subsequent victory in the Senate, given that body's present division, would be gravely impaired, possibly destroyed. Better to start the bill in the Senate. So it was officially announced on February 19 that hearings would be initiated, not before Sumner's Judiciary Committee, but before Ashurst's in the upper chamber. Simultaneously, Roosevelt reluctantly abandoned, once and for all, the indirection, the cleverness in which he had taken such delight, and prepared the direct appeal for popular support that he should have made at the outset. The first draft speech for the Democratic victory dinner was discarded. Corcoran, Cohen, Richberg, and Rosenman were set to work on a new one dealing exclusively with "the real mischief—the kind of decision which, as a studied and continued policy, had been coming down from the Supreme Court."[4] Nothing was said in it about overcrowded dockets or the mental failings of the aged. The same four men then drafted a fireside chat, now scheduled for delivery March 9, just five days after the victory dinner. It, too, would dwell wholly upon judicial obstructionism as disease, the bill as cure. And to each of these drafts Roosevelt personally made substantial contributions, working nearly as hard on them as he had upon his second inaugural.

His March 4 address was among the very best of his fighting speeches, and his delivery of it, to the audience before his eyes and to the unseen millions before their radio sets, was superb.

Having quoted the most memorable of his 1936 campaign speeches, with its listing of New Deal objectives and its reiteration of "for these things we have only just begun to fight," he passed in review the "vetoes" of key New Deal legislation that had been issued by the Supreme Court in the last three years. He condemned the use of legal fictions, shaped by interested motives, to prevent effective dealings with social and physical realities. "During the . . . past four years the nation has been overwhelmed by disasters of flood and drouth. Modern science knows how to protect our land and our people from the recurrence of these catastrophes and knows how to produce as by-product the blessings of cheaper electric power. . . . But how can we confidently complete . . . [the] Tennessee Valley project or extend the idea to the Ohio and other valleys while the lowest courts have not hesitated to paralyze its operations by sweeping injunctions? The Ohio River and the Dust Bowl are not conversant with the habits of the interstate commerce clause. But we shall never be safe . . . until we have somehow made the interstate commerce clause conversant with the habits of the Ohio River and the Dust Bowl." He closed with a powerful peroration ("one of the best that I have ever heard," said Harold Ickes) which had been suggested, even written in part, by popular economist Stuart Chase:[5]

> Here is one-third of a nation ill-nourished, ill-clad, ill-housed—NOW!
> Here are thousands upon thousands of farmers wondering whether next year's prices will meet their mortgage interest—NOW!
> Here are thousands upon thousands of men and women working for long hours in factories for inadequate pay—NOW!
> Here are thousands upon thousands of children who should be in school, working in mines and mills—NOW!
> Here are strikes more far-reaching than we have ever known, costing millions of dollars—NOW!
> Here are spring floods threatening to roll again down our river valleys—NOW!
> Here is the Dust Bowl beginning to blow again—NOW!
> If we would keep faith with those who had faith in us, if we would make democracy succeed, I say we must act—NOW!

His fireside chat of March 9, the first of his second term, was of similar quality. His rich voice, wonderfully coveying his living presence, came warm and friendly into ten million living rooms, there to argue for his proposal and against its detractors, earnestly, with the vibrancy of controlled passion.

> If by that phrase "packing the Court" it is charged that I wish to place on the bench spineless puppets who would disregard the law and decide specific cases as I wish them to decide, I make this answer—that no President fit for his office would appoint, and no Senate of honorable men . . . would confirm, that kind of appointees to the Supreme Court. But if by that phrase the charge is made that I would appoint and the Senate would confirm Justices worthy to sit beside present members of the Court who understand these modern conditions, that I will appoint Justices who will not undertake to override the judgment of Congress on legislative policy, that I will appoint Justices who will act as Justices and not as legislators—if the appointment of such Justices can be called "packing the Court," then I say that I and with me the vast majority of the American people favor doing just that thing—now.

A constitutional amendment was no practical alternative to his proposal. "Even if an amendment were passed, and even if in the years to come it were to be ratified, its meaning would depend upon the kind of Justices who would be sitting on the Supreme Court bench. An amendment, like the rest of the Constitution, is what the Justices say it is. . . ." Nor was his proposal any threat to personal liberties. On the contrary, it would "restore the balance" of "the three great branches of the Federal government" which the framers of the Constitution had intended, which the judiciary had "tipped out of balance," and upon which the maintenance of personal liberty depended. "You who know me will accept my solemn assurance that in a world in which democracy is under attack, I seek to make American democracy succeed."

Thus a highly personal appeal to the people from a President who, only four months before, had scored the greatest personal triumph in the history of presidential elections—and, surprisingly, dismayingly, it failed to work! Not, at least, as Roosevelt had counted upon its working.

A flood of approving letters and telegrams poured at once into the White House mail room, as always happened after a major presidential address, but no flood of protest poured onto the desks of opposition senators, which was the result most hoped for. No hitherto silent public figure of importance announced his conversion to the plan, nor did any who had declared himself against it announce a change of mind.

As for the Gallup poll, which by virtue of its accurate forecasting of the 1936 elections had established itself as the nation's chief oracle in such matters, it reported no decisive shift of public opinion toward the President's side of the issue. In the second week of February, Gallup's pollsters had begun asking a representative sample of the citizenry the following question: "Are you in favor of President Roosevelt's proposal regarding the Supreme Court?" Forty-five percent answered yes, 45 percent no, and 10 percent were undecided in the first of these weekly samplings. During the next two weeks, the reported support of the proposal had declined to 41 percent, while opposition increased to 48 percent and the undecideds to 11 percent, suggesting the cost to Roosevelt of his self-imposed silence on the issue. Gains for him were registered by Gallup following the two speeches, but these added up to no more than recovery of ground lost during his silent period. Two weeks after the fireside chat, which was also two weeks after hearings had opened before the Senate Judiciary Committee, the proposal's support and opposition were again of only equal strength, according to Gallup—45 percent for, 45 percent against—and this despite the fact that the administration had occupied the witness chair at the hearings during these same two weeks.[6]

Admittedly, the Senate hearings had not gone well for the administration. Cummings, the first witness, had done the cause no good by his persistence in the strategy of indirection which his chief had abandoned. Many were angered, few persuaded, by the attorney general's marshaling of statistical "facts" to "prove" that the caseload was too heavy to be borne by the federal judiciary, and especially the Supreme Court, as presently constituted; that "new young blood" was therefore urgently needed; and that this was the primary purpose of the proposed reform. Assistant Attorney General Jackson, who followed Cummings on the stand, undid some of the damage with a powerful argument frankly couched in terms of "the real mischief." But he was followed by a series of witnesses* who were so lengthily and cogently questioned by well-prepared opposition senators (the American Bar Association, predictably adamantly opposed to the bill, assigned legal experts to help in this preparation) that the ultimate value to the White House of their testimony was greatly diminished, sometimes destroyed. Almost every one of the witnesses had published statements in the past that contradicted, or seemed to contradict, the statements now made, and these contradictions the questioning fully exposed. Even more annoying to the White House's "General Staff" was the wordy nature of many of the questions. These caused Corcoran and his colleagues to suspect that the opposition, woefully unprepared to present its own case, was filibustering to postpone as long as possible the day on which its own first witness must appear—a suspicion rendered all the more plausible by the fact that the opposition had refused Corcoran's proposal, at the outset, to impose a four-week limit on the hearings, with two weeks allotted to each side. Hence Roosevelt's decision to cut off the administration's testimony at the end of two weeks, abruptly, with nearly half the scheduled administration witnesses as yet unheard.

II

THIS was on Saturday, March 20. On that same day, Burton K. Wheeler, who was to appear before the Judiciary Committee on Monday the twenty-second as the first witness for the opposition, called at the apartment of his old friend Mr. Justice Brandeis.

The two men had had especially close and frequent professional contacts during the last three years. In March 1935 the Senate had established, at Wheeler's instigation, a special subcommittee of the Wheeler-chaired Senate Interstate Commerce Committee, a subcommittee headed by Wheeler himself. Its assignment was to conduct a "thorough and complete" investigation of railroad financing—this following public charges (by historian Charles A. Beard, for one) that the nation's rail systems were under the control of a handful of New York bankers who, for their own profit, were driving them into bankruptcy. The subject was one on which Brandeis had become an authority while operating as "the people's advocate" early in the century, and Wheeler had naturally turned to him for advice at the outset of the investigation. One consequence of that advice, joined with Frankfurter's, had been the appointment of labor attorney Max Lowenthal as the subcommittee's counsel. Lowenthal was himself an authority on railroad finance—in 1933 he had published

---

*Professor E. S. Corwin, author of *The Twilight of the Supreme Court;* other leading authorities on constitutional law; one farm-organization representative; and several labor leaders.

*The Public Pays,* a penetrating and acerbic study of the receivership and reorganization of the Chicago, Milwaukee, and St. Paul Railroad—and he was a close friend and protégé of Brandeis. Ever since, during long and careful preparations for public hearings,* Wheeler had often consulted Brandeis concerning investigative strategy.

Until this March Saturday of 1937, however, he had scrupulously refrained from discussion of the court bill with the great jurist. He knew how pure of motive, how devoid of self-interest, were Brandeis's dealings with public affairs in general, and how high and stern was the Brandeisian code of honor. He assumed that Brandeis's commitment to the constitutional separation of powers was absolute (judges must *not* participate in the legislative process†); he feared, therefore, that he would give offense if he asked the justice for advice, much less for any help, in his fight against pending legislation that, if enacted, would greatly affect Brandeis's professional life. Yet Wheeler had been trying since early February to elicit a statement from the Chief Justice answering the charge that the Supreme Court was behind in its work. He had talked to Hughes about it face to face only the week before, in company with two senatorial colleagues; had then presented a formal request from the committee that the Chief Justice appear as a hearings witness; had been told that, though personally willing to testify, Hughes could not do so unless his court colleagues approved. A couple of days later, in a brief note to Wheeler, the Chief Justice declined the invitation to appear. And that had seemed an end to the matter. Only yesterday, however, Wheeler had been informed by his daughter of a social call paid her at her Alexandria home by Mrs. Brandeis, who, as she left, turned back to say pointedly: "You tell your obstinate father we think he is making a courageous fight." This encouraged Wheeler to believe that Brandeis might at least be willing to provide him with authoritative factual information about the state of the Court's work; and it was to ask for this that he came, with some trepidation, to the Brandeis home.

He need not have feared. Brandeis listened to him with total sympathy, then offered a suggestion of his own. Why not a letter from the Chief Justice to Wheeler answering the latter's questions—a letter that could be read into the hearings record? The upshot was a phone conversation between Wheeler and Hughes ("I'm calling from Justice Brandeis'," Wheeler was enabled to begin) during which the Chief Justice was persuaded with no great difficulty to

---

*As it turned out, the hearings were for the most part conducted, not by Wheeler, who became completely absorbed into the court-reform battle, but by the subcommittee's vice chairman, Harry S Truman of Missouri. They contributed much to Truman's education and brought him to national public attention for the first time.

†Actually, Brandeis, operating through his daughter and her husband, Paul A. Raushenbush, had participated quite actively in the drafting of Social Security legislation (see *FDR: The New Deal Years,* pp. 446–48). And, operating through Frankfurter, with whom he had a secret pecuniary arrangement, Brandeis constantly fed ideas into, and exerted influence upon, the politics of the New Deal (see Bruce Allen Murphy, *The Brandeis–Frankfurter Connection* [New York, 1983]). There is no doubt, however, that he did so in selfless dedication to the public good as he perceived it.

prepare a letter immediately, addressed to Wheeler, for Wheeler's use on Monday. Hughes set to work on it at once. Late in the following afternoon he placed the completed product in Wheeler's hands, saying with a broad smile: "The baby is born."[7]

And it proved to be, this "baby," a perfect instrument of Wheeler's purpose, its bombshell effect nearly as great as that of the President's court message, when Wheeler read it aloud next day in the crowded hearings room.

"The Supreme Court is fully abreast of its work," wrote Hughes flatly. "There is no congestion of cases upon our calendar. This gratifying condition has obtained for many years." The specific evidence of the Court's incompetence cited by Roosevelt-Cummings—namely, the Court's refusal to hear 717 of 867 cases submitted to it in petitions for certiorari the previous year—was summarily dismissed. "No single court of last resort, whatever the number of judges, could dispose of all the cases which arise in this vast country and which litigants would seek to bring up if the right of appeal were unrestricted." Traditionally, therefore, and in accordance with the expressed will of Congress, the Supreme Court granted review of lower-court decisions (when such review was not a clear matter of right) only in cases having great public interest. About 60 percent of the applications for certiorari were wholly without merit and should never have been made; another 20 percent had a certain plausibility, which, however, was quickly destroyed by critical examination. The remaining 20 percent were sufficiently substantial to survive preliminary analysis. These last cases were heard; and if the Court erred in granting such review, it was on the side of leniency. In sum, the Court as presently constituted was an efficient operation, and an "increase in the number of Justices" would certainly not increase its efficiency. On the contrary, "it would impair efficiency so long as the Court acts as a unit. There would be more judges to hear, more judges to confer, more judges to discuss, and more judges to be convinced and to decide." This last might be avoided, of course, by having an enlarged Court hear cases in division, a suggestion that had been made; but Hughes's opinion as Chief Justice was that such a procedure was forbidden by the Constitution. The Constitution, he said, provides for "one Supreme Court" and "does not appear to authorize two or more Supreme Courts or two or more parts of a Supreme Court operating in effect as separate courts." In conclusion, Hughes said that, though he had "not been able to consult with members of the Court generally" because of "the shortness of time," his letter had been specifically endorsed by Justices Brandeis and Van Devanter. Since Brandeis stood at the far left and Van Devanter at the far right of the Court's range of politico-economic attitudes, as everyone knew, their endorsements lent credence to Hughes's expression of "confidence" that his letter was "in accord with the views of the Justices."

All of which was immediately, immensely, and permanently damaging to the administration's cause.

It was also characterized by a sly trickiness on Hughes's part that was every bit as dubious, ethically, as the President's own actions. For as Justice Stone

insisted in a letter to Frankfurter nearly three years later (December 29, 1939),*
"the shortness of time" was no valid reason for Hughes's failure to consult his
colleagues "in connection with the preparation of a document which purported
to state" their views. True, the Court was in recess at the time of the letter's
preparation, but "all of its members were in the city" and "could have been
brought together for a conference on an hour's notice, or less." Three of the
justices—Sutherland, Cardozo, and Stone—lived "within five minutes' walk of
the residence of the Chief Justice" and all were at home on Sunday, March
21.[8] One must conclude that Hughes failed to consult because he feared the
consequences of consulting: He strongly suspected that his colleagues would
*not* unanimously approve what he said, or even his issuance of a public
statement of any kind on the question.

Certainly Stone and Cardozo emphatically disapproved of Hughes's giving
of an opinion as to the constitutionality of the Court's hearing cases in divisions. This was an "extra-official" or "advisory" opinion on a constitutional
question, and neither the Court as a whole nor any individual member of it
should ever issue such opinions. So said Cardozo and Stone to each other, and
to anyone else who asked—and so, as a matter of fact, said Hughes himself
in a book† he had published some years before.

In historical perspective, the Hughes letter, which opened public presentation
of the opposition's case (for weeks thereafter, opposition testimony made
newspaper headlines), appears as the turning point in the battle over the court
plan. From this point on, every significant Gallup-measured shift of public
opinion was away from support of the President and toward the opposition,
though the latter's gain was not equivalent to the former's loss since there was
a simultaneous increase in the proportion of undecideds. A similar erosion of
measurable support occurred in Congress, encouraged by the passionate phi-
lippic with which the aged Carter Glass answered the President's fireside chat,
over a national radio hookup, on March 29. ("I am speaking tonight from the
depths of a soul filled with bitterness against a proposition which appears to
me utterly destitute of moral sensibility. . . . The men and women of America
who value liberties . . . should . . . , with all the earnestness of their souls,
protest to Congress against this attempt to replace representative government
with autocracy."[9])

But this was neither foreseen nor even considered a serious possibility by
administration leaders in the days immediately following Wheeler's master-
stroke. Despite the woe that had come to Roosevelt from his initial "major
mistake," he yet retained one great advantage over his opposition: namely, the
popularly recognized necessity for a reversal of the trend of Supreme Court

---

*Stone had gone back to work just before the President's court message was delivered, having fully
recovered from the bacillary dysentery that had almost killed him the preceding autumn.
†*The Supreme Court of the United States* (New York, 1927), pp. 30–31, quoted by A. T. Mason,
*Harlan Fiske Stone* (New York, 1956), p. 451.

decisions and the fact that his bill was the one specific, concrete proposal toward this end on which immediate action could be taken. Moreover, he confidently expected that the margin of his advantage, which had admittedly been shrinking, would soon be expanding. All that had been lost from it, and more, would be regained when the Court's rulings on the Wagner Labor Relations Act and Social Security were announced, as assuredly they would be within the next few Monday decision days. These two laws directly benefited more millions of Americans, with less ambiguity as regards personal benefit, than any earlier New Deal measures save the emergency legislation creating WPA. Each had massive, fervent popular support (that of Social Security had been demonstrated by the failure of the attack upon it by Landon Republicans in the last election campaign; that of the Wagner Act was currently manifested in a wave of angry strikes against corporations that, with the aid of court injunctions, refused to obey it). Each was bound to be ruled unconstitutional by the same Court majority as had so ruled on railroad retirement, minimum wages, Guffey Coal, and others. And the popular outrage thus provoked would inevitably overwhelm the court bill's opposition.[10]

It didn't happen, however. In effect, the precise opposite happened—and began to happen (surprisingly and, from the White House point of view, dismayingly) just one week after the Hughes letter was published.

For on Monday, March 29 (the day of Carter Glass's radio speech), the Supreme Court reversed itself totally in its decision on the state minimum-wage law case, *West Coast Hotel Co.* v. *Parrish,* whose acceptance for review in the preceding October had gone unnoticed by either President or attorney general amid the election campaign.* Five to four, the Court upheld the Washington State law essentially identical with the New York law struck down, 5–4, in *Morehead* v. *Tipaldo.* Roberts made the difference. In *Tipaldo,* he had concurred in Butler's majority opinion, for which 1923's *Adkins* v. *Children's Hospital* was controlling precedent. In *Parrish,* he concurred in Hughes's majority opinion† that "the case of *Adkins* v. *Children's Hospital* . . . should be, and it is overruled." Thus the Constitution, specifically the due-process clause of the Fourteenth Amendment, had for Roberts, on the record, a meaning in March 1937 that flatly contradicted its meaning for him in June 1936—and the timing of his announced change of mind, less than two months after Roosevelt's court message, strongly suggested a causal linkage of the two events.

The inevitable conclusion was that Roberts's latest vote was determined, not by any discovery of new meaning in the Constitution or any concern for social justice, but by his anxious wish to defeat the court bill. Guided by the wily, foxy Hughes, he aimed to pull the rug out from under the feet of the President, toppling him. "With the shift of Roberts, even a blind man ought

---

*See pp. 11–12, 58.
†Predictably, the Chief Justice assigned to himself the drafting of this liberal, popular decision, as per the view of him described on pp. 44–45.

to see that the Court is in politics, and understand how the Constitution is 'judicially' construed," wrote Frankfurter from Cambridge on March 30 to Roosevelt, who had just returned to the White House from Warm Springs. "This behavior . . . comes on top of the Hughes letter. *That* was a characteristic Hughes performance—part and parcel of that pretended withdrawal from considerations of policy, while trying to shape them, which is the core of the mischief of which the majority have so long been guilty. That Brandeis should have been persuaded to allow the Chief to use his name is a source of sadness to me. . . ."[11] Quipped Thomas Reed Powell, Frankfurter's law-school colleague, "A switch in time saves nine."

And this interpretation seemed sustained when, two weeks later, on Monday, April 12, the Supreme Court announced its decision on three of the five Wagner Labor Relations Act cases, the most important being *NLRB* v. *Jones and Laughlin Steel*, which it had heard on February 10 and 11. The inordinate length of time (two months) intervening between the hearings and the decision announcement suggested that the draftsman for the majority was finding his task unusually difficult—and this interpretation, too, was sustained when the majority opinion was read by Hughes. Again the vote was 5–4, Hughes now joining with Roberts in flat, open self-reversal,* and it required the Chief Justice to assert that none of the long list of perfectly relevant precedents that had been confidently cited by Jones and Laughlin lawyers was "controlling here"—precedents defining all economic production (mining, manufacturing, agriculture) as local matters, hence exempt from congressional applications of the interstate-commerce clause—precedents Hughes himself had helped establish or maintain with quibbles about the "fundamental" distinction between "direct" and "indirect" effects of intrastate "transactions" upon commerce across state lines. "When industries organize themselves on a national scale," Hughes now said, "making their relation to interstate commerce the dominant factor in their activities, how can it be maintained that their industrial labor relations constitute a forbidden field which Congress may not enter, when it is necessary to protect interstate commerce from the paralyzing consequences of industrial war?"[12] Such a position, though its absurdity had not theretofore been discerned (on the record) by Hughes, was obviously untenable, and not only as regarded steel but also as regarded clothing (*NLRB* v. *Friedman-Harry Marks Clothing Co.*) and truck trailers (*NLRB* v. *Fruehauf Trailer Co.*). Hence and therefore, the collective-bargaining provision of the National Labor Relations Act was constitutional.

---

*The Chief Justice had almost equally reversed himself in *West Coast Hotel Co.* v. *Parrish*, but this was apparent only to close observers of the Court who understood those technical devices for complicating the simple and obscuring the obvious whereby lawyers make themselves "necessary," and expensive, to clients.

### III

Now came a time for decisions as fateful, and as revealing of Roosevelt's character and basic attitudes, as those that had produced his court bill.

On the morrow of the three NLRB decisions, the consensus of press and Congress was that the President had won not only a great victory but substantially the whole of his war for a more "enlightened" judicial interpretation of the Constitution. What Roosevelt should do, therefore, in the opinion of many senators, and of Joe Robinson specifically, was proclaim his victory to the world at large while communicating to the Judiciary Committee his terms of peace—"compromise" terms that (so some senators still believed) might actually have been prepared and intended from the first as a probable final settlement. By acknowledging his willingness to settle for less, Roosevelt could now safely tacitly admit that his initial call for six new justices had defined a bargaining position; but he must do this at once, according to Robinson, before the full impact of the Supreme Court reversal was felt, persuading New Deal supporters that no Supreme Court reform whatever was now needed. "If the President wants to compromise I can get him a couple of extra judges tomorrow," the Senate majority leader reportedly said to Joe Keenan on the afternoon of April 13.[13] His implication was that the day after tomorrow would be too late.

This general expressed consensus was not, however, what Roosevelt most heeded on the day after the Jones and Laughlin decision. He concentrated instead on an interpretation by his opposition of the Supreme Court's action —as if he feared that such an interpretation, whereby the Court, not he, emerged victorious from the strife, would be the one that prevailed in history. He also doubted that the present consensus included any significant number of "the people."

Thus, in his press conference of April 13, he spoke "off the record" about the "perfectly grand time" he had been having with that morning's "dear old *Herald-Tribune*." The New York paper's editorial comment upon the Wagner Act ruling was entitled "A Great Decision." This had reminded him of a *Herald Tribune* editorial entitled "Thumbs Down on the Wagner Act"— published, as Steve Early had confirmed, in September 1935,* after a "committee of very, very distinguished lawyers calling themselves the National Lawyers' Committee and operating under an organization known as the American Liberty League" had concluded from "a very careful analysis of the Wagner . . . Act" that "it was thoroughly and completely unconstitutional." The *Herald Tribune* had heartily approved this finding, "warning the country of what would happen if an act like that could possibly be found constitutional," said Roosevelt. "And now, this morning, they come out with 'A Great Decision.' Well, I have been having more fun." It was a malicious fun, however; far more disgust than joy was in it. And Roosevelt indicated no reason to feel

---

*To be precise, on September 21, 1935.

triumphant joy when, switching from "off the record" to "background" ("I am not to be credited in any way"), in answer to a reporter's question whether the court ruling would affect his "desire for a court reorganization bill," he said that "the majority opinion in the three manufacturing cases" seemed on "cursory reading" to apply only to those "three specific cases" and, as regarded these, "to the one phase of interstate commerce involved"—namely, "collective bargaining." There was no assurance that the "same legislative policy would be extended" to other progressive social legislation, especially since (as Roosevelt need not and did not say) the one-vote majority was provided by the highly erratic, unpredictable Roberts. And this fact was probably recognized by the general public. "My guess would be the feeling of the average man and woman on the street is, 'So far, so good, but—' and then, perhaps, the old phrase, 'So what—' " Ergo, the President's desire for passage of the court bill remained undiminished.[14]

Moreover, the long-term need "to make the judiciary as a whole less static by the constant and systematic addition of new blood to its personnel," as the President had put it in his court message, remained unaffected by the Supreme Court's wholly "political" and perhaps temporary turnabout. It was this argument for persevering with the bill in its present form that he used when, a few weeks later, his old friend Charles Culp Burlingham urged him, in view of recent developments, "to drop so much of the bill as relates to the Supreme Court." He replied: "I think you are looking a day or a week or a year ahead, while I am trying to look a generation ahead."[15] To other people he stated other seemingly objective reasons for continuing the battle on the same ground and terms as before.

But the essential root of what appeared to many his blind obstinacy, his stubborn refusal to face realities, would seem to have been a helpless feeling that he had no real choice in the matter. No opportunity for real compromise was now open to him. And for this, he himself was largely to blame. There could hardly have failed to grow in him a sense of personal affront from the moment of Wheeler's reading of the Chief Justice's letter. He whose greatest pride was his genius for political timing and maneuver, his mastery of political jujitsu, was being beaten at his own game by Charles Evans Hughes—who, Roosevelt was sure, had subsequently engineered the Roberts switch for the sole purpose of defeating the court bill. And he himself had placed in Hughes's hand the most potent of the weapons used against him. Worse still, by his two-year-old promise to Joe Robinson of the first available Supreme Court appointment he had drastically reduced the area of maneuver now available to him. If he settled for "a couple of extra judges," as Robinson urged, one of the two must be the conservative Robinson himself. This might well lead to 6–5 decisions as unreliable, as frequently discomfiting to him, as the prevailing 5–4 ones, for Roberts might still have the swing vote. If, on the other hand, he simply withdrew that portion of his bill pertaining to the Supreme Court, announcing that his proposal of it had now served its purpose, he might soon find himself more helpless than ever in the face of conservative Court intransigence. For as soon as a justice died or retired (such an event could not be far in the offing), Joe Robinson must be appointed in his place; and if the departed justice happened to be one of the liberal wing, Robinson's vote might well double the conservative majority. The New Deal would then be overruled 6–3 instead of 5–4, assuming that Roberts reverted, as he doubtless would, to his former conservative stance. In sum, formal "compromise" meant substantial defeat.

Roosevelt, with his Dutch up, adamantly refused to accept defeat.

He managed to maintain a flawless façade of good-humored confidence, perfectly hiding his doubts and fears while laughing, sometimes scornfully, at those of others. He even took an ostentatiously carefree vacation two weeks after the Wagner Act decisions, leaving his lieutenants to carry on in Washington as well as they could. He boarded his special train in Washington's Union Station on April 28, boarded the U.S.S. *Potomac* at New Orleans next day, cruised and fished for tarpon in the Gulf of Mexico for a fortnight, then entrained at Galveston for the return trip northward on May 13. To a press conference on his train that day, however, he spoke almost defensively of his holiday while talking "background" to the reporters. "The objective of these trips, you know, is not fishing. . . ." he said. "I don't give a continental damn whether I catch a fish or not. The chief objective is to get a perspective on the scene which I cannot get in Washington any more than you boys can." ("Right!" agreed one of the reporters, fervently.[16]) Yet the "perspective" gained evidently changed nothing of his view of the court bill, or of the strategy pertaining to it. He indicated as much when he arrived back in the White House next day.

There came to his office Robinson, Rayburn, Bankhead, upon his summons, that afternoon of May 14. All of them told him that the chance for passage of his bill in its present form was now virtually nil. They confirmed what Corcoran, Jimmy Roosevelt, and others of the White House inner circle had already told the President about the state of affairs in the Senate Judiciary Committee. When that committee went into executive session at the close of hearings in mid-April, eight members had declared themselves in favor of passage, seven had declared themselves against, and three had declined to commit themselves one way or the other. But two of the three had been Wyoming's O'Mahoney and New Mexico's Carl A. Hatch, each of whom was strongly opposed to the bill but hopeful of persuading the executive to modify it before the final tally was made. Their hope crushed by White House obstinacy, these two joined the declared opposition, O'Mahoney even assuming a leading role in it as ally of his Montana colleague Wheeler. The initially "doubtful" Pat McCarran of Nevada joined the opposition, too. It was therefore a foregone conclusion that the bill would be reported out of committee four days hence (the date, May 18, was already set) with a recommendation, by a vote of 10–8, that "it do not pass." Of course the Supreme Court might yet turn things around by striking down Social Security, but the possibility seemed remote in view of the minimum-wage and Wagner Act decisions. So Robinson, Bankhead, and Rayburn were agreed that the President should accept the best compromise they could arrange in the circumstances—either that or permit the bill to be put aside until the next session so that action could be taken on other proposed New Deal legislation, three items of which were of major importance.

Roosevelt refused even to listen to such advice.

At this juncture, external supports collapsing around him, he was forced to rely more and more exclusively upon inner resources—and he found these to be sadly diminished. Logical process failed him for lack of clearly true ideas with which to work, given his determination to persist in the course he had chosen. Manipulative shrewdness failed him for lack of solid, definite factors it could grasp. And his capacity for swift, sound judgments would in any case have been reduced by the vast anger that—born of frustration conjoined with guilt feelings; nourished by his imperious temper—seethed within him, painfully repressed. Thus an operation flawed at the outset by excessive willfulness became now, for him, a pure effort of will, and of a will imperfectly sustained by his religious faith. He could no longer believe with any serene assurance that his personal triumph in the current battle was God's intention. What happened would certainly be "for the best" in general and the long run, being a working-out of God's design, but it might well be "for the worst" so far as he personally was concerned. This dire possibility loomed ever larger in his mind as questions gnawed ever more deeply at the root of his confidence. Had he totally mistaken the signs and portents from on high? Was he now being punished for this by a withdrawal from him of divine guidance and favor? In proportion to such inward doubt was the increase in outward assertiveness. He whose strong normal inclination was to identify the will of the People with the will of God said over and over again to visitors in the Oval Room, "The people are with me! I know it!"[17] He had said this with a considerable measure of calm confidence in the opening days of the fight. He had asserted it in the face of mounting evidence that it wasn't so as the fight continued. It now became an incantation disturbingly similar in tone and sense to (despite the radical differences from) Woodrow Wilson's in 1919, when Wilson waged his hopeless, self-defeated campaign for American entrance into the League of Nations.

*"The people are with me!"*

He said it on this afternoon of May 14, flatly contradicting the judgment of the three who came to him in the Oval Room urging "compromise." He had just returned from a trip on which he had "seen a good many people—not only people in crowds," though crowds were not without communicative value ("for you get the feeling of a crowd"), "but people I talked to personally . . . down in Mississippi, in Louisiana, and a whole lot of people in Texas."[18] He asserted, at least by implication, that he knew the mood, the sentiment among Sam Rayburn's Texas constituency better than Rayburn did. He asserted that his visitors could yet lead his legislative forces to victory if only they held firm, if only they tried hard enough. His battle orders were unchanged.

Thereafter, hostile events crowded upon one another to march in swift unbroken ranks (as if they did indeed "conspire") against him, whose sense of timing, whose political expertise in general, deserted him utterly. Blindly he reacted to them, compounding ghastly errors as Wilson had done in 1919.

On the morning of May 18, Roosevelt found in his incoming mail a letter from Justice Van Devanter announcing an intention to retire from the bench at the close of the current court session. Roosevelt, who would have reacted with joy to this event had it occurred in early 1935, now winced under its impact, for it fell upon him (it had been timed by the opposition to fall upon him) as a grave double misfortune: It deprived him of one of his last potent popular arguments for his court bill, and it presented to him for immediate payment the promissory note to Robinson that he had, in effect, signed two years ago. That the payment must be made (Roosevelt could not get out of it) was demonstrated on the Senate floor as soon as news of Van Devanter's retirement arrived there: Republican as well as Democratic senators crowded around Robinson to congratulate him upon his impending elevation, making it clear that his appointment to the Supreme Court would be confirmed promptly and virtually unanimously, whereas failure to appoint him would spark a devastating explosion of congressional wrath.

It was as clear at the time as it is in retrospect that Roosevelt's single proper move at this point was to appoint Robinson to the Court at once, coupling this with the "compromise" agreement that Robinson himself had urged upon him, namely, a reduction from six to two of the number of additional justices called for by his court bill. On the tide of goodwill raised by this combine of honor and conciliation for the upper chamber, the revised bill would almost certainly have ridden to early victory, enabling Roosevelt to overbalance Robinson's conservatism on the bench with two liberal appointees. But when precisely this course was strongly recommended to him by Byrnes and by Pat Harrison of Mississippi on the afternoon of this same fateful May 18, Roosevelt was infuriated, being convinced that the two senators came to him as emissaries from Robinson, who sought thus to force him.

There followed two crucial weeks during which no communications flowed between White House and Senate majority leader, the latter fuming in a hurt, resentful anger that spread like contagion among his congressional colleagues —two weeks during which the Supreme Court knocked the last prop out from under the sagging support of the court bill by declaring constitutional (May 24) the unemployment-insurance-tax provisions of the Social Security Act, this by another 5–4 vote—two weeks during which factions began to form and a conflict situation to solidify in the Senate over the question of who should succeed to the majority leadership if Robinson did receive the promised appointment (New Deal liberals favored Alben Barkley of Kentucky; conservatives favored Pat Harrison)—two weeks at the end of which Roosevelt, in effect, capitulated, being forced at last to recognize the fact that, in its present form, his court bill was doomed. He summoned Robinson to the Oval Room (June 3), tacitly reassured him of the court appointment, transferred to him from Corcoran and colleagues the management of his court-bill forces, and gave him permission to arrange the best compromise possible.

Robinson, jubilant, at once recommitted himself heart and soul to the President's cause, settling promptly, with other administration Democrats, upon a proposal originally formally sponsored by Hatch, whereby the President was authorized to appoint a coadjutor justice for any justice who failed to retire at age seventy-five, though with the proviso that no more than one such appointment could be made in any one year. To this arrangement the White House perforce agreed. As for tactics, it was decided to introduce the revision as a series of amendments to the original bill.

But at once it became apparent, weeks before the revision could be put into final form, that Roosevelt had delayed too long. On June 7, the Gallup poll announced a reduction by 10 percent (from 45 to 35) in the number of Americans favoring the court plan. Opposition had increased from 45 to 50 percent, and the portion of undecideds from 10 to 15 percent, during the same period.[19] Congressional support had decreased at least proportionately. Clearly both houses of Congress were reluctant, and grew daily more reluctant, to pass any legislation that changed in any way the formal composition of the Supreme Court.

Nor did anything now happen to halt, much less reverse, the trend. Much happened, instead, to encourage it.

IV

VICE President Garner left Washington in early June to go to his Uvalde, Texas, home, where he would remain "sulking," as news commentators put it, for many weeks. He ignored all attempts by the White House, including a warm personal message from the President, to bring him back. The principal motive for his departure was his disgust with White House dealings, and refusals to deal, with the current wave of sit-down strikes; but he was also strongly opposed to Roosevelt's court-reform proposal and perceived a causal linkage between Roosevelt's fight for it and Roosevelt's attitude, in that season, toward militant labor. Hence Garner's departure from the capital was in good part what the public deemed it to be, the turning of a contemptuous back upon the President's court-reform effort; and this further reduced the already slim chances for passage of any revised court-reform bill. Garner's persuasive power over members of Congress, especially those of conservative or moderate bent, remained great.

As for the perception of linkage between Roosevelt's battle for court reform and his labor policy that spring, it was an accurate one.

The single largest financial contributor to Roosevelt's 1936 reelection campaign had been John L. Lewis's United Mine Workers. Lewis, his CIO now locked in mortal combat with both corporate America and William Green's American Federation of Labor, strongly and influentially supported the court bill, endorsing it in a CBS radio address heard by a national audience of many millions on May 14. On that occasion he described the Supreme Court as "a tyrannical and oligarchic tribunal, which arrogates to itself even the power of defying the wishes of the people of the United States." The "time of reckoning" was "at hand," he said. "I believe that the overwhelming majority of Americans are in favor of the President's Court plan. . . . The future of labor in America is intimately connected with the future of the President's proposal. . . ."[20] Roosevelt paid for this support with a policy of tolerance toward the sit-down strike tactic, and toward labor militancy in general, that was only somewhat less disturbing to him privately, personally, than it was outrageous to the business community's sensibilities, for it contradicted his own basic conservatism, his own fundamental commitment to the profit system. He was uneasy, too, in his relations with Lewis the man, whom he saw not only as an inspirational leader, a master of the kind of emotional oratory that provokes great crowd excitements, but also as an authoritarian personality who, lusting for power, was ruthless in his pursuit of it. Had Lewis not proved himself willing and able, in the past, to employ brutal means to achieve his ends, as Lenin, Mussolini, and Hitler had done on their way to totalitarian dictatorship? Were not avowed Communists and fellow travelers among the most effective CIO organizers, and were not several of them holders of high office in Lewis's organization? Was not Lewis therefore a potentially grave threat to Roosevelt's own power, and even to the survival of American democratic government, in this time of incipient and even, on occasion, actual class warfare?

Such uneasiness had been encouraged when, on the first day of 1937, Lewis issued a public statement saying in effect that Franklin Roosevelt owed his reelection to organized labor, especially to the industrial unions, and that labor had therefore a right to demand his solid support in its present struggle.[21] To this, Roosevelt's private reaction (he made no public response) had been what it always was when threatful pressures were applied to him: He was coldly angry, and grimly determined not to yield.

Yet he recognized, and would say in a public statement four years hence, that labor's current "excesses" were a natural reaction to the exploitation it had suffered in the past. They were also natural "growing pains" attendant upon the swift expansion of union power "under the new impetus of favorable legislation and a sympathetic government." He further recognized that these current labor "excesses" were not as great as those "of capital, of industry, of finance, in their own periods of rapid expansion." They were not even as great nor as criminal as the "excesses" being committed at that very moment by important segments of corporate America, in the opinion of a great many knowledgeable and fair-minded Americans if not of the President himself.

The sit-down tactic had been, from the business point of view, terrifyingly effective thus far. After violence had flared outside the worker-occupied Flint plants of General Motors on January 11, Michigan Governor Frank Murphy had sent National Guard units to Flint to restore law and order—but not by evicting the strikers and breaking the strike, which was the kind of action traditionally taken by officialdom in such situations. On the contrary, his aim was to protect the workers against the violence of police and sheriff's deputies who warred on the side of management—and the National Guardsmen, many of them, had unmistakably manifested their sympathy with the strikers. GM's management nevertheless continued adamant in its refusal of the United Auto Workers' wage and union-recognition demands, whereupon the UAW leadership boldly ordered the forcible seizure of yet another GM plant, a Chevrolet plant in Flint. This was on February 1. GM's response had been to obtain a court order for the eviction of the workers from the plant. Governor Murphy, however, refused to do what the court ordered. GM was paralyzed: During the first ten days of February, the giant manufacturer could produce, in the whole of its national enterprise, only 141 automobiles.[22] Brought thus to its knees, management then came to terms, the terms imposed by CIO–UAM in negotiations that Lewis personally conducted.

The auto workers' union now grew by leaps and bounds; it would grow nearly fivefold, from 88,000 in January to 400,000 in September.

And so, because of this triumph, did membership in the steelworkers' union, which was in process of formation by the Steel Workers' Organizing Committee (SWOC) of the CIO. A battle of titans, pregnant with possibilities of social-revolutionary violence, immediately impended as SWOC prepared to strike U.S. Steel, the largest of the steel corporations and the one historically most ruthlessly exploitive of its workers and most hostile to unions. But on March 2, before the threatened strike had begun, and to the stunned astonishment of a closely watching world, U.S. Steel's management caved in. An agreement was signed whereby wages were raised, working conditions improved, and the CIO steel union recognized as the workers' sole bargaining agent.

Immediately thereafter the wave of sit-down strikes rose to its greatest height, and so did industrial-union euphoria. Other giant corporations seemed now bound to abandon their stubborn insistence upon the open shop. Several of them soon did so, among them General Electric, Firestone, and RCA, all of which signed contracts with CIO unions. Ford, however, refused to budge, preferring to crush incipient unionism by whatever violent means were necessary—and side by side with Ford in this stand were Goodyear Rubber and the congeries of companies that made up so-called Little Steel.

Of these last, the chief was Republic Steel, headed by "rugged individualist" Thomas Girdler. Girdler reacted violently when CIO's SWOC struck Republic. Blood flowed. And nearly all of it was the blood of strikers.

The climactic violence occurred on 1937's Memorial Day, in South Chicago. There the authorities had issued a palpably illegal order prohibiting peaceful picketing at the gate of Republic Steel's mill. When the strikers, a considerable crowd of them, attempted to picket anyway, they were confronted by scores of heavily armed police. The strikers carried sticks and stones, the police guns and clubs—and when one of the strikers who was not in the forefront of the crowd arched a large stick over the front ranks toward the police lines, the nervous police fired three shots into the air. Some equally nervous strikers then

began to hurl their sticks and stones, whereupon the police opened fire at
point-blank range. Several strikers at once fell bleeding to the ground. The
others turned away and ran for their lives, pursued by police who fired as they
ran and savagely beat with their clubs those whom they caught or who stumbled and fell. Within minutes ten strikers were killed, thirty suffered gunshot
wounds, and twenty-eight were so severely beaten that they required hospitali-
zation. All the slain had been shot in the back. Only three of the police were
injured, none seriously.[23]

The "Memorial Day Massacre" (so designated by much of the press) undoubtedly strengthened labor's case in the court of public opinion. But it also
increased a widely prevailing fear that the escalating violence of the strife
between labor and management presaged actual social revolution, whose result
could be a "dictatorship of the proletariat" (this insofar as the administration
sided effectively with labor), or whose forestalling by the right wing might
result in a Fascist dictatorship or an assumption by the President of dictatorial
powers in which Fascist and Communist elements were mingled. Hence, the
overall effect of the labor-management strife upon public opinion was not
helpful, was indeed probably injurious, to the court-reform effort. It was
definitely so insofar as conservative allegations that Roosevelt lusted for dictatorial power were popularly believed.

And Roosevelt's sense of the currently predominant attitude among the
populace toward labor and management as they warred on each other, an
attitude he himself largely shared, led him to express it during his press
conference on June 29 in a way that made headlines. Asked for comment on
labor versus capital, as manifest by Little Steel versus CIO, he quoted *Romeo
and Juliet,* declaring a "plague o' both your houses." At once there was much
speculation in the press about a deterioration of what had theretofore been seen
as a warmly friendly relationship between the President and Lewis. Asked
about this in press conferences, Roosevelt repeatedly refused to comment.
Lewis, however, began to talk in July and August of forming a third political
party in which the industrial unions joined with dispossessed farmers and
unemployed workers to contest the 1940 election—though he also flatly denied
he had any such intention, saying he was convinced that either of the major
political parties could be expected to grant labor's just demands. Simultaneously he engaged in political organizing activities designed to strengthen the
liberal wing of the Democratic party and to reduce the potency of conservative
Democrats whose dominance of the House Rules Committee enabled them to
prevent floor votes on reform legislation. This organizing provoked expressions
of angry alarm by conservative Democrats, who denounced what they saw as
a planned joint effort by Roosevelt and Lewis to achieve absolute control of
the Democratic party by 1940; whereupon Roosevelt encouraged in subtle ways
the public's sense that he and Lewis had differences that rendered unlikely, if
not impossible, any such close Roosevelt-Lewis political alliance. Meanwhile,
it became clear that the CIO's initial effort to organize Little Steel was suffering
defeat; by September that defeat was an accomplished fact; and on the third

day of that month, in a network CBS oration heard by some twenty-five million people, Lewis let the world know that he placed much of the blame for this defeat upon the President of the United States. He employed Elizabethan rhythms and phrases, which issued far more naturally from his lips than they did from Franklin Roosevelt's. "Labor, like Israel, has many sorrows," he cried. "Its women weep for their fallen, and they lament for the future of the children of the race. It ill behooves one who has supped at labor's table and who has been sheltered in labor's house to curse with equal fervor and fine impartiality both labor and its adversaries when they become locked in deadly embrace." Asked, in his press conference next day, to state what his reaction had been to this, Roosevelt said: "There wasn't any."[24]

## V

BUT to return to mid-June 1937:

Some ten days after Garner had made his ostentatious departure from the Washington scene—that is, on June 14—the Senate Judiciary Committee's majority report on the court-reform bill was issued. It was a document (O'Mahoney its chief author) even more devastating to the court proposal and personally humiliating to the President than the Hughes letter had been. The committee majority (ten senators, including the author of the "compromise" measure, Hatch) damned the bill as "a needless, futile and utterly dangerous abandonment of constitutional principle . . . without precedent or justification," which had been "presented to the Congress in a most intricate form and for reasons that obscured its real purpose." If passed, the bill would accomplish not one of its stated objectives, but it "would subjugate the courts to the will of Congress and the President and thereby destroy the independence of the judiciary, the only certain shield of individual rights." As law, it would establish "the method whereby the people may be deprived of their right to pass upon all amendments of the fundamental law"; indeed, it was "acknowledged by . . . the bill's proponents as a plan to force judicial interpretation of the Constitution,* a proposal that violates every sacred tradition of American democracy" and "would . . . make this government one of men rather than of law. . . ."

Conclusion:

"It is a measure which should be so emphatically rejected that its parallel will never again be presented to the free representatives of the free people of America."[25]

And there was nothing the White House could do to soften the harsh impact of these words upon the public consciousness.

---

*Such "acknowledgment" totally discounted, of course, the deceitfulness of Roosevelt's original "mistake"—that is, the "intricate form" and the stated "reasons that obscured . . . [the] real purpose" in the President's court message. (Author's footnote.)

VI

EVERYTHING now depended, from the White House point of view, upon Joe Robinson, a big man of great physical force but also an essentially humorless man of towering passions (he took himself with special seriousness), and an elderly one (he was sixty-five), whose years of hearty living and insufficient physical exercise had severely strained that vital muscle, his heart.

On July 2, amid the sweltering heat of an unusually fervid Washington summer,* the substitute court bill was formally introduced to the Senate. Four days later, days spent by Robinson in strenuous and uncertain recruitment, the majority leader opened the floor debate with a long, passionate speech frequently interrupted by bitterly hostile questions, several of which deeply wounded his personal pride. He knew that his opponents were thoroughly prepared to filibuster the bill to death if they failed to gain, as they now had every hope of gaining by delaying tactics, enough votes to defeat it. He warned them that "ways will be found to meet their obstruction. It will not be tolerated." Next day, by raising a point of order at the first opposition question, he managed to invoke stringent and long-forgotten Senate rules limiting debate (he was enabled to do so by the fact that Nevada's senator Key Pittman, a presidential supporter, presided in the vice president's absence), thereby making himself the target of such vast and general wrath as had not agitated the Senate during the preceding decade. He had sound reason to believe the tactic had lost votes for the bill. By day's end he was, in the words of Alsop and Catledge, "purple and trembling."[26]

And this was but the beginning.

Day after day thereafter, the heat wave continuing relentlessly, the majority leader was the focus of a struggle that would have severely taxed the physical and emotional resources of a young athlete in perfect condition. Robinson's voice went hoarse with angry shouting. His vision blurred with weariness, with tension; his breath came short and hard, his blood-suffused face glistened with sweat, and his chest was intermittently stabbed with pain. When the long, hard week ended on Saturday, July 10—the proponents' initial arguments having been completed, the opponents' having just begun—Robinson was so utterly exhausted that a Sunday's rest could not restore him. On the following day, in the afternoon, while North Carolina's senator Josiah W. Bailey was making a powerfully effective argument against any tampering whatever with the Supreme Court, Robinson was forced by unprecedentedly excruciating chest pains to leave the floor.

He never returned.

*For the benefit of readers who have grown up in an air-conditioned America, this history has repeatedly emphasized the fact that there was little air-conditioning in the Washington of most of the 1930s. Drugstores, motion-picture theaters, portions of the White House, portions of the Capitol were among the few places where legislators and government officials might escape Washington's humid summer heat—a heat having, therefore, a considerable if unmeasurable effect upon American political events.

The small apartment in which he and his wife had lived for many years, across the plaza from the Capitol, was like an oven when he entered it, and it remained so through a smothering night. His wife was away, at their home in Little Rock, Arkansas. He was alone that night and (for the most part) all next day, too ill to go to the Capitol, yet anxious and fretful because he wasn't there. The fight had been going so badly! And the reports that came to him indicated it went yet worse today, for Bailey's great speech of yesterday seemed to have persuaded several waverers into the enemy camp. By nightfall Robinson was brought nearly, if not altogether, to crushing despair. Sometime during the black hours that followed, his heart broke: On the morning of Wednesday, July 14, his pajama-clad body was found upon the floor beside his bed, a copy of the previous day's *Congressional Record* at the fingertips of his right hand.

With him died any last lingering chance of passage for any bill touching upon the Supreme Court.

Before that fatal Wednesday was out, Wheeler had publicly demanded that the President now withdraw his bill "lest he appear to be fighting against God" —a statement that did the opposition no good at the bar of public opinion (even the bill's opponents thought it in wretched taste) but to which, as a psychological weapon, Roosevelt was at that moment peculiarly vulnerable. He reacted bitterly in private talk and, next day, released for publication a "Dear Alben" letter to Acting Majority Leader Barkley, wherein he condemned his opponents' callous attempt to use Joe Robinson's body, not yet buried, as a club with which to beat the court bill to death ("Advantage is being taken of what, in all decency, should be a period of mourning"[27]); asserted that the "principle" of the court bill was as sound and vitally necessary as ever, unaffected by Robinson's tragic end; and called upon Barkley to continue to struggle strenuously, uncompromisingly, until victory was won—a call so utterly at odds with real possibility that it distressed Barkley despite his pleasure in the President's public expression of confidence in him, and of warm personal friendship, amid the campaign for the post Robinson had vacated.

Yet even as Roosevelt issued this call to continued battle he was reluctantly facing the bitter fact that a clear majority of the Senate was now (since Robinson's death) firmly committed against any enlargement of the Supreme Court whatever. On the following day, Friday, July 16, he was forced to agree to an attempted face-saving stratagem whereby the "principle" of his original court proposal would be affirmed by Congress at the expense of any immediate practical implementation of it: The President would be authorized to appoint coadjutor justices to future Supreme Courts but none for any justice now sitting. Simultaneously, however, he vitiated the slender chances for such face-saving by adding two more errors to the unbroken series of errors he had made in his court-reform effort. First, he refused, despite the urgings of his closest advisers, to go personally to Little Rock for the funeral of the man who, having served him faithfully and well, had died in his service—a man for whose death he might be held, in some part, morally responsible. His refusal projected an image of himself as coldly ruthless, insensitive, and ungrateful beneath his outward show of warm friendliness and generosity. Second, in the afternoon of that Friday, he attempted to mollify with glaring mendacities an angry Pat Harrison, whose support he badly needed and who resented the "Dear Alben" letter as a virtual White House endorsement of Barkley for the majority leadership to which Harrison aspired. Face to face with the Mississippi senator in the Oval Room, the President blandly denied that he had any personal preference whatever between the rival aspirants (Harrison had "misinterpreted" the tone of yesterday's letter), also blandly asserted that neither he nor his lieutenants had or would "interfere" in any way with what was distinctly an internal Senate affair. Both the denial and the assertion were of course promptly published by Harrison (he had the President's permission to do so); each was promptly recognized as a deliberate falsehood by the several senators who had been talked to on this matter by Roosevelt or by White House aides; and each therefore reinforced an already widely pervasive image of Roosevelt as deceitful and untrustworthy.

The Robinson funeral was on Sunday, July 18. It was attended by Vice President Garner, who, thus ending his Uvalde "vacation," returned to Washington on the special train that carried back the congressional delegation and the representatives of the White House. On the train he convened meetings of both proponents and opponents of the court bill and assessed relative strengths, finding, as he had expected to find, that the bill's opposition was far stronger than its support.

Meanwhile, in Washington, Roosevelt suffered through one of the worst days he had had, emotionally, since entering the White House.

That day (Monday, July 19), began with his breakfast perusal of a newspaper column by General Hugh S. Johnson, former NRA administrator, who had become a syndicated columnist with a strong bias against the New Deal. The column said that Robinson's death had been in one respect fortunate for him: It spared him the knowledge that the President, for all his promises on the subject, had had no intention of appointing him to the Supreme Court. Guilt feelings may have augmented the cold fury this provoked in Roosevelt. He summoned Johnson to the White House. He read the offending column aloud to its squirming, red-faced author, commenting caustically upon it as he went along. Then he fixed upon the general a gaze of withering contempt.

"Hugh," he said, "do you know what fine, loyal old Joe Robinson would have said to you if you had written that while he was alive?"

Johnson muttered a barely audible no.

"He would have said, Hugh, that you are a liar, a coward, and a cad."

And Roosevelt repeated that statement, slowly, emphasizing the damning words.

Whereupon (or so Roosevelt told Ickes a couple of days later) Johnson, his face contorted, gasped out that he was "sorry, Mr. President, very sorry," and burst into tears.[28]

That same day saw the publication in the nation's press, under big front-page headlines, of a letter written to "My dear Senator Wagner" by New York's governor, Herbert Lehman, whom Roosevelt had regarded as both a personal friend and a close political ally—a letter urging Wagner, U.S. senator from New York, to vote against the revised court bill.

To this, also, Roosevelt's initial reaction was one of angry outrage. He thoroughly agreed with the sentiments expressed by Felix Frankfurter in a letter to him dashed off by Frankfurter that evening. "Some things just aren't done—they violate the decencies of human relations and offend the good taste and decorum of friendship," wrote Frankfurter, apropos the Lehman letter.[29]

Yet Roosevelt accepted with outward composure Garner's report to him next day (Tuesday, July 20) of the conclusions reached by the voting-strength assessments that had been made on the train.

"You're licked, Cap'n," Garner told him—not unhappily, one may be sure. "You haven't got the votes."[30]

Roosevelt neither argued nor gave sign of dismay. He shrugged. He smiled. Then he asked Garner to handle the details of his proposal's demise in ways that minimized the damage done party and administration.

He remained stubbornly, assertively "convinced" (he may even have said to Garner, good-humoredly) that "the people" were "with him" and would say so emphatically at his behest on some future date.

Next morning, Wednesday, July 21, the White House won its way with respect to the Senate majority leadership. By secret ballot, the Democratic caucus elected Alben Barkley to the post Robinson had vacated, but by the narrowest possible margin (38–37) and to the accompaniment of much ill will. Harrison supporters believed, with reason, that the President had "double-crossed Pat," and some of them, theretofore wavering on the court bill, promptly joined the opposition majority in order to avenge themselves upon him.[31]

Thus, finally and absolutely, Burton K. Wheeler's great day of triumph, Thursday, July 22, 1937, was assured.

In the morning of that day, the Senate Judiciary Committee adopted by voice vote a resolution requesting the full Senate to recommit "Senate Bill 1392, to reorganize the judicial branch of the government, with all amendment thereto," this in order to remove all provisions touching upon the composition of the Supreme Court, or of any lower court, while incorporating certain judicial-procedure reforms upon which there had been, from the first, general agreement. In the afternoon, the full Senate did recommit by a vote of 70–20, with five abstentions. The Judiciary Committee was instructed to report out the revised bill within ten days.

Ashurst's committee followed instructions. A week later it reported out favorably a bill, H.R. 2260, which had already passed the House (Hatton Sumners had done much to shape it) and which Garner now "jammed . . . through to passage, while the galleries grinned, in just fifty-seven minutes."[32]

Roosevelt signed it into law on August 26, five days after Congress had recessed, complaining as he did so that it left "entirely untouched any method of relieving the burden now imposed on the Supreme Court" (thus defiantly did he return to his original and thoroughly discredited contention) but approving its "several provisions which are definitely a step in the right direction."[33]*

VII

THERE remain to be assessed the short-term effects and the long-term historical significance of the court-packing effort.

Roosevelt himself, with an unwonted and therefore psychologically revealing defensiveness, claimed before the bar of history that, in the process of losing his battle, and because he fought it, he won his war against Supreme Court obstructionism. "The startling fact which did more than anything else to bring about the defeat of the plan in the halls of Congress," he said in 1941,[34] "was the clear-cut victory on the bench of the Court for the objectives of the fight. The Court yielded. The Court changed. The Court began to interpret the Constitution instead of torturing it. It was still the same Court, with the same Justices. No new appointments had been made. And yet, beginning shortly after the message of February 5, 1937, what a change!"

The crucial change, however, was of a single mind, the sadly muddled mind of Justice Owen J. Roberts—and we now know that the "Roberts switch" which became famous when the *Parrish* decision was announced on March 29, 1927, presaging Roberts's affirmance of the Wagner Act and Social Security, actually took place on December 19, 1936, some six weeks *before* the delivery of Roosevelt's court message. It was on this December 19 that Roberts, in voting conference with his fellow justices—all of them save Justice Stone, who, having fallen desperately ill on October 14, now lay "in a comatose state at his home"—joined with Hughes, Brandeis, and Cardozo to affirm the lower court's decision in *Parrish*, whereby the constitutionality of Washington State's minimum-wage law was upheld. The four conservative justices, of course, voted the other way. "If the decision had then been announced," Roberts explained some eight years later, "the case would have been affirmed by a divided court. It was thought that this would be an unfortunate outcome, as everyone on the Court knew Justice Stone's views." So the case was "laid over for further consideration when Justice Stone should be able to partici-

---

*The Judicial Procedure Reform Act of 1937 required lower federal-court judges to inform the government of any case pending before it involving a constitutional question, and to permit government attorneys to present evidence and argument on the validity of such question before the court ruled upon it. If the lower court ruled against the government in such a case, appeal to the Supreme Court was expedited by the act's provisions. The act also prohibited the issuance of an injunction on constitutional grounds by any single judge; three judges for this were required, at least one of whom must be a circuit judge. And no such injunction could remain in force more than sixty days. These were salutary changes in judicial procedure, but so deep did they lie in the shadow of Roosevelt's defeat on the Supreme Court issue that they went virtually unnoticed by the general public.

pate," which was not until February 1. Five days later, on the morrow of the court message, *Parrish* was again taken up in conference, with Stone voting as expected for affirmance. Hughes then assigned himself to write the majority opinion.[35]

Indeed, according to Roberts's own dubious testimony, his switch was being prepared, if not actually in process of being made, as early as March 1936, when the petition for certiorari was filed in *Morehead* v. *Tipaldo*.

It may be recalled* that *Tipaldo* came to the Supreme Court on appeal of a 4–3 decision rendered by the New York Court of Appeals in March 1935— a decision declaring unconstitutional the New York law establishing a minimum wage for women. *Tipaldo,* according to the New York court majority, was a case indistinguishable from *Adkins* v. *Children's Hospital* (1923) wherein a U.S. Supreme Court majority had struck down, as a violation of the due-process clauses of the Fifth and Fourteenth amendments, a 1918 District of Columbia statute establishing a minimum wage for women and children. The lawyers who had argued in defense of the New York law (Dean Acheson, representing the Consumers' League, had been a chief one of them) contended that *Tipaldo was* distinguishable from *Adkins,* made so by the experience and new factual information gained during the last dozen years; and it was upon this ground that the appeal from the New York court's decision had been made. However, only one member of the Supreme Court—namely, Chief Justice Hughes—had accepted such a distinction as valid and voted to grant certiorari because of it. The other eight justices had agreed with the New York court majority that *Tipaldo* was indeed ruled by *Adkins.* The three solid liberals (Brandeis, Cardozo, Stone) had then voted to grant the writ because they wished to overturn *Adkins;* the four solid conservatives (Sutherland, Van Devanter, Butler, McReynolds) had voted against granting the writ because they wanted *Adkins* to remain the law; and Roberts, in this instance, had sided with the liberals. The writ had been granted, by a vote of 5–4.

Why had Roberts done this?

By his own account, when the question of granting the writ was being argued in conference, Roberts had said flatly that he "saw no reason to grant the writ unless the Court were prepared to reexamine and overrule the *Adkins* case." His motive for voting to grant certiorari must then have been a desire to overrule *Adkins.* Yet when the time came to achieve this desire, Roberts had become, in effect, *Adkins*'s key defender. In the final decisive conference, he, by his own account, declared that, since "the State of New York . . . had not asked that the Adkins case be overruled but that it be distinguished" from *Tipaldo,* and since he "could find nothing in the record to substantiate such distinction," he was "unwilling to put a decision on any such ground." He therefore voted with the four conservatives for affirmance of the lower court's decision. He claims he told Butler, to whom the writing of the opinion was assigned, that he "would concur in any opinion [he implies his intention to

*Recalled, that is, by readers of *FDR: The New Deal Years,* pp. 614–15.

concur *only* in an opinion] which was based on the fact" that New York State
had not proved its contention of distinction. He further claims that Butler's
opinion "was originally so written." But after "a dissent had been circulated"
among the justices, Butler, infuriated by it, "added matter . . . seeking to
sustain the *Adkins* case in principle."

But surely this is disingenuous on Roberts's part. He seems at pains to
"prove" that as early as March 1936 he was convinced that *Adkins* was bad
law and should be repealed—and his effort so to "prove" has all the earmarks
of a desperately contrived defense against the charge, which he knew would
be prominent in the historical record, that his famous 1937 switch was politically motivated, being made solely for the purpose of protecting the Court
against a probable attempt to drastically limit its powers.

Actually, according to published evidence, Pierce Butler's original or unre-
vised draft opinion in *Tipaldo,* far from being narrowly focused on the question
of distinction, as Roberts implies, was an emphatic reaffirmation of the argument Sutherland had made in 1923 when writing the Supreme Court's majority
opinion in *Adkins.* We know this must be so because the Stone dissent, whose
"circulation" allegedly caused Butler to revise his draft into a defense of
*Adkins* "in principle," makes scathing reference to the "freedom of contract"
argument that was central to Sutherland's *Adkins* argument and was repeated
by Butler in *Tipaldo.* ("There is grim irony in speaking of freedom of contract
of those who, because of their economic necessities, give their services for less
than is needful to keep body and soul together," said Stone in his dissent.)

In any case, there was no necessity for Roberts to concur in what was
allegedly Butler's "revised" opinion; there was every reason why he should
not, assuming him to be as hostile to *Adkins* as his testimony implies. His
"proper course," as he himself admits, would have been to prepare a separate
opinion in which he based his affirmance of the New York court's decision
exclusively "on the narrow ground I had taken." But "I did not do so."[36]
Instead he silently affixed his signature to Butler's (and Sutherland's) outrage
of common sense and common decency.*

---

*Wrote Sutherland for the Supreme Court majority in *Adkins* v. *Children's Hospital:*

   The feature of this [District of Columbia] statute which . . . puts upon it the stamp of invalidity
   is that it exacts from the employer an arbitrary payment for a purpose and upon a basis having
   no causal connection with his business, or the contract, or the work the employee engages to
   do. The declared basis [for a legally enforced minimum wage for women] . . . is not the value
   of the service rendered, but the *extraneous circumstance* [emphasis added] that the employee
   needs to get a prescribed sum of money to insure her subsistence, health, and morals. The
   ethical right of every worker, man or woman, to a living wage, may be conceded . . . but the
   fallacy of the proposed method of attaining it assumes that every employer is bound, at all
   events, to furnish it. The *moral requirement* [emphasis added], implicit in every contract of
   employment, viz., that the amount to be paid and the service to be rendered shall bear to each
   other some relation of just equivalence, is completely ignored. The necessities of the employee
   are alone considered. . . . In principle, there can be no difference between the case of selling
   labor and the case of selling goods.

Seldom in American history has a single instance of one man's muddleheadedness had greater, deeper social impact.

But the point of all this, for our present argument, is that Roosevelt's court message had no such causal efficacy as he later claimed for it. One may well doubt that Roberts's change of mind occurred in exactly the way he describes, or as early as he suggests, in his obviously defensive testimony. One may well suspect that the political considerations he seems at some pains to deny— namely, an awareness that the Court gravely jeopardized its power and prestige by repeatedly frustrating the manifest popular will—weighed ever more heavily upon his judicial mind in the furious aftermath of *Tipaldo,* and that such considerations became decisive of his judicial opinions during and following the 1936 election campaign. (It was during this period that *Parrish* came up for review.) Yet the conclusion is inescapable that if Roosevelt had done nothing at all about the Supreme Court save keep the heat on it, as he did in January 1937 with his annual message and second inaugural, the Court would have changed in precisely the way it did change.

Indeed, Roosevelt himself seems to confess a feeling that this might be so, in his introduction to the 1937 volume of his *Public Papers and Addresses.* He there speaks of "the suggestion which came from some quarters that we do nothing about" the Supreme Court, then identifies this with the kind of "do-nothingism" that "brought us to the brink of disaster in 1932." He indicates that the "suggestion" came only from "those who mistrust democratic government" and "feared the will of the people as expressed on election day." But of course the *actual* counsel he received along these lines from the only "quarters" he listened to (people as anxious as he to remove the judicial roadblock to progressive legislation) was simply that he contain himself for a few months—that he wait and see what the Court would do in early 1937— before mounting, if this proved needful, what he himself calls a "frontal attack."[37] Roosevelt misstated the case, and it is hard to believe that his misstatement was not a deliberate, self-defensive distortion.

Hence, if one agrees with Roosevelt that his "message of February 5, 1937" was not only "one of the most . . . significant events of my administration" but "a turning point in our modern history," it is not for the reason he alleges.* It is because his sadly mistaken court-packing effort effectively ended the New Deal as a reforming, transforming social force—effectively destroyed the possibility that the New Deal could achieve those "practical controls over blind economic forces and blindly selfish men," could "create those moral controls over the services of science . . . necessary to make science a useful servant

---

*"For unless the Court had changed," he writes, "or unless some quick means had been found to give our democracy the power to work out its needs, there is grave doubt whether it could have survived the crisis which was bearing down upon it from within, to say nothing of the present 1941 threat against it from abroad." (Introduction to 1937 *Public Papers and Addresses,* pp. lxvi–lxvii.) The "bearing down . . . from within" of a "crisis" seems conclusive textual evidence that this prose is wholly Roosevelt's own; Rosenman had no hand in it.

instead of a ruthless master of mankind," that Roosevelt had named in his second inaugural as fundamental objectives of his administration.

VIII

AN immediate effect of the court battle was the failure in Congress of most of the administration's legislative program for 1937. This was in good part due to the failure of Roosevelt's celebrated sense of timing. His initial timing decision was that the court bill should take precedence over all else. There were, in his mind, two reasons: First, the court bill would pass more quickly if all administration energies were focused upon it; second, its passage would so strengthen his hand in dealing with his opposition that the success of the remainder of his legislative package, in Congress, would be assured. In late spring, when it became clear that his court bill was in serious trouble, he strove to reverse the order, on the assumption that passage of at least the most popular portion of his legislative package would facilitate passage of court reform. But by then what had begun as a war between President and Court had become a war between President and Congress, with the latter's alienation from the White House characterized by bitterest enmity. The power balance between left and right inevitably shifted rightward as the "Roosevelt coalition" came apart. Congressional liberals were in disarray, more divided and confused and demoralized than at any time since 1929. Congressional conservatives, on the other hand, always more cohesive (because more single-minded) than the liberals, were now more confident of their ability to obstruct and frustrate. As for Roosevelt personally, he was become for the moralist a cautionary tale, living proof that "pride goeth before a fall." When the congressional session began in January, he stood upon a higher pinnacle of power and prestige than any peacetime President before him had ever stood upon—had then seemed monarch of all he surveyed in politics and government. When the session approached its end, in August, he was so far cast down that the chances of congressional passage of anything he proposed were diminished by the very fact that *he* had proposed it.

Bits and pieces of his 1937 program had become statute law by adjournment day. Most had been substantially enacted early in the session. Some were of immediate importance. The Bituminous Coal Act did much to bring order out of the chaos to which the coal industry had been returned by the Supreme Court's invalidation of the Guffey Act in May 1936. The Bankhead-Jones Farm Tenancy Act made it easier for farm tenants to become farm owners by borrowing on easy credit terms from a federal farm-loan agency. This slowed somewhat the trend toward abolition of the family farm which technological advance (and AAA benefit-payment policies) continued to encourage. Renewal of the Trade Agreement Act enabled a continuation of the attempt, so fervently promoted by Cordell Hull, to make world peace through world free trade, pitting the tradesman's passion for profit against the warrior's lust for violence in the belief that the former would overbalance the latter. The Wagner Housing Act, for the passage of which Wagner was considerably more responsible than the President (the White House did not make it "must" legislation until June), established a United States Housing Authority empowered to make federal loans for the construction of low-rent housing and to make up the annual difference between such housing's maintenance cost and the rent paid by the housing's low-income inhabitants.*

Tax-reform legislation called for by the President in a special message delivered to Congress on June 1 was also passed, late in the session. The bulk of this message consisted of a letter to the President from Secretary of the Treasury Morgenthau (Roosevelt, who had had a hand in its preparation, quoted it in full)—a letter that announced and sought to account in part for "the failure of the receipts from the income tax on March 15 to measure up to the budget estimates." Some $600 million less in tax had been collected than had been confidently expected, and an immediate investigation of individual income-tax returns had shown much of this shortage to be due to the fact that taxpayers having "large incomes," also the hired help of expensive and ingenious tax lawyers, were employing numerous "devices" to avoid payment of the income taxes that Congress, in its latest tax legislation, had clearly intended them to pay. Several of the tax-cheat "devices" were described in the message in a way that shamed those who employed them, or would have done if these cheats had not remained cloaked in anonymity. There was aroused in the public at large the "feeling of indignation" which, said the President, "was mine" when he learned of all this. Through personal corporations established in the Bahamas, Newfoundland, "and other places where taxes are low and corporation laws lax"; through domestic personal holding companies whose income remained allegedly "undistributed" to those who set them up; through complicated insurance schemes involving the establishment of phony companies in foreign lands; through the incorporation of yachts, town houses, and country estates—through all these means, and several others, the very rich had challenged successfully "the power of the Government to collect uniformly, fairly and without discrimination, taxes based on statutes adopted by the Congress." ("Thus, one man's yacht is owned by his personal holding company, along with three million dollars in securities. He rents the yacht from his company for a sum far less than the cost of upkeep, and the company uses income from securities to pay the wages of the captain and crew, the expenses of operating the yacht, and the annual depreciation allowance. None of these

---

*The bill was much amended before being passed, and in ways disappointing to the bill's chief author since they severely limited the legislation's expansive effect upon low-rent housing. The Housing Authority, placed under Ickes in the Interior Department instead of functioning as the independent agency Wagner wanted, was authorized to make public-housing loans of $500,000,000, which was just half the amount called for in the original bill. Wagner had then to do battle with empire-builder Ickes for presidential appointment of Nathan Strauss, rather than foot-dragging Howard Gray of the PWA's housing division, to head the new agency.

items would be deductible if the individual owned the yacht personally.") The "long-term problem of tax policy" was wholly separate from this "immediate problem of glaring evasion and avoidance of existing law," said the President, adding that the latter involved "the decency of American morals" and called for "legislation at this session aimed at making the present tax structure evasion proof."[38] Congress responded with the Revenue Act of 1937, whereby the tax structure was rendered less vulnerable to wealthy cheats, if still far from "evasion proof."

Thus the administration's legislative successes in that session.

Four major administration proposals remained unpassed, however, and these the most important by Roosevelt's criteria. Also by history's.

A Fair Labor Standards Act had been introduced in late May by Alabama's senator Hugo L. Black after Roosevelt, having decided to reverse his temporal priorities, sent Congress a special message calling for such legislation. It proposed to set federal minimum-wage and maximum-hour standards for workers. Easy passage of it was assumed, in view of the rapid growth in labor organization and in popular recognition that the bitterness and ominous violence of the current struggle between labor and management must be moderated by governmental action if economic recovery were to continue. But the bill at once ran into strong opposition from Black's Southern colleagues, representing employers in a low-wage area. Pat Harrison attacked it vehemently on the floor of the Senate. It provoked divisive controversy in the ranks of labor itself, the AFL fearing it would encourage the CIO's drive for mass industrial organization. It contained a clause designed to protect the proposed wage-and-hour arrangements against foreign competition by raising certain tariff barriers, which promoted hostilities between protectionists and free-trade advocates in Roosevelt's own party. As a result, the bill passed the Senate only with great difficulty, and then languished in the Rules Committee of the House, where a coalition of Republicans and conservative Southern Democrats was strong enough to prevent its being reported for floor action.

A comprehensive farm bill had been proposed by the administration to fill the void left when the Agricultural Adjustment Act was invalidated by the Supreme Court—a void only partially filled by subsequent legislation alleging soil conservation as justification for limiting farm production. Of course the ultimate purpose of benefit payments for nonproduction of crops was not to save soil but to raise farm prices and, though nature had intervened to limit wheat and corn production drastically with the great drouths of 1934 and 1936, the individual incomes of drouth-stricken farmers had not been raised, whereas food prices had been, resulting in much consumer complaint. The administration's bill had at its heart an "ever-normal granary" device suggested to Secretary of Agriculture Henry Wallace, he claimed, by the biblical story of Joseph in Egypt: Surplus crops were to be stored in bumper years for release onto the market in lean years and also to even out the distribution pattern within any given year, thereby preventing drastic fluctuations in farm and consumer prices. Congress announced in midsummer, by joint resolution, its intention to enact such legislation but had failed to do so when, amid the bitter confusion following the court-reform defeat, it recessed.

The other two administration proposals were of yet greater long-term significance, being directly and importantly concerned with bringing technological power and its human consequences under humane controls—the overall aim, Roosevelt had suggested, of the New Deal.

One of these was the executive-reorganization bill, which had emerged from Brownlow Committee deliberations and which is discussed in the first chapter of this book.* It will be recalled that this bill proposed to "establish a budget and efficiency agency, a personnel agency and a planning agency."[39] The latter, labeled the National Planning Board, was central to the executive-reorganization scheme. It was to be the agency that supplied both executive and legislature with the information and ideas needed to deal realistically, creatively, with the environmental hazards, the natural resource hazards, that were encouraged by a causal linkage of technological change to private profit initiatives.

Through the National Planning Board proposal, executive reorganization was intimately joined with George Norris's administration-sponsored bill to create seven regional authorities. (It was largely because Norris was so deeply committed to this proposal, which must have active White House support for its passage, that he in tacit trade-off went along with the court-reform bill he initially opposed.) The authorities were to be modeled upon the TVA experience but, unlike the TVA, would have no direct administrative functions of their own. There were to be an Atlantic Seaboard Authority; a Great Lakes and Ohio Valley Authority; an agency "for the drainage basin of the Tennessee and Cumberland Rivers" (critics saw this as an invitation to trouble between the proposed agency and the TVA); an authority "embracing the drainage basins of the Missouri River and the Red River of the north"; one "embracing the drainage basins of the Arkansas, Red, and Rio Grande Rivers"; one "for the basins of the Colorado River and rivers flowing into the Pacific south of the California-Oregon line"; and, finally, an authority for the Columbia River basin.[40] Each of these agencies would be a planning body. Each would aim to coordinate or integrate, into a single overall program for its region, federal projects for flood control, soil and water conservation, hydroelectric power, irrigation, and river navigation.

The need for such coordination was compelling, and obvious to all who studied the consequences of the current distribution of water and water-related federal projects among competing specialized agencies. To the U.S. Army Corps of Engineers were assigned flood control and navigation. To the Bureau of Reclamation of the Interior Department was assigned irrigation.† The Federal Power Commission was concerned with the development of hydro-

---

*See pp. 19–28, 30.
†The Bureau of Reclamation and the Army Engineers quarreled continuously over the use of water in the upper reaches of the Missouri River system. In this drouthy region there was not enough water to supply both engineer navigation and reclamation irrigation.

electric power, the Public Health Service with halting the use of flowing streams as open sewers. The Soil Conservation Service and the Forest Service of the Department of Agriculture had to do with erosion control and the retention of precipitation in the soil for plant use, efforts directly connected with those of flood control and the prevention of silting, destructive alike of reservoir storage capacity and navigation channels, downstream. The silting problem also concerned Public Health. Thus each of these agencies had assigned to it a problem (or problems) ultimately insoluble in isolation from those assigned elsewhere, since all of them had as central theme the simple fact that water, precipitated unevenly upon the land, flows downhill and releases energy as it does so. Yet every one of these agencies, by the prevailing arrangement, was a sovereign power within its statute-defined field; each was characterized by bureaucratic jealousies and ambitions; each competed with the others for congressional appropriations; and each was backed in such competition by a special-interest pressure group.* The result was an incredibly wasteful chaos of water projects in every major river valley of the nation—a chaos that, to disinterested minds, argued unanswerably for some such "authority" device as Norris-Roosevelt proposed.

Moreover, it appears to a retrospective eye that this proposal (it was inaccurately dubbed a bill to create "seven TVAs"), along with executive reorganization, would have passed in 1937 with some (probably improving) modifications if Roosevelt had chosen to spend his vast post-election political capital upon them instead of upon his doomed court bill. As it was, neither had even been called up for floor debate by recess day, and the future for both was dark.

Roosevelt had lost control.

And it is one of the ironies of American history that this should have been caused by Roosevelt himself, just when the business community was forcing him to recognize, or to begin at long last to recognize, despite his personally conservative predilections, that some truly significant structural changes might have to be made in the American Way of producing and distributing goods, services, income, and decision-making power if the historic task (the God-assigned task) of his New Deal were to be accomplished.

The irony is compounded by the evident fact that Roosevelt, instead of blaming himself for having mistaken his will for God's in the court matter, interpreted his defeat as a sign that from now on he must be wary, that God intended him to be wary, of future head-on collisions with conservative busi-

---

*These pressure groups, of course, varied widely in numerical strength and effectiveness of organization. The Army Engineers' backing had proved, and would continue to prove, overwhelming. It was spearheaded by a National Rivers and Harbors Congress, whose immense power derived from the fact that its membership actually comprised many of those who were the objects of its pressure, namely U.S. senators and representatives (these were designated "honorary members" but were active participants, even serving as presiding officers) and all Army Engineer officers engaged in rivers and harbors work, as well as representatives of state and local governments, industrial organizations, trade associations, labor unions, and private contractors. The huge pork barrels it manufactured would still be rolling through legislative halls more than four decades later.

ness interests. His original tendency to identify "democracy" with "capitalism" (the profit system) was strengthened instead of weakened as it would otherwise have been. He was encouraged to make, in the future, "compromises" with big business that were actually surrenders of governing power— this in situations where he could almost certainly have won a battle for People against Property had he chosen to wage it.

Thus was further stimulated a process whereby America would come to resemble more and more closely the imperial Germany (a fusion of big business with big government) which Wilhelm II inherited from Bismarck*—a state wherein human choices and preferences were increasingly subordinated, for profit reasons, to the capabilities and "convenience" of the machine; a state whose very mind would be molded in large degree by electronic technology (television) harnessed to private profit-making; a state whose most crucial "decisions" would consequently consist, for the most part, of blind inertia or mechanical action-reaction. And all this without the general citizenry having any awareness of what had happened and was happening to them.

IX

NOR was it only of the external situation that Roosevelt had lost control; there was a failure, too, of self-control.

Throughout this long struggle he had seemed to most others to retain unflawed and in full force his sunny disposition. He had seemed to them to absorb repeated rebuffs and disappointments philosophically, with no reduction of his zest for life, his patience, his concern for the personal welfare of his subordinates, or his capacity for energetic and energizing fun. There was, however, a notable increase at this time of acerbity, of manifest disgust and anger, in his official operations as in his personal conversations and correspondence. It was with unwonted fury, streaked with vindictiveness, that he reacted to Morgenthau's disclosures to him of the afore-described tax cheating by the very rich. He regarded these disclosures as weapons to be used against the "enemies of reform," men who would, as he said to Morgenthau, create a Fascist America if they continued to have their way. He insisted that Cummings launch criminal proceedings against one wealthy man, "a son of a bitch" in Roosevelt's words, whose tax evasion was clearly provably illegal but whom the attorney general, for whatever reason, was reluctant to prosecute. (This man eventually went to the penitentiary.) He insisted that the names of rich tax cheats be published, and continued to insist on this against the considered opinion of Treasury and Justice lawyers that such publication would be illegal. Only with great difficulty was he finally persuaded to give up the idea.[41]

He also reacted with abnormal bitterness when banker J. P. Morgan, Jr., interviewed aboard the ship that had returned him from England in early June, told reporters, apropos of Roosevelt's special tax message, that "Congress

*See *FDR: The Beckoning of Destiny,* pp.372–75.

should know how to levy taxes, and if it doesn't know how to collect them, then a man is a fool to pay the taxes. . . . You only do what you are compelled to do by law, for it is never any pleasure for anyone to pay taxes." "What what do you think of J.P.M.'s exposition of Christianity when he landed the other day?" Roosevelt asked in a memorandum to his longtime friend Charles Burlingham, with whom he had had a recent argument about the ethics of America's businessmen and lawyers. "How many Englishmen occupying a similar position in London would express the same ethical viewpoint? . . . Finally, ask yourself what Christ would say about the American Bench and Bar were he to return today?"[42]

He rose to the bait with an expression of scornful disgust when Alexander Forbes, a distant cousin and Harvard classmate of his who was now professor of physiology at the Harvard Medical School, sent him a copy of a letter he had written to the Boston *Herald*—a letter defending the stand taken by Morgan. Tax-paying was a legal obligation, not a moral one, argued Forbes, and anyone was justified in taking advantage of whatever tax avoidance the law allowed, especially now when, obviously, private wealth was used far more "honestly and intelligently . . . to advance civilization" than was the tax money collected by government. "Look at the sorry spectacle presented by long rows of beneficiaries of the 'boondoggle,' leaning on their shovels by the hour, at futile projects, and contrast it with the great universities, museums, and research libraries which have come from the wise and generous giving of such as Morgan. . . ." Roosevelt in his reply branded Forbes "one of the worst anarchists in the United States. . . . You are saying in your letter . . . —'let every man who does not agree with the law violate it at his discretion.' "[43]

As for his fun, it became now, more than normally, exclusively of the practical-joke variety.

For instance, his anticipation of the late-June wedding of his namesake son and Ethel du Pont, daughter of Pierre S. du Pont,* was for him chock-full of a laughter that had more than a touch of malice in it. He saw in the approaching event a juxtaposition of incongruous elements that was both hilarious and wry, there being no more fervent right-wing Roosevelt-hater in all the land than Pierre S. du Pont; and his enjoyment was enhanced when Du Pont names appeared on the Treasury Department's list of wealthy tax cheats in May. This, conjoined with the special message of June 1, made it certain that the upcoming marriage ceremony in Delaware would be "a happy affair," chortled Roosevelt to intimates.

The wedding itself more than fulfilled his expectations of pleasure. It was one of the half-dozen most hugely publicized American weddings of the twentieth century, thanks to newsmen and a public that assessed its incongruities in the same way Roosevelt did. The President of the United States was as definitely the center of attention at these nuptials as an earlier President (Theodore Roosevelt) had been at those of Franklin and Eleanor Roosevelt

*See *FDR: The New Deal Years,* p. 661.

thirty-three years before, and FDR enjoyed himself quite as much as TR had done in 1904. "Rarely have I seen Father appear to have a better time at a social function . . ." James Roosevelt remembered many years later. "He . . . relished infiltrating the du Pont nest, flanked by such New Deal stalwarts as Harry Hopkins. . . . [He] enjoyed the rich food and champagne, and, as I remember it, kissed all the bridesmaids."[44]

One New Deal stalwart who might well have been but was not at that wedding was hard-driving Harold Ickes.

At Roosevelt's insistence, the secretary of the interior and WPA administrator Hopkins, between whom a long-smoldering quarrel over the division of federal funds between the PWA and WPA had burst into roaring flame in the summer of 1935, had gone with the President on a long vacation voyage aboard the U.S.S. *Houston* in the fall of 1935. This typically Rooseveltian tactic had worked well: Ickes and Hopkins had been surprised to discover a personal liking for each another, and this had prevented their subsequent clashes of ambition and policy from becoming such quarrels as had made headlines in the second and third years of the New Deal. Ickes himself, with Roosevelt's enthusiastic approval and facilitation, had arranged with Hopkins an April fishing cruise for the two, aboard federal revenue cutter *Saranac* (Morgenthau had placed the vessel at their disposal) in Florida waters. Ickes had returned from this apparently refreshed and relaxed, with friendly personal relations between him and Hopkins further strengthened. But in late May he had suffered a coronary thrombosis and had spent some weeks flat on his back in Bethesda Naval Hospital (a concerned Roosevelt had visited him there); he was still recuperating from this in late June.

Ickes was one of the few outside the innermost White House circle who sensed that Roosevelt, behind his show of calm confidence, good cheer, and imperturbability, was "punch drunk from the punishment . . . suffered recently" and "distinctly more nervous" than he had formerly been.[45] (This observation was made immediately after the court bill's demise.) And in actual fact, as has been indicated, the normal balance between arrogance and humility at the root of his good-humored behavior (his imperious Delano nature counseled arrogance; his religious faith, inspired by his father and by Peabody, counseled a species of humility) had been seriously disturbed. Inwardly he fumed, he raged against his humiliation. From festering psychic wounds there rose up into his mind a befogging poisonous passion for revenge upon those who had hurt and thwarted him. Which is to say that the vindictiveness that was a part of his natural response to the frustration of his will by other wills, and that had disastrously affected his decision-making at the outset of his struggle against the Supreme Court, now became a ruling passion.

This passion wholly determined his decision, almost certainly firmly made before that summer had ended, personally to purge from Senate and House in the primaries of 1938 those Democrats who had defeated his court proposal and otherwise obstructed his New Deal. He knew he could do so because, he asserted more strongly than ever, "the people are with me!"

And this passion largely determined the manner and substance of his choice of a replacement for Van Devanter on the Supreme Court, after Robinson's death.

Obvious to all informed folk were certain considerations that would guide the President's appointment of a new Supreme Court justice. First, in view of the emphasis that had been placed upon the infirmities of aged judicial minds, the new justice must be a relatively young man. Second, he should be a Southerner or Westerner, other things being equal, since these geographic regions were currently inadequately represented on the Court. Third, he must be a staunch liberal and loyal supporter of the administration. Fourth, he must be certainly confirmable by a Senate whose general attitude toward the White House was now rebelliously defiant.

One man who satisfied all four of these criteria was Solicitor General Stanley Reed, and Reed's appointment, confidently expected by many, was strongly favored by Corcoran.[46] Reed was a Kentuckian, fifty-two years old. He had performed well, since 1935, the thankless task of advocating and defending the government's position in cases before the Supreme Court; it was certainly not his fault that, prior to the spring of 1937, his efforts had almost invariably failed. He was highly respected nationally in the legal profession; he was urbane, courteous, cultured, sensitively considerate in his human relations; and he had no known enemies in the Senate. Indeed, he was generally well liked by the members of that body. His confirmation would assuredly be swift, easy, and free of rancor.

But did Reed's easy acceptability argue for his appointment, in Roosevelt's mind? It did just the opposite. It meant that Reed failed to satisfy a fifth criterion that, though unspoken, weighed at least as heavily with Roosevelt, in his present mood, as any of the four named above. This fifth criterion was, in a word, obnoxiousness. If possible, the appointment should be one the Senate would *have* to confirm, yet whose confirmation would be as gall and wormwood to many senators, to all conservatives. This practically meant that the appointee must be a member of the Senate itself, and a member whose support of administration measures, especially of the court bill from first to last, had been of such nature as to arouse strongly felt personal antagonisms. The antagonisms would count for nothing but helpless pain for those who felt them: Traditional "senatorial courtesy" precluded the possibility that a majority of the senators would vote against confirmation of any colleague.

By August, Roosevelt had narrowed the field of possibilities to two*—either Sherman Minton of Indiana or Hugo Black, the latter of whom, as an Alaba-

---

*He had also let it be known by then that he had asked the attorney general for an opinion on the legality of a recess appointment to the Court. This had provoked "a great deal of clamor in the Senate," as Ickes told his diary on July 29 and as Roosevelt intended. It meant that the Senate might have to delay its late-summer recess until Roosevelt decided upon a name (and the senators were eager to escape the broiling Washington heat)—either that or be presented with a fait accompli and the need, on reconvening, to hold dubiously constitutional hearings upon an already sitting justice.[47]

man, perfectly satisfied not only the fifth criterion but also the other four. Minton was approached on the matter; he promptly eliminated himself from consideration. He had said such harsh things about some of the present justices during the long court-reform battle that it would now be difficult if not impossible for him to work at all with the men he had attacked. He strongly recommended Black instead.

So it was Black's name that was sent to the Senate on August 13.

Fifty-one years old and looking younger, Black was greatly respected by his colleagues for courage, industry, tenacity, and the sharpness if not brilliance of a remarkably well informed mind. All the same he "would have unquestionably won the unpopularity contest in any secret poll of the upper house," according to a sympathetic biographer of him.[48] His was, it seemed from his record, an inquisitorial rather than judicial mind and temper. He had earned the bitterest enmity of conservatives, along with a reputation for ruthlessness, during his famous investigations of fraudulent shipping subsidies, fraudulent air-mail contract awards, and utility holding-company chicanery—investigations that had provided sound factual bases for important subsequent legislation but that had also raised doubts among civil libertarians concerning his commitment to the right of privacy, to the legal protections against unreasonable search and seizure. (Roosevelt himself had no high opinion of Black's abilities as a lawyer; he confessed as much to Ickes.[49])

Hence, the announcement of the appointment raised a storm of conservative protest quite high enough to gratify Roosevelt's malice; but it raised other protest as well—from socialist Norman Thomas and from the editors of liberal journals of opinion who feared Black's Alabama background and the racism this implied. Note was taken of his outspoken opposition to federal antilynching legislation. Consequently, he was denied the immediate confirmation without hearings that was customarily granted the appointment of an incumbent senator. Senator Hiram W. Johnson of California, for one, objected when Ashurst asked in formal motion for the unanimous consent necessary for this. Said the dour Johnson, erstwhile Progressive warrior, whose opposition to the court bill had been as deeply emotional as Carter Glass's: "Judging him [Black] by his disposition, he ought not to be . . . a member of the Supreme Court."[50]

During the six-hour debate over the confirmation on August 17, a question was raised about Black's membership in the Ku Klux Klan, it being known by all Southerners that he could not have won his first election to the Senate from the Alabama of 1926 without Klan support. Roosevelt had asked no such question during Black's secret night visit to the Oval Room on August 11— the night the President, impatient now to spring a dismaying surprise appointment upon the Senate, wrote Black's name into the Supreme Court nomination form. Homer Cummings had asked no such question either, earlier on, when he talked over his own list of candidates (Black's name prominent upon it) with the President. And no FBI investigation of Black's background had been ordered. But Idaho's Senator William Borah asked the question of Black directly, having been sent by his fellow senators to do so,* and received a careful reply. "I am not a member of the Klan," said Black, his tacit "now" implying he might formerly have been. Whereupon Borah returned to the floor to deny, or seem to deny (his words, too, were ambiguous), that Black was now or had ever been a Klansman.

The vote was then taken. Black was confirmed, 63–16.

"So Hugo Black becomes a member of the Supreme Court of the United States," wrote Ickes into his diary, "while the economic royalists fume and squirm and the President rolls his tongue around in his cheek."[51]

But this was by no means the end of the story.

On Monday, September 13, while Black and his wife were vacationing in Europe, the Pittsburgh *Post Gazette* began serial publication of a news feature by its ace investigative reporter, Ray Sprigle, based upon incontrovertible documentary evidence that Black had not only joined the Klan in 1923 but had "resigned" from it in 1926 with a letter signed "Yours I.T.S.U.B." The initials stood for "in the sacred unfailing bond" and meant that Black continued a covert allegiance to the body from which he was overtly separating himself. Clearly his "resignation" was designed to bemuse the non-Klan voting public as he entered that year's primary race; and his election had been celebrated by his local Klan chapter ("Klavern"), in Birmingham, as a victory for one of its own.

The Sprigle revelations provoked a national furor. There were immediate and loud calls for Black's forced resignation from the Court. Roosevelt, who had fought the Klan bravely in the 1920s (witness his Binghamton speech during his gubernatorial race in 1928†), was profoundly disturbed and again publicly embarrassed. He must have regretted the price he was now required again to pay for the secrecy with which he had made a major decision in order to spring it upon Congress and country as a shocking surprise. And there was little, if anything, he could do about it. At his press conference on September 14 he said he had had no prior knowledge of Black's Klan connection and now knew only "what I have read in the papers. Mr. Justice Black is in Europe. . . . Until such time as he returns, there is no further comment to be made."[52] This was taken to be a strong hint to Black that he had better be prepared with a public statement, and that it had better be a persuasive one, when he did return.

Three days after the press conference, Roosevelt delivered a nationally broadcast Constitution Day address substantially prepared for him by Felix Frankfurter, with some help from Tommy Corcoran.[53] It was a justification in historical terms of the stand he had taken and the course he had pursued in his campaign against the judiciary; his presentation of it indicated his intention to continue this pursuit.

The Constitution of the United States, said he, had been conceived as "a

---

*Black had, of course, absented himself from the Senate floor when he himself became the subject of debate.
†See *FDR: The New York Years,* p. 36.

layman's document, not a lawyer's contract," and as such it notably lacked "the 'whereases' and the 'parties of the first part' and the fine print which lawyers put into leases and insurance policies and installment agreements." But ever since this Constitution was adopted there had been "an unending struggle between those who would preserve . . . the Constitution as a layman's document," broadly conceived, and those who would, generally for their own selfish purposes, "shrivel the Constitution into a lawyer's contract"—that is, a legal document specifically designed to preserve existing institutions and routines unchanged, achieving rigidity and permanence amid and against the turbulent flow of time. To the extent that this aim was achieved, flexible responses to changing circumstances were denied; and the cost of the failure so to respond had often been, in American history, very high. The lawyers' view of the Constitution as a legal contract with slave owners, for instance, resulted in a Supreme Court decision that, with its implied repeal of the Missouri Compromise, removed the last safeguard against national civil war. And not only did it "cost a Civil War to gain recognition of the constitutional power of the Congress to legislate for the territories," it also "cost twenty years of taxation on those *least* able to pay to recognize the constitutional power of the Congress to levy taxes on those *most* able to pay"; it "cost twenty years of exploitation of women's labor to recognize the constitutional power of the States to pass minimum wage laws for their protection"; it "has cost twenty years already—and no one knows how many more are to come—to obtain a constitutional interpretation that will let the Nation regulate the shipment in national commerce of goods sweated from the labor of little children." Of course "it takes time to adjust government to the needs of [a changing] society. But modern history proves that reforms too long delayed or denied have jeopardized peace, undermined democracy and swept away civil and religious liberties." America could no longer tolerate twenty-year delays of desperately needed socioeconomic reforms, delays stubbornly imposed by lawyer-judges who *"read* into the Constitution language which the framers refused to *write* into the Constitution."[54]

Five days later, on September 22, Roosevelt boarded his special train, at Hyde Park, to begin a national tour that would take him to the Pacific Coast and back.

Meanwhile, in Paris, in London, wherever they went, Black and his wife were hounded by newsmen avid for a statement from him. He flatly refused to say anything until, having taken a slow steamer back from Ireland, he landed in Norfolk, Virginia, on September 30—and all he said then to the crowd of reporters was that, when he had a statement to make, he would "make it in such a way that I cannot be misquoted and the nation can hear."

He did so on the evening of the following day, October 1. Over three national radio networks, Black spoke, from seclusion in a friend's house, for precisely eleven minutes to a national audience that may have numbered fifty million people. He deplored the "planned and concerted attack" upon him, charging that it was "calculated to create racial and religious hatred." He pointed to his long and close personal friendships in Birmingham with Jews and Catholics. He then admitted what he could not deny—and not one whit more. He had indeed joined the Klan. "Before becoming a senator I dropped the Klan. I have had nothing to do with it since that time. . . . With this statement my discussion of the subject is closed."[55]

And it was. Black never referred to it publicly again.

Nor did Franklin Roosevelt.

And so it was, in a final prolonged spasm of ineptitude and consequent personal embarrassment, that the President came at last to the end of his long struggle against the U.S. Supreme Court.[56]

# BOOK TWO

⇥⤜⤛

# Falterings—
# The Bitter Years

# 4

###### ->->X<<-

# Lost Control: Events Take Command

I

STRANGE to say, the President, who on the evening of October 1, 1937, came to the end of the ninth day of his tour of the West, was among the very few Americans interested in public affairs who did not listen to what Justice Black had to say, over the radio, about his Klan connection.

The night before, spent in cabins belonging to the Lake Crescent Lodge on the northern edge of the Olympic National Park, had been for the President and his considerable party a literally chilling experience. The cabins were unheated; the temperature had dropped down into the forties, and many of the party had slept in their clothes. Few of them had shaved that morning, though Roosevelt himself had perforce done so. "This proves the old man can take it," he had joked as he was lifted into his car, one of a caravan of twenty-odd, early in the morning. He rode then southward, hour after hour, through some of the most beautiful mountain scenery in the world but saw none of it, alas. Heavy rain was falling. The air was thick with fog. Roosevelt's view was confined by shifting walls of mist to the huge firs and hemlocks that towered two hundred feet and more into the thick air immediately beside the road he traveled—a narrow road along which, nevertheless, the caravan moved at a steady pace of forty miles an hour or more. His schedule called for inspection stops on his way through the park, viewing Park Service and Civilian Conservation Corps projects; he was to speak briefly and informally at Aberdeen, and arrive in Tacoma at six-thirty that evening (nine-thirty Eastern Standard Time), which was precisely when Black was to go on the air.

He was actually well ahead of schedule when he arrived at Olympia, the state capital, late in the afternoon. There, however, he made an unscheduled and unexplained stop of more than half an hour at the governor's mansion; and when the journey was resumed, the rain having ceased, he rode, not in the sedan in which he had been sitting since morning, but in an open car—a shift allegedly made at the governor's suggestion, so that the people who would inevitably throng Tacoma's streets could see him. The caravan's speed was now drastically slowed; the cars crawled along the highway at little more than ten miles an hour. The President did not arrive at his special train, parked on a Great Northern siding in Tacoma's train yard, until more than an hour after Black's broadcast speech had ended.

He declined then to meet with the group of reporters who awaited him— reporters who clamored for a presidential statement about what Black had said. Instead, he sent James to explain that the open car in which he had been riding was unequipped with a radio. He couldn't comment upon what Black had said because he didn't know what Black had said. The reporters who received this information did so with rueful, knowing grins. They more than suspected that the President had been at some pains to avoid listening to what his troubled court appointee had to say.[1] (This same suspicion, as we may anticipate, would be manifest by the reporters who met with him at Hyde Park on October 6, a few hours after his tour had ended; nor would they be persuaded by his "explanation" of what had happened, which was that someone ["I think it was Jimmie"] had told him in the morning of October 1 that Black was "going on the air tonight at 6:30," but that he "never thought of it again" that day. "After we got away from Olympia the road was wet so we slowed the procession to prevent the policemen on motorcycles from going overboard," he would go on to say. "For that reason we had a slow run and instead of being in the open car for twenty minutes I was in it for exactly two hours and ten minutes. That is the actual, simple fact."[2])

By the time he reboarded his train at Tacoma, the Western trip had accomplished what was, for him, a sovereign purpose. "There was an old mythological character by the name of Antaeus, who was supposed, every time his foot touched the ground, to redouble his strength," he had said to a Boise, Idaho, crowd four days before. "When I go about the country after long weeks and months tied up in Washington . . . I feel that I regain my strength by just meeting the American people."[3] And certainly he had drawn strength from the sight and sound of the crowds that greeted him at his every stop. They were so large, so enthusiastic! They seemed to him as much so as any he had ever faced—and though he had thus far carefully refrained from any mention of the Supreme Court, much less of his defeated court bill, his speeches had evoked crowd responses confirmative of his repeatedly expressed belief that that failed struggle had not cost him popular support. "The people are [still] with me," their commitment to him as great as it been at the first of the year. He was encouraged, too, by the crowds' evident enthusiastic approval of the sentiments, the ideas that his speeches expressed.

The speeches, most of them informal and extemporaneous, had been numerous—four, on farm subjects, in Iowa on September 23; four more, on a miscellany of subjects, in Wyoming on September 24; another, at West Yellowstone in Montana on Sunday the twenty-sixth; and four, in Idaho and Oregon, on the following day. Two prepared speeches had been given in Oregon on Tuesday, September 28. One of the two had briefly dedicated a lodge, Timberline Lodge, on the slopes of Mount Hood, "as a monument to the skill and faithful performance of workers on the rolls of the Works Progress Administration." The other, a full-length address at the Bonneville Dam, had reiterated the environmental-conservation themes, along with an aversion to huge cities, that had been at the heart of his political thought and conception of government ever since he had first expressed them in public speech more than a quarter-century ago.* He had stressed the right and need of government "to interfere with" what some propertied men "miscall 'the liberty of the individual,' " saying that his own "conception of liberty does not permit an individual citizen or group of citizens to commit acts of depredation against nature in such a way as to harm their neighbors, and especially to harm the future generations of Americans." He had also stressed that the whole of the Columbia River watershed, including most of Washington, Oregon, Idaho, and a part of Montana, must be thought of "as a unit" and "in terms of the whole population of that area," not only "as it is today," but also "as we expect it will be fifty . . . years from now." And as he himself thought "of the Nation and the region fifty years from now" when making policy decisions about the use of the electricity generated at Bonneville, he was led to "venture the prophecy that . . . we will do everything in our power to build up the smaller communities of the United States," this because "many people are beginning to realize that there is inherent weakness in cities which become too large for the times[,] and inherent strength in a wider distribution of population. . . . There is doubtless a reasonable balance in all this and it is a balance which ought to be given more and more study." Careful overall regional planning was called for, not only for this Columbia River basin but also for "the other great regions of the Nation."

It was for this reason, he went on to say, that the establishment of "regional planning boards . . . for the purpose of coordinating the planning for the future in seven or eight natural geographical reegions" had been proposed in Congress. Many false and misleading statements about this proposal had been published. It had been said, for instance, "that this proposed legislation would set up all-powerful authorities which would destroy State lines, take away local government and make what people call a totalitarian or authoritarian or some other kind of of a dangerous national centralized control." The "exact opposite" was true. The proposed regional commissions would be "far more closely in touch with the needs of all the localities and all the people in their respective regions than a system of plans which originates in the Capital of the Nation." The proposal was for a decentralization, not a concentrated centralization, of planning process and power.

The Chief Executive, the various government departments, and the Congress itself will be able to get from each region a carefully worked out plan every year, a plan based on future needs, a plan which will seek primarily to help all the people of the region without unduly favoring any one locality or discriminating against any other. In other words, the responsibility of the Federal Government for the welfare of its citizens will not come from the top in the form of unplanned, hit or miss appropriations of money [he had in mind the aforementioned incredibly wasteful bureaucratic wars for congressional appropriations now being waged continuously among the Army Engineers, Reclamation, and other federal agencies having to do with natural

*See *FDR: The Beckoning of Destiny,* pp. 266–67.

resources], but will progress to the National Capital from the ground up—from the communities and counties and states which lie within each of the logical geographic areas. . . . By regional planning it will be vastly easier for the Executive branch and the Congress to determine how the appropriations for the following year shall be fitted most fairly and equitably into the total amount which our national pocketbook allows us safely to spend.[4]

Politics, a personal forceful politics of reward and punishment, threat and promise, had been practiced by him on his way west and would continue to be practiced on his way back home. He had pointedly not invited Nebraska's Democratic senator, Edward Burke, who had vigorously opposed the court-reform bill, to join the presidential party at any point along his train's long progress across Burke's home state on September 23 and 24. In Wyoming, his affability and self-control had been severely tested when that state's Senator O'Mahoney, whose scathing words in the unfavorable Senate committee report on the bill Roosevelt bitterly resented and whom he sought now to snub, boarded the special train (he had most emphatically *not* been invited aboard) as one of a formal welcoming committee. The test had been passed triumphantly: Roosevelt, giving no sign of being taken aback, greeted O'Mahoney with a smile, if possibly a wry one. During his speech stop at Boise, he had made a great display of friendship for Idaho's Republican senator Borah—a threatful reminder to Democrats who had fought his court bill that he valued support of his program more than he did party loyalty. The point was further emphasized during his passage through Montana on his way east. Not only was that state's Senator Burton Wheeler not invited to the special train, but his name went unmentioned in the extemporaneous talk Roosevelt gave at Fort Peck on October 3. Montana's senator James Murray, who had supported the court bill, was mentioned prominently.[5]

The two prepared addresses delivered on the following day, October 4—one of them at Grand Forks, North Dakota, in the morning; the other at St. Paul, Minnesota, in the evening—indicated a mind virtually made up on a question that had agitated both the White House and the general public ever since the first session of the 75th Congress adjourned with the bulk of the President's 1937 legislative program unenacted. Should a special session be called? One unspoken purpose of this Western trip had been to determine from the perceived mood of the general electorate whether or not such a session was likely to produce what the President wanted. That it probably would, being coerced by public opinion into doing so, was the conclusion Roosevelt had evidently reached; for each of his October 4 speeches stressed items that would appear on any special session's legislative agenda.

At Grand Forks he emphasized the urgent need for the "crop surplus control legislation" that had remained unpassed when the last congressional session ended. It was now "too late" for such legislation "to have any bearing on the winter wheat which is already in the ground," and if it were to have the desired acreage-reduction effect upon spring wheat and cotton plantings, "haste" was required. Cotton was "planted in late February or early March." Spring wheat was planted a month or so later. Clearly, if new legislation were "to affect the 1938 crops" it could not be postponed until January. "Even after a bill is passed and becomes law . . . it takes a month or two before it is humanly possible to set up the machinery . . . to carry out the provisions of the new law."

At St. Paul, where memories of the bloody labor strife of 1934 remained vivid,* Roosevelt spoke not only of the "pressing need for national legislation to preserve soil fertility and safeguard farmers' income," but also, and especially, of that legislation's twin piece, namely the "wage and hour legislation proposed for those industrial workers who are processing products that will move in interstate commerce. . . ." This legislation was "of course not intended to restore all of the National Industrial Recovery Act," struck down by the Supreme Court, but *was* "intended to restore certain fair standards for the workers of the nation," to "prevent over-long hours of work," to "establish a reasonable minimum wage," and "to end child labor in every state in the Union." This legislation, "as in the case of farm legislation, . . . will undoubtedly accomplish two great purposes, first, an increase in employment, and secondly, an increase in the total of the nation's income." National legislation along these lines was needed to achieve "uniform standards of pay and work" across the nation; and such uniformity was needed to prevent unfair and strife-engendering differences among local, state, and regional economies. "The more I study the subject the more I become convinced that it does not pay any community or any region to maintain low wages or low living standards."[6]

And these words, too, for all their plain sobriety, were enthusiastically received and loudly applauded by his audience.

The sound of crowd approval yet rang in Roosevelt's ears as he reboarded his special train at the St. Paul station in the evening of October 4 to begin his nighttime ride southeastward across Wisconsin. In Chicago, next morning, he was to deliver the last and by far the most important, historically, of all the speeches made on this trip.

II

THOUGH he had given no public sign of it—had seemed as exclusively concerned with domestic matters as his tour speeches had been—foreign affairs had been a major preoccupation of his ever since the tour began. Indeed, they had been thrusting themselves forcibly upon his consciousness, with an increasingly clamorous demand for attention, since the very first of the year—and during the summer the clamor had become loudly ominous.

In January 1937, the Spanish Civil War was at a bloody stalemate, Franco and his rebel forces, though continuously reinforced by Fascist Italy and Nazi

*See *FDR: The New Deal Years,* pp. 326–28.

Germany, had failed in their initial all-out effort to capture Madrid. Loyalist forces had not only blocked the drive upon the capital, they had driven the rebels back in several places, transforming Franco's attack into a prolonged siege. The narrow margin of this government success had been supplied at the last moment by Soviet Russia. In mid-October, a hundred Russian T-26 tanks, with their Russian crews, had been landed at the Mediterranean port of Cartagena. Russian planes and Soviet military "advisers" had also made their appearance. And since then, the Russian presence in Loyalist Spain had considerably increased. Moreover, International Brigades—volunteers recruited in several Western countries, including the United States,* under the aegis and through the agency of the international Communist party—had become elements of the government's army. These augmentations of the government's strength, however, were overmatched by the continuous and large increase of troops, planes, arms, and other war matériel supplied the rebels by Mussolini's Italy and Hitler's Germany. (According to Yvon Delbos, the French foreign minister, the French government had "positive information" in April 1937 that Franco's army consisted of 60,000 Italians, 15,000 Moroccans, and only 15,000 to 20,000 Spaniards [Delbos left out of this account the Germans, whose air force was of vital importance to the rebels] whereas the Spanish government forces were "composed entirely of Spaniards with the exception of 6,000 to 10,000 foreigners."[7]) The Spanish government remained in desperate need of the arms and other supplies denied them by the "nonintervention" policy of Britain and France, in which the United States effectively concurred. As the year wore on, therefore, though the stalemate before Madrid continued, rebel forces elsewhere made slow but steady gains.

Appalling atrocities were committed by both sides in this bitter struggle. But the consensus of impartial observers was that far more of them, and on a larger scale, were committed by the Fascist rebels, with their German and Italian allies, than by the Loyalists. Moreover, Franco's forces seemed to commit them, not as spontaneous isolated acts and not because the troops went out of rational control, but coldly, deliberately, as matters of policy. At Badajoz, for instance, where government resistance to rebels driving toward Madrid was especially fierce in August 1936, systematic officer-supervised executions of captured government troops, along with hundreds upon hundreds of noncombatants, had been carried out in the local bullring, night after night, for ten days after the town fell. *Chicago Tribune* correspondent Jay Allen had been told, and had reported the story, that upwards of four thousand people had

---

*American volunteers, most of them college students, traveled to France on passports stamped "NOT VALID FOR TRAVEL IN SPAIN"; slipped surreptitiously into the forbidden land (most of them crossed over the Pyrénées on foot); and enlisted in what became world-famous as the Abraham Lincoln Battalion. Their Stalinist Russian officers took ruthless, callous advantage of their idealism. Thus, in February 1937, out of 450 Americans thrown with little training into the fighting southeast of Madrid, 120 were killed and 175 wounded within a day or so. Ultimately, some 3,000 young Americans fought for Loyalist Spain or, as they saw it, for human decency against Nazi-Fascism. Most of them were killed.

been shot by Franco's forces in Badajoz between August 14 and August 24.[8]

The calculated terrorism of rebel forces as they drove into the ferociously defended Basque country of northern Spain had been especially horrifying to the civilized world. Its climax had been the murder from the air, on April 26, of the town of Guernica—a place of no military importance whatever, a market town containing no military installations and no factories producing war goods, and quartering no government troops. Only civilians were there—but these were there in great number on the bright clear morning of the twenty-sixth, a Monday, which was a market day. The streets and squares were jammed with people when, without warning, Nazi planes of the Condor Legion roared overhead, dropping bombs. They made repeated bombing runs, they reduced the town to smoking blood stained ruin, and they were followed by fighter planes which made low-level strafing runs, mowing down survivors with machine-gun fire. Many hundreds of defenseless human beings were thus slaughtered, more of them women and children than men. The event was shocking beyond belief to civilized folk in 1937, for it was in that year wholly unprecedented: Never before in the Western world had an open town been attacked from the air.

Guernica become at once a world symbol of Nazi-Fascist barbarism—was greatly aided in becoming so by its inspiration, immediate and impassioned, of one of the great works of art of the twentieth century. This was an allegorical painting in jagged grays and blacks and whites executed on a huge scale (it measured approximately twenty-six feet by twelve feet) and in a creative frenzy, in Paris, by Spanish-born Pablo Picasso. Virtually alone among Picasso's hundreds of works, this painting, "Guernica," had been left unsigned by its creator, as if to say it was the product, not of an individual talent, but of an outraged civilization. And immediately upon its display in June at the Paris World Fair, where it made a sensation, it became famous around the world.

By that time there had been changes in the American public's view of the Spanish conflict. They were increases in the intensity of feeling rather more than in the number of people having strong opinions on the subject, but they were not for that reason without political significance for Franklin Roosevelt. His problem in this regard, a problem that yet remained unsolved, was to determine precisely what the significance was, and what action was suggested by it. He had taken note, in January, of a Gallup poll in which two-thirds of those questioned had no preference between the two sides of the war; but he had also noted that 22 percent favored the Loyalists as against 12 percent for the rebels. In April, a *Fortune* poll had yielded almost the same results: Nearly two-thirds of those questioned had no preference between the two sides, but nearly 24 percent were pro-Loyalist and less than 12 percent pro-Franco.[9] Much increased, however, was the intensity of feeling on the part of those who had preferences. The partisanship had become increasingly passionate as the American Catholic hierarchy, with a very few exceptions among its members, strove to organize American support for Franco, making of such support an article of religious faith, while leftist organizations (the Socialist party, the American League Against War and Fascism, the American Friends of Spanish Democracy, among others) strove to organize support for the Loyalists, whom they saw as warriors for human freedom and civilization. This mounting emotional commitment was daily impressed upon Roosevelt, not only by his dealings with official business but also by his personal relationships within the White House itself.

There had been, for one thing, through the winter and early spring of that year, growing pressure upon him to do something about the congressional resolution imposing an embargo on arms shipments to Spain, legislation that applied exclusively to the Spanish Civil War and that had been adopted at his behest in early January. He was vehemently urged by Loyalist partisans to ask Congress to either rescind this action explicitly or enable him as President to do so in effect—the latter by rendering permissive rather than mandatory, in its revision of the Neutrality Act (the act must be renewed in the current session if it were not to expire), his application of an arms embargo to civil wars. He had been more than willing to do this. He wanted more discretionary power in the management of foreign affairs than he now had. He thoroughly agreed with the opinion expressed by Britain's chancellor of the exchequer, Neville Chamberlain, in a March letter to his American counterpart, Secretary of the Treasury Henry Morgenthau, Jr., that the neutrality legislation "in its present form constitutes an indirect but potent encouragement of aggression, and it is to be earnestly hoped that some way may be found of leaving sufficient discretion with the Executive to deal with each case on its merits."[10] Indeed, the neutrality law revision of 1937, as finally adopted, did give the President considerably wider discretionary powers than the earlier act had done. He was empowered to declare in effect a so-called cash-and-carry provision of the law, whereby a belligerent purchasing goods from the United States must itself transport the goods to their destination. He was also empowered to halt the shipment to belligerents of "certain articles or materials in addition to arms, ammunition, and implements of war" when, in his judgment, this was necessary "to promote the security or preserve the peace of the United States or to protect the lives of citizens of the United States"—a provision that, had it been in the 1935 neutrality law, could have been used to block the shipment of U.S. oil to Italy when Mussolini invaded Ethiopia.

But as spring came on and the court-reform bill stumbled in Congress toward its final fall, Roosevelt felt himself in no position to force a revocation of the congressional resolution applying exclusively to Spain. Also, he was by that time aware of certain advantages in having his hands tied: He was thereby relieved of the need to make decisions in an area that abounded in ambiguities, in uncertainties, in incalculable risks. So he had accepted with neither public protest nor any great personal regret a revised Neutrality Act that gave him the power to decide whether the act applied to any foreign civil war *excepting* the one now actually raging in Spain. ("The Spanish resolution . . . passed on January 8, 1937 . . . is not repealed by this act," declared the House sponsor of the joint resolution, shortly before the final vote was taken.[11]) And on May 1, 1937, immediately after signing the legislation, Roosevelt had issued the prescribed proclamation, forbidding American export of arms and munitions to either of the belligerents in Spain.

Such expediency, whereby he unprotestingly concurred in a policy that worked against the Loyalist triumph—which, he said in private talk, he personally wanted—did not go down well with his wife. Eleanor's commitment to the Loyalist cause was from the outset absolute, overt, fervent—and while she recognized her husband's need to proceed cautiously in this matter, with due respect for the potency of the Catholic Church within the Democratic party, and for the isolationism that a majority of the electorate continued (if more and more confusedly) to espouse, his caution often seemed to her excessive, if not actually cowardly and hypocritical. It led him into what she saw as betrayals of moral principle, and betrayals that resulted, on occasion, in an immediate increase of avoidable human suffering.

In May 1937, Eleanor gave her influential public support to a so-called Board of Guardians for Basque Refugee Children. Her longtime close friend, Caroline O'Day, now a New York congresswoman, was one of the board's directors, as were Mount Holyoke College president Mary E. Woolley and historian James T. Shotwell of Columbia University. Gardner (Pat) Jackson was board chairman. The organization's purpose was to transport five hundred homeless Basque children to the United States and provide homes for them with American families willing and able to take them in. The need for such effort was great. Tens of thousands of children had been evacuated from the Basque port city of Bilbao as Franco's forces advanced upon it. They had no place to go. And, in this country, there was no lack of families who volunteered the opening of their homes to such refugees. Nor was the U.S. government loath, at the outset, to cooperate in the effort. The Department of Labor, which had jurisdiction over the admission of refugees, and the Department of State, which must issue the visas necessary for such admission, moved quickly to implement the program. Facilitating instructions were promptly issued to U.S. embassy and consular officials in Spain and France.

But at this point the effort encountered, suddenly, strong opposition.

The Catholic hierarchy, which from the first had regarded this enterprise through hostile eyes, noting that its every officer and influential supporter was emphatically pro-Loyalist, now moved to prevent it. Representative John W. McCormick, a fervent Catholic Democrat whose Massachusetts constituency was equally so, publicly denounced the board as a tool of Communism and the refugee-rescue scheme as a Communist plot. Its design, he claimed, was to place Basque Catholic children in non-Catholic (if not godless) homes, and so wean them away from the church. He urged the Department of State to refuse the necessary visas.[12]

To such urging, the department was peculiarly sensitive: Its permanent staff contained a disproportionately large number of Catholics, graduates of a Catholic university with a curriculum specifically designed to prepare students for foreign-service careers. McCormick also exerted direct pressure upon the President—and the President was at that moment, for reasons of political expediency, as inclined to yield to such pressure as was the State Department. The result was that the whole effort came to naught, and an unknown number of refugee children whom the effort might have saved died instead of exposure, disease, and starvation. Eleanor was dismayed and disgusted.[13]

As for Roosevelt, the unease he felt with regard to his Spanish policy, amid his dark contemplation of the increasingly probable defeat of his court bill, could not have been reduced and may well have been increased by a letter he received at this time from Norman Thomas, head of the Socialist Party of America.

Thomas had just returned from an extensive European tour when he wrote the President, on June 9, to commend the "efficient service" he had received from embassy and consular officials in every country he had visited (Russia, Germany, France, Spain) but also, and chiefly, to voice his "personal concern . . . in the matter of the Spanish situation. Everything I saw or heard convinces me," he wrote, "that a state of real, if undeclared, war exists between the legitimate Loyalist government of Spain and Germany and Italy, or to be more accurate, Hitler and Mussolini. . . . If we are going in for the kind of neutrality policy that has been adopted, it seems to me that unless the German and Italian governments markedly change their policy we should apply the principle of neutrality against them. If we are not prepared to do that we should scarcely apply neutrality against Spain." He quoted a news article he had read in *Time* just before sailing from France—a report that "18 Rightist planes" reconnoitering on the Basque front had recently become lost in fog and forced to land in southern France. French officials had allowed the planes to return to Franco's forces but had noted that "twelve of the strayed planes were American-made Boeing fighters." Thomas conceded the possibility that the *Time* story was inaccurate. *Time* stories sometimes were, and U.S. embassy officials in Paris believed this one to be. But surely the matter was important enough to be investigated by Washington. For if the *Time* statement was correct, "surely neutrality has been outrageously violated in favor of Franco and the Fascists."* Thomas was "emphatically" not in favor of intervention by the "United States government as such in a European war," but he did "think that

---

*Thomas could and would have greatly strengthened his case in this regard had he known that the Texas Oil Company (Texaco) was at that very moment selling and shipping oil in large quantity to Franco's insurgents (not a drop went to the Loyalists) and would continue to do so for the duration of the war. At a Cabinet meeting on August 13, Attorney General Cummings reported that Texaco had been doing this "for several months," its tankers leaving Texas ports bound ostensibly for Antwerp but sailing instead (under sealed orders opened by the captain at sea) for rebel-held ports in Spain. According to Ickes, the President ordered the attorney general to "put a stop" to this, revoking the licenses of the ship captains involved "if necessary," and compelling Texaco "to pay damages under the law." Actually, nothing was done effectively to penalize Texaco for current violations of the neutrality law or to prevent continuance of such violations. The corporation ceased the delivering its oil directly to rebel ports but sent it instead by way of Italy. Texaco's head was a Norwegian-born "rugged individualist" named Torkild (Cap) Rieber.[14]

in its practical effect our neutrality policy thus far in the Spanish situation has tended not toward genuine non-intervention" but toward intervention on the side of Mussolini, Hitler, and Franco.[15]

Such argument, which was also being made at that time by several of the most prominent of America's isolationists, including North Dakota's senator Gerald P. Nye, chief author of the original neutrality legislation, was in accord with Roosevelt's own predilections. As President, however, he was forced to recognize serious legal as well as practical difficulties in the way of the indicated action. For one thing, as Thomas himself had noted, the de facto war between the Spanish government and Germany, and between the Spanish government and Italy, was not formally declared by any of these countries and was unlikely ever to be. The Spanish government was certainly in no position to declare war, and Mussolini and Hitler had nothing to gain and much to lose by doing so. For another thing, both Germany and Italy were formally committed to nonintervention in Spain and had official representation on the Non-Intervention Committee—a factor that, at least in the legalistic minds of the State Department staff, enormously complicated the situation in ways prejudicial to the contemplated action. For a third thing, the British and French (especially the British) were disposed to regard as dangerously "provocative" any U.S. embargo of arms and munitions shipments to Italy and Germany. They professed to see it pointing the way toward the general European war that must at all costs be avoided; and both U.S. ambassadors Robert Bingham (in London) and William Phillips (in Rome*) evidently shared this Franco-British attitude, for each of them advised Roosevelt, in written communications, not to take the action proposed.

All the same, Roosevelt not only answered the Thomas letter with thanks but also agreed to a personal interview with its author when the latter requested it—a fact that, publicized, encouraged a popular belief that Roosevelt was about to do what Thomas, with Nye and others, advocated. The interview took place on June 29. It was similar in tone and form to earlier interviews Thomas had had in the White House on difficult and highly controversial issues. Roosevelt did a great deal of the talking, and much of his talk was diversionary. It was with some difficulty that he was brought at last to listen "rather evasively" to Thomas's argument that a Loyalist victory was of vital importance to democracy everywhere; that if Franco won, the Spanish conflict could indeed become what many now saw it to be, namely, a prelude and dress rehearsal for World War II; that it was therefore in America's vital interest to aid the Loyalist cause by all means short of war; and that at the very least the United States should abandon a policy that gave unfair advantage to Mussolini, Hitler, and Spanish Fascism. Roosevelt, listening, nodded from time to time in seeming affirmation of what he heard. But then, instead of responding specifically to this, he "suddenly" and surprisingly began to talk about "what a great man Cardinal Mundelein was." The reference was to

*Sumner Welles had replaced Phillips as under secretary of state in the spring.

George Cardinal Mundelein of Chicago, one of the most liberal of the American Catholic hierarchy, and a man to whom Roosevelt often turned for support on political issues of concern to the church. Thomas, knowing this, quickly recovered from his surprise. He recognized the seemingly total non sequitur as actually highly relevant to the subject at hand. It revealed, as Thomas recalled in a later year, that "Roosevelt was primarily motivated [in his dealings with the matter at hand] by his feeling that he had to have the support of the Church on any move as great [and of as much concern to the church] as this, because it was so necessary to political strength" here at home.[16]

At any rate, Roosevelt made no overt effort to revise the American policy toward Spain. The Loyalists continued to be denied desperately needed planes, artillery, matériel of all kinds; and no real effort was made by Britain, France, or the United States to halt the flow of Nazi-Fascist "volunteers," air power, arms, and munitions to the rebels.

III

EIGHT days after Thomas's White House interview, Roosevelt's foreign-policy concerns were greatly augmented and further complicated by events in the Far East—events that abruptly ended the uneasy and imperfect armed truce that had prevailed between Japan and China since mid-1935.

Ever since early January 1937, Japan had been torn internally by a political struggle between democratic moderates, who sought a peaceful accommodation with China (though one that established Japanese dominance over that country), and aggressive militarists, who were bent upon the immediate conquest of China and its absorption into the Japanese empire. In this struggle, the militarists had been on the defensive, largely because the cost of maintaining Manchukuo as a puppet state, along with vast increases in military expenditures, forced the adoption of monetary and taxation policies that had deleterious effects upon the Japanese economy, lowering the general standard of living. The militarists badly needed an "incident" in China that would enable them to become identified in the public eye as avengers of the emperor's honor rather than destroyers of the economy; and as July came on, having tested and found wanting the will of Soviet Russia, and of the Western powers, to fight at that moment for their countries' Chinese interests, they were presented with such an "incident"—if, indeed, they didn't manufacture it.

On July 7, Japanese troops, after ten days of maneuvering provocatively near units of the Chinese 29th Army and well outside the zone of occupation assigned them by treaty, engaged in night maneuvers at Lukouchiao, some nine miles west of Peking. At a bridge there, the Marco Polo Bridge, in midnight darkness, a confused Sino-Japanese encounter occurred. Shots were fired. Casualties were inflicted. And the fighting thus initiated continued for three days on a small scale (few were killed or wounded on either side) while the Japanese made massive troop movements into North China, and the

Chinese countered with massive movements of their own. Soon thereafter the "incident" became full-scale war, with hundreds of thousands of troops involved on each side, though for technical reasons of international law there was not and would never be a formal declaration of war. There was not even, nor would there ever be, a severing of formal diplomatic ties between the warring nations. This fact complicated for Roosevelt and the State Department the question of whether or not the Neutrality Act must here apply.

And the complexity was increased when, on August 9, a Japanese navy officer and a seaman were shot and killed by Chinese guards as they allegedly attempted to force their way, as spies, onto a Chinese military airfield near Shanghai. At once, the Japanese moved massively upon Shanghai, which, with its population of three million, became the central focus of the war—and in Shanghai was a large International Settlement containing American civilians. Also at Shanghai were stationed a thousand American marines (there were some 2,200 U.S. troops altogether in China—500 marines in Peking and 700 infantrymen at Tientsin, in addition to the marines in Shanghai), present there in accordance with treaties negotiated immediately before and after the Chinese Boxer Rebellion of 1900. It was thus inevitable that there would be American casualties in this war, and almost at once, just four days after the fighting had spread to Shanghai, the inevitable occurred. On August 14, poorly trained Chinese aviators, attempting to attack Japanese warships in Shanghai's harbor, dropped their bombs instead on the International Settlement. More than eight hundred Chinese civilians and some forty foreigners were killed, including three Americans. The immediate U.S. government response was an urgent plea to American civilians to leave the war zone and, on August 17, the dispatch of 1,200 more marines from San Diego to Shanghai.

But in this case, unlike that of the undeclared international war in Spain, the President did not invoke the Neutrality Act. It was obvious that an embargo on arms and munitions shipments to the Far East would hurt China far more than it would Japan, and no such embargo was declared, though on September 14 Roosevelt did forbid the carrying of matériel to either of the belligerent powers on ships owned by the U.S. government.[17] The usual futile diplomatic gestures were made. A formal appeal was issued on July 16 by Secretary of State Hull and sent as an individual message to every national government in the world, urging each to comply with the treaties they had signed, especially those whereby they pledged themselves to abstain "from use of force in the pursuit of policy and from interference in the internal affairs of other nations." More than sixty nations promptly replied "favorably" to this appeal, including Japan, though the Japanese did stress the need, if the "objectives of those principles" were to "be attained," for "a full recognition and practical consideration of the actual particular circumstances" in the Far East. On August 23, in a press statement, Secretary Hull appealed to China and Japan to settle their dispute by peaceful means.[18]

Meanwhile, as he saw Mussolini and Hitler drawing together in ever closer cooperation in the prosecution of the Spanish war,* and as he considered the developing implications of Japan's signing of the Anti-Comintern Pact with Germany on November 26 of the previous year, Roosevelt cast around rather desperately for a foreign-policy move that would *not* be a meaningless gesture.

In May, Neville Chamberlain, who had been the strongman in Stanley Baldwin's Cabinet, became Britain's prime minister upon Baldwin's retirement. Roosevelt was inclined to welcome the change, knowing Chamberlain to be a stubborn and stalwart champion of peace. In June he issued, through Ambassador-at-Large Norman Davis, an invitation to Chamberlain to come to Washington for face-to-face talks about world conditions. Chamberlain's reply, through Davis, on July 8 (the day after the Marco Polo Bridge incident), was a polite but firm refusal of the invitation on the ground that the time was not ripe for it. Some resentment was aroused in the State Department by this seeming snub—a snub evidently expressive of Chamberlain's conviction that he alone was equipped by knowledge, skill, and character to deal with Hitler and Mussolini in ways that would make peace in Europe.[19]

Roosevelt may have felt some resentment himself. At any rate, seizing upon those portions of Chamberlain's letter to Davis that, if with a deliberate distortion of their intended meaning, gave him an opening for doing so, he on July 28 wrote directly to the new prime minister, saying he was "pleased to learn that you think it would be desirable to make a visit here . . . as soon as conditions appear to warrant your doing so; and also that we are in accord as to the importance of Anglo-American cooperation in the promotion of economic stability and peace in the world."[20]

And on the following day, July 29, he saw fit to reply at long last to a message of congratulation sent him, immediately after his reelection triumph last November, by Benito Mussolini. He had "delayed writing," he said, in the hope "that the world situation would clarify sufficiently for me to discuss with you measures looking toward the stabilization of peace among the nations. But the situation today seems no clearer than before, and, indeed, in some aspects the drift of events has been toward and not away from an ultimate crisis." He had, however, been "gratified in reading of your statements in favor of the principles of reduction of armament." Such reduction, and the lowering of international trade barriers, were "two things" that must "go hand in hand," the increase of international trade being necessary for an increased "employment in industry to take the place of employment in armament." He was, he went on,

---

*On September 25, 1937, Mussolini visited Hitler in Germany at Hitler's invitation—the first face-to-face meeting of the two dictators in three years. There was much pomp, ceremony, and military muscle-flexing on the part of the Nazis. Mussolini, resplendent in a new uniform specifically designed for the occasion, joined his host in a great display of personal as well as international friendship. Reading of all this in his railroad car in Montana next day, Roosevelt "rather glowered at the pictures of the two little men," according to Grace Tully (*F.D.R.: My Boss* [New York, 1949], p. 230).

confident, my dear Duce, that you share with me the fear that the trend of the present international situation is ominous to peace. And I am confident that you share with me the desire to turn the course of the world toward stabilizing peace. I have often wished that I might talk with you frankly and in person because from such a meeting great good might come. But we both realize the great difficulties that stand in the way—international difficulties as well as the distances of the Atlantic Ocean and the Mediterranean Sea.[21]

By the time he wrote this letter, he was toying with the idea of offering his services to fifty-five nations as a clearinghouse for the peaceful resolution of international disputes. The idea was opposed by Cordell Hull and Norman Davis; they thought it "wouldn't work," and they pointed out to Roosevelt a few weeks later that, in view of the revelation then just made of Justice Black's KKK connection, the White House could not at the moment politically afford a rebuff by foreign powers. They proposed instead that the President make a speech carefully designed to counter isolationist sentiment in the United States, and make it "in a large city where isolation was entrenched."[22] Chicago, home of Colonel Robert McCormick's arch-isolationist and arch-reactionary *Tribune* and the virtual capital of Midwestern isolationism, was obviously indicated.

The idea of making a dramatic foreign-policy speech had already occurred to Roosevelt. As early as July 8, the day Chamberlain wrote his letter declining the invitation to visit Washington—a day when the flare-up of crisis in the Far East dominated minds in the White House—Roosevelt said in conversation with Clark Eichelberger, head of the League of Nations Association, that he wanted to make a major address on foreign affairs that would not be "simply another speech" but "a dramatic statement" stressing the need of a "denial of trade to the aggressor" nation.[23]

On September 18, the idea became a decision. In conference with the President, Harold Ickes suggested that the President close out his Western tour with a speech in Chicago dedicating the Outer Link Bridge (on Lake Shore Drive, virtually in the shadow of the Tribune Tower) in that city, construction of the bridge having been a major PWA project. (Arrangements for this speech were promptly made.) During that same conversation, Ickes, by his own account, spoke of the international situation as being "just like a case of contagious disease in a community," adding "that the neighbors had a right to quarantine themselves against a contagious disease." Roosevelt looked hard at Ickes, nodding vigorously. "That is a good line," he said, and promptly wrote it down.[24]

Thus the terms "community" and "contagious disease" and "quarantine" were in the speech notes that Roosevelt had at hand on the evening of September 28, the day of his Bonneville Dam address in Oregon, when, on his special train, he began to dictate to his personal secretary, Grace Tully, a final draft of the speech he would give in Chicago. He also had at hand speech material sent him (it had arrived in his mail pouch from Washington that morning) by

Norman Davis. He worked on the draft, with Grace Tully, in snatches of time
from his crowded schedule during the days immediately following.[25]

This speech was in final shape when Roosevelt boarded his special train in
St. Paul in the evening. The neatly typed manuscript lay on a little worktable
within a few feet of his bed as, above an iron roar of wheels on rails that was
punctuated by the rhythmic clicks of a now inexorable destiny, he slept
through a dark night into the dawn of Tuesday, October 5, 1937.

IV

THE crowds were huge beyond belief. They jammed the sidewalks of the streets
through which the President rode, in warm October morning sunlight, from
the railroad station in Chicago. An estimated 750,000 people saw him smile
and wave from the rear seat of an open car as he made his way to the dedication
site at the Outer Link Bridge, where another fifty thousand awaited him. When
he stood at last at the lectern, his speech manuscript lying open before him,
the cheers, the applause, were deafening.

His acknowledgment of this approval was warmly grateful. But it was also
brief. Equally so were his bridge-dedicating remarks. The smile faded from his
face, the tone of his voice became grave, as he said that he had "chosen this
great inland city and this gala occasion to speak . . . on a subject of definite
national importance"—a subject unrelated (as he did not say) to the completion of this great PWA project.

He began by recalling how the "high aspirations expressed in the Briand-
Kellogg Peace Pact," signed by "more than sixty nations" fifteen years ago,
had raised up everywhere high "hopes for peace." But, alas, these had "of late
given way to a haunting fear of calamity" because of a "reign of terror and
international lawlessness" that now "seriously threatens the very foundations
of civilization." Large-scale aggressive violence, launched without warning or
declaration of war "or justification of any kind," resulted in "civilians, including vast numbers of women and children, . . . being ruthlessly murdered with
bombs from the air." In a time of "so-called peace," ships were being sunk by
submarines, and nations were "fomenting and taking sides in civil warfare in
nations that have never done them any harm." By the myriad, innocent people
were "being cruelly sacrificed to a greed for power and supremacy which is
devoid of all sense of justice and humane considerations."

And from this catastrophe the United States, for all its love of peace, could
not be isolated. "There is a solidarity and interdependence about the modern
world, both technically and morally, which makes it impossible for any nation
completely to isolate itself from economic and political upheavals in the rest
of the world. . . ." This was especially so "when such upheavals appear to be
spreading and not declining." Therefore, if civilization went down and barbarism triumphed "in other parts of the world, let no one imagine that America
will escape, that America may expect mercy, that this Western Hemisphere
will not be attacked and that it will continue tranquilly and peacefully to carry

on the ethics and arts of civilization." No, the threat to America was grave and immediate. What, then, should be done? He gave his answer slowly, stressing every key word: "The peace-loving nations [and the United States was certainly a peace-loving nation] must make a concerted effort in opposition to those violations of treaties and those ignorings of humane instincts which today are creating a state of international anarchy and instability from which there is no escape through mere isolation and neutrality."

Came then his use of the metaphor which Ickes had given him.

"It seems unfortunately true," he said, speaking even more slowly and emphatically, "that the epidemic of world lawlessness is spreading. When an epidemic of physical disease starts to spread, the community approves and joins in a quarantine of the patients in order to protect the health of the community against the spread of the disease."

He paused for a moment, to let the implication of these words sink into the minds of his listeners.

And what was this implication? Clearly it was that the three major aggressor nations in the world—Germany, Italy, and Japan—were "sick" with war lust ("War," he explicitly said, "is a contagion, whether declared or undeclared") and that "the concerted effort" of the "peace-loving" community of nations should be the imposition of a "quarantine" upon these aggressors. The "sick" nations were to be effectively expelled from the community of civilized nations, were to be isolated from and by "healthy" peace-loving nations through a severing of normal diplomatic and trade relations with them, until their sickness passed away. Vital questions were at once raised by this in critical minds. How was the severing of relations to be accomplished? Was a blockade to be imposed? And how could this be done "short of war," since a blockade was itself an act of war? The questions were left unanswered. But it was at any rate clear, at this point in his speech, that the President would have the United States join with other nations in "definite" collective security arrangements— pact arrangements that actively worked for peace and against aggression.

But from such clear implication the speaker seemed now to shrink or back away. Having defined—in, admittedly, very general terms—a ground upon which lovers of peace and civilization might firmly stand, he proceeded in his closing words, and in typical Rooseveltian fashion, to befog his meanings and blur his definitions, retreating thus into that swamp of ambiguity where he as politician so often dwelt.

"It is my determination to pursue a policy of peace," he declared with utmost earnestness.

It is my determination to adopt every practicable measure to avoid involvement in war.... We are determined to keep out of war, yet we cannot insure ourselves against the disastrous effects of war and the dangers of involvement. We are adopting such measures as will minimize our risk of involvement, but we cannot have complete protection in a world of disorder.... If civilization is to survive, the principles of the Prince of Peace must be restored.... Most important of all, the will for peace on the part of peace-loving nations must express itself to the end that nations that may be tempted to violate their agreements and the rights of others will desist from such a course. . . . America hates war. America hopes for peace. Therefore, America actively engages in the search for peace."[26]

The immediate crowd response was gratifying. "The reaction was deep and demonstrative and the President harkened to the roaring approval of the crowd with the same attentiveness a symphony orchestra leader directs toward the tuning notes of his musicians," remembered Grace Tully a dozen years later.[27]

Yet there evidently remained in him a rare amount (rare for him) of post-decision anxiety.

From the speaker's platform he rode to lunch with Cardinal Mundelein at the latter's residence, a luncheon date he had made for the double purpose of learning the cardinal's views on Spanish Civil War policy, and mitigating through the cardinal's influence such adverse reactions as there might be, among Catholics, to his appointment of a former KKK member to the Supreme Court. But as he lunched he was at some pains to "explain" to his host the "meaning" of the words he had spoken at the bridge, doing so in a negative way that drained the address's key words of nearly all their meaning. He did not "contemplate either military or naval action against the unjust aggressor nation," as Cardinal Mundelein recorded after Roosevelt had departed. Nor did Roosevelt's "plan . . . involve 'sanctions' as generally understood, but rather a policy of isolation, severance of ordinary communications in a united manner by all the governments in the pact," according to the cardinal.[28]

When Roosevelt returned to his railroad car in midafternoon, his first words to his personal secretary were "How did it go, Grace?"

He listened gratefully to Grace Tully's expressed belief that "it" had gone wonderfully well. There had been "a splendid reaction and appreciation of his meaning" by the audience, she said. He nodded slightly, then spoke as if he still had doubts.

"Well, it's done now," he said resignedly, and added, as if to reassure himself, "It was something that needed saying."[29]

V

AT Hyde Park next morning, as he prepared to meet reporters in a scheduled press conference, he reviewed with the closest attention press reports of the reaction, at home and abroad, to his speech.

He noted the unanimous opinion of editorialists, columnists, and quoted public figures that what he had said was of enormous importance. *The Washington Post* believed that the President's words, spoken at this time and in that place, could "well foreshadow a turning point in world history"—a turn toward the better, according to the *Post.* The *Chicago Tribune* disagreed with this last, of course. Convinced that the speech signified a radical shift of U.S.

foreign policy ("Americanism" was being abandoned in favor of "internationalism"), the *Tribune* deplored the change bitterly, as Roosevelt knew the Hearst newspapers would do. Chicago had been made "the center of a world-hurricane of war fright" by the President's fateful words, according to the *Tribune.* Arthur Krock of *The New York Times,* conceding the speech's importance, nevertheless wondered precisely what the importance was since, as Krock had ascertained, the State Department knew of no specific plan for implementing the President's words. (Secretary of State Hull, the *Times*'s Washington bureau chief had been told, was "shocked" by what the President had said; there had been no reference to a "quarantine" of "aggressors" in the draft speech sent out from the State Department to the President's special train.) *The Times* of London, similarly uncertain of the speech's meaning, concluded that "Mr. Roosevelt was defining an attitude and not a program," though an attitude the expression of which was indeed of great world importance, and an attitude the newspaper heartily approved of.[30]

In Geneva, the speech was similarly regarded as one of world-shaking import. News of its general nature had reportedly arrived in both London and Geneva several hours before the speech's actual delivery and had caused great excitement with its seeming announcement of America's new commitment to a policy of collective security. This was alleged to have had immediate influence upon League of Nations Assembly deliberations. It would encourage the Assembly to adopt that day a Far East Advisory Committee report presented to it the day before—a report that strongly censured Japan for aggression against China and proposed a special meeting of the signatories of the Nine-Power Treaty at the earliest possible moment "to seek a method of putting an end [to the Sino-Japanese conflict] . . . by agreement."[31] Japan, which had withdrawn from the League, and the United States, which had never joined, were among the signers of this 1922 treaty whereby China's independence and territorial integrity were "guaranteed" and the principle of the "Open Door" was reiterated. Clearly, as a direct consequence of what had been said in Chicago, the United States was being drawn toward active involvement in the League's dealings with the Far East crisis, and Roosevelt's reading about this was alarming rather than gratifying to him. He well knew that his heartening of the League of Nations would mean an equivalent disheartening of America's isolationists, and that this meant, in turn, an increased opposition to the administration on the part of outraged isolationist members of Congress. It was an increase of opposition which, in his present circumstances, he felt he could not afford.

His unease grew as he hunted through the papers that morning for statements of enthusiastic approval of his speech by Democratic leaders of Congress. He found none. This struck him as ominous: He knew that these congressional leaders had been asked by newsmen to comment on what he had said; their reluctance to do so could only mean that they were either doubtful about the words he had spoken or wholly disapproving of them.

Hence his response to the first question asked at his press conference a few hours later:

"Do you care to amplify your remarks at Chicago, especially where you referred to a possible quarantine?"

"No," he replied, flatly, dismissively.

But as the conference drew toward its close the question was again raised and stubbornly pursued, to Roosevelt's manifest displeasure, chiefly by Ernest K. Lindley, Roosevelt's biographer and the Washington correspondent of the New York *Herald Tribune.*

In view of the speech's "extreme importance," said Lindley, whose own views were isolationist, "I think it would be very valuable if you would answer a few questions or else talk for background."

Roosevelt demurred. He would say nothing on the subject "for background" (this would have enabled the reporters to write think pieces interpreting what he said, though without direct attribution). He would "only talk completely off the record." And when he did he followed the line of extreme caution, and obfuscation, that he had taken during his luncheon conversation with Cardinal Mundelein. He denied that there was any need to "reconcile the policy . . . outlined yesterday with the policy of neutrality laid down by the Act of Congress," as Lindley alleged there was; his words might even mean "an expansion" of the neutrality policy, he asserted; and when he was pressed to admit that his words implied, at the very least, "economic sanctions," he reacted almost angrily.

"Look," he said, " 'sanctions' is a terrible word to use. They are out the window."

All right, said the reporter, "call it concert of action on the part of peace-loving nations." Did that indicate "a likelihood that there will be a conference of peace-loving nations?"

"No," said the President, emphatically, "conferences are out the window. You never get anywhere with a conference." (He may have had in mind the proposed Nine-Power meeting, in which the U.S. must participate but the failure of which seemed to Roosevelt and his foreign-policy advisers a foregone conclusion.)

Evidently, then, the London *Times* was correct in saying that the Chicago speech expressed merely "an attitude without a program," a reporter concluded.

"It is an attitude, and it does not outline a program," agreed Roosevelt, adding defensively: "But it says we are looking for a program."

Lindley pounced on that.

If "any program is reached" it would have to be, surely, a "program" of collective security, and since neutrality and collective security were "on opposite poles," would not "our present Neutrality Act . . . have to be overhauled?"

Roosevelt was nettled.

"Put your thinking-cap on, Ernest," he said.

"I have for some years," replied Lindley, nettled in his turn—and he went on to reiterate his question concerning "how you can be neutral if you are going to align yourself with one group of nations."

To this, Roosevelt had no clear answer; and after much sparring, and backing and filling, whereby the word "quarantine" was rendered wholly meaningless within its present context, the press conference ended. The only solid printable news obtained by the reporters from the conference as a whole was that the President had nothing to say about Justice Black's radio talk, had no intention of meeting with the new justice when he arrived in Washington, and would determine "within the next week" whether there would be "an extra session of Congress," the overwhelming probability being that such a session would be called.[32]

In years to come it would be said by those close to Roosevelt (Sam Rosenman, for one)—and it would be intimated by Roosevelt himself—that he in his Chicago speech had moved too swiftly and far in advance of public opinion, had then found himself standing alone on politically untenable ground, and so had been forced reluctantly to retreat from that ground. "It's a terrible thing to look over your shoulder when you are trying to lead," he once remarked to Rosenman, apropos of this speech, "—and find no one there."[33]

Actually, there was manifest within a few days, in some of the most influential portions of the press, and in the White House mail, a considerable support within the electorate of the kind of collective security arrangement that Roosevelt had called for. Indeed, "much, perhaps most, of the country responded favorably" to what Roosevelt had said, concludes historian William E. Leuchtenburg after reviewing scholarly research on the subject.[34] It is true that most of this favorable response was to the President's denunciation of the aggressor nations; those favoring positive action of the kind Roosevelt had suggested were a distinct minority of the general public and of Congress. (A telegraphic poll of congressional members, taken by *The Philadelphia Inquirer* and published on October 9, showed a majority of two to one against U.S. cooperation with the League in the imposition of sanctions or in any other active intervention in the Sino-Japanese conflict.[35]) But among this minority were some of the most influential of the private citizenry—perhaps a *majority* of those well informed on world affairs—and some of the most powerful members of Congress as well. Late in the day following the Chicago speech, for instance, Key Pittman, the chairman of the Senate Foreign Relations Committee, published his conviction that an "economic quarantine" would end Japan's aggression against China within thirty days.[36]

One must conclude that there was, among the American citizenry at that time, enough support for a collective security policy, support from people able to persuade others of the rightness of their views, to be nurtured by bold, intelligent presidential leadership into a majority opinion—and quite possibly within a few weeks.

Which implies the further conclusion that it was not primarily for lack of followers, it was for lack of the requisite resolve, nerve, energy, and clarity of mind in the aftermath of his lost court battle, that Roosevelt, nursing with desperate hope isolationist sentiments of his own, failed at this crucial point to lead. Had he done so, he just *might,* even at so late a date, have given pause to Hitler, to Mussolini, to the militant imperialists of Japan. Certainly this leadership would have worked against the disastrous "appeasement" policy of the British and French, while preparing and easing the way of the democracies toward the kind of collective action that was ultimately required for the survival of Western civilization.

One can only conclude that Roosevelt made his flamboyant gesture toward internationalism in the first place from typically inconsistent motives, and that he then rendered the gesture an empty one from motives equally mixed. His, we know, was a mind and temperament (his was also the kind of manipulative political power) that thrives on the ambiguous, the contradictory. He instinctively shied away from the absolutely definite and unequivocal, feeling this to be a limitation of possibility, a closing-off of options, and so a threat to his freedom of action as well as a probable lessening of his capacity to perceive signs and clues (often slight signs, meant for him alone) from on high. We know, too, that he did sincerely wish to warn and educate his fellow countrymen about the threat to America of the rising tide of lawless international violence. This purpose alone would have been served, however, without the controversial "quarantine" remarks, which he himself, without consulting the State Department, inserted in the draft speech only a couple of days or so before going to Chicago. Why, then, the insertion? It rendered his statement more dramatic, of course, and he had told Eichelberger of his wish for such drama. It also served to test the political winds: The public's reaction to his words, carefully chosen to avoid committing him firmly to any policy, enabled him to determine how far he could safely or easily go in the direction of collective security.

And there may have been yet another motive, never to be publicly admitted —a motive quite commonly operative in the White House when its prestige and power are threatened by domestic troubles, as history shows—namely, a wish to divert popular attention from such troubles to foreign affairs over which the Chief Executive has, constitutionally, overriding power and from which, to the extent that a foreign threat is generally perceived, he can derive a united popular (patriotic) support. The German ambassador to the United States, Hans Dieckhoff, was inclined to give credence to this view of the matter, especially after it became obvious to him that the quarantine "threat" (so Dieckhoff dubbed it) was not, on Roosevelt's part, a truly serious one. "Possibly [the quarantine proposal] . . . was an attempt to drown out or silence the public discussion of the Black case, which was embarrassing to Mr. Roosevelt, by a spectacular fanfare in the field of foreign policy," said a memorandum from Dieckhoff to the Foreign Office in Berlin. "Roosevelt is a tremendously shrewd politician, and this might possibly have been his intention."[37]

VI

BUT the Black case embarrassment, if ever a factor in this Roosevelt decision, had ceased to be important by the date of Dieckhoff's memorandum. By then, Black's broadcast and Roosevelt's silence upon the subject had effectively removed it from the agenda of major popular concerns. Of far greater concern, as it would have been in any case by the second week of October, and becoming more serious with each passing day, was the state of the domestic economy.

Signs of a contraction of the economy had begun to appear even before Congress adjourned on August 21. Not only had stock prices then begun to decline, along with industrial activity, but also commodity futures sank to new lows while unemployment rose. Economists in Treasury's research division, though not yet convinced that a serious recession was under way, viewed the developing situation uneasily. From some of them to Morgenthau, who was on vacation in Hawaii, went a memorandum saying that the highly satisfactory level of business activity of the last year or so had depended upon a backlog of unfulfilled orders, that the backlog had now virtually disappeared, and that the void thus created must be filled by increased consumer buying if serious economic trouble were to be avoided. The memorandists professed no great anxiety, however—they professed a good deal less than they actually felt, one suspects—saying that the needed new purchasing power would be created by a lowering of interest rates and an increase in residential construction, provided these were not offset by reductions in government spending.[38]

But, alas for the persuasive effect of such argument, sharp reduction in government spending in order to achieve a balanced federal budget for fiscal 1939, was, as we have seen, the President's announced policy—a policy adopted against the strong protests of Federal Reserve Board chairman Marriner Eccles*—and no one was more fervently committed to this policy than Henry Morgenthau. The Treasury secretary, for all his experience of the New Deal, remained wholly conservative, orthodox, in his economic views. He saw the evident faltering of the economy as due to a faltering "confidence" on the part of businessmen; they were more "nervous" now, and consequently less inclined to make prosperity-breeding capital investments, than they had been at any time since November 1933 (so Morgenthau would say to fellow conservative Jim Farley a few weeks hence). To him, therefore, the research division memorandum was far less worrisome as a warning of developing economic illness than it was as a prescription of preventive medicine, for as a prescription it just might have enough influence upon Franklin Roosevelt, of whose constancy of purpose Morgenthau was never absolutely certain, to provoke a policy revision. This, in Morgenthau's opinion, could be disastrous. The proper prescription, precisely opposite that suggested by the memorandum, was an unwavering adherence to the established policy of budget-balancing through

*See *FDR: The New Deal Years,* pp. 663–65.

reduced spending. Only thus could the needed business "confidence" be "restored."[39]

When the Treasury secretary returned to Washington in mid-September, he found to his great relief that the President was seemingly as strongly committed to government economy as he had ever been. Roosevelt continued to insist upon budget-trimming by government agencies. He was delaying the expenditure of $23 million for new post-office buildings, had ordered Jesse Jones to reduce drastically the lending activities of the Reconstruction Finance Corporation, which Jones headed, and had encouraged Ickes's curtailment of PWA activity. (To Morgenthau's great surprise and delight, Ickes told him in September that PWA's expenditures ought to be cut in the interests of overall budget-balancing and that he, Ickes, "had urged that policy on the President.") Continuing along this line, Roosevelt now authorized Morgenthau to see what could be done to reduce the 1939 appropriations for RFC, the Resettlement Administration, and the Department of Agriculture as a whole (Resettlement was now a part of it)—and in the Cabinet meeting on Friday, October 8, he used data supplied him by Morgenthau to reiterate in the most emphatic terms his conviction of the necessity for a balanced budget, warning the department heads that they would have to cut by $300 million their combined budget requests for the coming fiscal year.[40] He continued to discount the mounting evidence of recession, though New York investment houses were now expressing concern over a perceived sharp decline in consumer spending. The stock-price decline, said Roosevelt in effect, was "apparently . . . only one of those corrective dips that occur even when the market is having an upward trend," as Ickes would record in his diary account of this Cabinet meeting.[41]

All the same, an apprehensive Morgenthau may have noted signs, in this same Cabinet meeting, that doubts were creeping into the all-too-open presidential mind—doubts that, in conjunction with Marriner Eccles's argument against the current policy, might weaken the President's "economy" resolve. For Roosevelt, during this meeting, having described the market slump as merely "corrective," had added thoughtfully that some of this "correction" did seem excessively "severe." He had also made significant reference to recent published statements by Secretary of Commerce Daniel Roper to the effect that, despite appearances, business conditions remained "fundamentally sound"—statements that were "Hooverish," said Roosevelt, and that he wished Roper would "stop giving out. . . ."[42] Moreover, he shrugged off Morgenthau's plea, in which Farley concurred, that he *not* call Congress into special session at this time but, instead, wait until the next regular session for the "reform" legislation he wanted. He seemed only too willing to risk what Morgenthau greatly feared, namely, that senators and representatives, having left Washington in a rebellious mood and been then subjected to constituent pressures on behalf of popular spending programs, would, if called back to Washington, take the bit in their teeth in headlong pursuit of resumed or even increased spending. That Roosevelt recognized the risk was clear. He took steps to mitigate it, obtaining from key members of the House Ways and

Means Committee promises to support, in the upcoming special session, any budget-balancing program he proposed.[43]

On Monday, October 11, 1937—the day on which Roosevelt signed his formal call (dated Tuesday, October 12) for a special session, to begin at noon on November 15—a huge wave of selling rolled over a stock market already drowning in a flood of sales. The selling continued in frightening volume through all the following week; *The New York Times*'s business index declined at an alarming rate, and so did index figures recording industrial activity. The most determinedly optimistic must now doubt that what was happening was a mere healthy "corrective" of a long-term bull market. It was all too reminiscent of the stock market's behavior in September and October of 1929.[44]

Then, on Tuesday, October 19, what had been unhappy reminiscence became in some respects a repetition, if on a much smaller scale, of the 1929 debacle. On that Black Tuesday of 1937, a total of 7,287,000 shares was traded on New York's exchange (over 16,400,000 were traded on Black Tuesday of 1929)—the largest number of shares since July 21, 1933*—and the stock price collapse on this and following days was sufficiently widespread to be a sharp reminder of the Great Crash. There loomed into the national mind the possibility of a renewal in full force of the Great Depression, and the Roosevelt administration, with this great trouble added to the injury inflicted by the court-reform defeat, found itself in by far the most serious political difficulty it had been in since taking office. Roosevelt personally was vulnerable to attack, to truly effective political attack, as he had not been since the New Deal began. For one thing, he must listen to harsh, jeering, and (in the circumstances) persuasive voices raised high to remind the general public of a boast he had made in Charleston, South Carolina, on an October Tuesday just two years before. "We are on our way back [from depression]," he had then said, "—not by mere chance. We are coming back more soundly than ever before because we planned it that way, and don't let anybody tell you differently."[45] Some planning! said the jeering voices; no doubt what was happening now had also been "planned . . . that way." In any case, if the Roosevelt administration were credited for the alleged "sound recovery" of 1935, it must be blamed for this "Roosevelt recession" of 1937 in the same way as the Republicans, having taken credit for the prosperity of the 1920s, could not avoid blame for the depression of the 1930s.

VII

PANIC fear swept over much of official Washington. Hard questions were raised about what had actually happened, why it had it happened, and who, if anyone, within the administration was to blame.

---

*Ten million shares were traded on July 21, 1933, as the speculative boom on that summer's as yet unregulated exchange came to its end. See *FDR: The New Deal Years,* pp. 136, 266.

To the last of these questions, the answer that came most readily, naturally, into conservative minds, and especially such minds within the Treasury and Commerce departments, was "Marriner Eccles." It was he, the Federal Reserve Board chairman—a man of shrewd intelligence, small physique, strong will, and peppery disposition—who had pressed hardest for an undistributed-profits tax on corporations, a measure adopted (though in a form far different from the one Eccles favored) by Congress in 1936. It was Eccles who had insisted upon, and forced through the Federal Reserve Board, an increase in bank reserve requirements last spring—a money-tightening, anti-inflation move which he himself might now regard as perhaps poorly timed. It was Eccles who had argued most strongly, and continued to argue, against federal budget-balancing at this time. In sum, therefore, it was Eccles who, of all men in high places, had done most to destroy or prevent a restoration of "business confidence," and who had thereby most discouraged the capital-goods expansion that truly sound economic recovery absolutely required.

To this indictment a harassed Eccles could only reply that what was happening was not primarily the result of a failure of capital goods to expand; it was primarily the result of a contraction of consumer purchasing power at a time when consumer-goods inventories had been overexpanded by speculative "forward buying" on the part of businessmen. To this contraction the government had contributed greatly. For one thing, there had been sharp reductions of relief and public-works expenditures in 1937 as compared with 1936, when a $1.7 billion soldiers' bonus, paid in a lump sum late in the year, had given a further boost to consumer buying power.* For another thing, there had been collected in 1937 a $2 billion Social Security tax, and virtually every dollar of this new tax came out of the pockets of people who would otherwise, perforce, have spent it in the consumer market. (Roosevelt had sternly opposed any funding of Social Security from general tax revenues [i.e., with money obtained through the graduated income tax]—any funding, in other words, that would increase the percentage of the national income going to those at the lower end of the income scale by reducing the percentage going to those at the upper end.) All in all, the federal treasury had accumulated a $66 million cash surplus during the first nine months of 1937 as compared with a $4 billion deficit in 1936, and such adherence to "sound business practice," in the absence of full employment, was catastrophic in effect. It proved once again that budget-balancing, far from being a requisite of prosperity, was in certain circumstances a recipe for disaster.† It was such a recipe at the present time. Loosed upon a helpless economy by fiscal conservatism were deflationary forces that savagely clawed down exchange prices and employment, day after day, week after week, and would continue to do so—there was every likelihood of a

---

*The bonus bill had been enacted over the President's veto in early 1936.
†The federal budget was in balance when the crash came in 1929, as Eccles was fond of pointing out.

return to the miseries of 1932–1933—unless bold, swift government action to restore consumer buying power was taken.[46]

Of all this (though he made no reference to the President's personal responsibility for grievous error), Eccles spoke with blunt candor when asked to do so by Roosevelt. The latter continued to listen with a sympathetic ear to his treasury secretary; he continued to share that worthy's basic conservatism in economic matters. But he was also acutely aware of the fatal dangers of his present political situation, he was convinced that the situation was at least partially the result of a business conspiracy (a "capital strike") against him, and he vividly remembered Eccles's flat prediction in late 1936 that to attempt a balanced budget while unemployment remained high would provoke severe recession. This, Eccles had said at that time, might lead the nation through economic misery into Fascism. (The possibility of the alleged business conspiracy's becoming a Fascist revolt was one of which Roosevelt spoke gloomily to close associates in the fall of 1937.[47]) Hence a Roosevelt invitation to Eccles to come to Hyde Park, in late October, for a frank tête-à-tête. And during this visit Roosevelt not only listened with flatteringly close attention to what Eccles had to say, he also responded affirmatively to Eccles's suggestion that, as a first step toward restored economic health, an expanded residential-construction program be launched through the Federal Housing Adminstration.

It was a somewhat reassured Eccles who left Hyde Park that day—an Eccles who believed Roosevelt was becoming convinced, at last, of the potency of deficit financing as a weapon against depression, and of the need, the desperate need, to use this weapon *now*. This belief was bolstered by the apparently persuasive effect upon the presidential mind of a memorandum written at this time by three New Deal economists who were strongly influenced by Keynes —namely, Lauchlin Currie of Eccles's own Federal Reserve staff, Leon Henderson of Hopkins's Works Progress Administration staff, and Isador Lubin, who was responsible for labor statistics in the Labor Department. The memorandum argued, with an abundance of supportive statistical data, that sharp reductions in government spending had indeed, as Eccles asserted, triggered the current recession, and that the only answer to recession, therefore, was a resumption of government spending. During a White House meeting which Eccles attended on November 8,* Roosevelt seemed to him wholly converted to what Eccles called "compensatory" economic activity by government; and two days later, when Eccles brought to the White House the draft amendments

---

*As a matter of fact, the Currie-Henderson-Lubin memo was written to provide the basis for discussion at this meeting—a meeting suggested and arranged by Harry Hopkins. In attendance, in addition to Hopkins, Eccles, and the three memo authors, were James Roosevelt and, incongruously, banker Paul M. Mazur of Lehman Brothers, the latter by James's invitation. The far from high quality of Mazur's mind is all too clearly revealed in his 1928 book, *American Prosperity: Its Causes and Consequences (FDR: The New York Years,* p. 113; see also p. 462, n. 4) and his contribution to this meeting, insofar as he made one, must have been a blurring of the otherwise sharply focused advice Roosevelt received. See Joseph P. Lash, *Dealers and Dreamers* (New York, 1988), p. 320.

of federal housing legislation that he had suggested at Hyde Park, and when Roosevelt expressed his awareness that this housing activity was but a first step toward ending the recession, implying that renewed large-scale government spending was in the offing, Eccles was convinced that the President had "seen the light."[48]

But all the while that Roosevelt was being counseled and seemingly persuaded by Eccles and company, he was permitting and even encouraging Morgenthau's preparation of an extended statement of the government's economic policy in the face of recession, a statement having as its central theme precisely that "government economy" that Eccles damned as, in the circumstances, ruinously deflationary.

During a Cabinet meeting on November 5—one of the very few Cabinet meetings during the whole of the New Deal in which the President asked for advice on substantive matters from Cabinet members—the treasury secretary, when asked by Roosevelt what the White House should do to solve the recession problem, stressed yet again the urgent need to "reassure business." Businessmen wanted to know whether "we [are] headed toward state socialism or are we going to continue on a capitalistic basis," said Morgenthau. Roosevelt responded irritably that he had "told them . . . again and again" of his and the New Deal's profound commitment to capitalism. "You want me to turn on the old record," said he—to which Morgenthau, echoed by Jim Farley, answered with a flat affirmative. "All right," said Roosevelt resignedly, ". . . I will turn on the old record."[49] This confirmed Morgenthau in his belief that the "old record" should be "turned on" at full volume when he addressed a meeting of the Academy of Political Science, an audience of conservatives (he would be introduced to it by Parker Gilbert of the House of Morgan), in New York City's Hotel Astor on the evening of November 10. Morgenthau had accepted the invitation in the hope of making his address a renewed commitment by the executive to the economic policy he favored. He would speak as the authentic voice of the administration; he insisted that every word of his draft speech be read and approved by the President. And every word had been by the time he stood up at the lectern, only a few hours after that White House meeting at which Roosevelt had given every indication, to Eccles, of being committed to renewed government spending.

Said Morgenthau:

> We deliberately used an unbalanced Federal budget [in 1933 and after] . . . to meet a great emergency. . . . The emergency no longer exists. . . . I am aware that there still remains a considerable volume of unemployment; that the speculative markets have recently been under severe pressure; and that our business indices have recently shown a declining tendency. I am further aware that some persons contend that another great spending program is [now] desirable. . . . But I have reached the firm conclusion that the problems which face us today are essentially different from those which faced us four years ago. Many measures are required for their solution. One of these . . . is a determined move toward a balanced budget. . . . We want to see private business expand. We believe that much of the remaining unemployment will

disappear as private capital funds are increasingly employed. . . . We believe that one of the most important ways of achieving these ends . . . is to continue progress toward a balance of the Federal Budget.[50]

The words shocked Marriner Eccles when he read them in his newspaper next morning. They also angered and disgusted him. "The contradictions between the afternoon and the evening position on November 10 made me wonder if the New Deal was just a political slogan," he remembered in print years later, "or if Roosevelt really knew what the New Deal implied from the standpoint of a recovery program. This is a harsh and ungenerous comment, yet it is what I thought at the time."[51]

### VIII

HARSH and ungenerous?

It was, certainly—and it was also untrue, insofar as the New Deal *was* considerably more than a slogan.

But Eccles's doubt about Roosevelt's grasp of the problems facing him at that time was wholly justified by facts. For Roosevelt did not know what "the New Deal implied" in the way of a recovery program, nor even what Eccles meant in statements of such implication—not, at least, with any solid, comprehensive understanding. He most "definitely" did not know ("definite" was his favorite modifier of "facts" tinged with doubt) what he himself should do about the recession. His natural optimistic tendency was to wait and see if "things" wouldn't work out of their own accord—but since they gave so few signs of doing so (he could see, in fact, no sign at all), his unease was profound. One suspects that deep within him was a vague but powerful feeling that he was being punished by God for having ignored or mistaken the Author's cues, for having misread the Author's lines. It had happened before. It had happened most horribly following the Lucy Mercer affair, when, in the darkest night of his polio ordeal, as he lay in the shadow of death upon a bed of agony, he had felt utterly abandoned by God. (He had confessed as much, years later, to Frances Perkins.[52]) This time, surely, his offense being far less, his punishment would be much milder. But at the very least he evidently now faced a winter of discontents—of miserable doubts and drift and helpless castings to and fro —more bitter and dangerous than the one he had suffered in 1934–35.

Such, one suspects, was his fundamental mood. But, if so, he continued stubbornly to deny its existence while revealing nothing of it to the world at large. For though his pride was hurt, and badly hurt, it, along with his religious faith, remained very much alive, and it would not let him wholly yield either to his own sense of guilt (never would he admit guilt) or to the hostile circumstances, the hostile men, by which and whom he was surrounded and besieged. He would admit only what he could not deny—namely, that everything at that moment was going wrong, at home and abroad, and that he himself, his physical self, seemed to be going to pieces also, as if breaking under the strain.

("There is no doubt that the President is showing the strain . . ." wrote diarist Ickes as November opened. "He looks all of fifteen years older since he was inaugurated in 1933. I don't see how anyone can stand the strain that he has been under."[53])

The conference of Nine-Power Treaty signatories, assembled under the auspices of the League of Nations for the purpose of negotiating a settlement of the quarrel between Japan and China, held its opening session in Brussels on November 3. Its utter futility was assured at the outset by Japan's refusal of her invitation to attend. When a second, more urgent invitation was issued her by the conference itself on November 6 and she again declined, the conferees could do nothing save adopt a general and, in the circumstances, cynical "declaration of principles," then adjourn. They did so a few days later, after listening to a closing speech by U.S. delegate Norman Davis in which he said that the conference's end did not mean the end of efforts to restore peace in the Far East. By that time—indeed, on the very day she received her second invitation to Brussels—Japan had signed with Nazi Germany and Fascist Italy a three-power anti-Communist pact, which is to say that the Nazi-Japanese pact of November 1936 now had Italy's signature appended to it. Roosevelt's hope that Mussolini might exert a moderating influence upon Hitler's ambition or might act in some way to restrain it was, by this, weakened almost to extinction. By that time, too, all Chinese troops had been driven from Shanghai, which was firmly in Japanese hands, and final preparations had been made for the capture by Japan's ground forces of Nanking, upon whose civilian population bombs continued to fall with horrible effect.

Hence the international situation was worse at the close of the Brussels conference than at the beginning, and in part because of the meeting. Demonstrated once again, redundantly, was the League's impotence in the face of events that continued to march relentlessly, at a constantly faster pace, across the darkening foreign scene toward new world war—a war Roosevelt now believed, or told H. G. Wells he believed, would begin in 1941 (Wells predicted it beginning in 1940).[54]

The domestic scene also darkened, in Roosevelt's vision, and here, too, the march of events was ominous.

On November 15 the extraordinary session of Congress was opened with a presidential message acknowledging frankly that "a marked recession . . . following a fairly steady advance for more than four years" had occurred since the regular session's adjournment in August. (Unlike Herbert Hoover, Franklin Roosevelt proposed to "face facts" and state them honestly.) He had "sought to avail" himself during the last two months "of the wisdom and advice of" businessmen big and little, "and of representatives of agriculture and labor"—conferences that increased his awareness of the complexity of the "economic problems which today face all nations." (Was not this implying of foreign causes for domestic woes a bit "Hooverish"?) They could not be "cured" by "single answers and simple slogans." The many "suggestions" and "recommendations" he had received were too often "at complete variance" one with another to add up to a program proposal; but they did in sum "make it clear that we have enough wisdom in the country today not only to check the present recession but also to lay the ground work for a more permanent recovery." Certainly, the "fundamental situation" today was far different from that of 1929, thanks to New Deal reforms, and "with the exercise of ordinary prudence, there is no reason why we should suffer any prolonged recession, let alone any general economic paralysis."

Of what the government should do to check recession, however, Roosevelt said nothing specific; he made only a few general remarks on the subject. An obviously "immediate task," he said, "is to try to increase the use of private capital to create employment. Private enterprise, with cooperation on the part of government, can advance to higher levels of economic activity than those reached earlier this year." This would assure balanced budgets. (Later in his message he said that he would soon submit to Congress a federal budget for the next fiscal year "which I expect can be brought within a definite balance.") But the government "cannot let nature take its course without regard to consequences. If private enterprise does not respond, government must take up the slack." Moreover, the "course" of "nature" must not be permitted to develop business combinations, or perpetuate existing ones, so huge that they threatened democratic freedoms. There was need for "special tax consideration" for small business. "In this way we may also find assistance in our search for a more effective method of checking the growing concentration of economic control and the resultant monopolistic practices which persist today in spite of anti-trust statutes." Roosevelt reminded his listeners that "this Administration has pledged itself . . . to carry on with a wide social program pointed toward higher living standards and a more just distribution of the gains of civilization." (These words expressed Roosevelt's reaction to what he perceived as big business's conspiracy against him—that is, a "capital strike"— and the specific mention of antitrust law signified a new tack for him, a further shift toward Brandeisianism. It was at once recognized as doing so.) Much of this social program was "already in effect, but its continued and complete success depends on a wider distribution of an immensely enlarged national income."

Hence his summoning of this extraordinary session.

It was called, not to attack the recession problems that had arisen in recent weeks, but to enact the four major bills left over from the regular session, proposals essential to the realization of the broad purposes of the New Deal. He made an extended statement (this was the bulk of his speech) about each of these—the agriculture bill, the wage-and-hour bill, the executive-reorganization bill, the bill to create seven regional authorities and a national planning body—then closed with words indicative of his awareness that he faced in this congressional session a New Deal–frustrating coalition of Republicans and conservative Southern Democrats, solidified during and by the Supreme Court battle, and now stronger and more sullenly hostile to him than ever before. He made an attempt, a fairly lame attempt, to mitigate conservative animosity. He tried, halfheartedly, to appeal to the materialistic self-interest—the acquisitive instinct, the concern for private property and fear of its loss—that is the motivating essence of political conservatism in a capitalistic society. Said he: "What these four subjects promise in continued and increased purchasing power—what they promise in greater efficiency in the use of government funds —are intelligent foundations for the other plans for the encouragement of industrial expansion with government help. What they promise in social contentment is an almost necessary basis for greater security of profits and property. . . . For the sake of the Nation. I hope for your early action."[55]

But he had, in actual fact, very little such hope: He could take no cheer from the evident immediate effect of his words upon those he wished to persuade, and before the day was out his inner gloom was rendered darker still by physical illness.

He had felt unwell when the day began. By day's end, his sickness was focused and defined by throbs of pain, the whole of his consciousness centering upon the inside molar on the right side of his mouth whence spread, as it seemed, a pulsing anguish of failure, despair, ruin, death. His toothache was the worst he had suffered since the shattering of one of his front teeth in a boyhood accident on Campobello—and simultaneously, perhaps consequently, he suffered a "gastro-intestinal upset" (so news reports dubbed it) of considerable severity.[56]

There followed two days of misery for him as efforts were made to save the abscessed tooth. Then, on a day when he was scheduled to address a meeting of the presidents of land grant colleges at Mount Vernon (Secretary of Agriculture Wallace read the address in his absence), the tooth was extracted. By that time the infection had spread through his gum. The surgery spread it through his body. He remained bedridden, feverish and in pain, for several days, and was forced to postpone a week-long vacation cruise in Florida waters which he had planned to follow hard upon the special session's opening. He also had to cancel plans to spend Thanksgiving, at the close of his vacation, in Warm Springs. Even after he had risen from his bed and resumed a fairly normal work schedule, on November 23, he was confined to the White House, far from well. The infection was as stubbornly persistent and sullenly hostile to him— his gum very sore, his cheek badly swollen—as the conservative coalition, which, it was now clear, had the special session's majority in thrall.

For by then the President's four major legislative proposals, and the housing bill that had been added to them, were obviously in grave trouble. Washington newsmen were reporting that the rebellious mood that had characterized the assemblage at its opening had continued unabated through the days that followed. Nor was Roosevelt himself in any shape, physically or mentally, to do anything to put down this rebellion; he could only put as brave a face as possible on the matter, giving others no sign that he was seriously worried by it. He was letting Congress "have its head," he told close associates, confident that sooner or later, quite possibly before this special session ended, the members would run into so much trouble they would have to turn to him for help.[57] What objective basis he had for this belief he did not say.

Meanwhile, in part as an ostentatious display of calm confidence but even more because he really needed to get away from Washington's late-fall chill into summer warmth and sunlight, to recuperate, he revived plans for the cruising holiday that his illness had frustrated.

Late in the night of Saturday, November 27, he and his party (it included, for the train trip, Betsey Roosevelt, Missy LeHand, and Florida senator Claude Pepper) boarded the President's special train in Washington's Union Station. At midnight the train pulled out. On Monday morning, November 29, it arrived in Miami.

IX

Alas, the holiday fishing cruise failed of its purpose—failed almost as miserably as everything else in that opening season of failure.

Roosevelt was, of course, in no festive mood at the outset. To his already sufficiently heavy load of concerns had been added, during the last few days, great apprehension over an unspecified but allegedly drastic aggressive action to be taken by Japan in the far Pacific on or about December 1; this was highly secret information that had come to him from three confidential sources abroad, one of them, presumably, the highly respected British intelligence service.[58] Amid such anxieties he could borrow little comfort from the two other principals of his party, who were Harry Hopkins and Harold Ickes, for they were in no happier mood than he. Nor could he borrow it from his other shipboard companions (they included military aide Colonel "Pa" Watson; presidential physician Ross McIntire; presidential secretary James Roosevelt; and Assistant Attorney General Robert Jackson, who was in charge of the antitrust division of the Department of Justice and whose inclusion in the party indicated to some observers the President's intention to implement soon, legislatively and in other ways, the antimonopoly sentiments expressed in his last message to Congress). The mood of these companions was inevitably affected by that of the three principals—and in any case, the deficiency of good cheer was too great to be supplied by their efforts, either at the outset or as the days passed.

Ickes had been asked to come on this trip just forty-eight hours before it began, and had accepted the invitation only because he felt unable to refuse it, the President having phoned him personally to say, in a rare if jocular admission of personal insecurity, that "he wanted someone to hold his hand."[59] The invitation, tantamount to an order, came "at a very inconvenient time," the interior secretary complained to his diary. He had a major address to prepare for the delivery at the annual banquet of the American Civil Liberties Union in New York on December 8. He was trying to heal wounds that had been given his relations with bureau chiefs in his department by certain internal-espionage devices (they included wiretaps) he had employed to root out

and prevent the graft and corruption for which Interior was historically notorious and to which PWA, by virtue of its emergency status and the amount of
money it administered, was peculiarly vulnerable. He was anxiously involved
in congressional lobbying activities, and in a power struggle with Henry Wallace, to obtain the transfer of the Forest Service from Agriculture to Interior,
this on behalf of his grand ambition, the creation and heading of a Department
of Conservation which, under the Brownlow Committee's executive-reorganization plan, would handle all natural-resource conservation activities. Moreover, though he was very tired (he had not yet fully recovered from his heart
attack) and needed rest and relaxation, he would never have chosen an ocean
voyage for this purpose. A poor sailor, he was very far from having such love
of the sea, such belief in the recreative and therapeutic value of shipboard life,
as Franklin Roosevelt had. He was, in fact, generally uneasy and often miserable aboard ship—and it was with a sinking heart, premonitory of seasickness,
that he saw tied up at the Miami dock on Monday morning, awaiting the
party's boarding, not the navy cruiser or other large ship he had expected, but
the relatively tiny presidential yacht *Potomac*—a vessel that would certainly
pitch and roll, sickeningly, in even a moderate sea.[60]

An equal anxiety, though unrecorded, must have been felt on the same score
by Harry Hopkins, who was at that time in far worse shape physically and
emotionally than Ickes was. He had suffered a shattering tragedy in his personal life during the summer and fall.[61]

In January 1937, Barbara Duncan Hopkins, Harry's wife for the last six
years and the mother of his five-year-old daughter, Diana, had discovered a
lump in one breast, had consulted a doctor in New York City who diagnosed
cancer, had then at once undergone surgery. From the mastectomy itself her
recovery had been swift and complete; by late spring, after the family had
moved from the Wardman Park apartment where they had been living to a
rented house in Georgetown, she felt so well, so abundantly full of life, that
she and Harry dared hope that a recurrence of malignancy, said by the doctors
to be a statistical probability with this kind of cancer, would not in her case
happen. Then, in midsummer, she had come down with what at first seemed
to be an attack of pleurisy but was quickly diagnosed as cancer, now spread
so widely that nothing could be done to save her. Shortly before dawn on
October 6, with her sobbing husband at her hospital bedside, she died.

The widower's immense grief was exacerbated by feelings of guilt.

Hopkins was only somewhat less fatalistic in basic attitude than Franklin
Roosevelt, though his fatalism differed in nature from Roosevelt's—was, in
fact, more like that of Louis Howe, minus Howe's sense of the world as
theater.* What Roosevelt identified with God and supported with a strong
religious faith was by Hopkins called simply luck or fortune and supported by
belief in a natural order that underlay and determined all events, all phenomena. Hopkins's living faith was, in this sense, considerably more "scientific"

---

*See Davis, *FDR: The Beckoning of Destiny,* pp. 286–87.

than Roosevelt's. But it was also, in a curious mingling of incongruities, far more puritanical than Roosevelt's (puritanism was in fact notably absent from the latter), Hopkins having been raised by his mother in a strict and narrow Calvinism. There yet remained in Hopkins enough religion to make him now feel, deep down, that he was in some degree responsible for this death—that he had caused it, at least in part, by his sinful disregard of right conduct ("natural-right" conduct). Barbara was his second wife. His previous marriage, complicated at the outset by religious differences (his first wife was Jewish), ended in divorce in 1931, after three sons had been born of it. For the failure of his marriage he, a man of tender conscience and great compassion, had blamed himself bitterly, even morbidly. Since young manhood he had thought of himself, he had encouraged others to think of him, as a rakish fellow —a racetrack and poker-table gambler, a nightclub habitué, fond of liquor and fast women. It was a generally bright and happy self-perception or self-deception, essentially innocent (he lacked the time, the money, the physical capacity, or even the urgent desire for great dissipations) yet pleasurably spiced with a sense of sin. It turned dark and sour, however, when his "luck" ran out: He then stood self-convicted of a criminally selfish hedonism. He felt that his marriage had come to grief in good part because of his love, and ruthless pursuit, of pleasure. But during the years since his divorce and his immediately following second marriage, he had come to believe that all was forgiven. This second marriage was gloriously happy. Physically attractive, affectionate, outgoing, Barbara Hopkins, a former Bellevue Hospital nurse who had been a secretary in the New York Tuberculosis Association when Hopkins (then executive director of that agency) first met her, understood her husband's work and fully shared his social-welfare commitments. She also greatly aided his government career by simply being herself in her relations with other people, for this made her popular in Washington, despite her small liking for formal society. More important, it also made her a White House favorite. Roosevelt was fond of her; so were Rex Tugwell, Ickes, and virtually every other key New Deal figure. And Eleanor Roosevelt not only became her warm friend but also bestowed upon little Diana a grandmotherly love. But now this "good luck" or "fortune" had, in its turn, gone bad, had been lost to malignant death, and Hopkins was so distraught, so utterly devastated, that his intimates feared he might never recover.

He acceded to Eleanor Roosevelt's insistence that Diana come live in the White House until other living arrangements for her and her father could be made. He managed, somehow, to continue running the WPA in his own uniquely efficient administrative style; his job, though now severely hampered by budget cuts, was again of crisis importance as unemployment grew and relief rolls lengthened. He did his work well and was grateful for it as a distraction from grief, a kind of numbing drug. But sometimes during his workdays he spoke of Barbara to others (to Missy LeHand, for one) as though she were yet alive, and when he was alone in the Georgetown house, at night and on weekends, he spent hours sitting motionless before her photograph—

was found doing so by people who visited him at home. Moreover, he became daily more convinced of the likelihood that his own life was nearing its end. Ever since September 1936, when he had experienced difficulty eating while on a presidential-campaign speaking tour of the west, he had felt unwell. He now believed he had stomach cancer (his father had died of it). (The belief would be justified in the event, as we may anticipate here. On December 20, just three weeks hence, Harry Hopkins would be lying on an operating table in the Mayo Clinic in Rochester, Minnesota; some two-thirds of his cancerous stomach would be removed in what the public would be told was surgery for ulcers.) Thus it was with a stomach far more queasy than Ickes's that he boarded the *Potomac* at the Miami dock on the morning of Monday, November 29.

And before the first vacation day ended, both Hopkins and Ickes were nauseatingly aware of the ship's movement.[62] After an afternoon's slow progress (slow for trolling purposes) down the Florida coast, the *Potomac* headed out to sea, bound for the Dry Tortugas islands, and the farther out she went the more she was tossed by roughening water. Hopkins and Ickes, sharing the ship's largest cabin, were more than happy to retire to it, and to an early bed, from the after-dinner poker table around which all of the President's party save the President himself were seated. The sea grew more and more rough during the night. The yacht pitched and rolled so badly that even Roosevelt was distinctly uncomfortable, his normally strong stomach having been weakened by his illness. He did not protest, therefore—he seemed as relieved as his guests —when the captain of the ship ordered its mooring at the dock at Fort Jefferson until the seas grew calmer.

For several days thereafter the *Potomac* remained at Fort Jefferson. Most of the party went ashore at one time or another to visit the historic fort where Dr. Samuel Mudd, who had set John Wilkes Booth's broken leg after Booth's assassination of Lincoln, was for several years imprisoned. There was much fishing from small boats off the island shore, much lazy socializing, a great effort (overall) to have a good time. But there was all too little unforced, unalloyed pleasure in warm sunlight (the skies were overcast much of the time), and Roosevelt himself was unwontedly listless, withdrawn from his guests, through all save the last day or so of the vacation. He kept much to his cabin. Even on deck he socialized relatively little with his companions, reading instead or working (playing) with his stamps, or simply sitting in silence for an hour at a time, dozing or staring vacantly out to sea. He did participate, after the first night, in the after-dinner poker games, but only for an hour or so. All in all, he was so far different from his usual self, he wore so much the aspect of a man who had been beaten and had given up, that his companions worried about him. They worried, too—at least Hopkins, Jackson, and Ickes did—over what was now happening to the New Deal and would certainly increasingly happen if the White House continued to give way to congressional government, continued to fail to exercise strong leadership in the face of economic recession and political reaction. All that had been accomplished in the way of progressive reform was threatened by the political servants of big business who, in 1940, with Roosevelt's name absent from the ballot, might well capture the White House itself.

Ross T. McIntire, the President's personal physician, was worried for a different reason. The doctor greatly feared that the tooth infection, persisting in the gum, would spread to the bone—a development that could have grave consequences indeed, requiring a scraping of the jawbone—and it was at his urging that Roosevelt decided on December 3 to cut short by two days his fishing cruise and go directly from his Florida landing to Washington, canceling a brief speech scheduled for Warm Springs and another that was to have been made at Gainesville, Georgia.

Yet he seemed almost his usual buoyant self to the reporters who interviewed him in a press conference held on his special train as it rolled northward toward Washington. It was noted that he lacked the suntan he usually had after an ocean-fishing vacation, but he dealt with questions as adroitly and good-humoredly as he usually did, if also less communicatively than usual. (The reporters were given, in fact, no substantial news whatever; the President declined to answer questions about the Far Eastern situation, or the fate of his legislative proposals to the special congressional session, or the revision of antitrust law with which Robert Jackson was presumed to be concerned.[63]) And in actual fact, Roosevelt did feel better, physically, when he arrived at the White House on the afternoon of December 6 than he had for a long time. He at once underwent examination by the dentist who had extracted his tooth (Commander Arthur H. Yando of the Navy Dental Corps)—an examination that revealed, to everyone's relief, no need for further surgery. The infection had certainly gone deep into his gum, but it had not quite touched the bone, and it was now retreating.[64]

X

BUT the soreness of his gum, along with the continuing parade of dire events with which he must deal, remained great enough to encourage, through the remaining weeks of 1937, Roosevelt's unwonted irritability—and though his show of high spirits and good humor remained quantitatively unchanged, his humor was different in quality from that he displayed in his truly happy times. It continued to be disproportionately of the practical-joke variety, the kind of malicious humor that had dictated in part the way in which the Supreme Court battle was initiated as well as the nomination of Hugo Black to take the place of Van Devanter on the Court. Currently, it played a part in his choice of a replacement for Robert W. Bingham as ambassador to the Court of St. James's, Bingham having been forced by illness, in the fall, to leave London and return to his Kentucky home, where he soon died.

The story of this last choice, rendered abnormally important by the crisis in world affairs amid which it was made, is especially revealing.

Early in 1937, Joseph P. Kennedy, who had been chairman of the Securities and Exchange Commission during the first year of its existence,* had reluctantly accepted appointment to the chairmanship of the newly established Maritime Commission, imperfectly designed by New Deal law to rescue America's merchant marine from chronic depression. This was an important, pioneering task, but impossible in the absence of regulatory powers much greater than the current law provided. (Kennedy proposed a bill granting such powers; it was opposed by Secretary of Labor Perkins; Roosevelt refused to take a stand on the matter; and a despairing Kennedy concluded, despite his hatred of socialism, that outright government ownership was the only solution to the merchant marine's problems.) In any case, the commission chairmanship was not a big enough job to endow Kennedy with the kind of fame and prestige he wanted for himself and his sons. He continued to yearn for the Cabinet post he believed he should have been given in 1933; he made use of James Roosevelt, with whom he had associated in a lucrative liquor-importing enterprise immediately after Prohibition's repeal and who remained a close social friend, as his conduit to the President; and as soon as he learned that the London ambassadorial post would soon be vacant he let the President know, through James, that he wanted it.[65]

To Roosevelt, the idea of naming an Irish Catholic to the Court of St. James's—and a crusty, combative, remarkably undiplomatic Irishman at that—was initially so hilariously outrageous, according to son James, that "he almost toppled from his wheelchair" with laughter.[66] But as he thought about it, remembering the arrogance with which Chamberlain had refused his recent invitation to come to Washington for talks, he became more and more "intrigued with the idea of twisting the lion's tail a little," as James later put it. Moreover, the ruthlessly ambitious and profoundly conservative (even reactionary) Kennedy was for Roosevelt a serious problem. His wealth, his persuasive power over the Catholic hierarchy, his strategic position as a pro-Roosevelt big-business man (he could partially deflect or substantially augment the hostile fire focused upon the New Deal by the big-business community), his considerable abilities and personal charm—all these made Kennedy a force to be reckoned with, and especially so because he had rendered services to the Roosevelt campaigns of 1932 and 1936 that, by the law of political give-and-take, *did* deserve greater reward than they had thus far received. His recognized deserts gave him a certain power over Roosevelt. And the latter resented the creditor demands that Kennedy made of him, resented Kennedy's use of James to influence (or attempt to influence) presidential policy, resented and distrusted Kennedy personally, deeming him (as he said

---

*This appointment, made in belated payment for Kennedy's service to Roosevelt's first presidential campaign, was itself not wholly free of practical jokery, Kennedy having made the bulk of his large fortune through precisely the kind of Wall Street operations outlawed by the Securities and Exchange Act. "Set a thief to catch a thief," Roosevelt had said to members of his inner circle who expressed outrage. See *FDR: The New Deal Years,* pp. 369–71.

to Morgenthau) "a very dangerous man—too dangerous to have around here [i.e., in Washington]."[67]

Hence his decision, reluctantly made, to send Kennedy to London—where, as he told Morgenthau, he would have him "watched hourly" so that he could be "fired . . . the first time he opens his mouth and criticizes me."[68]

Hence, too, the manner in which he made the appointment, this being a practical joke whereby the prideful, willful, power-hungry Joe Kennedy was forced to admit, in a humiliating way, that Roosevelt was his master.

Roosevelt had son James bring Kennedy to the presidential office one autumn day. He greeted Kennedy with a special warmth. "Joe," said he, "would you mind standing back there by the fireplace so I can get a good look at you?" Kennedy, puzzled, did so. The President looked him up and down, then said, "Joe, would you mind taking down your pants?" Kennedy, and James, who remained in the room, "couldn't believe our ears." Surely, Roosevelt was kidding? He insisted, however, that he was serious—he wanted to confirm the truth or falsity of something he'd been told by a man who'd once seen Kennedy in a bathing suit—whereupon Kennedy, rather incredibly (clearly he wanted this post very much indeed), pulled down his suspenders and let his trousers drop to the floor.

He stood then, red-faced with embarrassment, while Roosevelt stared at his bare legs. Roosevelt shook his head ruefully; what he had been told was, alas, true, he said. "Joe, you are just about the most bowlegged man I have ever seen." If photographs appeared in newspapers and newsreels of him wearing "knee britches and silk stockings," as protocol would require him to do during his ceremonial acceptance by the British monarch, he and the country he represented would become "a laughingstock" around the world. Roosevelt was sorry, but "you're just not right for the job, Joe."

According to James's remembrance, Kennedy "without batting an eye" asked if he could have the appointment if he were given permission from the British government to wear "a cutaway coat and striped pants" at the induction ceremony. Roosevelt said he could, provided the permission were given within two weeks' time. But there was no chance of that, he added, deadpan, the British being such sticklers for ceremonial tradition. Actually, of course, Kennedy obtained the required permission without difficulty; it was granted in an official document placed in the President's hands before the two weeks were up.[69]

The appointment was made known to the world on December 9, in a bylined scoop by Arthur Krock in *The New York Times,* Krock having been given the news by his good friend Kennedy (perhaps Kennedy now got some of his own back) along with permission to print it from James as presidential secretary. Roosevelt, who loathed Krock, was furious. In a press conference, some time later, he charged the *Times* bureau chief with "hastening the death of Ambassador Bingham" by this premature disclosure.[70]

Three days later, on December 12, the importance of this appointment—that is, the importance of the influence Kennedy would have in the London embassy upon Anglo-American relations—was increased by an event on the opposite side of the globe.

On December 10, Japanese forces in China launched an all-out offensive against Nanking. By then, the Chinese government offices in that capital had been moved to three inland cities, the Chinese Foreign Office being established in Hankow. To the latter place the U.S. ambassador to China, Nelson T. Johnson, had also gone on November 23 with the bulk of his embassy staff. He had left behind, however, several attachés to conduct routine embassy business and render service to American citizens who yet remained in the abandoned capital. The only armed protection for them was a single U.S. Navy gunboat, the *Panay,* anchored off Nanking's waterfront in the Yangtze River.

This protection was meager: The *Panay,* separated by hundreds of miles from the nearest support units of the U.S. Asiatic Fleet, was well enough armed against surface attack, but her sole armament against a far more likely attack from the air consisted of eight antiquated .30-caliber Lewis machine guns, left over from the Great War. It was in recognition of the ship's vulnerability to air attack that, when Japanese shells began to fall on the city's waterfront on December 11, several large American flags, one of them measuring twenty-six feet by thirty-two feet, were spread flat across her top deck, marking her unmistakably, to eyes in the sky, as a U.S. vessel. The *Panay,* with embassy staff members, newspaper correspondents, and a Universal newsreel cameraman aboard, and accompanied by three Standard Oil Company river tankers, which had placed themselves under her protection, then sailed several miles upstream, well out of the zone of shell fire. On the morning of the following day, she and the tankers moved yet farther upstream, anchoring a full twenty miles from Nanking.

The skies over east central China that day were bright and clear. Japanese warplanes, afar off, were sighted by the *Panay* in the early afternoon. The planes seemed to be headed elsewhere, however. The *Panay*'s crew was not called at once to general quarters. Then, abruptly, the planes veered in a swooping dive toward the gunboat, beginning a bombing and strafing attack that continued for more than an hour, with the belatedly manned Lewis machine guns chattering away through most of that time in utter futility. Not until the *Panay* was a ruined vessel, obviously sinking (soon thereafter she rolled over and went down), did the attack upon her cease. The planes then focused their lethal attentions upon the three defenseless Standard Oil vessels. These had got under way when the attack on the *Panay* began and were steaming upstream as fast as they could go, which wasn't fast enough. By the end of another hour, two of these vessels were burning and the third, the only one of the three to survive, was beached.

There were many casualties, Two *Panay* crew members, the captain of one of the river tankers, and an Italian newspaper correspondent were killed.

Seventy-four people were wounded, many of them seriously, including the *Panay*'s captain, Lieutenant Commander James Hughes.[71]

In part, perhaps, because he had been warned that a world-challenging act of aggression by Japan was scheduled for early December, and had pondered the response he should make to it, Roosevelt was able to rise to this crisis with an emotional calm and mental poise that were quite remarkable, given the state of his political fortunes and spiritual health at that time. His calm, his poise, and his projection of these through the mass media were soothing to a shocked, frightened, and angry American public. There were, of course, loud demands by bellicose patriots for an immediate declaration of war upon Japan. Among those making them most vehemently was the very ill secretary of the navy, Claude Swanson,* speaking for most of the U.S. Navy's admirals. Even Harold Ickes, who called himself a pacifist, voiced a conviction that "war with Japan is inevitable sooner or later" and that "right now" might be "the best possible time."[72] The President's realistic appraisal of the situation led, however, to a different conclusion.

For one thing, the U.S. Navy, for all the admirals' bellicosity, was not ready for a major war in the Pacific, and certainly not for the two-ocean war that the treaty linkage of Nazi-Fascism to Japanese militarism portended. Time was needed to complete the shipbuilding program that had been launched by Roosevelt early in his administration—a program he now planned to augment significantly in his budget proposals for the upcoming fiscal year.

For a second thing, there came to Washington immediately after the first news of the *Panay* attack an expression of profound apologies for it by Foreign Minister Koki Hirota of Japan, who called upon U.S. Ambassador Joseph C. Grew in Tokyo to make them personally. (Hirota said that the Japanese naval commander in Shanghai took full responsibility for a tragic "mistake": The Japanese aviators, flying too high to see the American flags, had believed they were attacking Chinese vessels.)

For a third and most important thing, though anti-Japanese feeling, racism very much a part of it, had long run high across the nation, the American public, with its hard core of isolationist and pacifist sentiment, was not mentally or morally prepared for war—was, indeed, quite emphatically committed, in the main, to the avoidance of war even at the risk of what historic convention called honor. Roosevelt was told by Senator Ashurst of Arizona that a war resolution, presented to Congress now, would win not a single vote in the Senate—and that the mood in the House was at least equally pacifistic was indicated by the fact that Democratic representative Louis Ludlow of Indiana found the moment right to force a House vote on a proposed constitutional

---

*The seventy-five-year-old Swanson, suffering from high blood pressure and other circulatory problems, had been almost an invalid when appointed to the Cabinet in 1933. By 1938 he had to be carried into Cabinet meetings. He clung to his post, however, and Roosevelt "hadn't the heart to let him go," as he (FDR) confessed to former secretary of the navy Josephus Daniels.

change in the method of declaring war, one that would drastically affect the handling of America's foreign affairs.

This highly controversial Ludlow Amendment, the support of which at that moment could be construed as a vote of no confidence in Roosevelt's management of the Far Eastern crisis, and also as a measure of isolationist reaction to the Chicago quarantine speech, provided that Congress could declare war through simple majority vote of both houses *only* if the United States were actually invaded by a foreign foe. In all other cases, to become valid, a congressional declaration of war would require the approval of the electorate in a nationwide referendum. Ludlow had made the proposal three years ago when Mussolini's military operations against Ethiopia had just begun; at that time the conjoined peace movement and fear of war, spurred by exposures of war-fomenting by armaments manufacturers, was at its height in America, This height had been measured by Gallup's Institute of Public Opinion in November 1935, when a nationally representative sample of Americans was asked precisely the question which Ludlow had raised: "In order to declare war except when our country is invaded—should Congress be required to obtain the approval of the people by means of a national vote?" Seventy-five percent of those in the sample who had formed an opinion answered yes; 25 percent said no. Nevertheless, Ludlow's bill had languished in committee ever since, its doom sealed, as it appeared, by the executive's adamant opposition to it. Ludlow, however, encouraged by the fact that Gallup polls in 1936 and 1937 had shown that a huge if somewhat smaller majority of the public continued to favor his proposal, had for many months been circulating a petition to force discharge of his bill from committee and had managed to obtain 205 signatures on it, just thirteen short of the number needed, when the *Panay* attack occurred. Within two days thereafter, these thirteen were obtained. Thus the proposal, utterly disastrous to the executive's conduct of foreign affairs, as Roosevelt insisted in private communications to congressmen (he cautiously refrained from much public comment on the matter), would be acted upon by the House as one of its first items of business in the upcoming regular session, and all signs pointed toward a close vote.[73]

Conceivably, had the public mood been radically different, Roosevelt the politician, in his currently precarious circumstances, just might have given furtive consideration to the vast increase of presidential power that comes from war patriotism and war-waging; it is even conceivable, if highly unlikely, that this consideration would then have become a decisive factor for him. As it was, sharing as he largely did the predominant mood, he was determined to avoid war now.

On December 13, he instructed Secretary of State Hull to tell the Japanese ambassador in Washington that he, the President, was "deeply shocked and concerned"; he "requests that the Emperor be so advised"—this last in recognition of the fact that the military power in Japan had gone largely out of the control of elected officials and that the sacred Emperor was the nation's ultimate unifying authority.* He also "hoped" that the Japanese government would present to the United States "a. Full expressions of regret and proffer of full compensation; b. Methods guaranteeing against a repetition of any similar attack in the future."[74]

Simultaneously, fumblingly, with his usual disregard for logical consistency, Roosevelt cast about for "a technique of fighting without declaring war" and that wouldn't "lead to war"—something that could be called quarantine rather than economic sanction but that, to the extent that he was ever explicit about it, was precisely the latter. On December 16, for example, he said to Sir Ronald Lindsay, Britain's ambassador in Washington, that he wanted "a systematic exchange of secret information" between the U.S. and British navies, and concerted plans for a blockade of Japan, to be effected by the two powers as soon as "the next grave outrage occurred"; and on the following day he told his Cabinet that such a blockade, extending from the Aleutians to Britain's naval base at Singapore, would bring Japan to her knees within a year. But from such forcefulness he promptly backed away—had done so even before the end of the day on which he spoke of it in Cabinet meeting. By then he had decided simply to send a U.S. Navy officer to London for "technical discussions" of cooperation between the U.S. and British navies in case the two powers became involved in war with Japan.[75]

His main worry at that time was over the failure of Tokyo to respond promptly to his *Panay,* protest, an anxiety fed by his now certain knowledge that the attack on the gunboat had been a deliberate act of war. With the bravery characteristic of those engaged in his hazardous profession, Norman Alley, the Universal newsreel cameraman aboard the *Panay,* had remained on the ship's deck during the whole of the attack in order to film the incident. He had had five thousand feet of film negative with him when the U.S. Navy rushed him from China to the United States via destroyer and China Clipper airplane. As soon as it was developed, this film had gone to Washington, where it was at once screened in the White House for Franklin Roosevelt. It conclusively disproved Japan's official claim that the Japanese airmen had flown too high to be able to distinguish American vessels and Chinese. Alley's camera had caught Japanese planes strafing the vessel at masthead height, so low that the pilots' faces could be seen. The anger this aroused in Roosevelt was great. It was overbalanced, however, by his concern that, shown uncut to the general public, the film would have an option-closing inflammatory effect upon public opinion, possibly forcing him into the belligerency he now desperately wished to avoid. He therefore asked Universal executives to eliminate the strafing

---

*According to the 1937 volume of *The United States in World Affairs,* published by the Council on Foreign Relations, the original draft of the presidential instruction to the secretary of state, a draft prepared in the State Department, used the word "suggests" instead of "requests." Roosevelt substituted the latter word "in his own handwriting . . . and with remarkable diplomatic flair . . . [gave] a copy of his memorandum, so revised, to the press for photographic reproduction" (p. 233).

footage from the newsreel shown in theaters across the land—a request to which the executives, with some natural reluctance, agreed.[76]

But he could not revise or censor in this way the Japanese reply to his note. It would perforce go into the public mind as written. And the longer it was delayed the greater his fear that the Japanese military authority was refusing to yield to civilian authority on this crucial matter, that the note was being dictated by the very men responsible for the incident, and that it would therefore prove impossible to accept.

What should or could he then do?

Hence his great relief when, on December 24, Foreign Minister Hirota's reply was received. The reply reviewed in detail the findings of an allegedly thorough investigation of the *Panay* incident—findings known by Washington to be factually inaccurate insofar as they "confirmed" Hirota's original description of the attack as a tragic blunder by air force pilots. Roosevelt, Hull, and Grew, having in hand the newsreel film, could and did let Japan's government know that they knew the formal note's "explanation" to be false. But the note also expressed profound regrets, said that the aviators responsible would be severely punished, pledged that Japan's air force would henceforth go to great lengths to avoid injury to American lives and property in China "even at the sacrifice of a strategic advantage in attacking the Chinese troops," and promised full indemnification for death, personal injury, and property damage. Next day, Secretary of State Hull formally instructed Ambassador Grew to notify the foreign minister in Tokyo that his note of explanation and regret was accepted and that a bill for indemnification was being prepared for presentation to his government by the United States. (In April 1938, a check for $2,214,000 was received from Japan.)[77]

XI

BY that time, the special congressional session had come to its sorry end. On December 21, at five P.M., with only eight members in the Senate chamber and fewer than a hundred on the House floor (the bulk of the membership had left Washington by then, going to their homes for the holidays), the session was adjourned sine die, without having enacted a single one of the four bills it had been summoned to pass and with only "transitory action," as the press described it, on the housing bill proposed by Senator Wagner and supported by the White House. There was not the slightest sign that Congress, having been given its head, was running into such trouble that it would soon call upon the President for help. There was instead conclusive evidence that the President had lost control over his own party and that he was now more than ever at the mercy of a hostile combination of conservatives who eschewed party labels in order to vote their pro-business, anti–New Deal sentiments. And, thanks mostly to a lack of firm, consistent liberal leadership by the President, this loss of conservative support was not offset by a gain of liberal support.

Nor could he anticipate an easing of his legislative problems in the months to come. The coalition of "little people" or "average Americans"—farmers and industrial workers, professional people and small-business men—which had constituted his political base was rapidly disintegrating. With it was going the power he had formerly been able to wield through his discernment and occupation of points at which opposing interests were balanced. Imbalance was everywhere. Agricultural policy was increasingly at the mercy of the American Farm Bureau Federation (Rex Tugwell had warned Roosevelt that it would be, because of the way in which the AAA was set up and administered)—that is, at the mercy of the bigger farmers and their business allies, who had little concern for the small family farm, were even hostile to measures that strengthened small farmers or farm tenants or consumer organizations, and were opposed to the New Deal in general insofar as it aimed toward any real change in farm income distribution. They wanted, simply, more income for themselves. Organized labor was embroiled in bitter civil war: John L. Lewis of the CIO, the "Huey Long of the labor movement" as some called him, was rapidly becoming a major threat to Roosevelt's leadership. And as Roosevelt's labor and farm support was thus weakened, big-business hostility to both labor and the New Deal was stronger than ever—and bore more and more, in Roosevelt's eyes, the earmarks of a developing American Fascism. For large corporations now made war, increasingly bloody war, upon their workers, following the pattern established by such as Tom Girdler of Republic Steel last Memorial Day. They employed labor espionage and subversion; they stockpiled arms and munitions; they allied themselves with organized crime as they recruited strike-breaking gangs of thugs—private armies whose only allegiance was to those who paid them. The possibility, the threat, of a Fascist coup appeared to Roosevelt not only real but growing as the economic recession continued with no end in sight. Since September 15, more than 1.8 million people had been added to the ranks of the unemployed, and WPA analysts predicted an additional million unemployed by mid-January.

As for foreign affairs, dominated by the growing strength of Fascism abroad, never had they posed graver threats to the United States, and never had the presidential power to respond to them been more seriously challenged. Soon, now, a Congress gone almost completely out of the administration's control would be debating, then voting upon, the Ludlow Amendment.

## XII

SMALL wonder that Christmas Day in the White House, in this year 1937, was less exuberantly cheerful than any other there since the New Deal began. Also, the family gathering was smaller.[78]

Last night, the President had made a brief radio broadcast to the nation, during which he referred to the angel's song of "peace on Earth, good will toward men"—had also, in pursuance of what had become a family tradition, read aloud an abridged version of Dickens's *A Christmas Carol* to assembled family and houseguests. Equally traditional would be his celebration of this joyous day. Soon his bedroom was invaded by three excited little girls: the two children of Betsey and James (Kate, aged five; Sara, aged two), and the motherless five-year-old Diana Hopkins, whose father, on this Christmas Day, was reported to be "doing well" following his drastic, life-threatening surgery. Roosevelt greeted these children with the heartiest of Merry Christmases, then presided over the opening of the gift-stuffed stockings that had been hung beside his fireplace the night before. His breakfast followed, after which he donned formal morning dress (striped trousers, cutaway coat, winged collar) to attend Christmas services at the Church of the Covenant. Accompanying him were his mother, his eldest and youngest sons, his daughter-in-law Betsey, and his half-sister-in-law (the widow of James [Rosy] Roosevelt), among others. At noon was the traditional children's Christmas dinner. Then, in the afternoon, seated before the family Christmas tree, the grown-ups opened gift packages and cards sent them from all over the nation and around the world. The day closed with the traditional family Christmas dinner, the President seated at one end of the long table, his mother at the other, and Roosevelt carving the traditional roasted turkey.

Three of the immediate family were absent. Son Elliott, with his second wife (the former Ruth Chandler Googins) and their two children, remained in Fort Worth, Texas, where Elliott had recklessly plunged into the radio broadcasting business and was now at grave risk of drowning in a sea of financial troubles. Daughter Anna and her second husband, newspaperman John Boettiger, remained in Seattle with the two children of her first marriage, and to them had gone by airplane, a couple of days ago, Eleanor Roosevelt, She had done so, evidently, on sudden impulse (the press had been told on December 22 that she would, of course, spend Christmas at her husband's side), and not without raising questions in the minds of the most knowledgeable close observers of the Roosevelt family lives. This was the second Christmas in a row on which she had absented herself from White House holiday festivities—and this year she had no such excuse as had justified her going last year to a Boston hospital in which Franklin Junior lay seriously ill. Nor would the latter, the President's namesake son, be at the Christmas dinner table this evening. Though he and his bride of six months, the former Ethel du Pont, were in the White House this morning, they would not be going with the others to church and would leave at noon to go to Greenville, Delaware, there to visit for several days in the home of Mr. and Mrs. Eugene du Pont.

That the family should be thus scattered on this Holy Family day was consistent with a general loosening of ties, these last two years, among members of what had been in 1933 a remarkably close-knit, though oddly assorted, group of Roosevelt intimates.

Between a husband and wife who had long ceased to be intimately joined, the distance had markedly increased since and because of the death of Louis Howe. As has been said, the wizened, sickly, devoted Howe, being loved and absolutely trusted by Eleanor as well as Roosevelt, had been a means of communication between the two that, removed, proved irreplaceable; he had also been a vital glue, holding together with bonds of mutual affection not only these two but also the most intimate longtime friends of each: Missy, Grace Tully, Marion Dickerman, Nancy Cook, Earl Miller. Through Howe there had even been effected a wary truce between Lorena Hickok, who had become the most intimate of all Eleanor's friends since 1932, and the two women (living together) who up till then had been the most intimate—namely, Nancy and Marion—though "Hick," as she was known to all her acquaintances, could never abide either Marion or Nancy personally, nor they her. The truce was now ended—and gaps were opening, widening, between Eleanor and the two women with whom she had been associated in the running of Todhunter School, the building of Val-Kill Cottage, the establishment and operation of the Val-Kill furniture factory, and (primarily with Nancy Cook) the handicrafts portion of the pioneering federal homestead project at Arthurdale, West Virginia.

It was Hick, a newspaper reporter when she first met Eleanor—Hick aided and abetted by Howe, a newspaper reporter when he first met Roosevelt—who had done most to encourage Eleanor into what had become during the last four years her primary pursuit, that of communicating the "woman's point of view" from White House to general public via regularly scheduled press conferences to which only women reporters were invited, and well-paid lecture tours arranged by Colston Leigh, America's premier lecture impresario. It was to Hick, traveling the country as observer for Harry Hopkins, that Eleanor had addressed, as diary letters, the plain, concise accounts of her daily activities upon which was modeled her famous newspaper column, "My Day," begun in January 1936 and now distributed daily by United Features Syndicate to scores of newspapers with millions of subscribers across the land. Eleanor herself, thus encouraged into increased independence and self-sufficiency, had proposed in the summer of 1936 to her literary agent, George Bye, that she do an autobiography and had then, being urged on by him, begun work on it while in the midst of her husband's campaign for reelection, dictating in snatches of time to her secretary and friend, Malvina (Tommy) Thompson. Incredibly, in just six months, by which time the early chapters were being serialized in the *Ladies' Home Journal* (the magazine paid $75,000 for first serial rights), the manuscript had been completed. *This Is My Story* had been published by Harper & Brothers some six weeks ago and was a smashing success critically and commercially, being greatly praised by reviewers for its "classic simplicity" of language, its living wisdom, and its "astonishing frankness." She had indeed been remarkably frank and plain-speaking about her unhappy childhood, her English schooling, her coming-out and marriage, her experience of motherhood, her emotional reactions to her husband's prolonged polio ordeal. But she had made many changes in the last, in response to her husband's criticisms (she had submitted the manuscript to him for review and censorship), and had been extremely reticent about the most important parts of her emotional life since the Great War, leaving wholly out of account the Lucy Mercer affair, of course, and making only oblique and fleeting references to her unhappy relationship with her mother-in-law. She had also substituted her husband's language for her own in that portion of the manuscript dealing with his struggle to get into uniform during the war.[79]

It is therefore a President with an at least vague sense of loneliness, of incompletion and unfulfillment in his personal life, who goes through one by one the scheduled items of this traditional day.

Behold him as he enters the Church of the Covenant at midmorning, with his indomitable and seemingly ageless mother at one side of him, his son James at the other, and, having swiftly, unobtrusively unlocked the steel braces on his withered legs, sits or is eased down by his son's strong arm into the fourth pew. He remains sitting, with no changes of expression on his solemn face, while hymns are sung, prayers are spoken. Then he listens to a sermon not designed to comfort him or lighten his heavy burden of anxieties, delivered by the Reverend Mr. Peter Marshall, a young man (he is thirty-five) who is destined for national fame in years to come. It opens, this sermon, on an unhappy, even bitter note, describing the President's quoting of the angel's song, in the Christmas Eve broadcast from the White House, as "ironical," the song itself as "the lost refrain." "Christmas comes to mock us for our infidelity," says earnest, youthful Peter Marshall. "It is Christmas Day in Spain—and machine guns rattle in the hills. It is Christmas Day in China—and shrapnel is falling in the rice fields." All over the world it is Christmas—and "little children are being taught to wear gas masks." Nor is bitter irony absent from Washington itself this day. Here in the capital "many are shivering, many are weeping." He drives his painful point as hard and deep as he can into the mind, the spirit of the listening President, crying: "Peace on earth! Good will toward men! Say the words [to yourself] over and over and you will be shocked at the hypocrisy of a world celebrating in solemn manner something it has not taken to heart."[80]

Do the words yet ring in the President's ears as, his left arm looped through the crooked right arm of James, his right hand clasping an ivory-handled cane, he poses for news photographs in the church's entrance hallway? His photographed face, like those of his sons, is unwontedly grim.

In the afternoon, soon after the children's Christmas dinner, he joins eagerly, happily in a three-way long-distance phone conversation with those of his immediate family who are absent from the White House—his wife and daughter and grandchildren in Seattle, his son Elliott and family in Fort Worth. That night he presides over the Christmas feast; he carves the Christmas turkey, with, as it seems, all the gaiety and zest of old.

But some of the old spark is absent.

He lies lonely in his bed as the last hour of that Christmas Day glides into the troubled past and draws him toward an even more troubled future.

And beyond the curtained windows of his bedroom, the night that is scattered and diminished by city lights and by these held a little way above the dark soil, the pavements, the crowd of buildings, is a deep dark night, heavy with responsibilities and full of dread.

# 5

⇢⇢✕⇠⇠

# Drifting: The Politics of Indecision amid World Crisis

I

ROOSEVELT had twice before suffered through long winters of discontent since entering the White House. Each had followed hard upon an election victory of unprecedented magnitude whereby, as it seemed to the public at large, he was rendered invulnerable and virtually omnipotent politically. "He has been all but crowned by the American people" was William Allen White's published comment upon the midterm election victory of 1934; and even greater had been Roosevelt's reelection triumph of 1936. Yet the winters of 1935 and 1937 had been alike characterized for him by frustration and defeat; each had been at its end remarkably barren of accomplishment, and in both seasons the failure had been rooted, most of it, in his own psychology, his own state of mind.

In 1935 he had not profitably employed the great power in his hands because he had not known what to do with it. Faced by the necessity to choose between two fundamental tendencies of the New Deal that, incongruously intermingled since the first inaugural, now diverged widely, he had for a long time been unable to do so.

The root cause of failure in 1937 was precisely the opposite. In January of that year he had known exactly, definitely, what he wanted to do. He had then acted too swiftly, too boldly, with an excess of hard will, a deficiency of well-informed idea, and had thereafter stubbornly persisted in error, as we have seen, until most of the governing power in his hands at the opening of the year had been dissipated. Much of it had gone into the hands of his enemies.

And it was in this weakened political condition that he entered now, in January 1938, upon a third winter of discontent whose bitterness should have been in some ways harsher and harder for him to bear than that of 1935, or even that of last year, had been. For his was now a double disability: It was both psychological and circumstantial. Not only was his range of choice more severely limited by his politico-economic environment than it had been at any other time since March 1933, but he also suffered, as in January 1935, from his own indecisiveness. As in 1935, he faced the necessity to choose between two divergent, even contradictory basic policies and was for a long time unable to do so. He floundered between the fiscal orthodoxy of Morgenthau (identified with conservatism) and the fiscal heresy of Eccles and the Keynesians (identified with liberalism), making option-maintaining gestures toward Eccles now and then but clinging stubbornly, in practice, to Morgenthau orthodoxy in the hope that it would prove justified by developing circumstance. Meanwhile, economic conditions grew steadily worse.

Nevertheless, he was able to dissemble such bitterness as he felt more effectively, more completely than he had done in 1935. There were, perhaps, three reasons for this. One was that his present indecision had to do with governmental tendencies less profound and sweeping than 1935's had been. Another was that he now knew who his chief enemies were: There was no possibility of persuading big business to support any element of the New Deal that served the general good at the expense of its own special privilege; insofar as he strove for social reforms, he could expect from big-business men in general nothing but the most vicious enmity. Third, and most important, was his belief that the upcoming midterm elections would prove his loss of power to be temporary, even illusory, since his support among the general electorate remained as great as ever. Having recovered from the illness that had darkened the last weeks of autumn, he displayed to even his closest associates in the most trying circumstances very little of the irritability he had quite often manifested all through the winter of 1935 and occasionally in 1937. He remained, as in his palmiest days, incredibly patient, seemingly wholly free of fearful doubt, almost unfailingly cheerful. And when troubled subordinates came to him with their complaints and anxieties, as he continued to encourage them to do, he served up to them portions as generous as before of the morale-boosting joie de vivre—the revivifying, energizing zest, the optimistic confidence, the hearty laughter—of which his own supply was, it seemed, inexhaustible.

II

ONE who came to him with troubles in early 1938 was balding, scholarly-appearing, deceptively mild-mannered David E. Lilienthal of the Tennessee Valley Authority. Lilienthal's troubles were grave indeed. They threatened not only the very existence of Roosevelt's own favorite New Deal agency but also a drastic limitation of the New Deal's whole effort to master the private utilities, develop public power, provide the general citizenry with electricity at reasonable prices, and plan nationally and regionally the use of natural resources.

Readers of earlier volumes of the present work* may recall that the TVA at its inception embodied two ideas or concepts, one inclusive of the other.

The first idea—first in time and in immediate practical efficacy—had come from the fact that, as a war project in 1917–1918, a great hydroelectric dam had been built by the federal government at Muscle Shoals on the Tennessee River. All through the 1920s and early 1930s, this dam had stood idle, the object of bitter contention between the advocates of public power, who pressed for its use as a federally owned and federally operated facility, and private utility interests, who were, of course, adamantly opposed to any such development.

*FDR: The New York Years, pp. 413–15; FDR: The New Deal Years, pp. 90–94.

The fight for government operation had been led by Nebraska's great Progressive (nominally Republican) Senator George E. Norris. Into every congressional session for a dozen years Norris had introduced legislation that would accomplish his purpose, gaining increasing popular support for it but being defeated year after year by a Republican, pro-business Congress and executive. Then had come the election triumph of Franklin Roosevelt who, as New York's governor, had fought hard and with some success for public ownership and development of hydroelectric power sites and to force private utilities to lower their rates. In January 1933 the President-elect had visited the great Wilson Dam at Muscle Shoals and, with Norris at his side, publicly committed himself not only to "national" operation of the facility but also to "national" development of "the Tennessee Basin as a whole."[1]

And this last, the development of the whole of the Tennessee River and its watershed as a multipurpose national project, was the second idea, the overall concept, embodied in the TVA. Roosevelt had stressed it in the special message to Congress calling for the legislation whereby the authority was established. Muscle Shoals realized but a small part of the hydroelectric-power potential of the Tennessee basin, he had then said; a realization of the whole of this power potential was equally but a small part of the proposed development of the entire valley. Flood control, soil-erosion control, the restoration of soil productivity with cheap fertilizers (the original purpose of the Wilson Dam was to provide power for the manufacture of nitrates, used in explosives), reforestation, the establishment of small industries in rural communities, the retirement of marginal agricultural land—all these were comprehended in the valleywide job to be done. "In short, this power development of war days leads logically to national planning for a complete river watershed involving many states and the future lives and welfare of millions. It touches and gives life to all forms of human concern."[2]

That last sweeping sentence was reflective of a searching conversation Roosevelt had had with Arthur E. Morgan during the 1932–1933 interregnum. Morgan, a tall, lean, thin-faced man who appeared to be what in fact he was, the very type of a high-minded Yankee (though born in Cincinnati) schoolmaster, was by professional training a civil engineer. As a young man, he had become famous in his professional field for his planning and dam construction while head of the Miami Conservancy District, an agency created to prevent recurrence of a disastrous 1913 flood of the Miami River in Ohio. But unlike the generality of engineers he was no narrowly focused specialist. He was more concerned with what he called human engineering than he was with civil engineering. And he had so well demonstrated his social and educational concerns during his conservancy-district operation that the small but prestigious Antioch College in Yellow Springs, Ohio, some twenty miles east of the conservancy-district headquarters in Dayton, asked him to become its president, an offer he had promptly accepted. Thus it was not primarily as a flood-control engineer but as an administrator, a progressive educator, a recognized authority on the economy, the people, the social life, and the environmental problems of the central portion of the Ohio Valley (it includes the Tennessee basin) that Morgan, then fifty-five years old, was consulted by President-elect Roosevelt in early 1933. The two men had got on famously. Each had inspired the other with stupendous visions. Both were convinced that the Tennessee Valley development could and must become a conclusive demonstration, on a scale unprecedented, of what multipurpose regional planning could achieve in the way of creative harmony between man and nature. It could and must become a shining model for civilized mankind, lighting the way toward watershed planning all over the world.

Hence, when he signed the TVA bill into law in mid-May 1933, Roosevelt had already decided that Morgan would be chairman of the three-member committee that was to administer the TVA—and Morgan, certainly, was eager for the appointment.

On the evidence, Roosevelt's original conception, which coincided with Morgan's own, was that Morgan, while of course applying to the TVA enterprise his expertise as dam-builder and flood-control engineer, would be the agency's top executive, uniquely administratively responsible for the enterprise as an organic whole. He was to oversee, in terms of general pattern, the work of the other two directors, each of whom was a specialist in one of the two major areas of the TVA's total concern. But this conception of administrative priorities was not expressed in the language of the organic act—language that instead indicated that the three directors had equal shares of the agency's total executive authority and were equally responsible for the agency's overall direction. Nor (typically) did Roosevelt, when he appointed the other two directors, make explicitly clear to them his conception of TVA priorities and their administrative implementation. Almost certainly, the conception was far from clear in Roosevelt's own mind.

Of these other two directors, one was Harcourt A. Morgan (no relation to Arthur), a former dean of agriculture at the University of Tennessee, who since 1919 had been president of that institution. His initial understanding was in accord with the language of the act. He would be primarily responsible for the agricultural phase of the TVA's operation, with special emphasis upon the manufacture and distribution of cheap fertilizer, and upon the improvement of farming techniques through educational demonstration projects. But at the same time he would have a voice equal in force to the chairman's and to that of the third committee member in the determination of general agency policy. At age sixty-six, however, he did not lust after personal power and glory. He had not done so when young. Remarkably sweet-tempered, pacific and cooperative, kind and considerate in his relations with other people, he was both temperamentally and by professional experience an organization man, a practical man, at home with the compromising indirections of committee politics. He distrusted grandiose "visions"—they seemed to him to get in the way of one's perception of hard facts—and was consequently inclined to shy away from visionaries. Certainly he was no radical social reformer, was not inclined toward TVA programs that *might* improve the situation of small landowners, tenant farmers, and blacks, but would certainly provoke a dangerous hostility to the agency on the part of the large landowners and Southern white racists of the Tennessee basin. To farmers and the farm problem in general his approach was pretty much that of the extension service of the U.S. Department of Agriculture (the director of the service in Tennessee had reported to him when he was dean of agriculture)—an approach strongly influenced insofar as it was not determined by the conservatives who dominated the American Farm Bureau Federation.

David E. Lilienthal, the third director, was a DePauw University and Harvard Law School graduate who had become one of Felix Frankfurter's favorite students at Harvard. "You could not . . . have given Mr. Morgan a better associate . . . than Lilienthal," wrote Frankfurter to Roosevelt on June 6, 1933. "That's a team that's bound to produce results." And the professor had gone on to speak of the rarity of "such a combination of training, courage, understanding and youthful ardor as Lilienthal represents."[3] Certainly Lilienthal was young—thirty-two years younger than Harcourt Morgan, twenty-one years younger than Arthur Morgan—and certainly he was ardent in his commitment to public service. He had begun his professional career as a labor lawyer in the Chicago law firm of Donald Richberg, had a few years later established a lucrative law firm of his own in Chicago, but had then abandoned it, in 1931, at a considerable sacrifice of income, to accept appointment by Wisconsin's young governor Philip La Follette to the chairmanship of the Wisconsin Public Service Commission. It was the national reputation he had made in the field of public-utilities regulation during his two Wisconsin years —a reputation for personal courage, devotion to the public weal, and practical effectiveness—that had led, in part through Felix Frankfurter's hearty recommendation, to Roosevelt's naming him a TVA director.

But Frankfurter could not have been more mistaken in his prediction that Arthur Morgan and young Lilienthal would be "a team." They never were. At their very first meeting, on May 29, 1933, in Chicago's Palmer House, whence Lilienthal had been summoned from a fishing trip in northern Wisconsin by an urgent phone call, there was a lack of understanding, a failure of sympathetic connection, between the two men. Though Lilienthal had realized that he must be "investigated" thoroughly before being offered a government post as high as the one for which (so press speculation had told him) he was being considered, he was a bit resentful of the fact that one of Arthur Morgan's colleagues, an Antioch College dean, had been asking probing questions about him in Madison and Chicago, and had then questioned him directly on various matters, without saying frankly why he did so. The resentment was not reduced by Morgan's conduct of the Palmer House interview; the older man did not come to the point until, after three long hours of "general inquiries" and "exploratory discussion," Lilienthal forced the issue by rising to take his leave. Why the reluctance on Morgan's part? Was he doubtful about the man he was interviewing? In his journal a few days later, Lilienthal described the TVA chairman, unenthusiastically, as "a very tall man of 55 years who has brought himself up through various channels of activity through tremendous energy and imagination."[4]

And even before he attended his first committee meeting as TVA director, Lilienthal was given reason to wonder about the soundness of the chairman on the issues with which Lilienthal would primarily deal: those of the TVA's power policy and relationship with private utility interests.

The young man's experience in the field of utility regulation, a harsh experience in many ways, had taught him to expect nothing of private utility managers save ruthless acquisitiveness, a single-minded pursuit of immediate profit at whatever cost to the public at large. It was therefore glaringly evident to him that the TVA and the utilities would become bitter adversaries if the TVA insisted upon providing its hydroelectric power to the public at a fair price—that is, with a profit margin calculated at a reasonable percentage of the actual production cost instead of as a percentage of vastly inflated capital values. Indeed, TVA proponents and private utility interests had already clashed noisily. During hearings on the TVA bill in Congress, Wendell Willkie, president of Commonwealth and Southern (this Wall Street holding company controlled Georgia Light and Power, Alabama Light and Power, and Tennessee Electric Power, the three major utilities companies in the Tennessee Valley), had vehemently protested the bill's provision that the TVA not only generate electricity but also deliver it directly to consumers over its own transmission lines. Willkie, who wanted the TVA to deliver its power to the private utilities at the generating sites—this power to be then transmitted to users over company lines at a price reflective of the capital values recorded on Commonwealth and Southern's books—had cried out in anguish that what Norris proposed would render worthless some $400 million of his corporation's securities. It would be tantamount to a seizure of private property by the government without compensation. His testimony had not persuaded Congress—the bill had been enacted as proposed, its transmission-lines provision intact—but this was assuredly not the end of the story. Commonwealth and Southern seemed bound to challenge the transmission-lines provision in the courts, if not the constitutionality of the whole TVA enterprise, and it was in full recognition of this virtual certainty that Lilienthal had accepted appointment to the TVA board. He knew that prolonged and savage legal battles probably lay ahead for him.

Hence his unease when Senator Norris told him, in Washington, four days before the first TVA committee meeting on June 16, 1933, that he (Norris) had had to complain to the President about Arthur Morgan's conduct during a tour of Muscle Shoals and other portions of the Tennessee basin shortly before Memorial Day. On this tour, Morgan had "visited with the [private] power representatives but had failed to meet with a number of people who had been carrying on the fight, in the public interest, as Senator Norris saw it, for a number of years," to quote Lilienthal's journal.[5] This boded ill, in Norris's view, for the TVA as producer and distributor of electricity in the public interest. Roosevelt had countered Norris's fears by saying that, while Chairman Morgan was clearly no expert in the utilities field, he had a great vision of what regional planning could do, overall, in the Tennessee basin. (In this assessment, the senator had concurred, as he may or may not have indicated to Lilienthal in late May 1933. Though deploring not only the chairman's naïveté with regard to "the Power Trust" but also his brusque manners and abrupt speech, whereby important people were needlessly offended, Norris had been vividly impressed by Morgan's high idealism and vision of what the project could become. "When you get on the inside of the man," he would write to the influential editor of the *Chattanooga* [Tennessee] *News* as late as October 1935, "you find one who is . . . perhaps as near perfect as a human being can become."⁶) As for Morgan's lack of public-power expertise, Roosevelt went on to say, it would be supplied on the TVA board by Lilienthal, if that young man could be persuaded to become the third TVA director. The appointment "would be a ten-strike," Roosevelt had said, adding that he was going to phone Madison right away to arrange a meeting between Lilienthal and Morgan. And, indeed, it had been only an hour or so thereafter that Lilienthal, reached by phone on the shore of a northern Wisconsin lake, had begun his all-day automobile drive to Chicago.⁷

Unease was compounded—it became actual alarm on Lilienthal's part—during the first board meeting of the three directors. Chairman Morgan at that meeting read aloud a letter he had just received from Wendell Willkie in which Willkie asked to meet with the chairman "to discuss problems common to the Authority and to his [Willkie's] corporation," as Lilienthal recorded in his journal. Lilienthal reacted to this with some of the resentment that Arthur Morgan had earlier aroused in him. Surely he himself should be invited to participate in any such conversation as Willkie proposed—and surely the chairman, who had not indicated as much, should now do so! Morgan didn't. Consequently, there had "followed a considerable discussion as to what the attitude of the board should take toward the private utilities, etc. While fundamentally we may be in agreement, there was some difference of opinion [Lilienthal put it mildly] as to tactics and strategy expressed as between myself and Chairman Morgan, with Harcourt Morgan acting as mediator. This will require a good deal of working out."⁸

Actually, as Lilienthal already more than suspected, his disagreement with the chairman was not merely over tactics and strategy. It was fundamental. For a time, a year or more, harsh frictions were prevented by a full exercise of Harcourt Morgan's conciliatory lubricating talents, and by the fact that each of the directors was at the outset overburdened with initiating efforts in his own field of special expertise—Arthur Morgan in construction, land planning, and education; Harcourt Morgan in agriculture and fertilizers; Lilienthal in power, transportation, and legal relations—and that the three fields were complementary. But from the first, Harcourt Morgan was far more strongly attracted by Lilienthal's views and personality than he was by the chairman's —he voted with Lilienthal when, at a very early board meeting (in August 1933), it was decided 2–1 that each director would have complete autonomy in his own special field—and in any case, given the personalities and depth of conviction of the men involved, the disagreement could not be long suppressed or denied.

Like Harcourt Morgan, Lilienthal was instinctively distrustful of visionaries, who, as he saw it, soar high above the ground of common sense on wings of idealistic (or nonsensical) imagination. He was especially impatient with "great visions" that, in his view, were intoxicating and addictive—befogging issues, inspiring vast schemes for human betterment, and inhibiting practical small-step dealings with those particulars, those individualities, of which the "real" world is made. He was inclined, in fact, to equate social-welfare planning with totalitarianism. There was, he claimed, "something about planning that is attractive to" people (clearly, in Lilienthal's opinion, Chairman Morgan was one of them) who possess "a vague and diffuse kind of mind given to grandiose pictures not of this world"—people "who are in a hurry but are . . . hazy as to where they want to go."[9] Such people were, he thought, incipiently fascist, or communist, whether they knew it or not.

Not that Lilienthal was opposed to planning per se. He was as convinced as Rex Tugwell that efficient use of advanced technology, such technology as was involved in the central manufacture and network distribution of electricity, required large-scale planning and organization, and that such planning should be done in the public interest and not primarily in the selfish interest of business and businessmen. The public-authority device was, in his conviction, a sound approach to the problem. But he had a profound aversion to the kind of large-scale socioeconomic planning whereby the individual person tends to become an object to be manipulated, fitted into a general scheme for his own good, willy-nilly. He was committed, instead, to what he called grass-roots democracy (the phrase may actually have been coined by him), meaning a community initiated by and growing out of the individual people living in it, its overall functioning the active voluntary cooperation of these individual people living on the land—this as opposed to a "democracy" regionally planned by an elite few for many "others" and imposed upon the latter from above.

He was vitally concerned, in other words, to ensure that the planning and organization were truly human and neither an elite's design nor a machine-determined design upon, and against, human freedom. To him, human freedom was the end, the goal, the focus of a good society. It was also exclusively individual, an indissoluble amalgam of individual right and individual responsibility, the service and enhancement of which were the proper purpose of every social organization. And to human freedom as an end, he took, as a means, the approach of Brandeis and Frankfurter, stressing local control of economic life to the maximum degree consistent with the efficient use of advanced technology. Hence the enthusiasm with which he seized upon the portion of the Authority's organic act that instructed the TVA, as it distributed the power generated by its dams, to give priority to municipal light and power companies, farmer and other cooperatives, and nonprofit agencies in general. Lilienthal saw this as a socially healthful exercise in decentralization. It would strengthen local organization in the valley, freeing the people on the land from bondage to those giant utilities, controlled from Chicago or Wall Street, which had theretofore refused to these people any electricity whatever. If this required war with Commonwealth and Southern, so be it.

Naturally, his basic views being what they were, he was wholly at odds with Arthur Morgan's "do-good human-engineering" proposals for the Tennessee Valley. As Lilienthal once said to Senator Bob La Follette, apropos his unhappy relationship with the chairman, he most emphatically did not "believe that . . . the way to get a better living for people [is] by human engineering them." ("Welfare work and economic revision," he added, "are two different things—I don't have much confidence in the first."[10]) When he learned in late June 1934 that "Mrs. A.E. had some scheme on to make mountain type furniture [that is, have the TVA manufacture such furniture] to be sold [by the TVA] to our employees," he was thoroughly "riled." Was not the employee bound to feel and resent the fact that pressure to buy was being exerted upon him by his employer? So outraged was young Lilienthal that he ridiculed the idea in a board meeting, doing so in a way that caused everyone at the meeting to laugh—everyone, that is, save the chairman. Arthur Morgan, as seen by Lilienthal, "got gray, clasped his hands before him, and started in on me." Said the chairman, revealingly: "We don't want to pick their furniture for them, but many of these people have never known anything except what they have had up in the hills [of Appalachia]," and so on, as Lilienthal recorded in his journal.[11]

And in this instance, as in many others, Lilienthal would surely have been deemed right and the chairman wrong by most Americans. Arthur Morgan was too much inclined to make of the TVA a schoolmaster in his own image. He would have the federal Authority deal with the valley as a great schoolroom in which educational projects, à la Antioch College's famous "learning through doing" curriculum, resulted in local cooperatives, small-industry development, improved health and welfare services, prosperous subsistence farms employing soil-conserving methods, and the replacement of rural slum dwellings with decent housing. Even a considerable measure of an old-time teacher's disciplinary authority would be exercised in this schoolroom if the chairman had his way: He favored a law which would deprive a farmer of his land if he failed to adopt erosion-control measures; he would have liked the TVA to discourage actively such traditional mountaineer recreations as tobacco-chewing and whiskey-drinking.[12]

But there are, of course, two sides to every quarrel, and some people, pondering this one overall and in depth, found truth and justice to be by no means wholly on Lilienthal's side of it. Certainly, young Lilienthal, with his hard, precise, knife-sharp, activist's mind, and with his instinct for combat (boxing, in which he excelled, had been his favorite sport at DePauw), was overly contemptuous of his older colleague's very different mind and temper. Indeed, his published words indicate that, during his five years of direct official relationship with Morgan, he lacked not only sympathetic feeling for the latter's basic attitudes but also any real understanding of the philosophy behind Morgan's program proposals and priorities. Yet in the opinion of many people as hardheaded as Lilienthal, and equally committed with him to human freedom, the philosophical case to be made for Arthur Morgan's general approach had sufficient merit to justify its respectful consideration by anyone concerned to find a proper balance between freedom and organization, between individual liberty and community authority, in a technologically advanced and advancing democracy. Indeed, Lilienthal himself, in a highly influential best-selling book that he wrote about the TVA five years later (*TVA—Democracy on the March* was published in March 1944), gave signs of recognizing this and of having been far more strongly influenced in attitude and thought by Arthur Morgan than he ever admitted or, perhaps, realized.

The philosophical case for the TVA chairman's approach was based on a concept of freedom that in turn was based on a concept of the human person, or of the nature of "individuality," that differed radically from Lilienthal's. The latter, in the critical view of those who shared Arthur Morgan's mind-set, was essentially a *spatial* concept and, as such, too limited, too exclusive, too materialistic in its definitions. It made of the individual person a discrete, sharply defined entity—a tightly wrapped package of energy (the wrapping impenetrable) possessed of "properties" also sharply defined—an entity utterly unique, wholly itself, exclusive of all else. The individual person, however, is in reality not only spatial but temporal, the latter being the truly vital dimension. He must therefore be viewed, not as a completed entity, a static being, but as a process, a continuous becoming, essentially identical with the path or channel he follows (or forges) through space-time; he must be seen as a stream of being connected with the environment in somewhat the same way as a river is connected, by a continuous web of water, with the land through which it flows. Which is to say that the living self actively involves (internalizes) its environment—its social, economic, and cultural, as well as physical, environment—while being also marginally but continuously absorbed *into* that environment. And this means that human freedom is not the kind of exclusive independence that Lilienthal stressed—is not merely a property of the individual person, not just a capacity possessed by him—but a certain kind of interdependence and interaction between the individual and the world around him. It involves a dependence upon, even an actual merging with, the impinging environment. It is, in sum, a harmonious, active relationship between, and involving some measure of interpenetration of, self and world.

Arthur Morgan never articulated his philosophy in this way. ("He was a man with a mission, deeply apprehended, yet largely inarticulate, so intensely nursed in the passionate depths of his personality that it came to rule his life and undermine his judgment," according to Francis Biddle.)[13]* But it was in accord with the described sense of the self as process, and of the world as organism, that he sought and gave the highest priority to harmonious relationships among the various elements of Tennessee Valley life while at the same time insisting that such harmony, what Tugwell called "a concert of interests" (this in a famous paragraph contributed to one of Roosevelt's 1932 campaign addresses), could be achieved only through overhead planning and control. A musical concert requires a conductor. It also requires a plan, a composition. And though the TVA's composition, in Morgan's view, must be "democratic" in the sense that there was "voluntary general agreement" with it,[14] the composing must be done, the concert must be conducted, largely by the Authority itself. Only thus, through the exercise of a large measure of regional authority, could the TVA succeed as the great social experiment of which Roosevelt had so often publicly spoken—a weaving together of all strands of the Tennessee basin's life, economic, educational, cultural, governmental, in a seamless web according to a pattern of natural harmony.

Of these many strands, electricity, power for the people, was of course a major one—a fact recognized by Congress when it specifically assigned the bulk of the agency's large appropriation to river engineering and power development. But power was definitely *not* the dominant theme, the central purpose, of the whole enterprise as originally conceived. And to prevent its becoming so, or being made so through conflict between the TVA and the utility interests already operating in the valley, was a primary concern of the chairman from the very outset. At the August 1933 board meeting in which Lilienthal and Harcourt Morgan proposed and won, over Arthur Morgan's objections, complete autonomy for their separate parts of the TVA program, the chairman warned earnestly against "the warfare of the duplication of [electricity] facilities" and the consequent "hard feeling and bitterness" between the TVA and the utility corporations. Such hostility was bound to make the TVA "less effective" and "less representative of what economic planning can accomplish" than it would otherwise be;[15] and it could be avoided, the chairman thought, if only Lilienthal were less blindly antagonistic to utility executives in general, to Wendell Willkie in particular (Morgan himself seems to have been peculiarly vulnerable to Willkie's personal charm)—if only he were more willing to negotiate compromises in a spirit of sweet reasonableness. The young man had, in the older man's view, rather more than his fair share of the aggressiveness, the ruthlessness, the penchant for sharp practice, that bigoted prejudice deems typically "Jewish."

Inevitably, within a few months after the TVA's launching, the Lilienthal-Morgan disagreement, which had not yet become personal and acrimonious,

---

*Francis Biddle, of the historically famous Biddles of Philadelphia, was involved as a New Deal lawyer in the 1938 governmental investigation of TVA management that was invited by the Morgan-Lilienthal quarrel.

made its way to the White House, where alone resided a finally decisive authority over the matter at issue. And there Franklin Roosevelt, originally sharing the chairman's "visionary" approach to Authority policymaking and program-making, clung for as long as he could to his original implicit conception of Arthur Morgan as "first among equals" on the TVA board. He initially supported the chairman's efforts to make peace between the TVA and the private utilities, despite the fact that he had come, through bitter experience, to distrust and dislike utility-corporation executives as greatly as Lilienthal did.

When the chairman proposed in 1933 that the TVA and Willkie's Commonwealth and Southern agree to a division of valley territory between them, with the TVA delivering power directly to consumers in some areas but indirectly through Commonwealth and Southern in other areas, Lilienthal vehemently protested. He was sure such an arrangement violated the spirit if not the letter of the Norris Act (for one thing, it rendered null and void the clause requiring preferential service to municipalities and other nonprofit organizations); he was equally sure that the pledged word of a private-utility executive was not to be trusted in any matter of this kind. But his opposition was overruled by Roosevelt's evident belief that the proposal should be given a fair trial. Lilienthal therefore, in early 1934, reluctantly negotiated an agreement with Willkie whereby the Authority not only purchased from Commonwealth and Southern certain local companies that could be linked together in an areawide power network but also promised not to sell TVA power to consumers outside the network area—consumers, that is, who were now buying from Commonwealth and Southern—for a period extending at least three months beyond the date Norris Dam was completed.

Alas for Arthur Morgan and his great dream, the arrangement made no peace between private and public power interests in the valley. Barely six months after the agreement was signed, the utilities pulled the rug out from under the chairman, and justified Lilienthal's cynical view of the value of their pledged word, by instituting a stockholders' suit against the Alabama Power Company to prevent its carrying out the signed agreement, this on the ground that the Authority had no constitutional right to enter into such an agreement, having no constitutional right to sell electricity at all. Lost by the TVA in federal district court, some nine months later, the case went by government appeal to the U.S. Supreme Court, which ultimately ruled 8–1 that, though this particular deal was legal (the Authority could sell power generated at the Wilson Dam to the Alabama Power Company), the "question of the constitutional right of the Government to acquire or operate local or urban distribution systems" remained open, to quote Chief Justice Hughes's majority opinion. So did the question of the legal "status of any other dam or power development in the Tennessee Valley, whether connected or apart from the Wilson Dam."[16]

And by the time this limited decision was handed down, in February 1936, the dissension within the TVA board, with Lilienthal and Harcourt Morgan voting against the chairman on virtually every question that arose, was beginning to be noised abroad and to have deleterious effects upon the morale of TVA employees, these being inevitably increasingly divided between supporters of Lilienthal and supporters of Arthur Morgan. The situation worsened as open warfare flared between the utilities and the Authority. A volley of lawsuits was now fired by the former against the latter, each suit challenging the constitutionality of the law that had created the TVA. The utilities also began to build transmission lines in areas not previously served by them but in which TVA transmission lines were now going up. And an increasingly desperate Arthur Morgan, blaming Lilienthal for his and the TVA's troubles, began a campaign to prevent the obnoxious young man's presidential reappointment to the board in June 1936, when Lilienthal's first term expired. (By law, TVA directors had nine-year terms but to prevent the simultaneous expiration of all three terms, which would have prevented continuity of administration, the terms of the first appointees were staggered, Arthur Morgan being appointed for nine years, Harcourt Morgan for six, Lilienthal for three.) Arthur Morgan brought to the White House, in May 1936, an administrative reorganization plan that would give him as chairman the authority he had believed he would have when he accepted the appointment (there would be a general manager of TVA operations, to be nominated by the chairman; all policy questions must be decided by unanimous vote of the board); he also told the President that if Lilienthal were reappointed, he, Arthur Morgan, would be compelled to resign his post (Lilienthal was continuously "undermining" him, building up an organization against him, and so on).

Roosevelt was then preparing to fight for reelection and could ill afford the full public exposure of TVA board dissension that the chairman's resignation would produce, especially in view of the fact that he was then hoping and planning to establish other TVA-like watershed authorities across the nation. So he first prevailed upon Lilienthal to make an effort to patch up the quarrel with the chairman. This effort failed. Then, as he had told Lilienthal he would do, he persuaded both Harcourt Morgan and the editor of the Chattanooga *News* (George Fort Milton) to plead with the chairman to stay on, following this up with a session of his own with Arthur Morgan during which he talked to him "like a Dutch uncle," telling him "that I am going to send . . . [Lilienthal's] name in, and that he must be ready to take responsibility for delaying and perhaps disrupting not only TVA but the whole future. The issue of the Government's efforts to conserve human resources is at stake."[17]

The reappointment was made.

Arthur Morgan did not resign.

But he began now to take his case to the public in ever more strident and unjust ways—ways that revealed grave flaws in his character, wiped out Roosevelt's confidence in him, and, astonishingly, actually allied him with those who would destroy the TVA altogether. "To understand this complete about-face . . ." explained Francis Biddle in a later year, "it is essential to realize this strange delusion of certainty that at times attacks the vicar of God on earth." (Biddle had described Arthur Morgan as having "the strength and smaller weaknesses of the American zealot.") "We find this self-delusion in other great Americans—and Morgan had a touch of greatness about him—in Woodrow Wilson, for instance. . . . Arthur Morgan confused policies with principles; and when he reiterated that he would never compromise with principle he meant that he would not yield to someone who disagreed with him on policy."[18] As early as January 1935 he had contributed to *The New Republic* an article in which he described Lilienthal, without explicitly naming him, as a man "ruled by a Napoleonic complex" who was determined to destroy the utility companies instead of cooperating with them in the "spirit of tolerance and reasonableness" which was "a public obligation."[19] He began now to give speeches (to the American Economic Association on December 30, 1936; to the National Rivers and Harbors Congress on April 26, 1937) and to write magazine articles (in *The New York Times Magazine,* in January 1937; the *Saturday Evening Post,* in August 1937; and the *Atlantic Monthly* for September 1937) in which he, though stressing the necessity for evenhanded honesty and fairness in relations between the private utilities and the government, effectively sided with the utilities against his own agency's power policy—this at a time when the Authority was involved in critical litigation with the power companies. In his *Atlantic Monthly* article the TVA chairman cast aspersions upon the personal honesty, and impugned the motives, of both Lilienthal and Harcourt Morgan. On February 14, 1938, he wrote to Texas representative Maury Maverick a letter—eventually published in *The New York Times*—attacking Lilienthal as one who engaged in "evasion, intrigue, and sharp strategy with remarkable skill and the malevolent habit of avoiding direct responsibility which makes Machiavelli seem open and candid." He finally, on March 3, 1938, spread across the morning newspapers of the land a charge that Lilienthal and Harcourt Morgan had mishandled a claims case against the TVA (it had to do with allegedly commercially valuable marble underlying land flooded by one of the TVA's dams) in a way typical of their lack of "honesty, openness and fairness."[20]

Lilienthal was in Washington that Thursday morning. He was at once summoned to the White House, to Roosevelt's bedroom, where he found the President of the United States stretched out in his underwear on his bed. "He has that amazing assurance and nonchalance and complete lack of self-consciousness that made it seem appropriate to be discussing matters of high policy with a gentleman in his B.V.D.'s, and particularly a man whose legs are shrivelled up," wrote Lilienthal in his journal that night. The interview that followed was conducted while Roosevelt was being dressed in formal morning attire by his valet, preparatory to lunching, as he gaily put it, with the sultan of Muscat.* He began by asking, with a fierce mock scowl: "What in hell are we going to do about Arthur Morgan? He's out again." Lilienthal replied that

---

*"I thought this was a gag of some kind and retorted in kind," wrote Lilienthal in his journal that day, "and he seemed to be injured to think that I doubted there was such a thing as a Sultan of Muscat."

perhaps the only "thing to do" was "saw wood"—that is, keep on "doing our job and producing results"—but added that he was prepared to resign his post "if you feel that my presence on the board is embarrassing to you." By that time, the President, "with much straining of the neck and facial contortions," had put on the stiff stand-up collar and was tugging at his necktie. He stopped this to say, "Don't be silly. The only embarrassment is the embarrassment of having a befuddled old man on our hands."[21]

Four days later, in morning conference with the vice president, the speaker of the House, and the majority leader of the Senate, Roosevelt was told by the former that he had simply "got to do something about this TVA business" which was "getting worse all the time and will be in every congressional campaign in the country" this coming autumn. Asked by the President what he would recommend, Garner replied: "Well, Captain, I think you ought to fire the whole three of them and appoint a new board." No, said Roosevelt. Two of these three were doing a good job; it was only Arthur Morgan who was "always raising hell and obstructing the others," and it was therefore Arthur Morgan who would have to go. But how, in view of the substantial support the chairman was being given by press and public, and by many liberals as well as conservatives in Congress, could he be removed without grave further damage to the TVA and the administration? Roosevelt's answer, suggested by his successful handling of the dangerous Jimmy Walker case in 1932,* was explained by him to Lilienthal ("this is what I want to get your ideas about") late in the afternoon of the same day.

"Suppose I were to call all three of the directors to come here to my office," said Roosevelt, "and say to them, 'Now here you, Chairman Morgan, have made grave charges of dishonesty and what not against your colleagues, and you, H. A. Morgan and Lilienthal, have filed a statement with me saying that the chairman is obstructing the work of the board, etc. Now I want you to state the facts that support those charges, and I will ask the questions and I will be the judge.' I will say to Morgan, 'Now I don't want any opinions and I don't want any speeches. I want the cold facts.' And when he starts going off into his usual harangue and personalities, I will just stop him and say, 'I don't want that—I want the facts.' And I will turn to you and Dr. H.A. and say, 'What is the answer to these charges, and again I want the facts, not opinions.' And I will say, 'What are the facts supporting your charges?' What do you think of that?"

Lilienthal thought it was "a grand idea."[22]

And so it was that, five days later, at eleven o'clock in the morning of Friday, March 11, Harcourt Morgan, David Lilienthal, and A. E. Morgan were ushered from Marvin McIntyre's office into the President's, in the White House's Executive Office Wing, to begin what turned out to be (in Lilienthal's words) "six gruelling hours." They were far more so for Arthur Morgan than for anyone else in the room. He knew he stood on untenable ground—knew, or

---

*See *FDR: The New York Years,* pp. 353–55.

sensed, that a public exposure of this fact was the real purpose of the hearing
—and the death of the great dream of his life, coupled with the unadmitted
realization that he himself bore some responsibility for it, was for him an
unbearable agony. For the last year and more, his nights had been often
sleepless, his food often tasteless. He had lost much weight. His clothes hung
loosely on his gaunt frame; and his face, though suntanned, was so haggard
it gave an impression of paleness. He was so obviously in spiritual agony, so
clearly on the verge of nervous collapse, that both Lilienthal and Harcourt
Morgan, despite their angry resentment of the harm he had done, felt "terribly,
terribly sorry for him" (again to quote Lilienthal's journal). Not so hard-
crusted Harold Ickes, who was present at the President's request, in the event
that his testimony was needed, and whose fund of personal compassion and
psychological acumen was in any case severely limited. Ickes subsequently told
his diary that Roosevelt's patience with the TVA chairman during the hours
of questioning was "more than I can understand," since "Morgan's attitude
was really insolent. He declined to produce facts in support of his charges
[Morgan asserted that a presidential hearing was 'not the proper tribunal for
a trial of facts'; he would present his factual evidence, he said, only to a
congressional committee] . . . , repeatedly he made a stereotyped reply to
questions propounded by the President for the purpose of throwing light on
the subject matter; . . . and [on one occasion], when the President interposed
to ask a further question, Morgan asked him not to interrupt until he had
finished." All this was recorded verbatim by a court reporter who had a
stenotype perched on her knees, the record being placed in the hands of eagerly
waiting newspaper reporters as soon as it had been transcribed.[23]

Thus it became at once clear to all reasonable men, including those who
shared the chairman's view of what the TVA might become as a great experiment in overall regional planning, that Arthur Morgan was indeed (though
barely sixty years of age) a sadly "befuddled old man," that he had in fact no
solid evidence in support of his defamatory charges, and that the President
consequently had no choice but to remove him forthwith from the TVA board,
for cause. This Roosevelt did, effective March 23, 1938, after having held two
more fruitless hearings, his grounds being that "Arthur E. Morgan was con-
tumacious in refusing to give the Chief Executive the facts, if any, upon which
he based his charges of malfeasance against his fellow directors, and in refusing
to respond to questions of the Chief Executive relating to charges of obstruction made against him by his fellow directors."[24]

III

ALL this did no good, certainly, for the public image of Franklin Roosevelt's
favorite New Deal agency. The effect on the morale of the TVA staff was
definitely bad, though at its lowest TVA employee morale remained remarkably high.

Nevertheless, in the Tennessee Valley itself, actual measurable progress toward the Authority's specific river-engineering and agricultural goals was neither prevented nor even appreciably slowed by the furor at the top. Moreover, this progress was being made at abnormally low monetary costs. This was due in good part to a so-called "force account" system whereby, instead of letting jobs out on contract, the TVA hired its own steamfitters, bulldozer operators, bricklayers, and all other professional as well as skilled and common labor. It was due also to a no-price-trading policy adopted by the board for the TVA's land acquisition. The policy was adopted when Chairman Arthur Morgan pressed for establishment of a TVA "code of conduct" for real estate dealers, defining their "proper function in organized society," a proposal that the other two board members deemed "inappropriate."[25] Avoided by these devices was the graft and corruption that seem endemic in the private construction industry—this along with such cost-boosting real estate speculation as had plagued the region in the 1920s when an offer by Henry Ford to buy Muscle Shoals from the government (at a bargain price, of course) seemed certain to be adopted by a Republican Congress. Roosevelt knew that the hard-cash cost–benefit ratio was so strongly favorable to the TVA, becoming more so with every passing month, that the agency had growing support in conservative quarters initially hostile to it.

Twenty-one major TVA dams, out of an ultimate thirty-three—each a clearly defined element of an integrated valleywide flood-controlling, navigation-developing, and power-generating plan—were under or about to begin construction in 1938. Several of the largest were already completed or nearly so. From them long and ever longer lines of transmission towers, strung with wires, marched across the land. The elevating effect of the electricity they carried upon the quality of life for hundreds of thousands in the valley was already immense; it would be so for millions by the time the Authority had brought the Tennessee and its tributaries wholly under control, harnessed to human purposes as was no other great river system in the world. Fewer than a quarter-million people in the area were served by electricity in 1933, and virtually all of those lived in towns or cities; less than 3 percent of the valley's farms were wired when the TVA was launched. By 1938, well over two million would be served by TVA electricity brought them through 160 local distributors owned by them—110 municipal systems, fifty rural cooperatives. By then, too, per capita electricity use in the valley would be twice the national average, while the price per kilowatt-hour, though set at a rate deemed fair in terms of cost of production, would be half the national average. The TVA would by then have taught private-utility executives what, to justify the high salaries they voted themselves, they should have been able to figure out for themselves, or so one would think—namely, that lowered rates that stimulate greatly increased electricity sales, along with increased purchase of all manner of electric appliances, result in increased total profits. It was a lesson the learning of which benefited both the utilities and those who bought from them, nationwide.

The dams served equally well the purpose of flood control in an area that because of mountainous terrain, high rainfall, and heavy runoff was peculiarly vulnerable to devastating inundations. Stream-flow management would become tighter, more efficient with every dam and reservoir completion, until, by the mid-1950s, the TVA's hydraulic engineers would be able to handle a twenty-odd-inch rain falling over twenty consecutive days upon thousands of square miles of hill and valley, forest and field and town, and do so in a way that prevented any flooding whatever anywhere downstream. Similarly successful were the dams, the locks, and the accompanying channel-dredging in making the Tennessee and its major tributaries navigable by boats drawing as much as nine feet, thereby reducing shipping costs and stimulating industrial development. By the mid-1950s, two billion ton-miles of freight would move annually on the Tennessee—a river that in 1933 had carried only thirty-two million ton-miles. And to these strictly commercial uses of reservoirs and waterways were added recreational uses—boating, fishing, swimming—that not only made life more enjoyable for valley dwellers but also attracted a profitable tourism.

Meanwhile the TVA's agricultural program continued apace, aided by CCC camp labor. Phosphate and nitrogen fertilizers, about the use of which Harcourt Morgan probably knew as much as any man in the world, were cheaply manufactured in TVA plants and distributed to farmers at cost for their use in restoring fertility to worn-out soil. Contour strip farming, terracing, the grassing of waterways, the installation of farm ponds and gully-control dams, above all the application of complete farm land-use plans whereby every acre was assigned the use (crop or wood or pasture) for which it was naturally best fitted—these greatly reduced soil erosion while enhancing the beauty of the countryside. Through the extension service's demonstration projects, wherein individual farmers cooperated with agricultural experts, spread knowledge of the latest improvements in farm crops, land management, farm machinery— and to the last of these, the TVA's inventive mechanical engineers made, in their laboratories, direct contributions, including a cheap electric barn hay drier, a portable thresher, and, as Arthur Schlesinger, Jr., records, "a new side-hill terracing disk" and "a new cottonseed-oil cooker."[26]

In every phase of this work, under the successive chairmanships of Harcourt Morgan (he succeeded A.E. in that post) and Lilienthal (he was the dominant board member even during Harcourt's tenure), the TVA involved the people of the valley as participants in project planning and execution to the maximum degree possible. They so participated, for the most part, through organizations that had been long established in the valley when the TVA began—an arrangement that, as some critics complained, amounted to an underwriting rather than a needed revision of prevailing patterns of economic and political power distribution in the valley (certainly it was so insofar as the TVA allied itself with the land grant colleges and the agricultural extension service) but that contributed greatly to the Authority's political support and immediate practical effectiveness. With these existing organizations and institutions, the TVA formed partnerships by means of written contracts. These, in Lilienthal's words, were "more than a definition of legal obligations." Their drafting and signing encouraged "consideration of specific issues under existing conditions, but within the broad framework of the common purpose of strengthening the region"—this "instead of abstract talk about 'cooperation' between local and federal agencies." As a result, local and state government, local and state institutions of widely varying kinds (library boards, school boards, wildlife-protection societies, conservation commissions, and so on), far from being superseded or weakened to the point of extinction, as the TVA's opponents had predicted they would be, were much strengthened. In sum, according to Lilienthal, the TVA's "democracy at the grass roots" was an inspiring demonstration of how "man as an individual" might be preserved, even strengthened, against the "fatally impersonal" pressures of "huge factories, assembly lines, mysterious mechanisms, standardization" and other institutional consequences of technological advance.[27]

From all this it becomes clear that the TVA, though it failed to become the life-transforming regional experiment that Arthur Morgan (and Roosevelt) had originally envisaged, was a good deal more than "the Tennessee Valley Power Production and Flood Control Corporation" which, according to Rex Tugwell, it "should have been called" after 1936.[28] And for this, much credit is due the TVA's first chairman. "An excellent engineering staff . . . was assembled under his leadership, and a good many of his unacceptable proposals . . . stimulated decisions endorsing similar goals but employing methods more compatible with TVA's assignment," writes Marguerite Owen[29]—but more important was the unadmitted, perhaps unperceived influence of his vision, his implicit organismic philosophy, upon young David Lilienthal's mind, as we have already suggested. It was in some considerable degree a negative influence, with Lilienthal reacting against Arthur Morgan, defining his own individualism in opposition to Morgan's stress on organization and centralized controls. "Is it inescapable that such a task of resource development [as the TVA faced] be carried on only by highly centralized government direction?" Lilienthal asked in his *TVA—Democracy on the March.* "Must it inevitably be run by a privileged elite of managers or politicians? Yes, say the defeatists about democracy, the cynics, the disillusioned and frustrated liberals, the believers in force, the disbelievers in men." No! said the TVA, resoundingly, in practice, according to Lilienthal, who obviously numbered Arthur Morgan among the elitists, the antidemocrats. But elsewhere in his book, and indeed as a central theme of it, he stresses (to quote one key chapter's title) "A Seamless Web: The Unity of Land and Water and Men"; in his chapter on "Democracy at the Grass Roots" he quotes Roosevelt's sentence, in the 1933 TVA message to Congress, about a regional approach that "touches and gives life to all forms of human concern"—and here Arthur Morgan's evident organismic influence is wholly positive.[30]

In a summary of the first TVA chairman's contribution to this most exciting of the New Deal's new departures, Marguerite Owen quotes, with regard to the chairman's dismissal, a former member of the TVA's legal staff—a man who had suffered under Arthur Morgan's directorship, having incurred the chairman's wrath during the TVA's court battle with the utilities and been hindered in that battle by the chairman's obstructionism. "It was essential for the chairman to be removed," this man said, with feeling. "But," he added, reflectively, "it was just as necessary for him to be appointed. The President was right both times."[31]

IV

WHEN a weary David Lilienthal walked with Harcourt Morgan off the White House grounds late in the afternoon of Friday, March 11, 1938, upon conclusion of the presidential hearing that resulted in Arthur Morgan's dismissal from the TVA, he came face to face with an equally weary Secretary of State Cordell Hull, evidently on the way to conference with the President. Hull, whose normal facial expression was of ineffable sadness, appeared on this occasion both gloomy and agitated. He had reason. His, too, had been "quite a day," as he said to Lilienthal, for "Germany has just taken over Austria." And Hull went on to warn, despairingly, that Germany was "becoming the 'colossus' of Europe," as Japan was of the Orient, and that "between them they will try to rule the world." The success of this attempt was not improbable, in Hull's dark vision at that moment; the "desperado" nations would continue to capitalize on the evident fact that "peaceful nations" would not "fight under any circumstances."[32]

*Anschluss*, the political union of Germany and Austria, had been deemed a "natural" historical development by a multitude of Germans on both sides of the Austro-German border; it had been devoutly wished for, worked for, even before the unification of Germany in 1870. (Bismarck, however, for shrewd power-balance reasons, had opposed the incorporation of Austria into the new Reich.) It would doubtless have been accomplished when the Habsburg monarchy collapsed at the end of the Great War (the Constituent National Assembly for the new postwar state of German Austria actually proposed on March 12, 1919, a political union with Germany) if the victorious Allies, at Versailles, had not forbidden it. Adolf Hitler, himself a native Austrian, had proclaimed it a "task to be furthered by every means our lives long"—this in the very first paragraph of *Mein Kampf*—and he had ruthlessly, brutally attempted it in July 1934, when Austrian Nazis, whose party had been outlawed as violently subversive of the state, murdered Austrian chancellor Engelbert Dollfuss in his Vienna office.* At that time, Hitler, whose government had encouraged if not actively participated in this crime, deployed a so-called Austrian Legion, consisting of several thousand troops, on the Bavarian side of the Austrian border. He was thus prepared mentally and physically to march upon Austrian

---

*The Dollfuss regime had brutally destroyed left-wing opposition parties in 1934. The Austrian Social Democrats continued to be outlawed by Dollfuss's successor as chancellor.

territory within the hour—but he was equally prepared to draw back, should the risks of action appear too great. He knew that he was operating at the outermost limits of his power. Reichspresident Paul von Hindenburg, though mortally ill, had not yet died (he did so a week later), which meant that Hitler had not yet combined in his own person the offices of president (head of state, supreme commander of the armed forces) and chancellor. His awe-inspiring "genius" had not yet been demonstrated by his winning of the great gamble of Rhineland occupation. There yet remained in 1934 an effective opposition to his foreign policy, on the part of top officials of the Foreign Office and top generals of the army—formidable figures who deemed him reckless to the point of insanity in view of Germany's actual military capability vis-à-vis the nations that would be allied against her in a general European war. Hence, when Mussolini's prompt response to the Dollfuss murder was the massing of four army divisions at the Brenner Pass, Hitler's equally prompt reaction was to retreat. Instead of the triumphant proclamation of the birth of Greater Germany which had been prepared for press release in Berlin, there was issued, on the day after Dollfuss's death, an official statement deploring the "cruel murder" and describing what had happened as a purely "internal" Austrian affair.

There was, however, during the immediately following months and years, no slackening of the effort by Austrian Nazis to destroy the Austrian republic, nor any lessening of the encouragement of such "internal" effort by Berlin. Instead, both were increased in proportion to Hitler's gain in power. The latter was both swift and great, of course, being abundantly fed by the weakness, the cowardice, the stupidity, the duplicity of key policymakers and decision-makers in London and Paris. By 1937 only four Germans in high official posts —Hjalmar Schacht, the economics minister; Baron Konstantin von Neurath, the foreign minister; Field Marshal Werner von Blomberg, the war minister; and Colonel General Werner von Fritsch, army Commander in Chief—stood in the way of the Führer's absolute and total control of Germany's domestic and foreign affairs; and by early February 1938, these four were also out of the way, three of them removed from their posts through nasty, mendacious intrigues of the kind characteristic of Nazi party politics. They were replaced, of course, by men wholly subservient to the Führer.

By then, too, Mussolini's capacity for effective opposition to Hitler's Austrian ambition was much reduced. (So was his wish to oppose; Hitler's protestations of eternal friendship, joined with great parades of German might before the Duce's eyes, had had their desired effect.) His unexpectedly difficult and expensive Ethiopian adventure, followed by his massive intervention on Franco's behalf in the Spanish Civil War, forced upon him the bitter realization that his military strength was unequal to his ambition and was certainly now far less, relative to Hitler's, than it had been in 1934.

Hence, in Hitler's judgment, the time of *Anschluss* had now arrived.

On February 11, 1938, Kurt von Schuschnigg, who had succeeded Dollfuss as Austrian chancellor, arrived at the Berghof, Hitler's mountain retreat at

Berchtesgaden, in response to an invitation from Hitler for a discussion of "misunderstandings and points of friction" that "persisted" between the Reich and the Austrian government. The invitation, coming after a year of increasing terrorist violence (bombings, murders, kidnapings, bloody riots) by Austrian Nazis against the Austrian republic, had been tantamount to a command. Having obeyed it, Schuschnigg was forced to endure, on February 12, two hours of threatening verbal abuse from a frequently ranting, raving Hitler, following which the Austrian was presented with a draft "agreement" that was in effect a virtually total surrender of Austrian sovereignty. The Austrian Nazis were to be accorded recognition as a legitimate political party; all Nazis imprisoned for criminal violence against the state were to be released; the Austrian Nazi leader Arthur Seyss-Inquart was to be named Austria's interior minister, with control of the police; another leading Austrian Nazi was to become minister of war; close working relations between the Austrian and German armies, with interchange of officers, were to be established; yet another leading Austrian Nazi was to be appointed minister of finance, an office in which he would preside over the initiation of a program "for the assimilation of the Austrian into the German economic system."[33] Schuschnigg protested these hard terms. Hitler refused to soften them in the slightest. And Schuschnigg, perforce, signed the surrender document.

Returned to Vienna, the Austrian chancellor, while Austrian Nazis stepped up their terror campaign, cast about desperately for some means of saving at least a nominal independence, some vestiges of sovereignty, for his country. He finally seized upon the idea of a national plebiscite, to be held on Sunday, March 13, wherein the Austrian people would be asked whether they were in favor of "a free, independent, social, Christian and united Austria," answering yes or no. There could be little doubt that a question so phrased would be answered "yes" by a majority of the citizenry, thus giving the lie to Hitler's assertion that union was being vehemently demanded by a huge majority. So within an hour after he learned of it, Hitler resolved forcibly to prevent the proposed plebiscite by immediate military invasion. This began on March 11. There was no resistance by the Austrian armed forces. Next day, Hitler himself drove in an open car into Austria where, in every village he passed through, and in Linz, where he had spent his school days and now spent the night, he was greeted by huge welcoming crowds, delirious with joy. On Sunday the thirteenth, Austria was formally declared a province of Greater Germany; and on the following day, Hitler made his triumphant entry into Vienna, where the popular response to his coming appeared fully to justify his assertion that he came, not as a conqueror, but as a liberator. ("I have in the course of my political struggle won much love from my people," he would say in a public speech twelve days later, "but when I crossed the former frontier [into Austria] there met me such a stream of love as I have never experienced."[34])

Hitler's only serious worry, as he made his final decision in this crisis, was over a possibly negative reaction on the part of Mussolini. On the eve of the invasion he sent by special messenger, traveling by air to Rome, a lengthy letter to the Duce explaining and justifying, with his usual untruthfulness, what he was about to do: Schuschnigg had failed to carry out the "more than moderate" terms of the "agreement" he had signed at Berchtesgaden; instead, the Austrian and Czechoslovakian governments were conspiring to restore the Habsburgs to power in central Europe and then attack Germany; meanwhile "Austria was approaching a state of anarchy." In the face of all this it was impossible for Hitler "as Führer and Chancellor of the German Reich" to "remain passive"; he must "restore law and order in my homeland." But the Duce, who must remember the "steadfastness" of the "sympathy" shown by Hitler during "a critical hour for Italy" (i.e., during the crisis over Ethiopia), could rest assured that the action now being taken was wholly "one of national defense" and posed not the slightest threat to the "definite boundary . . . between Italy and us."

He seems to have awaited Mussolini's reply to this with a greater anxiety than one would have expected in the circumstances—though these circumstances did include an expression of annoyance by the Italian foreign minister, Count Galeazzo Ciano, in mid-February, over the fact that Rome had not been given prior notice of the Berchtesgaden meeting with Schuschnigg. When Hitler's special messenger phoned him from Rome on the night of March 11 to report that Mussolini, with whom the messenger had just had a personal conference, "accepted the whole thing in a very friendly manner," sending the Führer his personal regards, Hitler vented an almost hysterically joyous relief. "Then please tell Mussolini that I will never forget him for this!" he cried into the phone. ". . . Never, never, never, no matter what happens! . . . I shall be ready to go with him through thick and thin. . . . I shall make any agreement [with him]."[35]

V

ON March 9, two days before *Anschluss,* Franklin Roosevelt in the White House addressed a letter to Dublin, to John Cudahy, his astute former ambassador to Poland, who, having begged for the apparent demotion (Irish Catholic Cudahy felt deep attachment to the Auld Sod), was now minister to Ireland. "Dear John," he wrote. "Your analysis of what happened in England is the best I have seen." He then made comment upon what had happened, events consequent upon a Birmingham businessman's trader instinct operating, untrammeled by ethical sensitivity, at the highest level of the British government —and as he did so he used words somewhat revealing, perhaps, of his own pragmatic morality. He said that "someone" had "remarked" to him that, if "a Chief of Police makes a deal with the leading gangsters and the deal results in no more holdups, that Chief of Police will be called a great man—but if the gangsters do not live up to their word the Chief of Police will go to jail." He added: "Some people are, I think, taking very long chances—don't you?"[36]

Certainly he himself, he felt, had earned the right to say "I told you so" to Neville Chamberlain (not that he ever would) if the enormous gamble now being taken by the prime minister was lost disastrously. Roosevelt had tried to prevent it.

On the day after his "quarantine the aggressors" speech, during his press conference at Hyde Park, he had dismissed impatiently the idea of "a conference of peace-loving nations," saying, "You never get anywhere with a conference."[37] But within a day or so thereafter he was responding positively, even enthusiastically, to a proposal put to him by Under Secretary of State Sumner Welles which, though it called for no immediate formal international conference (Welles stressed this point), logically implied a conference of some sort in the end. What Welles recommended would be, if nothing else, a grand theatrical gesture of a kind most attractive, as the under secretary well knew, to the large histrionic element of Roosevelt's personality. The whole of Washington's diplomatic corps was to be summoned to the White House on November 11—Armistice Day—for a purpose undisclosed. Great suspense would, of course, be generated among the diplomats, if not the general public, during the period between the invitation to the meeting and the meeting itself. Once assembled, the official representatives of foreign governments were to be presented with a dramatic review by the President of the present sad state of world affairs, then surprised by an urgent appeal from him for a "unanimous agreement" by all nations "at the earliest date" upon certain basic principles of international conduct, this along with broad general agreements upon the ways in which the principles could be carried into practice. Methods of achieving disarmament, international economic welfare, and a "maximum respect" for "humanitarian considerations" in the waging of war were to be considered and agreed upon. The President was to close his appeal with an assurance that, if the governments of the world were (to quote Welles) "favorably disposed to his major proposals, the government of the United States would, if they wished, request a number of other governments to join in drawing up tentative proposals which would be submitted to all nations as a basis for universal agreement." He was to "make it clear," however, that he was *not* "proposing any general international conference." It was Welles's belief that, through "its impact upon Japan," this worldwide appeal would of itself alone increase the relative strength of peace-seeking nations at the then upcoming Nine-Power Conference in Brussels.[38]

Revealing of Roosevelt's highly personal, idiosyncratic administrative technique, also of its advantages (it encouraged a free flow of ideas and information from those who had them to the President) and grave disadvantages (it hampered the practical implementation of ideas by promoting disorder and quarrelsomeness), is the fact that Sumner Welles felt free to take this plan of his across the street to the White House without first obtaining the approval of Cordell Hull, his official superior, who bore the top public responsibility, under the President, for the conduct of America's foreign affairs.*

---

*In his *Seven Decisions That Shaped History* (New York, 1951), Welles says (pp. 22–23) that, after he'd prepared his proposal in full detail, including the implementing documents, and was about

Like Roosevelt, who was ten years his senior, Welles was a son of privilege, the scion of a wealthy and historically distinguished family (he bore the name of his granduncle Charles Sumner, the Massachusetts abolitionist senator; one of his paternal ancestors was Gideon Welles, Lincoln's secretary of the navy; his palatial Washington residence is now the home of the prestigious Cosmos Club). Tall and handsome, as trim of figure as Roosevelt had been before the polio attack, he was intimidatingly aristocratic in manner, seeming cold and aloof, if not actually disdainful, in his general attitude toward the ordinary run of mankind. Few if any press photographs of him show him warmly smiling.[39] With Roosevelt, however, his relationship had the warmth of personal friendship buttressed by much shared experience. His mother and Roosevelt's had been the closest of friends. Aged twelve, he had been a page in service of the groom at the wedding of Franklin and Eleanor in 1905. He was, like Roosevelt, an alumnus of Groton and Harvard. His entrance into the Foreign Service in 1915 had been facilitated by Assistant Secretary of the Navy Roosevelt. He and Roosevelt the President were consequently perfectly at ease, swiftly and sympathetically communicative, in each other's company.

No such intimacy was possible between Roosevelt and Hull, who differed as radically in mind and temperament as they did in social background. In fact, Roosevelt, who thoroughly enjoyed Welles's swift intelligence and succinct speech, was often bored almost to distraction by Hull's fussy cautiousness and ponderous step-by-step style of argument. He also valued highly the service Welles had rendered him as adviser on Latin American affairs during the 1932 election campaign; it was allegedly through Welles that the "good neighbor" phrase had come into the first inaugural address; it was certainly through him that the phrase, originally descriptive of the administration's foreign policy in general, became attached exclusively to its policy toward Latin America—a policy of which Welles was a principal architect.

Roosevelt had not hesitated, therefore, during a major State Department reorganization last spring, to name Welles under secretary, though he could not but have known that this appointment was, to say the least, distasteful to Cordell Hull. Nor had he done anything thereafter to discourage an increase in the number and importance of Welles's direct personal contacts with him, bypassing the secretary—he had, indeed, done the opposite—which meant that the under secretary, operating virtually autonomously in dealing with a President determined to keep the reins of foreign policy firmly in his own hands, became, in the eyes of many, a more powerful figure in the administration,

---

to present it to the President, with whom he had already arranged an appointment, he "talked it over" with Hull, who, though he "evinced" no "intense interest in the subject . . . certainly made no objection." It was "with profound discouragement" that Welles learned "next day," through Norman Davis, that Hull's "original tepid acquiescence" had "changed to violent opposition." The historian is compelled to note that making "no objection" to a proposal hardly constitutes even a "tepid" endorsement of it.

exerting a greater influence upon America's international relations, than Cordell Hull.

It was an appearance that the secretary of state resented, naturally.

It was also deceptive.

A good gray man, Hull in his sober unimaginative way was an intelligent idealist of the Wilsonian school, totally committed to international free trade as the prime prerequisite of world peace, and willing to sacrifice much, including himself, to this overly narrow and exclusive conception of peacemaking. Thus encumbered by principle, he was vulnerable to personal hurt by the adroit, pragmatic politician in whose Cabinet he served—and certainly he was much put upon by the President of the United States. He bore with long-suffering patience repeated snubs and humiliations—was utterly resigned to them, as it seemed, though they accumulated in a weight sufficient to justify another kind of resignation, that of his Cabinet post, in the opinion of a good many informed observers. This seemingly endless patience and Christian meekness were, however, more appearance than reality. Hull had no abnormally masochistic inclination to turn the other cheek when slapped in the face. He had in fact great personal pride, a hot temper, and a good deal of the feuding Tennessee mountaineer's ability to hold and nurse a grudge, secretly, tenaciously, until an opportunity for effective vengeful action presents itself. Raymond Moley, who like Welles was a highly influential presidential adviser and a nominal subordinate of Hull's, had discovered this to his sorrow during the London Economic Conference of 1933*—had discovered, too, that Hull was far from being as powerless within the administration as he often seemed to be. A former representative and senator from Tennessee, he had in fact a very considerable persuasive power where the President needed it most for long-term administrative success, and where such as Welles and Moley had little: namely, in the halls of Congress.

Perhaps Hull saw an opportunity for revenge when he learned, belatedly, of Welles's proposal for the President's Armistice Day and then of the President's eager embrace of it. But if so, this was by no means his sole motive for registering what Welles later described in print as an "almost hysterical opposition" to the whole idea.[40] It was out of conviction and commitment to perceived truth that Hull protested the "project" as "illogical and impossible" in that it would play directly into the already strong hands of Japan, Italy, and Germany. Each of these "desperado" nations had repeatedly demonstrated its contempt for treaties, for pledged words; each, after five years of strenuous effort, was now armed to the teeth; and one of them, Nazi Germany, through Hjalmar Schacht, had actually suggested "something similar to what Welles had in mind" nearly ten months ago—"Hitler to submit proposals to France and Germany which would guarantee European peace, secure present boundaries, reduce armaments, establish a new, workable League of Nations, abolish sanctions, and obtain colonies for Germany." For though nothing of actual

*See *FDR: The New Deal Years*, pp. 161–98.

peacemaking importance could be achieved "just by sitting down around a table for a day or two and talking," the fact that such "talking" was going on would tend "to lull the democracies into a feeling of tranquillity . . . when their utmost efforts should be devoted toward arming themselves for self-defense." Certainly, if the President remained determined to go ahead, he should give up the notion of springing his idea as a dramatic surprise upon the British and French governments. They were "at that moment engaged in delicate negotiations with Germany and Italy" aimed at "keeping alive and functioning the Nonintervention Committee for Spain." To thrust "so ambitious a project upon them without warning might seriously embarrass them."[41] Moreover, if the President did not receive prior assurance from them that what he proposed had their support, he himself might be seriously embarrassed.

By this protest, or (more precisely) by the vehemence with which the secretary and others immediately afterward made it, Roosevelt was persuaded to forgo the Armistice Day dramatics. He was not persuaded that Welles's idea was a bad one. It was the timing he was doubtful about. His perception of the congressional and popular reaction to his vaguely worded "quarantine" proposal was not such as to encourage another flamboyant gesture toward collective security at that moment. He was acutely aware of the danger of provoking strong organized opposition by pacifists and isolationists.

A few weeks later, this awareness was made even more acute by the success of Congressman Ludlow's attempt, in the immediate aftermath of the *Panay* incident, to force a House vote on a motion to discharge from the Judiciary Committee the Ludlow Resolution, which called for a constitutional amendment whereby a national popular referendum would be required to validate any declaration of war by Congress. Passage of the motion would mean a prolongation of pacifist-isolationist agitation for the amendment through many months, perhaps many years,* with an equivalently prolonged hampering of the executive's conduct of foreign affairs. The vote was to be taken, it will be remembered, as the House's first order of legislative business in the upcoming congressional session—and until the motion was defeated, the hands with which Roosevelt made collective security gestures were, he felt, tied.

He therefore made defeat of the motion a top-priority item on his legislative agenda when the new congressional session opened, deploying for this purpose all the forces available to him. He personally addressed to Speaker of the House Bankhead a public letter saying that "the proposed amendment would be impracticable in its application and incompatible with our representative form of government." It would "cripple any President in his conduct of our foreign relations" while encouraging "other nations to believe that they could violate American rights with impunity." He fully realized "that the sponsors of this proposal sincerely believe . . . it would be helpful in keeping the United States out of war," but he was himself "convinced it would have the opposite

---

*A two-thirds vote of both houses of Congress, then ratification by the legislatures of thirty-six states, were required for the adoption of a constitutional amendment.

effect."[42] He received unexpected, strong, and warmly welcomed support for this stand from Alf Landon, his Republican opponent in the 1936 presidential election—also a not-so-unexpected strong support from former Republican secretary of state Henry Stimson—and when the vote was taken on January 10, 1938, the motion was indeed defeated. The vote was far closer than Roosevelt would have liked (188 voted for committee discharge, 209 voted against), but the event encouraged him, on the following day, to revive, at Welles's behest, the project which the under secretary had proposed last October.

There was one important tactical revision. This time, before the plan was actuated, the British prime minister was to be consulted and his approval sought.

We should pause here for a close look at this prime minister, since the psychology and moral character of the Right Honorable Neville Chamberlain, operating at the fulcrum of the world's balance of politico-military power, were and would continue for years to be a major determining factor in the international affairs with which Roosevelt must now increasingly deal.

Chamberlain was descended from a London family described in 1829 as "the highest sort of tradesmen, plain, honest and sincere"[43]—a family that, removed from London to Birmingham, obtained for itself a disproportionate share of the wealth produced by that city's rapidly expanding industry during the last half of the nineteenth century. It did so through Neville's father, Joseph, who employed acquisitive methods bitterly condemned by ruined competitors as ruthless and unfair. But Joe (everyone called him Joe), having retired rich from business at age thirty-eight, also won great respect, honor, and fame thereafter as, first, Birmingham's mayor, then member of Parliament from Birmingham, then Cabinet officer in the ministries of Gladstone, Salisbury, and Balfour. As colonial secretary under Salisbury, Chamberlain, who had entered Birmingham's local politics as a Radical, became the most vociferous of Tory imperialists, calling so loudly for aggressive action in South Africa after the Jameson Raid that the Boer War, when it came, was dubbed by many "Joe's War." He was a surpassingly able man, intelligent, strong of will, forceful of personality, but he was also a man in whom moral commitment was inversely proportionate to ambition, the latter being immense. "He has not persuaded himself that he has any convictions," Salisbury once complained of him to Balfour, "and therein lies Gladstone's infinite superiority."[44]

Son Neville, though he evinced none of Joe's fighting temper (he was, indeed, notably pacifistic) and had none of the personal warmth that made Joe attractive to Birmingham's workingmen, had inherited a fair measure of his father's ability and much of his father's basic character. Tall, thin, stiff, reserved, almost invariably sober of face—a man whose overwhelmingly prudential concerns were epitomized by his carrying, even when the sun shone, an umbrella against the rain that, in the English climate, just might fall unexpectedly—he had a colossal ego, supreme self-confidence, a stubborn will, and an impregnable self-righteousness. His loving concern for his fellowman did not extend far beyond his immediate family, and his empathic sensitivity extended hardly at all beyond his social class; his capacity for moral outrage was, as a result, severely limited. His strictly orthodox pieties *were* outraged by the godlessness of Soviet Russia; he loathed Communism far more than Fascism. He had little imagination. Personal property and profit were the lodestones of his conduct of private affairs, and his conduct of public affairs was grounded in an unexamined assumption that all men, including the kind who become totalitarian dictators, are similarly guided by rational materialistic self-interest, are similarly inclined toward profitable trade.

On the evening of Tuesday, January 11, Welles called personally at the British embassy in Washington to tell the British ambassador, Sir Ronald Lindsay, in strictest confidence, what the President had in mind. He gave into Lindsay's hand, for telegraphic transmittal through secure diplomatic communication channels, a highly secret personal letter (Welles stressed the need for secrecy) from Franklin Roosevelt to Neville Chamberlain. In it, Roosevelt said that, if he had the "cordial approval and whole-hearted support of His Majesty's Government," he would work out tentative substantive proposals with representatives of some of the "small powers," then warn the governments of France, Germany, and Italy of what impended, then present the plan publicly to the whole of the Washington diplomatic corps in a White House meeting on January 22. He stipulated that no other government be told of this communication, or told that any action of this nature was contemplated. He asked for a reply no later than January 17.[45]

The telegraphed letter, accompanied by a communication from Lindsay urging a cordially approving response to it, was received and decoded in the Foreign Office on the afternoon of January 12. Copies were sent that evening to Chamberlain, who was at Chequers, the official country residence of the prime minister. He read them next morning. It happened that Foreign Secretary Anthony Eden, who profoundly disagreed with his superior's conception of the proper way to deal with Hitler and Mussolini, and who for two years had been doing his utmost to strengthen Anglo-American ties, was out of the country at that time. (He had departed a few days before for a brief holiday on the Riviera.) And Chamberlain did not see fit to tell him by telegraph or phone that the President had made a proposal of major importance, much less to ask his return and advice. Instead, Chamberlain at once phoned the permanent under secretary of the Foreign Office, Sir Alexander Cadogan, to say that he personally was not in favor of what Roosevelt proposed (he in fact deemed the "plan . . . fantastic and likely to excite the derision of Germany and Italy," as he wrote in his diary a couple of weeks later) and to ask Cadogan to consult with the government's chief industrial adviser, Sir Horace Wilson, who he knew would agree with him. Cadogan was then to prepare a draft reply for Chamberlain's consideration when he returned to London that evening.[46]

Cadogan did his drafting that day on the assumption that, before a final draft was transmitted to Washington, what he wrote would be reviewed not only by the prime minister but also by Eden, who would be summoned home for this from the South of France. He delicately phrased Chamberlain's objection that the President's proposed initiative might complicate and compromise discussions which His Majesty's Government were prepared to open soon, first with Italy, then with Germany, and suggested, even more delicately, that the President might therefore wish to "defer his initiative until the result of our talks became known." He concluded, however, with an assurance of Britain's wholehearted support if the President, having considered the suggestion of postponement, rejected it and decided to go ahead immediately.

These closing words did not please the prime minister when he read them that evening. He would not promise support for the President if the latter insisted upon proceeding with this "fantastic" scheme, thereby placing at risk Chamberlain's own plan to make general European peace through appeasement of and accommodations with the dictators. He shrugged aside Lindsay's assertion that this presidential "initiative" was "invaluable" and that "destructive criticisms" of it, or stated "reservations" concerning it, would "accomplish very little in favour of anything you may wish to put forward" while doing great harm to the close Anglo-American ties that the Foreign Office had been struggling to achieve. Clearly, Roosevelt's good opinion was less valuable to Chamberlain—he deemed it less important in world affairs—than Hitler's or Mussolini's. He would not even agree that the foreign secretary must at least be informed of what was happening before the reply was dispatched. There wasn't time, he said; the President had demanded a reply not later than the seventeenth, and it was now late in the thirteenth. He therefore completely redrafted the message, and sent it off that very evening.[47]

In it he spoke of "the great dangers that beset us" and, somewhat condescendingly, made grateful acknowledgment of the President's good intentions with regard to them. But, he went on to say, "it may be permissible to look forward to some improvement in the immediate future"—if only, as his following words clearly implied, he were not inhibited in his own peacemaking effort by foolish if well-intentioned meddling. He indicated the extent to which he was prepared to go in the case of Italy, saying that, in the upcoming talks, "His Majesty's Government would be prepared . . . to recognize *de jure* the Italian conquest of Abyssinia (by which Signor Mussolini sets great store) . . . if they found that the Italian Government, on their side, were ready to give evidence of their desire to contribute to the restoration of confidence and friendly relations." His "fear" was "that if the President's suggestions are put forward at the present time, Germany and Italy may feel constrained to take advantage of them, both to delay the consideration of specific points which must be settled if appeasement is to be achieved and to put forward demands over and above what they would put forward to us if we were in direct negotiation with them."[48]

Early next morning, Friday, January 14, Cadogan, without asking the prime minister's permission, phoned Eden to say that important developments, not describable "over the open line," required the foreign secretary's "instant return." Eden started his journey at once, arriving that evening in England where, shocked and dismayed by the information he received, he immediately set about repairing, so far as he could, the damage done Anglo-American relations. This damage was considerable, as Eden gathered from a brief message from Lindsay—a message saying that the President was to make a written reply to the prime minister on Monday, the seventeenth; that in it he would indicate a willingness "to postpone his scheme 'for a while' "; but that, according to Welles, the President felt "a little disappointed." The latter was a gross understatement, as Lindsay and Eden surmised. Eden at once wired Lindsay to say he "was sure" the prime minister would be "very grateful for the President's . . . willingness to postpone . . . for a while" but that he, Eden, feared "the President may be registering disappointment" over what seemed "a negative attitude on our part." This last was not, in Eden's stated conviction, "the impression" that the prime minister "intended to convey."[49]

But, of course, it *was* precisely the impression intended, and Roosevelt was more than "disappointed." He was angered and disgusted by what he felt to be another snubbing put-down by Neville Chamberlain. He was also convinced that the lengths to which Chamberlain was willing to go to appease the dictators were outrageous, and he indicated as much in his reply to the prime minister, received in London in the early morning of Tuesday the eighteenth. After agreeing to "a short postponement" (Chamberlain described this in his diary as "a somewhat sulky acquiescence"), he raised strong objections to Britain's granting de jure recognition to Italy's Ethiopian conquest, saying it would have a most harmful effect on American public opinion and would further encourage Japan's treaty violations in the Far East. Considerably stronger representations to this effect were made to Lindsay, upon Roosevelt's instructions, by both Welles and Hull. Hull said de jure recognition would be regarded by "the desperado nations" as a "virtual ratification of their policy of outright treaty wrecking." Welles said it "would rouse" in the United States "a feeling of disgust; would revive and multiply all fear of pulling the chestnuts out of the fire; and it would be represented as a corrupt bargain completed in Europe at the expense" of America's Far Eastern interests.[50]

By all this, Chamberlain was given slight pause. He agreed, under pressure from Eden, to hold secret Cabinet discussions of the matter. As a consequence of these, he modified his initial stand to the extent of sending a brief message to Roosevelt: "I warmly welcome the President's initiative and I will do my best to contribute to the success of his scheme whenever he decides to launch it." But this fell short of the "cordial approval and whole-hearted support" for which the President had originally asked, and it was followed by a lengthy message to Roosevelt in which the prime minister, stressing the crucial importance to Britain of "an appeasement in the Mediterranean situation," set forth reasons why, in his view, de jure recognition might be necessary to achieve it.[51] He was determined to proceed with the Italian talks.

At this point, Eden proposed to resign his office. Despite the international furor it was sure to cause, this proposal was not personally distressing to

Chamberlain: He would appoint in Eden's place Viscount Halifax, whose commitment to the policy of appeasement was almost as strong as his own. But he pointed out to Eden that, because of the secrecy that Roosevelt had enjoined, the resignation could not be publicly grounded in disagreement over the Roosevelt initiative.

Three weeks later came Schuschnigg's forced surrender to Hitler at Berchtesgaden. (Said Chamberlain, when questioned on this in the House of Commons: "What happened [at Berchtesgaden] is merely that two statesmen agreed upon certain measures for the improvement of relations between their two countries. . . . It appears hardly possible to insist that just because two statesmen have agreed on certain domestic changes in one of the two countries . . . the one country has renounced its independence in favor of the other."[52] Obviously, since there was no audible or visible protest from Rome, Mussolini was prepared to acquiesce, if he had not already acquiesced, in Hitler's Austrian scheme. This meant total failure for British efforts to create a division between Italy and Germany whereby Hitler might be restrained. Nevertheless, Chamberlain remained determined to press ahead with de jure recognition; he would do so despite Italy's failure to give any solid assurances that it would withdraw from war-torn Spain or do anything else toward a peaceful settlement of international problems.

This provided Anthony Eden with an issue on which he could resign his post. He did so on February 20, 1938.

The event came as a great shock to a public that had had no warning that it impended. Its repercussions were worldwide. There was rejoicing in Berlin and Rome, where Hitler and Mussolini had long deemed Eden a mortal enemy and had made no great effort to hide that fact. There was dismay in the democracies among those most deeply committed to human freedom and profoundly opposed to Nazi-Fascism. Winston Churchill, who was at his country home, Chartwell, when a midnight phone call informed him of what had happened, has recorded his emotional response to the news:

> I must confess that my heart sank, and for a while the dark waters of despair overwhelmed me. . . . From midnight until dawn I lay in my bed consumed by emotions of sorrow and fear. There seemed one strong figure standing up against long, dismal, drawling tides of drift and surrender, of wrong measurements and feeble impulses. . . . Now he was gone. I watched the daylight slowly creep in through the windows, and saw before me in mental gaze the vision of Death.[53]

There were many in America who had much the same reaction.

Eden, a physically handsome man of the same general type as Sumner Welles, tall, youthful at age forty-one, slender, aristocratic of manner, highly intelligent, was one of the relatively very few of his English social class and generation to survive years of active service on the Western Front during the Great War. He was reputed to be the model for the central character of *Lost Horizon,* James Hilton's best-selling novel of 1933—the idealistic British statesman (Ronald Colman played him on the motion-picture screen) who was kidnaped and transported to Shangri-La, a utopian community hidden in a remote central Asian mountain valley, there to be preserved against world catastrophe in order to become himself a savior of civilization, a restorer of it, after the coming world war was ended. For Eden had indeed stood up these last years, in many an American vision, as a lonely heroic figure, a tower of strength and wisdom and virtue raised against the sea of cowardly and perfidious mediocrity that had washed and continued to wash over England.

VI

THESE, then, were the events in England the analysis of which, in a letter by the American minister in Dublin to the President of the United States in Washington, was judged by the latter, on March 9, "the best I have seen." And *Anschluss,* three days later, might well have confirmed Roosevelt in a flatly negative view of the "long chances" Chamberlain was taking.

It failed to do so, however. Logic and Roosevelt's own experience of life joined in damning the policy of appeasement as inevitably disastrous—and it was repugnant to him personally. He could not possibly personally embrace it. But neither could he reject it totally, unequivocally. After all, it just might succeed.

He refused, therefore, to issue any public statement about the Austrian takeover that might jeopardize "certain political appeasements in Europe" (the phrase is from a Roosevelt letter to Hull, January 21, 1938). Nor would he permit Hull to make meaningful official comment on the event. All Hull was allowed to say publicly, in a statement issued on March 19, was that the "extent to which the Austrian incident, or any similar incident, is calculated to endanger the maintenance of peace and the preservation of principles in which this Government believes is, of course, a matter of serious concern to the Government of the United States."[54]

But by that time Roosevelt felt a need for some response by the administration to horrifying reports of what the Nazis were doing to the Jews of Vienna in the immediate aftermath of *Anschluss*—reports printed under the blackest of headlines on the front pages of newspapers and commented upon with forceful eloquence by a morally outraged Dorothy Thompson in her syndicated column and weekly national radio broadcast. "Adolf Hitler has left behind him in Austria an anti-Semitism that is blossoming far more rapidly than ever it did in Germany," reported a *New York Times* correspondent in a dispatch dated March 16. (The "blossoming" was due in part to a young and ambitious SS officer named Adolf Eichmann, who was assigned the task of dealing with Austria's Jews and was anxious to demonstrate to his superiors in Berlin his special talent for the "solution" of the "problem.") "This afternoon the Jewish quarter of Leopoldstadt was invaded by triumphant crowds that called families from their homes and forced them to kneel and try to scrub from pavements slogans such as 'Heil Schuschnigg' which were part of the former Chancellor's plebiscite campaign." Far worse followed. Jewish men, women, and children were robbed, beaten, forced to perform all manner of humiliating acts while taunting crowds and smiling police looked on. Their homes and businesses were pillaged. Jews by the score, by the hundred, were arrested and imprisoned on flimsy charges, or no charges at all; and Austrian borders were so tightly sealed, not only by the Reich authorities but by those of neighboring Italy, Switzerland, and Czechoslovakia, that there was no escape. In Vienna, the suicide rate rose to two hundred a day. Said a *New York Times* story on March 20: "The death carts of the Anatomical Institute [in Vienna] are busy daily collecting the bodies of those poisoned by their own hands or by those nearest and dearest to them. Death seems to them the kindest gift for those . . . for whom once smiling Austria has become a vast prison. . . ." Could this be Vienna, the correspondent asked, "with its truck-loads of palefaced citizens being hurried through the streets to vanish through the great gates of the central prison—for many of them the first stage of the journey to the concentration camp?"[55]

There was bound to be growing pressure for a revision of American immigration laws and policies that would permit Jewish refugees to come to America, pressure exerted not only by such influential Jews as Rabbi Stephen S. Wise but also by leading Protestant clergymen. But though failure to respond to this pressure could do some political damage to an administration avowedly liberal, yielding to it could do truly major damage, in the judgment of the State Department and the White House. There was wide and deep hostility among the general public to any increase in immigration quotas in a time of rising unemployment, and especially to the throwing wide open of American doors to foreign Jews. Anti-Semitism was pervasive in the United States (it was especially so among the career diplomats of the Foreign Service) and had strong ties with isolationism. Father Charles E. Coughlin, the "radio priest," was telling his enormous audiences that Jewish internationalists plotted to involve the United States in a war that would make huge fortunes for Jewish financiers.

Hence the swift ease with which Roosevelt acquiesced in a device presented him by Sumner Welles whereby, without provoking as much conjoined isolationist and anti-Semitic wrath as any truly substantial proposal was bound to do, the appearance of attempting to help the Jews would be sufficiently convincing to appease those who demanded that something be done. Welles proposed that the President summon an international conference on the refugee crisis—a conference whose announced purpose was to aid Jewish emigration from Hitler's Greater Germany. The announcement was made by the President at Warm Springs on March 25. He said that invitations had been issued to thirty-three countries, including twenty Latin American republics, but that none "would be expected or asked to receive a greater number of emigrants than is permitted by its existing legislation." The actual rescue work would be done, for the most part, by private agencies. The precise date and place of the conference would be decided by conference-planning committees representing the various governments and the private charitable organizations. (In his Königsberg speech on that same March 25, Adolf Hitler said: "I can only hope and expect that the other world, which has such deep sympathy for these criminals, will at least be generous enough to convert this sympathy into practical aid. We, on our part, are ready to put all these criminals at the disposal of these countries, for all I care, even on luxury ships."[56])

The announcement had its intended and expected effects.[57] The American Jewish Committee, the Hebrew Sheltering and Immigrant Aid Society, the Federal Council of Churches, and numerous charitable groups hailed the proposal as "a great humanitarian act," and there was an immediate expression of eagerness by such groups and by prominent individuals to work hard for the conference's success. Nor was this chorus of approval offset by any loud outcry from those who would certainly have opposed a truly substantive proposal; the vitiating promise of no increase in immigration quotas muffled hostile criticism.

A couple of weeks later (April 16), in utter disregard of the strong protests that had been made by the U.S. executive, Chamberlain's government granted de jure recognition to the Ethiopian conquest in an Anglo-Italian agreement signed in Rome. Chamberlain insisted that the grant was part of a "general settlement" of Mediterranean problems, and was morally and practically justified by its context. In fact, Mussolini reciprocated this legal blessing upon his ruthless aggression only by renewing his disclaimer of territorial or economic ambitions in Spain, along with his obviously false statement of commitment to nonintervention in that country's civil war. He actually withdrew from Spain none of the Italian "volunteer" forces fighting there. And the spuriousness of this "settlement" was at once perceived in the White House and State Department. Within an hour or so after he learned of the event in Rome, Roosevelt was writing thanks to John Cudahy for letters in which the latter sharply criticized Chamberlain's appeasement policy and the so-called Cliveden Set (Joseph Kennedy was in effect a member), which sponsored that policy. "Over here there is the same element that exists in London," said the President to "Dear John." "Unfortunately, it is led by so many of your friends and mine. They would really like me to be a Neville Chamberlain—and if I would promise that, the market would go up and they would work positively and actively for the resumption of prosperity. But if that were done, we would only be breeding more serious trouble four or eight years from now."[58]

Also virtually simultaneously with the British-Italian pact-signing, Roosevelt, in response to a congressional resolution the adoption of which he had encouraged, published a list of the nations currently in violation of treaties with the United States—a list obviously intended to cast doubt upon the value of the pledged words of these nations; Italy's name was high on the list. Nevertheless, when pressed by Chamberlain and British foreign secretary Halifax for "some public indication of his approval of the agreement itself and of the principles which have inspired it," Roosevelt obliged with a statement saying that the United States looked upon the agreement "with sympathetic interest because it is proof of the value of peaceful negotiations." If "sympathetic interest" was not the same as the "approval" sought, it had, upon the general public, the same effect. "In one breath we praise the British for getting together with the Italians; in the next breath we imply that the Italians are treaty breakers and unworthy to be dealt with on a footing of equality," complained the assistant secretary of state for Western European affairs to his diary.[59]

By that time it was clear that Czechoslovakia was the next item on Hitler's agenda for conquest.

The Versailles Treaty had drawn the boundary between Germany and the Czechoslovak Republic along a natural mountainous frontier, one well suited to defensive fortification by the Czechoslovaks vis-à-vis the Germans. And this frontier had indeed been made a strong defensive line. But behind it, as a part of Czechoslovak territory agreed upon by the victors at Versailles, was the Sudetenland, the population of which was predominantly German. Some 3.25 million Germans lived there. They were, by historical tradition, hostile to the Czechs. Their "liberation" from Czech "tyranny" became now, in the aftermath of *Anschluss,* Hitler's major announced foreign-policy concern. His agent in Czechoslovakia, Konrad Henlein, whose Sudetenland German party had been secretly subsidized by Berlin since 1935, in the amount of fifteen thousand marks a month, was ordered by Hitler personally, in late March 1938, to make "demands . . . which are unacceptable to the Czech government," and to up the ante whenever and whatever the Czechs conceded.[60] Hitler was resolved to "settle" the Czech "problem" by military force if "necessary," despite the fact that nearly all high-ranking German generals were adamantly opposed to an action that seemed to them certain to spark general European war. For France was pledged by treaty to defend Czechoslovakian sovereignty against any foreign aggresion; the Soviet Union was pledged by treaty to come to Czechoslovakia's aid *if* France did so (this "if" loomed ever larger as appeasers came increasingly to dominate French foreign policy*); and Britain could hardly stand idly by if France became mortally threatened.

As April gave way to May, Hitler's sinister design was manifest in increasingly vociferous mass agitation by Sudentenland Germans. The Chamberlain

---

*Édouard Daladier, the Radical Socialist who succeeded Léon Blum as French premier, had led his party into Blum's Popular Front coalition. But after the Chamber of Deputies granted him powers denied Blum, including (temporarily) the power to rule by decree, the refusal of the Socialists and Communists to join his government enabled (or, perhaps, drove) him to move steadily rightward. Georges Bonnet, who became foreign minister in the Daladier government, was a peace-at-any-price appeaser. (See William L. Shirer, *The Collapse of the Third Republic* [New York, 1969], pp. 337–38.)

government, in response, was preparing new and yet greater sacrifices of honor, of human decency, of ordinary common sense upon the unholy altar of dictator appeasement. And Roosevelt's proposed peace initiative, which had been originally postponed for one week (that is, from January 22 to January 29), was perforce wholly abandoned.

# 6

⟶⟩⟩✕⟨⟨⟵

# Drifting: To a Decision of Sorts

ROOSEVELT'S dealings with domestic affairs during the winter and early spring of 1938 were as wavering, uncertain, and ineffectual as his dealings with foreign policy. This was due in some measure to his perception of a causal linkage between these two areas of concern—a perception that worked against truly decisive action, on his part, in either of them. The perception emerged from, or was at any rate sharpened by, his analysis of the House vote on the Ludlow Resolution in early January 1938.

In his State of the Union message just one week before that vote was taken, he had addressed to a sullen, divided, and rebellious Congress a reaffirmation of the New Deal "in a world of high tension and disorder." He had stressed the necessity, in the present sad state of the world, to "keep ourselves adequately strong in self-defense," thus presaging a call for increased armaments expenditures—for naval expansion especially. He had restated the administration's commitment to natural-resource conservation and agricultural-production controls, to pending minimum-wage and maximum-hour legislation. to work relief (as distinct from "the dole"), to "the reorganization and improvement of the administrative structure of the government," and to the principle of a balanced budget. "I am as anxious as any banker or industrialist . . . that the budget of the United States Government be brought into balance as quickly as possible," he had declared, but not by "permitting any American who can and is willing to work to starve because the Federal Government does not provide the work," and not by cutting relief expenditures so drastically that those unable to work were starved. He proposed instead to eliminate or curtail "non-essential" government expenditures while at the same time working to raise the national income "to the point that the taxes [on it] . . . will be sufficient to meet the necessary expenditures of the national government." "We have raised the nation's income from thirty-eight billion dollars in the year 1932 to about sixty-eight billion in the year 1937," he said. "Our goal . . . is to raise it to ninety or a hundred billion dollars. . . . As the Congress is fully aware, the annual deficit, large for several years, has been declining in the last fiscal year and this. The proposed budget for 1939 . . . will exhibit a further decrease in the deficit, though not a balance between income and outgo."[1]

He made no specific reference to the economic recession, which continued with no sign of recovery and which contributed greatly to Congress's current unhappiness with the administration, but he more than hinted that one cause of it was, in his opinion, "the concentration of economic control [in the hands of big business] to the detriment of the body politic—control of other people's money, other people's labor, other people's lives." These concentrations could not, in many cases, "be justified on the ground of operating efficiency, but have been created for the sake of securities profits, financial control, the suppression of competition and the ambition for power over others," he said, thus indicating his intention to follow through on that promise or threat of new anti-monopoly activity that had been implied by his inclusion of Robert H. Jackson in his last fishing-cruise party, and by his prior approval of an immensely publicized speech that Ickes had delivered over a national radio network only a few days before (December 30, 1937). The speech, the first draft of which had been written by Cohen and Corcoran, capitalized on the popular mood generated in part by Sinclair Lewis's best-selling anti-Fascist novel of 1935, *It Can't Happen Here,** and by Ferdinand Lundberg's current nonfiction best-seller, *America's Sixty Families,* a thundering if dubiously accurate description of the iron control over the nation's economy, mass communications, and political life allegedly exercised by the five dozen wealthiest American families.[2]

Overall, the annual message indicated no intention to halt the administration's domestic reform effort, much less to retreat from reforms already made, which meant that Roosevelt, if the effort were to succeed, must rally behind him forces sufficiently strong to overcome the coalition of Southern Democrats and Republicans that for the last year had stood as a stone wall against any liberal advance.

And what made the vote on the Ludlow Resolution so frustratingly significant in this context was the fact that the margin of defeat for the discharge motion—that is, the margin of victory for the administration—was supplied by precisely those Southern Democrats who normally joined with Republicans in opposition to the New Deal, whereas a major portion of those forces that could normally be counted upon to support New Deal domestic policy were, in this instance, because of pacifistic and isolationist sentiments, joined with congressional Republicans in a vote against the administration. As Rexford Tugwell put it: "The chief strength of the opposition to his [Roosevelt's] foreign policy came from the sources he counted upon to uphold his domestic measures. It looked as though he might have to choose between them. It amounted to this: he could risk collective security to get domestic reform, or he could risk domestic reform to get an acceptable foreign policy."[3] The dilemma, this necessity to choose between alternatives equally unpalatable, was especially paralyzing to one of Roosevelt's temporizing, compromising, pragmatic disposition and aversion to rigorously logical thought.

Nor was it only through analysis of the House's Ludlow debate and vote that the practical connection (or contradiction) between social reform and collective security was revealed. It was also emphasized in Roosevelt's mind by Senate debate (it opened simultaneously with the Ludlow furor in the House)

---

*A dramatization of this was one of the most successful of Hallie Flanagan's WPA Federal Theater Project productions. Ickes's speech was entitled "It Is Happening Here."

of an antilynching bill originally introduced by Wagner and Costigan in 1934 —a bill that, if it became law, would make lynching a federal crime and would be enforceable by the Justice Department and the federal courts.

That the bill *would* become law if it ever came to a vote, that it commanded a large majority in the Senate and a much larger one in the House, was obvious from the moment of its 1934 introduction.[4] It was strongly favored by most of the nation's New Deal supporters and was most emphatically supported by the National Association for the Advancement of Colored People (NAACP) as well as by Northern liberals who were continually morally outraged by the refusal of Southern states to enforce laws protecting black citizens' rights. The only effective opposition was that of the Southern Democrats, including some states'-rights Southerners of otherwise liberal inclination—a minority opposition, clearly, but a passionately flaming one, fueled by the fearful, hateful guilt feelings that had characterized Southern white attitudes toward black people ever since the Republic's founding. From the outset, therefore, the Southern strategy was to prevent a floor vote on the bill by every possible parliamentary trick and maneuver. It was a strategy unlikely to succeed in the House, which had no such tradition of unlimited debate as prevailed in the Senate, and its failure there was in this case assured by a lynching that took place in Duck Hill, Mississippi, in April 1937, just as House floor consideration of the bill was getting under way. The lynching was especially atrocious: Two young black men were seized, dragged into woods, and there chained to trees and tortured to death with blowtorches while a howling crowd of whites cursed and taunted them. Photographs were made of the dead bodies, sagging against the chains that yet bound them, their sides cooked by the torches. The pictures appeared in the national press. And as they did so, while the full initial shock of the atrocity was being felt, the antilynching bill came to a vote and was approved by the House 2–1.

Two months later, as 1937's bitter and acrimonious regular congressional session drew toward its close, the Senate version of the bill was reported out favorably by the Senate Judiciary Committee. The chances that it would ever come to a floor vote in the upper house appeared at that time to be almost nil, however, since the President's refusal to endorse it enabled the Senate's Southern leadership to place it at the very bottom of the Senate calendar. It was expected to die there, in effect, and would no doubt have done so if Senate majority leader Joseph Robinson, than whom the bill had no stronger opponent, had not himself died at that point, worn out by his futile battle for the President's court-packing scheme. Alben Barkley of Kentucky, who replaced Robinson as majority leader, was, of course, like all others of the Southern senatorial contingent, opposed to antilynching legislation. But he was yet new and inexperienced in upper-house leadership. And on a day in the second week of August, as he was trying to bring the stormy session to an orderly close, he suddenly found himself in a position where he had to recognize Robert Wagner when the latter rose to move the immediate consideration of his bill. Nor would Wagner withdraw his motion under the hot and heavy pressure that was at once applied to him by the speaker, by Southern senators who threatened to debate the motion until Christmas if that were necessary to prevent a vote, and by Senate colleagues who, though they would vote for the bill if permitted to do so, were anxious above all to end this unhappy session and leave steamy Washington. Not until the speaker proposed a resolution to make consideration of antilynching the first order of business in the next regular session did Wagner relent; he and the NAACP were convinced that they had a better chance at the beginning of a session than at the close of one to defeat the inevitable Southern filibuster against the bill. The resolution was adopted.

And when floor debate of the bill opened on January 6, 1938, Wagner and his allies had reason to believe they would prevail over the Southern opposition. They were well prepared to argue their case, and that case, concurred in by a large majority of the national public, was far stronger morally, logically, factually, and in terms of legal precedent than was the clearly diversionary and disingenuous constitutional ("states' rights") argument of the Southerners. No fewer than fourteen of the sixteen Republican senators joined a large majority of the Senate Democrats in already publicly recorded support of the bill. Moreover, Wagner and the others felt that the time wasted by North Carolina's "tobacco senator," Robert Reynolds, in a two-day travelogue of South America, Europe, Asia, and the South Seas, and by other filibusters in similarly obstructionist fashion, actually aided the bill's supporters—for surely the White House, unable to proceed with its legislative agenda until this matter was disposed of, must eventually be forced to press for a motion for cloture whose passage by the required two-thirds majority would bring the filibuster to an end and enable the bill to pass.

But when a cloture motion was made in late January, after three weeks of Southern filibuster, Roosevelt did nothing to aid its passage. Indeed, even had he wished to do so, he might have felt unable to aid it at that juncture. The fear of a Roosevelt "dictatorship" that had been aroused by the attempted court-packing, and that now militated against executive reorganization, would be strengthened by any perceived presidential attempt to "interfere" with the operation of a hallowed Senate tradition. Certainly such fear was skillfully played upon by the Senate minority leader, Oregon's Charles McNary, as he led all but one of his Republican senatorial colleagues to vote against the cloture motion on January 27. On the Senate floor he made a ringing declaration of sacred principle. "I am not willing to give up the right of free speech," he cried. (Cynical observers recalled that McNary had voted for cloture on nine earlier occasions.) "That right is the last palladium . . . it may be the last barrier to tyranny."[5] A number of Democratic senators who favored antilynching made similar endorsements of free-speech principles. The cloture motion then went down to defeat, 51–37. The filibuster continued.

And as it did so, the tide of circumstance that had initially seemed to flow toward the antilynching bill's passage began to turn the other way.

The major cause of this turn was the continuing and deepening economic recession; it forced changes in the general public's assessment of political priorities, changes unfavorable to Wagner's cause. The feeling grew that the endless antilynching debate wasted, on behalf of a measure not immediately imperative, time and effort that should be devoted, that must be at once devoted, to what now rapidly became a truly major economic crisis. This impatience with the Senate came to be focused, ironically, not on the filibustering opponents of the antilynching bill, but on its proponents. Nor were Wagner and his fellow warriors aided, as House supporters of the bill had been the previous spring, by the effects upon public opinion of an atrocious lynching —or, indeed, of any lynching at all. Southern whites had, evidently, tacitly declared a moratorium on lynching until assured there would be no future federal interference with such pleasures. (One young black man, at least, a mill hand in Greensboro, Alabama, definitely owed his life to a local official who pointed out to the lynch mob that if they killed this "nigger" they'd undercut heroic efforts currently being made on behalf of their "states' rights" by their elected representatives in Washington.[6]) Wagner, increasingly blamed for causing Congress to fiddle while Rome burned, was pressed increasingly to give up an evidently futile struggle.

And this pressure was not mitigated—it was, on the contrary, covertly and indirectly augmented—by the White House. Roosevelt had never shown any eagerness to extend his New Deal effectively into the area of race relations. He had never in any specific case manifested a civil-liberties commitment strong enough to stand up against his wish or need for city machine or Southern white votes. And as the antilynching bill furor lengthened, with no end in sight, while the economy sagged and events abroad marched relentlessly toward new world war, his sense of domestic policy–foreign policy dilemma (collective security abroad balanced against social reform at home) was sharpened. On February 10 he addressed a request to the House for a $250 million supplemental appropriation to enable the WPA, whose employment lists were lengthening, to continue operating until June 30. Promptly passed by the House and sent to the Senate, this emergency bill might have been used to force cloture on the antilynching bill debate if Roosevelt had indicated that he favored passage of the latter. Instead, though Mississippi's notorious racial bigot Senator Theodore Bilbo had announced a speech that would take him a month to deliver, the President remained silent when Wagner made his second cloture motion. On February 16 cloture was again defeated, and by a margin only five votes smaller than the one that had defeated the earlier motion.

Senate Majority Leader Barkley then used the emergency appropriation bill, labeled "urgent" by the White House, to force Wagner to withdraw the antilynching proposal; he moved on February 21 the immediate consideration of the administration measure. Wagner made a last desperate effort on behalf of his own bill, moving an amendment of the Barkley motion that would permit consideration of antilynching to be renewed on March 28. The Southerners at once threatened a filibuster of this amendment as stubbornly prolonged as that against antilynching itself; the White House gave no sign that it would do any more toward cloture on this matter than it had done with regard to antilynching; and Wagner, perforce, surrendered. On February 21 he withdrew his antilynching motion and the six-week filibuster came to an end.

II

IN his February 10 letter to Speaker Bankhead, the President said that, though 1,950,000 people were on WPA "rolls today," the funds made available to WPA on January 1, 1938, "would permit the employment of an average of only 1,700,000 persons for the six months ending June 30, 1938." He might have added that the work-relief program, even with this additional quarter-million people on WPA's payroll, aided less than a fifth of the number currently unemployed. On January 1, the unemployed had totaled nearly eleven million, according to both AFL and National Industrial Conference Board estimates; by March 1, they totaled over eleven and a quarter million, according to the same agency estimates.

And every other reliable index of business and industrial activity was also indicative of grave economic illness. Railroad freight loadings were sharply lower than they had been in the same months of last year. Automobile sales were down 50 percent and would remain so for the first five months of the year. The iron and steel industry operated at only a little more than half capacity: Monthly pig-iron production, which had averaged 3 million tons in 1937, was down to a little more than 1 million; steel production, which had totaled 45,875,521 tons for the first ten months of 1937, reached only 21,123,872 tons for those same months of 1938. The Federal Reserve Board's index of industrial production fell 39 points between August 1937 and April 1938, standing at 119 in the former month and at 80 in the latter. *The New York Times*'s index of business activity fell during the same period from 111 to 75. Consumer prices, increasingly managed by the supply side of the economy, showed no equivalent decline, but commodity prices, indexed at 80.9 in January 1938, sank slowly but steadily through February, March, and April, standing at 78.1 as April ended. As for security prices, they were dramatically lower than they had been last year: The security-market index, which was at 143.8 in February 1937, sank to 87.6 in February 1938, to 81.9 in March, to 78.5 in April. Overall, the U.S. economy, during these opening months of 1938, lost two-thirds of the gains made since March 1933.[7]

Yet Roosevelt, as he made his futile gestures toward collective security in the face of crisis abroad, and as he dealt (much more effectively) with the TVA's administrative crisis, took no definite action in the face of a national crisis that threatened to destroy utterly not only the economic gains made under the New Deal but also the presidential capacity to govern. He was acutely aware of the threat. He did not know what to do about it. If he saw merit in each of the two broad and widely divergent courses of action that were pressed upon him by advisers, courses determined by radically different conceptions of what had gone wrong, he also saw grave hazards. Balanced against each other, the alternatives canceled each other out: He was unable to think his way through either of them to a conclusion that felt "definitely" more "right" than the conclusion reached when he considered the other. And so he continued to drift on a sea of troubles, tossed this way and that by waves of contradictory advice, as the long winter wore itself away.

His Brandeisian advisers joined with his own observations and predilections to persuade him, as we have seen, that one cause of the recession might be a "capital strike" against the New Deal, a strike rendered effective by big-business monopoly. But if monopolistic business were truly a major cause of the recession, if big business were in fact this powerful, then a direct attack upon it would do nothing to solve the immediate recession problem. It would, on the contrary, make solution more difficult, perhaps impossible. Indeed, in view of the exposures just made (in a report issued in late December 1937) by the La Follette civil-liberty committee of the Senate—exposures of industrial espionage and preparations for all-out bloody war by giant corporations against labor unions—a truly threatful move by government against concen-trated private power could provoke precisely that organized big-business reac-tion toward a Fascist America of which Ickes, in his network broadcast, had warned.

Best to be cautious in this matter.

And ambiguous in word and deed.

At any rate, Roosevelt *was* ambiguous and even self-contradictory in his immediate dealings with the monopoly question. Within twenty-four hours after lecturing Congress, in his annual message, on the evils of excessive "concentrations of economic control," he lectured his press conference on the evils of a lack of intelligently planned production and distribution on the part of big industry—a kind of planning that became possible only through *in-creased* concentration of economic control. He said he had talked "to a very large steel manufacturer the other day" and had asked him why "you suddenly dropped [production] from 90 percent to around 28 percent" of capacity. The steelman allegedly replied that, because automobile manufacturers had made more cars in the first half of 1937 than their dealers could sell, they had abruptly revised their orders for steel drastically downward. Also, the rail-roads had last spring ordered and demanded immediate delivery of "all the steel rails they needed for a full year." This meant that "all through the summer we were working seven days a week, turning out steel rails," and now "they do not need, or want, any more for another nine months." The steelman deemed this behavior "highly unintelligent." So did Franklin Roosevelt. But could government "do anything to prevent this type of unintelligent business operation?" asked a reporter. Roosevelt thought it could. He referred to the NRA codes whereby "the heads of all the companies in a given industry" were enabled "to sit down around a table with the Government" and, on the basis of their own and government statistics, "figure out . . . what the probable demand of the country would be for a period of six months or a year ahead." He emphasized that he was not advocating the immediate reenactment of

NRA; he fully realized that antitrust legislation now on the books might prevent the kind of planning he'd described. He knew, too, that "[a] lot of people are afraid of it." But he personally "would very much favor making it a completely legal thing to do: to meet around a table and find out, with the help of the Government, what the demands are, what the purchasing power of the country is, what the inventories are."[8]

In this he followed the lead of "national planners" who had played an important role in the so-called "first" New Deal but, considerably discredited by the NRA experience, had given way to the piecemeal social reformers of the "second" New Deal. Two of the foremost exponents of such "planning" —that is, of a renewed emphasis upon the kind of government-and-business cooperation that NRA had attempted and of which AAA, in its increasing real effect, was a current manifestation—were Bernard Baruch, who had headed the War Industries Board of the Great War, and Donald Richberg, who had headed NRA during its last months of existence. Richberg, now senior partner in a leading Washington law firm headed by Joseph E. Davies, was the more influential of the two. In a series of letters and memoranda addressed to the President and to business leaders, he argued that the "true side of the New Deal," as opposed to the "false side" of the antibusiness reformers, was represented by NRA and AAA, being grounded on "the foundation principle of our political economy," namely, "the self-regulation of commerce and the fixing of wages and prices by competition." It limited government to whatever regulation of competition was necessary to remove "excesses" and ensure "fairness." But "excesses," in the Richberg lexicon, included the "unintelligent business behavior" (the failure to coordinate production activities in accord with a realistic overall plan) that Roosevelt referred to in his January 4 press conference—which is to say that the Richberg conception of "competition" most emphatically did not rule out "cooperation" of a kind to which "fanatic trust busters" were vehemently and, in Richberg's view, stupidly opposed.[9] Such cooperation between business and government was, in fact, the heart of Richberg's prescription for economic recovery; and the obviously necessary first step toward it must be a reconciliation of business with the New Deal.

To effect this reconciliation became Richberg's major effort in early 1938.

He persuaded Roosevelt to hold in the White House on January 11 a morning meeting with a group of leading industrialists, among them such formidable longtime foes of the New Deal as Alfred Sloan of General Motors, steelman E. T. Weir, Colin Chester of the National Association of Manufacturers, and Lewis Brown of Johns Manville. (On the afternoon of Friday, January 14, Roosevelt told his Cabinet "that this conference [with the industrialists] would not have been possible if it had not been for the speeches of Bob Jackson and Harold Ickes. . . . Prior to the speeches these businessmen refused even to come to talk to me." Ickes, who had been unhappy over Roosevelt's seeming shift away from antimonopoly toward a rapprochement with big business, beamed.[10]) The meeting went well, Richberg thought. He was encouraged to believe that machinery for new business-government cooperation along NRA lines might soon be in place; he was further encouraged when, on January 17, Roosevelt talked with General Electric's Owen D. Young, Morgan partner Thomas W. Lamont, and the CIO's John L. Lewis in a White House meeting arranged by Tugwell and Adolf Berle.[11]* Richberg's high hopes had a brief life, however. They were soon replaced by deep despair as Roosevelt listened to antitrust "left-wing advisers" (Richberg's description) with what seemed a greater sympathy and responsiveness than he had shown the counselors of business-government cooperation. By late January, after the President in a press conference and in other ways had revealed that his anti–holding company attitudes and distrust of big business in general remained unchanged, Richberg, whose mood swings were always swift and wide, was saying gloomily to his friend Raymond Clapper, a syndicated newspaper columnist, that the end of free enterprise was at hand and "the days of democracy are numbered."[13]

A few days later, Roosevelt received a letter from John Maynard Keynes in which the English economist argued almost as strongly as Richberg did, though with far different motivation and intent, for a more conciliatory attitude toward business on Roosevelt's part.

In this unsolicited letter, dated February 1, 1938,[14] Keynes sharply criticized the President's past and current dealings with utilities corporations. All utilities really ought to be nationalized, in Keynes's opinion, since efficient energy supply was so absolutely necessary to public welfare and since utilities were rendered naturally monopolistic by the technology involved. But if Roosevelt deemed the time not yet ripe for this, there was no point in "chasing the utilities around the lot every other week." Far better to "make peace on liberal terms" —terms that guaranteed fair earnings on new capitalization and fair recompense for stockholders in case of future nationalization. Similarly with the railroads. (Here Keynes may have been influenced by a speech delivered on the Senate floor, December 20, 1937, by Missouri's Harry Truman, reporting the findings of a very thorough investigation of railroad financing conducted by the aforementioned subcommittee of the Senate's Interstate Commerce Committee, nominally chaired by Montana's Burton K. Wheeler.† It was a scathing, fact-loaded criticism of railroad financing, of giant railroad holding corporations formed by "greedy" financiers to "milk" and wreck the operating lines; it made front-page news all across America.[15]) The railroads, too, should be nationalized, said Keynes, but if the administration was unprepared to move toward this now, it should certainly "take pity" upon a current railroad management that drowned in the flood of water poured by past managers into

*Berle, currently head of New York City's planning commission, under Mayor La Guardia, indicated to Roosevelt at the close of this meeting that he would accept the appointment as assistant secretary of state that the President, to the acute displeasure of Cohen and Corcoran, had wanted to make for several months. The appointment was confirmed by the Senate in March. Like Moley, his predecessor in that post, Berle functioned as a presidential adviser on a wide range of problems, though initially with special emphasis on financial and general economic concerns.[12]
†See pp. 75–76.

railroad capital structures. Why? Because one root of the present business recession was clearly psychological, said Keynes, in partial agreement with Morgenthau, Richberg, and others who stressed "business confidence" as a prime prerequisite to economic recovery. The President discouraged recovery, in Keynes's view, by his treatment of businessmen as public enemies.

"Businessmen have a different set of delusions from politicians," lectured Keynes,

> and need, therefore, different handling. They are, however, much milder than politicians, at the same time allured and terrified by the glare of publicity, easily persuaded to be 'patriots,' perplexed, bemused, indeed terrified, yet only too anxious to take a cheerful view, vain perhaps, but very unsure of themselves, pathetically responsive to a kind word. You could do anything you liked with them, if you would treat them (even the big ones), not as wolves and tigers, but as domestic animals by nature, even though they have been badly brought up and not trained as you would wish. It is a mistake to think that they are more *immoral* than politicians. If you work them into the surly, obstinate, terrified mood, of which domestic animals, wrongly handled, are so capable, the nation's burdens will not be carried to market; and in the end public opinion will veer their way.

The central argument of Keynes's letter, however, was the one also made by Eccles, Currie, Leon Henderson, Mordecai Ezekial: Public underconsumption rather than industrial overproduction was the cause of the economic slump. If true recovery were to be achieved, the federal government must spend more, much more; it must engage in deficit financing on a far larger scale than the New Deal had ever done. A vast expansion of public works was needed, especially housing construction (the administration's past dealings with the "housing problem," said Keynes bluntly, were "wicked"), in addition to the steps toward easier credit, gold desterilization, and increased relief spending that the administration had taken or was now beginning to take.

It was an eloquent letter, but it had no more influence upon Roosevelt than Keynes's earlier advice had had. For one thing, Roosevelt was convinced by his presidential experience of big-business men that Keynes's description of their essentially harmless nature, their "pathetic" responsiveness to "kind" words, was highly inaccurate—at least, when applied to the American variety (possibly it fit the English gentlemen with whom Keynes was personally acquainted). For another thing, the tone and style Keynes employed, as in earlier communications to the President, militated against his purpose, being far more likely to irritate than to persuade the man he addressed. Keynes did not flatter as Frankfurter did. Instead he seemed impatient with Roosevelt's lack of information, even (subtly) contemptuous of Roosevelt's mental processes.

Roosevelt's response was ostentatiously perfunctory. Without commenting upon its contents, he handed the letter over to the secretary of the Treasury, asking him to draft a reply for presidential signature. And Morgenthau, one may be sure, accepted the assignment happily; it seemed to signify a continued support by Roosevelt of the antispending budget-balancing to which Morgenthau was so fervently committed. The blandly insincere reply then drafted, and signed by the President without demur or revision, was tacitly insulting to John Maynard Keynes. "It was very pleasant and encouraging to know that you are in agreement with so much of the Administration's economic program," the letter said. "This confirmation coming from so eminent an economist is indeed welcome. Your analysis . . . is very interesting. The emphasis you put upon . . . housing . . . is well placed."[16] No reference whatever was made to the main point Keynes had made: the urgent, immediate need for a vast increase in federal spending.

At the time he did this drafting, Morgenthau held, and continued to hold for weeks to come, a highly ambivalent attitude toward the war being waged for the President's approval between the antimonopolists and the "national planners." On the one hand, he "seemed to think that an antimonopoly approach would take the President's mind off the arguments of the spenders," as Ellis W. Hawley has written,[17] and he encouraged it to the extent of initiating an intradepartmental investigation of collusive bidding by big business for government contracts. On the other hand, as chairman of an interdepartmental committee for the study of prices he approved a three-and-a-half-page memorandum drafted, for the most part, by Gardiner C. Means, co-author with Berle of *The Modern Corporation and Private Property*, which seemed to imply the need for national planning, by government and business cooperatively, to bring prices "into balanced relation to one another." A reluctant Roosevelt was persuaded by Wallace and Morgenthau to release this memorandum to the press and did so on February 18, not as a direct presidential statement but as one approved by him and by the Federal Reserve Board. He reviewed it for reporters that day, with commentary and accompanying charts, in one of the most masterfully handled of his press conferences. He drew from it, however, stated conclusions so general, so vague, that most of the reporters were left more confused than before about his overall intentions with regard to the recession.

For instance, the memorandum made a sharp distinction between prices that were "rigid" (they were notably so in the steel, cement, and plumbing industries) and those that were "fluid" or "flexible," the latter being determined by what was left of the "free" market, the former being managed by corporate executives who, instead of cutting prices when faced with declining demand, cut production (which meant, also, employment). Roosevelt spoke of "easy credit," the "new farm bill," and the "new housing bill" as ways of "stiffening up the fluid prices," as a reporter remarked. But when this same reporter asked "about methods to give fluidity or flexibility to rigid prices," Roosevelt said merely: "Now you are asking about the industries that are more monopolistic. We . . . are not ready to 'shoot on it.' It is a big problem."[18]

The "new farm bill" to which Roosevelt referred was actually, by February 18, not a bill but a law. Four days before, the House by a vote of 264–135 had accepted the conference report on the comprehensive farm bill that had failed to pass either the regular or special congressional sessions of 1937,* a report already accepted by the Senate, 56–31. Designed to replace 1936's stopgap Soil Conservation and Domestic Allotment Act, the new measure, signed by Roosevelt on February 16, accorded more closely with the views of the "national planners" than with those of the Brandeisian antimonopolists. It authorized the secretary of agriculture to make national acreage allotments for wheat, corn, cotton, rice, and tobacco on the basis of domestic and export market demand and of the need for commodity storage in "fat" years for release to the market in "lean" years—Wallace's "ever-normal granary" idea. Like its immediate predecessor, the new law provided for "benefit payments" ("conservation payments" in the 1936 act) to "cooperating" farmers out of general tax revenues, but for the first time explicitly added "parity payments" aimed at making up the difference between current agricultural commodity prices and those prevailing during the so-called "normal base period" of August 1909–July 1914. The distribution of the total national acreage allotments among the several states and counties was to be made through the administrative machinery already in place (that is, state and county AAA committees), mostly on the basis of past acreages.[19] The long-term effect would be of a piece with that of the original AAA: that is, a continuing gradual surrender of free individual choice to blind technological determinism in the agricultural economy. There would be some slowing, perhaps, but no halting (indeed, AAA actually assured a continuation) of the trend away from the small family farm toward the large agribusiness farm.

As for the "new housing bill," it was a modification of the Wagner housing bill passed the previous August, designed to liberalize provisions for the making of federally insured loans for the construction of low-rent housing. Only so-called transitory action upon it had been taken during the special session, final or complete action being blocked by a proposed amendment that would have effectively rendered the new law null and void. The amendment would have required the payment to labor of the "prevailing wage" in any given locality by builders, contractors, or subcontractors whose operations were financed by a federal housing loan. And since to determine just what the "prevailing wage" was for every locality in the nation would have been a virtually impossible task, yet bonds purchased by private lenders could become worthless upon any future court finding that the construction funded by them had employed labor not paid the prevailing wage, the market for such bonds would be wiped out.[20] The obstacle had not been surmounted, and the bill had been returned to Senate committee when the special session ended. But the measure, minus the crippling amendment, went through both houses with overwhelming majorities early in the regular 1938 session.

*See p. 101.

III

ON March 14, Morgenthau, lunching alone with the President, as he normally did on Mondays, spoke of two major economic proposals that had been made to the White House within the last two weeks. One came from Joseph Eastman, chairman of the Interstate Commerce Commission, for a reorganization of American railroad corporations—a proposal made in response to the sensational exposures by the Wheeler-Truman subcommittee of financial chicanery ruinous to operating railroad lines. Eastman's was a revival of a 1933 plan for a drastic overhaul of railroad financial structures, whereby water would be squeezed from railroad stock, and called for national planning by government to eliminate the current "foolish" duplication of rail facilities and services. The other proposal, by William O. Douglas of the Securities and Exchange Commission, was originally made by Berle in 1934; it would create a permanent system of government industrial banks to aid, primarily, small business. Roosevelt told his treasury secretary that he was not ready to move on either proposal (two days later he would turn both over to Morgenthau for "review" and "study"). Nor was he ready, he indicated, to move on any other proposal of real substance.

A small tight smile of pleased comprehension appeared upon Morgenthau's rarely smiling face.

"As I see it," said he, "what you are doing is just treading water . . . to wait to see what happens in the spring."

"Absolutely," Roosevelt replied.[21]

Certainly, neither railroad reorganization nor improvement of the nation's credit structure was among Roosevelt's major concerns at that moment. Weighing far more heavily on his mind were his concerns over the executive reorganization bill and the Public Utilities Holding Company Act of 1935.

The fate of the latter was now being decided by the nine justices of the U.S. Supreme Court. None of the utility holding companies had registered with the SEC as the law required; all asserted the Act to be unconstitutional; and, to prove the contrary, the SEC had sued to enjoin one of the largest utility holding companies, Electric Bond and Share, from violating the registration provision. Argument on this before the Court had been completed some time before. The justices, having deliberated, should by now be preparing their opinions. These would surely be announced very soon—perhaps as early as next Monday. It is true that Roosevelt's worry over what the majority opinion would say was now considerably less than it would have been last fall, for arch-conservative seventy-five-year-old Justice George Sutherland, who most certainly would have voted for the utilities, had retired from the bench in January.* But even with Sutherland out of the way here was, as regarded this case, a sufficient worry in Roosevelt's mind.

---

*He was replaced by Stanley Reed, whose own vacated post of solicitor general had been filled by Robert H. Jackson. The Jackson appointment seemingly signified the President's intention to pursue vigorously the antimonopoly policy tacitly announced in the annual message.

Far greater, however, was Roosevelt's anxiety over his executive-reorganization proposal. The fate of the bill embodying the Brownlow Committee's recommendations* was now being decided in the halls of Congress, and there had been mounted against it an opposition that rivaled in extent and fervor the opposition to last year's court-packing proposal. Indeed, it included the same conservative enemies of Roosevelt personally and of the New Deal generally; it employed essentially the same major basic argument—to wit, that the proposed bill was designed to create a Roosevelt dictatorship. It also comprised a good many people who were generally supportive of the administration, as the opposition to court-packing had done, including AFL officials and even some social-welfare workers who, though they trusted Roosevelt, were afraid that a future executive could and would employ his reorganization powers to abolish or curtail agencies they deemed essential to the well-being of labor and of the economically disadvantaged generally. There was opposition from the Catholic hierarchy, who feared that the bill if enacted would lead to the establishment of a federal Department of Education, and that this new federal bureaucracy, dedicated to the strengthening of secular education, would become a force inimical to Catholic parochial schools. There was fear on the part of conservatives, many Democratic politicians, and many moderates that the enacted bill would result in the elevation of Harry Hopkins to the Cabinet as secretary of the proposed Department of Welfare; from that post he, the "reckless spender," the ruthlessly ambitious political operator, might launch a successful campaign for presidential nomination in 1940. Fear was, indeed, the dominant emotion whereby the the bill's chief opponents were motivated, and in their campaign they employed fear tactics of the most extreme sort. Full-page advertisements in newspapers, special town meetings replete with emotional oratory, syndicated columns and radio speeches by famous pundits, lead editorials in most of the daily press, deluges of telegrams addressed to congressmen and senators—all these played upon such alarm as Massachusetts's Senator Walsh expressed when he likened passage of the bill to the "plunging of a dagger into the very heart of democracy."[22]

Two weeks later, on March 28, one of these two causes of anxiety was erased from Roosevelt's mind and the other somewhat reduced. On that Monday the Supreme Court upheld the SEC registration provision of the Public Utilities Holding Company Act† and the Senate passed the executive-reorganization bill. The margin of administration victory on the latter issue was, however, as small as it could possibly be. It consisted of a single vote. And, astonishingly to the well-informed, among the senators who voted against the measure was New York's Robert Wagner.

The closeness of this vote was jarring to Roosevelt. It might presage fatal

---

*See pp. 19–28, 130.

†The ruling did not result in immediate implementation of the Holding Company Act. The SEC seemed to many observers to move with extreme cautiousness to achieve the act's stated goals. Not until 1940 did it initiate hearings on the corporations' "programs for simplification."[23]

trouble for the bill in the House, which had not yet acted on the matter, thanks mostly to the reactionary representative John J. O'Connor. A fervent opponent of the bill, O'Connor had maneuvered skillfully to keep it bottled up in the Rules Committee, which he chaired.

Equally jarring was Wagner's disaffection (so Roosevelt deemed it). How on earth could this most loyal supporter of the administration, this most stalwart of New Deal liberals, actually a principal author of the New Deal insofar as his name was on much of its most important legislation—how on earth could he vote against a clearly necessary progressive measure to which the President had committed all the power of his office, all the prestige of his person? One may be sure that Roosevelt pondered this question most earnestly. One may be equally sure that he found its answer in the pressures that had been brought to bear upon the New York senator. Of these, a principal one was exerted by the Catholic Church—a political pressure to which Roosevelt was himself extremely sensitive. Wagner had been born and raised a German Lutheran, but he had married an Irish Catholic girl thirty years ago (the wedding ceremony was performed in a Catholic church) and had ever since been strongly attracted to the Catholic religion and the Catholic discipline (in 1946 he would join the Church formally). Another opposition pressure that Wagner acutely felt was that of union labor, he being labor's chief champion in the Senate.

There is evidence, however, that inner conviction was at least as important as outer pressure in determining Wagner's astonishing vote. His was a mind that made no such sharp and arbitrary distinctions as pragmatic Roosevelt habitually made between ends and means, "ideals" and "methods," the "big picture" and "mere" detail. Leon Keyserling, who was Wagner's administrative assistant in the 1930s, writes: "He [Wagner] believed that basic decisions as to administrative structure could not be separated from those fundamental questions of substantive policy and program which would remain subject to initial control by the Congress."[24] He knew from long experience that the bureaucratic machinery which carries out policy is also machinery that necessarily interprets policy and, to that extent (often a very wide extent), makes it. Hence Wagner's conclusion that the proposed reorganization would not merely increase executive "efficiency"; it would do what its opponents asserted and the President denied it would do, namely transfer legislative power from Congress to the executive. And this conclusion was linked with certain doubts that Wagner justifiably had about the strength and depth of the present chief executive's commitment to liberalism, a commitment that was necessary, in Wagner's view, to curb this same executive's undoubted appetite for power.

By this time (March 28), Roosevelt had been in Warm Springs for five days. Leaving Washington on his special train on March 22, with news of another stock-market slump preying on his mind, he had interrupted his southward journey to make a speech indicating that he was again more than half persuaded of the need for renewed federal spending. It was concrete human necessity that he most clearly recognized, however, not that need for "compensatory spending" which the Keynesian economists stressed. In Gainesville, Georgia, at a celebration of the rebuilding of the town following a tornado that had devastated it, he said:

Today, national progress and national prosperity are being held back chiefly because of selfishness on the part of a few. If Gainesville had been faced with that . . . selfishness your city would not stand rebuilt as it is today. . . . This nation will never permanently get on the road to recovery if we leave the methods and the processes . . . to those who owned the Government of the United States from 1921 to 1933. They are the kind of people who, in 1936 [Gainesville's tornado year], were saying: "Oh, yes, we want nobody to starve"; but at the same time insisted that the balancing of the budget was more important than making appropriations for relief. And when I told them that I, too, wanted to balance the budget but that I put human lives ahead of dollars and handed them the government estimates and asked them just where they would cut the appropriations, inevitably they came back at me and said, "Mr. President, that is not my business, that is yours."

He mentioned only in passing the importance of "buying power" to "efficiency" and to "many other kinds of better things—better schools, better health, better hospitals, better highways."[25]

A few hours later he was joyously welcomed by his friends and neighbors in Warm Springs and plunged at once, joyfully, into the heated swimming pool, the socializing, the picnicking that were essential features of his Warm Springs life and by which he was revitalized, re-created, as he was nowhere else.

He remained headquartered in his resort cottage, the Little White House, for the remainder of the month.

IV

AND it was there and then that the logic of events developed at long last a conjunction of the spending and antimonopoly arguments to form a single pressure upon the presidential mind—a pressure great enough to overcome both Roosevelt's personal commitment to financial orthodoxy and the influence upon him of the budget-balancers joined with that of the planners.

Of the many elements that came together to form this finally decisive pressure, four may be distinctly discerned.

One was an early March memorandum to the President from Marriner Eccles, wherein the chairman of the Federal Reserve Board argued for increased federal spending in a way far more likely to persuade politican Roosevelt than the way taken in Keynes's letter. "We appear to be launched on a severe depression . . ." wrote Eccles, after reminding the President of his earlier warnings. "Big Business is utilizing the opportunity to drive for repeal [of the New Deal] and inaction. . . . The conciliatory attitude adopted by the Administration [toward business] has borne no fruits. . . . I urge you to provide the democratic leadership that will make our system function. Only in that way can the growing threat of Fascism be overcome. Congress should be provided with a reflation program, *now.* "[26]

A second element was an event that occurred almost simultaneously with the Eccles memorandum—namely, the sensational disclosure that Richard Whitney, the arrogantly aristocratic president of the New York Stock Exchange, who had led the fight against the legislation creating the Securities and Exchange Commission and remained one of the bitterest of big-business foes of the New Deal, was a common thief—common, that is, in the techniques he employed, uncommon in the amount he stole. The bankruptcy of his prestigious brokerage firm, Richard Whitney and Company, revealed that the head of the firm had systematically looted clients' accounts in a futile effort to cover his own market-gambling losses. (Whitney was subsequently convicted on several counts of embezzlement and sent to prison.) The event was a blow to the big-business community, which had been gaining back some of the prestige it had lost in the crash of 1929;[27] and by the same token it lessened the persuasive power over the presidential mind of probusiness advocacy.

A third element in the new pressure on Roosevelt was another sharp downturn in stock prices that were already far below those of last spring and summer, having drifted downward since the October break on a volume averaging some 27 percent less than last year's.* There had been an immediate positive stock-market response to the President's release on February 18 of the Morgenthau committee's memorandum. The business community evidently interpreted it, more certainly than the reporters did, as a move by the executive toward government-business cooperation. But this had proved a distressingly brief interruption of the prevailing downward trend. Hitler's seizure of Austria and announced intention to "liberate" Sudetenland Germans had been a severe securities-price depressant in the third week of March: Wall Street averages went down 3 points on March 16, lost another point on the seventeenth, went down nearly 2 points the next day, and, having gained back 1¾ points on the twenty-first, dropped nearly 3 on the following day and 3 points more on March 23. But the worst breaks came on March 25 (stock averages fell 4 points on high volume) and March 29 (the averages fell yet another 4 points), with declines of more than a point on March 30 and, again, on March 31. These market declines could not be attributed to events abroad; they undeniably reflected and presaged a further deterioration of the domestic economy as a whole, and they destroyed the last vestiges of Roosevelt's hope for a "natural" or laissez-faire recovery.

The fourth decisive element, coincident with the third, was the return to action of Harry Hopkins, whose absence from Washington and the President's counsels since mid-December may well have caused Roosevelt's period of indecision to be considerably longer than it would otherwise have been.

---

*According to the *Statistical Bulletin,* Standard Statistics, Inc., the average price of ninety stocks (twenty railroads, fifty industrials, and twenty public utilities) for March 1938 was 81.9 as compared with 143.7 for the same month in 1937, a loss of over 37 percent.[28]

· · ·

Certainly Roosevelt had missed Harry Hopkins personally, He enjoyed Hopkins's companionship immensely, and felt closer to Hopkins than he did to any other top New Deal official save (in a very different way) Henry Morgenthau. He saw in the younger man's attitude toward life, in his cynical idealism (or idealistic cynicism), similarities to the Louie Howe he had first known in the 1910s and had loved as he loved few others. He admired Hopkins's unique administrative talents and political realism, his commitment to the relief of needless human suffering; and when Roosevelt looked ahead to the 1940 election, he found himself focusing more and more upon Hopkins as a possible successor to him in the White House, incredible though this would have seemed to most outside observers if they had known of it.

During the most dangerous period following Hopkins's surgery for "ulcers" at the Mayo Clinic three months before, Roosevelt had asked for and received almost daily medical reports from Hopkins's doctors. He had responded with joyful relief to the news, conveyed in a letter from Hopkins to Marvin McIntyre, that no bad "post-operative effects" were occurring and that a "complete cure" was expected. (Actually the sick man had been told by his doctors that the odds against cancer recurrence were, in his case, no better than two to one.) "Missy has told me that you telephoned [her] on Saturday night," wrote Roosevelt to Hopkins on January 11. "I am sorry I had not returned from the [Jackson Day] speech, as it would have been grand to have talked with you. . . . We all had great fun with Diana [Hopkins's daughter] at Christmas time. She is a lovely youngster and stole the show that day. As you know . . . she is now at Jimmy's 'political' farm in Massachusetts where Jimmy and Bets say they are all having a grand time. . . . Do keep us in touch. . . ."[29]

And Hopkins had indeed kept in touch, not only with the White House but also with the developing national political and economic situation.

Discharged from the clinic, he journeyed south to convalesce, pausing for a few days in New Orleans as the guest of John Hertz, founder of the Yellow Cab Company, then establishing himself for two months in the Palm Beach home of Joe Kennedy, who had not yet departed for London where he would take up his duties as ambassador in March.* Considering the seriousness of

---

*Hopkins's increasing socialization with the very rich, his evidently growing fondness for luxurious pleasures that only the very rich could afford, was eyed askance by Eleanor Roosevelt. She and Secretary of Labor Frances Perkins had been instrumental in bringing Hopkins to Washington, and then into her husband's personal orbit. He was her warm friend before he became Franklin's; she continued to regard him as more her friend than Franklin's and to do all she could to advance him, in the White House and elsewhere. But she deplored his hedonism, feared it as a corrupting influence upon his character, and feared it also as a strengthening bond between him and her husband. For was it not closely akin to that playboy element of her husband's character, which was manifested (to cite one example) in a fondness for cruising, with companions as frivolous as they were wealthy, aboard Vincent Astor's luxury yacht? Was it not precisely this seeking of pleasure without regard for duty or obligation which had led to Franklin's infatuation with Lucy Mercer and the ruination of her marriage? And would not a strengthening of any such bond of fun between Harry and her husband mean a proportionate weakening of the bond of

the surgery he had undergone, Hopkins's recovery in Southern warmth and sunlight was remarkable both for rapidity and seeming completeness. Within a fortnight after his operation he was feeling far better physically than he had for many years, and this sense of restored physical health increased in the following weeks while his mind, freed of immediate attention-absorbing concerns, moved with abnormal swiftness and clarity of vision over the current national scene.

He was no more pleased than any other dedicated New Dealer by what he saw. Like Eccles, Ickes, Corcoran, and many a lesser light, he had become increasingly alarmed since the beginning of the recession by the President's prolonged basic policy indecision, and by the forceful moves of business into the power vacuum thus created. ("I see no signs of returning confidence on the part of the President," wrote a gloomy Ickes in his diary on March 28, after Roosevelt, in Warm Springs, had told him in a long-distance phone conversation that he was "feeling fine" and would be "coming back full of fight." Ickes could only hope "that if he finally wins his reorganization bill, as now [after the Senate action that day] seems quite likely, he will show some signs of fight."[31]) Like Eccles, Ickes, and Keynes, among others, Hopkins saw Roosevelt's prolonged inaction as a threat not just to the New Deal but to the very survival of democracy in an increasingly totalitarian world. ("I am terrified," Keynes had written Roosevelt in his February 1 letter, "lest progressive causes in all the democratic countries should suffer injury, because you have taken too lightly the risk to their prestige which would result from a failure measured in terms of immediate prosperity. There *need* be no [such] failure."[32]) Hopkins had been especially troubled by the amount and character of the opposition to executive reorganization, and by Roosevelt's seeming weakness in the face of it. For Hopkins was indeed slated to become the first secretary of social welfare, once the reorganization was made; and there had begun to grow in him a secret hope that this Cabinet post would lead to his becoming, with Roosevelt's blessing, his party's nominee for the presidency in 1940.

He was almost equally concerned over the fate of the Fair Labor Standards Bill (the Wage and Hour Bill, as it was commonly called), whose passage he deemed essential to the completion of the New Deal's labor legislation. This bill, it may be recalled, had been introduced by Hugo L. Black, then senator from Alabama, and William P. Connery of Massachusetts, then chairman of the House Labor Committee, in May 1937. It had at once run into fierce opposition from many of Black's Southern colleagues, who represented the low-wage employers of their region. (Southern white racists also feared the racial-equality implications of the proposal.) There had been opposition, too, from officials of the AFL, who feared that the legislation would weaken the appeal of unionization to presently unorganized workers while at the same

friendship between herself and Harry? She viewed such prospect with dismay, for she valued this friendship highly.[30]

time conferring advantages upon industrial unionism in the war between the CIO and AFL. Nevertheless, after much revision, the weakened bill had passed the Senate. In the House, however, it remained bottled up in John J. O'Connor's conservative Rules Committee when the acrimonious first session of the 75th Congress adjourned. It yet remained there at the end of the special session. And by January 1938, when the second regular session opened, with Black gone from the Senate to the Supreme Court and Connery gone from the House (he died in late 1937), many of the bill's supporters had become convinced that their cause was hopeless.

Hopkins, however, was by no means despairing. A decisive victory won in January by liberal Lister Hill over the reactionary Tom Heflin in a contest for Black's vacated senatorial seat, in Alabama, encouraged his belief that Roosevelt's political potency, and the New Deal's, were far greater than was now commonly believed by professional politicians. This in turn encouraged his optimism concerning the reelection chances of Senator Claude Pepper, an ardent New Dealer, who was running in the Florida Democratic primary against a conservative who was strongly backed by Florida's business community and who was making opposition to wage-and-hour legislation a plank of his campaign platform. Pepper could win with White House support—he could win big, Hopkins was convinced; and that victory would greatly aid congressional approval of the Wage and Hour Bill. Hopkins said as much to Jimmy Roosevelt when the latter came down in early February to visit his good friend Joe Kennedy. On February 6, having consulted his father by phone, Jimmy did indeed announce, in Palm Beach, that Pepper was the administration's candidate.

No, Hopkins was not despairing. With the highest ambition possible in American politics now added to his normal ambitions and concerns for the general welfare, he was more hopefully motivated than ever before. And by the time his prescribed convalescent period approached its end (his doctors had informed the White House that he must not return to work until April), he had settled upon some very definite conclusions about what should be done, politically as well as economically, to turn things around. He was preparing to argue for these at the White House when he received from there an invitation to come to Warm Springs as the President's guest for the last two days of March, thence to ride back to Washington with the President on the presidential special.

On Wednesday, March 30, the President heartily welcomed Hopkins in the Warm Springs cottage and congratulated him upon his healthy appearance. Hopkins came well armed with facts and figures about the economic situation, and with policy arguments written and oral. Before leaving Palm Beach, he had arranged to meet in Atlanta with three men whose economic expertise was greater than his but whose view of the situation in general was much the same as his. One of the three was the notably tough, outspoken, hard-driving Leon Henderson, who late last fall had argued in a letter to Hopkins that deficit financing and antimonopoly should be regarded, not as alternative policies, but as complementary elements of any sound recovery plan.[33] Another of the three was Beardsley Ruml, the burly, brilliant treasurer of the R. H. Macy Company, a tax expert whose recovery recipe joined "compensatory spending" to "incentive" tax-cutting, with the latter especially stressed. The third man was deputy WPA administrator Aubrey Williams, Hopkins's close friend, the most dedicated and consistent of liberals, who with the WPA staff had developed in considerable detail, during the winter now ended, a list of work-relief projects among which choices could be made for immediate launching if federal money became available for them. With these three men, Hopkins had spent a crowded day of discussion and memorandum-writing. The results were in the memoranda that he carried in his briefcase across the threshold of the Little White House next day; soon afterward the President was perusing them.

But this President, Hopkins happily discovered, actually required very little persuasion to go the way Hopkins wished him to go. He was already well headed in that direction. He raised no argument against the most important of these memoranda, being now as convinced as Hopkins had long been that his laissez-faire economic policy, with its wishful reliance on "free-market" forces to bring about "natural" recovery, wasn't working and must be abandoned. Budget-balancing would have to be indefinitely postponed again; large-scale federal spending would have to be resumed at once. And Roosevelt especially welcomed the concrete work-relief proposals, with price tags attached, that Williams had worked out, for they would help in the estimation and justification of new appropriations from Congress. Thereafter the talk between him and Hopkins had to do mostly with the practical political implementation of the basic decision now made. It included much talk about the "purging," in upcoming primary elections, of reactionaries from the Democratic contingent in Congress. Roosevelt had contemplated such a purge ever since the defeat of his court scheme, and Hopkins enthusiastically endorsed the idea.

With decision came liberation. A heavy weight was lifted from Roosevelt's mind; his long-oppressed spirits could again rise.

He continued to be anxious over the fate in the House of the reorganization bill, however, and spoke of this to Hopkins. On the day after the bill squeaked through the Senate, he had felt compelled to answer publicly the "charges in several newspapers" that the bill "would make me a Dictator." He had released to the press a letter to an anonymous "friend" in which he said that he was "as much opposed to American Dictatorship as you are, for three simple reasons. A. I have no inclination to be a dictator. B. I have none of the qualifications which would make me a successful dictator. C. I have too much knowledge of existing dictatorships to make me desire any form of dictatorship for a democracy like the United States of America." The sole purpose of the bill, which was "similar" to those recommended by "seven or eight of my immediate predecessors in the Presidency," was "to make the business end, i.e., the Executive branch, of the Federal Government more business-like and more efficient."[34]

But this letter had done little or nothing to reduce an opposition now actually hysterical. Two days hence, for instance, the editorial page of the Washington *Star* would declare that "passage of this bill would pave the way to sovietizing the United States."[35] Moreover, the issue now transcended that of the bill per se. In view of the enormous energies that had been invested on both sides of it, the issue might well be a make-or-break one for the administration as a whole.

All the same, when Roosevelt boarded his special train, with Hopkins beside him, on Friday, April 1, he was in better psychological shape, overall, than he had been for over a year.

An hour or so later, when the train passed through Atlanta, Ben Cohen and Robert Jackson boarded it. Cohen had with him a memorandum on which he and Corcoran had collaborated at Charleston, South Carolina, during preceding days—a memorandum arguing, as Henderson had argued, that renewed spending must be joined with a drive for restored market competition and flexible prices (that is, against monopoly and rigid prices) if spending were to increase mass purchasing power as effectively as it should. In the present state of managed prices in key industries, far too many federal dollars spent for recovery would end up, not in the hands of mass consumers, but in the already overstuffed pockets of upper-income groups. This, of course, was an argument in which Jackson concurred, and Roosevelt, whose own public opposition to monopoly had mainly stressed the threat that concentrated economic power poses to personal freedoms and political democracy, listened to it with a sympathetic ear. He did not, however, commit himself to trust-busting on any grand scale. Indeed, the recent appointment of Yale University's Thurman Arnold to head the antitrust division of the Justice Department seemed indicative of a belief on Roosevelt's part that trust-busting was a highly dubious exercise, for Arnold in his 1937 masterpiece of Veblenian irony, *The Folklore of Capitalism,* had ridiculed antitrust laws and the recurrent efforts to enforce them as sentimental gestures toward a dead past. Yet the Arnold appointment might also indicate an intention to move vigorously toward a federal control over giant business combinations sufficient to bring fixed prices into reasonable balance with flexible ones, for Arnold had damned antitrust law as not only sentimental but also a "protective rock" against the kind of governmental control over huge combinations that was both practical and necessary for the general welfare.[36] (It should perhaps be said here that Arnold, during the recently concluded Senate committee hearings on his appointment, had attempted in complicated, opaque language to deny what *Folklore* said much more sharply and clearly about antitrust law. He had been given a hard time by Senator Borah, to whom the Sherman and Clayton acts were sacred text. Nevertheless, he had been confirmed as assistant attorney general and was now about to launch the most vigorous effort ever made by the Justice Department to enforce the laws he had ridiculed.[37])

During his conferences on the train, Roosevelt went only so far as to approve a recommendation Leon Henderson had been making for years—that Congress be asked to launch a wide and deep study of the monopoly problem. Such a study, the findings of which would presumably provide a solid basis for reform legislation, would take a long time—many months, possibly years—and for that very reason was unlikely to be strongly opposed by conservatives, who feared immediate drastic action by government toward economic structural reform.[38] It was a time-honored device, as Thurman Arnold, among many others, had pointed out: If you can't or don't want to act on an issue but want to give the appearance of action, appoint a commission to study the matter.

The presidential special arrived in Washington on Saturday, April 2.

Six days later, on the morning of Friday, April 8, Harry Hopkins testified before a special Senate committee set up to investigate unemployment and relief. His testimony reflected the conclusions reached during the discussions at Warm Springs and on the returning train. The recession was caused, he said, by a decline in mass purchasing power brought about by the excessively high prices now being set by monopolistic industry. To promote recovery, therefore, government must act not only to increase consumer purchasing but also to increase competition "on a scale that we have not known for many years."[39]

And while Hopkins thus testified before the senators, he himself became a decisive issue in the minds of many representatives as the House debate on executive reorganization entered its final hours. On the day before, Hatton Sumners, chairman of the House Judiciary Committee, who had been denied direct access to the White House ever since he had publicly declared his opposition to the court-reform bill, had told House Speaker Bankhead and House Majority Leader Sam Rayburn that reorganization would probably be defeated unless the President removed from it the provision for a new public-welfare department, this because of the fear of Harry Hopkins as the new department's head. Why didn't the President submit the new department proposal as a separate bill? Reorganization would then be supported by twenty-five House members now prepared to vote against it, according to Sumners's estimate. Rayburn believed and said that Sumners was probably right. But he also said that any such approach to the President as Sumners suggested would be futile, the presidential mind being firmly made up and closed over this matter. Well, then, said Sumners, shrugging, "the bill will have to take its chances."[40]

Technically, what the House was debating on Friday the eighth was a motion to recommit the reorganization measure to the hostile Rules Committee, in effect killing it. The final vote was taken that night, and the motion won, which is to say reorganization lost, by eight votes. There were loud cheers in the gallery and on the floor when the result was announced.

The defeat was gleefully described by fervent anti–New Dealers, and by a majority of the opinion columnists of press and radio, as a vote of no confidence in the word, the character, the leadership of Franklin Roosevelt. What the "investing public" thought of it was indicated by stock-market performance: Stock prices were 2 to 6 points higher (they averaged 4.25 points higher) when the market opened on April 9 than they had been at the close on April 8, though there was no further advance as that day's trading continued.

It was a hard knock for Roosevelt, and he seemed to some of his close associates to wilt under the blow. He at once dashed off a brief letter to "Dear Sam" thanking him for "the fine fight" and asserting, against much contrary evidence, that "the question presented" had been "solely one of policy. Therefore the legislative developments of yesterday offer no occasion for personal recrimination, and there should be none." To this he appended in his own hand a thank-you note to Bankhead, couched in terms indicating that he intended no further fight on this front.

Harold Ickes and Tommy Corcoran were outraged when Steve Early showed them the signed but yet unmailed letter in Missy LeHand's office on Saturday morning. Ickes burst out that no such defeatist note should be struck; the President was "through" if he "takes this lying down." What Roosevelt ought to do was summon a special Cabinet meeting and let the members know that he was disgusted by the failure of some of them to go all out for this measure, and that he expected them to do so in an immediately upcoming battle to force the bill out of committee and onto the floor again. Consider, for instance, the fact that "practically all" of the "representatives particularly close to the department of agriculture had voted for recommittal." Was not that clear evidence that "Henry Wallace . . . could have saved the bill" all by himself? Why hadn't he? Obviously because he wanted at all costs to prevent transfer of the Forest Service from Agriculture to Interior. Corcoran, who sympathized with his friend Ickes's ambition to transform Interior into a Conservation Department headed by himself, agreed that the President had "now to show whether he is going out of office like Herbert Hoover or like Andrew Jackson." A few minutes later, the interior secretary voiced these views to Roosevelt himself in the Oval Office. ("I hit him with words, telling him he couldn't accept such a defeat. . . . I begged him to . . . fight.") He had little evident persuasive effect. Roosevelt finally agreed to remove from his Rayburn letter the personal postscript to the speaker, with its past-tense reference to reorganization, inserting instead in the body of the letter a request that Rayburn "also thank the Speaker." That, however, was the sum total of his concession to Ickes's wrath.[41]

V

In the evening of the following day, Sunday, April 10, Roosevelt had another interview with a hurt and angry Cabinet member.

Treasury Secretary Morgenthau had left Washington for a much-needed vacation at Sea Island, Georgia, a day or so after Roosevelt's departure for Warm Springs. He had then felt secure in his belief that the President, remaining true to his (and Morgenthau's) principles of "fiscal responsibility," had finally, if not as emphatically as Morgenthau would have liked, rejected the advice of the "spenders." This comforting belief was disturbed by a phone call from Henry Wallace on April 4. The President had returned from Warm Springs "rarin' to go," said Wallace; he had instructed Wallace to work with RFC head Jesse Jones on a federal program for housing, flood control, industrial loans, and rural rehabilitation, all of which would cost a great deal of money. Two days later, Morgenthau learned that the President also proposed large increases in WPA and CCC appropriations; that a revival of the Public Works Administration, with development of a national superhighway system as major project, was contemplated; and that the Treasury Department's research division, which the White House seemed not to have consulted, was opposed to increased public-works expenditures because they "would create anxiety within the business community." He was therefore himself in a state of anxiety when, during his train ride from Sea Island to Washington, he composed a "Memorandum for the President" in which, facing the bitter fact that a balanced budget for the coming year was now "out the window," to use a favorite phrase of Roosevelt's, he strove to keep as small as possible the inevitable deficit increase. Like Roosevelt, Morgenthau was naturally inclined toward a shotgun or scattershot attack on large problems. The attack proposed in this memorandum, which was conceived as the draft of a statement by the President on long- and short-range administration policy, included a little of almost everything that had been suggested thus far—a spending and lending program, though severely limited; the creation of a transportation authority (earlier Morgenthau had suggested to Roosevelt a Department of Transportation with Jesse Jones as its first secretary, a suggestion Roosevelt had seemed to approve); monopoly investigation and prosecution; the taxation of securities now tax-exempt; renewed efforts to eliminate governmental waste and inefficiency; desterilization of more gold; wage-and-hour legislation; and measures specifically aimed at fostering business "confidence" and thus increasing private employment.[42]

Morgenthau was rather proud of this effort when he reviewed it in typescript, upon his arrival in Washington. But when he carried it into the Oval Office a few hours later and saw waiting for him not only the President but also Hopkins and Jimmy Roosevelt, he had a sinking feeling that he had wasted his time and his energy.

Nor were his spirits lifted by Roosevelt's casually cheerful greeting.

"We have been traveling fast this last week," said the President, "and you will have to hurry to catch up."

"Mr. President, maybe I never can catch up," Morgenthau replied, gloomily.

"Oh, yes, you can—in a couple of hours."

Roosevelt smiled reassuringly, then launched into a presentation of what he proposed to do.[43]

It was a lengthy recital, and virtually every word of it fell as a stone's weight upon Morgenthau's spirits, dragging him down into the depths of despair. For one thing it was tacitly insulting to the treasury secretary, insofar as he had been excluded from decision-making within his own area of official responsibility. For another, it broke a promise that, Morgenthau felt, Roosevelt had implicitly made him. He read aloud his own memorandum after Roosevelt had finished, though doing so now seemed to him useless. Worse than useless. Then he said, in answer to a direct question by the President:

"What you have outlined not only frightens me but will frighten the country. How much is it going to cost?"

"Oh, we have all that . . . we have all that," said Roosevelt with airy impatience, though he named no cost figure.

"Please, Mr. President," pleaded an almost tearful secretary, "don't decide on this until you sleep on it."[44]

Yet he sensed that the decision was already made,

And the more Morgenthau thought about this during his own sleepless night, the more hurt and angry he became. Next morning he revealed his emotion to a meeting of his staff as he commented upon "what I heard last night," saying that "it just scared me to death," that it "hadn't been thought through," that Roosevelt at Warm Springs had been "stampeded" by the spenders. He vented the hurt given him by the fact that "they [Hopkins, Jimmy, the President] had a conference—lasted an hour before I came—in advance of my coming," which suggested that what "they" mainly talked about was ways and means of "handling" him to prevent his making any effective opposition to what "they" were determined to do. "I think the whole thing is finished, and there hasn't been a single person in the Treasury that knows a single thing about this."[45]

A few minutes later he was again in the White House, attending a conference in which the President told congressional leaders of the increases in emergency relief expenditures that the administration proposed to make: $1.25 billion more for WPA, $150 million for the Farm Security Administration, $50 million each for CCC and the National Youth Administration. Morgenthau was not called upon for a statement but, just as the meeting was about to adjourn, he made one anyway. The congressional leaders might be interested to know what these proposed spending increases would do to the federal deficit, he interjected, not without sarcasm. Taking into account the continuing steep decline in federal revenue (it would fall some $900 million below the January estimate, Treasury now believed), the proposed new spending would add, said Morgenthau, at least $3.5 billion to the deficit for 1939!

This had some of the immediate shock effect which Morgenthau intended.

It also angered Franklin Roosevelt.

At the outset of his weekly luncheon with the treasury secretary, immedi-

ately after the congressmen had left the Oval Room, Roosevelt said coldly that
Morgenthau had had no right to inject the deficit matter into the conference
without having first spoken to the President about it. He had been deliberately
mischievous, calculatedly obstructionist. And Roosevelt's voice rose, the palm
of his hand slapped hard the table at which they sat, as he said that, whether
determined by humanitarian considerations or by practical political necessity,
the top priority for the administration right now was relief for the unemployed.
This *must* be provided immediately, whatever its monetary cost. As for Morgenthau's reiterated belief that the final decision on this matter had been taken
behind his back, it was simply dead wrong.

"You can call Steve Early, and he will tell you that *nothing* is settled. You
are just jumping to conclusions."

"No use getting angry," Morgenthau protested, miserably. "No use yelling
at me. . . ."[46]

He was especially hurt by Roosevelt's implicit charge that he was indifferent
to the sufferings of the unemployed, or at any rate placed a higher priority on
a balanced budget than on relief of human suffering. He was in fact, as
Roosevelt well knew, more sensitive to the sufferings of others, and less inclined to interpose obstructive "theory" between compassionate impulse and
its practical efficacy, than were most of his New Deal colleagues.*

On the evening of the following day, Tuesday, April 12, the Treasury secretary was again in the Oval Room, this time to review and discuss the recovery
message that the President was to send Congress on Thursday. In attendance
were all the top officials directly concerned with fiscal and economic matters
—Hopkins, Eccles, RFC Director Jesse Jones, Budget Director Daniel Bell—
plus Interior's (and PWA's) Ickes, Secretary of State Hull, Postmaster General
Farley, Jimmy Roosevelt, and Steve Early. Despite his conviction that the final
policy decision had been made and was irrevocable, Morgenthau had armed
himself with a memorandum (Herman Oliphant, his chief adviser, had pre-

---

*A few weeks hence he would be embroiled in controversy with Henry Wallace and would be aided
by Eleanor Roosevelt as he struggled to revive the program of the Surplus Commodities Corporation. "I think from the day we started killing pigs, there has been a curse on this Administration,"
he would write in his diary on May 14. "The thing I'm trying to do now, instead of spending $100
million to grow less wheat, I want them to buy wheat and make it up into flour for people who
need it." He and Surgeon General Thomas Parran, whose Bureau of Public Health was in the
Treasury Department, and who had conducted a study of national dietary deficiencies, wanted
also to have surplus wheat used as cattle feed, distributing the consequent meat and dairy products
to the unemployed. The proposals were opposed by the secretary of agriculture because they would
allegedly depress farm prices. Moreover, said Wallace, substituting wheat for corn as cattle feed
would have bad political repercussions in the Corn Belt. Morgenthau also found, to his surprise
and disgust, that Harry Hopkins opposed any direct distribution of foodstuffs to the needy, on
the ground that such charity was humanly demeaning and might weaken work-relief and wage-
increase programs. (Hopkins's surprising stand on this matter is one of several seeming manifesta-
tions of the distorting effect his secret ambition was having at this time upon his value judgments,
his sense of priorities.) Only through strenuous effort would Morgenthau be able to stimulate
Wallace's distribution to the urban needy, through the Surplus Commodities Corporation, of
surplus wheat, beans, potatoes, dried prunes, and other fruits and vegetables, along with butter
and dried skim milk.[47]

pared it) that proposed, instead of increased spending, a purely monetary solution to the recession problem. More gold desterilization and the desterilization of close to $1 billion of government-held silver seigniorage, a devaluation of gold by another 10 points, the deployment of nearly $500 million held by Treasury as a working balance, the lowering of bank-reserve requirements by the Federal Reserve, inflation of the currency by some $3 billion under the Thomas Amendment to the Agricultural Adjustment Act of 1933*—these devices in tandem would stimulate business and increase employment without increasing the deficit. A desperate Morgenthau presented this to the conferees with all the argumentative force he could muster. But its only effect, utterly dismaying to him, was the addition of these monetary proposals to the increased-spending program that Hopkins outlined at that same meeting and that, by meeting's end, had become the main substance of the upcoming message.

It was near midnight when the meeting broke up.

And as Morgenthau went home to bed, there rang in his ears Daniel Bell's estimate, gloomily communicated to him at the meeting's close, that 1939's deficit would now exceed $4 billion, would perhaps go as high as $5 billion! Some $2 billion of this could be offset by desterilization and Social Security receipts, but there would remain between $2 billion and $3 billion, at the very least, to be raised by Treasury through securities sales on the financial market.[48] Could the market take it?

Morgenthau, at any rate, could not.

A war of contraries in his soul made horrid the pitch-dark hours of early morning (it was now Wednesday the thirteenth) as he tossed and turned on a sleepless bed. On one side were, of course, his commitments to fiscal orthodoxy, joined with the hurt he felt over the way Roosevelt had treated him. On the other side was his commitment to the administration's overall purpose and program, joined with the love and need he had for the man who had so greatly hurt him. His emotional attachment to Franklin Roosevelt, his psychological dependence upon him, were greater even than Ickes's. Since 1915, Roosevelt had been Morgenthau's neighbor and close friend. For more than a decade, Roosevelt had been the sun to his earth, warming him, vitalizing and energizing and magnetically compelling him, opening him up to fresh joyful experience, whose natural tendency was toward tight and tense self-closings. They had so much in common, these two. They shared patrician, benevolently paternalistic attitudes toward the Common Man; a love of country living amid the woods and hills, the fields and meadows of the Hudson Valley; and a love for the great slow tidal river, the mighty Hudson, which, though Morgenthau's home was not, like Roosevelt's, upon its bank, was thematic in both their lives and might serve as metaphor for, or symbol of, the stream of their fate, their destiny. Moreover, Morgenthau's wife, Elinor, a working associate of Eleanor Roosevelt in Democratic politics and in women's and civil-rights causes all

*See *FDR: The New Deal Years,* pp. 104–7.

through the 1920s, was as wholly absorbed into the Roosevelt life and career as he was.

Thus the agonizing inner contradiction. It was clearly impossible for him, Henry Morgenthau, to continue in an office for which he had been tacitly branded unfit by the man who had appointed him. He must resign at once. But it was equally clear that he could not tear himself away from Franklin Roosevelt in this fashion without rending his own vital fabric; to resign his post would be a suicidal act. A little later on that same morning of Wednesday the thirteenth, the suicidal act came very close to actual performance.

In a hastily arranged White House interview for which midmorning time was snatched out of a segment originally assigned to Bernard Baruch, a wan, tense Morgenthau told the President that he was "seriously thinking of resigning." Roosevelt, rather surprisingly, seems to have been surprised. Certainly he was dismayed. He was under enormous immediate work pressures that day. His message to Congress, to be delivered tomorrow, was yet far from being in final form; the drafting of the fireside chat he had scheduled for Thursday evening had not yet even been begun; an emergency phone call to Sam Rosenman in New York had brought him down for this difficult speechwriting chore. And Morgenthau, Roosevelt well knew, was no such chronic tactical "resigner" as Harold Ickes was. Roosevelt protested bitterly—all the more bitterly, perhaps, because of guilt feelings, for he knew he should have consulted his treasury secretary by phone while the latter was yet at Sea Island. He told Morgenthau that he had done "a grand job" at Treasury and that he needed him, but then charged his friend with yielding to a personal "pique" as petty as its consequences would be enormous and disastrous, should Morgenthau persist. By resigning now, on this issue, Morgenthau would not only wreck the administration's legislative program in the current congressional session, he would also destroy the Democratic party, assure the rise of a dangerously potent and extremist third party, and "go down in history" as a coward who had "quit under fire."

Morgenthau, almost physically ill, countered with a reiteration of his belief that the spending program could ruin the country. He flatly denied that personal pique was his prime motivation, though personal pique was surely justified by the way in which he had been treated. It was patently unfair of the President to ask "your general, in charge of finances, to carry out a program when he had nothing to do with the planning."

The meeting ended in impasse, with the President insisting that Morgenthau simply could not resign and the treasury secretary saying that he saw, in the circumstances, no alternative.[49]

Yet both must have known, deep down, even as the emotional fires raged highest within them, that the outcome of this quarrel was foreordained. For in the war of contraries within Morgenthau's soul, one side, that of love and psychological dependence, was far stronger than the other and had only to be reinforced by Roosevelt's expression of a complementary need and personal affection in order to prevail. The White House interview that day was the climax and substantially the end of Morgenthau's rebellion. Before the day was ended, he reluctantly, but also with great relief, accepted Roosevelt's conclusion: It was indeed impossible for him to resign.

The special message calling for a $3.7 billion spending and lending program was delivered to the Hill, fresh from the Government Printing Office, at noon next day. At ten-thirty that night, after a nap followed by a light dinner in bed, Roosevelt sat before a cluster of radio microphones in the White House and, with his familiar "My friends," began an unusually lengthy fireside chat, his first in five months. The final script for it had not been completed until after six o'clock, just four hours ago. ("This was the quickest job of speech writing that I ever had anything to do with," said Rosenman who, with Corcoran and Hopkins, had labored all day at it, working on a rough draft that had been completed by Roosevelt and his writing team at two-thirty the morning before.[50])

Barely a month had passed since Hitler's taking over of Austria, less than a week since the fall of Blum's Popular Front government in Paris and its replacement by an appeasement-minded government headed by Édouard Daladier. Even as the President spoke, Hitler intensified his pressure upon Czechoslovakia, and Franco's Spanish rebels closed in on the Mediterranean coast town of Vinaroz, completing a bloody drive that split Loyalist Spain in two. Roosevelt was impelled to stress, both in the message and in the fireside chat, the importance of American economic recovery to the preservation of American democracy in "a troubled world." He even essayed in his words to Congress a rare (for him) statement of commitment to free speech, though in muddled language that indicated a far from total commitment. He spoke of "schools of thought" existing "elsewhere" which "contend that . . . free speech and the free exchange of views will destroy democracies."* His own "conviction, on the contrary, is that the United States retaining free speech and a free exchange of views can furnish a dynamic example of successful government, *provided* [emphasis added] the Nation can unite on practical measures when the times call for unified action." For, he went on to say, the "driving force of a Nation lies in its spiritual purpose, made effective by free, tolerant *but* [emphasis added] unremitting national will." In the fireside chat he said that he had "waited patiently to see whether the forces of business itself would counteract" the economic "setback" and was acting as he now did only because "aggressive government steps" were obviously immediately necessary. He outlined these "steps" in considerable detail, then justified them in terms of the threats facing free governments. "Democracy has disappeared in several other great nations," he said, "not because the people of these nations disliked democracy, but because they had grown tired of unemployment and insecurity. . . . History proves that dictatorships do not grow out of strong and

---

*Corcoran's original draft probably had the totalitarian "contenders" asserting that democracy was doomed because free speech made decisive governmental action impossible.

successful governments, but out of weak and helpless ones. . . . Therefore, the only sure bulwark of continuing liberty is a government strong enough to protect the interests of the people, and a people strong enough and well enough informed to maintain its sovereign control over its government."[51]

Two weeks later (April 29) he sent to Congress his message on monopolies and the concentration of economic power. "Unhappy events abroad have retaught us two simple truths about the liberty of a democratic people," the message began. "The first truth is that liberty is not safe if the people tolerate the growth of private power to the point where it becomes stronger than that of their democratic state itself. That, in its essence, is Fascism. . . . The second truth is that the liberty of a democracy is not safe if its business system does not provide employment and produce and distribute goods in such a way as to sustain an acceptable standard of living." Such provision and distribution were militated against in the United States by excessive concentrations of private wealth and power. Roosevelt cited highly disturbing statistics gathered by the Bureau of Internal Revenue and the Natural Resources Committee. One-tenth of 1 percent of all America's corporations owned 52 percent of the national total of corporate assets; less than 5 percent owned 87 percent of these assets. One-tenth of 1 percent of the corporations obtained half the net income of corporate America; 4 percent obtained 84 percent of the net profits. Nor was the "danger of this centralization . . . reduced or eliminated, as is sometimes urged, by the wide public distribution of their securities." Stock ownership was also concentrated "in the hands of a tiny minority of the population." Even in 1929, which was "a banner year for distribution of stock ownership," three-tenths of 1 percent of the population received 78 percent of the dividends reported by individuals to Internal Revenue. And the distorted national pattern of personal income distribution reflected the concentration of capital ownership. In 1935–1936, 47 percent of all American families and single-individual households had incomes of less than $1,000 a year while "at the other end of the ladder a little less than 1½ percent . . . received incomes which in dollars and cents reached the same total as the incomes of the 47 percent at the bottom." He quoted Daniel Webster, though without naming that great Whig orator: "The freest government, if it could exist, would not be long acceptable if the tendency of the laws were to create a rapid accumulation of property in a few hands, and to render the great mass of the population dependent and penniless."[52]

But having thus defined the problem, he went no further in proposals for its solution than he had done during his train ride back from Warm Springs. Congress, he said, should revise antitrust law in ways that would make it more practically enforceable. For instance, "identical bids, uniform price increases, price leadership, higher domestic than export prices, or other price rigidities might be accepted as *prima facie* evidence of unlawful action"; and, as a "deterrent to personal wrong-doing, I would suggest that where a corporation is enjoined from violating the law, the court might be empowered to enjoin the corporation for a specified period of time from giving any remunerative employment or any official position to any person who has been found to bear responsibility for the wrongful corporate action." Congress should also make possible a "more rigid scrutiny through the Federal Trade Commission and the Securities and Exchange Commission of corporate mergers, consolidations and acquisitions than that now provided by the Clayton Act to prevent their consummation when not clearly in the public interest; more effective methods for breaking up interlocking relationships and like devices for bestowing business by favor." Certainly the federal government should have a greater control over bank holding companies.

His major proposal, however, was the one he had agreed to on the train. He called for an appropriation of $500,000 for a "thorough study of the concentration of economic power . . . and the effect of that concentration upon the decline of competition." The study should include examination of the prevailing industrial price system and pricing policies to determine their effect on trade, employment, consumption, and long-term profits—also, the "effects of tax, patent and other government policies."[53]

Raymond Moley, observing it all as a journalist from a post well outside the administration he had once intimately served, saw "this request for a study" as a mere playing for time, a putting off of "the adoption of a guiding economic philosophy," and a sop to "nagging subordinates" who recognized "that an administration which was of two minds" regarding the relationship of government to business "would contradict itself into disaster." Certainly, the request was, as Moley saw it, "the final expression of Roosevelt's personal indecision" about "this all-important question."[54]

VI

WE may anticipate here the enactment and the effect of the legislation that came out of these two messages. Each of the two bills was extensively debated, the spending bill especially; each was revised by each house in ways that required much work in conference committee; but in the end, each went through both houses with a large majority, and on June 16, the last day of that congressional session, was sent to the President's desk for signature.

During the following six and a half months, WPA expenditures were some half-billion dollars more than they had been during the last half of 1937 ($1.5 billion as compared with $1 billion), while AAA expenditures were four times as great as they had been during the same period of the year before—and there were proportionately large increases in public-works spending. To this were added large increases in defense spending, Congress having passed the administration's $1.2 billion naval-expansion bill on May 13.

The immediate effect upon the national economy was as Eccles and his fellow "spenders" had predicted: The decline was halted, and recovery begun. It was a moderate recovery, gaining back by year's end only part of the ground lost during the last half of 1937 and the first half of 1938—which is to say that, though human misery was far less than it had been in early 1933, genuine prosperity remained for Roosevelt, as it had for Hoover, "around the corner." In its *Guaranty Survey* of December 27, 1938, the Guaranty Trust Company of New York noted that the

> significant contrast between the present situation and that a year ago lies not in the level of activity but in the trend. At the end of 1937, industrial output and trade volumes had been decreasing steadily for nearly five months at one of the swiftest rates on record . . . and business had become aware that it was undergoing not a minor adjustment but a major recession. . . . At present, on the other hand, activity has been increasing continuously for nearly seven months, although at a pace by no means equaling that of the decline.

The "revival" had "apparently regained at least half the ground lost in the recession." For instance, automobile production between January 1 and December 1 of 1938 totaled only 2,101,209 units as compared with 4,482,740 and 3,955,405 for the corresponding periods of 1937 and 1936, but the November 1938 production was 372,358 units, as compared with 360,055 for the same month of 1937. Similarly with pig-iron production: It totaled only 18,774,000 tons in 1938 as compared with 36,612,000 tons in 1937, but the production for December 1938 was 2,270,000 tons, as compared with only 1,494,000 for the corresponding month of the year before.[55]

The unemployment figures were less satisfactory by far. The decline in employment, which, beginning in September 1937, had been precipitous in that month and the three that followed, and had continued through the first six months of 1938, though less steeply, was halted in July 1938. The upturn that then began caused employment increases in August and September that were greater than the normal seasonal gain. The factory-employment index in October stood 9 percent higher than it had in June, but it remained 17 percent below what it had been in October 1937, and in that earlier month the employment situation had been far from satisfactory. In early December 1938, an authoritative estimate presented to the Temporary National Economic Committee* "gave the total of employed persons in October 1938, including agriculture but excluding relief work [that is, WPA and CCC employment], as about 44,231,000 and the total labor supply as about 55,000,000, the estimate of unemployment thus being somewhat less than 11,000,000." It was further estimated "that the volume of industrial production would need to rise about 40 percent above the level of the latter part [that is, the relatively prosperous part] of 1938 to reduce unemployment to the same percentage of the working population as in 1929. Such estimates are rough approximations . . . but serve to indicate the gravity and persistence of the problem of unemployment."[56] And this stubborn persistence in turn served to indicate to some makers of public opinion, six years after the New Deal began, that the unemployment problem just might not be soluble within a "mature" capitalist economy—that

*See p. 232.

high unemployment must from now on be accepted as a permanent feature of American society.

People of the Brandeisian persuasion, however, resisted this despairing conclusion. They continued to insist that unemployment could be greatly reduced, if not eliminated, by a strict enforcement of antitrust law and a consequent restoration of "free competition." The President had spoken for these when he said in his message to Congress that the "basic purpose" of his program was "to stop the progress of collectivism in business and turn business back to the democratic competitive order. . . . Once it is realized," he had gone on to say, "that business monopoly in America paralyzes the system of free enterprise on which it is grafted . . . action by the government to eliminate these artificial restraints will be welcomed by industry throughout the nation. For idle factories and idle workers profit no man."[57]

Others, having less faith in free-market solutions, hence more inclined toward "national-planning" solutions, challenged the dark conclusion about unemployment with basic questions. If high unemployment was "inevitable" in an industrially advanced capitalist system, what in that system made it so? Was the causal factor a *fundamental* contradiction inherent in highly industrialized capitalism—a contradiction between, on the one hand, individual private profit as prime economic motivation and, on the other hand, the ever closer, ever tighter economic interdependencies, and the consequent need for large-scale planning and organization, which technological advance implies? If so, were not truly *fundamental* structural changes needed to tame a monstrous and growing technology that was now out of control, and to harness it to truly human personal needs, truly humane social purposes? And must not these be changes that expressed and emphasized the generous, cooperative, spiritual elements of the human person instead of the selfish, acquisitive, physically appetitive elements upon which the prevailing system placed its greatest emphasis?

The people who asked such questions were, along with the Brandeisians, the same people who had pressed hardest for the unprecedentedly wide and deep study of American business that issued from Roosevelt's antimonopoly message, and who now hoped for the most from it.

What Roosevelt had originally intended was an inquiry conducted by the executive branch of government. What Congress enacted was legislation, introduced by Wyoming's senator Joseph C. O'Mahoney, establishing a joint legislative-executive committee of inquiry. It was composed of three senators (O'Mahoney, Borah of Idaho, William King of Utah), appointed by the vice president; three congressmen (Texas's Hatton Sumners, Tennessee's B. Carroll Reece, Iowa's Edward C. Eicher), appointed by the speaker of the House; and six representatives of executive agencies appointed by the respective heads of those agencies. They were Thurman Arnold of the Justice Department, Herman Oliphant of the Treasury Department, Isador Lubin of the Labor Department, Richard Patterson of the Commerce Department, William O. Douglas

of the SEC, and Garland Ferguson of the Federal Trade Commission. Leon
Henderson was named the committee's executive secretary. And when this
Temporary National Economic Committee (TNEC) opened public hearings
on December 1, 1938, the probability seemed great, to the well-informed, that
antitrust sentiment would dominate its proceedings and find ultimate expression in definite, fact-informed proposals for new legislation to reduce corporations' size and to halt, then reverse, the prevailing trend toward bigness.
Certainly a large majority of the committee and its staff were on record as
alarmed by, and hostile to, current monopolistic trends, being convinced that
these threatened not only the nation's economic well-being but also the essential liberties of private citizens. Indeed, of the TNEC's congressional members
only Senator King, and of the executive branch only Commerce's Patterson,
were staunch defenders of the big corporation as necessary and good. But, as
has been indicated, there were immediate basic disagreements among the
antitrust majority about the nature of the problem and its proper solution.
These disagreements, which might have been removed (resolved in a "higher
synthesis") had they been squarely faced and fairly argued, did not in fact
diminish as the work proceeded. This rendered impossible even a truly comprehensive conception of the prevailing situation. For the ground the committee was assigned to cover, comprising nothing less than the essential workings
of the whole of American industry, commerce, and finance, was huge beyond
individual or committee understanding in the absence of clear, generally accepted ideas about that ground's elemental composition.

None could fault the committee for lack of diligence and energy, however.
The hearings, which began on December 1, 1938, continued, with interruptions,
until late April 1940, by which time there had been accumulated an enormous
amount of information about every portion and aspect of American business.
Thirty-one large volumes (seventeen thousand printed pages) of testimony
were published. To these were added forty-three published monographs prepared by various agencies at the bidding of the TNEC and bearing such titles
as *Technology in Our Economy, Control of the Petroleum Industry by Major
Oil Companies, Economic Power and Political Pressures, Patents and Free
Enterprise, Who Pays the Taxes?, The Distribution of Ownership in the Two
Hundred Largest Non-financial Corporations,* and *Taxation, Recovery, and
Defense.* As source material for future students of the economy, this published
work, stored on library shelves, was to prove invaluable.

But since the committee remained as divided of mind and counsel at the end
of its study as it had been in the beginning, there issued from all its mountain
of labor, in preliminary and final reports dated July 17, 1939, and March 31,
1941, respectively, only a few feeble mice of legislative recommendation. Moreover, virtually every published conclusion of the committee majority about
basic concerns was dissented from, in published statement, by a committee
minority.

Perhaps the most important majority recommendation was for legislation
authorizing the FTC to forbid any corporation's acquisition of the assets of a

competing corporation unless that corporation could prove that the acquisition increased efficiency, was in the public interest, and did not "substantially decrease competition."[58] But it came as a surprise to many people that the FTC did not *already* have, under the Clayton Act, the power here recommended for it; and it would have been an even greater surprise to informed observers if, should the recommended legislation be enacted, the result was a prevention of further increases in concentrated economic power. For the FTC, which was to be the final judge of the merits of the cases made by acquisitive corporations, had throughout its history proved notoriously reluctant to exercise the regulatory powers in its hands. To such informed observers it would appear that Congress, by assigning to the FTC the task of deciding whether a proposed merger was monopolistic, would shift to a regulatory body of the executive branch a function constitutionally assigned to Congress itself. What Congress ought to do—what the framers of the Constitution had quite clearly intended Congress to do in such matters—was define legislatively the evil to be removed and prevented, then define with precision the means of remedy, then state the penalties to be imposed for violations of the law.

Most of the other final TNEC recommendations were innocuous when not trivial. There was TNEC "commendation and approval" of such government programs for "the less privileged" as food stamps, slum clearance, low-cost housing, "the extension of hospital and medical facilities, and the development of vocational and cultural opportunities." Legislation was recommended "establishing a committee on federal-state relationships, charged with the responsibility of collecting current information as to trade practices among the states and with a duty of devising ways and means of preventing uneconomic barriers to trade"—also legislation "to deal [just how remained unspecified] with the control now exercised by foreign governments and their industry over American concerns through patent laws." No federal regulation of life-insurance companies was required "at present," said the TNEC majority, but "officers and directors of insurance companies operating in more than one state" should be prevented "from using their positions for improper personal gain directly or indirectly."[59]

Thus the great monopoly investigation proceeded and ended as Raymond Moley, on the basis of his sour view of it, would have predicted when it began. The immense research effort proved to be typically New Dealish, typically Rooseveltian, insofar as it blurred fundamental issues and refused basic decision, this on the eve of a world war whose pressures, if the status quo were maintained, would create an America dominated by big business, and at the mercy of irresponsible private power exercised through giant corporations, as America had never been before, not even in the palmiest days of the New Economic Era.

Long before the final TNEC report was issued, Thurman Arnold had ceased to attend committee meetings with any regularity. He was too busy with the actual enforcement of antitrust law to be much interested in a "study group" that was merely "grinding out academic monographs."[60] And during his first years in the Justice Department, when he was fully supported by the President, he scored remarkable successes. He was enabled by additional appropriations to increase the number of lawyers in the antitrust division from forty-five to more than three hundred—an increase required by his decision to proceed on a case-by-case basis.* Thereafter, operating in a blaze of publicity, to which he personally was not at all averse, Arnold initiated criminal prosecutions in unprecedented numbers, conducted them with unprecedented vigor, supplemented them with a highly creative use of the consent-decree device, and thus actually effected some slight reduction in "concentrated private economic power," a reduction reflected by lower prices, in several instances, as competition was increased. Arnold did so in the area of automobile financing by negotiating consent decrees with Ford and Chrysler whereby these corporations agreed to abandon requirements that their dealers do business with stipulated finance companies. He did so through criminal indictments of two huge dairy corporations, Borden and National Dairy Products. According to Arnold, the greatly publicized Borden investigation alone resulted in a dramatic drop in the price of milk (from thirteen cents a quart to nine).[61] His bold move against the Aluminum Company of America (ALCOA), though it failed to break up that Mellon corporation, helped encourage competition by new concerns in the theretofore monopolized field of aluminum production, thus stimulating production and lowering prices. This was of immense importance to the war economy, which was by that time being developed.

Alas, however, for the long-range effectiveness of Arnold's antimonopoly effort, the President would withdraw his support from it just as it seemed about to effect some truly important market changes. As the 1930s gave way to the 1940s, and as we shall see in considerable detail as this history proceeds, national security through rearmament took precedence over all else in Roosevelt's mind—a collector's mind, which, though remarkably acquisitive of facts and ideas, could deal with these only as distinct and separate items, applying to them a system of priorities that was wholly external to them. The President began to look upon the antimonopoly effort as not merely less important by far than the defense effort but actually inimical to it. He rejected, or did not recognize at all, the possibility that antimonopoly could be made a part of the defense effort in ways that not only increased war production but also preserved or increased democratic freedoms in America. Hence, when Arnold requested increases in the Antitrust Division budget for 1941 and 1942, increases essential to the completion of highly important cases for which preparations were already made, his requests were denied.

In sum, this first serious attempt to enforce antitrust law in ways that truly released free-market forces in industrial America would prove a failure, overall. And there would not be effective development and application of the

---

*The alternative to this, clearly impractical, would have been a comprehensive, industrywide attack by the Justice Department upon monopolistic practices.

alternative to Brandeisianism, namely, national economic planning in the public interest, implemented through increased and strengthened federal regulation. Prevailing trends would continue. The management of giant corporations would have an ever wider and ever tighter control of the economic, the social, the political life of America. And since corporate management was itself increasingly "managed" by technological imperatives, the large-scale effect would be an accelerating growth of technological tyranny. In more and more ways, the individual person would become subordinate to the machine. He would be ruled by the "laws" of machine "efficiency," would function actually as an adjunct of the machine insofar as his consumption of machine products in ever increasing volume, whether he really wanted to or not and regardless of disastrous environmental effect, was an essential of the profit system's survival.

VII

BUT to return to the closing weeks of the second regular session of the 75th Congress.

Two major pieces of legislation were enacted, in addition to the spending and antimonopoly bills, in the late spring of 1938. One of them seemed to many observers a further manifestation of Roosevelt's loss of political potency. The other was, at the very least, a resounding echo of the New Deal effectively ended the year before by Roosevelt's disastrous court-packing effort. It is an echo that yet reverberates down the corridor of years.

The first of the two to be passed, namely, the revenue act of 1938, was displeasing to the President because it virtually nullified the graduated tax on undistributed corporate surpluses, which had been imposed (more in principle than in fact) by the revenue act of 1936; and it abandoned altogether the graduated-tax principle by imposing a flat 15 percent tax on capital gains.

Admittedly, 1936's revenue act had been, in its central portions, an effort to achieve social and economic reform goals through exercise of the federal taxing power. It had been, in part, an "anti-bigness" measure, designed by Brandeisians to discourage inordinate corporate growth, to encourage a decentralization of economic power. And it had been initially supported by some small-business men while being bitterly and unanimously attacked by big business. In practice, however, the undistributed-profits tax, insofar as it had had any effect at all during the last year (the graduated rate imposed was not great enough to have much effect), seemed to have done more to prevent the building-up of necessary reserves by small businesses than to discourage tax-dodging and excessive growth by large ones. For this reason there developed a considerable opposition within the administration itself to the present tax law, if not to the whole undistributed-profits-tax idea, and this disagreement was not along the usual lines of conservative versus liberal. Such administration conservatives as Jesse Jones of the RFC, Joseph Eastman of the ICC (the tax worked against needed railroad refinancing, Eastman believed), and Joseph

Kennedy were, of course, opposed to the tax, but so were Hopkins and Eccles, both of whom now thought that, by inciting a "strike by capital," the tax had helped bring on and might now be prolonging the recession. Such fiscal conservatives as Treasury's Morgenthau and Oliphant, on the other hand, concerned with revenue enhancement as well as antimonopoly, favored not only retention of this tax but also a sharp increase in its progressiveness (that is, in the steepness of the tax-increase gradient), In 1936, as the economic historian Ellis W. Hawley writes, these fiscal conservatives had "argued that the tax would strike a blow . . . particularly against the managerial elite that controlled investment decisions, limited investment opportunities, and deprived stockholders of any decision as to how their funds would be used." Two years later, they still believed that the tax worked toward a "democratization" of corporate finance, "forcing large corporations to compete for their new funds in the money market, and restoring financial control to the stockholders."[62] To prevent hardship for small businesses, they now favored, as did the President, modifications of the 1936 act whereby small business would have preferential treatment.

Congress, however, in the aftermath of the court battle and in the midst of a recession, was in no antibusiness or social-reform mood, as we have seen. The revenue bill passed by the House on March 11 by the overwhelming vote of 203–97 did contain a greatly modified undistributed-profits tax provision, and this was restored to the bill in conference committee after the Senate had completely eliminated it, but the restoration was for a specified and severely limited period (1938–1939) only.

Hence, as finally sent to the White House, the bill presented the President with a dilemma.

He discussed it on May 27 in a nationally broadcast high school commencement address at Arthurdale, West Virginia. Arthurdale was the federal subsistence homestead project that had been famous (or notorious) since the summer of 1933 as "Eleanor's baby,"* and this was Roosevelt's first visit to it. But he greeted his audience as "old friends because you are Mrs. Roosevelt's old friends and . . . I have heard so much about you." He spoke of the administration's overriding purpose and effort to improve the material life of ordinary American citizens. But the newsworthy portion of his speech had to do with the "new tax bill" which Congress had passed "last week." It contained, he said, "many good features—improvements in tax administration, the elimination of a number of nuisance taxes . . . , the lightening of the tax burden on small corporations, in accordance with what I recommended to the Congress last fall." The bill also "retains the principle" of the undistributed-profits tax, but only the principle: "The penalty for . . . large corporations for withholding dividends to their stockholders has been made so small—only two and a half percent at the most—that it is doubtful, very doubtful whether it will . . . eliminate the old tax avoidance practices of the past." As for the "progressive

*See *FDR: The New Deal Years,* pp. 349–55, 373–75.

tax principle with respect to capital gains," it was wholly eliminated. "Small capital profits and large capital profits" were to be taxed at exactly the same rate. "That, my friends, is not right." More than 80 percent of the capital gains reported were "profits made in the stock market—profits made not by developing new companies, not by starting new industries the way they are being started in Arthurdale, oh, no, but profits made by buying stocks of old companies, buying them low and selling them high, or by . . . selling stocks short—selling stocks you do not own—and then buying them at a lower price."

Hence his dilemma: "If I sign the bill—and I have until midnight tonight to sign it—many people . . . will think I approve the abandonment of an important principle of American taxation. If I veto the bill, it will prevent many of the desirable features of it from going into effect." He had therefore decided neither to sign nor to veto. "For the first time since I have been President," he announced, "I am going to take the third course which is open to me under the Constitution. At midnight tonight the new tax bill will automatically become law; but it will become law without my signature or my approval."[63]

The other major piece of 1938 legislation was the Fair Labor Standards Act —the wage-and-hour law.

We have told of the despair of many of the supporters of this measure in January 1938, of Harry Hopkins's refusal to despair, and of Hopkins's insistence that an all-out fight for the measure would win. Another who refused and insisted in this way was Senator Wagner. Indeed, Wagner's support of the bill was so emphatic, so constantly reiterated, that much of the general public believed him to be its author. In this instance, thanks in part to Hopkins's influence, he had a firm ally in the President. Compromises, some of them excruciatingly painful to the bill's proponents, were made during the legislative debate. A North–South wage differential was written into the bill, then taken out, then partially effected in other ways. Exemptions were inserted in distressingly large number. But there remained the essential principle of a floor under wages, a ceiling over hours, governmentally guaranteed in ways that protected otherwise defenseless unorganized workers—and to the statutory embodiment of this principle Roosevelt committed himself almost as strongly and actively as he did to the battle for executive reorganization.

He resorted, as of old, to wily stratagem.

Senator Claude Pepper's aforementioned battle for renomination in Florida's Democratic primary, to be held on May 3, had by early April attracted national attention. Its outcome was deemed a measure of Roosevelt's current strength at the polls, hence a prophetic judgment upon the upcoming midterm elections; for the White House, as we have said, had endorsed Pepper as the administration's candidate in early February. Ever since, Pepper's opponent, riding high the current wave of anti-Roosevelt reaction and playing heavily upon regional fears and prejudices, had proclaimed more and more loudly his opposition to the Wage and Hour Bill. (He also reportedly told backwoods crowds in tones of pious horror that Pepper had been guilty of "celibacy" before his marriage and addicted to "monogamy" ever since.) And, as April advanced, the belief had grown among professional politicians, political commentators, and the public at large that Pepper's defeat was virtually certain. Pepper himself, however, remained confident that he would win if only he obtained enough campaign money. Money was his problem; his opponent's campaign funding was great, his own meager. He said as much to his friend Tommy Corcoran (he and Corcoran had been classmates at Harvard Law School), and Corcoran, who had the greatest respect for Pepper's political acumen, passed the information on to Roosevelt. The latter at once authorized the secret raising of money for Pepper by Corcoran who, with the aid of others of Roosevelt's inner circle, did so very effectively. (According to historian James MacGregor Burns, "at least $10,000 was turned over to Pepper's campaign managers by Roosevelt's assistants, who had got the money from a radio corporation executive on the basis of another deal.") He also easily persuaded Pepper to make the wage-and-hour bill his own major campaign issue. Pepper argued for it fervently in his every speech thereafter.[64]

And on May 3, Claude Pepper did win the Florida primary, and by a wide margin, his renomination being, of course, tantamount to reelection in that one-party state.

The effect, according to an exuberant Corcoran and Cohen, was to make Claude Pepper "the father of the Fair Labor Standards Act."[65] The bill had been reported out of the House Labor Committee, now chaired by New Jersey's Mary T. Norton, on April 21. It had gone then to the Rules Committee. To tear it out of this committee's conservative clutches required 218 House member signatures on a discharge petition. They were obtained in just two hours and twenty minutes after the petition was opened for signatures on the morning of May 6.[66] Two weeks later, on May 24, after twelve hours of stormy debate, the House passed the bill, 314–7. This was not the end of its troubles. The House version now differed greatly from the bill the Senate had passed a year ago, and the resolution of the differences required a pitched battle in conference committee between Southern supporters of a North–South wage differential and supporters of the AFL version, which the House had passed. Further compromises had to be made. But the regional wage differential was not in the bill that the conference committee finally reported and that then sailed through the House, 291–89, on June 14. It went through the Senate on that same day without even a recorded vote.

The new law reestablished the ban on child labor, which had been first written into 1933's ill-fated National Industrial Recovery Act. It established a minimum wage of twenty-five cents an hour for the first year of the act's operation, of thirty cents for the next six years, and forty cents thereafter, and a workweek maximum of forty hours to be effective after two years (a forty-four-hour week was permissible the first year, a forty-two-hour week the second), with overtime to be compensated at 1½ times the normal rate. The act was to be administered by a Wage and Hour Division of the Labor Department, which was to be advised by committees representing each interstate industry.*

As things turned out, this measure was the last of the New Deal's major social reforms; it was also one of the most important—almost as important, in long-term effect, as Social Security. Indeed, Isador Lubin, the brilliant Labor Department statistician, thought it more important than Social Security. He claimed that, "in its philosophical base" and in the number of people it affected (that is, the great mass of unorganized workers), it was "the most vital social legislation" in the nation's history.[67]

Also enacted during the closing days of the session, in greatly weakened form, was the Food, Drug, and Cosmetics Bill, which in its strong original form had been known, and damned by business interests, as the "Tugwell Bill." It replaced the 1906 Food and Drug Act, which was repealed, and it improved considerably upon the consumer-protecting provisions of the earlier law. It provided that no new drug could go on the market without "adequate testing"; that, with some exceptions, all ingredients of foods, drugs, and cosmetics must be named on containers; that all habit-forming drugs be clearly labeled; and that the strength, quality, and purity of drugs be noted on containers. But it contained numerous loopholes through which corporate lawyers could operate to frustrate its purposes, and it said nothing about false and misleading advertising, whose definition and prohibition, in the original proposal, had provoked furious opposition by the advertising industry, the drug and cosmetics industries (cosmetics especially), and the proprietors of press and radio.

## VIII

As Arthur Krock of *The New York Times* surveyed the Washington scene on June 16, the day Congress adjourned, he was amazed by the extent of Roosevelt's recovery of power over the legislative body during the last two and a half months. It was a power that had seemed irretrievably lost in late 1937 and early 1938. Roosevelt had accomplished what Krock called a "historic feat" and "a political miracle," by "regaining control of a balky Congress in the middle of his second term [when there is normally a marked loss of presidential power over legislators] and during a growing depression [which, one would think, should have increased the power loss]." "But perhaps there is a reasonable explanation of the paradox," Krock went on to say, adding wishfully that "such future control by Mr. Roosevelt over Congress" was not likely "to be witnessed." Roosevelt was amused in his turn, and grimly amused (Krock was

---

*It would become traditional, in the years ahead, for Congress to adjust the minimum wage to inflation by setting it at half the current average hourly wage in private employment—a tradition followed by all administrations until that of Ronald Reagan. The minimum was $3.35 an hour in 1981; it remained at that figure until 1989.

almost if not quite his least favorite journalist), when he read Krock's "reasonable explanation" while breakfasting next morning. It ran as follows:

> The chief victims of the depression are the least numerous classes of the population. Obviously they have fewer votes than the classes less affected, or actually benefitted, by what has happened to employment and industry in this country. Organized labor, with considerable ability to marshal its members at the polls, acknowledges a political debt to the President. The very poor, chief beneficiaries of relief (and these include the bulk of the Negroes who in 1936 held the political balance in several great States), have not wavered in their gratitude for Washington's generous, unexacting [*sic*], helping hand. These constitute, in the view of Congress, the majority of voters. . . . Therefore, the depression has—at least temporarily—made the President seem politically stronger.[68]

Roosevelt himself saw the matter in a somewhat different light, we may be sure.

He knew that the theretofore ebbing tide of his political fortunes had turned because of his forced and belated recognition that those who were the "chief victims of the depression" in Krock's view (that is, the business community) were unwilling or unable to do what was necessary to turn things around. He had then made the decision to resume spending; and, as part and parcel of this decision, begun to exert firm and forceful leadership on behalf of those who were *in actual fact* the most "numerous classes of the population" and the depression's "chief victims," namely, people of middle and low income and those (the unemployed, the disabled, the indigent elderly) who had no income at all. He knew, too, that one reason he had not suffered the normal loss of power over Congress was that congressional members were uncertain about his plans for 1940. He just might run for an unprecedented third term. He might feel compelled to do so by the developing world crisis, according to some leading opinion-makers, since, they said, he alone among all possible candidates would have, two years hence, the world prestige, the experience, and the practiced skills adequate for successful presidential dealings with that crisis. Roosevelt himself had taken care not to erase this modicum of uncertainty from the public and congressional minds. He had reiterated on every suitable occasion his wish and intent to retire to private life in January 1941, but never had he said flatly, unequivocally, that he would retire. He had learned from Theodore Roosevelt's mistake in announcing, immediately after the 1904 election, that he would "under no circumstances" be a candidate for reelection in 1908, this because of his reverence for "the wise custom which limits the President to two terms." The announcement had made Congress much less responsive to White House wishes, following the 1906 midterm elections, than it would otherwise have been.

Running again in 1940, however, seemed to him so remote a possibility in this spring of 1938 that it entered hardly at all into his plans for the years ahead.

He was concerned far more with his and the New Deal's place in history.

More than a year before, while in the midst of his Supreme Court battle, he had arranged for the preparation and publication of his public papers and speeches in multiple volumes. The almost incredibly efficient and industrious Sam Rosenman had taken on the formidable task of compiling and collating the voluminous material, adding this to his duties as judge on New York's Supreme Court and as frequent speechwriter for the President. Roosevelt himself devoted much time, thought, and effort to the project, contributing, in collaboration with Rosenman, lengthy first-person notes upon the documents and the context of events within which they were composed. The first fruits of this labor, five large volumes entitled *The Public Papers and Addresses of Franklin D. Roosevelt 1928–1936,* appeared in the early spring of 1938. They were very handsomely published and as handsomely reviewed in the press. Much praise was bestowed upon the editorial performance, which was indeed excellent, if sometimes a bit more "judicious," out of a wish to present the President's words in the most favorable light, than future historians would like it to be. "I want to tell you how much I like the books," wrote Roosevelt to Rosenman, adding that "the book reviews have been exceptionally good" and that this, he hoped, "would be some slight compensation for the months of drudgery which the editing entailed."[69]

During these months Roosevelt was also initiating a project he described as "ambitious" in a letter to Harvard historian Samuel Eliot Morison on February 28—namely, the creation of "a repository for manuscripts, correspondence, books, reports, etc. etc., relating to this period of our national history." Without such a single repository, "this material will be available [only] in scattered form—throughout libraries and private collections. . . . For example, my own papers should, under the old method, be divided among the Navy Department, the Library of Congress, the New York State Historical Division in Albany, the New York City Historical Society, and various members of my family." Such scattering militated against the writing of accurate, comprehensive histories. "If anything is to be done in the way of assembling a fairly complete collection in one place, the effort should start now, but it should have the sanction of scholars." He suggested that Morison "run down here some day within the next week or two to talk this over with me." Morison did so, of course. Thus began the process of establishing on a sound scholarly basis the Franklin D. Roosevelt Library at Hyde Park. Public announcement of the project would be made at a press conference on December 10 of that year. Construction of the library building, the public was informed, would be financed by private donations; the land on which it stood, adjacent to the rose garden on the grounds of the Big House at Hyde Park, would be donated by the Roosevelt family; and the facility would be under the administrative control of the archivist of the United States. To it, Roosevelt would assign all his papers since his entrance into politics in 1910, his personal library, and all his various collections of naval prints, books, pictures, ship models, and memorabilia. To it also would come, as Roosevelt hopefully suggested in his announcement, "such other source material relating to this period in our history as might be donated . . . in the future by other members of the present Administration."[70]

Roosevelt was actively concerned, too, during this season, with physical arrangements for his personal life after his retirement from office.

In the mid-1920s, Eleanor Roosevelt with Nancy Cook and Marion Dickerman, her two closest friends of that time (and for some nine years thereafter), had had built for them at Hyde Park, under Roosevelt's close personal supervision, a fieldstone house which had since become famous as Val-Kill Cottage. It stood in a lovely spot beside a placid stream on land that was Roosevelt's own, bought with his own money—land to which he had given the three women a joint life interest (it was to revert to his estate upon the death of the last survivor). It adjoined the Hyde Park acreage owned by Roosevelt's mother but was a mile and a half away from the Hyde Park mansion. This separation was one of its great advantages for Eleanor, Nancy, and (to a somewhat lesser extent) Marion, for the formidable Sara Delano Roosevelt yet ruled the Big House with undiminished vigor, and ruled in a fashion not conducive to loud, careless, informal fun or even, for such as Eleanor, to quiet relaxation. Roosevelt himself, it would seem, had some of this same sense of advantage. Certainly, at Hyde Park, he had gone to Val-Kill for his most relaxing times these last dozen years. He had often swum in the pool he had insisted the "girls" must have; it was on the cottage grounds, not the lawn of the Big House, that he had presided over his most crowded, exuberant, and publicized picnics, including the annual one for newspaper reporters; and he had often spoken of emulating "the girls" by building a "dream cottage" of his own, a retreat where he could "get away from it all" when he came to Hyde Park. He'd not even have a telephone in it.

He now moved actively toward the realization of this dream. He had recently added to his personal landholdings a forty-two-acre tract that adjoined both Val-Kill and his mother's acreage. It comprised a wooded hill rising 410 feet above the Hudson, and it was atop this Dutchess Hill, as it was called, that the cottage was to be built. Incredibly, considering how crowded were his days, he involved himself almost as deeply in this new construction project as he had been in that for Val-Kill Cottage. Sometime in February he carefully sketched the floor plan and exterior design (a traditional Hudson River Dutch farmhouse design, like Val-Kill's) of a house whose central portion and two wings totaled ninety feet in length. He estimated the cost at $15,000 and was determined to spend no more than that. The primary building material, like that of Val-Kill, would be fieldstone derived from fences that in Dutch and English colonial times had divided meadows and pastures and cultivated fields in what was now a wooded wilderness. He then called upon the expertise of architect Henry J. Toombs of New York City and Atlanta—the same architect he had worked with on Val-Kill Cottage and on the new buildings at Warm Springs. By July 1, the building contract having been let to the lowest bidder (precisely $15,000 by a Montclair, New Jersey, firm), the site was being cleared of trees.[71]

And on that day, a Friday, the project, which was to be completed by November 1, was announced to the public via newsmen who were taken to the hilltop by the President, driving himself there in his hand-controlled Ford. He was the architect, he boasted to the reporters; he had called upon Toombs to "assist" only because he had feared "being caught practicing without a license." On the following day he was back again atop Dutchess Hill for a picnic of hot dogs ("dripping with mustard") and cold beer at which the guest of honor was Crown Princess Louise of Sweden, whose husband was then undergoing treatment in a New York hospital for a kidney ailment. "The hot dogs were served at the insistence of Mrs. Eleanor Roosevelt, wife of the President," reported *The New York Times* next day. "Mrs. James Roosevelt, the President's 83-year-old mother, . . . had wanted to serve pork sausages on finger rolls, but these were ruled out by her daughter-in-law, the hostess of the day." Added to the menu were chicken and ham sandwiches for Sara Delano Roosevelt, who never ate hot dogs and doubtless deemed their very name distasteful but did, at that picnic, accept a glass of beer.[72]

IX

ROOSEVELT had less anxiety regarding politics than he had had when, on April 13, he so vehemently protested Morgenthau's threat to resign from the Cabinet. He had then been worried over the effect the disaffection of the La Follette brothers, Wisconsin's Governor Phil and Senator Bob, might have upon his political fortunes, these two having parted company with him because of the spending cuts that he was in process of restoring on that April day. A new party, the National Progressives, was to be launched on April 28 by Phil La Follette in, of all places, the livestock pavilion of the university's college of agriculture, and it was this that had caused Roosevelt to fear, as he had said to Morgenthau, that the latter's threatened resignation would split the Democrats and assure the rise of a potent extremist movement. Fortunately, from Roosevelt's point of view, the La Follette party's launching had been hastily, carelessly improvised, with more attention paid to outer trappings than to inner workings. The La Follettes had failed to consult beforehand with leading liberals throughout the country, had concentrated fairly exclusively upon Midwestern liberalism with its strong flavor of isolationism, had thus defined their effort as regional rather than national, despite the new party's name. Moreover, young Phil had employed at the launching ceremony a pageantry that struck many as ominously imitative of Nazi-Fascism, as if he aspired to become himself an Americanized *duce* or *Führer.* His speech on that occasion had been a good one. He had argued, persuasively to many, that a new, solidly liberal party was indeed needed, the liberal cause having been betrayed by the vacillations, the fumbling inconsistencies, of the New Deal. But as Adolf Berle noted in his journal (he came to Madison as La Guardia's representative and

Phil La Follette's personal friend, but with Roosevelt's permission) the National Progressive program, while "interesting," was "so little worked out as not to be really subject to analysis," the "only clear-cut" item of it being "government ownership of the banking system which I think is sound and will have to come."[73] And behind young Phil as he spoke was the new party's emblem, dedicated with great ceremony that day: a twenty-foot-wide banner bearing at its center a blue cross within a red circle. Roosevelt, watching from afar, was relieved. The new movement, he was convinced, would not move very far.

He himself concentrated on the midterm elections, He planned, first, to justify in a public speech his departure from that pledge of nonintervention in state primaries which, in former years, he had based tacitly or implicitly on the separation-of-powers principle of the Constitution. Thereafter he would very actively and personally intervene with a vengeance. The result he confidently expected was the retirement to private life, through primary defeat, of Democratic senators and representatives who had, in his words, "betrayed" the "liberalism" so overwhelmingly mandated by the electorate in 1936, he being that liberalism's personification. He would then be enabled to march in triumph through the last two years of his term and virtually to appoint his White House successor, as Andrew Jackson had done.

Who would his successor be?

In its October 2, 1937, issue, *Collier's* magazine had placed Harry Hopkins's name high on its list of possible Democratic presidential nominees in 1940. Those who knew that Roosevelt had used *Collier's* before to launch trial balloons might wonder if he were now doing so again, but they probably dismissed the idea as incredible, Hopkins seeming to them so incredible a choice. Immediately thereafter, Hopkins's grave health problems prevented for several months much serious thought about his future political role; he seemed to have been removed from the political game. In the spring, however, when Hopkins's return to Washington coincided with a vigorous renewal of White House decisiveness and leadership, there was a resurgence of speculation about his political future—and Roosevelt encouraged it with gestures indicating that Hopkins was a favorite whom he was determined to promote. He had been told that one factor in the defeat of executive reorganization had been congressional dislike of Harry Hopkins, congressional hostility to Hopkins as Cabinet member. "There's more than one way to skin a cat," Roosevelt said to Hopkins when, on April 29, eleven days after reorganization's defeat, he insisted that Hopkins accompany him to that afternoon's Cabinet meeting. He insisted that Hopkins attend the next Cabinet meeting also—a meeting not held until Friday, May 13, Roosevelt having returned the day before from an eleven-day cruise to the Sargasso Sea aboard a new navy cruiser, the U.S.S. *Philadelphia*. Thereafter, Hopkins was a fairly regular attendant at Cabinet meetings.[74]

At some point during this period, Hopkins had a momentous private interview with the President. (Its precise date remains unknown because Hopkins failed to date the copious record he made of it immediately after it ended.[75])

At the interview's outset, Roosevelt told Hopkins that he wanted to retire in January 1941, in part for financial reasons. His mother was using up capital to pay for the upkeep of Hyde Park and the New York City house because his presidential salary was too low to enable him properly to share this expense. He couldn't absolutely rule out the possibility of running again, but it was very slight, whereas his personal wish to return to Hyde Park and assume the management of the family estate was very great. This, of course, raised the question of his successor—someone who, as a candidate, would strengthen the Democratic party as a liberal party, and, in the White House, continue and extend the New Deal. He named several possibilities, canceling out each of them. Cordell Hull was "too old," Harold Ickes "too combative," Jim Farley too parochial (he knew nothing of world affairs) and conservative. Indeed, from Roosevelt's point of view, Farley was "clearly the most dangerous" aspirant because politically "the strongest." There was talk of Farley's running for governor of New York in the fall. If he did so, and won, he would be a formidable presidential candidate, and if he then won the White House he would preside, one could be sure, over a resurgence of conservatism in the country. That must not be allowed to happen. Other names were then mentioned: Henry Wallace; Michigan governor Frank Murphy; Wisconsin senator Bob La Follette; Pennsylvania governor George Earle. Each was dismissed for one reason or another (with respect to Bob La Follette, Hopkins noted, "fine —later—Secretary of State soon").

There remained Hopkins himself. He had, to be sure, some liabilities as a candidate, and Roosevelt reviewed them. First and foremost was the health question. This was not, in Roosevelt's view, a serious hazard as far as the election campaign was concerned, for the public had been given no hint that Hopkins had cancer; they believed that his operation was for ulcers. Newsmen had reported him completely recovered, and the Mayo Clinic had told Roosevelt that the chances were (to quote Hopkins's handwritten notes) "2 to 1 against recurrence." But the health question was certainly one Hopkins himself should consider seriously, keeping in mind that the presidency was a man-killing job. (Here Roosevelt made one of his rare references to his own health problem, saying that he could have walked without a brace on his left leg if he had continued with his recovery program in 1928 instead of running for the governorship of New York; he did not say he regretted his decision to run.) A second liability was the fact that Hopkins had been divorced. This, too, was not a serious hazard, for his second marriage was known to have been an unusually happy one, which indicated that the failure of his first marriage was due to no grave and ineradicable character defect. After all, Grover Cleveland, amid mores much more puritanical than those of the present day, had been elected despite the revelation that he was the father of an illegitimate child.

On the positive side was the fact that Hopkins was most emphatically a liberal, had proved his ability to handle huge administrative assignments efficiently, had also proved to be politically realistic and adroit, and (the prime essential) could, in politician Roosevelt's opinion, be elected. He would have to plan his campaign carefully, with close attention to timing. He must not get out in front too soon, for then his opponents would be enabled to organize against him before his own organization was strong enough to resist their attack. Meanwhile he must do what he could, without dangerously compromising his liberal position, to reduce his conservative opposition and win over moderate conservatives. To this end, Roosevelt proposed to appoint Hopkins secretary of commerce, replacing Dan Roper, before the end of the year—an appointment bound to cause a furor in the business community, but one that would enable Hopkins to prove in direct dealings with influential businessmen that, contrary to portrayals of him in the conservative press, he was not a wild-eyed radical, did not have horns and a tail. There were other things the President could do to promote Hopkins's candidacy, things covert and subtle as well as things wide open to the public gaze, and Roosevelt promised to do them.

One may be sure that it was a bemused and excited Harry Hopkins who walked out of the White House that day.

And it is a bemused historian who seeks this day to understand what Roosevelt was actually doing in this interview—what his deepest motive was. The inquiring mind stumbles jarringly over Roosevelt's seemingly confident assertion of Hopkins's electability. Did Roosevelt honestly and truly believe that Hopkins had it? Certainly most contemporary observers would have said that Hopkins was the least electable of all the New Deal's top officials. He was a very questionable figure in the eyes of a great many middle-class voters, disliked and distrusted by them as a Machiavellian who pursued power ruthlessly, using relief funds (CWA and WPA jobs and projects) lawlessly to gain political objectives. Frequently sardonic in manner and speech, addicted to wisecracks that sometimes backfired dangerously, addicted also to shortcuts to get jobs done, he seemed to many to be far too much in a hurry, far too little committed to a strict observance of law. Others thought they saw a fanatic gleam in his preternaturally piercing eyes, one that boded ill for democratic forms and procedures to the extent that power came into his grasping hands. His physical appearance, unlike Roosevelt's (despite the latter's withered limbs), did not inspire confidence. He had been thin to the point of emaciation last fall; he remained much underweight, in appearance at least, which suggested that, if he did not suffer from pathogenic infection, he was ravaged by dissipation. And the sense of his being in fact dissipated was fed by his self-proclaimed fondness for racetracks and nightclubs—a fondness that of course, especially in a high government official, outraged the pious of the Bible Belt. These were negatives in abundance, surely, viewed in terms of vote-getting, of popular leadership. And did Roosevelt actually cancel them out with positives in his shrewd politician's mind? Did he intuitively see through them to a reality hidden from others and know, in consequence, that, once the voters were acquainted with Hopkins as the campaign would enable them to be, they would, most of them, find him as attractive as his staff did and as Roosevelt himself did? Or was there operative here, deep in Roosevelt's psyche, a secret wish to prove to himself as well as to contemporary commentators and future historians that, though he tried earnestly to find a suitable successor (one who could be elected), there simply was none to be found and that, therefore, *he* must run again?

Certainly some of the uses made of Hopkins during the primary campaigns of that spring and summer, with Roosevelt's approval if not at his instigation, were incongruous with the expressed presidential desire "to build Hopkins up" for 1940. For example, the White House insisted, through Tommy Corcoran, that Hopkins, as a native Iowan, make a statement favoring Representative Otha Wearin in a race Wearin was making against Senator Guy Gillette in the Iowa Democratic primary. Gillette had incurred Roosevelt's wrath, and Hopkins's also, by voting against the court-reform bill and the wage-and-hour bill, and for crippling amendments to the failed executive-reorganization bill. Hopkins protested to Corcoran that he had almost no political clout in Iowa (he was on bad terms with Iowa's senior senator, Democrat Clyde Herring). His endorsement of Wearin could therefore do that worthy no good, and it would inevitably provoke renewed charges that he, Hopkins, used the WPA for political purposes. He protested in vain. He perforce made, in as mild a form as he could, the desired statement (if he were able to vote in the Iowa primary he "would vote for Otha Wearin on his record," Hopkins said). The consequences were precisely what he had predicted: no help for Wearin, harm for himself. He became at once the target of bitter attacks on the Senate floor, typically from Montana's Burton Wheeler, who declared that "Congress in appropriating for the relief of the underprivileged never intended that these funds should be utilized to slaughter a member of this body." And Guy Gillette, far from being "slaughtered," was helped to an easy victory over Otha Wearin in Iowa's early-June primary.[76]

On the afternoon of Monday, May 9, the day of Roosevelt's return to the White House from his Caribbean cruise, Ickes and the President talked of events abroad, in whose darkening shadow all domestic political affairs must now be planned and conducted. Ickes brought up the question of the embargo on the shipment of arms and munitions to Loyalist Spain. It should never have been imposed, said he, with emphasis. It should be lifted at once.

Pressure to do precisely this had been increasing for many months, as it became more and more widely recognized that the embargo worked wholly to Franco's advantage and, in fact, probably provided the margin between victory and defeat for Spain's legitimate government. But this same recognition on the part of Catholics and others who wanted Franco to win had, of course, produced an increasing counterpressure to retain the embargo. In late January 1938, for instance, sixty members of Congress signed a message to the Loyalist Cortes, declaring their support of Spanish democracy and thus clearly implying their support for a lifting of the embargo, But several of these congressmen quickly backed away from this stand when faced by the wrath of Catholics led, most prominently in this case, by Democratic senator David I. Walsh of

Massachusetts. Immediately thereafter, sixty prominent Americans, among them former secretary of state Henry L. Stimson and former ambassador to Germany William E. Dodd, signed a petition to the President calling for revision of our Spanish policy—and none of these later repudiated his signature or tried to explain it in ways pleasing to pro-Franco elements. In following weeks, embargo-repeal sentiment spread, strangely enough, among isolationists in the Midwest and West; this sentiment was fed by a traditionally powerful antipathy to Perfidious Albion, which, through the Chamberlain ministry, was dictating (as the isolationists felt) our Spanish policy. North Dakota's Senator Nye was deemed the very personification of pacifistic isolationism; it was out of his committee to investigate the armaments industry that (at Roosevelt's instigation, ironically*) the 1935 Neutrality Act had come; yet on May 2, Gerald Nye introduced to Congress a resolution to repeal the Spanish embargo.[77]

Ickes had referred to this as a most hopeful event when, three days before his talk on this subject with the President, he was visited in his office by Jay Allen, the former Chicago *Tribune* foreign correspondent, who had been fired for reporting facts about the Spanish conflict that contradicted the *Tribune* publisher's reactionary opinions. Allen, outraged by the continuation of the embargo, had vehemently voiced a belief that Roosevelt was being "imposed upon" in this matter by pro-Franco "career men" in the State Department. Ickes said that this might be true but that there were signs that the President was about to change course. One such sign was a sensational front-page story in the May 5 *New York Times* headlined: ROOSEVELT BACKS LIFTING ARMS EMBARGO ON SPAIN; CONGRESS AGREES IT FAILS. Jay Allen didn't believe it. The story, its substance unattributed to any named persons, had been "deliberately planted," Allen was convinced, "to stir up the Catholics to protest" in such organized numbers that it would be "impossible for the President to act" as the *Times* story said he intended to do.[78]

That Roosevelt himself might have connived in such "planting" did not occur to Allen as a possibility, but it may have occurred to Ickes when, on May 9, he learned from the President's own lips that the White House planned to do nothing about the embargo. Loyalist Spain wouldn't be able to obtain arms and munitions from us now in any case, the President said; they couldn't be delivered through France, now that the Popular Front government there had fallen and the border between France and Spain would soon be tightly closed. Ickes countered with a statement of what Jay Allen had told him—namely, that the French "would probably close the border" only because "there were no munitions coming in from the United States to make it worth while to keep it open." Thus pressed, the President "finally" told Ickes that Speaker Bankhead and Majority Leader Rayburn of the House had been in to see him that morning and had told him that the "Democratic members of Congress" were "jittery" about this matter because, said the President, "frankly . . . to raise

*See *FDR: The New Deal Years,* pp. 554–62.

the embargo would mean the loss of every Catholic vote next fall." A disgusted Ickes wrote in his diary three days later that "the cat [thus released from] the bag . . . is the mangiest, scabbiest cat ever," one that proved "up to the hilt . . . that the Catholic minorities in Great Britain and America have been dictating international policy with respect to Spain."[79]

As regards this matter of aid to Loyalist Spain, a curious incident occurred some six weeks after the above-described White House conference. It is told of in a letter handwritten from Ambassador Bullitt in Paris to the President on June 21, 1938. Marked "personal and confidential," as was virtually every communication from the dramatic ambassador to the President, save those marked "personal and secret," the missive began, "This is a very private letter which requires no answer," and went on to say that, a few days before, the ambassador had received a telegram from Eleanor announcing the imminent arrival in Paris of her brother Hall Roosevelt and asking Bullitt to "do anything I could for him." Bullitt was therefore not surprised to receive a phone call from Hall shortly after noon of this day, the twenty-first.

He was surprised, however, by what Hall had to say when he arrived in the ambassador's office at four-fifteen.

> He said that he, acting through Harold Talbott of Cleveland, had managed to gather for the Spanish Government approximately 150 new and second hand planes of various makes—all of which he specified. He said that he had discussed this transaction with you [the President] and that it had your entire approval. He stated that you and he and Jimmy had discussed all the details and that you had agreed to wink at the evasion of the Neutrality Act involved because of your interest in maintaining the resistence of the Spanish Government against Franco, and on Monday, June 13th, had sent for Joseph Green, who is in charge of such matters in the Department of State, and had ordered him to permit the export of these planes and to accept such falsified papers as might be presented and not to scrutinize the entire matter too carefully.

Informed by Bullitt that the embassy had received no notice "from the Department . . . that the policy of our Government" opposing "absolutely the giving of licenses for shipments of planes to Spain via France" had been changed, Hall "replied that you had thought of writing me; but that since he would arrive in Paris as quickly as a letter you had preferred to have him explain the matter to me by word of mouth."

This seemed, of course, utterly incredible and, clearly, Bullitt did not believe it.

> I informed Hall . . . that the French Government had closed the frontier to Spain absolutely; that the French Government had a real hope that the volunteers might be withdrawn at last from both sides in Spain and the British were pushing for an armistice pending the withdrawal of volunteers. I told him that I could not imagine a moment more unpropitious for an attempt to organize the shipment of planes to Spain in contravention of the wishes of the British and French Governments and of our own Neutrality Act.

Bullitt also told Hall that, on the morning of this very day, the Spanish (Loyalist) government's ambassador to France had "berated" French foreign minister Georges Bonnet for having agreed "to the closing of the French frontier to military shipments," just as the Spanish government was enabled "to buy more than one hundred planes in the United States at once for immediate delivery to to Spain via France." The Spanish ambassador had, further, asserted to Bonnet "that you [Roosevelt] personally had approved the sale of these planes . . . and that you were arranging for the evasion of the Neutrality Act involved in their shipment to Spain, knowing fully that their destination would be Spain." Bullitt, told of this by Bonnet, had "expressed . . . skepticism" and promptly, at noon, telegraphed what he had heard to the State Department, asking if there had been, thus abruptly, a policy change. Of this, too, Hall was informed by Bullitt, who added that he had as yet received no reply. Hall then said "he would come to see me tomorrow morning and that he would telephone to Jimmy with great discretion this afternoon and say that the situation seemed to have changed since he had left America."

Shortly after Hall had left him, Bullitt received replies from Washington to his telegram of inquiry. Joseph Green phoned to say

> that there had been no change whatsoever in the opposition of our Government to the shipment of planes to Spain via France; that our Government was fully aware of the attempt that certain people were making to ship a large number of second-hand planes to Spain and had definitely decided to refuse export licenses for such planes. Later I received a telegram from the Department signed Welles, Acting, which confirmed Green's statements. Tomorrow I shall show Hall the telegram signed by Welles.

Bullitt closed: "I have not the slightest desire to know what lies behind this expedition of Hall's, and I am writing this letter for your own eye and no one else's, merely because I feel that since your name has been used by the Spanish Government in its conversations with the French Government, you ought to have a full account of the facts."[80]

What is one to make of all this?

On the one hand, arguing for the truth of what Hall had to say, is the circumstantial detail of his account joined with the fact that Roosevelt certainly had no conscientious aversion to the devious, the indirect, but, instead, had a penchant for intricate secretive games (a species of practical jokery) wherein his opponents were fooled and foiled rather than put down in open combat.

On the other hand, Roosevelt had no such passionate commitment to the Loyalist cause as Eleanor had—no such recognition of this "civil war" as an international conflict between democracy and Fascism wherein victory for the latter might well mean destruction for the former in a renewed world war. He *was* acutely conscious of the political strength of the Catholic Church, along with his need for Catholic votes in the midterm elections, as he had indicated to Ickes. And, for all his fondness for intricate games, he was not likely to engage in one whose risks were enormous and whose loss could destroy utterly his power over foreign affairs. He was, as Walter Lippmann once observed, an extremely cautious politician.

Finally, arguing strongly if not conclusively against the truth of Hall's story, is the fact that Hall, approaching his fiftieth birthday, had gone the way of his and Eleanor's father and of one of their maternal uncles: He had become hopelessly alcoholic, with no such capacity to drink heavily without palpably impairing his mental processes as his uncle Theodore Roosevelt is said by some to have had.[81] Franklin Roosevelt, knowing this, would almost certainly not have trusted Hall to carry out a mission so delicate and fraught with danger as this one.

On May 12, 1938, Ickes had another highly confidential talk with the President, the subject this time being the succession of 1940. Replying to Ickes's assertion that Roosevelt might, as "the democratic hope of the world," be forced by the international situation to run again, the President said that he certainly didn't want to. He was, he remarkably added, "slowing up." But "where are we going to find a candidate . . . who would measure up from a liberal point of view and who could hope to win the nomination?" asked Ickes. Whereupon Roosevelt proceeded to "go over the list," dismissing each name in turn. He began with Ickes, "since you are here." Ickes was "too didactic, too likely to blow up." Ickes agreed, adding that he lacked "the elements" needed for a successful campaign—an assessment he hoped the President would disagree with, as the President promptly did. Ickes, said Roosevelt, made highly effective speeches and would be able to "make a good campaign." He went on down the list. Henry Wallace was "too aloof." Handsome Paul V. McNutt, former governor of Indiana, now high commissioner of the Philippines, was ethically insensitive (as governor he had organized "2 percent clubs," which in effect taxed state employees to raise campaign funds; he had called out the National Guard to break strikes) and too conservative. Governor Earle, though he had been a staunch supporter of the New Deal, did not "measure up" in other ways. Senator Barkley was too long-winded and lacked "a sense of proportion." Bob Jackson, though he had sound liberal qualifications, lacked the necessary political experience. Of Bob La Follette, Roosevelt spoke as he had done to Hopkins, naming him as a possible secretary of state in 1941—a strange judgment, in view of Bob La Follette's strong and already manifest isolationist view of foreign relations.

This seems to have completed Roosevelt's list, and the remarkable thing about it, the thing most revealing of Roosevelt's shrewd assessment of the man he talked to, is that Harry Hopkins's name was not on it. Nor did Ickes mention Hopkins. Perhaps this was because Ickes wished not to suggest such a possibility to a President who had not thought of it. More likely, indeed almost certainly, Hopkins's name simply did not occur to Ickes in the context of that discussion. The idea of Harry as Roosevelt's successor (Harry in the White House!) was, at that early date, too outlandish.

X

YET at that time, the relations between Ickes and Hopkins were at their warmest, their most cordial. Hopkins was at some pains to make them so, and Ickes was in a generally far mellower mood than he normally was, thanks to an impending happy event of central importance to his personal life.

For Ickes, a widower since the death of his unbeloved first wife in 1935, was to be married on May 24, in Dublin, Ireland, to Jane Dahlman, an in-law of his first wife and a niece of John Cudahy, the U.S. minister to the Irish Republic. She was staying with her uncle as she awaited the arrival of the bridegroom-to-be; and Cudahy was doing his best, in vain, to dissuade her from a marriage almost certain, in his view, to be unhappy. His opinion was grounded on the vast discrepancy between her age (she was twenty-five) and that of the man she would marry (he was sixty-four)—an embarrassing discrepancy, which accounted for the extreme secrecy with which the wedding arrangements were being made. Both Ickes and his bride-to-be sought to avoid all publicity of the event until it could be presented as a fait accompli. With Roosevelt's connivance in the matter of passport and visa, Ickes was to sail incognito on May 18 aboard the *Normandie* (he was on the ship's passenger list as "John L. Williams"), would dine privately during the voyage and try hard to avoid recognition during his rare appearances on deck, and would debark at Southampton, whence he would go by train and boat to Dublin. The marriage ceremony was to be performed within hours of his arrival, in the Adelaide Street Presbyterian Church.

In the event, all went according to plan, save that John Cudahy surprised and dismayed the bride and groom by refusing to attend the ceremony. The reason he gave, at which a hurt and angry Ickes scoffed as "the flimsiest kind of an alibi," was that he, a devout Catholic and a U.S. minister to a Catholic country, would put himself in an "embarrassing position" by attending a wedding in a Protestant church.[82] This did nothing, one may be sure, to soften Ickes's harsh view of the church as, politically, a dangerously reactionary institution whose influence upon America's foreign affairs was disastrous.

# 7

✦➤X<✦

# A Summer of Dust and Weeds

NEVER had the phrase "fireside chat" seemed less appropriate. The very thought of sitting before a glowing fireplace was antipathetical to most of the tens of millions of Americans who listened to the President's speech, broadcast to them through a cluster of microphones set up in the White House's Diplomatic Reception Room. For on this night of June 24, 1938, Washington sweltered in relentless steamy heat, much of the rest of the country was also suffering an unusually high heat wave, and the words the President poured into the millions of listening ears were not designed to cool, to soothe. They were fighting words, drafted by the new speechwriting team of Tom Corcoran, Ben Cohen, and Sam Rosenman, with Corcoran providing much of the fire.

The speech began with a brief reference to things left undone by the second regular session of the 75th Congress—a Congress "elected in November, 1936, on a platform uncompromisingly liberal." Most notably, it had "refused to provide more businesslike machinery for running the Executive Branch of the Government." On the other hand, "the Congress, striving to carry out the platform on which most of its members were elected, achieved more for the future good of the country than any Congress between the end of the World War and the spring of 1933." Roosevelt mentioned these "accomplishments": the creation of "a new Civil Aeronautics Authority" and of a "United States Housing Authority to help finance large-scale slum clearance" and low-rent housing; additional WPA and PWA funding; "important additions to national armed defense"; the monopoly investigation; the agricultural act; the reduction of taxes on small business and the easing of RFC loan policies—laying special stress on the "Fair Labor Standards Act, commonly called the Wage and Hours Bill." It was, with the possible exception of the Social Security Act, "the most far-reaching, far-sighted program for the benefit of workers ever adopted here or in any other country." Belligerent words followed: "Do not let any calamity-howling executive with an income of $1,000 a day, who has been turning his employees over to the Government relief rolls in order to preserve his company's undistributed reserves, tell you—using his stockholders' money to pay the postage for his personal opinions—that a wage of $11 a week is going to have a disastrous effect on all American industry." A softening of the indictment followed: "Fortunately for business as a whole, and therefore for the Nation, that type of executive is a rarity with whom most business executives heartily disagree."

But this was not the sum total of Roosevelt's expressed scorn for the political mentality and morality of the business community. "From March 4, 1933, down, not a single week has passed without a cry from the opposition 'to do something, to say something, to restore confidence,'" said Roosevelt.

There is a very articulate group of people in this country, with plenty of ability to procure publicity for their views, who have consistently refused to cooperate with the mass of people, whether things were going well or badly, on the ground that they required more concessions to their point of view before they would admit having what they called 'confidence.' . . . It is my belief that the mass of the American people do have confidence in themselves—have confidence in their ability, with the aid of Government, to solve their own problems. It is because you are not satisfied, and I am not satisfied, with the progress we have made in finally solving our business and agricultural and social problems that I believe the great majority of you want your own Government to keep on trying to solve them. . . . I need all the help I can get. . . . And now, following out this line of thought, I want to say a few words about the coming political primaries.

Came then the two portions of the speech that made headlines in next morning's newspapers. The first was the President's announcement of his intention to fight for the nomination of liberals and the defeat of conservatives in his own party's primaries. He began it with a reference by implication to the dual role that he as White House occupant was required to play—that of national chief executive and that of national party leader. He sought, by implication, to distinguish between the obligations attached to the former and the rights and duties attached to the latter:

As President of the United States, I am not asking the voters of the country to vote for Democrats next November as opposed to Republicans. . . . Nor am I, as President, taking part in Democratic primaries. As the head of the Democratic Party, however, charged with the responsibility of carrying out the definitely liberal declaration of principles set forth in the 1936 Democratic platform, I feel that I have every right [he meant, also, every obligation] to speak in those few instances where there may be a clear issue between candidates for a Democratic nomination involving those principles, or involving a clear misuse of my own name.

The second most newsworthy part of the speech was a (for Roosevelt) unusually strong statement of commitment to the principle of free speech— a statement he presented as a continuation and necessary part of his announced determination to fight for liberals and liberalism.

He said, with heavy emphasis upon the key words:

And I am concerned about the attitude of a candidate or his sponsors with respect to the rights of American citizens to assemble peaceably and to express publicly their views and opinions on important social and economic issues. There can be no constitutional democracy in any community which denies to the individual his freedom to speak and worship as he pleases. The American people will not be deceived by anyone who attempts to suppress individual liberty under the pretense of patriotism.[1]

· · ·

What made this latter so newsworthy was the fact, clear in the public mind, that the unnamed "anyone" at whom the shaft was aimed was Mayor Frank Hague of Jersey City, New Jersey—a pompous strutting hard-faced man (he seldom smiled, and almost never when his picture was being taken) who carried himself always with the ramrod stiffness he thought befitted an iron-fisted boss of a locally omnipotent city machine. Nor was Hague's influence merely local. He was a power in New Jersey state politics and he was vice chairman of the Democratic National Committee—a party post only two steps below Franklin Roosevelt's as national party head.

He had been much in the news since last May 1 in ways that, by late June, were embarrassing to a President now embarking on a crusade for congressional liberalism. "*I* am the law in Jersey City," he once proclaimed when charged with breaking the law. To the Jersey City Chamber of Commerce he said: "As long as I am mayor of this city the great industries of the city are secure. We hear about constitutional rights, free speech and the free press. Every time I hear these words I say to myself, 'that man is a Red, that man is a Communist.' You never hear a real American talk in that manner."[2] None could deny him the virtue of consistency, if consistency is a virtue in such cases. In his rule of his city, Hague abundantly practiced what he preached. For instance, very soon after it was launched he damned the CIO as a Communist organization and refused to permit its organizers to operate in Jersey City. (It was of this stand, and in response to legal action brought against him for it by the CIO and the American Civil Liberties Union, that he spoke to the Chamber of Commerce the above-quoted words.) But neither could anyone deny that he delivered the vote of his bailiwick to Democratic candidates—national, state, and local—with rare efficiency on election days. He had done so for Roosevelt and Roosevelt supporters every two years since 1930. And the administration reciprocated with patronage that strengthened the Hague machine. Roosevelt had appointed no one to a federal judgeship or a federal district attorneyship in New Jersey who had not been personally endorsed by Mayor Hague, and he continued along this cooperative line despite increasingly loud protests by liberals. Harry Hopkins, too, had found the mayor useful in the handling of unemployment relief in New Jersey; he remained on good terms with him—a "plus" for Hopkins as presidential candidate, in Roosevelt's view.

But latterly the boss had made, before a national audience, so blatant a display of his "philosophy" and method of governing that Roosevelt, for all his trying, could not wholly publicly ignore it.

Several weeks before May 1 last—May Day being the traditional date for left-wing political and labor demonstrations—the local Socialist party had applied to Jersey City's director of public safety for permission to hold a mass meeting in the city's Journal Square. The meeting was intended to be a direct challenge to Hague's dictatorship and it derived a special newsworthiness from the fact that Norman Thomas was to be the principal speaker. As expected, the application for a permit was promptly refused by the public safety director, a Hague henchman named Daniel Casey. He did so, he said, in order "to avert trouble threatened by the Catholic War Veterans." (Casey was himself a Catholic veteran.) Thomas then announced that, permit or no, the meeting would be held and he would exercise his constitutional right to address it.

Physical as well as moral courage was required of Thomas when May Day evening arrived. He rode in an open car through Jersey City streets to the square. More than two thousand people were assembled there; they loudly cheered his appearance. But also assembled there was a small army of Hague's notoriously brutal police; and when Thomas dismounted from the car and mounted the platform, a squad of these police mounted with him. They roughly seized him, dragged him into a police car, and drove him, with others who had come with him, to the Jersey Central Railroad Ferry Slip. He and the others were hustled aboard a ferryboat about to depart for New York City and warned not to show themselves again in Jersey City. Meanwhile, in Journal Square, the police were at work dispersing the crowd with billy clubs, fists, and kicking feet. Violet Thomas, Norman's wife, was struck in the face by a policeman. The secretary of the Workers' Defense League of New Jersey had his glasses shattered by a policeman's club. Dozens of others were struck and kicked.[3]

A few days later, in a radio speech that made national news, Norman Thomas called the attention of the President of the United States to this latest outrage of American liberties by a machine boss with whom that President was politically allied. He called for presidential action. "You are hero and leader to millions of Americans," he said. "You have repudiated for yourself, your party and your country the degradation of lands where men are slaves of dictators. . . . Is it only foreign dictators whom we are to fear and fight?"[4] Roosevelt made no reply, took no action. Nor did he when, on June 4, in Newark, which is less than ten miles from Jersey City, another meeting that Thomas attempted to address, this one in Newark's Military Park, was broken up by Hague's minions. Just as Thomas rose to speak, a marching brass band came down the street, loudly playing patriotic music to drown out his words. The band halted, continuing to play, while an organized mob of hoodlums carrying placards ("The Working People of Our City Are Contented—REDS KEEP OUT," and so on) pelted Thomas and others on the platform with eggs, decayed vegetables, and light bulbs. When Thomas insisted upon continuing the meeting, calling upon Newark's police to provide protection, the police instead declared the meeting adjourned, in the interest of law and order. Next day, newspapers all over the country carried a photograph of Norman Thomas at the instant an egg splattered on his face.[5]

Alf Landon, the Republican whom Roosevelt had so soundly trounced in 1936's election, voiced in two public speeches, at Rochester and Watertown, New York, his outrage at this violation of civil liberty. He damned Frank Hague as an enemy of freedom and praised Norman Thomas as a defender of it, referring to both by name. As for Thomas, he had by then filed a complaint in federal court and called for a U.S. Department of Justice investigation of his April 30 kidnaping and deportation. Thus the tide of protest against Hague-style fascism continued to rise. And in the face of it, the very least a President could do who proclaimed himself a liberal embarking on a new liberal crusade was let the public know that he disapproved of what Hague had done. Hence the three sentences on civil liberty in a fireside chat. They served Roosevelt's purpose. They broke an embarrassing silence with high notes of liberal music while committing Roosevelt to no action whatever.

But it was action that Norman Thomas called for.

On the morning following the speech, he dashed off on his typewriter a double-spaced letter to the President saying that, while he had read "with gratification and approval" the words that "general opinion" saw as "your answer to" the fascism of Frank Hague, and had "also read with . . . approval your declaration of your right . . . to support liberals in the Democratic primaries," it was "surely . . . equally important that you as leader of your Party should not countenance a little Hitler as its vice-chairman." He therefore "respectfully" pressed three questions: "When will you as President . . . stop supporting Hague by giving him the federal patronage which is so great a part of his strength? When will you as President . . . instruct your Attorney General to make a real and not farcical investigation of Hague's rule . . . ? When will you as leader of the Democratic Party act to rid the Party of its fascist vice-chairman . . . ?"

During the ten days that followed, the President addressed, in Wilmington, Delaware, the tercentenary celebration of the first Swedish emigration to America; laid (on June 30) the cornerstone of the U.S. government building at the New York World's Fair, to be held in 1939; and addressed on the same day the annual conference of the National Education Association in New York City. "If the fires of freedom and civil liberty burn low in other lands, they must be made bright in our own," he told the assembled educators. "If in other lands the press and books and literature of all kinds are censored, we must redouble our efforts here to keep them free." But he made no reply to Norman Thomas.

So, on July 5, Thomas addressed a second letter to the President. He had just come, he said, "from an appearance before the Federal Grand Jury in Newark, New Jersey," wherein he had asked for a postponement of any consideration of his charge that his "forcible deportation from Jersey City" violated federal law (specifically, the so-called Lindbergh Law, which made kidnaping across state lines a federal offense) until "a proper investigation" of the matter had been made by the U.S. Justice Department—a request to which the grand jury had acceded. During the proceedings, Thomas had received the "astonishing information" from the assistant district attorney in charge of grand jury work "that the Attorney General had refused to authorize any investigation although requested to do so by the District Attorney's office." Thomas therefore requested the President to "direct the Attorney General to change his attitude on the case" since "this attitude . . . is clearly an obstruction of justice. . . . I am making this request . . . on my own responsibility as an

American citizen and not under the direction of any lawyer, because I believe
that the issues involved go to the root of any support of civil liberty in
America."

As soon as he had read this missive, Roosevelt sent it, along with the earlier
one from Thomas, to the man of whom Thomas complained. Attorney General
Homer Cummings was asked to prepare a reply for presidential signature
and to do so "as soon as possible" because the President "would like to sign
it before his departure tomorrow evening." Instead, Cummings prepared a
draft letter to be signed by one of the presidential secretaries since, in his
opinion, it was not "desirable" for the President "to answer these letters
personally." Cummings also, in his cover letter, blandly explained his own
inaction and not-so-blandly commented upon Norman Thomas's character.
"In view of the fact that Mr. Thomas had . . . taken decisive steps, under advice
of counsel, to prefer criminal charges against Jersey City officials," wrote
Cummings,

> it seemed to me that no particular action was required by the Department of Justice
> pending such proceedings. . . . I have reason to doubt . . . whether he has any faith
> in his complaint that he was kidnaped under the terms of the Federal Statute. That
> Statute, as you know, was under consideration by the Supreme Court . . . in the case
> of Gooch v. U.S., . . . which seemed to indicate that to support a Federal prosecution
> there should not only be an interstate kidnaping or transportation, but that it should
> be for the purpose of benefit, gain, or advantage to the kidnaper. . . . To say the least,
> Mr. Thomas is a very unreasonable person and, in my judgment, one of the most
> mentally dishonest men in public life and his primary purpose in bombarding you
> and me with letters is for propaganda and public consumption.

As for the draft letter, it tersely advised Thomas to have his attorney
communicate directly with the attorney general so that "the matter" could be
handled "in orderly fashion." Roosevelt made but one tiny change in it before
turning it over to Marvin McIntyre, who would sign it. The Cummings draft
addressed Thomas as "Dear Sir"; the letter McIntyre signed addressed him as
"My dear Mr. Thomas."[6]

A few hours later, Roosevelt was aboard his special train, bound for Marietta, Ohio, there to begin a long speaking tour designed to remove Democratic conservatives from Congress and replace them with Democratic liberals
in the upcoming party primaries.

II

FOR the next nine days he lived in his railroad car at the end of his special
ten-car train (it was fortunately air-conditioned against the summer heat) as
he made his arduous way, with many an abrupt zig and zag, across the
continent. During those nine days he made twenty-seven speeches in as many
different cities and towns, all of them dedicated, if generally in subtle ways,
to the purpose he had announced in his fireside chat.

In Marietta, Ohio, he celebrated the 150th anniversary of the "establishment of the first civil government [in the U.S.] west of the original thirteen states," Marietta having been founded in 1788 by settlers sent west by the Ohio Company. Among them was "a representative of the national government . . . to administer the Northwest Territory under the famous Northwest Ordinance." He traced similarities between that pioneering enterprise and the New Deal, inserting at a suitable point words approving Ohio senator Robert J. Bulkley. They were no more enthusiastic, these words, than Bulkley's support of the New Deal had been, but they might serve (in the event they did serve) to assure Bulkley's victory over an even less New Dealish Democrat in what promised to be a close primary race.[7]

Far different was his speech a few hours later at Covington, Kentucky. "Some Republicans have suggested that I come to Kentucky on a political mission," he began. "But I assure you the only reason is because I cannot get to Oklahoma without crossing Kentucky." He then devoted the whole of his address to a glowing endorsement of Alben Barkley, who was being strongly challenged in the upcoming primary by Kentucky's governor Albert B. (Happy) Chandler. The always wide-grinning and brashly assertive Chandler (he managed to insinuate himself into the seat beside the President's in the car that led the parade to the speaker's stand, a seat Roosevelt had intended for Barkley) was a man of dubious liberal credentials and equally dubious ethical standards, but, worst of all, his election to the Senate would mean, almost certainly, the elevation of Pat Harrison to the post of Senate majority leader, which Barkley now held. The latter prospect was so frightful in Roosevelt's eyes that he had accepted John L. Lewis's offer of CIO help for Barkley, coupled though this was with a tacit tit-for-tat demand that the administration help toward Pennsylvania primary victory a CIO man, Thomas Kennedy, whose candidacy for the Pennsylvania governorship (the incumbent, Earle, had announced for the Senate) was badly splitting the Pennsylvania Democrats.[8] Said Roosevelt: "His [Barkley's] outlook on affairs of Government is a liberal outlook. He has taken a major part in shaping not only the legislation but the actual policies of the last six years. I have no doubt whatsoever that Governor Chandler would make a good Senator . . . but I think my good friend, the Governor, would be the first to acknowledge that as a very junior member of the United States Senate, it would take him many, many years to match the national knowledge, the experience and the acknowledged leadership in the affairs of the Nation of that son of Kentucky, of whom the whole Nation is proud, Alben Barkley." Later on that same July 8, in Louisville, Kentucky, which had suffered greatly from an Ohio River flood the year before, Roosevelt's extemporaneous remarks were wholly about flood control. But Alben Barkley did not go unmentioned. "The people of the Ohio Valley . . . I am sure, approve our intentions—under a well-coordinated plan— to make the Ohio Basin flood proof. . . . In this work of planning and coordinating work on a vast scale, I want to acknowledge the splendid assistance I have received from the senior Senator from Kentucky. This is a national problem. We need people of national experience with a national point of view to carry it out."[9]

Presidential speechmaking, it should here be noted, was not the administration's only major effort at that time to ensure Alben Barkley's survival as Senate majority leader. Thomas L. Stokes, a Scripps-Howard syndicated columnist who had written much in favor of the New Deal, was reporting at this time, in a series of articles,* WPA activity on Barkley's behalf that was clearly an unethical if not illegal use of work-relief organization and appropriations. Hopkins felt compelled to order an investigation by the WPA headquarters staff. Not surprisingly, the investigators found little wrongdoing, none of a serious nature—a fact that provoked cries of "whitewash" from conservatives.[10] The whole episode did damage to Hopkins's presidential hopes, confirming as it seemed to do a popular impression of him as a cynical, Machiavellian "operator." For the Stokes pieces remained convincing. Few were the politically sophisticated people who doubted that WPA officials were doing all they could safely do, that summer, to encourage WPA employees to vote and work for Barkley, not Happy Chandler; that their activity was condoned if not initiated by the White House (probably through Tommy Corcoran); and that this activity was of great importance, perhaps decisively important, to the outcome of the Kentucky primary.

From Kentucky the President went to Oklahoma City where, on July 9, he again spoke of water control, with specific reference to a large federal dam project on the Grand River. "It was due to the persistent effort of my old friend Senator [Elmer] Thomas [who faced a formidable primary challenge] . . . that that particular project is definitely underway, and I might say the same thing about other projects on other watersheds of this State." But the main thrust of his speech was the central theme of his liberal crusade—that the most important state problems were elements of national problems, they could not be solved without national planning and action, and he mentioned Thomas only in passing as he pursued this theme. The Grand River project that Thomas had helped along, for instance, was in Roosevelt's words

> a vital link in the still larger problem of the whole valley of the Arkansas—a planning task that starts far west in the Rocky Mountains, west of the Royal Gorge, and runs on down through Colorado and Kansas and Oklahoma and Arkansas to the Mississippi River itself and thence to the sea. The day will come, I hope, when every drop of water that flows into that great watershed, through all those states, will be controlled for the benefit of mankind, controlled for the growth of forests, for the prevention of soil erosion, for the irrigation of land, for the development of water power, for the ending of floods and for the improvement of navigation.

A national problem, too, was unemployment—a problem the federal government attacked in ways that "assisted communities in the erection of much-

*Stokes was awarded a Pulitzer Prize for them, in 1939.

needed public improvements. . . . Senator Thomas has been of enormous help
. . . in keeping me advised as to the needs of your State, and as to how we,
in Washington, could help meet them. I am told by him that the Works
Progress program in Oklahoma is leaving permanent monuments all over the
state . . . and that in the matter of new schoolhouses in cooperation with WPA,
this State has made a greater record than any other State in the union."[11]

In Texas, where Roosevelt gave seven informal talks in two days, no senatorial seat was at stake that year, but he created and seized upon an opportunity
to humiliate Senator Tom Connally, who had opposed the court-reform bill.
In Connally's presence, he announced to a crowd gathered around the presidential car's rear platform that he was appointing to a federal judgeship a man
whom Connally had not recommended—and Roosevelt had no need to mention this lack of recommendation to his immediate audience (he did not do so,
of course), for newspaper and radio commentators were quick to point out that
the appointment was a slap in the senator's face. Of Texas's liberal contingent
in the House, the most liberal, Maury Maverick, was most seriously threatened
with primary defeat. His flamboyant liberalism had earned him the enmity of
his fellow Texan Vice President Garner, whose absence from the presidential
train as it moved through the state (he sent "regrets" from Uvalde) was
everywhere noted. In 1936, Garner had urged his many friends in San Antonio
(Maverick's hometown) to vote for Maverick; now he was quietly passing the
word that he wanted Maverick crushed by a conservative named Paul Kilday,
whose campaign speeches damned Maverick as a "friend and ally of Communism." Roosevelt therefore, during his passage, bestowed especially warm
smiles upon Maury Maverick. He also warmly publicly smiled upon young
Lyndon B. Johnson, who at age twenty-nine had won a special election to enter
the House only the year before, and upon Representative W. D. McFarlane,
who was a friend and ally of Johnson.[12]

In Colorado on July 12 he made three speeches, each brief and all informal,
without once mentioning that state's senator Alva Adams, another Democratic opponent of the court bill. This was a humiliating experience for Adams,
who stood behind the President on the special car's rear platform while the
speaking was being done.

In Nevada on the following day the President spoke in four towns, including
Reno, without once mentioning the archconservative Democratic senator Pat
McCarran, whose primary defeat he devoutly wished for but knew to be
impossible. McCarran, however, unlike Adams, gave no sign of discomfiture.
Uninvited, he climbed aboard the presidential special at its first Nevada stop,
rode across the state in it, and, despite being treated by the President with what
the latter wrote James Roosevelt was "due courtesy" (that is, coldness), led
the crowd at every stop in a cheer for FDR.[13]

Not that such cheerleading was needed. Beginning with his first stop, in
Ohio, the trip had been a triumphant procession across the continent. The
crowds had been huge and enthusiastically responsive to his every word, his
every gesture; and it was clearly the man, Franklin Roosevelt, who was ap-

plauded, cheered, even revered. James MacGregor Burns tells of "a little old woman" in Marietta who "symbolized much of the popular feeling when she knelt down and reverently patted the dust where he had left a footprint."[14] Moreover, as Roosevelt moved through Nevada, he was given tangible reason to believe that his personal popularity was being translated into the kind of primary vote he wanted. From his son Elliott, with whom and whose wife he had visited in Fort Worth, he received on July 15 the news that, in Oklahoma, Elmer Thomas was winning in the Democratic primary and Governor W. H. (Alfalfa Bill) Murray, a reactionary who affected the rhetorical and personal style of a Populist, was losing—was running third, as a matter of fact, in a three-man race. "I am having a grand trip," wrote Roosevelt that day to Nevada senator Key Pittman, who remained in Washington and who had provided him with a memorandum to guide his public actions and speech across the state. "The memorandum," Roosevelt said, "has been helpful"; then he went on to poke fun, typically heavy-handed fun, at Pittman's latest scheme for fattening Nevada's silver interests at the expense of the rest of the world. "Nothing doing on the silver business," wrote Roosevelt. "—Scrugham tells me [James G. Scrugham was meagerly populated Nevada's sole representative in the House] they have found a new manganese process and that at the next session we will pass a bill demonetizing silver and substituting manganese. . . . Not only will the United States Treasury be saved but so will Brazil. That is why the Chairman of the Foreign Relations Committee will introduce it and call it the Pittman World Currency Act of 1939."[15]

On the following morning, Thursday, July 14, he arrived in San Francisco, where he spoke at Treasure Island, site of the Golden Gate International Exposition, which was to be held in 1939 simultaneously with the New York World's Fair. He exulted over "the wonderful reception" he had received "all along the line of march" to the speaker's platform, and over the "two great bridges [the Golden Gate and the Bay] which I saw today for the first time. Those bridges form a magnificent illustration of the new saying that 'what nature has put asunder, man can put together.' " He said:

> Confidence that in the year 1939 the United States and all the Western Hemisphere will be at peace is shown by the fact that in this Nation two great international expositions are to be held. It is our hope and our expectation that that confidence is well placed—and that the very fact of holding these two expositions means an added impetus to the cause of world peace. Great gatherings of such a nature make for trade, for better understanding and for renewed good will between the Nations of the world.

But he also said that "in another two hours" he would be reviewing the United States fleet then anchored "in this great American harbor"—a fleet that was "not merely a symbol" but

> a potent . . . fact in the national defense of the United States. Every right-thinking man and woman in our country wishes that it were safe for the Nation to spend less

of our national budget on our armed forces. All know that we are faced with a condition and not a theory—and that that condition is not of our own choosing. Money spent on armaments does not create . . . wealth, and about the only satisfaction we can take out of the present world situation is that the proportion of our national income that we spend on armaments is only a quarter or a third of the proportion that most of the other great nations . . . are spending at this time.* We fervently hope for the day when the other leading nations of the world will realize that their present course must inevitably lead to disaster.[16]

The Democratic party situation in California was, as so often in that state, far too confused to be dealt with in simple terms of liberal versus conservative; and Roosevelt, in his three speeches there (he spoke in Los Angeles and San Diego on July 16), made no reference to party politics. He did refer in each of them to "my old friend, Senator McAdoo," but that was as close as he came to promoting McAdoo's candidacy for renomination. After all, William Gibbs McAdoo was deemed no true liberal by those who remembered his lucrative legal service to Edward L. Doheny, one of the great oil thieves of Teapot Dome, and his tacit welcoming of Ku Klux Klan support in the disastrously deadlocked Democratic National Convention of 1924. Nor could McAdoo's opponent in the primary race be labeled "conservative." He was, on the contrary, dangerously, irrationally radical, in the view of all conservatives. His name was Sheridan Downey. In the tradition of Townsend and Upton Sinclair, though with a much closer affinity to the former than to the latter, he had attracted national attention as leader of a so-called "$30 Every Thursday" movement. His name was not mentioned by the President, publicly, in California.

On Saturday, July 16, the Western tour came to an end in the naval base at San Diego. There the President, Commander in Chief of the nation's armed forces, was piped aboard a warship, the U.S.S. *Houston,* to begin a four-week vacation cruise for which he had made plans in early February.

### III

ON the day before Roosevelt left Washington on his Western tour there opened at the Hotel Royal in Évian-les-Bains the international conference on the refugee crisis that the White House had initiated in March.† The conference closed on the day before Roosevelt sailed from San Diego; it had by then accomplished all that could be reasonably expected of it, given its terms of reference and its circumstances.

---

*In his last press conference in Washington he had minimized the boost America's current rearmament could give to economic recovery, saying that "in some countries in Europe" 45 to 50 percent of the total national income went into armaments whereas in America the percentage would run no higher, even with the increased expenditures, than 15 or 16 percent. "Therefore it is not to be compared with the economic effect in those countries" where the percentage was more than three times higher. (Author's note.)
†See pp. 196–97.

Thirty-four nations, with Nazi Germany not included (for obvious reasons), had received conference invitations from the State Department. Thirty-two had accepted. Only Fascist Italy (again, for obvious reasons) and the Union of South Africa had declined, though the latter would send an observer.

But several of the acceptances had been of a qualified nature.

France stipulated that the whole of the conference be held in executive session—that is, with press and public excluded—and that the British, French, and U.S. delegations meet together prior to the conference "to assure a unity of views." For the French wondered and worried about Roosevelt's motives in all this. The conference agenda proposed by the United States called for the organization of a new international agency, an Intergovernmental Committee on Refugees (IGC). This was evidently one of the meeting's chief purposes, in the American view. But the League of Nations had already established a Commission for Refugees from Germany (it had become a kind of wastebasket into which, with a show of "doing something," scraps of the unsolved refugee problem could be cast). Why didn't the United States cooperate in the work of this commission instead of creating a new international agency? Premier Daladier believed, and later said to Neville Chamberlain, that Roosevelt was merely making a humanitarian gesture "to soothe an aroused public opinion,"[17] but Daladier was not himself soothed by his recognition of this alleged fact. With his colleagues, he worried lest the conference focus the pressure of opinion too intensely upon France, which had already accepted more than 200,000 refugees and had, as the chief French delegate would inform the conference, "reached, if not . . . passed, the extreme point of saturation."[18]

Britain stipulated that Palestine, mandated to it by the Versailles Treaty, and currently in violent turmoil (some 30,000 British troops would be stationed there by the end of 1938), must not be discussed at the conference. Yet the establishment of Palestine as a national Jewish homeland had been for decades the goal of the Zionist movement; moreover, the British government had formally declared (the Balfour Declaration of 1917) that they favored such establishment and would "use their best endeavors to facilitate the achievement of that object, it being clearly understood [this was the joker, of course] that nothing shall be done which may prejudice the civil and religious rights of existing non-Jewish [i.e., Arab] communities in Palestine." It was precisely toward Palestine that Nazi-terrorized Jews by the tens of thousands turned in desperate hope of survival. The recent immigration of thousands of them was at the root of the current Palestinian turmoil.[19]

The tone, the manner in which several other countries accepted their invitations betrayed their wariness of involvement in an enterprise that might seriously antagonize Hitler's Germany. This was true not only of European but also of South American countries. These last had close and profitable commercial ties with Germany, and feared that these might be jeopardized by a conference that was, by its very nature, a criminal indictment of Hitler's conduct of German internal affairs. Indeed, it was fear of Hitler that had caused traditionally neutral Switzerland, home of the League of Nations headquarters, to decline the "honor" of holding this meeting on Swiss soil—a refusal that surprised and dismayed the conference organizers, who had taken Swiss acceptance for granted. "It would be preferable," said the Swiss, firmly, "for the conference to meet in some other country where the situation is more suitable to the special problems which will be discussed."[20] Hence the choice of Évian as meeting place (it was a small city on the French shore of Lake Geneva, hitherto famous chiefly for bottled spring water)—a decision in which France concurred with no show of enthusiasm.

Thus it was clear from the outset that the conference, if it was to have any success, must be strongly led along paths clearly defined by the nation that had summoned it. This in turn required on the part of the U.S. executive a bold, frank leadership whereby, in preparation for the conference, the American public was educated as to the nature and dimensions of the refugee crisis, and educated in a way that mobilized the people's generous humanitarian instincts in sufficient strength to overcome the fears of the immigration restrictionists —fears that expanded immigration would deprive Americans of employment, fears that were accompanied by no small degree of covert anti-Semitism. These fears were strong. Typically, on the eve of Évian's opening, the New York State Veterans of Foreign Wars, at their annual encampment, resolved against admitting any refugees to the United States and for suspending all immigration for ten years.[21] Yet the humanitarianism was there also to be mobilized. There was an outpouring of it through popular outrage over increasingly horrifying reports of Nazi Jew-baiting and of the desperate people who congregated by the thousands daily before the German and Austrian consulates of the United States and other countries in the forlorn hope of obtaining visas that would enable them to escape an otherwise certain doom. But far from focusing this sentiment in politically effective ways, the White House and State Department worked to dissipate it, this being their major (if of course highly secret) reason for summoning the conference in the first place. Consider the White House handling of a petition, bearing 120,000 signatures, that was presented to it on June 7, 1938, by delegates of a Jewish political-action organization. It proposed "that the unused [immigration] quotas from any country be made available for the admission of refugees from other countries," to quote Arthur D. Morse, thus multiplying the number of refugees who could enter the United States. The petition was accepted with coldly formal politeness by presidential secretary Marvin McIntyre, who then sought the advice of Sumner Welles. "Personally," wrote McIntyre to Welles, "I do not see much necessity for any reply except that a more or less courteous but stereotyped answer signed by me may head off insistence in the future for a specific reply. What do you think?" Sumner Welles was of the same opinion.[22]

In other words, integrity and sincerity of purpose were notably absent from the U.S. government's preparations for the conference. Notably present were a great concern for formal (and false) appearances along with a carelessness, even a calculated evasion, of substantial realities. For instance, when leaders of American private organizations concerned with the refugee problem were invited to the White House to confer with the President on April 13, the invitees, who were to constitute the impressively titled President's Advisory Committee on Political Refugees, included the chairman of a so-called National Coordinating Committee, a representative of the National Council of Churches, the chairman of the American Committee for Catholic Refugees from Germany, the president of the National Council for Catholic Men, and a former League High Commissioner for Refugees from Germany (he was James G. McDonald, who had resigned in disgust over this commission's calculated impotence in the face of vast and increasing human suffering). Presumably representing the American Jewish community were Bernard Baruch and Henry Morgenthau. But neither of these two had ever been an active participant, much less a leader, in Jewish organizational life. Uninvited, amazingly, was Rabbi Stephen S. Wise, who was not only the most prominent of American Jewish leaders and the most outspoken champion of the victims of vicious anti-Semitism, but also reputedly a good personal friend of Roosevelt's. The omission, whether careless or deliberate on the part of the State Department, was a glaring error that had at once to be corrected. Rabbi Wise became one of the advisers. Even so, the composition of the advisory committee, reflective of the composition and mind-set of the State Department's career staff, was incongruous with the problem the committee was to deal with, insofar as it overrepresented non-Jewish organizations (especially Catholic organizations) and underrepresented Jewish ones—this despite the fact that the great bulk of the actual and would-be refugees from Nazi barbarity were Jews. One authoritative estimate had it that, in July 1938, there were 660,000 refugees from Hitler. Of these, 300,000 were Jews, 285,000 were Christians "tainted" (as defined by the Nuremberg Laws) with Jewish blood, and 75,000 were Catholics.[23]

A month later, after Roosevelt had tried and failed to persuade Hamilton Fish Armstrong, head of the Foreign Policy Association and editor of its magazine, *Foreign Affairs,* to chair the advisory committee, James G. McDonald was appointed to that post. Whereupon, as Henry L. Feingold writes, Roosevelt "seemed [to forget] . . . that such a committee existed and it worked almost exclusively through the State Department. . . ."[24] Appointed head of the U.S. delegation was Myron C. Taylor, former head of U.S. Steel, who had long been on friendly personal terms with Roosevelt. His was a prestigious name, and he was given an impressively high rank and a grand title: "U.S. ambassador extraordinary plenipotentiary." Moreover, he was a man of ability who was sincerely committed to the rescue of the victims of Nazi persecution. But he knew when he accepted his post that any considerable resettlement of refugees in his own country was out of the question. The preface to the conference agenda prepared by the State Department stressed, as the original conference invitations had stressed, that the United States could make no change in its immigration laws and did not expect other countries to change theirs either. Presumably, then, the myriads of violently dispossessed must be settled in countries that did not now narrowly restrict immigration and that contained large amounts of empty land. Taylor could only hope, as others did, that Mexico, Central and South America, Australia, and the African colonies of European powers would provide the needed homes.

This hope proved vain.

At Évian, where the exclusion of press and public enabled frank talk by the delegates, Britain and France at once made it clear that they could accept few refugees on their home soil and that their overseas possessions were unavailable for large-scale resettlement. Of all the European nations, only Holland and Denmark were willing to accept as many refugees as they possibly could, but it was physically impossible for them to accept very many; the Dutch and Danes had already accepted more refugees than their small and densely populated homelands could easily accommodate. Underpopulated Australia, which had been advertising for immigration from the U.S. and Britain, stated bluntly that, having at present no "racial problem," it was "not desirous of importing one." Canada said that, because of its persistent unemployment problem, it could take few immigrants, and that most of these must be farmers and farm workers—a meagerly helpful stance since most of the Jewish refugees were urban business and professional people. Argentina's delegate declared that his country had done all it could do, having accepted already one and a half times as many refugees as had the United States and twice as many as all other South American countries combined. Brazil would say only that it "might" admit a small number of agricultural workers to the state of São Paulo, while four Central American countries (Nicaragua, Honduras, Costa Rica, Panama) issued a joint statement declaring flatly that they would accept no "traders or intellectuals." In all Latin America, only Mexico, the Dominican Republic, Colombia, and Peru indicated a willingness to accept refugees in significant numbers, and they, too, limited their acceptance to agricultural labor.

As for the United States, whose President had been so applauded for summoning this conference, it "prides itself," said Myron Taylor to the assembled delegates, "upon the liberality of its existing [immigration] laws and practices. . . . I might point out that the American government has taken steps to consolidate the German and former Austrian quotas so that a total of 27,370 immigrants may enter the United States on the German quota in one year." This meant, of course, no increase in total U.S. immigration—and in fact there were only 17,868 German and Austrian immigrants in the whole of fiscal 1938. Of these, 11,917 were Jews.[25] Myriads of others were denied visas by American consular officials, acting in accordance with U.S. immigration laws, because they were destitute, or nearly so, having been stripped of their property by the Nazis. In the first year after Hitler became chancellor, German emigrants were allowed to take with them 75 percent of the value of their property. This was lowered to 15 percent a couple of years later, and to 5 percent in 1938. Hence, by that time, a large majority of the would-be immigrants were unable to satisfy officials that, having arrived in America, they would not become public charges. The policy seemed, in the tragic circumstances, outrageous to many Americans of goodwill. Anne O'Hare McCormick spoke for them in her *New*

*York Times* foreign-affairs column, published two days before the conference opened:

> It is heartbreaking to think of the queues of desperate human beings around our consulates in Vienna and in other cities waiting in suspense for what happens at Evian. But the question they underline is not simply humanitarian. It is not a question of how many unemployed this country can safely add to its own unemployed millions. It is a test of civilization. . . . Can America live with itself if it lets Germany get away with this policy of extermination, allows the fanaticism of one man to triumph over reason, refuses to take up this gage of battle against barbarism?[26]

Evidently, America could.

In sum, Évian's sole tangible achievement was the establishment, against initial British opposition, of the aforementioned Intergovernmental Committee on Refugees, to be permanently headquartered in London. The stated argument in favor of establishing the IGC, which would operate outside the League of Nations, was that, in view of Hitler's hostility toward the League, the new agency would be better able than any League agency to negotiate with Germany on the refugee problem. The argument proved untrue. When the new negotiating attempts were made they would be frustrated by Germany's continued refusal to modify its emigration-restricting policy. Instead, the would-be receiving countries must change *their* immigration laws, abolishing their immigration restrictions, insisted the Nazis. The result was that the IGC, through all the years of its existence, accomplished nothing toward a solution of the hugely growing, the increasingly agonized refugee problem.

IV

THE warship on which Roosevelt sailed from San Diego, Saturday, July 16, 1938, was one with which he was intimately familiar. In the summer of 1934 he had lived for six weeks in the same ship's quarters he now occupied, the admiral's quarters of the flagship U.S.S. *Houston,* as he made a fourteen-thousand-mile voyage down the Atlantic coast, through the Panama Canal, across the Pacific to Hawaii, then back to the Columbia River and up that and the Willamette to Portland. This time, his voyage reversed the direction followed four years before and was some thousands of miles shorter.

His original plan for this trip, outlined in an early February memorandum to his naval aide, Captain Walter B. Woodson, had been to go by train from Washington to Mexico City for a day of ceremonial Good Neighborliness, then motor down to Acapulco, where he would board ship. From Acapulco he would go directly to Cocos Island, there to remain two days; thence to the Galápagos Islands for five or six days; then from the Galápagos "through Panama Canal to Mobile or Pensacola, allowing for two six or eight hour stops —one off the northwest coast of Colombia in the Pacific and the other at New Providence Island, a short distance north of Colón."[27] His Western speaking trip, not contemplated in early February, had of course changed his point of departure from the United States; a serious break in the normally friendly relations with Mexico caused him to cancel his official visit to the Mexican capital. Otherwise, the originally planned itinerary was generally followed.

The trouble with Mexico, which, as we shall see, Roosevelt did something to soothe within twenty-four hours after putting out to sea, had became acute with the abrupt March 18 announcement by Mexico's president, Lázaro Cárdenas, that his government was expropriating all American, British, and Dutch oil property in Mexico and would henceforth itself operate the oil industry in the public interest.

Cárdenas had been born and raised a peon. He had therefore had abundant personal experience of poverty and human exploitation. It had added fervor to his strong, true belief in the continuing Mexican Revolution, which he sought now to advance far more rapidly than General Plutarco Calles, a more conservative predecessor, had done. In the three years of his presidency, he had in fact, and in the words of Whitney Shepardson of the U.S. Council on Foreign Relations, "done more than all his predecessors since 1920 in carrying out the economic program of the revolution. He had speeded up the redistribution of estates among landless peons on a basis of communal ownership; he had sought to provide more adequate credit facilities for farm cooperatives; and he had taken steps to obtain a betterment of wages and working conditions in industry."[28] Part and parcel of this effort had been government encouragement of industrial unionism, with the result that the Confederation of Mexican Workers, or CTM, which was a "vertical" union not unlike John L. Lewis's CIO, had grown by leaps and bounds. One of the CTM's chief affiliates was the Mexican Petroleum Workers' Union; and it was out of a contract dispute between this union and the oil companies that the oil-expropriation decision had emerged.

The process had been prolonged.

In early November 1936, the union had presented to eighteen foreign oil companies a single standard contract and threatened to strike all the companies if they did not join together to open, within ten days, a general negotiating conference whose agenda was limited to the union demands. The companies agreed to hold a general conference but insisted that its agenda not be limited to the union's demands. To this the union would not agree, but just before the strike deadline it postponed the walkout until late May 1937. No settlement having been negotiated by that time, the strike began, causing considerable hardship and great inconvenience to the general public. The angry reaction was such as to cause the union to suspend the strike after twelve days. It called then for government adjudication, as provided for by a section of Mexico's labor law having to do with economic controversies that "by their special nature" could not be settled through ordinary negotiating procedures. The quarrel thus came under the jurisdiction of a federal Board of Conciliation and Arbitration (it was somewhat similar in function to the U.S.'s National Labor

Relations Board, though more powerful) which appointed a "commission of experts" to study and report on the matter. This commission completed its investigation and submitted its findings within a suspiciously short time— indeed, with a speed absolutely astonishing, considering the length of the report (nearly a million words, counting exhibits and appendices) and the drastic nature of its recommendations: The findings were in the federal board's hands by early August, less than two months after the "experts" were appointed!

The gist of the report was a comparison of the Mexican and U.S. oil industries, stressing wide discrepancies between the two in wages and profits. Thus, though production per oil worker was higher in Mexico than in the United States, the wage paid Mexican workers was much lower than that paid U.S. workers; this largely accounted for the fact that it cost five times as much to produce a barrel of oil in the United States as it cost to do so in Mexico, Moreover, the gap between the two national wage levels steadily widened. The real wage of the Mexican oil worker had allegedly declined 16 to 22 percent since 1934; the real wage of the U.S. oil worker had allegedly increased 8 percent during the same period. Naturally, therefore, American oil-company profits in Mexico were much higher than they were in the United States. In 1935, the companies in the United States had made a mere 1.2 percent on their capital investment, whereas in Mexico they had made 16.8 percent. These findings, the accuracy of which was vehemently denied by the American oil companies in testimony before the federal board, provided the basis on which the board awarded the union a basic wage increase of 27 percent, a workweek of forty-five hours, liberal vacation and pension allowances, and other benefits, all to be retroactive to the date the strike began. Taken together, these made unprofitable (they were deliberately intended to make unprofitable) the private operation of Mexico's oil industry. Nor could the oil companies obtain redress through the Mexican Supreme Court. Unlike Roosevelt, Cárdenas had been able to "pack" the Supreme Court with appointees who would rule as he wished, with the result that when the oil companies petitioned the court for an injunction against enforcement of the board's award to the union, their petition was promptly (on March 1) denied.

Even this rapidity of legal action was too slow for the revolutionary-minded Mexican president, however. Only two and a half weeks after the Supreme Court action, and at a time when most observers thought Mexico's most extreme next move would be to force the oil companies into receivership, Cárdenas made his expropriation announcement, doing so in a dramatically emotional radio address delivered at ten o'clock at night. The announcement struck U.S. ambassador Josephus Daniels like (in his own words) "a bolt from the blue." For the announced action admittedly disregarded procedures established under Mexican law. "Elaborate legal proceedings" would "unduly prolong a situation that must, for the honor of the nation, be decided at once," explained Cárdenas. And, after all, had not the oil companies themselves, with their private police and their subversive political activity, including the covert subsidizing of influential portions of the Mexican press, been operating for a long time in flagrant disregard of Mexican rights and Mexican law? Cárdenas assured Loyalist Spain, to whose cause Mexico was committed, that this move would benefit it. On January 1, 1937, he had proudly proclaimed the recent shipment by his government of $11,500,000 worth of guns and ammunition to the Loyalist government. He now proclaimed that the nationalized oil industry, unlike the foreign-owned oil companies, would not simply sell oil "to the highest bidder" but would always take into account the effect any oil sale would have upon "nations engaged in conflict."[29] (It must be said that Cárdenas broke this promise almost on the morrow of his making it. Absolute necessity, determined by that economic interdependence of the world's peoples that is so dangerously contradicted by unlimited national sovereignty, forced him to do so, and in ways economically damaging to the three countries whose oil companies had been ousted from Mexico. Germany and her cosigners of the Tripartite Pact provided almost the only market for Mexican oil following the expropriation; by the end of 1938, the Mexican government would perforce be selling most of its oil to Germany and much of the rest to Italy and Japan, taking payment for 60 percent of it in goods that Mexico would otherwise have purchased, in good part, from the Americans, the British, and the Dutch.)

All this presented the Roosevelt administration with a diplomatic problem as difficult as it was grave. It was of course necessary for the administration to insist that American citizens receive just and fair compensation for their expropriated property, as stipulated in Mexican law. It was equally necessary, or more necessary, that this insistence be made in ways that did not destroy the credibility of Good Neighborliness. For if there were any hint of a return by the United States to "dollar diplomacy," the fragile democracies of Latin America would be tempted toward the totalitarian arms of Communist Russia (in the case of Mexico) or Nazi Germany (in the case of Central and South American countries). Ambassador Daniels stressed the point in his advice to the President, saying: "The upholding of . . . [the Good Neighbor] policy . . . is of the highest consideration in a mad world where Pan American solidarity may save democracy. Oil sought not to smear it."[30]

Hence the delicate blend of firmness with sympathetic respect in the Roosevelt-approved note that Secretary Hull dispatched to Mexico City nine days after the expropriation announcement and that Ambassador Daniels then presented personally to Cárdenas. The Mexican government's right as well as its sovereign power to expropriate was unquestioned, the note said. But it added, in the tone of an "of course" reminder, that "the properties of nationals so expropriated are required to be paid for by a compensation representing fair, assured and effective value to the nationals from whom these properties were taken." The note further reminded the Mexican government that there had been a series of as yet uncompensated expropriations, mostly of land owned by American ranchers and farmers, in recent years, and that these added to a problem for which, "because of the very friendly relations existing between the two governments," a solution would, it was hoped, be soon found by the

Mexican government. The note was effective. The Mexican president quickly responded with a note to Josephus Daniels saying that the U.S. attitude "reaffirms once more the sovereignty of the peoples of this continent which the statesman of the most powerful country of America His Excellency President Roosevelt has so enthusiastically maintained"; that this attitude had "won the esteem of the people of Mexico"; and that "Mexico will know how to honor its obligations of today and its obligations of yesterday."[31]

Roosevelt's own public response to all this evinced more sympathy for the Mexican government's problems than for those of the oil companies—an attitude strikingly at variance with that of past administrations. He was informed of the Cárdenas reply on the last day of his spring vacation in Warm Springs. Speaking of the expropriation to his press conference on that same day, he said that the administration's chief concern was for small American farmers and ranchers whose lands in Mexico had been expropriated during the last three years, people who had invested their all in these properties and would lose it all if not compensated. The oil companies were in no such dire straits. They were legitimate businesses deserving of compensation, of course, and the administration would insist that they be compensated for the actual amount they had invested in their Mexican facilities, minus normal operational depreciation. They had no right to demand payment, however, as they were inclined to do, for the loss of prospective profits. As for those who by hook or crook had acquired hundreds of thousands of acres of Mexican land for a pittance (during the Porfirio Díaz dictatorship, William Randolph Hearst had acquired a Mexican ranch larger than Rhode Island) and now claimed full market value for the expropriated holdings, they were on their own, the President indicated. The U.S. government was not going to act as their collection agent.[32]

The response of the Chamberlain ministry in Great Britain to Mexico's action was very different. In 1935, after prolonged negotiations, Mexico had agreed to pay a stipulated sum to Britain for certain losses suffered by British nationals during the Mexican Revolution. The payments were to be made in installments of 361,737 pesos, and one of these had come due in January 1938. When, by the second week of May, it remained unpaid, the British in a blunt note not only demanded immediate payment but coupled the demand with remarks to the effect that Mexico's untrustworthiness in such matters deprived its expropriations of any legal or moral justification. Mexico's prompt reply was a note enclosing the installment payment with the comment that "even some powerful states and those which have ample resources [as Mexico patently did not] cannot pride themselves on the punctual payment of all their pecuniary obligations"—a pointed reference to the fact that Great Britain had defaulted on its war debt to the United States. Simultaneously, the Mexican Foreign Office, "in view of the very unfriendly attitude of the British government," announced the breaking-off of diplomatic relations between Mexico and Britain.

Clearly, the Rooseveltian attitude, though it infuriated American businessmen with Mexican interests, was far more likely to serve those interests than the British hard line was serving British businessmen, It relieved and gratified Lázaro Cárdenas, who was therefore pleased to send personal representatives out to sea to welcome the President of the United States to Mexican waters on Sunday, July 17, 1938. And Roosevelt was in turn pleased to welcome these representatives aboard the U.S.S. *Houston* as highly distinguished guests and to convey through them to Cárdenas warm personal regards along with clear indications that he had a sympathetic understanding of the Mexican president's politico-economic goals, also that he was certain the current problem would be solved in ways satisfactory to both Mexico and the United States.*

Of all Roosevelt's presidential holiday cruises thus far, this of the summer of 1938 was perhaps the one he most needed for relaxation, recreation, restoration of body and spirit. It was also perhaps the most completely successful in satisfying those needs.

He took with him no one who would tax him with weighty affairs of state. From his Washington staff, he asked only military aide Pa Watson, who was one of the most relaxed and relaxing men in his troubled world. He also took with him a distinguished scientist, Dr. Waldo S. Schmitt of the United States National Museum of Natural History (a part of the Smithsonian Institution), "with the objective of making a survey of the fishes, marine invertebrates, flora, and other biological specimens in the many out-of-the-way places we visited," as he himself later wrote. This greatly added to the interest, the excitement, of the voyage, and to its fun, for Dr. Schmitt was not only diligent and effective in the performance of his scientific duties but also proved a good companion in conversation and sport. (On the first day of the voyage, Roosevelt, as he recounted to a Hyde Park crowd a month later, asked the scientist if there were "any particular thing or animal that you would like to find?" The doctor had replied that "the one thing" he was searching most ardently for was "a burrowing shrimp." But why leave Washington for that? asked Roosevelt. "Washington is overrun with them. I know that after five years."[33]) For several days they enjoyed fine weather and excellent fishing along the Mexican coast and at Socorro Island, where a new species of burrowing shrimp was indeed found. At Clipperton Island a calm sea enabled the scientist to land with a party of *Houston* crew volunteers to "collect many fine specimens of marine and plant life and birds, and to shoot a wild pig which we duly ate!" as Roosevelt wrote in a diary letter addressed to Eleanor ("Dearest Babs"). A two-day sail straight southward then brought them to islands remote from well-traveled sea-lanes but central to the history of biology—the Galápagos astride the equator, the islands that contributed so greatly to the development of Darwin's theory. There they spent a week "going from island to island," barren islands, for the most part, but "full of color, for they are all volcanic." They had "good

---

*It would be, though in August 1938 that event was yet far distant. Complicated negotiations extending well into the following year would be required, negotiations that would test severely the long-suffering patience of Secretary of State Cordell Hull.

fishing" there and, because the water was very cold (the Humboldt Current flows from the Antarctic through these islands), the fish were "excellent eating." Schmitt added much from the islands to his scientific eollections. "My only complaint," wrote Roosevelt, "is that the weather here on the Equator has been too cool. Also one has no feeling of the tropics—no lush vegetation —it might be Nantucket Island, only not so green. Still it is all interesting— especially remembering that the tortoises [the giant turtles after whom the Spaniards named the islands], iguanas etc. are the oldest living form of the animals of 15,000,000 years ago." The *Houston* arrived at Cocos Island, a day's sail northeastward from the Galápagos, on Monday, August 1—a day rendered memorable for all aboard, and especially for General Watson, because in the afternoon "Pa got a sailfish . . . —the only one & he is asking to succeed Pershing as General of the Armies." So said Roosevelt in a note to Marvin McIntyre in the White House. "I take it you have a screamingly funny time over primaries!" he added. "Here we don't care who wins." Months later, that day would be also remembered as the one when Doctor Schmitt discovered, on Cocos, "a new palm . . . which is not only a new species but constitutes a new genus, It has been given the name 'Rooseveltia Frankliniana,' " as Roosevelt proudly noted in the 1938 volume of his *Public Papers and Addresses.* On the following day, in the morning, a destroyer brought mail out to the *Houston,* the first mail since leaving San Diego (though news and messages had of course come via radio) and, as Roosevelt wrote Eleanor, it seemed "queer to resume contacts!" He had been so happily, totally cut off from them.[34]

But during this carefree time he did make final plans for a trip to Canada that had been scheduled months before. On August 18 he was to go to Kingston, Ontario, at the head of the St. Lawrence River, to be honored with a degree from Queen's University and to make an acceptance speech. On that same day he would go by automobile to the Thousand Islands, to dedicate the newly completed International Bridge at its American terminal in Clayton, New York. At the close of the diary letter he mailed Eleanor on August 2, he invited her to accompany him on this trip. He would be back in Washington on August 12, he said, and his "thought" was that they "go direct from there the eve of the 17th" to Kingston, leave the Thousand Islands on the evening of the eighteenth, "and get to H.P. the A.M. of the 19th and stay there 10 days!" From the Canal Zone a couple of days later he wrote to her again, saying he had "wired you today about the plans for Canada. . . . I do hope you can come." (He also gleefully reported that he had "caught a 230 lb. shark yesterday—1 hr. and 35 minutes—so I win the pool for Biggest Fish!") But his two letters crossed one from her in the mail, and hers told him that "John [their youngest son, married in mid-June to Anne Clark at Nahant, Massachusetts] would like to meet me in N.Y. on the 18th & spend the 19th getting what he wants [for his and his bride's new home] out of storage. If you don't have to have me in Canada will you wire *at once*? . . . I don't want to go anywhere I don't have to go until my lecture trip which starts October 18th." He did wire her, saying she didn't *have* to accompany him, and she, in another letter written immediately upon receipt of his "two letters this morning" (they were "grand" and told "so much that is interesting about the trip. What a big shark!"), said that she, with "Johnnie" and Anne, would be in Hyde Park to greet him on the nineteenth.[35]

V

HE was in high spirits—suntanned, relaxed, exuding confidence in himself and his cause—when, having debarked at Pensacola on the morning of Tuesday, August 9, he addressed informally the great welcoming crowd that awaited him there. The outcome of the primaries already held was generally satisfactory to him. To Elmer Thomas's victory in Oklahoma had now been added Barkley's in Kentucky, both of them by wide margins—and these were the only two races in which he had thus far invested substantial portions of his personal prestige. Clearly his frown had not withered the candidacies of Adams in Colorado and McCarran in Nevada; the former had won his primary, the latter was obviously on the way to winning his; but this could hardly be interpreted as evidence of a loss of political potency. After all, he had spoken publicly against neither man. He had only frowned, and with no ferocity.

But now began the most difficult and dangerous part of his liberal crusade.

His special train took him northward into Georgia, to Warm Springs, where he spent a happy Wednesday before proceeding, next day, to Barnesville some thirty miles to the northeast. Normally a sleepy country town of some four thousand people, far outside the mainstream of current history, Barnesville was transformed for a few hours on this one day into a bustling center of national attention. No fewer than fifty thousand people were gathered before the stage on which Franklin Roosevelt was to play, under the hot August sun, a triple role: that of Georgia citizen, by virtue of his second home in Warm Springs; that of President of the United States, concerned about the South as the nation's "Number One economic problem—the nation's problem, not merely the South's"; and that of party politician determined to lead his party toward liberal goals. The situation was highly dramatic; it had been deliberately designed to be so. Behind Roosevelt as he rose to speak sat Georgia's senator Walter F. George, a leading figure in that conservative coalition of Republicans and Southern Democrats that stood like a high, spiked wall between the President and his legislative goals. Also on the platform sat George's opponent in the Georgia Democratic primary, U.S. Attorney Lawrence Camp, a rather shy, self-effacing young man whose liberal convictions were strong but whose desire to challenge the formidable George was (or had initially been) very weak. He had been talked into doing so by representatives of the White House. Thus this staged meeting was inherently confrontational, a fact that had been advertised, and it was in the expectation of exciting theater that most of the vast throng had come to this place. They therefore waited in suspense as Roosevelt rose and, with a wide but brief smile, propped himself against the podium. Their suspense was intensified by the manner (grave, deliberate, subtly portentous) in which the address's opening words were spoken.

Since the ostensible occasion of this meeting was the dedication of a new Rural Electrification Administration project at Barnesville, these opening words told of how Roosevelt had first come to Warm Springs "fourteen years ago" as "a Democratic Yankee, a comparatively young man"—of how his "new neighbors" had then "made him feel so much at home that he built himself a house, bought himself a farm," and had "been coming back ever since"—and of how there had been "only one discordant note in that first stay of mine at Warm Springs," a note that grated harshly upon his mind when he read his first monthly electricity bill for "my little cottage."* This bill informed him

> that the charge was eighteen cents per kilowatt hour—about four times as much as I was paying in . . . Hyde Park, New York. That light bill started my long study of proper utility charges for electric current, started in my mind the whole subject of getting electricity into farm homes throughout the United States. So, my friends, it can be said . . . that a little cottage at Warm Springs, Georgia, was the birthplace of the Rural Electrification Administration. . . . Electricity is a modern necessity of life, not a luxury. That necessity ought to be found in every village, in every house and on every farm in every part of the United States. The dedication of this [REA] . . . project in Georgia today is a symbol of the progress we are making—and we are not going to stop.[36]

To all this Walter George listened impassively but, one may be sure, with no great pleasure. He was a handsome, graying, sixty-year-old man whose manner was so intimidatingly formal that even his wife addressed him as "Mr. George." He perfectly "looks the part of a southern statesman who never thought to let his hair grow long or to sprout a goatee," according to *Time* magazine.[37] His reserves were so great, his gravity so unrelieved by humor, that he seemed more than a little pompous to many people. And he would almost certainly have voted against legislation creating a Rural Electrification Administration had such a bill been presented to the Senate in 1935.† Officials of the Georgia Power Company were among his closest friends (so were officials of the Coca-Cola Company in Atlanta). Georgia Power had strongly backed him in his every senatorial election campaign; it did so now, in 1938. And Georgia Power, in common with the rest of the utilities industry, had fought tooth and nail against the rural cooperatives, organized under the aegis of REA, through which electric power was being wired into country homes that had been theretofore denied it by the utilities industry.

Even less to George's liking were Roosevelt's following words.

---

*Actually, the cottage was not completed until early 1927, more than two years after Roosevelt's first stay in Warm Springs.

†The REA was created by executive order through exercise of the huge grant of legislative authority made to the President by the omnibus work-relief bill enacted early in 1935. See *FDR: The New Deal Years*, pp. 490–92.

The first of them quoted from a message he had delivered last July 4 to a conference on economic conditions in the South, a conference of "distinguished, broad-minded Southerners" whom he had invited to Washington. It was in this message that he had identified the South as the "Nation's Number One economic problem." Why? Because the South's gross "economic unbalance" created "unbalance" in the nation as a whole. He now had in hand the report of this conference—it had been delivered to him when he landed at Pensacola—and it succinctly listed in fifteen categories the South's very many serious socioeconomic troubles. (Significantly, neither Roosevelt nor the conference report made any mention of unjust and inhumane race relations, the institutionalized degradation and exploitation of black people by white, as a prime essential of the South's "feudal system"—Roosevelt in his bitter Gainesville speech of last March had equated this feudalism with fascism— though the system was clearly a root cause of Southern poverty, ignorance, and general backwardness.) The grouped listing of problems in the conference report indicated that "many steps . . . must be taken to solve the problems." And since the problems involved "interstate relationships" within the South, as well as relations between the South and the nation as a whole, few of these steps could be taken successfully by a state government alone.

It is not an attack on state sovereignty to point out that this national aspect of all these problems requires action by the Federal Government in Washington. . . . Such action . . . must be vigorously supported by Senators and Representatives whose constituents are directly concerned with Southern economics and Southern social needs. Translating that into more intimate terms, it means that if the people of Georgia want definite action in the Congress of the United States they must send to that Congress Senators and Representatives who are willing to stand up and fight night and day for Federal statutes drawn to meet actual needs.

In other words, they must send liberal congressmen, liberal senators.

"Here in Georgia, however," Roosevelt went on, speaking very slowly, deliberately, "my old friend, the senior Senator from this State, cannot possibly . . . be classified as belonging to the liberal school of thought. . . ."

Whereupon, Walter George, though he had known what was coming (he and the President had recently exchanged letters), was observed to stiffen in his chair, to lift his head a little higher, to set his jaw more firmly. There appeared upon his finely chiseled countenance a slight, grim smile.

The speaker continued:

"Let me make it clear that he [the senator] is, and I hope always will be, my personal friend. He is . . . beyond any possible question a gentleman and a scholar. . . . [But] on most public questions he and I do not speak the same language. To carry out my responsibility as President, it is clear that if there is to be success in our Government there ought to be cooperation between members of my own party and myself—cooperation, in other words, within the majority party, between . . . the Legislative branch and the head of the other branch, the Executive. . . . The test is not measured, in the case of an individual, by his every vote on every bill. . . . [but]

rather in the answer to two questions: first, has the record of the candidate shown
. . . a constant active fighting attitude in favor of the broad objectives of the party
and of the Government as they are constituted today; and, secondly, does the
candidate really . . . deep down in his heart believe in those objectives? I regret that
in the case of my friend, Senator George, I cannot honestly answer either of these
questions in the affirmative.

The case was different with the man Roosevelt regarded as George's chief
primary opponent. (Also running for the Senate seat was the foul-mouthed,
reactionary racial bigot Eugene Talmadge, former governor of the state, but
Roosevelt devoted to him just three contemptuously dismissive sentences.)
Lawrence Camp, having served in the state legislature and as state attorney
general for four years, and having "made a distinguished record in the United
States District Court," was "not only a public servant with successful experience but . . . a man who honestly believes that many things must be done and
done now to improve the economic and social conditions of the country, a man
who is willing to fight for these objectives. . . . I have no hesitation in saying
that if I were able to vote in the September primaries in this State, I most
assuredly should cast my ballot for Lawrence Camp."

Then Roosevelt, a broad smile on his face, turned to Walter George with
his right hand extended. The senator stood up to grasp it.

"Mr. President," said the senator with his customary formal courtesy, shaking hands, "I regret that you have taken the occasion to question my Democracy and to attack my record. I want you to know that I accept the
challenge."[38]

And from the huge throng there burst a roar of mingled hand-clapping and
cheers. None, however, could say how much of this applause was mere emotional reaction to a highly dramatic moment; neither could anyone say how
the rest of it was apportioned between approval of Franklin Roosevelt's stand
and approval of Walter George's.

From Barnesville that afternoon the President journeyed to Athens,
Georgia, where he received an honorary degree from the state university and
spoke again to a huge crowd about Georgia's and the South's grave problems.
All of them, he stressed, were "intimately dependent" for their solution "upon
economic conditions: higher wages, higher farm income and more profits for
small businessmen." All of them called for action by the national government
"to eliminate discriminations between one part of the country and another, to
raise purchasing power and thereby create wealth in those sections where it
is far too low, to save [sic] the waste and the erosion of our natural resources
. . . , to take the lead in establishing social security," and also to lead the people
away from demagogic reaction and toward sound, rational progressivism. "At
heart Georgia shows devotion to the principles of democracy," he concluded.
"Georgia, like other states, has occasional lapses; but it really does not believe
in demagoguery or feudalism [he obviously referred first to Talmadge, second
to George], even though they are dressed up in democratic clothes. . . . To be
a part of you is [for me] a great honor and a great privilege."[39]

An hour or so later he spoke from the rear platform of his railroad car to yet another huge crowd, this one in Greenville, South Carolina. He did so very briefly, extemporaneously, since, having already delivered two speeches that day, he had not had "time nor opportunity to prepare a third." But he seized the opportunity to swipe at South Carolina's conservative Ellison D. (Cotton Ed) Smith, who, for the first time in decades, faced a serious primary challenge. Smith, opposing the Wage and Hour Bill, had said that in his state fifty cents a day could support a family—a remark quoted far and wide as evidence of Cotton Ed's commitment to the ruling planter class, his indifference to the plight of the working class. "Before I stop—and I believe the train is pulling out in a minute or two," said Roosevelt, "—I want to suggest two things to you." The first was a promise he had made South Carolina's governor that he would visit the state capital later that year. "The other thing is that I don't believe any family or man can live on fifty cents a day."[40]

This parting shot was loudly, laughingly applauded.

## VI

ELEANOR'S last letter to her husband had spoken of a long spell of "rain, damp & heat" along the Eastern Seaboard, saying that this had been very "trying." The weather was bound to improve, of course, but she doubted he would "find . . . Washington very pleasant."[41] She was right. He had abundant reason to be grateful for the air-conditioning that Louie Howe had insisted upon installing in six rooms of the family quarters on the second floor of the White House, including the Oval Room, as soon as he had had his first taste of Washington's summer heat in 1933.* Roosevelt was also glad of the central air-conditioning that had been installed in the Executive Office Wing in 1930, when the wing was rebuilt following a ruinous Christmas Eve fire.[42] This helped him through the five work-crowded days that intervened between his return to Washington on Friday, August 12, and his departure for Kingston, Ontario.

His first newsworthy act was to add Representative O'Connor of New York and Senator Millard Tydings of Maryland to his list of purge targets. He did so in a press announcement within a dozen hours after his arrival at the White House. Two days later, in a radio address on the third anniversary of the passage of the Social Security Act, he thanked "publicly, as I have often thanked privately," four members of Congress whom he credited with "carrying" this act through the House and Senate, the first-named of them being Congressman David J. Lewis of Maryland, "known as one of the American pioneers of the cause of Social Security." Lewis was giving up virtually certain reelection to the lower house in order to run as the White House's candidate for the Senate seat of Millard Tydings. (Of the other three congressional members given public thanks on this occasion, only New York's Senator

---

*But Roosevelt made as little use of air-conditioning as he could; he believed it aggravated his chronic sinus infection.

Wagner deserved them. Irritating to those well informed on Social Security's history were the accolades to "Senator [Pat] Harrison of Mississippi and Congressman [Robert L.] Doughton of North Carolina, who carried the bill successfully through the Senate and the House." Neither of the two had been a champion of Social Security; neither had made any major effort on its behalf in Congress. Secretary of Labor Frances Perkins was duly and deservedly thanked, but strangely unmentioned was Harry Hopkins, whom Roosevelt was supposed to be building up to succeed him in the White House. Yet Hopkins had probably done more than anyone else in government, save Madam Perkins, to promote the Social Security idea and overcome, insofar as it *was* overcome, Roosevelt's excessively conservative conception of, and attitude toward, social insurance in general in 1935.[43])

On the following day, in his press conference, he "sounded off" (as a reporter put it) against both Tydings and O'Connor, reading to the assembled newsmen a lengthy editorial from a liberal paper which became, upon his reading it, "my statement" and, as such, directly attributable to him. "If men like Senator Tydings . . . said frankly: 'I no longer believe in the platform of the Democratic Party as expressed in the New Deal; I am running for reelection as a member of the Republican opposition . . . ,' there would be no . . . excuse for President Roosevelt to intervene against them," said the editorial statement.

> The issue would be clear. The voter could take his choice between the New Deal and Tydings' record of consistent opposition to it. But Tydings . . . wants to run with the Roosevelt prestige and the money of his conservative Republican friends both on his side. That's why we welcome the report that Roosevelt help is going to be given to Tydings' opponent . . . and to James H. Fay, candidate for the nomination in the Sixteenth Congressional District of New York. Fay is running against . . . one of the most effective obstructionists in the lower house. Week in and week out [John J.] O'Connor labors to tear down New Deal strength, pickle [as his chairmanship of the rules committee greatly helped him to do] New Deal legislation.[44]

During these five days Roosevelt had also to put into final shape the draft speeches that had been prepared in the State Department for his delivery at Queen's University and at the International Bridge dedication ceremony.

The original draft dedication speech had been prepared in whole or in large part by Adolf A. Berle, who also wrote out and submitted to the President at this time his formal resignation from the post of assistant secretary of state, which he had accepted, with some reluctance, six months before. "I made the date at your pleasure in September," said Berle's cover note, "but I hope to get away for a holiday about September 1."[45] (In the event, overwhelmed by the hugely breaking wave of the Czechoslovakian crisis, Berle would have to forgo his September holiday—and his resignation, after having been accepted "with real regret" by the President, would be withdrawn at the latter's urgent request. Berle was destined to remain assistant secretary of state for nearly six more years.) His most active concern since coming to Washington had been the revival of the long-proposed but also long-dormant St. Lawrence Seaway project. This included not only the construction, through the St. Lawrence and around rapids, of a channel wide and deep enough to permit ocean vessels to dock at Great Lakes cities, but also the construction of a number of great hydroelectric plants at suitable points along the river.

Since this must be a joint undertaking by Canada and the United States, a special treaty between the two countries was required. The Hoover administration had negotiated one in late 1932,* submitting it to the Senate for ratification in the last month of that year. After languishing in committee during the remainder of the lame-duck session and through all the New Deal's first year, the treaty had been rejected by the Senate in 1934, despite Roosevelt's support of it. The opposition was grounded wholly in special regional economic interests. Atlantic seaboard cities were opposed out of fear they would lose to Chicago and other Great Lakes cities much of their overseas traffic. Railroad companies opposed the treaty because it would, they thought, drastically reduce Eastern rail freight traffic. And, of course, utilities corporations opposed the hydroelectric portions of it as they did all proposals for public power development. But there was also strong organized support for the project, especially from agricultural and industrial interests in the Midwest, and Roosevelt refused to concede its death in 1934. Instead, he promptly announced his intention to negotiate a new treaty—an intention not acted upon, however, until the 1938 "Roosevelt recession" forced the renewal of federal spending, whereupon the seaway became, in Roosevelt's view, a public-works project that would spur economic recovery as well as add greatly and permanently to the nation's wealth.

By that time, Berle was in the State Department and in a position to press the matter, not only within the administration, but also with William Lyon Mackenzie King's government in Canada. By June 1938 he could report to Roosevelt that a treaty with Ottawa was definitely in the works.[46] And this bridge-dedication speech, which he had wholly or mostly drafted, and which Roosevelt now worked into final form, was designed to further the process.

Determinative of the final form of the Queen's University speech were the smoldering fires of Europe, in whose lurid light the revision was made. By mid-August Hitler's will to effect a "solution" of the Sudetenland problem within the next few weeks, even if it cost a general war, was dreadfully apparent. A fatal pronouncement on the subject when the Führer addressed the annual Nazi party rally at Nuremberg in mid-September was dreadfully anticipated. Roosevelt's draft speech revision, whereby the original's coherence was destroyed and a major foreign-policy statement inserted, was his response to the threat thus posed to the Western Hemisphere. That he had worked with reckless haste on both drafts became apparent to critical ears when the speeches were delivered, and to critical eyes when they were printed.

At Queen's University on August 18, following the ceremony of his investiture with the degree of doctor of laws *honoris causa* by the university chancel-

---

*See *FDR: The New York Years,* pp. 99–101.

lor, he first told the immense crowd before him of the pleasure he felt at "being once more on Canadian soil where [on Campobello Island] I have passed so many happy hours of my life [his mother and son James were on Campobello at that very moment]," He spoke of his "gratitude for being admitted to the fellowship of this ancient and famous university." He spoke of civilization as being "not national" but "international," of ideas as "the common inheritance of all free people," and of the ever closer interdependence of all peoples, all nations, whereby war was made ever more threatening to civilization's survival. No longer could "we in the Americas" be isolated from the quarrels of Europe and Asia. "Instead, we in the Americas have become a consideration to every propaganda office and to every general staff beyond the seas. The vast amount of our resources, the vigor of our commerce and the strength of our men have made us vital factors in world peace whether we choose it or not." In what were evidently his own words, he spoke of how Canada and the United States, "in friendship and in entire understanding, can look clear-eyed at these possibilities [there had been no prior mention of 'possibilities'; what they were his present listeners and future readers could only guess], resolving to leave no pathway unexplored, no technique undeveloped which may, if our hopes are realized, contribute to the peace of the world. Even if these hopes are disappointed, we can assure each other that this hemisphere at least shall remain a strong citadel wherein civilization can flourish unimpaired"—which was a fairly flat contradiction of his earlier assertion of a worldwide interdependence that, by clear implication, made isolation from events overseas impossible for both Canada and the United States.

He spoke then the inserted words that gave this speech its immediate and historic importance—spoke them slowly, heavily emphasizing the key phrases. "The Dominion of Canada is part of the sisterhood of the British Empire," he said. "I give to you assurance that the people of the United States will not stand idly by if domination of Canadian soil is threatened by any *other* Empire."[47]*

There rolled up from the great crowd a mighty wave of applause.

An hour or so later he arrived by automobile at the bridge he and Prime Minister King of Canada were to dedicate. There was a ceremony at the Canadian terminus, then King crossed over with Roosevelt to the American terminus at Clayton, New York—and there, with the prime minister of Canada seated behind him, the President of the United States made in his address a strong argument for the earliest possible revival of the St. Lawrence Seaway project.

"The St. Lawrence River is more than a cartographic line between our two countries," he said. "God so formed North America that the waters of an inland empire drain into the Great Lakes Basin. The rain that falls in this vast area finds outlet through this single natural funnel. . . . Therefore we stand as trustees for two countries of one of the richest natural assets . . . anywhere in

*Italics added.

the world. The water that runs underneath this bridge spells unlimited power, permits access to raw materials both from this continent and from beyond the seas. . . . Yet up to now the liquid wealth . . . has run in large part unused into the sea." Surely "we can agree upon some better arrangement than merely letting this water contribute a microscopic fraction to the level of the North Atlantic Ocean." Surely the time had come for action "by our two governments" on a much "larger scale" but of the same kind as had made "the bridge we here dedicate," action that brushed aside the protests of the "prophets of evil." Among such "prophets" were the railroads. He himself was "very clear" that they "are wrong" to fear "that the St. Lawrence Waterway will handicap our railroad systems on both sides of the border." It would instead "create new . . . business," generate "more railroad traffic than it takes away." He was equally if not more emphatically "clear" that the great river's electric power must not only be developed by the two governments, it must remain the property of the citizenry of the two countries and be used to provide cheap electricity.

He made ironical reference to, without naming, the Niagara-Hudson Corporation, which had been formed in 1929 through the merger, under Morgan Bank auspices, of the three largest electric-power systems in New York, and whose directors now looked northward through greedy eyes:

> A conception has been emerging in the United States which is not without a certain magnificence. This is no less than the conviction that if a private group could control the outlet of the Great Lakes Basin on both sides of the border, that group would have a monopoly in the development of a territory larger than many of the great empires of history. If you were to search the records . . . you would discover that literally every development of electric power, save only Hydro-Ontario [government-owned and -operated], is allied to, if not controlled by, a single American group.

The immense social cost, the immense social danger "resulting from the ownership by any group of the right to dispose of wealth which was granted to us collectively by nature itself," was, in the present instance, obvious. "To put it bluntly, a group of American interests is . . . gradually putting itself into a position where, unless caution is exercised [he meant governmental action by Canada and the United States], they may in time be able to determine [for their private profit] the economic and social fate of a large area" in both Canada and his own country. Hence the urgent necessity for action now.

He concluded: "I look forward to the day when a Canadian Prime Minister and an American President can meet to dedicate, not a bridge across this water, but the very water itself, to the lasting and productive use of their respective peoples. Until that day comes, and I hope it may be soon, this bridge stands as an open door. There will be no challenge at the border and no guard to ask a countersign."[48]

On the following day, at his press conference in the Big House at Hyde Park, he faced imperturbably a barrage of questions about the import of his statement, in Kingston, that the United States "would not stand idly by" if any "other empire" than the British "threatened" the "domination" of Canadian soil. The morning papers had been full of speculation about it, some asserting that the President was dramatically widening the scope of the Monroe Doctrine. Roosevelt denied that this was so. All he had done was emphasize what had always been the doctrine's application to Canada, doing so in circumstances which, as he did not need to add, made such emphasis a warning to Berlin.[49]

That his interpretation of the doctrine was historically correct was agreed in the ensuing editorial comment upon it. Americans were reminded that Canada in 1823 was still a British colony and that Austria, Prussia, and Russia in unholy Holy Alliance were rumored to be plotting the forcible restoration to Spain of her former American colonies. It was as a warning against any such design, to which Great Britain was, of course, adamantly opposed, that Monroe, relying upon the British navy for the implementation of his policy, shaped the famous message he delivered to Congress on December 2 of that year. "With existing colonies or dependencies of any European power we have not interfered nor shall we interfere," he said; but any extension by the European autocracies of their form of government "to any portion of either continent" of this hemisphere would constitute a threat to the peace and security of the United States. The threat was answered by threat in the muted language of diplomacy. This country, said its President, could not and would not "behold such interposition, in any form, with indifference."

The fact that the doctrine would never have been promulgated but for Great Britain's control of the Atlantic plus the assurance that this control would be exerted on behalf of the stated policy, and that the doctrine could still (in 1938) be effectively implemented only with the aid of the British navy, gave to Roosevelt's Kingston words a foreign-policy significance that, had it been clearly recognized by the leaders of isolationism, would have made the speech much more loudly controversial than it ever became. For what Roosevelt unmistakably implied was a kind of Monroe Doctrine in reverse. Our fate as a nation was so intimately bound up with Britain's that if Britain went down our own survival as a free people would become highly doubtful. Therefore, the United States could not permit Britain to go down.

VII

ALWAYS, for self-renewal and a reconnection of self with world, of present with past, he returned to this house beside the river, to these gardens, orchards, fields, meadows, woods, to Val-Kill, to Dutchess Hill where his "dream cottage" was now a-building, to the river itself.

And because he so returned—because, too, of a 1935 novel by a lushly rhetorical Whitmanesque writer who died in 1938 at the height of his fame (the fame has since been much reduced, alas)—this river was for many, in those years, a simile of the American experience. "The Hudson River is like . . . the flames of color on the Palisades, elves' echoes, and old Dutch and Hallowe'en," chanted Thomas Wolfe. "It is like the Phantom Horseman . . . and great fires of the Dutchmen in winter time. . . . The Hudson River is like old October and tawny Indians in their camping places long ago. . . . It is like the Knickerbockers and . . . the Rich Folks, and the River People, the Vanderbilts, the Astors, and the Roosevelts. . . ."[50] Nor was the river only simile, even in Thomas Wolfe's feverish and decidedly unphilosophic mind. It was also symbol and metaphor—a symbol of destiny, a metaphor for history.

Out of a remote mountain wilderness down a widening and increasingly populous valley, swelling as it drank dark time out of the earth, growing upon what it secretly drained away of a pastoral America that now ceased to be, year by year, mile by mile, the great river flowed in increasing flood. And here at Crum Elbow, around the hills of Hyde Park, it flowed with a ponderous immensity of power against the far-inland-reaching tides of the sea, yet was by these so gentled that its flow became a slow drift around the bend and south again toward the world-city harbor where Liberty's torch thrust heavenward. The salt of the sea intermingled here at Crum Elbow with fresh water, and this sea salt might be deemed portentous of the river's death since, beyond the harbor, which at this point was near and soon, the river at ebb tide must lose itself utterly in the ocean, as Time is lost in Eternity. Hence this present moment of Crum Elbow was darkly shadowed by fatal destiny for anyone who felt that he himself was of the river, that it was the very substance of his being (becoming) as well as the medium of his connectedness with the world.

Thus the symbolic, metaphorical river suggested by Wolfe's poetic imagination.

But this was not, we may be sure, the river seen on a warm lazy sunlit August Sunday afternoon in 1938 by the man whose identification with it in the public mind was in part responsible for Wolfe's rhapsodically extended soliloquy—the one man who of all Americans was best placed to influence the symbolic river's rate and weight of flow, and even that river's course as a stream of national and world event.

It was the actual, physical Hudson River that Franklin Roosevelt saw, and saw only, we may be sure, when he looked down upon it, across sloping orchard and meadow and wildwood, from the south porch of Hyde Park's Big House. He saw a shimmering blue expanse of reflected sky, with glitters of reflected sunlight dancing across it, and what the sight evoked in him, insofar as it was evocative, was not metaphysically symbolic meaning but actual personal memory. Perhaps he had a flashing regret, quickly suppressed, that he could not now go down to the water's edge, as he had so often done on long strong legs in years past. Perhaps he did now go down to it through memory, down to a great block of ballast limestone half submerged at the foot of the railway bed's steep bank where he had stood many times as a boy looking out into the Hudson's wide channel and imagining the upstream sailing there of Henry Hudson's *Half Moon* on a September day in 1609. He might now imagine, too, James Roosevelt's *Half Moon,* the yacht on which Franklin as a boy had learned to sail at Campobello, burning there in that same channel one October day in 1898, its auxiliary fuel tank having exploded while it was being towed to its winter dry dock. (Groton schoolboy Franklin, reading of this with horror in a letter from his mother, had promptly, angrily demanded to know, in a letter home, why no men had been aboard to douse the flames.) And perhaps then he went through memory and imagination from that rock up the embankment and across the railroad right-of-way into the woods, a virgin remnant of the immense forest that had stretched inland for a thousand miles with scarcely a break in it when Henry Hudson sailed here, where a dank green twilight was perpetual beneath the merged crowns of ancient pines and where there was a religious silence, the kind of softly echoing quiet found in those great dim Gothic cathedrals whose architectural inspiration, within the overall shape assigned them by the tree of Christ's death, was precisely such a forest (a sacred grove) as this. Franklin Roosevelt loved these woods. The great thick-trunked trees, some of them already tall when the Republic was born, were his lifelong friends, and memories by the hundred embraced them. In one of them, from one of the boughs swinging low over an outcropping of granite, the boy Franklin, on a chilly day forty years earlier, had shot a winter wren to add to his collection of mounted Hudson Valley birds. He remembered it vividly because, when he came up to the house to get his collector's gun, not having had it with him when he first glimpsed the wren, his mother had scoffed at his godlike confidence that the bird would still be there, waiting for him, when he returned.

Yes, his view of the river on that August afternoon may have been thus evocative.

But certainly that view was of a piece, in its shimmering brightness, with the view he then had of his summer as a whole thus far. It had been, as he looked back over it, a richly green and smiling summer for him personally, despite the smoldering fires and smoke clouds rising over Europe—a summer prosperous for his political fortunes and for nearly every endeavor over which he had any measure of control or perceived responsibility.

It had begun in what even his enemies described as great personal triumph. The humiliation of early April, when Congress rejected the executive-reorganization bill, had been balanced in the public mind, if not erased from it, by the victory of the Wage and Hour Bill six weeks later—a victory implying a revivified New Deal on the march toward further subordinations of special interest to general welfare, corporate management to national government, Property to People. And during his speaking tour the green smile had remained on summer's face. The political increase for him had been, if anything, an accelerating process. Brightly had the sun shone upon a West and South that were obviously rebounding from the steep economic recession of last fall, winter, and early spring, and the crowds that welcomed him had never been greater nor more enthusiastic. Even such actual clouds as blotted the sun once or twice during the trip had spread good cheer rather than gloom. They had blessed thirsty soil with rain as part of the natural cycle whereby landscapes that had been virtually desert when he viewed them during the great 1934–1936 drouth—landscapes harsh of outline, monotonously metallic—were now softly watercolored in myriad shades of living green and gold. And even for this he might be given, he felt, some credit and much thanks by the people of the plains, with great profit to him politically. For had he not made soil and water conservation a top priority of his administration? Had he not insisted upon shelter-belt plantings across a formerly treeless, windswept land, and upon great projects that would soon dot formerly arid countrysides with man-made lakes? And had not desperately needed rain accompanied his personal visits on well-publicized occasions, as if he commanded the heavens (Franklin the Rainmaker) on behalf of communities in dire need? In Texas on this last trip, for instance, when he spoke at Amarillo, a capital of the recent Dust Bowl, he and his audience had been soaked by an unpredicted and gaily welcomed downpour.

And the summer continued to smile upon him during the first few of his ten days at Hyde Park.

They were happily crowded days. He spent much time in his hand-controlled Ford, driving around the estate, generally with Missy LeHand beside him, to view the fields and meadows farmed for him by Moses Smith, the large acreage of new tree plantation he had ordered over the last dozen years, the cottage that neared completion on Dutchess Hill ("Top Cottage," he began to call it), and the virgin woods along the river. He improved his acquaintance with his son John and John's bride, Anne, whom he much liked —also his relationship with Eleanor, whose career as a journalist and lecturer and promoter of causes (women's rights, Negro rights, Loyalist Spain, the American youth movement) had now hit the full stride that would be maintained through all her remaining White House years. On August 21, at the annual baseball game between a team of White House correspondents and a scratch team assembled by newsman Lowell Thomas (the game was held at Thomas's estate in nearby Pawling) Franklin and Eleanor Roosevelt were excited spectators, if also somewhat disappointed ones. For, as Eleanor wrote in her column next day, "Johnny played with the Washington side, and they lost the game, which was a sad blow."[51]

That same August 21 was the publication date of a new book by Eleanor, an advance copy of which had been placed in her husband's hands when he arrived at Hyde Park from Canada. One of three anthologies of her writings to be published that year (the other two were *It's Up to the Women* and *This Troubled World*), this book was entitled *My Days,* being made up of selections from her syndicated column, "My Day," which now appeared six days a week in seventy-five newspapers having a total of more than four million readers. The popular success of these writings, especially of the column, along with the success of her lecture tours (astonishing, since she had a quavering, high-pitched voice ill suited to public speech), advanced her husband's political fortunes insofar as they strengthened and energized a liberal support that might otherwise have been lost to the White House by Roosevelt's Spanish

policy, his silence and inaction regarding race relations, his refusal in general
to take political risks on behalf of civil rights. Her lectures and writing also
continued to serve him as trial balloons for liberal ideas, and she as a lightning
rod. For Eleanor drew to herself the bolts of conservative wrath that necessarily accompanied her attraction of liberal support and that, had they directly
struck his political habitation, might have damaged it severely. She spoke for
herself, he could and did continue to insist when others complained to him
about something she'd said or done; she had a mind of her own, with which
he did not always agree; she had an American citizen's right to speak her mind,
whereas he had no right, constitutional or moral, to trammel it.

He was appreciative of this service she rendered him. He was grateful to her,
and proud of her, too, as she was of him in a different way, with greater moral
reservations. Their relationship was now firmly set in the mold that had been
shaped for it by character and circumstance through the trauma of the Lucy
Mercer affair; Eleanor's subsequent and consequent war for independence;
Roosevelt's long struggle against his polio crippling, followed by his triumphant political career; the vital personal friendship with both of them of Louis
Howe; the friendship, with its secret passionate essence, between Eleanor and
Lorena Hickok; the continuing close relationship between Roosevelt and
Missy, which may or may not have had (it probably did not have, on Roosevelt's part at least) a secretly passionate essence; and, as the conclusive shaping
circumstance, Louis Howe's fading out of life into death during the last two
years of the first presidential term. In their public lives they were a team,
complementary, mutually reinforcing in the face of growing world crisis. He
was team captain, no doubt of that. A subordinate role was perforce accepted
by her, if with considerable secret resentment. But she was considerably less
subordinate, she was far more nearly an equal player, than she had been during
the Albany years. In their private lives—though no active vestige remained of
the romantic love they had presumably once had for one another; and despite
their vital differences, their often sharp disagreements—they were close
friends, or as close as Roosevelt's nature permitted (he "was really incapable
of a personal friendship with anyone," Missy LeHand once said, astonishingly,
to the journalist Fulton Oursler[52]). Each had an immense respect for the other's
special strengths and abilities.

It was in some sense as trial balloonist, in another as New Deal publicist
in service of what she knew to be her husband's desire, that Eleanor began her
column of August 22 (the one that told of the baseball game) as follows:

It was good to see Mr. Harry Hopkins yesterday and to have him spend the night
with us. He is one of the few people in the world who gives me the feeling of being
entirely absorbed in doing his job well. So many of us do things because they are
thrust upon us or because it seems to be our duty to do them [ten days before, she
in her column had spoken of herself as "having been a shy child with very little
personality and having become accustomed to do things because they were expected
of me and not because I wanted to do them"]. He seems to work because he has an
inner conviction that his job needs to be done and he must do it. He would not

undertake a job at all [the presidency, for instance?] unless he felt that he could really accomplish something which needed to be done.[53]

But though it was indeed "good" for Roosevelt to have Hopkins at Hyde Park—though, as always, he thoroughly enjoyed Hopkins's company—it was through Hopkins, with his latest "inside" news and assessment of the primary campaigns, that discordant notes were introduced into the theretofore sweet harmony of Roosevelt's Hyde Park days. They were notes of doubt. The assertive confidence ("The *people* are with me!") that had sustained him during the last days of the Supreme Court fight, and during the long winter of discontent that followed—a confidence reinforced by the closing acts of the last congressional session and by the enthusiastic response to him of every crowd he had faced during the transcontinental tour—this confidence began to wane.

For neither of the two primary candidates to whom he had committed to the fullest his personal prestige, his persuasive power, was doing at all well. Camp, in fact, was doing very badly in Georgia; he made no headway whatever against George. Lewis still had a chance against Tydings in Maryland, but all indications were that he was much further behind the incumbent than he should have been at this point to make his victory probable. Tydings proved under pressure to be a remarkably adroit as well as confidence-inspiring politician. He refused to engage his opponent on the issue the latter (and the President) had raised, that of his anti–New Deal voting record. He spoke instead, and effectively, of "outside interference" in his state's internal affairs, of the "invasion" of Maryland's sacred soil by "carpetbaggers," and he proclaimed in grand Southern oratorical style that Maryland would never permit "her star in the flag to be 'purged.' "[54] Roosevelt's perturbation, masked by the unflawed good cheer of his manner, was revealed by his acts. On the day after Hopkins's departure he addressed a memorandum to Marvin McIntyre in the White House: "Will you call Breck Long* and ask him how he can help in Maryland both personally and financially?"[55] He also, on that same August 23, delivered to his press conference a homily on political morality for which the chief incitement was a "recent letter by the Republican State Chairman of Georgia . . . calling on all Republicans in . . . Georgia to enter the Democratic primary" where, of course, they would vote for George. This violated the principle and frustrated the purpose of the direct primary, making it less expressive of the will of rank-and-file party members than the "old-fashioned boss-controlled" nominating convention had been. The grievous abuse was widespread. In Idaho, for instance, the Republican primary vote in 1936 "was about 42,000 and the Democratic primary vote was about 55,000" whereas "this year the Republican primary vote was only 30,000 and the Democratic

---

*Breckenridge Long, whose mother was of the politically famous Breckenridge family of Kentucky and whose father was of the only somewhat less politically famous Longs of Virginia, had been Roosevelt's ambassador to Italy from 1933 to 1936. He was married to the very wealthy granddaughter of Francis Preston Blair, Jr.; the Blair family had been a major power, first in Democratic politics, then in Republican, before and during the Civil War.

primary vote was about 85,000"—proof positive that the direct primary system had been corrupted "by the entrance of 15,000 or 20,000 Republicans into the Democratic primary." (He found it "interesting" in this connection "that the Tory press of this country" had thus far "overlooked a very interesting opportunity to work for . . . political morality.") When a reporter pointed out that Democrat John J. O'Connor was now entered in the New York Republican primary, then asked if this was "in the same category" as the Georgia and Idaho episodes, Roosevelt replied: "Certainly, Democrats ought not to enter Republican primaries. . . . It is a question of A, B, C morality. . . ."[56]

In the immediately following days he completed plans for a speaking foray into Maryland over Labor Day weekend, a two-day stump-speaking effort whose strenuousness measured the intensity of his concern for Tydings's defeat.

On Monday evening, August 29, he boarded his train at Hyde Park station. On the following morning he was again in the White House.

VIII

THERE had by now begun, as he would later realize, a reversal of fortune whereby what had theretofore been for him a green, smiling summer was almost wholly transformed—retroactively, retrospectively—into a summer of dust and weeds. At its end, as the November election results would unmistakably reveal and as his election eve speech (anticipating these results) would tacitly recognize, he knew or felt himself to be politically impotent as he had not been since entering the White House—weaker, even, than at the end of the court fight.

He insisted that Jim Farley, Democratic party chairman, accompany him during his foray into Maryland. He sought thus to persuade the public that he spoke for the Democrats nationally, not just for Franklin Roosevelt, as he strove to read Tydings out of the party. And the non–ideologically conservative Farley, though he thought the "purge" effort in general a very bad idea, joined this portion of it willingly enough since Tydings was guilty, in Farley's view, of flagrant party disloyalty.

Roosevelt m ʻde six speeches in Maryland on Sunday and Monday of that long Labor Day weekend. Five of them were informal, innocuous, and brief. But in his single prepared address, nationally broadcast from the little town of Denton on Labor Day, he pulled out all the stops.

"For a dozen years or more prior to 1933, the Federal Government had not moved forward at all . . ." he said. "In a nation-wide effort to catch up, to bring the distant past up to the present, a whole series of new undertakings had to be launched. . . . During this process there were of course many people both in private and public life who did not like to do the things that had to be done." They admitted the existence of abuses, but "if improvement could not come without Government action, then they wanted no improvement. . . ." People like that were conservatives or reactionaries, whereas those "who feel that the past should be brought up to the present by using every legitimate means to do the job, including Government" were liberals or progressives. "Any man . . . has a right to be honestly one or the other. But the Nation cannot stand for the confusion of having him pretend to be one and act like the other."

So much for Millard Tydings!

Fortunately, Maryland Democrats had a choice in the upcoming primary between this false liberal and the genuine article. Nearly thirty years ago, "thanks to the pioneering of a young Maryland legislator, the first workmen's compensation act ever to be passed in the United States was adopted by Maryland. . . . Later on in the halls of Washington a young congressman pushed and pleaded until he got a parcel post law on the statute books of the United States. . . . Many years later it became clear that the problem of dependent old age was a trying one. . . . Once again the representative from the Free State of Maryland took the lead and, thanks to his pioneering, decent security of life is ensured today to millions of our people." Of course everyone in Maryland knew of whom he spoke, he said. "But in forty-seven other states there are people . . . who are listening to what I am saying on this Labor Day, and for their benefit the name of that man is Representative Lewis of Maryland." He, Lewis, had not only "seen visions" but had "lived to make his dreams come true." Having risen "from humble circumstances" he had grown "in vision and effectiveness in the fertile soil of American opportunity and the American tradition of equality." Nor "has he ever forgotten that he learned to read and write at the knee of a Christian minister in Sunday School. That is why perhaps he has lived the life of the Good Samaritan. . . ."[57]

But as he spoke, though the crowd before him was responsive, Roosevelt derived from it none of the warming glow he was accustomed to feeling in such circumstances.

He felt increased unease when he returned to the White House and took stock of his situation. Never before had he transformed a national holiday address, nationally broadcast, into a local political stump speech. Seldom, if ever before, had he made a local stump speech so blatantly tailored to parochial sentimentalism. And in so doing he evinced a self-contradictory motivation. Confidence in the power of his personal appeal was mingled with a species of desperate fear. He risked too much. So obviously did he stoop to conquer— so low and so shortly before the decisive event did he stoop—that the event of failure must find him yet humbly bowed before the eyes of a national public, his helplessness emphasized by his attitude.

Eight days after his Labor Day speech, Maryland's primary was held. In it, Millard Tydings defeated David Lewis by the humiliatingly large margin of sixty thousand votes.

A few days later, in Georgia's three-man primary race, the humiliation was even greater: Roosevelt was emphatically rebuffed by the electorate of his "second home" state. For not only did Lawrence Camp trail far behind Senator George, he ran also behind Eugene Talmadge.

And in South Carolina Cotton Ed Smith seemed actually to have been helped at the polls by Roosevelt's swipe at him. So averred at least some analysts of Smith's narrow victory over the White House candidate, former governor Olin Johnston. (Johnston, it must be said, could hardly have passed as a liberal in any region save the South. Attacked by Smith for an insufficiently ardent support of white supremacy, he proclaimed himself far more committed to that sacred cause than Smith was. "Why, Ed Smith voted for a bill that would permit a big buck nigger to sit by your wife or sister on a railroad train!" he cried in tones of horrified outrage.[58])

Nor did candidates whom the President had conspicuously favored fare much better in other states. Lyndon Johnson won in Texas, and clearly Roosevelt's blessing was a favorable factor in Johnson's geographically huge but sparsely populated and poverty-stricken district. But other liberal Texans upon whom Roosevelt had smiled, including the nationally famous Maury Maverick, went down to defeat. Elsewhere, in state after state, the Democratic senatorial primaries chose conservatives over liberals by decisive margins— Guy Gillette (early) in Iowa, Pat McCarran in Nevada, Augustine Lonergan (destined for defeat in November by his Republican opponent) in Connecticut. Only in California were there liberal primary victories that attracted national attention. There, Sheridan Downey was nominated for the Senate, Culbert Olsen for the governorship, Jerry Voorhis for the House. These victories, however, had been gained with little help from the President. Indeed, Roosevelt would remain publicly silent about Olson and Downey, while the Republican opposition capitalized upon his evident lack of interest in (if not secret opposition to) their candidacies, until the last day of October. He then, in a public letter to journalist George Creel, endorsed both candidates, while reiterating his opposition to "$30 every Thursday."[59]

All eyes now focused on New York's Sixteenth District, the normally conservative Silk Stocking District, where the Democrat most frustrating to House liberalism, by virtue of his chairmanship of the Rules Committee, fought for his political life against James H. Fay, a popular member of Ed Flynn's Bronx organization whom Hopkins and Tommy Corcoran had persuaded, with some difficulty, to make the race.

He fought with the strength of furious desperation, did John J. O'Connor. He faced a White House effort that, for a single congressional seat, was uniquely great and fervent. Tommy Corcoran had by mid-September spent a month in New York City (he moved into a Hotel Windsor apartment that had long been leased by Ben Cohen; it happened to be located in the Sixteenth District), there to devote to a ferocious ward-and-precinct campaign all his time and immense energy, all his skill in ruthless covert operations, all the power and prestige that accrued to him as presidential agent. Roosevelt himself had persuaded a reluctant Ed Flynn, the Bronx organization boss, to help out, though with the stipulation by Flynn that he not be required to work with Corcoran, whom he disliked and distrusted. And Corcoran proceeded to add to that dislike and distrust by secretly, dangerously mobilizing federal employees in the district on Fay's behalf; he went so far as to ask Morgenthau, who flatly refused, to order Internal Revenue Service agents in the Sixteenth District to work against O'Connor. On Sunday morning, September 18, forty-eight hours before primary day, a top news story was a personal statement by Roosevelt endorsing Fay.[60]

It then appeared, however, that all this frantic effort was in vain. On primary eve, O'Connor still seemed to be ahead.

Hence the jubilation with which Tommy Corcoran informed Roosevelt by phone, late on primary night, that the effort had not failed. O'Connor had lost to Fay by a narrow margin. He had won the Republican primary and might well be elected as a Republican in November, but he would no longer be Rules Committee chairman. "Tommy," said Roosevelt (by Corcoran's account), ". . . I have never had such a lift in my spirits in my life. I'm eternally grateful and I will never forget it." To Fay he wrote next day, "Harvard lost the schedule but won the Yale game,"[61] meaning that O'Connor's removal overbalanced the sum of the preceding primary defeats. He made the same analogy to others while continuing to insist that the effort had been "necessary," that its long-term effect would be a more emphatic definition of the national Democracy as a liberal party, and that he had not the slightest regret over having done as he had done.

This, however, was a whistling at midnight amid the tombstones of buried hopes, and it must have sounded quavering and off-key in his own ears. In the glaring light of day there could be no blinking the fact that the campaign for liberalism, judged by its own avowed purpose, had been (to quote Farley) "a bust."[62] Moreover, a major contributor to the "bust" had been the "purge" label attached to Roosevelt's effort by his opponents—a fact of especially ominous significance for a President of the United States in the world situation of September 1938. Hitler's bloody purge of early Nazis and Stalin's of Old Bolsheviks—these had been analogously called into the American public mind. Thus reinforced in that mind were those fears of a "Roosevelt dictatorship" which had defeated executive reorganization a few months before. There was in this an implied linkage of domestic politics to foreign affairs that boded ill for Roosevelt's capacity to lead the nation through the world crisis that impended.

IX

NOR was it only in his public life that this once bright and happy season became, during its closing weeks, a summer of dust and weeds. Harsh discord came into his private family life also, beneath the smooth and smiling surface it continued to present to the world. His eldest son was brought near to death largely because of services to the President which Eleanor had begged him not to permit, much less insist upon, and for which she now bitterly if silently reproached him; and a great friendship of his wife's, vital to her development and of some importance to his own career, came to an end.

On June 23, the day before his fireside chat declaring war upon conservative

Democratic candidates in the upcoming midterm primaries, Roosevelt had responded publicly to loud protests against the labor-organizing tactics (especially the sit-down strike) employed by John L. Lewis's CIO, protests that were accompanied by demands for new federal statutes to enforce labor-union "responsibility" to the "general public" (meaning, in context, the employers). Roosevelt had done so with typical well-calculated indirection by announcing from Hyde Park his appointment of a nine-member commission to study industrial relations in Great Britain and Sweden, two countries where labor and management were far less violently opposed than they were in the United States. It was widely assumed, and as widely published, "that one of the purposes of the inquiry was to pave the way for amendment of the National Labor Relations Act to place labor on a par with management in its responsibilities for preserving industrial peace," to quote *The New York Times* of June 23, 1938. This assumption had not deterred William Green's designation of a representative of the AFL to serve on the commission, when he was asked by Secretary of Labor Perkins to do so, but Lewis, after initially agreeing to designate a CIO representative, had quickly changed his mind. "Conspicuously absent from the [commission's] personnel list," therefore, "was a representative for the Committee for Industrial Organization," as the *Times*'s Felix Belair, Jr., pointed out. Among the nine appointees were Lloyd K. Garrison, dean of the Wisconsin law school; three representatives of business, including General Electric's Gerard Swope, who was named commission chairman; and Eleanor's longtime friend and colleague in the Todhunter School, Marion Dickerman.

The commissioners had sailed for England on June 28, going from England to Sweden a few weeks later. They had found in the two countries what most of them expected to find but were now able factually to describe in their report to the President: namely, that British and Swedish industrial relations were generally happier than American ones because the industrialists in those countries (especially the Swedish) had long recognized the right of labor to organize and bargain collectively on an industrywide scale, something American industrialists continued violently to refuse to do. The commissioners' return to England in early August was by ship to Hamburg, thence by train southward through Germany and France. There was a nasty episode in Germany. Gerard Swope, a Jew, told that all passports would be examined at the next train stop, discovered that his was misplaced somewhere in his luggage. He was accustomed to exercising authority, he was normally notable for self-possession, but he was white-faced and trembling by the time he found the missing document, He did so just as dark-uniformed Nazi officials came down the aisle toward him. There was another nasty episode in London, at a luncheon for the commissioners hosted at the American embassy by Ambassador Joseph P. Kennedy. The ambassador may or may not have known that Swope was Jewish, but he should certainly have known that the members of such a commission as this were unlikely to be admirers of Adolf Hitler or of Nazi "discipline" and "order." Kennedy himself *was* an admirer, or indicated at table that he was while also expressing contempt for certain slack "soft" features of British and American democracy. Again Swope became white of face, this time with rage. In a note passed to Marion Dickerman, his table companion, he proposed that they two leave the table at once. She, with difficulty, dissuaded him, though she was as furious as he was.[63]

The ship on which the commission returned to the United States docked in New York on August 18, the day of Roosevelt's important foreign-policy pronouncement in Kingston, Ontario. On the following day, Marion and Nancy Cook, who met Marion at the dock, were at Hyde Park, arriving there almost simultaneously with the President's return from Canada—and within a few days thereafter, Roosevelt, always remarkably sensitive to psychological environmental pressures, became aware that something had gone seriously wrong between Eleanor and her two co-owners of Val-Kill Cottage.

He had long known, of course, that the "E.M.N." intimacy that had inspired the building of the cottage was considerably lessened after Eleanor moved into the White House.

As First Lady, she had initially involved her two friends in as many of her activities as she could. She had ordered furniture for the White House family quarters to be made in the Val-Kill Industries shop, which Nancy ran; had continued covertly to help in the work of the Women's Division of the New York Democratic party, which Nancy ran as executive secretary; had involved both women (Nancy especially) in the Arthurdale project; and had continued actively to concern herself with Marion's administration of the Todhunter School, whose ownership she shared with the two friends. But there were necessarily a great many activities in which Eleanor could not involve the other two, among them the writing and lecturing that became increasingly important to her. But in this last (the initiating of the "My Day" column, for instance), Lorena Hickok was involved, and the passionate friendship Eleanor formed with Hick during the 1932–1933 interregnum* was not merely exclusive of the "M.N." portion of the former triumvirate but strongly antithetical to it. Hick's original wariness and distrust of the "Val Kill ladies" became a profound loathing after a single overnight stay in a cottage guest room. She refused ever to go to the cottage again, having been snubbed and made to feel that her hostesses deemed her too coarse and crude and ugly to associate with such gentlewomen as they. The loathing was mutual. Nancy and Marion found Hick "impossible" and were fearfully resentful of Eleanor's attachment to her.

Then had come the death of Louis Howe, who had held things together in the Roosevelt household as none other could do; it was followed within a month by the death of Val-Kill Industries. A news release dated May 14, 1936, said that, according to "an announcement made by Mrs. Franklin D. Roosevelt," the Hyde Park furniture-making enterprise would be "taken over and operated by one of the expert craftsmen, Otto Berge," while the weaving enterprise would "continue under the direction of Nellie Johannesen." By late

*See *FDR: The New Deal Years,* pp. 175–82.

1936, Eleanor, who felt a need for a home of her own where she could entertain visitors who had no relationship with, or were unfriendly to, Nancy and Marion, had proposed that she take over the unused shop building for that purpose. By late June 1937 the necessary remodeling had been done and the move made into what Eleanor intended to be, and which actually became, her primary dwelling for the rest of her life.

Simultaneously, the ties that had formerly so strongly and closely bound Eleanor to the Todhunter School, necessarily much loosened by Eleanor's move from New York to Washington, became weakened to very near the breaking point—and this just as Marion, the school principal, was launching or attempting to launch an extremely ambitious expansion program. A new and larger building for the school was found, priced at $100,000. Bernard Baruch, whose niece was a Todhunter pupil, promised help with the financing. A professional fund-raiser was hired. But in the fall of 1937 serious questions arose about the possibility of obtaining clear title to the wanted building; fund-raising was stymied by the sharp economic recession; and Eleanor, who despite her co-ownership of the school had taken no active part in all this (she deemed the project wholly Marion's and Nancy's), began to think that it might be wise for her to sever her connection with Todhunter altogether. Something of this last was revealed, or at least hinted at, in Eleanor's response to curriculum and fund-raising plans that Marion sent her (she was in Chicago at the time) in early November 1937. Eleanor, having replied to Marion with a few suggestions concerning the curriculum, then sent the report and plan to her husband, seeking his advice, something she rarely did regarding activities of her own that had no connection with her husband's political operation. "Will you look at this?" she wrote him. "I have turned down the pages and marked such places as I think you should read. I confess I think this is a tremendous task and wish I could be as optimistic as they [Marion and Nancy] are! However, if the market goes up it may not be so bad." Four months later, asked to contribute a statement for use in a fund-raising brochure, she did so with less enthusiasm than the fund-raising professional desired. She was asked to strengthen the statement by adding a sentence to the effect that Todhunter would be a major interest of hers after she left the White House. "I am terribly sorry," she replied, "but as I do not intend to make the school one of my major interests, I feel it very much wiser to be absolutely honest. It will be one of my interests, but as I have no idea of what my other interests may be or where they will take me, I regret that I cannot change my statement." She was greatly relieved when, a few weeks later, chiefly because of the continuing recession, the expansion plan was laid aside.[64]

On the night before Marion left Hyde Park for her journey overseas, she and Eleanor had a long conversation about Val-Kill arrangements and about Todhunter's future. The two evidently disagreed on certain points, but they parted affectionately. ("I knew we had some problems ahead, but not ones that seemed impossible of solution," Marion later wrote of this talk.) Bon voyage gifts of flowers and a check were sent by Eleanor to Marion's ship cabin next day. Affectionate letters were exchanged between the two while Marion was abroad. And when Marion talked to Nancy by transatlantic phone from Hamburg, only three days before boarding ship in England for the homeward voyage, Nancy was her usual self. All was well at Hyde Park, with her as with Eleanor, she reported.

But all was obviously not well with the Nancy who met Marion at the New York dock on August 18. Her appearance was shocking—her cheeks pale, her eyes bloodshot, her eyelids swollen with weeping—and her manner was distraught, even hysterical. When she tried to reply to Marion's immediate anxious questioning she burst into tears. All that Marion was able to learn from her, between her sobs, as they drove up to Hyde Park, was that she and Eleanor had had, sometime during the last few days, "a long and tragic talk" (so Marion later described it) during which each "had said things that ought not to have been said." Nor could Marion learn more than this in the days that followed. Nancy broke down whenever questioned on the subject. As for Eleanor, she refused now even to speak to Marion in private, being always "too busy" to grant Marion's requests for a private interview.[65]

This remained the state of affairs at Val-Kill when Roosevelt, who felt its impact without (in all probability) knowing any of the particulars, left Hyde Park at the last of August for Washington. And there also, in the private life of the White House, he encountered breakup and dissolution.

The reader may recall Eleanor's vehement protest in late 1936 against her husband's appointment of son James to the White House secretarial post vacated by Howe's death.* She had prophesied dire consequences. What she had feared was now reality. The son, though unequipped to fill Howe's role of adviser, had provided Roosevelt some of the relaxed, easy, intimate companionship that Howe had given. The cost, however, was outrageously high. Virulent animosity was focused upon the son by his father's political enemies from the moment he assumed his office. He had been ridiculed in the process as the "crown prince" whose ineptitudes justified the label "clown prince." Loud and reiterated accusations of personal dishonesty and official incompetence had been made by anti–New Deal politicians and journalists. And all this had proved to be unbearable by him, weakened as he was by the self-acknowledged fact that during his years in the insurance business in Boss Curley's Boston he had indeed capitalized upon his filial relationship with the President in ways that were morally questionable. (He had, for instance, while a partner in the insurance firm of Roosevelt and Sargent, accepted the presidency of a New Jersey firm called National Grain and Yeast, a $25,000-a-year position offered him by the company's owner, one Frank Hale, solely because he was his father's son. Moreover, he retained this post after he became suspicious, if he did not actually know, "that the grain was going into bootleg alcohol, the yeast company was just a front, and I [James] was a front for it all." He had resigned his position, after enjoying "about eighteen fat months," only

*See p. 5; also, *FDR: The New Deal Years,* pp. 669–70.

because an agitated Henry Morgenthau had gone to the President with information about Hale's connections with the underworld.[66]) He suffered pangs of guilt that he had done grave injury to his father, and these ate like acid into his inward self. Since childhood, he had had chronic "stomach trouble"—he himself believed it to have been initiated by an alcoholic and sadistic English nanny, hired by his imperious grandmother; one day when he was a young boy, the nanny punished him for impertinence by forcing him to eat spoonful by spoonful a pot of hot mustard*—and in late May 1938 this trouble was so aggravated by prolonged tension that it became serious indeed. He was rushed to the Mayo Clinic in Rochester, Minnesota, where he was found to be suffering from a gastric ulcer. He was hospitalized for three weeks, placed on a strictly bland diet, then sent to Campobello for what was supposed to be months of complete rest and relaxation, but may not have been, since Sara Delano Roosevelt attended him. When he returned to Mayo's for a checkup in early September it was found that the ulcer was worse, with malignancy a fearful possibility. Surgery was necessary—major, dangerous surgery, scheduled for Monday, September 12, as Eleanor, who had gone from Hyde Park to her son's bedside, informed her husband by phone.

An anxious Roosevelt, having canceled all the appointments that had been made for his next few days—including his attendance at a birthday party for his uncle Fred Delano at Algonac (this was the Delano family seat, Sara's birthplace, at Newburgh)—again boarded his special train on Thursday evening, September 8, bound this time for Rochester.[67]

James's wife, the very attractive Betsey Cushing Roosevelt, of whom the President was especially fond, had not gone with her sick husband to Minnesota; she, too, had to be summoned by phone or telegraph. What this signified was another breakup, a further dissolution consequent upon the White House secretarial arrangement. A rather weird tangle of emotional relationships had developed within a few months after James entered his father's service. Betsey had put herself out to be charming to the President, who was indeed charmed by her. She was pretty, gay, vivacious, flirtatious ("a tease," said James sourly), and more than willing to perform White House hostessing functions, which Eleanor was seldom present to perform (the glamour "went to her head," said James sourly). This may have aroused secret resentment in Missy. It certainly aroused resentment in Eleanor, whose distaste for Betsey seems indicated by the fact that, from first to last, she never bothered to learn the proper spelling of her daughter-in-law's first name (it was always "Betsy" in Eleanor's correspondence). And such resentment as Eleanor and Missy felt was more than matched by that aroused in James himself. The son became actually jealous of his father, or of the attentions his wife lavished upon his father, and became thus emotionally allied, strangely, with his mother against his wife. There began a quarrel that drove like a knife to the very heart

*See *FDR: The Beckoning of Destiny.* pp. 205–6.

of what had been, in former years, a gloriously happy marriage. Husband and wife began to move in different social circles, making separate and incompatible sets of social friends. By this late summer of 1938 James's marriage was well on the way to ending, as Anna's and Elliott's first marriages had already ended, in divorce.[68]

"Betsy arrives tomorrow A.M. early & I go to meet her, after that I expect to feel somewhat out of place!" wrote Eleanor on September 8 from Rochester to Lorena Hickok in New York (Hick was then working on public relations for Grover Whalen and the New York World's Fair, a job Eleanor had helped her obtain). "F.D.R. gets in Sunday A.M. [September 11] with his retinue [it included Harry Hopkins as well as Missy] & I dread it. . . . Elliott is coming [from Fort Worth] which will be nice, tho a bit hard on him for he's opening his new [Texas radio] network on the 15th. . . . I'm glad he's doing it tho' and that FDR asked him for he gets a 'left out' feeling so often. . . ."[69]

By the time Roosevelt's train arrived on Sunday morning, the doctors, greatly fearing a rapidly spreading malignancy, had decided not to wait until the next day but to operate at once. Wrote Eleanor to Hick that night: "I met the train at 9:30. He [FDR] saw the doctors and the X-rays, saw Jimmy & by 10:30 they began. It was over at 1:30 & nothing malignant found & his condition is good. Betsy has had the jitters & I've felt . . . as cold as ice which is always my reaction."

The relief was immense. Two days later was Missy's birthday, an event celebrated with a luncheon for her at which the whole of the sizable presidential party gathered in Roosevelt's private railroad car. "I am taking a [birthday] cake," said Eleanor in a morning note to Hick. "James is doing very well but while I spend a good deal of time in the hospital I don't go in [James's room] much for there are so many doctors & F's visits & Betsy flitting in & out that I feel he must make a great deal of effort. The less now the better for his future. He really ought to be quite well after he has completely got over the effects of this operation."[70]

And we may here anticipate his complete, if slow, physical recovery. His official White House service was forever ended, however. So was his marriage to Betsey. From Rochester he went to a California ranch for convalescence, taking with him as his nurse the woman, Romelle Schneider, who had nursed him at Mayo's. ("I fell for her," he later wrote. "Maybe it's easy for a sick man to fall for his nurse."[71]) Within a few months he was divorced from Betsey, who was given custody of their two young children.

X

No happier, and only slightly if at all less consequential in the private life of the White House, was the end of the "E.M.N." arrangement at Val-Kill.

Roosevelt returned to Hyde Park from Washington at the last of September for a long week's stay. Badly worn by the intense pressures of the immediately preceding weeks, he needed the full use of Hyde Park's recreational and restorative capacity. And so, on the first Sunday of that Hyde Park week, a large picnic was arranged for him at Val-Kill Cottage.

It was, through most of the late afternoon and evening, a picnic like scores of earlier ones at Val-Kill. There was the usual animated talk, loud laughter, boisterous activity, and abundance of plain good picnic food. But for Nancy, Marion, and Eleanor there was from the first a darkness beneath the bright cheerful surface, a darkness where tigers lurked.

Among the picnic guests was Eleanor's alcoholic brother Hall, who was nearly six years her junior. Her relationship with him was more maternal than sisterly, she having assumed after her mother's death (when Eleanor was eight) much of the role her mother would or should have played. Not only did she love him dearly, she was also fiercely protective of him who, God knew, greatly needed protection, chiefly from himself. He was drunk at this picnic. He was so drunk he didn't know what he was doing when, as night fell, he played with his son Danny in what was known at Val-Kill as Marion's garden. He lifted the young boy high above the ground, then threw him down hard. The boy screamed in agony. Dr. Herman Baruch (Bernard's brother), a picnic guest, examined him and declared his collarbone to be broken.

What followed was a nightmare for Marion Dickerman.

Missy phoned the hospital emergency ward in Poughkeepsie. Hall, somewhat sobered by shock and dismay, insisted he would drive his son in himself. The boy, terrified of his father, begged Marion to come along, which she did, though badly frightened herself. And Hall then promptly drove them into a ditch as he tried to make the turn from the end of the long driveway into the post road. The accident, which luckily injured no one, was witnessed by a state trooper who was on guard as part of the President's security and who then took them to Poughkeepsie in his own car. Eleanor had not witnessed the accident in the garden; she learned of it only when told of the driving accident; and she seems then to have lost her self-control completely. She at once asserted to all within the sound of her voice that Marion was the one who had driven into the ditch. She phoned Marion at the hospital and talked to her "in a way I had never heard before," berating her in tones of cold accusatory fury, blaming her for everything that had happened and slamming down the receiver before Marion could defend herself. Marion was in a state of shock when she returned to the cottage. She went to her room where, soon, Missy came to her. The President knew it was Hall who had driven into the ditch, Missy said, for the state trooper had told him so. The President "doesn't want you to be hurt," Missy said.

But Marion was already hurt, and though the President's concern gave her some relief from pain, the hurt was so deep, so terrible that she would never fully recover from it.[72]

She tried repeatedly during the following weeks to have a private interview with Eleanor. The latter refused to talk to her, on this subject or any other.

For Eleanor was agonizingly disillusioned by things Nancy had said during their "tragic talk," things for which she blamed Marion as well since she deemed these two to be as one in such matters. And she was now, consequently, in full exercise of what she herself admitted was a deplorable trait, namely, her tendency to withdraw wholly into herself when hurt, assuming the role of martyr as she raised a wall of silence against those she thought responsible, refusing all their efforts to communicate. She called it her "Griselda mood." It was cruelly vengeful. For all its seeming passivity, it was the most devastating kind of psychological aggression when focused upon people of sensitive conscience who deeply cared for her. It raised conscience as a fifth column (Franco's phrase had become everywhere current by mid-1938) within the targeted psyche; it aroused, as it was intended to arouse, guilt feelings and self-doubt. The suffering it inflicted upon Nancy and Marion was proportionate to the great intimacy and affection that had formerly bound them and Eleanor together. And these two lacked that plethora of vital connections and activities, of corridors and tools of power, through which Eleanor could divert, assuage, and attenuate her own psychic pain. Eleanor could be sustained not only (if especially) by her relationship with Hick, which indeed had contributed much to the weakening of "E.M.N.," but also by a number of other intimacies, including her warm, close friendship with her personal secretary, Malvina Thompson.* Nancy and Marion had each other but now only each other in intimate relationship. They must therefore suffer from this breakup a relatively pure, undiluted pain.

It was a rending pain, as Eleanor moved to dissolve the lifetime property arrangement wherein Val-Kill Cottage had been initiated and to obtain an absolutely clear legal title to the former shop building which was now her home. She proposed to pay for the shop with her share of Val-Kill Cottage and of a Todhunter School reserve fund into which she, Marion, and Nancy had paid some of their portions of the school's profits for many years. Marion objected. The reserve fund was not the private property of the three school owners, share and share alike, she insisted, but had been set up as a school trust. It was the property of the school. Hence it could not legally be divided and used as Eleanor wished. By this, Eleanor was outraged. If the school fund was not the property of the three contributors to it, why had each of them paid income tax on her contribution to it every year? In cold fury she wrote from the White House to her erstwhile friends, saying that never before "in all our relationship" had she "wanted anything, nor suggested anything about the cottage or the school." Now, however, she had "a distinct preference and as you do not care to handle it in the way I wish, I have decided to turn over to you now, instead of at my death, my entire interest in the cottage, the shop building and the other buildings. . . . In view of what has happened I . . . wish

---

*The aversion to men that ran as a leitmotif through the lives of Eleanor's closest associates was very slightly contradicted in the case of Malvina Thompson by her marriage in 1933 to Frank J. Scheider. He played a small and shadowy role in his wife's life during the next few years, her life being almost totally absorbed into Eleanor's, and was in process of divorce from her in September 1931.

also to withdraw entirely from the school. I will give you both with great pleasure my share of the school fund. . . ." In the future she would come to Hyde Park only "when the President is at the big house and I will stay at the big house."[73]

Marion and Nancy of course resisted this punitive, masochistic generosity. A telegram from Marion in late October pleaded for an interview. Eleanor refused ("every minute . . . is filled"), saying she was "leaving everything in Harry's hands"—"Harry" being Harry Hooker, Roosevelt's former law partner, whom she now retained.[74] In desperation, and (we may be sure) "great reluctance," as Marion wrote to Hooker, the two women turned to Roosevelt himself for advice in early November. He suggested, as Marion recorded, "that all the furniture in the shop which is jointly owned . . . shall belong to Eleanor exclusively during her lifetime; and the cottage and all jointly owned furniture within it shall be considered cottage property and shall belong to Nan and me, or to the survivor, exclusively, during our lives, or the life of the survivor."[75] This seemed to Marion and Nancy a fair and reasonable arrangement.

Eleanor, however, refused to agree to it. In a letter which at last (November 9, 1938) gave Marion her version of the "tragic conversation," she wrote that she would

> only live in the shop building if there is a tangible settlement of the cash values involved in Nancy's accounts. I have made this perfectly clear to both of you over a long period, and last summer I had a talk with Nan. She may not have told you that at that time I told her, that for a long time I had been conscious of the fact that we three viewed certain things in very different ways. She told me, for instance, that while we were working in the committee, in the school, and in the industries together, you had both always felt that whatever was done was done for the sole purpose of building me up. My whole conception was entirely different. I went into the industries because I felt that Nan was fulfilling something which she had long wanted to do. I would never have done it alone. I had neither the knowledge nor the background nor the interest.
>
> I went into the school because I had an interest in education and in young people and being fond of you I was anxious to help you in what you wished to do. It gave me an opportunity for regular work which I was anxious to have. I went into the political work because Louis was anxious to have me do something to keep up Franklin's interest in a field which he eventually hoped Franklin would return to. I had no personal ambitions of any kind and I have none today.
>
> Nan told me that all my friends sensed a great difference in me and many of them felt a change of attitude just as you and she had felt it. This is probably true and I am free to say that I also have felt a change.[76]

In another letter to Marion, written on that same day, Eleanor resigned from the school.

During the following weeks and months, through the remainder of 1938 and into the spring of 1939, a financial settlement was worked out, through Hooker, whereby Eleanor received the clear title she demanded; but there were no direct communications between Eleanor and either Marion or Nancy. There was a final exchange between Eleanor and Marion in mid-May. Marion wrote on May 16 saying that, since her return from the overseas trip, she had "never had a chance to talk to you about anything." She was aware of but a single "instance" in which she had "displeased" and that "was on the night I went to the hospital with Danny. My judgment in that instance may not have been wise. My motive however was a kindly one. I have never understood why you spoke to me that night as you did. Your letter telling me to see Harry Hooker seemed like a bad dream. Three times I asked to see you in order to talk matters over. Each time you refused. I know nothing of what has brought this on my head save the incident to which I refer, and that, unless far more was implicated than I know of, seems rather out of proportion to what went before."

Eleanor replied in a typewritten letter within an hour or so after reading this.

What you did for Danny that night . . . was not what called forth my displeasure. I was displeased because you did not let me know that Hall had reached a point where this could happen. I, of course, realize that probably not being familiar with gentlemen under those conditions except under different circumstances, you did not realize what was happening. It might have been possible for me to prevent Hall taking the car had I known in time. That would at least have obviated the danger that the situation in the ditch caused, or anything else which might have occurred if you had got beyond the ditch.

But the real, the ultimate source of her "displeasure" was obviously that "long and illuminating talk with Nan" to which she again referred with bitterness. She had been "made to feel that you and Nan felt that you had spent your lives building me up." She had been "a little appalled" by "what was in Nan's mind, and of course must have been in yours." She made cryptic reference to "certain things" that "came back to me through Franklin which made me realize many things which I had never realized before." She concluded with a stated belief "that we can have a very pleasant and agreeable relationship at Hyde Park" in the future, enjoying "many things" together there, "but not on the same basis that we had in the past." Whatever work she did "in the future" would, of course, "be along entirely different lines which will not bring me into close contact with either of you in your work." She would always wish "both you and Nan well in whatever you undertake."[77]

To this, Marion made a succinct reply. She had had "no part" in "your talk & Nan's last summer" and felt she "should be allowed to speak for myself." She had never had the " 'building up' idea" and had "never heard anyone use the expression before this summer except Louis, then I did not take it seriously. . . . I have been busy with the school & have put all that I have . . . into it & I thought of your connection in the same way." She had accepted Eleanor's decisions regarding both the school and the Hyde Park setup and "unless you wish to refer to this matter again I shall consider it closed for I have found nothing in it but disillusion and unhappiness. Needless to say . . . I shall always wish you success in what ever you may care to do." She signed the letter "Affectionately."[78]

Thus ended what had been for more than a dozen years the closest and most vitally important of Eleanor's friendships—an ending whose pain was great but was made easier to bear by the sense the three women had of its triviality in comparison with the anguish of world history in which they were all by that time (the ghastly spring of 1939) deeply involved.

Nancy and Marion continued to live at the cottage, in close proximity to Eleanor's house. On the latter's ground was raised, however, a high fence (Marion bitterly dubbed it a "spite fence")—and though Eleanor continued to involve her former friends in Hyde Park social affairs and to make use of Nancy's organizing talents when picnics were arranged for visiting dignitaries, there was never again an intimate personal communication between the "E." and the "M.N." of the former triumvirate.

# BOOK THREE

❊❊❊

# Into the Valley of the Shadow of Death

## 8

#### ⟶⟫⟩✕⟨⟨⟵

# *New World War Becomes Inevitable*

### I

THOUGH chronology is indeed "the key to narrative," as Winston Churchill has said,* it can also be fatal to narrative clarity if too slavishly adhered to by the historian faced with "a throng of events . . . marching abreast." He does well at such juncture to separate and classify, then deal with each class chronologically—and this is what we have done, and now do, with the tragically decisive events of 1938. All through the spring, summer, and early autumn of that year events were taking place in Europe that had a considerable and pervasive influence over the American domestic affairs told of in the last chapter, and even directly impinged on these now and then, but remained in sum distinct and separate. These European events constituted a different story, so to speak; certainly they did for the pragmatic, opportunist, collector's mind that dominated the White House.

It is this story, and that of Roosevelt's continued tangential and ineffective relations with European affairs, that we have now to tell. For the two streams of event are about to flow together, the two stories are about to become one, a single drama having Roosevelt as a central character, and this drama we cannot understand without knowledge of precisely what happened, and how wickedness, stupidity, and cowardice caused it to happen, in the Europe of 1938.

### II

SUSPENSE over Czechoslovakia began building as soon as Adolf Hitler turned his baleful gaze upon that unhappy land following *Anschluss* in mid-March. As we have said, he then instructed his henchman, Konrad Henlein, head of the Sudeten German party, to make increasing demands upon the Czech government and never to be satisfied by the concessions the Czechs would make. Accordingly, in an address at Carlsbad on April 24, Henlein presented Prague with eight demands. The most important was for "full liberty to Germans [in Czechoslovakia] to proclaim their Germanism and their adherence to the [Nazi] ideology of the Germans"[1]—in other words to establish a Sudeten Nazi state which would, of course, promptly declare its independence from Czechoslovakia and its union with Germany. Despite urgings by London

*On p. 407 of the one-volume edition of *The World Crisis* (London, 1931).

and Paris for "utmost concessions," the demand was rejected by the government headed by Dr. Edvard Beneš in Prague.

Nine days after the Carlsbad speech, Hitler arrived in Rome for a week-long official visit. His purpose was to demonstrate to the world that the Rome-Berlin Axis was not in the slightest impaired by *Anschluss* and would not be by the impending "solution" of the Sudetenland "problem." He sought assurances as to the latter from Mussolini but had to wait several days before he could even broach the subject. Mussolini saw to it that Hitler with his large entourage (it numbered 125) was lavishly entertained, that Italian troops marched in Prussian goose-step when they passed in review before Hitler, and that both Hitler and the world were treated to impressive displays of Italian naval and air power as well as Italian art and opera. ("What a show it must have been!" wrote Roosevelt from the White House on May 18 to Ambassador William Phillips in Rome, going on to make apropos comment upon the ominously imitative pageantry and emblem with which Phil La Follette had just launched his new party: "Most of the country" thought the emblem "a feeble imitation of the Swastika. All that remains is for some major party to adopt a new form of arm salute. I have suggested the raising of both hands over the head, followed by a bow from the waist. At least that would be good for people's figures."[2]) But Il Duce made a point of the fact that, unlike der Führer, he was not formally head of state. He owed allegiance to King Victor Emmanuel. It was therefore the diminutive king, his tall queen beside him, who functioned as Hitler's official host, and neither the king nor the queen made the slightest effort to hide the dislike and contempt they both felt for this Austrian upstart who by odious means had made himself master of a state they persisted in regarding as a hostile power.[3] Not until the fourth day of the grandiose Roman festivities was German foreign minister Joachim von Ribbentrop enabled to present to Italian foreign minister Ciano the draft treaty of an alliance, a treaty Mussolini had already decided to sign—and not until a day or so after that was Hitler, in a private talk with Mussolini, assured of Italy's indifference to the fate of Czechoslovakia.[4]

Meanwhile, Henlein visited Paris and London to present his case to the governments of Chamberlain and Daladier. He was evidently persuasive. Within a day after his talk with Chamberlain, the prime minister granted a luncheon interview, at Lady Astor's Cliveden estate, to Joseph Driscoll of the *Herald Tribune*, the gist of which was reported in a dispatch printed in the New York paper on May 15. It shed "official light on the real British attitude" toward Czechoslovakia, saying that, since geographical realities made effective fighting for the Czechs impossible for Britain, as for France and Russia, the Czechs in the end would either have to accept a Swiss-type cantonal system (the Sudetenland would become a largely self-governing canton) or cede the Sudetenland to Germany. It was the latter alternative that, according to Driscoll, the British were inclined to favor.[5] Henlein also had a conversation, on May 13, with Winston Churchill, during which, according to Churchill's written summary of it, the German spelled out his Carlsbad demands in terms considerably softer than they had seemed in their original form or than Chamberlain, judging from Driscoll's dispatch, was willing to accept. For instance, what had been originally a demand for full autonomy for the Sudeten Germans now became "local autonomy, that is to say, they should have their own town and county councils, and a diet in which matters of common regional concern could be debated within definitely delimited frontiers." Czech troops would continue to man the frontier fortifications to which "of course" they would "have unlimited access." When the Czech ambassador in London, Jan Masaryk, was informed of these terms he pronounced them acceptable as a basis for settlement, and Churchill himself found them so. "A peaceful solution . . . compatible with the independence of the Czech Republic was by no means impossible," he wrote, "if there were German good faith and good will." But of the latter, he added, "I had no illusions."[6]

His cynicism on this score was at once abundantly justified by events.

Immediately upon Henlein's return to the Sudetenland, his party's agitation against the Prague government, an agitation not without violence, was intensified. Simultaneously, in Berlin, Joseph Goebbels intensified his thoroughly mendacious propaganda campaign against Czechoslovakia. And on May 20, a Friday, with municipal elections in the Sudetenland scheduled for Sunday, two of Henlein's followers were reported killed as Nazi electioneering demonstrators clashed with Czech police. Huge *red* headlines proclaimed the alleged "murders" in German newspapers. On that same day there were rumors of massive German troop movements toward the Bohemian frontier, rumors that gained credence from the fact that they contained precise details and that Hitler's dramatic surprises had always been timed for weekends. Eleven infantry and four armored divisions were said to be on the march. A lightning-swift coup on the order of *Anschluss* seemed in the making.

President Beneš's response was immediate and forceful. Without consulting beforehand his French ally, he called an emergency meeting of his Cabinet and defense chiefs, whence issued that night an order for immediate partial mobilization of Czechoslovakia's armed forces. By dawn of Saturday, May 21, some 400,000 troops of the notably well-trained and well-equipped Czech army were manning the well-prepared frontier fortifications.

This show of decisive will and courage forced the hands of the appeaser governments in Paris and London, tied to Prague as these hands were, in the eyes of the world, by solemn treaty obligations. They were obligations that both France and Russia had categorically declared their determination to honor as recently as mid-March (Blum was then still the French premier). Both Paris and London warned Berlin in diplomatic language that a military attack on Czechoslovakia would mean general war, though the British ambassador in Berlin, Sir Nevile Henderson, whose pro-Nazi sympathies were obvious to all (he was a warm personal friend of Reichsmarschall Hermann Göring), made his warning statement as weak as possible. "I warned His Excellency [Joachim von Ribbentrop]," he wrote in his memoir of his mission to Berlin, "that France had definite treaty obligations to Czechoslovakia and that, if these had to be fulfilled, His Majesty's Government could not guarantee that they would not be forced by events to become themselves involved."[7] The German government replied with vehement denials that there was any truth whatever in the rumors, and the weekend then passed without invasion or, indeed, further excitement. The Sudeten municipal elections were held without incident and won, for the most part, by Henlein's party.

During this crisis weekend, Roosevelt was urged to intervene both by his new ambassador in Berlin, Hugh Wilson (he had replaced William Dodd in early 1938), and by Bullitt in Paris. Wilson suggested merely "representatives" by the President to both Berlin and Prague on behalf of a "peaceful settlement." But the dramatically emotional Bullitt, under pressure from the notoriously reactionary and appeasement-minded French foreign minister, Georges Bonnet, recommended that the President summon to the White House the British, French, German, and Italian ambassadors and issue through them an "urgent invitation to Chamberlain, Daladier, Hitler, and Mussolini to send representatives at once to The Hague to work out a peaceful settlement of the dispute. [The omission of Russia's Stalin and Czechoslovakia's Beneš from the list of invitees is notable.] . . . You should also make a personal appeal . . ." Bullitt continued, "[saying] that we are the children of all the civilizations of Europe . . . ; that we cannot stand by and watch the beginning of the end of European civilization without making one last effort to stop the destruction; that you are convinced that the only result of general European war today would be an Asiatic despotism [fear and hatred of Communist Russia was the root of Bullitt's European policy] established on fields of dead." He admitted that "the conference in The Hague would probably have to recommend a plebiscite" whereby Czechoslovakia would be stripped of the Sudeten territory and that consequently, Roosevelt "would be accused . . . of selling out a small nation in order to produce another Hitler triumph. [But] I should not hesitate to take that brick on my head and I don't think you should either if, thereby, you could avoid a general European war." A cautious Roosevelt, however, did hesitate, and before he could make up his mind what, if anything, to do, the crisis had ended.[8]

To the world, which had been badly scared, it appeared that at long last Hitler's bluff had been called. Great relief and renewed hopes for peace sprang from the perception that the Führer, faced, as he had been by Mussolini in 1934, with unwavering opposition, had now as then backed down. Nor can one doubt that he would have done so, would have been forced to do so, had he actually planned to invade Czechoslovakia that weekend. He had had, however, no such intention. This became evident to knowledgeable observers before the weekend was over. When military attachés of foreign missions in Berlin personally reconnoitered Saxony and Silesia on Saturday the twenty-first, as they were encouraged by Berlin to do, they found no unusual military activity. How, then, had the frightening rumor originated? Had trickster Adolf Hitler, he who had openly and even boastfully extolled the efficacy of the Big Lie as a means of manipulating people and events, himself been tricked? He believed so, certainly. He was convinced that Dr. Beneš had "invented the lie" of German troop movements to justify a display of "brute force" in the Sudetenland, this not only to intimidate Sudeten Germans who were about to go to the polls but also, and mainly, to humiliate Adolf Hitler personally.[9]

For five days, he brooded in dark fury over this "intolerable provocation." Then, on May 28, though the world at large would not learn of it till a decade had passed, he abruptly summoned to the Berlin Chancellery a group of top generals and admirals, top Foreign Office officials, and top Nazi officials, and declared to them his "unshakable will to wipe Czechoslovakia off the map." This action, he stressed, was an essential element of German grand strategy. Germany must conquer living space in the east. Czechoslovakia, if it continued to exist, would threaten the rear of German forces moving against Poland and Russia. And circumstances were now propitious for the launching of Case Green, as the military plan for a lightning attack on Czechoslovakia was code-named (the plan, frequently revised and updated, had existed since June 1937). Treaty or no, France, he asserted, would not fight for Czechoslovakia unless absolutely assured that Britain would join her in war against Germany; and Britain would give no such assurance. As for Russia, she would act only if France did so; and Italy, he had just been assured by Mussolini, had no interest in the Czechs. Hence his order: "(1) that preparations . . . be made for military action against this state by October 2; and (2) the immense and accelerated expansion of our defensive front in the West."[10]

The meeting's format permitted no spoken protest against this fateful decision, nor even any discussion of it. Yet there was strong, even desperate opposition to it on the part of officers in Germany's armed forces, including General Ludwig Beck, chief of the army General Staff, and General Franz Halder, Beck's deputy. They found it impossible to believe that France and Britain would not march if Czechoslovakia were invaded. Ordinary prudence and common sense required them to preserve a European balance of power that now favored the West but would be drastically altered in Germany's favor if Czechoslovakia were "wiped off the map." Obvious to the German generals was the fact that the combined military strength of France and Britain joined with Czechoslovakia's was much greater than Germany's—and to this capability must be added whatever force Russia could bring to bear, she having declared repeatedly and categorically her determination to honor the Franco-Russian treaty. There were, of course, serious geographical and political barriers to Russia's effective participation, but there were also indications that these, at least so far as Rumania was concerned, were not insurmountable. Indeed, Czechoslovakia of herself alone was no negligible factor in the military equation. She had an army of a million and a half men, the strongest fortress line in Europe, a small but thoroughly up-to-date air force, and a formidable armaments industry focused on the vast Skoda munitions works. Her defensive capability, despite the exposure of her southern flank by the *Anschluss,*[11] was probably great enough by itself alone to challenge for months the full strength (thirty-five divisions) that Germany could bring against her—an offensive strength achievable only through a virtual denuding of the West Wall,* where a mere five divisions would remain to face the hundred divisions France could bring against it. Moreover, this West Wall was as yet a misnomer; it existed only as pieces of a wall connected by fieldworks (trenches, barricades, mine fields, and so on) and it could not possibly be completed, however heroic the efforts, for at least another year. In sum, the gamble Hitler was taking, the loss of which would mean Germany's destruction, was enormous to the point of insanity, in the view of the German General Staff.

That this view was not at once made emphatically known to Hitler was not the fault of the staff chief, Beck. Even before the decisive May 28 meeting, he had written a memorandum to General Walther von Brauchitsch, the recently appointed top commander of the German army, saying flatly that an attack on Czechoslovakia would inevitably mean a general war, which Germany could not win, her overall "military-economic situation" being actually "worse than it was in 1917–1918," when she collapsed under Allied pressure. This memo was followed by others from Beck to Brauchitsch, disputing the argument Hitler had made on May 28, disputing also, point by point, the substance of subsequent Case Green directives. Beck intended these, or the gist of them at least, to be transmitted by Brauchitsch to Hitler. The army commander failed to transmit them, evidently out of fear.[12]

Even so, during the weeks immediately following the May 28 proclamation of "unshakable will," the Führer suffered qualms, which, though never openly confessed, were revealed in word, deed, and general demeanor. He retreated to the Berghof, his alpine aerie above Berchtesgaden on the Austrian border. He spent virtually the whole of that summer secluded there in a state of nervous excitement—a state wherein long fits of tense solitary brooding (Nietzsche's superman amid dark clouds of Wagnerian music) were alternated with bursts of feverish activity. In June, he ordered that the usual autumn troop maneuvers begin in August this year, so that the army would be in top fighting form by late September. He fumed that work on the West Wall was not proceeding rapidly enough. By his order some 400,000 industrial workers were drafted, placed under strict military discipline, and sent to labor upon the fortifications, their vacated industrial jobs being filled, thousands of them, by women who had been earlier forced out of the labor market by Nazi gender policies. Still the work did not go fast enough. He demanded and promptly received detailed reports on Czech fortifications, armament, state of readiness, and ultimate mobilized strength, then worried about the overall military potency that these reports revealed. In a special "general guiding directive" for Case Green, issued in mid-June, he so far wavered in the direction of his generals' anxieties as to say that he would "take action against Czechoslovakia only if . . . firmly convinced . . . that France will not march and that therefore England will not intervene."[13]

He continued to assert, however, that France's marching required prior

*Known to the Allies as the Siegfried Line.

assurance that England *would* then intervene—and on this point he was himself repeatedly reassured, his secret doubts laid to rest, by the words and acts of Neville Chamberlain.

As a matter of fact, through the whole of that long, tense summer, and especially during the first part of it, the chief resource of Hitler's heroic spirit was the British prime minister's dogged determination to appease him. This last, which faltered not at all under great pressures, was made known to Hitler in his remote aerie through repeated clear signals; and these signals were invariably given, as if deliberately, at precisely those moments when his resolve was most in danger of weakening.

We have told of the revealing dispatch by Joseph Driscoll published in the New York *Herald Tribune* in mid-May. Two weeks later (on June 1), in the immediate aftermath of the war scare of May 20, Chamberlain evidently reiterated in off-the-record remarks to a group of British correspondents the views he had expressed to Driscoll. For on June 3, *The Times* of London, notoriously a mouthpiece for the Baldwin-Chamberlain portion of the Tory party, published a leader (editorial) urging "self-determination" for minorities upon the Czech government "even if it should mean their secession from Czechoslovakia." The German embassy in London promptly reported to Berlin that the *Times* leader expressed Chamberlain's views.[14]

This greatly helped Hitler to stand firm when he at last learned the extent and seriousness of his generals' opposition to his Czech policy. That was in the third week of July, after Beck had climaxed his series of memos to Brauchitsch with one (on July 16) saying that "the Supreme Commander of the armed forces [Hitler] *must*" be "urgently" asked to cease his war preparations "and abandon the intention of solving the Czech question by force until the military situation is fundamentally changed" because "at the present time," in the view of "all the highest officers of the General Staff," this situation was "hopeless." There was in this a clear undertone of threat, of rebellion, and Brauchitsch, who shared Beck's assessment of the military situation, was sufficiently disturbed by it to do what Beck had wanted him to do with earlier memos— namely, show it to the Führer. It was shown in an edited version: The portion of it dealing with international political factors was deleted; only the purely military argument, that of balance of power, remained.[15]

Hitler, too, was disturbed by the memo. He remained wholly unpersuaded, convinced that psychological factors rendered accurate estimates of relative military strengths essentially irrelevant to the present situation's outcome. But he was well aware of the dangerous implications of the Beck memorandum, and he brooded over it intermittently for some weeks. He then summoned to the Berghof, on August 10, not Beck or Halder or any other of the disaffected top officers, but generals of the second rank—service and army commanders who were younger and more ambitious for promotion than the top men, hence more vulnerable to what the Columbia Broadcasting System's Berlin correspondent, William L. Shirer, later called the Führer's "persuasive oratory." He "treated" his guests on this occasion to an excellent dinner followed by nearly three hours of "oratory," at the close of which he invited or permitted questions and comment. He was then infuriated to discover that he had been far from totally persuasive. The ranking officer present was a general who had just been designated Chief of Staff of the German Army of the West; he dared challenge directly his Führer's estimate of the strength of the West Wall. With the five divisions available to man it, it could be held for three weeks at most, this general said. The French would overrun Germany before Czechoslovakia could be disposed of. Hitler, typically, flew into a rage, shouting: "I say to you, Herr General, the position will be held not only for three weeks but for three years!"[16]

Thereafter he held no meetings with his generals in which they were permitted to ask questions or voice opinions. Nor did any of them attempt to force their opposing views directly upon him, an attempt they recognized as dangerous to their careers, if not ultimately their lives. Beck had proposed orally to Brauchitsch, when he presented his last memo, that he and Brauchitsch and all the other top generals resign in a body if Hitler persisted on the present course. That would put a stop to this madness. But as it turned out only Beck resigned, this on August 18, and even he yielded enough to Hitler's will, or to his own conception of honor and patriotism, to limit his resignation's effectiveness as protest. Hitler, if relieved to have Beck out of the way, was concerned over the effect knowledge of the resignation might have upon the public, the officer corps, and, most importantly, upon decision-makers in London and Paris. He therefore ordered the utmost secrecy regarding it (official announcement of Beck's departure would not be made till late October), and Beck obeyed the order strictly. If dismayed that not one of the top generals who agreed with him had done or would do as he had done (he was especially disillusioned and embittered by Brauchitsch's spinelessness), he made no further effort to persuade them that they should.[17]

Nevertheless, his three months of increasingly strong protest through official channels was not without effect along the line he so desperately pursued. Pro-Nazi before Hitler came to power, he was now convinced that Hitler's removal was essential to Germany's survival, and he therefore welcomed the serious approaches made to him, for the first time, by members of an anti-Hitler movement, small but potent, which had been developing piecemeal since 1933. The earliest members of this movement were civilians, among them scions of several of the most distinguished and aristocratic of German families. They aimed from the first at Hitler's overthrow and the seizure of governing power but were only too aware that by themselves they could not possibly succeed against the elaborate apparatus for internal espionage, brutal coercion, and psychological terror whereby the Nazi party ruled the state. Only the army possessed the necessary physical force—and for nearly five years the loosely organized civilian disaffection had not been matched by any equivalent disaffection among the army officer corps. By the summer of 1938, however, in large part because of Hitler's drastic reorganization of the armed forces command in February of that year, an active anti-Hitler movement had developed among ranking army officers, and there was a drawing together of the two groups, civilian and military. Both approached Beck. He joined with them. And since he was greatly respected and absolutely trusted by everyone, there was a coalescence and consolidation under—or around—him. By the time of his resignation he was a leading figure in a definite conspiracy.[18]

Enlisted in it were three generals holding three key commands, those of Berlin and environs, of the garrison at Potsdam, and of an armored division so positioned in Thuringia that it could block any attempt by S.S. troops in Munich to move on Berlin. The plan was to arrest Hitler and seize control of the German government as soon as the final order was given to attack Czechoslovakia. The attack would, of course, be halted. Hitler, brought before a People's Court (these were a Nazi creation, a part of the Nazi apparatus of repression), would be convicted in typical People's Court fashion of incompetence to govern, if not actual treason, and then disposed of through imprisonment or, more probably—necessarily—death. Germany would be ruled thereafter by a military dictatorship until a republican government of conservative nature could be formed.[19]

But meanwhile, unfortunately for the conspirators and for world peace, Chamberlain's will to appease was relentlessly operative.

In late July he told Parliament that he was sending to Czechoslovakia as special agent of the British government a former Cabinet minister, Lord Runciman, a fervent appeaser, whose mission was to seek peaceful settlement of the differences between Prague and Konrad Henlein. He did so "with the full concurrence of Herr Hitler," as was publicly said at the time.[20] Inevitably there was suspicion among the well-informed that Runciman's actual purpose was to negotiate, not a compromise, but a surrender—that his real mission was to persuade the Prague government to do whatever Hitler wanted done with respect to the Sudetenland, this by a threat to withhold British support from Czechoslovakia if, in consequence of a refusal to do this, Germany attacked her. "Runciman's whole mission smells," wrote correspondent Shirer into his diary on the day (August 4) of the viscount's arrival in Prague. "It was a shabby diplomatic trick," he remembered twenty years later.[21]

Simultaneously, the Chamberlain government discounted to the point of nullity every sign and specific warning that the appeasement policy was leading to catastrophe. It also rebuffed the desperate efforts of the German anti-Hitler conspirators to make meaningful, policy-determining contact with it.

On August 18, the date of Beck's resignation and two weeks after Runciman's mission began, an emissary of the German conspirators, General Ewald von Kleist, traveling under a false passport secretly issued by Admiral Wilhelm Canaris, chief of intelligence of the German armed forces, who was one of the conspirators, arrived in London. His arrival was preceded by a telegram addressed to the British Foreign Office by Ambassador Henderson in Berlin, saying that "it would be unwise for him to be received in official quarters."[22] Kleist *was* received, however, by Sir Robert Vansittart, chief diplomatic adviser to the foreign secretary, who was personally strongly opposed to appeasement and who made an immediate detailed report to Halifax and Chamberlain of what the emissary had to say. The gist of this was that Hitler was determined to strike in late September; that the only slight chance of deterring him was to convince him absolutely that Britain and France would fight for Czechoslovakia's survival; and that, if Hitler then still persisted, decisive preventive action would be taken by the German General Staff. Would Britain support Czechoslovakia with armed force? Kleist wanted to know—and received no answer from Halifax or Chamberlain. He also talked with Winston Churchill, however, and Churchill assured him, in a letter Kleist took back to his fellow conspirators, "that the crossing of the frontier by German armies or aviation in force" would, he was certain, "bring about a renewal of the World War" because "England will march with France. . . . Do not, I pray you, be misled upon this point."[23] Three days later (August 21), the British military attaché in Berlin was called upon by an agent of the conspirators and told: "If by firm action abroad Hitler can be forced to renounce his present intentions, he will be unable to survive the blow. Similarly, if it comes to war the immediate intervention by France and England will bring about the downfall of the regime."[24] Hitler's situation was hopeless, in other words, provided Britain and France stood firmly by their treaty obligations. His "unshakable will" had placed him in a fatal position from which he could neither advance nor retreat. When Henderson forwarded this communication to London he accompanied it with his own expressed opinion that it was "clearly biased and largely propaganda."[25]

By the first of September, weeks of talks presided over by Runciman had produced concession after concession by the Czech government but none by Konrad Henlein (he wanted more, always more), yet the Czechs remained firm in their determination to fight rather than agree to the dismemberment of their country. Preparations proceeded feverishly in Germany, desperately in Czechoslovakia, and reluctantly in France and Britain for the war which it was now feared Hitler might announce in his closing speech at the annual Nazi party congress at Nuremberg, on September 12. Equally feverish and desperate were the counterwar preparations of the German anti-Hitler conspirators—and on September 5 the Chamberlain government received yet further evidence of this conspiracy's vitality and potency.

The first secretary of the German embassy in London, Theo Kordt, called that day upon Vansittart to impart, at grave risk to his own life, information that had come to him, deviously, from his brother, Dr. Erich Kordt, who was Ribbentrop's Chief of Staff. Both brothers were active conspirators. Theo Kordt's information was that Halder, Beck's successor as German army Chief of Staff, had now become one of the active conspirators; that army Commander in Chief Brauchitsch, though not a part of the conspiracy, was aware of it and would do nothing to hinder it; that Baron Ernst von Weizsäcker, who as under secretary of state for foreign affairs was Ribbentrop's second-in-command, was in sympathy with the conspirators' purpose; that Hitler's order to mobilize for the invasion of Czechoslovakia on October 2 would probably be issued on

September 16; and that its issuance would be the signal for decisive action by the conspirators, according to plans now definite and detailed.

This information seemed to Vansittart of such urgent importance that he arranged to have Kordt convey it at once, personally, to Sir Horace Wilson, Chamberlain's right-hand man, whose office was adjacent to the prime minister's at 10 Downing Street. Wilson, in his turn, was sufficiently impressed, despite himself, to arrange at once an interview between Kordt and Foreign Secretary Halifax, at 11 Downing Street. Halifax listened imperturbably; his sole comment to Kordt at the interview's close was that Kordt's communication was "most interesting."[26]

All the same, what he had heard so agitated Halifax that he, for once, took independent action, instructing Nevile Henderson, who was then at Nuremberg as observer of the Nazi party rally, to seek an immediate audience with Hitler and warn him officially that, if Czechoslovakia were invaded, there would be general war, for Britain would certainly act with France. Henderson, however, at once protested these instructions with a vehemence that seemed to Alfred Duff Cooper, then First Lord of the Admiralty, "almost hysterical."[27] The ambassador was under earlier highly secret instructions from the prime minister that, in his view, contradicted those Halifax now issued. He had been summoned from Berlin to London for "consultations" immediately following, and because of, the Kleist mission to London; had then been initially told by the prime minister to warn Hitler that aggression against Czechoslovakia would have grave consequences and to prepare the way secretly for "personal contact" between Chamberlain and Hitler at some early future date. He had easily persuaded the prime minister to rescind the first of these instructions; he had since happily pursued the second. But to what avail? he now asked. The effect of doing what Halifax requested would be, he cried desperately, "opposite . . . to that desired." An official warning of Hitler must necessarily be a public warning; its heeding would therefore be a public humiliation which Hitler in his present mood and situation would not, could not accept. He'd be driven "right off the deep end" into "immediate aggression."[28]

It was an argument, or assertion, with which Chamberlain perfectly agreed. Halifax was overruled.

Two days later, on Wednesday, September 7, *The Times* of London published a leader which, though it may have been composed by *Times* editor Geoffrey Dawson, not only employed the maddeningly circumlocutory style of Neville Chamberlain's public speech but also expressed, this time more definitely and in circumstances that gave it a far more decisive weight, the policy view that had been identified with Chamberlain in the above-quoted *Times* think pieces of the previous mid-May and early June. Said *The Times:*

If the Sudetens now ask for more than the Czech Government are ready to give in their latest proposals, it can only be inferred that the Germans are going beyond the mere removal of disabilities for those who do not find themselves at ease within the Czechoslovak Republic. In that case it might be worth while for the Czechoslovak

Government to consider whether they should exclude altogether the project, which
has found favour in some quarters, of making Czechoslovakia a more homogeneous
state by the cession of that fringe of alien populations who are contiguous to the
nation to which they are united by race.[29]

What the Czechs should "consider," in other words, was the giving up to
Germany of more than a fifth of their country's citizenry and the whole of its
Bohemian fortress line.

"A more appropriate moment and method for raising general hell could
hardly have been chosen" was the disgusted comment on this editorial by a
spokesman for the U.S. Council on Foreign Relations.[30] The Czech and French
governments immediately demanded that the British issue an official disclaimer, and the Chamberlain government complied with a statement saying
the *Times* leader "in no way" represented "the view of His Majesty's Government." *The Times* itself, however, stood firmly by its expressed view, which
continued to be viewed by the knowledgeable as that of the Chamberlain
ministry. On the following day, along with a leader warning Hitler against the
use of military force to achieve his ends, the paper printed a summary of the
opinions it had expressed on the Sudeten crisis since May, proving thereby that
it had consistently advocated, as a "solution if others failed," the cession of
the Sudetenland to Germany.[31]

III

IT is notable that, throughout the Austrian and Czechoslovak crises, Chamberlain stubbornly resisted every effort by the Soviet Union, through Commissar of Foreign Affairs Maxim Litvinov, to join with Britain and France in
shaping what Churchill had already called a "Grand Alliance" against Hitler.
Litvinov's efforts toward such an alliance, by means of the League of Nations,
had been strenuous, numerous, and, in the face of Chamberlain's opposition,
utterly futile.

They continued to be.

On September 2, in a personal conversation obviously intended for report
to the British Foreign Office, the Soviet ambassador in London, Ivan Maisky,
told Winston Churchill what Litvinov had said to the French chargé d'affaires
in Moscow the day before. In the last few months "the policy of the Rumanian
government has been remarkably friendly," Litvinov had said, according to
Churchill's detailed memorandum on this conversation, delivered to Halifax
next day. Litvinov had expressed the opinion that "the best way to overcome
the reluctance of Rumania" to permit the passage of Soviet troops "would be
through the agency of the League of Nations." He went on: "If . . . the League
decided that Czechoslovakia was the victim of aggression and that Germany
was the aggressor, that would probably determine the action of Rumania in
regard to allowing Russian troops and air forces to pass through her territory."
He advised that a meeting of the Council of the League be at once "invoked

under Article II, on the ground that there is danger of war." But what if the vote of the League Council were not unanimous? asked the French chargé. Litvinov answered that he thought "a majority decision would be sufficient" and that Rumania would vote with the majority. Halifax's response to this, in a September 5 note to Churchill, was that "at present" he "did not . . . feel that action of the kind proposed under Article II would be helpful."[32]

In private conversations, the prime minister expressed the opinion that Russia, in any case, was of little importance militarily—less valuable as a military ally, in fact, than Poland. Soviet armed strength had never been great, in his view; it had now been almost destroyed by Stalin's purges; it would certainly collapse quickly under attack by Nazi Germany. And this consummation was not one that the prime minister was inclined to deplore. On the contrary, he welcomed it. Such, at least, was the conclusion of analytical observers at the time, a conviction published in U.S. journals of opinion (for instance, by Frederick L. Schuman in *The New Republic*) as in those of England and France. The crushing of Communist Russia was precisely what Chamberlain and his fellows of the Cliveden Set secretly wished for and aimed to accomplish through their foreign policy, these analysts said. Otherwise appeasement, viciously stupid when measured against the moral standards and practical interests of the democracies, became totally and hopelessly insane.

Consistent with this conclusion were Chamberlain's attitude toward America and his policy dealings with the American government. If the United States figured at all in his European strategic calculations at this time—if he assigned the slightest weight to American opinion and power as actual influences, much less potentially determinative ones, upon the course of European affairs—he gave no public sign of it.

We have seen how he dealt with Franklin Roosevelt's "peace initiative" of early 1938, a Rooseveltian gesture toward Anglo-American rapprochement and collective security in general that would have become considerably more than a gesture had Chamberlain welcomed and wholeheartedly cooperated in it. We have seen how this enabled Chamberlain to replace anti-appeasement Eden with pro-appeasement Halifax as foreign secretary. He now stood equally firm against an effort by Churchill, late in the summer of 1938, to enlist the personal prestige of the President of the United States in a renewed world peacemaking role—an effort that aimed also to breathe life back into a dying Franco-Russian alliance.

"Would it not be possible," Churchill asked in a memorandum addressed to the foreign secretary on August 31,

to frame [this week] a Joint Note between Britain, France, and Russia stating (a) their desire for peace and friendly relations; (b) their deep anxiety at the military preparations of Germany; (c) their joint interest in a peaceful solution of the Czechoslovak controversy; and (d) that an invasion by Germany of Czechoslovakia would raise capital issues for all three Powers? This Note . . . should be formally shown to Roosevelt by the Ambassadors of the three Powers, and we should use every effort to induce him to do his utmost upon it. It seems to me not impossible [thus did

Churchill ingratiatingly employ the rear-end-forward style of speech habitually employed by Chamberlain] that he would then himself address Hitler, emphasizing the gravity of the situation, and saying that it seemed to him that a world war would inevitably follow from an invasion of Czechoslovakia, and that he earnestly counselled a friendly settlement.

Such a "process," Churchill went on to say, evidently with the Kleist mission in mind, "would give the best chance to peaceful elements in German circles to make a stand, and . . . Hitler might find a way out for himself by parleying with Roosevelt."[33]

Halifax's reply to this, if any, was a mere acknowledgment of receipt. In his war memoirs, Churchill makes no mention of it.

## IV

ON the day Churchill's memorandum was being written, Roosevelt was exploring with Morgenthau and other Treasury officials, in the White House, a plan for depositing French and British gold in the United States, converting this gold into dollars, then enabling the British and French to use these dollars to purchase American-made arms and war matériel—this possibly conjoined with the imposition of "countervailing duties" on German imports.[34] He himself had asked Morgenthau to develop such a plan, the effect of which would be to tie the United States to Britain and France in a limited but concrete alliance against Germany. He now enthusiastically endorsed, orally, what Treasury proposed, expressed a desire to act upon it at once, and might have done so if a fussily cautious Cordell Hull, asked for his approval, had not instead voiced grave reservations. Hull was fearful that the proposed action would injure the trade policy to which he was religiously committed. He "would have to sleep on it," he said. Whereupon Roosevelt himself, having ordered Hull not to show the plan memoranda to anyone in the State Department, decided also to "sleep on it."[35] But clearly, Roosevelt's personal desire was to do all that he deemed possible to strengthen the stand of the European democracies against Hitler.

Hence an irony in his situation vis-à-vis European affairs at this time—an irony, not without bitterness, that he may or may not have recognized. For to the extent that he wished to steer America away from isolationism toward collective security (the extent is incalculable; he was ambiguous and ambivalent in his dealings with this as with most fundamental issues)—to the concomitant extent that he would persuade the European democracies away from appeasement toward joint international action against Nazi-Fascist aggression —he found in his way, as a serious obstacle to such purpose, the man whom he had so blithely named, exclusively for reasons of domestic politics, to the highly sensitive and important post of U.S. ambassador to the Court of St. James's.

Within weeks after Joseph Patrick Kennedy's arrival in London he had become a regular guest at Clivedon and a warm personal friend of "Neville." By the summer of 1938, he had acquired a reputation for personal anti-Semitism, a consequently excessively sympathetic "understanding" of Germany's "Jewish problem" (witness the already recounted embassy-luncheon experience of the Gerard Swope party); and by late August, as the Czech crisis mounted toward climax, he was doing all he could, and far more than an ambassador should, to commit the President and his country to continued isolationism joined with support of the Chamberlain ministry. On August 30, during an hour-long interview with the prime minister, he gave fervent expression to his personal view that general war *must* be avoided, then went on to say (on what authority no one knows; one cannot rule out the possibility of Roosevelt's having actually said something of the sort) that the President had decided "to go in with" Chamberlain and would approve whatever course Chamberlain chose to follow with respect to Czechoslovakia. During that same interview, Chamberlain in his turn evidently disclosed to his good friend his own determination to compel Czechoslovakia to agree to Hitler's terms. For on the following day, in a transatlantic telephone interview given, incredibly, as an "exclusive" to the Hearst-owned *Boston American* (that is, to all subscribers to Hearst's International News Service), Kennedy told his fellow Americans that he had just returned to the embassy from the British Foreign Office, that "things aren't as bad as they seem," and that the "thing to do here [in London] and in the United States is not to lose our heads." The British people were united "very strongly" behind the Chamberlain ministry, he said, and "no war is going to break out during the rest of 1938."[36]

By the time he gave this interview he had prepared and cabled to the State Department the draft of a speech he was to give at Aberdeen, Scotland, on September 2. One paragraph of it dealt by clear implication with Czechoslovakia: "I should like to ask you all if you know of any dispute . . . in the world which is worth the life of your son. . . . Perhaps I am not well informed . . . but for the life of me I cannot see anything involved which could be remotely considered worth shedding blood for." In his cover message, Kennedy requested immediate approval of the draft, doing so in such fashion as to indicate he would brook no departmental censorship of it. Whereupon the secretary of state not only told the ambassador to delete the references to Czechoslovakia but also said that the President, having been consulted in the matter, concurred in this instruction. Simultaneously, Hull made a sharply worded protest against the Hearst newspaper "exclusive" that Kennedy had granted—and Roosevelt, days later, let the ambassador know in a mildly reprimanding personal note to "Dear Joe" that he, too, was "greatly disturbed" by this.[37]

Nor were these the only specific public evidences, as August gave way to September, that Kennedy was "beginning to go Walter Hines Page on us and run foreign affairs all by himself," as Berle noted in his diary.[38]* The British press reported on September 1 that Foreign Secretary Halifax had asked Kennedy what the United States would do if Britain did go to war over Czechoslovakia. The report angered Roosevelt. "It is a nice kettle of fish!" he said wrathfully to Morgenthau. The obvious design of Chamberlain and Halifax was to make America in part responsible, in the eyes of the world, for whatever they decided to do. If the British went to war over Czechoslovakia it would be because America promised support of such action; if they did not, it would be "because we held back." For the dire consequences of either course, the Roosevelt administration would be blamed. Why hadn't Kennedy at once denied the story and berated the British press for inaccurate reporting? he wanted to know, then answered his own question with a voiced suspicion that Kennedy was himself the story's source—that the ambassador was deliberately leaking information to the British press in the service, not of Roosevelt's foreign policy, but of Chamberlain's. As for Chamberlain, he was "slippery" and not to be trusted in any circumstances.

"Who would have thought that the English could take into camp a red-headed Irishman?" asked Roosevelt disgustedly. "The young man needs his wrists slapped rather hard."[39]

These remarks were made during what turned out to be the decisive conference on the Treasury gold-deposit and countervailing-duty plan that Morgenthau had presented to him the day before. The decision was, in form, typically tentative. Roosevelt said that the plan memoranda were in the "middle drawer" of his desk from which he could "always get them out in a minute." But, as Morgenthau had said to his staff the day before, "if we are going to do anything" with deterrent effect on Germany "the time to do it is in the next forty-eight hours. . . . And it ought to be out in the papers . . . and the President ought to send for the German diplomatic representative."[40] Instead, Roosevelt again consulted Hull—the effect also (though this went unmentioned that day) consulted any bold move toward collective security might have, not only on his Democratic primary "purge" campaign, about which he was justly worried, but also upon the midterm elections in November—and, having so consulted, he did nothing about the mounting European war crisis.

Nor did he do anything in this regard during the twelve days that followed, days shadowed by anxiety over what Hitler would say in his long-dreaded Nuremberg speech and by even greater anxiety, for Roosevelt personally, over the outcome of James's dangerous surgery. As always, he was buffeted by contrary waves of foreign-policy advice. These waves, however, rode a deep, strong tide that flowed consistently, persistently, and (for the purely pragmatic politician) overwhelmingly against any openly committed involvement of the United States in what Bullitt and others called the "mess" in Europe. Britain and France must pull their own chestnuts out of the fire this time. America

---

*Page, U.S. ambassador to Britain during the Great War, did all he could to involve the United States in the war on the Allied side.

must not be bamboozled into doing so, as she had been during the Great War.

Writing from Paris on August 17, when Hitler seemed (he wished for the moment to seem) hesitant, Bullitt had voiced what we now know to have been the totally mistaken opinion that "fear of the United States is unquestionably a large factor in Hitler's hesitation." He went on: "If, in September, Europe should again appear to be on the verge of war, a quiet conversation between you and the German Ambassador in the White House might have more effect in deterring Germany . . . than all the speeches you or anyone else could make." All Roosevelt would have to do was "recite a few facts" about the hostility toward Germany of American public opinion and the consequent "possibility that the United States might be drawn in" to a general war as she had been in 1917. But that the United States must not be "drawn in" was Bullitt's constant theme. On August 31 he wrote that, if war began, "the result will be such a devastation of Europe that it will make small difference which side should emerge the ostensible victor. I am more convinced than ever that we should attempt to stay out and be ready to reconstruct whatever pieces may be left of European civilization."⁴¹ On the following day (September 1), Adolf Berle addressed to the President a personal memorandum earnestly warning against "emotional thinking" based on a horror of Hitler and Hitlerian "methods." One must instead, in this situation, think "historically," recognizing the fact that the breaking-up of the Austro-Hungarian Empire had been recognized as a "mistake" by "one branch of the American Delegation" at the very conference, the Versailles Conference, where the deed was done.

> Our emotion is obscuring the fact that were the actor anyone other than Hitler, with his cruelty and anti-Semitic feeling, we would regard this as merely reconstituting the old system, undoing the obviously unsound work of Versailles and generally following the line of historical logic. . . . It seems to me . . . that we should be developing a north–south axis [that is, a firm defensive alliance of North and South American countries], and not be swung off base by either diplomacy or emotion. In this connection, requests from Halifax to Kennedy asking continual consultation and the similar moves by the French Foreign Office could easily and insensibly make us substantially "an associate power" [Wilson had insisted during the Great War that the United States was not one of the Allies but "an associate power"] before we know it.⁴²

V

CAME Monday, September 12, 1938.

As evening shadows fell across the huge open-air stadium at Nuremberg there was vast pageantry, a stark, somber, vividly exciting pageantry, dramatic in its contrast of the bright with the dark, the vital with the deathly, but ominous and terrifying also for all lovers of life and liberty, since it was darkness and death that predominated. Hundreds of thousands were gathered there, yet in a human sense no one was there. No definite person. The scene was all of dark masses, uniform, totalitarian under the huge swastika banners, mankind dehumanized because deindividualized. Until, abruptly, a single man did appear. He entered the stadium before the ranked masses, his individuality not only defined by the empty space that surrounded him but emphasized by the spotlight that followed his progress across open ground to the podium steps. He marched with slow, deliberate stride, looking neither right nor left. His right hand was upraised but seemingly carelessly, perfunctorily, even absent-mindedly. The gesture seemed more a wave than a salute, for his elbow and fingers remained bent. Not so the arms and hands that immediately sprang up in a huge forest from the dark masses. These were stiffly straight. And with them sprang also from the masses, in a single frightful roaring voice, a triple chant: "Sieg heil! Sieg heil! Sieg heil!" Then silence. Adolf Hitler mounted the podium. He turned to face the Nazi horde, the clustered microphones. And the Nuremberg throng continued to wait in silence, as much of the population of the civilized world waited with bated breath beside millions of radio sets, for der Führer's decisive words.[43]

But, as it turned out, the words were *not* decisive. They poured out in turgid endless stream; they spread in turbulent flood across landscapes of the mind for lack of any defining channel through which they might flow to a conclusion. Hitler was raving mad over the "lie" that "Herr Beneš" had "invented" last May, and the "crimes" committed against the Sudeten Germans by the Czechs. There must be (he repeated this several times) full Sudeten German "self-determination." By his order "the most gigantic fortifications that ever existed" were under construction "in the west," consisting of "17,000 armored and concrete fortifications . . . laid out in three and partially four lines, of a total depth of fifty kilometers." They would be completed before winter, though actually their full "defensive capability" was "already in existence."

But Hitler never came to the point that the world awaited with such dread. Instead, he trailed off into vague generalities about History, evidently in search of the right note on which to end his speech. He never found it. At last, he simply quit.[44]

The peace-loving world's reaction to this flood of words mingled relief that war had not been made with disappointment that peace had not been either. There was a slight resurgence of hope amid a continuing dreadful suspense, a mingled mood that found editorial expression in the free-world press. Thus *Le Temps* in Paris said that though Hitler "left matters in an indecisive state, . . . he did not close the door against a peaceable solution." The London *Times* said the speech, "though not altogether reassuring, was not violently disturbing."[45]

This slight sense of relief and resurgence of hope were strengthened for many critical observers by the outcome of a crescendo of violence which began in the Sudetenland within a dozen hours after the last limping words of the Nuremberg tirade were spoken. The sun had barely risen over the border town of Eger on Tuesday, September 13, when two Czech policemen, attempting to carry out an order to search a hotel for small arms believed cached there by

Henlein's Sudeten German party, were fired upon without warning by Nazis occupying rooms on an upper floor. One policeman was killed instantly. The other fled on foot. Prague reacted promptly, forcefully. Czech troops with armored cars and mortars were called in. A firefight followed, in which another Czech policeman and eight of the ten Nazis in the hotel were killed. By afternoon, all through the Sudetenland, mobs of Henlein's followers, incited by Hitler's Nuremberg demand for Sudeten German self-determination, were clashing bloodily, first with police, then with Czech troops as Prague declared martial law for the whole border district. By nightfall twenty-one had been killed and scores wounded, but Konrad Henlein had fled to Germany and the Czech government was in firm control of the Sudetenland for the first time since the crisis began.[46]

On that same Tuesday, in the presidential railway car parked at Rochester, Minnesota, an anxious Roosevelt discussed with Harry Hopkins the state of America's military defenses and the need for a great strengthening of American arms. He had listened to the Nuremberg speech over the radio in this car the day before, with Hopkins seated beside him, and had not been in the slightest soothed by it. "The President was sure then that we were going to get into war . . . ," Hopkins later asserted.

Yet the country was woefully unprepared physically for the crisis it faced. As of June 30, 1938, the U.S. Army had a commissioned-officer strength of 12,472, not counting Philippine Scouts and retired officers on active duty; it had an enlisted strength of 163,800, not counting Philippine Scouts. More nearly adequate to defense needs, but inadequate still in view of growing Japanese strength in the Pacific, was the U.S. Navy as it would be when the current naval construction program was completed. Roosevelt's special concern, however, was over the American air arm. He was convinced, according to Hopkins, "that air power would win the war." Which meant that America's air arm, pitifully weak at that moment, must be vastly strengthened as rapidly as was politically and physically possible. Moreover, Britain and France, the latter especially, would almost certainly seek to buy warplanes from the United States—and the United States, in its own defense interest, should be prepared to supply their need. If prevailing isolationist sentiment made this impossible to do openly, or too dangerous politically, some way to do it secretly might be found. But just what was the warplane-manufacturing capacity of the United States, actual and potential? Roosevelt didn't know; he had no solid data for even an educated guess. He bemoaned the fact. Whereupon Hopkins may have suggested that he himself gather the needed information. At any rate, Roosevelt decided then and there that Hopkins should go at once to the West Coast, where much of the aircraft industry was concentrated, and obtain, under a thick cloak of secrecy, factual information on which the President could base an expansion program having precisely numbered goals.[47]

A few hours later, Cordell Hull, phoning from his Washington apartment, where he and Berle had dined together alone that evening, told the President that, according to a late-afternoon phone call from Bullitt in Paris, Daladier and Chamberlain were considering a direct personal approach to Hitler; they might journey to Berlin within a couple of days to confer with him.[48]

On the following day, James being now wholly out of danger, according to Mayo doctors, Roosevelt bade farewell to "my friends" of Rochester in informal remarks delivered from the rear platform of his railway car. Because of the European crisis he was going "straight through to Washington" instead of stopping at "my house on the Hudson River."[49]

And by that time, Chamberlain in London, evidently rebuffing Daladier's proposal of joint talks, had sent a telegram to Hitler saying: "In view of the increasingly critical situation [that is, the Czechs had shown their determination to defend themselves and Hitler had again shown slight signs of wavering], I propose to come over at once to see you with a view to finding a peaceful solution."[50] Hitler, prepared for this offer by Nevile Henderson, promptly invited the prime minister to come to Berchtesgaden.

So at eight-thirty in the morning of Thursday the fifteenth, accompanied not by the foreign secretary but by his great friend Sir Horace Wilson and no other adviser, Chamberlain boarded an airplane for the first time in his sixty-nine years of life, flew to Munich where Henderson greeted him, then went by car with Wilson and Henderson to the Berghof. There he and Hitler conferred for three hours, the two of them alone save for an interpreter, a German who took no notes of the conversation. (The impression the dictator made on Chamberlain, he told his sister, was that "in spite of the hardness and ruthlessness I thought I saw in his face . . . here was a man who could be relied upon when he had given his word."[51]) On Saturday, September 17, he was back in London where, evidently well satisfied with his trip, he at once reported to the Cabinet and consulted with his ministers regarding the position he would take when, as it had been agreed he would do, he returned to Germany for a second meeting with Hitler.

By Thursday evening, Roosevelt was returned to Washington. He could not then know, nor know the next day, precisely what had been said and agreed to at Berchtesgaden. But the general nature of the conversation and the substance of the conclusion reached were obvious. Chamberlain had been informed by blaring radio broadcasts within minutes after his landing in Munich that the temporarily exiled Konrad Henlein now demanded an immediate plebiscite in which Sudeten Germans voted on the question of making the Sudetenland a part of the Third Reich. There was no question what the result would be. And this result was favored, plebiscite or no, by Lord Runciman in the long-awaited report he presented to the British Cabinet on the seventeenth. Runciman recommended the "immediate and drastic action" of transferring to Germany "the predominantly German districts" of Czechoslovakia.[52] No one in Washington doubted (Kennedy's reports from London clearly indicated) that Sudeten German "self-determination" was what Chamberlain was agreeing to "in principle" during his talk with Hitler. Nor could there be any doubt that a majority of the British Cabinet would approve such agreement.

During his own Cabinet meeting on Friday the sixteenth, while Chamberlain was yet in Germany, and again, more emphatically, in an hour-long conversation with Ickes on Saturday afternoon, Roosevelt expressed disgust. "The once-proud British lion seems now to have its tail thrust firmly between its legs, when its Prime Minister . . . rushes to plead with the ex-corporal, ex–house painter who is now bossing Germany," the Hitler-hating interior secretary had told his diary on September 15. The President thoroughly agreed. With British and French concurrence, Hitler would now get what he wanted from the Czechs who, in Roosevelt's opinion, would be unable to resist Germany's might for long if they refused to yield to Franco-British pressure and fought alone, as it then appeared they would do. No doubt Poland and Hungary would also demand slices of Czechoslovakia. Soon what had once been a strong, prosperous democracy, and democracy's champion in central Europe, would lie prostrate, dismembered, on ground dark with gore. "In the President's graphic language, England and France, during and after this international outrage, will 'wash the blood from their Judas Iscariot hands,' " wrote Ickes in his diary.[53]

There had been for many days a virtually continuous crisis conference in the State Department, the agenda provided by a flood of cables and phone calls from the European capitals. This conference now became what "might . . . be called the 'death watch' of Europe," as Berle wrote on the evening of Monday, September 19.[54] Only somewhat less continuous, being interrupted by only the most necessary other business, were the crisis sessions in the Executive Office and Oval Room—and these, too, perhaps even more than those in the State Department, were dark with doom, poignant with regret, angered by frustration. For Roosevelt could no longer blink the fact of his gravely weakened domestic political position. The negative returns on his purge attempt were now all in; he must expect to face in January a Congress even less agreeable to him, or with him, than the one he had had to face at the first of the present year. And as the digests of cables that poured in unceasing stream onto the President's desk kept him au courant with events in London and Paris and Prague—events that outraged logic, morality, and every principle of civilized intercourse between sovereign states—he felt ever more acutely his helplessness in the face of onrushing catastrophe.

French premier Daladier, accompanied by French foreign minister Bonnet, came to London on Sunday the eighteenth. By noon of the next day these two had collaborated with Chamberlain and Halifax in a draft of proposals to be at once presented to the Czech government, proposals calling for the cession to Germany of all territory having a population more than 50 percent German. Nothing was said about a plebiscite (one for the Sudeten Germans would lead to plebiscites for the Slovaks and Ruthenians, the French had argued), nor about the strongly fortified defensive line that must go with the Sudeten Germans into the cruel hands of Czechoslovakia's mortal enemy. There was just a hint of shamefaced apology, along with a most emphatic call for prompt Czech surrender, in the following words: "Both the French and British Governments recognize how great is the sacrifice thus required of Czechoslovakia. They have felt it their duty to set forth frankly the conditions essential to security. . . . The Prime Minister must resume conversations with Herr Hitler not later than Wednesday [September 21], or sooner if possible. We, therefore, feel that we must ask for your reply at the earliest possible moment."[55]

If Roosevelt had not actually read a cabled copy of these proposals he was evidently very accurately informed concerning them when, on that Monday the nineteenth, just a few hours after the proposals were drafted, he engaged in a highly secret tête-à-tête with the British ambassador in Washington, Sir Ronald Lindsay. Total secrecy was imperative, Roosevelt stressed at the outset, for if isolationist leaders learned of what he was about to say, he could be impeached. He then spoke of the Anglo-French proposals to Czechoslovakia as "the most terrible remorseless sacrifice" ever demanded of a sovereign state and gave it as his opinion that the Czechs would not, could not agree to them —though he added, characteristically, that if Chamberlain's policy *did* somehow "work" he would "be the first to cheer." It was on the assumption that the policy would fail that he went on to outline a very general plan for getting American aid to the British and French in opposition to Germany, a plan he had reviewed in his talk with Ickes last Saturday afternoon and with Morgenthau earlier on that very day. It called for the adoption by the British and French of precisely the military strategy that Adolf Hitler wanted them to employ, and counted upon their employing, in case of hostilities. The two allies should stand on the defensive in the west, said Roosevelt, since their chance of mounting a successful attack was at best 60–40 in view of Germany's reported military superiority, especially in the air. They should impose a strict blockade, insist that other nations respect it, and at the same time let the world know that they based this strategy "on the loftiest humanitarian grounds . . . the desire to wage hostilities with a minimum of suffering and the least possible loss of life and property." Evidently he did not ask himself what such a strategy would do to the Czechs, against whom, in the absence of pressure from the west, Hitler could hurl the whole of his military force. His exclusive concern at the moment was with American domestic politics as related to foreign affairs. If the strategy he proposed were adopted, and especially if Britain and France could adopt it without an outright declaration of war, he would be able, he believed, to persuade the American people to respect the blockade and perhaps even to supply the Allies with arms and munitions. (Roosevelt also spoke of the possibility of a world conference "for the purpose of reorganizing all unsatisfactory frontiers on rational lines," according to Lindsay's report to the Foreign Office in London, but the suggestion "was not strongly emphasized."[56])

Meanwhile, in Prague, the Czech government was agonizing over the Anglo-French proposals.

The document containing them had been given to Edvard Beneš by Sir Basil Newton, the British minister in Prague, early in the afternoon. The Czech president, worn out by the constant tensions and recurrent terrors of the preceding weeks, and by consequent sleeplessness, had been shattered momentarily by the new blow. He had railed bitterly against this "betrayal," saying that to give the Sudetenland to Hitler would be tantamount to giving Czechoslovakia as a whole to him. But soon he pulled himself together, saying coldly that his government would reply as soon as possible.[57]

Through all the rest of that day, and night, and most of the next day (Tuesday, September 20), London and Paris waited with fuming impatience while Beneš desperately considered his options, consulted his Cabinet, and tested the strength of Russia's commitment to a "Stop Hitler" policy. Through the Soviet minister in Prague, two questions were addressed to Moscow where, evidently, they provoked a considerable discussion, since answers to them were not forthcoming until a half-dozen frantic hours had passed. But by evening Beneš had received specific reassurance of the Soviet Union's determination to march with France if France fulfilled her treaty obligations—had also been assured by Moscow of the Soviet Union's support of a Czech appeal for action by the League of Nations if Hitler attacked and France did *not* fulfill her treaty obligations. Whereupon the Czech foreign minister handed Newton a note rejecting the Anglo-French proposals and making the counterproposal that the Sudeten issue be submitted to arbitration under a German-Czech treaty signed in 1925 and never since rescinded. He also pointedly reminded France of her treaty obligations and of the damaging effect the reduction of Czechoslovakia would have on French security.[58]

The emotional effect of this missive upon the heads of government in London and Paris was a mixture of anger, dismay, guilt feeling, and fear, with anger predominating. The practical effect was the issuance of what amounted to an Anglo-French ultimatum to Czechoslovakia—an effect encouraged by a total failure of nerve and honor on the part of Beneš's ranking subordinate, Dr. Milan Hodža, the Czech prime minister.

Just two days ago, broadcasting a speech saying no to Henlein's plebiscite demand, the sixty-year-old Hodža, described by John Gunther as being "rather pro-German (but not pro-Nazi)," had struck correspondent William Shirer "as being very high-strung and nervous. . . . He showed visibly the strain of the last days. Is he . . . weakening, I wonder?"[59] He now not only weakened, he collapsed into such hysterical fear, late in the night of September 20, that he betrayed both his country and his president personally. He summoned to his office the French minister in Prague, Victor de Lacroix. Agitatedly, he told this diplomat that the only way to save the peace was to obtain immediately a telegram from Paris saying bluntly that if Czechoslovakia persisted in her present course France would deem herself released from her treaty obligations. President Beneš wished desperately to receive such a message, lied Hodža, and had approved Hodža's asking for it. Within the hour, it being now after midnight in London, this lying information was in the hands of Bonnet and Halifax. The message to Halifax was accompanied by a recommendation from Newton that Beneš be told to accept the Anglo-French proposal "without reserve and without further delay failing which His Majesty's Government will take no further interest in the fate of the country."[60] A few minutes later, Chamberlain and Daladier were apprised of the new development. Within an hour they had concurred in fateful, threatening instructions, which were dispatched at once to their representatives in Prague.

It was two-fifteen in the morning of Wednesday, September 21, when Newton and Lacroix routed Beneš out of bed. Upon the judgment and strength of will of this Czech president depended, quite literally at that moment, the fate of the Western world. He was a short, slightly built, sharp-featured man of fifty-three—a highly cultivated intellectual who, like his predecessor in the Czech presidency, the legendary Jan Masaryk, was at once a fervent national patriot and a "good European." He was committed to the League of Nations and to the ultimate creation of a United States of Europe. He had a remarkably orderly mind, much efficient energy, and great moral courage. But he was in poor physical shape to receive the news his callers now brought him, having had only an hour or two of fitful sleep after a number of virtually sleepless days and nights. And at the first words spoken by Lacroix ("The French Government at least was sufficiently ashamed of this communication to instruct its Minister to make it verbally," wrote Churchill[61])—words saying that there was not the slightest chance of arbitration under the 1925 German-Czechoslovakian Treaty—he reeled as though struck by a club. A sobbing groan burst from his lips. Tears ran down his cheeks as Lacroix went on to say that Beneš *must* accept the Anglo-French proposals "before producing a situation for which France and Britain could take no responsibility."[62] Perhaps he learned from Lacroix, in that black hour, of his own premier's treachery. If so, he must have felt like a solitary walker upon a remote beach who finds himself sinking helplessly into quicksand. His two callers pressed for an immediate decision. In a quavering voice, Beneš promised one by noon of that day.

And, indeed, by noon of the twenty-first Newton was told unofficially, by Hodža, that the Czech government was in the process of accepting the proposals.

Actually the issue was still in doubt at that time, for there was acrimonious disagreement in the Cabinet and among the Czech army command. The discussions that had begun at dawn continued into late afternoon. Before they ended, the Soviet Union's Litvinov had addressed the League of Nations, saying: "When, a few days before I left for Geneva, the French Government . . . inquired as to our attitude in the event of an attack on Czechoslovakia, I gave . . . a clear and unambiguous reply: 'We intend to fulfill our obligations under the Pact, and together with France to afford assistance to Czechoslovakia by the ways open to us. . . .' " The Czechoslovak government, in response to a formal inquiry two days before, had been given the same assurance, said the Russian foreign minister.[63] A rested Beneš, in full control of his nerves, might have seized upon this speech to support an unequivocal demand that France abide by her pledged word ("I have always believed that Beneš was wrong to yield," wrote Churchill[64])—and certainly, in such a stand, he would not have stood alone within his own government. Up to the very last a strong minority of responsible officials, including top army commanders, preferred war to national suicide, and it is probable that a majority of the general Czech population was of the same opinion.

Alas, Beneš was now beyond the breaking point.

A few hours later, the French and British having been notified of Prague's acceptance of their proposals, the Czech government, in an official communiqué, told the world what had happened: "We relied upon the help that our friends might have given us but when the question of reducing us by force arose [and it became evident that general war might ensue] . . . our friends . . . advised us to buy peace and freedom by our sacrifice. . . . The President of the Republic and our government had no other choice, for we found ourselves alone."[65] In London, at that same time, Winston Churchill issued a press statement: "The partition of Czechoslovakia under pressure from England and France amounts to a complete surrender of the Western Democracies . . . [and] will bring peace and security neither to England nor to France. On the contrary, it will place these two nations in an ever-weaker and more dangerous situation. The mere neutralization of Czechoslovakia means the liberation of twenty-five German divisions, which will threaten the Western Front; in addition it will open up for the triumphant Nazis the road to the Black Sea. . . ."[66]

On the following day, humiliated beyond bearing, the entire Czech Cabinet resigned. A new nonparty "government of national concentration" was formed under Beneš's continued presidency, its premier (significantly) the general who had commanded the heroically famous Czech forces in Siberia in 1918.

And on that day, September 22, Chamberlain, umbrella in hand, flew again to Germany.

This time he flew less than half as far as he had before: He landed at the aerodrome in Cologne, for the Führer, in gracious consideration of the prime minister's advanced age, condescended to meet his guest at Godesberg on the Rhine. The two men shook hands in a hotel there at five P.M. They entered at once into what Chamberlain had every reason to expect would be a pleasant meeting, its agreeable conclusion being foregone. For had he not accomplished in an incredibly brief time, overcoming serious obstacles, all that Hitler had said needed to be done to solve the Sudeten problem permanently? He was enabled to tell the German chancellor that all arrangements for the peaceable transfer of the Sudeten territory to Germany had been made. Only procedural details remained to be worked out, and for these, and the assurance of an orderly transfer, he proposed the use of an international commission.

He then leaned back in his chair with, as it seemed to the German interpreter, a self-satisfied air, evidently expecting from his host words of gratification, if not of praise and thanks to him personally for all he had achieved.[67]

Nothing of the sort was forthcoming.

"There was a slight pause," writes Nevile Henderson, who sat at Chamberlain's side during this meeting, "a silence in which Hitler appeared for a moment to be making up his mind."[68]

And there is reason to believe that Hitler was indeed balanced then "on the razor's edge," as he himself had put it in a recent conversation, and in that instant did decide finally, narrowly, upon the dangerous tactical maneuver he now employed.

Breakfasting that morning in the garden of the hotel where this meeting took place, correspondent Shirer had seen Hitler from close up as he walked past Shirer's table on his way "down to the edge of the Rhine to inspect his river yacht." The correspondent noted that, both on his way down and on his way back a few minutes later, the "great man" took mincing "ladylike" steps that were very unlike his normal stride and that "every few steps he cocked his right shoulder nervously, his left leg snapping up as he did so"—clearly a "nervous tic" of appalling proportions. There were also "ugly black patches under his eyes," leading Shirer to conclude that "the man is on the verge of a nervous breakdown." Other observers at that time reached the same conclusion. Some believed that the breakdown had already occurred and Hitler was now actually certifiably insane. It was said that on one recent day, in a fit of hysterical rage against "Herr Beneš," he had flung himself facedown upon the floor and chewed the edge of a carpet—an unlikely story which Shirer for one, "after seeing him this morning," found it possible to believe.[69]

There were yet others, however, who discounted totally these evidences of hysterical collapse, and these others included German officials who had long worked closely with the Führer. Far from seeing in him a shattered man, they saw a man of iron nerves who, considering his circumstances, remained remarkably self-possessed, self-controlled. His notorious temper tantrums were for the most part, in their view, carefully calculated appearances rather than true emotional outbursts; they were tactical elements of a coldly conceived strategy of terror, when not a mere letting-off of steam such as any man might indulge in who was under very heavy pressures of personal responsibility, might even deliberately indulge in order to retain his sanity, his basic and general self-control.

There could be no doubt, at any rate, that Hitler was now under the most extreme possible pressure. He had of course breathed an atmosphere of crisis from the moment he launched his political career. He himself had done all he could to generate crisis of the kind, the only kind, in which his kind of politics could thrive. He had also always aimed, was by his totalitarian personality compelled, toward that outermost limit of possible triumph which is also, by the same token, the abysmal edge of utter catastrophe. Which is to say that at every major step of his career he had been precariously balanced between the most brilliant success and the blackest failure. Seldom had he been (he did not wish to be) in an easy situation, permitting relaxation and enjoyment. But never before, not even when he moved troops into the Rhineland, had the strain been as severe, the stakes as high, the situation as desperate, the fatal dangers for him personally as great as they now were. He absolutely had to win the tremendous gamble in which he now engaged if he and his regime were to survive, since it was he alone—even among his own party leaders, save for such sycophants as Ribbentrop and Goebbels—who had at the outset believed it a gamble that *could* be won. He alone had insisted upon making it. Assuredly, he knew nothing concrete of the conspiracy that had been organized against him. But he was only too acutely aware that the existence of such a conspiracy was more than possible, that he had now advanced too far to be able to retreat without a fatal loss of prestige, and that it was impossible for him to advance any further if he were firmly opposed. He knew as well as his generals did that Germany was not strong enough militarily to mount a successful attack upon Czechoslovakia and at the same time hold the line against attack in the west. He must therefore rise to glory or sink into ignominious death upon the exceedingly narrow ground where he now stood.

Small wonder if he, at this climax of one of the most amazing and consequential exercises of individual willpower in all history, hesitated a brief moment, silently measuring one more time the quality of the Birmingham businessman seated opposite him, before adding, as he now proceeded to do, one more gambling chip to a stack already terrifyingly high.

He broke the silence with words that were spoken "decisively," according to Henderson—"quietly, almost regretfully," according to the German interpreter—saying that what the prime minister had accomplished, though it was more than he had believed possible within the allotted time, was "no longer of any use."[70] The situation had changed since the Berchtesgaden meeting. The Sudeten Germans, having been placed under Czech martial law, were suffering at this very instant more insult, humiliation, and fatal injury than ever before. He had just received a report from Eger that twelve German hostages had been shot! Moreover, both Poland and Hungary had within the last two days laid claims to Czechoslovakian territory and he, Hitler, was required by his friendship with these two states to support their claims. Hence, the leisurely timetable for territorial transfer which Chamberlain had just outlined was unacceptable. The Sudeten territory must be ceded to Germany at once, must be occupied by German troops at once, with the frontier line to be established by plebiscite at a later time.

Chamberlain, according to Henderson, expressed "surprise and indignation," though the latter was evidently, given his circumstances, quite astonishingly mild, He was, he said, "both disappointed and puzzled." He had "risked his whole political career" to achieve what Hitler "had demanded" at Berchtesgaden ("on leaving England that morning he actually had been booed!"); it was politically impossible for him to return to London with a demand for more. There followed what Henderson describes as "three hours of somewhat exacerbated debate" during which the prime minister kept his temper admirably (or contemptibly, depending upon one's point of view) while Hitler, at least ostensibly, repeatedly lost his. The session ended with Hitler insisting upon immediate occupancy of the Sudetenland, by military invasion if necessary, and Chamberlain insisting that what Hitler demanded was impossible.[71]

The next day was the most doom-shadowed, its air the heaviest with foreboding, of all the days in Europe since July 1914, and it was but the first of a

succession of days equally gloomy, equally fraught with terror. From Godesberg the news went out that the talks between the German chancellor and the
British prime minister had broken down. In Prague, the newly formed Czech
government ordered full military mobilization—a move that neither Paris nor
London felt able any longer to oppose—while in both England and France
feverish preparations were made for defense and shelter against air attack and
gas attack. Written messages were exchanged between Chamberlain and Hitler
that day, with the former yielding to the latter only to the extent of saying that
he would "as mediator" transmit to Czechoslovakia the terms Hitler proposed,
provided these were put into writing, with an accompanying map. Chamberlain concluded his second missive coldly, saying: "I do not see that I can
perform any further service here. I propose therefore to return to England."[72]

There was a final three-hour meeting in Hitler's hotel suite that night,
beginning at ten-thirty. At its outset Hitler handed Chamberlain the requested
memorandum outlining his terms. It was in fact an ultimatum demanding that
the Czechs begin their evacuation of the Sudeten territory on September 26
(that is, within forty-eight hours) and formally cede it to Germany on September 28, a timetable utterly impossible for the Czechs to follow. Chamberlain,
with Henderson at his side, protested firmly, thus continuing the first true
opposition to Hitler's will he had ever shown. And in the end, after hours of
wrangling, with much emphasis upon the difficulty and rarity of his doing such
a thing, Hitler made a "concession." His revised memorandum set the "single
date" of October 1 for Sudetenland evacuation (October 2 had been, of course,
the target date for Case Green since the previous May) but specified that the
evacuation must be completed on that day; that all fortifications and transportation facilities be left intact; and that "no foodstuffs, goods, cattle, raw materials, etc., are to be removed." This last meant that hundreds of thousands of
Czechs, forced out of their Sudeten homes, could take with them only the
clothes on their backs and such personal belongings as could be carried in their
hands. Hitler also set a deadline of two P.M. on September 28 for Czech
acceptance of these terms. Chamberlain gave every sign of gratitude and relief
over this "concession." He promised to transmit the memorandum to Prague,
it being understood that his doing so would mean to the Czechs that he urged
them to accept its terms. Then, at one-thirty in the morning of September 24,
the two men said their farewells at the hotel door. They did so with a show
of cordiality that astonished correspondents who watched it, among them
Shirer, who was in the hotel porter's booth barely twenty-five feet away.[73]

VI

THE culmination of this complicated process of ineptitude, perfidy, cowardice,
and evil was reached during the next five days.

When Chamberlain met with his Cabinet on Saturday, September 24,
shortly after landing at Heston airport, he encountered unexpectedly strong
opposition to the Godesberg terms. The First Lord of the Admiralty, Alfred

Duff Cooper, damning Hitler as totally untrustworthy, proposed immediate general mobilization; other Cabinet members supported him, and the prime minister barely managed to postpone a decision on this until the French, whose premier and foreign minister were to return to London on the evening of the following day, had been consulted. Two more Cabinet meetings held on that following day (Sunday the twenty-fifth) revealed a split of opinion so deep, so wide, that it could not be bridged. Duff Cooper wanted to reject the Godesberg terms out of hand and, surprisingly, was at least tentatively supported by Halifax, who complained that Hitler has "given us nothing" but was "dictating terms . . . as though he had won a war." Chamberlain and those who joined him in the desire to put pressure upon the Czechs to accept the terms felt stymied. As for the Czechs, Ambassador Jan Masaryk told Chamberlain flatly on Sunday: "Against these new and cruel demands my government feels bound to make their utmost resistance and we shall do so. . . ."[74]

When the French delegation headed by Daladier arrived, it proved more inclined toward Duff Cooper's position than toward Chamberlain's. A stormy session lasted well into the early morning hours of Monday the twenty-sixth, by which time it had been agreed that Chamberlain should make one last effort to prevent general war. He was to send Sir Horace Wilson to Berlin as his personal emissary with a letter to Hitler pleading for orderly, peaceful implementation of the agreed Berchtesgaden terms. If Hitler replied to this negatively, Wilson was to warn the Führer that Britain and France would certainly act together as the latter honored her treaty obligations to Czechoslovakia. This warning was called by Chamberlain an "ultimatum" and he was at great pains to instruct his envoy precisely as to when and how it should be delivered.[75]

Meanwhile, in Washington, the State Department's "death watch" had been meeting in somber, yet agitated session. On Sunday morning, September 25, Roosevelt had received no response from London to the suggestion of a "defensive war" strategy that he had made in his secret talk with Ambassador Lindsay. He had instead been repeatedly and emphatically informed by both Kennedy and Bullitt that neither France nor England was materially or psychologically prepared to fight any kind of war against Germany. And since an agreement in principle had been reached between Prague and Berlin, since questions of mere "method and detail" were all that remained unsettled, it seemed to him that the voice of reason, if loudly enough raised, might yet save the peace. He proposed to become himself that loud-speaking voice—and it was this proposal that the "death watch" discussed and approved this Sunday morning. Adolf Berle and J. Pierrepont Moffat of the State Department were assigned the task of drafting what Roosevelt should say. They labored all afternoon. Berle wanted the statement to be more than an appeal for a continuation of negotiations; he wanted it to be "a definite suggestion that we would use our good offices" to help effect "revision of the Versailles Treaty." And this "definite suggestion" was in the draft that Hull took to the President at six o'clock that evening. Hull, however, strongly advised the President against any offer to help facilitate Versailles revision, feeling it to be "too dangerous"—and Roosevelt, whose assessment of the limits of the politically possible was at that moment even narrower than usual, agreed. The "suggestion" was therefore excluded from the final draft, which, addressed to the heads of government of Czechoslovakia, Germany, Great Britain, and France, was issued at one-thirteen A.M. Washington time on Monday, September 26.[76]

The message, obviously aimed specifically at Adolf Hitler, began: "The fabric of peace . . . is in immediate danger. The consequences of its rupture are incalculable. . . . [But] the lives of millions of men, women and children in every country involved will most certainly be lost under circumstances of unspeakable horror. . . . The social structure of every country involved may well be completely wrecked." There followed a series of non sequiturs adding up to a desperate plea unsupported by any indication that the government in Washington was itself willing to take any concrete action whatever to make peace:

> The United States has no political entanglements, It is caught in no mesh of hatred. Elements of all Europe have formed its civilization. The supreme desire of the American people is to live in peace. . . . During the present crisis [they] . . . and their Government have earnestly hoped that the negotiations for the adjustment of the controversy . . . might reach a successful conclusion. . . . On behalf of the 130 millions of people of the United States of America and for the sake of humanity everywhere I most earnestly appeal to you not to break off negotiations. . . ."[77]

It was at almost the precise moment that this message was received in London that Wilson took off for Berlin. His selection for so delicate a diplomatic mission seemed strange even to him ("a bit much," he told Leonard Mosley long afterward[78]) and his feeling that he was out of his depth was certainly not diminished when, accompanied by Ambassador Henderson, he was received by Hitler that Monday afternoon. The Führer was to address a huge throng in the Sportspalast just three hours hence. He had worked himself into that hysterically excited state in which he customarily gave his speeches. It was in this state that he had read Roosevelt's appeal to him—an appeal more likely to increase than diminish his sense of power, his will to exercise it—and even before Chamberlain's letter had been completely read to him he flew into a rage of such awesome proportions that Wilson was intimidated by it. The envoy decided to postpone delivery of the warning message (the "ultimatum") until the great man was calmer, more "reasonable."

This meant that it was an unwarned Hitler who screamed into radio microphones in the Sportspalast that evening his determination to take the Sudetenland by force if it were not given him on October 1. He made a coarse, vituperative attack upon Beneš personally, blaming him for everything. He did, however, throw in a sop for the appeasers: He spoke of England, France, and Chamberlain personally in accommodating terms and emphatically asserted, twice, that the Sudetenland was "the last territorial demand I have to make in Europe." (He had said this to Chamberlain at both Berchtesgaden and

Godesberg.) Only Germans were wanted in the Third Reich, he insisted, adding contemptuously: "We want no Czechs!"[79]

A few hours later—that is, early in the morning of September 27 in Berlin; early in the evening of September 26 in Washington—Hitler sent off his reply to Roosevelt's appeal. It was intransigent, being substantially a review of German grievances. The artificial creation at Versailles of the Czechoslovak state by the victors over Germany had been a criminal act. "Never in history has the confidence of a people been more shamefully betrayed" than was Germany's confidence in Woodrow Wilson's word. And never had a people suffered more outrage, indignity, and misery than the Sudeten Germans had suffered, and continued to suffer, at the hands of the "Government of Prague." It was Hitler's "conviction that you, Mr. President, when you realize the whole development of the . . . problem from its inception . . . , will realize that the German Government has truly not been lacking either in patience or a sincere desire for a peaceful understanding. . . . It does not rest with the German Government, but with the Czechoslovak Government alone, to decide, whether it wants peace or war."[80]

Roosevelt had been given the gist of this via a phone call from the State Department by the time he went to bed near midnight of the twenty-sixth. He was yet asleep in the White House when, in the morning of September 27 in Berlin, Sir Horace Wilson again talked to Hitler.

Predictably, Wilson opened the brief talk by referring gratefully to the very few accommodating words Hitler had spoken in the Sportspalast. "I congratulated him upon the ovation he had received, but he brushed it aside," the envoy recalled long afterward. "Then I delivered the ultimatum, but he hardly seemed to notice it now."[81]

All the same, this warning letter became a factor, one among several, decisive of Hitler's next act.

For while Wilson flew back to a London where trenches were being dug in the parks, gas masks were being issued to civilians, and an order for the general mobilization of the British fleet was being prepared for issuance that night, Hitler in Berlin was subjected to new, desperately intense pressures against his war policy by those who would have to execute it. Delegates of the German army General Staff had called at the Reich Chancellery the day before to protest this policy. Hitler had refused to see them. They and their colleagues then prepared on behalf of the staff an eighteen-page memorandum arguing in the most forceful terms, with supporting factual evidence, that the morale of the German people was too low to sustain prolonged war; that the army, woefully lacking in war matériel and trained officers, was too weak to win any but a short, strictly local war; and that there was small likelihood the Czech war could be short enough to be locally contained. Even if they fought alone and unaided, the Czechs were strong enough militarily to resist a German assault on the Sudetenland fortifications for at least three months, since the Germans must in any case maintain covering forces on the French and Polish borders, plus 250,000 troops in Austria to guard against popular uprisings and a possible Czech offensive in that direction. Before those three months had passed, the British and French governments would almost certainly be forced by public opinion into declarations of war.[82] This memorandum was delivered by special messenger to the Chancellery, where Hitler read it in the late afternoon.

Nor was it only the army that now protested his Czech policy in accents of despair. By the time he had digested the army staff memorandum, Hitler had scheduled for ten that night an interview with the chief of Germany's naval forces, Admiral Erich Raeder, who had begged for it (he knew the British fleet was being mobilized) with an urgency leaving no doubt that he would proclaim Germany to be as unprepared to wage successful war on the ocean as she was on land.[83]

And there also waited in the wings the anti-Nazi conspirators, of whom Hitler of course knew nothing specifically but of whose possible existence he could not but have been, on this Tuesday the twenty-seventh, more acutely aware than ever before. They, the conspirators, had been shocked beyond belief by Chamberlain's capitulations at Berchtesgaden and Godesberg—had been dismayed and disconcerted. Was the Führer's "genius," his marvelous "intuition," to triumph once again over concrete realities and ordinary common sense? But the stiffening of French and British attitudes after Godesberg, coupled with the renewed determination of the Czechs to fight for their survival, gave the conspirators new heart. Whether they would actually have struck according to plan, had Hitler persisted, is a question forever unanswerable; but certainly they yet remained poised at that time to strike with lightning swiftness, seizing the reins of German government, and Hitler personally, within an hour after the order for Case Green was issued, as it was expected to be issued, at two P.M. on Wednesday, September 28.[84]

That evening, Chamberlain made a radio address to the English people (though broadcast worldwide)—an equivocating, "on-the-one-hand-yet-on-the-other" speech that could have done nothing to reduce Hitler's contempt for him personally but that seems finally to have convinced the Führer that he had gone as far as he could possibly go with the tactical maneuver he had decided upon at Godesberg. "How horrible, fantastic, incredible, it is that we should be digging trenches and trying on gas-masks here because of a quarrel in a far-away country between people of whom we know nothing," said Chamberlain, adding that he "would not hesitate to pay even a third visit to Germany, if I thought it would do any good." On the other hand, if he were "convinced that any nation" aspired to world domination "through fear of its force, I should feel that it must be resisted. . . . But war is a fearful thing. and we must be very clear, before we embark on it, that it really is the great issues that are at stake."[85]

Shortly thereafter came clear signs that Hitler hesitated at the brink of the abyss. Chamberlain received from him a reply to the personal letter Horace Wilson had delivered, a reply in which the Führer relaxed ever so slightly the rigid, uncompromisingly aggressive posture he had theretofore maintained. He did not specifically modify the timetable imposed at Godesberg, but, by offering to guarantee jointly with France and Britain the new frontiers of a truncated Czechoslovakia, and to consider anew the manner of the Sudetenland transfer, he hinted that modification was possible. A few hours later (at two A.M. on September 28), German radio broadcast an official denial of reports that Germany would mobilize on September 29—a denial that was repeated to British press representatives by the official German news agency shortly before noon of that day.

By then Chamberlain had seized the opportunity he perceived in Hitler's communication.

"After reading your letter," said the prime minister in a personal message to Hitler, "I feel certain that you can get all essentials without war and without delay. I am ready to come to Berlin at once myself to discuss arrangements for transfer with you and representatives of the Czech Government, together with representatives of France and Italy if you desire. I feel convinced that we could reach agreement in a week."[86]

He also telegraphed a personal message to Mussolini, saying: "I trust your Excellency will inform the German Chancellor that you are willing to be represented, and urge him to agree to my proposal, which will keep our peoples out of war."[87]

There was feverish activity in Washington, too, on Tuesday the twenty-seventh. At a morning conference of top State Department officials the decision was made, according to a diary entry written by Berle at one o'clock that afternoon: "(1) to send a telegram instructing all our representatives to request their governments to telegraph Berlin suggesting the continuance of negotiations; (2) to draft a personal appeal from the President to Mussolini; (3) to work out, if possible, an answer to Hitler."[88]

All three decisions were approved by Roosevelt and acted upon immediately.

The President's reply to Hitler, of which the initial draft was a collaborative effort by Sumner Welles and Berle, was sent off shortly after Roosevelt had listened to Chamberlain's address (with approval, according to eyewitness accounts) at midafternoon, Washington time. "The question before the world today . . . is not the question of the errors of judgment or of injustices committed in the past," the message said, referring to Hitler's list of Versailles grievances. "It is the question of the fate of the world today and tomorrow." Roosevelt reiterated his earnest appeal for continued negotiations, adding to it, in watered-down form and wholly by implication, the proposal for Versailles revision that had been removed from the initial appeal. "Present negotiations still stand open. They can be continued if you give the word. Should the need for supplementing them become evident, nothing stands in the way of widening their scope into a conference of all the nations directly interested in the present controversy. Such a meeting to be held immediately—in some neutral spot in Europe—would offer the opportunity for this and correlated questions to be solved in a spirit of justice, of fair dealing, and, in all human probability, with greater permanence." Roosevelt expressed his "unqualified conviction that history, and the souls of every man, woman, and child whose lives will be lost in the threatened war, will hold us and all of us accountable, should we omit any appeal for its prevention." But he continued to refuse to run the slightest domestic political risk. "The Government of the United States has no political involvement in Europe, and will assume no obligation in the conduct of the present negotiations," he said, then proceeded to vitiate this concession to American isolationist sentiment with a concession to American internationalist sentiment, adding: "Yet in our own right we recognize our own responsibilities as a part of a world of neighbors."[89]

If this communication had any effect whatever upon Hitler's decision-making there is no evidence of it. The message to Mussolini may have had some slight effect insofar as it reinforced Chamberlain's appeal—an appeal that prodded the Italian dictator toward action he would almost certainly have taken in any case, since his national interests and personal circumstances virtually demanded it. At any rate, Mussolini, at eleven on the morning of the twenty-eighth, did phone his ambassador in Berlin, instructing him to ask for an immediate interview with the chancellor. "Tell him the British government [the U.S. government went unmentioned] asked me . . . to mediate in the Sudeten question," said Mussolini. "The point of difference is very small. Tell the Chancellor that I and Fascist Italy stand behind him. He must decide. But tell him I favor accepting the suggestion."[90] This provided Hitler with a way to step back from the brink. He promptly employed it. "Tell the Duce," he said to the Italian ambassador at noon, "that I accept his proposal."[91] Messages were then telegraphed by Hitler to Chamberlain and Daladier proposing that they meet with him and Mussolini at Munich next day, Thursday, September 29.

Chamberlain was approaching the end of a speech in the House of Commons, wherein he reported Mussolini's approach to Hitler in response to the prime minister's personal appeal, when, shortly before three in the afternoon, he was handed a note from Halifax. He read it in a glance, then said with as wide a smile as his naturally stiff and sober countenance ever permitted: "That is not all. I have something further to say to the House yet. I have been informed by Herr Hitler that he invites me to meet him at Munich tomorrow morning. He has also invited Signor Mussolini and Monsieur Daladier. Signor Mussolini has accepted and I have no doubt Monsieur Daladier will accept. I need not say what my answer will be. . . ." The relief from extreme tension was explosive. The normally staid House erupted in wild cheering amid which were heard the shouted words "Thank God for the prime minister!"[92]

An hour or two later there arrived at No. 10 Downing Street a personal message to the prime minister from the President of the United States. It consisted of just two words: "Good man."[93]

The salient conclusions of the Munich conference next day were all foregone, and numerous exhaustive narrative descriptions and analyses of it have been published. Suffice it here to say that a halfhearted attempt was made by Chamberlain and Daladier to add Beneš to Hitler's list of invitees. Hitler flatly refused to do so. He did permit a Czech delegation of two, namely, the Czech minister in Berlin and an official of the Prague Foreign Office, to come to Munich as "observers," their sole actual function being to receive directly from the representatives of their country's "friends" and "allies" the sentence of crippling mutilation which these, in concert with Czechoslovakia's avowed enemies, imposed upon their country. No one seems to have thought of proposing that the Soviet Union be invited, or even permitted to send observers. And, in the absence of any active Czechoslovak or Soviet representation, the four heads of government were able to reach agreement with remarkable ease and swiftness. The conference opened at half past noon on the twenty-ninth. Its memorandum of agreement, the terms of which were essentially those of Hitler's Godesberg ultimatum, was signed at a little after one o'clock in the morning of the thirtieth. There were two minor variations from the Godesberg dictum. One was a slight extension of the timetable for Czech evacuation and German occupation of the Sudetenland; this was now to proceed in five stages beginning on October 1 and ending on October 10. The other provided that an international commission determine the final Czech frontiers, as Chamberlain had proposed at Godesberg.

When the Czech delegates were presented with a copy of this document, at one-thirty A.M., they were permitted to ask no probing questions concerning it, much less protest the terms. They had already been told bluntly, three hours before, by an Englishman who had been a member of Lord Runciman's mission to Prague, that if the Czechs did not accept what was being decided "you will have to settle your affairs with the Germans absolutely alone. Perhaps the French may tell you this more gently," the Englishman had added, "but you can believe me that they share our views."[94]

Some ten hours later, near noon of Friday, September 30, Chamberlain and Hitler met in Hitler's flat for a tête-à-tête, which Chamberlain had asked for shortly after the conference adjourned. The two were alone save for the German interpreter, Paul Schmidt, who later reported in an official German Foreign Office memorandum that Chamberlain, for all his physical weariness, was in an expansive, talkative mood whereas Hitler was pale, moody, abstracted. The prime minister spoke at length of his hopes for the future, which looked bright to him because of the agreement just reached. He was sure Germany would be "generous . . . in the implementation" of the agreement; the Czechs would not be "so unreasonable as to make difficulties"; and the four powers could now cooperate to end the Spanish Civil War, reduce armaments, promote economic prosperity, and even come to terms with Soviet Russia. He then presented Hitler with a note he had written in the hope that it could be immediately published as a joint Anglo-German statement. It said that the German chancellor and the British prime minister "agreed . . . that the question of Anglo-German relations" was of first importance to the two countries and to Europe; that "the Agreement signed last night" symbolized "the desire of our two peoples never to go to war with one another again"; and that "the method of consultation shall be adopted to deal with any other questions that may concern our two countries." Hitler listened intently as the interpreter translated this and then—with some slight reluctance, as it seemed to the interpreter, but certainly promptly and without demur—signed the declaration.

This was the famous paper that Chamberlain held aloft triumphantly before the deliriously happy crowd that welcomed his return at Heston airport at five-thirty that afternoon. He was wildly cheered by London crowds solidly lining the streets through which he rode to No. 10 Downing Street. And there, at the prime minister's official residence, a huge throng refused to disperse until he had addressed it from an open window, saying: "This is the second time in our history that there has come back from Germany to Downing Street peace with honor.* I believe it is peace in our time."[95]

VII

THERE was, of course, in the following days, a mighty surge of relief through the Western democracies, and of a hope and will to believe that the prime minister's assessment of Munich's consequences was correct. There was also manifest, initially, a disposition in the White House to claim for Roosevelt an important share of the credit for averting war. (In his diary entry for September 30, Berle noted wryly that Steve Early was telling the press that, during the crisis, "all drafting was done by President Roosevelt, who virtually assumed control of the State Department." In a radio speech on October 3, Sumner Welles, after telling of the President's part in the events leading up to Munich, asserted that "today, perhaps more than at any time during the past two decades, there is presented the opportunity for the establishment by the nations of the world of a new world order based upon justice and upon law."[96]) But this White House effort was tentative and short-lived. For it was clear from the first that the feeling of relief from immediate danger, not real belief or even solid hope that a permanently peaceful settlement had been made, was the dominant popular reaction. From the first, also, this relief was qualified by the strong feeling throughout the Western world that the Munich Agreement, Chamberlain to the contrary notwithstanding, was no triumph of national honor. Immense sympathy for the Czechs, who suffered so greatly, so unjustly, was joined with a realization that, if this injustice was "necessary," it was made so by a national weakness that was deplorable, even contemptible. Hence a

---

*The "first time" was in 1878 when Prime Minister Disraeli, speaking to a crowd from the same window of Number 10 at which Chamberlain now appeared, proclaimed that he had brought back from the Congress of Berlin "peace with honor." Chamberlain's evocation of Disraeli in this context was perhaps unfortunate for his prestige among the knowledgeable. The contrast between Disraeli's conduct during the crisis of 1878 and Chamberlain's during the crisis of 1938 could hardly be greater. Disraeli dominated the Congress of Berlin, despite the fact that the formidable Bismarck presided there and acted for the Germany he had just unified.

sense of national guilt and shame, though meagerly expressed, was not absent from the jubilant popular mood in both France and England.

On Sunday, October 2, Poland, whose historic inability to manage its domestic and foreign affairs with intelligent morality had contributed greatly to its national misfortunes, took advantage of Czechoslovakia's helplessness to seize that country's Teschen region—this despite the widely recognized probability that Poland was the next country on Hitler's hit list and might soon desperately need the support of democratic public opinion, which it now outraged.

On that same day, Alfred Duff Cooper introduced one of the very few discordant notes in the then-swelling chorus of British praise for the prime minister by resigning his Admiralty post in protest against the Munich Agreement.

And this discordant note was amplified in ways highly influential of American public opinion by the speech with which Winston Churchill, on October 5, closed a three-day debate in the House of Commons upon a motion to approve "the policy of His Majesty's Government by which war was averted" and to support "their [the Government's] efforts to secure a lasting peace." The motion was certainly "couched in very uncontroversial terms," Churchill remarked with sarcasm. Nevertheless, expanding upon the criticism made in his press statement of September 21, he controverted the motion's premises and opposed its adoption with vehement eloquence: "We have suffered a total and unmitigated defeat," he declared, going on to ridicule the assertion made during the debate by arch-appeaser Sir John Simon, chancellor of the exchequer, that Hitler, faced by an adamant Chamberlain, had been forced into retreat, something the Führer had never done before "in any degree." Actually "the difference between the positions reached at Berchtesgaden, at Godesberg and at Munich" could be "very simply epitomized," Churchill said.

One pound was demanded at the pistol's point. When it was given, 2 pounds were demanded at the pistol's point. Finally, the dictator consented to take 1 pound 17s. 6d. and the rest in promises of good will for the future. . . . It must now be accepted that all the countries of Central and Eastern Europe will make the best terms they can with the triumphant Nazi power. The system of alliances in Central Europe upon which France has relied for her safety has been swept away, and I see no means by which it can be reconstituted. The road down the Danube Valley to the Black Sea . . . has been opened. . . . And do not suppose that this is the end. . . . This is only the first sip, the first foretaste of a bitter cup which will be preferred to us year by year unless, by a supreme recovery of moral health and martial vigor, we arise again and take our stand for freedom as in the olden time.[97]

The House then, on October 6, adopted by overwhelming majority the motion before it.

VIII

HITLER'S triumph at Munich of course totally discomfited his domestic opposition while virtually deifying him in the eyes of the German people. It also totally discomfited Maxim Litvinov as the Soviet Union's commissar for foreign affairs, since it declared the utter failure of his policy—a policy aimed at forming a united front of the Western European democracies and the Soviet Union against Nazi-Fascist aggression. (There was a plaintive if not desperate note in Litvinov's own words spoken to the French ambassador in Moscow some two weeks after the Munich conference: "Henceforth the USSR has only to watch, from the shelter of its frontiers, the establishment of German hegemony over the center and southeast of Europe. And if by chance the Western Powers finally decide to wish to stop it, they must address themselves to us. . . ."[98]) Munich thereby destroyed utterly, unless Hitler died, what had been up till then a steadily diminishing chance to avert the ultimate catastrophe. Renewed world war became inevitable now. And this inevitability was as horrifyingly evident in prospect to many a disinterested and well-informed mind as the confirming event would soon become to everyone in retrospect.

It was also evident, as our narrative has shown, that this "victory . . . was won upon the narrowest of margins," to quote again from Churchill's October 5 speech. Small changes in any of a number of psychological factors—a slight increase in Chamberlain's human compassion and capacity for moral outrage, for instance; or in Beneš's nervous control under extreme pressures despite sleeplessness; or in Daladier's political power and commitment to France's national honor; or in Roosevelt's logical intelligence and willingness to run immediate risks in pursuit of perceived long-term good—could have resulted in a defeat for Adolf Hitler that would have doomed him and his Nazi party while setting in train a series of events pointed toward an orderly and peaceful correction of Versailles's grievous errors.

But our narrative has not sufficiently stressed, perhaps, the importance of a common denominator among such psychological factors as are listed above —namely, a paralyzing fear of Germany's air force. Dominant in the mind of every top political leader of the democracies was a grossly exaggerated estimate of Germany's strength in the air compared with that of the Soviet Union, Czechoslovakia, France, and England. Thus when Chamberlain's plane flew up the Thames during his return from Godesberg he, according to his own account, imagined what would happen if German bombers took the same route a few days hence: "I asked myself what degree of protection we could afford to the thousands of homes which I saw stretched out below me. And I felt that we are in no position to justify waging war today in order to prevent a war hereafter."[99]

How had this inflated estimate gained such currency among democracy's official leadership? It had done so in some considerable part through an American hero whom we have encountered before in this history. On that earlier occasion he had challenged Franklin Roosevelt (and bested him, as many believed) in public dispute.* He was destined soon to challenge the President again in a dispute of worldwide consequence. His personal character and role in the Munich crisis are therefore worth our brief but close attention, especially since he is a symbolic personality, significant of that dynamic relationship between man and machine whereby modern history has been largely determined.

Charles A. Lindbergh had, in his own view, no reason to love either the Common Man or egalitarian democracy as a social system. Ever since May 1927, when he at age twenty-five flew an airplane alone from New York to Paris, he had had focused upon him a popular hero-worship unprecedentedly massive, intense, and ferocious. It was streaked with morbidity; it would dehumanize its object, transforming him wholly into object, if not stubbornly, relentlessly resisted. He happened to be a shy person, a natural loner with a passion for order, efficiency, and personal privacy that was joined through feeling and logical consistency with a strong if (by him) unrecognized attraction toward coercive power. And because he was as he was and America's commercially manufactured popular culture was as it was, his fame became his mortal enemy. It made impossible his quiet appearance in any public place —a restaurant, a theater, or on a city street. It was directly responsible for the kidnap-murder of his firstborn, namesake son. It made an obscene spectacle of the trial and conviction of one Bruno Hauptmann for the murder of his son. And it threatened the life of his second-born son, or so he believed, when, in late December 1935, he sought refuge from it by fleeing his native land. With his wife and infant son he secretly embarked in New York upon a small freighter bound for England, where privacy was more highly valued and respected than in the United States. He and his family lived for more than two years in a secluded house, rented from Harold Nicolson, M.P., at the edge of a Kentish village forty miles from London.[100] Theirs was a rather reclusive life, though with frequent sorties into the highest English society: They dined in Buckingham Palace; they became frequent guests of the Astors at Cliveden.

Then, in June 1938, they moved to a much more remote and solitary place, a gray stone manor house on a rocky islet off the coast of Brittany. They did so because the islet, named Illiec, was joined at low tide to a somewhat larger island, St. Gildas, where lived for the warmer part of each year Lindbergh's chief mentor and closest personal friend of that time, a famous and highly controversial scientist named Dr. Alexis Carrel. Lindbergh had worked with Carrel at New York's Rockefeller Institute for Medical Research, developing a so-called and hugely publicized "mechanical heart" (actually, an aseptic glass pump in which whole excised organs could be kept alive through a rhythmic washing with nutrient and waste-removing fluids). He had also imbibed, as one with a natural thirst for it, a goodly portion of the famous scientist's philosophical and political views. These were of a reactionary nature, for Carrel was a dramatic authoritarian personality with a totalitarian

*See *FDR: The New Deal Years,* pp. 358–61.

mind. He was convinced that egalitarian democracy was "scientifically" unsound. He had said in a 1935 book, *Man, the Unknown* (it had been a best-seller
in America), that petty criminals should be "conditioned" with the whip,
"followed by a short stay in hospital" and that the insane, those guilty of
serious crimes, and others of the "unfit" should be "humanely and economically disposed of in small euthanistic institutions supplied with proper gases."
For "society should not hesitate to organize itself with reference to the normal
individual," he said, and "sentimental prejudices must give way before such
a necessity." His chief personal ambition was to establish a great institute for
the "scientific" creation of a human elite possessed of the "quality of Leadership."[101]

Thus Lindbergh was psychologically prepared to see what Nazi leaders
wanted him to see, and to draw from what he saw the conclusions his Nazi
hosts wanted him to draw, when he accepted an invitation from Hermann
Göring to visit Germany in the summer of 1936 (the Olympic Games were held
in Berlin that year) for the express purpose of inspecting and judging Germany's air power. The invitation had been issued through the military attaché
of the U.S. embassy in Berlin, a Major Truman Smith, whose judgment in this
matter, if not his personal motivation, must later seem highly suspect to
historians strongly committed to the American democracy. For Smith urged
Lindbergh to accept the invitation on the grounds that, by doing so, he,
Lindbergh, could add greatly to American military intelligence of German
strength in the air; he worked out, in cooperation with Lindbergh and the Nazi
government, the Lindbergh tour itinerary; and he accompanied Lindbergh on
a tour of more than half Germany's aircraft factories, the largest of her
aeronautical research facilities, and most of her major air bases. The still-
youthful aviator (he was then thirty-four) and his wife, Anne, were royally
received and entertained as guests of the Nazi state. They greatly enjoyed
themselves, as was evident in photographs of them broadly smiling (rarely in
recent years had Lindbergh smiled in an American press photograph) taken
by Hitler's friend and official photographer, Heinrich Hoffmann, in the company of such as Göring. And Lindbergh returned to England enormously
impressed, even awestruck, by what he saw as the actual and potential strength
of Germany's air arm. The impression was deepened, the awe increased, by
what he saw in subsequent visits to Germany in 1937 and 1938.

His 1938 visit was preliminary to the launching of a project that was self-
assigned, though evidently encouraged and certainly facilitated by the U.S.
War and State departments. His aim was to gather "all the data possible on
comparative air strength among the major powers," to quote his close friend
C. B. Allen.[102] With Anne, Lindbergh flew from England to Russia, landing
in Moscow on August 17 and spending the next two weeks as a guest of the
Soviet government touring airplane factories, aviation schools, and military air
bases scattered through the European portion of the Soviet Union. His Russian
tour was followed by a week in Czechoslovakia, on the second day of which,
"after the visits I have made to aviation establishments here, . . ." he concluded

"that Czechoslovakia is not well equipped in the air."[103] From Prague he flew to Paris, where, on August 9, he and Anne were dinner and overnight guests of Ambassador Bullitt at the latter's rented country house in Chantilly.

The Bullitt dinner was of some historical importance. French air minister Guy La Chambre was a guest, and to him and his host Lindbergh made scarifying report of Germany's air power, as he had witnessed it, compared with that of Russia, Czechoslovakia, France, and England. According to his published diary entry for that Friday, September 9, he estimated Germany's current warplane production to be between 500 and 800 a month (6,000 to 9,600 a year), France's at 45 a month (540 a year), and England's at around 70 a month (840 a year). There is some reason to believe, however, that the German figure he reported in the original diary entry was revised downward when the author prepared his war diary for publication in 1970, by which time the true production figures were known. Certainly Roosevelt, in a memorable conversation at Hyde Park some six weeks later, estimated German warplane production at 40,000 planes a year—an enormously inflated figure clearly derived from Lindbergh via Bullitt and Kennedy. "The French situation is desperate. Impossible to catch up to Germany for years, if at all," says the published diary entry. " . . . One is forced to the conclusion that the German air fleet is stronger than that of all the other European countries combined."[104] (We now know that Germany produced in 1938 approximately 7,500 aircraft of all types, only 3,300 of which were warplanes. She would produce 4,733 warplanes in 1939—a total of 8,033 for the two years. The British production figures were 2,827 combat planes in 1938 and nearly 8,000 in 1939—a total of nearly 11,000 for the two years.[105]) La Chambre, already deeply depressed by what he had learned of the French air force, over which he had exercised civilian control for barely eight months, sank more deeply into a slough of despond, whence he issued a full report to Daladier and Bonnet of what Lindbergh had said. Thereafter, in virtually every meeting with French and British officials, Bonnet cited Lindbergh's estimates to support his contention that war with Germany must be avoided at all costs.[106]

The British appeasers, too, found Lindbergh and his report useful to their cause. Nine days after the hero and his wife had returned to their island home he received an "urgent telegram from Ambassador Kennedy" asking "Anne and I to come to London as soon as possible." The two flew to England next day, and lunched with the ambassador on the day after that (September 21; Chamberlain was preparing to meet Hitler at Godesberg). Then, evidently at Kennedy's request, Lindbergh drafted a letter to Kennedy "on the military situation in Europe" and, certainly at Kennedy's request, talked to "some of the British officials." Kennedy cabled the Lindbergh letter in full to the State Department.[107]

For these services, Nazi Germany was grateful.

Eleven days after the signing of the Munich Agreement, Lindbergh, with his wife, was again in Berlin where, on the evening of October 19, he was guest of honor at a stag dinner in the home of U.S. ambassador Hugh Wilson.

Wilson, a typically suave career diplomat, was far too sophisticated to permit himself strong moral feelings (he frankly confessed he preferred "good manners" to "sincerity"[108]). His personal attitude toward such as Hermann Göring and Joseph Goebbels had, in consequence, none of the horror, disgust, and contempt which these creatures had aroused in William Dodd, his predecessor in Berlin. Several ranking Nazis were Wilson's guests that Tuesday evening, Göring among them, and Göring provided the high point of the evening's festivities when he unceremoniously presented Lindbergh with the Service Cross of the German Eagle with Star, "by order of the Führer." This was the second-highest of all German decorations. It had been created for the express purpose of honoring foreigners who "deserved well of the Reich." And the "general assumption" among diplomats and newsmen in Berlin was that Lindbergh's role in the events leading up to Munich had been "one factor in Chancellor Hitler's decision," according to *The New York Times*. That the hero had accepted this "honor" outraged democratic public opinion on both sides of the Atlantic. By doing so he "expressed approval of the Nazi" regime, said C. R. Miller, director of the Institute of Propaganda Analysis, and the only effective counterpropaganda would be for him now to return the medal. Instead Lindbergh let it be known that he was as pleased to receive this decoration as he had been to receive any other given him by a foreign government.[109]

# 9

# The Abdication of Leadership: 1938's Elections, and After

I

"ON the eve of another election, I have come home to Hyde Park and am sitting at my own fireside in my own election district, my own county and my own state."[1]

Thus Franklin Delano Roosevelt began his radio address to the nation on this evening of Friday, November 4, 1938. It was as if he sought self-definition, sought to sharpen his awareness of his own identity, through a precise placement of himself in space and time. And almost certainly, as he sat in his wheelchair in the Big House's living room, waiting to go on the air, he did need a renewed self-assurance and did gain some of it from immediate sights, sounds, and odors, and the memories connected with these, memories that not only defined but also permeated his essential self. We know, at any rate, that he was in a serious, even somber mood that evening, and had every reason to be. His summer of dust and weeds had come to a violent end in a hurricane that was horrible both in actuality and in its portentous symbolism: A huge black storm came roaring up the Atlantic coast to slam deep into New England, wrecking beach towns, leveling forests, killing more than seven hundred people, on the day that Czechoslovakia was forced to agree to its own dismemberment. And the autumn that followed had not thus far been happier, had in fact been a season of virtually unrelieved gloom. Of course he had not and would not give signs to others that the gloom had entered his inner self, coloring his basic mood and outlook. His displayed disposition remained as sunny as ever, his laughter as frequent and hearty, his manner as zestfully jaunty. Nevertheless, there was spread before his mind's eye, under skies darkened by the smoke of Europe's smoldering fires, domestic political landscapes of almost unrelieved desolation, swept by cold winds against which his disguising and dissembling outer self gave insufficient protection. He had inwardly to brace himself against it, at a great cost in flexibility and capacity for decision.

All his domestic calculations were shadowed by the dark events abroad. They called urgently for action he felt it impossible for him to take since they also sharpened, in his perception, the horns of the dilemma Rex Tugwell had remarked on the occasion of the Ludlow Amendment vote. It was essentially the same dilemma (nationalism versus internationalism) that had tormented him during the months of preparation for the London Economic Conference, for these events seemed to require him to make a conclusive, mutually exclusive, and utterly repugnant choice between New Deal continuance and collective security.* They increased opposition to collective security on the part of those most strongly supportive of the New Deal, and vice versa—or so, at least, it appeared to him. Other people, of course, took a different view. He was well aware they did. These others asserted loudly, in effect, that the horns of his perceived dilemma were actually not sharpened but instead blunted by the terrors Hitler had loosed upon the world, and that one of the horns—namely, the opposition to collective security—could be shorn wholly away and the dilemma thus removed if only the President exercised strong, bold, unequivocal leadership toward what he knew to be right and necessary. Surely what he knew could be taught the multitude. And surely the White House provided a "bully pulpit," the best possible platform, for such pedagogy. Roosevelt did not doubt the truth of these two statements, a truth that was implicit in his conception of the American democracy. He *did* doubt, to the point of total nonbelief, that he himself, with his prestige and credibility at their lowest point since the New Deal began, could now use the "bully pulpit" effectively in this way. He saw all too clearly the fatal risks attending any such decisive speech and action as the proponents of collective security urged upon him, and concluded that it was not only far safer but probably absolutely necessary for his own political survival to do now as he commonly did when dealing with fundamental issues: wait upon events to do the necessary teaching while he cautiously aided and abetted the process, enhancing each major event's persuasive power over the public mind, through carefully calculated words and deeds.

As for the events in Europe, there was not the slightest indication that they would soon (or ever) assume a brighter hue. His hopeful belief that the Munich Agreement might lead to the building of a solid foundation for European peace had been, he now recognized, a spasm of wishful thinking which, though shared by most Americans (a Gallup poll revealed a large American majority's approval of the agreement), had not been shared, evidently, by any save Neville Chamberlain of the four signers at Munich, not even at the moment of their signing.† Certainly the dictators had not shared it; neither Hitler nor Mussolini

---

*See *FDR: The New Deal Years,* pp. 122–23, 153–57, 183–93.

†That this "wishful thought" was not soothingly dominant over the American public mood—that the mood remained one of insecurity and apprehension, streaked with hysterical fear—seemed demonstrated by popular reaction to a radio broadcast made over the Columbia Broadcasting System on Sunday evening, October 30, 1938, by a theater group headed by a young and brilliant actor-producer named Orson Welles. The broadcast, one of a long-scheduled series, was of H. G. Wells's science fantasy *The War of the Worlds.* It was presented as a series of news bulletins of the kind (portentous-voiced H. V. Kaltenborn and Edward R. Murrow were past masters of it) that had kept people glued to their receiving sets during the Munich crisis; these told of spaceships from Mars landing, first in New Jersey, then in spots scattered over the nation, each disgorging alien monsters armed with lethal weapons against which defense was impossible. The immediate reaction by a large minority of the American public was blind, unreasoning terror. In some communities people ran from their homes by the thousand to mill about the streets in helpless

gave any sign of deviating from the aggressive policies that had led to Munich. And Daladier realized "fully" when he arrived back in Paris from Munich, according to an October 3 telegram from Bullitt, that the agreement was "an immense diplomatic defeat for France and England." Daladier predicted "a fatal situation . . . within a year" unless France recovered "a united national spirit," Bullitt reported.[2]

But was not France at that very moment in a "fatal situation"? The question weighed heavily upon the back of Roosevelt's mind during this waiting moment, for it imposed upon him an immediate problem. It was not just "national spirit" that France lacked. She needed warplanes, desperately. And it was the latter need, along with a devious scheme for satisfying it, that Bullitt had stressed in a late-September telegram from Paris. The scheme, evidently the brainchild of Air Minister La Chambre, proposed the establishment of huge French factories for warplane production in Canada, "possibly just opposite Detroit and Buffalo, so that American workmen living at home could be utilized readily," to quote the Bullitt message. "He [La Chambre] asked me for suggestions as to persons to take in hand this immense program of plane construction on the success or failure of which, in his opinion, the outcome of the war would depend." The scheme was of course a roundabout way of using American mass-production technique to make up the current deficiencies of France's miserably unproductive aircraft industry (France's plane manufacture was plagued by labor strife, inefficient piecemeal production methods, and obsolete designs). The Canada plan required for its success the shipment in large quantity of "machine tools and plane parts and instruments from the United States to Canada." The French air minister therefore wanted to know the extent to which such export was possible "without violating the Neutrality Act." Bullitt's own expressed belief was "that we should go to the extreme limit compatible with a reasonable interpretation of the law. . . ."[3]

Two weeks later, on Thursday, October 13, Bullitt himself, home for a much-needed vacation, was in the White House to present a typically dramatic oral report on the frightening European situation and the threat it posed to U.S. security. He made much and effective use of the Lindbergh estimates of relative air strengths and production among the nations Lindbergh had toured during the summer. Roosevelt admitted to being deeply disturbed. In his press conference on the following morning, when a reporter commented upon his "snappy" appearance in a new suit, he replied that he was "not feeling snappy," having "sat up [late] last night hearing the European side of things from Ambassador Bullitt." He must delay indefinitely a promised statement on current budget planning, he had gone on to say, "for the reason that new developments . . . require a complete restudy of American national de-

---

confusion. Highways leading from several Eastern cities became clogged with the cars of people fleeing they knew not where.

fense. . . ." Difficult problems of mass production, necessarily involving an increased standardization of weapons and equipment, must be solved. Asked if he intended to establish an organization similar to the War Industries Board of 1918, and to create a service-unifying Department of Defense, he had replied somewhat testily that he was not now concerned with the "details" of the "machinery for running" an expanded national-defense effort. "What I am doing now is studying a plan to meet needs under rather new world conditions."[4]

And by "needs" he had emphatically meant those "immediate needs" of France, the satisfaction of which neither the Congress nor the general public was prepared, in that hour, to recognize as integral and important to U.S. security. Two days later, on Sunday, October 16, at Hyde Park, he discussed with Bullitt, Hopkins, and others, not only the plan for Canadian factory production of French planes, but also a tentative plan of his own to produce fifteen thousand planes a year (at the moment, American plane production added up to little more than a hundred planes a month) in eight new factories, government-built and operating under license, located in areas of high unemployment. Hopkins, with WPA money available for assignment to such construction, said he was ready to begin at once if money could be found for purchase of the needed land. All this had delighted Morgenthau when Roosevelt told him of it a few days later—and to Morgenthau had been delegated responsibility for implementing the expansion plan, this through an executive order assigning to Treasury's procurement division authority over aircraft purchasing policies.[5]

By the time this order was issued, Roosevelt, at Bullitt's urgent behest, had received at Hyde Park Bullitt's good personal friend, Jean Monnet, a French political economist and international financier (he had become the European partner of a New York investment bank in 1925) who, during the last years of the Great War, had demonstrated a rare genius for administering large-scale international efforts. Monnet, as Roosevelt was reminded by Bullitt, had "organized and directed the Inter-Allied Maritime Transport Council, the wheat and shipping pool and all the vast other Inter-Allied organizations . . . when he was only twenty-eight,"[6] and had thereafter, from 1919 to 1923, been deputy secretary general of the League of Nations. A dapper, balding, sprucely mustached man of fifty years, unimpressively bank-clerkish in appearance and self-effacing in manner, yet precise and forceful of speech, Monnet was now in America as head of a French mission to purchase military aircraft from U.S. manufacturers. The enterprise was one that Roosevelt was eager to aid and that he moved quickly to facilitate, albeit with great secrecy; it was, indeed, one of the incitements of his proposal to expand hugely U.S. production of military planes, in part through direct government manufacture. He had concluded that such expansion, if not the precise means he proposed to achieve it, was immediately politically feasible and that French air needs might be supplied from it, perhaps in part through Bullitt's Canadian scheme. Meanwhile the politically risky business of the Monnet mission—that is, the display and sale to the French of American military aircraft of the latest design—must be expedited with the greatest possible discretion and reticence.

Even greater was the secrecy required, in Roosevelt's view, by another, closely related problem of collective security that was at the back of his mind on this evening of the first Friday of November. Just two weeks ago, on Friday, October 21, he had sat in this room alone with an old Scottish friend, Sir Arthur Murray, a top railroad executive in Scotland who was very much a part of the British Establishment.[7] Twenty years earlier, when Roosevelt was assistant secretary of the navy, Murray had been assistant military attaché at the British embassy in Washington. The two young men had had social and working contacts with each other. In consequence, Roosevelt knew Murray to be a man of discretion with some experience in clandestine operations; in 1917–1918, Murray had occasionally served as a conduit for secret messages between the head of British intelligence in the United States and Colonel House, Woodrow Wilson's great friend, when Wilson wished to communicate directly with British Cabinet officers. It was as conduit of a personal message to Chamberlain and, through Chamberlain, to British air minister Kingsley Wood, that Roosevelt now employed his friend, confiding to him a communication so desperately in need of total secrecy that he dared not trust it to either British ambassador Lindsay or his own ambassador, Kennedy. Murray must see Chamberlain privately and deliver the message to Chamberlain only, Roosevelt had insisted, though the delivery need not be wholly oral. To ensure accuracy, Murray might and did make copious notes of what Roosevelt had to say. And what Roosevelt had to say—what he most emphatically desired the prime minister to hear—was that, "in the event of war with the dictators," Chamberlain would have "the industrial resources of the American nation behind him" insofar as "he, the President, was able to achieve it."[8] Specifically, he as President would do everything possible to assure overwhelming British and French air superiority over Germany and Italy by supplying all the materials and parts needed for military aircraft production: cylinder blocks, spark plugs, steel, wood, aluminum skin for wings. He would also discuss at once with Canadian premier Mackenzie King the feasibility of a proposal to establish airplane assembly lines in Canada. The American industrial effort thus implied would, of course, be huge. It would have to be to overcome Germany's immense lead (it was during this conversation that Roosevelt reportedly estimated current German airplane production at forty thousand a year, a figure derived from Lindbergh via Bullitt). But Roosevelt believed the effort could and would be made, enabling him to divert to Britain and France, within a year or two, the equivalent in parts of twenty thousand warplanes annually from the stream of supply to the U.S. Army and Navy.

Roosevelt's purpose in sending this message was clear in his own mind. He sought to strengthen not only Chamberlain's hand in dealings with the dictators but also Chamberlain's will to deal with them in the firm, stern way required to deter them. But he, Roosevelt, could not but be unhappily aware that the total secrecy he insisted upon, a secrecy dictated by his perception of domestic political necessity, gravely reduced his message's effectiveness. Only if Hitler knew substantially what the message said, and Chamberlain knew that Hitler knew, was there likely to be either a strengthening of the prime minister's will to stand firm or a weakening of the Führer's will to aggress. Thus rose up stubbornly into the back of his mind a nagging question: Was he not risking far more by this secret personal diplomacy than could possibly be gained by it? He awaited Chamberlain's reply, which for secrecy's sake was to be conveyed to him through Murray, with considerable anxiety.

Nor was secrecy the only immediate contradiction of this latest of his moves toward collective security. His purpose was also contradicted by a speech delivered in London on October 19, just two days before the Murray visit, by his own ambassador to Great Britain—a speech designed to strengthen, not Chamberlain's will to resist the dictators, but Chamberlain's will to accommodate them, and a speech that consequently reinforced Roosevelt's conviction that what he wished to communicate to Chamberlain could not be sent through normal diplomatic channels with any assurance that it would not be distorted or reduced in force by the manner of its delivery. It might even be leaked to the press. (When, on November 2, he sent a lengthy letter to George VI in Buckingham Palace, outlining plans for an American visit by the king and queen,[9] he confided no copy of it to his ambassador. He would continue to bypass Kennedy completely in this matter and would not be distressed, though he would of course endeavor to smooth ruffled feathers, when Kennedy expressed a hurt resentment at being thus snubbingly ignored.)

October 19 was Trafalgar Day in London, celebrating Lord Nelson's great victory of 1805, and Joseph Patrick Kennedy was invited to address the annual Navy League dinner, held that evening. It was a signal personal honor. Never before had an ambassador received such an invitation. And Kennedy had prepared carefully for the occasion, devoting nearly three weeks to the writing of an address he intended to be an expression of gratitude to the Chamberlain government for averting war during the September crisis. He knew that his sentiments were anathema to anti-appeasers. He had attempted to keep expected critical repercussions well below the explosive point by emphasizing that his appeasement-approving words were his personal view, not an official one. This had enabled State Department reviewers to clear the speech for delivery, when he cabled a draft of it to Washington, despite its sharp divergence from the policy the President had seemed to define in his "quarantine" speech and in numerous words and gestures since. (After all, had not Roosevelt himself said and done a number of things inconsistent with the "quarantine" speech's main thrust? The ambassador, and the State Department reviewers of his speech, could cite Roosevelt's "Good man" telegram to Chamberlain on the day before Munich, and the White House's initial eagerness, on the morrow of the pact-signing, to claim a major share of the credit for what had happened, as evidence that the President was in general support of Chamberlain's policy.) "It has long been a theory of mine," Kennedy had said, that it is unproductive for both the democratic and dictator countries to widen the division now existing between them by emphasizing their differences. . . . Instead . . . they could advantageously bend their energies toward solving their common problems by an attempt to re-establish good relations on a world basis. It is true that the democratic and dictator countries have fundamental divergencies of outlook. . . . But there is simply no sense, common or otherwise, in letting these differences grow into unrelenting antagonisms. After all, we have to live together in the same world. . . .[10]

Within twenty-four hours after this personal "theory" had been thus publicly exposed, Kennedy was the object of furious attacks in the press on both sides of the Atlantic. The London *Times* was almost alone in its public praise of the speech, saying in its characteristically woolly style that the ambassador encouraged "an atmosphere in which the policy of the Munich declarations can work itself out toward its proper consummation." Elsewhere, Kennedy was damned for vicious stupidity, moral blindness, cynical expediency, anti-Semitism, pro-Nazism.[11] Surely no civilized man of decent instincts and honorable motives, concerned to defend democracy and given Kennedy's access to accurate information, could seriously propose "cooperation" at this late date with Adolf Hitler and his regime of murder, torture, terror, and calculated deceit! So cried fervent anti-Nazis. Cooperation in what? they asked. The "solving" of the "Jewish problem" through the torture-murder of Jews? The absorption into the Reich of what remained of Czechoslovakia? The Nazification of the Balkans as Hitler marched triumphantly to the Black Sea? The destruction of the Soviet Union? Ah, yes! No doubt this last was an enterprise in which big-business man Kennedy, like Chamberlain, would be glad to "cooperate," so long as Hitler did the bloody work! Thus the anti-Nazis. But even leaders of the isolationist bloc in Congress, men formerly supportive of Kennedy and inclined to build him up for a possible presidential nomination in 1940, were dismayed by this speech. It seemed to them clear evidence that the ambassador, having become a pliant tool of perfidious Albion, was now more a spokesman for the British prime minister than for the American President, and was, therefore, a betrayer of the basic tenets of American isolationism.

Roosevelt the politician had at once moved to correct any popular impression that Kennedy on October 19 spoke for the administration. "Our business now is to utilize the desire for peace to build principles which are the only basis of permanent peace," he had told the New York *Herald Tribune* Forum in a radio address on October 26. They were principles that precluded any cooperation in the designs of men and nations committed to the conquest of other peoples, other nations.

Peace by fear has . . . no more enduring quality than peace by the sword. *There can be no peace* if the reign of law is to be replaced by a recurrent sanctification of sheer force. *There can be no peace* if national policy adopts as a deliberate instrument the threat of war. *There can be no peace* if national policy adopts as a deliberate instrument the dispersion all over the world of millions of helpless and persecuted wanderers.... *There can be no peace* if humble men and women are not free to think their own thoughts, to express their own feelings, to worship God. . . . You cannot organize civilization around the core of militarism and at the same time expect reason to control human destinies.[12]*

These words were deemed by press commentators a public rebuke of Joe Kennedy. They were recognized as such by the ambassador who, in private talk, angrily called them "a stab in the back."[13] And they were, as rebuke, but a feeble echo of the angry disgust with Kennedy that Roosevelt had felt, and had expressed in the bosom of his official family, when first he learned what his ambassador had said. Yet from the ensuing furor, Roosevelt the politician might gain instruction regarding the ingredients, and the changing proportions of their mixture, in the seething brew that was the American public's attitude toward European affairs. In his intuitive rather than logical fashion he might examine that portion of the brew called isolationism—might strive to discern and measure the relative strengths in it of reasoned convictions, Anglophobia, Nazi-hatred, Nazi-sympathy, anti-Semitism, fear of war, conscientious objections to war, and the reactive pacifism and cynicism that were a legacy of the Great War's murderous command stupidities and lying official propaganda. He might try to discern changes in the ambivalent attitude of the American public toward Nazi-Fascist aggression—might seek to measure shifts in the balance between the growing conviction that America must *at all costs* stay out of war and the growing conviction that Hitler must *at all costs* be stopped. He might also derive some comfort from the fact that Kennedy's words had evidently lost the ambassador the support of many a conservative isolationist who had theretofore favored him for the 1940 Democratic presidential nomination. The threat to Democratic party liberalism that the ruthlessly ambitious Irishman posed for 1940 was somewhat reduced.

God knew, at any rate, that politician Roosevelt was in sore need of all the comfort he could get as he awaited his cue to speak into the microphones clustered before him—had need for recourse to his deepest religious faith, with its conjoined sense of the rhythms of political history, of the ebb and flow of it, the flood tide of liberalism eternally recurrent. He may have read historian Walter Millis's pronouncement in the current issue of the *Yale Review* that the New Deal, as election year 1940 approached, "has been reduced to a movement with no program, with no effective political organization, with no vast popular party strength behind it, and with no candidate."[14] Certainly he was acutely aware of the impression the American public now had of his loss of governing power, and aware that the impression was an accurate one. In every former election campaign he had seemed at the last in majestic control of events; in this of 1938 he remained as obviously and even abjectly at the mercy of events

*The recurrent phrase was italicized by the emphasis which Roosevelt gave it in his speech delivery.

as he had been when the active interparty campaign began. Ever since his "purge" offensive failed so dismally, he had been continuously on the defensive. The main thrust of his every purely political public statement latterly had been, not an affirmation of his faith and purpose, but a denial that what his enemies alleged was true.

On October 26 he had denied the charge by the Republican candidate for governor of Pennsylvania that he stayed aloof from that state's Democratic campaign because he was "unwilling to put his hands in that muddy water." Pennsylvania's Governor Earle was 1938's Democratic senatorial candidate and "in my own relations with the Earle administration I can truthfully say that I have found it at all times willing and eager to help in carrying into effect a liberal program for social and economic justice." Three days later he had sent a telegram to the chairman of a volunteer committee for the reelection of Farmer-Laborite Elmer Benson to the governorship of Minnesota. Polls indicated that Benson faced defeat by Republican Harold Stassen, a personable young man who was far less conservative than his party. "If the political writers of Minnesota newspapers are inferring that I have deliberately withheld approval from or disapproved of the candidacy of your progressive governor, they are of course misinterpreting my attitude," said the telegram. "I have repeatedly indicated the high esteem in which I hold Governor Benson and the interest I take in his efforts to develop liberal governmental policies in Minnesota." In California, as we have seen, he denied that his outspoken opposition to "$30 every Thursday," joined with his failure hitherto to endorse publicly the state's Democratic senatorial and gubernatorial candidates, meant that he was "indifferent" to the fate of these candidates. Sheridan Downey, having a liberal "temper of mind," should go to the Senate, and Culbert Olsen, of similar mind, belonged in the governor's chair, said Roosevelt on the last day of October; but the belatedness of this endorsement testified to the reluctance with which it was made, and since both Downey and Olsen had by that time become clear front-runners in their races *without* the President's blessing, the latter now seemed a face-saving maneuver. Just three days ago, on November 1, Roosevelt had sent a telegram to the Democratic national committeeman in Wisconsin, where Senator F. Ryan Duffy, running for reelection, lagged far behind both the Republican and Progressive senatorial candidates. The telegram in effect denied that its author was indifferent to Duffy's fate, saying that he, Roosevelt, had "previously indicated his interest" in Duffy's campaign: "Ryan always has cooperated loyally. He is a real friend of liberal government."[15]

The most emphatic and nationally newsworthy of all these defensive statements was on behalf of Michigan's governor, Frank Murphy, whose reelection campaign was imperiled by charges that he had been a willing tool or at best a dupe of the Communist party in his dealings with the 1937 sit-down strikes against General Motors in Flint, Michigan. The charges had been made in testimony before a new congressional investigative body called, strangely, the House Un-American Affairs Committee. It had been authorized on May 26,

1938, to investigate subversive activities in the United States—primarily, the House majority had assumed, Nazi-Fascist activities. The committee chairman, however, had other ideas.* He was a blocky, smooth-faced, cold-eyed, unscrupulous, ruthlessly ambitious young Texas Democrat named Martin Dies, whose political career had been advanced by fellow Texans Vice President Garner and Majority Leader Rayburn.[16] He knew what would most please his Texas constituency; he therefore conceived his primary duty to be the "revelation" of Communist and fellow-traveler influence over New Deal agencies, over liberalism in general. WPA's Federal Writers' Project and Federal Theatre Project had been his first targets, during the summer, when they had been "proved" under sensational newspaper headlines to be dominated by Communists who had made them virtually propaganda arms of Moscow. These "disclosures" had of course done nothing to decrease the dustiness, the weediness of Roosevelt's summer, but the discomfort they had caused him was small compared to that of late October, when the committee abruptly and unexpectedly turned its attention to the Michigan sit-down strikes. The President was prepared with an extended written reply when a reporter asked on October 25 if he were "concerned" about the charge that Michigan's governor had engaged in "treasonable activities in the settlement of the . . . strikes." He was indeed "very much disturbed," he said,

> . . . not because of the absurdly false charges made . . . against a profoundly religious, able and law-abiding Governor; but because a Congressional Committee . . . permitted itself to be used in a flagrantly unfair and un-American attempt to influence an election. At this hearing the Dies Committee made no effort to get at the truth. . . . On the threshold of a vitally important gubernatorial election, they permitted a disgruntled Republican judge, a discharged Republican City Manager and a couple of officious police officers to make lurid charges . . . without attempting to elicit from them facts as to their undeniable bias and their charges and without attempting to obtain from the Governor or, for that matter, any responsible motor manufacturer, his version of the events. . . . Governor Murphy never said a word in condonation of the sit-down strike or any illegal practice. But the Governor was informed by officials of the National Guard that any attempt . . . forcibly to eject the sit-down strikers at Flint would result in bloodshed and riot. Knowing these facts, the Governor labored in the open, in the American way, to bring about a prompt settlement of the labor trouble without resort to violence.[17]

From each of these political brushfires, as it was thus clumsily, imperfectly damped down, rose up puffs of smoke to merge with the smoke clouds drifting in from Europe over Roosevelt's mental skies.

These last were thus further darkened.

And their gloom was reflected in the address whose opening words have already been quoted and which Roosevelt, responding to cue, began now to make to the nation:

---

*In his book, *The Trojan Horse in America* (New York, 1940), Dies devoted twenty-three chapters totaling 303 pages to Communist and other left-wing activities, and only five chapters totaling forty-two pages to Nazi-Fascist subversion.

I have changed my mind about the nature of some problems of democratic government over the past few years as I have had more and more experience of them. I
had never realized how much my way of thinking had changed until the other day
when I was watching the finishing touches being put on a simple cottage I have
recently built. . . . Just watching the building go up made me realize that there was
a time not so long ago when I used to think about problems of government as if they
were the same kind of problems as building a house—definite and compact and
capable of completion within a given time. Now I know that the comparison is not
a good one. Once you build a house you always have it. . . . [But] a social or an
economic gain made by one Administration . . . may, and often does, evaporate into
thin air under the next Administration.

Thus the "march of progress" begun during the seven years of Theodore
Roosevelt's presidency was halted, then reversed by the succeeding Taft administration. Similarly with the New Freedom of Woodrow Wilson; its
"achievements" were "liquidated under President Harding." And now, again,
at a time when democratic government everywhere in the world was threatened by totalitarian aggression—at a time when it was therefore more important than ever before that the American democracy be "a positive force in the
daily lives of its people . . . militant enough to maintain liberty against social
oppression at home and against military oppression abroad"—the New Deal
was being challenged by conservatives and reactionaries bent on returning the
nation to the old order of social injustice and economic exploitation. In words
to which he gave special emphasis he linked "old-line Tory Republicanism"
with fascism and communism as a triple threat to "our form of government,"
venturing "the challenging statement that if American democracy ceases to
move forward as a living force, seeking day and night by peaceful means to
better the lot of our citizens, then Fascism and Communism, aided, unconsciously perhaps, by old-line Tory Republicanism, will grow in strength in our
land."

Since he was speaking from Hyde Park, in his "own election district . . .
county . . . state," the only specific races he referred to were those of New York
senator Wagner, New York governor Lehman, and New York representative
James M. Mead, who ran for the short-term senatorship occasioned by the
death in June of Royal S. Copeland. He cited the numerous "Wagner Acts"
—for labor relations, Social Security, housing—and Mead's expertise in railroads, aviation, and civil service, along with his "unflagging support of every
liberal measure that has come before the Congress." But he spoke at greatest
length of Herbert Lehman. Lehman's challenger was a handsome velvet-
voiced young Republican named Thomas E. Dewey who had recently gained
national fame as Manhattan's racket-busting district attorney. Roosevelt,
without pronouncing Dewey's name, expressed doubt that the young man's
zeal and success as a "local" prosecutor qualified him for the governorship of
"the most complex state in the Union," an office whose powers Lehman had
exercised superbly for a half-dozen years. "We need more active law enforcement, not only against the lords of the underworld, but also against the lords

of the overworld. It is right—wholly right—to prosecute criminals. But that is not enough, for there is the immense added task of working for the elimination of present and future crime by getting rid of evil social conditions which breed crime. Good government can prevent a thousand crimes for every one it punishes."

Roosevelt then spoke the words most expressive of his mood that night— words from which he, or Sam Rosenman with his approval, would draw the identifying title of this speech when it was printed in the 1938 volume of his public papers and addresses.

"The fight for social justice and economic democracy has not the allure of a criminal jury trial," he said; "it is a long, weary, uphill struggle—and those who give themselves unsparingly to it are seldom acclaimed at my lady's tea or at my gentleman's club."[18]

II

FOUR days later, on Tuesday, November 8, he again sat in the Big House library, this time beside a radio receiving set out of which came the unhappy election news he had expected. It was, alas, worse news than he had expected, far worse for the administration than it might seem to the ill-informed to be.

True, both Wagner and Mead won their Senate races in New York, and Lehman was reelected governor. But Wagner's victory margin was narrow, while that of Lehman, theretofore the most popular governor in New York history, was so tiny (64,394 out of 4,718,178 votes cast) that the outcome could be interpreted as a defeat for Rooseveltian liberalism. Certainly it boosted young Dewey's presidential-nomination chances, and Dewey, an immensely effective public speaker, would be, if nominated. a far more formidable opposition candidate in 1940 than Landon had been in 1936 or Hoover in 1932. In California, Downey and Olsen won handily, as they had been expected to do, but elsewhere every candidate whom Roosevelt had specifically latterly endorsed—Benson in Minnesota (brilliant Harold Stassen, winning the governorship by a huge margin, became another potential Republican presidential candidate), Duffy in Wisconsin (where Progressive Phil La Follette's bid for gubernatorial reelection was emphatically rejected), Earle in Pennsylvania, Murphy in Michigan—went down to defeat. The defeat of Frank Murphy was the most galling of all to Roosevelt, for Murphy, like Wagner, was the quintessential New Dealer, and his rejection seemed to indicate that the demagogic reactionary Martin Dies was more persuasive of the Michigan electorate than was the President of the United States. Of the thirty-three contested governorships, the Republicans won eighteen, a gain of eleven for them. The Democrats won but fifteen.

Of course, Democrats would continue to have comfortable majorities in both houses of the 76th Congress. Of the 435 members of the House of Representatives, 262 would be Democrats, 169 Republicans (there would be two Progressives, one Farmer-Laborite, one American Laborite). Of the 96 members of the Senate, 69 would be Democrats, 23 Republicans (there would be four senators of other parties). But this was for the Republicans a gain of 81 House and 8 Senate seats—a near doubling of their strength in the lower chamber (the solidly liberal bloc there was reduced by 50 percent)—and it was a far greater strengthening of conservatism in both houses than the uninterpreted figures indicated, since many of the elected Democrats were indistinguishable on ideological grounds from Republicans and could be counted upon to vote with the Republicans on every issue of liberalism versus conservatism in domestic affairs. Moreover, one of the new Republican senators was Robert Taft in Ohio, President Taft's son, compared to whose social and political views those of the conservative Democratic incumbent, Robert Bulkley, could be deemed almost radical. The dismal failure of Roosevelt's primary campaign against Democratic conservatives had evidently been a symptom of a dramatic rightward shift in the mood of the national body politic—a shift in turn symptomatic of a widespread distrust of Roosevelt's leadership; and this, again in turn, was a consequence of the Supreme Court battle, whereby such distrust was bred in not a few New Deal Democrats. The returns boded ill for the implementation of the decision for collective security in foreign affairs which Roosevelt had personally firmly made by October's end. He now felt even more strongly than before that he could act upon this decision only in cautious, devious, covert, severely limited ways. The formidable Robert Taft's election had, in this regard, an ominous significance. Almost all congressional Republicans and many congressional Democrats were fervently isolationist, and Taft's extreme isolationism, along with his coldly passionate hatred of Roosevelt and every element of the New Deal, was notorious. He would be from his first day in office a powerful spokesman for conjoined isolationism and reaction.

In the face of all this it required some hardihood for Roosevelt to claim, as he did to his associates on the morrow of the election, that the outcome had been determined, not by a national trend, but by a congeries of local accidents and was "on the whole helpful." He said so to Josephus Daniels ("Dear Chief") who wrote from Mexico City that he had found the election returns "unexpected and depressing." Roosevelt replied that he was

wholly reconciled to last Tuesday's results. . . . We have eliminated certain individuals and certain intra-party fights which were doing positive harm. Curley in Massachusetts is, I hope, finally out of the picture, Quinn and O'Hara in Rhode Island tried to murder each other and both are dead! Cross was too old a story in Connecticut and Lonergan was a reactionary. Jersey City's Frank Hague was slapped down in New Jersey and the Pennsylvania row brought inevitable defeat. In Ohio, Davey, the worst of our Governors, wrecked the whole ticket. . . . We have on the positive side eliminated Phil La Follette and the Farmer-Labor people in the Northwest as a standing Third Party threat. They must and will come to us *if* we remain definitely the liberal party. Frankly, I think we will have less trouble with the next Congress than with the last.[19]

When a reporter asked him during his November 11 press conference if he would "not encounter coalition opposition" in the new Congress he replied jauntily, "No, I don't think so." "I do!" the reporter snapped back, provoking laughter that evidently disconcerted a President who knew only too well that the reporter's prediction was accurate. He tried to reply that the reporter couldn't see the forest for the trees but it came out: "The trees are too close to the forest."[20]

III

THAT the election results further narrowed Roosevelt's already narrow estimate of the politically possible was demonstrated, in the days immediately following the election, by his response to events abroad—events that presented a moral as well as a political challenge to the American government.

On the morning of November 8, election day, most American newspapers reported on their front pages that in Paris on the preceding day a distraught seventeen-year-old Jewish boy named Herschel Grynszpan had gone armed with a pistol to the German embassy, had asked to see the ambassador, had instead encountered the embassy's third secretary, Ernst vom Rath, whom he at once shot several times. He was promptly arrested by the French police.[21]

What incited Grynszpan's desperate act was the sudden brutal mass expulsion by the German government, on October 28, of Polish Jews who had long resided on the German side of the present German-Polish border. Some ten thousand men, women, and children were seized and, deprived of all possessions save ten reichsmarks ($4) and the clothes they wore, jammed into trucks and trains that took them to the border. There they were put down on neutral soil between the frontiers. It was a frozen, hostile soil. The weather was bitterly cold; the sudden Jewish influx was decidedly not welcomed by the surprised, hence unprepared, and generally anti-Semitic Poles. All of these dispossessed suffered horribly. Among them were the parents and siblings of Herschel Grynszpan, who learned of their miserable plight from a letter his father managed to get into the mails. The boy, who had himself only recently fled from the family home in Hanover, was in a highly nervous state, preyed upon by anxiety, homesickness, dread, and rage. His father's letter drove him to the edge of insanity.

Under police interrogation he broke down.

"Being a Jew is not a crime," he sobbed. "I am not a dog. I have a right to live and the Jewish people have a right to live."[22]

Vom Rath, mortally wounded, lay unconscious in a Paris hospital for two days during which, in Germany, Goebbels's propaganda machine did all it could to whip the all-too-susceptible German public into a vengeful fury against the Jews. In the afternoon of November 9, Vom Rath died. That evening instructions were issued by Goebbels for "spontaneous demonstrations" to be "organized and executed" during the night, and shortly after midnight on the morning of November 10 urgent teletyped orders went out from Reinhard Heydrich, Himmler's chief subordinate as head of the S.S. and Gestapo, to all police and S.S. stations, implementing these instructions.[23]

What followed, known at once as *Kristallnacht* (the "Night of Broken Glass") because of the vast shattering of windows (an estimated $1,250,000 worth of window panes was broken), horrified the civilized world. "A wave of destruction, looting, and incendiarism unparalleled in Germany since the Thirty Years' War, and in Europe generally since the Bolshevist revolution, swept over Great Germany today as National Socialist cohorts took vengeance. . . ." reported *The New York Times*'s correspondent in Berlin in a story datelined November 10. "Beginning systematically in the early morning hours in almost every town and city in the country, the wrecking, looting and burning continued all day. Huge but mostly silent crowds looked on and the police confined themselves to regulating traffic and making wholesale arrests of Jews 'for their own protection.' " Scores of Jews were murdered, thousands maltreated. Twenty thousand were arrested and sent to concentration camps. Nearly two hundred synagogues were burned; more than eight hundred shops were destroyed and seventy-five hundred looted; more than a hundred dwelling houses were totally destroyed. Nor was this the end of the obscene story. On November 12 a government committee in Berlin of which Göring was chairman issued a public statement holding the Jews responsible "for all the damage . . . resulting from the people's resentment toward the agitation of international Jewry against National Socialist Germany during November 8, 9 and 10, 1938." On that same day the German government imposed a fine of one billion marks ($400 million, approximately) on Germany's half-million Jews as "atonement" for Vom Rath's murder. Moreover, it was decreed that the Jews must bear all costs of the repair of their damaged property, that these repairs must be made immediately, and that all private insurance-company payments to Jews for *Kristallnacht* damages to their property, under the terms of the policies for which they had made premium payments, were to be made to the state, which would return part of them to the companies.[24]

It would be difficult to overestimate the height of the wave of revulsion against Nazi Germany that now swept over the American public. Father Charles E. Coughlin, whose rabble-rousing activities had since 1936 become more and more violently anti-Semitic, condoned the Nazi violence as a necessary defense against "Jew-sponsored" communism, but his was almost the only influential American voice so raised publicly. Virtually every major U.S. newspaper damned what the Berlin government had done as "lynching," "a throwback to barbarity," an act of "indecency and brutality" before which "humanity stands aghast and ashamed."[25] Within days, public meetings of religious and civic groups in nine of the largest American cities, including Father Coughlin's Detroit, adopted resolutions, addressed to the State Department and the White House, calling for a strong U.S. government response to the atrocities. So did dozens of similar meetings in smaller cities across the land. Thirty-six of the most famous American writers addressed to the President a telegram calling for a severance of trade relations with Germany. "We feel we no longer have any right to remain silent," the telegram said; "we feel that the American people and the American government have no right to remain silent. . . . We feel that it is deeply immoral for the American people to continue to have economic relations with a country that avowedly uses mass murder to solve its economic problems."[26] The signers included John Steinbeck, Thornton Wilder, Robert Sherwood, Eugene O'Neill, Van Wyck Brooks, Pearl Buck, Robinson Jeffers, and Dorothy Thompson, whose fervently anti-Nazi newspaper columns and weekly radio broadcasts powerfully influenced American public opinion and who may have been the actual author of this missive. The German ambassador in Washington reported to Berlin on November 14 that "a hurricane is raging here," that "without exception" the American public was "incensed against Germany." He went on: "Even the respectable patriotic circles which were thoroughly . . . anti-Semitic in their outlook also begin to turn away from us."[27]

And on that same November 14, within the State Department itself, where strong moral feeling was generally frowned upon as a hazard to "realistic" policymaking, there was an outburst of moral outrage. Assistant Secretary of State George S. Messersmith, who had served as American consul-general in Germany during Ambassador Dodd's tenure in Berlin, then as American minister to Austria during that country's closing days as a sovereign state, addressed to Hull a memorandum describing had happened as "an irresponsible and mad act" by the German government "that our Government cannot [let] pass unnoticed. . . . The time has come, I believe, when it is necessary for us to take action beyond mere condemnation." If this were not done "we shall be much behind our public opinion in this country." The specific action he proposed "as a token of our disapproval of this wholesale inhumanity" was the summoning home of Ambassador Hugh Wilson for report and consultation, an action considerably milder than a flat recall, which would have implied a complete break in diplomatic relations. Such action, Messersmith hastened to add, could have no adverse effect on the work of the London-based Intergovernmental Committee on Refugees (the establishment of the IGC, it will be remembered, had been the sole tangible achievement of the Évian Conference) since it seemed clear that the German government had no intention of meaningful cooperation with that body.[28]

It happened that, earlier on that very day, Hull had received a lengthy and gloomy telegram from George S. Rublee, the extremely able lawyer and international negotiator who had recently been appointed director of the IGC—a missive in which Rublee said that the "attack on the Jewish community in Germany on the one hand and the indifference of the participating governments to the fate of the victims on the other hand has brought the affairs of the Intergovernmental Committee to a critical state where, in our opinion, immediate action is required if the President's initiative [in calling the Évian Conference in order to set up the committee] is to lead to a positive result. . . ." Rublee added that his "chances of being received [by German officials to negotiate the refugee problem] are receding."[29]

It may be that the conjunction of these two messages caused Hull to act with unwonted swiftness. At any rate, he went at once to the White House. On the following day Roosevelt read to his press conference a brief statement: "The news of the past few days from Germany has deeply shocked public opinion in the United States. . . . I myself could scarcely believe that such things could occur in a twentieth century civilization." He said he had asked the secretary of state to order his Berlin ambassador home at once to report on the situation, and that Wilson would embark on the S.S. *Manhattan* "Thursday, the day after tomorrow." But no formal protest had been made to Germany, he said in reply to a reporter's question; nor was he able to say to where Jews in massive numbers might emigrate from Germany, despite having "given a great deal of thought" to the matter. "The Intergovernmental Committee on Refugees is at work trying to extend its help to take care of an increasingly difficult situation." What about the United States itself as a haven? a reporter asked. Would the President "recommend a relaxation of our immigration restrictions so that Jewish refugees could be received in this country?" "That is not in contemplation," the President replied; "we have the quota system."[30]

Two days later (November 17), British ambassador Lindsay called upon Under Secretary of State Welles to present a way in which the number of German Jewish refugees admitted to the United States under the quota system might be multiplied by four. His Majesty's Government, he said, was willing to give up the bulk of the 65,000 places allotted English immigrants annually by the quota (in 1938 only four thousand of the places had been filled), enabling these to be added to the German quota, which was less than half the English one. Scores of thousands of people could thus be rescued from degradation, brutality, death. Far from welcoming the proposal, Welles rejected it out of hand. Quotas, he said, were not the property of the nations to which they were assigned but were specifically established by U.S. law. They could not be arbitrarily shifted from one nation to another. There were also "objections from the standpoint of policy," Welles went on, according to his report of this conversation. "I reminded the Ambassador that the President had officially stated once more only two days ago that there was no intention on the part of this Government to increase the quota already established for German nationals. I added that it was my strong impression that the responsible leaders among American Jews would be the first to urge that no change in the present quota for German Jews be made."[31]

On that same Thursday, Secretary of Labor Perkins discussed with the President a proposal to permit the immediate entry to the United States of all the German immigrants permitted by the German quota for the coming three years, 82,000 in all. She emerged from their conference to tell reporters that "a cautious approach is necessary to be certain we are doing the right thing and that the American people will cooperate," according to Arthur Morse.[32] Her proposal, in other words, had been turned down.

She was better able to sway the President in another matter, as was revealed at the White House press conference next day (November 18). A reporter referred to printed speculation during the last three days (there had been a great deal of it) that the President, despite his disclaimer, was considering a "lowering of immigration barriers for the benefit of German refugees." The reporter wanted to know if the President had changed his mind. Roosevelt replied with a flat no. There was, however, "one other factor . . . which I did not hear about until yesterday," namely that there were between twelve thousand and fifteen thousand German nationals, many of them formerly Austrians, who were in this country on visitors' permits issued by the Labor Department. A considerable number were employed by colleges, universities, research institutions, and the like. These visitors all traveled under German passports which "because of a recent decree [of the German government] . . . will be cancelled as of the thirtieth of December, this year." In other words, these people must, by December 30, be back in Nazi Germany where a great many of them, "who are not all Jews by any means," had reason to dread their treatment by their government. "It is a question of concentration camps, et cetera and so on." They were not here under a quota, but their visitors' permits could legally be extended by the labor secretary for six months and then, apparently (the law set no limit on the number of consecutive extensions), for six months more, and so on indefinitely. Roosevelt added cautiously that these "visitors" could not, "as I understand it, apply for American citizenship." He had asked Secretary Perkins to grant the initial six-month extensions and would present "the facts to the Congress . . . when it meets. I have no doubt that the Congress will not compel us to send these twelve or fifteen thousand people back to Germany, any more than the Congress compelled us to send a large number of the old Russian regime back to Russia after Russia was taken over."[33] (This presidential decision, it should be pointed out, was as patently illegal as the shifting of quotas from one country to another, or from one year to another, would have been. After December 30, the affected German nationals would have no valid passports, hence no valid visas to be extended, for the latter were legally dependent upon the former. Clearly, the Roosevelt administration could surmount or bypass legal obstacles to the achievement of humanitarian goals, as we know it could and often did in its pursuit of other goals, when the will to do so was present and the President deemed it reasonably safe politically.)

Meanwhile, in London, Joseph Kennedy had seized and was exploiting to the full an opportunity he perceived in the current furor to wash away on a tide of favorable personal publicity the effects of the bad publicity he had received for his Trafalgar Day speech. On November 15, *The New York Times* reported in a lengthy front-page story that Kennedy had persuaded Chamberlain to make the statement that Chamberlain issued that day, regarding the Jews in Germany—his first public statement on the refugee crisis. The statement said that, since the presence of Jews in Germany incited German persecution of them, and since this constituted a threat to world peace, a removal of the Jews from Germany for resettlement elsewhere was advisable. Roosevelt, asked about this in his press conference that day, replied: "I cannot comment on the report, because I know nothing of what has been happening in London."[34] On the following day, *The New York Times* announced on its front page what it called a "Kennedy Plan" for a total emigration of German Jews, who were to be resettled in areas of the world at present underpopulated. The "plan" was virtually identical with the loose, vague proposal discussed at Évian, it was wholly devoid of specifics, and its public exposure surprised both the IGC and the State Department, though the latter *had* let Kennedy know that Chamberlain's silence on Nazi persecution of the Jews was inflaming American public opinion against Britain's appeasement policy.[35] A few weeks later, *Life* magazine editorialized that "if his [Kennedy's] plan . . . succeeds, it will add new luster to a reputation which may well carry Joseph Patrick Kennedy into the White House"[36]—an opinion that did nothing to increase Roosevelt's affection for Kennedy and much to encourage his conviction that his ambassador's operation in this case was a personal publicity stunt. However, by the time the *Life* editorial appeared, the "plan"—after arousing false hopes in myriads of tormented Jews, and confusing the staff of the IGC, to whose efforts the ambassador had theretofore paid slight and mostly negative attention—was fading out of the news.

Roosevelt himself, all through this period, was toying with the possibility "of establishing Jewish colonies on uninhabited or sparsely inhabited good agricultural lands," as he wrote to the famous geographer Isaiah Bowman, president of Johns Hopkins University, on November 2. He asked Bowman to explore this possibility (the geographer did so at some length, though he deemed the resettlement scheme unfeasible). In late November, he sent to London as his personal representative on refugee matters Myron Taylor, who had headed the U.S. delegation to Évian, saying in his letter of instruction that "the time has come when a special effort must be made to make the [IGC's] . . . work really effective. . . . It is essential to create the proper spirit in the countries of potential settlement and to lead them to see this problem as one which is humanitarian in its urgency but from which they can draw ultimate practical benefit. . . . I do not believe it either desirable or practicable to recommend any change in the quota provisions of our immigration laws. We are prepared, nevertheless, to make any other contribution which may be in our power to make."[37]

The whole of this episode is revealing of Roosevelt's priorities among the options he perceived to be open to him in this late autumn and early winter of 1938. The priorities, in turn, reveal something of Roosevelt's mental qualities and moral character.

As a cold-eyed politician, he measured against each other the popular outrage engendered by the Nazis' Jew-baiting and the popular opposition to any revision of the 1924 immigration act. He saw the latter to be, in terms of political potency, far greater than the former. The moral outrage was a violent agitation of public opinion, certainly. It was an energy that might have been organized into a substantial enduring force by a President who had in hand an abundance of political capital and was willing to use up a significant portion of it to achieve this end. But Roosevelt's capital, especially his persuasive

power over Congress, was now sadly depleted—was probably considerably
smaller in his estimation than it would have proved to be in reality, had he
opted for bold action—and in these perceived circumstances he saw the agitation as relatively superficial, a transient phenomenon in the absence of energy-
organizing leadership. Immigration-restrictionist opinion, on the other hand,
was a long-existent, powerful reality. It was a fluid compound of passionate
nativism, "patriotism" of the D.A.R.–American Legion variety, economic
(unemployment) anxieties, and, in this instance, a pervasive and virulent anti-
Semitism, which ran deep and strong through the body politic. The latest
public opinion polls showed nearly 70 percent of the American people opposed
to any liberalization of immigration law or policy. (The percentage opposed
actually rose, to 83 percent, during the four months following *Kristallnacht*.[38])
To challenge this tide of public opinion directly was, in his present circumstances, impossible for Roosevelt, whose remarkable self-control and instinct
for power included a tight rein upon moral feelings—which in this case seem
not to have been enormously strong.*

That they were not is further attested to by his response, or lack of it, to
a conscience-challenging event, which we may here anticipate.

In mid-May of 1939 there would sail from Hamburg, Germany, bound for
Havana, a ship of the Hamburg-American line, the *St. Louis,* aboard which
were 936 passengers, all but six of them Jewish refugees.[40] These were almost
the last Jews ever to receive passports from the Nazi government and each of
them had, along with a passport, an official permit to land in Cuba, signed by
Colonel Manuel Benites, Cuba's director-general of immigration. The permits
had been purchased for approximately $150 apiece from Hamburg-American,
officials of which had earlier obtained thousands of blank forms from Benites's
representatives at a price considerably less than $150. Alas, they were worth-
less, and were known by Hamburg-American officials to be worthless, before
the *St. Louis* sailed. On May 5, Cuban President Federico Bru had signed a
decree invalidating them—a fact that had been at once made known to the
management of Hamburg-American but had not been communicated by that
company's responsible officials to the Jewish passengers, nor even to the *St.
Louis*'s captain, Gustav Schroeder. It was not until the ship approached
Havana that radiograms from the Cuban government informed the captain,
who in turn informed his passengers, of the ugly fact. One of the refugees
collapsed upon receipt of this news, died, and was buried at sea to keep the
Cubans from using the presence of his dead body aboard as a health excuse
for turning the ship away. Schroeder proved at this juncture to be a civilized
man, a man remarkable among German administrative officials, in that year,
for compassionate courage and moral sensitivity. Arrived at the Havana dock,

---

*There is a shrugging acceptance of deplorable "inevitability" in his comment upon the anti-
Semitic decrees Mussolini imposed on Italy in July and August 1938. "What a plight the unfortunate Jews are in," he wrote to Ambassador Phillips in Rome on September 15, 1938. "It gives them
little comfort to remind them that they have been 'on the run' for about four thousand years."[39]

he labored mightily on behalf of his panic-stricken passengers, focusing upon the callous and corrupt Cuban officials all that he possessed of coercive and persuasive power. His arguments, his pleas fell on deaf ears. Only those refugees who had visas authorized by the Cuban government's State, Treasury, and Labor departments could come ashore, and there were but twenty-two who had had the wit and money ($500 per visa, plus legal fees) to obtain them. These twenty-two duly landed, along with four Spaniards, come to visit, and a Cuban couple returning home. Only one of the unauthorized passengers was permitted ashore. He was a lawyer, a decorated German veteran of the Great War who had survived a concentration camp—though he was somewhat crippled by the beatings he had received there—and who was pulled from the water beside the ship and rushed in critical condition to a Havana hospital after he plunged overboard, having slashed his wrists. The remaining Jews, including the wife and two children of the man who had attempted suicide, remained aboard when Schroeder, repulsed by the Cubans but determined not to return to Hamburg until every possible means of rescuing his otherwise doomed human cargo had been exhausted, cruised slowly northward, hovering off the Florida coast within sight of Miami. There the ship was met and closely watched by a U.S. Coast Guard cutter, to prevent any refugee's reaching American soil by boat or swimming.

By that time, the plight of the *St. Louis* passengers had become front-page top-headline news in the American press. So were the strenuous but vain efforts made by the Jewish Joint Distribution Committee and other concerned groups to persuade Washington officials that the ship should be permitted to land its passengers in New York. Seven hundred and thirty-four of the refugees possessed United States immigration-quota numbers—and this fact was published—but they would be permitted entry as part of Germany's immigration quota only at some future date. Surely, in this unique case, the date of permitted entry could be advanced! Editorialists called upon the President to exercise his authority toward this humane end. He did not do so. On June 6, the *St. Louis* at last sailed toward Europe (it would proceed slowly, to provide a maximum of time in which to reverse course if the Cuban or American government changed its mind), and that night a committee of the now-despairing passengers addressed a plea for help directly to Franklin D. Roosevelt in the White House, stressing that among those aboard were "more than 400 . . . women and children."[41] They received no reply.

One of the things Roosevelt as President might have done, as a general and potent aid for the victims of Nazi barbarity, was to interpret immigration law administratively in such a way as to make less strict the means test that U.S. consular officials were currently applying, as they had been for the last eight years, to applicants for visas. In September 1930, Herbert Hoover, fearful of rising unemployment-relief costs, had ordered consular officials to refuse a visa not only to anyone who was not at present self-supporting but also to anyone who might, at any time in the future, become a public charge. Since then, tens

of thousands of German and Austrian Jews, stripped of their property by Nazi
decree, had been denied visas because they could not prove themselves self-
supporting. All Roosevelt would have had to do to change the situation and
save thousands of lives was rescind the Hoover order and issue a new, more
lenient interpretation of his own. This he did not do. He was determined to
conserve every bit of his depleted political capital for expenditure on matters
he deemed of supreme importance, and the Jewish refugee crisis was not one
of these.

IV

NATIONAL defense, on the other hand, was paramount.

In the concluding sentence of his November 14 letter to Josephus Daniels
about the election results, Roosevelt said that "at the present time" he was
working "on national defense, especially mass production of planes. . . ." And
within three or so hours after this letter was dictated he was presiding over
a crucially important conference in the Oval Office, called for the purpose of
launching his plan for a huge expansion of U.S. air power. Among those
attending were Treasury Secretary Morgenthau, Treasury Solicitor Herman
Oliphant, WPA Administrator Hopkins, Assistant Secretary of War Louis
Johnson, Solicitor General Robert H. Jackson, Army Air Force General
Henry H. (Hap) Arnold, Army Chief of Staff General Malin Craig, and Craig's
newly appointed deputy, Brigadier General George Catlett Marshall, whose
present position automatically made him a candidate for the post Craig would
vacate at the end of a four-year term on September 1, 1939.

Roosevelt began the conference with a review of the relative air strengths
of the European democracies and the Axis powers. He was no longer proud
of what he had done to promote the Munich accord: "Hitler would not have
dared to take the stand he did" the previous summer if the United States had
then had five thousand warplanes and the capacity to produce ten thousand
more within the next few months. This hemisphere now faced a greater danger
of attack from across the Atlantic than at any time since the Holy Alliance
of 1815. Roosevelt concluded that the nation should therefore have an air force
large enough to defend the hemisphere "from the North to the South Pole."
The actual need, he said, was an air force of 20,000 planes and an annual
production capacity of 24,000, but since he doubted Congress would appropriate more than half the money needed for this, his immediate concrete proposal
was for 10,000 planes and an annual production capacity of 12,000. To achieve
the latter, he proposed the supplementing of private manufacturing capacity
with government-built and government-operated plants.[42]

There was nothing tentative about Roosevelt's presentation; he made it as
of a program firmly decided, to which he was personally profoundly committed. He asked for opinions after he had completed his presentation, but he did
so in a way that solicited approval and discouraged criticism. The replies he
received were accordingly noncommittal, soothingly so, when not warmly

approving—until, at last, as if in afterthought, he turned to the deputy Chief of Staff, the man responsible for preparation of the army budget.

"I think I've made a pretty good case for my program," he said to Brigadier General Marshall with a broad smile. "Don't you think so, George?"

Most of the eyes in the room turned to George Marshall, a tall, trim-figured man of fifty-seven years (he would be fifty-eight on the last day of that year), austere of countenance and demeanor, who sat erect (he didn't lounge) upon a lounge against the wall and who responded to the President's smile with none of his own. Replied Marshall, coldly: "I am sorry, Mr. President, but I don't agree with that at all."

Roosevelt was visibly taken aback; his mobile countenance registered a dismaying realization that the general resented the use of his first name, evidently deeming it patronizing as well as deceitful in its implication of intimate acquaintance. (Never again would he address the general as "George.") Then, without asking for elucidation from Marshall, he closed the meeting. As the conferees filed out of the office, some of them cast commiserating glances upon the deputy Chief of Staff; in the hallway outside they "bade me goodbye and said that my tour in Washington was over," as Marshall remembered twenty years later.[43]

It was a judgment in which he may at that moment have concurred, and with less regret than he would have felt if his introduction to the Roosevelt mind on that afternoon had been a happier one. He had in fact been appalled by the President's presentation—an emphasis upon combat-plane production so exclusive of other needs as to render virtually useless, for national defense, the planes thus procured. What good would be a mass of warplanes without trained pilots to fly them, airfields to fly them from, guns and ammunition with which to arm them, mechanics to service them, barracks to house the needed personnel—matters of which the President spoke not at all? Indeed, Roosevelt had at one point disparaged the building of barracks, saying it would do nothing to deter Hitler, whereas thousands of new planes would do a great deal. Weeks would pass before the general fully realized that Roosevelt had been less than candid when he said why a vast expansion of America's air arm was immediately, urgently necessary. No more than Marshall did the President actually believe this hemisphere to be in imminent danger of attack from across the Atlantic; he had spoken as if it were because he did not want (did not dare) to reveal his real intention, which was to supply Britain and France from the stockpile of planes he proposed to build. These two nations might thereby be sufficiently strengthened in the air to deter Hitler and Mussolini or, if war came, to defeat them without the actual fighting assistance of the United States. His plan was thus actually a design for keeping America out of impending war and, as such, might conceivably have won the support of many who now considered themselves isolationist, had he frankly disclosed and strongly argued for it.

But even after Marshall became aware of the President's hidden purpose he remained convinced that the plan, as proposed, was radically unsound. Roosevelt greatly overestimated the decisiveness of air power in modern war. "Military victories are not gained by a single arm . . ." Marshall had said in a speech at the Air Corps Tactical School two months before, "but are achieved through the efforts of all arms and services welded into an Army team." Hence Marshall more than doubted that a vast increase of British and French air strength would, of itself alone, assure their victory over Germany and Italy, though it might, if soon obtained, stave off defeat. As for the U.S. Army's immediate task, it was, as he had stressed in that same speech, "to maintain a conservatively balanced force for the protection of our territory against any probable threat during the period the vast but latent resources of the United States, in men and material, are being mobilized."[44] And he would continue to insist upon a balanced development of America's armed forces as, in pursuit of his assigned duties and of the office of Chief of Staff (he very much wanted it), he made his precarious way through the confusion, the acrimonious bureaucratic muddle, into which the growing national defense effort was cast by White House ambiguities and indecisiveness,

The muddle, a serious hazard to Roosevelt's openly avowed rearmament policy and an even more serious one to his unavowed collective-security commitment, had two main sources. One was the executive order assigning authority over aircraft purchasing to the Treasury Department's procurement division. This provoked no loud protest from the relatively well nourished Navy Department, but it at once embroiled Treasury and a long-starved War Department in a bitter quarrel over the dimensions of their respective bureaucratic turfs. The other trouble source was an equally bitter quarrel within the War Department itself, between Secretary of War Woodring and Assistant Secretary Johnson.

Harry Woodring was a conservative Democrat from Kansas, a rather tightly buttoned-up authoritarian personality, highly though narrowly principled. He had been a prosperous small-town banker before entering his state's gubernatorial election contest in 1930 and winning it. He had lost to Alf Landon when he ran for reelection in 1932 (a rabble-rousing quack medical "doctor," running as an independent, drained scores of thousands of votes away from the Kansas Democractic party that year) and had then, in 1933, been named assistant secretary of war, this as a reward for services he had rendered Roosevelt's preconvention campaign in 1932. As assistant secretary, he had, in a *Liberty* magazine article,* aired views about the proper role of the U.S. Army in domestic affairs which had decidedly fascistic implications, provoked loud controversy, and caused him to be summoned to the Oval Office to explain himself. He "explained" by saying he hadn't meant what he had plainly said. ("Our Army," he had said, "happens to be the only branch of the Government which is *already organized and available not only to defend our territory but also to cope with social and economic problems in an emergency* [the italics are Woodring's own]. . . . It is my opinion that the Army *should* take over

*Issue of June 6, 1934.

immediately some of the activities which are now being handled by some of the new executive agencies. Whether or not it is true . . . that the C.C.C. camps are the forerunners of the great civilian labor armies of the future, I believe that activity should be expanded and put under the control of the Army. . . . Let us speak frankly! *If this country should be threatened with foreign war, economic chaos, or social revolution, the Army has the training, the experience, the organization, and the men to direct the country in the national interest* [again, the italics are Woodring's own].") Woodring was also known to be a fervent isolationist, utterly committed to the spirit and letter of the Neutrality Act. Nevertheless, in September 1936, a few weeks after the death of Roosevelt's first war secretary, George A. Dern, he had been named Dern's successor.[45] He was extremely jealous of his authority, which was continuously gravely challenged by his principal assistant. And for both reasons he was fiercely determined, as were most of the army's top officers, to retain in the United States every gun, every shell, every item of matériel, and especially every warplane, which the rearmament program produced. All these were desperately needed by the nation's armed forces, he insisted; none could be spared for shipment abroad.

No less conservative than Woodring but very different in temperament, style, and policy commitment was Louis A. Johnson, from West Virginia, who had succeeded Woodring as assistant secretary and was, ex officio, in charge of army procurement and economic-mobilization matters. The fact that the duties of his office had been specifically defined by the National Defense Act of 1921 meant, he insisted, that he was not subordinate to the secretary but was directly responsible to the Congress and the President, and he operated accordingly from his first day in office. Formerly a highly paid corporation lawyer (he had lobbied fervently on behalf of his clients against the holding-company bill) and national commander of the American Legion, he was talkative (excessively so), gregarious, aggressive, tactless, ruthlessly ambitious, and openly contemptuous of the secretary, whose authority he strove continually to undermine and whom he aimed soon to replace.[46] Ambition if not conviction inclined him to side with the White House in its opposition to the Neutrality Act and in its as yet imperfectly revealed commitment to collective security, though, in his need to remain on good terms with career army officers, he would prove only somewhat less unhappy than Woodring was over any supply to France of American aircraft of the latest design.

Obviously, the quarrel between these two could be ended only by a presidential removal of one or both of them from office, but Roosevelt's penchant for divide-and-rule administration, coupled with his aversion to any direct personal infliction of pain, militated against his taking such action. He was rumored to be on the verge of doing it in mid-November. It was then said that he would remove Woodring, who might be named minister to Canada, and put Johnson in the Cabinet. But he had not so acted when, on November 20, he departed for Warm Springs to renew, after a two-year lapse, his traditional Thanksgiving with fellow polio victims.

· · ·

At Warm Springs he did his usual exuberant speechmaking and expert turkey-carving. He conferred with both Hugh Wilson and William Phillips on conditions in Germany and Italy. He answered a long letter from an aged, ailing General Pershing in which that American Expeditionary Force commander of 1917–1918 cautiously protested a lack of balance in the current expansion of air power at the evident expense of the ground forces (Pershing had been asked by Marshall to do this). "I am having a study made of the ammunition situation and also artillery—especially the anti-aircraft guns. . . . ," Roosevelt replied. "I am having the General Staff study the ground forces that are necessarily connected with increased air operations."[47]

On his way back to Washington from Warm Springs, on December 5, he accepted an honorary degree from the University of North Carolina and there made a speech to students and faculty in which he counseled patience for those who pursue the liberal dream ("liberal forces" would "come to life again," after the temporary setback of the last election, "with more strength than . . . before") and ridiculed the view of him that was imposed on the public mind by a hostile press and radio. "You have heard for six years that I was about to plunge the Nation into war; that you and your little brothers would be sent to the bloody battlefields of Europe; that I was driving the Nation into bankruptcy; and that I breakfasted every morning on a dish of 'grilled millionaire,' " he said. "Actually I am an exceedingly mild-mannered person—a practitioner of peace, both domestic and foreign, a believer in the capitalistic system, and for my breakfast a devotee of scrambled eggs."[48] At his press conference in Washington next morning he said that "as a general proposition national defense ought to be paid for on a pay as you go basis [that is, from immediate tax increases if needed] because it is not a self-liquidating project in any way"; denied the validity of an alleged War Department report that U.S. airplane production was "far behind [other countries] technically" ("not technically," said Roosevelt); and said he did not plan to include natural-resource conservation measures in the national-defense proposals he would soon present to Congress.[49]

A week later (on December 13), having on an intervening day made the press conference announcement regarding the Franklin D. Roosevelt Library at Hyde Park, of which we already know, he received in the Oval Office Britain's former foreign secretary, Anthony Eden, who, with the unenthusiastic acquiescence of the Chamberlain ministry, had accepted an invitation to address the annual conference of the National Association of Manufacturers in New York, was receiving a hero's welcome in America, and was accompanied to the White House by Sumner Welles (though not, significantly if unsurprisingly, by the British ambassador). "We spoke for three-quarters of an hour, freely if somewhat discursively," wrote Eden in his memoirs. "I sensed that the President may have been slightly embarrassed about how to take this visitor who was not in agreement with his own country's foreign policy. In any event he was correct in avoiding that topic, while expatiating on the inferiority of the air-power of Britain and France compared with Germany's. He kept insisting that we should strengthen ourselves in the air, and described his own intention to increase the armaments of the United States."[50]

On the day following Eden's White House visit, Arthur Murray, in London, was finally able to deliver to Neville Chamberlain personally, orally, confidentially, Roosevelt's highly secret promise to do all within his presidential power to provide material aid to Britain in case of war with Germany. The meeting between Murray and the prime minister had been long delayed by Foreign Secretary Halifax's reluctance to arrange it; Halifax knew Chamberlain was not eager to hear what Murray had to say, and expressed to Chamberlain his regret that he had been unable "to ride him [Murray] off seeing you." But according to Murray's letter to Roosevelt, dated December 14, the meeting itself went well. The prime minister "derived a real feeling of encouragement from the messages and tokens of your sympathetic attitude, and from the sense of friendly contact with yourself that these messages and tokens brought."[51] No supporting evidence that this was so was provided by Chamberlain himself, however, then or later. Roosevelt consequently remained doubtful of the prime minister's goodwill, resented the apparent lack of it, and must have sighed with relief that there had been no news leakage of this risky and evidently futile venture into secret diplomacy.

Part and parcel of the overall national-security effort during this period was a "Declaration of the Solidarity of America" which was proposed by the United States and adopted by the eighth Pan-American Conference of twenty-one American republics, held in Lima, Peru, from December 9 to December 27, 1938. The U.S. delegation, headed by Secretary of State Hull, included Alf M. Landon, the 1936 Republican presidential candidate, who was appointed to give a bipartisan coloring to this portion of U.S. foreign policy. He proved a most fortunate choice for that role, according to Adolf Berle, who managed the delegation's staff work. (Landon knew that "he knew nothing . . . of the subject matter," noted Berle in his diary, "and therefore conceived that his job was to back up the Secretary whenever possible and be as pleasant to everyone as he could. As a result, he was an immense favorite in Lima. . . .") The Lima Declaration, as it was called, implemented the sentiments Hull expressed (the expression was probably drafted by Berle) in his speech at the conference opening: "Each and all of us desire passionately to live in peace with every nation of the world. But there must not be a shadow of a doubt anywhere as to the determination of the American nations not to permit the invasion of this Hemisphere by the armed forces of any power or any possible combination of powers." The declaration was finally adopted unanimously (though weakened because of the obstructionism of Argentina, whose government included fervently pro-Nazi elements); it not only "reaffirmed . . . continental solidarity" but also stipulated means by which it might become practically effective. If the "peace, security or territorial integrity of any American Republic" were threatened by an overseas power, all the republics were pledged to consult with one another regarding forcible resistance to such a threat.[52]

However, as Christmas came on, Roosevelt did nothing about the danger-ously debilitating quarrel within the War Department, despite its increasing threat to defense efforts. He made other Cabinet changes, two of them. And one of these should have been more difficult than the removal of a troublesome, not-very-likable Woodring.

Certainly it was painful for Roosevelt to request, in late November, Homer S. Cummings's resignation from the attorney generalship. Cummings was a pleasant man who, though his excessively clever implementation of his supe-rior's wishes with regard to the Supreme Court had proved politically disas-trous, had served the White House with total loyalty and general efficiency. Obviously deeply hurt, he insisted that he be permitted to resign, ostensibly because he wished to resume private law practice, well in advance of the general Cabinet shake-up which, Roosevelt said, impended.[53] Roosevelt agreed. He was still at Warm Springs when he announced "with great regret" that Cummings would leave the Cabinet in January. At his first press confer-ence after his return to Washington he neatly parried questions about Cum-mings's successor. When would Governor Murphy's appointment go to the Senate? he was asked. Or, alternatively, when would Bob Jackson's? "Gosh, they [the questions] are getting better and better . . . ," Roosevelt replied. "I am going to have all these questions framed. . . ."[54] But he in fact intended Murphy for the post, provided he was assured by Senate leaders that his *other* Cabinet appointment would be confirmed.[55]

This other was the long-planned, highly controversial naming of Harry Hopkins as secretary of commerce, to replace the seventy-one-year-old Daniel Roper. Roper cheerfully accepted Roosevelt's decision to retire him; the Presi-dent "regretfully" accepted the resignation on December 15, to be effective December 22; and on December 23, Hopkins, having resigned as WPA admin-istrator, was appointed Roper's successor.* Of course, the announced eleva-tion of "Spendthrift Harry" sparked an explosion of wrath in the business community, many of whose members deemed the appointment personally insulting to them. The Chicago *Daily News* editorialized: "Surely, this is the most incomprehensible, as well as one of the least defensible, appointments the President has made in his six and one-half years in the White House."[56] The explosion, however, was less violent, and certainly far less noisy, than it would have been if the appointment had not been made just two days before Christ-mas and if Hopkins had not been personally liked, and been generally known to be liked, by several highly influential big-business men. This last fact was commented upon by Roosevelt when he told Ickes of Hopkins's impending

---

*Hopkins's departure from the WPA had slight consequence for relief. It was only insofar as WPA and national-defense projects coincided that Hopkins had latterly taken much active administra-tive interest in the agency he nominally headed. Day-to-day administration had for months been handled by the two key second-level executives, Aubrey Williams and Francis Harrington, who now became, briefly, rivals for the top spot. Harrington won. He was an army colonel and could therefore, Roosevelt assumed, work more easily with the army than Williams could on the WPA's national-defense projects.

elevation. "Harry does get along well with the economic royalists," agreed Ickes, who still refused to take seriously the rumors that the President intended Hopkins to be his White House successor ("Harry . . . told Tom Corcoran the other day that he realized he was merely being used as a stalking horse so far as the Presidency is concerned," Ickes noted in his diary on December 18). "There is something debonair and easygoing about him that makes him personally attractive; he seems to like to accept invitations to expensive homes; he loves horse racing and poker and women and, except for his social-service and relief records, he would be highly acceptable to this class." (Ickes added: "Of course I believe that, fundamentally, Harry is a liberal with a real concern for the underprivileged.")[57]

On Saturday, December 24, at eleven o'clock in the morning, Hopkins was sworn into his new office in a ceremony in the White House Oval Room. The President read his new Cabinet member's commission slowly, with more than usual feeling. Justice Stanley Reed, whom Roosevelt had named as Sutherland's successor on the Supreme Court earlier that year, administered the oath. "Harry looked pale and thin [he was, in fact, feeling far from well], but . . . his clothes were in good order," noted diarist Ickes who, with his young bride, was the only Cabinet member present. "I suspect that Harry has really sloughed off his sloppy habits preparatory to living up to his new job."[58] All those present knew that the appointee faced rough questioning during the upcoming Senate Commerce Committee confirmation hearings and would be furiously attacked on the Senate floor. His purportedly partisan handling of relief funds would be assailed. Much would be made of something he was alleged (by Arthur Krock) to have said to companions at a New York racetrack last fall—namely, "We will tax and tax, and spend and spend, and elect and elect"—a remark he flatly, publicly, vehemently denied he had ever made. He would be forced to admit that once, in his zeal for New York City reform, he had registered as a Socialist prior to a city election—also that he regretted some of the speeches he had made. "I do not want to imply I withdraw the contents of those speeches," he would say, "but if I had the road to go over again I would not have made them as relief administrator."[59] Nevertheless, by the twenty-fourth, Roosevelt was assured by W. Averell Harriman of Union Pacific, a personal friend of both Roosevelt and Hopkins, that the Commerce Department's Business Advisory Committee, of which Harriman was the appointed chairman, would unanimously endorse this nomination,[60] and there was virtually no doubt that Hopkins would ultimately be confirmed. (In the event, he was, by an almost straight party vote of 58 to 27, on January 23, 1939.)

The White House Christmas of 1938 was the exuberant, sentimental, strictly traditional family celebration which it had always been and would always be for the Roosevelts. Eleanor Roosevelt, whose absence last year had occasioned much comment, was this year at her husband's side. So, as always, was his mother, the matriarchal Sara, who at eighty-three seemed to some slightly more feeble than she had been last year, but *very* slightly; certainly she was as forceful, as domineering a personality as ever. A yet pale and weak Jimmy

Roosevelt (his thirty-first birthday had been celebrated in the White House on Friday the twenty-third) was also present, with the lovely wife from whom he was becoming estranged and their young children, Sara and Kate. Eleanor's brother Hall was there. Hopkins and daughter Diana were there; they had been staying in the White House since Friday evening, both being now fully accepted members of the Roosevelt family.* The White House's second floor was again loud with excited, romping children. On Christmas Eve the whole large White House party accompanied the President to the traditional lighting of the national Christmas tree in Lafayette Square, where he spoke of the Lima Conference as a sign and promise of peace "in the spirit of Christmas" throughout the Western Hemisphere. Afterward, back in the White House, he gave his traditional actor's reading of Dickens's *A Christmas Carol.* On Christmas Day, as always, there was church attendance in the morning, and Roosevelt's hearty, fun-inspiring presiding over the unwrapping by the children of their Christmas gifts, then the children's Christmas dinner. The dinner for adults, with Roosevelt carving the traditional meats, was held later in the afternoon.

V

TWO days after Christmas, Harry Hopkins, unwontedly neatly clad in suit and tie, seated himself for the first time behind his enormous and as yet clean desk in the commerce secretary's intimidatingly large, luxurious, walnut-paneled office and, as almost his first act there, phoned General Marshall at the Munitions Building to ask if he might come over to see him. Marshall, more mindful of protocol than Hopkins, said he instead would come to Hopkins.

The general then came gratefully, wearing the civilian clothes he always wore and encouraged fellow officers to wear in Washington, this in deference to the anti-militaristic prejudices of congressmen and senators who must vote on the army budget.

He also came well prepared.

He had been deputy Chief of Staff for only a few days (he assumed these duties October 15, 1938) when he read an excited memorandum from Colonel Arthur R. Wilson, who as War Department representative had accompanied Hopkins during the latter's secret autumn tour of West Coast airplane factories. From it, Marshall gathered that Hopkins was highly critical, not only of a "sleepy" War Department, but also of some of his own WPA officials for permitting millions of relief dollars to be spent on useless make-work projects when they could and should be spent on projects for national defense. "Mr. Hopkins thinks that the War Department should present [in the budget for

---

*It was only a few days before this Christmas that Eleanor Roosevelt came to Harry's Georgetown house with her suggestion that he name her Diana's guardian in his will. For all his public protestations to the contrary, he had sad reason to believe his health was again failing and he was, as Eleanor knew, very worried about what might happen to his daughter if he died. He promptly, gratefully acted upon this suggestion.[61]

whose preparation Marshall was responsible] a big program which will include the manufacture of modern armament, airplanes, perhaps the employment of men in all arsenals so they can go at top speed—all this without regard to the present rules of relief labor and material . . . ," wrote the colonel. "The point is that Mr. Hopkins has the ear of the President as no other man. . . . The Chief of Staff or the Deputy [should] get an appointment with him [as soon as possible]. . . ."[62] This memorandum had been followed onto Marshall's desk, some days later, by one addressed by Colonel Wilson to Marshall himself, "urging [with some specifics] that more use be made of relief funds to further national defense."[63]

Hence the general's gratefulness, and hence his mental preparation, for the long hour he now spent alone with the new commerce secretary—an uninterrupted hour of animated talk, most of it Marshall's, during which a curious Hopkins learned why Marshall had responded so negatively to the President's air-power expansion proposal, and learned also, in considerable vivid detail, of the army's appalling unpreparedness, in every branch, for war. The unpreparedness was worse than Hopkins had surmised. He was so disturbed by it that he pressed the general to go at once to the President with his story. This Marshall declined to do (his code of conduct would not permit his so usurping a staff chief's function) but was more than willing to have Hopkins do; and the latter did do it, being persuaded by Marshall's argument for a swift and huge, but also balanced, expansion of the armed forces,

This meeting had an immediate practical consequence. Because of it, as Arthur Wilson remembered a decade later, "several millions of dollars of WPA funds were [at once] transferred secretly [legally?] to start making machine tools for the manufacture of small arms ammunition. This . . . one move put the production of small arms ammunition at least one year ahead [of what it would otherwise have been] when England . . . started to place orders in this country for the manufacture of small arms ammunition."[64]

But more important to history than the practical effect was the impression these two remarkable men made upon each other at this first of their personal interviews, for from it grew a mutual trust, admiration, and personal affection that would considerably influence coming great events.

Such mutuality appeared to a surface view, and at the outset, highly unlikely. It is true that Hopkins at that moment, in fitful service of an ambition he could never quite take seriously, was making a rather pathetic attempt to acquire the conformist bourgeois respectability that Marshall appeared naturally to personify; but he and the general nevertheless remained two very different men. They differed greatly in physical appearance. Hopkins, whose health, of which he was unconscionably careless, was again failing, as has been said, looked much sicker than he felt—ravaged, emaciated, burning-eyed. The notably self-disciplined Marshall, on the other hand, who rigorously adhered to a health regimen, was and looked healthy. His plain, rather stern countenance, though devoid of superfluous fat, as was his trim figure, was far from hollow-cheeked, and the gaze of his sky-blue eyes was the opposite of fervid, being instead coolly appraising. (Even when angry, that blue-eyed gaze was likely to be, not hot, but icy cold, frozen by the effortful control which Marshall exerted over the quick temper with which he, a redhead before he grew gray, had been born; it had a freezing effect upon those who suffered it.) Equally great were the differences between these two in manners, tastes, personal habits, personal behavior. Indeed, they were so widely different in these respects that any direct relationship between them must have, one might think, a confrontational character, as when the disheveled encounters the orderly, hedonism faces asceticism, and corner-cutting Machiavellianism comes hard against an unswerving straight-arrow honesty. But threading through all these differences, and underlying them, were similarities. There was a sharing of fundamental values and commitments, a consequent mutuality of abhorrences and aversions. For instance, though each man was personally ambitious, longing and scheming for advancement, each was also highly endowed with what Thorstein Veblen calls the "instinct of workmanship," joined with what is commonly called a sense of duty. Both had a compulsion to perform their assigned roles well, such performance being for each an end in itself—excellence for its own sake. This imparted to their personal ambition a selfless quality. They did not seek advancement primarily for egoistic reasons, not for power per se or to obtain wealth, social prestige, luxury, though Hopkins was evidently far more attracted to the last than Marshall was. They sought it in order to be able "to do a job" which they felt they could do better than others could. The two also had in common their decidedly prosaic, logical minds, minds relatively devoid of intuitive or imaginative faculties, minds that sought always the most direct route to the practical heart of a matter and were irritably impatient with anything that diverted or distracted from this straight line. A concomitant of all this was a shared abhorrence of the meretricious, a loathing of the pretentious and the incompetent, which expressed itself sometimes in harsh, even cruel rejections. Finally, both men, like the President they served, were possessed of a rare stoic courage, a fortitude that could endure great pain and adversity without giving way; and each greatly appreciated this quality in the other, knowing that it made the other a man who could be absolutely counted upon in dire circumstances. Thus the threads of similarity. Eventful time soon wove them into a strong bond of friendship— and Marshall, whose reticence was notable (rarely did he reveal any personal feeling whatever), would give expression to his end of it in numerous written communications addressed to Hopkins during the years ahead. "You have been a source of confidence and assurance to me ever since our first meeting in December 1938," he would write on Christmas Eve 1941. A year later he would write: "Your presence . . . has always been a great reassurance, and I pray for . . . your health, and damn your indiscretions." On other occasions he wrote to thank Hopkins for his "stalwart and invaluable support" and to express profound admiration of Hopkins's steadfastness under an unremitting fire of unfair criticism, and of Hopkins's selfless life-spending gallantry in the service of his country.[65]

He, the general, badly needed Hopkins's support in the winter and early spring of 1939. He had found when he arrived in Washington that the influence of the current Chief of Staff had suffered nearly fatal wounds from the cross fire between Woodring and Johnson ("They have crucified my husband," said a bitter Mrs. Craig to Marshall's wife, Katherine, when the latter made her initial formal call[66]). And since the President remained astonishingly passive in this matter, never requesting from Woodring the resignation he told others he wished for (he did strongly hint to Woodring his wish for it, but the stubbornly tenacious, thick-skinned Woodring would not take the hint), this cross fire continued with unabated intensity over the mine field Marshall must traverse. The Department of War had, alas, become precisely that, a war theater in which "Johnson men" faced "Woodring men" in tumultuous enmity —this while unprecedented challenges from abroad were calling for the most coolly calculated decisions, crucially important decisions, by those responsible for the American defense effort. Marshall "had to work like lightning, compromise endless disagreements, [and] sit in on most difficult scenes"[67] through one grueling week after another as he perforce assumed some of a staff chief's functions without having a staff chief's authority, or even the rank proper for his assigned post (he must give orders to officers who outranked him, his promotion to general having been unduly delayed by an unfriendly Chief of Staff MacArthur). His struggles for a rational balance in the development of America's armed strength, also between the matériel needs of the U.S. Army and those of America's potential allies in Europe, without becoming involved on either side of the Johnson-Woodring feud (he worked well with Johnson but owed official loyalty to Woodring and gave it in full)—these struggles severely tested his strength and strained his nerves.

For though his loyalty to the secretary remained firm, Marshall had to adjust his operation to the ebb and flow of battle, the waxing and waning of relative opposing strengths, in the intradepartmental war. Johnson, the aggressor, held initially formidable strategic advantages over his opponent. He had vigorously advocated a ten-thousand-plane army air corps, with heavy reliance on heavy bombers, since early 1938 (his advocacy had influenced the President); he strongly favored, whereas a puritanical Woodring opposed, the use of relief funds for national defense; and he gave signs of being more willing than Woodring to approve plane purchases by France, not primarily because a strong French air force would increase American security but because French purchases would stimulate the needed expansion of U.S. plane-producing capacity. It was for this reason that he had been invited to the November 14 conference whereas Woodring was given no prior notice of it; and it was he, not Woodring, who on the morrow of that conference ordered Craig to prepare as quickly as possible a detailed two-year rearmament program incorporating the ten-thousand-plane air-force proposal but also providing for industrial mobilization and for the ground force specified by an already developed Protective Mobilization Plan. This was, though distorted, the kind of balanced development to which Marshall was committed, and in the ensuing labor, which was intensely concentrated within severe time limits, Marshall had a great part. The program, bearing a total price tag of $1.8 billion ($1.289 billion for the air corps, $421 million for ground forces, $122 million for industrial preparedness) was delivered to the White House on December 1. Roosevelt at once reacted negatively to it, as Johnson ought to have expected. He summoned to the White House the assistant secretary, the Chief of Staff, and the deputy Chief of Staff, among others of his military advisers, and berated them for their gross distortion of his original rearmament proposal. Had he not told them at the November 14 conference that he could not ask of Congress more than $500 million for army rearmament? Had they no sense of political realities? He sent them back to their desks to prepare a program that cost no more than a half-billion. One effect of this was a temporary shift in the balance of power between Johnson and Woodring. Johnson was out of favor with the White House for the moment; Woodring, for the moment, was in. But the balance was certain to tilt back toward Johnson in the not-distant future.[68]

In these shifting circumstances, of which the one constant was the personal animosity of secretary and assistant secretary, Marshall's strategy for achieving appointment as Chief of Staff was subtly, acutely conceived. Thirty-two of the generals on the list of eligibles—twenty-one major generals, eleven brigadiers—outranked him, but this naked fact gave no accurate sense of his chance for advancement. It was an established rule that no man could become Chief of Staff who would reach age sixty-five before his four-year term ended. When this rule was applied to the list of eligibles, twenty-nine of the top thirty-three were eliminated. Actually, then, Marshall stood, not thirty-third, but fifth in the line of seniority; and of the four who outranked him only one appeared to have a better (though, it seemed to most observers, a much better) chance than he. This one was Major General Hugh A. Drum, who was the most senior on the eligible list, had been a leading candidate when Craig was appointed, was far better known to the general public than Marshall was, had long been waging an open and intense campaign for the appointment, and had a number of powerful political friends, including Postmaster General Farley, whose support was commonly deemed decisive. In the face of such seemingly great odds, Marshall sought a support of himself that was not solidly concentrated and highly publicized but, instead, widely scattered and not publicized at all —a support whose elements remained discrete, independent of one another, until they came together in focus upon the ultimately decisive point, the mind of Franklin Roosevelt. By early 1939, as he himself later remembered: "Johnson wanted me for Chief of Staff, but I didn't want Woodring to know he was for me. Craig was for me but [because Craig did not stand high in Roosevelt's estimation] I wanted it kept from the President. Woodring was for me, but I didn't want others to know." Pershing, still widely regarded as the nation's first soldier, whose opposition would certainly have kept Roosevelt from appointing Marshall, was emphatically for him. Most important of all, Hopkins was for him, and Hopkins not only poured into the presidential ear, at favorable moments, the Marshall argument for balanced force development but also disposed Roosevelt to think well of Marshall personally, something Roosevelt on his own was increasingly inclined to do. With all this going for him, Marshall was at great pains to avoid "publicity . . . or 'build-up' as it is called." He had been from the moment he was named deputy chief. When a newspaperman friend of Woodring's wished to launch a publicity campaign on his behalf in October 1938, this to counter the huge publicity that Hugh Drum at his own instigation was receiving, Marshall pleaded with him not to do so: "The well-known fact [in Army circles] that I attended strictly to business and enlisted no influence of any sort at any time . . . has been my greatest strength in the matter of future appointment, especially as it is in contrast with other most energetic activities in organizing a campaign and in securing voluminous publicity. Therefore it seems to me that at this time the complete absence of . . . publicity . . . would be my greatest asset, particularly with the President. . . ." And when, in February 1939, Pennsylvania's senator Joseph F. Guffey wished to enter a direct plea on Marshall's behalf at the White House, "I had the damndest time to keep him" from doing it. "I said you will destroy me. Let things take their course and perhaps I will get it."[69]

Of the chief executive who would ultimately make the decision, Marshall's opinion remained for obvious reasons highly dubious. His view of Roosevelt the man was elevated by the fact that Roosevelt harbored no resentment of his blunt truthfulness at the November 14 conference ("I want to say in compliment to the President that that didn't antagonize him at all"[70]), also by the fact that Roosevelt was so greatly admired, even loved, by the acute, realistic, phony-hating Hopkins. But the general continued to measure the President far short of greatness as, aided in this by Hopkins's advice, he made shrewd assessments of Roosevelt's mental and temperamental characteristics, and of the ways in which the possessor of such characteristics could be most efficiently handled. Thus, in advance of a visit Roosevelt made to the army's Infantry School in the winter of 1939, Marshall, who may have been the instigator of this visit, was enabled to give sound warning advice to the school's commandant. He wrote: "I make this suggestion—that . . . no one press him to see this or that or understand this or that; that whatever is furnished him in the way of data be on one sheet of paper, with all high-sounding language eliminated, and with very pertinent paragraphed underlined headings; that a little sketch of ordinary page size is probably the most effective method, as he is quickly bored by lengthy papers, by lengthy discussions, and by anything [more than] . . . a few pungent sentences of description. You have to intrigue his interest, and then it knows no limit."[71] While making such assessments, Marshall armed himself and shaped a defensive strategy against the threat, as he deemed it, of the President's famous charm—a threat to which he was by nature considerably less vulnerable than most men were. His relations with the President were calculatedly distant, impersonal. He kept them as stiffly formal as possible, then and later, invariably refusing Hopkins's urgings that he go to Warm Springs or Hyde Park for private talk with the President in the latter's most relaxed and happy moods. He feared that, in informal conversation, at the dinner table, for instance, he might feel compelled by politeness to agree, at least tacitly, with expressed presidential military opinions or judgments he knew to be mistaken, and that his subsequent freedom to speak and act according to his own professional lights might thus be seriously impaired. He also shaped during this time tactical defenses against Roosevelt's discursiveness, remaining silent when Roosevelt invited diversions from the subject at hand, and even refusing to smile at the President's jokes—a risky tactic, surely! This reduced Roosevelt's enjoyment of Marshall's company—the conduct of business with the general became for him an uncommonly bleak and humorless exercise—but it increased his respect for Marshall the man. It also sharpened in Marshall's favor the contrast between him, who with quiet efficiency "stuck strictly to business," and the ceaselessly publicized, importuning, self-promoting Hugh Drum. ("Drum, Drum," Roosevelt was heard to complain as 1939's spring came on, "I wish he would stop beating his own drum."[72])

We have already violated our main story's chronology in order to give an uninterrupted account of George C. Marshall's rise toward fame. We may as well continue the violation and tell of his final emergence from obscurity into the intensifying light of history.

On the last of March 1939, Roosevelt arrived at his cottage in Warm Springs for a stay of ten days. His sole companions in the house were Missy LeHand and Hopkins. The latter had then been for several weeks too ill to attend to his duties in the Commerce Department but, after a few relaxing days in the warmth of the Georgia sun and that of Roosevelt's radiant personality, felt (he said) "ever so much better." The three lunched together. They shared the cocktail hour together, though neither Missy nor Hopkins would drink the "vile concoction" of gin and grapefruit juice which was the President's "current favorite."* They dined together. And during these companionable hours, "personal and public business" was "discussed with the utmost frankness."[74] One item of it was the question of Craig's successor. Before Roosevelt left Warm Springs for Washington on April 9, the question was answered: George C. Marshall would be the new army Chief of Staff.

Marshall was not informed of this fact, however, until two weeks later, Roosevelt having been caught up during those weeks in a veritable hurricane of crisis event. On Sunday afternoon, April 23, the general was summoned by phone to the White House. He met with the President in the Oval Room. "It was an interesting interview," Marshall acknowledged long afterward. "I told him I wanted the right to say what I think and it would often be unpleasing. 'Is that all right?' He said, 'Yes.' I said, 'You said *yes* pleasantly, but it may be unpleasant.' "[75] The public announcement of the appointment was made by

---

*Hopkins's opinion of Roosevelt as bartender was shared by most who had experience of his "Children's Hour." Wrote Hopkins: "He makes a first rate 'old fashioned' and a fair martini—which he should stick to—but his low and uncultivated taste in liqueurs leads him woefully astray."[73]

the White House on April 27, Marshall having asked that it be delayed until he had left Washington for a flying official trip to the west coast.

Thereafter, Marshall functioned practically as acting Chief of Staff, though he did not nominally take the post until July 1, when Craig went on a two-month terminal leave. He became formally the Chief of Staff on September 1, 1939—precisely the day on which that office abruptly acquired an importance it had not had since the end of the Great War.

VI

ON January 2, 1939, Frank Murphy was appointed attorney general, an appointment that might be vehemently protested by Martin Dies but would certainly be swiftly confirmed by the Senate as a whole. He accepted the post with the understanding that he would soon be shifted to the War Department, replacing Woodring. Murphy, as Roosevelt had stressed in public comment, was a profoundly religious man; his idealistic liberalism, with its emphasis upon individual human freedom, was rooted, he himself believed, in his Christian faith. It is therefore conceivable that Roosevelt had Murphy in mind, as an influence conjoined with the spirit of Christmas, when, at various times over the holidays, he dictated to Grace Tully (herself a devout Catholic, as were both Murphy and Missy LeHand) additions to and revisions of the annual message he was to deliver to the new Congress. At any rate, this address to Congress and the nation in the morning of Wednesday, January 4, emphasized religion as few other of his public speeches had done.

A world war "has been averted," he began, but "world peace is not assured. All about us rage undeclared wars. . . . All about us grow more deadly armaments. . . . All about us are threats of new aggression. . . ." Three "institutions indispensable to Americans" were threatened by these "storms from abroad." The first was religion, which, he asserted, "is the source of the other two—democracy and international good faith.* Religion, by teaching man his relationship to God, gives the individual a sense of his own dignity and teaches him to respect himself by respecting his neighbors. Democracy, the practice of self-government, is a covenant among free men to respect the rights and liberties of their fellows. International good faith, a sister of democracy, springs from the will of civilized nations of men to respect the rights and liberties of other nations of men. In a modern civilization, all three . . .

---

*History teaches a different lesson—that religion breeds strife and tyranny far more often than it does peace and freedom. Witness, in our time, the tragic horrors of fused religion and tyranny in Franco's Spain; in the ayatollahs' Iran; and in Mussolini's Italy, Hitler's Germany, and Stalin's Russia insofar as Fascism and Nazism and Communism were religious passions. Witness the strife of Muslim versus Hindu in India, of Jew versus Muslim and Muslim versus Christian in the Middle East. Witness the dangerous stubborn opposition of the Catholic hierarchy and Protestant fundamentalists to a desperately needed limitation of world population growth. If history be a cautionary tale, one moral to be drawn from it would seem to be that sober thought must curb or prevent religious fervors, else mankind and the planet Earth will be destroyed by the effects of a rampant scientific technology.

complement and support each other." The destruction of any of the three meant, Roosevelt went on to say, the destruction of the other two. "There comes a time in the affairs of men when they must prepare to defend, not their homes alone, but the tenets of faith on which their churches, their governments and their very civilization are founded. . . . We know what might happen to us of the United States if the new philosophies of force were to encompass other continents and invade our own." With an oblique reference to the Lima Declaration, he initiated what promised to become a bold verbal move toward collective security: "We have learned that God-fearing democracies . . . which observe the sanctity of treaties and good faith in their dealings with other nations cannot safely be indifferent to international lawlessness anywhere. They cannot forever let pass, without effective protest, acts of aggression against sister nations." But having thus advanced two steps toward what he felt to be necessary, he promptly retreated two steps, then advanced one step, and finally ended the passage in typical ambiguity. Thus: "Obviously they [the God-fearing democracies] must proceed along practical, peaceful lines. But the mere fact that we rightly decline to intervene with arms to prevent acts of aggression does not mean that we must act as if there were no aggression at all. . . . There are many methods short of war, but stronger and more effective than mere words, of bringing home to aggressor governments the aggregate sentiments of our own people." He did not say what these methods were, contenting himself instead with a far from emphatic indication of his wish to revise drastically, if he could not abolish, his country's Neutrality Act. "At the very least, we can and should avoid any action, or any lack of action, which will encourage, assist or build up an aggressor. We have learned that when we deliberately try to legislate neutrality, our neutrality laws may operate . . . unfairly—may actually give aid to an aggressor and deny it to the victim. The instinct of self-preservation should warn us that we ought not to let that happen any more."

He turned then with somewhat more confidence, hence with somewhat greater clarity of expression, to national defense and socioeconomic reform, adroitly joining the two as aspects or elements of a single enterprise. An "adequate defense" required "armed forces and defenses strong enough to ward off sudden attack against strategic positions and key facilities"; it also required such "organization and location of those key facilities" as would enable them to be "immediately utilized and rapidly expanded to meet all needs without danger of serious interruption by enemy attack." (He would, he said, "send you a special message making recommendations for those two essentials" within the next few days.) But no less important to "adequate defense" was

> the underlying strength of citizenship—the self-confidence, the ability, the imagination and the devotion that give staying power to see things through. A strong and united nation may be destroyed if it is unprepared against sudden attack. But even

a nation well armed and well organized from a strictly military standpoint may . . . meet defeat if it is unnerved by self-distrust, endangered by class prejudice, by dissension between capital and labor, by false economy and by other unsolved social problems at home. . . . Our nation's program of social and economic reform is therefore a part of defense, as basic as armaments themselves.

He made swift review of "what the seemingly piecemeal" activities of the New Deal had contributed to "realistic national preparedness," concluding that never before had there "been six years of such far-flung internal preparedness in our history. And this has been done without any dictator's power to command, without conscription of labor or confiscation of capital, without concentration camps and without a scratch on freedom of speech, freedom of the press or the rest of the Bill of Rights." Much remained to be done, however. There must be "better provision for our older people under social security legislation" and "better care" for the "medically needy," a reorganization "of the executive processes of government" (he gave no special emphasis to this), major improvements "in the railroad and general transportation field," and the development of means for resolving peacefully, along progressive lines, the chronic strength-sapping quarrel between management and labor. There was need, too, for "consideration of relatively small tax increases to adjust inequalities without interfering with the aggregate income of the American people"— a use of the taxing power, in other words, to effect a more just distribution of the total national income while also stimulating activities that would increase that total income from its current level of $60 billion annually to $80 billion.

His following words indicated that, if he had learned little from Keynes's argument, he had learned much from last year's "Roosevelt recession." He now described federal expenditures as "investments" in the national economy, which must not be curtailed "at the moment [when] we seek to increase production and consumption." If we were to balance the budget on the basis of the current $60 billion economy, we must cut federal spending by a third. (The Republican congressional contingent interrupted him at this point with loud applause which he smilingly acknowledged.) This would mean a drastic reduction of "aids to agriculture and soil conservation, veterans' pensions, flood control, highways, waterways and other public works, grants for social and health security, Civilian Conservation Corps activities, relief for the unemployed, or national defense itself." To make such cuts would invite economic disaster, as the experience of 1937–1938 should have made obvious to all, whereas "if government activities are fully maintained, there is a good prospect of our becoming an eighty billion country in a very short time. With such a national income, present tax laws will yield enough each year to balance each year's expenditures."

He closed with a not very apt quotation of Lincoln's impassioned though futile plea to Congress for a compensated emancipation of slaves, saying that the present American generation, in its aforementioned "rendezvous with

destiny," must " 'nobly save or meanly lose the last best hope of earth. . . . The
way is plain, peaceful, generous, just—a way which if followed the world will
forever applaud and God must forever bless.' "[76]

Many who listened critically to this message heard, as its dominant note,
a wary cautiousness. Here was no bold new proposal, nor any strong argument
for proposals formerly made but as yet unenacted—for executive reorganization, as one instance, or neutrality-law revision, as another. Even the argument
for a strengthened national defense, though the need for this was already
generally agreed, was very guardedly made. And the same cautiousness was
evident in the annual budget message delivered next day (it proposed a $9
billion budget, $3 billion of it deficit-financed) and in the special national-
defense message, delivered on January 12. To those who had attended the
November 14 White House conference, the defense message sounded the cautious note especially loudly, for it revealed that the Commander in Chief, in
the face of strong opposition from balanced-force advocates and several senators, had drastically revised the program he had originally boldly advanced.
No mention was now made of a 10,000-plane air corps sustained by a 12,000-
plane annual production capacity, at an initial cost of a half-billion for this
alone. Called for instead, as an addition to the budget for fiscal 1940, was a $450
million appropriation for new army needs, $65 million for new navy needs, and
$10 million for training civilian air pilots ($525 million in all), with $300 million
of the army appropriation to be used to strengthen the air arm. "This should
provide a minimum increase of 3,000 planes for the Army," said the President,
"but it is hoped that orders placed on such a large scale will materially reduce
the unit cost and actually provide many more planes." Of the navy appropriation, $44 million was to be used "for the creation of strengthening of Navy
bases in both oceans" and $21 million "for additional Navy airplanes and air
material tests."[77]

During the whole of that January 1939, Roosevelt openly made but a single
important decision to which any immediate political risk might appear to be
attached, and this was a decision already unconscionably delayed by an excess
of prudence, or so Roosevelt's liberal advisers believed. A half-year had passed
since the great and gentle Benjamin Cardozo had died. Immediately following
this death, in July 1938, a poll of leading members of the American bar showed
Felix Frankfurter to be overwhelmingly favored as Cardozo's successor on the
U.S. Supreme Court. Legal scholars made a public point of the fact that the
vacated seat was historically the "scholar's seat," having been occupied before
Cardozo by Joseph Story and the junior Oliver Wendell Holmes. Prominent
cultural leaders, editorialists on important newspapers, and syndicated columnists published their opinion that, for this seat, Frankfurter was now clearly,
on his record, the best-qualified man in America. "President Hoover indicated
that a seven-dollar night letter that I sent him a day or two before Cardozo
was named had weighed somewhat in the balance," wrote William Allen
White to Roosevelt in early October. "If I could have one word to say to you
now it would be to urge the appointment of Felix Frankfurter to succeed

Cardozo."[78] But Roosevelt, who dearly wanted to make this appointment, received also much contrary advice. It was presumed by political advisers that powerful Western senators would oppose Frankfurter because he came from the already overrepresented East. Roosevelt himself had publicly asserted, during the court-reform battle, "that no two Justices should come from the same judicial district" (he reminded White of this in his answer to the latter's letter[79]), and Frankfurter not only came from the same judicial district as Brandeis but also, like Brandeis, was a Jew. ("Old Isaiah" must soon retire; he himself had indicated as much; and then, as Roosevelt told the professor, Frankfurter could be safely named to the top bench.) Attorney General Cummings opposed Frankfurter on the the grounds that the appointment would encounter grave Senate confirmation difficulties. Even some of the most wealthy and powerful of Frankfurter's coreligionists, including Arthur Hays Sulzberger of *The New York Times*, urged Roosevelt in a group visit to his office not to make the appointment because, in the present world situation, it might inflame anti-Semitic passions across the land—advice that Roosevelt heavily discounted as cowardly and that disgusted Frankfurter when he learned of it.[80]

It was not until Nebraska's George Norris had waged a public, personal campaign on Frankfurter's behalf and thereby removed the threat of serious Western-senator opposition, that Roosevelt at last decided. On Thursday, January 5, it was publicly announced that Frankfurter's commission as associate justice had been signed and sent to the Senate. The news sparked spontaneous joyous celebrations among key New Dealers in Washington—and not only among those whom Frankfurter had recruited for the administration. Ickes was lunching with Frank Murphy in the Interior Department "when in came Tom Corcoran with two magnums of champagne and soon there was a party of us three, Harry Hopkins, Bob Jackson, Bill Douglas, David Niles, 'Missy' LeHand and Peggy Dowd," as Ickes recorded in his diary. ". . . Bob Jackson [the solicitor general, who argued government cases before the Court] was particularly joyous. . . . [It meant that] regardless of who may be President during the next few years, there will be on the . . . Supreme Court a group of liberals under aggressive, forthright, and intelligent leadership."[81]*

Relief was a major component of this rejoicing—a release from the fear they had had that Roosevelt would not, in this case, depart from the pattern of conservative appeasement into which the main bulk of his current overt operation was fitted. No further reason for such rejoicing was provided during these opening weeks of the new year. Roosevelt hesitated. He procrastinated. The indirection, the secretive deviousness which he had practiced intermittently in more prosperous times, often, it seemed, for the sheer fun of dramatic surprise and role-playing, was now practiced by him almost continuously out of,

---

*None of these celebrants would have then believed possible what in fact happened—that Felix Frankfurter became the most conservative member of the "Roosevelt Court," especially with regard to cases involving individual civil liberties.

clearly, a felt grim necessity. On occasion, his reluctance to meet opposing forces head-on became extreme to the point of cowardice.

Thus it was with regard to the slashing frontal attack upon Martin Dies and the House Un-American Affairs Committee that Ickes, having twice received specific approval of this enterprise from the President, zestfully but carefully prepared for national radio broadcast on Friday evening, January 6. Ickes was convinced that Dies had gone as far as he had only because he had not been strongly opposed, and that this fighting speech, called "Playing with Loaded Dies," would so undermine his credibility that his committee's funding by the House would be drastically curtailed, perhaps cut off altogether. If, on the other hand, Dies were *not* openly opposed, he would continue to feed upon the irrational prejudices and fears of an ill-informed public and might grow into a political force strong enough to injure the American democracy fatally. Had not both Mussolini and Hitler come to power through Red-scare tactics? Might not Dies "put his pieces together in the same pattern"? "Most of his witnesses have been scalawags, or worse," Ickes had found. "One is a racketeer, one is a psychiatric case, and three or four have criminal records. Moreover, I have affidavits to the effect that Dies has been getting away for years without paying taxes in Texas which he is supposed to pay." Hence his astonishment, dismay, and angry outrage when, on Monday, January 2, he received an agitated phone call from White House press secretary Steve Early saying that the President had just learned of Ickes's planned speech and begged him "for God's sake not to do it." By then the speech had been nationally advertised in the press. The failure to deliver it must therefore be generally interpreted as a retreat motivated by fear. The net effect would be an increase of Dies's credibility with the general public. Ickes demanded of Roosevelt an explanation. It was that the situation had changed. Dies now had the House votes needed to assure his receipt of $100,000 to continue his "investigation," for a year, but Rayburn believed that, if Ickes were called off, "a little quiet maneuvering" could effect a reduction in both the appropriation and the time extension.[82] Ickes, disgusted, was sure this wouldn't happen. (It didn't. On January 8, 1939, two days after Ickes's speech would have been given, *The New York Times* said editorially: "Legislators admitted privately that they cannot afford, for political reasons, to vote against [the committee's] continuance."[83] And so it did continue, not just through 1939–1940 but year after year after year, dangerously polluting and corrupting democratic processes, destroying the careers and wrecking the lives of scores of people, and pointing the way for future vicious demagoguery.)

Simultaneously, the public's response to the annual message proved more alarming than gratifying to the President. The address was promptly dubbed the "Methods Short of War Speech" and, as such, won but a questioning, tentative approval from the advocates of collective security. What, precisely, had the President meant by this key phrase? *The New York Times* assumed he meant a hard push toward lifting the arms embargo, and asserted editorially, on January 5, that the speech therefore marked "a turning point" in the administration's foreign policy. But the paper also remarked, significantly, that the President had presented no specific proposals for a neutrality-law revision.[84] Senator Pittman publicly assumed, as he had done immediately after the Chicago "quarantine" speech, that the President advocated "moral, commercial, and financial sanctions"—actions that the senator apparently approved of. Leading pacifistic isolationists, on the other hand, were very sure what the President meant and were loud in their condemnation of it. Far from being revised in the way the President intended, neutrality legislation should be strengthened to assure an arms embargo "on all countries at all times," said the influential Frederick J. Libby of the National Council for the Prevention of War. *The New Republic* said that the proposed neutrality-law revision would "free the President to lead us into war," something the President seemed only too willing to do. The freshman Republican senator Robert A. Taft, making himself at once the chief spokesman of his party's conservative majority, pronounced the speech's "logical conclusion" to be "another war with American troops again sent across the ocean."[85] Roosevelt, having intuitively measured these opposing pressures, was confirmed in his fear that his position on this matter was already dangerously advanced and that any bold, forthright move by him toward embargo repeal was likely to be politically disastrous, further splitting the Democrats while simultaneously solidifying and augmenting the strength of his Republican opposition.

He was consequently all too vulnerable to the advice he received in a lengthy memorandum, dated January 11, from the bibulous Nevada silverite, Key Pittman, chairman of the Senate Foreign Relations Committee, which numbered among its members Idaho's Progressive Republican William E. Borah, California's Progressive Republican Hiram Johnson, Wisconsin Progressive Robert La Follette, and Michigan Republican Arthur H. Vandenberg, all stalwart isolationists. Pittman, whose own foreign-policy convictions, insofar as he had any, inclined toward isolationism, advised that the administration present no neutrality bill of its own, and that the President and the State Department maintain strict silence on this matter until the committee had held lengthy public hearings on the numerous neutrality bills being presented to the new Congress. These hearings would fully expose the various views on neutrality and enable a valid assessment of overall public opinion regarding it. Pittman might then "be able to bring about a satisfactory compromise in the Committee," whereas his "position as a compromiser would be weakened" were he to present "bills and resolutions at this time setting forth" his own "present opinions as to the character of the legislation that should be adopted."[86]

This advice was, in effect, a proposal that Roosevelt abdicate presidential leadership on a matter of supreme national importance at a time when a lack of leadership might have fatal consequences for the nation. It was rendered further suspect by Pittman's dismal past record as a congressional agent of administration policy in foreign affairs. Nevertheless, having conferred with the ever cautious Hull, Roosevelt accepted the proposal, though with the understanding that Pittman would begin the hearings within a couple of weeks, as Pittman then publicly announced he would do.[87]

He failed to do so, however. On January 19, he announced an indefinite postponement. His committee's members were too fully occupied with other legislative chores to attend properly to this one, he said. The real, unspoken reason was different. It was that Pittman and his committee colleagues blanched and fled the issue (their vote to postpone was unanimous) when faced by an abrupt intensification of the quarrel between the American left and the Roman Catholic Church over the Spanish war embargo—a quarrel that had raged ever since the issue between Franco and the Loyalists in the Spanish Civil War had become sharply defined in the American public mind.[88]

# 10

*The Coming-on of World War II:*
*Part One*

I

IN April 1938, it will be remembered, Franco's drive to the sea split Loyalist Spain in two—Catalonia (Barcelona) to the north, Valencia to the south. There followed a terrific battle along the Ebro, ending in a stalemate that lasted through the summer into the fall and, as it continued with no end in sight, convinced many that Franco could never prevail and would collapse with the withdrawal from him of even a small portion of his foreign aid. But there was no such withdrawal. Actually, during these weeks and months, Franco was gathering new strength for a final decisive attack (some 40,000 of the best Italian troops continued to serve as "volunteers" under his command, despite Mussolini's promise to withdraw) while the legitimate government's forces, starved for matériel, grew weaker.

In Loyalist Spain there was, during this time, an increasingly desperate need for food—a need that was far less in what was now called Nationalist Spain where, indeed, after the harvest of 1938, there was actually a wheat surplus. News of this need provoked, in the United States, an increasingly loud cry for American relief shipments. The cry was answered by the American Red Cross very softly and cautiously. The organization's new (Roosevelt-appointed) president, Norman H. Davis, was only too aware that the Catholic Church hierarchy, with its peculiarly political definition of Christian charity, would inevitably damn the feedings of starving Loyalists as giving aid and comfort to the godless enemies of pious, devout Francisco Franco. Roosevelt and his administration were similarly cautious for similar reasons. During the summer and fall of 1938, however, a scheme for using government-held surplus commodities to relieve starvation was worked out by the State Department, the Department of Agriculture, and the Red Cross. At a nominal cost, the federal Surplus Commodities Corporation supplied the Red Cross with sufficient wheat (some 250,000 bushels) to make sixty thousand barrels of flour, worth on the current market $250,000. The U.S. Maritime Commission carried the flour to France on its ships free of charge. The American Friends Service Committee accepted the shipments and distributed them to overseas representatives of the American Red Cross, also free of charge. The Red Cross bore only the cost (some $66,000) of milling the wheat, transporting the flour to seaports, and loading and unloading it at dockside. But this was the absolute maximum that the Red Cross budget could bear in this one cause, said the organization's administrators, pointing to other urgent commitments; nor would they, in their fear of a wrathful church, undertake any special campaign for popular contributions to Spanish relief. Yet the terrible fact remained that sixty thousand barrels was but a fraction of what was needed to prevent starvation in Spain during November and December and that the need grew daily and enormously as winter came on.[1]

It was at this point that Roosevelt personally took a hand in the matter. By the spring of 1938 he had become acutely aware that his Spanish policy, which was in fact the British and French policy of lopsided "nonintervention," was doing grievous harm to the cause of democracy in Europe. By December 1938 this unhappy awareness had become streaked with feelings of guilt. Yet he was only slightly more willing to run political risks for the Spaniards whose suffering was augmented by his policy than he was to run them for the Jews who could be rescued by his reinterpretation of immigration-quota law. He went as far as he felt it possible for him to go when, in the second week of that month, he established a fund-raising Committee for Impartial Relief in Spain —a private committee to which he appointed fourteen wealthy and prominent citizens representing a wide range of foreign-policy views. Included on it were Chicago's General Robert E. Wood, president of Sears, Roebuck and Company, whose isolationism was vehement and notorious; Marshall Field III, who strongly favored collective security; Toledo's John D. Biggers; Fort Worth's Amon Carter; and Mrs. Henry Goddard Leach, Roosevelt's and Eleanor's (especially Eleanor's) longtime social friend. To head the committee he chose, evidently upon Norman Davis's advice, a leading New York City Catholic layman named George MacDonald.[2] He addressed to MacDonald on December 19 a letter outlining what needed to be done. An estimated "500,000 bushels, representing about 100,000 barrels of flour per month, will be required for the next six months to meet the minimum needs of the women and children [in Spain] for bread alone," the letter said. The Surplus Commodities Corporation would "make available . . . this quantity . . . to be processed into flour at the same advantageous terms" as before, and the Maritime Commission would transport it to France free of charge, as before. The committee's task was to raise approximately $500,000 to pay the milling and other necessary costs, every dollar of which would "furnish food for relief to the value of some four dollars." Similar letters went to the thirteen other committee members.[3]

Alas, this attempted solution proved no solution at all.

From the moment its creation was announced, the "impartial" committee was furiously attacked as pro-Loyalist by the Catholic press and by individual spokesmen for the church. It was as if the church hierarchy, committed to a Franco victory at whatever human cost, were as convinced as the British Foreign Office is said to have been in mid-November "that Franco could not win unless he were able to starve out the Loyalists"[4] and that food, therefore, was war matériel whose shipment to Spain violated neutrality. Then, two days before Christmas, came the launching of the long-dreaded drive toward Barcelona, a drive that, abundantly supplied with arms and munitions, made swift and steady progress against a valiant but ill-armed opposition. The event sparked a last desperate effort by Loyalist sympathizers in the United States to obtain American arms for the Spanish government. They proclaimed the third week of the new year to be "Lift the Embargo Week"; they poured by the hundred into the capital from all over the country to lobby and demonstrate. Franco's American supporters, or their spokesmen in the Catholic hierarchy, countered with a "Keep the Embargo Week." Both sides engaged in massive letter-writing and telegram-writing campaigns. The Senate Foreign Relations Committee was inundated within a few days by more than 35,000 letters and thousands upon thousands of telegrams (three thousand in one morning)—a "conflicting avalanche . . . from both sides" which, Pittman explained to J. Pierrepont Moffat of the State Department, "convinced individual senators [members of the Foreign Relations Committee] that they were in too hot a spot to sit with ease and that the sooner they could get off it by avoiding the issue, the happier they would be."[5] Inevitably, the Spanish relief committee's work became enmeshed in this controversy, with the Catholic press charging that the relief effort was part and parcel of the embargo-repeal effort. And MacDonald himself (clearly Roosevelt "had chosen the wrong Catholic" to head the committee, remarks Richard P. Traina[6]) was at once persuaded that this was so, that he had been duped into the role of front man for an evil operation. He issued a denial that he bore any personal responsibility for the committee's work, stayed away from his committee chairman's office, made no monetary contribution from his own ample personal resources to the fund the committee struggled to raise, and permitted this last fact to be publicized. Soon thereafter, having destroyed the committee's fund-raising capability, he ostentatiously resigned his post and refused to sanction the appointment of a successor.

From first to last, a mere $50,000, barely a tenth of the low goal the President had set, was raised by this effort to feed starving Spain.[7]

Meanwhile, Franco's forces drove ever closer to Barcelona. Since these forces included 40,000 of the Italians Mussolini had promised to withdraw, the moment seemed remarkably inopportune for a new display of friendship for the Italian dictator by the British prime minister. Nevertheless, Neville Chamberlain chose that moment to act, again, upon his belief that Il Duce might join him in pleas to der Führer not to aggress any more. Having wangled an invitation, he journeyed to Rome, with Halifax, arriving on January 11. He left two days later, disappointed by Mussolini's flat refusal even to talk about Hitler's intentions but heartened by the exuberant welcome he had received from the Italian people and convinced that, overall, his visit had advanced "the cause of peace." Evidently the U.S. ambassador, Phillips, agreed, for he wrote Roosevelt that the meeting was "a good move" resulting in "a pleasanter atmosphere" in Rome. The assessment made by Count Ciano, the Italian foreign minister, was different. He told German foreign minister Ribbentrop by phone, within an hour or so after the meeting had ended, that the whole affair had been "a fiasco, absolutely innocuous." As for Mussolini, he in private talk dismissed Chamberlain and Halifax with contempt. "These men are not made of the same stuff as Francis Drake and the other magnificent adventurers who created the Empire," he said to his son-in-law, Ciano. "They are after all the tired sons of a long line of rich men."[8]

With Barcelona's fall on January 25, followed by the total collapse of the Loyalist army in Catalonia, the last hope for a Loyalist victory was destroyed, and Roosevelt's guilt feelings grew more painful. He had reason for them. He knew himself to be personally responsible for the joint resolution whereby, on the first day of its existence, the 75th Congress imposed without debate (unanimously in the Senate; 406–1 in the House) the Spanish embargo*—which, as he now freely confessed, should never have been imposed. The mistake, he insisted defensively, had been an honest one. He told his Cabinet in late January 1939 that "we [the 'we' implied that his listeners had joined him in the decision-making] acted in perfectly good faith and in the belief that we were working in our own interests." All the same, the embargo had violated historic American principle and international law inasmuch as the Loyalist government was the legitimate, freely elected government of Spain. The policy we should have followed was "to forbid the transportation of munitions of war in American bottoms" while permitting such shipments in vessels of foreign registry. Had this been done, as Ickes wrote into his diary, "Loyalist Spain would still have been able to come to us for what she needed to fight for her life against Franco—to fight for her life and the lives of some of the rest of us, as events will very likely prove."[9]

Nor was this initial mistake all that Roosevelt had, in this matter, to feel guilty about. Last spring, he had been presented with a golden opportunity to correct what by that time he knew to have been a mistake. Pacifistic isolationist Gerald Nye had introduced in the Senate (May 2, 1938) his joint resolution calling upon the President "to raise the embargo against the Government of Spain," with the proviso that all shipments be on a cash-and-carry basis. The resolution made no reference to the insurgents, upon whom, therefore, the embargo would continue to apply. This was precisely what Roosevelt now told his Cabinet should have been done in the first place. Yet he had opposed the resolution, which almost certainly would have been adopted had it had his support. Instead, Roosevelt approved the negative reply Hull made to the request from Pittman, as Foreign Affairs Committee chairman, for administration policy guidance.† Nye had run some political risk in proposing his resolution. He was up for reelection in the fall; he faced a strong opponent in William Langer (who ran as an independent); and he had a large number of German Catholics in his North Dakota constituency. He had run this risk in part from Anglophobia (the administration's Spanish policy had been shaped, he be-

---

*See pp. 15–16, 29, 30–31.
†The circumlocutory language of this missive was perfectly expressive of the fuzzy, timid, dishonest minds it bespoke. Said Hull's letter: "In view of the continued danger of international conflict arising from the circumstances of the [Spanish] struggle, any proposal which at this juncture contemplates a reversal of our policy of strict non-interference which we have thus far scrupulously followed, and under the operation of which we have kept out of involvements, would offer a real possibility of complications."[10]

lieved, in the British Foreign Office) but mostly out of a conviction that the embargo was dishonest and unjust, serving "neither neutrality nor non-intervention."[11] Roosevelt, with the same conviction, had weighed it light against the "political reality" of church opposition—the fact, for instance, that pro-embargo petitions sponsored by the Catholic hierarchy and bearing more than a million signatures were received by Congress in immediate opposition to the Nye resolution. He had heeded also a vehement protest from Catholic and pro-Franco Joe Kennedy, who claimed that lifting the embargo would gravely injure Anglo-American relations.[12]

It was this "political realism" with which her husband answered, in practice, what seemed to her questions of moral right or wrong—it was this that idealistic, passionately pro-Loyalist Eleanor Roosevelt found difficult, even impossible, to forgive. She deemed it cynical, cowardly, dishonest, hence profoundly *un*realistic in that it was bound to have precisely the consequence her husband now deplored. From the outset, she had added what she could to the pressure upon him to do what he privately admitted was the right thing to do; and she did nothing now to ease his pangs of conscience. Her cold anger with him at this time became evident to Leon Henderson when, one evening after Barcelona's fall, he came at her invitation to dine at the White House. Her husband occupied his usual place at the head of the table. She, however, spoke as if he were not there as, turning to her guest, she said, "You and I, Mr. Henderson, will someday learn a lesson from this tragic error over Spain. We were morally right, but too weak. We should have pushed *him* harder." She nodded toward her husband, who made no response. His silence seemed to Henderson an admission that this verbal chastisement was deserved.[13]

II

AND indeed these closing days of January and opening ones of February 1939 might have seemed to Roosevelt days of reckoning during which he was marked by fate for chastisement, deserved or not. Almost simultaneous with Barcelona's fall came a disastrous practical realization of the risk inherent in the devious secrecy with which he had dealt, out of grim necessity, as he felt, with the French warplane-purchasing mission. The risk, of course, was of disclosure—that the veil of secrecy might by circumstance be torn away and the truth exposed, naked, quivering in its vulnerability, to a withering glare of hostility.

Jean Monnet, returning from America to Paris in November 1938, had reported to his superior, Premier Daladier, that France might obtain delivery of as many as a thousand American-made warplanes of the latest design by the end of July 1939 if orders for them were placed within the next few weeks. Daladier had authorized this purchase, provided that the planes met French air-force specifications and that firm delivery dates were assured. Monnet then returned to the United States, accompanied by three aviation experts. With his friend Ambassador Bullitt, he at once (December 16, 1938) called upon Morgenthau, who, it will be recalled, had been assigned administrative authority over aircraft purchases by the U.S. Army and Navy and upon whom devolved, therefore, a corresponding authority over any sale of U.S. planes to foreign powers. Morgenthau thereupon asked for and received from the White House specific formal permission to facilitate the Monnet mission, the order to this effect being signed by the President on December 21, 1938, with the stipulation that "for reasons of state . . . [it] be kept as confidential as possible." Morgenthau told Monnet the next day that the President was "anxious" to give the French "every opportunity . . . to purchase these planes in such volume as to meet their needs, providing their arrangements can be completed and orders given and deliveries made with sufficient promptness so as not to interfere with U.S. army orders for the same type of planes." Also stressed by Morgenthau and agreed to by Monnet was the need for "absolute secrecy."[14]

Soon thereafter, Monnet's aviation experts evinced their desire to inspect a newly designed, Douglas-manufactured, twin-engined light bomber, the DB-7, destined for some fame a few years later as the American army's A-20 (the "Boston," as it was called). Woodring, at the instigation of U.S. Army Air Corps officers, refused to permit this French inspection, saying the plane had been produced to meet air-corps specifications, had been partially funded with government money, and was "loaded" with technical military secrets. But was the air corps definitely committed to the purchase of this plane? Woodring had to admit that it was not—that the army had not accepted it and no purchase order could be placed until weeks or months had passed. Clearly, then, a French order now would not delay delivery of the plane to the air corps later but, on the contrary, would speed this by ensuring the necessary expansion, now, of Douglas's plane-manufacturing capacity. All the same, at a White House meeting (January 16, 1939), of Morgenthau, Woodring, Louis Johnson, and Ambassador Bullitt, the President as Commander in Chief had flatly to order the plane's release for French inspection before the necessary instructions were wired by General Arnold to military authorities at Los Angeles.[15]

Four days later, two of Monnet's aviation experts were shown the Douglas bomber. Both were colonels in the French air force but both came dressed in civilian clothes and were careful to speak only English. One of the two, Colonel Paul Chemidlin, was a test pilot. He was riding in the plane when Douglas's test pilot, overreacting to Chemidlin's expressed doubts about the plane's maneuverability, began to put it through a series of dangerously low-level acrobatics. Suddenly, from a height of only four hundred feet, the plane spun out of control and crashed in a parking lot, demolishing nine automobiles and injuring ten bystanders. The Douglas pilot, attempting to parachute, was killed. Colonel Chemidlin, badly hurt, was pulled from the wreckage just before it burst into flames. His fellow colonel forgot, in the intense excitement of the moment, that he was to speak only English, and burst into voluble French.

The secret was out.[16]

It created a sensation, of course.

Army air corps commander General Arnold was at that time testifying before the Senate Military Affairs Committee, in secret session, regarding the air corps's needs for the coming fiscal year. Several of the most fervent congressional isolationists sat upon this committee, among them Gerald Nye and Missouri's Bennett Champ Clark. It was the latter who digressed from the subject at hand, on January 26, to ask Arnold pointedly how it happened that a representative of the French Air Ministry was in the "secret" bomber that had crashed. Arnold, notably lacking in political sophistication, replied that the Frenchman "was out there under the direction of the Treasury Department with a view of looking into possible purchase of airplanes by the French mission." The actual formal authorization of this, he quickly added, had come from the War Department, and all secret equipment had been removed from the plane before it was shown. Clark was outraged. Was the secretary of the Treasury now "running" the air corps? he wanted to know. When Arnold floundered in his attempt to answer, Clark proposed to summon both Morgenthau and Woodring before the committee at once to explain this mysterious, highly suspicious business.[17]

On the following morning, both *The Washington Post* and the New York *Herald Tribune* gave a garbled account of what "a witness" had told the Military Affairs Committee in "secret" session, namely, that "permission to ride in a new, test plane which embodied military and technical secrets, had not been obtained from any officer of the Army or from the War Department, but from the Treasury."[18] A few hours later, in his press conference, Roosevelt was asked if "this Government [had] taken any steps to assist or facilitate France in buying planes in this country." He replied, mendaciously, "As you put the question, no." The French, for obvious reasons, "wanted to buy planes over here," he went on, and their doing so would serve America's defense needs. At the present moment, most of the plane-manufacturing plants in this country were idle. "One of the largest engine companies just the other day laid off 1500 men." French orders would "start the . . . plants going, especially if those orders come in very quickly so that they will be completed before our larger program can be authorized and actually get under way. The French Government did want [to order] planes and we told them . . . it would be an excellent idea for them to do so." As for the plane that had crashed, it "had not been accepted by the United States Government" and might never be. "It was purely a manufacturer's plane . . . flown at the time at a public municipal airport by the company." But why was the Treasury Department involved in all this? the reporters wanted to know. The President replied that Treasury was of course "interested in building up" the foreign trade of the United States and that "in the procurement of planes and a great many other things, the Procurement Division of the Treasury works in very close cooperation with the Army procurement system and the Navy procurement system."[19]

On that same day the same questions were asked of Morgenthau and Woodring as they testified before the Senate Military Affairs Committee. Clark demanded to know from Morgenthau what the Treasury Department had to do with showing a French aviation expert "a plane supposed to embody the very latest development . . . for American national defense." Morgenthau replied with a detailed if selective history of the matter, stressing that the plane-inspection order had gone from the secretary of war through General Arnold to Los Angeles and that the plane was the sole property of the Douglas Company, had not yet been entered into competition for army orders (Clark objected that the company was about to do so, according to Arnold's testimony) and could hardly be called "secret" since it was flown from a municipal airport where anyone could see it ("It was secret enough," objected Clark). Woodring, under grueling questioning by both Clark and Nye, was forced to admit that, though he had acted in this procurement matter under instruction from the Treasury secretary, the latter had acted under instruction from the President. Had the army been opposed to this cooperation with the French? asked Nye, who by then knew it had been. Woodring perforce admitted that the army air corps had been originally opposed but that "everyone [was] . . . in accord before the French went to the West Coast." The crucial question then became whether the French plane order could actually be filled by July 1, 1939, so as not to interfere with the satisfaction of U.S. Army needs, Arnold having testified the day before that the air-force program, if it got under way at midyear, as expected, would require all the planes American manufacturers could produce for the next two years. Woodring was compelled to admit that, in his opinion, the French order could *not* be filled within the specified time, and that he had said so to Morgenthau.[20]

All this was fuel for a raging fire of controversy.

*Now* America knew what the President meant by "methods short of war"! He meant secret conniving methods of entangling the United States in sick Europe's broils in ways that would make our ultimate involvement in war inevitable—methods that, insofar as they revealed military secrets to a foreign power, came dangerously near being, if they were not actually, treasonable! So cried isolationist legislators, editorialists, columnists, radio commentators, public speakers.

The personal attacks, as always in such cases, hardened Roosevelt's will. He demonstrated once again that the hesitation, the extreme caution that characterized his decision-making in politically risky situations was due to no lack of personal courage. Once a decision was made it was firmly made (though the decision itself was often ambiguous) and he persisted in it under the heaviest hostile fire, retreating only when doing so was absolutely necessary for political survival. His Dutch was now definitely up. At his next meeting with his Cabinet he let its members know that the furor had effected no change in his plane-selling policy, and would not. He told Morgenthau "to proceed as before" with the French, letting them "buy what they want."[21]

But he did at once attempt to damp down the fire that raged in Congress, running a new calculated risk, a serious one, as he did so. He summoned to the White House on Tuesday, January 31, the entire Senate Military Affairs

Committee for an "extra confidential" conference of which the substance was a remarkably full and frank exposition by him of his thinking about foreign affairs.

This thinking, and the form in which he presented it to the senators, was influenced by a conversation he had had in the White House, three weeks before, with Britain's Lord Lothian, who was being groomed to replace Sir Ronald Lindsay as British ambassador to the United States (Lindsay had long made known to the Foreign Office his wish to retire from his post in early 1939). Lothian had painted for the President a dark picture of the world the United States must live in if the British empire collapsed, and had indicated that collapse, in the absence of strong American support, was a distinct possibility. Without the "very powerful outpost line" of British military and naval defenses, the United States would be hard put to maintain her democracy, her commitment to the principles of liberty and justice, against the powerful totalitarian forces which would then press upon her. Therefore, since Britain was no longer the democratic world's center of gravity, this having been shifted by world events to America, the United States must now assume obligations and responsibilities formerly borne by the empire.[22]

Such talk had not gone down well with Roosevelt. His negative reaction to it would be reinforced a little later by a letter from the English historian G. M. Trevelyan to Harvard historian Roger B. Merriman, who sent an extended excerpt from it to the President on February 10. Trevelyan defended Chamberlain's appeasement policy, saying it was dictated by necessity, but concluded that Britain, if forced into a war to defend Western civilization, would make "a jolly good fight" of it. "I wish the British would stop this 'we who are about to die, salute thee' attitude," Roosevelt would write Merriman on February 15.

> Lord Lothian was here the other day, started the conversation by saying he had completely abandoned his former belief that Hitler could be dealt with as a semi-reasonable human being, and went on to say that the British had been for a thousand years the guardians of Anglo-Saxon civilization—that the scepter or the sword or something like that had been dropped from their palsied fingers—that the U.S.A. must snatch it up —that F.D.R. alone could save the world, etc., etc. I got mad clear through and told him that just so long as he or Britishers like him took that attitude of complete despair, the British would not be worth saving anyway. What the British need today is a good stiff grog, inducing not only the desire to save civilization but the continued belief that they can do it. In such an event they will get a lot more support from their American cousins. . . .

This letter, passed on by Merriman to Trevelyan, who in turn sent it to Foreign Secretary Halifax, came close to costing Lothian his ambassadorial appointment. Not until Lindsay had assured the Foreign Office that Roosevelt was a remarkably even-tempered man who tended in later recall "to exaggerate what is said to him and what he says in reply"—not until Roosevelt himself had assured Lindsay he would welcome Lothian as Lindsay's successor—not until then would this historically important appointment be made, in April 1939.[23]

But for all his deploring of Lothian's attitude, Roosevelt had been immediately impressed by the main outline of Lothian's argument. He had been even more impressed when, shortly after the Lothian interview, he read the document (Kennedy had sent it to him from London) whereby this argument was originally shaped—a nine-page memorandum that Sir Maurice Hankey* had prepared for Lothian's guidance. And it was somewhat upon the Hankey argument that he modeled his own as, on the last day of January, he addressed the senators seated before him.

"I do not belong to the school of thought that says we can draw a line of defense around this country and live completely and solely to ourselves," he began.[24] "I always think of what happened in another Administration." In 1807, responding to the quarrel between Britain and Napoleon's France during which each forcibly forbade American commerce with the other, Congress (at Jefferson's instigation, though Roosevelt didn't say so) passed embargo legislation prohibiting virtually all U.S. overseas commerce. "Of course the damned thing didn't work. In the first place, it was practically unenforceable and, in the second place, the country began to strangle. . . . The net result was that . . . we got into the War of 1812. . . ." He interrupted his discourse at this point to stress the importance of keeping "confidential" what he was about to say. Confidentiality was necessary because "we . . . don't . . . want to frighten the American people . . . at this time or any time. We want them to gradually realize what is a potential danger. . . ." But the danger was not in fact merely potential; it was actual and immediate. The United States faced a "definite" threat of world domination by Germany, Italy, and Japan—a threat that had begun "with the first anti-Comintern Pact" three years ago and had increased as that pact "was strengthened almost every month" into what amounted "to an offensive and defensive alliance." Faced by such threat, what should the United States do? One answer, of course, was to attempt another retreat into complete isolation, as in Jefferson's time, and hope that revolts and assassinations would soon eliminate Hitler, Mussolini, and the militaristic regime of Japan. But such isolationism was even less likely to work today than it had been then, for the nations of the world (though Roosevelt did not specifically say so) were much more interdependent economically now. Nor was there any solid basis for believing that the totalitarian regimes would collapse in the foreseeable future; at the moment, they marched from triumph to triumph. The other and sensible answer was to attempt to prevent "by peaceful means" the domination of the world. How? By clearly recognizing and strengthening as much as possible America's "first line of defense," against Japan in the Pacific, against the Nazi-Fascists in the Atlantic.

Where and what, then, was this "first line of defense"?

---

*It may be remembered that Hankey was the man described by Britain's Tom Jones, in conversation with Louis Brownlow, as the perfect type for the American President's secretariat: "a man of high competence, great physical vigor, and a passion for anonymity." See p. 25.

In the Pacific, of which Roosevelt said little that day, it consisted of "a series of islands, with the hope that through the Navy and the Army and the airplanes we can keep the Japanese . . . from dominating" the entire ocean and denying us "access to the west coast of South America." In the Atlantic, of which Roosevelt said much that day, it consisted of "the continued independent existence" of some eighteen European nations, large and small, four of them countries whose independence was already seriously compromised if not practically destroyed by Hitlerian aggression. (Could Czechoslovakia and Hungary be truly called independent? Rumania? "It is scared pink." Poland? "Poland I call a 'mugwump' nation because so far it has sat successfully on a fence with its mug on one side and its wump on the other, hoping and praying that [it] . . . won't be attacked by either Russia or Germany.") The other fourteen, including Finland, the Scandinavian countries, Holland, Belgium, Yugoslavia, Greece, and, most important, France and Britain, were as yet truly independent states. None of them would be, however, if France and England went down. They would "drop into the basket of their own accord" because "it [would be] . . . silly for them to resist." Africa would "automatically" fall "because Africa is ninety-five percent colonial." Then would come the turn of Central and South America, as "Brother Hitler suggested in [his] speech yesterday."* A Hitler dominant over Europe could make Argentina subservient to him by refusing to buy its wheat and meat unless it not only accepted payment in whatever goods he specified but also permitted German domination of its military. In Brazil the Nazis already had, according to secret information obtained by the administration, "an organization [of the 250,000 Germans living there] which . . . even today [could constitute] a very serious threat to the Brazilian Government." Colombia, next door to the Panama Canal, and Venezuela, only two and a half hours by air from Miami, could then easily fall under German domination. In Central America there was not a country wherein a "revolution" could not be bought by a foreign power "for between a million and four million dollars." As for Mexico, "you know the situation" there.

In sum, the United States would be closely encircled by immensely strong hostile powers within a very few years (had not Nazi Germany been transformed in just six years from one of the weakest powers to the very strongest in Europe?) if it failed to do all it could to build up, now, its "first line of defense." Hence the administration's policy of helping "any government which we know, on the doctrine of chances, will never be an enemy of ours . . . to rearm against . . . the dictators of this world." Hence, specifically, the decision to sell to the French right now all the airplanes of latest design they wished to buy, so long as they paid "cash on the barrel head" and their orders could

---

*Hitler's speech to the Reichstag on January 30, 1939, the sixth anniversary of his rise to power, was also notable as the first definite public hint of his "Final Solution" of the Jewish "problem." If "the international Jewish financiers in and outside Europe" succeeded "in plunging the nations once more into a world war," he shouted, the result would be "the annihilation of the Jewish race in Europe."

be filled without delaying the buildup of America's own air forces. "I am frankly hoping that the French will . . . get the fastest pursuit planes we can turn out. . . . I hope they will get the best heavy and medium bombers they can buy in this country." Similarly with the British, whose purchasing mission was, he thought, buying three or four hundred planes.

One beneficent and crucially important effect of this would be to "test out" within the next few months the ability of American private manufacturers to mass-produce airplanes. Such a test would enable an informed decision on whether government plants were needed for our defense effort. Germany had right now an immense plane-producing capacity. "We think [they] . . . have enough mass production factories to turn out forty thousand planes a year on a three-shift basis," though the figure might be "only" thirty thousand. (Lindbergh's inflated estimate, one is glad to note, was not having its intended effect.) What was the current U.S. capacity? "At the present time we *think* our . . . airplane factories," if put on a mass-production basis, might "turn out nine or ten thousand planes a year. None of them has ever been in mass production, so we do not know."

He closed his discourse, grim-faced, on a somber note.

"I cannot overemphasize the seriousness of this situation," he said.

III

As a virtuoso performance, this exposition was reminiscent of the case for executive reorganization that Roosevelt had presented, a little over two years ago,* to congressional leaders predisposed to oppose him in this. It had, however, no such immediately overwhelming impact upon his listeners as that earlier exposition had had. They did not now, as then, leave his presence, at meeting's end, in a helpless daze, convinced either that his policy was correct or that they could not successfully resist his will. This was partly because his present argument, assuming the inevitability of an unlimited "domino effect" upon nation-states, as if these last were inert objects rather than organizations of living people who might make choices different from those he predicted— this argument was less persuasive per se than that he had made for executive reorganization. But the lack of overwhelming impact was also due, and much more, to the fact that the aura of invincibility that had surrounded him two years ago was now wholly dissipated.

---

*The two very different expositions had a basic similarity in that both were concerned, essentially, with the same fundamental question of government—namely, the question of the proper relationship, for democratic purposes, between freedom and organization. Scientific technology rendered increasingly obsolete one after another of the existing social and economic arrangements—those of "private" business enterprise, those of national sovereignty—as it relentlessly advanced toward either world government or world destruction. Could Organization be so shaped and used, in these circumstances, as to preserve and enhance Freedom? If so, "freedom" must evidently be institutionally redefined in ways that made Man, not Machine, the author of Organization. (See pp. 22–23.) Executive reorganization had to do with the national governmental side of this fundamental question; collective security had to do with the international side.

He was sharply questioned when the meeting was opened for discussion. Isolationist Robert Reynolds of North Carolina, whose conservative principles were outraged by the "red" Mexican government's expropriation of American-owned oil properties, promptly challenged Roosevelt's statement that the Mexican "situation" was known to all. Hitler was said to be obtaining, through barter arrangement with Mexico, some $17 million worth of the expropriated oil. Reynolds had recently introduced in the Senate a resolution calling for an investigation of the matter, and he sought now to force from Roosevelt an admission that such an investigation was needed to "ascertain facts" that might be inimical to our national security. Roosevelt's answer was brusque. Suppose the discovered facts were as Reynolds suspected, "what the hell are you going to do about it?" If we retaliated by further reducing our already slender purchases of Mexican silver, and by discouraging tourism in Mexico, the Mexican government would simply sell their silver to somebody else, if at a lower price, and sell more oil to Germany to make up whatever was lost through the U.S. action. Economic necessity would compel them to do so. (He did not mention the gravely wounding effect such U.S. action would have upon hemispheric solidarity.) "Every country in the world has the right to expropriate property. Our point of view is that if a government . . . takes property, it has got to pay . . . a reasonable sum for it. Mexico has agreed to pay a reasonable sum for it. Today the situation is solely a question of getting them to pay." Negotiations toward that end were under way. They were bound to take time, given the Latin American temperament and the disposition of American oil corporations to ask exorbitant prices—prices that included potential profits. Nevertheless, progress was being made, and the Senate investigation which Reynolds proposed could only slow it.

Sharper still, penetrating indeed to the very heart of the matter, was the question asked by isolationist J. Hamilton Lewis of Illinois. "There is a little matter I would like to clear up," he said, with evident sarcasm. Did the President "intend to leave the impression" that the United States had the "duty" to "maintain the independence of these nations you described . . . by whatever efforts may be necessary?" "No. No!" replied an immediately alarmed Roosevelt: "Listen: I probably saw more of the war in Europe than any other living person." He attempted to justify this amazing assertion by telling of his 1918 three-month official tour, as assistant navy secretary, of the Azores, Great Britain, Ireland, and the Continent. "I covered the whole coast of France. . . . I spent days on the Belgian front, on the British front, on the French front, and on the American front. I was an observer in the push up the Veale. I saw the operations in Italy. Therefore, you may be quite sure [of my personal conviction] that about the last thing that this country should do is ever to send an army to Europe again." It was a too-hurried, overly agitated reply. It did nothing to restore his diminished credibility with the isolationists before him. He would have done far better to answer Lewis with a forthright yes, thus affirming what his listeners would in any case continue to believe true since it was the only logical conclusion from his presentation. He could then

have gone on to argue with persuasive consistency, not only before the committee but also (later) before the general public, in a fireside chat, that the strengthening of our "first line of defense," *now,* was our best if not only chance to
prevent a world war in which our involvement, one way or another, was
inevitable. His answer of "no" not only contradicted his argument but was also
cowardly. For if the independent existence of Britain, France, and sixteen
other European states truly constituted America's first line of defense, and if
the collapse of that line meant that we would almost certainly have to fight
for our national survival against great odds, becoming ourselves a totalitarian
state in the process, then surely we must maintain that first line by whatever
means were required, including, as a last resort, armed force. Were we so
lacking in courage, in self-respect, in commitment to "the tenets of [our] faith,"
that we were unable to defend ourselves against unmitigated evil? Must we rely
on others to fight for our lives?

The isolationist senators left Roosevelt that day (Nye, Clark, and Reynolds
walked out together) shaking their heads in disbelief and disagreement with
him. One of them, Nye, questioned by newsmen outside the White House,
deplored the "extra confidentiality" with which the meeting had been invested.
"To be confined by secrecy when there is so much to be said is distressing,"
he said. In an eleven-page memorandum to himself, written immediately thereafter, he stated a conclusion shared by others: first, that the President had
called this secret session primarily to prevent public disclosure of embarrassing
correspondence regarding the French mission; and second, that the President
was "determined to utterly ignore the neutrality law" in order to give "aid [to]
the so-called democracies" in a coming European war. ("Get the uniforms
ready for the boys" was his bitter last sentence.) Next day, on the Senate floor,
he strongly protested the secrecy that had been imposed upon "a matter which
quite properly might have been wide open to the press and to the public." He
himself would attend no more executive sessions of the Military Affairs Committee, he said, "until . . . a reasonable part of the record, devoid of any military
secrets . . . , shall be available to the public." He would not again be placed
in "a position that is intolerable" and contrary to "what ought to be practice
under a democratic representative form of government."[25]

But by the time Nye spoke, the particular secrecy he deplored had been
effectively dispelled. *The New York Times* on that morning of Thursday,
February 2, reported under big front-page headlines that the Military Affairs
Committee had been told by the President, according to an unidentified senator, that they should "regard France as the actual frontier of America in an
apparently inevitable showdown between democracies and dictatorships."[26]
Other press reports on the same day were that Roosevelt had proclaimed
"America's frontier" to be "on the Rhine." This created a sensation greater
than the original exposure of the French purchasing mission had made.

The immediate effect abroad, on both friend and foe, was, as Ambassador
Cudahy would soon write from Dublin, "a good one." The British and French
were heartened, while "the violent outpourings from Italy and the vitriolic

abuse of the German press indicate how much Mussolini and Hitler have been disconcerted and how deeply has registered the spectacle of a French-British front with the support of the United States in the background." Thomas W. Lamont of J. P. Morgan and Company phoned Roosevelt from New York to tell him of the grateful enthusiasm with which the City of London at once reacted to the report of what he had said; Britain's financial community was convinced "that your attitude has constituted a real deterrent to the dictators." A few days later, Lamont sent on to Roosevelt an excerpt from a letter just received from the poet laureate of England, John Masefield, a "great friend" of the Lamonts. "I do not suppose you will ever realize what a profound sensation President Roosevelt's words to the Senators have made throughout Europe. . . ," Masefield wrote. "Just as we expected war at any moment, or if not war, a crisis . . . leading to the brink of war, he has said things which have perhaps altered history. The effect here has been so great that I marvel they have not rung the church bells over it. . . . The prestige of America has never stood so high. . . . You [Americans] have a chance now [through solidarity with the European democracies] to remake the world order; the best chance that the world has ever had of getting a decency to live in, and a Humanity to work for."[27]

Nor did the general populace in the United States react negatively to what was presumed to be Roosevelt's European policy. On the contrary, to judge from the results of two Gallup polls taken during the furor, most Americans accepted as valid the major premises of his policy argument and were therefore prepared to accept his policy conclusions if these were fairly and fully presented to them. The first of the two polls showed 65 percent of the poll sample favoring the sale of airplanes to France and Britain while 44 percent favored legislation prohibiting such sales to Germany.[28] In the second poll, voters were asked: "If Germany and Italy go to war against England and France, do you think we should do everything possible to help England and France, except go to war ourselves?" Sixty-nine percent answered yes; 31 percent answered no. Only 6 percent said they had no opinion on the matter. Gallup also asked those surveyed: "If Germany and Italy defeated England and France in a war, do you think Germany and Italy would then start a war against the United States?" Yes, answered 62 percent. No, answered 38 percent.[29]

But Roosevelt did not wait for such returns as these before reacting to the furor himself.

He might well have done so—might well have felt constrained to silence for a few days, at least, in order to measure the real, as distinct from the immediately apparent, overall effect of what was, after all, an essentially truthful report of his personal belief and policy. He might have concluded, as he waited, that the chief source of his current trouble was the devious secrecy he had theretofore practiced and that, therefore, he should from now on be more open, frank, straightforward, more willing to trust other people and take them into his confidence, as he dealt with problems of national defense and foreign affairs. He at once arrived, instead, at a precisely opposite conclusion—that his troubles, born of plain bad luck, were greatly augmented by his pressured departure from the tactics he had previously followed. He had been too frank with the senators, too open, too trusting, and now paid the cost of a mistake he would not make again. Domestic politics was his primary concern and, in the looming shadow of the 1940 elections, he must play his defense and foreign-policy cards even closer to his chest than before.

He promptly acted upon this conclusion.

Angrily, publicly, he denied that he had said to the senators anything like what he had been quoted as saying. At his press conference on February 3, having refused to say whether or not Germany and Italy could obtain U.S. planes on the same cash-on-the-barrelhead terms as applied to France (he had told the committee members he would "do everything I possibly can . . . to prevent any munitions from going to Germany or Italy or Japan"), he branded the "frontier on the Rhine" statement a "deliberate lie" and gave the reporters permission to quote him. "Some boob got that off," he added. When it was suggested that the "Rhine frontier" statement, if not made by him in precisely that form, might as a "catch phrase" accurately sum up what he had said, he emphatically denied it. He also termed "100 percent bunk" the charge that, out of a fear of adverse public opinion, he had imposed secrecy upon matters that should be openly discussed. The "only element of secrecy" that had been imposed was upon "one or two pieces of—you could not even call it information—matters which have been reported to us, which we have reason to believe are true" but which were far from certainly so, matters which, if revealed by the White House, would needlessly alarm the public. Asked if he intended "a statement or speech or fireside chat in the near future" to clear up a growing public "confusion" about evidently changing U.S. foreign policy, he flatly denied that there had been any change. We as a nation opposed "entangling alliances," favored worldwide free trade, were "in complete sympathy with any and every effort . . . to reduce armaments," and were "sympathetic with the peaceful maintenance of political, economic and social independence of all nations in the world." That was our foreign policy "and it is not going to change."[30]

Roosevelt's "usual charm" (so Nye disgustedly called it in his memo to himself) and force of personality evidently won the immediate personal sympathy of most of the newsmen at this press conference, but their reports of what he said did nothing for his credibility among those who read them with critical eyes and well-informed minds. These suspected what Military Affairs Committee members knew to be a fact: that the President, feeling forced to back down, told lies as he did so. The same conclusion was drawn overseas by those who were well informed about the general situation and were logically realistic rather than blindly wishful in their thinking. Neville Chamberlain must be counted among the latter. He deemed Roosevelt's "frontier" statement an "ingenious" response to a British plea, made some two weeks before, for a White House gesture toward solidarity with the British and French—a gesture that might help to deter Hitler, who was believed at that moment to be contemplating a descent upon Holland. The prime minister persisted in this notion despite Roosevelt's clear indication that it was untrue. His belief contributed in a minor way to the euphoric optimism that, incredibly, was his from early February until the Ides of March. ("I . . . am going about with a lighter heart than I have had for many a long day," he wrote to his sister, Hilda, on February 19, 1939. "All the information I get seems to point in the direction of peace and . . . I believe we have at last got on top of the dictators."[31]) The realistic Prime Minister Eamon De Valera of Ireland took a very different view. He was sure, and told Cudahy, that Roosevelt's "disavowal" of what he was reported to have said gave Hitler and Mussolini "reason to believe . . . that American public opinion will not tolerate any other than an attitude of the most rigid neutrality."[32] They would therefore, as they prepared new aggressions, derive more encouragement than discouragement from the episode as a whole. Roosevelt's enmity they had long recognized. It was now exposed to them as weak and wavering, so stymied by domestic political opposition that it could be contemptuously ignored.

Nor did the press conference "disavowal" halt, or even greatly quiet, the domestic furor. This continued loud for a long time. At the instigation of its isolationist members, the Senate Military Affairs Committee continued the investigation of the bomber crash in secret sessions for another fortnight, at the end of which it released testimony proving absolutely that Roosevelt had acted "against the judgment and over the protests of the war department" when he authorized the Douglas attack bomber's "demonstration to the French air mission. . . ."[33] During the weeks that followed, Roosevelt was under almost continuous attack from isolationist spokesmen for pursuing secretly a foreign policy of his own that, in its "unneutrality," differed greatly from the one he publicly avowed, and even more from the one Congress, with his signature of approval, had legislated.

## IV

THREE of the unhappy consequences of this unhappy episode deserve special mention.

One was a prolongation of the defense-threatening internecine War Department quarrel. In the eyes of fervent isolationists, Harry Woodring emerged a hero from the plane-crash furor, a stubborn defender of American arms against those who would give them away, and one of the very few in the whole of the administration who insisted upon operating in accord with the spirit as well as the letter of the neutrality law. By removing him from office at this juncture, Roosevelt would not only have increased the wrath focused on him by isolationist politicians but also have spread further fear among the general public that he was determined to get America into war. With 1940 in the offing, he dared not do it. So Woodring stayed on, and Louis Johnson stayed on, and the bitter war between the two went on. It enormously complicated Morgenthau's facilitation of plane purchases by France. On the very day (January 31) of the risky presidential meeting with the Senate Military Affairs Committee, a strained and irritable Roosevelt, in a long conversation with Morgenthau, angrily chided the latter for presenting to the Cabinet at its last meeting the draft of the executive order that Treasury had prepared, and Roosevelt had signed, placing all military purchasing under Treasury's procurement division. "That was too much of a shock to Woodring" and needlessly provoked "a terrible row," Roosevelt charged. Morgenthau replied "that Louis Johnson [had known from the first] . . . all about what we were doing . . . but . . . withheld the information from Woodring. It seems to me that most of the difficulty I have met with is on account of the constant clash between Woodring and Johnson." This further annoyed Roosevelt. "You know I have plans to clear up that situation," he said testily. But when were these plans to become effective? Morgenthau wanted to know. "Mr. President," he said with some heat, "you can take six months or a year to clean up some other situations . . . but in the case of the war department . . . [in view of the dangerous international situation] it is a matter of days to get the thing in order."[34] He pleaded in vain. The days passed—they would add up to weeks, the weeks to months, and the months, incredibly, to a year and a half—with no presidential action on the War Department mess. Thanks to this mess, General Marshall, directing army rearmament, reorganization, and expansion from the staff chief's post, would often be harassed to the very limit of his endurance. Thanks to it, and to chaotic conditions in America's plane-manufacturing plants as they advanced toward mass production, barely half of France's total order of airframes (planes without engines) and only a third of her order for engines would be delivered by 1939's Labor Day. (However, all the ordered Douglas bombers would be delivered by then, as would most of the basic trainers and half the dive-bombers ordered.) It was largely due to Morgenthau's "firmness of attitude," as Jean Monnet called it, sustained by Roosevelt's firmness of purpose but hampered by Roosevelt's fluctuations of mood and tactic, that the French purchase mission succeeded to the extent that it did.[35]

A second effect of the furor, akin to the first, was a tightening of Joseph P. Kennedy's theretofore loosening grip upon the post he held. For months there had been rumors in Washington among wishful-thinking liberals that the President was so displeased with his isolationist, appeasement-minded ambassador to the Court of St. James's that he was on the point of recalling him. Jim Farley, no liberal, was of the same opinion. When it was announced at the end of November 1938 that Kennedy was returning to America for Christmas and a lengthy vacation, Farley told Morgenthau (who already knew) that Roosevelt was "terribly peeved with Joe," adding that Kennedy's return "probably" meant "the beginning of the end."[36] And indeed there is every reason to believe that Roosevelt's meeting with "Joe" in the White House immediately after the latter's landing in New York was notably lacking in warm cordiality. Roosevelt continued angry over Kennedy's attempts to commit the administration irrevocably to Chamberlain's policies, and over Kennedy's "grandstanding" with regard to the Jewish refugee problem.

Kennedy's spirit was bruised by press criticism of him emanating from people close enough to the President to speak the presidential mind, and by the fact that he was continually bypassed by the White House and State Department on matters clearly within his ambassadorial jurisdiction, particularly the upcoming visit to the United States of their Majesties King George VI and Queen Elizabeth. Following the meeting, Kennedy went with his son Jack* to his winter home in Palm Beach where he booked passage for England on February 23 and settled in for a prolonged holiday broken only by a brief visit to Washington, in mid-January, to testify (with Bullitt) in favor of rearmament at a joint executive session of the House and Senate Military Affairs committees. He did not cease, however, to make newspaper headlines, and these were not of a kind conducive of Roosevelt's goodwill. The Kennedy's Palm Beach home became, in the words of a Boston *Herald* correspondent, "a virtual publicity bureau" designed to serve, as this reporter surmised, the ambassador's 1940 presidential aspirations. (Press and radio commentators Walter Winchell and Boake Carter, the latter a notably bitter and mendacious right-wing critic of Roosevelt, were among his houseguests.) Almost certainly, Roosevelt wished at that time to remove Kennedy from his sensitive post, and sought politically safe ways and means of doing so.[37] He found none. And when the furor over the French plane mission broke out he felt compelled to abandon the idea altogether. Kennedy, who had a considerable following among Catholics and businessmen, would not peaceably accept public humiliation. A "red-headed Irishman," abnormally sensitive to personal slights and belligerently competitive, he would launch an attack upon administration policies, foreign and domestic, which could disastrously split the Democratic party between conservatives and liberals and assure a conservative presidential victory (Kennedy's, possibly?) in 1940. Roosevelt heeded, therefore, strong hints from the Chamberlain government in late January that Kennedy's early return to London would be welcomed. He phoned Kennedy in Palm Beach during the first week of February to suggest, charmingly, flatteringly, that Kennedy cut short his holiday and return at once to London. Kennedy remained no less susceptible to Roosevelt's personal appeal than most people were; he also had no wish to risk an open break with the President at that time. He acted promptly on the suggestion. When the *Queen Mary* sailed for England on February 9, he was aboard.[38] He would remain ambassador to the Court of St. James's for nearly two more years.

A third effect of the plane-crash furor, and the most grievously unhappy of the three, was a prolongation of Roosevelt's abdication of presidential leadership toward neutrality-law repeal or revision, which meant a prolongation of the handling of this crucially important matter on behalf of the administration by the unreliable and essentially isolationist Key Pittman.

---

*John F. Kennedy and his elder brother, Joseph P. Kennedy, Jr., who was destined to die a hero as a navy pilot in World War II, had at their father's request taken leaves of absence from Harvard, where they were students, to serve on the ambassador's personal staff.

On February 13, Utah's Elbert D. Thomas introduced in the Senate a resolution that would grant the President authority to forbid the export to belligerent nations of *all* supplies and raw materials (oil and so on) as well as arms, but would also give him the authority, with congressional approval, to lift the embargo against nations that were the victims of aggression. This, of course, was the authority Roosevelt wanted. He knew that this so-called Thomas amendment had influential, organized support—had in fact been drafted by a Committee for Concerted Peace Efforts, on which were representatives of fifteen national organizations, including the League of Nations Association (of which Roosevelt had once been a member), the General Federation of Women's Clubs, the American Association of University Women, and the American Youth Congress.[39] He was impressed by a *New York Times* editorial on February 15 saying that the resolution, if adopted, would "abandon, in clear-cut cases, that indifference to the moral issue of aggression which is implicit in the present law and is in reality a counsel of cowardice and a bankruptcy of American idealism." He was yet more impressed, three weeks later, by a letter to the *Times* from Henry L. Stimson, wherein this former secretary of state strongly if indirectly supported the Thomas amendment, saying he was "unalterably opposed to the doctrine preached in many quarters that our Government and our people must treat the nations of both sides of this great issue [democracy versus dictatorship] with perfect impartiality; that, for example, we must sell to a nation that has violated its treaties with us . . . the very instruments with which to continue its wrongdoing as freely as we sell to its victim the instruments for its self-defense."[40] But the furious reaction to his "confidential" explanation of his foreign policy, and his consequent public denial of that policy, caused Roosevelt to fear that his expressed approval of the Thomas amendment might hinder rather than help its passage while further diminishing the political capital with which he faced onrushing 1940. He therefore maintained total public silence on the matter in the weeks immediately following the amendment's introduction—a silence perceived by the general public, alas, as a negative attitude on his part toward the measure.

He maintained, in fact, a total silence about neutrality law in general throughout this period, save for a single comment forced from him by a stubbornly insistent reporter at his press conference on the day Stimson's letter was published. This reporter almost literally put words into his mouth. " 'Has the neutrality legislation of the last three years contributed to the cause of peace?' " asked Roosevelt, repeating in paraphrase the question the reporter had put. "If one can answer . . . with a 'yes' or 'no,' I would say, 'No, it has not.' " The reporter pressed further. Would America not be stronger if we had had no such law? "We might have been stronger if we had not had it," Roosevelt admitted.[41] This was caution in the extreme, surely. Even so, it prodded Pittman into announcing, next day, that his Foreign Relations Committee would begin to consider within the next ten days—that is, within two months after he had first promised early hearings—the various neutrality proposals that had been made. This in turn prodded a still fuming Gerald Nye to threaten a filibuster if the administration attempted "to repeal or emasculate" existing neutrality law. The Senate would be kept in session "all summer," he warned. To this, the White House made neither overt nor covert response, whereupon Pittman lapsed again into passivity. He not only failed to bring up neutrality-law revision at the Foreign Relations Committee's meeting on March 15, he also told reporters afterward that, to his knowledge, no interest in such revision had been manifested by the Senate. None of his committee colleagues had so much as mentioned the subject to him, he asserted.[42]

By that time, Roosevelt had suffered (in the second week of February) and recovered from another of the viral respiratory attacks which so often laid him low during periods of indecision and frustration. He was very much under the weather on the day Thomas introduced his resolution. He still was on the following day, February 14, when he received from the venerable Louis Brandeis, "Old Isaiah," the latter's long-expected letter of resignation from the Supreme Court. He felt but little better on the day after that, when he dictated his unwontedly irritable remarks about Lothian and British defeatism.

But on February 16 he felt some relief from stress as he turned away from defense and foreign-policy questions to deal with those of natural-resource conservation—a field dominated by matters of fact among which he could walk with a sure footing; a field wherein the issues, the problems, the indicated solutions were relatively clear and definite; a field relatively free of passionate assertiveness. He transmitted to Congress that day two reports prepared by technical experts for the National Resources Committee. One had to do with water pollution by sewage and industrial wastes, and its abatement through treatment plants—a task "primarily [the responsibility] . . . of municipal government and private industry" but one whose performance would be greatly aided by federal loans and grants-in-aid and by a central agency to coordinate educational, research, and enforcement activities, as Roosevelt said in his transmittal letter. He recommended congressional legislation providing for these. The other report was a comprehensive study of the nation's energy resources. For this he prepared a cover letter advocating an integrated national energy policy that took full account of the interconnectedness of the problems of coal, oil, natural gas, and water power use and conservation.[43]

Even greater was the relief with which, next day, the flu bug having departed, though leaving him pale and worn, he boarded his special train for a long-planned journey to Key West, Florida. There he embarked on what had become his favorite cruise ship, the U.S.S. *Houston,* for another fortnight of rest and recuperation in the warm sun, the balmy salt air of the Caribbean.

His trip was by no means all holiday. On the day of his embarkation he made two brief radio speeches from Key West, one of them opening the San Francisco World's Fair (the Golden Gate Exposition) on manmade Treasure Island, the other extending greetings to a "Pan-American Hernando de Soto Exposition" in Tampa. In both speeches he stressed the value of such expositions as examples and promoters of friendly international relations. (Treasure Island, he said, was an outstanding example of "territorial expansion without aggression." The Tampa exposition, he said, exemplified the solidarity of the Americas, proclaiming "to all the world that in the Western Hemisphere ... the institutions of democracy . . . must and shall be maintained.""⁴⁴) Nor was the voyage that followed altogether a pleasure cruise. On January 13, 1939, the entire U.S. fleet had made a mass transit of the Panama Canal, concentrating in the Atlantic for the first time in five years in order to conduct, off the northeast coast of South America and in the Caribbean, a so-called Fleet Problem XX. This was a fleet action in defense of America's East Coast against an imagined attack from across the Atlantic, and the flagship *Houston* took part. A windswept Franklin Roosevelt, Commander in Chief of the army and navy, bareheaded and wearing what would become famous as his naval cloak (one of the most published photographs of him was taken at this time), observed a closing portion of the "battle" from the *Houston*'s quarterdeck.

While aboard ship, he also dealt with two problems that were important but, fortunately, easily solved. One was the choice of a Supreme Court justice to replace Brandeis. Even before his departure from Washington, even before the expected Brandeis resignation was received, Roosevelt had virtually decided that the post should go to forty-year-old William O. Douglas, a fervent liberal who currently was on leave from his Sterling Professorship of Law at Yale in order to serve as chairman of the Securities and Exchange Commission. This decision was now made firm. Douglas's nomination would be announced March 20, 1939. The other problem was presented him in a letter, dated February 23, from a harassed Steve Early. "This concerns . . . your secretariat," wrote Early, "—a problem . . . I believe more important to you than you perhaps realize." Marvin McIntyre, the appointments secretary, whose cadaverous appearance accorded with his actual poor health, had been hospitalized, and his "physical condition makes it extremely doubtful, in my opinion, that he will be able . . . to carry on unless he is given [frequent] . . . periods of rest." Jimmy Roosevelt's illness-forced resignation of his secretarial post left young James Rowe, Jr., in charge of it, and Rowe was not sufficiently well known and trusted to function there "in a helpful way." Consequently, a tremendous load of work and responsibility descended upon Press Secretary Early, and "no one of the three secretaries to the President . . . can single-handedly and efficiently carry on the work of these three offices." He proposed that Colonel Edwin M. (Pa) Watson, the President's military aide, who was at Roosevelt's side aboard the *Houston,* be named presidential secretary. "Pa is well known and well liked. Most senators and members of Congress love him. . . . His appearance is imposing and his personality is happy and pleasing."⁴⁵ Roosevelt, whose affection for Watson was akin to (if different from) that he had felt for Gus Gennerich, at once accepted and acted upon this suggestion. Watson would resign his army post and assume his new duties on March 13, he having on that day become eligible for, and received, promotion from colonel to brigadier general.

But if not wholly free of work, of problem pressures, Roosevelt's cruise was mostly so—"quiet but interesting," as he wrote in a shipboard letter to his mother in New York City. "The weather is heavenly," he went on, "and I hope to get in an hour or two of fishing [there is no record of his having done so]. It will be grand to find you at the White House on my return."[46] And certainly he seemed fully restored to health, the tired lines erased from his suntanned face, his buoyant zestful energy replenished, as the *Houston* sailed from the "battle" zone toward Charleston, where he would debark. On the way he received a radiogram from James F. Byrnes. "Sorry I cannot be in Charleston to welcome you to a good state and a good city," said the South Carolina senator. "For ten days the Senate has been debating war but formal declaration has been withheld because of inability to agree on whom we will fight. Know you have not spent two weeks studying war tactics . . . for nothing and possibly your return may solve question. . . ." Roosevelt replied: "Sincerely hope Nye, Vandenberg, and Borah will not force us into war before I get back. Charleston Navy Yard needs three or four days' notice before any actual declaration."[47]

V

ROOSEVELT returned to the White House in the morning of March 4, which happened to be not only the sixth anniversary of his first inaugural as President but also, according to the Supreme Court, the one hundred and fiftieth birthday of the Congress of the United States. (The Constitution replaced the Articles of Confederation in the first minute of March 4, 1789, said the Court.) The event was honored by a joint session of Congress attended by members of the Supreme Court, the diplomatic corps, and the President of the United States, who delivered his address on the occasion within two or three hours after his train pulled into Union Station. In the address, he reminded his listeners that the first official meeting of the federal Congress had actually not taken place on March 4, 1789, because, thanks to travel difficulties, a quorum could not be attained until a month later. He spoke "of the counting [in early April 1789] of the ballots unanimously cast [by the electoral college] for General Washington; of his notification; of his triumphal journey from Mount Vernon to New York; and of his inauguration as first President on April 30." He opined that the risk-filled "evolution of permanent substance out of nebulous chaos" (that is, the creation of a national constitutional democracy out of thirteen quarrelsome sovereign states) could be fairly described as "the eighth wonder of the world," then asserted that the present state of our democracy gave "no encouragement to the belief that our processes are outworn" and must give way to "forms of government which for two thousand years have proved their tyranny and their instability alike."[48]

But as he made this assertion, may he not have felt at least a twinge of doubt about its truth? Did his contemplation of those seated before him sustain an unflawed confidence in the American democracy's capacity for wise, timely, decisive action? Certainly he faced now a federal legislature less responsive to the executive, less willing to deal reasonably with what he perceived to be harsh necessities, more determined to frustrate his policies for the sole purpose of discomfiting him personally, than any he had faced before. And certainly his experience of this Congress in the immediately following days could have done little to strengthen a conviction that democracy would survive, much less prevail, in the present and coming struggle with the dictatorships for world power.

Virtually the whole of his legislative program was in great trouble during these March days. Of all his proposals, only that for a greatly increased defense appropriation was clearly on its way to easy early passage without important amendment.

He had proposed an extension of the $2 billion currency-stabilization fund, along with presidential power to fix the gold value of the dollar. It encountered strong opposition in the House from those who would strip the President of his power to determine dollar value. In March, the measure seemed likely to pass the House in a form satisfactory to the administration, as indeed it did, but certain to encounter grave difficulties in the Senate, where silverite senators led by Key Pittman, whose chairmanship of the Foreign Relations Committee gave him key importance to presidential conduct of foreign affairs, was bound to fight for a far higher price for silver in terms of gold than was consistent with market reality. (Ultimately, the fund would be extended, as would the President's power to determine dollar value, but only after fiscally outrageous concessions had been made to Pittman and the other Senate silverites.)

Roosevelt had proposed an increase of $800 million in the Housing Administration's loan authorization, and of $45 million in housing subsidies. This appeared in March to be headed for defeat in the House. (The appearance would prove to be the reality.)

He had proposed an appropriation of $875 million to the WPA to enable government employment of an estimated three million people able and willing to perform useful work who could not find jobs in the private sector, Congress in February had appropriated only $725 million to the WPA; the need for the whole of the originally requested amount had latterly increased, and the President had every reason to doubt that the fact-supported plea for an additional WPA appropriation that he was currently preparing, and would make on March 14, would be persuasive. (It wasn't; the proposal's rejection, accompanied as it was by a refusal to fund the Federal Theatre Project, which the Dies Committee had so viciously attacked, would be perceived as a major defeat for him.)

Roosevelt had most emphatically proposed some form of additional tax to finance the "parity" payments to farmers that Congress had approved in 1938 and then promised, in a gentleman's agreement with the White House, to finance in a way that did not drain the federal treasury. In March, the agricultural appropriations bill was well on the way toward passage, but nothing was being done to finance parity payments, thanks in good part to the political clout of the American Farm Bureau Federation as the agent of agribusiness

—a clout for which the administration's way of achieving crop and livestock reductions in 1933 was largely responsible. (The bill would pass in this fiscally irresponsible form in late June, and Roosevelt would sign it on the last day of 1939's fiscal year only because, if he did not, "the Department of Agriculture and the Farm Credit Administration will stop functioning tomorrow."[49]) Roosevelt had proposed amendments to the Social Security Act whereby old-age benefit payments and the number of people covered were increased, and basic changes were made in Social Security financing. The House Ways and Means Committee was holding seemingly endless hearings on this, though ultimate passage of the measure in a satisfactory form seemed certain, thanks not to Roosevelt's persuasive powers but to the overwhelming popular support that Social Security had generated. (The amended bill would indeed pass with overwhelming majorities in both houses, in July.)

Finally, there was the executive-reorganization bill. This was a measure directly related to the question of democracy's viability since its failure to pass would condemn the President to continued overwhelming executive inefficiency while foreign dictatorships marched swiftly toward world domination. Yet executive reorganization was threatened with a fatal maiming as March advanced.

It will be remembered that Roosevelt, acting upon the Brownlow Committee's report, had originally proposed this measure in January 1937;* that the House had passed it in approximately its original form in 1937's regular session but, thanks to the Supreme Court battle, too late for the Senate to act upon it before the session ended; that the reintroduced bill had in 1938 become the object of furious attacks within and outside Congress as a measure designed to grant dictatorial powers to an untrustworthy President who longed for them; and that it had nevertheless narrowly passed the Senate in that session, only to meet defeat in the House—this despite the fact that the Democratic majority was much greater in the House than in the Senate. The smarting memory of this humiliating personal defeat, conjoined with the failure of the congressional-primary "purge" campaign and the subsequent victory of conservatism in the midterm elections, had dictated to the President a radical change of strategy with regard to reorganization in the 76th Congress. He barely mentioned the subject in his 1939 annual message, then dropped it altogether from his public discourse and maintained a strict hands-off policy with regard to it in his dealings with Congress. (Overtly, that is; his legislative agents had done some covert prodding, cajoling, promising, threatening.) The consequence had been legislative deliberations that provoked little public controversy in the process of producing a drastically revised bill. Stripped from it were all of the most controversial and, in the President's view, some of the most desirable, of the original proposals, including the creation of new departments of public works and welfare, the replacement of the Civil Service Commission by a single civil service administrator, the expansion of the civil service

*See pp. 32–36.

to include all federal jobs of a non-policy-determining nature, and the abolition of the offices of comptroller general and general accounting, their functions to be transferred to the Bureau of the Budget. But the revised measure did retain considerable portions of the vital core of the original proposal, enough of them to cause the President to favor strongly the measure's passage. It established the Executive Office of the President. It gave the President the six administrative assistants ("with a passion for anonymity") he so greatly needed. And it empowered him to investigate the whole of the executive branch of the government to determine bureaucratic inefficiencies, redundancies, and overlappings, and to propose corrections of these through transfers, abolitions, and consolidations of existing agencies and functions.

There remained to be determined, in these March days, the method by which the reorganization plans were to become practically effective. The initial idea of having the President effect reorganization by simple executive order was emphatically rejected. If dictatorial executive power were to be avoided, Congress insisted, the legislature must retain the right to review and act upon every proposed executive reorganization. But how could Congress do this without also retaining a power to obstruct and frustrate reorganization proposals that, exercised, would defeat the central purpose of the legislation? The answer, incorporated into the bill that emerged from committee for floor debate and vote, was an article that provided for congressional review of any reorganization plan but also imposed a two-month time limit upon congressional dealings with it. Congress might reject the plan in toto (no insertions, deletions, or other changes in the plan could be made) within sixty days after its submission, but if it failed to do so, the plan became effective. This arrangement, regarded by some public-affairs management experts as a stroke of genius, was prudent, certainly, in that it guarded against an excessive shift of organizational power from legislature to executive or from the latter to the former—and Roosevelt had become converted to it, convinced it could be made to work satisfactorily. There were many in Congress, however, who didn't want it to work. A House amendment that would have invalidated a reorganization plan by a negative vote in *either* chamber required for its defeat (209–193) some fairly intense covert activity on the part of the White House. Even more intense covert activity was required to defeat a Senate amendment that would have required specific approval of any reorganization plan by *both* houses.

As a matter of fact, this last, crippling amendment had actually passed the Senate, 46–43, before covert White House manipulations resulted not only in its reconsideration but also in a vote switch whereby it was finally defeated by just two votes, 46–44. One of the two was that of New Mexico's Dennis Chavez, who had initially voted for the amendment. (No doubt "promises were made to Chavez," Ickes told his diary, "because he is that kind of statesman."[50]). The other was that of Missouri's Harry Truman, who had been absent from the Senate when the initial vote was taken and who, in response to two emergency phone calls—one from Jim Farley, one from Steve Early in the White House—made a dangerous night flight from Missouri through a snowstorm to Washington to cast his deciding vote.[51]

Roosevelt would exercise the powers the Reorganization Act gave him with a very deliberate speed. Not until April 26 did he submit to Congress his Reorganization Plan Number 1, designed to reduce drastically the number of agencies reporting directly to the President, and to improve overall management. Reorganization Plan Number 2, submitted on May 9, further reduced the number of independent agencies while regrouping in more logical fashion agencies formerly scattered helter-skelter, by accident and impromptu improvisation, through the executive branch. "In these days of ruthless attempts to destroy democratic governments, it is baldly asserted that democracies must always be weak in order to be democratic at all; and that, therefore, it will be easy to crush all free states out of existence," said the President to Congress as he introduced the first of his plans.

> Confident in our Republic's 150 years of successful resistance to all subversive attempts upon it . . . nevertheless we must . . . make sure that the people's Government is in condition to carry out the people's will, promptly, effectively, without waste or lost motion. . . . We are not free if our administration is weak. But we are free if we know, and others know, that we are strong; that we can be tough as well as tender-hearted; and that what the American people decide to do can and will be done, capably and effectively, with the best national equipment that modern organizing ability can supply in a country where management and organization is so well understood in private affairs.[52]

Both plans went into effect on July 1, 1939, a resolution to disapprove them having failed to pass Congress.

By them, the Bureau of the Budget, formerly in the Treasury Department, became a part of the Executive Office of the President. So did the National Resources Committee, formerly an independent agency, which was renamed the National Resources Planning Board and to which were transferred from the Commerce Department the functions of the federal Employment Stabilization Office. Established in the Executive Office were three new agencies: a Federal Security Agency, a Federal Works Agency, and a Federal Loan Agency. Each of these consolidated a number of agencies that had formerly been independent or distributed among the various departments. Thus the Federal Security Agency comprised the Social Security Board (formerly in the Labor Department), the U.S. Employment Service (formerly in Labor), the Public Health Service (formerly in Treasury), the Office of Education (formerly in Interior), the National Youth Administration (originally in the WPA), and the formerly independent Civilian Conservation Corps. In the Federal Works Agency were consolidated the staffs and functions of the WPA, the PWA, the Bureau of Public Roads (formerly in Agriculture), the Public Buildings Branch of the procurement division of Treasury, the Board of Buildings Management of the National Park Service (in Interior) insofar as this was concerned with public

buildings operated for other departments of agencies, and the U.S. Housing
Authority. In the Federal Loan Agency were consolidated the Reconstruction
Finance Corporation (RFC; formerly independent), the Federal Home Loan
Bank Board, the Federal Housing Administration, the Electric Home and Farm
Authority, the Farm Credit Administration, the Commodity Credit Corpora-
tion, the Federal Mortgage Corporation, and the Export-Import Bank. Trans-
ferred to the Foreign Service of the State Department were the Foreign
Commerce Service (formerly in Commerce) and the Foreign Agricultural
Service (formerly in Agriculture).

The reorganization resulted in estimated savings of $20 million annually
and, far more important, when joined with the addition of the six assistants
to the President's staff (though Roosevelt made haste very slowly indeed as he
filled these posts), greatly increased the efficiency of executive operation. They
did so despite Roosevelt's administrative idiosyncrasies. And they did so on
the eve of events that made such efficiency a vital element of the American
democracy's survival.

Among the matters of concern to Roosevelt, in the crowded days immediately
following his return from his cruise, were Harry Hopkins's health problems,
now grown serious again.

Hopkins, unhappily going through the motions prescribed for a politician
aspiring to presidential nomination, had made his maiden speech as secretary
of commerce on February 24, in the capital of Iowa, his native state. He made
it at a black-tie dinner meeting of the Des Moines Executive Club, whence it
was nationally broadcast by radio—an effort to woo businessmen by implicitly
repudiating those central portions of the New Deal with which Hopkins had
always before been actively identified. It was promptly dubbed "Hopkins's
acceptance speech" by Jim Farley, who had been given some reason to believe
that his own aspirations to the presidency had Roosevelt's personal blessing.
"With the emphasis shifted from reform to recovery, this Administration is
now determined to promote that recovery with all the vigor and power at its
command," Hopkins said. Labor, he said, "must fully realize that under our
economic system, businessmen have to make money to hire workers." And
businessmen could make money, he said, only if they had more than the
"minimum volume [of business] . . . necessary to break even on fixed ex-
penses."[53] It was a poor speech, almost wholly the product of hands and minds
other than the speaker's own, and its delivery was as poor as its content,

One major reason for this was that Hopkins, as he spoke, was physically ill.
He was suffering "a touch of flu" (so he invariably described his illnesses), as
he had been for weeks. He felt so miserable when he returned to Washington
that, having been urged to do so in a letter from his worried brother Lewis,
who was in medical practice in Tacoma, Washington, he went at once to New
York City for examination by a specialist there, one Dr. Johnson. The specialist found no sign of a recurrence of "my former trouble," a relieved Hopkins
then wrote to his brother, nor of anything else especially sinister. The specialist

was evidently more alarmingly frank, expressing worried puzzlement over Hopkins's condition, in a letter he wrote to his medical colleague in Tacoma, for Dr. Lewis Hopkins was moved to address a personal letter to Roosevelt in which he begged the President to "add the real weight of your request that he [Harry] follow Dr. Johnson's advice," which was that Hopkins impose upon himself a strict ascetic regimen, including a special diet and "much more rest." Dr. Hopkins was "sure Harry will not do [so] without your orders."[54]

Roosevelt acted at once upon this request. Bernard Baruch was persuaded to invite Hopkins down for a two-week visit at Baruch's huge country estate, Hobcaw Barony, in South Carolina. Roosevelt then, as he wrote Dr. Hopkins on March 13, had his "long talk with Harry on the necessity for his doing as the Doctor advised. He was grand about it and left the following night for South Carolina."[55]

VI

WE have seen how Roosevelt, from the moment he assumed his presidential duties, had suffered a gradual yet constantly accelerating encroachment of foreign affairs upon work time and attention he would have preferred to devote to domestic affairs. This was thanks mostly to the simultaneous rise to power of Adolf Hitler. But it was not until this opening month of his seventh year in the White House that foreign affairs achieved that absolute dominance over domestic concerns that they were destined ever after to retain in his mind. A specific day can be named on which this occurred: Wednesday, March 15, 1939 —the day, ironically, on which Key Pittman proclaimed his Senate Foreign Relations Committee's lack of interest in Neutrality Act revision.

For on that day Adolf Hitler, totally violating the Munich Agreement, marched his troops unresisted into Bohemia and Moravia while Hungarian troops, with his permission, seized Ruthenia. He came in person to Prague, where he proclaimed Czechoslovakia to be now a German protectorate. At once, the anti-Semitic decrees of Berlin went into effect. At once the brutal Nazi apparatus for repression and oppression, whereby every frank exponent of human freedom and decency was liable to imprisonment, torture, and death, went into action. And thus was completed, somewhat sooner than even the most pessimistic had expected, that destruction of the Czech Republic that had been begun in the spring of 1938 and in which Chamberlain's Britain and Daladier's France had cooperated.

Neville Chamberlain's immediate reaction was precisely what one would expect of him. He told the House of Commons in the afternoon of the fifteenth that, since the Slovaks had on the day before formally declared their independence of the government in Prague (the Slovak Diet had done so under extreme pressure by the Nazis), the Czech Republic whose boundaries had been guaranteed at Munich no longer existed by the time the Germans marched. "His Majesty's Government cannot accordingly hold themselves bound by this [Munich] obligation," he said. "It is natural that I should bitterly regret what

has now occurred, but do not let us on that account be deflected from our
[appeasement] course. Let us remember that the desire of all the peoples of the
world still remains concentrated on the hopes of peace."⁵⁶ This time, however,
Chamberlain's words found no credence even among most of those who, as late
as the day before, had supported his appeasement policy. He faced, from one
end of Britain to the other, and in the Dominions, a rising storm of moral
outrage—an emotion he personally seemed incapable of feeling. Even the
London *Times,* even Sir Nevile Henderson, seem to have felt it, for the former
joined in the chorus of press denunciation of Hitler, if less emphatically than
other papers, while the latter telegraphed from Berlin that "the cynicism and
immorality of the German action defied description." Henderson also suggested that he be recalled. In the Foreign Office, Cadogan, the under secretary,
who had theretofore shared some of the euphoria emanating from Chamberlain, was abruptly, completely converted to the dark view of Hitler and the
future that the hitherto ignored Vansittart (he had seldom been included in
foreign-policy meetings) had taken all along. So was Halifax, who addressed
personally to German ambassador von Dirkson words decidedly not in accord
with any spirit of conciliation—words so harsh, in fact, that Dirkson softened
them in his report to Berlin. Halifax also urged upon the prime minister the
necessity for an immediate total reversal of course if the government were not
to fall.⁵⁷

By all this, tradesman politician Chamberlain was forced to reconsider. He
was scheduled to speak on March 17, his seventieth birthday, in his hometown
of Birmingham. He had in hand a speech about his ministry's efforts toward
improved social services and economic recovery. But on the train carrying him
from London to Birmingham, with the urgent advice of Halifax ringing in his
ears, he virtually scrapped the prepared speech and wrote a new one of wholly
different nature, a speech concentrated on Hitler's flagrant violation of the
Munich Agreement and of the repeated Hitlerian assertion that the Reich
should and would incorporate none but the Germans who, by blood, belonged
in it. The Sudetenland was "the last territorial demand I have to make in
Europe," Hitler had said. "We want no Czechs," he had said. And the prime
minister now asked "how . . . these events this week" could be "reconciled with
these [earlier] assurances." Obviously they could not be. "Who can fail to feel
his heart go out in sympathy to the proud, brave people who have so suddenly
been subjected to invasion, whose liberties are curtailed, whose national independence is gone?" he asked ["*You* can!" some might have answered], then
went on to reject the German claim that disorders within the Czech Republic
had necessitated the German action. "If there were disorders, were they not
fomented from without? . . . Is this the last attack upon a small state or is it
. . . a step in the direction of an attempt to dominate the world by force?"⁵⁸

Thus was the end of appeasement announced to the world.

There followed frantic efforts in London to shape and implement a new
policy of collective security. The governments of France, Russia, Poland,
Turkey, and Rumania were asked for suggestions. Most of them replied in

ways indicative of the distrust of Britain that Chamberlain's management of affairs had created during the last eighteen months. Moscow, through Maxim Litvinov, voiced a suspicion that Britain sought to tie the Soviet Union's hands with commitments that left Britain's hands free and, to test this suspicion, proposed an immediate conference, perhaps in Bucharest, for the purpose of forming a six-power pact of mutual defense. The proposal found no favor in Chamberlain's Britain. Any astute British statesman would at that point have taken into account the implications of an address Stalin had presented to the Eighteenth Congress of the Communist Party on March 10. It was an address remarkably devoid of those denunciations of Nazi-German barbarism that had become standard public Soviet rhetoric, an address that instead denounced, as attempts to foment war between Germany and Russia, recent reports in the Western democratic press of German designs upon the Soviet Ukraine. Such attempts, Stalin had said with emphasis, were futile. The Soviet government would not "allow our country to be drawn into conflict by warmongers accustomed to have others pull their chestnuts out of the fire for them."[59] But Chamberlain, as we know, was the opposite of astute; and when Britain consulted Poland on the Litvinov proposal, Poland rejected it outright. In Warsaw's view the Soviet Union was a worse enemy than Germany, this despite ever stronger evidence that Poland, threatened on her southern as well as her western border now that Czechoslovakia was part of the Third Reich, was next on Hitler's list of national victims. (Hitler's demands for Danzig [now Gdańsk], liquidating the Polish Corridor, grew louder by the day; Lithuania, under threat, surrendered Memel to Germany on March 23, Hitler going there by battleship—he arrived seasick—to accept the surrender in person.) And Chamberlain, presented with a choice between Poland and Russia as military ally, found no difficulty in choosing the former. For one thing, Poland was in his view the more formidable power. "I must confess to the most profound distrust of Russia," he wrote at this time in a private letter (March 26). "I have no belief whatever in her ability to maintain an effective offensive, even if she wanted to. And I distrust her motives."[60]

The upshot was a hurried, ill-considered unilateral guarantee by Britain of Poland's independence. The prime minister who five and a half months before had wantonly cast away the shield raised against Hitler by a strong Bohemian fortress line, a well-trained Czech army of a million and a half, an air force far from contemptible, and the vast Skoda armaments works—this prime minister rose in Parliament on March 31 to say: "I have now to inform the House that . . . in the event of any action which clearly threatened Polish independence and which the Polish Government accordingly considered it vital to resist with their national forces, His Majesty's Government would feel themselves bound at once to lend the Polish Government all the support in their power. They have given the Polish Government an assurance to this effect."[61] It was an assurance that Britain's hands were now tied to Poland's, with the latter as prime mover. The question of peace or war for both Britain and France, since France's hands were certainly tied to Britain's in this matter, was now to be answered, not in London or Paris, but in Warsaw, and by some of the most dim-witted, morally obtuse characters on the contemporary political scene.

There was no direct communication between Chamberlain and Roosevelt during these hectic days nor, indeed, much mention of U.S. attitudes and acts in the council rooms of Whitehall. Chamberlain continued to weigh lightly U.S. influence upon current European affairs. Halifax weighed it only somewhat more heavily. And in any case the two were well aware that the Roosevelt administration, shackled as it was by neutrality law and struggling futilely, as it appeared, to break those shackles, would decidedly not welcome at that moment any attempt to associate the American government with a British foreign policy whose final shape was still in process of determination.

As for Washington, its divided mind (fervently solid isolationism versus a slowly growing tendency toward interventionism) ensured a mouse-birthing mountain of agitated discussion in White House and State Department. Hull was vacationing in Florida. It was Welles as acting secretary of state who, after consulting the President, prepared the single official U.S. government comment upon the Czech takeover. It was issued on March 17 over Welles's signature—a predictable, ritualistic, impotent condemnation of "the acts which have resulted in the temporary [Roosevelt inserted the adjective] extinguishment of the liberties of a free and independent people with whom, from the day when the Republic of Czechoslovakia attained its independence, the people of the United States have maintained specially close and friendly relations. . . . It is manifest that acts of wanton lawlessness and of arbitrary force are threatening world peace and the very structure of modern civilization."[62] (Significantly, Welles did not consult Hull by phone on this, as he should and could easily have done, nor did he, upon whom was focused intense press attention that week, make the slightest effort to associate his superior publicly, by nominal reference, with what he was doing. This provoked a brief but dangerous flare-up of angry enmity out of the chronic personal tension between secretary and under secretary. Assistant Secretary Berle had imposed upon him, in the following week, "a difficult piece of buffer work," as he wrote in his diary. "There is such a thing as having too capable an Assistant from the point of view of the Chief. Yet actually the men complement each other completely; and it is essential that they work together in complete confidence."[63]) Welles also presided over lengthy State Department discussions of whether or not diplomatic relations with Germany should be completely severed. The predictable answer, in the circumstances, was no. The view that prevailed was expressed by pacifistic isolationist Berle: "Breaking relations of itself means little; there would follow increasingly strained relations, Nazi excesses, demand for reprisals here, and we should slowly drift into a state of war without shooting. Further, we might excite hopes in France and Great Britain that in case of ultimates we would go to war—a process which would be futile. . . . [We] should have stimulated a course of action . . . we were not prepared to see through."[64] Roosevelt accepted this conclusion. Though Hugh Wilson was never to return to Berlin as ambassador, the U.S. embassy there would remain officially open until December 11, 1941.

Roosevelt's primary concern in these last weeks of March—his primary foreign-policy concern of the year, in fact—was voiced at his press conference on the day the Welles statement was issued. It was neutrality law. Hitler's latest aggression increased the urgent necessity for revision of this law, he indicated; prompt congressional action was required. On the following day (March 18) he received from R. Walton Moore, a State Department counselor, a letter saying that Senator Pittman had spent more than two hours in Moore's office on the preceding afternoon, outlining and having put into proper legal form a neutrality bill of his own "which if enacted would be a substitute for the existing law." It provided that "within thirty days after an armed conflict begins [whether or not there was a formal declaration of war], the President shall issue a proclamation confining all American shipments to the belligerent countries to foreign vessels under the cash and carry plan." American vessels were to be barred from entrance into such zones of danger as the President might designate. No mention of civil wars was made. Several key provisions of the 1937 act were included in the draft legislation—the prohibition of American credits to belligerents, for one; the prohibition of the arming of American merchant vessels, for another. On Sunday, March 19, Pittman announced and described his proposal in a national network radio broadcast. "We are interested in seeing that there is maintained in Europe a substantial balance of power," he said, "because if any one group obtains absolute power over Europe and Asia then we are faced with the defense of the Monroe Doctrine in Latin America." On the following day he formally introduced his bill in the Senate. It was *not* an administration measure, he stressed; it embodied his own independent views, not those of the State Department or White House; and he labeled it the Peace Act of 1939, obviously hoping thus to blunt attacks upon it as a step toward economic "entangling alliances" that presaged our involvement in war.[65]

The tactic proved futile, of course. Even before the bill's introduction, Idaho's leonine Borah, the ranking Republican on the Foreign Relations Committee and a former chairman of it, responded to Pittman's radio address with a Sunday evening press statement condemning the proposed repeal of the arms embargo. Actually, he said, the embargo should be made more inclusive, to cover not just arms but all war matériel. And what Borah aimed for was embodied in a bill at once introduced, in response to Pittman's, by Nye, Clark, and Washington State's Homer Bone. Utah's Thomas and Florida's Claude Pepper countered with an effort to revive the Thomas amendment. Several other Foreign Relations Committee members favored a total repeal of neutrality law, according to a poll taken by the *Times*, while a majority of the committee had yet to decide among the presented alternatives. "In this confused picture," as Robert A. Divine writes in his *The Illusion of Neutrality*, "only one fact stood out clearly—the failure of the administration to put forth its own neutrality program had created a hopeless tangle of conflicting proposals which ruled out any chance for a prompt decision by Congress."[66]

Roosevelt's only specific, expressed reaction to Pittman's bill was determined by the loud and desperate protests at once made by the Chinese against the discriminatory effect of the cash-and-carry provision upon China vis-à-vis her Japanese invader. These were conveyed to Washington through a message from the U.S. embassy counselor in Chungking. Roosevelt referred to it in a memorandum to the secretary and under secretary of state on March 28, going on to say: "I think that before the bill gets too far it should be called to the attention of Senator Pittman that while the cash and carry plan works all right in the Atlantic, it works all wrong in the Pacific. The more I think the problem through, the more I am convinced that the existing Neutrality Act should be repealed in toto without any substitute. I do not mind if you pass this word to Senator Pittman and the leaders." But Pittman had already had it pointed out to him, by R. Walton Moore, that the proposed legislation "would place Japan at an advantage over China." His reply had been that "independent legislation" would be enacted, in his opinion, to prevent American shipments of war matériel to Japan. And Pittman had also told Moore that there was not "any possibility of an outright repeal of the present law, with nothing substituted therefore"; nor was there "the slightest prospect of any measure being adopted expressing the aggressor theory [that is, enabling the President to discriminate between aggressor and victim nations]." The effect of Roosevelt's memo was therefore nil.[67]

# 11

**-»>X«<-**

# The Coming-on of World War II:
## Part Two

I

ROOSEVELT'S sense of helplessness was acute. Frustration fretted his every day, almost his every hour. Not since the early stages of his struggle for recovery from polio, save perhaps during the latter stages of his Supreme Court battle, had his vital reserves been so severely tested, so heavily drawn upon. And there was no lessening of tensions as the spring of 1939 came on, though there was some lessening of his confusion, his indecision, as the torrent of events rose ever higher and, seizing him, bore him onward toward ends unknown while drowning one after another of his options.

The experience was, for him, not dissimilar in some essentials to that of the spring of 1933 when, amid universal ruin and collapse, he had presided over the birth of the New Deal. Now as then, with no more than a guiding oar in hand, he rode a small raft down destiny's turbulent stream. ("Never in my life have I seen things moving in the world with more cross currents or greater velocity," he wrote in a personal letter on March 25, 1939.[1]) But there was a difference. In the spring of 1933, the stream had been like the ebb of a storm-tossed tide that, far from drowning options, heaved them up from the depths in multitude—a tide that must surely turn into flood (such was his faith) as these options, a select few of them, were exercised. What he now rode, and on a frailer raft than he then had had, was not a streaming tide but a narrowing river, which he knew, despite his assertive wish, would never slow, could never reverse itself, but must rush faster and faster into a rock-strewn rapids whose roar sounded ever louder in his ears. His world was ruled by inevitability. He could no longer try something with any assurance that, if it failed to work, something else would turn up that *would* work. All that turned up now was more of the same trouble, and all he could now do was repeat the futile gestures against impending catastrophe that he had earlier made—this while maintaining his balance upon his raft.

It was a balancing act almost as difficult as that of the summer and fall of 1930 when, striving for a gubernatorial reelection victory of a kind helpful to his 1932 presidential candidacy, he had appeased Tammany crooks and wooed liberal reformers simultaneously.* Yet he performed it with a magnificent élan, as he had not quite been able to do in 1930 but had emphatically done in the spring of 1933, plying his guiding oar with skill for the most part, though on occasion with a life-threatening clumsiness, as we have seen. He did not flinch

---

*See *FDR: The New York Years,* pp. 167–81.

as he was borne rushingly onward. He continued to display to the watching
world nothing of fear or despair but, instead, a kind of grim gaiety that was
contagious—this along with an absolute confidence that an appropriate response would be found for every challenge, and all would come out right in
the end. The jagged rocks would be survived. The raft would come at last to
rest beyond the white-foamed rapids upon water that was still and blue under
cloudless skies. For God the Cosmic Author, whose stellar agent he was, was
good and kind and moved always, if often in mysterious ways, toward ultimately beneficent goals. Such remained Roosevelt's simple, unquestioned
faith. And again, as in the darkest year of the Great Depression, it would
become a factor of some decisive importance in the history of the world.

With its temperamental effects, it compensated considerably for grave deficiencies in the mental side, the intellectual portion, of his performance—
compensated, at least, to an extent sufficient for his maintenance of position
at the vital center of things. The evidence indicates that, deep down,* he was
aware of mental limitations, that this awareness bred deeply hidden psychic
insecurities, and that these insecurities in turn encouraged the mendacity and
deviousness that again and again led him into great trouble. But the insecurities were counteracted and generally overcome by his sense of himself as a
chosen one who, as such, had relatively little need for profound thought, for
intellectual brilliance, since God, the supreme intelligence, directed him
through signs and cues intended for him alone. His failures, therefore, were
not of logical thought, in his view, but of perception; they were failures to note
or accurately interpret the signs, the cues. And it was this deepest sense of
himself that enabled him, exercising his remarkable talents as role-player, to
impress upon great masses of people, and upon most of those who had face-to-
face dealings with him, an image of wisdom, of sure confidence, in situations
of whose elements his actual mental grasp was feeble or nonexistent. It also
enabled him to act at last, overcoming paralysis, even when there were no
perceived clues, no perceived signs, and the consequences of his act might be
hugely disastrous. For even in such cases his act was not, in his belief, a solitary
personal one. Always he was accompanied and sustained by the Divine Other.

Nevertheless, he could now maintain his balance, his élan, his exemplary
courage, only by taking holidays more frequent than they had formerly been.
On the last of March, barely three and a half weeks after his return from the
Caribbean cruise, he went to Warm Springs, as has already been mentioned.
This was a typically Rooseveltian holiday, more crowded with activities than
most people would have found restful. He left Washington early in the after-
noon of Wednesday the twenty-ninth. On the following day, while victorious
Spanish Nationalist troops were completing in twilight and darkness their

---

*That is, below the level at which he collected facts, classified them, retained them, used them
to buttress argument—a level on which he operated with a facility of which he was justifiably
proud. For it was a truly remarkable facility, displayed continuously, and sometimes with awesome effectiveness, in his press conferences.

occupation of fallen Madrid, he moved through Georgia's morning into Alabama's afternoon, delivering three brief extemporaneous talks in Alabama (at Opelika, at the Tuskegee Institute, and at Alabama Polytechnic Institute in Auburn) before returning to Georgia. He slept that night in his Warm Springs cottage, awaking in the morning to news of the British and French commitment to Poland's defense. An hour or so later, seated in his hand-controlled car in front of his cottage, with Missy LeHand and a thin, pale Harry Hopkins beside him, he made to the reporters clustered around him an innocuous "background, not for attribution" comment on this latest European development. A line had been drawn, he indicated, which Hitler could not cross without risk of general war. But he switched abruptly from this somber tone to a laughingly carefree one. He was driving down to the pool, he said, where he would "make [Harry] take a bath," Hopkins not having had one "for two months." Asked if he had "been discussing anything with the secretary of commerce," he replied: "Yes. Last night we discussed the relative merits of bridge and poker. We came to no conclusion."[2]

And in that same hour, from his as yet unmoved headquarters at Burgos in northern Spain, Francisco Franco, peerless champion of Catholic Christianity, was ordering for Madrid the ruthless reprisals against helpless opponents that were his standard way of celebrating his Christian victories. He would celebrate now with less inhibition and for a longer period than before. Republican Loyalists and those suspected of Loyalism were executed by the hundred that day and would be every day, in Madrid, in Barcelona, in other cities, for many months to come. Ultimately, tens of thousands would, on Franco's orders, be lined up against walls and shot.

The U.S. government had earlier made a typically futile effort to forestall this acceleration of slaughter. In February, while Roosevelt was cruising aboard the *Houston,* he was informed that sixteen governments had already recognized Franco's regime as Spain's legitimate government and that Britain, France, and the Netherlands were on the verge of doing so. On March 1, in preparation for U.S. recognition, Roosevelt had approved the recall of Claude Bowers from his post as ambassador to the Spanish Republic and, simultaneously, had approved instructions to Bullitt, who was again in Paris, to seek assurances from Franco's official representative in France that there would be no Nationalist reprisals. Franco's response had been a "weasel-worded assurance" (so Hull described it) that was at once revealed by his acts to be a totally false one. This, however, did not prevent nor long delay Washington's establishment of full diplomatic relations with Franco's regime, for the hope remained in Washington that Franco, despite his great debts to Mussolini and Hitler, might remain neutral in the probable coming war if properly encouraged to do so. On April 1, in his Warm Springs cottage, Roosevelt signed the legally required proclamation lifting, at long last, the Spanish arms embargo. (He also on that day dedicated, with appropriate ceremony, new medical and hospital buildings that had been added to the Warm Springs Foundation.) On April 3 he approved the decision to grant de jure recognition to Franco's

government, the announcement to be made next day.* (And on that same
April 3 he signed into law the reorganization bill and the national-defense
appropriation bill, though protesting the attachment to the latter of a rider
giving "the same retirement and pension privileges to reserve officers and
enlisted men who may be disabled while on temporary thirty day duty as is
accorded to regular officers and enlisted men of the Army. . . . It seems a pity
that without . . . study this clause, which will cost the Government a large sum
of money, has been tacked onto an emergency defense measure to which it has
no relationship whatsoever."⁴)

And the swelling, narrowing torrent roared on.

Albania, after a long campaign of subversion conducted by Italy, was invaded by Italian troops, who encountered no organized resistance, on Friday
(Good Friday) April 7. Albania's King Zog fled with his wife and newborn
child to Greece, where he was not welcomed. The event was intended by
Italian foreign minister Ciano to demonstrate Rome's ability to act independently of Berlin, but it was perceived by the world at large as, in Halifax's
words, another "step in a wider movement for the achievement of the expan-
sionist aims of the Axis powers, who, it must be presumed, are acting in
collusion."⁵ It provoked from Washington, after a lengthy phone conversation
between Hull and Roosevelt in Warm Springs, another futile protest. The
invasion, said Hull's public statement, was "unquestionably an additional
threat to the peace of the world" and as such "seriously concerns all nations."
It was "scarcely necessary to add," he concluded, "that the inevitable effect
of this incident, taken with other similar incidents, is further to destroy confidence and undermine economic stability in every country in the world, thus
affecting our own welfare."⁶

It was the economic effect that Roosevelt stressed in his Warm Springs press
conference on that same Saturday, April 8. In remarks attributable, not to him
personally, but to "sources close to the White House," he referred to the only
"three alternatives" that would remain open to the Western democracies if
totalitarian nations continued their aggressions. Faced with the fact that the
dictatorships "can and do work their people much longer hours and for much
lower pay" than the democracies while engaging in world trade only though
"the barter system," the democratic nations might, one, "build the old Chinese
Wall around themselves" and retire from world trade altogether, thereby
"necessarily" reducing their standards of living; two, reduce wages and increase work hours in an effort "to compete in the world market," a device also
reductive of standards of living; or three, "subsidize the export of . . . products

---

*In another instance of Rooseveltian deviousness, Bowers, who was passionately committed to
the Loyalist cause and whose trenchant pen might prove immediately embarrassing if he used it
to attack the administration's Spanish policy, was encouraged to believe that the State Department
acted without Roosevelt's permission when it granted diplomatic recognition to Franco. This and
the promise of a new ambassadorial appointment (his financial need was great) evidently persuaded Bowers to make no public comment on the matter at that time. He was soon named U.S.
ambassador to Chile.³

as a national policy." If the United States opted for the last, the subsidy would have to be paid out of the federal treasury and, though initially limited to a few products, would soon be extended by a log rolling Congress to virtually all products, at an enormous cost that must result either in an economy-crushing national debt or in an equally crushing burden of taxation. "That is an angle of the present international situation that ought to be given a lot of consideration because it affects . . . not only industries and industrial workers . . . but . . . also . . . farmers and all of the agricultural end of the country." In response to a reporter's question, he suggested that they, the reporters, "go back to the famous Senatorial conference" wherein he had argued that "our national safety and prosperity" were so bound up with "the continued politi-cal, economic, and social independence" of "the small nations of the world" that the disappearance of any one of them was a blow to American security. ("That is all there was to the Senatorial conference," he added, defensively and inaccurately.) All this was of course designed by him for isolationist consump-tion, and he insisted to the reporters that there was "a swell story for you" in it. The reporters themselves were not so sure. "I think we ought to be able to write something on that," one of them replied, dubiously. The President encouraged him. "You are doing all right," he said.[7]

On the following day, Easter Sunday, Roosevelt and his party boarded his special train to begin the return to Washington. From the rear platform of his personal car he addressed a few farewell words to "my friends of Warm Springs."

"I have had a fine holiday here with you all," he said. "I'll be back in the fall *if we do not have a war.*"[8]

The closing words were not italicized by Roosevelt's delivery of them, which was casual, matter-of-fact, and he may have been surprised by the degree to which they were italicized by their historical context in the public mind. At any rate, big headlines featured them in next morning's newspapers—and by the time his train arrived in Washington on that Monday, April 10, virtually every editorialist, every columnist, every radio news commentator in the na-tion had publicly pondered or was preparing so to ponder what the President had meant, precisely, by "we." Did he mean "we" as citizens of the world or, scarifyingly, "we" specifically as citizens of the United States?

Roosevelt did not elucidate.

II

FOR his attention was by then wholly absorbed into the preparation of a much more important public statement.

On the day of Mussolini's Albanian invasion, when Roosevelt was in Warm Springs, he had at first toyed with, then finally decided to act upon, the idea of addressing a personal but very public letter from himself as President of the United States to Hitler as chancellor of Germany and Mussolini as premier

of Italy. He had little hope that more mere words would at this late date have
a deterrent effect upon the dictators, nor was he willing to risk anything
beyond mere words; but he felt that the latter, carefully chosen to give the
impression of boldly committing the United States to something while in fact
committing it to nothing, just might force from Hitler and Mussolini verbal
expressions of their absolute disregard for international law—either that, or
statements of their devotion to such law so patently false they would embarrass
the dictators in the eyes of their own people. With this purpose in mind he had
at once made a rough draft of what he wished to say. En route from Warm
Springs to Washington, he revised what he had written. And at five o'clock
in the afternoon of April 10 he handed the product of this labor to Cordell Hull,
who was so impressed by the expressed firmness of the presidential decision
to proceed along these lines that, for all his cautiousness, he raised no objections. Instead Hull at once went into conference on the draft letter with Moffat,
Berle, and Norman Davis in his State Department office.[9] There ensued hours,
adding up to days, of discussion and redrafting, then of more discussion and
more redrafting, in the State Department and the White House.

Amid these labors, on Tuesday evening, April 11, Berle, who did much of
the State Department drafting, conferred by phone with Roosevelt, who was
endeavoring in the Oval Room to "strengthen" the latest State Department
version of his original letter, a version he deemed "a little weak." But what
was uppermost in the President's mind at that moment, Berle discovered, was
not the draft letter but a report just received from London to the effect that
the British government, concerned about Japan's evident intention to strike
southward soon against Indochina and the Dutch East Indies, might be about
to move much of the British fleet from the Atlantic and Mediterranean to
Singapore. Roosevelt was very sure this would be a bad mistake. The main task
of the British fleet at that time must be to guard the sea-lanes from Gibraltar
to Suez. Berle agreed. But London's decisions about British fleet dispositions
were necessarily affected by Washington's decisions about American fleet
dispositions, and Roosevelt decided that night, evidently during his phone talk
with Berle,[10] that the U.S. Pacific Fleet, at present joined with the Atlantic
Fleet for maneuvers intended to end in a grand review opening the New York
World's Fair, should be returned at once to San Diego. An order to this effect
was issued next day and was at once seen by the world (including especially
Berlin and Rome) for what it was—a move to maintain Britain's sea strength
against Germany and Italy by relieving her of the necessity for a strengthened
defense against Japan.

Berle was also involved in, having written the first draft of, an address
Roosevelt delivered to the governing board of the Pan-American Union on
Friday, April 14, the union's forty-ninth birthday. In it, Roosevelt stressed the
value of the union not only as a peacemaking and peacekeeping enterprise in
this hemisphere but also as a defensive alliance against aggression from across
the seas and as a model for the organization of world peace.

Pledges designed to prevent aggression, accompanied by open doors of trade and intercourse, and bound together by common will to cooperate peacefully, make warfare between us [in the Americas] as outworn and useless as the weapons of the Stone Age. We may proudly boast that we have begun to realize in Pan American relations what civilization in intercourse between countries really means. If that process can be successful here, is it too much to hope that a similar intellectual and spiritual process may succeed elsewhere? Do we really have to assume that nations can find no better methods of realizing their destinies than those which were used by the Huns and Vandals fifteen hundred years ago?

But he warned those nations overseas that employed such outmoded methods that they had better not attempt to use them against this hemisphere.

The American peace we celebrate today has no quality of weakness in it! We are prepared to maintain it, and to defend it to the fullest extent of our strength, matching force to force if any attempt is made to subvert our institutions, or to impair the independence of any one of our group. Should the method of attack be that of economic pressure, I pledge that my country will also give economic support, so that no American nation need surrender any fraction of its sovereign freedom to maintain its economic welfare. This is the spirit and intent of the Declaration of Lima: the solidarity of the continent.

He closed with references to that decreased international distance and increased interdependence that result from technological advance.

Beyond question, within a scant few years air fleets will cross the ocean as easily as today they cross the closed European seas. Economic functioning of the world becomes therefore necessarily a unit; no interruption of it anywhere can fail, in the future, to disrupt economic life everywhere. The truest defense of the peace of our hemisphere must [consequently] . . . lie in the hope that our sister nations beyond the seas will break the bonds of the ideas that constrain them toward perpetual violence. By example we can at least show them the possibility.[11]

Immediately following his delivery of this address, Roosevelt, back in the White House, held a final conference with Sumner Welles concerning his own redraft of Berle's last redraft of the personal messages to Hitler and Mussolini. Within an hour or so he had in hand, neatly typed, the final draft—a suitably noncommittal document, its essential timidity cloaked in the desired seeming boldness—which was dispatched to Berlin and Rome at nine o'clock that night, Washington time.*

After a brief review of the acts of aggression committed during the last few years, and an assertion that the United States pleaded for peace "not through

---

*The missive to Berlin was directly addressed by the President of the United States to the chancellor of Germany, whereas the one to Rome, addressed to the Italian premier, was signed by the U.S. secretary of state—this because Hitler was formally head of the German state, while Mussolini was but head of government, serving, nominally, at the pleasure of King Victor Emmanuel.

selfishness or fear or weakness" but "with the voice of strength and with friendship for mankind," the message asked the dictators, with Hitler obviously the primary one of the two, "to make a statement of policy to me as head of a nation far removed from Europe in order that I, acting only with the responsibility and obligation of a friendly intermediary, may communicate such declaration to other nations now apprehensive as to the course which the policy of your Government may take." The policy statement requested was "assurance that your armed forces will not attack or invade the territory or possessions of" some thirty-three European and Middle Eastern nations, each of which was specifically named. (They included the presumably immediately Axis-threatened nations of Poland, Rumania, Hungary, Greece, and Holland, along with the small Baltic states and Switzerland, and, of course, the major powers: Russia, France, Great Britain.)

> Such an assurance clearly must apply not only to the present day but also to a future sufficiently long to give every opportunity to work by peaceful methods for a more permanent peace. I therefore suggest that you construe the word "future" to apply to a minimum period of assured non-aggression—ten years at least—a quarter of a century, if we dare look that far ahead. If such assurance is given by your government, I shall immediately transmit it to the governments of the nations I have named and I shall simultaneously inquire whether, as I am reasonably sure, each of the nations enumerated above will in turn give an assurance for transmission to you.

These "reciprocal assurances . . . will bring to the world an immediate measure of relief." And in this atmosphere of relief, "I propose that . . . two essential problems shall promptly be discussed" (in an international conference?): those of, one, "progressive relief from the crushing burden of armament"; and two, the "opening up [of] avenues of international trade to the end that every nation in the world may be enabled to buy and sell on equal terms in the world market." In such discussions "the Government of the United States will gladly take part."[12]

It was Roosevelt himself who, in his press conference the next morning, announced to the world the dispatch of these identical messages. He did so with great care, reading the missive aloud word for word to the reporters and interpolating a weakening "interpretative" comment upon every portion of it which, to the extent of its actual meaningfulness, collided head-on with isolationism. Thus, having read with careful emphasis his promise to act as "a friendly intermediary" between the dictators and the nations he had named, he paused to stress heavily the difference of meaning between "intermediary" and "mediator." "You see the point?" he went on. "Of course there will be a danger—this is of course off the record—that some of our friends on the Hill and some newspaper owners will try to make it appear that I will mediate. There is nothing in it at all. I am the post office, the telegraph office—in other words, the method of communication." When he read the sentences promising American participation in discussions of "two essential problems," he warned the newsmen: "Now, be careful! Be careful!" There was, he emphasized, "nothing new" in the promise to discuss with other nations either disarmament or the "economic side of international problems." We had already "done a great deal of conferring" on these matters. "So," he reiterated, "there is nothing, absolutely nothing, that we have not been doing right along." In response to reporters' questions, he said the letters had been received in Rome and Berlin at three o'clock that morning, their time, and that there had been no prior consultation concerning them with "Great Britain, France or any other nation in the world."

He terminated the press conference abruptly.

"You 'got a mouthful,' " he said; "better run."[13]

But of course, for all his cautious deprecation of its newsworthiness, the message made, as he intended it to make, top headline news all over the world. It had no effect whatever upon the torrential course of world affairs.

The governments and general publics of the European democracies expressed cordial approval of what the President had done. This was predictable. In France, according to the Paris correspondent of *The New York Times,* there was a widespread belief that the President, if the dictators responded negatively to his appeal, was prepared "to go one step farther and offer aid in some form to the victims of their aggression."[14] But in Berlin and Rome, also predictably, the message was received with contempt. Its sender was privately derided by Göring, by Mussolini, as the victim (the message being evidence) of a brain disorder connected, perhaps, with his polio paralysis. And no direct reply came to Roosevelt from Rome. Mussolini merely let the public know that he was uninterested in "Messiah-like messages" and deemed "absurd" the request for a ten-year peace guarantee.[15]

Hitler, on the other hand, though he told associates he was reluctant even to acknowledge his receipt of a "communication from so contemptible a creature as the present President of the United States,"[16] gleefully seized upon what he perceived to be a glorious propaganda opportunity. On April 17, by his order, a telegram went out from his government to the governments of all the nations named in Roosevelt's message save Britain, France, Poland, Russia, and Syria. Each of the recipients was asked two questions: Did it feel threatened by Germany? Had it authorized Roosevelt to make the proposal he had made? In swift due course, the desired negative answers were received from all those addressed (Belgium and the Netherlands among them), with the notable exceptions of Rumania and Switzerland. Hitler then prepared an address and delivered it to the Reichstag, which he called into special session on April 28 for the sole purpose of hearing and demonstratively responding to it. The two-hour speech, broadcast over hundreds of radio stations around the world (every major network in the United States carried it), was listened to by more people (literally hundreds of millions) than was any other speech he ever made.

It began with the usual tirade against the crimes of Versailles, proceeded to denounce as "mere inventions of the international press" reports that Germany planned to attack Poland, but then also, with Hitler's usual contempt for logical consistency, declared that the Polish-German ten-year nonaggression pact (initiated by Hitler himself in 1933) was voided by the new mutual-assistance treaty between Britain and Poland. Why? Because the British-Polish arrangement would "under certain circumstances [that is, *if Germany attacked Poland!*] . . . compel Poland to take military action against Germany." The 1935 Anglo-German Naval Treaty was also voided by Britain's new "policy of encirclement," the policy manifested by the British-Polish arrangement. The speech then proceeded to answer one by one some nineteen points which, according to Hitler, Roosevelt had raised in his letter. For instance: "Mr. Roosevelt declares that . . . all international problems can be solved at the council table." Yet "it was America herself who gave the sharpest expression to her mistrust in the effectiveness of conferences" when she refused to join the League of Nations, this despite the fact that the League had been "created in accordance with the will of an American President." Germany, on the other hand, had been eager to join at its outset this "greatest conference in the world" and had done so as soon as the bar against her membership raised at Versailles had been removed. "It was not till after years of purposeless participation that I resolved to follow the example of America and likewise leave the largest conference of the world. Since then I have solved the problems concerning my people which . . . were unfortunately not solved at the conference table of the League of Nations—and, too, without recourse to war in any case."

But the central point of Roosevelt's "curious telegram" was, of course, the one calling upon him, Hitler, to give assurances to some thirty-three named nation-states "that the German armed forces will not attack, and . . . invade" them. *"The answer"* (*Antwort*) was that, as he had taken pains to ascertain (he told of the communications he had had with the named nations), none of those whom Roosevelt had cited felt threatened by Germany, nor had a single one of them authorized the President of the United States to speak for it or intercede in any way in this matter.

> The German government is nevertheless prepared to give each of the States named an assurance of the kind desired by Mr. Roosevelt . . . provided that the State wishes it and itself addresses to Germany a request for such an assurance together with appropriate proposals. . . . And I here solemnly declare that all the assertions which have been circulated in any way concerning an intended German attack or invasion on or in American territory are rank frauds and gross untruths, quite apart from the fact that such assertions, so far as the military possibilities are concerned, could have their origin only in a stupid imagination.

Hitler's peroration was an exercise in ironic sarcasm whose heaviness and length seemed grossly excessive to most non-Germans but that, like the earlier reference to the League, was shrewdly designed to appeal to America's Roosevelt-hating isolationists. And it did so appeal. Some leading congressional isolationists enjoyed this Hitlerian "humor" almost as much, it would soon appear, as did the Reichstag, whose roaring approval of it now rang in the world's ears.

Mr. Roosevelt! [said Adolf Hitler.] I fully understand that the vastness of your nation and the immense wealth of your country allow you to feel responsible for the history of the whole world and the history of all nations. I, sir, am placed in a much more modest and smaller sphere. . . . I once took over a State which was faced by complete ruin, thanks to its trust in the promises of the rest of the world and to the bad regime of democratic governments. . . . Since then, Mr. Roosevelt, . . . I have regarded myself as called upon by Providence to serve my own people alone and to deliver them from frightful misery. Consequently, during the past six and one-half years, I have lived day and night for the single task of awakening the powers of my people. . . . I have conquered chaos in Germany, re-established order and enormously increased production in all branches of our national economy, by strenuous efforts produced substitutes for numerous materials that we lack, smoothed the way for new inventions, developed traffic, caused mighty roads to be built and canals to be dug, called into being gigantic new factories and at the same time endeavored to further the education and culture of our people. I have succeeded in finding useful work once more for the whole of the 7,000,000 unemployed [in 1933],* in keeping the German peasant on his soil . . . , in once more bringing German trade to a peak. . . . As precaution against the threat of another world war, not only have I united the German people politically, but I have rearmed them [and] . . . endeavored to destroy sheet by sheet that Treaty which in its 448 articles contains the vilest oppression which peoples . . . have ever been expected to put up with. . . . I have re-established the historic unity of German living space and, Mr. Roosevelt, I have endeavored to attain all this without spilling blood and without bringing to my people, and consequently to others, the misery of war. I, who twenty-one years ago was an unknown worker and soldier of my people, have attained this, Mr. Roosevelt, by my own energy. . . . You, Mr. President, . . . stepped [in 1933] to the head of one of the largest and wealthiest States in the world. You have the good fortune to have to feed scarcely fifteen people per square kilometer in your country. [Germany had to feed 140.] You have at your disposal the most unlimited mineral resources in the world. . . . Consequently . . . you perhaps believe that your intervention and action can be effective anywhere. . . . My world, Mr. Roosevelt, in which Providence has placed me . . . is limited to my people! I believe, however, that this is the way in which I can be of most service to that for which we are all concerned, namely, the justice, well-being, progress and peace of the whole human community.[17]

The effect of this interchange upon American public opinion was not what Roosevelt, when sending his missive, had hoped for, but neither was it all that he had feared. The initial response to the presidential message had been generally and surprisingly favorable. Isolationist attacks upon it were blunted by the "watering down" that Roosevelt had accomplished in his April 15 press conference. Many "who on principle objected to any involvement in European matters were ready to applaud a noncommittal appeal to reason and an invocation to peace," as William L. Langer and S. Everett Gleason have written.[18] After Hitler's reply was broadcast, however, it appeared that the whole of the interchange had done nothing to clear away obstacles in the path of Neutrality Act revision or repeal, and might even have added to them. The *Christian*

*The implicit invidious comparison of New Order with New Deal was obvious, especially to Roosevelt-haters. The number of U.S. unemployed, 15,653,000 in March 1933, was 11,145,000 in March 1939, according to American Federation of Labor estimates. (See *The American Year Book 1939* [New York, 1940], p. 613.)

*Century,* an influential organ of American Protestantism, deplored the President's having "taken his stand before the Axis dictators like some frontier sheriff at the head of a posse." The liberal Catholic *Commonweal* blamed him for ignoring "the wrongs committed by post-war England and France . . . [which] contributed to the impoverishment of the Axis powers." And some of the most prominent of congressional isolationists were very sure, and said privately, that Roosevelt in this encounter had been worsted by Hitler, and deserved to be. "Hitler had all the better of the argument," gloated Hiram Johnson in a letter to his son. "Roosevelt put his chin out and got a resounding whack. I have reached the conclusion that there will be no war. . . . Roosevelt wants to fight for any little thing. He wants . . . to knock down two dictators in Europe, so that one may be firmly implanted in America." Gerald Nye said somewhat the same thing publicly. "Mr. Roosevelt will not like it" (Hitler's speech), Nye told reporters, "but let it be remembered that he invited at least part of what was said. Certainly nothing said by Hitler can be taken as an insult to the American people, and it might be that a reasonable approach to Germany by our government now would invite better understanding and bring some rest to the world."[19]

III

SOME informed observers of the European scene, closely studying Hitler's April 28 speech, remarked a curious and perhaps significant fact: Not once, in a two-hour harangue of which approximately half dealt with Central and Eastern European concerns, was mention made of Russia or bolshevism. In his last major speech preceding this one, at Wilhelmshaven on April 1 (two days after the signing of the Anglo-Polish pact), der Führer had had much to say about the threat posed to civilization by the "Jewish bolshevist pest," about the triumph of Nationalist Spain over "devastating bolshevism" in that country, and about the "essential" difference between the "philosophical community" of fascist Italy and national-socialist Germany and the "nonhomogeneous body" which would be formed if "democratic Britain and the bolshevist Russia of Stalin" were to draw together. He betrayed some apprehension over, while at the same time ridiculing, the possibility that such a combination was in process of formation. Were there, then, "no philosophical or ideological differences of any kind between England and Soviet Russia"? If not, "how correct, indeed, is my position toward Marxism and communism and democracy!"[20] Nothing of this sort was said to the Reichstag on April 28.

And this fact, taken in conjunction with what Stalin had said on March 10, suggested to a very few analytical minds in the Western democracies a theretofore unthinkable idea, one that shook, if it did not shatter, the very foundations of current thought about European affairs. A basic given of such thought, determining most of the conceived pattern of European event as this had developed since the Great War, was the implacable enmity between Communism and Nazi-Fascism, and between their national embodiments. The very raison d'être of Fascism and Nazism was Communism, insofar as they had been conceived and shaped in antithetical (though also imitative) response to the latter. Hence the vast reluctance and inertia that had to be overcome by the new thought as it forced itself upon a very few minds; and hence the need to shape this thought in question form only. Were Stalin and Hitler now warily feeling each other out with a view to burying the ideological hatchet? Was there a real possibility that this hatchet might be buried deeply enough and long enough for the two to reach an effective economic and military agreement? Worst of all, were secret negotiations now actually under way toward a Russo-German accommodation whereby Germany would be enabled to crush Poland and then, if Britain and France honored their treaty obligations, turn full force against the West? The answer to the first two questions, in the minds that raised them, was a highly tentative yes. The answer to the third was an even more tentative no, a very temporary no. For, though definite negotiations between Russia and Germany were almost certainly not now under way, they might be very soon. Much, if not all, depended on how Britain and France responded to Russia's latest diplomatic initiative.

On April 17, near midnight, the British ambassador in Moscow had been summoned to the Kremlin to receive from the hand of Maxim Litvinov a written proposal for a triple alliance of Britain, France, and Russia. It would be a mutual-assistance pact—each signatory would be obligated to act against an aggressor upon any one of them—but it would also be a guarantee by the three to come to the aid of any Eastern European state between the Baltic and the Black Sea (Britain had by this time extended to Rumania and Greece the same guarantee she had made to Poland) that was attacked. Litvinov had then summoned home for consultations the Soviet ambassadors to Britain and France. Obviously, what Litvinov proposed was essential to the practical meaningfulness of the guarantees already extended from London and Paris to Eastern Europe. Without Russian cooperation, Britain or France could do virtually nothing in direct aid of Poland, Rumania, Greece, or any Balkan country attacked by Germany. With such cooperation, on the other hand, they might regain much of the advantage over Hitler that had been thrown away at Munich. Hitler might again find himself in a fatal position, as he had been the previous summer before the stupidity and cowardice of the Western leaders, upon which he so heavily counted, came to his rescue—a position untenable for more than a few weeks or months, yet one from which he could neither advance nor retreat without destroying the Nazi regime and losing, in all probability, his life. (Wrote Churchill: "Hitler could afford neither to embark upon the war on two fronts, which he himself had so deeply condemned, nor sustain a check. It was a pity not to have placed him in this awkward position. . . ."[21]) Made clear, too, by the speed with which Hitler escalated the Polish crisis, and by the anxious impatience Litvinov evinced as he thrust his written proposal into the British ambassador's hand, was the need for a prompt, encouraging reply to Moscow from London and Paris.

No such reply was made, however. Profoundly prejudiced against the Soviets, distrustful of their motives, contemptuous of Russia as a military power, and, above all, persistent in his conviction that the destruction of Communist Russia remained Hitler's ultimate goal, Chamberlain, with Halifax, paid reluctant, leisurely, and desultory attention to the Litvinov document. There were consultations with Polish leaders, who deemed Nazism far preferable to Communism, and Russian "protection" a greater danger than German expansionism. There were consultations with Rumanian leaders, some of whom were of the same mind as the Poles. There was leisurely consideration of possible counterproposals of a kind Poland could accept. And there was action aimed at implementing, if only potentially, Britain's foreign guarantees: On April 27, thanks to relentless pressures exerted upon a stubbornly resistant Chamberlain by War Minister Leslie Hore-Belisha, the most popular and forceful member of the British Cabinet, Britain introduced the first peacetime military conscription in all her history. Toward Moscow, however, concerning the alliance proposal, London maintained silence as the passing days added up to weeks. Not until May 8, a full three weeks after Litvinov's note was handed to the British ambassador, did the Chamberlain ministry reply to it.

But by that time, Litvinov was not on hand to receive it. Victimized by London's prolonged silence, following as it did a long series of rebuffs by London, he had on the night of May 3 been abruptly relieved of his duties as Soviet foreign minister ("by his own request," said a back-page news brief in the Soviet press next morning) and replaced by V. M. Molotov, who, as Soviet premier, was known in the West to be one of Stalin's closest associates and trusted confidants. Molotov's appointment was the top-featured news of May 9 in the Soviet press—and the well-informed of the watching world took note of the fact that, unlike Litvinov, this new commissar of foreign affairs was not a Jew. A major impediment to the establishment of amicable relations with Hitler's Germany had been removed. Did this mean that such relations were now in process of being established?

The possibility seems not to have been recognized by Neville Chamberlain. On May 10, *Izvestia,* official organ of the Soviet government, sharply criticized the British reply to the Litvinov proposal as unacceptably lopsided in that it would oblige Russia to come at once to the aid of Britain and France if they became involved in war in consequence of their guarantees to Poland and Rumania, but would not obligate them to do the same for Russia if she became involved in war in consequence of her guarantees to her immediately neighboring states, guarantees which the counterproposal specifically obliged her to make but which, it must be added, were emphatically not welcomed by most of these neighbors, who deemed them dangerous to their sovereignty. Three days later, Molotov formally rejected the counterproposal on the grounds *Izvestia* had stated, insisting instead upon a triple alliance extending guarantees to the Baltic states as well as to Poland and Rumania. There followed a month during which no British move toward Russia was made but during which, also, it was made clear to Chamberlain that such a move was urgently desired by an overwhelming majority of the British public and Parliament.

Finally, in mid-June, Chamberlain sent a special envoy to Moscow to negotiate with Molotov. The move, vitiated by its belatedness, was further vitiated by Chamberlain's choice of envoy. If the mission were to be deemed by Moscow a serious and sincere effort, the envoy should be a man whose rank approximated Molotov's—and, indeed, Moscow had let it be known that Foreign Minister Halifax would be welcomed. Halifax chose not to go, however; and when Anthony Eden, whose prestige was high in Russia, volunteered his services, his offer was rejected. Instead, there was chosen one William Strang, an able but second-rank career official of the Foreign Office whose negotiating authority was severely limited by both his rank and his instructions. Molotov deemed this personally insulting. He received Strang coldly and did nothing thereafter to lessen, and much to increase, the difficulties in the way of a firm triple alliance. The negotiations dragged on, and on, with the Russians interposing so many obstacles to an agreement that their desire for one was called into question—this while subtle signs multiplied that the Soviet leadership, desperately seeking safe haven from the storm about to break over Europe, might indeed be dealing covertly with Germany at the same time as it ostensibly strove for a Western alliance.

Meanwhile, Hitler, undeterred and seemingly unperturbed by the prospect of new world war, pressed relentlessly toward an early "solution" of the "Polish problem."


IV


FOR Franklin Roosevelt and millions of his fellow Americans there were two bright spots, one much brighter than the other, amid the deepening gloom of that spring of 1939. The first was a brave gesture toward the future, the second a ceremonial reaffirmation of ancient national ties.

On April 30, the hundred and fiftieth anniversary of George Washington's inauguration as first President of the United States, the nation's thirty-second President formally opened the New York World's Fair. It was the greatest such fair in history. For three years it had been a-building in Flushing Meadow, atop a garbage dump (the Past? the Present?) in the New York borough of Queens, and it now asserted with awesome impressiveness and defiant optimism, and at an ultimate cost of over $170 million, that there was a shining "World of Tomorrow" (circa 1960) beyond the terror, the persisting depression, the flames, the bloodshed of the present day—a world of peace, happiness, beauty, prosperity, and, above all (or as the sum of all), limitless technological power harnessed in service of the Common Man. Two thematic structures were supposed to convey this message. One was a slender swordlike pyramid, dubbed the Trylon, thrust seven hundred feet into the air. The other, beside it, was "the world's largest perfect sphere," two hundred feet in diameter, dubbed the Perisphere. (Eleanor Roosevelt, who accompanied her husband and mother-in-law to the gala opening, and whose beloved friend, Lorena Hickock, was fair president Grover Whalen's assistant in charge of press publicity, wore that day a tan dress on which was printed in white a pattern of the fair's Trylon-Perisphere emblem.[22])

Within the Trylon were the two longest escalators in the world, up one of which some five million people would ride during the next two years to a bridge that arched between the Trylon and the Perisphere. They would cross that bridge into the hollow Perisphere, where, from revolving platforms, they would view for precisely five and a half minutes, until the platforms ejected them onto the bridge in the light of the present-day, a wondrous city of the future, "Democracity," modeled in meticulously detailed miniature. It was most emphatically a planned city, created not by individualistic private enterprise but cooperatively, collectively, by and through government. It consisted of a central metropolis of beautiful buildings, which was exclusively a workplace. The population lived in apartment buildings, surrounded by spacious lawns and gardens, which rimmed the metropolis, or in towns scattered through a wide, planned greenbelt wherein, also, were factories surrounded by landscaped open space. The whole was tied together by a network of express highways five hundred feet wide and minor roads three hundred feet wide, along which the populace could swiftly, safely shuttle from home to workplace, from workplace to home. Democracity was undoubtedly impressive. It was less memorable, however, and would be seen by far fewer people, than General Motors's famed "Futurama." The brainchild of America's most gifted theater stage designer, Norman Bel Geddes, and built at a cost of $7 million, Futurama comprised "500,000 buildings, 10 million trees (of eighteen species), and 50,000 cars, of which 10,000 were in motion."[23] Like Democracity, it featured a metropolis whose elements came together according to an overall plan of a kind individualistic entrepreneurship could not possibly produce, though the whole of the exhibit was of course intended by GM's corporate executives to be a paean to untrammeled private enterprise. Its buildings were of seven standardized heights, were so spaced that none of them shadowed another, and were arranged in self-contained blocks between which were pedestrian ways soaring high above the city traffic. This ideal city was, however, a much smaller proportion of the total exhibit than was the case with Democracity. Futurama also "showed unspoiled countryside, the vastness of America, the variety of the land, the beauty of its terrain," as Alice G. Marquis has written. "It implied a perpetual frontier, a frontier that in the future would become more accessible than ever by automobile. Some people might have to —or even want to—live in cities, it suggested, but the American rural ideal was but a Sunday drive away."[24] And this drive would be made in perfect safety along fourteen-lane main highways, each car moving in the lane designated for its speed (the outer-lane speed was as high as one hundred miles an hour), with transition lanes between the main ones; and each car would be equipped with a radio beam device at its front and rear which would keep it automatically at a safe distance from the car ahead and the car behind. No car would need headlights: At dusk, light strips along the highway lanes would wink on as a car approached, and off as it passed. Significantly, Futurama would be viewed, not collectively by people standing up in close-packed lines, as Democracity would be, but individualistically, each visitor seated comfortably in an upholstered chair as he or she was borne noiselessly, smoothly, in fifteen minutes, from daybreak to nightfall, across the wondrous America of 1960.

Central to the fair's geography, comprising a goodly portion of the fairground's 1267.5 acres, was a so-called Court of Peace, a vast oblong area along the sides of which were ranged the pavilions of sixty nations, many of them lavish indeed (the Italian pavilion cost $5 million, that of the Soviet Union $4 million). Included were most of the nations then in existence: two whose nationhood had been extinguished by Nazi-Fascist aggression within the last few weeks (the national flags above the Czech and Albanian pavilions flew at half-mast); one, Poland, that was threatened with imminent invasion; one, Japan, which was at the moment bloodily engaged in the rape of a neighbor; and every nation that could be classed as "major" save China, Spain, and Germany. The last, in view of the bitter popular protest its symbolic presence would certainly provoke, had not been invited to participate.

It was in this Court of Peace, upon a "Plaza of Freedom," that the speaker's platform had been erected. The great crowd assembled before it on this opening day was only too aware of the contradiction between the future the fair depicted and the future that, according to all present signs, actually immediately impended. The crowd's mood, therefore, was as mixed and mingled as the shifting moods of that day's weather. At dawn the sky had been bright and clear; Trylon and Perisphere had gleamed in brilliant sunlight through much of the morning. But the sky above Franklin Roosevelt's bared head, when he rose to speak, was darkly, sullenly menacing, threatening the chill rain that by late afternoon would leave "the crowd's spirit . . . broken," as *The New York Times* reported next day.* Nor was the President's speech of a kind likely to dispel any prevailing gloom. He confessed at its outset that he'd seen few of the fair's abundant wonders—only enough of them to justify his congratulating "all of you who conceived and planned the Fair and all you men and women who built it." And the words that followed were lame, banal, perfunctory, mostly concerned with the fact that "the permanent Government of the United States" had begun with Washington's first inaugural here in New York City a century and a half ago. Not till near the end of his discourse did he refer to the symbolism of the Court of Peace. He said then that the participation of sixty nations in this great international exposition was "a gesture of friendship and good will toward the United States for which I render most grateful

---

*The dismal weather might later be taken to presage the fair's abysmal financial failure. Less than a fifth as many admission tickets were sold on the fair's opening day as Grover Whalen had predicted (198,000 as compared with 1,000,000); only a fifth as many would be sold over the fair's two-year life as had been predicted. Purchasers of fair bonds would eventually receive a return of but 20 cents on every dollar invested and might deem it distressingly apropos that the chairman of the $28 million fair-bond drive wherein they had made their purchases in 1936 was Richard Whitney, the former New York Stock Exchange president who, by the time the fair opened, was a convicted embezzler serving time in Sing Sing (see p. 215).

thanks." He said that visitors coming here from abroad would "receive the heartiest of welcomes" and would also find "that the eyes of the United States are fixed on the future. Yes," he concluded, "our wagon is still hitched to a star. But [unlike an earlier star?] it is a star of friendship, a star of progress for mankind, a star of greater happiness and less hardship, a star of international good will, and, above all, a star of peace."[25]

One circumstance alone made memorable, in after years, this uninspired performance: It was the first presidential address ever to be broadcast live over television. A single cumbersome TV camera focused upon Roosevelt as he spoke. Its picture, marred by "white streaks," as *The New York Times* reported, was seen on perhaps two hundred nine-inch television screens scattered within fifty miles of the broadcasting station.

The second bright spot of that season of gloom was, for Roosevelt especially, very bright indeed, in that it accomplished precisely and almost flawlessly what it had been designed to do. And Roosevelt himself was its chief designer.

While in Canada last August to deliver his Queen's University and International Bridge dedicatory speeches he had been informed by Canada's prime minister, Mackenzie King, in strictest confidence, that King George VI and Queen Elizabeth of England were contemplating a ceremonial visit to Canada in the summer of 1939. He had at once (August 25, 1938) addressed to the King in Buckingham Palace a personal letter expressing his earnest hope that, should such a visit take place, "You will extend [it] . . . to include the United States" because this would "not only . . . give my wife and me the greatest pleasure" but also "be an excellent thing for Anglo-American relations." He reminded the king that "an International Exposition is to be held in New York City" and pointed out that "you could come from Montreal or Ottawa to New York" in "only an overnight journey." His hope and wish at that time seem to have been that the royal couple, after briefly visiting the New York fair, would choose to "avoid the [summer] heat of Washington" and the strenuous ceremony of a state visit to the capital, coming instead to "our country house at Hyde Park which is on the Hudson River . . . for three or four days of very simple country life . . . with no formal entertainments."[26] On November 2, 1938, he joyfully replied to a letter from King George indicating that "the visit is a definite possibility." He had, he said, discussed the matter with Britain's Ambassador Lindsay, and the two were "agreed it would probably be advisable for you and Her Majesty to pay a formal visit to me at the Capital." He strongly objected, however, to Lindsay's calling the visit to Washington "the principal part of the plan," as Lindsay had done in an "informal memorandum" to him, a copy of which he enclosed. Lindsay "does not even refer to your coming to stay with Mrs. Roosevelt and me at Hyde Park," Roosevelt complained. "I know you will not mind my telling you that in my judgment, to the American people, the essential democracy of yourself and the Queen makes the greatest appeal of all. Probably the official visit to the Capital should be made, and also a visit to New York, but if you could stay with us at Hyde

Park for two or three days, the simpliciy and naturalness of such a visit would produce a most excellent effect—in addition to giving my wife and me the greatest possible pleasure in getting to know you both."[27]

Thereafter, delighted by the chance to manage this one glittering event amid the dark multitude that were in effect managing him, he did so with boyish zeal and zest. The event was without precedent. Never before had a reigning English monarch set foot in this country born of rebellion against an English monarch. And the pleasure Roosevelt took in the ceremony was of the kind he had taken in Groton play-acting and annually took in his Cuff-Links Club parties and national birthday celebrations. But, as in the case of the fund-raising birthdays, he had also a serious purpose. He strove to make the royal visit the most popularly effective demonstration possible of the closeness of Anglo-American ties—a show mingling aristocratic glamour with democratic home-folksiness, in which the Common Man of both Britain and America could wholeheartedly vicariously participate and which, by that token, was bound to weaken exclusive, isolationist sentiments. He was at pains to avoid all that would make the event politically controversial. When it was suggested that the British prime minister or foreign secretary might accompany the royal couple, he flatly opposed the idea. The show of warm friendship should be *purely* that, he insisted. Spectators should be left free to draw their own conclusions as to its Anglo-American foreign-policy implications. On the other hand, he encouraged Mackenzie King to accompany the royal party because his doing so would emphasize in the public mind, and in a noncontroversial way, the Monroe Doctrine implications of his Queen's University address.

Of the careful planning that ensued, virtually no detail escaped Roosevelt's watchful, measuring, revising eye. In mid-January, having "just received word from Canada that they are expecting you [King George] and Her Majesty to arrive at Niagara Falls, Ontario, at about 4:00 P.M. on Wednesday, June 7," and to reenter Canada on the morning of Monday, June 12, he enclosed with a personal letter to the king an itinerary and agenda for the U.S. visit which he himself had worked out and which, in the event, with minor alterations, was followed. He asked for and obtained from Bullitt, the latter having obtained through the British embassy in Paris (Kennedy in London was thus snubbingly bypassed), recommendations for the care and feeding of Their Royal Majesties which were so excessively detailed that they seemed ludicrous to both Bullitt and Roosevelt but which were at once transmitted to the White House social secretary, Mrs. Helm, with the request "that you show [them] . . . to Mrs. Roosevelt" while warning her they were "confidential." In mid-May, he asked Eleanor to obtain for him a complete list of all members of the royal party who, as guests of the Roosevelts, were to attend services in Hyde Park's St. James Episcopal Church on Sunday morning, June 11. Since the royal party numbered sixty people and the church would hold only 150, the St. James rector was to "distribute to the regular congregation these extra seats by ticket so that no outsiders will be able to get in." He personally arranged the service itself, easily prevailing upon Henry St. George Tucker, the presiding bishop of the Protestant Episcopal Church, to conduct it with the assistance of the St. James rector and "Mr. Smith, the Rector of the Little Church of England church at our summer home at Campobello Island, N.B.," as he wrote to the bishop on May 17. On June 3, five days before the royal couple were to arrive in Washington, he bombarded Mrs. Helm with no fewer than six separate one- or two-sentence memoranda concerning the guest list "for the Tea on Friday afternoon" (why was Lady Nunburnholme not on it, since she "is staying in the house"?), the seating arrangement around the great horseshoe table for the state dinner in the White House on the evening of June 8, and the guest list for the picnic lunch to be given for the royal couple at his new Hilltop Cottage at Hyde Park following Sunday church services ("The picnic list . . . is O.K. [Marion Dickerman and Nancy Cook were on it*] except for one change . . .—The Secretary of the Treasury and Mrs. Morgenthau come before Bishop Tucker").[28]

This presidential attention to detail paid off. From the moment the king and queen were formally welcomed to the United States by Secretary of State and Mrs. Hull at Niagara Falls in the late afternoon of June 7, until they boarded the royal train at Hyde Park station for their return to Canada on the night of June 11, everything that was humanly controllable marched straight and true along the path so carefully planned for it. Washington's weather, alas, was not only uncontrollable but uncooperative. Bright sunlight filled the days of June 8 and 9 (there were thundershowers on the evening of the eighth), but so did sweltering heat—the thick, humid heat that so often blankets the capital in summer. That no one collapsed of it during the crowded garden party at the British embassy on the afternoon of June 8 nor during the formal dinner and following musical entertainment in the White House that night was part of the good fortune attending the whole of this affair. (Ickes's young wife, Jane, who was six months pregnant, almost collapsed during the after-dinner musicale in the East Room, where popular radio singer Kate Smith, the incomparable Marian Anderson, and operatic baritone Lawrence Tibbett performed. "I really think the President ought to do something about air-conditioning the White House, especially the public rooms," fumed Ickes in his diary three days later. ". . . I cannot forget that I strongly urged the President to let us air-condition the White House as a PWA project in 1933 but he would not give his consent."[29])

By that time the royal couple had captivated both their immediate audience and, through press and radio, their national one. The king was a naturally shy, perhaps excessively conscientious young man (he had with difficulty mastered an embarrassing stammer) whose virtuous domesticity and selfless devotion to public duty contrasted sharply with the willful selfish hedonism of his elder brother, the abdicated Edward VIII, now the exiled Duke of Windsor. George's diminutive physical stature surprised those who, from his photo-

*Nancy Cook's informal snapshots were the only photographs taken at this picnic, no others being permitted. They remained unpublished until the early 1970s.

graphs, had expected a much taller man—Roosevelt and Eleanor towered over him and his wife, who was yet shorter than he, when the four stood together —but he had presence and a trim figure, and carried himself well. His queen's physical appearance also surprised those who saw her in the flesh and, from her photographs, had expected a less attractive woman. She struck a great many as actually pretty. Each of the two had a real dignity joined, seemingly without effort, to spontaneous graciousness and a "democratic" manner, and this made a highly favorable popular impression, which was reinforced next day when they went with the Roosevelts up the Potomac on the presidential yacht to Mount Vernon and, on the way back, at Arlington, laid a wreath (the king did) on the tomb of the Unknown Soldier. The impression was deepened beyond possibility of erasure in the following two days. On Saturday, June 10, they briefly visited the New York fair, then motored up the Hudson to Hyde Park where, for a day and a half, they became simply family friends of the Roosevelts come from abroad to visit in the latter's country home. The world was promptly told, though the press, how the king and President, after an informal family dinner in the Hyde Park Big House that evening, sat up until one-thirty in the morning, alone together, talking about "everything under the sun"—a conversation ended only when Roosevelt, placing his hand on the king's knee, said, "Young man, it's time for you to go to bed!" The shining event's culmination and symbolic apotheosis was the typically Rooseveltian picnic served the royal couple at Hilltop Cottage next day. Hot dogs, potato salad, baked beans, and strawberry shortcake were the featured foods, the only publicized food, though actually there was a substantial array of fancier fare of which the queen partook (her mouth was "too small" to encompass a hot dog, according to Marion Dickerman).

The farewell scene at Hyde Park's railroad station that night was poignant, sharpened by awareness of what this young couple returned to—a war-shadowed England, a London on which bombs might soon come raining down, a Buckingham Palace that might soon become a ruin. Someone started singing "Auld Lang Syne" as the royal couple boarded the royal train. The crowd gathered by the tracks joined in. And as the train pulled out Roosevelt's vibrant tenor voice was heard calling after it, "Good luck to you! All the luck in the world."[30]

## V

As for Roosevelt, he returned from his happy Hyde Park weekend to a Washington where his own luck, as pertaining to his primary concern of that sultry season, was bad—and bad mostly because of his excessive reliance upon it. For four long months, jealously hoarding what remained to him of his former governing power, fearful of another disastrous public display of impotence, and (most important) far from clear in his own mind what should be done, he had remained publicly passive and silent concerning Neutrality Act revision. He had assigned to Key Pittman, who was the very embodiment of haphazard

randomness, the management of this key enterprise, contenting himself with
a mild public hint now and then that repeal of the arms embargo might be a
good idea. In sum, he had trusted to luck—had waited upon events to fall of
their own accord into the pattern he felt was the right one, or at least to point
the way he should go. The result, by the end of April, was chaos. A disgusted
and disheartened J. Pierrepont Moffat of the State Department indicated in his
diary, as May opened, that after weeks of hearings the Foreign Relations
Committee was no nearer to reporting the Pittman bill, one way or the other,
than it had been at the outset. Pittman had little or no control over his
committee. Individual senators, in the absence of word from White House or
State Department, fed their fact-starved minds on rumors and guesses about
the administration's wishes. Moffat, during his visits to the Senate, heard
"everything from a rumor that the Administration wants complete repeal to
the rumor that the Administration wants nothing done," as he noted in his
diary on May 3.[31]

Yet at that very moment Moffat was engaged with a half dozen other high
State Department officials, and with Hull himself, in a belated effort to supply
the crying need for a clear statement of administration policy on this matter.
He and they were putting into final form written testimony to be presented by
Hull personally to a closed session of the Foreign Relations Committee. It was
arduous labor, demonstrating once again the foolish inefficiency of committee
drafting. Every phrase, almost every word and punctuation mark, was questioned and debated before being approved. And when the task was at last
completed, after nearly a fortnight of toil, Pittman, upon being shown the draft
testimony, promptly and roughly pronounced it worthless as a persuasive
instrument. Hull would do better to cancel his appearance before the committee than to present this to it, said the senator, adding that if Hull *did* appear
it could not be in closed session. Committee members now demanded an open
hearing; Borah and Hiram Johnson, especially, were eager to quiz the secretary
publicly concerning the relationship between Neutrality Act revision and administration policy toward Britain, France, China. A hurt and angry Hull had
then canceled his appearance—a move that denied isolationists an opportunity
to sway public opinion, certainly, but at the cost of further confusing the
American public, further encouraging the aggressive mood in Berlin, and
further increasing alarm and dismay in the foreign offices of London and Paris.

The culmination of this futile exercise had come on May 16 when, abruptly,
without warning, the erratic and wavering Pittman announced in a letter to
Hull that he was again postponing for several weeks any further consideration
of neutrality legislation by his committee. This was tantamount to postponing
action on it by the Senate as a whole until the next session of Congress opened
in January 1940. Pittman's stated reason was as shocking and infuriating to
Hull as the act itself: The secretary, whose war anxieties were lifted higher and
higher every day on the flood tide of alarming cables pouring in from Europe,
had now to read that, according to the Foreign Relations chairman, "the

situation in Europe does not seem to induce [*sic*] any urgent action on neutrality legislation."[32]

By then, however, Roosevelt with Hull's concurrence had begun to hedge the bad bet he had made on Pittman.

For many weeks, beginning in March, New York's representative Sol Bloom, chairman of the House Foreign Affairs Committee, had been begging the administration to permit him to initiate in his committee a neutrality bill that had the administration's blessing. His wish had been opposed by State Department officials, including most definitely Cordell Hull, who felt that Bloom was unreliable and untrustworthy. How Bloom could have been deemed less reliable than Pittman, considering the latter's record, makes an interesting question, answerable in large part by the fact that Bloom was most emphatically a Jewish "character," one as if designed (self-designed) to focus upon himself the anti-Semitism that then permeated the upper echelons of the State Department. Admittedly, he was no foreign-affairs expert: He had prospered as a sheet-music publisher, then increased his fortune through shrewd real-estate deals, before entering Congress in 1923, and he had not since made any serious study of international affairs. His committee chairmanship had come to him solely through seniority, when Representative Sam D. McReynolds, an administration stalwart, was forced by illness to relinquish his post in the fall of 1938. Admittedly, also, Bloom notably lacked the diplomatic temperament, the diplomatist's manner. A flamboyant, extroverted, urban type, brash, uninhibited—an exhibitionist whose antics were sometimes amusing but often merely ridiculous—he grated harshly upon such as prim, cautious, homespun Hull.[33]

It had therefore been with extreme reluctance that the secretary on March 10, immediately following the forced cancellation of his Pittman committee testimony, and after consultation with Roosevelt, permitted a high State Department official to attend a closed session of Bloom's committee and there present to it, for study, a draft neutrality bill. A couple of days later, Roosevelt had granted Bloom an interview during which the proposal to shift the administration's primary neutrality-revision effort from Senate to House was discussed. And on May 19, three days after the total collapse of Pittman's feeble effort, the decision to do what Bloom had long urged was perforce made. Bloom was summoned to the White House that day, along with Hull, House Speaker Bankhead, House Majority Leader Rayburn, and other House leaders, there to hear from the President that he, the President, was now determined, at long last, to fight openly and all-out for a neutrality bill that repealed the arms embargo while retaining, perhaps, the cash-and-carry and combat-zone provisions of the 1937 act. When Bankhead and Rayburn warned him that arms-embargo repeal would be extremely difficult to achieve, Roosevelt reiterated that the effort to do so must be made, and at once, since repeal would in his belief actually prevent the outbreak of European war or, if it did not, "would make less likely a victory for the powers unfriendly to the United States."[34]

The responsibility which now devolved upon Sol Bloom brought out qualities in him which, in the present situation, counted heavily against his disabilities. They included mental agility, great energy, much courage, and an anti-Nazi fervor that, fed by his sense of personal peril, made him a more dedicated and tenacious warrior for collective security than Pittman or many State Department officials would ever be. He introduced as his own the administration bill (it had been substantially drafted in the State Department) on May 29 and initiated consideration of it by his committee in executive session on June 5. On the following day the committee voted to repeal the arms embargo, though on a close count (11–9). On the day after that several restrictive amendments proposed by the arch-reactionary, arch-isolationist Republican Hamilton Fish (he represented Roosevelt's own congressional district) were defeated. The momentum thus established might well have resulted in a favorable committee report on the bill on June 8 and approval by the full House in the following week if, ironically, it had not been interrupted by the visit of the king and queen of England. A committee majority voted to suspend further consideration of the measure for the duration of this visit, and the smooth sailing that the Bloom bill had theretofore had was never after resumed. When the committee reported the bill favorably on June 13, it was on a straight party vote, twelve Democrats against eight Republicans.

And with the bill thus clearly become a partisan issue, the threat posed to it by Democratic disaffections, in view of Republican conservative cohesiveness, became acute. Strenuous efforts to prevent such disaffections were made during the two weeks before floor debate began on June 27. For one thing, Bloom was persuaded not to manage the floor fight for the bill himself but, instead, to let Texas's Luther Johnson do so. A more experienced floor manager than Bloom, Johnson was not prone as Bloom was to misguided humor. And Johnson, loyally assisted by Bloom, performed well. By the evening of June 29, a series of amendments designed to preserve mandatory neutrality had been defeated by large majorities. House passage of the bill in the form desired by the administration seemed certain.

Then came disaster.

Late in the night of the twenty-ninth yet another crippling amendment was proposed, this by Republican John M. Vorys of Ohio, who described it as a "compromise" between total repeal of the embargo and total retention of it. Arms and ammunition were to be embargoed, but not "instruments of war," with the latter loosely defined to include airplanes and other things that had peaceful as well as military uses. The intended effect was, of course, the evisceration of the bill as an administration measure—and after a brief debate this amendment, too, was voted down. Its defeat, however, was by a show of hands, and Hamilton Fish, after a pause in the proceedings, demanded an accurate record vote. Tellers were called in. And to the astonishment and dismay of administration forces (many Democrats, assuming that the hand vote was conclusive, had left the chamber) the Vorys amendment was then adopted by a majority of two, 159–157. Next day, desperate efforts were made to remove this amendment. They failed. The Republican ranks held firm, and the 150 of them who voted to retain the amendment (only seven voted against doing so) were joined by sixty-one Democrats to defeat the repeal attempt, 214–173. The bill, with the arms embargo thus restored, then passed the House, 200–188.[35]

Roosevelt's anguish was palpable. One of the Democrats who voted for the Vorys amendment was New York representative Caroline O'Day, a staunch liberal of strong pacifist convictions who had long been one of Eleanor's and his close friends. To her Roosevelt addressed on July 1 a "Dear Caroline" letter which, for all its restrained language, she recognized as a bitterly angry rebuke:

> I think it may interest you to tell you in great confidence that two of our Embassies abroad tell us this afternoon that the action of the House last night has caused dismay in democratic peaceful circles. The anti-war nations believe that a definite stimulus has been given Hitler by the vote of the House, and that if war breaks out in Europe . . . an important part of the responsibility will rest on last night's action. I know you always want me to be frank with you and I honestly believe that the vote last night was a stimulus to war and that if the result had been different it would have been a definite encouragement to peace.[36]

On that same day he addressed to Attorney General Murphy a memorandum enclosing a note just received from Ickes, advising him to announce that under the Constitution "his was the duty and obligation to conduct foreign affairs and that he proposed to do so without any assistance from Congress"—a position that Vice President Garner, a bit surprisingly and quite possibly from ulterior motives, had urged upon the President during the June 30 Cabinet meeting. "As you know," said the memo, "the V.P. [argues] . . . that the President should not be bound at all by legislation [that] . . . offends his constitutional powers. If we fail to get any Neutrality Bill, how far do you think I can go in ignoring the existing act—even though I did sign it?!"[37] (That he dared not openly ignore it to even a slight degree, whatever his constitutional powers, he doubtless realized before Murphy had so much as read this missive.) Several other items of his correspondence testify to the anger, born of frustration, that he felt at this time, and to the hardening of combative liberal resolve that was the obverse of his increased bitterness toward conservative enemies. Thus, in a memo to Leon Henderson on July 1, he asked the latter to check a report from the Treasury Department "on the 'spendable income' of very rich people in comparison with the 'net income' on which they report and pay personal Federal and State income taxes." He was, he said, "fed up" with "very rich people who say they . . . pay 75 or 80% of their income in personal income taxes" when in fact they had huge "spendable incomes" on which they paid no income tax at all.[38] On July 7, he addressed to Wilbur

Cross, former Connecticut governor, now editor of the *Yale Review,* an ill-considered "personal protest" against an article in that quarterly's current issue, entitled "Mr. Hopkins and Mr. Roosevelt," by fervently anti-Roosevelt isolationist John T. Flynn. He had, he said, "watched" Flynn for "many years and . . . he has always, with practically no exception, been a destructive . . . force. Therefore . . . John T. Flynn should be barred . . . from the columns of any presentable daily paper, monthly magazine or national quarterly."[39]

By that time, the amended Bloom bill had gone to the Senate Foreign Relations Committee, which meant that the administration's neutrality-law-revision hopes were again in the slippery, fumbling hands of Key Pittman. And Pittman was operating true to form. A few days before, he had been very substantially bribed by Roosevelt not only to support a continuation of presidential power to fix the gold value of the dollar* but also to deal expeditiously with neutrality legislation. For months there had been before Congress a proposal by the Western silver bloc, headed by Pittman, to raise to 77.57 cents an ounce the price (currently 64.64 cents) that, under the terms of the Silver Purchase Act, the Treasury was required to pay for domestic silver. In effect, the proposal was of a dramatic increase in what was already an outrageously high federal subsidization of Western silver interests (silver could be bought on the world market for 41 cents an ounce), and Roosevelt had flatly, stubbornly opposed it. Then, on the last day of June, just as his two-year dollar-devaluation power was about to expire, Roosevelt gave in. He let it be known that he was willing to "compromise" on a silver price of 71 cents.[40] Whereupon Pittman promised that final action on the Bloom bill, with removal from it of the Vorys amendment, would be taken by his committee at its Wednesday, July 5, meeting. He failed, however, even to bring the bill up for consideration that day: Too many committee members were too busy with other urgent legislative matters to pay proper attention to the neutrality issue, he explained. Final action, he now promised, would be taken on Saturday, July 8. But on July 8 he announced that so many committee members were out of town for the weekend that final action must be deferred until Tuesday, July 11. This dawdling gave isolationist senators Nye, Clark, and Johnson ample time in which to organize a solid bloc of thirty-four senators who were "unalterably opposed to repeal or modification of the present Neutrality Law" and were prepared to filibuster if the administration measure came to the floor on a favorable committee report.

Yet with respect to the action of the committee itself, the White House, on the eve of the decisive day, was cautiously optimistic. Of the committee's twenty-three votes, eleven were firmly committed to the administration bill, ten were firmly against it, and the two members who had not publicly committed themselves one way or the other were Democrats known to favor repeal of all neutrality legislation. These two, however, were Georgia's Walter F.

*See p. 416.

George and Iowa's Guy M. Gillette, each a major target of Roosevelt's purge attempt last summer, each a bitter political foe of the President. They were therefore vulnerable to the plea that Bennett Clark made to them in a very private conversation among the three on the night of July 10—a plea, not that they vote against the Bloom bill, but that they vote for a postponement of consideration of it until the next session of Congress. In Europe, a surface calm had for some weeks masked those ominous undercurrents of which the State Department's coded cables made daily report—a fact that made superficially plausible Clark's assertion that general European war was *not* imminent, Roosevelt and Hull to the contrary notwithstanding, and consequently there was no urgent need for immediate congressional action on neutrality. Had not Pittman himself admitted as much?

When the committee meeting opened next day, Clark at once moved to postpone the Bloom bill's consideration until 1940. His motion was at once seconded. The vote on it was at once taken. And the motion carried, 12–11, with George and Gillette voting with the majority.* The meeting was then adjourned, barely a quarter-hour after it had been called to order.[42]

Roosevelt's fury, amid the sullen sultry heat of a Washington July, was now compounded. He immediately prepared a message to Congress denouncing in intemperate language "those who scream from the housetops that this nation is being led into war, . . . that this government is being tricked into the support of any group of foreign nations. . . ." Those making such false allegations "deserve only the utmost contempt and pity of the American people," he continued. It was with difficulty that Cordell Hull, at the cost of himself suffering a searing blast of presidential heat, persuaded Roosevelt not to send this tirade to a Congress that could only have been further alienated by it— and after a United Press correspondent somehow learned of the stormy session during which Hull accomplished this feat, Roosevelt publicly blasted the press service for disseminating to its subscribing newspapers a dispatch saying he and Hull "were reported in Administration quarters today to have disagreed on the language of a neutrality message." The United Press, employing the "obvious subterfuge" of attribution to an anonymous source, "has been guilty of a falsification of the actual facts," the President stormed in a written statement issued on July 13. "If called upon to give the source . . . they will decline to give it—another usual subterfuge. . . . It is, of course, impossible for the White House to deny every false story. This latest episode, however, represents the limit of any decent person's patience." The press had been "informed continuously for the past 36 hours that the President and the Secretary of State have not decided, up to the present time, whether he will

---

*The three other Democrats voting with the majority were Clark (of course), Indiana's Frederick Van Nuys, and North Carolina's Reynolds. Progressive Robert La Follette of Wisconsin, Farmer-Laborite Henrik Shipstead of Minnesota, and five Republicans made up the remainder of the majority.[41]

address any Message to the Congress or what the next step of the Administration on neutrality will be," he concluded.[43]

But if the decision on this matter had not by then been made, it certainly was within two or three hours thereafter, for on the following day the President addressed to Congress a brief, mildly worded message to which was appended, as a document having "my full approval," a "Statement on Peace and Neutrality by the Secretary of State," this last being substantially the written testimony that Hull had been dissuaded from presenting to Pittman's committee in May. It was a lengthy statement, covering more than five single-spaced typewritten legal-sized pages. In it, Hull argued that the present so-called Neutrality Act was in fact grossly unneutral, being heavily weighted on the side of aggressor nations unfriendly to the United States; that repeal of the arms embargo would strengthen friendly nations in their stand against the dictators; and that U.S. involvement in war would be guarded against to the fullest extent possible by the following means. One: prohibiting American ships from entering combat zones. Two: restricting travel by Americans in combat areas. Three: requiring that all U.S. exports to belligerent nations "be preceded by the transfer of title to the foreign purchasers." Four: retaining existing legislation "respecting loans and credits to the belligerent nations." Five: regulating "the solicitation and collection in this country of funds for the belligerents." Six: continuing "the National Munitions Control Board and the licensing system with respect to the importation and exportation of arms, ammunition, and implements of war."[44]

The hopeful purpose of this was, of course, to incite the Senate as a whole to override the Pittman committee's action.

It was a forlorn hope. But in a final effort to achieve it, Roosevelt arranged for the night of July 18 an informal meeting in the Oval Room of a half-dozen Senate leaders.[45] Three of the invitees were Republicans, each shrewdly assessed by his host in terms of the role he might play, the kind of influence he might exert, in the discussion. Minority Leader Charles L. McNary of Oregon, for instance, was a man whose tolerant cynicism, hence flexible convictions, might effectively offset the massive moral egotism and impregnable self-assurance of that bulwark of isolationism, William E. Borah, who was also present and was, indeed, a principal focus of Roosevelt's attention. The third Republican, Vermont's Warren R. Austin, could be counted on to support the administration's argument, for he, an earnest, studious man, possessor of a New England conscience, was virtually alone among congressional leaders of his party in a fervent commitment to collective security. (Austin was sure much of the current international trouble stemmed from America's failure to join the League of Nations.) Majority Leader Alben Barkley was there, of course, and Key Pittman, along with Garner, Press Secretary Early, and Cordell Hull, who was in effect the President's co-host. Roosevelt was at pains to make the gathering a friendly one. As his guests filled their glasses from the plentiful supply of wine, whiskey, gin, vermouth on a sideboard against the wall, he jokingly disagreed with the vice president as to the proper proportions of bourbon and dry vermouth in an old-fashioned. Each guest was urged to remove his coat (Roosevelt and Hull were both in shirtsleeves); each promptly did so, for the night was typically hot and humid. By nine o'clock, when the discussion began, the prevailing mood was relaxed, convivial, as Roosevelt wanted it to be.

Hence the no doubt deliberate shock of his introduction of the topic of the evening. It might "be the proper thing to open this meeting with a prayer," said he solemnly, "for our decision may affect the destiny of not only our own people but of all the peoples of the world." He offered no prayer, however. He plunged at once into an hour-long review of the events—the Nazi-Fascist aggressions, the democracies' yieldings to these aggressions—whereby Europe had been brought to the verge of a world war which, he stressed, could now break out at any moment. He spoke of his own efforts to save the peace and of how these had been hampered and weakened by existing neutrality legislation. "But now," he concluded, "I've fired my last shot. I think I ought to have another round in my belt."

He turned to Hull.

And Hull's extended remarks were even more grim and much more emotional than the President's had been. War, the secretary insisted, was now absolutely certain and would come very soon unless the arms embargo were repealed, whereas with such repeal there was a fifty–fifty chance that war could be averted. Those who opposed repeal, far from serving the cause of peace and American security, were encouraging a general war whereby this country's vital interests if not her very survival would be threatened. Hull looked toward Roosevelt for a confirmation of his statement. And Roosevelt, leaning forward and speaking very earnestly, said that the peace and security of the United States were indeed endangered by the extreme isolationism of Senator Nye.

"There are others, Mr. President!" roared the lion of Idaho.

Roosevelt, though he had noted Borah's increasing restiveness during the latter part of his own discourse and throughout all of Hull's, was nevertheless startled by this outburst.

"What did you say, Senator Borah?" he asked.

"I said there are others, Mr. President. Senator Nye is not alone. . . ." And he went on to assert dogmatically that "there is not going to be any war in Europe," at least not soon, and that "all this hysteria is manufactured and artificial."

Quickly Roosevelt turned to the secretary of state who, he saw, was about to respond explosively to what amounted to a personal insult.

"Cordell, what do you say to that?" he asked calmly, soothingly.

And Hull, fighting for self-control, said he wished that "Senator Borah would come to my office and look over the cables coming in. I feel satisfied he would modify his views."

Whereupon Borah augmented his insult, saying he had his own sources of

European information which he deemed "more reliable than those of the State Department,"* and they told him emphatically "that there is not going to be any war."

This was the climactic point of the evening. Hull, white-faced with anger and on the verge of helpless tears, lapsed into silence as others in the room were canvassed for their opinions. Of the Republicans, only Warren Austin spoke in support of the President's position, saying "the time has come to repeal this impossible act."

It was near midnight when Garner, with a point-blank question, forced Barkley to admit that he did not have enough votes to override the Foreign Relations Committee and bring Bloom's bill to a floor vote. Others in the room, questioned by Garner, agreed with Barkley's assessment. The vice president then closed the discussion with the same words he had used at the end of the battle over court reform.

"Well, captain," he said, "we might as well face the facts. You haven't got the votes and that's all there is to it."

Roosevelt accepted the verdict with outward good humor, as he had done when Garner pronounced the verdict on court reform. He did feel, however, he said pleasantly, that the public had a right to know where lay the responsibility for this decision. "There'll be no difficulty about that!" said Borah assertively. Swiftly, during the last minutes of July 18, two brief statements for the press were prepared with the assistance of Steve Early, then hurried downstairs for release to reporters waiting in the White House pressroom. One was by Barkley, with McNary's concurrence, saying simply that the senators at the meeting were agreed that "no action on neutrality can be obtained in the Senate at the present session" and that neutrality legislation would be considered in the next session. The other, drafted by Roosevelt, said: "The President and the Secretary of State maintained the definite position that failure by the Senate to take action now would weaken the leadership of the United States in exercising a potent influence in the cause of preserving peace . . . in the event of a new crisis in Europe between now and next January."[46]

VI

WHEN Congress adjourned on Saturday, August 5, ending a session that had been for the White House an almost uninterrupted procession of woe, a tired, worn Roosevelt took with him to Hyde Park the residue of that woe in the form

---

*He did not say what they were. According to Cordell Hull's *Memoirs,* p. 656, Borah's source was an obscure pro-Axis press service in London, but Donald Cameron Watt, in his *How War Came,* p. 268, says flatly that Borah's "sources . . . consisted simply and solely of Claud Cockburn's *The Week* [it was Cockburn who, in his exposé periodical, had labeled the Cliveden Set] and reflected the beliefs and suspicions of West European Communists, fellow-travelers, and all who shared their ineradicable distrust of the Chamberlain and Daladier governments." Cockburn was a member of the British Communist party. Watt cites Robert Maddox, *William E. Borah and Foreign Policy.*

of more than three hundred last-minute bills which must be signed or vetoed. These he dealt with during the following week. He also conferred daily by phone with Sumner Welles on the deteriorating European situation. He had, therefore, relatively few relaxing hours during which he could drive over the estate, check on his tree plantings, talk over farm-management matters with Moses Smith, visit with friends. But he was buoyed by anticipation of the sea voyage he had long planned to take in northern waters, aboard the U.S.S. *Tuscaloosa*. And by Friday, August 11, he was able to chortle in a letter to James that all the bills had been dealt with and he would be "off tomorrow morning." He would, he said, "be . . . somewhere near the North Pole for the next ten or twelve days, then Washington, then return to Hyde Park on August 29th and stay 'till about September 10."[47]

But as he wrote this he was only too aware that his travel plans were at the mercy of events abroad. Indeed, on the following morning, just as he was about to leave to board his ship in New York City, he received from Bullitt in Paris a telephone message so fraught with intimations of immediate war that he at once phoned Welles for assurance that his northern voyage was really feasible. He concluded from what Welles told him that he had "a couple of weeks" in which "to get a rest" but reminded Welles that he would return at once to Washington if the situation required it.[48] He boarded the *Tuscaloosa* a few hours later, sailed through the next days in leisurely fashion along the New England coast, paused briefly on Campobello amid happy scenes of his boyhood and young manhood, some of which were also scenes of his greatest misery, then sailed northward along the coast of Nova Scotia, fishing, relaxing, his days alternating sunshine with mist and rain but filled, always, with a blessed quiet and coolness.

He was denied any complete relaxation of the spirit, however. Ominous messages came to him daily from Welles.

August 16: "Telegrams from all sources this morning demonstrated a distinct increase in tension and augmented possibilities of an early crisis."

August 17: "Moscow [embassy] reports that, acting under instructions . . . the German ambassador saw Molotov on August 15th to deliver a message from Hitler to the effect that the German government would be prepared to discuss any territorial question in eastern Europe with the Soviet government, and that the conversations should begin upon an early occasion. . . . Molotov is reported to have informed the German Ambassador that his government would welcome these conversations if there could be reasonable assurance that they might lead to concrete results, which might include a non-aggression pact."*

---

*This development came as no surprise to Roosevelt. Two of his former ambassadors to Moscow, Bullitt and Joseph E. Davies (the latter was now ambassador to Belgium), had repeatedly warned him that a Nazi-Soviet pact became more probable with every British and French rebuff of Soviet overtures. When newly appointed Soviet ambassador Constantine A. Oumansky returned to Moscow on leave in early July, he carried with him a personal message from Roosevelt to Stalin saying that "if his [Stalin's] government joined up with Hitler, it was as certain as that night

August 18: "The German press in terms distinctly reminiscent of those employed . . . regarding Czechoslovakia describes the ruthless terror to which Germans in Poland are being subjected. . . . An American oil representative confidentially informed the Paris embassy that German interests have been frantically endeavoring to purchase for immediate delivery quantities of diesel oil and gasoline. Payment in foreign exchange offered and the firm was told that August 27th, the date on which it could promise delivery at a gulf port, was too late."

August 19: "Tass communique [in Moscow] conveys an impression of Soviet dissatisfaction with the progress of the [military] conversations [between the British, French, and Russians]."

August 20: "The Polish ambassador [in Berlin] is reported to have said that he would have 'no right' to talk to Hitler [about Danzig and the Corridor] under the present conditions of German pressure, since this would be construed as a sign of weakness not only in Germany but also in England where certain elements were still trying to bring about 'appeasement' and 'sell out' Poland."

August 21: "Bullit has just telephoned me to say he has information from two . . . authoritative sources that Germany will break loose on Thursday or Friday of this week [i.e., August 24 or 25]. . . . If [after further checking] the . . . outbreak of war seems . . . as imminent as Bullitt's reports indicate . . . you may decide to hasten your return to Washington."[49]

And Roosevelt did so decide. On August 21, informed that Ribbentrop was about to depart for Moscow, he turned the *Tuscaloosa* southward and sailed thereafter, slowed by fog along the New England coast, to Sandy Hook, New Jersey, where he debarked and entrained for Washington, arriving on September 24. Welles met him at Union Station. By that time a ten-year nonaggression pact between Nazi Germany and Communist Russia had been signed; there had been a great show of friendship between the two countries at a celebratory banquet in the Kremlin (Stalin had toasted Hitler's health, Ribbentrop had toasted Stalin); Hitler was demanding from Poland as the price of peace not only Danzig but also the Corridor, immediately; and drafting had begun, was almost completed, on last-minute appeals for peace to the king of Italy, the Polish president, and the chancellor of Germany by the President of the United States. The messages were dispatched not long after Roosevelt returned to his desk. They had their expected effect upon the course of events—that is, none at all.

The first ring of the phone beside Roosevelt's bed brought him instantly awake. He switched on the lamp and glanced at his watch as he put the receiver to his ear. It was ten minutes to three in the morning of September 1, 1939.

---

followed day that as soon as Hitler had conquered France, he would turn on Russia," to quote Davies's diary entry for July 18, 1939. See Davies, *Mission to Moscow,* p. 450.

"Who is it?"

"This is Bill Bullitt, Mr. President."

"Yes, Bill."

"Tony Biddle has just got through from Warsaw, Mr. President. Several German divisions are deep in Poland, and fighting is heavy. Tony said there were reports of bombers over the city. Then he was cut off. He tried to get you for half an hour before he called me."

"Well, Bill, it's come at last. God help us all."[50]

# BOOK FOUR

·→»×«←·

# Confusion and Division
## in the
## Darkening Valley

# 12

### ➜⫸✄⫷

# The Root of Event: Nationalism
# and Science

I

WHAT was it that had now "come at last"? Let us pause here to consider the question, since doing so will refresh our understanding of Roosevelt's role in its coming and perhaps deepen our understanding of his part in what was now to come.

At the time, what happened was generally regarded as a renewal of the war of 1914–18, and indeed that war might be truly said never to have ended, in the sense of reaching a conclusion or settlement of its basic issues. It had merely been suspended until one of the combatants, having collapsed of exhaustion, regained sufficient strength to renew the struggle. That Germany *would* renew the struggle had been virtually ensured by the "peace" that the Allies, themselves on the verge of collapse when joined by the United States, imposed upon her at Versailles*—a "peace" whose perfection of economic stupidity was unmarred by the slightest hint of economic realism, a "peace" whose perfection of nationalistic vengefulness was but slightly marred by the establishment of a toothless League of Nations, a "peace" that was otherwise quite marvelously devoid of rational dealings with the deepest of the war's root causes.

This deepest root, from which all the others branched out, was unlimited national sovereignty. The horrors growing from it increased in proportion to the widening contradiction between it and the economic interdependence of all nations, all peoples, that technological advance creates. Every year since the seventeenth century had seen an increase in man's capacity to produce goods; to transport these, and himself, around the world; to acquire, process, store, and communicate information; and to destroy both his own works and himself with ever more powerful weapons of war. In almost every year this increase had been greater than in the year before; the Law of Acceleration, as Henry Adams conceived it, applied everywhere and almost without interruption. Consequent was an increased necessity for cooperation among human beings and institutions—an ever closer and tighter cooperation over wider and wider geographic areas as new technology promoted more and narrower functional specialties and multiplied the ways in which these must fit together in order to become practically effective. Against all this stood the mutual exclusiveness of nation-states, each a law unto itself, each with its own currency system, its own tariffs or unfettered right to impose them, its own armed forces,

---

*"This is not peace," commented France's Marshal Foch when the Versailles Treaty was signed. "It is an armistice for twenty years."[1]

and its own sacred flag with all that this symbolized of assertive, belligerent, egoistic national will. Politics opposed economics, patriotism opposed reason, and the world community, which science and technology implied with increasing emphasis, was thereby violently denied.

The contradiction had not gone unrecognized during those decades when the world tragedy of 1914–18 was being prepared. As the Western world hurtled at accelerating pace through the age of steam into the age of electricity and internal combustion in the last half of the nineteenth century, increasing myriads of people all over the civilized world had shared Tennyson's vision of a future in which all "battle flags were furled" in "the Parliament of Man, the Federation of the World"—shared this and begun, considerable numbers of them, to view as a possible model for ultimate global organization the American Union of States, though a far looser, more decentralized union than was the United States that emerged from the Civil War. It would be a One composed of Many ("e pluribus unum"), but the One would be wholly the Many's creature, a central authority wherein were pooled only those elements of sovereignty, military and economic, whose very raison d'être was to make war. Each of the Many would retain its distinctive cultural identity and full freedom to express and develop this fully. Was not such a Federal Republic of the World at least conceivable? Indeed, was not the main flow of history overwhelmingly in that direction?

Thus a growing and growingly insistent "peace movement" had accompanied and opposed the swelling tide of British, French, and American imperialism all through the 1880s, the 1890s, the early 1900s. There had been formed an International Peace and Arbitration Association in London, an Interparliamentary Union in Paris, a Universal Peace Union in the United States, each dedicated to the proposition that technological advance ("progress") had made war not merely obsolete but a major threat to the very survival of civilization and that, therefore, the great task of the closing nineteenth century and opening twentieth was the disarmament of nations and the pooling of their sovereignty, or at least the hitherto lawlessly belligerent portion of it, in international organization governed by international law. The movement had been by no means confined to misfits and soft-headed visionaries. Enlisted in it and supplying a large part of its financial resource were people of great prestige and wealth and power. Two of them were mighty industrialists —the American steelmaker Andrew Carnegie; the Swedish inventor and explosives manufacturer Alfred Nobel—whose products contributed hugely to the destructiveness of war. And with its energies and finances so supplied, the peace movement had grown strong enough to force the reluctant statesmen of nationalism, including the vociferously belligerent Teddy Roosevelt and his friendly admirer, the German kaiser, to agree to the participation of their governments in a great international peace conference held at The Hague as the 1800s ended and the 1900s began. The conference was planned to be a permanent enterprise, with its sessions spaced eight years apart, and from the first two of these, in 1899 (when twenty-six nations were represented) and 1907 (when forty-four were), issued numerous conventions, each with numerous articles, dealing with the treatment of war prisoners, outlawing various war practices (the use of poison gas, for one; the launching of explosives and projectiles from balloons, for another), and presumably laying the foundations for a solid body of international law. No action was taken, however, toward the establishment of international law-enforcement machinery and procedures, or toward disarmament. On the agenda of the 1907 meeting was a proposal to create a permanent Court of International Justice (a world court), staffed with permanent judges to which disputes between nations could be submitted for lawful decision—a proposal made, incidentally, by the chief delegate from the United States—but this had not been acted upon when the conference adjourned. It was to be taken up at a third Hague session in 1915.

The Great War destroyed much of what had been noblest and best in the nineteenth century along with, thankfully, much of the smug hypocrisy and cloying sentimentality that permeated Victorian culture. But it did not destroy the peace movement. The idea of peacemaking and peacekeeping through international organization was vividly present at Versailles in the person of Woodrow Wilson, as we all know. Passionately committed to his vision of a world in which all differences between nations were settled through rational discourse around the conference table, he seized the historic moment to make his vision the shining hope of a suffering humanity throughout war-ravaged Europe. When he came to Europe in 1919 to shape jointly with the fervently nationalistic leaders of the Allies the future of the world, he was hailed almost as the new messiah. His political potency at Versailles had been enormous. Under pressure, however, he proved a sadly flawed vessel for hopeful historic transformation. He had a proud heart, an imperious temper; his highest statesmanship was frustrated as much by his own egoistic willfulness and consequent penchant for narrow partisanship as it was by the ruthless "realism" of his Versailles and Washington colleagues. He had a fuzzy mind, manifest in his addiction to the vacuous rhetoric of popular "idealism" with its heavy reliance upon such undefined terms as "honor," "moral," "the right," "the good." He managed to make his conception of a League of Nations an integral part of the Versailles Treaty, but he did so by paying an excessive price—namely, his acquiescence in other elements of the treaty whereby internationalism was offset and contradicted by an increase of fervent nationalism. Indeed, he personally contributed greatly to the latter with his insistence upon the "principle of self-determination." This principle, as we have seen, was not permitted by the Allies to apply to Austria when its German population tried to unite with the German Reich following the breakup of Austro-Hungary, but otherwise "self-determination" ran rampant across the map of Europe, resulting in the emergence of nine new nation-states out of the former empires of Russia, Germany, and Austro-Hungary. In 1919, Finland, Estonia, Latvia, Lithuania, Poland, Austria, Czechoslovakia, Hungary, and Yugoslavia sprang up to join the ranks of sovereign powers, each with its own army, its own currency, its own exclusive patriotism, and, alas, its own vulnerability to the territorial ambitions of one or more of its Great Power neighbors.

In earlier volumes of this history we have traced the events subsequent to and consequent upon Versailles. We have seen how the League of Nations was almost fatally wounded in its earliest infancy by the refusal of the United States to join it, or even to join the world court that was established under the League's aegis; how the Weimar Republic was similarly wounded by the attempts of the Allies to obtain payment of the exorbitant war reparations they had demanded of Germany; and how the economic problems of Europe were exacerbated by the insistence of the United States upon the full payment to her of war debts contracted by the Allies, the maintenance of high U.S. tariff walls against the entry of goods whose export alone made debt payments possible, and the total separation of war-reparation payments from war-debt payments, though their actual linkage in Europe was obvious. We have seen, further, how Republican taxation and fiscal policies during the 1920s resulted in a gross distortion of America's national income-distribution pattern, with too high a percentage of the total income going to too small a percentage of the total population; how the disastrous effect of this upon mass-consumption markets was for a time obscured and postponed by massive, reckless private American lending abroad, chiefly to Germany; how in general economic nationalism, especially rising tariff barriers, sparked militarism (imperialism) in such "have-not" nations as Japan and Italy; and how this militarism and its violent expressions were accelerated, and the rise of Hitler to power made possible in Germany, when the inevitable American market crash of 1929 abruptly terminated American lending abroad and triggered a world economic depression. We have seen, too, in close-up detail, how a slim but very real chance to reverse the tragic trend was destroyed when Franklin Roosevelt, forced to make a choice between economic nationalism and economic internationalism at the outset of the New Deal, and without knowing in any deep sense what he was doing, opted for nationalism and wrecked with his "bombshell" message the 1933 World Monetary and Economic Conference.*

Thereafter, the tide of aggressive nationalism rose overwhelmingly. The League of Nations drowned in it as Italy, Germany, and Japan canceled their memberships, and Britain and France chose not to use League machinery for collective security in any effective way but to adopt instead the essentially nationalistic policies of "appeasement." In the United States, as the League floundered and sank, even the peace movement became increasingly, confusedly nationalistic insofar as it lost faith in internationalism and sought to embrace both isolationism and antifascism. Roosevelt himself was not only confused on this matter but also contributed greatly to the general confusion. Especially did he do so in March 1935 when, abruptly and astonishingly, he suggested to the Nye Committee that it turn its attention away from the problems of wartime industrial mobilization and war profiteering, for the

*See *FDR: The New Deal Years*, pp. 122–31, 153–57, 161–63, 182–98.

solution of which the committee was then preparing legislation, to the problem of maintaining U.S. neutrality should war break out overseas.* It was a maneuver perfectly in accord with the general pattern and practice of Roosevelt's New Deal in that it was designed to scatter into futility energies of popular opinion that, concentrated, might effect real change in the politico-economic power structure of the nation. Journalistic and Nye Committee exposures of war profiteering by big business, and of the covert activities and blatantly false "patriotic" propaganda whereby armaments manufacturers sought to frustrate efforts toward disarmament and peacemaking, had aroused great popular excitement, outrage, and determination to "do something about it." The political potency of the various well-organized peace groups was greater than ever before or since. There was in consequence a "definite threat" (so Roosevelt perceived it) of congressional legislation whereby the armaments industry would be nationalized and arrangements made to conscript capital as well as men if war came. Roosevelt's maneuver, whereby the Nye Committee's attention was diverted to neutrality legislation (the subject was wholly outside the committee's original terms of reference), achieved its immediate purpose. It headed off the perceived threat. But it did so by distracting and scattering the internationalist portion of the antiwar movement, which had formerly ardently embraced the League of Nations idea, while concentrating and strengthening its opposite, the isolationist portion. The price was very high, as we have seen: It may even have included, as Roosevelt was arguing in the summer of 1939 it did include, a last chance to head off new world war.

The persistence and growing malignancy of limitless nationalism meant the persistence and growing malignancy of the contradiction between it and the internationalizing implications of scientific technology. For, all this while, science was continuing its discoveries apace, and new technologies were being born of these, augmenting the constructive and destructive power in men's hands at a rate terrifying, in the circumstances, to thoughtful men who deeply cared about civilization. Men's minds remained fixed in the social, economic, and political molds of an age when the human body supplied of itself alone a major portion of the total work energy of society, an age when the maximum distance across which a man's eyes and ears could see and hear was the total range of his capacity to receive immediate information. But by the time the Great War began, heat-engine technology born of thermodynamic theory had reduced to very modest proportions, in terms of overall economic process, the importance of individual bodily strength, while communications technology born of electromagnetic theory had rendered infinitesimal the individual's range of unaided sight and hearing compared to that of machine extensions of these.

*See *FDR: The New Deal Years,* pp. 550–62.

II

SOME of the shapes of the accelerating technological advance after the Great War were determined by the military side of the very nationalism that the advance, as a whole, outmoded. This was true of radar ("*r*adio *d*etecting *a*nd *r*anging"), which may be said to have had its beginnings in 1922 when two research scientists in the employ of the U.S. Navy, one working with a high-frequency radio transmitter on the west bank of the Anacostia River, the other with a radio receiver on the east bank, in Washington, D.C., found their experiments irritatingly interfered with whenever a river steamer crossed the line of sight between transmitter and receiver. This at once suggested the placement of high-frequency transmitters and receivers aboard naval vessels to alert any two of them, despite darkness or fog, when a third vessel passed between them. Subsequent developments led to the assignment to the U.S. Naval Research Laboratory in 1931 of a project, classified secret, of course, aimed at "Detection of Enemy Vessels and Aircraft by Radio." From this emerged pulsed radar, upon which the U.S. Army also began experimental work in 1935. Simultaneously, secretively, experiments along the same line, suggested by similar accidental observations, were conducted in the interests of the military in Germany, France, and England, with the greatest progress toward the development of airborne and microwave radar being made in England. By 1939, a coastal chain of radar stations, linked to a central control station by an elaborate telephonic communications system, was in process of being established in England, enabling the detection of aircraft incoming from the Continent while they were yet sixty miles from the English shoreline, and the plotting of their courses on large maps at a central control station from which counteractive strategy could be directed. This and the use of airborne radar to detect submarines when they surfaced, as they must for battery recharge, et cetera, or to detect them even when they remained submerged but thrust a snorkel above the surface, were destined to play decisive roles in the upcoming struggle.[2]

The secretive military side of nationalism also determined a considerable portion of the way in which advances were made in aircraft design and equipment between 1919 and 1929. There was great improvement in airplane engines and—as a result of research into the fluid dynamics of drag—in the design (streamlining) of airframes, with the result that airplanes of the latest design in 1939 could fly much faster and higher and farther with a single fuel load than could the bombers and fighters of the Great War. They were also commonly several times as large. Simultaneously there was born and developed through its primitive stages a new technology aimed at freeing man from his bondage to the surface of the earth—namely, rocketry. Though rockets were invented by the ancient Chinese, who used small ones to frighten their enemies in war, though they were developed in the first years of the nineteenth century into actual weapons by a British artilleryman who had been in the Orient (their use against Fort McHenry by the British in 1814 inspired Francis Scott Key's

"Star-Spangled Banner," as everyone knows), and though they were a prominent part of every American's Fourth of July experience in the late nineteenth
and early twentieth centuries, it was not until a Worcester, Massachusetts,
physicist named Robert Hutchings Goddard became obsessed with the notion
of using rockets for upper-atmosphere and space exploration that their wonderful, frightening possibilities began to be realized. Goddard published his
first theoretical and speculative paper on rockets in 1919. It attracted little
attention. He then proceeded to the actual design and making of rockets. His
first experimental one, remarkable for its use of liquid rather than solid (gun-
powder) fuel, was launched two hundred feet into the air from an open field
in Auburn, Massachusetts, on a March day in 1926, with an explosion so loud
it terrified people for miles around, Thereafter, financially aided by a grant
from the Guggenheim Fund for the Promotion of Aeronautics, Goddard
removed his experiments to a desert place in New Mexico, where by 1935 his
rockets attained a speed of 540 miles an hour and a soaring height of a mile
and a half. By 1939 he had developed rocket steering devices, gyroscopes to
keep rockets on course, and, most important, the idea (which he patented) of
multistage, or booster, rockets, whereby rocket speed, range, and fuel efficiency
were multiplied. And by that time Goddard's work, virtually ignored by the
American military and naval establishment, had been closely studied and was
being rapidly built upon by German scientific technologists, notably Wernher
von Braun.[3]* The rocket would become a major part of Hitler's stock of "secret
weapons" in years to come. Its "red glare" would ominously light the closing
scenes of the European war.

But the historically most important of the scientific advances made between
1919 and 1939, that of nuclear physics, had nothing to do with nationalism save
insofar as individual scientists involved in it had their work interrupted during
the 1930s by nationalistic violence. The advance per se was a wholly intellectual
endeavor conducted in accord with the openness, the emphatic rejection of
secretiveness, that had been the hallmark of pure science since the 1600s.

In an earlier volume of this history† we mentioned the remarkably fruitful
research into the nature of the atom that was proceeding by leaps and bounds
during the years of Roosevelt's launching of the New Deal.[4] Let us here
recapitulate and amplify by saying that this line of research was initiated when
a German professor of physics, Wilhelm Röntgen, announced his discovery of
X rays in a paper mailed on New Year's Day 1896 to every leading physicist
in Europe. The announcement at once stimulated Henri Becquerel, a physics

*Charles A. Lindbergh, fascinated by what he had read of Goddard's rocket work, came to
Worcester to talk personally with the physicist and was instrumental, through his friendship with
Harry Guggenheim, in obtaining for Goddard the grant money he needed. There is reason to
believe that Lindbergh, during his long visits to Nazi Germany, helped stimulate Nazi officialdom's interest in rocketry and thus government support of Braun's work. The latter made creative
use of the Goddard patents, which America's military ignored. "Goddard's experiments in liquid
fuel . . . enabled us to perfect the V2 years before it would otherwise have been possible," Braun
once said. (See Leonard Moseley, *Lindbergh* [New York, 1976], p. 344.
†*FDR: The New Deal Years*, pp. 214–16.

professor at the Paris Museum of Natural History, to conduct experiments that, in late February 1896, revealed the radioactivity of uranium. The name "radioactivity" was suggested for the phenomenon by Marie Curie, née Manya Skłodowska, a native of Warsaw in what was then Russian Poland, who had come to the Sorbonne in Paris to study physics, had there met and married French physical chemist Pierre Curie, and now, having demonstrated that thorium, too, was radioactive, began with her husband the prolonged, difficult, and physically laborious analysis of pitchblende, the principal ore of uranium, samples of which emitted rays even more strongly than did pure uranium. By the turn of the century Marie Curie, with Pierre's indispensible help, had isolated three new radioactive elements, namely, polonium, actinium, and radium, the latter the most intensely radioactive of all substances. Meanwhile, in Cambridge University's Cavendish Laboratory, a young New Zealand native named Ernest Rutherford had defined in the emanations of thorium and uranium two particles or rays (at the subatomic level, discernible entities manifest both particle and wave characteristics) which he dubbed simply "alpha" and "beta," each of the former bearing two positive charges (it was in fact the helium atom minus its electrons) and each of the latter having a single negative charge (it was, in fact, a highly energized electron). Shortly thereafter a Frenchman, P. V. Villard, discovered among these emanations a third ray, dubbed gamma, which is like the X ray but has a shorter wavelength and greater penetrative power.

It occurred to Rutherford in the early 1900s that the alpha particle, by virtue of its combination of mass with what seemed in those years a remarkably high energy (it shot out at a substantial fraction of the speed of light), might be a useful tool for probing the secrets of atomic structure. He soon devised means of collecting alpha particles emitted by radium, shaping a beam of them, directing this beam against very thin metal foils, then measuring their deflection by the atoms they encountered in their passage through the foil. The scattering turned out to be much wider than could be accounted for by the then most widely respected theory of the atom, that of J. J. Thomson. Thomson, discoverer of the electron, described the atom as a collection of electrons (he called them negatively electrified corpuscles) embedded "in a sphere of uniform positive electrification," like plums in a pudding. Evidently, the atom's positive charge was *not* evenly distributed through its spherical body but was instead concentrated at some central point. One day, Rutherford almost off-handedly suggested to one of his students an experiment in which alpha rays that bounced back from the target material toward their source could be detected. He most emphatically expected from this a wholly negative result. Such "bouncing back" would be "almost as incredible as if you fired a 15-inch shell at a piece of tissue paper and it came back and hit you," to quote Rutherford himself. Yet it happened! Some of the rays, a very small percentage of them, did bounce back! The only possible explanation was that the backward-deflected rays had encountered positively charged entities at least as massive as they. Moreover, since but a tiny percentage of the alpha particles were widely deflected, and of these but a tiny percentage bounced backward, the positively charged entities, for all their mass, must make up but the tiniest fraction of the atom's total volume. Rutherford thus made, in 1911, the greatest of his long list of great discoveries—namely, the atomic nucleus, which makes up virtually the whole of an atom's mass but occupies only about 1/100,000th of its volume.

There followed intensely concentrated efforts to develop a theory of atomic structure that explained the experimental evidence. The solution to the problem, or, more precisely, the basic design for what became over the years a highly complicated but experimentally confirmed solution, was worked out in 1913 by a twenty-eight-year-old native of Copenhagen named Niels Bohr. In 1910 he had come to Manchester University, where Rutherford then headed the physics department (a half-dozen years later he became head of the Cavendish in Cambridge), to work for a few months under Rutherford, returning then to the university in Copenhagen, where he immediately experienced, as if a gift from the gods, a dazzling series of intuitions that proved, upon his testing of them by rigorous logic against the experimental evidence, to be wondrously explanatory of former mysteries. He shaped from these a mathematical model of the atom in which the classical mechanics of Newton was replaced by the quantum theory then being developed, especially by the German theoretical physicist Albert Einstein, out of the radiation formula discovered in 1900 by the German physicist Max Planck. Initially, Bohr's model was only of the hydrogen atom, the lightest and simplest of all atoms, but he subsequently and with great difficulty managed to encompass the heavier atoms in his theory in a way that explained and revised Mendeleyev's periodic table of the elements, linked chemistry to physics indissolubly, and set physics upon a new and immensely fruitful course.

What had emerged from all this by the time of Roosevelt's first inauguration was an experimentally verified picture of the atom as an infinitesimal nucleus whose positive charge was determined by the number of protons in it (the name "proton" was bestowed by Rutherford upon this nuclear particle) and precisely matched the number of electrons that the nucleus held in thrall. These last dashed around it at enormous speeds in fixed shells or orbits. In the outermost shell were the atom's trading counters in its combinant (chemical) transactions with other atoms. Only in the case of hydrogen, whose nucleus was a single proton, was the nucleus a solid integrity. In all other elements it was a composite which, as it increased in mass, tended toward instability and spontaneous disintegration—tended to become, in other words, naturally radioactive. Moreover, naturally stable atoms could be disintegrated if the bombarding alpha particles, instead of being deflected by the charged nucleus, penetrated the nuclear interior. They had done so in a late 1918 experiment of Rutherford's, shattering the nitrogen nucleus; and he had subsequently, with Englishman James Chadwick, the most brilliant of his associates at the Cavendish, managed to disintegrate a good many other of the lighter elements. The two had had no luck, however, with heavier elements, because the positively charged alpha lacked the energy necessary to overcome the electric repulsion of the heavier nuclei's multiple protons; it was repulsed before reaching the nuclear surface, jarring nothing loose. But Rutherford, in a 1920 lecture, had spoken of the possible existence of another nuclear particle having the same mass as a proton but bearing *no* electrical charge. Such a particle would explain the fact, then just being discovered, that the same element, defined as "the same" by its chemical properties, commonly exists in forms of different atomic weight (they came to be called isotopes), a fact difficult to explain by the then prevailing assumption that the nuclear mass was determined solely by protons. This unknown particle would be difficult to detect experimentally, Rutherford predicted, precisely because of its lack of charge. And so it proved to be. It remained undetected when, in 1930, two German physicists, Walther Bothe and Herbert Becker, who were studying gamma radiation by bombarding beryllium with alpha particles, jarred loose from their sample a mysterious radiation that was unaccompanied by proton emission and had a penetrative power much greater than that of gamma rays, theretofore the greatest known.* James Chadwick at once suspected that the mysterious radiation, which easily passed through *several inches* of lead, might be the neutral particle Rutherford had predicted, and in 1932 he proved experimentally that this was indeed the case. The nucleus of the heavier elements, then, was composed not only of protons but also of these newly discovered particles, dubbed "neutrons" by Chadwick, each of which had a mass very slightly greater than the proton's and derived its penetrative power, not from any remarkable energy (in the Chadwick experiment it had had only moderate energy), but from its electrical neutrality whereby it could pass unslowed and undeflected through electromagnetic fields. This penetrative power included that of entering the nucleus it struck and, if its energy was sufficiently low and/or the nucleus sufficiently massive, being trapped or "captured" there, with shattering effects upon that nucleus. The neutron was, in short, uniquely suited to atom-probing functions and was immediately theorized so to be by a young Italian physicist named Enrico Fermi, who lived and worked in Rome.

In January 1934, Fermi, like every other nuclear physicist, was greatly excited by an announcement that, at the Radium Institute in Paris, Irène and Frédéric Joliot-Curie† had, through alpha-ray bombardment, made several light elements (boron, magnesium, aluminum) temporarily radioactive—an epochal discovery whose implications Fermi prepared at once to explore experimentally. He reasoned that, if alpha rays produced this effect on light elements, neutrons would be likely to produce it on heavier ones, especially if these neutrons were sufficiently slowed to facilitate their actual absorption by

---

*It perhaps need not be pointed out that a ray or particle's penetrative power is not of itself alone useful for nuclear disintegrative purposes. Mass is also necessary, and the gamma ray, like the X ray and the electron, has virtually no mass.

†Irène, daughter of Marie and Pierre Curie, had married French physicist Frédéric Joliot; the two of them took the name Joliot-Curie and formed a working scientific partnership as productive as that of Marie and Pierre Curie had been.

the nuclei they struck. With great ingenuity, he developed from radon, the radioactive gas emitted by radium, a neutron source providing at first a beam of a hundred thousand neutrons a second, later nearly a million. He shot these through substances whose atomic nuclei were of approximately the same mass as the neutron, thus achieving a series of "elastic collisions," like those of two billiard balls, whereby part of the neutron's energy was imparted to the struck particles. He was thus enabled to regulate the speed or energy of neutrons and study the effects of bombardment by those of "fast," "moderate," and "slow" speeds. The event proved the validity of his hypothesis: The absorption of a neutron by a nucleus produced a nuclear imbalance requiring the emission of rays by the nucleus in order to achieve a new balance between itself and its shells of electrons. The bombarded element became, in other words, radioactive, a "radioisotope" of its former self, and was ultimately transformed into a different element, one of higher atomic number and weight. For instance, aluminum, ordinarily a stable element with an atomic number (or positive nuclear charge) of 13 and an atomic weight of 27, became radioactive aluminum-28 when it absorbed a neutron and, finally, after stabilizing itself through emission of a beta ray, became silicon-28, with an atomic number of 14. In these 1934 experiments, Fermi with his associates induced temporary radioactivity and transmutation in no fewer than forty of the sixty elements he subjected to neutron irradiation. When he came to the heaviest element then known, uranium, atomic number 92, however, his results were inconclusive. He set up his experiment on the assumption that uranium, though naturally radioactive, would like aluminum be transformed into a new and heavier element (a "transuranic" product) when it absorbed a neutron and, as it did so, would emit a more penetrating radiation than formerly. To separate this expected radiation from that of normal uranium he enclosed the bombarded sample in a shield of aluminum foil—a shield or screen just thick enough (.003 inch) to stop natural uranium emissions while permitting those of the presumed new elements to pass through. This shield prevented Fermi's instruments from recording the burst of released energy which they would otherwise have recorded and which would have alerted him to the fact that something strange indeed was taking place. What he did observe was strange enough: Under neutron bombardment, uranium seemingly gave birth, not to a single substance, but to several, which Fermi assumed to be heavier transuranic elements.

Determining precisely what these were became the task set for themselves in 1935 by German radiochemist Otto Hahn and Austrian physicist Lise Meitner, working together (they had long been a famous team) in Berlin's Kaiser-Wilhelm Institute. They launched a long series of uranium investigations in which they were soon joined by a young German chemist named Fritz Strassmann. By that time, virulent nationalism was seriously impeding and threatening to distort what had theretofore been an intellectually creative international effort having nothing to do with politics or patriotism. The sick supernationalism of the Nazis had disrupted and crippled the German physics community, of which approximately one-fourth had been Jewish as the 1930s opened.

Einstein, in anticipation of Hitler's rise to power, emigrated to America in late 1932, accepting appointment to Princeton's new Institute for Advanced Study. The Nazi civil-service law of 1933 dismissed every German Jew from German university faculties; other anti-Semitic laws threatened and scattered a brilliant coterie of young Hungarian Jewish scientists then working in Germany, including mathematician John von Neumann and physicists Leo Szilard, Edward Teller, and Eugene Wigner. All of those named found, like Einstein, refuge in American universities. So did Enrico Fermi when Italy's newly decreed anti-Semitic laws became, in late 1938, an active threat to his wife, Laura, who was Jewish, and to his two half-Jewish children (Fermi himself was "pure" Italian). In December the Nobel Prize awarded Fermi for his neutron-bombardment discoveries enabled him to take his family with him to Stockholm for the award ceremony and from there, using his prize money, to New York City. Arriving on January 2, 1939, he joined Columbia University's physics faculty. Lise Meitner was in Stockholm when the Fermis passed through. She, too, was Jewish by birth (few of her colleagues knew this, she having been baptized a Protestant), but her Austrian citizenship had formerly protected her against Hitler's anti-Semitic decrees. *Anschluss* in March 1938 abruptly thrust upon her a decidedly unwanted German citizenship. Four dangerous months later, with her research grant canceled, her dismissal from the institute imminent, and the uranium experiments as yet yielding strange and inconclusive results (it then appeared that neutron bombardment produced *ten* different transuranic products, none absolutely certainly identifiable in terms of the periodic table), she fled Germany, going via Holland and Denmark to Sweden, where a post in Stockholm's Physical Institute of the Academy of Sciences had been obtained for her by Niels Bohr.

It was in Sweden, therefore, in the last two weeks of 1938, that Meitner learned, through letters from Otto Hahn, that he and his partner Strassmann had identified what appeared to be a radioisotope of barium among the products of their slow neutron bombardment of uranium. She was as astonished and initially bewildered by this as Hahn and Strassmann were. Far from being heavier than uranium, barium is approximately half as heavy and has little more than half uranium's nuclear charge. Hahn begged her for a physical explanation but she was unable to come up with one before he and Strassmann, having run an experiment proving conclusively that the radioisotope was indeed barium, felt compelled to send a cautiously worded report of their observation to a German scientific periodical, which published it on January 6, 1939.

Meanwhile, Meitner had been joined for the Christmas holiday in Sweden by her nephew, physicist Otto Frisch of Bohr's Institute of Theoretical Physics in Copenhagen (Frisch, too, was a refugee from Hitler's greater Germany), and the two of them had pondered excitedly the Hahn-Strassmann observation. They applied to it Bohr's latest (1937) model of the atomic nucleus. This described the nucleus as a tightly packed composite of protons and neutrons which, because of the delicate balance within it of the "strong force" and the electrical repulsion of like-charged protons, behaves like a liquid drop. It has surface tension, which, as in the case of a falling drop of water, draws it into spherical shape; and it tends to shiver and shake, as a drop of water does, when acted upon by an outside force. If a slow neutron struck an already wobbly uranium nucleus, theorized Meitner and Frisch, and so transferred some of its energy to it, the protons in that nucleus might be sufficiently pushed apart to enable electrical repulsion to replace the strong force, which normally holds the nucleus tightly together but which operates only across extremely tiny distances. The nucleus would then split apart, with each part at once pulled spherically together into a new nucleus as the strong force again became dominant over the electrical. The process would involve the release of (for a single atom) an enormous amount of energy. Why? Because the two parts into which the uranium was split had less mass in the aggregate than the original nucleus had had, and this difference would be translated into energy in accordance with Einstein's mass–energy equation, $E = mc^2$, where $E$ is energy, $m$ is mass, and $c$ is the velocity of light. Using this equation, Meitner calculated the energy release per split atom at about 200 million electron volts, and this was the energy release actually measured by Frisch when, returned to Copenhagen, he conducted an experiment that confirmed physically the chemical observation of Hahn and Strassmann, completing it in the early morning hours of January 14, 1939.

Three days later, two momentous papers by Meitner and Frisch (who collaborated by long-distance phone)—one of them physically explaining Hahn and Strassmann's chemistry, the other reporting Frisch's confirming experiment—were airmailed to *Nature* in London. In them the atom-splitting process was called nuclear fission, a name suggested to Frisch by the liquid-drop model and by the fact that a water droplet dividing under impact does so in much the same way as bacteria do in what microbiologists call binary fission.

But even before the Meitner-Frisch papers were published—before they were even mailed, in fact—the stupendous news they contained was spreading like wildfire through the American physics community. Niels Bohr had been on the verge of sailing for the United States to work for a term at Princeton's Institute for Advanced Study when told by Frisch, just returned to Copenhagen, of the conclusion he and his aunt had reached in Sweden. ("What idiots we have all been!" Bohr cried, smiting his forehead with an open hand. ". . . This is just as it must be!") On the evening of January 16, 1939, the day Bohr's ship docked in New York, a physicist colleague of Bohr's, who had accompanied him from Copenhagen and now preceded him to Princeton, told a group of physicists there what had happened—this to Bohr's consternation since he had promised to make no public disclosure until Meitner and Frisch had published. Fermi, with his wife, greeted Bohr at dockside but did not hear the news until the following day, via Princeton. Soon thereafter, not having been told of Frisch's confirming experiment (Bohr himself did not yet know how this had come out), Fermi suggested to Columbia's Herbert Anderson a similar experiment, which Anderson successfully completed (the second nu-

clear fission ever deliberately experimentally achieved) in the basement of
Columbia's Pupin Hall late in the night of January 25.

Neither Bohr nor Fermi knew of this successful completion when, in the
following afternoon (Thursday, January 26), they took their great news to an
annual conference on theoretical physics assembled in a lecture hall of George
Washington University just a few blocks from the White House. Most of the
leading physicists in America were in the audience that Bohr, followed by
Fermi, informally addressed. The words they spoke, the equations they
chalked upon a blackboard, created a sensation. Several of Fermi's listeners,
his discourse being more sharply focused and easier to follow than Bohr's, were
brought to their feet. They were young scientists who left the room hurriedly
while Fermi yet spoke, for all the world like newspaper reporters rushing from
an uncompleted press conference in the hope of scoring a news scoop. Some
rushed to laboratories in Washington and Baltimore, others to phones where
they placed long-distance calls to their home institutions. Each was eager to
be the first to perform an experiment which, unknown to him, had already been
twice (in two different ways) completed.

Among the possibilities mentioned by Fermi in his talk was that the uranium
nucleus, as it split in two, would emit two or three fast neutrons. Indeed, he
thought such emission probable in view of the enormous kinetic energy imparted to each nuclear fragment, an energy more than sufficient to "boil off"
a neutron or so. He said no more about this that afternoon—it was only an
educated guess, after all—but its potential significance was as obvious to his
listeners as it was exciting and, to such widely synthesizing minds as Bohr's,
frightening in the present state of the world. Each of the neutrons shooting into
a dense collection of uranium atoms might knock around among them until
sufficiently slowed down to be captured by a nucleus, with resultant fission.
This fission, releasing more neutrons, could produce more fissions. In other
words, the fission of a single nucleus might set off a self-sustaining chain
reaction. If each fission in the chain produced *more* than one other fission the
reaction could proceed with lightning rapidity. In less than a millionth of a
second, every nucleus in, say, an ounce of uranium might be shattered, releasing energy, from this one ounce, equivalent to that of six hundred pounds of
exploding TNT.

There followed, in the minds and laboratories of physicists working in the
United States, a burst of mental energy almost as explosive as that of the above
hypothetical ounce. Within four weeks, the fact of uranium fission had been
further confirmed experimentally at Johns Hopkins University, the Carnegie
Institute of Washington, and the University of California at Berkeley. Far
more important, Bohr and Princeton physicist J. A. Wheeler had theoretically
determined (the theory would be experimentally confirmed a few months later)
that neutron bombardment produced fission in the rare light isotope of uranium having an atomic weight of 235 (U-235) but *not* in the heavy isotope
(U-238), which constitutes 99.3 percent of all the uranium found in nature. The
common isotope of uranium, when it captured neutrons, acted just as Fermi

had expected uranium to do in his earlier experiments: It shot out two beta rays and became a new element, soon dubbed "plutonium," with an atomic number of 94 and an atomic weight of 239. This new element, theorized Bohr and Wheeler, would probably prove as fissionable by slow neutrons as was U-235. As for the emission of two or more neutrons with each fission, experiments by Leo Szilard and young Walter Zinn in Columbia's Pupin Hall, and by the Joliot-Curies in Paris, proved in March 1939 that this did happen, which meant that an explosive chain reaction could occur if a sufficiently large mass (a "critical mass") of pure U-235, or of plutonium, could be brought together. The chief obstacle to this, if uranium were used, would be the formidable difficulty of separating U-235 from U-238. Since isotopes of the same element are chemically identical they cannot be separated from one another by chemical means, and the weight difference between U-235 and U-238 was far too slight to indicate any simple means of physical separation. Nevertheless, it seemed distinctly possible that the obstacle could be overcome, perhaps within a few years, and that all the other great obstacles to the development of an atomic explosive could be overcome, *if* the government of a highly industrialized nation-state devoted to the task a sufficiency (it would have to be a vast quantity) of its available material and mental resources.

### III

WE may be sure that the dreadful possibility of atomic weaponry in Hitler's arsenal, and his arsenal alone, had been recognized by Niels Bohr shortly after Frisch told him of the Hahn-Strassmann observation and the Meitner-Frisch interpretation of it. He regarded it initially as a very remote possibility, one that would be denied altogether if physics retained the unlimited freedom and openness of communication that presently obtained and that he was at great pains to preserve. But the governments of Hitler and Mussolini were of course implacably hostile to freedom, openness, internationalism in any form. They could be counted upon to make physics a rigorously closed national enterprise, serving their aggressive purposes alone, if ever they recognized its power potential. Bohr, therefore, must deem ominously significant, in its political context, the fact that Hahn and Strassmann had scored their breakthrough in the Kaiser-Wilhelm Institute only a few blocks from Hitler's Chancellery; that Max Planck, Werner Heisenberg, and a group of some of the most talented younger physicists in the world still lived and worked in the Third Reich; and that one of the best of these younger physicists, Carl F. von Weizsäcker, was the son of Baron Ernst von Weizsäcker, Ribbentrop's second-in-command, who was the reputed brain of Germany's Foreign Office,

We may therefore imagine, with much probable accuracy, some of Bohr's thoughts and feelings as his taxi rolled eastward along G Street in Washington, D.C., late in the afternoon of January 26, bearing him away from the momentous physics conference at George Washington University toward his hotel. His was a mind very different from Enrico Fermi's. The latter, akin to that of Ernest Rutherford, was like a knife, sharp, penetrating, capable of swift, precise distinctions between what was essential and what nonessential in any given problem. Or it was like a searchlight, which brilliantly illuminates whatever it is focused upon and which focuses upon one spot at a time, undistracted and uninhibited by what is hidden in the surrounding sea of darkness. Fermi's ability to isolate a fact or idea, severing its connections with other things at precisely the right points for his immediate purpose, was a major factor in his phenomenal experimental skill and success. Bohr's mind, on the other hand, was intensely engaged by precisely those interconnections that individual experiment necessarily ignores. If he eschewed metaphysics, he did so in ways that betrayed his strong attraction to it (he confessed that Hegel had strongly if indirectly influenced his thought); and if he abhorred the arbitrary imposition of "system" upon phenomena, seeing this as a kind of intellectual arrogance discouraged by his own upbringing in a small country with no delusions of grandeur, he was nevertheless in constant search of system, in the philosophic sense, among the phenomena themselves and was quick to recognize its emergence. For instance, he was acutely aware of the dangers hidden in the concept of causality. Very consciously, when speaking of processes or sequences, he avoided those lurking implications of force, of creativity, of motive power operating through temporal gaps between events, which commonly distort descriptions of the natural world. Instead of "principle," he used "point of view" or "argument"; instead of "laws of nature" he spoke of "regularities of the phenomena." Yet he constantly strove for conceptual universality in his approach to both science and politics (he thought much about politics) and had developed an "argument" for "complementarity" which he applied to both endeavors, aiming to achieve a "harmonious synthesis" of opposites (these, by the argument, became separate aspects of the same reality) that owed much, and obviously, to Hegelian dialectic. Thus there was a profound and, for him, painful irony in the fact that he, whose life voyage had been a quest for unity, integrity, harmony, now brought to America from a disintegrating Europe news of a fundamental force of physical *dis*unity which, in the hands of nationalistic politicians, might destroy the world. Small wonder that the famous "Copenhagen spirit," whose essence was a creative optimism, and which normally spread over Bohr's laboratories as an emanation from Bohr himself, had manifestly departed from him when the Fermis greeted him at the dock in New York. To Laura Fermi he "seemed to have aged" greatly during the few weeks since the Fermis had visited him in his home on their way to Stockholm. "He stooped like a man carrying a heavy burden," she wrote. "His gaze, troubled and insecure, shifted from one to the other of us."[6] And a gloomy anxiety may well have been his dominant mood as his taxi passed the White House this wintry day and he looked toward it through the iron fence (it was spiked like the Prussian helmets of 1914–1918) that bordered the White House yard.

Certainly we ourselves may perceive an ironic symbolism in his spatial location at that moment. His taxi moved eastward. Lafayette Square was at his left hand. And across that square stood the Hay-Adams House. It was but a wink of time ago, in the long sweep of history, that Henry Adams on a wintry day stood at a window in his home, where the hotel now stands, and looked toward the White House where, in 1905 as in 1939, a Roosevelt who was "pure act" (Adams's phrase) wielded executive power. Adams's mind was then struggling toward the climax of his ironically conceived *Education*—struggling to shape the "Law of Acceleration," which, applying to the increase in the amount of man-utilized force or power in the world, was to be central to his "Dynamic Theory of History." Radium, just discovered, indicated that there would be no slowing of the rate of increase in power during the century then opening. On the contrary, there would be a veritable "explosion of new power." Immense energy "leaped from every atom" and "man could no longer hold it off." "Forces grasped his wrists and flung him about as though he had hold of a live wire or a runaway automobile. . . ." But Adams did not believe that man would be a fatal victim of this rampant power. Beneath his elaborate surface show of personal failure and general pessimism he, at sixty-seven, remained imbued with nineteenth-century optimism, the nineteenth century's faith in "progress." He had no serious doubt that man would soon have the live wire hooked up, the runaway car under control, and he considered it probable that "every American" living in the year 2000 would "know how to control unlimited power," would think "in complexities unimaginable to an earlier mind," and would "deal with problems altogether beyond the range of an earlier society." Soon, perhaps on that very day, turning from the window to his writing desk, Adams would pen the famous closing sentence of his *Education,* the sentence in which he wonders what he and his two closest friends (John Hay, Clarence King) might see if they were permitted to return to life in 1938, their centennial year: ". . . Perhaps then, for the first time since man began his education among the carnivores, they would find a world that sensitive and timid natures could regard without a shudder."[7] How grotesque these words would have seemed to Niels Bohr had he read them in his taxi! He who had just lived through the year 1938 was a far from timid man, but he could not regard the world without a shudder. Adams's implied prophecy of atomic energy under human control might be on the verge of coming true; but there was no clear sign that the other phenomenon he prophesied, a citizenry capable of dealing rationally with "unlimited power," would come true in time to prevent unlimited catastrophe. Certainly, in this first month of 1939, the wire remained live, the machine unmastered. Not only was man's physical power growing far more rapidly than his political intelligence, it was almost wholly divorced from the latter. Moreover, this last might be more emphatically true in the Western democracies, in America particularly, than it was in Hitler's Germany—where, conceivably, there was, through young Weizsäcker, a swiftly communicative blood tie between physics and the highest government officialdom. Nothing of the sort obtained in the United States.

What effective communication was there between physics now speeding past the White House and politics immobile behind a desk in the West Wing's Oval Office? There was none at all.

IV

IN March 1939, as soon as the possibility of a controlled atom-splitting chain reaction had been experimentally confirmed, a group of the émigré physicists in this country began reluctantly but also with desperate fervor to agitate against the total openness, the immediate publication of every bit of newly discovered truth, to which each and every one of them had been formerly fervently committed. Included in the group were the Italian Fermi; the Hungarians Szilard, Wigner, Teller; the Austrian Victor F. Weisskopf—men who had personal experience of the viciousness of totalitarian nationalism. They began to press toward twin objectives: restrictions upon the publication by physicists in the Western democracies of developments in nuclear physics that might help the dictatorships toward atomic explosives; and governmental support of such developments in America.

As regards the first objective, one leading American physicist, Harvard's Percy W. Bridgman, had already announced (in a January 1939 issue of *Science,* official organ of the American Association for the Advancement of Science) his decision "from now on not to show my apparatus or discuss my experiments with the citizens of any totalitarian State," this because a "citizen of such a State is no longer a free individual, but he may be compelled to engage in any activity whatever to advance the purposes of that State." But Bridgman's decision, though immediately praised by the famous humanist Christian Gauss of Princeton, had been roundly condemned as a betrayal of the basic principle of free inquiry by most American scientists and also, if somewhat less emphatically, by Niels Bohr. On the same ground, these scientists now opposed the émigré group's publication-restriction efforts—efforts that were in any case rendered futile for the time being when the Joliot-Curies in Paris, who worked at the cutting edge of nuclear physics, flatly refused to join in them.

As regards their second objective, the émigré group was frustrated by the apathy and ignorance of American military and naval officialdom. Fermi, for instance, made a direct approach to the Navy Department in Washington on March 17, it being generally acknowledged that the navy was more receptive to new ideas than the army. This was on the day after Hitler took over the whole of Czechoslovakia—and Fermi knew that Czechoslovakia had the only considerable deposits of uranium in Europe. He was armed with a cautiously worded letter of introduction addressed to Admiral S. C. Hooper in the office of the chief of naval operations by George Pegram, physics professor and graduate dean at Columbia, but instead of the admiral he saw two youthful lieutenant commanders. These listened politely as the Italian, handicapped by imperfect English, struggled to impress upon them the significance of the new discoveries. When he had finished they asked him politely to keep them informed of future developments. But after he had left, the story goes, one of the two turned to the other and said, "That wop is crazy!" Probably this story is apocryphal. That it accurately indicates the naval officers' evident attitude, however, is attested to by the fact that Fermi himself felt he had been personally insulted and was so fumingly angry over it that he vowed never again to attempt to deal with army or navy officers. For agonizing months thereafter the émigré scientists noted helplessly one seeming sign after another that the physicists and chemists of Nazi Germany were being concentrated in the Kaiser-Wilhelm Institute, where they worked on uranium.

By the summer of 1939, Leo Szilard had became convinced that Albert Einstein, who had long been a personal friend of his, was the only physicist in America with sufficient popular fame and prestige to gain a sympathetic hearing from high American government officials. So on a day in mid-July 1939, Szilard, accompanied by Wigner, went by automobile (Wigner drove; Szilard had never learned to drive) to the remote cottage on the Long Island shore where Einstein was in summer retreat. There they obtained from him a promise to write, or at any rate sign, whatever letter or letters might be needed to effect Szilard's purpose—a promise that pacifist humanitarian Einstein regretted years later as the "one great mistake of my life."[8] A few days thereafter, Szilard was persuaded that the only way to achieve his purpose with the necessary speed was by a direct approach, with an Einstein letter, to the President personally, Franklin Roosevelt being famously committed to "experiment" and reputedly remarkably open to new ideas.

Szilard was persuaded of this by Dr. Alexander Sachs, the Russian-born economist whom we have encountered before in this history* and to whom Szilard was introduced by a former member of the German Reichstag, now a refugee from Hitler's Germany, named Gustav Stolper. Sachs not only kept up with scientific developments, Stolper told Szilard, but was said also to have easy access to the White House. The immediately following interview between the economist and the physicist went very well. Quickly grasping the importance of what Szilard was trying to do, Sachs at once "took the position, and completely convinced me, that these were matters which first and foremost concerned the White House and that the best thing to do, also from the practical point of view, was to inform Roosevelt," Szilard wrote to Einstein. "He [Sachs] said that if we gave him a statement he would make sure it reached Roosevelt in person."[9] Subsequently, Einstein agreed with Szilard that Sachs himself should be their intermediary, and by early August there was in Sachs's hands, to be delivered by him to Franklin Roosevelt in person at the earliest possible moment, a somewhat clumsily worded letter dated August 2, 1939, and signed "A. Einstein"—a letter destined to become one of the most famous in history.

It said, in part:

*See *FDR: The New Deal Years,* pp. 240, 245, 268.

In the course of the last four months it has been made probable—through the work of Joliot in France as well as Szilard and Fermi in America—that it may become possible to set up nuclear chain reactions in a large mass of uranium,* by which vast amounts of power and large quantities of new radium-like elements would be generated. Now it appears almost certain that this could be achieved in the immediate future.

This new phenomenon would also lead to the construction of bombs and it is conceivable—though much less certain—that extremely powerful bombs of a new type may thus be constructed. A single bomb of this type, carried by boat or exploded in a port, might very well destroy the whole port together with some of the surrounding territory. . . .

In view of this situation you may think it desirable to have some permanent contact maintained between the administration and the group of physicists now working on chain reaction in America. One possible way of achieving this might be for you to entrust with this task a person who has your confidence and who could perhaps serve in an unofficial capacity. His task might comprise the following:

(a) To approach government departments, keep them informed of further developments, and put forward recommendations for government action, giving particular attention to the problem of securing a supply of uranium ore for the United States.

(b) To speed up the experimental work, which is at present time being carried on within the limits of the budgets of the university laboratories, by providing funds. . . .

I understand that Germany has actually stopped the sale of uranium from the Czechoslovakian mines which she has taken over. That she should have taken such early action might be understood on the ground that the son of the German Undersecretary of State, von Weizsäcker, is attached to the Kaiser Wilhelm Institute in Berlin, where some of the American work on uranium is now being repeated."[10]

When Sachs received this letter, the man to whom it was addressed was in Hyde Park, his time wholly absorbed in the task of signing or vetoing the hundreds of bills pushed through Congress during the last days of the session just ended.

Ten days later, Roosevelt boarded the *Tuscaloosa* for his troubled vacation cruise into far northern waters.

And before a personal interview between Sachs and Roosevelt could be arranged upon the latter's return to Washington, Hitler's legions were raging across Poland, war upon Germany had been declared by Britain and France, and Roosevelt was fully occupied by the urgent, immediate problems of a still predominantly isolationist America's relations with general war in Europe. Alexander Sachs recognized this fact. He repeatedly reminded Missy LeHand and Pa Watson that he had requested an interview and that the information he wished to convey to the President was of the utmost importance, but he bided his time with far more patience than did an increasingly anxiety-ridden Szilard. When the latter, accompanied by Wigner, called upon Sachs at the

---

*Clearly, Szilard and Einstein were thinking at that time of an explosive chain reaction in natuin the separated light isotope U-235.

close of September and discovered that the Einstein letter and the memorandum he had prepared to accompany it yet remained in the economist's hands, he wrote Einstein (October 3) saying there was "a distinct possibility that Sachs will be of no use to us" and that "Wigner and I have decided to accord Sachs ten days grace."[11]

## 13

### Storm, Followed by Thick Fog

I

WITHIN minutes after he received the news of Germany's attack on Poland, shortly before three o'clock in the morning of Friday, September 1, 1939, Franklin Roosevelt began imparting it by phone to Hull, Woodring, Welles, Acting Secretary of the Navy Charles Edison, and William Haslett, who was acting press secretary in Steve Early's absence. His phone calls were immediately consequential. Before the last one was completed, automobiles were racing through Washington's theretofore quiet and deserted streets. Lights were flashing on at State, War, and Navy, and in Washington's news bureaus, where grim-faced and agitated men gathered to perform tasks long prescribed for this event and to decide what else must be immediately done.

At the Navy Department, the chief of naval operations conferred with the navy secretary on the disposition of the Atlantic and Pacific fleets. At the War Department on Constitution Avenue, George C. Marshall, the acting army Chief of Staff, who would be sworn in as Chief of Staff Craig's successor a few hours hence, conferred with the war secretary and the assistant secretary on the alerting of America's military outposts and on immediate steps to be taken toward strengthening the nation's dangerously weak ground and air defenses. At State the decision was made to release at once, though formal declarations of war had not yet been made by Great Britain or France, an appeal by the President to those countries, and to Germany, Poland, and Italy, to refrain from air bombing of civilians. The appeal had been suggested by Bullitt just one week ago for release "immediately after the first shot" was fired, had then been drafted by Welles and approved by Roosevelt, and was on its way to Europe before dawn of this day.[1] Fortunately or unfortunately, State had not now to deal with the question of Germany's great liner, the *Bremen,* whose sailing from New York had been delayed for days while U.S. officials searched her, as the vessel of a potential belligerent, to make certain she carried no contraband and could not be transformed at sea from passenger ship into commerce raider. The search had been conducted, at the President's suggestion, in very leisurely fashion to induce a maximum of Nazi discomfort and of likelihood that the great ship would not be able to reach her home port before she became a legitimate prize of war for Britain or France. An inquiry into the matter, polite but more than hinting at an imminent formal protest, had been made in a call upon Assistant Secretary Berle by the German chargé d'affaires on the day before yesterday. A few hours later, Republican senator Styles Bridges of New Hampshire had loudly, publicly denounced the ship's holding as an action calculated by the administration to involve the United States in the coming war even before that war began.[2] But yesterday afternoon the ship had been at last permitted to sail. Without passengers, she now raced for home across the open sea, where surely the British navy could and would be shadowing her, prepared to capture her as soon as war was declared by Poland's allies. (In the event, she remained unshadowed, uncaptured.)

By five o'clock in the morning, in well-lighted offices all across town, the appropriate machinery of government, fueled by excitement and lubricated by custom, was working or prepared to work in the highest gear.

At the controlling center of this great machine, however, in the White House, no light burned. All was peace and quiet and restful dark in the presidential bedroom, where the iron-nerved President of the United States indulged his unique capacity for turning off, for letting go, for putting aside for the time being—a capacity that, seemingly unimpaired by the most feverish excitements, the most fearful pressures, never ceased to amaze his closest associates. Having completed his last phone call, Franklin Roosevelt simply switched off his waking mind as he did his bed lamp, lay back upon his pillow, and went off at once into sleep.

At six-thirty he was awakened by a second call from Bullitt, in Paris; Bullitt had just talked with Premier Daladier and been told that France would certainly honor her treaty commitment to Poland. It had been far from certain she would do so, in view of her betrayal of Czechoslovakia; it may have remained yet doubtful in Roosevelt's mind that she would. But if Daladier spoke truth, a general European war was certain to begin—when? within hours? days? (Soon Roosevelt would learn of an offer by Mussolini to mediate between Berlin and Warsaw by means of an international conference. It was an offer obviously made to provide an out for Italy from her Pact of Steel with Germany but it might provide a means and excuse for delaying war action in London and Paris until Poland no longer existed, rendering all treaties with her meaningless.) Was there a time limit in the ultimatum France had supposedly served upon Hitler? Bullitt didn't say. Roosevelt didn't ask. He simply thanked "Bill" for the news, replaced the receiver, and went off again into sleep. But not for long. Shortly after seven A.M. he was awakened by a call from Kennedy who, at the embassy in London, had just learned of the invasion. For the last week, Kennedy had been trying with no success to persuade Washington to bring pressure upon Poland to make "concessions" to Hitler, having been urged toward this course by Sir Horace Wilson, Chamberlain's closest adviser. The ambassador was now utterly despondent. He took it for granted that the Chamberlain ministry could not avoid a declaration of war and this, as Kennedy now indicated to Roosevelt and would later say flatly to Hull, meant "the end of the world, the end of everything." Roosevelt didn't believe it. He said so cheerily, doing his best to comfort "poor Joe."[3]

But this time, when he'd hung up, Roosevelt did not lie back in his bed. He rang for his valet, and breakfast.

At his press conference some three hours later he was his usual buoyant, jaunty self. "What time did you get up?" he asked correspondent Earl Godwin as the newsmen began filing in. "About 3:00 . . . , right after you aroused the nation," said a sleepy-looking Godwin, who wondered "if anybody got Borah up." Roosevelt wondered, too. "Where is he?" he asked, registering astonishment when someone said, as he thought, that Borah had gone to Poland. Actually, Borah had gone to Poland Springs, Maine, Roosevelt was informed, whereupon he registered mild disappointment over the loss of a perfectly marvelous news story. As for his own news, he told the assembled reporters, he really had none "that you do not know already." He couldn't now say "when Congress will be called"—that he did not say "if" was duly noted—when the neutrality proclamation would be issued, and so on. He must await developments "on the other side." Meanwhile, he hoped the newsmen would avoid making alarming news out of mere rumors or wild surmises, of which there were bound now to be a great many. For instance, Hull had just told him of a false report ("if it was printed it would be a pity") that "we had sent out a general order for all American merchant ships to return to American ports. Now that kind of thing is confusing to the public mind. . . ." To avoid such confusion, to relieve fearful anxieties, to reassure—such was his own primary intent at this juncture. When asked the inevitable question, the one "uppermost in the minds of all the American people today," as the asking reporter put it—namely, "Can we stay out?"—Roosevelt replied with careful emphasis: "I not only sincerely hope so, but I believe we can; and . . . every effort will be made by the Administration so to do." He gave the reporters permission to quote this statement directly.[4]

There followed, in Washington, a mysteriously prolonged period of suspenseful waiting for decisive developments "on the other side." German armor struck deep into Poland, Polish ground forces were being slashed to pieces, the initially inadequate Polish air force was being annihilated, and Polish civilians reportedly died by the thousands under a rain of German bombs. The watching world was appalled by the swift and terrible effectiveness of a new kind of warfare, the *Blitzkrieg,* or "lightning war," in which striking force was multiplied by the speed and utter ruthlessness with which the blows were delivered by plane and tank and motorized transport. But from Britain and France, though both ordered general mobilization of their armed forces on the morning of September 1, there issued no declarations of war as Friday gave way to Saturday, September 2, and hour after hour of that Saturday passed by. The lengthening pause was increasingly filled with an angry, disgusting rumor that another "Munich" was being attempted, a rumor that seemed sustained by fact when Chamberlain, after two postponements, addressed to the Commons on Saturday evening a self-centered speech clearly expressive of his personal anguish over the failure of his efforts for peace but maddeningly vague, even obfuscating, about what His Majesty's Government proposed now to do. He spoke of the Italian mediation offer, and of France's (that is, Foreign Minister Bonnet's) aversion to immediate action, as if these were a sufficient cause and justification of inaction on his part. But now, even among members of his

Cabinet, Chamberlain stood almost alone, and stripped for the moment of all dignity. When the Labour opposition spokesman rose to answer him he was loudly urged by a leading Tory to "speak for England" and did so briefly, forcefully, with great effect: "An act of aggression took place thirty-eight hours ago. The moment that act of aggression took place one of the most important treaties of modern times automatically came into operation. . . . I wonder how long we are prepared to vacillate . . . when Britain, and all Britain stands for, and human civilization are in peril." The Commons' approving response to this was of such magnitude and vehemence that no government could stand which opposed it. Two hours later, in a hastily summoned Cabinet meeting at 10 Downing Street, Chamberlain bowed at last to the inevitable.

At eight o'clock Sunday morning, September 3, London time, a British ultimatum, demanding by eleven A.M. a German statement that she would at once begin withdrawing her forces from Polish soil, else Britain would declare war upon her, was delivered to Ribbentrop by Sir Nevile Henderson. At eleven-fifteen Chamberlain told the British people in a radio broadcast that "this country is now at war. . . ." He spoke as a heartbroken old man ("a dithering old dodderer with shaking voice and hands," according to one observer) already mortally ill (cancer, as yet undiagnosed, would kill him fourteen months hence), and neither his radio address nor the one he made to Parliament could be deemed a ringing call to arms. Each was, instead, an egoistical apologia. "You can imagine what a bitter blow it is to me that all my long struggle for peace has failed," he said to the British radio audience. "Yet I cannot believe that there is anything more, or anything different that I could have done. . . ." To Parliament he said: "Everything I have worked for, everything I have hoped for, everything I have believed in in my public life has crashed in ruins. There is only one thing left for me to do: that is to devote what strengths and powers I have to forward the victory of the cause for which we have to sacrifice so much."[5] But he did not on that day resign his high office, as many or most of his listeners would have been more than willing for him to do.

Five hours later, the final French ultimatum to Germany expired. France also was at war with Germany.

And some seven or so hours after that, on Sunday evening in Washington, Roosevelt addressed to "the whole of America" a brief fireside chat in which he sounded again that soothing note of reassurance he had struck during his press conference two days before. Curiously, for it was decidedly out of character for him, he also echoed, if faintly, the note of personal sorrow, defeat, and regret which Chamberlain had sounded. He echoed, too, faintly, Woodrow Wilson's speechifying attempts at the opening of the Great War to hold America aloof from war's destruction in order to retain for America and himself the post of final arbiter, of world peacemaker:

Until four-thirty this morning I had hoped against hope that some miracle would prevent a devastating war in Europe and bring to an end the invasion of Poland by

Germany [he began]. For four long years a succession of actual wars and constant crises have shaken the entire world and have threatened in each case to bring on the gigantic conflict which is today unhappily a fact. It is right that I should recall to your minds the consistent and at times successful efforts of your Government in these crises to throw the whole weight of the United States into the cause of peace. In spite of spreading wars I think we have every right and every reason to maintain as a national policy the fundamental moralities, the teachings of religion and the continuation of efforts to restore peace—for some day, though the time may be distant, we can be of even greater help to a crippled humanity.

He repeated his press-conference caution against the spread of false rumor, then went on: "You must master at the outset a simple but unalterable fact in modern foreign relations between nations. When peace has been broken anywhere, the peace of all countries everywhere is in danger." Nevertheless:

Let no man or woman thoughtlessly or falsely talk of America sending its armies to European fields. At this moment there is being prepared a proclamation of American neutrality. This would have been done even if there had been no neutrality statute on the books, for this proclamation is in accordance with international law and . . . American policy. This will be followed by a Proclamation required by the existing Neutrality Act. And [he emphasized these words, in obvious reference to Neutrality Act revision] *I trust that in the days to come our neutrality can be made a true neutrality.*

At this point he departed from the example set by Wilson in 1914. He said that, though this "nation will remain a neutral nation," he could not ask "that every American remain neutral in thought as well. Even a neutral has a right to take account of the facts. Even a neutral cannot be asked to close his mind or his conscience." The operations of mind and conscience must be severely limited by the American commitment to peace, however; they must not be permitted to motivate as their logical consequence words and deeds that might involve the United States in the war. "I have said not once, but many times, that I have seen war and I hate war," he closed. "I say that again and again. . . . As long as it remains in my power to prevent, there will be no blackout of peace in the United States."[6]

Significant of his political purpose was Roosevelt's distinction, in this speech, between the two neutrality proclamations he was to issue—the one that accorded with long-established international law, the other forced upon him by the rigidities of the Neutrality Act. Both of them, and an accompanying package of draft executive orders, had been for days in the Oval Office's active file; Berle had delivered them to him a week ago in anticipation of the seemingly inevitable. But not until September 5 were the two proclamations issued, a delay that expressed Roosevelt's opposition to the arms embargo while providing Britain and France more time in which to obtain shipments of arms and war matériel from the United States. He dared not go further in an exercised "unneutrality." The American public's pacifistic mood seemed at that moment virtually universal and utterly impregnable. It was manifest in the reaction, or remarkable lack of it, to the top war news of September 4 in the American press, namely, that twenty-eight American citizens were among the 112 who had lost their lives when the British passenger liner *Athenia,* outward bound for Canada, was torpedoed by a German U-boat off the coast of Scotland six hours after Britain's declaration of war, three hours before Roosevelt began his fireside chat. The event provoked nothing of the belligerent outrage that the sinking of the *Lusitania* had caused in May 1915. If anything, it strengthened the public's determination to resist such dangerous passions. The expressed majority opinion was that Americans so foolish as to sail into a war zone on a belligerent's vessel must do so at their own risk. There were isolationist and pro-German Anglophobes in the United States who even professed to believe the Nazi government's assertion that the *Athenia* was sunk, not by a German torpedo, but by a bomb secretly ordered aboard her by Winston Churchill, who sought thus to foment war between the United States and Germany.[7]

This last was an absurd charge, of course, too absurd to be countenanced for an instant by well-informed and sober-minded people. It had little impact upon the general public, who forgot it within a few days after it was made. But it may have been the immediate cause of a presidential action having great and fortunate consequence for the defenders of civilization against barbarism.

For Roosevelt may have been reminded, first, that the same absurd charge had been leveled against Churchill in the immediate aftermath of the *Lusitania*'s sinking, when Churchill was First Lord of the Admiralty in London while Roosevelt was assistant secretary of the navy in Washington; and second, that Churchill was now again at the Admiralty (he had been appointed to that Cabinet post by Chamberlain, reluctantly, in response to pressures impossible to resist, on the day Britain declared war on Germany*). This in turn may have reminded Roosevelt that, in October 1933, in the eighth month of the New Deal, he had received as a gift a copy of the first volume of the multivolume *Marlborough: His Life and Times,* Churchill's biography of his most illustrious ancestor, John Churchill. It bore upon its title page a handwritten inscription by its author: "To Franklin D. Roosevelt . . . , with earnest best wishes for the success of the greatest crusade of modern times." There was, then, some slight basis or precedent for a special personal relationship between the President and the man most likely to become Chamberlain's successor as his Majesty's first minister. So on September 11, 1939, Roosevelt addressed to "My dear Churchill" a brief note: "It is because you and I occupied similar positions in the World War that I want you to know how glad I am that you are back again in the Admiralty. Your problems are, I realize, complicated by new factors but

---

*At a tension-relieving stag dinner and poker party at the White House on the night of Saturday, September 2, Ickes had provoked a roar of laughter from the President when he said with a straight face that, according to Senator Borah's private sources of foreign intelligence, which were superior to those of the State Department, Chamberlain was enlarging his cabinet "so he can give Joe Kennedy a place on it."[8]

the essential is not very different. What I want you and the Prime Minister to know is that I shall at all times welcome it if you will keep me in touch personally with anything you want me to know about. You can always send sealed letters through your pouch, or my pouch." He added that he was "glad you did the Marlboro [*sic*] volumes before this thing started—and I much enjoyed reading them." Aware of the troubles that might boil up out of a personal correspondence exclusively between a head of state and a subordinate official of another state, Roosevelt was careful to write the prime minister on that same day, saying, "My dear Mr. Chamberlain: I need not tell you that you have been much in my thoughts during these difficult days and further that I hope you will at all times feel free to write me personally and outside diplomatic procedure about any problems as they arise. I hope and believe we shall repeal the embargo within the next month and this is definitely a part of the Administration's policy." He did not mention to Chamberlain the message he was sending Churchill, but the latter, upon receipt of his message, at once disclosed its contents to the prime minister and, in Cabinet meeting, dwelt upon the advantages Britain would gain from the personal correspondence the President invited. On October 4 Chamberlain replied to his letter from the President, writing that in "his own view . . . we shall win . . . by convincing the Germans that they cannot win. . . . I believe they are already halfway to this conviction and I cannot doubt that the attitude of the United States of America, due to your personal efforts, has had a notable influence in this direction. If the embargo is repealed this month, I am convinced that the effect on German morale will be devastating." On the following day, with the permission of his government, Churchill sent through the U.S. embassy in London a short message stressing Britain's wish to respect "a safety belt extending outward from 300 to 1,000 miles around the [Western] hemisphere except for Canada"—a belt that had just been proclaimed, at U.S. instigation, by a meeting in Panama of the foreign ministers of all the republics of the Americas. The message, like those which followed, was signed "Naval Person," a code name valueless as a disguising device but, intentionally, puckishly amusing.[9]

Thus began a correspondence of great historical importance, which would extend over five and a half years and comprise, ultimately, nearly two thousand messages—1,161 from Churchill to Roosevelt, 788 from Roosevelt to Churchill —plus hundreds of phone conversations. It effected a de facto alliance between the U.S. and British governments long before that alliance was an openly acknowledged reality.

The *Athenia* was barely mentioned in the presidential press conference of September 8, the main news of which was that an executive proclamation of "limited national emergency" would be issued during the noon hour.

Roosevelt explained at some length what such "emergency" meant. He did so in soothingly deprecatory terms. Had he declared a national emergency "without any limitation," as a number of statutory provisions authorized the executive to do in dire circumstances, "scare headlines might be justified because, under that, the Executive could do all kinds of things." But there was now need to do only "a few . . . simple and minor things within peacetime authorizations." There was need for an immediate moderate increase in the number of army and navy personnel on active duty, and two executive orders for the calling up of reserves would be among the four to be issued immediately following the emergency's formal proclamation. Even with the added personnel, Roosevelt stressed, the army would remain well below its authorized peacetime strength of 280,000, the navy well below its authorized 180,000. Approximately a third of the nation's presently out-of-commission destroyers —that is, thirty or so—would be recommissioned and used for patrol duty. A third executive order would "merely carry out the existing law which says, 'In the event of a national emergency there is appropriated $500,000 to the State Department for the aid of Americans in foreign countries.'" The fourth order "relates to what you might say is a combination of neutrality and national defense" in that it would strengthen "certain investigative agencies" in order to guard more effectively against sabotage and other forms of subversion. And that, said the President, was the sum total of the proclamation's significance. There was absolutely "no thought, in any shape, manner or form, of putting the Nation, either in its defenses or in its internal economy, on a war basis. . . . We are going to keep the Nation on a peace basis. . . ."[10]

Five days later, on September 13, he formally summoned Congress to convene in extraordinary session at noon on Thursday, September 21.

II

THE ground for this had been and was being carefully prepared. Steps had been taken to counter the massive effort to arouse public opinion against embargo repeal that was being mounted by such groups as the National Keep America Out of Foreign War Committee, organized by Hamilton Fish the previous spring, and by the Women's National Committee to Keep the United States Out of War. On the day after the call for a special session went out, Roosevelt was told by Press Secretary Early that the Republican 1936 presidential candidate, Alfred M. Landon; Landon's running mate in 1936, Colonel Frank Knox of the Chicago *Daily News;* and Hoover's secretary of state, Henry L. Stimson, had all agreed to support the President's neutrality-law revision with public statements, and that Harvard president James B. Conant and Massachusetts Institute of Technology president Karl Compton had agreed to organize support of the President's proposal among the nation's leading educators. Effective pressure had been brought to bear upon several Democratic congressional members who had deserted the administration during the vote on the Vorys amendment. In general, the chances for the success of his cause seemed to Roosevelt good. A number of congressmen other than those who had been pressured by the White House—Republicans as well as Democrats formerly opposed to embargo repeal—had now changed their minds or were on the verge of doing so, according to a letter to Roosevelt from the State Department's counselor, R. Walton Moore. A Gallup poll published on September 3 showed that there had been a gain of 3 percent (from 47 percent to 50 percent) in popular support of embargo repeal since a poll taken last spring, and one could logically assume that this support increased as the terrifying efficiency of the German military machine continued to be demonstrated in Poland and more and more people consequently realized the importance of French and British arms to U.S. security. "My own personal opinion is that we can get the votes in the House and Senate but that the principal difficulty will be to prevent a filibuster in the latter," Roosevelt concluded in a letter to Moore on September 11.[11]

The President's chief concern at that moment was the antirepeal publicity campaign of the "peace bloc," as the isolationists now called themselves. It was to open with a national radio broadcast by Senator Borah on September 14. This presented no very serious problem to the White House. The senator's credibility as a foreign-policy expert had been severely damaged in the public mind by his emphatic eve-of-war assertion that war would not occur; and Frank Knox, whose newspaper was famous for its brilliant foreign correspondents, and who had been well educated by them in this field, was to issue a statement rebutting Borah as soon as the latter had spoken. His paper would follow this up with a front-page rebuttal editorial. Roy Roberts of the *Kansas City Star* would also rebut with a front-page editorial.[12] But Borah's speech was to be followed, on the evening of the fifteenth, by an address broadcast over all three of the major networks by Charles A. Lindbergh, and Roosevelt, who had an all too vivid remembrance of what had happened when, in 1934,* he and the aviator last came together in head-on collision, found this worrisome indeed.

It was of course true that the Lindbergh who returned to America from his self-imposed European exile in April 1939 was considerably less a popular hero than the Lindbergh of five years before. His fame had been tarnished by his evident fondness for Nazi Germany. But when he sailed into New York harbor aboard the *Aquitania* he yet retained a good deal of the glamorous appeal he had had for the multitude ever since his epochal flight of 1927; and in recent months some of the tarnish had been removed from his fame. Immediately upon his return his apologists began to claim that he had accepted his notorious Nazi medal for secret reasons which would prove to have been highly honorable, even heroic in service of his country, when the "true story" could at last be told—a claim that gained plausibility when, within a week after his return, he, a colonel in the army air corps reserve, reported to the corps commander, Major General H. H. (Hap) Arnold, for undisclosed active duty in Washington. His famed reclusiveness, his notorious avoidance of crowds or indeed of public appearances of any kind over the last eight years, now added an eager curiosity to the glamour which invested him in the popular view; for assuredly he would not now be courting publicity were he not profoundly,

*See *FDR: The New Deal Years,* pp. 358–61.

fervently committed to the cause for which he spoke. An unanswered question was the effectiveness of his speech delivery; he had never before made a full-length radio broadcast. But it was likely that his still boyish earnestness and sincerity, coupled with the attractive image of him that remained in the popular mind, would more than compensate for whatever deficiencies there were in his speaking style. Certainly his radio audience would be immense.

Thus Roosevelt knew he was being formidably challenged in an area of mass communication of which he had long been master, and we may be sure he pondered seriously the question of what to do about it. One option, of course, was simply to order the flier to remain silent or, at least, to submit his draft speech to the White House for prior review. An army colonel was subject to such orders from his President and Commander in Chief. But if this option was even considered by Roosevelt it was at once rejected as inevitably politically counterproductive. Colonel Lindbergh had asked for relief from his active status so that he might speak his mind as a private citizen, and the relief was granted him by the War Department, with evident reluctance, on September 14. Was another perceived option then acted upon? It was, according to Lindbergh's published diary: In the afternoon of the next day, only a few hours before his scheduled broadcast, Lindbergh was very privately informed by his great friend Major Truman Smith, who had it from Hap Arnold, who had it from Woodring, who presumably had it from the White House, that if he canceled his broadcast or refrained from opposing administration policy in it, he would be named to the Cabinet as "secretary for air," a new post the White House proposed to create specifically for the purpose, evidently, of appointing him to it and thereby muzzling him.[13] According to comments by Lindbergh's friends (he himself makes no mention of this), the attempted bribe was accompanied by a threat. The hero was allegedly told that if he *did* oppose administration policy his income-tax returns for the last several years would be scrutinized by Internal Revenue with a microscopically critical eye. Such tactics were not out of character for Roosevelt, one must admit—they had been employed against Huey Long, for one—but if they were employed in this instance they manifest a rare lack of psychological acumen on Roosevelt's part. Far from being merely futile, they were as if designed to harden Lindbergh's stubborn will.

At nine-forty-five P.M. EST on Friday the fifteenth, the hero spoke through microphones set up for him in Washington's Carlton Hotel to an audience as large as that which had listened to the President's fireside chat twelve days before. Lindbergh's delivery, in a pleasant voice having the timbre and vibrancy of a clarinet, proved more than adequate for his purpose. He began with words seemingly indicative of an intention to organize and lead a great national movement. "In times of great emergency, men of the same belief must gather together for mutual counsel and action. . . ." he said. "I speak tonight for those people who feel that the destiny of this country does not call for our involvement in European wars." He made thereafter no direct reference to neutrality law or embargo repeal, but his implicit opposition to the latter was obvious

and strong. The core of his message was ominously racist: "These wars in
Europe are not wars in which our civilization is defending itself against some
Asiatic intruder. There is no Genghis Khan or Xerxes marching against our
Western civilization. This is not a question of banding together to defend the
white race against foreign invasion. This is simply one more of those age-old
struggles within our own family of nations—a quarrel arising from the errors
of the last war—from the failure of the victors of that war to follow a consistent
policy either of fairness or force." (He said nothing of the "errors" of the
defeated in that war.) He espoused the "hard-headed realism" of those who
would rule moral feeling out of account in the conduct of "practical" affairs,
saying we "must not permit our sentiment, our pity, our personal feelings of
sympathy to obscure the issue. We must be as impersonal as a surgeon with
his knife." He condemned "foreign propaganda [emanating from the White
House?] to the effect that our frontiers lie in Europe" and, rather strangely for
one whose fame derived from a solo flight across the Atlantic in a now
long-obsolete single-engined airplane, argued that "even [with] . . . modern
aircraft" we need have no fear of attack from over the seas. America's historic
task was to "carry on Western civilization," he closed. "This is more important
than the sympathies, the friendships . . . of any single generation. This is the
test before America now."[14]

His speech loosed a flood of mail upon radio station WOL in Washington,
its original sponsor. It raised a storm of controversy. There were immediate
bitter personal attacks upon Lindbergh as pro-Nazi, by Ickes and other administration spokesmen who dismissed with contempt the claim that his clandestine pre-Munich activities, for which Hitler had rewarded him, were really
secret services to his own country. He was as vehemently defended by spokesmen for a weird conglomerate of elements, many of which were otherwise
strongly opposed to one another. There were Norman Thomas socialists,
Midwestern Progressives, Communists and fellow travelers, business leaders
who hated Roosevelt, the German-American Bund, other American fascist
organizations, Father Coughlin with his *Social Justice* magazine, and Christian pacifists (the *Christian Century* was eloquent in his defense while attacking
the administration's "smear tactics")—all joined by anonymous myriads who
yet worshiped at the shrine of Lindy, the Lone Eagle. On balance, the public
response was deemed highly favorable by the self-styled "peace bloc." Immediately following the broadcast, and for two weeks thereafter, a flood of letters,
postcards, and telegrams, demanding retention of the arms embargo, poured
into the offices of senators and representatives. Most of the mail was individual
and spontaneous (form letters made up only 15 percent of it, according to one
analysis) and most of it came from the Midwest. The deluge was effective. One
Republican congressman who the previous spring had strongly favored embargo repeal now came out publicly against it, saying that of 1,800 letters and
telegrams he had received in the last few days only seventy-six were in support
of embargo repeal. A Republican senator who had formerly inclined toward

repeal let it be known that he was now inclined against it. Yet other members of Congress who were formerly for repeal began to waver.

Lindbergh himself was highly pleased. Fulton Lewis, Jr., the archreactionary radio commentator who had arranged this broadcast, easily persuaded him to repeat his performance. A second broadcast was scheduled for the evening of October 13 over the Mutual Broadcasting System, the network of Colonel McCormick's right-wing, propagandistic *Chicago Tribune.*[15]

Meanwhile, Roosevelt prepared to open, with his message to the special congressional session, his side of what would become known to history as the Great Debate. The final preparations were hasty. On short notice, in an endeavor to give his effort a bipartisan flavor, he summoned to the White House for conference on September 20 not only congressional leaders of both parties but also the 1936 Republican candidates for president and vice president. Knox and Landon came, however, in the expectation of being informed about, and participating in a discussion of, the international situation. They had been led to believe they would be. Hence their angry disappointment, their feeling that they were being used, when the discussion was confined to the President's upcoming speech, and to congressional strategy for neutrality-law revision. (Landon was actually personally offended; Berle had to attempt to mollify him, over cocktails, the following evening.[16]) It was not until the morning of the twenty-first, the day of its delivery, that the final draft message was completed. In his bedroom, propped upright by pillows as he lay in bed, Roosevelt worked, with Sam Rosenman, against the pressure of an immediate and absolute deadline, piecing the speech together out of a confusion of earlier drafts: one by Corcoran and Cohen; one a rough draft Roosevelt himself had dictated; one a rewrite by Hull and Berle of this first rough draft; one a loose compendium of key elements of these which Rosenman had assembled the day before. The pages were sent one by one to Grace Tully for typing, with the last page not okayed until the noon hour, just as Congress was being formally convened "to receive such communication as may be made by the Executive."[17]

Two hours later an unsmiling, even grim-faced President entered the Capitol chamber and made his slow, arduous way on steel-braced legs to the podium. The applause that greeted him was but a polite ripple. He barely acknowledged it as he placed upon the lectern before him the reading copy of a speech that, for all the frantic haste of its final preparation, was, as a tactical maneuver, shrewdly and artfully designed. "I have asked the Congress to reassemble . . . in order that it may consider and act on the amendment of certain legislation which, in my best judgment, so alters the historic foreign policy of the United States that it impairs the peaceful relations of the United States with foreign nations," he began. ". . . I proceed on the assumption that every member of the Senate and the House . . . , and every member of the Executive Branch . . . are [sic] equally and without reservation in favor of such measures as will protect the neutrality, the safety and the integrity of our country and at the same time keep us out of war. . . . Let no group assume the exclusive label of 'peace bloc.' We all belong to it." He reviewed the administration's efforts "within our traditional policy of non-involvement" to avert "the present appalling war," and went on: "Having thus striven and failed, this Government must lose no time or effort to keep our nation from being drawn into the war. In my candid judgment we shall succeed in these efforts."* But *only* if we abandoned the failed effort "to legislate neutrality," he implied—for the legislation now in force "may actually give aid to the aggressor and deny it to the victim." We must return to our traditional reliance on international law. Roosevelt referred to the disastrous results of America's only previous departure from this, "the so-called Embargo and Non-Intercourse Acts" adopted during the Napoleonic Wars. "It is merely reciting history to recall to you that one of the results . . . was the burning in 1814 of part of this Capitol in which we are assembled today. Our next deviation by statute from the sound principles of neutrality, and peace through international law, did not come for one hundred and thirty years. It was the so-called Neutrality Act of 1935. . . . I regret that the Congress passed that Act. I equally regret that I signed that Act." There followed words that soothed, or were intended to soothe, the prevailing fear of U.S. involvement in the war while carefully avoiding any direct reference to his purpose of aiding Britain and France in their struggle. The nearest he came to such reference was his statement that the embargo

had the effect of putting land powers on the same footing as naval powers, as far as sea-borne commerce was concerned. A land power which threatened war could thus feel assured in advance that any prospective sea-power antagonist would be weakened through denial of its ancient right to buy anything anywhere. This, four years ago, began to give a definite advantage to one belligerent as against another, not through his own strength or geographical position, but through an affirmative act on the part of the United States. Removal of the embargo is merely reverting to the sounder international practice, and pursuing in time of war as in time of peace our ordinary trade policies. . . . The step I recommend is to put this country back on the solid footing of real and traditional neutrality.

But in fact, as he didn't say and must have hoped no one would notice, this recommended "step" comprised three measures that departed widely from "traditional neutrality" as practiced by the United States prior to 1935. Two of them—the barring of American merchant vessels from designated combat zones, and the denying of "war credits to belligerents"—were borrowed intact from existing neutrality law. The third, the requirement that "the foreign buyer . . . take transfer of title in this country to commodities purchased by

---

*On the night before, Cordell Hull had pressed him to declare that never under any circumstances would we go to war. "Can you guarantee that?" Roosevelt had replied, looking hard at him. "Can I guarantee that?" Berle then opined that no one could "guarantee the future" eight months ahead and that "all we can do now is say that until the Atlantic line is seriously threatened or crossed, we will not go to war." This statement was then dictated by Roosevelt into the speech draft but was evidently removed next day. See Berle, *Navigating the Rapids,* p. 257.

belligerents," was equally at odds with "our ordinary trade practices." The three, however, provided "far greater safeguards than we . . . have ever possessed, to protect American lives and property from danger," Roosevelt insisted. And most emphatically they were not, and must not be permitted to become, a partisan issue. "Our acts must be guided by one single, hard-headed thought—keeping America out of this war. In that spirit, I am asking the leaders of the two major parties in the Senate and in the House of Representatives to remain in Washington between the close of this extraordinary session and the beginning of the regular session on January 3, 1940. They have assured me they will do so; and I expect to consult with them at frequent intervals. . . ." His closing words seemed, strangely, to echo Lindbergh's argument: "We must appreciate in the deepest sense the true American interest," he said. "Rightly considered, that interest is not selfish. Destiny first made us, with our sister nations in this Hemisphere, joint heirs of European culture. Fate seems now to compel us to assume the task of helping to maintain in the Western world a citadel wherein that civilization may be kept alive.* The peace, the integrity, and the safety of the Americas—these must be kept firm and serene."[18]

So many telegrams poured into the White House mail room the following morning that the staff had been unable to count them (besides, they were still flooding in) when Roosevelt was asked about them at his press conference. According to "the tabulation kept by the telegraph office last night and up to ten o'clock this morning, they were pro [i.e., for embargo repeal] with the exception . . . of eight or ten, and two of these were not in exact opposition," Steve Early told Roosevelt and the assembled reporters. The telegrams had "come in spontaneously; they were enthusiastic and the volume was in excess of any received after any of your recent speeches," which included the September 3 fireside chat. (A reporter asked Roosevelt if he was aware "that there is a large and increasing volume of telegrams and messages against your proposal." "Oh, yes," replied Roosevelt dismissively.)[19] In following days there were further evidences of the speech's persuasive impact. Polls taken at the outbreak of war had shown the American people evenly divided on the question of repeal. By mid-September, 57 percent of a national Gallup poll sample favored repeal. Sixty percent did so immediately following the President's speech. As for that body of opinion, congressional opinion, which was of immediate decisive importance, it too was evidently favorably impressed; on September 28, the Senate Foreign Relations Committee reported the revised Pittman bill, 16–7, and there were clear signs that, in both House and Senate, the tide of opinion flowed now toward the administration's position. The presidential message, as a tactical maneuver, must therefore be counted successful.

---

*America's task was "to preserve the things we love and mourn the passing of in Europe. . . ." Lindbergh had said. "The gift of civilized life must still be carried on."

But would it have been less so, and would it not have better served Roosevelt's long-term strategic purposes, if it had more frankly expressed his real motives?

The speech "set the tone for the ensuing debate" in a way that "for the next six weeks" required the administration to carry on "the elaborate pretense that the sale of arms to the Allies was but an accidental by-product of a program designed to keep the United States clear of the war," Robert A. Divine has written.[20] Despite this, the real, intended effect of repeal was repeatedly frankly recognized during the debate in ways that manifestly did no harm to the administration's cause. On October 3, Henry Stimson, in pursuance of his promise to cooperate with the administration, phoned Cordell Hull to read him the central portion of the radio network speech he was scheduled to make on the evening of October 5. This central portion said unequivocally that the embargo must be repealed so that Britain and France could be helped in their war against Hitler's Germany. Hull listened, aghast. On the day before, Borah had opened the "peace bloc" side of the Senate floor debate with a direct challenge to the administration's contention that the arms embargo was a departure from international law. There was "no rule of international law . . . which in any way denies the right of a nation to prohibit the sale of arms and munitions," he had said, whereas repeal of the embargo after its announced application to the current hostilities would be not merely a gross breach of neutrality but actually "an act of intervention." And intervention through the provision of aid to Britain and France was precisely the administration's intention, claimed Borah.[21] Now, to Hull's consternation, Stimson proposed to concede to the enemy this crucial point. Excise the offending words! At least blunt their cutting edges! So pleaded the secretary. Stimson flatly refused; if he were not permitted to speak his mind freely he would not speak at all, he said, and hung up. Hull then conferred agitatedly with State Department colleagues and was forced to conclude that Stimson's appalling frankness could hardly do as much harm as the publicized cancellation of his broadcast would do, whereupon he phoned Stimson and withdrew his objections. The speech was delivered as written. Significantly, it went over well, so well that tens of thousands of printed copies were soon being nationally distributed by a pro-repeal publicity committee chaired by the famous Republican editor of the Emporia (Kansas) *Gazette,* William Allen White. White himself, in a nationally broadcast speech in mid-October, stressed support for the democracies against Hitler as the main reason for embargo repeal.[22] Nor was this argument absent from the congressional floor debate. It was repeated by several senators who were bitterly hostile to Roosevelt and the New Deal. Conservative Democrat Edward R. Burke of Nebraska could "see no justification on any ground for permitting a law to stand which favors Hitlerism" and declared his intention to vote for repeal because it "would go far toward insuring victory for the European democracies." The fervently isolationist Robert A. Taft surprised many by saying he would vote for repeal because the embargo "favors the aggressor against the peaceful nation." The conservative

Tennessee Democrat Kenneth McKellar also said bluntly that he would "vote for repeal of the embargo because it operates to injure two of the great democracies of the world, France and England."[23] The designated congressional spokesmen for the administration, however, scrupulously adhered to the President's line of argument. They made no mention of arms and munitions for the Allies, fearing, as Roosevelt did, the potency of the charge that they, as pawns and dupes of the armaments industry and international financiers, would transform America into a giant "merchant of death."* Echoing the President, they stressed, instead, the risk of war involvement that inhered in the embargo's "unneutrality."[25]

A price was paid for this subterfuge. When further steps were required, in the future, to maintain Allied resistance to Hitler, they would encounter an isolationist argument against them whose strength would have been somewhat reduced had it been squarely met and overcome by administration counterargument in this autumn of 1939 but that remained, in the event, undiminished. Roosevelt would then be faced with the need to fight his battle all over again with the chances for victory smaller, perhaps, than those he now had. He might then feel compelled to fight not at all but, instead, to wait upon decisive events—a passivity whose tragic effect could be a prolongation of the war, if not an Axis victory.

In the stormy debate that followed the special message, Roosevelt personally took no public part. Having placed his definition of the issue squarely before Congress and public, he imposed upon himself and his official family a strict rule of silence on this matter. When the governor-general of Canada, Lord Tweedsmuir (John Buchan, author of *The Thirty-Nine Steps*), proposed to "slip down inconspicuously" to Hyde Park for a visit, Roosevelt responded negatively, giving two reasons: "The first is that you could not 'slip down inconspicuously.' . . . [The visit] would be bound to be front page news. . . . The second reason is that I am literally walking on eggs and, having delivered my message to the Congress, and having good prospects of the bill's going through, I am at the moment saying nothing, seeing nothing and hearing nothing."[26] He was particularly concerned to prevent the explosive question

---

*A convoluted irony inheres in the fact that (a) the popular fear and distrust of munitions makers and international financiers as warmongers, and (b) the consequences of Roosevelt's 1935 maneuver whereby the Nye Committee was encouraged to frame the original Neutrality Act, were now fused in opposition to Roosevelt's present purpose. As has been pointed out, his cynical 1935 move was designed to counter the Nye Committee's moves toward nationalization of the armaments industry along with other legislation (the drafting of capital as well as men, etc.) aimed at "taking the profit out of war." Had such Nye Committee legislation been passed in 1935, a principal 1939 argument against embargo repeal could not have been made. Yet it is *also* true that Roosevelt's present cause was served by his prevention in 1935 of meaningful anti-profiteering legislation: The big-business men who would make money out of trade with the Allies were generally lined up on his side of the current controversy and accounted largely for the support he received from Republican legislators. "On September 26, the National Republican Club, whose members included many prominent industrialists and financiers, voted 46 to 6 to back the administration's neutrality program," writes Divine.[24]

of a third presidential term for himself from becoming entangled with that of embargo repeal. Suspenseful speculation about his 1940 intentions had now been mounting for months, dominating more and more of the nation's political news, conditioning more and more of the nation's political action. So when Landon, on September 23, eschewing the statesmanship he had theretofore practiced with regard to foreign affairs, injected partisanship into the current debate by issuing a public call upon the President to remove party politics from the repeal issue by removing himself from the 1940 presidential race, Roosevelt not only refused to reply himself but also refused to permit any administration spokesman to reply. Ickes was at that moment scheduled to participate the following week in the popular radio network program "Town Meeting of the Air." He proposed to answer Landon "very vigorously" in his address. Roosevelt forbade his doing so, saying, "Wait until we get this neutrality legislation before we discuss any political subject."[27]

Behind this wall of silence, however, was much covert activity. Clark Eichelberger, who as director of the League of Nations Association had encouraged Roosevelt to make what became the famous "quarantine" speech of October 1937, had for many months, with no encouragement from the White House, been agitating for embargo repeal. He had received no reply to his telegram to the President, at the outbreak of the war, offering the services of his organization (it had been renamed the American Union for Concerted Peace Efforts) in a renewed fight for repeal. But he was now encouraged by the State Department, at Roosevelt's request, to form the aforementioned national committee to develop and lay before the public the case for repeal. It was officially named, cumbersomely, the Non-Partisan Committee for Peace through Revision of the Neutrality Act but immediately became known as the White Committee after William Allen White was with some difficulty persuaded to serve as its chairman. Some two hundred prominent Americans had consented to serve on it by October 2 when, on the day on which Senate debate of the Pittman bill began, its formation was announced in a national radio network broadcast by White himself. On the evening of that same Monday, Bishop Bernard J. Sheil of the Chicago archdiocese of the Catholic Church delivered a strong pro-administration radio address which, as a matter of fact, was largely scripted by Tommy Corcoran, sent to Chicago for that purpose by a President greatly concerned, as always, to woo Catholic support for his program.* Al Smith, in a move aimed at overcoming that Irish Catholic opposition to repeal which was rooted in anti-British prejudice, had spoken over the radio the night before, urging all Americans to back their President on this issue.[28]

On October 13, when Lindbergh made his second network broadcast, his audience was smaller than the one he'd had the month before, but huge all the same. His speech sounded the racist note more strongly and ominously than

---

*Actually, Roosevelt had arranged for this with Cardinal Mundelein, whose sudden unexpected demise (he was found dead of a heart attack in his bed on the morning of October 2) meant the loss to him of one of the most valued of his political allies.

his first address had done, employing tortured logic to proclaim that embargo repeal could not aid European democracy because democracy was not the issue of the present war. "This is a war over the balance of power in Europe," he said, "—a war brought about by the desire for strength on the part of Germany and the fear of strength on the part of England and France. . . . Our bond with Europe is a bond of race and not of political ideology. . . . It is the European race we must preserve; political progress will follow. Racial strength is vital —politics a luxury. If the white race is ever seriously threatened, it may then be time for us to take our part for its protection, to fight side by side with the English, French, and Germans. But not with one against the other for our mutual destruction."[29] These strange words were clearly no argument for retention of the arms embargo—an end by then very unlikely to be achieved in any case, as must have been realized even by a speaker whose contemptuous distrust of democratic public opinion militated against his accurate measurement of it. Roosevelt need have no concern over the words' effect upon the immediate issue. But what, then, *did* they mean? What was their purpose?

A possible and disturbing answer was suggested when a Lindbergh article entitled "Aviation, Geography, and Race" appeared a few days later in the November 1939 issue of *Reader's Digest.* "It is time to turn from our quarrels and to build our White ramparts again," proclaimed the aviator to the *Digest*'s millions of readers. Western civilization depends "on a united strength among ourselves; . . . on a Western Wall of race and arms which can hold back either a Genghis Khan or the infiltration of inferior blood; on an English fleet, a German air force, a French army, an American nation, standing together as guardians of our common heritage, sharing strength, dividing influence." Roosevelt, considering this assertion in its historical context, could only conclude that Lindbergh favored and was working for a negotiated peace between the Allies and Nazi Germany. (High-placed appeasers, including Ambassador Kennedy, were at that moment intensely though covertly active in London toward this end, as Roosevelt was acutely aware.) "Western civilization" could then stand armed and ready for war against the "Yellow Peril" of Asia and the Communist threat of Russia, the two being linked, in Lindbergh's view: He deemed Soviet Russia more an Oriental despotism than a Western power. And what would be the basis of this negotiated peace? Lindbergh indicated its nature when he said in his article that "men must be accorded rights equal to their ability," and that "no system of representation can succeed in which the voice of weakness is equal to the voice of strength."[30] Was it not obvious after two months of conflict that Nazi Germany's "ability" was vastly superior to that of her opponents? Was it not obvious that Hitler, not Chamberlain or Daladier, now spoke with the "voice of strength"? What Lindbergh obviously contemplated, therefore, with complacency if not approval, was a settlement whose terms would be dictated by Adolf Hitler.

The speech and article conjoined went far toward convincing the President that Lindbergh, nursing secret political ambitions of his own, was an implacable enemy of democracy and, in the present confused and divided state of the nation, a dangerous one. Roosevelt's instinct for power made him highly sensitive to the power drives of other people; his political experience and Christian commitment to democracy enabled him to measure with uncommon accuracy, in terms of democratic values, the malignant potency of such drives; and he now recognized (felt intuitively) in Lindbergh's cold, reclusive temperament—he sensed in Lindbergh's superficially "scientific" but basically sentimental and ill-informed mind—a mystical "think-with-your-blood" yearning of the hero toward a totalitarian pyramid of power with himself, this particular hero, at its apex.

"If I should die tomorrow," the President would say with wrathful earnest vehemence to Morgenthau in a black hour seven months hence, "I want you to know this. I am absolutely convinced that Lindbergh is a Nazi."[31]

III

UP to the time Roosevelt opened his side of the Great Debate on September 17, and for two weeks or so thereafter, the events of the European war encouraged in America a mental climate increasingly favorable to Roosevelt's neutrality-revision program.

The hapless Poles were speedily and bloodily sacrificed not only to the might and skill of Germany's armed forces but also to their own rulers' thickheadedness. During the weeks immediately preceding the invasion, these rulers had faced the Nazi menace with a haughty outward defiance but, out of fear of taking "provocative" action, had failed to order a general mobilization of their country's armed forces until August 31, less than twenty-four hours before the Nazis, without bothering to issue a declaration of war, launched their attack. In consequence, at dawn on September 1, only 600,000 troops of Poland's (on paper) two-million-man army—that is, thirty infantry divisions, eleven horse cavalry divisions, and a single mechanized brigade, backed by an inferior artillery and an effective air force of only 450 planes, most of which were obsolete—stood on the line to meet the assault of more than a million German troops (counting reserves and occupying forces), all well trained, armed with modern weaponry, skillfully commanded, and covered and preceded in attack by 1,400 modern warplanes. Moreover, the line on which the Poles stood was stupidly drawn. The whole of the mobilized Polish force was unevenly distributed along the 1,750 miles of German-Polish frontier, with no strategic reserve behind them. A third of the troops were concentrated in the Danzig corridor or immediately adjacent areas, where they virtually invited a crushing flank movement and envelopment by Nazi forces driving west and south from East Prussia and, simultaneously, east and south from Pomerania. In general, the Polish troop dispositions were as if designed to ensure the Poles' being sliced into pieces by swift, armor-heavy, concentrated enemy thrusts, the pieces surrounded, then destroyed.

And that is what happened, with greater rapidity than even the most sanguine Germans had expected.

Within forty-eight hours, by which time the Polish air force had been eliminated, most of the planes having been destroyed on the ground without ever having become airborne against the enemy, nine German columns were deep into Polish territory, driving from Slovakia, Silesia, and Pomerania across the flat Polish plain toward a convergence at Warsaw. By September 5, Kraków had fallen. On the next day, German troops were in a suburb of Warsaw from which, however, they were forced to retreat temporarily. On September 15 the encircled Polish army in the Poznań area was being crushed, and a wide-swinging pincer movement from the southeast and northeast had reached Brest-Litovsk (where the Germans had imposed a merciless treaty upon the new Bolshevik regime in March 1918) a full 112 miles *east* of Warsaw. Two days later the Polish state ceased to exist. As many of its leaders as could had by then fled the country to establish, in Rumania (they would later flee to London), a Polish government-in-exile. Besieged Warsaw continued to resist but was being subjected to unprecedentedly massive and ruthless bombing from the air. Elsewhere, as those Polish troops belatedly mobilized on August 31 were thrown into the battle, there were scattered pockets of resistance, but these were obviously doomed. And from the east there moved in, against almost no resistance, some forty divisions of Soviet troops to meet the Germans amicably along an agreed line stretching north and south through Brest-Litovsk, this in accordance with the Nazi-Soviet agreement of the month before. On September 23 Germany announced that all organized Polish resistance had ceased. Four days later Warsaw surrendered. In less than a month a once proud nation-state whose leaders had boasted of a military potency which, indeed, had been deemed by Chamberlain greater than that of the Soviet Union, was utterly destroyed. The first great battle of World War II had ended in absolute and total Nazi triumph, and many of the German people who had displayed no enthusiasm for the war when Hitler began it, who indeed had reacted glumly, sullenly, with gloomy foreboding, to the show parades of troops marching toward the Polish border, now greeted the returning troops with delirious joy and a renewed faith in the "genius" of der Führer.*

But it was Stalin, not Hitler, who gained the most from this conquest, and with virtually no bloodshed by his troops. On September 29, a "boundary and friendship" treaty was signed by the Germans and Russians, whereby a new German-Soviet frontier was established along, roughly, the Curzon Line of 1920. By this treaty, the Soviets gained nearly half of Poland's territory, containing most of Poland's oil fields but only 13 million of its prewar population of 35 million—a population that, as the Russians had learned from hard experience, was extremely troublesome to govern, being stubbornly, unappea-

---

*Germans living in Berlin and other large cities were considerably less prone to such patriotic fervors than were Germans who lived in smaller towns or in the country. George Kennan, who in 1939 served as administrative officer in the U.S. embassy, tells of standing on the Pariserplatz in Berlin among a crowd who watched "with a reserved, sullen silence the troops returning from the successful completion of the Polish campaign." See Kennan's *Memoirs, 1925–1950* (New York, 1967), p. 108.

sably patriotic and rebellious. The treaty also caused Berlin to order the immediate evacuation of 86,000 German citizens living in Latvia and Estonia while acquiescing in Russia's imposing upon these countries, and upon Lithuania also, treaties of "mutual assistance" whereby they would soon be occupied by Soviet armed forces. Thus would be extinguished the sovereignty of three out of the four Versailles-created Baltic states, all three to be absorbed soon again into the Russian empire. Simultaneously, again with Germany's reluctant acquiescence, pressure was brought to bear by Moscow upon Finland, the fourth of the Versailles Baltic states, to cede to Russia a sufficient portion of the Karelian Isthmus to place Leningrad, with its 3.2 million people, beyond the range of artillery along the Finnish border running from Lake Ladoga to the Gulf of Finland—though, if other terms of the treaty Moscow proposed were accepted, there would *be* no guns along that border. The frontier was to be demilitarized. Also, the Soviet Union demanded a thirty-year lease on the port of Hangö, on the southern Finnish coast, so that Russia could establish a naval base there at the mouth of the Gulf of Finland. The Finns, acutely aware of their danger, stated their willingness to accept all these terms save the last. The leasing of land to a foreign power for war purposes would be, they declared, both an abdication of their national sovereignty and a violation of their status as a neutral nation. They refused to do it. Whereupon the Soviet press, and the Communist press in other countries, including most emphatically the *Daily Worker* of New York City, launched a bitter propaganda campaign against the Finns of much the same kind as Hitler had employed prior to his invasions of Austria, Czechoslovakia, and Poland.

Such events as these were, to repeat, conducive to an American popular mood favorable to repeal of the arms embargo. They impressed upon the American mind an image of terrifying Nazi military might linked, as it seemed, with the tremendous inertial weight of Russia's armed masses. They raised the ghastly specter, should Britain and France be struck down by Germany's mailed fist, of a completely Nazified Europe, backed by Russia, glaring across the Atlantic while fomenting anti-U.S., pro-totalitarian revolts and coups in Latin America. Great persuasiveness was thus added to the argument that the United States' first line of defense did indeed lie in Western Europe and that this line could be breached, even wiped out altogether, unless the United States strengthened it with American-made war matériel and other goods.

What followed, however, had an impact of a different kind, raising renewed questions, doubts, hesitancies, indecisions in the public mind. Were France and Britain really seriously at war with Germany? There had been, and was, little evidence in the West that they were.

Virtually everyone had expected massive air raids upon London, and counterraids by the British air force upon the Ruhr, heart of Germany's industrial might, within a few hours or at most a few days after war was declared. Actually there had been no air raids whatever in the west. Virtually everyone had expected France to relieve the pressure on Poland by launching a massive attack upon Germany's West Wall, which must surely be relatively lightly held, being stripped of troops in order to provide a sufficiently large strike force in the east. (French general Maurice Gamelin, with a hundred French divisions under his command, thirty-five to thirty-eight of them battle-ready, had in fact promised Poland that he would attack by September 17 when, as would be learned after the war, only twenty-four or twenty-five German divisions manned the West Wall, and these not of the first class.) No such attack had taken place. Actually no land fighting of any kind had occurred in the west. Only at sea had there been war action between Allies and Nazis. During the first week after her war declaration, Britain lost to German U-boat torpedoes eleven merchant ships having a combined tonnage of 64,595—nearly half the weekly tonnage lost in April 1917, when submarines came close to severing Britain's Atlantic lifeline. Thereafter, however, the weekly tonnage lost had declined rapidly; it was only 4,646 during the fourth week of the war; which seemed to indicate that the U-boats were ordered by Hitler, in late September, to "go slow" while attempts were made toward a negotiated peace.

Der Führer made an open bid for such a peace in a speech to the Reichstag, meeting in the Kroll Opera House in Berlin on October 6, this after three weeks of increasingly loud "peace" propaganda issued by press and radio from Berlin, and of tentative peace feelers extended from Berlin to London via a shadowy figure, a Swedish businessman named Birger Dahlerus, who had high connections in both capitals. Said Hitler to the Reichstag and the world: "My chief endeavor has been to rid our relations with France of all trace of ill will. . . . I have refused even to mention the problem of Alsace-Lorraine. . . . I have devoted no less effort to the achievement of Anglo-German understanding. . . . I believe even today that there can only be real peace in Europe and throughout the world if Germany and England come to an understanding. . . . Why should this war in the West be fought? For restoration of Poland? Poland of the Versailles Treaty will never rise again. . . . What other reason exists? . . . No, this war in the West cannot settle any problems." Those problems, which comprised arms reduction, colonies, and "the Jewish problem," among other things, could be settled only by a conference of the principal European powers. Hitler proposed that such a conference be held "after the most thorough preparation." If this offer were rejected, of course, and "the opinions of Mssrs. Churchill and followers should prevail," Germany would fight furiously and victoriously. "There will never be another November 1918 in German history."[32] Three days later, after Daladier had replied inconclusively that France would not lay down her arms until a "real peace and general security" was guaranteed, but before Chamberlain had replied at all, Hitler met with his top generals and presented them with a directive for the conduct of the war that called for an "attacking operation . . . through the areas of Luxembourg, Belgium, and Holland" to be carried out "at as early a date as possible." Accompanying this order was a detailed historical analysis of the situation. Der Führer read it aloud. The attack, it said, must be made "if at all possible, this autumn" since time, working against Germany and for her enemies, was of the essence. Circumstances (created by his own "genius," he might have added) had enabled the Polish campaign to be fought, actually, as a one-front war. The campaign in the west could be similarly fought if launched within a few weeks or, at most, a few months and completed with lightning speed. But the opportunity for this was fleeting. "At present all reasons speak against Russia's departure from neutrality" but the prevailing situation could be drastically "altered" within a year or perhaps in as short a time as "eight months." Certainly "no treaty or pact" could be counted upon as insurance against a Russian attack. Had not the "trifling significance of treaties . . . been proved on all sides in recent years"? No, the "greatest safeguard against any Russian attack lies . . . in a prompt demonstration of German strength."[33]

But none of this ominous design upon the near future was visible or audible to the American public. The public did see and hear Chamberlain's rejection of Hitler's proposed peace terms. It was made in a speech in the House of Commons on October 12. Hitler's terms were "vague and uncertain," said Chamberlain, devoid of "suggestions for righting the wrongs done Czechoslovakia and Poland," and not to be trusted because "the present German Government" could not be trusted. If Hitler wanted peace he must provide "convincing proof" through "acts" that he did so.[34] These were tough words. They were softened for Americans, however, and rendered doubtful for them, by the past history of the man who spoke them, joined with the highly visible and puzzling fact that peace was not being interrupted by any act of war along the whole of the Western Front. William L. Shirer and other correspondents, visiting the front in October, reported German and French troops going about their daily work, building up their respective defenses along the Maginot and Siegfried lines in full sight of one another across no-man's-land, without a shot being fired on either side. Shirer called this, in his diary, a "queer sort of war."[35] The Germans began referring to it as *Sitzkrieg,* the French as *drôle de guerre.* Senator Borah, continuing his impassioned leadership of the "peace bloc" despite his failing health (he would die, aged seventy-four, in the first month of the coming new year), called it the Phony War.

The effects of this upon American popular opinion were measured in a small but steady erosion of support for embargo repeal following its high point of 62 percent in a Gallup poll taken in the last week of September. In early October, support was down to 60 percent, and it declined slowly but steadily thereafter, though it never fell below 56 percent before this portion of the Great Debate was ended by congressional action in early November.[36]

As for the debate itself, its chief focus as the October days passed was the cash-and-carry provisions of the Pittman bill. These, as Pittman originally defined them, applied not only to shipments to the belligerent powers across the North Atlantic but also to shipments to British and French colonial possessions, and to other belligerent ports, in Africa, South America, and the Far East. American shipping interests protested loudly that such rigid and broad restrictions upon American overseas trade would have a "calamitous" effect upon the American economy. Republican senator Wallace H. White, Jr., of Maine, and other senators damned cash-and-carry as a "surrender of American rights" whereby American agriculture and business would be deprived of their export market.[37] Economists of the Treasury and State departments agreed, and the administration joined in the protest, if cautiously, and wholly behind the scenes. By early November the bill had been amended to limit cash-and-carry, in effect, to the North Atlantic. Normal trade practices were to be permitted for shipments to belligerent ports across the Pacific and South Atlantic.

Final action on the amended bill, after it was reported by conference committee, was taken on November 3. The Senate then passed it 63–30, the House 243–172. And thus was the arms embargo finally repealed, an occasion of great rejoicing in London and Paris as well as in the White House.

IV

IT was on one of the early days of the so-called Phony War, at a midpoint in Roosevelt's period of self-imposed public silence, that Dr. Alexander Sachs was at last granted the private interview that he had been seeking since early August. He was ushered into the Oval Office by presidential secretary Pa Watson late in the afternoon of Wednesday, October 11, 1939, there to be warmly greeted by a President who was obviously in a relaxing mood as his so-called Children's Hour (the cocktail hour) approached.[38]

"Alex!" cried Roosevelt, as if the sight of his visitor were a delightful surprise. "What are you up to?"

The forty-six-year-old Sachs was himself a loquacious man whose prose, written or spoken, was often so elaborate (he "adumbrated" his "theses" from a "pluralism of sources," et cetera) as to require translation into ordinary English to be understood by common folk. He had personally experienced the loquacity with which Roosevelt commonly protected himself against unwelcome demands for a decisive attentiveness. And he now sensed a threat to his serious purpose in the President's present mood. He therefore responded to the President's greeting with a plaintive plea.

"Mr. President," said he with an impudent grin, "I want you to know I paid for my trip to Washington. I can't deduct it from my income tax. So won't you please pay attention?"

Roosevelt, with a laugh possibly somewhat rueful, nodded his assent.

As to precisely what followed there are quite widely differing published accounts, each having Sachs as its primary source (no third person was present at the meeting; Roosevelt left no written record of it). One account has Sachs asking for and good-humoredly receiving permission to read aloud three documents he has come to deliver personally into the President's hand—Einstein's letter, Szilard's memo, a letter from Sachs himself—this to make absolutely sure that what they say is suitably impressed upon the ear-minded President. He does so, slowly, emphasizing key points, then hands the documents to Roosevelt who at once peruses the Einstein letter carefully. Another, later account has Sachs reading, not the Einstein letter, but two memoranda of his own composition, one of them giving the gist of what Einstein said and the other "adumbrating" Sachs's own geopolitical views, no doubt from the "vantage point of cultural-technological history." Yet another account has Sachs reading only his own eight-hundred-word summary of the Einstein letter and concluding with a quotation from a 1936 lecture by the English physicist Francis Aston.* The quotation was "Personally, I think there is no doubt that sub-atomic energy is available all around us, and that one day man will release and control its almost infinite power. We cannot prevent him from doing so and can only hope he will not use it exclusively in blowing up his next door neighbor." The conclusion of this account is that Aston's last words echoed in Roosevelt's mind and determined the sentences with which he closed the interview, sentences upon whose deliverance all accounts are agreed.

"What you are after," said the President to Dr. Sachs, "is to see that the Nazis don't blow us up."

"Precisely," said Dr. Sachs.

The President then pressed a button, summoning Watson.

"Pa," said Roosevelt, handing over the two letters and Szilard's memorandum, "this requires action!"

What directly followed from this, however, was "action" of a remarkably passive and dilatory kind. It belied what later became a widely held assumption (Einstein himself evidently held it) that the Einstein letter initiated a process, which might otherwise never have begun, leading directly to later momentous decisions.

Actually, there was directly incited only a very small, tentative, almost inconsequential step toward a truly effective working relationship between science and government. A presidential Advisory Committee on Uranium was established within the National Bureau of Standards, which was part of the Commerce Department. The committee's government members were an army ordnance expert, a navy ordnance expert, and the bureau's elderly director, Dr. Lyman J. Briggs, with the last as chairman. Briggs, who gave his name to the committee, was a physicist by training. His specialty, however, was soil physics, and it had been long since he had done any active research in this restricted field. For more than forty years he had been in government service, operating through much of that time in administrative capacities. To the young physicists who now dealt with him he seemed to possess in full measure the bureaucrat's protective coloration, the grayness that results from a habitual fear and refusal of risky personal black-or-white decisiveness. When they (Szilard, Teller, Wigner) and Sachs met with the committee for the first and last time on October 21, they were unable to infuse in its chairman any of their

---

*It was one of the items anthologized in *Background to Modern Science,* a book edited by Joseph Needham and Walter Pagel, of which Sachs is said to have brought a copy with him.

sense of urgency, of fatal danger. As for the two ordnance experts, their natural skepticism about the possibility of a fantastically powerful new explosive was rendered personally offensive, to Wigner especially, by the contemptuous manner in which the army representative expressed it. Nor can it be said that the White House encouraged Briggs toward speed of movement, much less toward bold new departures. Roosevelt seems never to have dealt with Briggs directly during the whole of the committee's independent existence, but always and only through the presidential secretary.[39]

The written report of the October 21 meeting which the chairman made to the President on November 1 recommended the funding of research into the possibility of using a controlled chain reaction to power submarines, adding that if the reaction turned out "to be explosive in character" it might "provide a possible source of bombs with a destructiveness far greater than anything now known." Seventeen days later Briggs was told by Watson that the President had read the report and wished to keep it on file. By then, $6,000 of federal money had been granted for the purchase of purified graphite, needed as a "moderator" of neutron speed, for use in experiments by Fermi and Szilard to find out whether a controlled, self-sustaining chain reaction could be induced in natural uranium (99.3 percent U-238, 0.7 percent U-235). The size of the grant was determined by the absurdly low estimate of need which a rattled Edward Teller, under sharp questioning by one of the ordnance experts, gave off the top of his head, and regretted ever after that he had so given. Six thousand dollars would buy less than a fifth of the amount of pure graphite actually required for a large-scale experiment, Szilard complained to Briggs in a letter dated October 26. At least $33,000 worth of the graphite would be needed.[40] But $6,000 remained all that was forthcoming from the federal treasury, and its appropriation constituted the sum total of the Briggs Committee's concrete action as 1939 gave way to 1940 and the spring of 1940 came on. "It seems an incredible fact, in retrospect, that between the end of June 1939 and the spring of 1940, not a single experiment was underway in the United States aimed at the possibilities of a chain reaction in natural uranium," said Szilard in a later year.[41]

When Roosevelt established by executive order a National Defense Research Committee in mid-June 1940, under circumstances to be described later, the by then nearly moribund uranium advisory committee was made a part of it. Briggs remained the chairman. And nothing continued to happen under the aegis of the Briggs Committee as the long hot political summer of 1940 wore on.

"In retrospect it is evident that the effect of the appointment of the Government's Advisory Committee on Uranium was to retard rather than advance the development of American uranium research," writes Arthur Compton, the Nobel laureate in physics who would make major contributions to that research in the years just ahead. "Its appointment seemed to imply that the nation's interests with regard to fission would be looked after. That such was not the case became quickly apparent to those at New York, Princeton, and Washington who found in the government committee no substantial help for their work."[42]

But to say this is not to say that the famed Einstein letter had no important effect whatever. The letter did strongly suggest to the presidential mind a fateful possibility. It somewhat prepared that mind to receive later information on which to base later fateful decisions. And it is at least conceivable that these exceedingly high-risk decisions would not have been made had not the presidential mind been thus early prepared for them. It is also conceivable that, had Harry Hopkins's health not failed again disastrously in the summer of 1939— had he remained actively, not merely nominally, the secretary of commerce during the autumn and winter of 1939–1940—the Briggs Committee would have become far more effective than it was. For Hopkins from the outset of his tenure as a Cabinet member took a special interest in the work of his department's Bureau of Standards and, as we shall see, at once recognized the importance to national security of a close working relationship between science and government when a practical proposal to achieve this was presented to him.

V

WITH the Phony War there began for America a strange period of suspense and doubt and unreality. The war that was not a war was equally a peace that was not a peace, and it cast across the Atlantic into American life a fog of ambiguity through which one walked almost somnambulistically, seeing images that dissolved as one approached them, only to reappear farther on. Nothing was simply, substantially, itself. Everything was also something else, a something else that might prove contradictory of what apparently it was. For hidden forces, hidden motives, were, it seemed, everywhere at work. The mental climate accorded well with certain natural predilections of Franklin Roosevelt, and his major operations during this period were not of a kind to dispel the fog. They had, indeed, and deliberately in many cases, a precisely opposite effect.

We have seen that his foreign policy as publicly defined by him during the embargo-repeal debate had one dominant purpose—namely, "to keep our nation from being drawn into the war." This purpose was to be achieved through the practice (a return to the practice) of a "true neutrality" which just happened, wholly inadvertently, to be heavily weighted on the side of the Allies against Hitler's Germany. Certainly "no person in any responsible place in the national administration . . . has ever suggested in any shape, manner or form the remotest possibility of sending the boys of American mothers to fight on the battlefields of Europe." Yet "God-fearing democracies . . . cannot forever let pass . . . acts of aggression against sister nations." "We know what might happen to us of the United States if the new philosophies of force were to encompass the other continents and invade our own. We no more than other nations can afford to be surrounded by the enemies of our faith and our humanity." All the same, and again, we "must be guided by one single hard-headed thought—keeping America out of this war."[43] Thus did the White House, out of its own confusions and concern with 1940 election politics, flatly reflect instead of attempting to remove the fearful confusions of the public mind. It thereby generated in the United States a fog that merged with that generated overseas—a fog that grew ever thicker across the whole field of foreign affairs as the Phony War was lengthened by weeks, then months.

Overtly during this period, American foreign policy remained almost in a state of suspended animation, paralyzed by its avowed neutrality. Covertly, however, the administration pursued to the outermost limits of perceived possibility an exclusively pro-Allies policy, making highly creative executive interpretations of legislative language as it did so.

For instance, there was much subterfuge and attempted subterfuge designed to circumvent the cash-and-carry provisions of the new Neutrality Act. The provisions, despite the legislative revision of Pittman's original proposal, remained extremely onerous, certainly, to American shipping interests—more so to them, at that moment, than to Britain and France, both of which (Britain especially) were slow to place the large orders that Roosevelt had hoped would give a shot in the arm to the yet ailing economy. American merchant vessels could now legally sail the Atlantic only to Mediterranean ports, and to African ports south of the Canary Islands, while avoiding on the way all designated combat areas. No U.S. ship would sail to Irish, British, French, Belgian, Dutch, German, Danish, Baltic, or Swedish ports, or to any Norwegian port south of Bergen. The practical effect was greatly to augment the strength of Germany's naval blockade of Britain; it was as if a huge concerted U-boat attack had sunk every U.S. vessel bound for or returning from an Allied port. Naturally, as U.S. ships remained with empty holds in U.S. harbors and thousands of American sailors and dockworkers were forced into the ranks of the unemployed, which were already unacceptably large without them, export businesses and maritime unions rose up in angry protest. The administration made devious response. The ink was scarcely dry on the offending statute when Admiral Emory S. Land,* chairman of the U.S. Maritime Commission, approved the transfer of fifteen Standard Oil tankers to Republic of Panama registry and, at the same time, initiated an effort to transfer nine ships of the United States Line, which the commission controlled, to the same registry. Though they continued to be American owned and operated, the ships, sailing under Panama's flag, would presumably not be subject to the Neutrality Act. The scheme appealed to the President. He quickly approved it. So did the secretary of state initially, having been apprised of the President's approval. The supercautious Hull soon backed away, however. He told his morning press

---

*The admiral was a first cousin of Lindbergh on the latter's mother's side. He totally and vehemently disagreed with Lindbergh's political views and activities, as his Columbia Oral History Office transcript makes clear, though Lindbergh gives no hint of this in his published war diary.

conference that he "assumed an attitude of opposition to the proposal" because "I am extremely desirous, as I know every official is, of preserving the absolute integrity of every phase of the Neutrality Act, and especially the combat area phase of it. . . ." Soon thereafter, William Allen White wrote Roosevelt a personal letter protesting that he would never have worked as he had done for the embargo-repeal bill had he known that its cash-and-carry provision, the price of its passage, was to be administratively violated. Missouri's Senator Truman, though personally primarily concerned at that moment to ensure Britain's survival, also deplored such deviousness and proposed to prevent it with legislation specifically prohibiting the transfer of American ships to foreign registry for the duration of the Neutrality Act.[44] Roosevelt then perforce changed *his* mind. The Maritime Commission withdrew its application for the registry transfer. But at the same time the commission proposed to sell laid-up United States Line ships to Britain and France, both of which were interested in buying them. This occasioned an urgent meeting of Hull with State Department staff, in which it was decided that these ships could *not,* under the terms of the Neutrality Act, be sold directly to a belligerent but could be sold to a nonbelligerent who might in turn sell them to a belligerent. Subsequently, with the approval of State and the unpublicized concurrence of congressional leaders of both parties, eight ships of the United States Line were sold to a private corporation in Belgium. A number of privately owned American vessels were also permitted to be sold directly to Britain and France, with the understanding that they were not to be used to commit hostilities against another belligerent.

Similar in purpose to the above were the administration's dealings, or attempts to avoid dealing, with British violations of America's rights, under international law, as a neutral on the high seas.

On the day after the British declaration of war, Cordell Hull and Lord Lothian, whose diplomatic skills and lubricating personality now proved him a most fortunate appointment to Britain's Washington embassy, conferred on ways and means of avoiding such high-seas incidents as had exacerbated British-American relations in 1914–1916. Subsequently there was worked out, and formally adopted by the British on November 21, a so-called "navicert" system whereby British representatives examined the cargoes of American ships while these were yet in American ports, then issued to ship captains certificates supposedly protecting their vessels against being stopped at sea and searched for contraband by the British navy. Nevertheless, incidents occurred. U.S. ships were stopped and boarded at sea in increasing numbers, their cargoes searched, their mail censored. Some of them were forced by British naval vessels into British ports, where the Neutrality Act's combat-zone provisions forbade them to go, and there detained sometimes for as long as three weeks while especially exhaustive searches of their cargoes along with censoring reviews of their mail were conducted. The State Department did its best to avoid protesting these indignities officially, publicly. "I knew that Hitler, not Britain, had started the war, and that a German victory would be dangerous to the best interests of the United States," writes Hull in his memoirs. "Hence it would be poor policy to arouse public opinion in the United States against Britain. . . ." But others had a different view. U.S. shipping interests were increasingly outraged, and their cause was gleefully championed by the strong Anglophobic element of American isolationism, notably Colonel McCormick's *Chicago Tribune.* Isolationist members of Congress made floor speeches about it, singling out for especially angry condemnation Britain's censorship of U.S. mail. And in January 1940 the State Department was at last compelled to hand to the British government a series of protesting notes. Roosevelt took cognizance of the matter in his personal correspondence with Churchill, writing with evident reluctance on February 1: "I would not be frank unless I told you that there has been much public criticism here. The general feeling is that the net benefit to your people and France is hardly worth the definite annoyance caused to us." He himself somewhat deprecated this feeling, however, going on to say: "That is always found to be so in a nation which is 3,000 miles away from the fact of war." Churchill replied that he had ordered the fleet "not to bring any American ships into the zone you have drawn around our shores" but that his order was being strongly opposed by "many other departments" which had "become much concerned about the efficiency of the blockade. . . . All our experience shows that the examination of mails is essential to efficient control as only in this way can we get the evidence of evasion." Soon thereafter two "blockade experts," one from England, one from France, arrived in Washington as representatives of London and Paris. They engaged in friendly, lengthy discussions of the situation with U.S. representatives while, at sea, unhappy incidents continued to occur. They did so, however, with a gradually diminishing frequency. "By degrees," wrote Hull, "our difficulties with Britain were smoothed out."[45]

Far different—more absolutely literal, with rigidity replacing flexibility—was the practical definition of "neutral rights" that Washington applied to Germany's naval operations.

The German surface navy of September 1939 was much less formidable than that of August 1914, as Churchill was glad to note. It had no great battleships, though two, *Bismarck* and *Tirpitz,* were under construction and would be completed within a year or so. The most powerful immediately available fighting ships were two light battle cruisers, *Scharnhorst* and *Gneisenau,* of 26,000 tons each, and three superbly designed and armed "pocket battleships," *Admiral Scheer, Deutschland,* and *Admiral Graf Spee,* of 12,000 tons each. Of these, *Graf Spee* and *Deutschland* had escaped the British blockade by sailing from their home ports in August, a week or more before that blockade went into effect. They were far out at sea on September 3, when they began to operate under orders to "disrupt . . . enemy merchant shipping by all possible means" while avoiding engagement with "enemy naval forces," even of inferior strength, unless such engagement "should further the principal task."[46]

*Deutschland* was then near Greenland, well positioned to do much damage to Britain's lifeline across the northwest Atlantic. She, however, interpreted her orders so cautiously that she sank but two ships, both of them small, before dangerously running the Allied blockade on her return to Germany in November. By then, however, she had also captured in the North Atlantic an American freighter, *City of Flint.* This was in October, while congressional debate over embargo repeal raged at its height. *City of Flint* was known to the American public for her heroic rescue of passengers cast into the sea when the torpedoed *Athenia* went down, and, despite the fact that at least half her cargo, destined for Britain, was indubitably contraband of war, the U.S. government, so prone to ignore British infractions of a neutral's sea rights, reacted with swift acrimony to her seizure. Much of this wrath was diverted to Soviet Russia when it, though nominally a neutral in the Allied-German conflict, seemed to function actively as a German ally by permitting the captured ship, under a prize crew, to put in at the far-northern Russian port of Murmansk. The situation was not eased by Soviet ambassador Oumansky in Washington; he was an insultingly suspicious and abrasive personality who fully exercised in this instance his remarkable capacity for antagonizing nearly all who had to deal with him. But the quarrel was eventually resolved to Washington's satisfaction. The German government, extremely anxious at this juncture to avoid a serious dispute with the United States, ordered the prize crew to sail *City of Flint* from Murmansk to a Norwegian port, where Norwegian authorities could and promptly did take her in charge. She was then released to her American crew.[47]

Much bolder than *Deutschland,* and frighteningly effective as a commerce raider, was *Graf Spee.* Between the outbreak of war and the second week of December she preyed ruthlessly upon the sea-lanes of the South Atlantic, sinking ship after ship with swift strikes from which she fled with such speed and artful dodging that none of the powerful British and French forces relentlessly hunting her (they comprised five heavy cruisers, four light cruisers, two aircraft carriers, dozens of destroyers) caught sight of her. Not, that is, until the morning of December 13. She then approached the wide mouth of the River Plate, which divides Uruguay from Argentina, where three British cruisers were patrolling just outside the wide American neutrality zone proclaimed by the Panama convention of American foreign officials. The British, having long expected *Graf Spee* where so many good targets were available to her, had the advantage of surprise. They needed it. *Graf Spee,* more heavily armored than the British vessels, mounted eleven-inch guns and, had she been early aware that she faced an eight-incher-armed cruiser and two six-incher-armed ones instead of, as she thought, a light cruiser and two destroyers, would have changed course and probably destroyed or incapacitated at least one of the cruisers before coming within range of the guns of any of the three. As it was, she drove straight toward the eight-incher and was fired upon by the latter before she herself opened fire. In the fierce ensuing action, the last of it fought well within the River Plate, far inside the proclaimed neutrality zone, the eight-incher was so severely damaged that she could no longer fight, and both the six-inchers were so badly mauled that the British flotilla commander broke off the action with the intention of continuing it after nightfall when darkness would make the odds between him and his enemy more nearly even. *Graf Spee,* which had also suffered grave injuries (between fifty and sixty hits had been scored upon her), then sailed full speed for Montevideo, where she put in to repair herself, to land her wounded, and to take on supplies. Just outside the harbor hovered the two British cruisers that had dogged her passage. They were soon joined by a cruiser mounting eight eight-inch guns (the one that *Graf Spee* had incapacitated mounted only six of these) which had raced up during the preceding two days from the Falkland Islands. Other much more powerful British warships were on their way. Thus *Graf Spee*'s position was hopeless. Her commander petitioned the Uruguayan government for an extension of the seventy-two hours during which, by international law, she might remain in the port. At the same time, he cabled Berlin to ask for instruction regarding the grim alternatives he faced. Should he accept *Graf Spee*'s internment for the duration of the war? Or should he scuttle his ship? He was told *not* to accept internment but to endeavor by all means to extend the time limit upon the ship's stay at Montevideo. If that endeavor failed, the ship should be destroyed.

Meanwhile, Washington, through the American legation in Montevideo, had brought pressure upon the Uruguayan government to adhere strictly to international law in the case of *Graf Spee.* Neighboring Argentina and Brazil were persuaded to do the same (Argentina, one must assume, did so with some reluctance). Uruguay then denied the German request for an extension of the time limit, and *Graf Spee,* her men transferred to a German freighter in the harbor, was sailed beyond the harbor breakwater into the broad River Plate and there, in the evening of December 17, blown up. (On the nineteenth, her captain, disgraced, as he felt, by his loss of his ship, committed suicide.)[48]

A week later, the United States joined the other American republics in a formal protest to both Britain and Germany against the battle's flagrant violations of the neutrality zone. The protest by Washington to London was, however, *purely* formal. The administration tacitly accepted as valid the argument that Naval Person made in a "strictly secret and personal" message to the President on Christmas Day 1939—namely, that the British navy deserved thanks rather than condemnation for eliminating a major threat to American commercial interests. As for Roosevelt personally, he read with an avid and approving interest official Admiralty accounts of the River Plate action, sent him by Churchill. In personal messages he congratulated Naval Person upon a famous victory.[49]

By this time, the fog of ambiguity and uncertainty that blanketed for Americans the whole scene of foreign affairs had been much thickened by strange events in northeastern Europe.

The diplomatic negotiations between Russia and Finland, initiated by Moscow on October 5, 1939, ground on in wheel-spinning futility all through October. In the first week of November, Moscow ominously charged Finnish troops with firing upon Russian border patrols and demanded that Finland withdraw all her troops from the border. Finland refused to do so unless Russia did likewise. On November 13 the negotiations were broken off. On November 28 the 1934 nonaggression pact between Russia and Finland was denounced by Moscow. And on December 1 Russian planes bombed Viipuri and Helsingfors while five separate Russian forces, in numbers far greater than the Finns could muster, attacked along the long Versailles-drawn Russo-Finnish border, which stretched from the Barents Sea southward to Lake Ladoga and thence westward, barely twenty miles north of Leningrad, across the Karelian Isthmus to the Gulf of Finland.

What immediately followed astounded the world.

Moscow had evidently counted upon massive Finnish defections to a puppet "people's government" which it established just across the border from Russia on December 1 and which was headed by a long-exiled Finn. The invading troops, nearly all of whom were of the Leningrad garrison, were more abundantly supplied with propaganda leaflets than with adequate winter clothing. Their ill-coordinated attacks were determined by a war plan prepared, not by the general staff in Moscow, but by the headquarters and staff of the Leningrad Military District—a clear indication that Stalin and his closest associates expected an easy conquest, if not immediate Finnish capitulation. Instead, all five of the columns were disastrously repulsed. Finland's troops, motivated by ferocious patriotism and a virulent hatred of Communist Russia, proved well trained and well equipped to fight in the gloom and bitter cold of a northern winter. Under the supreme command of Marshal Carl Gustav von Mannerheim, after whom the formidable main line of Finnish fortifications across the Karelian Isthmus was named, they were skillfully handled, exploiting to the full their advantage of interior lines and a heavily forested lake-studded terrain beautifully suited to the defensive. They employed highly effective hit-and-run tactics (especially effective were their ski patrols, clad in white uniforms that were almost invisible against the snow) as elements of a soundly conceived strategic plan. The result was, for the Russians, an unbroken series of bloody, humiliating defeats (small companies of Finns stopped and slaughtered whole regiments), which ended only when, in early January 1940, the Russian forces initially committed were so depleted and exhausted that they could no longer continue the offensive. They were drawn back into a defensive posture.

But how could and why should any of this be happening? The question, rising without answer in the American public mind, added to the confusions of that mind, and to its sense of living in an unreal world wherein nothing and nobody could be totally trusted. Russia, it was said, sought to correct errors in the arrangements made at Versailles whereby its defensive position against attack from the west and north was greatly weakened. Leningrad, for special instance, was exposed almost naked to attack from the north down the Karelian Isthmus. But surely Russia did not truly believe that Finland, a country of few people (less than 3.7 million), meager resources, and forbidding climate, a country whose government had pursued a friendly policy toward

Russia when other Baltic states cooperated in arrangements clearly aimed against Moscow, would of herself alone attack her! Surely Finland could do so, in the prevailing circumstances, only as an ally of Germany—which, in that case, would be the instigator and predominant force of the enterprise. But were not Communist Russia and Nazi Germany now friends? Had they not signed, only a little more than two months ago, a pact saying so? Had not Stalin then toasted Hitler, and Ribbentrop Stalin, in a glow of good-fellowship? In accord with what must have been specific articles of the pact (though they remained unpublished), had not the two powers partitioned Poland and clearly defined their separate spheres of influence in Eastern Europe? The mental confusion that gave rise to such questions was not reduced by the response of the Western democracies to the Soviet aggression. The League of Nations, so slow to act against earlier German and Italian aggressions, acted now with astonishing swiftness. Ignoring an "explanatory" note from Moscow, the League on December 14 expelled the Soviet Union (the only nation ever to be expelled as "unworthy" of membership) and authorized League members to give Finland whatever assistance they wished; Britain and France, which had found it impossible to aid Poland by mounting ground and air attacks against Germany, now made prompt and serious efforts to obtain from Norway and Sweden free passage of Franco-British forces and supplies across them to Finland. The Scandinavian countries, which believed their survival to depend upon their maintenance of strict neutrality, refused the desired permission, whereupon consideration was given by the British government (though the general public knew nothing of this) to a proposal to seize the far northern Norwegian port of Narvik and from it force a passage for Finnish aid. This would kill two birds with one stone, as Churchill argued, Narvik being the principal port from which shipments of Scandinavian iron and steel were made to Germany; its seizure would sever a supply line vital to Germany's war effort.[50] The British government finally decided against the proposal as too risky, but did so reluctantly. Meanwhile, France manifested an extreme eagerness to send an expeditionary force to Finland, making a strenuous search for ways and means by which this might be done. Premier Daladier in fact staked his political life on the mounting of an attack, via Finland, on the Soviet Union; he would fall from power, replaced by Paul Reynaud, when these efforts failed. What did all this mean? Did London and Paris continue to deem Stalin's Russia, not Hitler's Germany, the prime enemy of Western Europe? Was the Phony War but a continuation of Britain's appeasement strategy and, as such, the prelude to a German drive eastward, which would be tacitly supported, or at least not interfered with, by the British and French?

As for the American government's response to the Finnish crisis, it did nothing to clarify the public mind. Indeed, administration policy on this matter was largely determined *by* that mind as perceived in the White House.

On October 11, after receiving an appeal from the president of Finland, and when the American public was manifesting a mighty surge of sympathy for that threatened country, Roosevelt cabled Soviet president Mikhail Kalinin

calling "attention to the long-standing and deep friendship which exists between the United States and Finland" and expressing "the earnest hope" that
the Soviet Union would "make no demands on Finland which are inconsistent
with the maintenance and development of amicable and peaceful relations
between the two countries, and the independence of each." Kalinin replied
curtly on October 16, saying that the "present negotiations" with Finland were
"being conducted in conformity" with long-defined "reciprocal relations" between the two countries" and that "[d]espite the tendentious versions which
are being disseminated by circles evidently not interested in European peace,
the sole aim of the negotiations . . . is a strengthening of friendly cooperation
between the two countries. . . ." On December 1, Roosevelt issued public
statements expressing "profound shock" over "Soviet naval and military
bombings within Finnish territory," stressing the "respect and warm regard"
America had for Finland, appealing to both belligerents to desist from the
"ruthless bombing of civilians," and suggesting that Americans not sell airplanes or plane-manufacturing materials to belligerents who bombed civilians,
this last being an extension of the futile "moral embargo" he had earlier
declared.[51] But he also took cognizance of the fact that, in political potency,
the virtually universal sympathy Americans had for Finland measured small
against their fear of becoming involved in the war; he took cognizance, further,
of the evident fragility of the proclaimed friendship between Moscow and
Berlin, and of the advisability of doing nothing that might encourage the
growth of that "friendship" into something truly real and strong. He had
refrained from declaring Russia a belligerent in the war between Germany and
the Allies when Russia invaded eastern Poland, in consequence of which no
Neutrality Act restrictions had been placed upon trade with her (Soviet purchases in the United States between December 1, 1939, and February 1, 1940,
with the "moral embargo" presumably in full force, were twice those for the
same period of 1938–1939). Neither had he formally protested against Russian
occupation of the three small Baltic republics. And he now refused officially
to recognize the existence of war between Russia and Finland, hence issued
no neutrality proclamation with regard to it. He also declined to propose the
severing of diplomatic relations with Moscow.

He did propose to aid Finland to the limit of perceived acceptance of this
by the general electorate, this limit being a narrow one. He ordered Morgenthau to halt the sale of aluminum and molybdenum to the Soviet Union,
though such sales were perfectly legal, as Morgenthau pointed out. He asked
Congress to return the interest payment of $235,000 that Finland had just
made on its World War I debt to the United States (the fact that Finland, alone
among the European debtors, had never missed such a payment was much
commented upon in the American press) and prodded RFC's Jesse Jones into
arranging a $10 million credit for Finland. But this was as far as he dared go.
The Finnish ambassador in Washington, protesting that $10 million "does not
help us very much," asked for a $60 million credit and $20 million in war
matériel ("We need . . . guns and airplanes and shells").[52] Instead, Roosevelt,

in a letter to the Senate president and House speaker on January 16, 1940, recommended an increase of credits for Finland from RFC and the Export-Import Bank "to finance the purchase of agricultural surpluses and manufactured products, not including implements of war." He specified no amount but, by warning against "the creation of precedents which might lead to large credits to nations in Europe," seemed to ensure that any increase granted would be a modest one.[53] Congress, left to its own devices and subjected to a barrage of isolationist warnings against the dangers of European involvement, then dawdled on the matter week after week.

While it did so there assembled in Washington, in the second week of February 1940, a meeting (a pilgrimage, it was called) of another congress, the American Youth Congress. This had for several years been a democratic socialist organization of young people dedicated to social reform and welfare. Its leaders had been encouraged, befriended, and defended against Dies Committee attacks by Eleanor Roosevelt. But latterly, and especially since the signing of the Nazi-Soviet Nonaggression Pact, there had been signs that this leadership was increasingly dominated by young Communists who adhered strictly to policy lines laid down in Moscow. The Youth Congress's formerly vociferous antifascism had become strangely muted, the struggle against Hitler had become an "imperialist" war, and the organization's leadership now joined incongruously with Republican isolationist extremists in bitter opposition to American rearmament and aid to the Allies. In New York City, shortly before the Washington pilgrimage, there was a Youth Congress council meeting in which resolutions were adopted condemning the President for sacrificing social programs to rearmament, for attempting to aid Britain and France at the risk of American war involvement, and, most emphatically, for advocating aid to Finland in her war against the Soviet Union. This last was especially revealing and disturbing to Eleanor, who, though she did her best to defend the young people in argument with her husband, also urged him to state the case for his policies in person to the youth group in a major broadcast speech. He did so during the noon hour of February 10—a day of gloom and chill and rain. Some 4,500 youthful marchers had come bearing placards (SCHOOLS NOT BATTLE-SHIPS, and so on) up Constitution Avenue through the White House gates onto the South Lawn where, cold and wet, they listened to an address, delivered from the south portico, that was for them as unpleasantly uncompromising as the weather. After citing statistics on the nation's economic progress since 1932, the President warned his young listeners not, as a group, to "pass resolutions on subjects which you have not thought through." He referred specifically to the New York City meeting's "stand against the granting of American loans to Finland . . . on the ground that such action was 'an attempt to force America into the imperialistic war'" against Russia. This, he said, was "unadulterated twaddle" obviously inspired, as his following words clearly indicated he believed, by Moscow propaganda. His belief was confirmed by the flurry of boos and hisses, quickly suppressed but then repeated, which greeted his statements that the "Soviet Union, as everybody who has the courage to face the fact knows, is run by a dictatorship as absolute as any other dictatorship in the world. It has allied itself with another dictatorship, and it has invaded a neighbor so infinitesimally small that it could do no conceivable possible damage to the Soviet Union, a neighbor which seeks only to live in peace as a democracy, and a liberal, forward-looking democracy at that."[54]

A few days later the Senate finally passed a bill that increased the capital of the Export-Import Bank but made no mention of Finland, and that also specified that the total credit to any one country could not exceed $30 million and that none of this could be used for the purchase of arms, munitions, or other implements of war. The measure then went to the House, where it languished through the remainder of February.

But by that time, Finland's cause was clearly hopeless.

The Russian pullback of early January 1940 had been followed by a pause of over a month in the action. Stalin, who had hoped and expected to force his will upon Finland without using and thereby exposing his best troops and most advanced armament, now ordered a major effort which did just that. Russia's top general, S. K. Timoshenko, was placed in command of the Finnish front. The attempt to invade the northern wilderness in major force was abandoned in favor of a massive direct assault on the Mannerheim Line. There was assembled before that line an attacking force vastly outnumbering the Finnish defense, supported by huge masses of cannon and bombing planes. On February 11, 1940, the new attack was launched. Heavy Russian artillery subjected the Mannerheim to the heaviest barrage since that the Germans had laid upon Verdun on February 21, 1916. Three hundred thousand large-caliber shells blasted the Finnish fortifications within a twenty-four-hour period, and the furious cannonade continued for days thereafter, accompanied by heavy bombing from the air of supply depots and railway junctions behind the Finnish line. By the end of the month that line had been breached. Ten days later the key port of Viipuri, second-largest city in Finland, was invested. On March 11, the Finns, having lost some 25,000 troops killed, which was a significant percentage of their total armed force (the Russians had lost upwards of 200,000 killed), asked for an armistice. An envoy was sent to Moscow to receive Stalin's terms. These were much harsher than those offered five months before. Some sixteen thousand square miles of Finnish territory, the bulk of it on the Karelian Isthmus, but enough of it on the Rybachi Peninsula to ensure Russian control of the port of Petsamo and the nearby nickel mines, was ceded to the Russians. They also gained the thirty-year lease on the Hangö naval base which they had originally asked for in October 1939.

But Finland yet remained an independent nation, and the Soviet Union had seemingly revealed to all the world a contemptible military weakness consequent, as everyone thought, upon Stalin's ruthless mid-thirties purges. Moreover, Moscow and the world were now assured that if in the future a Russo-German conflict did occur, as many predicted it would, the formidable Finns were likely to become a German ally.

This last added to the mental confusion of Americans. For as a potential ally of Nazi Germany was not heroic little Finland also a potential enemy of the United States?

VI

CONFUSION was compounded in the the general public mind, and mingled with a good deal of consternation in the minds of the well-informed in both America and the European democracies, when Roosevelt announced at his press conference on February 9, 1940, that Under Secretary of State Sumner Welles would "proceed shortly to Europe to visit Italy, France, Germany and Great Britain" as the President's personal emissary. The visit had as its sole purpose the "advising [of] the President and the secretary of state as to present conditions in Europe." Welles would have no authority "to make . . . proposals or commitments in the name of the Government of the United States" and all "statements made to him by officials of the Government" would be "kept in strictest confidence and . . . communicated by him solely to the President and Secretary of State." This raised very serious questions of intent, destined never to be answered with absolute certainty. Was the President dissatisfied with the copious information he received daily from the four countries through established diplomatic channels? Asked this by a reporter, Roosevelt replied that, "instead of having four separate minds reporting on separate things," it "might be a good thing" to have "one mind" see and report on "all the conditions in all the countries." Asked if Welles would "be in a position to discuss . . . your personal view or the views of this Government on a possible peace," Roosevelt replied brusquely, as he always did when a query cut too close to the bone. "There you go," he said. "Now, do not get didactic." He had already stated the "sole" purpose of the Welles mission, said he.[55]

According to Welles himself, who in all probability originally proposed this enterprise (Hull, taking a dim view of it, was sure Welles had done so), Roosevelt wished to "find out what the views of the four governments might be as to the present possibilities of concluding any just and permanent peace." According to Assistant Secretary of State Breckinridge Long, Roosevelt hoped the mission would delay Hitler's expected spring attack upon the West by a few weeks, giving the Allies more time in which to obtain war supplies from America. He admitted to Welles that "the chances seemed to him about one in a thousand that anything at all could be done to change the course of events," but added that he felt he would be remiss if he did not seek to open a way for that one chance. The question of whether Moscow should be included in the Welles itinerary, since the Nazi-Soviet pact to some extent involved Russia in the German war with the West, had been considered but answered in the negative, the President feeling, according to Welles, that such a visit now, while Russia was attacking little Finland, could serve no "useful purpose."[56]

The four selected capitals, when asked in early February if they would receive Welles in the indicated capacity, replied, of course, in the affirmative

(Welles writes that Rome, Paris, and London responded "cordially"), but none did so with enthusiasm. Berlin's reply was coldly formal; and both Paris and London coupled their affirmations with indications of anxiety. To Daladier and Chamberlain, as to Cordell Hull, it seemed that the timing of this enterprise, whose only purpose could be to encourage a negotiated peace, was in the highest degree unfortunate. All signs were that peace could now be achieved only through surrender to Adolf Hitler, whose pledged word could not be trusted in any case. Indeed, by that time the British and French governments should have been convinced (though Chamberlain evidently was not) that der Führer, behind his smokescreen of peace talk, was determined and fully prepared to launch a blitzkrieg against the West at a very early date. On January 10 a staff major of the German 7th Airborne Division, flying from Münster to Bonn, had lost his way in bad weather and made a forced landing on Belgian territory. He had been taken into custody by Belgian authorities before he was able to burn vital secret papers he carried with him. These papers, copies of which the Belgians at once sent to London and Paris, were in fact the complete operational plans for an attack upon France through Luxembourg, Holland, and Belgium, bypassing the Maginot Line.* It was with this information in hand that Chamberlain, writing to Roosevelt in early February, described the Welles mission as a "sensational intervention" likely to become an "embarrassment to the democracies from which Germany . . . will reap advantage." In another message a few days later, the prime minister worried about the effect the Welles mission might have upon British and French negotiations with the Scandinavian countries, which were then under way. But Roosevelt's replies to such criticisms seem to have been persuasive, for on February 24 the prime minister, addressing the House of Commons on "peace aims," and apropos the upcoming Welles visit, said: "We for our part should be ready to seek a settlement with any Government that had subscribed to these aims and given proof—proof that can be relied upon —of their sincerity."[57]

In America, announcement of Welles's mission encouraged a slight, desperate, and (in the circumstances) politically unhealthy hope among the multitude that a dramatic release from the looming horror of war might be imminent. Its most palpable effect, however, was a new storm of criticism focused upon the White House. Isolationists denounced the trip as another attempt by Roosevelt to involve the United States in the war; pro-Allies interventionists damned it with equal fervor as an attempt to encourage the embattled democracies to accept from Hitler terms of surrender.

Welles debarked in Naples on February 22, accompanied by J. Pierrepont Moffat, and was in Rome, the first stop on his trip, next day. He had a lengthy

---

*The incident caused Hitler to "drop the original operational plan entire" and order the preparation of a new one. See B. H. Liddell Hart, *History of the Second World War* (New York, 1970), p. 37, quoting the account of General K. Student, Commander in Chief of the German airborne forces.

conversation with Foreign Minister Ciano, who expressed emphatically "his contempt and hatred for Ribbentrop" and, in Welles's words, "an underlying antagonism toward Hitler." The emissary then, in the company of Ambassador William Phillips and Ciano, conferred with Mussolini, who seemed to Welles "fifteen years older than his actual age of fifty-six . . . ponderous and static rather than vital . . . heavy for his height . . . [;] his face in repose fell in rolls of flesh." He was obviously "laboring under a tremendous strain. One could . . . sense a leaden oppression." Welles surmised that the Italian dictator was then agonizing over the question of whether or not to abandon neutrality and enter the war as a full partner of Hitler; and since a principal aim of Welles's trip was to encourage Italy to remain neutral, the envoy was depressed by the hatred of Britain and France that Il Duce expressed. Nevertheless, responding to a direct question, Mussolini said with emphasis that he did believe it possible for successful peace negotiations between Germany and the Allies to be held "at this moment"—and he evinced a great and approving interest in the handwritten personal letter from Roosevelt which Welles handed him and which he, who had trouble deciphering Roosevelt's script, handed in turn to Ciano to be read aloud. This letter was, in Welles's words, "of outstanding importance" in that it emphasized "the satisfaction which the United States . . . would derive from a continuation of Italian neutrality and expressed [Roosevelt's] . . . emphatic desire to meet personally with" Mussolini. (Writes Welles: "The President believed—and I am . . . confident . . . he was right—that if he and Mussolini could meet in some relatively remote spot, such as the Azores, he could very probably persuade Mussolini" to remain neutral.) When Ciano read aloud that the President hoped for an early face-to-face meeting with him, Il Duce nodded vigorously and said he himself had hoped for such a meeting for a long time. He feared, however, that there "were too many miles of ocean between us to make it possible." Welles quickly interjected that "there are halfway points which would halve the distance," whereupon Mussolini said, thoughtfully, "Yes, and there are ships to take us both there." He would, he said, "answer this [letter] personally." (He was evidently dissuaded from doing so by German foreign minister Ribbentrop, who made a hurried trip to Rome immediately following the Welles visit to Berlin.)

Far less friendly, indeed cold to the point of hostility, was the American envoy's reception in the German capital, whence he journeyed from Rome. There he was subjected to a two-hour harangue from Ribbentrop, an outpouring the envoy characterized as "an amazing conglomeration of misinformation and deliberate lies" delivered with a "pomposity and absurdity of manner [which] could not be exaggerated." On March 2, he had an interview with Hitler, in which the latter laid heavy stress upon his oft-expressed desire for an understanding with Britain, but also asserted that the aim of Britain was the total destruction of Germany and that "I can see no hope for any lasting peace until the will of England and France to destroy Germany is itself destroyed." Later interviews with Rudolf Hess and with Göring confirmed

Welles in a belief that Mussolini now had no influence in Berlin, that in Berlin "all decisions had already been taken," and that the only thing that could now give Hitler pause was an absolutely solid assurance that the United States would support the Allies to the extent of entering the war on their side if that proved necessary to prevent their defeat. Such assurance was of course impossible, given the present state of American public opinion. It was therefore a gloomy Welles who proceeded to Paris, where his gloom was deepened by the evidence he saw all around him of a pervasive, vicious anti-Semitism, and of the undermining of French morale by Goebbels's propaganda. Morale was said to be especially low among upon the bored French troops who were held inactive, virtually prisoners, along the Maginot Line. It was upon these that Goebbels concentrated his propaganda barrage. Nor was Welles's gloom much reduced by his visit to London, though he was there convinced that British morale was high and that the former appeasers who remained dominant over the British government, Chamberlain and Halifax particularly, were now adamantly anti-Nazi and determined to accept no "peace" that left Hitler in power in Berlin.

From London, pausing in Paris on the way, Welles went again to Rome, where he once more had interviews, insignificant ones, with both Ciano and Mussolini. He found the Italian dictator in much better shape, physically and mentally, than he had been two weeks earlier. It was as if he had "thrown off some great weight." Did this mean he had now made his crucial decision? Had he now firmly committed himself to Hitler's cause? Welles pondered these questions at the time and was later convinced by events that the answer to both of them was yes. He sailed from Naples for New York on March 20.[58]

By then, Roosevelt had attempted to quiet the most disturbing of the rumors that the Welles mission had provoked—namely, that the administration was prepared to negotiate a "peace" that left Hitler in possession of the gains he had achieved though naked aggression, a "peace" certain to be but a brief pause in Hitlerian violence. "Today we seek a moral basis for peace," he said in a radio broadcast on March 16. "It cannot be a real peace if it fails to recognize brotherhood. It cannot be a real peace if the fruit of it is oppression, or starvation, or cruelty, or human life dominated by armed camps. It cannot be a sound peace if small nations must live in fear of powerful nations. It cannot be a moral peace if freedom from invasion is sold for tribute. It cannot be an intelligent peace if it denies free passage to that knowledge of those ideals which permit men to find common ground. It cannot be a righteous peace if worship of God is denied." Upon Welles's return, the President issued (March 29) a public statement saying that "though there may be scant immediate prospect for the establishment of any just, stable and lasting peace in Europe, the information made available to this Government as a result of Mr. Welles' mission will undoubtedly be of the greatest value when the time comes for the establishment of such a peace."[59]

Which is to say that, as Roosevelt had anticipated, this enterprise had not had the slightest effect upon the course of European event. In the United States, its chief effect was the addition of another modicum of fog to the already heavily befogged mind of the general public as it viewed the European scene.

## 14

#### ➳➤✕◄ᵏ

# *The Sphinx. The Hurricane*

BUT it was with regard to domestic politics that Roosevelt added most greatly, during this period, to the general sense of breathless suspension in a void, of helpless waiting upon decisive event. He did so in part out of circumstantial necessity, in part out of calculated design, in part out of sheer indecision.

As a presidential election year began, the national political scene was dominated by the burning question of whether or not the President would run for an unprecedented third term. It was a question only he could answer. He did not do so. Instead, week after week, month after month, artfully, teasingly, often playfully, he alternately encouraged flatly opposed views of his intention. He repeatedly evinced a mischievous enjoyment of the mystery surrounding him, especially of the efforts of newsmen and columnists to discern in his every utterance, however casual, a hint of his election plans. When he spoke at the laying of the cornerstone of the Roosevelt Library at Hyde Park on November 19, 1939, having expressed the hope that the building would be in use by the spring of 1941, he added a further hope that his "good friends of the press" would "give due interpretation to the expression of my hope that, when we open the building to the public, it will be a fine day." When a reporter in a press conference near the end of 1939 pointedly wished him "an eventful 1940," he laughingly responded, "Don't be so equivocal!" At the annual Gridiron Dinner of the National Press Association in December 1939, the backdrop for one of the spoofing skits was a papier-mâché sphinx eight feet tall, its face that of a wide-smiling Franklin Roosevelt with a long-stemmed cigarette holder clamped at a jaunty angle between his teeth. Roosevelt promptly arranged to have it stored for exhibit in the museum of the a-building Roosevelt Library. Some weeks later a cartoon in *The Washington Post* showed a Roosevelt-visaged sphinx with one paw resting on papers labeled "THIRD TERM?" and the other on papers labeled "WELLES REPORT?"[1] And in the immense dark cold shadow cast by this sphinx, this candidacy that might not be one, every frank and open bid for the Democratic nomination was blighted, denied the light energy required for healthy growth.

Yet a good many of these candidacies had been deliberately encouraged, in one way or another, by the President himself.

We have seen how, as early as the spring of 1938, Roosevelt had virtually anointed Harry Hopkins as his successor. The then recognized chief hazard to Hopkins's candidacy was, of course, his precarious health. But Roosevelt had been easily persuaded by Hopkins's assertion that his health at that time, following his recovery from the Mayo operation, was better than it had been in a dozen years, and that, according to the doctors, the chances were against a recurrence of the cancer that had occasioned the operation. He was persuaded, too, that Hopkins's electability remained unimpaired by the Mayo operation, the public having been told that it had been, not for cancer, but for ulcers. The covert White House buildup of Hopkins had therefore begun and been persisted in even after Hopkins's health began again to fail as the spring of 1939 came on. By late April, however, he was too sick to go to his office for several weeks, and in June, meeting with reporters during a temporary and partial recuperation, he tacitly removed himself from further consideration for 1940 (he seems still to have harbored secret hopes for 1944) by publicly advocating a third term for President Roosevelt. By August 17, his forty-ninth birthday, he was again desperately ill; his body, underweight to begin with, was shrunk to skin and bone. Five days later he returned to Rochester, where Mayo Clinic doctors ran test after test in a futile effort to determine why it was that his digestive system could not adequately absorb proteins and fats. In a few days, the Mayo doctors, baffled, gave up on him; they predicted his death within a month or so. But at that point, Franklin Roosevelt, whose personal experience of illness (his own and Louie Howe's) had made him skeptical and defiant of dire prophecies by physicians, intervened to save the life of his friend. At Roosevelt's order, Hopkins was brought from Rochester to Washington in late September and there placed in a government hospital in the care of a team of U.S. Navy physicians headed by the navy's surgeon general. He remained under their care for months, the subject of a long series of exhausting, frequently painful, and always unpleasant experiments whereby enough of the nature of his "deficiency disease" was finally discovered to enable the development of a nutritional regimen to overcome it, or at least hold it at bay. He began slowly, as the spring of 1940 came on, to gain back some of the weight and strength he had lost. But he had now to operate upon very slender margins of strength and energy; the days of his self-distorting political ambition were forever ended.[2]

Among others who had reason to believe that their presidential aspirations had Roosevelt's blessing, and who remained in the race, was handsome young, though silver-haired, Paul V. McNutt, former Indiana governor. He had been crossed off Roosevelt's private list in the spring of 1938 as "too conservative," also ethically dubious, but a presidential campaign had got under way for him during his service, by presidential appointment, as high commissioner of the Philippines. It was well financed, well organized. When McNutt returned to the United States in early May 1939 he was popularly regarded as a frontrunner for the Democratic nomination, if Roosevelt did not run. And when, having resigned as high commissioner, McNutt was in July named administrator of the newly created Federal Security Agency, it was widely assumed, and evidently by McNutt himself, that his elevation by Roosevelt to so high and powerful a post meant White House approval of his presidential ambition, despite the fact that Roosevelt promptly described him to reporters as but one of a dozen or so "charming" young Democrats who might be deemed presidential material, and despite the further fact that Ickes, who presumably knew the presidential mind, pooh-poohed the claims of presidential support made by "McNutt's friends."[3] Soon thereafter, however, the McNutt candidacy, its vulnerability increased by administrative decisions made by him as Federal Security head, began to bleed heavily from the wounds that Ickes and his fellow liberals inflicted. It faltered. It faded.

The case of Robert Jackson was very different. This "charming young man" was often mentioned with enthusiasm by Roosevelt in private but reported talk as a "true liberal" and potential President. He, too, became a national figure through presidential appointment. In January 1940 he was named attorney general, succeeding Frank Murphy, who went to the U.S. Supreme Court, there to occupy the seat vacated by the death of "Old Guard" Pierce Butler, who had died in November 1939. No organized campaign on Jackson's behalf had thus far developed, but he was often mentioned in the public prints as "available" and it was generally believed that his name might well go before the convention in circumstances favorable to his nomination, should the President not run.

Another "true liberal," with more impressive credentials, was Secretary of Agriculture Henry Agard Wallace. His liberalism had become somewhat bolder and more solid since the day when he acquiesced in the purge of Jerome Frank and friends from the USDA.* An authentic intellectual, yet also practical, he had from the first administered his huge department, with the indispensable help of Paul Appleby, in a highly imaginative, creative way—and his active governmental interests had greatly broadened in recent years. He was a persuasive communicator, an eloquent, incisive writer whose well-informed views on foreign affairs, though he was a native of the heartland of isolationism, were strongly internationalist. Some of his personal predilections seemed to Roosevelt as questionable as they were incongruous with the clearheaded reasonableness that characterized Wallace the geneticist, Wallace the businessman. There was the secretary's shifting faddishness in matters of food and exercise, for one thing. There was his highly unorthodox religiosity, for another, manifest in a strong attraction toward weird forms of Eastern mysticism. But Roosevelt, whose wide tolerance was of a piece with his almost incredible patience, shruggingly dismissed these as minor deviations from the sound main line of the secretary's operation. He was also inclined to discount the dislike of Wallace frankly expressed by urban professional politicians. It was more than offset, in Roosevelt's view, by the strength of Wallace's support among the agricultural community, and by his unacknowledged yearning for presidential power, sensed by Franklin Roosevelt. The yearning for such power by a man of Wallace's stamp often indicated (again, in Roosevelt's view) a capacity to exercise it effectively. At various times, therefore, the President had specifically encouraged the secretary's ambition.

*See *FDR: The New Deal Years,* pp. 475–80.

He had also encouraged, if with a highly questionable sincerity and without explicitly pledging his support, Cordell Hull's presidential ambition, though it was far from certain that Hull, who felt his age (he was sixty-eight) and was in poor health, really had any. Roosevelt told the secretary of state on several occasions that he hoped he would become his White House successor[4]—and Hull, if he chose actively to run and Roosevelt to retire, seemed the most likely of all possible Democratic candidates to win both nomination and election. He could hardly be deemed a "true liberal." He was conservative by temperament, always fussily cautious and often to the point of political cowardice. He shared with a majority of the Southern Democrats an aversion to the more "radical" elements of the New Deal. But he remained acceptable to the liberal wing of the party as a compromise choice while commanding strong support from the conservative wing, and he was probably, of all possible Democratic nominees save Roosevelt himself, the most electable. Hull, however, had made it clear that he would not actively seek the nomination; to do so, he said, would be incompatible with the dignity and duties of his present office. Also, as he candidly privately admitted, he doubted that his health could withstand the strains of the presidency. This rendered safe for Roosevelt, in the sense of doing nothing to limit his own options, whatever specific encouragement he gave to Hull's running.

Jim Farley at age fifty-one was in the prime of his life and, in good part because he was known to be no New Deal reformer, remained immensely popular with the party's professional politicians, especially big-city politicians. He, too, had reason to believe that, despite the handicap of his Roman Catholicism, his candidacy was regarded by Roosevelt with favor. In circumstances that made his words seem an approval of Farley's ambition, Roosevelt had said emphatically, responding to a specific question from Farley, "Of course I will not run for a third term."* But at the same time, in July 1939, Roosevelt had asked the liberal Cardinal Mundelein to try to talk Farley out of entering the 1940 race. The cardinal, while on a trip east, had done so, telling Farley that in his opinion Roosevelt *must* run again and that if Farley felt otherwise, and sought the nomination himself, he could not count on the cardinal's support.[5] The interview had had no deterrent effect. Farley had begun thereafter to pursue the nomination frankly, fervently, employing to their full extent his considerable manipulative skills, honed by long political experience. As he did so, he consulted frequently with both Hull and Vice President John Nance Garner. The three differed widely in their political views. They had in common, however, a resentment of numerous snubs and slights each had suffered from the White House; and they were united in their opposition to a third term for the President.

The last of these three, Garner, had most emphatically not received the slightest encouragement from the White House to run. Roosevelt disliked him personally as he did few men. In his eyes, Garner's Santa Claus appearance

---

*Farley italicizes the statement in his embittered *Jim Farley's Story* (New York, 1948).

(white-haired, bushy-browed, blue-eyed, round-cheeked, red-complexioned) belied a basic instinct and mind-set that, in their lack of generosity, their unmitigated commitment to private pecuniary interests, were those of an unreconstructed Ebenezer Scrooge. The two men had ceased to be on truly friendly terms well before the first Roosevelt term ended. Personal animosity, unwontedly bitter on Roosevelt's part, had begun to characterize their relations during Roosevelt's ill-fated court-reform attempt of 1937. And by the summer of 1939, the President was taking actual delight in such jibes as John L. Lewis's hugely publicized and politically damaging description of the vice president, during testimony before the House Labor Committee, as a "labor-baiting, poker-playing, whiskey-drinking, evil old man."[6] Nor had Garner sought or evinced the slightest desire for the President's approval. It was in an adversarial mood vis-à-vis Roosevelt, it was primarily for the purpose of blocking the movement toward a third-term presidential nomination, that the vice president formally announced his candidacy in December 1939 and began at once to run, almost in tandem with Farley, near the front of the Democratic pack, being strongly supported by the party's conservative wing and by a sizable portion of the nation's conservative press.

The bemusement of the general public, its sense of the perceived world as a fearful phantasmagoria wherein no substantial reality could be discerned, was heightened by all this. Ordinary citizens, for whom politics was necessarily a concern far secondary to that of making a living, sought in vain for solid reality amid the shifting appearances of the domestic political scene. They could find no certainty there until Roosevelt unequivocally declared his intention, and Roosevelt had not done this even in private communications to his closest intimates. For instance, when Eleanor, lunching alone with Hopkins in late May 1939, forcefully expressed her personal anxiety lest Roosevelt run again, Hopkins had "the distinct impression that she has no more information on that point than the rest of us."[7] And, as the election-year winter passed and the portentous spring of 1940 came on, the mystery remained as great among those closest to Roosevelt as it was for all others.

His political enemies of course thought they knew his mind precisely. Almost universally they assumed that he was playing, throughout this period of suspense and illusion, a deep, shrewd, and duplicitous game. They told themselves and others that he had never for a moment considered not running again in 1940—that everything he now said and did with regard to the upcoming campaign was deliberately designed to promote his reelection. His repeated "private" expressions of a wish to retire to Hyde Park were intended to provoke, as they did provoke, louder and louder cries that he *must* run again, that the survival of the civilized world depended upon his doing so. His encouragement of numerous others to seek the nomination had the same aim of rendering him "indispensable": The competing candidacies would cancel each other out, the candidates would kill each other off, and the party politicians, increasingly united by a growing fear of losing office, would turn to him as their only hope of official survival.

But this hostile view of the matter, though containing considerable portions of truth, would seem on the whole, and on the evidence, mistaken. Roosevelt, as early as his second inauguration, may have contemplated in the deepest recesses of his psyche the possibility of seeking a third term, and been careful thereafter to preserve the possibility intact (he never closed out an option irrevocably if he could avoid doing so; besides, doubts about his 1940 intentions constituted a substantial element of his influence with Congress). But, on the evidence, he in his conscious mind took it for granted as late as the late summer of 1938 that his second term would be his last. The two dominant events of the autumn of 1938—namely, the Czechoslovakian crisis and the triumph of conservatives in the midterm elections—forced him to reconsider and further postpone any final decision. He simply didn't know what he should do, as 1938 gave way to 1939, nor yet as 1939 gave way to 1940. He did definitely know by the latter date what he would *like* to do, what he wished he could do: He longed to retire to Hyde Park and there resume his personal management of private affairs that had suffered from his enforced long neglect of them. He made financial arrangements for such retirement: In late January 1940 he signed an open-ended contract with *Collier's* magazine for unspecified services at an annual salary of $75,000, the salary he received as President of the United States. In his aforementioned informal talk at the Hyde Park library cornerstone laying he said:

> Half a century ago a small boy took especial delight in climbing an old tree, now unhappily gone, to pick and eat ripe sickle pears. That was about one hundred feet west of where I am standing now. And just to the north he used to lie flat between the strawberry rows and eat sun-warmed strawberries—the best in the world. . . . In the summer with his dogs he dug into woodchuck holes in this same field. . . . The descendants of those same woodchucks still inhabit this field and I hope that, under the auspices of the National Archivist, they will continue to do so for all time . . . [and] that this Library, and the use of it by scholars and visitors, will come to be an integral part of a country scene which the hand of man has not changed very greatly since the days of the Indians who dwelt here three hundred years ago.[8]

The nostalgic yearning to come home again is manifest. He frankly admitted to a few intimates that he was tired. He had said to Ickes, a bit surprisingly, that he was "slowing down" physically and mentally. "He has not the same zest for administrative detail that he had and is probably quite frankly bored," Eleanor had said to Hopkins.[9] And in his own conversations with Hopkins, during which the two discussed retirement plans, he eagerly anticipated the peaceful happy hours he would spend in the office he had designed for himself in the new library where, amid his catalogued and indexed papers, and with Hopkins assisting him, he would "write history."

His establishment of the library showed how greatly he was concerned with history, especially with his own standing in it—and his cold-eyed survey of the current political scene gave him no reason to believe that this standing would be elevated by his running for a third term. It was more likely to be lowered. Running on domestic issues alone, or even primarily, as he would have to do should the Phony War continue, he could have no assurance of victory. The "Roosevelt coalition" of triumphant 1932 and 1936 was now in sad disarray, in good part because of disaffections from its agricultural and labor components. The farmers who had most prospered from AAA policies, and the agribusiness interests served by a Department of Agriculture increasingly subservient to the Farm Bureau, had mostly reverted to the Republicanism or conservative Democratic politics natural to them. The schism between the CIO and the AFL in the ranks of organized labor also meant a loss of political support for Roosevelt to the extent that this could be effected by the leader of the CIO—and the CIO was by far the more liberal and militant of the two great labor organizations. Speaking in Columbus, Ohio, on January 24, John L. Lewis had shockingly declared his hostility to the President, saying that the leaders of the New Deal had "not preserved faith" with American labor and that, if the Democratic convention were "coerced and dragooned" into renominating Roosevelt, "his candidacy would result in ignominious defeat."[10]

Considering all factors, Roosevelt felt forced to admit that Lewis might be right. Indeed, the possibility seemed increased almost to the point of probability as the spring of 1940 came on. Anxious to preserve their limited dollar reserves and unable to borrow from the United States because the Neutrality Act forbade it, the Allies by March had not placed anywhere near enough war-goods orders with American firms to stimulate industrial production significantly. As a matter of fact, the industrial-production index of the Federal Reserve Board, which had stood at 128 (an all-time high) in December 1939, had fallen to 119 in January, to 109 in February, and was down to 105 in March. Unemployment remained well over ten million, a million more than it had been in March 1937. And every poll showed that the President's popularity, having climbed immediately after the outbreak of war (it always did in moments of acute international crisis), had now slumped to or near the lowest point it ever reached. The polls showed, too, that the American people remained by a huge majority opposed on principle to breaking the anti-third-term tradition and were, if by a smaller majority, specifically opposed to a third term for Roosevelt. Moreover, the Republicans, by early 1940, had already fielded four formidable candidates—New York's Thomas E. Dewey, Ohio's senator Robert A. Taft, Michigan's senator Arthur Vandenberg, Indiana's and Wall Street's Wendell L. Willkie (admittedly a long shot)—each of whom appeared far more attractive to the general electorate than Hoover had been in 1932 or Landon in 1936. From all this it seemed clear that, even if Roosevelt managed to win reelection, his victory was likely to be both narrow and hollow. Following it he would face a Congress as recalcitrant, as frustrating of his initiatives, as the one he had been so unhappily dealing with these last two years.

The prospect was the opposite of enticing. Far better to retire in January 1941 with his high place in history secure, as he felt sure it would be. What earlier consecutive six years in American governmental history had wrought as many improving changes in American government and in the lives of ordinary Americans as Roosevelt's first half-dozen years in the White House had done? Nor need this be the end of the political story for him. There was no absolute requirement that his retirement be permanent. If the Republicans won next fall and the unfettered business community, with its usual combination of greed and stupidity, made its usual mess of the economy in the process of trying to dismantle the New Deal, he might emerge from retirement in 1944 to run again for the White House, hopefully with far more success than Eleanor's "Uncle Ted" had had in 1912.[11]

It would, then, have been easy for him to make up his mind absolutely and finally by April 1940 if purely domestic issues had constituted the sum total of his political concerns. They didn't, of course. Offsetting all of the above were the imperative demands made by the world crisis upon presidential leadership. Welles's detailed and authoritative reports of the European situation convinced the President in late March that the Phony War was almost certainly about to end. In a matter of weeks, perhaps of days, all hell was likely to break loose on the Western Front, and who other than himself was equipped by knowledge and experience to meet the challenges that would then be made to the White House? It had been dinned into his ears for nearly two years now, by earnest voices for which he had great respect, that only he could supply the necessary leadership and that he was morally obliged to do so. The expected end of the Phony War would increase this din to a deafening volume.

In the third week of March he was attacked by a "stupid flu germ" which, though it did not incapacitate him, was "most annoying," as he wrote to Illinois governor Henry Horner, and continued to be for nearly two weeks.[12] It increased the weary suspense with which he awaited the decisive event.

II

MEANWHILE, his experience of the second regular session of the 76th Congress had done nothing to reduce his personal reluctance to run, his eagerness to retire.

We have noted the extreme caution with which he dealt with embargo repeal and with aid to Finland. The same degree of caution characterized his annual message, delivered on January 3. In it he continued his equivocation with regard to America's proper attitude toward the European war. "I can understand the feelings of those who warn the nation that they will never again consent to the sending of American youth to fight on the soil of Europe," he said.

> But, as I remember, nobody has asked them to consent—for nobody expects such an undertaking. . . . I can also understand the wishfulness of those who oversimplify the whole situation by repeating that all we have to do is mind our own business and keep our nation out of war. But there is a vast difference between keeping out of war

and pretending that this war is none of our business. . . . I ask that all of us . . . think things through with the single aim of how best to serve the future of our own nation. I do not mean merely its future relationship with the outside world. I mean its domestic future as well—the work, the security, the prosperity, the happiness, the life of all the boys and girls in the United States as they are inevitably affected by such world relationships. For it becomes clearer and clearer that the future world will be a shabby and dangerous place to live in—yes, even for Americans to live in —if it is ruled by force in the hands of a few.

But from this suggestion that Americans might have to choose between living in such a world and taking forceful action to prevent its creation he at once backed away: "The time is long past when any political party or any particular group can curry or capture public favor by labeling itself the 'peace party' or the 'peace bloc.' That label belongs to the whole United States and to every right thinking man, woman and child within it." He plumped unequivocally for but two things: a renewal for three years of the Trade Agreements Act (the reciprocal trade act), which would otherwise expire in June; and increased appropriations (he did not say by how much) for national defense. He made not a single new program proposal.[13]

Equally cautious was his budget message next day.

In it he revealed to the general public for the first time the extent of his mental grasp of those Eccles-Keynesian economic principles he had seemed to espouse and express in his budget message of last year. In the opening three years of the 1930s, he said, the fiscal policy of the government "was exceedingly simple in theory and extraordinarily disastrous in practice. It consisted in trying to keep expenditures as low as possible in the face of shrinking national income. Persistence in this attempt came near bankrupting both our people and our Government."* Then, in the spring of 1933, had come a governmental fiscal policy "more realistically adapted to the needs of the people. All about were idle men, idle factories, and idle funds, and yet people were in desperate need of more goods than they had the purchasing power to acquire. The Government deliberately set itself to correct these conditions by borrowing idle funds to put idle people and idle factories to work." This reversal of fiscal policy "had a profound effect": Within four years the national income was raised nearly 70 percent, "from 42 billion dollars in 1933 to 72 billion dollars in 1937, the largest absolute rise for any four years in our history, not even excepting the rise during the World War." Tax revenues during this period rose from $2 billion to more than $5 billion and "it seemed that the Federal Government would be able safely to balance its budget [for fiscal 1939] on the basis of a national income of 75 billion dollars. . . ." Alas (as Eccles, Lauchlin Currie, and others, pointing to an unemployment figure that remained well over nine million, had emphatically warned him, though this he did not say), the budget-balancing attempt proved calamitous. The overly abrupt reduction

*He himself had persisted in it during his first weeks in the White House. See *FDR: The New Deal Years,* pp. 57–58.

in government expenditures, combined with the "over-optimism which led . . . business to expand production and raise prices too sharply for consumers' purchasing power to keep pace," triggered a recession. To prevent its feeding upon itself and growing into "another depression" he had, "in the spring of 1938, . . . recommended a further use of Government credit and the Congress acted on my recommendation. The soundness of this realistic approach to a fiscal policy related to economic need was again strikingly demonstrated." Within nine months "productive activity turned up."

But having thus stated persuasively the case for Eccles-Keynesian principles, Roosevelt proceeded to reveal how very limited, tentative, and slippery was his mental grasp of them. The argument was plausible, certainly, but he could not down a suspicion that it was also sophistical, designed to justify a yielding to wicked temptations. He continued to share with his conservative political opposition a yearning for a balanced budget wherein alone, according to his deepest feeling, resided economic virtue. And this made it impossible for him to perceive the scale upon which the principles he had just described must be applied in practice to achieve a true and full national economic recovery. He *did* perceive only too clearly, indeed with a magnifying clarity, the scale of the political opposition he currently faced and the consequent political necessity, as he saw it, for a maximum possible "economy in government" joined with a maximum possible concession to isolationist sentiments. Hence his statement that the "wise exercise" of the fiscal policy he had just described "imposes grave responsibility on the Government"; having used "its credit to sustain economic activity in periods of economic recession," government must have "the courage to withold it and retire debt in periods of economic prosperity." But hence also the unseemly and risky haste with which, encouraged by the December 1939 industrial-production index figure, and in anticipation of the boosting effect that Allied war orders were likely soon to have upon American employment figures, he described as actual an "economic prosperity" that was in reality only potential. Though "employment still lags considerably below the level of 1929," he said, we currently enjoyed "the highest levels of production and consumption in our history" and this "made it possible for us to consider a substantial lessening of Government expenditures on activities not immediately essential for national defense." Whereupon he called for a national-defense appropriation of $1.8 billion, which, in the circumstances, was an astonishingly modest increase over the appropriation for the current year and, as he admitted, "far less than many experts on national defense think should be spent." As if to emphasize his hasty departure from deficit financing, he called for special taxes "to finance the national defense expenditures," despite the fact that virtually the whole of the proposed defense-budget increase was offset by a cut of a half-billion dollars in the appropriation for work relief ($1.3 billion was now asked for this)—this at a time when the number of unemployed was but a few hundred thousand smaller than it had been at the bottom of the 1937–1938 recession. Substantial cuts were also proposed for agricultural programs ($900 million for the coming fiscal year), public works

($1.1 billion), and pensions, retirements, and assistance programs ($1.2 billion).[14]

It was a budget determined far less by perceived need than by perceived congressional and public mood, and it pleased few in the administration. It had been protested by many administration officials with greater than usual vehemence when it was being put into final shape. George C. Marshall had been the chief of the "experts" who argued strongly against the drastic cuts made by the White House in the army budget he had proposed. Once the White House decision was made, however, Marshall refused to engage in recriminations and imposed a restraining patience upon his staff, saying it was probable "that events in Europe will develop in such a way as to affect congressional action." To his friend Douglas Southall Freeman, biographer of George Washington and Robert E. Lee, Marshall wrote that "the pressure from home is so heavy for economy that the legislators are genuinely embarrassed and they have my sympathy." At the same time he made determined and effective efforts, in speeches and published statements, to persuade the public that the United States was dangerously unprepared to deal with the emergencies that were sure to arise from "chaotic world conditions."[15] Thus he evinced a self-mastery, a principled subordination to civilian control, a breadth of vision, and a political acumen (closely akin to Roosevelt's in some respects) that were exceedingly rare in a professional soldier and would make him invaluable, in the post he occupied, to President and country in the years ahead.

A very different objection had been raised, during the budget message's preparation, by Marriner Eccles. On grounds both humane and economic he had protested the cut in work relief, saying that not more than three of the ten million or so unemployed "had ever been cared for by the government even before relief appropriations were cut" and pointing out that the present cut could only mean a further contraction of a market demand for consumer goods that was already contracted by continuing unemployment. In response to this, Roosevelt had more fully revealed than he normally did the devious intricacies of his mental dealings with political tactical problems—revealed also the caution-breeding, leadership-denying narrowness with which he measured the limits of the politically possible. Eccles, he admitted, was "absolutely right" about the inhumanity of the work-relief cut. But "with the war in Europe likely to spread" he *must* provide more money for the military and, "since Congress simply will not support an increase in the total budget," the "relief budget is the only place from which I can transfer the additional funds needed by the military." The President was sure, however, that "Congress will support further relief appropriations as pressures [to do so] develop on all sides. In this roundabout way, I hope ultimately to take care of the unemployed." Even so, he went on, "despite the immediate decreases in relief appropriations, it is going to be extremely difficult to get the Congress to pass the military budget." Eccles had disagreed. He saw the situation as a challenging call for presidential leadership. He argued that the President, if he forcefully "presented all the factors to Congress," could obtain a sufficient increase in the total budget to permit the needed military appropriation *without* cutting relief. "But," writes Eccles, "Roosevelt remained unconvinced. . . ."[16]

And whether or not presidential leadership could in this case have made a difference, what actually happened convinced Eccles himself "that I was wrong, and Roosevelt was absolutely right."[17] Neither of the only two measures for which Roosevelt in his annual message had plumped unequivocally had easy sailing through Congress, despite the fact that prudent common sense in the circumstances argued overwhelmingly for each of them. The Trade Agreements Act was generally agreed to be an enlightened measure that had worked well during the years of its operation and that gained enhanced value as a servant of American economic and security interests in the present world situation. Few outside observers had expected the act's three-year extension to encounter much opposition. Yet from January through March it was the subject of bitter congressional debate, and the issue was yet in doubt when, on April 5, it came up for final Senate vote. It then passed the upper chamber with only a five-vote margin. In the House it encountered less opposition but was passed by no great majority. Even more surprising to many observers, and dismaying to all who were concerned about an obviously endangered national security, were Congress's dealings with a proposed military budget that, in view of the current international situation, had already been cut to the bone. In a House Appropriations Committee hearing on February 23, Marshall pleaded to no immediate avail for an orderly, step-by-step approach to necessary national preparedness, which was possible only if the full $1.8 billion military budget were approved. A month later the military appropriations bill was in deep trouble in the House and, reportedly, would encounter even greater hostility in the Senate. According to syndicated columnist Hugh Johnson, one senator said flatly that he and his colleagues "were going to cut the hell out of the army's appropriation." On April 3, the House committee reported an army appropriation 10 percent *smaller* than Roosevelt in his budget message had asked for, cutting from Marshall's list of minimum necessities a proposed air base at Anchorage, Alaska, and reducing by two thirds (from 166 to 58) the requested number of military planes.[18]

### III

BUT now came the first blows of the hurricane—the "hurricane of events," as Roosevelt would call it[19]—that had been preparing in Europe ever since the fall of Poland and of which an increasingly ominous noise, deep-sounding, had reached clear across the Atlantic into ears not deafened by the high shrill clamor of immediate self-interest.

On the very day (April 3) of the House committee's maiming of the army appropriation bill, the British Cabinet met in London to approve a Churchill-sponsored project code-named WILFRED—a scheme to, first, mine the Norwegian Leads, waters that must be traversed by ships sailing between Scandinavia and Germany; second, land a British brigade, accompanied by a French contingent, at Narvik, with orders to advance to the Swedish border; and third, send other Allied forces to Stavanger, Bergen, and Trondheim, denying these ports to the Germans, who were bound to respond violently to this action. WILFRED was both tactically bold and strategically wise; in the process of dealing a truly crippling blow to the German war economy, it might substantially destroy Germany's surface fleet by compelling the latter to engage an Allied naval force immensely superior to it. But the scheme's implementation had been too long delayed, partly by a surpassingly strange action-inhibiting optimism on Chamberlain's part but mostly by a scrupulous reluctance to violate Norwegian sovereignty. No such scruple hampered Adolf Hitler. Prodded by the German Admiralty, he had so far anticipated the British move that forces of slender strength, yet ample for the task, were at that very moment poised in northern German ports, along with the shipping to transport them and the warships and air power to cover them, for a lightning assault upon Norway and also Denmark—along whose border German troops were likewise poised—to be followed by the occupation of both countries. Final orders for the operation had already been issued—were issued by Hitler on April 2; the attack was to begin at precisely five-twenty A.M. Norwegian time (four-twenty Danish time) on April 9, 1940.

In the black shadow of this immediately impending event, some signs of the imminence of which had been reported to him by British intelligence, Neville Chamberlain stood up on the evening of Friday, April 5, to address an audience of fellow Conservatives. He promptly revealed that he had learned little of his own weaknesses from his long series of disastrous errors; he remained as addicted to the "positive thinking" of the tradesman, and almost as egoistically willful and wishful, as ever. It required therefore no wide Atlantic to muffle, for him, the ominous noise from the Continent; the narrow North Sea and yet narrower English Channel sufficed. And what he saw with his optimistic vision was neither shadow around him nor darkness ahead but only bright sunshine, everywhere. "After seven months of war I feel ten times as confident as I did at the beginning," said he in buoyant tones. He reminded his listeners that Germany had been "increasing her armed forces on land and in the air with feverish haste" for many years before the outbreak of war, while England "postponed as long as any hope for peace remained." In consequence, when the war began,

> German preparations were far ahead of our own, and it was natural to expect that the enemy would take advantage of his initial superiority to make an effort to overwhelm us and France before we had time to make good our deficiencies. Is it not a very extraordinary thing that no such attempt was made? Whatever may be the reason—whether it was that Hitler thought he might get away with what he had got without fighting for it, or whether it was that after all the preparations were not sufficiently complete— . . . one thing is certain: he missed the bus.[20]

Hitler missed the bus! In little more than three days thereafter the phrase became a bitter mockery which, added to the throng of earlier deeds and words

that had become bitterly mocking, must pursue hapless Chamberlain thence-
forth down memory's lane to the very end of it.

For Hitler, who had not once ridden a bus these last dozen years, nor
perhaps the last twenty, had no need of one in the predawn darkness of April
9 when, almost flawlessly performing a masterpiece of blitzkrieg planning, his
troops struck without warning across the Danish border and, simultaneously,
his transports and accompanying naval vessels, covered by warplanes, abruptly
appeared in the harbor of Oslo and off every major Norwegian port—Arendal,
Kristiansund, Stavanger, Bergen, Trondheim, and even, astonishingly, Narvik,
which was a thousand miles to the north of Kristiansund. Four British cruisers
covered seven destroyers engaged in mine-laying operations in waters near
Bergen; two British cruisers covered four mine-laying destroyers off Narvik's
fjord. How, then, could it be that the German ships were not intercepted and
destroyed? Later it would be attested by naval experts that such deliverance
for the Germans was not improbable amid the turbulent seas, the mist, the
early darkness that characterized this April 9 in the North Atlantic. But at the
end of this day the general public knew only the gross facts—that all Denmark
was now occupied by the Germans, who had encountered no resistance save
for a brief skirmish with the king's guard (though token, for honor alone, the
resistance was not without bloodshed. Several guardsmen were killed); that
Britain's vaunted naval power, in this crucial moment, had counted for remarkably little; and that, in consequence, every important town and city in
Norway was in German hands, though Norwegian resistance continued and
would continue wherever possible in the name of a king and government soon
to flee to exile in London. The event had been facilitated, typically, by disgusting treachery on the part of a handful of Norwegian Nazis headed by one
Vidkun Quisling. He, an army major and former Norwegian minister of war,
had cooperated with Berlin in the planning of his country's destruction; his
name would ever after be synonymous with "traitor" in every language.[21]

What followed reflected no more credit upon the present British government's capacity to wage war than the initial event had done. First Lord of the
Admiralty Churchill told the House of Commons on April 11 that "Herr Hitler
has committed a grave strategic error" by making "a whole series of commitments upon the Norwegian coast for which he will now have to fight . . . against
Powers possessing vastly superior naval forces and able to transport them to
the scenes of action more easily than he can."[22] But this optimistic assessment
presupposed swift, bold use by the Allies of their naval strength, to devastate
the committed German naval forces and to effect amphibious assaults upon the
lightly held Norwegian ports, Narvik and Trondheim especially, before these
could be adequately reinforced. It presupposed, in other words, the immediate
launching of the landing portions of WILFRED, on a much larger scale. And
this didn't happen. Orders were issued, canceled, reissued, revised, in good
part because of the Admiralty's reluctance to expose its fighting ships, uncov-
ered or very thinly covered in the air, to a superior German air power solidly
based on land. Thus an attack by the four cruisers and seven destroyers near

Bergen upon German warships and transports in Bergen's harbor was canceled at almost the last possible moment by an Admiralty order in which Churchill concurred, at midmorning of April 9, because the risk of exposing the cruisers to air attack was deemed too great. (There was risk, certainly. It was demonstrated that very day when British naval dive-bombers off the aircraft carrier *Furious* sank in Bergen's harbor, with three direct bomb hits, the German cruiser *Königsberg,* a loss the Germans, who contemplated a possible invasion of England in the months ahead, could ill afford. But risks must be run in war; this one measured small against the profit that would have accrued from the operation's success, smaller still against the risks the Germans now boldly ran; and Churchill soon regretted his concurrence in the refusal of it.) Confused and confusing signals from London meant confused British operations in Norwegian waters and on Norwegian land. The counterstrokes to Hitler's enterprise were delivered by the British in scattered, hesitant, piecemeal fashion and, on land, met everywhere with humiliating failure. Churchill, who initially favored conceding central and southern Norway to the Germans for the time being and concentrating British forces upon the key strategic port of Narvik, soon concurred in a division of the British Expeditionary Force between Narvik and Trondheim, neither of which was frontally assaulted and neither of which was ever firmly gripped by the British. Trondheim, indeed, was never reached at all; the British troops assigned to take it were small in number, inadequately equipped, devoid of air cover, and, having landed at small ports to the north and south of the target port, were soon so badly mauled in a hopeless situation that they had to be withdrawn, with considerable difficulty. Narvik was seized after many weeks, from a greatly outnumbered German force, by British troops landed in difficult country on either side of the town, but had then to be immediately evacuated because of climactic events far to the south.

This failure of British amphibious warfare was somewhat offset by wounds inflicted upon the German fleet, which lost (in addition to *Königsberg*) the cruiser *Karlsruhe,* the pocket battleship *Lützow* (formerly *Deutschland*), a dozen or so destroyers, at least nine transports, and a number of submarines, and suffered severe damage to powerful *Admiral Hipper* and *Gneisenau*—an overall injury to German sea power that would have inhibiting effect upon Hitler's planned invasion of England in the months ahead.

None could deny, however, that, overall, the Norwegian campaign had been for the British a debacle, and the British people's response to it mingled a compound of angry disgust, resentment, even suspicions of treason, with a horrid anticipation of worse to come and a dread lest similar ineptitudes, greeting this worse to come, resulted in the extinguishment of British liberties. A swirling black storm of negative emotion focused upon the Chamberlain ministry. On May 7, 1940, a three-day debate of the war situation, demanded by the government opposition, opened in the Commons. During it Chamberlain was repeatedly taunted with his "Hitler missed the bus" phrase. There were addressed to him in verbatim quotation, and not by a Labour opponent but by a longtime Tory friend, the words of scorn with which Oliver Cromwell dismissed the Long Parliament: "You have sat too long here for any good you have been doing. Depart, I say, and have done with you. In the name of God, go!" Against this the prime minister made feeble defense, typically egoistic in its plea for the support of "my friends," and was promptly rebuked by an aged and ailing Lloyd George, whose last major address in Parliament this was. "It is not a question of who are the Prime Minister's friends," said the former prime minister, head of the British government during the last years of the Great War. "It is a far bigger issue. He has appealed for sacrifice. . . . I say solemnly that the Prime Minister should give an example of sacrifice, because there is nothing which can contribute more to victory in this war than that he should sacrifice the seals of office."[23] Chamberlain perforce did so on May 10, having tried in vain to persuade his Labour opposition to join him in a national coalition government—perforce also made the obvious choice of the man to succeed him (he wishing it could be Lord Halifax), naming that man to the king, who then promptly, in the evening of May 10, summoned Winston Leonard Spencer Churchill to Buckingham Palace and there commissioned him to form a new government.

So it was that by London's midnight of this momentous day a new government in which Labour participated was formed; a broken, cheerless, almost friendless Chamberlain, whose cancer death would come within six months, had announced his resignation in a radio broadcast to the nation; and Churchill, after eight eventful months at the Admiralty preceded by a decade of exile in what he had called "the political wilderness," was at age sixty-six his Majesty's first minister and also, by his own decision, minister of defense. Supreme governing power over the British nation and people was now in his hands.

And those hands did not tremble, though well they might.

For it was amid what had now become, abruptly, the hurricane in full force, black and terrible, that they grasped the controlling levers of a yet building and faltering machine, a machine for which the fuel was severely limited, but which must function at once with fullest efficiency if Britain were to survive. At four o'clock in the morning of this Friday, May 10, 1940, Hitler had launched his long-expected, long-dreaded assault upon the West. German troops and armor had thrust far into Luxembourg and, preceded by remarkably daring and skillful paratroopers, across the frontiers of Holland and Belgium, countries whose neutrality Germany was pledged to respect. Everywhere total tactical surprise was achieved. Already, as Friday gave way to Saturday, May 11, Luxembourg was occupied, Belgium in dire straits, and, despite defensive flooding by opened dikes, the Dutch army was being broken into pieces. At the very moment Churchill was told by Chamberlain of his impending elevation there awaited him in his Admiralty office Dutch ministers just arrived by air from Amsterdam, "haggard and worn, with horror in their eyes," come to plead for immediate British naval assistance. He heeded the plea with multitudinous urgent Admiralty orders. Yet he, the new prime minister, going to bed "at about 3 A.M." in the morning of May 11, did not have anxiety as his dominant emotion, and certainly not trembling fear, but, instead, "a profound sense of relief. . . . I felt as if I were walking with Destiny, and that all my past life had been but a preparation for this hour and this trial." In his bed, "though impatient for morning," he slept soundly, dreamlessly, having "no need for cheering dreams."[24]

Nor was any great anxiety aroused in him by his view of the battlefield situation during the next three days. The opposing forces seemed evenly matched in numbers (actually 136 German divisions faced 135 Allied divisions in Flanders) and the French, reputed masters of the military art, with 1.3 million men on the line between Switzerland and the Channel, supplemented in a key sector by a British Expeditionary Force of some 350,000, were prepared to counter with long-prepared strategy (Plan D) what the Germans had been long expected to do. In accordance with this Plan D, the Allied forces were so deployed that their heaviest weight was in the northwest of France, between the Oise River and the Strait of Dover—a strong left arm, which was supposed to swing swiftly into Belgium and there join up with the Belgian army in a counterattack, which, it was hoped, would become a flanking action against any overly vehement German advance centrally toward France. Relatively lightly held, and by troops not of the first quality, was the line between the Meuse River and Longwy at the western end of the Maginot (wherein and behind which, between Langwy and Switzerland, stood more than half the French army, immobile). For this line fronted the Ardennes, which, heavily forested, hilly, with few and poor roads, was deemed by the French impassable by the tanks and motorized transport of any large modern army.

And this Plan D, ordered into execution by General Gamelin at dawn of May 10, seemed on the evening of May 12 to have proceeded satisfactorily. The French had advanced up the left bank of the Meuse River to Huy, some sixteen miles east-northeast of the fortress city Namur, which the Belgians still held, and elsewhere the Allies stood on or close to the phase lines specified in the operational schedule. Hence it may well be that Churchill spoke simple truth when he told the House of Commons and the world on the morning of May 13, in his first public speech as prime minister, that he took up his task "with buoyancy and hope." It was, however, the earlier words of that same address which would be remembered in history, words whereby the man who spoke them became at once recognized everywhere in the free world as the voice, the inspiration, the very personification of that England of stouthearted free men which Baldwin, Chamberlain, and their ilk had come close to burying in a quaking bog of bourgeois mediocrity. Said Winston Churchill:

> I have nothing to offer but blood, toil, tears, and sweat. . . . You ask, what is our policy? I will say: It is to wage war, by sea, land, and air, with all our might and with all the strength that God can give us: to wage war against a monstrous tyranny, never surpassed in the dark, lamentable catalogue of human crime. . . . You ask: What is our aim? I can answer in one word: Victory—victory at all costs, victory

in spite of all terror, victory however long and hard the road may be; for without victory there is no survival.[25]

Through the rest of that Monday, May 13, the Flanders battle, though growing in intensity, continued to arouse in London and Paris no great anxiety.

Next day, however, came the beginning of a blitzkrieg compared to which that of Poland was pale and puny. Everywhere, taking skillful advantage of their superiority in tanks and planes (though individually their planes were in part outmatched by the British Hurricane fighters*), the Germans attacked all along the line, and everywhere, save in the Wavre–Louvain sector held by the BEF, they sent the Allies reeling backward. The hardest German blow, however, was struck by masses of heavy tanks and motorized transport thrusting down through the "impassable" Ardennes against the weakest portion of the French line which, shredded, its rear communications cut by the swift-moving tanks, abruptly ceased to exist. By the fifteenth a fifty-mile gap had been opened between the left and right wings of the Allied army—black news that came to Churchill via his bedside phone at seven-thirty or so in the morning of that day from Paul Reynaud in Paris. Speaking in English "and evidently under stress," the French premier said flatly that the battle, now only in its fifth day, was already lost. "We are beaten!" he declared.[26] The French 9th Army had collapsed in the Sedan area, opening a gap through which massed German tanks and armored cars, preceded by dive-bombers, were pouring at speeds unprecedented in warfare. The message was a wail of despair, and it thrust anxieties in abundance, and of the most terrible nature, upon Winston Churchill.

He promptly involved Franklin Roosevelt in them—which meant also that Harry Hopkins became involved, and almost to the full extent that Roosevelt permitted himself to be. For it so happens that on May 10, the day of Hitler's launching of the western assault, Hopkins felt sufficiently strong after his long illness to put in an appearance at his Commerce Department office ("his second . . . there in ten months," writes Robert Sherwood[27]) and to dine that evening at the White House—where, however, his strength departed and, "feeling miserable," he was persuaded by the President to stay the night. Established in the White House room that Lincoln had used as a study, Hopkins was destined to live there for three and a half years, and was already (abruptly) the most intimate personal assistant—as he had long been, perhaps, the closest friend—that Roosevelt had had since the death of Louis Howe. To him were shown and with him were talked over all the most important of the cables that poured daily into the President's office, and we may be sure he was soon aware of, if he didn't actually see, the one that arrived during the noon hour of this May 15 in Washington—a "most secret and personal" message to the President from *Former* Naval Person, sent through the U.S. embassy at six in the evening London time.

---

*Spitfires were not committed to this battle until May 20.

"Although I have changed my office, I am sure you would not wish me to discontinue our intimate, private correspondence," it began, going on to say that, though the "scene has darkened swiftly," with the "small countries . . . smashed up . . . like matchwood" and the enemy's "new technique" of warfare "making a deep impression upon the French," he himself believed "the battle on land has only just begun." The gravity of the situation was, however, undeniable.

We must expect . . . that Mussolini will hurry in to share the loot. . . . We expect to be attacked here ourselves, both from the air and by parachute and air borne troops in the near future, and we are getting ready for them. If necessary, we will continue the war alone and we are not afraid of that. But I trust you realize, Mr. President, that the voice and force of the United States may count for nothing if they are withheld too long. You may have a completely subjugated, Nazified Europe [continental Europe] established with astonishing swiftness, and the weight may be more than we can bear.

There followed six specific requests: one, for "the loan of forty or fifty of your older destroyers to bridge the gap between what we now have and the large new construction" now under way; two, for "several hundred of the latest types of aircraft, of which you are now getting delivery"; three, for anti-aircraft equipment and ammunition "of which again there will be plenty next year, if we are alive to see it"; four, for facilitation of British purchases of steel and other materials from the United States ("our ore supply is being compromised from Sweden, from North Africa, and perhaps from northern Spain. . . . We shall go on paying dollars as long as we can, but I should like to feel reasonably sure that when we can pay no more, you will give us the stuff all the same"); five, for a "visit of a United States squadron to Irish ports" to discourage "possible German parachute or airborne descents in Ireland"; six, for whatever U.S. naval movement is necessary "to keep the Japanese dog quiet in the Pacific, using Singapore in any way convenient."[28]

To which, next day, when Churchill had gone to Paris to try to hearten the French and concert a retrieval of the desperate military situation, Roosevelt made vague and cautious reply. As regarded the loan of forty or fifty destroyers, "a step of that kind could not be taken except with the specific authorization of the Congress and I am not certain that it would be wise for that suggestion to be made to the Congress at this moment. . . . Furthermore, even if we were able to take the step you suggest, it would be at least six . . . weeks . . . before these vessels could undertake active service under the British flag." As to supplying aircraft, "everything within our power" was being done. Regarding anti-aircraft equipment and ammunition: "If Mr. Purvis [Arthur Purvis, the very able head of the British purchasing mission in the United States] may receive immediate instructions to discuss the question . . . with the appropriate authorities here in Washington, the most favorable consideration will be given to the request made in the light of our own defense needs and requirements." Satisfactory arrangements had already been made by Purvis for "the purchase of steel in the United States," believed Roosevelt, who pointedly gave no hint of what the United States might do when Britain's dollar reserves were exhausted. To the suggestion that a U.S. naval squadron visit Irish ports "I shall give further consideration." As for use of the British naval base at Singapore by U.S. fighting ships to ward off Japan, "the American fleet is now concentrated at Hawaii where it will remain at least for the time being."[29]

A most unsatisfactory reply, from Churchill's point of view! It did nothing to relieve his immediate anxieties, which daily increased in crushing weight and number. Nor did relief come from the President's promptly reported replies to Lord Lothian when the British ambassador, in face-to-face meeting, made urgent representations to him,

By May 20 it had become impossible for the Allied forces in Belgium and northwest France to retreat southward, as they were belatedly ordered to do, there to meet and halt the westward-driving Germans; already those Germans had flanked and undercut them on their right (German armor captured Abbeville near the French coast this day) while at the same time pressing them relentlessly backward along the whole of their eastward-facing front. They were being squeezed into an ever smaller pocket. In England orders were given for the swift assemblage of all available small craft (private yachts, fishing vessels, and the like) to be used to evacuate from Channel ports the BEF, and the trapped Belgian and French forces beside it, should this become necessary, as now seemed almost certain. Questions horrible for Britain to contemplate were now forced upon her: Was Belgium about to collapse? Was France? If the French armies were forced to surrender, would the French government continue the fight from her overseas possessions, establishing herself in North Africa and joining her powerful fleet to Britain's? Or would she become a German province, with her fleet joined to Germany's and, probably, Italy's also? Sweeping changes had been made at the top of the French political and military pyramid, but these were of dubious import: Inert Gamelin had been replaced by active Maxime Weygand as French Commander in Chief, but Marshall Henri Philippe Pétain, aged hero of the Great War's Verdun, had become vice president of France's war council, making him in effect Reynaud's second-in-command if not, in view of his vast prestige, Reynaud's equal in influence—and Pétain, with greasy-slippery Pierre Laval at his side, was known to have strongly totalitarian and anti-British views. Certain it was, as Churchill had observed firsthand in Paris, that the morale of the French, notoriously low at the beginning of the war, was now at or very near rock bottom.

It was in the black shadow of these events, it was amid the acute anxieties of these questions, that Winston Churchill, at one P.M. London time of this same May 20 (eight A.M. Washington time), dispatched to Franklin Roosevelt a second desperate plea for immediate concrete aid. "I understand your difficulties but I am very sorry about the destroyers," he wrote. "If they were here in six weeks they would play an invaluable part. . . . Our intention is whatever happens to fight on to the end in this Island and, provided we can get the help for which we ask, we hope to run them very close in the air battles in view of individual superiority. . . . In no conceivable circumstances will we [the present British administration] consent to surrender." But, Churchill warned, if the present administration should "go down" and be replaced by men of different temper who must "parley amid the ruins," Roosevelt should not "be blind to the fact that the sole remaining bargaining counter with Germany would be the fleet, and if this country was left by the United States to its fate no one would have the right to blame those responsible if they made the best terms they could for the surviving inhabitants. Excuse me, Mr. President, putting this nightmare bluntly."[30]

To this ominous, threatening note, Roosevelt made no written reply. He promptly employed its grim warning, however, in his efforts to persuade the War Department to make generous estimates of the number of planes and amount of other war matériel that could be spared from America's meager stockpiles for immediate shipment overseas—efforts that were resisted by Harry Woodring, by Hap Arnold, even in some degree by George Marshall, and would be by the isolationist contingent in Congress to the extent of its ability to obstruct them.

For Roosevelt paid now in heavier coin than ever before the price of his overhasty retreat from the ground he *seemed* to be occupying with his "quarantine" speech in 1937; of his failure ever since to present in full to the American people frankly, boldly, forcefully, his perceptions and conceptions of his country's security needs; also of his failure, at a different level of responsibility, to resolve the long energy-sapping, action-frustrating quarrel between Woodring and Johnson in the War Department, a quarrel that yet continued. Public opinion, which he had been more concerned to reflect than to inform and mold, was woefully unprepared to deal realistically with the grave threat now facing the nation, and the people's psychological unpreparedness hampered and frustrated him at almost every turn. (Had the bootless question of what might have been entered his mind at this crisis moment, as we may be sure it did not, he would have replied that he could not have done other than he did in the past—nor can anyone deny that his doing "other" without loss of his power to govern at all would have severely tested his leadership capacities, especially the precision of his vaunted sense of timing. All the same, it was the undone, with its consequent psychological unpreparedness, that now threatened to undo him and the country.) He felt that he approached the limit of his narrowed range of possible immediate action when, on May 16, the day of his reply to the first of Churchill's pleas, he went before Congress to request an increase of $1.4 billion ($732 million for the army, $408 million for the navy) in the national-defense appropriation he had originally called for in his budget message. Certainly he startled virtually everyone that day, and provoked the ridicule of many, by proposing to increase America's capacity to produce military and naval planes from its present twelve thousand annually to fifty thousand. He dared increase the risk of this bold proposal by no more than a hint that large portions of the increased production were intended for the

Allies. "For the permanent record," he said, "I ask the Congress not to take any action which would in any way hamper or delay the delivery of American-made planes to foreign nations which have ordered them or seek to purchase new planes. That, from the point of view of our own national defense, would be extremely short-sighted."[31] Immediately provoked by this were inhibiting questions, publicly asked, about the distorting effect the proposed $2 billion defense appropriation might have upon American industry. Can "the present machinery of the country . . . digest the thing without something very drastic in the way of [plant] expansion?" Roosevelt was asked in press conference on May 17, replying that "if we cannot do this program in time of peace" we certainly could not do what would be immediately necessary if America were actually attacked. "And anyone who says that, might just as well advocate no national defense at all on the grounds that the country could not handle it."[32]

IV

COMES the predinner hour of May 26, a Sunday evening, and a cocktail hour presided over in the Oval Room of the White House by a President who, almost unprecedentedly, mixes the drinks mechanically, unsmilingly, almost silently for a small group that includes his wife, Hopkins, Missy, his secretaries, all of whom are as cheerless as he. None engages in the lighthearted banter normally characteristic of such occasions. Most of the group have just listened with no pleasure to a CBS radio broadcast by Charles Lindbergh in which he, who formerly stressed the overwhelming importance of air power in the modern world, has pooh-poohed Roosevelt's call for fifty thousand warplanes, dismissing it as "hysterical chatter." It is true that "the power of aviation" was "greatly underrated in the past," the aviation hero has just said, but "we must be careful not to overestimate this power [now] in the excitement of reaction." "Air strength depends more upon the establishment of intelligent consistent policies than upon the sudden construction of huge numbers of airplanes," he pontificates. Also: "If we desire peace, we have only to stop asking for war."[33] Roosevelt's reaction to this is an irritable disgust proportionate to his recognition that Lindbergh's popular following remains disturbingly large. Encouraged by it is the gloom, the foreboding already weighing down Roosevelt's spirit—a mood further encouraged by a sheaf of dispatches from London, from Paris, delivered now into his hands by Pa Watson.

He learns that the whole of the 300,000-odd BEF and some 25,000 of the French 1st Army are now trapped with their backs to the sea at Dunkirk, whence, this day, some few thousand have been evacuated to England. It is believed that no more than 45,000 can be taken off the beaches and borne to Britain during the next two days, and that two days is probably all the time the Allies will have in which to carry out this Operation Dynamo. (No troops at all could have been evacuated but for a strange order, radioed in the clear [British intelligence listened to it] on May 24, halting a German armored drive that, had it continued, would have cut the Allies' line of retreat to the sea.[34]

It must be assumed that the armored drive will shortly be resumed, ending the possibility of further evacuation.) "I believe that the British, Belgian, and French armies in Flanders will be obliged to surrender within two or three days," says a telegram from Bullitt, who adds that within six days the German mechanized divisions will "have been reformed for the march on Paris," the occupation of which is expected "in about ten days."[35] On the twenty-fourth, the Belgian line was broken on either side of Courtrai, and the British fear that King Leopold, convinced that the Belgian army's position is hopeless, contemplates an unconditional surrender to the Germans, a move that will nakedly expose the BEF's left flank to the enemy. In no part of the great battlefield do Weygand's brave orders have effect. They cannot be obeyed. Confused, demoralized French troops are surrendering by the thousand, sometimes without having fought at all—indeed, half the French army will never see action, thanks to the Maginot Line and the troop dispositions of Plan D. There has as yet been no response to a message sent by Roosevelt that afternoon via Hull through Bullitt to Reynaud and Daladier, saying that "if the worst comes to the worst, we regard the retention of the French fleet as a force in being as vital to the reconstitution of France . . . and to the ultimate control of the Atlantic and other oceans and as a vital influence toward getting less harsh terms of peace. That means that the French fleet must not be caught bottled up in the Mediterranean. . . . The same thought is being conveyed in the strictest confidence to the British regarding the British fleet."[36]

Thus, in sum, the hard and heavy burden imposed by the cables upon Roosevelt's mind as he scans them, then hands them to Eleanor, to Hopkins.

"Bad," he mutters. "All bad."[37]

But, some two hours later, nothing of despair is seen by the newsreel camera's eye nor heard by the radio microphones in the hot, stuffy diplomatic reception room downstairs as Roosevelt delivers a fireside chat on national defense to an audience of scores of millions across the land. What rides out on the airwaves into listening ears is calm confidence, determination, and life-affirming, death-defying fortitude packaged in a singing tenor voice that is marvelously warm, intimate, soothing, encouraging, a voice inspiring hopeful action even when it speaks of the millions of civilians who, driven from their homes by "bombs and shells and fire and machine gunning," now "stumble on" in helpless misery over the roads of Belgium and France. "The American Red Cross, that represents each of us, is rushing food, clothing and medical supplies to these destitute civilian millions. Please—I beg you—. . . give . . . to your nearest Red Cross chapter . . . as generously as you can." Having said which, as a last-minute tacked-on preliminary to his prepared text, Franklin Roosevelt begins to talk, not to the American people as a whole, but to each and every one of them personally, saying: "Let us sit down together again, you and I, to consider our own pressing problems. . . ." The shocking events of the last two weeks, he goes on, have been a "rude awakening" for those Americans who formerly believed that what happened in Europe was "none of our business." With disillusionment has come to some (not including *you,* of course) "fear, bordering on panic." These now moan that "we are defense-less" in a hostile world and "that only by abandoning our freedom, our ideals, our way of life, can we build our defenses adequately, can we match the strength of the aggressors." Not so, says Franklin Roosevelt, in a surging voice. The United States is strong militarily, and will soon be immensely stronger, thanks to the defense program now being initiated. The great danger is that, "as this [rearmament] program proceeds," we will fail to maintain intact that which our guns and planes and ships are intended to defend—that which in fact underlines and gives "strength, sustenance and power" to our "physical armament"—namely, "the spirit and morale of a free people." In these last seven years "we have carried on an offensive on a broad front against social and economic inequalities and abuses which had made our society weak. That offensive should not now be broken down by . . . those who would use the present needs of physical military defense to destroy it. There is nothing in our present emergency to justify" the abandonment of collective bargaining, the lowering of the minimum wage, or the increase of working hours beyond present statutory limits. Instead, work should soon be given to "tens of thou-sands . . . now unemployed." Neither should there be, there must not be, any reduction in old-age pensions and unemployment insurance, or any "retreat from . . . conservation of natural resources, assistance to agriculture, housing, and help to the under-privileged." Conversely (Roosevelt stresses this point), a greedy, acquisitive minority must not be permitted to profit from the misery of millions. "Our present emergency and a common sense of decency make it imperative that no new group of war millionaires shall come into being in this nation as a result of the struggles abroad. The American people will not relish the idea of any American citizen growing rich and fat in an emergency of blood and slaughter and human suffering."[38]

All of which is comforting and inspiring to common folk and to those New Dealers who have feared an abrupt repeal of liberalism. It is far less so for the latter, however, than it would have been had it not been preceded in this same chat by words of very different import, words pregnant with meaning for the future and, as such, noted with anxiety by Ickes, Harry Truman, Thurman Arnold, and all knowledgeable others who fear a renewed and increased domination of America by big business. "The Government of the United States itself manufactures few of the implements of war," the President has said. "Private industry will continue to be the source of most of this matériel; and private industry will have to be speeded up to produce it at the rate and efficiency called for by the needs of the times. . . . It would be unfair to expect industrial corporations or their investors to do this [make the required capital investment for immediate plant expansion, and so on], when there is a chance that a change in international affairs may stop or curtail future orders a year or two hence. Therefore, the Government of the United States stands ready to advance the necessary money. . . ." So far, so good, most American liberals would agree, provided such money advances are accompanied by sufficient governmental controls to prevent their use for concentrated private profiteering. Will they be so accompanied, in Roosevelt's conception? Doubts and alarms are raised in informed minds, in all who remember the 1935 Nye Committee's exposures of big-business profiteering during the First World War, when Roosevelt says:

> The details of all this are now being worked out in Washington, day and night. We are calling on men now engaged in private industry to help us in carrying out this program, and you will hear more of this in detail in the next few days. . . . The functions of the business men whose assistance we are calling upon will be to coordinate this program—to see to it that all of the plants continue to operate at maximum speed and efficiency. Patriotic Americans of proven merit and of unquestioned ability in their special fields are coming to Washington to help the Government with their training, their experience and their capability.[39]

All of which strongly suggests to suspicious, critical minds that, as in Woodrow Wilson's Washington with its "dollar-a-year" men, the foxes are being called to the capital to guard the chicken coop and fatten up the chickens in preparation for their own hearty repast. The President more than hints at a revival of the industrial-mobilization system of 1916–1918, a system whereby American "war millionaires" were made by the score, big-business domination of the American economy was greatly advanced, and foundations were laid for a military-industrial complex (so to be called in a later year) destructive of a true free-market economy and highly dangerous to civil liberties and political democracy.

Two days later it becomes clear that the 1916–1918 system *is* being revived, and precisely in its original form. In his press conference of May 28, Roosevelt speaks of the remarkable response of the American public to his Sunday night talk, a "flood of mail and telegrams" from people "offering help . . . [and] personal services" and enclosing checks for the Red Cross. (The response is so much to him personally, to his personal leadership, that it affects considerably his thinking about a third term.) He also studiedly minimizes the impact that war abroad and rearmament at home must have on American consumer-goods production. But his big news for the day is his announcement that he is reestablishing the Council of National Defense, originally provided for by a 1916 statute that remains unrepealed.* The council is a Cabinet committee consisting of the secretaries of war, the navy, agriculture, commerce, labor, and the interior, who "meet [with him] every Friday anyway." Also appointed is an Advisory Commission of the Council (so named in the organic act), which will be a far more important body than the council in that, like the commission Wilson appointed in 1916, it will function, not as a merely advisory body, but as an executive one. Indeed, as between the council and the commission, it is the former that will be primarily "advisory" insofar as the latter operates with its advice and consent. The commission will both plan and carry out a major portion of the overall industrial-mobilization program. Its seven members,

*See *FDR: The Beckoning of Destiny,* pp. 415, 421–22, 498–99.

who are to "serve without compensation," are Edward R. Stettinius, Jr., board chairman of United States Steel, charged with managing the supply of industrial materials; William S. Knudsen, president of General Motors, who will handle industrial production; Sidney Hillman, president of the Amalgamated Clothing Workers of America, who will deal with employment matters; Ralph Budd, board chairman of the Chicago, Burlington, and Quincy Railroad, whose responsibility is transportation; Chester C. Davis, former AAA administrator, currently on the board of governors of the Federal Reserve System, who will handle agricultural matters; Leon Henderson, currently of the Securities and Exchange Commission, who is to deal with price stabilization; and Harriet Elliott, dean of women at the University of North Carolina, whose concern is consumer protection. Of these seven, only Knudsen and Stettinius will have from the outset full-time commission jobs, though Hillman's job may be almost full-time. The others will serve only part-time.[40] Each member will, of course, be provided with necessary staff, key members of which will be of the commissioner's own choosing.

Meanwhile and thereafter the dark, flame-shot hurricane roared to its climax in Belgium and France, with only a single narrow space of sunlight opening for the British amid the thickening gloom.

The mysterious three-day halt of the German armored drive northward toward Dunkirk enabled the trapped British and French troops to retreat in good order toward the Channel and consolidate their eastward- and southward-facing defenses. The British troops managed also, with heroic effort, to cover defensively their exposed left flank after King Leopold, with no prior warning to his allies, abruptly made his final decision to surrender to the Germans and simultaneously acted upon it early in the morning of May 28. By then in full swing was Operation Dynamo, that masterpiece of British phlegm and improvisation known to history as the Miracle of Dunkirk (Heaven-sent? Remarkably smooth seas were an important part of it) conducted under the calmly efficient overall direction of a vice admiral who, with a staff of sixteen, was ensconced in a command post (a single large room) carved into the white cliffs of Dover. A fleet of nearly nine hundred widely varied craft—speedboats, yachts, Channel ferries, tugs with strings of barges attached, lifeboats, passenger ships, naval vessels; all save the naval ships were manned by civilian volunteers—crisscrossed the Channel, often under attack from the air, to pluck from Dunkirk's harbor and beaches and carry off to English ports 26,000 French troops and the whole of the BEF save those who had to fight to the last to cover the withdrawal. Necessarily left behind, alas, was the whole of their armament and equipment, but 338,226 troops had been borne to England by June 4, when the remnant of the BEF (the Germans claimed 40,000 prisoners) was forced to surrender, and Dunkirk became a German port. The operation would not have been possible without temporary domination of the local sky by the Royal Air Force which, battling against great numerical odds, had decisively defeated the Luftwaffe: Hurricanes and

Spitfires had knocked down three or four German bombers and fighters for every plane lost of their own.

This last was emphasized by the British prime minister when, on this same June 4, he delivered to Parliament an address that, broadcast to America, had great impact upon the American mood and mind and a very considerable influence upon the decision-making of Franklin Roosevelt. The prime minister warned against assigning "to this deliverance the attributes of victory," since "wars are not won by evacuations," but went on to assert that there was indeed "a victory inside this deliverance." It was won in the air by the British air force, it boded ill for any plan "Herr Hitler" might have "for invading the British Isles," and it provided realistic justification for Britain's confidence in ultimate victory, whatever now happened on the Continent. Voicing a magnificent defiance that would ring down the corridors of history into the ears of generations yet unborn, Winston Churchill growled and roared:

> We shall go on to the end, we shall fight in France, we shall fight in the seas and oceans, we shall fight with growing confidence and growing strength in the air, we shall defend our island, whatever the cost may be, we shall fight on the beaches, we shall fight on the landing-grounds, we shall fight in the fields and in the streets, we shall fight in the hills; we shall never surrender, and even if, which I do not for a moment believe, this island or a large part of it were subjugated and starving, then our Empire beyond the seas, armed and guarded by the British Fleet, would carry on the struggle until, in God's good time, the New World, with all its power and might, steps forth to the rescue and the liberation of the Old.[41]

Apocryphal is the story that Churchill closed his series of "we shall fight" assertions with a whispered aside to a colleague: "Yes, and we shall hit them over the head with bottles, for that is all we have"—apocryphal, yet perfectly consistent with appalling reality. For though British industry worked night and day to make good the Dunkirk losses, the fact remained that the uniformed defenders of the British Isles were themselves for the moment defenseless, lacking virtually every item needed to make them effective fighting men. Hence the imperative need for the New World to "step forth" now, *at once*, in aid of the Old—and hence the great good fortune for freedom's cause that it was doing so, in some significant degree. Even as Churchill spoke, arms and munitions for the British army were being loaded onto British ships at U.S. docks. Flat orders imposed by the White House upon an initially reluctant War Department and army had been carried out with remarkably swift efficiency by General Marshall and his staff. In less than forty-eight hours was compiled a complete list of American reserve ordnance and munitions stocks that could at once be sent to England without denying arms to the 1.8-million-man army called for, in case of war, by the army's long-made mobilization plan. The list was approved by Marshall on June 3, the day before Churchill's address. Included on it were 500,000 Enfield rifles, which had been stored in grease since World War I; 900 75mm field guns; 50,000 machine guns; 130 million rounds of rifle ammunition; a million rounds of ammunition for the 75s, and quantities of TNT and smokeless powder, in addition to an assortment of bombs. Also on June 3, to save precious hours of time, arrangements were made to sell these stocks for $37,619,556.60 to a single large company, the United States Steel Export Company, which was to resell them at the same price (had in fact already resold them) to the British Purchasing Commission. This particular export company was selected for the transaction because Edward Stettinius, Jr., board chairman of United States Steel until the afternoon of this June 3, was in Washington to assume his duties as National Defense Council commissioner in charge of "industrial materials."[42] He could and did facilitate matters—an instance of the immediate advantage (it may also hint at a grave long-term danger) of having such "dollar-a-year" men as he in charge of industrial mobilization.

Simultaneous, too, with Churchill's brave words in the Commons were British deeds that testified to their truthfulness. Despite the increasing probability that France would soon fall, two newly formed British divisions, the only ones now fully armed and combat-ready on the island, were ordered to France, and went there in the days immediately following, along with the French troops evacuated at Dunkirk. ("Looking back on it, I wonder how . . . we had the nerve to strip ourselves of the remaining military formations we possessed," Churchill later wrote.[43]) Almost as soon as they were committed to battle in France, however, they found themselves in a hopeless position and had to be withdrawn in a small-scale Dunkirk operation.

For on June 5, having regrouped with astonishing swiftness after their westward drive to the sea, the German forces, a hundred divisions strong, launched what would within days become a four-pronged drive southward into the heart of France, with hard- and swift-driving armor as the gouging, boring spearhead of each prong and with the whole covered by dive-bombers, other bomber types, and machine-gunning fighters, which encountered virtually no resistance from the French air force; their resistance by outnumbered British fighter planes was limited by the fact that fighter planes in maximum possible number were vital to Britain's defense against any attempted invasion. One German prong curved around the north end of the Maginot Line, through Verdun and Châlons toward far distant Lyon; a second drove southward through Rheims toward equally distant Vichy; a third headed directly toward Paris, thence to move on toward Châteauroux; a fourth, with branches soon to shoot westward into Normandy and Brittany, pressed southward toward Tours and beyond. All these made swift progress. By June 10, with the Germans pouring across the Marne, it was clear that Paris, which was promptly declared an open city, must soon fall; the French government fled southward to Tours. And on that day, jackal Mussolini moved in to take his bites out of mortally wounded France, sending 400,000 Italian troops to invade the very lightly defended French Riviera. On that day, too, France's premier, Paul Reynaud, cabled the U.S. President: "Today the enemy is almost at the gates of Paris. We shall fight in front of Paris, we shall fight behind Paris; . . . and if we should be driven out . . . we shall establish ourselves in North Africa to continue the fight. . . . May I ask you, Mr. President, to explain all this yourself to your people [and at the same time] . . . declare publicly that the United States will give the Allies aid and material support by all means short of an expeditionary force. I beseech you to do this before it is too late. I know the gravity of such a gesture. Its very gravity demands that it should not be made too late."[44]

At the University of Virginia in Charlottesville a few hours later, Roosevelt, in doctoral cap and gown, delivered a long-scheduled commencement address wherein he spoke, not without a cold grim anger, of "those [Americans] who still hold to the now somewhat obvious delusion that we . . . can permit the United States to become a lone island . . . in a world dominated by the philosophy of force." Such an island would be like a prison wherein people are "handcuffed, hungry, and fed through the bars . . . by the contemptuous, unpitying masters of other continents." And it must be said that, though the pressures upon him were intense, Roosevelt himself, responding to these, felt somewhat like a man just released from prison: The education of the American public by threatful event had so far proceeded, he felt, as to give him freedom to make bolder, less equivocal, more concrete public commitments to collective security than he had ever dared make in the past. He did so in deeds when he ordered the arms and munitions shipments now being made to England; he did so now in words, at Charlottesville, as he restored to his prepared speech text a statement he had earlier removed from it at the State Department's behest. "On this tenth day of June, 1940," he said, in a voice dripping with scorn, "the hand that held the dagger has struck it into the back of its neighbor." The statement, causing the address to be ever after remembered as the "stab-in-the-back" speech, was made highly inspiriting to both Churchill and Reynaud by two things: First, Roosevelt had permitted Reynaud to publish his (Reynaud's) message to the White House of June 10, wherein the French premier said, "This very hour another dictatorship has stabbed France in the back"; second, Roosevelt's repetition of the phrase seemingly enhanced the meaning of his following words: "In our [new] American unity, we will pursue two obvious and simultaneous courses; we will extend to the opponents of force the material resources of this nation; and at the same time, we will harness and speed up the use of those resources in order that we ourselves . . . may have equipment and training equal to the task of any emergency and every defense. All roads leading to the accomplishment of these objectives must be kept clear of obstructions. We will not slow down nor detour. Signs and signals call for speed—full speed ahead."[45]

"We all listened to you last night and were fortified by the grand scope of your declaration. . . ." wrote Churchill to Roosevelt on June 11. "The hope with which you inspire them [the French] may give them the strength to persevere" despite the impending fall of Paris. But hope must be sustained by deeds: Reiterated was the immediate need for destroyers, though Churchill scaled back the number requested from "forty or fifty" to "thirty or forty." "Nothing is so important. . . . We can refit them very rapidly. . . . Not a day should be lost."[46] To which Roosevelt made no written reply. He did reply to Paul Reynaud on this June 11, saying in part, "Your message of June 10 has moved me very deeply. As I have already stated . . . this Government is doing everything in its power to make available to the Allied governments the material they so urgently require, and our efforts to do still more are being redoubled. This is so because of our faith and our support of the ideals for which the Allies are fighting. . . . I am . . . particularly impressed by your declaration that France will continue to fight . . . even if it means slow withdrawal . . . to North Africa. . . ." A copy of this awaited Churchill upon his return, on June 12, from a flying trip to Tours, where he had gone (his fourth flight to France since mid-May) in a desperate effort to ensure that, should the defense of metropolitan France become impossible, the French government would indeed fight on with the French fleet and as many French troops as could be got away to North Africa. Having received no such assurance, he was in need of encouragement. He seized avidly upon the President's words, which he wishfully interpreted to mean that the United States was on the verge of entering the war. He promptly said so in a message to Reynaud: "If France on this message of President Roosevelt's continues in the field and in the war, we feel that the United States is committed beyond recall to take the only remaining step, namely, becoming a belligerent in form as she already has constituted herself in fact. The Constitution of the United States makes it impossible . . . for the President to declare war himself, but, if you act on his reply now received, we sincerely believe that this must inevitably follow." He privately noted, however, with perturbation, that the Roosevelt message was not the public declaration that Reynaud desired. It was labeled "secret." And the prime minister at once protested this secrecy, writing Roosevelt:

> While we were flying back here your magnificent message was sent [to Reynaud] and Ambassador Kennedy brought it to me on my arrival. The British Cabinet were profoundly impressed, and desire me to express their gratitude for it, but, Mr. President, I must tell you that it seems to me absolutely vital that this message should be published tomorrow, June 14, in order that it may play a decisive part in turning the course of world history. It will, I am sure, decide the French to deny Hitler a patched-up peace. . . . He needs this peace in order to destroy us and take a long step toward world mastery. All the far-reaching plans, strategic, economic, political, and moral, which your message expounds may be still-born if France cuts out now. Therefore I urge that the message should be published now.[47]

Roosevelt, however, had now reached the outermost edge of the perceived possible, had indeed gone well beyond what he recognized as safe limits, and, instead of going further, drew back. "As I asked Ambassador Kennedy last night to inform you, my message . . . to the French Prime Minister was in no sense intended to commit and did not commit the Government to military participation in support of the Allied governments." Only Congress had the constitutional authority to make such a commitment. His primary concern, as he composed his message, was, he said, "the French fleet and its disposition for future use. I regret that I am unable to agree to your request that my message be published since I believe it imperative that there be avoided any possible misunderstanding in regard to the facts set forth above. . . ." As soon as he had read this, Churchill dictated and immediately sent off the longest, the most desperate, the most direfully warning, and the most demanding of all his messages to Roosevelt thus far.

> I am grateful to you for your telegram, and . . . have reported its operative passages to Reynaud. . . . He will, I am sure, be disappointed. . . . I understand all your difficulties with American public opinion and Congress, but events are moving downward at a pace where they will pass beyond the control of American public opinion when at last it is ripened. . . . I am personally convinced that America will in the end go to all lengths but this moment is supremely critical for France. A declaration that the United States will, if necessary, enter the war might save France. Failing that in a few days French resistance may have crumbled and we shall be left alone.

The consequence of this might be that, in a few weeks or months, the present British ministers would be swept out of office by a shattered, starving, demoralized people who, in their misery and despair, listened to Hitler's promise of easy terms and proposed to accept them. A pro-German government, disposed to buy peace with the British fleet, might be "called into being." This would be catastrophic for the United States. The British fleet "joined to the fleets of Japan, France, and Italy and the great resources of German industry" would place "overwhelming sea power . . . in Hitler's hands." The United States of America would then face "a United States of Europe under the Nazi command far more numerous, far stronger, far better armed than the [N]ew [World]." Churchill closed with a reiterated plea for the overage destroyers; their immediate delivery was "a matter of life or death."[48]

Perhaps, even at this last hour for the Third French Republic, the Rooseveltian gesture-statement called for by Churchill and beleaguered Reynaud might have accomplished what Reynaud hoped, what Churchill asserted it would do. Since the gesture-statement was unmade, however, all we can be sure of is that this *is* absolutely the last hour for France and the Franco-British alliance.

The darkness of that hour is stygian.

But not unbroken.

It is shattered and dissolved for a single flashing instant by a lightning bolt, an astonishing lightning that is worth our attending to, since it may light the way Europe must go in years ahead if, surviving this war, European civilization survives for long—the way toward a United States of Europe far different from the one Hitler would make, being a federal republic founded on democratic principles.

It is Sunday, June 16, 1940. The French government, forced by the advancing German hordes to flee Tours, has settled itself in Bordeaux whence, on the night before, it has dispatched to London a request for relief from an Anglo-

French agreement that neither Britain nor France will ever seek a separate peace with Hitler. A French Cabinet majority, beating down Premier Reynaud's resistance, is now determined to ask for armistice terms. Churchill, in a message approved by his Cabinet, makes to Reynaud a stern reply:

> Our agreement forbidding separate negotiations, whether for armistice or peace, was made with the French Republic, and not with any particular French administration or statesman. It therefore involves the honour of France. Nevertheless, *provided, but only provided, that the French fleet is sailed forthwith for British harbours pending negotiations* [italicized in Churchill's war memoirs], His Majesty's Government give their full consent to an inquiry by the French Government to ascertain the terms of an armistice for France. His Majesty's Government, being resolved to continue the war, wholly exclude themselves from all part in the above-mentioned inquiry. . . .[49]

But uppermost in Churchill's mind as he sends this message during the noon hour is the urgent immediate need for some dramatic move that will strengthen Reynaud's position vis-à-vis those of General Weygand, Pétain, and the other defeatists on the French Cabinet.

A startling proposal to this end has been worked out by the intellectually bold and remarkably efficient Jean Monnet, whom we have met before in this narrative. Yesterday he discussed and revised his proposal in a long talk with the British Foreign Office's Sir Robert Vansittart and the French ambassador; it has been written down, clearly, concisely, in the form of a proposal by the British government to the French; and Monnet, accompanied by the French ambassador, has presented it that morning to a forty-nine-year-old French general, one Charles de Gaulle, an ally of Reynaud's who has flown over from France at dawn that day for the express purpose of facilitating with Britain the continuation of the war by a Reynaud government headquartered in Algiers. A very tall, stiff beanpole of a man, rigid, upright, humorless, this De Gaulle has international fame in military circles as the creator of ideas about the use of mobile armored striking forces which, having been ignored by the top French military command, are now being terrifyingly applied by the Germans to the conquest of France. None can doubt his high intelligence, his fertile imagination, his receptivity to new ideas. But he is, one would think, the last man in the world to be at all receptive to this idea of Monnet's, for he is a passionate French nationalist whose patriotism is a religous devotion to what he deems the unique Spirit of France, the unique genius of her people, whereas Monnet's idea is a declaration of an "indissoluble union" of the United Kingdom and the French Republic. "The two Governments declare that France and Great Britain shall no longer be two nations, but one Franco-British Union," says the declaration. "The constitution of the Union will provide for joint organs of defence, foreign, financial, and economic policies. Every citizen of France will enjoy immediately citizenship of Great Britain; every British subject will become a citizen of France." Nevertheless, nationalist De Gaulle reads this with sympathetic eye and listens with sympathetic ear to what Monnet has to say. He regards it as a wildly impractical scheme (Monnet admits that it bristles with practical difficulties) but one whose expression at that moment, signifying British solidarity with the fighting French, may restore strength and vigor to Reynaud's fading power and prestige.

That it will do so is, indeed, the argument that Monnet presents to De Gaulle and that De Gaulle in turn presents to Winston Churchill during lunch with the prime minister this day, a luncheon arranged precisely for this purpose of persuasion. It is in the Carlton Club. De Gaulle is accompanied by the French ambassador. And Churchill, whose nationalism is fully as passionate as De Gaulle's, is quickly persuaded. He presents the proposal to the British Cabinet at a meeting summoned to consider it at three o'clock that afternoon. Embellished with florid war propaganda authored by Churchill, it is approved and phoned by De Gaulle to Reynaud, who is elated by it, being convinced it will enable him again to dominate the French Cabinet and prevent the armistice. He is abruptly disillusioned. The Cabinet meeting in Bordeaux, a little after five that afternoon, is dominated by Weygand, who asserts that within three weeks "England will have her neck wrung like a chicken," and by Marshal Pétain, who says a union with Great Britain would be "fusion with a corpse." The union proposal is not even put to a vote. It perishes under a withering fire of scorn, of mockery.[50]

And with it dies the Third Republic.

Reynaud is seen, immediately after the Cabinet meeting, by the U.S. ambassador who accompanied the French government on its flight from Paris. This ambassador is not William Bullitt. In a typically dramatic gesture of heroism, and against the urgings of the State Department and of Roosevelt personally, Bullitt has chosen to remain in his beloved Paris at the risk of death (so he assures others) at the hands of the Germans or of the "Communist mob" which he "expects" to take over Paris should the legitimate French government flee the city.[51] It is J. Anthony Biddle, the former ambassador to Poland, who is in Bordeaux as Bullitt's deputy, and it is he who reports to Washington that Reynaud, following the Cabinet meeting, is in a state of collapse. "If ever a confident courageous little man lost his nerve, it was Reynaud," says a June 16 telegram from Biddle to Washington that night. "He turned literally ashen gray in panic and you would never have known him to be the same man of two weeks earlier."[52] An hour or two later, at a renewal of the Cabinet meeting, Reynaud does resign. He is replaced by aged Henri Philippe Pétain.

Next day, while the U.S. Senate is adopting a resolution "refusing to recognize any transfers of territory in the Western Hemisphere from one non-American power to another," Hull dispatches to Biddle an urgent cable:

> The President desires that you obtain immediately an interview with Admiral Darlan [Jean François Darlan, French minister of marine] . . . and state that the views of this Government with regard to the disposition of the French Fleet have been made very clear to the French Government on previous occasions. The President desires you to say that in the opinion of this Government, should the French Government,

before concluding any armistice with the Germans, fail to see that the fleet is kept out of the hands of her opponents, the French Government will be pursuing a policy which will fatally impair the preservation of the French Empire and the eventual restoration of French independence and autonomy. Furthermore, should the French Government fail to take these steps and permit the French Fleet to be surrendered to Germany, the French Government will permanently lose the friendship and good will of the Government of the United States.[53]

This stern missive is delivered not only to Darlan but to the French foreign minister, angering both of them but forcing them to present it to the full Cabinet, which promptly decides that "the fleet should under no circumstances be turned over to the Germans and if surrender [of it] were part of the German terms, the armistice should be rejected."[54]

On June 22, 1940, in the Forest of Compiègne, in the very railway car in which the Germans were compelled to sign the armistice of 1918, a jubilant Hitler personally presides over the signing of surrender terms by France. They are harsh. More than half of metropolitan France—all the northern part of it, including Paris, and the whole of the Atlantic coastal area from Belgium to Spain—becomes a German province. France must bear the cost of German occupation. Unoccupied France is to be governed by a regime friendly to Germany. But the French fleet, neutralized of course, yet remains anchored in French ports—at Toulon and in Algeria.

Britain now stands alone in arms against the Hitler barbarians.

V

IT was on one of the last days of this hurricane's roar that the aforementioned National Defense Research Committee* was established by presidential order.

The prime mover of this enterprise, though it had been agitated for by key members of America's National Academy of Sciences ever since the Munich Agreement of 1938, was Vannevar Bush, an inventive electrical engineer who had formerly been dean of electrical engineering at the Massachusetts Institute of Technology, had become vice president of that institution, and was now president of the Carnegie Institute, in Washington. He had, in fact, resigned his MIT position and gone to Washington in large part to facilitate that organized research cooperation between the federal government and American scientists which he, President Karl Compton of MIT, Compton's Nobel laureate physicist brother, Arthur, and President James Conant of Harvard (a former chemist), among several others, had long recognized as essential to the success of any American war effort. In Washington, Bush's determination had been hardened by his extensive exposure to the pro-German, isolationist views of Charles Lindbergh. Bush was chairman of the National Advisory Committee for Aeronautics; Lindbergh was a committee member, and the two men had several lengthy private conversations during which the flier expatiated upon

*See p. 507.

German superiority in the air and in scientific organization. Bush's response to this was to work out on paper a plan whereby American engineers and scientists could have their research funded and be provided with guidelines by the national government for defense purposes. He talked it over with a friend of his, a brilliant young attorney named Oscar Cox who, though engaged in private law practice in Washington, had been occasionally called upon by the White House for special chores. Cox at once found a way through which Bush's proposal could be given legal structure—namely, by establishing a National Defense Research Committee as a working element of the newly reactivated Council for National Defense. Cox also told Bush that the best way to approach the President on such a matter as this was through Harry Hopkins who, now living in the White House, increasingly operated as Roosevelt's virtual alter ego. He arranged an interview between Bush and Hopkins.[55]

Bush approached this interview with no enthusiasm. He was a spare, lean New Englander whose engineer's education had been highly and narrowly specialized and whose natural instincts were conservative; his socioeconomic views inclined strongly to the right. He admired "big operators" in industry. He heartily disapproved of social workers as a type ("a bunch of long-haired idealists or do-gooders," in his own words) and was prepared to dislike Hopkins personally. Hence the surprise with which he at once recognized Hopkins to be as hardheaded, as realistic, as committed to "getting things done" expeditiously, as was he himself—a man utterly loyal to his chief, utterly devoid (by this time) of personal ambition, possessed of a shrewd wit and much personal charm; a man, moreover, who was mentally prepared by his brief experience with the Bureau of Standards and the Patent Bureau of the Commerce Department to understand and act upon what Bush proposed.

On June 12, 1940, Bush met Roosevelt for the first time, in an Oval Office interview arranged by Hopkins and to which Hopkins accompanied him. He presented to the President a single-page four-paragraph memorandum describing and naming a National Defense Research Council. Roosevelt read it, then reached for his pen and scrawled upon it the magical "O.K.—FDR" which caused doors to open and wheels to turn in Roosevelt's Washington. The interview, for which Hopkins had obviously prepared his chief, was opened and closed in little more than five minutes.

With Hopkins's advice, Bush then wrote a formal letter for the President's signature, addressed to himself, appointing him committee chairman and outlining his and the committee's functions. Among the letter's paragraphs was this: "Recently I appointed a special committee, with Dr. Briggs of the Bureau of Standards as Chairman, to study into the possible relationship to national defense of recent discoveries in the field of atomistics, notably the fission of uranium. I will now request that this committee report directly to you, as the function of your Committee includes this special matter, and your committee may consider it advisable to support special studies on this subject. . . ."[56]

# 15

# *Sorting Things Out*

I

ON the evening of Wednesday, June 5, 1940, the day the Germans launched their full-scale attack southward into France, there gathered in the State Dining Room of the White House some fifty young men and women, each a leader in one or another of the organizations constituting the left-leaning American youth movement. Many of them were tense, and their physical situation did nothing to relax them; for all of them, as well as Eleanor Roosevelt and Harry Hopkins, who accompanied them, were seated none too comfortably, considering the length of time they expected to sit there, in hard-seated straight-backed chairs. It was a meeting consequent in some degree upon the unhappy one last February between the President and the American Youth Congress on the White House's South Lawn. He, the President, had then displayed an irritable impatience with what he deemed the mingled ignorance and arrogance of his young listeners; had been booed by some of them, it will be remembered, for daring to describe Stalin's Russia as a ruthless dictatorship preying upon innocent democratic Finland; and had ever since felt unease over his unwontedly brusque behavior on that occasion, as well as regret over the breach then revealed between himself and politically minded young people with whom he had been accustomed to believe he had a special rapport and whose friendly support he, with and through his wife, had certainly been at pains to cultivate. The unease and regret had latterly grown in proportion to the likelihood that he as Commander in Chief of the nation's armed forces might soon be demanding great, even fatal, sacrifices of America's youth. Hence he accepted with surprising alacrity a suggestion by his wife, who had it from youth leader Joseph P. Lash (he was becoming one of her closest friends), that he engage with a select youth group in a frank question-and-answer discussion of the national problems that most greatly concerned them. He had promised three hours of his precious time on condition that those invited be, as Eleanor wrote to Joe Lash, people "whom we can trust not to go out and talk about it."[1]

What ensued was revealing of Roosevelt's basic mental and emotional attitude toward the problems he then faced—revealing also, again, of salient features of his personality and character which, already influential in world-historical event, would perhaps soon be more so than ever. Wheeled in, he greeted the young people with a warm smile, as guests in his home. The horrendous news from France weighed heavy on his mind, yet he gave full courteous attention to these guests, doing his best, which was generally

enough, to put them completely at ease. He betrayed not the slightest annoyance later on when his courtesy encountered rudeness, as it did from time to
time. He remained unprovoked by questions put to him rhetorically, questions
that were in effect hostile arguments delivered at excessive length in an abrasive manner; and he dealt patiently, kindly, respectfully, not only with hostile
questions, but also with those which, if friendly enough, betrayed a woeful lack
of information and acumen on the part of him or her who asked them. A pale,
thin Harry Hopkins, seated beside him, though answering as well as he could
the questions that were referred to him, often showed an irritable impatience
with the young people's lack of understanding. Roosevelt himself never did.
The whole of his effort was educative in intent. He manifested a flattering
eagerness to learn from his guests, to be understood by them, and to reach with
them a common ground of understanding.

What troubled the young people most, and provided the main thrust of their
questioning, was Roosevelt's perceived abandonment of the New Deal in the
face of foreign threats. They protested his subordination of social concerns
wholly to those of national defense despite the fact that the barest beginnings
had yet been made toward a solution of social problems. Grave economic and
welfare deficiencies continued for "one-third of a nation"—deficiencies in
education, housing, food, health care, wage rates, working conditions, employment opportunity. Rampant racial bigotry, legalized over large areas, imposed
second-class citizenship upon black Americans, who were systematically humiliated, deprived of their constitutionally guaranteed civil rights—including
(or especially) the right to vote—and subjected to fatal violence if they dared
challenge "white supremacy." Racial bigotry extended into the armed services,
each of which rigidly enforced racial segregation and discrimination. And none
of this was now being addressed in any meaningful way by a White House and
Congress that were spending billions of tax dollars for new battleships, for
warplanes, for armaments of all kinds, and were in process of raising new taxes
and the statutory debt ceiling to enable the spending of billions more. Moreover (this was heavily stressed), the White House was calling big-business men
to Washington to manage the expenditure of these billions, men who could be
counted upon to grab huge profits and increased power for themselves and
their corporations from such expenditure. It was a move tantamount to turning over to business reactionaries the whole of the economy, the whole of the
nation itself. And was not all this flatly contradictory of Roosevelt's own
recently spoken words? Had not he himself insisted that social welfare was an
integral part of national defense, being essential "to the spirit and morale of
a free people"? Had he not emphasized the indecency of war profiteering,
whereby a new crop of "war millionaires" would be raised up out of soil
manured with the lifeblood and dead bodies of human beings? Why, then, was
he not backing his words with deeds?

Roosevelt replied with disarmingly frank talk of the practical difficulties
with which, under extreme pressures, he must daily deal. It was true that social
welfare and national defense were of equal importance but it "is a little difficult

in our system to pursue two equally important things with equal emphasis at the same time." He faced in this time of peril two powerful enemies of human freedom, totalitarian dictatorship abroad, blindly selfish reaction at home, and he proposed to defend the national good against both of them; but it was impossible to do so simply by taking rigid, uncompromising stands upon moral principle and then making ringing public pronouncements about them. As a practical matter, to get anything done in a world of contradictions, one had to pick and choose, shifting immediate priorities in accord with shifts of immediate circumstance.

As he spoke, he was reminded of Abraham Lincoln—the Lincoln who had been forced in this house to deal responsibly with both black slavery, which he knew to be an unmitigated evil, and the splitting apart of a Union he had taken a solemn oath to preserve. The immense evil and the national disunion had been causally connected and Lincoln was acutely aware of how closely they were. Yet he had postponed his dealings with the former in order to concentrate upon the latter until circumstance enabled him to deal with both of them simultaneously as fused elements of a single problem. Thus reminded, Roosevelt invoked Lincoln in his answer to the longest, the most eloquent, and in some ways the most irritating of the question-speeches made that night. Having asked the "young man" who made the speech whether he had "read Carl Sandburg's *Lincoln*" and learned that the young man had not, Roosevelt said: "I think the impression was that Lincoln was a pretty sad man because he couldn't do all he wanted to do at one time, and I think you will find examples where Lincoln had to compromise to gain a little something. He had to compromise to make a few gains." Lincoln was, in other words, "one of those unfortunate people called a 'politician' " who, realizing that "he couldn't get it all at once" ("nobody can"), was saddened by that fact but nevertheless managed "to get a great many things for this country" by concentrating on what was possible. Perhaps the young man before him "would make a much better President than I have," Roosevelt concluded, pointing up while also softening what was essentially a stinging rebuke of youthful arrogance. "Maybe you will someday." But if "you ever sit here you will learn that you cannot, just by shouting from the housetops, get what you want all the time."[2]

Soon thereafter the allotted three hours were up, and Roosevelt, his cigarette holder with his last cigarette of the day tilted upward at a jaunty angle, was wheeled from the room into the elevator that took him to the second floor. He left behind a group of young people who, if charmed by him, remained yet dubious of his purposes and far from relieved of their anxieties. A number of them said so, as midnight came on, to Hopkins, who defended the President's position with some show of irritation, stressing the proven accuracy of Roosevelt's sense of timing, and to Eleanor, who defended her husband far more gently, kindly, patiently.*

---

*Five days later, replying to a thank-you letter from Lash, Eleanor reiterated her defense of her husband's basic strategy in current dealings with social welfare and national defense: "I . . . think

Both of the Roosevelts were continually reminded of the Civil War President during these dark June days.

Eleanor felt that Lincoln's ghost nightly prowled the halls of the second floor and haunted the room where Hopkins slept. When, late in the night before the youth-group meeting, Joe Lash and a young woman friend of his arrived at the White House, where they were to be overnight guests of hers, she at once took them to the Mall, there to share with her two night scenes that never failed to move her. One was the lighted Washington Monument mirrored in the Reflecting Pool; the other, more meaningful for her, was the giant figure of Lincoln who sits brooding, his strong sad craggy countenance illumined as if by an inner light, in his marble-columned memorial. Having returned to her White House sitting room, she conversed with her young guests well into the early morning hours, telling them, among other things, how this second floor was alive with historical presences, and that she believed she had actually heard Lincoln pacing the floor, sometimes, in the darkest hours of the night.[4]

We may be sure that her matter-of-fact, invincibly prosaic husband heard no such thing, but it is a more than merely plausible conjecture that Lincoln was called often and vividly into his consciousness all through this period. The period was, for him, a rare if not unique time of self-examination and self-definition. He struggled to make, being now at last forced to make finally and irrevocably, the most difficult personal career decision of his entire life—far more difficult than his decision to run for elective office in 1910, considerably more so than his decision to run for the New York governorship in 1928, the latter having been more a passive yielding to outer pressures than his present decision could be. And as he struggled he did well to consult as guiding example a preceding President who, though as widely different from him in overall temperament, personality, and character as any man could be, shared much with him in the way of war circumstances, attitudes toward historic challenge, strategies of decision-making, and religious faith.

There was, for major instance, Lincoln's conception of the nature of power and his attitude toward its personal exercise. Like Roosevelt, he was sharply aware that he was far more determined by the flowing tides of history than he was determinative of them, and that he would have been only somewhat less so even had he assumed the absolute dictatorial powers that were at times pressed upon him and that, like Roosevelt, he shunned. "I claim not to have controlled events," he wrote in April 1864, "but confess plainly that events

---

many of you young people are not recognizing the fact that while you cannot be sure of the future, there are immediate things that have to be handled now and we have to go on feeling confident in our ability to go on fighting for the other things in the future. I could tell you plenty of things about the way everyone of us here has to fight reaction every day and be on the look-out but that does not mean we must not use the people who sometimes unconsciously would push us back. They know nothing else and they may learn. . . ."[3]

have controlled me." Yet as he said this he fully realized that he was no mere puppet of events, no utterly helpless chip borne toward mysterious ends upon history's stream. He himself was an event decisive or influential in other events in proportion to such real power as circumstance had placed in his hands. And the power in his hands, deriving from the office he occupied, was, Lincoln admitted, substantial. It imposed upon him commensurate responsibilities. "In the very responsible position in which I happen to be placed, being a humble instrument in the hands of our Heavenly Father, as I am, as we all are, to work out his great purposes," wrote Lincoln in September 1862,

> I have desired that all my works and acts may be according to his will, and that it might be so I have sought his aid; but if, after endeavoring to do my best in the light which he affords me, I find my efforts fail, I must believe that for some purpose unknown to me he wills it otherwise. If I had had my way, this war would never have commenced. If I had had my way, this war would have ended before this; but we find it still continues, and we must believe that he permits it for some wise purpose of his own, mysterious and unknown to us. . . .

The close resemblance of this to Roosevelt's uncomplicated and unquestioned religious faith is obvious. Each man was helped to bear his heavy burden by his belief that the *ultimate* responsibility for what followed from his personal effort, provided this effort was the best he could make, was not his but God's. Lincoln's sense of personal responsibility was greater than Roosevelt's, certainly, as his sense of history was more complex and profound. He was no such actor as the Franklin Roosevelt who pleased and manipulated his audiences, enlarged his externalized personality, and expanded his experience of life, while at the same time diminishing his morally responsible essential self, by playing widely various roles on what he, with his naturally histrionic temperament, conceived to be history's stage. Lincoln manifested no superstitious faith in chance events as signs or cues. He did not much rely upon cues. He turned inward instead, consulting observations that had been thoughtfully transformed into conscience-soaked ideas while drawing also upon other inner resources that, richer than Roosevelt's, including as they did a first-rate mind, were part and parcel of an integrity, a simple purity of being, which Roosevelt notably lacked. But Lincoln's dealings with Sumner and the abolitionists clearly reveal that he, like Roosevelt in *his* dealings with isolationists and interventionists, conceived a major portion of his historic task to be the accurate measurement of the limits of the possible, this in order subsequently to operate within them to achieve beneficent change. And also like Roosevelt, he saw the limits of the possible to be those of prevailing public opinion. "Our government rests in public opinion. . . ." said Lincoln. "With public sentiment nothing can fail; without it nothing can succeed. . . . Any policy to be permanent must have public opinion at the bottom—something in accordance with the philosophy of the human mind as it is."[5] The politician who ignored this foundation for action or tried to press far beyond it must see the whole structure of his effort collapse in ruin around him. The successful politician waited patiently upon events, including events which he himself encouraged, to develop the public opinion that would sustain the action he wished to take.

II

ROOSEVELT'S response to a May 16 telegram from Grenville Clark had been in accord with this. Clark had been a fellow clerk of his in the law offices of Carter, Ledyard, and Milburn from 1907 to 1910 and was now senior partner in the rich and powerful Wall Street firm of Root, Clark, Buckner, and Ballantine. He had been one of nine men, all in their fifties or sixties and all of great social distinction, who had met informally at New York City's Harvard Club on May 8.* They constituted the executive committee of an organization officially entitled the 2nd Corps of the Military Training Camp Association (MTCA)—a nostalgic remnant of the Plattsburg Movement of elitist lawyers and businessmen, which, initiated in this same Harvard Club immediately after the sinking of the *Lusitania* in 1915, had established a military training camp for themselves at Plattsburg, New York, and agitated for military conscription nearly two years before the United States entered the Great War. On the assumption that the present Allies' war was equally that of the United States, this small group had taken a large decision: They proposed to revive a dominant Plattsburg theme by agitating for the immediate adoption of national compulsory military training and service, the first peacetime draft in American history—and this in a presidential-election year. To this end they arranged a second, much larger meeting to be held in the Harvard Club on May 22 and attended by some one hundred carefully selected invitees, men whose social prestige, conservatism, and generally Anglophilic sentiments matched their own. Among these were Colonel Henry L. Stimson; Colonel Frank Knox; Colonel William J. Donovan; former Arizona congressman Lewis Douglas, who had been Roosevelt's first budget director; and Judge Robert P. Patterson of the U.S. Circuit Court of Appeals. It was as chairman of the planning committee for this second meeting that Clark addressed his telegram to the President. It said that some of "the old Plattsburg crowd" considered "recommending and supporting compulsory military training" and wondered "whether, as a matter of timing, it is opportune to put it forward publicly at this time." Roosevelt replied two days later that he saw "no reason why the group you mention should not advocate military training, but if it is to be called 'compulsory' I am inclined to think that there is a very strong public

---

*Among them were Langdon Marvin, who had been a law partner of Roosevelt's in the 1920s; Julius Ochs Adler, general manager and vice president of *The New York Times;* and lawyer Philip A. Carroll of the famous Carroll family of Maryland (the paternal grandmother of Lucy Mercer, the great romantic love of Roosevelt's life, was a Carroll). A Harvard sophomore when Roosevelt entered college, Clark had been automatically accepted into membership by Porcellian, the ultraprestigious Harvard club whose unexpected rejection of Franklin Roosevelt had been painfully, yet fortunately educative of him. (See *FDR: The Beckoning of Destiny,* pp. 155–56.)

opinion for universal service of some kind so that every able-bodied man and woman would fit into his or her place." That is, the service should not be exclusively military but should include vocational training for entry into defense industries as well as other occupations, something Roosevelt and his wife had long had in mind. This answered Clark's specific question in no discouraging way while at the same time expressing no enthusiastic approval of what Clark's group proposed to do. Certainly it constituted no presidential endorsement.[6]

And neither did Roosevelt's reply three days later to another Clark telegram, this one asking his reaction to three draft resolutions which the May 22 meeting was to act upon. The first of these called for conscription as "the only measure that will suffice to protect this country in the present war situation." The second called for "immediate and concrete measures, short of war, in aid of the Allies, including the sale of army planes." The third called for cooperation with those who joined with Frank Knox in advocacy of "Air Plattsburgs" wherein selected civilians (presumably of the committee members' "own kind") could be trained as army pilots, an idea Knox had championed in his Chicago *Daily News.* All three of these, and especially the second, were proposals whose promotion Roosevelt must have welcomed. Yet he made to Clark a noncommittal reply. With regard to the second, he pointed to the "difficulty of proposing a concrete set of measures 'short of war' " that was politically feasible, since one had to consider "what one can get from Congress"; he expressed neither approval nor disapproval of what Clark and the others were doing.[7]

Why he did not was indicated in another of the messages he sent out on that same day. He had received a letter from Helen Rogers Reid, wife of the publisher of the New York *Herald Tribune,* in which she pressed him to come out at once for compulsory military service. His unwontedly eloquent reply expressed a generally Lincolnian idea in distinctively Lincolnian prose. "You say you have been a pacifist all your life, but now you are for universal service," he wrote. "From what extremes do pendulums swing for us as individuals. Governments, such as ours, cannot swing so far or so quickly. They can only move in keeping with the thought and will of the great majority of our people. . . . Were it otherwise the very fabric of our democracy—which after all is government by public opinion*—would be in danger of disintegration." Next day, in the evening, the hundred or so distinguished men who gathered in the Harvard Club's Biddle Room not only adopted all three of the draft resolutions —the first and third unanimously—but added to them a fourth, calling for immediate expansion of both the Regular Army and the National Guard to their full authorized strengths, pending conscription.[8]

Thereafter the movement toward compulsory military service gathered mo-

---

*Lincoln would have said, not that public opinion *governs* the United States, but that it is the source and limit of governing power. The difference between the two statements indicates the difference between principled political leadership and mere political opportunism.

mentum swiftly, spurred by the dire events in Europe. It did so with no help from Roosevelt personally. On May 28, he at Clark's request had invited Clark, Julius Adler, and Judge Patterson to meet with him in the White House on May 31; but on May 29, as more news of the Allied disaster in Flanders poured in and he prepared to ask Congress on May 31 for another billion dollars for national defense, he canceled the meeting, suggesting that Clark and the others meet instead with Hopkins. Clark rejected the suggestion; he and the others would wait until the President personally had time for them. He then awaited the May 31 presidential message to Congress with some eagerness, believing that in it the President would surely indicate the urgent need for conscription.* Instead, Roosevelt made a single vague, general reference to the government's emergency personnel requirements: "The expansion of our defense program makes it necessary that we undertake immediately the training and retraining of our people, and especially our young people, for employment in industry and in service in the Army and Navy."[9]

Nor did Clark receive encouragement from the U.S. Army. He had taken for granted Army Chief of Staff Marshall's enthusiastic approval of his enterprise, but when he and Adler conferred with the general on this eventful May 31 the two were shocked, dismayed, and angered (Clark especially was) by Marshall's courteous but cool reception of them. Hemispheric defense was the army's primary task, said Marshall, a task whose active performance might be required very soon (there were well-founded rumors of an impending Nazi coup in Uruguay), and for this a rapid *but orderly* increase of both manpower and efficiency was imperative. A sudden influx of raw recruits en masse would disrupt the process; the officers to train them were not yet available. Certainly a draft would soon be an absolute necessity, but was it wise to hit Congress with a demand for it right now, when the administration was pressing for one huge increase in military appropriations after another, and congressional isolationists, as they voted on these, watched sharp-eyed for the slightest sign of interventionist sentiment on the part of the administration? Marshall doubted it. More important, Roosevelt evidently doubted it. And Marshall, who had a principled commitment to the subordination of the military to civilian authority and knew he did not yet have the President's full confidence, deemed it no part of his obligation as staff chief to join in an agitation for legislative policies not specifically approved by the President and Commander in Chief. He said so, provoking a lecture from the decidedly unpolitic Clark during which the general's concern over Uruguay was ridiculed as an outrageous distortion of priorities in the face of the threat to American security posed by France's imminent fall. Clark lectured the general on the moral obligation that, in Clark's view, a professional in any field has to his client; Marshall, he said, was derelict of duty in not pressing upon the President military policies

---

*It was expertly estimated that approximately 750,000 men would be required to adequately maintain the airfields, service the planes, provide necessary armament and intelligence, train the pilots, and fly the planes of a 50,000-plane air force.

that, as a professional soldier, he knew to be right and necessary. Marshall's face reddened. It was only through a terrific effort of self-control that he managed to end the interview politely, abruptly, and coldly, *very* coldly, instead of in a hot flare of wrath.[10]

Yet Clark, as the leader of this endeavor, persevered with the bulldog tenacity characteristic of him, his driving energy perhaps increased by his angry disgust with what he perceived as a mindless, gutless inertia in the highest reaches of the American military. The pro-conscription agitation initiated in New York City abruptly became a national movement when, on June 3, a so-called National Emergency Committee (NEC) of the MTCA was established, chaired by Clark. Its thousand prestigious members, representing the nine MTCA corps areas into which the country was divided, became at once intensely active in all corners of the land. A vigorous national publicity campaign was launched under the direction of a former *New York Times* reporter who had been publicity director for the New York World's Fair. On June 10 there met in New York City's Century Club a group of men who, like William Allen White, were members both of the White Committee and of the Century but who, unlike White, were convinced that the fullest possible U.S. aid to the Allies would not be sufficient to save the free world, that active intervention in the war was necessary. They said so out loud that day, making headlines by adding their names to a public call for an immediate declaration of war by the United States upon the Axis powers. This call had been made the day before by "30 Notables," as newspaper headlines put it, including Lewis Mumford, Walter Millis, Herbert Agar, educator Stringfellow Barr, and retired admiral William H. Standley. Insofar as the Century Group's bold interventionism was perceived to be linked to the conscription agitation, it did the latter no good at that moment in Congress. And such linkage was bound to be perceived, since it certainly existed: Many of the most prominent agitators were Century Club members;* several of them, including nonmembers, actually joined the group as, in following weeks, it expanded to include some fifty men. All this activity achieved a specific focus when, on June 20, a conscription bill, euphemistically labeled a selective service bill, was introduced in the Senate by Nebraska Democrat Edward R. Burke (he had been targeted for oblivion by Roosevelt during the 1938 purge attempt, it will be remembered), and in the House next day by New York Republican James W. Wadsworth.[11]

At the outset of this intense activity, Clark had necessarily run head-on into the mess at the top of the War Department, and been appalled. He had long known of it, of course. The general public had long known of it and shared by a considerable majority Clark's view that Secretary of War Harry Wood-

---

*Among them were Grenville Clark, Lewis Douglas, Dean Acheson, and Henry L. Stimson. (Interestingly, Philip Kerr, who was now Lord Lothian and, as British ambassador to the United States, lobbied the Century Group to support Churchill's request for old-aged U.S. destroyers, had been a "Centurion" since 1936. Franklin Roosevelt had been one since 1922.)

ring, with his meager leadership capacities, was unfit for the office he occupied
in such times as these and that the excessively ambitious Louis Johnson, with
his ceaselessly intriguing insubordination, probably was also. But the mess
Clark now encountered was worse than he had imagined. He at once moved
with characteristic vigor to clean it up.

He lunched on May 31 at the Supreme Court Building with Justice Felix
Frankfurter, an old friend and fellow member of the Harvard Law School class
of 1906. They listed and discussed possible candidates for Woodring's post,
quickly concluding that the new secretary of war in the bipartisan Cabinet
which Roosevelt had long talked of forming should be their greatly honored
and trusted longtime friend, Henry L. Stimson.[12] Though a staunch Republican, highly conservative in his social and economic views, Stimson was totally
at odds with the isolationist wing of his party. As Hoover's secretary of state,
he had worked hard, if with little success, for collective-security action against
Japan's aggressions in the Far East; he had come out strongly in support of
the collective-security policy seemingly implicit in Roosevelt's "quarantine"
speech; he had the confidence and respectful admiration of myriads of Americans across the land, regardless of party affiliation; his had been one of the
dominating voices at the May 22 Harvard Club meeting; and he had repeatedly
inveighed against any political partisanship that impeded the swift buildup of
America's military defenses. True, he was elderly, and his age counted against
him. He would be seventy-three this coming September and had seemed to
Clark frail, and certainly very tired, during the Harvard Club meeting.[13] This
disability would be offset, however, if Stimson were provided with a strong,
vigorous assistant, a man whom Stimson liked and absolutely trusted and who
was yet in the prime of his life. Such a man was forty-nine-year-old Robert
Patterson. A distinguished lawyer with a distinguished war record (he had
been awarded the Distinguished Service Medal for heroism in action during
World War I), Patterson had, said Frankfurter to Roosevelt a few days later,
"a most extraordinary clarity and rapidity of mind" along with "unflagging
industry and great capacity for mastering complicated facts." He was, moreover, said Frankfurter, "free from the doubts and inhibitions which afflict even
many good men . . . in matters . . . calling for decision which would recoil upon
the actor in case of error."[14]

The quotations are from Frankfurter letters dated June 4 and 5, by which
time Frankfurter was sure, and had said to Clark, that their nomination of
Stimson had "struck fire" with Roosevelt during Frankfurter's face-to-face
conversation with the President on June 3. That it had indeed done so seems
indicated by admiring references that Roosevelt rather gratuitously made to
"Harry" Stimson (few of Stimson's associates called him "Harry") during the
youth-group meeting of June 5.[15]

But for a fortnight thereafter, inhibited not only by his extreme aversion to
the direct infliction of pain but also by what seemed to others his overestima-
tion of isolationist Woodring's political potency, he took no action on the
matter, despite repeated prodding by both Morgenthau and Frankfurter. Not

until the narrowly principled Woodring directly challenged presidential authority by refusing, on June 17 and again on June 18, to approve the sale of a dozen B-17 bombers to Britain (he claimed, as he had consistently claimed, that such sales violated even the revised Neutrality Act and stripped the United States of needed defenses)—not until then did Roosevelt finally act. On the morning of June 19 he requested Woodring's resignation, saying that "a succession of events both here and abroad" made Cabinet changes necessary and offering Woodring in consolation the governorship of Puerto Rico. Woodring at once submitted a resignation letter in which he refused the governorship and, evidently for public consumption, pleaded for continuation of Roosevelt's "pronounced non-intervention policy." Roosevelt made a soothing reply: "Don't worry about maintaining the non-intervention policy. We are certainly going to do just that—barring, of course, an attack on the validity of the Monroe Doctrine." He then refused to release for publication either Woodring's letter or his own (the correspondence was "too personal," he said) but went to great lengths to placate Woodring, exercising to its fullest extent his beguiling personal charm and hinting at possible future preferments. He thus managed to prevent Woodring's immediate active participation in isolationist political attacks upon the administration, attacks that would have reduced the chances for election victory in the fall.[16]

The need for a new navy secretary had long been only somewhat less great and urgent than that for Woodring's replacement. Charles Edison, who, after serving six months as acting secretary following the death of Claude Swanson, had been named Swanson's successor in January 1940, seemed to Roosevelt much too much under the thumb of the admirals, had priorities that evinced slight awareness of the magnitude of the threat posed to American security by European events, lacked force of personality, and was seriously handicapped by the deafness he had inherited from his father, the great inventor. Few and meager had been his contributions at Cabinet meetings. But the personnel problem he presented had been easily solved. Roosevelt had persuaded him to run, with the administration's blessing, for the governorship of New Jersey, this to offset the power of Jersey City's Boss Hague. Hence, the navy post had been open since May.[17] So when Roosevelt in the morning of June 19 phoned Frank Knox to renew an offer he'd made months before of a Cabinet post, he was free to offer the publisher the choice between navy and war and, rather incredibly, did so. Fortunately, as Roosevelt must have confidently expected, the navy was chosen by bluff, hearty, extremely likable Knox, a former Rough Rider and Bull Mooser who had loved TR and seemed to many (including Roosevelt) to have many of TR's traits.

Roosevelt then immediately phoned Stimson to offer him the War Department post. Stimson, though prepared by Clark and Frankfurter to accept the offer, did not at once do so. He asked for a few hours in which to consult his wife and law partners. And when he phoned the White House at seven o'clock that evening he first made sure that Roosevelt knew of his public commitment to compulsory military training (it had been a main theme of a commencement address he had delivered at Yale on June 16) and of an NBC radio address he had given on June 17, entitled "America's Interest in Britain's Fleet," wherein he argued that, since Britain's defeat would expose the United States to fatal danger, the U.S. simply could not afford to let Britain fall. Roosevelt, who had read both of these addresses in *The New York Times,* expressed a noncommittal "sympathy" with Stimson's views on conscription and a wholehearted approval of the radio talk. Stimson then accepted the Cabinet appointment with the explicit understanding that, within a few days, Judge Patterson would be appointed to replace Louis Johnson as assistant secretary.[18]

This last didn't happen, however, as we may here anticipate.

Roosevelt had repeatedly encouraged not only Johnson's hard-driving efforts toward industrial mobilization ("Go ahead!" he had said. "I'll back you up") but also Johnson's ambition to become secretary of war. The announcement of the Stimson-Knox appointments on June 20 (the day the Burke-Wadsworth selective service bill was introduced) was therefore, for Johnson, an especially bitter blow. There ensued "a scene" between Johnson and Roosevelt "which must have been painful," as Berle recorded in his diary after a distraught Johnson, on June 25, had told him of it. "The President . . . told him that he recognized his commitment to make Louis Secretary of War, but the political situation had not worked out that way. Louis . . . thereupon offered his resignation, assuming that Stimson would want his own assistants. The President [violating his commitment to Stimson] declined the resignation, saying that they could not [had not the time to] educate a new Assistant and Louis had to go on and do the work, and all would be well."[19] But of course all was not well. Stimson took over as secretary on July 10, his appointment having been confirmed by a Senate vote of 56 to 28 the day before, this after committee hearings during which he endured sharp hostile questioning from Taft and other isolationists. Johnson yet remained assistant secretary—had, indeed, been acting secretary following Woodring's departure. And Johnson's continuation in office "kept a much disorganized Department in a continual state of disorganization," as Stimson complained to a friend. The new secretary protested to the White House, several times. Roosevelt counseled patience. Gradually thereafter, as day after day passed by, Stimson realized that Johnson intended to stay on, might have been encouraged by the White House to do so, and evidently believed that Patterson was to be brought in as the secretary's special personal assistant. Stimson then (on July 19) wrote a stiff letter to the President, saying it was imperative that Patterson come in *at once* as assistant secretary. But more days passed with no White House action on the matter. Finally, a near desperate Stimson turned to Morgenthau, with whom he had worked closely on the procurement of planes and other supplies for Britain— and Morgenthau at last triggered the needed action on July 23 by phoning Roosevelt, then at Hyde Park, and eliciting from him a firm promise to request Johnson's resignation forthwith. Roosevelt couldn't bring himself to do so himself, however: He had Pa Watson convey the doomful message. And upon hearing the bad news, "Louie broke down and cried like a baby," as Watson said to Morgenthau soon afterward.[20]

Johnson's resignation and Patterson's appointment were announced on July 26.

### III

MEANWHILE, in this presidential-election year, the political pot had been boiling faster and faster. The announcement of the Knox and Stimson appointments came just four days before the formal opening of the Republican National Convention in Philadelphia, and it caused the pot to boil over with, for many an orthodox Republican, scalding fury. Party professionals of isolationist bent, led by national committee chairman John D. M. Hamilton, damned Roosevelt for perpetrating the dirtiest political trick in all American history, aided and abetted by unspeakable treachery on the part of Knox and Stimson, whom Hamilton reportedly read out of the party. But of course other Republicans, some of the most prestigious of whom had been actively involved in the event, as we have seen, loudly and publicly cheered it. Knox and Stimson had "done the patriotic thing," editorialized William Allen White, and if his fellow Republicans in the face of the Nazi-Fascist threat to civilization permitted themselves to "bleat like sheep for peace at any price, my beloved party will not even carry Maine and Vermont."[21]

Yet there could be no doubt, even among such as Grenville Clark, Henry Stimson, and White, that the maneuver weakened the election chances of the Republican party in a presidential year by exposing and accentuating the bitterness of the split between that party's isolationist and internationalist wings. At the same time it strengthened Roosevelt's candidacy if he chose to run, while also seemingly indicating that he certainly *would* run, by enabling him to present himself to the electorate as a unifying figure—one who, recognizing the isolationist–interventionist split in his own party (it was considerably less wide and bitter than that in the Republican party, Democratic isolationism being relatively much weaker), firmly subordinated partisanship to pursuit of the national good. There was equally no doubt that this aspect of the matter, viewed and assessed by Franklin Roosevelt, had played a part in his calculations.

The Philadelphia convention of 1940 was one of the relatively few Republican national conventions, from 1908 until today, that were authentically dramatic. These quadrennial Republican exercises have been for the most part cut-and-dried affairs—spectacles of which nearly all the elements have been both predictable and artificially colored, having as their main purpose the packaging in attractive disguise of candidates and programs which, frankly exposed to public view, would be seen to serve very few at the expense of very many. This is because the Republican party in its highest echelons has long been (perhaps since its first shaping in the Grant years) a single-interest party with, consequently, a single mind—increasingly so as economic power has become increasingly concentrated in a contracting number of giant corporations. It has little need to make up its mind on fundamental issues through public debate and deliberation since its mind, being identical with the big-business pocketbook interest, is always essentially made up. But the 1940 convention was different. The American business community, united as always in its hostility to liberal domestic policies, was that year split apart in its view of foreign affairs, and as a result of this, and of the emergence during the pre-convention campaigning of a potent candidate utterly unlike any the Republicans had ever fielded before, the Philadelphia show acquired a rare spectator appeal. It had suspense. Those who watched awaited eagerly (not knowing, for a change) what would come next, and became genuinely interested in how it all would turn out.

The uniquely different candidate was dark horse Wendell L. Willkie. Earlier in this narrative we have seen him operate as president of the giant utility holding company Commonwealth and Southern, have seen him fight tooth and nail (he went at everything *hard*) against the electric-power policies of the TVA and the mandatory "death sentence" clause of the Wheeler-Rayburn Anti–Holding Company Bill of 1935.* He was still fighting a rearguard action against the mandated liquidation of Commonwealth and Southern in early 1940. This had naturally given him high standing among Roosevelt-hating businessmen but was not likely to recommend him strongly to the common man, much less surround him with the aura of a folk hero. Yet a folk hero of sorts he had become.

He had some qualifications for such a role, including immense personal magnetism. Physically, he was a bearlike figure of a man, more than six feet tall, broad of face, broad of shoulder, deep of chest, who, however, was not at all athletic, partly because he had had little time for sports but mostly because he lacked the necessary physical coordination. He most notably lacked a sense of rhythm, which lowered his appreciation of music and prevented his ever learning to dance. Being a lover of good food who exercised too little, he was somewhat overweight and would have been much more so had he not been a chain-smoker of cigarettes. This last manifested a note that sounded insistently through his personality into the few ears attuned to such vibrations: the note of incipient hysteria. Thus the general impression he made was somewhat like that of the late Huey Long, whose dimple-chinned countenance his own somewhat resembled—was much like that of the NRA's Hugh Johnson, whom he also resembled physically and who, in his syndicated newspaper column, was among the first to tout him as a presidential candidate. It was an impression of torrential energy pressing always against the bounds of its control and sometimes bursting through them. He paid little attention to his appearance —his hair was generally tousled, his suits often looked as if they'd been slept

---

*See *FDR: The New Deal Years,* pp. 92–93 and 531; and pp. 168, 169, and 301–2 of the present volume.

in—and his rural Midwestern manners, though courteous, were markedly informal. He did not lack social adroitness. He was an interesting conversationalist, witty, well informed, incisive, and honestly interested in what others had to say. Most people, men and women, found him personally abnormally attractive.

Of his basic moral character, much was explicable in terms of his family background and upbringing. Born and raised in modest circumstances in the small town of Elwood, Indiana, he was of pure German-American stock, all four of his grandparents having emigrated from Germany before the Civil War[22] to escape the freedom-denying reaction that accompanied and followed the Congress of Vienna and the crushed revolutionary movement of 1848. His hard-driving mother, née Henrietta Trisch, was a vivid champion and exemplar of personal freedom—her own, primarily. She was a flouter of inhibiting conventions—had been the first woman in her hometown to smoke cigarettes publicly and the first to wear French high heels; she was the first woman ever admitted to the Indiana bar, and one of the first in her state actually to practice law, this in partnership with her lawyer husband, Hermann. She did so while mothering six children—four boys, two girls—of whom Lewis Wendell (he later reversed the names) was, in 1892, the fourthborn. She was, from all accounts, a not very lovable personality. Her assertive independence was evidently joined to a typically Germanic power lust. She brooked no opposition that she could overcome; she strove to dominate, exercising "a dread power at the family hearth," as a biographer has written. She also "continuously dinned into [the] . . . young minds" of her children her ambitions for their "success."[23]

But her famous son's resultant success anxiety was fortunately mitigated, and on many an occasion overcome, by a generosity of spirit and a passion for democracy and simple justice, which evidently came to him through his father. Hermann Willkie was a first-rate lawyer who in an urban environment could have commanded large fees but, as Joseph Barnes writes, "had no ambition to be anything more than he was [a small-town lawyer], to get anywhere, to pile up a fortune."[24] Though a far gentler personality than his wife, he was by no means meek and mild. He had strong opinions, he expressed them strongly, and since they were often not those of the "best people" of the town he was regarded by them somewhat askance. He was, for instance, a fervent Bryan Democrat who provoked controversy by defending labor organization and crusading for the free-speech rights of the exponents of unpopular causes. He was committed to helping the exploited and ill-used of our society. In religion, though he became with his wife a pillar of the local Methodist church, he was essentially agnostic—had become so when he rebelled against the Catholic faith in which he had been raised—but he was nonetheless concerned, as was his wife, to develop in their children solid moral values, along with a strength of character great enough to resist vicious temptations, and was happy to have Methodism help in this. Most important, both he and his wife were great readers who built up a home library of some seven thousand books and inculcated in all their children, in young Lewis Wendell especially, a love of reading and of learning, and an immense respect for those engaged in intellectual pursuits.

Maternal influence seems evident in the Wendell Willkie who, upon receiving his A.B. and law degrees at Indiana University, chose to practice remunerative corporation law. Beginning in the legal department of the Firestone Tire and Rubber Company in Akron, Ohio, then switching to partnership in a leading Akron law firm, then moving to Wall Street as general counsel of a giant utilities holding company, he roared up the pathway to success through the Roaring Twenties with enormous energetic drive, his eyes always wide open and fixed upon the main chance. He *had* to win his courtroom cases! He *had* to rise, to get ahead! But paternal influence is also discernible—in the Willkie who remained an outspoken Democrat and thus set himself at odds politically with most of those who could advance him in the business world (Harvey Firestone once told him that, though he liked him, he didn't think he'd "ever amount to a great deal" because he was a Democrat and "no Democrat can ever amount to much"[25]); in the Willkie who, at the high tide of the Ku Klux Klan's power in Ohio, organized and led a successful fight to eliminate Klan influence from Akron's school administration; in the Willkie who dared challenge in public speech, during a 1929 utilities-executive conference, the arrogant and then seemingly omnipotent utilities magnate Samuel Insull, when Insull proposed ways and means of silencing "radical agitators" who dared criticize big-utility executives; and in the Willkie who (though here his mother's influence is also evident) sought out and won admission to New York City's prestigious intellectual circles, including membership, as of 1937, in the Century Club.* Of First Amendment principles his manifest understanding was more profound, as his commitment to them was far stronger (it was, indeed, absolute), than Franklin Roosevelt's.

Willkie's emphatic move into the ranks of big-business men, which coincided with his move to New York City in 1929, had no initial effect upon his political views or party affiliation. He attended the 1932 Democratic convention, not as a delegate but as an influential supporter of utilities lawyer Newton D. Baker, whose internationalist views he wholly shared. He voted for Roosevelt that year and made a very modest financial contribution ($150) to the Roosevelt campaign. But Roosevelt's power policy soon alienated Willkie, of course, and, though remaining a registered Democrat, he voted for Landon, if with no enthusiasm, in 1936. By then he was, as regards party politics, a deeply divided man. He approved the New Deal's labor, welfare, and conservation programs, argued publicly that Social Security should cover all citizens, even favored the TVA as a power-development and regional-planning enterprise, objecting only (if vehemently) to its power-distribution policy. In 1937's New York City mayoralty campaign he voted for Fusion candidate Fiorello

---

*The Century Association (to use its official name) constitutionally defines itself as an organization "composed of authors, artists, and amateurs of letters and the fine arts."

La Guardia. A year later he still considered himself a Democrat, referring in a major public speech (October 1938) to the Democratic party "of which, incidentally, I am a member." He voted that year for Democrat Lehman against Republican Dewey in New York's gubernatorial race, a race Lehman narrowly won. But he disliked and deeply distrusted Franklin Roosevelt personally, and was more and more convinced that the Democrats under Roosevelt's leadership had forsaken the true liberal philosophy which, grounded in individual liberty, was concerned to prevent *all* liberty-threatening concentrations of power, whether in governmental or private hands. Under Roosevelt, the federal government, and especially the office of the presidency, was growing, Willkie thought, too big, too powerful. Roosevelt's foreign policy, on the other hand, insofar as it was a collective-security policy, commanded his wholehearted allegiance. He remained strongly committed to the League of Nations idea, was thus wholly opposed to the dominant foreign-policy attitude of the Republican party.

It was therefore with extreme reluctance, and very belatedly in view of the ambition soon to consume him, that he finally formally switched his party allegiance. "If he's a Republican—is he?—you can't wholly count out Willkie [as a 1940 presidential possibility]," wrote Arthur Krock in an influential *New York Times* column on February 23, 1939. Krock went on to say that "1940 will be a little early to bring out a utilities man. But if anything like that can be put over, I'd watch Willkie."* Not until several weeks after this did Willkie register as a Republican, and he did so then "partly because of the urgings of his son and his wife," as Ellsworth Barnard has written.[26]

Thereafter his public speech and published writing, joined with the personal magnetism that attracted people to him as individuals and in crowds, focused upon him an increasing popular attention. He had early discovered in himself a rare talent for impromptu, extemporaneous public speaking—an ability to adapt an unprepared public speech to the immediate mood and interests of the audience he addressed while at the same time saying something substantial (he did have something to say) with force and sincerity. He had abundantly exercised this talent in Akron. He continued to do so, before much larger audiences, after his 1929 move to New York, where he also fully exercised his considerable journalistic ability (he contributed articles and book reviews to such serious journals as *Atlantic Monthly* and *New Republic,* also popularly written pieces to the mass-circulating *Reader's Digest* and *Saturday Evening Post*). By early 1940, the hinting and whispering about him as a potential Republican political figure had become a full-voiced and ever louder demand that he enter the presidential race. Willkie initially regarded such talk as absurd in view of the fact that he had gained his prominence as a top executive in an industry notorious for exploitive arrogance and corruptive political

---

*The phrases "bring out" and "put over" may seem to some indicative of the way in which Republican presidential candiates are typically chosen by the party's top echelon and of the contempt for the average voter's intelligence that is implicit in this process.

influence. But he was repeatedly reminded that, way back in January 1938, he was generally deemed to have "won" a nationally broadcast radio debate on national issues with the extremely able and articulate Robert H. Jackson; he had thereby allegedly greatly discouraged an administration buildup of Jackson as potential Democratic presidential nominee. And by late mid-1939 the published talk of him as presidential material, by columnists, magazine-article writers, and prominent public speakers, was so loud that *Time* magazine mentioned it, though calling it "mildly fantastic," in a July 31, 1939, issue, having his picture on its cover and dealing at length with the TVA–Commonwealth and Southern battle, now ended with the TVA's purchase of the latter's operating facilities.[27] He could not blink the fact that, as April 1940 came on, though his name had not been entered in a single primary, he as potential Republican presidential nominee was evoking more spontaneous popular excitement than were the declared and organized candidacies of Dewey, Vandenberg, or Taft, the three front-runners.

The excitement increased with Willkie's appearance on April 9, 1940, as guest of the extremely popular network radio show "Information Please." On it, a guest matched wits and measured his fund of general information against those of four permanent panel members, each famous in a different field, with literary critic Clifton Fadiman of *The New Yorker* as master of ceremonies. It was a challenging exposure of mind and personality to a huge public, and several big-name guests had been embarrassed by its revelation of appalling gaps in their information—also of sluggish mental operations. Willkie, however, scored a triumph. Both the panel and the national audience were impressed by the quickness of his intelligence (he traded wisecracks on equal terms with the urbane and witty Fadiman), by the amount and variety of his general knowledge, and by the warm friendliness of his person. On that same April 9, lawyer Oren Root, nephew of Grenville Clark's law partner Elihu Root, Jr., declared for Willkie's candidacy, doing so because of Willkie's stand for all-out U.S. aid (short of war) for the Allies, and mailed out to Harvard, Yale, and Princeton alumni some two thousand copies of a printed statement of support for Willkie, each with spaces for fifteen signatures. The response was such that five days later, Root sent out an additional twenty thousand copies of the statement and soon thereafter took leave of absence from his law firm in order "to organize the people's demand for Willkie." Almost overnight, Willkie clubs sprang up all across America.

This Root activity was apparently the final, decisive shove for Willkie. Certainly he needed none further. In May, he plunged into the race with both feet, both of them churning at a furious pace, and the pace never slackened from then on to the race's end. Since primary elections as a way of securing convention delegates were unavailable to him, and knowing he could expect no help from the party bosses, he at once set out to woo the Republican rank and file along with anti-Roosevelt Democrats. He did so strenuously, making within five weeks some fifteen or twenty speeches to largely Republican crowds in at least fourteen widely scattered cities. They were effective speeches. Each of them set its fire of enthusiasm. And these were soon fanned into a sheet of flame across the land by a loosely organized coalition of so-called passionate amateurs of politics who, however, were highly skilled professionals in the fields of public relations, of advertising, of journalism. They represented, these professionals—indeed, they were most of them employees of—some of the most powerful publishers in America, including Roy Howard of the Scripps-Howard newspapers; Henry Luce of *Time, Life,* and *Fortune* (Russell Davenport resigned as managing editor of *Fortune* to devote himself full-time to Willkie); the Cowles brothers, John and Gardner Jr., with their Minneapolis papers, their Des Moines *Register and Tribune,* their *Life*-rivaling picture magazine, *Look;* and Ogden and Helen Reid of the New York *Herald Tribune.* Hence the "spontaneous" eruption of Willkie support was beautifully planned and shrewdly directed. Bragged one of the public-relations men later on: "It should never be forgotten that the 'Willkie boom' was one of the best engineered jobs in history."[28]

This was a new phenomenon in America's national political life, and one that numerous observers, seeing it as precedent-setting, heartily deplored. It seemed to them dangerously manipulative, diverting into artificial channels while also interestedly changing the character of public information which, as the lifeblood of democracy, should flow freely and unpolluted through neutral communication facilities into the public mind. None could deny, however, that this "amateurish" labor, abundantly aided by Willkie's strenuous exercise of his own talents, passed the pragmatic test triumphantly. It "worked" on its own terms; it produced its intended effect.

On May 8, a Gallup poll of rank-and-file Republicans showed Willkie in fourth place among Republican presidential contenders. Dewey was in first place, with 67 percent of the sample vote, Vandenberg in second with 14 percent, Taft in third with 12 percent. Willkie had at that time the support of a mere 3 percent, according to Gallup—hardly enough to make him a truly viable candidate. But in the three following polls, spaced eight days to two weeks apart, Dewey's percentage declined to 52 and Vandenberg's (precipitously) to 12, while Taft's increased to 13 and Willkie's to 17, putting him in second place. He remained second in a poll published on June 21, just three days before the Philadelphia convention opened, but by then his percentage of the poll sample's vote had climbed to 29, while Dewey's had declined to 47. Both Taft and Vandenberg were seemingly out of the race, if party rank-and-file opinion prevailed (by no means a foregone conclusion), their shares having declined to 8 percent piece.[29] On the following day, June 22, Willkie went to Philadelphia where, by the time the convention formally opened, he had already won through personal contacts a considerable number of formerly uncommitted delegates.

What followed was an irony delicious or bitter, depending on point of view, but extreme, certainly, from any point of view.

Willkie's descent upon the city, portrayed in a widely reprinted newspaper cartoon as that of a tornado, was viewed with emotions ranging from distaste

to horror by members of the Republican Old Guard who, as always, had the
convention's formal procedures under their control. Willkie's efforts to persuade them into his camp were at the outset emphatically rebuffed. (Famous
in later years became the response made by former senator James E. Watson
of Indiana when Willkie, a fellow Hoosier and, indeed, Indiana's favorite son,
sought his support. "You're a good Methodist, don't you believe in conversion?" asked Willkie, alluding to his former membership in the Democratic
party. "Yes, Wendell," replied Watson. "If a whore repented and wanted to
join the church I'd personally welcome her and lead her up the aisle to a pew.
But, by the Eternal, I'd not ask her to lead the choir the first night!"[30]) Other
delegates, however, jarred to the roots of their being by the fall of France and
the implications of the Knox-Stimson appointments, were susceptible to
Willkie's charm and persuaded by his arguments. He had the courage of
convictions far more appealing to the ordinary citizen who commonly voted
Republican than they were to the party's bosses, against whom some delegates
were inclined to rebel. And he expressed these convictions with breathtaking
frankness. "I don't know Joe Pew," he had said to a reporter shortly before
the convention opened, referring to the millionaire oilman who dominated the
Republican organization in Pennsylvania and presumably controlled that
state's seventy-two convention votes, "but I am 100 percent against his policy
of turning the Republican Party back to the days of Harding and Coolidge."[31]
Persuasive, too, were the number and fervor of the pro-Willkie letters, postcards, and telegrams that every delegate received from fellow residents of his
community. Delegates' names and addresses had been distributed by local
Willkie clubs and had been published in the local press, along with admoni-
tions to exert pressure. The result was a considerable number of such communications addressed to delegates before they left home, then a veritable flood
of them after the delegates were in Philadelphia. Nor could any delegate have
been wholly immune to the influence of the galleries. These were packed with
Willkie supporters who loudly cheered every mention of his name and often
booed almost as loudly the names of his rivals. By all this it was borne in upon
delegates, who might otherwise have resisted the fact, that Willkie was a truly
interesting, even exciting personality—immensely more attractive than dry,
colorless Robert Taft or than prosecuting attorney Thomas Dewey, whose
sharp-edged personality seemed to many to have been stamped out of sheet
metal—and should therefore be more electable by far than his rivals.

What persuaded individual delegates had coercive effect upon the convention's key decision-makers, hence upon the convention as a whole. The convention, initially resisting, was driven to conform with popular Republican
opinion. On the first nominating ballot Willkie polled 105 votes, more than
expected but far behind Dewey's 360 and well behind Taft's surprisingly small
189. He remained in third place, though with a substantial gain in votes, after
the second ballot. On the third ballot, he replaced Taft in second place, with
259 votes compared to Dewey's 315. He then took the lead, and doomed
Dewey's chances, by polling 306 votes against Dewey's 254 on ballot number

four; he made further gains on ballot five, and, at the close of the sixth ballot, at one-thirty in the morning of Friday, June 28, 1940, was officially proclaimed the Republican candidate for President of the United States.

It was an exhilarating personal triumph, certainly, and dramatic in its impact upon the national public. But it was won far more on grounds Willkie shared with Roosevelt and the New Deal than upon those he shared with the hard core of his own party. Indeed, the latter grounds were hard to discern —if, in fact, they existed. Frankly flatly opposed to the isolationism that dominated his party's congressional delegation, he was almost as frankly and flatly opposed to every other of that delegation's major differences from the New Deal. Moreover, with respect to personality, he had been nominated because of qualities (charm, warmth, compassion for the underdog) that more closely resembled Franklin Roosevelt's than they did those of any of his rivals. And this rich irony was further enriched by the selection of his running mate. For vice president, the convention chose, with Willkie's concurrence, Charles L. McNary of Oregon, the Senate minority leader. McNary was an isolationist, an opponent of the administration's reciprocal trade agreement policy, which Willkie strongly supported. Coming from the electricity-starved Northwest, he had been a strong supporter of the TVA and the administration's power policy in general. And he had been a leader of the initial convention opposition to Willkie's candidacy.

It now became Willkie's task to convince the American public that the differences between him and Roosevelt as personalities, and between his philosophy of government and that of the New Deal, approximated those between life and death. The challenge was daunting. His initial response to it, in the formal acceptance speech he would deliver in his old hometown of Elwood in mid-August, would be widely deemed inadequate. It was "a synthesis of Guffey's First Reader, the Genealogy of Indiana, the collected speeches of Tom Girdler, and the *New Republic,*" according to Norman Thomas, who would again be the Socialist party's presidential candidate. "He agreed with Mr. Roosevelt's entire program of social reform—and said it was leading to disaster."[32]

IV

NEVERTHELESS, Roosevelt at once recognized Willkie as a formidable candidate, by far the best vote-getter the Republicans could have chosen in this year of terror and turmoil. He also recognized that the choice of McNary as running mate, for all its logical inconsistency with respect to issues, was a good one in terms of vote-getting potency. He said so at his Cabinet meeting on June 28, where his judgment was emphatically agreed with by both Ickes and Jim Farley. He then proceeded to expound as a possible basis for his own party's countercampaign the "theory that Willkie represents a new concept in American politics—the concept of the 'corporate state'" on the order of Fascist Italy.[33] It was a theory wholly contradictory to the opposition candidate's character and convictions, as Roosevelt would learn when he knew Willkie better, but it was by no means inconsistent with the way in which Willkie's nomination had been brought about—a way giving ample grounds for a belief that this "new" Republican was but an attractive front for big-business reactionaries who intended to use him, whether he realized it or not, to achieve reactionary aims. Joined with Willkie's perceived formidability as vote-getter, this belief became a final congealing factor in the hitherto fluid mishmash of conflicting emotions and ideas that had swirled through Roosevelt's head whenever he contemplated, during this last year, the possibility of seeking a third term. A congealing factor was urgently needed; an irrevocable decision must be made within a few days. The 1940 Democratic National Convention was to open in Chicago on Monday morning, July 15.

So it was that Roosevelt came to the last portion of his long moment of truth —the most testing such moment, perhaps, since his polio crisis of the early 1920s—and much evidence indicates the way in which he finally sorted things out in his mind and reached, at last, a conclusion.

Of one thing he had long been certain, as we have seen. He yearned to retire from his high office. He had had his fill of personal power and glory; he wanted now to relax and enjoy. Aside from playing with his stamp collection, whereby he was imaginatively transported to distant places and injected into different climes and cultures, his favorite recreation these last weeks had been, as it would also be in the months ahead, his review with Harry Hopkins in elaborate detail of plans for his and Harry's retirement. He talked of "starting an entirely new kind of country newspaper, a new kind of college, and even a new kind of roadside hot-dog stand," as Robert E. Sherwood has written. For years, ever since his winters aboard his houseboat *Larooco* in the early 1920s, he had had in mind the purchase of a Florida key, Channel Key, which lies about halfway along the line of islets between Key Largo and Key West, in order to establish upon it a fishing retreat. He had begun recently talking about this as a definite possibility for himself and Hopkins; he would soon make definite moves toward purchase of the key, would design on paper a cable-anchored structure wherein he and Hopkins could survive South Atlantic hurricanes more comfortably and far more certainly than either of them could the eventful hurricanes now sweeping the White House.[34] For Roosevelt, though generally immunized by Christian fatalism against health anxieties, could not totally ignore a warning sign given him a few months ago—a sign that his health just might be dangerously compromised and liable to collapse if subjected to the pressures of another four years of the presidency. No hint of this had reached or would ever reach the general public, but one evening the previous February, while at table alone with Missy and Bill Bullitt in the White House, he had gone suddenly pale and limp, then lapsed into momentary unconsciousness. A distraught Missy had at once summoned Dr. McIntire, who took charge while she and Bullitt withdrew. McIntire later told them in evidently soothing tones, though Missy remained unsoothed, that the President had suffered "a very slight heart attack."[35]

Roosevelt might well have regarded this as a sure sign from on high that his personal desire coincided with the divine will had it not been embedded, alas, in such an abundance of signs to the contrary—signs delivered to him, not as mistakable hints (McIntire had assured him his health was basically sound) but as hard, bludgeoning facts. The incredibly swift fall of France was a fact. The consequent desperate situation of Britain was a fact. The grave danger in which this placed the United States was a fact. The need for an immense national effort to meet the threat was a fact. And so, as a result, was the need for an experienced leader in the White House who could do what Lincoln had done when last this nation's very survival was at stake—a leader who could maintain the American Union against all forces that would split it apart, a leader who could take a united nation into war should this prove necessary, as almost certainly it would, while preserving intact both the liberties guaranteed by the Bill of Rights and the social gains that the New Deal had made. Who other than Franklin Roosevelt could this leader be?

Thanks largely to his own sphinx-riddling operations, as he may or may not have admitted to himself, there was now no other Democrat of sufficient standing and ability to take on Wendell Willkie in an election contest with any assurance of victory. Cordell Hull was no doubt the Democrat other than himself most likely to win but, elderly and showing his age, he was a far less exciting and attractive personality than Willkie. Moreover, if he did win, he was likely to do so on terms less liberal, as regards domestic policy, than those that Willkie, at least, avowed. A Hull victory in such times as these would mean a sharp turn to the right for the Democratic party—a return of it very swiftly to the business domination, indistinguishable from that of the Republicans, that had characterized its top leadership in the days of John W. Davis and John J. Raskob. This would certainly happen if Jim Farley won the White House. With these two eliminated, there was left, as a major Democratic contender, only John Nance Garner, and he had been dismissed by Roosevelt long ago (in talk with Farley) as "simply impossible." As for what would happen to the country under a Willkie presidency, Roosevelt remained in early July of the same mind he had expressed immediately following Willkie's nomination. This "new" Republican might personally be in some respects the "true liberal" he claimed to be, but if he were he would find himself isolated in his own party, frustrated and defeated at every turn by that party's dominating forces. Look at what had happened to earlier Republican leaders who had favored human values over property values—TR, Robert La Follette, George Norris. Each had been either driven from the party or, like William Allen White, rendered ineffective within it. And in such times as these, under such pressures as he would face with the advice of such slickly cynical manipulators of popular opinion as had "engineered" his nomination, a President Willkie would almost certainly preside over the birth of a cold, monstrous, machine-like Corporate America which, organized for war, would have as its dominant if hidden purpose the maximization of big-business profits.

Thus the case as it presented itself to Franklin Roosevelt during the final days of his deliberations. Thus the case he in turn presented to Justice Felix Frankfurter whose opinion he sought, in lengthy conversation, on one of these final days. He then asked Frankfurter to draft a memorandum stating the case as he, Frankfurter, saw it. Frankfurter at once did so, delivering it a few days later in person and in longhand to the White House, along with a typewritten memo from lawyer-poet Archibald MacLeish whom Roosevelt, upon Frankfurter's glowing recommendation, had appointed librarian of Congress in the late spring of 1939 and whose ideas on this third-term matter Frankfurter had, in strictest confidence, requested.

"The task of safeguarding our institutions is two-fold," wrote Frankfurter. "One must be accomplished . . . by the Armed Forces of the nation. The other, by the united but diversified efforts of the . . . men and women of the country, individually and banded together in trade unions and farm granges, trade associations and cooperatives, and in that common effort of all of the people which is Government. For we must continue to pursue our two great actions at the same time: we must be ready to defend the right of our democracy to continue to exist; we must have a democratic society worthy of survival." Roosevelt's eight-year record protected him against the charge that, in running again, he strove

to seize power as a "strong man." You would in fact be protecting the nation from . . . convulsions, dangers and upheavals . . . that could indeed lead to the establishment of arbitrary power in Washington by men no longer responsible to the values of democracy and the wishes of Lincoln's common people. . . . You can gladly submit your purpose, your achievements, and your record to the judgment of your countrymen for a third term in the midst of unprecedented conditions that impose their own duties and obligations. A President must continue in office when the voice of the people calls him to the continuing task.

The enclosed MacLeish memo concurred in the necessity of Roosevelt's running for a third term but argued that he "should not 'accept a call' " from the people. "Undoubtedly the actual truth is that he will be doing precisely that. But to put it that way is to lead with the chin. I can see the cartoons from here." What Roosevelt had better do was respond to the call of duty, laying aside "in the face of the public danger" his wishes and plans for a return to private life. No man summoned by a majority of his party and of the electorate to serve in the nation's highest office in such parlous times as these could in good conscience ignore the summons. . . .[36]

So the decision that was widely believed to have been made many months ago was now in fact at last made.

Roosevelt would run again.

But he would do so on his own terms. Party leaders and party bosses, desperate to keep the Democratic party in office, had been begging him for months to run. He would make it clear to them that he now did so as a self-sacrificial act and that he expected them, in their turn, to sacrifice "politics as usual" to the urgent necessity to unite a free, democratic, and progressive

America, and arm her, in opposition to the only serious foreign threat to her survival that she had ever faced. He would state conditions; he would adamantly adhere to them. The party platform on which he ran must be a brief, clear statement of liberal principles with the slightest possible of necessary concession, in its foreign-policy plank, to the extreme antiwar sentiment which yet widely prevailed in the land. This plank might well consist of a single sentence: "We do not want to become involved in any foreign war"; or "We are opposed to this country's participation in any wars, unless for the protection of the Western Hemisphere"; or "We are in favor of extending aid to democracies in their struggle against totalitarian powers, within the law."[37]

The question of who should be Roosevelt's running mate was one that may have remained open, if very narrowly, even as the convention began, but he was determined from the first that he alone would do the choosing. No vice presidential candidate would be foisted upon him by convention managers for the sole purpose of "strengthening the ticket" or mollifying party conservatives. He would accept neither RFC's Jesse Jones nor House Speaker William B. Bankhead. Most emphatically he would not accept Garner. They were all too conservative. He unenthusiastically but seriously considered Cordell Hull, who would probably be the best vote-getter of all the available candidates, had high standing with Congress, and saw eye to eye with him on international affairs. He soon abandoned the idea, however. For if he must assume the immense probability that he would live well beyond another four years (else why was the need for him to seek a third term so impressively indicated by factual signs?), he must also concede the distinct possibility that he would fail to do so (else why had he been presented with that single emphatic sign of his mortality?). In the latter case, every argument against the choice of Hull for first place applied with only slightly less force to the choice of him for second. Elderly, conservative on domestic issues, of uncertain health, Hull, moreover, in conversations with Roosevelt, had said flatly that he did not want the vice presidency; he preferred to remain secretary of state. Roosevelt personally liked the ingratiating Senator James F. Byrnes of South Carolina, who was frankly and fervently a candidate for the post, but Byrnes had very dubious liberal credentials, strong labor opposition, and, as a white supremacist in one of the most racist states in the Union, the even stronger opposition of black Americans who constituted an important voting bloc in Northern cities. Moreover, Byrnes was a born Catholic who had left the Church and thus incurred what Rosenman calls "a double-disadvantage politically; for not only would anti-Catholic bigots oppose him, but Catholics themselves might resent his change of religion."[38]

Roosevelt finally decided, largely because of that doubt about his own life span, that his vice president must be a man still in the prime of life and in excellent health, who had truly strong liberal and internationalist convictions along with an acute sense of world history and of the role America should play in it. This man, Roosevelt concluded, was Secretary of Agriculture Henry Agard Wallace.

That conclusion was probably reached during the first week of July. For at the end of that week, during a memorable conversation with Jim Farley, of which an account is given below, he reviewed the quite lengthy list of vice presidential possibilities, dismissing one after another of them on grounds of ideology or health or old age while adding to that list, surprisingly for Farley, the name of Henry Wallace. What did Farley think of Wallace for the post? Not much, Farley promptly, emphatically replied: Wallace would detract from the strength of the ticket, for he did not have the support in the Farm Belt that Roosevelt thought he had, and he would cost Roosevelt votes in the East. Moreover, he was personally a strange character, a "mystic" whose mental and emotional stability seemed, to such eyes as Farley's, highly questionable: "I think you must know that the people look at him as a wild-eyed fellow." To this, Roosevelt made no reply. He went on, instead, to make the only reference he ever made, in talk with Farley, to his physical condition. "The man running with me must be in good health because there is no telling how long I can hold out," he declared with astonishing frankness. "You know, Jim, a man with paralysis can have a breakup at any time." Whereupon he unbuttoned and pulled up his shirt (the two were sitting alone in shirtsleeves) to show him a large lump under his left shoulder which, he said, consisted of misplaced flesh and muscle. The sedentary life imposed upon him by his "affliction" was not conducive to long and healthy living. Therefore: "It's essential that the man who runs with me should be able to carry on." Farley was later convinced that Roosevelt had by then "already made up his mind on Wallace and had determined not to disclose his choice until the last minute in order to keep the field of vice-presidential candidates in line for [i.e., unwilling to oppose] the third term."[39]

Clearly these deliberations of Roosevelt's were permeated by the fears, the anxieties that Roosevelt's young guests had so earnestly expressed during his night meeting with them on June 5 and that, if in far lesser degree, were also his own. As he dealt with them, he now as then consulted the exemplary Abraham Lincoln, giving special heed to Lincoln's famous letter to Horace Greeley at the outset of the Civil War. In that letter, Lincoln stated plainly the scheme of priorities that determined his policy and that, he believed, was itself determined by the "solemn oath" he had taken "to preserve, protect, and defend the Constitution of the United States." Lincoln's top priority was the preservation of the Union. To it he firmly subordinated the abolition of slavery, despite his personal wish "that all men everywhere could be free." Roosevelt's top priority was essentially the same. He must preserve the Union against all forces, internal and external, that would destroy it. And since at the moment, the overwhelmingly threatening forces were external, he must for the moment subordinate domestic reform to the necessity for swift rearmament. In his conception (a conception radically different, incidentally, from that of trust-buster Thurman Arnold or small-business champion Harry Truman), swift and massive rearmament required immediate employment and total dependence upon the American industrial-corporation structure as it now existed, which meant contractual arrangements between the government and such giant corporations as U.S. Steel, General Motors, Ford, Du Pont, Monsanto. Hence Roosevelt's revival of the Council of National Defense. But he had no intention of turning the national government over, even temporarily, to big business. If not adamantly determined, he at least actively hoped to maintain or develop countervailing forces, regulatory and power-distributive forces, that would keep big business sufficiently in check and the liberal reform movement sufficiently alive and strong to shape in its spirit and form the America that must emerge triumphant from her present trials. To this end Roosevelt would keep the reins of ultimate power firmly grasped in his own hands.

V

IT was shortly before one o'clock in the afternoon of Sunday, July 7, a steaming-hot day, that Jim Farley arrived at the Big House in Hyde Park for the interview we have mentioned.[40] He responded to an invitation from Roosevelt, who extended it in the hope that Farley might be persuaded to withdraw his name from consideration for presidential nomination in Chicago and, instead, continue as a Cabinet member and as national party chairman. For since Roosevelt must run again, he wanted very much for appearances to coincide with the reality of the matter as he conceived this reality to be: namely, that he was being drafted into the service of his country as truly as any future conscript in the armed forces would be. He wanted to be unanimously chosen by the convention on the first ballot, to be nominated by acclamation. And this could happen only if Farley withdrew. In that case Garner, whose candidacy had gathered very meager national support but was backed by the sizable Texas delegation, would almost certainly also withdraw before the first ballot was counted. And these two, thanks to Roosevelt's refusal to declare himself one way or the other, were the only Democrats who entered the convention with any pledged delegate support whatever—aside, of course, from Roosevelt himself who, if his name were placed in nomination, was assured of more than the majority needed for a first-ballot victory.

A few minutes after Farley's arrival, the President returned from church services at St. James. Soon thereafter luncheon was served in the dining room, presided over as always in the Big House by the President's mother, eighty-six-year-old Sara Delano Roosevelt, who was still the legal owner of this property. Roosevelt sat at the opposite end of the table from her. Eleanor was seated as one of the guests ranged along the table's sides, the others being (with Farley) Missy LeHand, Steve Early, Hopkins, and a young man who was Hopkins's secretary.

There was some serious talk at the luncheon table about the implications for the United States of the fall of France. Because of a dramatically decisive event at sea off French North Africa four days before, and because of Churchill's words as he reported the event to Parliament and the world just three days ago, Roosevelt was then in process of revising upward his estimate of Britain's chances for survival, which had been not more than 50–50 when France signed the German armistice terms. At Oran on July 3, after vain attempts to persuade the French admiral there either to join his ships with those of the Royal Navy in continued war against Germany or to sail them with reduced crews to the French West Indies for demilitarization, a British naval task force had attacked in a brief but fierce fight three French battleships. Two had been destroyed, a third had been severely damaged. Simultaneously, at Alexandria, a French admiral was forcibly persuaded by British admiral Sir Andrew Cunningham to incapacitate for fighting purposes the French warships anchored there. Action by the British against the great French battleship *Richelieu* at Dakar was expected at any moment. All this had immensely impressed Roosevelt with the grim determination as well as the ability of the Churchill government to fight on—an impression deepened by the prolonged standing, cheering ovation the prime minister had received in the House of Commons on July 4, at the close of his report of the action. At table, Roosevelt spoke of it as abundantly justifying the American policy of all-out aid to the British.

Of domestic politics he said, at table, not a word.

Nor did he, for a considerable time, in the narrow high-ceilinged room that was the President's Hyde Park study and where, following lunch, after having had press photographs taken of them delightedly smiling at each other, Farley and Roosevelt were alone together for more than two hours. The hot, still air in that small room was stifling. As soon as the photographers left, the two men removed their jackets (Roosevelt's white, Farley's dark; he had attended Mass before driving up along the west bank of the Hudson). They nevertheless remained as uncomfortable physically as Roosevelt seemed to be, in Farley's view, mentally. For the President talked at random of a multitude of irrelevant things for a long half-hour, smoking one cigarette after another (the blue haze of smoke added nothing to nonsmoking Farley's comfort), before coming at last to what both men knew was the point of this interview. It was with no assistance from Farley that Roosevelt at last took the plunge into what was evidently, for him, hot water. He reminded Farley, who needed no reminder, of the conversation the two had had almost precisely a year ago in this same room during which Roosevelt had said, in what Farley remembered as "an impressive whisper," that *"of course, I will not run for a third term"** — something he claimed not to have told another living soul and which he had asked Farley to keep to himself in deepest secrecy since his presidential power, especially his power over the legislative branch and consequent influence upon foreign governments, would be weakened the instant his intention became publicly known. It was this last fact, he now said, that had prevented his doing what he and Farley had last summer agreed he would do: write a letter in January 1940 to the party chairman of North Dakota (which held one of the earliest primaries) announcing that he was not a candidate for reelection. The

*Italicized in *Jim Farley's Story*, p. 186.

war had come, and "to have issued such a statement would have nullified my position in the world and handicapped the efforts of this country to be of constructive service in the war crisis," said the President. Admittedly his efforts in this regard had had little or no effect. "We bullied Mussolini in every way possible and tried to get the influence of the Pope to keep Italy from getting into the war, but Italy went in. So I would probably have been better off if I had said I didn't want to run. I still don't want to run. I want to come up here." And with a sweep of his left arm he indicated that "up here" included his new hilltop cottage retreat and the Franklin D. Roosevelt Library, of which the building had been completed but which would not be formally opened to the public for another year. "Jim," he repeated, "I don't want to run—and I'm going to tell the convention so." He would do it in a letter to some party official or prominent delegate known to be close to him (Jim Farley, perhaps?) to be read to the convention. He looked questioningly at his guest. Well, if the President said flatly and unequivocally that he *would not run,* said Farley, who was cynically convinced that the President would do no such thing, then he would not be nominated—and Farley went on to state emphatically his own principled opposition to a third term; his conviction that if, after eight years under Roosevelt's leadership, "the party has no other candidate" than Roosevelt, the party "deserves to lose"; and that, thanks to the way he, Farley, had been treated (here his bitterness, his resentment showed) "the time has passed when any opinion of mine can have any bearing on the convention."

The smiles, as Farley writes, were now gone. The two men looked hard at one another.

"Jim," said Roosevelt after a brief pause, "what would you do if you were in my place?"

"In your position I would do exactly what General Sherman did many years ago—issue a statement saying I would refuse to run if nominated and would not serve if elected."

Roosevelt shook his head.

"Jim," he said, "if nominated and elected I could not in these times refuse to take the inaugural oath, even if I knew I would be dead within thirty days."

The statement, if precisely quoted, may seem to critical historians one of appalling irresponsibility, but it "made a powerful impression" upon Farley, who wrote five years later: "I can see him now, with his right hand clasping the arm of his chair as he leaned back, his left hand bent at the elbow to hold his cigarette and his face and eyes deadly earnest."

This substantially closed the interview, though there was considerable rambling, inconsequential talk thereafter. Roosevelt knew he had failed of his purpose: Farley was not going to withdraw and he, Roosevelt, was therefore not going to be nominated by acclamation. All Roosevelt could now do was end the conversation on the warmest possible personal note.

"Jim," he said, as he shook hands with his departing guest, "no matter what happens, I don't want anything to spoil our long friendship."

"That goes for me, and I mean it sincerely," Farley said.

On the following morning, Farley left for Chicago.

Harry Hopkins was in Chicago three days later.

# 16

>>X<<

# 1940's Presidential Election Campaign

I

As the delegates gathered that week for the Democratic National Convention, to open in the Chicago Stadium on Monday the fifteenth,[1] it was common knowledge among them that Farley, national party chairman or no, was not "the man to see" for final guidance on the substantive matters with which the convention must deal. The Farley headquarters in the Stevens Hotel was seldom crowded, was often empty of visitors, both during the days immediately preceding the convention's formal opening and during the days that followed. Not so the headquarters of Harry Hopkins, which was across the street in suite no. 308–309 of the Blackstone Hotel.* This suite was seldom empty of visitors; to it delegates trekked, singly and in groups, in a steady stream, seeking instruction and advice. For it was known that Hopkins was the only man in town who could communicate immediately and directly at any time with the President; he had a direct telephone line to the White House, the phone having been installed in his bathroom because it was only there that he was assured complete privacy. The natural assumption, therefore, was that Hopkins came to the convention as the President's man, knowing precisely what the President intended to do and wished the convention to do. Certainly no other knew. Even after the convention had been called to order by the temporary chairman at noon of Monday, even after the keynote address had been delivered that night, the wearily prolonged and maddeningly frustrating riddle of the Roosevelt sphinx remained unsolved, and oppressed the minds of the party faithful. The fact did nothing to lighten Farley's dark mood, and much to increase the bitterness of his cynicism, since, during the Hyde Park conversation, Roosevelt had "definitely" promised him that Bankhead would read at the very outset of the convention a letter "definitely" stating the President's fervent desire not to run.

In point of fact, Hopkins when he boarded the train for Chicago did have with him a handwritten note from Roosevelt to Bankhead in which "Dear Will" was asked, during the keynote speech, to "say something for me which I believe ought to be made utterly clear." The "something" was a typically

---

*One of the rooms of the Hopkins suite at the Blackstone was the notorious "smoke-filled" one in which the Republican bosses of 1920 decided that Warren Gamaliel Harding was sufficiently mediocre and malleable to be their President of the United States. Hopkins had rented a second suite in Chicago, at the Ambassador East hotel, which also had a telephone line that bypassed the hotel switchboard and where he could retreat from the convention's turmoil, but he was seldom there during his week in the city.

"sincere" statement of total untruth: "You and my other close friends have known and understood that I have not today and have never had any wish or purpose to remain in the office of President, or indeed anywhere in public office after next January. You know and all my friends know that this is a simple and sincere fact. I want you to repeat this simple and sincere fact to the Convention."[2] Hopkins had had serious misgivings about this note when Roosevelt gave it to him. More serious still were his misgivings about a revision of it which Roosevelt and Rosenman drafted on the Saturday afternoon preceding the convention's opening (this while cruising up the Potomac on the presidential yacht *Potomac*) and which Hopkins received next day. For in this revision Roosevelt added to his original words others that strengthened his statement of personal preference and specifically released his pledged delegates from their pledges. Late that night, Rosenman in his White House bedroom was awakened by a rather frantic phone call from Attorney General Jackson and Frank Walker,* saying that the consensus of the President's Chicago friends was that the message Roosevelt had sent should not be delivered. Early the following morning, Hopkins was on the phone to Roosevelt's bedroom, saying the same thing to the President himself. No presidential message at all should be delivered; it was too dangerous. And what Hopkins said was earnestly seconded during the same phone call by, in succession, Byrnes, Walker, and Chicago's Mayor Kelly. Roosevelt was unmoved. The message *must* be read, he insisted. But he was at last persuaded, with difficulty, to have Alben Barkley do it during the speech he was to deliver upon taking over the convention's permanent chairmanship on Tuesday evening, rather than have Bankhead do it on Monday night. House Speaker Bankhead was neither an inspiring orator nor truly one of Roosevelt's "close friends," whereas Barkley was both. Moreover, Bankhead would not begin speaking until ten o'clock at night and might not close till near midnight. By that time his national radio audience would be small. Barkley, on the other hand, would speak early on Tuesday evening.[3]

As a result of this postponement, Tuesday was a very bad day at the convention. Fortunately, Chicago was having a spell of unusually cool summer weather. Had the city been sweltering in the kind of humid heat that had blanketed it during the 1932 Democratic convention, truly disastrous things might have happened to the Democrats there. As it was, the considerable number of delegates who made up the Farley-Garner anti–third term coalition were in an ugly mood, resentful of Hopkins's assumed power over the convention delegation as a whole and furious at the way he exercised it. Certainly Hopkins made little effort to placate or persuade those he regarded as Roosevelt's enemies. They were, simply, enemies, in his view, who must be circumvented or outmaneuvered or knocked down in direct confrontation. (Harry seemed to be "making all his usual mistakes," remarked Eleanor Roosevelt to

*Frank Walker, an Irish-American Catholic from Minnesota, was a former executive director of the National Emergency Council who would soon succeed Farley as postmaster general.

her friends at Val-Kill Cottage, where she listened with them to radio reports of the proceedings; "he doesn't seem to know how to make people happy."[4]) Even delegates who were as profoundly committed to a Roosevelt third term as Hopkins was were angered by what they deemed his arrogance, his ruthlessness, his deafness to their views, their advice. They knew that Rosenman was now at Roosevelt's side; they assumed, as every press and radio commentator assumed, that he was there to craft with Roosevelt the latter's acceptance speech; and they were therefore sure that Roosevelt was taking far too much for granted and that they themselves were being contemptuously manipulated.

Harold Ickes, for instance, whose general feeling about Hopkins was always ambivalent, alternately friendly or hateful (seldom evenly balanced between the two) depending upon whether his touchy ego was being currently salved or abraded—Ickes was convinced that Hopkins's maladroit Chicago operation would be catastrophic for Roosevelt, the party, the country, the world. On Tuesday morning, at the single strategy conference he was invited to attend during the whole of the convention, he said flatly, belligerently to Hopkins, Byrnes, and Bob Jackson "that if the Republicans had been running the convention in the interests of Willkie, they could not have done a better job" than Roosevelt's presumed friends were now doing.[5] A few hours later, he addressed a lengthy "personal" telegram to Roosevelt saying that, though he had

> sought out no political leader nor any of your friends [in Chicago] . . . they have been coming to me in increasing numbers because they are convinced, as am I, that this convention is bleeding to death and that your reputation and prestige may bleed to death with it. . . . A world revolution is beating against the final ramparts of democracy in Europe. . . . In such a situation you are the only man able to give the country that quality of moral leadership without which we cannot hope to save our institutions. . . . Here in Chicago are more than nine hundred leaderless delegates milling about like worried sheep waiting for the inspiration of leadership which only you can give them.* . . . And yet control of this convention [the convention machinery] is in the hands of men who are determined to destroy you at any cost. . . . The Farley coalition is actually beginning to believe that someone other than yourself can be nominated. Failing this, their objective is to create such a situation that (a) you will not accept the nomination or (b) the chances of your success will be gravely compromised.

In these circumstances the election of Willkie was a distinct possibility and "Willkie means fascism and appeasement."[7]

Another Cabinet member in Chicago who was profoundly unhappy that day over the way things were going was Frances Perkins. She, too, felt that Hopkins was mismanaging, and that Jim Farley, whom she personally liked and to whom she felt the party and Roosevelt owed a great deal, was being shabbily

---

*Writes Ickes in his diary entry for July 5, 1940: "When I saw the President on Tuesday [July 2, 1940] I asked him whether we were to be permitted to go to Chicago without a program, without a floor leader, without knowing who was going to make the nominating speech. He grinned at me and said that he was 'trusting in God.' "[6]

treated. She phoned Roosevelt in the early morning to voice her concerns, saying the convention's mood was so surly, so churlish, that only the President, by coming out to address it personally, could retrieve the situation. He refused to come. He had made his decision; he was sure it was the right one: "If I go, people will get promises out of me that I ought not to make. If I don't make promises, I will make new enemies. If I do make promises, they'll be mistakes." Instead: "How would it be if Eleanor came? You know Eleanor always makes people feel right." The labor secretary thought this an excellent suggestion. "Telephone her," said Roosevelt. "I'll speak to her, too, but you tell her so that she will know I'm not sending her on my own hunch. . . ." Madam Perkins promised to do so at once; she also said that Jim Farley was hurt by the fact that everyone around Hopkins seemed to know the contents of a message the President was rumored to be delivering to the convention that night but that Farley did not know. Something ought to be done to soothe his hurt feelings. The result was that, shortly before that evening's convention session opened, Farley, who had been in his fairly quiet headquarters office all afternoon, received a phone call from the President who said he'd "been trying to reach" him all afternoon. He wanted Jim to know "that Alben has that statement we talked about. I decided it would be best to release it after the permanent organization was set up. . . . I think you'll agree when you think it over." But he did not read the statement to Farley.[8]

The evening session at the close of this bad day was one that lifted Ickes's drooping spirits (though he, disgusted, remained in his hotel that night) and injected, briefly, some hopeful life into the convention majority.

In his rather dull speech of the night before, Bankhead had made several perfunctory references to the President and the administration, none of which provoked much audience response. He had (carefully? deliberately?) made no mention of Roosevelt's name. Neither did orator Barkley in the course of a typically electrifying speech during which repeated references to New Deal triumphs evoked enthusiastic audience response—not, that is, until he mentioned the magic name incidentally, if not inadvertently, and sparked a spontaneous floor demonstration that threatened to prevent the climax toward which he had been carefully building. It was a climax that would ensure, he believed, an approximation of a Roosevelt "draft" so close to the real thing as to be indistinguishable from it. He shouted, waving his arms. He pleaded in stentorian tones. He banged his chairman's gavel with all his might. He finally managed to restore order by calling into the microphone for a doctor, claiming that a woman had been injured.[9] He then went on with a speech that held his audience in thrall for another half-hour or so before he closed it, as planned, with the President's message.

He said:

I and other close friends of the President have long known that he has no wish to be a candidate again. We know, too, that in no way whatsoever has he exerted any influence in the selection of delegates or upon the opinions of delegates.

Tonight, at the specific request and authorization of the President, I am making this simple fact clear to the Convention.

The President has never had, and has not today, any desire or purpose to continue in the office of President, to be a candidate for that office, or to be nominated by the Convention for that office.

He wishes in all earnestness and sincerity to make it clear that all the delegates to this Convention are free to vote for any candidate.

That is the message I bear to you from the President of the United States.[10]

There followed a long moment of silence during which the delegates looked at one another confusedly, trying to understand what was happening.

They needed to be told what their response should be.

And they promptly were; this stunned silence had been anticipated and carefully prepared for.

In a small basement room of the stadium, huddled before a microphone hooked up to numerous loudspeakers scattered around the convention hall, sat a little man with a big voice, a remarkably big voice, who now used it full force, crying into the microphone and thence booming out over the great hall above: *"We want Roosevelt!"* Small scattered demonstrations began at once in various parts of the vast floor, delegates seizing their state standards and marching into the aisles with them. *"Everybody wants Roosevelt!"* boomed the voice. The demonstrations swelled, and the galleries, packed by Mayor Kelly with Roosevelt supporters, began to empty out onto the floor. *"The world needs Roosevelt!"* and then, again and again, *"Roosevelt! . . . Roosevelt! . . . Roosevelt!"* in a voice of such penetrating force that it could be clearly heard above the vast noise that now filled the hall. Shouting, whistle-blowing, standard-waving delegates poured by the hundred into the aisles to mingle with thousands from the galleries, and the band played "Happy Days Are Here Again," and the organist played "Franklin D. Roosevelt Jones," and cheerleaders led impromptu group cheering—a pandemonium that roared on and on and on for nearly an hour, continuously incited and goaded by that mysterious stupendous voice. Reporter Warren Moscow of *The New York Times* soon discovered the owner of it. It belonged to one Thomas D. McGarry, Chicago's superintendent of sewers, a Kelly man—whereupon it was dubbed the "voice from the sewers" by Roosevelt's enemies, a label yet attached to it in American political history.[11]

On the following evening, Wednesday, July 17, the convention in a single session disposed of the two major items on its agenda: the selection of the Democratic candidate for President; and the adoption of the party platform on which this candidate would run. The latter, having been prepared and revised in the White House, was the brief document, uncompromisingly liberal in tone and substance, which Roosevelt wanted, and of it only the foreign-policy plank provoked much controversy in the convention's Resolutions Committee, chaired by New York's Senator Wagner. This controversy, however, was fierce. A sizable group of isolationists, led by Montana's Senator Wheeler and Massachusetts's Senator Walsh, insisted upon a plank saying:

"We will not participate in foreign wars. We will not send our armed forces to fight in lands across the seas." This was wording that Roosevelt could not in good conscience accept (how could any man guarantee, in such times as these, that the United States would not have to fight on "foreign fields" for her very survival?); yet if he rejected the plank in toto he would lay himself open to the charge that he intended to lead the United States into the war as Britain's ally. Rosenman suggested adding to the second of the two statements a proviso, "except where necessary to protect our American interests," but this, because it opened the way for debilitating debate over how our "interests" were to be defined, failed to pass muster with the President. Roosevelt finally wrote out in his own hand, as an addendum to the second statement, a proviso so ambiguous as to be meaningless, namely, "except in case of attack." To this ambiguity, Wheeler and Walsh, after much hard talk with Byrnes, finally agreed.[12]

With the platform adopted, the formal nominating procedure began. Roosevelt was nominated in a lackluster speech by Alabama's Lister Hill; Farley in an even less effective speech by Virginia's ancient Carter Glass; then Garner, Maryland's Millard Tydings, and Hull. The demonstration following Hill's speech nomination was satisfactorily enthusiastic but, as Ickes told his diary, "the crowd had pretty well shouted itself out the night before." It sat with manifest impatience through the seconding speeches and the brief and pitifully small demonstrations accorded Farley and Garner. The outcome of the balloting was awaited with suspense only by those delegates who knew of Hopkins's assertion, as the convention opened, that Roosevelt would refuse the nomination if more than 150 votes were cast against him. The first ballot results were: Roosevelt, 946½; Farley, 72½; Garner, 61; Tydings, 9½; and Hull, whose name had not been placed in nomination, 5. Thus the vote in opposition to Roosevelt totaled 148. So at ten-thirty-eight P.M., Chicago time, of this Wednesday, July 17, 1940, Roosevelt became for the third time the Democratic party's presidential nominee, and shortly after midnight, upon the motion of party loyalist Jim Farley, the nomination was declared unanimous.

By this time, the euphoria of the night before had been dissipated; the dominant conference mood was again unhappy, shot through with anger, resentment, and rebelliousness. The delegates went to bed smarting with a sense of having been used, and determined that as they went about their main business of tomorrow, the choosing of the vice presidential candidate, they would go their own way. They had been given reason to believe that, in this portion of its business, the convention would be truly a free and open one. Wide open. For there were a great many men who were frankly "available" and campaigning more or less vigorously for the second spot. Byrnes, Paul McNutt, Jesse Jones, Bankhead, Sam Rayburn, Louis Johnson, Lloyd C. Stark of Missouri, Scott Lucas of Illinois, and no fewer than ten others were known or believed to want it; and several of these were sure that they had the President's blessing to the extent, at least, that he had given them a "green light" (the convention hall was full of such "green lights," someone told

Johnson when he bragged that he had one), or that he, the President, would be, as he had said, "happy" to run with them. Hence the furious outrage with which the convention learned, via Hopkins, on Thursday morning, that it was no more free to choose the second man than it had been to choose the first. Not only had Roosevelt made the choice, but his choice, Henry Wallace, was almost, if not quite, the least acceptable to the delegates that he could have made. Hopkins himself, when he phoned Rosenman early Thursday morning to make certain that Wallace was still the man, expressed some anxiety about it. There were at least ten vice presidential candidates who now had more delegate support than Wallace on his own could ever gain, he said. There would be "a hell of a lot of opposition"; a "cat-and-dog fight" was in the offing. "But I think [which meant Hopkins wasn't sure] that the Boss has enough friends here to put it over."[13]

What followed was perhaps the worst day of Hopkins's life in politics. He must absorb, hour after hour, the hatred, the vituperation that delegates of conservative persuasion would have liked to focus directly upon Roosevelt, but dared not. Roosevelt himself found the day decidedly unpleasant. He spent much of it answering phone calls protesting his decision. There was an especially vicious call from Bankhead, who was bitter over the President's snub (as he felt it), loathed Wallace's liberalism, and was, as party politician, outraged that a man who had been a Republican before he entered the Cabinet, and had never been an organization Democrat, was now slated for the second-highest office in a Democratic administration. Jimmy Byrnes, his courtier instincts momentarily overbalanced by the hurt of thwarted ambition, phoned to protest and was with some difficulty persuaded, at last, to "go along," as he put it, and help put Wallace over. There was even a protesting call to Roosevelt from his wife, according to Farley's later account. Eleanor had been flown to Chicago on Thursday morning in a small private American Airlines plane from Wappingers Falls, which was some fifteen miles from Hyde Park, and had been met at the airport by Farley, who drove her alone into Chicago and the Stevens Hotel. "On the way he [Farley] told me that Franklin . . . had never told him who was his choice for vice-president," wrote Eleanor. "I was horrified to realize that things had come to this pass between these two men, because I had always had a feeling of real friendship for Jim Farley." And according to Farley, who listened to her end of the conversation, she in her phone call to her husband said: "Franklin, I've been talking to Jim Farley and I agree with him Henry Wallace won't do. . . . I know, Franklin, but Jesse Jones would bolster the ticket and win it business support. . . ." That she, with her strong liberal views, could have preferred Jones over Wallace seems unlikely, and her own memory of the incident was that she expressed no opinion of her own ("I never expressed a preference or an opinion on matters of this kind") but simply passed on to her husband what Farley had said to her, she being anxious to do what she could to heal a breach that she deemed deplorable for both men, for the party, and for the country. At any rate, Roosevelt was highly irritated and showed it to Farley after she, at his request, had turned the phone over to him. There was no point in arguing further about it, said the President: Wallace was his choice and would remain his choice. To which Farley replied that Jesse Jones was *his* choice, and would so remain. "I am going out and vote for Jones if he will run, and if he won't I'll vote for Bankhead," said Farley; "but I feel the Democrats want a Democrat and I do not consider Wallace one."[14]

It was a grim Franklin Roosevelt who that night, in the Oval Room of the White House, listened to radio reports of the Chicago proceedings. Spiritually solitary at that moment, he was by no means physically alone in the room. Steve Early, Rosenman, Missy, Grace Tully, Ross McIntire, Pa Watson with his wife, and several others were there. But Roosevelt had little communication with them. He had had a card table set up before him, and sat there playing solitaire while he listened to the reporting from Chicago.

During the afternoon, which was when the balloting for vice president had been originally scheduled to take place, one after another of the seventeen or so earlier candidates for the post had either withdrawn from the race or been dropped by his supporters. Often the withdrawal speeches were openly embittered and aggrieved. Only McNutt, Bankhead, and Wallace were yet in the running as the evening session began in noisy turmoil and confusion—turmoil, however, that was temporarily almost wholly (miraculously) abated when Eleanor Roosevelt arose to speak. She was admired and respected by both the conservatives and liberals of the party—was trusted by them to speak truth as she saw it, pure and unadorned, with no artful dodges. The delegates, the jammed galleries, listened with close attention to her words. They were few and simple. She spoke of the immense burden her husband was being asked to bear. If he "felt that the strain of a third term might be too much . . . and that Mr. Wallace was the man who could carry on best in times such as we were facing," surely he was "entitled to have" Wallace's help. In these times, "no one should think of himself but only of the job which might have to be done."[15] In the relative calm and quiet that followed her words, McNutt, his name having been formally proposed, made a brief emphatic speech saying that under no circumstances would he accept the nomination. An infuriated Bankhead, however, did not withdraw, and the warm enthusiasm that greeted the speeches nominating him and seconding the nomination contrasted sharply with the boos and hisses with which Wallace's nominating speeches, and indeed all mentions of his name, were greeted.

As the balloting began it was obvious that the race would be a close one, and as it proceeded, very slowly, with seemingly endless "explanations" of vote, the likelihood that Wallace would lose became emphatically clear. In Chicago, Byrnes, Hopkins, and other friends of Roosevelt circulated among the delegates, warning them that Roosevelt had not yet made his acceptance speech and might well refuse to do so if Wallace went down ("For God's sake, do you want a President or a Vice President?" was Byrnes's frantic plea). In the White House's Oval Room, a grim-faced Roosevelt laid aside his cards and asked Missy for a notepad and a pencil. As swiftly as his hand could move he covered five pages with his scrawl, then handed them to Rosenman, asking him to "clean it up" quickly because "I may have to deliver it very quickly." The statement that Rosenman "cleaned up" and Roosevelt in turn swiftly revised —which Grace Tully then typed and Roosevelt again revised in minor ways —was addressed to "Members of the Convention." It is so pure an expression of Roosevelt's sense of basic issues, and of his mood at this climax of his long moment of truth, that it is worth quoting here extensively:

> In the century in which we live, the Democratic Party has received the support of the electorate only when the party . . . has been the champion of progressive and liberal policies and principles of government. The party has failed consistently when . . . it has fallen into the control of those interests . . . which think in terms of dollars instead of in terms of human values. . . . The Democratic Convention, as appears clear from the events of today, is divided on this fundamental issue. Until [unless?] the Democratic Party through this convention makes overwhelmingly clear its stand in favor of social progress and liberalism, and shakes off the shackles . . . fastened upon it by the forces of conservatism, reaction and appeasement, it will not continue its march to victory. It is without question that certain political influences pledged to reaction in domestic affairs and to appeasement in foreign affairs have been busily engaged behind the scenes in the promotion of discord since this Convention convened. . . . I cannot, in all honor, and will not . . . go along with the cheap bargaining and political maneuvering which have brought about party dissension. . . . It is best not to straddle ideals.

Whereupon he echoed Abraham Lincoln's "house divided" speech, saying:

> I wish to give the Democratic Party the opportunity to make its historic decision clearly and without equivocation. The party must go wholly one way or wholly the other. It cannot face in both directions at the same time.
> By declining the honor of the nomination for the Presidency, I can restore that opportunity to the Convention. I so do.[16]

This labor completed, Roosevelt went back to his game of solitaire.

In Chicago, Wallace, who had fallen well behind Bankhead in the early balloting, caught up as the vote proceeded, and emerged at last with 627 votes out of some 1,100 cast.* No one moved that the nomination be made unanimous, and Wallace was virtually ordered by Hopkins, in harsh tones, not to deliver the acceptance speech he had prepared. Wallace, eager to confront his enemies head-on, very reluctantly obeyed. Wrote Farley: "There is no doubt in my mind that Mrs. Roosevelt's appearance and her speech about the burdens of the presidency in critical times saved the day for the President."[17]

The humid heat that Chicago at that time fortunately escaped was oppressively present in the Oval Room that night, for Roosevelt, fearing the effect of air-conditioning on his sinus problem, had not ordered it turned on. His

---

*Had Bankhead won and Roosevelt not then withdrawn, the Democrats would have been forced to repeat very hurriedly the vice presidential nominating process before election day. House Speaker William P. Bankhead died on September 15, 1940.

shirt was soaked with sweat, strands of his hair were plastered against his moist brow, and his facial expression was of weary relief, not elation, as he pushed himself away from the card table and was wheeled into his bedroom. But having bathed, changed clothes, and combed his hair, he appeared wholly relaxed and at ease when, at twelve-twenty-five in the morning of Friday, July 19, 1940, speaking into a cluster of microphones in the White House's Diplomatic Reception Room, he began his address accepting the unprecedented third-term nomination.

He spoke, he said, "with a very full heart" and "mixed feelings," giving first, and at length, that explanation of his delay in announcing a decision about running again of which we already know. He spoke of "the efforts I made to prevent war from the moment it was threatened and to restrict the area of carnage, down to the last minute," efforts in which he had persisted "in the face of appeaser fifth-columnists who charged me with hysteria and war-mongering." He spoke of the steps that had been and were being taken "to implement the total defense of America"; of the men and women of exceptional ability and high position who had answered his call to service in the government ("Regardless of party, regardless of personal convenience, they . . . answered the call"); of the necessity for an increasingly massive influx of manpower into government service to be trained in the supply and maintenance of the materials of war as well as in the use of weaponry in combat ("For every individual in actual combat service, it is necessary for adequate defense that we have ready at hand at least four or five other trained individuals for non-combat services"); and, very cautiously and tentatively, with no specific reference to the Burke-Wadsworth bill, of a consequent need for manpower conscription. "Because of the millions of citizens involved in the conduct of defense," he said, "most right-thinking people are agreed that some form of selection by draft is as necessary and fair today as it was in 1917 and 1918." He spoke then of his own "draft," drawing some of his language from the MacLeish memo, which Frankfurter had sent him:

> Lying awake, as I have, on many nights,* I have asked myself whether I have the right as Commander-in-Chief of the Army and Navy, to call on men and women to serve their country or to train themselves to serve and, at the same time, decline to serve my country in my own personal capacity, if I am called upon to do so by the people of my country. In times like these . . . the compass of the world narrows to a single fact. The fact which dominates our world is the fact of armed aggression, of successful armed aggression, aimed at the form of Government, the kind of society that we in the United States have chosen and established for ourselves. . . . [This war] is not an ordinary war. It is a revolution imposed by force of arms, which threatens all men everywhere. It is a revolution which proposes not to set men free but to

---

*The truth of this statement was laughingly challenged by members of his personal staff who were sure there was never a time or circumstance in which he could not go to sleep when he wanted to. But one historian, at least, believes Roosevelt in this instance spoke literal truth. Certainly, if ever there was a period in his life when anxious doubts assailed and defeated sleep in the darkness of his nights, that period was now. (Author's note.)

reduce them to slavery—to reduce them to slavery in the interests of a dictatorship which has already shown the nature and extent of the advantage it hopes to obtain. That is the fact which dominates our world and which dominates the lives of . . . each and every one of us. In the face of [it] . . . no individual retains or can hope to retain the right of personal choice which free men enjoy in times of peace. He has a first obligation to serve in the defense of our institutions of freedom—a first obligation to serve his country in whatever capacity his country finds him useful. . . . Only the people themselves can draft a President. If such a draft should be made upon me, I . . . will, with God's help, continue to serve with the best of my ability and with the fullness of my strength.

He thanked the convention delegates for their selection of Henry Wallace "for the high office of Vice President. . . . His first-hand knowledge of the problems of Government in every sphere of life and every single part of the nation—and indeed of the whole world—qualifies him without reservation. His practical idealism will be of great service to me individually and to the nation as a whole." He spoke warmly of "my old friend Jim Farley," sending him, "as I have often before and shall many times again, my most affectionate greetings."

As for the presidential election campaign of "the next few months," it must of necessity "be different from the usual national campaign. . . . Events move so fast in other parts of the world that it has become my duty to remain either in the White House itself or at some nearby point where I can reach Washington and even Europe and Asia by direct telephone—where, if need be, I can be back at my desk in the space of a very few hours." The establishment "of the new defense machinery" required him "to spend vastly more time in conferences," as did the "constant cooperation between the Executive and Legislative branches" consequent upon the fact that Congress had been compelled by the crisis "to forego its usual adjournment. . . . I do expect . . . to make my usual periodic reports to the country through the medium of press conferences and radio talks. I shall not have the time or the inclination to engage in purely political debate. But I shall never be loath to call the attention of the nation to deliberate or unwitting distortions of fact, which are sometimes made by political candidates."[18]

## II

AND indeed, between mid-July and early autumn of 1940, the demands made by the world crisis upon the time and energy of a chief executive who was loath to delegate authority, being determined to keep every rein of power tightly gripped by his own hands, were virtually all-consuming.

There was a dizzying elevation of national-defense appropriations, a dizzying acceleration of the processes of armed-forces expansion and industrial mobilization. Roosevelt, who in his budget message of January 1940 had given it as his considered judgment that $1.84 billion "was a sufficient amount" for national defense "for the coming year," and whose estimate was being drastically revised downward by Congress when Hitler invaded Norway, had asked Congress for over a billion more on May 31, as we have seen, and promptly received it. On July 10 he asked for nearly $5 billion more, saying to Congress that a partial defense was no defense at all: "If the United States is to have any defense, it must have total defense. We cannot defend ourselves a little here and a little there. We must be able to defend ourselves wholly and at any time."[19] Which meant, in the present state of the world, a two-ocean navy, an army of millions, an air force of tens of thousands of planes. This second supplemental appropriations request was also promptly granted. With the signing of a third supplementary bill on October 8, the appropriations and contract authorizations for immediate and future spending on national defense voted by Congress since the second week of June reached the staggering total of $17.692 billion.[20] (The amount would be more than doubled during the year ahead.) There was also on the statute books by then the administration's special tax measure designed to place this huge defense effort, to some degree, on a pay-as-you-go basis. The latter fact surprised many New Dealers, especially those of isolationist sentiment, who were inclined toward a cynical view of the alacrity with which men who had bitterly opposed government welfare expenditures, saying they dangerously unbalanced the budget, sprang to the support of naval and military expenditures many times as great. No doubt a sincere patriotism was operative here, but would this expression of it have been quite so emphatic if patriotism and private profit had not conveniently coincided? Such cynicism increased the sourness with which many a New Dealer viewed the ready access to the White House that Roosevelt's patriotic big-business men at once had, contrasting it with the difficulties they themselves now encountered when they sought to approach the throne.

But the point for us here is that the active management of all this vast effort was concentrated in the White House. The Defense Commission (so the Advisory Commission of the Council of National Defense was promptly dubbed) remained technically strictly advisory. Each of its members—William Knudsen, industrial-production advisor; Edward Stettinius, Jr., industrial materials; Ralph Budd, transportation—had his own operation and reported upon it directly to the President. The President was the one who was advised; he was the one who decided; and his daily burdens, with the consequent necessity for him to stay within or in immediate contact with the White House at all times, were greatly increased.

All this, of course, implied a huge recruitment of young Americans into service in the armed forces, and that in turn implied the passage, as swiftly as possible, of the Burke-Wadworth selective service bill. This was, of course, another burdensome problem for the President, its weight increased by the fact that 1940 was a presidential election year. He continued to deal with it gingerly, making sure of bipartisan support and coalesced interventionist-isolationist support before he made a final, open commitment. He was concerned to prevent any massive organization against conscription on the part of the yet powerful pacifist groups, which were predominantly liberal politically—an opposition that had begun to organize when, in a June 7 press conference, Roosevelt expressed approval of a *New York Times* editorial that day in which conscription was vigorously advocated. He had then at once retreated, saying in his next press conference, "I did not . . . intend to imply that there should be compulsory military training for every boy in this country." He did believe, he said, that the times called for more disciplined American youth and that the country was coming "to some form of universal government service" which would include but by no means be confined to military service.[21] Of this notion (he had been encouraged in it by Clarence Pickett of the Friends Service Committee; Sidney Hillman, labor adviser on the Defense Commission; and Eleanor Roosevelt), he was now promptly disabused. Universal service was more strongly opposed than compulsory military service. Congressional conservatives damned it as socialistic regimentation; Minnesota's young governor, Harold Stassen, who belonged to the relatively liberal wing of his party, poured withering fire upon it during his keynote address to the Republican National Convention. Roosevelt, however, did not then turn at once openly toward the military draft; he maintained a careful distance between the White House and Grenville Clark's group, being convinced that the measure had a better chance of passage if he were known or believed to have virtually nothing to do with it. Not until mid-August, after Willkie in his acceptance speech had come out forthrightly for the measure, did Roosevelt clearly indicate that he favored it, whereupon administration forces pressed hard if quietly for its passage.

The measure then swiftly gathered strength, much of it through the skillfully organized efforts of Clark's national emergency committee. It continued to be vehemently opposed by pacifist organizations, to be strongly opposed by a majority of the Republicans in Congress, despite its endorsement by their party's standard-bearer, Willkie. When the Senate passed its version on August 28, twelve Republicans voted against it, eleven (including a reluctant McNary) for it. In the House, New York Republican Hamilton Fish proposed a crippling amendment, limiting the armed-forces increase to 400,000 and delaying the act's implementation for sixty days, during which time the army must attempt to achieve the limited increase through voluntary enlistments. House Republicans voted, 144–22, for this amendment. In the final vote on the House version, which contained the amendment, on September 7, 112 Republicans voted against it, 51 for it. In conference committee the Fish amendment was removed, after much loud wrangling, and on September 14 the final version of the bill, substantially that which the Clark group had originally prepared, passed the Senate, 47–25 (seven Republicans voted yes, ten no), then passed the House, 232–124 (forty-six Republicans voted yes, eighty-eight no). Roosevelt signed it into law two days later.[22]

Part and parcel of these national-defense problems was that of supplying aid to Britain. It was the single most time-consuming matter of all those with which the President had to deal during that crowded crucial summer. The decision had already been made to provide Britain with the maximum possible assistance within the limits of America's national-security needs, but this in its turn raised a fundamental question exceedingly difficult to answer. Since Britain's survival, and American security, were by no means distinct and separate matters—Britain's war effort was in fact an integral part of America's defense against Nazi-Fascist aggression—just what were the limits of America's security needs insofar as these did *not* coincide with Britain's? What were the chances that Britain would be invaded and crushed within the next few months even if she received all possible American aid? If Britain went down, all the war matériel she had received from the United States could fall into German hands. America's danger would then be vastly increased while her actual defense capability was reduced by precisely the amount of aid she had given. Hence very close calculations of relative risks and cost–benefit ratios were required of the American executive, and they must be made under the pressures of—even, to some extent, in terms of—a bitter partisan political contest. For it was Roosevelt's conviction that true American security, the very survival of the United States as a free society committed to humane goals, depended upon the defeat in November of those forces of "corporate statism" that were backing Wendell Willkie.

On July 31, renewing a correspondence that had lapsed, with a single minor exception, since June 15, Churchill addressed a "Strictly Secret and Personal" message to the President:

> It has now become most urgent for you to let us have the destroyers, motor boats and flying boats for which we have asked. The Germans have the whole French coast line from which to launch U-boats, dive-bomber attacks upon our trade and food, and in addition we must be constantly prepared to repel by sea action threatened invasion in the narrow waters, also to deal with breakouts from Norway toward Ireland, Iceland, Shetlands, and Faroes. Besides this we have to keep control of the exit from the Mediterranean, and if possible the command of that inland sea itself, and thus to prevent the war spreading seriously into Africa.

As Churchill had repeatedly stressed before, a large-scale construction of destroyers was under way, but until it was completed a year from now, the gap in Britain's defenses, which only the United States could fill, yawned dangerously wide. In just the last ten days, air attacks, to which destroyers were "frightfully vulnerable," had sunk four British destroyers and knocked seven others out of commission. "We could not keep up the present rate of casualties for long, and if we cannot get a substantial reinforcement, the whole fate of the war may be decided by this minor and easily remediable factor." He pleaded for "50 or 60 of your oldest destroyers," saying: "Mr. President, I must tell you that in the long history of the world, this is a thing to do now."[23]

But it was also a thing impossible for Roosevelt to "do now," at once, by a simple, affirmative wave of his hand. His hands, he felt, were tied. He was constitutionally bound to respect the expressed wishes of the legislative branch; and Congress had passed, and Roosevelt had signed, a measure, originally proposed by Senator Walsh, Democrat of Massachusetts, which said in effect that destroyers could be sent to Britain only if the navy certified that they were of no use to U.S. defense.* Naval officials, alas, had not long ago certified the precise opposite of this. In order to prevent the scrapping of these overage vessels on the ground that they were a useless expense to the taxpayer, top navy officials had in congressional testimony asserted that the destroyers were potentially valuable for U.S. defense and should be retained in repair. Therefore, as Roosevelt initially saw it, special legislation would be required to effect the destroyers' transfer. The proposal of such legislation would certainly incite furious isolationist opposition. This would not only add renewed and amplified charges of warmongering to the hazards already faced by Roosevelt's reelection campaign, it would also delay unconscionably the sending of the destroyers—and time, as Churchill had indicated, was of the essence of this matter. On July 10, with a massive onslaught upon Channel shipping and Britain's southern ports, the German air force had launched what at once became known as the Battle of Britain, obviously intended to prepare the way for invasion and occupation of the island. British fighter squadrons more than held their own in daily air battles against superior numbers, but as July gave way to August, and all through the first two weeks of August, the Germans continued to concentrate on Channel shipping and the destroyers which protected that shipping against U-boats. The number of available British destroyers continued to be reduced—by sinkings, by crippling wounds. Much further destruction of the destroyer shield would expose Britain's sea lifelines, helpless, to submarine torpedoes which could cut them to pieces—and if that happened, a starving Britain might collapse before the British destroyers now being built could come down the ways. The American destroyers presently immobile in American ports, doing no good to anybody, could make at this juncture, if properly employed, the difference between death and survival for freedom's cause, but the time in which they could do so, as Churchill warned, was rapidly running out.

Roosevelt, as has been indicated, had lately been revising steadily upward his estimate of Britain's chances of survival as a sovereign power, which is to say he had been revising steadily downward his estimate of the accuracy and judgmental value of the reports he received in steady stream from his ambassador in London. Joe Kennedy's dispatches were uniformly darkly pessimistic: Britain's only hope of escaping appalling slaughter and ruin lay in a negotiated peace, the opening for which was indicated in Hitler's July 19 radio statement (he called it an "appeal to common sense") that a continuation of the war would result in Britain's annihilation for no good reason ("I can see no reason why this war should continue," Hitler had said).[24] Roosevelt's conclusion was, by early August, precisely the opposite: Britain not only could but would defeat Germany's attempt to invade her if, indeed, such an attempt were actually made. It would not be, it could not be, unless Göring's air force were assured of absolute command of the skies above the Channel and the English

---

*Actually, the measure was an amendment tacked onto the last naval-appropriations bill, else Roosevelt would not have signed it into law.

coastal areas where the invasion forces would land. Such assurance was certainly not forthcoming from the Battle of Britain as it had thus far proceeded. In a later year, when German official records became available, it would be learned that between July 10 and August 3 the Royal Air Force destroyed 183 German planes in the skies above England and the Channel while losing but 59 planes of its own[25]—and the reports Roosevelt received at the time, based upon the optimistically inaccurate reports of RAF pilots, indicated a much greater imbalance than this in favor of the British. Hence Roosevelt need not ask himself whether or not the requested destroyers should be supplied (to strengthen a Britain able and determined to fight on was to increase American security); he need only concern himself with how it could be done.

This was a question sufficiently difficult, surely. Roosevelt's first step toward answering it was to make sure that the American public was fully informed of Britain's desperate need. (Gallup polls would soon show 62 percent of the American people in favor of letting Britain have the destroyers.) Then, in a Cabinet meeting on August 2, he listened responsively to a proposal made by his new navy secretary, Frank Knox, who on the night before had discussed it at length with British ambassador Lothian and had found Lothian personally in favor of it. Lothian had by now communicated the idea to the Churchill government. The proposal was of a destroyers-for-bases deal. The British had naval bases scattered along the Atlantic coast, especially in the West Indies, which in American hands would continue to serve British security interests while greatly strengthening America's hemispheric defenses. Why not trade these for the destroyers Britain so desperately needed? This would enable the administration to present Congress with a deal manifestly advantageous to the United States—and if the Republican presidential candidate endorsed it, rendering it a nonpartisan proposal, swift and favorable congressional action upon it was likely. The proposal was strongly backed in the Cabinet meeting by Stimson, Ickes, and Wallace; whereupon Roosevelt at once, from the Cabinet room, phoned William Allen White to ask this chairman of the six-hundred-chapter Committee to Defend America by Aiding the Allies to obtain his organization's approval of the proposal. He also asked White to serve personally as intermediary between himself and Wendell Willkie to the end that Willkie not only publicly personally approved the deal but also pressured Republican members of Congress to approve it with their votes. White quickly agreed to do as he was asked.

Willkie, however, refused to go along. By the time White talked to him, he had been informed of the proposed deal by Archibald MacLeish via MacLeish's friend and former editorial associate on *Fortune,* Russell Davenport, and had expressed himself as personally in favor of it. He said so to White. But he had reasonable doubts about his influence over the Republican delegation in Congress; he feared that the discord between him and his adopted party's Old Guard would be increased in ways harmful to his election campaign if he agitated on this issue; and he was wary, being profoundly distrustful, of Franklin Roosevelt. Instead he issued on August 9 a public statement saying: "My general views on foreign policy and the vital interests of the United States in the present international situation are well known. As to specific executive and legislative proposals, I do not think it appropriate for me to enter into advance commitments and understandings." White hastily wired the President (August 11) to say "it's not as bad as it seems. I have talked to both of you on the subject during the last ten days, I know that there is not two bits difference between you on the issue pending. But I can't guarantee either of you to the other, which is funny for I admire and respect you both. . . . But I've not quit and as I said it's not as bad as it looks."[26]

Nor *was* it bad, overall.

The Century Group was taking a decisive hand in the matter. It had induced the aged and ailing General Pershing to make a national network radio broadcast on August 4 in which he, the commander of the AEF in World War I, warned the American people that "all the things we hold dear are gravely threatened"; asserted that Americans could best defend their heritage by aiding Great Britain in every possible way, at once, "before it is too late"; and pointed out that one way to give immediate important aid was to place at the disposal of the British or Canadian governments "at least fifty of the overage destroyers which are left over from the days of the World War"—a recommendation at once seconded by three retired naval officers: Admirals Harry Yarnell, William Standley, and Yates Stirling, Jr.[27] On August 11, the day of White's wire to Roosevelt, there appeared in *The New York Times* a lengthy letter to the editor signed by four of the Century Group's most distinguished members: Charles Culp Burlingham, Dean Acheson, George Rublee, and Thomas D. Thacher, each a lawyer famed for legal acumen, each a longtime personal acquaintance of Roosevelt's, and two of them former associates of his in the administration. They argued persuasively in their letter that the President need not seek special congressional approval of the destroyer transfer to Britain; he possessed abundant authority under the Constitution, and under existing legislation, to do so by executive order. Immediately thereafter their view was concurred in by Attorney General Jackson in a formal preliminary legal opinion. The group then fully exercised its considerable ability to stimulate public support of such presidential action (Walter Lippmann and Joseph Alsop argued for the deal in their syndicated columns) and undertook to obtain assurances from Willkie that he would not attack the destroyers-for-bases exchange once it was announced. Willkie's campaign headquarters made a commitment to that effect on Friday, August 30.

By then, in exchanges of cables and phone messages between the President and Churchill, a final serious difficulty had been removed.

Roosevelt wanted to present this deal to the American people as a "Yankee horse trade" in which he, the shrewd tradesman, got for the United States by far the best of the bargain. Obviously a few dozen ancient, obsolete war vessels were a laughably puny price to pay for a number of strategically placed naval bases with a monetary value of hundreds of millions of dollars. Few if any senators or congressmen would dare oppose it. Equally obvious was the fact that presenting the deal in this light to the British Parliament and public would be politically disadvantageous, dangerously so, for the Churchill government. The prime minister, therefore, wanted the destroyer transaction and the base leases to be kept distinct and separate from one another, with the declared motivation for both placed "on the highest level," that of human love, human friendship, a common humanity. The United States gave the destroyers to her great and good friend because that friend needed them; Great Britain gave the base leases to her great and good friend because that friend needed them.

"His Majesty's Government are entirely willing to accord defence facilities to the United States on a ninety-nine years' lease-hold basis," Churchill told Parliament on August 20,

> and we feel sure that our interests no less than theirs, and the interests of the Colonies themselves and of Canada and Newfoundland, will be served thereby. These are important steps. Undoubtedly this process means that these two great organizations of the English-speaking democracies, the British Empire and the United States, will have to be somewhat mixed up together in some of their affairs for mutual and general advantage. For my own part, looking out upon the future, I do not view the process with any misgivings. I could not stop it if I wished; no one can stop it. Like the Mississippi, it just keeps rolling along. Let it roll. Let it roll on—full flood, inexorable, irresistible, benignant, to broader lands and happier days.[28]

It was a speech pregnant with long-term world-historical implications, but it was also highly discomforting politically to Franklin Roosevelt at that moment. He at once called into conference Secretaries Knox, Stimson, and Hull, the last of whom expressed the acerbic view that chronically perfidious Albion was again "crawfishing." This provoked from Stimson a strong plea for a sympathetic understanding of beleaguered Britain's position. "The great thing is not for either side to forget the other one's troubles and get into recriminations which will take the spirit—the high spirit of grand policy—out of the entire transaction," he said. All the same, as Lord Lothian was informed, it was "utterly impossible" for the President simply to give the destroyers to Britain. He must have certification from navy officers that these destroyers were not essential to national security, and these officers, in view of their recent testimony before Congress, could not so certify without a quid pro quo. The two transactions could not be kept separate; they must be linked.

A way out of this impasse was suggested by the State Department's legal adviser, Green H. Hackworth, during a conference in Hull's office on the morning of August 24. "Since the British had not stated precisely what bases they intended to lease to us, why not divide them into two parcels? The first would comprise the bases in Newfoundland and Bermuda. These Britain could lease to us as an outright gift. The second would comprise the bases around the Caribbean, strategically more valuable to us because of their nearness to the Panama Canal. These could be leased in consideration of the cession of the fifty destroyers."[29]

If not wholly pleasing to either Churchill or Roosevelt, this was a formula easily acceptable by both of them.

The destroyers-for-bases deal was announced to Congress and the world in a special presidential message on Tuesday, September 3, 1940.[30]

III

WILLKIE had promised not to attack the transaction after it was announced. But a loud chorus of Republicans promptly dubbed it, and damned it as, an "act of war"—which, in the absence of a declaration of war, no President had the legal authority to perform—and only Congress, under the Constitution, could declare war. If Willkie did not actually break his promise by joining in this chorus full voice (it was soon a harsh rasping voice) he certainly seriously cracked it by joining in sotto voce (though intending to be heard). On September 4, he issued a public statement saying: "The country will undoubtedly approve of the program to add to our naval and air bases and assistance given to Britain. It is regrettable, however, that the President did not deem it necessary in connection with this proposal to secure the approval of Congress. . . . We must be extremely careful in these times, when the struggle in the world is between democracy and totalitarianism, not to eliminate or destroy the democratic processes while seeking to preserve democracy." Three days later, after he had conferred with Vandenberg and other Republican stalwarts, this temperate language no longer sufficed. Willkie now described the deal as "the most dictatorial and arbitrary act of any President in the history of the United States."[31]

The difference in tone between the two statements measures the difference between the unofficial campaign Willkie had theretofore been conducting and the official one he began after its formal opening on September 16 in Coffeyville, Kansas.[32]

The earlier tone had been that of a conscientious, civilized man who meant it when he told one of his summer audiences that never during the campaign would he say anything he did not believe to be true. In this mode and mood he had attacked Roosevelt's conduct of domestic affairs, in general, for ineptitudes and dishonesties that, betraying the liberal principles espoused by the New Deal, resulted in glaring economic failures, notably in the continuing high rate of unemployment. He had damned the administration for stifling economic initiatives and preventing the vast increase of material wealth that could come from a proper employment of available technological resources. With respect to foreign affairs, he had attacked Roosevelt as an isolationist, instanced by the wrecking of the World Economic Conference in London in 1931 —also as an appeaser, instanced by the President's role (as Willkie understood it) in the events leading to the Munich Agreement. He blamed Roosevelt for the fact that the United States in the summer of 1940 was appallingly unprepared militarily for the crisis she faced. He blamed Roosevelt, too, in the third week of August, for failure to lead on the issues of peacetime conscription and all-out aid to Britain.

But three things, none of them within Willkie's control, rendered politically ineffective his attacks upon his opponent and his efforts to assume for himself a credible leadership role.

One was the fact that he, eager to fight, was denied a tangible and present opponent and must therefore spend his tremendous energies shadow-boxing around an otherwise empty ring. Roosevelt, in keeping with the statement he had made in his acceptance speech, ostentatiously disdained "politics" in times like these. He was far too busy with important affairs to engage in such trivial pursuit. He remained in the White House making major news daily, or he journeyed to Chattanooga to dedicate a giant new TVA dam, or he made greatly publicized "inspections" of defense facilities; but never once did he reply to anything Willkie said, or respond to any of Willkie's numerous demands for a debate on fundamental issues, or even publicly mention Willkie's name. For instance, during congressional debate of the Selective Service bill, Democratic senators John H. Overton of Louisiana and Richard B. Russell (neither of them a liberal) proposed an amendment that could have enabled the government to draft capital as well as men in certain circumstances. Designed to blunt the charge that private property was deemed too sacred to be confiscated while human beings were being forced to risk their lives, the amendment would have given the secretaries of war and navy blanket authority to seize industrial properties.* Willkie impulsively blasted this as an attempt to "sovietize" the economy and demanded to know where Roosevelt stood on the "fundamental" issue. Roosevelt refused to say. Willkie suffered damaging ridicule. A Democratic senator proposed as the Republican campaign song "I Didn't Raise My Dollar to Be a Soldier";[33] and Ickes, who had already dubbed Willkie "the barefoot boy from Wall Street," shot new barbs of the same kind into his public image.

The second factor that rendered Willkie's opening campaign politically ineffective was the reactionary and isolationist record that had been made and, even as he spoke, continued emphatically to be made by the Republican congressional delegation. As Walter Lippmann wrote in his column for August 19: "Mr. Willkie cannot make speeches advocating conscription and the policy of extending to Great Britain 'the material resources of the nation,' and expect the people to follow him if his own party does not follow him. . . . The party cannot offer the country a national leader for the next four years if in the weeks after he accepts the nomination they reject and repudiate his leadership."[34] The Republican record left the Republican standard-bearer helplessly exposed and vulnerable, early and late, to the more than plausible charge that his election victory was ardently desired and actively worked for by Nazi-Fascist agents

---

*The amendment was subsequently made more specific, hence more limited: Industrial plants could be seized in the unlikely event that their owners refused to accept government contracts. Thus clarified and weakened, the amendment was in the bill Roosevelt signed on September 16.

and supporters in the United States. "The Republican candidate is not an appeaser and not a friend of Hitler," said Henry Wallace. "I'll say, too, that every Republican is not an appeaser. But you can be sure that every Nazi, every Hitlerite, and every appeaser is a Republican."[35] It was on this ground that Dorothy Thompson outraged the owners of the New York *Herald Tribune,* whose syndicate distributed her column, by announcing for Roosevelt on October 9. Five days later, in a column the *Herald Tribune* refused to print (other papers did print it), she asserted that, though Willkie "as a character and a patriot" had "nothing to do with the case," a "systematic" campaign against Franklin D. Roosevelt" was being directed from Berlin and Rome through "the entire Fascist setup in this country, including a large section of the Italian and German press."[36] Very few Americans who believed—or even deemed it at all likely—that a vote for Willkie would be a vote for Hitler were likely to vote Republican that year.

The third factor injurious to Willkie's campaign was a rapidly improving domestic economy. British orders of war goods from the United States, slow in coming and meager in amount during the Chamberlain ministry, now came in flood, and to their stimulating effects upon the economy were added those of the American rearmament effort. By late summer, industrial plants long idle were gearing up for new production, and unemployment rolls were beginning to shrink rapidly—by 400,000 in August, by another 500,000 in September, according to official estimates. Willkie's charge that Rooseveltian mismanagement of the economy was prolonging the depression ceased to have much persuasive force.

Small wonder that polls which in June had shown Roosevelt leading Willkie with 60 percent of the vote continued to do so in September. What could Willkie do about it? Either he confessed his utter helplessness and conceded the election—something he could not honorably do, something his temperament made it utterly impossible for him to do—or he must make drastic changes in his campaign strategy. He of course did the latter. And these changes, as he gradually made them, were inevitably of a kind that brought him into ever closer alignment with the ruling powers of the party he presumed to represent.

Accompanying this shift of strategy was the aforementioned change in the tone of Willkie's campaign. The new tone was the strident one of a man whose sole commitment is to victory in a contest he has entered—victory at whatever cost to truth and fair play. Was not he himself victimized by the foul play of his opponents? In mid-September, in a Los Angeles suburb, he was struck by a tomato thrown by a high school student. Thereafter, in other cities across the land, in working-class districts, he became the target of a wide assortment of thrown vegetables in various states of decay—also of eggs, light bulbs, and other articles—and was told that at least some of this injury-threatening rowdiness was organized and paid for by Democratic city bosses. Seldom in prior American political history had passions been as strong and bitterly negative as those on both sides of this campaign. And as Willkie's incredibly strenuous campaigning continued without letup day and day out, week after week—as, living on his campaign train with little sleep, he became more and more tired and less and less certain of what his "crusade" (so he called it) was all about—as his voice went hoarse after the first day of his official campaign, a symptom of profound psychological insecurities, some thought, and was soon thereafter reduced to a rasping croak (a throat specialist was summoned aboard the train to prevent total voice collapse)—as all these things happened, hostile circumstance conspired with his deeply inbred success-anxiety to overwhelm his initially conscientious reasonableness. He had never had control of his political situation; he now lost control of himself.

Simultaneously, one brake upon his ruthless pursuit of "success" was removed or much loosened by the progress of the Battle of Britain. By the last of September it was evident that the Royal Air Force was winning the battle —might, in fact, have won it. In August, the RAF had reportedly destroyed 1,133 German aircraft in the skies over England while losing only 360 planes of its own; the same ratio of nearly three to one was being maintained through September, during which month, reportedly, 1,108 German planes were destroyed as against 361 British.[37] Göring had failed to break Britain's air shield; he seemed to be admitting as much by shifting his main attack from daylight fighter-plane assaults and daylight bombing to heavy night bombing of London and other cities.* Hence no immediate land invasion of Britain was likely to be attempted or, if attempted, to succeed. Clearly, Britain was not only determined but also able to defend herself, and Hitler's triumph, if still ultimately inevitable, was indefinitely posponed. Political potency was thereby restored to charges of "warmongering" hurled at Roosevelt—charges that during the summer he had been drained of such potency, to a considerable degree, by fear that major Nazi-Fascist aggressions against this hemisphere might be launched very soon.

It *may* have been by inadvertence that Willkie injected the war issue into the campaign in late September. He *may* have been primarily concerned to impugn Roosevelt's honesty in general, and deficit financing in particular, when he said in a public speech: "If his [Roosevelt's] promise to keep our boys out of foreign wars is no better than his promise to balance the budget, they're already almost on the transports." Inadvertent or not, the remark opened a wide crack in a dam holding back floodwaters of popular emotion; and soon the dam gave way altogether, loosing a torrent upon which Candidate Willkie began to ride willingly, if not happily, since it roared, apparently, toward November victory. Noting the sudden leap upward for him in the polls, egged on by John D. M. Hamilton and other professional right-wing Republicans,

---

*This shift was made in specific response to the bombing of Berlin by some eighty RAF bombers on the nights of August 25–29. "The Berliners are stunned," wrote William L. Shirer in his diary entry for August 26, 1940. "They did not think it could happen. . . . Goering [had] assured them it couldn't." See Shirer, *Berlin Diary* (New York, 1961 paperback edition), p. 361.

he who had damned Roosevelt as an "appeaser" during the summer began damning him in October as a "warmonger," a man whose ambition for dictatorial powers made him a greater threat to America's peace than Adolf Hitler. Before long, Willkie was going so far as to hint that "secret agreements" to get this country into the war had been entered into, and to predict that "on the basis of his [Roosevelt's] past performances with pledges to the people, you may expect war in April 1941, if he is elected."[38]

Abruptly, Roosevelt's hitherto comfortable victory margin in the polls began to shrink and a flood of telegrams, letters, and phone calls descended upon the White House, many of them from people whose political judgment had proved accurate in the past and all of them predicting a Roosevelt defeat unless he entered the campaign at once, and vigorously.

He did so.

A White House press release announced on October 18 that, in response to "a systematic program of falsification of fact by the opposition," and pursuant to the promise he had made in his acceptance speech, the President "has . . . decided to tell the American people what these representations are and in what respect they are false. With that purpose in mind, the President will make five speeches between now and election day."[39]

Roosevelt was of course much involved covertly in the campaign through all the post-convention weeks and months before he became overtly active in it; and one portion of this covert involvement was portentious of the "dirty tricks" that would become a staple of Republican presidential electioneering in the 1970s, '80s, and early '90s. The very worst of these "tricks" would be exposed to the general public some forty years later, by a historian of remarkable persistence and sleuthing skill. . . .[40]

Immediately following press reports of his supposedly off-the-record explanation of his foreign policy to the Senate military affairs committee on January 31, 1939—the reports in which he was alleged to have said that America's "frontier" was "on the Rhine"—an infuriated Roosevelt and press secretary Steve Early had cast about for some way in which the President could be protected absolutely against the perpetuation, in the historical record, of such "lies" as this. An answer to the problem was provided when, evidently at the original instigation of White House official stenographer Henry M. Kanee, and after many months of skilled hard work, an experimental mechanical voice-recording device employing film sound tracks was developed by technicians of the Radio Corporation of America. It was personally presented to the President as a gift, in late June 1940, by the executive head of RCA, David Sarnoff. Dubbed the RCA Continuous-Film Recording Machine, the device (it was the first and last of its kind) was installed in a booth in the basement of the White House's executive wing, immediately beneath the Oval Office—a booth to which only the White House stenographer had access; it was kept securely locked against everyone else. From it wires ran upward through the office floor to a button switch hidden in a desk drawer at Roosevelt's left hand, thence to a microphone concealed in a lamp on the presidential desk, so that Roosevelt could turn the microphone on or off, activating or deactivating the recording device surreptitiously.[41]

He was thus physically prepared secretly to record (if imperfectly, due to mechanical deficiencies) whatever was said by him and others in the Oval Office. He was, however, unprepared spiritually to do so in any wholesale fashion. His game-playing, fun-streaked penchant for secrecy and deviousness here collided with, and was halted by, his sense of justice and fair play, his gentleman's code of honor, and his remarkably acute sensitivity to political risks. He permitted Kanee to test out the device through a secret voice recording of his press conferences in late summer and early autumn; this was no honor-code violation since, as every reporter knew, verbatim stenographic records were kept of every press conference. He evidently further experimented by recording or permitting Kanee to record a few of his office conversations with personal aides and members of Congress, though some of these preserved recordings may have been unintended, the microphone having been inadvertantly switched on or not switched off. But the equipment was very sparingly used for these three months or so and, after 1940's election day, was evidently not used at all. It was subsequently dismantled, never again to be reassembled.[42]

The microphone was open, however, on a day in late August 1940 when Roosevelt talked with one of his assistants, Lowell Mellett, in the Oval Office. He had been informed that Republican campaign strategists had somehow managed to get their hands upon, and were trying to persuade a Republican newspaper to publish, a cache of letters written by his running mate, Henry Wallace, to one Nicholas Roerich, a White Russian mystic, cult leader, and presumed expert on central Asian agriculture with whom, according to Wallace's later testimony, Roosevelt's mother, Sara, was much taken.[43] Wallace had employed Roerich as head of a 1934–1935 department of agriculture expedition in search of drouth-resistant grasses in Manchuria and Mongolia. Some of the letters, bearing the salutation "Dear Guru," were more than embarrassing: The extravagance of the mystical occult language they employed called into question the mental and emotional stability of the man who wrote them. Published, they would harm, perhaps gravely, the Roosevelt reelection campaign. And it was ways and means of forestalling such publication that Roosevelt talked about in rambling, ambivalent, and ambiguous fashion while the microphone listened and the basement machine recorded.

*"Now, now,* if they want to play dirty politics in the end, we've got our own people," said he to Mellett, going on to refer to "this story about the *gal"* that "is spreading around the country." The "gal" was Irita Van Doran, book reviewer of the New York *Herald Tribune* ("awful nice gal," said Roosevelt, "writes for the magazine and so forth and so on"), with whom Willkie, allegedly estranged from his wife, had allegedly been having an affair for many years. Roosevelt, convinced that the allegations were true (". . . there is the *fact,"* he said), was also convinced that "so far as the Old Man [that is, he

himself] goes, we can't use it." The story could, however, be "spread . . . as a word-of-mouth thing . . . by some people *way down the line.* . . . I mean the Congress speakers, and state speakers, and so forth. *They* can use the raw material." He was reminded of the famous "trial" of New York City mayor Jimmy Walker on charges of corruption which he, Roosevelt, as governor of New York, had conducted in Albany in 1932.* Walker, born and raised a Catholic, had at that time a mistress with whom he was "living openly . . . all over New York . . . an extremely attractive little tart." He and his wife were separated. And Walker "hadn't been in church in five whole years." But "Jimmy . . . paid his wife ten thousand dollars to come up to Albany . . . on a Friday afternoon, after my trial had finished for the week," and live with him "in the same suite in the hotel, and on Sunday the two of them go to Mass in the Albany Cathedral together. . . . *Now, now,* Mrs. Willkie may not have been *hired,* but in effect she's been hired to return to Willkie and smile, and make this campaign with him."[44]

As it turned out, whether because the Republicans feared the kind of retaliation Roosevelt spoke of or because (as Rosenman believed) a high-minded Willkie refused to stoop so low, the so-called "Guru Letters" were not published during the 1940 campaign.

What followed reflected no credit upon either Roosevelt or his opponent (Willkie's extremist language became more extremist still). It was, indeed, as regards foreign policy, a downward action–reaction spiraling, for both of them, into depths dark and dangerous for the American people.

Roosevelt's first campaign speech was on October 23 in Philadelphia. In it, after contrasting his administration's eight-year record in domestic affairs with the Republicans' twelve-year record from 1920 through 1932, he poured contempt upon the irresponsible charge that "secret agreements" with other powers had been entered into and that "this Administration wishes to lead this country into war. That charge is contrary to every fact, every purpose of the past eight years. . . . To Republicans and Democrats, to every man, woman, and child in the nation I say this: 'Your President and your Secretary of State are following the road to peace. . . . It is for peace that I have labored; and it is for peace that I shall labor all the days of my life.' "[45]

Two nights later he, with some thirty million other Americans, listened to John L. Lewis as this founder of the CIO, in a radio speech carried by all three radio networks and heard over some 350 local stations, castigated him, with the vigor of virulent personal hatred, in a peculiarly ugly tirade. Having charged Roosevelt with dictatorial ambitions, declared his support for Wendell Willkie, urged organized labor to "sustain" or "repudiate" his leadership in this matter, and promised to resign as CIO president if he were not so "sustained"—having done all this, Lewis addressed the young men of his audience, saying: "You, who may be about to die in a foreign war, created at the whim of an international meddler, should you salute your Caesar?" He then addressed the mothers in his

*See *FDR: The New York Years,* pp. 300–302, 304–5, 353–55.

audience: "May I hope that on election day [you] . . . with the sacred ballot, [will] lead the revolt against the candidate who plays at a game that may make cannon fodder of your sons?" But Roosevelt had heavily counted in advance on the adverse effect that Lewis's speech would have on his, Roosevelt's, reelection chances. He had foreseen that Lewis's virulence would probably be so extreme as to alienate independent voters—had been assured that labor's rank and file, recognizing Lewis's power-lust as clearly as the White House did, shared the White House's fear of it. And in the event, though Willkie promptly wired Lewis to thank him and compliment him on "the most eloquent address I ever heard," and though Herbert Hoover told Lewis "that the speech will resound over years to come," the popular reaction to Lewis's negativism was itself generally negative while most of organized labor, including a huge majority of the members of his own CIO, promptly denounced him bitterly as "traitor" and "turncoat."[46]

Roosevelt's concern over the adverse effect that Joe Kennedy's public speech would have.

Much more serious was, particularly if the ambassador, now flying back to the United States via Lisbon, thence by Clipper across the Atlantic, should resign his ambassadorial post and then endorse Willkie in a radio network broadcast. That Kennedy, infuriated by a long series of White House and State Department snubs, planned to do precisely this had been reported to Roosevelt as a more than plausible rumor in the second week of October. The rumor had become front-page news in the national press on the day of Roosevelt's first campaign speech, which was also the day of Kennedy's departure from London. Roosevelt found it highly worrisome. A full-scale Kennedy attack a few days before the election upon the administration's foreign policy, and upon Roosevelt personally, was certain to lead America into the war, would probably cost Roosevelt the election, the race being as close as it was. Roosevelt promptly took steps to prevent the threatened dire event. There awaited Kennedy in Lisbon a note from the President requesting him to come at once to the White House when he arrived in the United States and, in the meantime, to make no statements to reporters. Another presidential note awaited Kennedy when he landed in Bermuda, this one inviting him and his wife (she would meet him in New York) to come to the White House as overnight guests immediately upon his arrival. This invitation was reiterated with great cordiality by the President in direct conversation when, within an hour after landing in New York on October 27, Kennedy phoned the White House.[47]

"Ah, Joe, old friend, it is good to hear your voice," Roosevelt reportedly boomed. "Please come to the White House tonight for a little family dinner. I'm dying to talk to you."[48]*

Kennedy accepted the invitation, of course, and thereby provided the occa-

---

*Young Lyndon B. Johnson later told Arthur Krock that he was with the President when the Kennedy phone call came through and that, as Roosevelt hung up the phone, he drew his finger, as if it were a razor, across his throat.

sion, while becoming (as he would later believe) the victim of one of the most remarkable triumphs of the famous Roosevelt charm. Fellow guests at the dinner table were Senator and Mrs. Byrnes, with whom the Kennedys had warmly friendly social relations. They joined with Roosevelt to provide a sympathetically responsive audience as the ambassador, encouraged to do so, gave untrammelled expression to his abundant grievances. Roosevelt, indeed, was more than sympathetic: He fully shared Kennedy's resentments, was outraged by the State Department's circumvention of the London embassy (he claimed not only to have had no part in this but also to have been, until now, unaware of it), praised Kennedy's performance as ambassador, avowed his continued great personal affection for Joe, and strongly hinted that Joe's support of him now would lead to his support of Joe's presidential candidacy in 1944. Before the evening was over, Kennedy, who may have entered the White House intending to do what rumor had said he would do, had instead promised to do as Roosevelt wished.

He did so in a highly effective radio speech on October 29. He let it be known in advance that he personally, and not the Democratic National Committee, was paying for his radio time, thus heightening popular suspense over what he might say and greatly expanding his radio audience. To this audience he frankly admitted that "there have been disagreements between the President and me" but went on to measure them small against the necessity for retaining in office, in these parlous times, a strong and experienced leader. He said that "if we rearm fast enough we will stay out of war," assured his listeners (despite his own doubts about it) that Roosevelt had entered into no secret agreements with the British government, and closed with "I urge the reelection of Franklin Roosevelt."[49]

On the evening before (October 28), just a few hours after Mussolini had launched from Albania an unprovoked invasion of Greece, Roosevelt had addressed a huge rally in Madison Square Garden. Without mentioning Willkie's name, he assailed Willkie's assertion that the administration had failed adequately to build up America's armed defenses and so exposed the nation to grave threats from abroad. In fact it was the Republicans in Congress, he said, who had "played politics" with national defense, opposing in huge majority every measure designed to increase national security. "In March, 1939, the Republican Senators voted 12 to 4 against the bill for $102 million to buy certain strategic war materials which we did not have in this country. In March, 1939, the Republicans in the Senate voted 11 to 8 against increasing the authorized number of planes in the Navy. In June, 1939, Republicans in the House voted 144 to 8 in favor of reducing the appropriations for the Army Air Corps." And what of the claim by "Republican campaign orators and leaders" that they, too, favored aid to Britain? Where stood the congressional Republicans when repeal of the arms embargo, to permit aid to the Allies on a "cash-and-carry" basis, was presented to them? "In the Senate the Republicans voted 14 to 6 against it. In the House the Republicans voted 140 to 19 against it. . . . And just to name a few, the following Republican

leaders, among many others, voted against the act: Senators McNary, Vanden-
burg, Nye, Johnson, and (now wait, a perfectly beautiful rhythm) Congressmen Martin, Barton, and Fish."* Great Britain would never have "received
one ounce of help from us," he said a little later, "if the decision had been left
to Martin, Barton, and Fish"—and this time, as he chanted the refrain, his
audience delightedly chanted it with him. He placed his greatest emphasis,
however, in this speech, upon his efforts over the years to maintain true
"neutrality" in a world of growing dangers, going so far as to mention favorably the Neutrality Act of 1935! He called it one of the "steps" whereby "your
government undertook to eliminate certain hazards which in the past had led
us into war"![50] On the following day, against the insistent and even frantic
urgings of political advisers, he personally presided over the drawing of the
first draft numbers under the newly passed Selective Service Law. "This is a
most solemn ceremony," he told a national radio audience. "It is accompanied
by no fanfare—no blowing of bugles or beating of drums. There should be
none."[51] He then stood grave-faced to one side before clicking still photographers and whirring newsreel cameras while a blindfolded Secretary Stimson
fished out of a huge glass goldfish bowl the historic cobalt-blue capsule.

But he overbalanced this brave act with its opposite when, next day, riding
his special train to Boston, with frequent interruptions for rear-platform appearances, he worked with his new team of speech writers upon the address
he would give that night in the Boston Garden. This new team, destined to
remain together as key members of the President's official family from then
on, consisted of Rosenman, Hopkins, and playwright Robert Sherwood, whom
Hopkins had recruited in the early summer. And as the four men worked
together, with Missy and Grace Tully at hand to type and retype the speech
draft, each of them felt acutely the pressure of the messages pouring in from
frightened politicians all over the country—messages delivered in bundles at
every train stop—saying that the President would lose the election unless he
flatly guaranteed to "American mothers" that their drafted sons would be well
fed and housed in military camp, would be well cared for there in every way,
but would *never* have to fight. A bone-tired Franklin Roosevelt yielded to these
importunities. He had not intended to repeat the peace plank of the Democratic platform in this speech, and when he was handed a telegram from Ed
Flynn (he had replaced Jim Farley as campaign manager) insisting that the "no
foreign wars" pledge be emphasized in Boston he protested: "How often do
they expect me to say that? . . . I've repeated it a hundred times." To which
Sherwood replied that "evidently you've got to say it again—and again—and

*Joseph W. Martin of Massachusetts was minority leader of the House; Bruce Barton was a New
York City advertising man who had written a best-selling book, *The Man Nobody Knows,* describing Jesus Christ as a genius of advertising and salesmanship who, had he lived in modern-day
America, would undoubtedly have been a leading member of the Rotary Club; Hamilton Fish was
the Dutchess County aristocrat whose personal hatred of neighbor Franklin Roosevelt was the
dominant emotion of his political life and who saw no reason why good Americans could not get
along with Adolf Hitler.

again." So he wrote into his speech the words that, a few hours later, he would speak to his huge audience with utmost emphasis and earnestness: "Very simply and very honestly, I can give assurance to the mothers and fathers of America that each and every one of their boys in training will be well housed and well fed. Throughout that year of training, there will be constant promotion of their health and their well-being. And while I am talking to you mothers and fathers, I give you one more assurance. I have said this before, but I shall say it again and again and again: Your boys are not going to be sent into any foreign wars." When Rosenman reminded him that the platform added a proviso, "except in case of attack," Roosevelt responded irritably: "If somebody attacks us, then it isn't a foreign war, is it? Or do they want me to guarantee that our troops will be sent into battle only in the event of another Civil War?"[52]

The words were destined to plague him "again and again and again" during the coming months. So would the flat statement he made during extemporaneous remarks in Buffalo on November 2, when he was on his way to Cleveland to deliver on the following night the last of his five formal campaign addresses. His Buffalo statement was: "Your President says this country is not going to war."[53]

IV

IT is the last hour of Monday night, November 3, 1940, and Franklin Delano Roosevelt, with his considerable entourage, is again at Hyde Park—the single spot in the whole of that wide world he now bestrides (with withered legs) where he feels truly at home. Outside the windows facing him, reaching out dark and flat under the night sky to the Albany Post Road, are the bluegrass lawn, overarched by great elms and maples, and the wide fields and meadow, over which he had roamed and played as a shy, solitary, overmothered, highly privileged little boy. Behind him is the back wall of the mansion where, furtively, through gaps in the Georgian mantle that he (with his mother's permission) imposed upon it decades ago, peeks out the old Victorian Hudson River–bracketed Springwood that was his father's house and his own boyhood home. Beyond it are orchard and meadow and the remnants of ancient forest, a wilderness of ancient firs and pines, sloping down to the great river of his life, the mighty Hudson.

"Once more I am in the quiet of my home in Hyde Park on the eve of Election day," he says to his fellow Americans through the microphones clustered before him.

> I wish to speak to you not of partisan politics but of the Nation, the United States of America, to which we all owe such deep and inborn allegiance. As I sit here tonight with my own family, I think of all the other American families—millions of families all through the land—sitting in their own homes. They have eaten their suppers in peace, they will be able to sleep in their homes tonight in peace. Tomorrow

they will be free to go out to live their ordinary lives in peace—free to say and do what they wish, free to worship as they please. Tomorrow, of all days, they will be free to choose their own leaders who, when that choice has been made, become in turn only the instruments to carry out the will of all the people. . . . Dictators have forgotten—or perhaps they never knew—the basis upon which democratic Government is founded: that the opinion of all the people, freely formed and freely expressed . . . is wiser than the opinion of any one man or any small group of men. . . . Your will is a part of the great will of America. Your voice is a part of the great voice of America. And when you and I stand in line tomorrow for our turn at the polls, we are voting equals.

He urged his listeners to exercise their Heaven-blessed right to vote. "Last Saturday night, I said that freedom of speech is of no use to the man who has nothing to say and that freedom of worship is of no use to the man who has lost his God. And tonight I should like to add that a free election is of no use to the man who is too indifferent to vote." He closed with a prayer he remembered from the Episcopalian Book of Common Prayer that Rector Endicott Peabody had used at Groton long ago, a prayer that itself closed as follows: "Endue with the spirit of wisdom those to whom in Thy Name we entrust the authority of government, that there may be peace and justice at home, and that, through obedience to Thy law, we may show forth Thy praise among the nations of the earth. In the time of prosperity, fill our hearts with thankfulness, and in the day of trouble, suffer not our trust in Thee to fail; Amen."[54]

He went to bed that night knowing that the latest Gallup survey showed Willkie so close to him in popular support, as of a couple or so days ago, that he might well by now have overtaken and surpassed him—though the less widely known Roper poll, taken somewhat later than Gallup's and that he liked to believe was the more accurate, had him ahead by a margin nearly as wide as it had been in early summer. Neither poll disturbed his sleep. With Eleanor and his mother he voted next day at Hyde Park's town hall, posing good-humoredly for photographers. When a photographer asked him to wave, he asked, "At what?" When the reporter replied, "At the trees," he demurred, saying he never waved at trees "unless they have leaves on them," yet waved nevertheless at trees that were leafless.

There was the usual election-night party of family, staff members, and friends in the Big House that night. Roosevelt was seated in the small family dining room off the big dining room. A tablet on the table before him, pencil in hand, he listened to radio reports of the election returns, also read them on snatches of teletype brought him now and then from the AP, UP, and INS machines that chattered away in a corner of the dining room; he added the figures as he jotted them down. He was in his shirtsleeves, alone at that point save for brief visits from Eleanor, other family members, and a tense and nervous Henry Morgenthau, who was in and out constantly. Mike Reilly, chief of the Secret Service staff responsible for Roosevelt's safety, sat beside the open door. The President seemed his usual relaxed genial self. It was early in the evening. The returns were yet too meager and mixed to show a definite trend, though the evident Willkie strength in New York and other large cities was somewhat greater than expected.

Suddenly, Roosevelt spoke sharply to Reilly.

"Mike, I don't want to see anybody in here," he said.

Surprised by the tone of voice, Reilly was astonished to see that Roosevelt had broken into a heavy sweat. Was he ill? Or had he noted something that upset him? Reilly at once concluded it was the latter—the only failure of nerve on Roosevelt's part that he had ever witnessed, or ever would.

"Including your family, Mr. President?" asked Reilly.

"I said '*anybody*,' " Roosevelt snapped.

So Reilly closed the door and stood outside it, after telling Eleanor Roosevelt her husband's wish. Soon he had to turn away an angrily protesting Morgenthau, which gave him mingled pleasure and pain, since he didn't much like fussy nervous Morgenthau, yet was acutely aware that Morgenthau was his boss (the Secret Service was a part of Treasury) and not the kind who ever forgot that he was.[55]

The door remained closed and Reilly on guard for an indefinite period, perhaps as long as forty minutes.

We may imagine, as earlier historians have imagined,[56] what went on in Roosevelt's mind during this time of solitude. Something seen or heard in the returns had convinced him that he had lost the election—that the end had come of the road he had entered with his race for the New York legislature thirty years earlier. Nor was it, alas, for him, a personally honorable end; he had to feel shame over his final performance, the sacrifice of principle to an expediency that proved not even expedient. Yet what else could or should he have done, given the enormity of the alternative to his victory in this election? The race was so close, the outcome so important! And had he done other than he did, would not the margin of his defeat have been much wider than it now appeared to be, hence more decisive of sad change in American life? As it was, with Willkie's narrow victory, he must now be forced to witness, in all likelihood, the ruin of the America to which the New Deal had been dedicated and which it had striven to build; and this meant, in a world of totalitarianism, the loss of what Lincoln had called the "last best hope of Earth." For now, more than ever, Roosevelt was sure that his defeat would mean the triumph of forces of immense evil in American life, forces that flourished in a world environment increasingly favorable to them, forces aimed straight at the kind of civil strife out of which, in other lands, the corporate state had arisen. Wendell Willkie was but a puppet of these forces, to be used and then cast aside.

"There is something very ominous in this combination that has been forming within the Republican Party between the extreme reactionary and extreme radical elements of this country," he had said in Brooklyn five days ago.

There is no common ground upon which they can unite—we know that—unless it be their common will to power, and their impatience with the normal democratic processes to produce overnight the inconsistent dictatorial ends that they, each of them, seek.

No elements in American public life have made such attacks upon each other in recent years as have the members of this new unholy alliance against each other. . . .

[W]e must remember what the collaborative understanding between Communism and Nazism has done to the processes of democracy abroad.

Something evil is happening in this country when a full-page advertisement against this Administration, paid for by Republican supporters, appears—where, of all places?—in the *Daily Worker,* the newspaper of the Communist Party.

Something evil is happening in this country when vast quantities of Republican campaign literature are distributed by organizations [they were right-wing organizations] that make no secret of their admiration for the dictatorship form of government.[57]

Such cynical and obviously strictly temporary cooperation between extremes fundamentally and passionately opposed to one another was not only reflective of the cynical and, to Roosevelt's mind, obviously strictly temporary accomodation between Hitler and Stalin; it was also only too reminiscent of the collaboration between German Nazis and German Communists in the frustration and ultimate destruction of the Weimar Republic. It gave a measure of disturbing plausibility to a report brought to Roosevelt only a few days ago of a secret meeting between representatives of the German government and men purporting to speak for Willkie wherein it was allegedly agreed that the United States, if Willkie became President, would compel Britain (by witholding aid from her, and despite candidate Willkie's public stand on the matter) to accept the peace terms Hitler had proposed. In return for this, according to the report, Germany would guarantee an unchallenged hegemony by the United States over the Western Hemisphere.[58]

"Those forces [of the extreme right and left] hate democracy and Christianity as two phases of the same civilization," Roosevelt had gone on to say in Brooklyn. "They oppose democracy because it is Christian. They oppose Christianity because it preaches democracy.

"Their objective is to prevent democracy from becoming strong and purposeful. We are strong and purposeful now and intend to remain so."[59]

But were we? And did we?

Evidently not.

Yet the election returns continued to pour into his ears, his eyes, his mind, and soon their import drove from that mind most of the darkness that had oppressed it. Evidently the early returns had misled him. The voting trend he had thought he discerned, if ever present, had now wholly disappeared. Its opposite was increasingly emphatically evident. Willkie was *not* winning! He, Roosevelt, was! This trend was not as yet absolutely irreversible; there still remained, and would for hours remain, an ever fainter statistical possibility that Roosevelt's electoral college victory margin would be erased by late returns. Clearly Willkie himself remained unpersuaded of defeat, since no concession message had come from him. Hence Roosevelt's feeling of immense relief over catastrophe averted was not unqualified. But the black cloud of utter terror and despair in which, almost unprecedentedly, he had been lost for a long moment was now dissipated as abruptly as it had been formed.

He called out to Mike Reilly. The door was opened. It remained wide open for the remainder of a crowded, festive evening.

Toward midnight, responding to a commotion on the wide lawn outside, Roosevelt clicked into rigidity the steel braces on his legs and, one hand grasping the arm of Franklin Junior, moved stiffly out of the Big House's front door onto the portico, there to greet a jubilant crowd of Hyde Park friends, neighbors, well-wishers.

He knew by then that he had carried his own district, the third Hyde Park district, 426 to 309.* This delighted him, for the district was heavily Republican and he had not carried it in 1932 or 1936. But not until two-thirty in the morning was he sufficiently assured of his victory to go peacefully to his bed, the nature of his relief expressed in his good-night statement to his wife's young friend, Lash: "We seem to have averted a *Putsch,* Joe," he said.[60] Not for eight or so hours after that would he receive a somewhat grudgingly worded message of concession and congratulation from his opponent. And not until the evening of November 6 would he know the exact proportions of his victory—that of the nearly fifty million votes cast in this election, the largest voter turnout in American history up till then, he had won 27,243,000, Willkie 22,304,000, which was five million more than Landon had won in 1936 (Roosevelt's plurality was the smallest any presidential election winner had had since Woodrow Wilson in 1916); and that of the electoral college vote he had won 449 from thirty-eight states compared to Willkie's 82 from ten states.

Lacking this knowledge, Roosevelt had still quivering deep within him a slender, shrinking streak of anxiety as, at midnight, he faced the happy throng on the lawn. He gave no sign of it, however, in face or manner. It was a confidence of victory unflawed by the slightest doubt that he projected as he smiled down upon the sea of faces—faces that were themselves smiling, and ruddy in the light of the flaming, smoking victory torches that most of his visitors carried. The crowd responded with a roar of laughter when he pretended surprise at seeing them there, a similar torchlight parade having ended here in celebration of every Democratic presidential election victory in the last six decades, and of every Roosevelt election victory since 1910. He himself roared with laughter when a young boy held up a placard on which OUT AT THIRD had been crossed out and SAFE ON THIRD lettered above it.

In the brief informal remarks that followed, he claimed to remember the torchlight parade onto these grounds in celebration of Grover Cleveland's first election in 1884 ("but the family say I do not. . . . I was one and a half years old at the time") and wondered aloud if the present occasion would be remembered fifty-eight years from now by his grandson (he, Franklin Junior's son, was now one and a half), who perhaps watched these proceedings from "up

---

*He did not carry the whole Town of Hyde Park, however, losing 1,363–1,422. Dutchess County voted against him by a substantial margin, 32,318–25,591.

there in that room." This speculative cast into the wide river of time brought to mind an acute awareness of the river's present turbulence, of the fatal dangers to the Republic of this turbulence, and of the awful responsibilities of a President who must somehow guide the ship of state, intact, through the raging waters to a safe shore.

The awareness shaped his final words.

"We are facing difficult days in this country, but," he said—and his use of the conjunctive has rich psychological implications, "I think you will find me in the future just the same Franklin Roosevelt you have known a great many years."

He gave one reason why this was so—perhaps the main reason, in his view. "My heart has always been here," he closed. "It always will be."[61]

Then, with another wide smile, and a farewell wave to the crowd, he turned and, again grasping the arm of his son, made his way back into the mansion past his wife, Eleanor, his aged mother, Sara Delano—past an exulting Harry Hopkins and the wives of sons Franklin and John, all of whom had stood behind him while he spoke. The crowd broke up. Its members, yet noisily laughing and chatting, moved slowly off the lawn into the driveway that ended in the historic road running north toward Albany, running south toward the world city at the Hudson's mouth, and toward a hazardous future lighted, not by the controlled and cheerful flames of hand-held torches, but by the raging spreading flames of world-consuming war.

## Afterword

This history, now grown to four volumes, with a fifth and final volume yet to come, "is concerned less with the discovery and presentation of hitherto hidden facts about Franklin Roosevelt and his years than it is with comprehending in interpretive ways, and from a clearly defined point of view, factual information that has long been at hand in vast [intimidatingly vast] bulk." Thus I wrote in a foreword to the notes for the second volume. I added "my hope and belief . . . that such comprehension may help us better understand what is happening in American life today." This hope and belief are stronger now than they were then; for again and again as I've worked on the third and fourth volumes I've had further impressed upon me how very much of what is happening today in America and, indeed, the world, is consequent upon decisions that Roosevelt made—including (or especially) his decisions to do nothing save drift with the tide of circumstance—during the twelve crisis years in which he, as President of the United States, occupied a pivotal position in world affairs.

I also wrote, in the foreword to the notes for volume two, of a decision of my own, which was that I not include in the printed book the extensive bibliography I had prepared. "It would add at least ten pages to a work already sufficiently lengthy while serving, so far as I can see, no useful purpose. Most of the titles on my list are necessarily the same found in the literally hundreds of Roosevelt–New Deal bibliographies already printed and readily available to students, including that for *FDR: The Beckoning of Destiny, 1882–1928,* which is the first volume of the present history. Moreover, though several works consulted for general historical context and thematic program are not specifically cited in the following notes, most of the titles I used *are* so cited."

The same decision holds for the present volume.

# Notes

*Book One:* **The End of the New Deal**

**One: The Pride That Goeth Before a Fall?**

1. Raymond Moley, *After Seven Years* (New York, 1939), pp. 342, 350.

2. *The Public Papers and Addresses of Franklin D. Roosevelt* (13 volumes; New York, 1938–1950), vol. 5 (1936), pp. 568–69. These volumes are hereinafter cited as PPA 1936, PPA 1937, etc.

3. *Ibid.*, p. 72.

4. Author interview with Benjamin V. Cohen, Winthrop House, Washington, D.C., March 4, 1974.

5. Actually, the news stories summarized in the following pages, and which I have Roosevelt reading on Sunday morning, January 3, 1937, appeared in two successive issues of *The New York Times*, that of January 2 and that of January 3. As a general rule, I deplore any sacrifice of absolute factuality to the convenience of narrative in the writing of history (I am unaware of having done so at any other point in this history), but in the present instance the sacrifice seems to me very slight, resulting in no loss of historical truth, while the gain in narrative convenience is great. Indeed, Roosevelt may in fact have reviewed both papers on January 3.

6. *New York Times*, January 3, 1937.

7. PPA 1936, p. 644.

8. Harold L. Ickes, *The Secret Diary of Harold L. Ickes: The First Thousand Days, 1933–1936* (hereinafter, *Thousand Days*) (New York, 1953), p. 704.

9. *New York Times*, December 10, 1936. Kenneth S. Davis, *FDR: The New Deal Years, 1933–1937* (New York, 1986), p. 661.

10. PPA 1936, pp. 191–92.

11. Peter Wyden, *The Passionate War* (New York, 1983), p. 69, quoting Claude D. Bowers letter.

12. D. W. Brogan, *The Era of Franklin D. Roosevelt* (New Haven, Conn., 1950), p. 192.

13. Biochemist Stanley, in this 1935 research, worked with the tobacco mosaic virus, mashing up infected tobacco leaves and employing with rare skill techniques for extracting the virus and concentrating it in pure form. What astonished him and the scientific world was the fact that the virus he obtained was in crystalline form. This seemed clearly to indicate that the virus was simply dead protein, for theretofore nothing alive had ever been crystallized, and it was assumed that "life and crystallinity" were "mutually contradictory," as Isaac Asimov has written. "Life was flexible, changeable, dynamic; a crystal was rigid, fixed, strictly ordered." But when Stanley redissolved the virus crystals in liquid he found them to be as infectious as before, which is to say they grew and reproduced as only living things were assumed to be able to do. Years later, it was discovered by two British biochemists that the tobacco mosaic virus was *not* pure protein. It was 94 percent protein and 6 percent ribonucleic acid (RNA) —was, in other words, a nucleoprotein, which is "the stuff of genes, and the genes are the very essence of life." Subsequently, all other viruses were found to be nucleoproteins, "containing RNA or DNA or both." See Isaac Asimov, *The Intelligent Man's Guide to the Biological Sciences* (paperback ed.; New York, 1964), pp. 185–88. See also Davis, *FDR: The Beckoning of Destiny* (New York, 1972), pp. 651–53.

14. *New York Times,* January 2, 1937. Louis Brownlow, *A Passion for Anonymity,* vol. 2 (Chicago, 1958), p. 382. During his 1932 election campaign, in his notoriously ultra-conservative address in Pittsburgh, Roosevelt, having castigated Herbert Hoover for "an unbalanced budget," announced his own determination to balance the budget in part "by reorganization of existing departments, by eliminating functions, by abolishing many of those innumerable boards and those commissions . . . which . . . have grown up as a fungous growth on American government." Thus Roosevelt in 1932 had publicly espoused what Senator Byrd was proposing in 1937 as the main purpose of executive reorganization. See Davis, *FDR: The New York Years* (New York, 1985), p. 371.

15. Brownlow, *op. cit.,* p. 314.

16. *Ibid.,* p. 327, quoting the Merriam memorandum submitted to the President in October 1935.

17. *Ibid.,* p. 344, quoting the letter sent to Brownlow on March 20, 1936, by Roosevelt. The language of this letter, as Brownlow remarks, "is somewhat odd, since it was determined not by the President but by somebody on the staff of Mr. [John Raymond] McCarl, the comptroller general," in conference with "a staff member of the Bureau of the Budget." Roosevelt in conversation with Brownlow deplored the letter's "English" and resented the fact that he, the President of the United States, was "compelled [by the pre-auditing powers assigned the comptroller general by the Budget and Accounting Act of 1921] . . . to submit his letters in advance to the comptroller general," an office he hoped to abolish, through executive reorganization, as worse than useless.

18. Barry Dean Karl, *Executive Reorganization and Reform in the New Deal* (Cambridge, Mass., 1963), p. 215.

19. Brownlow, *op. cit.,* p. 336.

20. PPA 1936, pp. 669–70, 672–73.

21. Brownlow, *op. cit.,* pp. 347–48.

22. *Ibid.,* pp. 357, 381.

23. *Ibid.,* pp. 270–72.

24. *Ibid.,* p. 384.

25. This description of Brownlow's reaction to, and conclusion concerning, Roosevelt's psychological state is, admittedly, an inference from the tone and wording of the chapter entitled "The President and Congress" in *ibid.*

26. Harold L. Ickes, *The Secret Diary of Harold L. Ickes: The Inside Struggle* (New York, 1954) (hereinafter *Inside Struggle*), p. 32.

27. *Ibid.,* p. 31. PPA 1936, p. 639.

28. PPA 1936, pp. 639–42.

29. Ickes, *Inside Struggle,* pp. 32–33.

30. Robert Dallek, *Franklin D. Roosevelt and American Foreign Policy, 1932–1945* (New York, 1979), p. 136.

31. New York *Herald Tribune,* January 7, 1936.

32. Ickes, *Inside Struggle,* p. 45.

33. Brownlow, *op. cit.,* p. 389.

34. *Ibid.,* p. 396.

35. *New York Times,* January 13, 1937.

36. PPA 1936, pp. 670–72.

37. *New York Times,* January 17, 1987.

## Two: The Initiation and Anatomy of a Tragic Error

1. James MacGregor Burns, *Roosevelt: The Lion and the Fox,* p. 291, suggesting (though he never explicitly makes) an assessment of FDR's "gambler" psychology akin to my own assessment, opens his chapter entitled "Court-Packing: The Miscalculated Risk" with "Was it an omen?" —referring to the weather.

2. Samuel I. Rosenman, *Working with Roosevelt* (New York, 1952), p. 144.

3. *Ibid.*

4. PPA 1937, pp. 1–5.

5. Philip Dunne, ed., *Mr. Dooley Remembers* (Boston, 1963), p. 303.

6. The quote is but part of a sentence that goes on to say: ". . . and the judiciary is the safeguard of our liberty and our property." Governor Hughes made the remark in an extemporaneous speech on May 7, 1907, but essentially repeated it in a formal address, September 5, 1908, saying, "The Constitution, with its guarantees of liberty and grants of Federal power, is finally what the Supreme Court determines it to mean." Quoted by Samuel Hendel, for one, in his *Charles Evans Hughes and the Supreme Court* (New York, 1951), p. 12.

7. "When Charles Evans Hughes is a liberal, he proclaims it to the world. When he is a reactionary, he votes silently and allows someone else to be torn to pieces by the liberal dissenters. . . . One can only guess what the reputation of Mr. Hughes would be, if, in the fifty-one cases in which he helped create a reactionary majority, he had exposed himself sixteen times to the dissenting logic of Mr. Justice Stone. . . . Not once has he [Stone] had an opportunity to analyze an opinion written by the Chief Justice himself." Irving Brant, "How Liberal Is Justice Hughes?" *New Republic,* July 21, 1937. Quoted by Alpheus T. Mason, *Harlan Fiske Stone: Pillar of the Law* (New York, 1956), p. 316.

8. Ickes, *Thousand Days,* p. 704.

9. Rosenman, *op. cit.,* p. 141.

10. Max Freedman, ed. *Roosevelt and Frankfurter, Their Correspondence, 1928–1945* (Boston, 1967), p. 378.

11. Rosenman, *op. cit.,* pp. 145–46.

12. Letter and bill are in PPA 1937, pp. 60–66.

13. The direct quote is from the Message to Congress of February 5, 1937, PPA 1937, p. 53, but closely similar if not identical language was employed during the January 30 conference.

14. Joseph Alsop and Turner Catledge, in their indispensable and brilliant *The 168 Days* (New York, 1938), say, p. 33, that Cummings had originally noted the McReynolds quote while he and his special assistant, Carl MacFarland, were writing their history of the Justice Department entitled *Federal Justice,* published in the fall of 1936. The quote appears on p. 531 of the Cummings-MacFarland volume.

15. Rosenman, *op. cit.,* p. 147.

16. *Ibid.,* p. 149. Italics mine.

17. Author interview with Benjamin V. Cohen, Winthrop House, Washington, D.C., March 4, 1974. See also Alsop and Catledge, *op. cit.,* pp. 36–37.

18. Rosenman, *op. cit.,* p. 147.

19. Cohen interview, March 4, 1974.

20. Alsop and Catledge, *op. cit.,* p. 37.

21. Kenneth Burke, *Attitudes Toward History,* vol. 2 (New York, 1937), p. 61. Writes Henry Adams of his feeling about the Supreme Court in 1870, when the Court declared the Legal Tender Act unconstitutional: "Although, step by step, he [Adams] had been driven, like the rest of the world, to admit that the American society had outgrown most of its institutions, he still clung to the Supreme Court, much as a churchman clings to his bishops, because they

are his only symbol of unity; his last rag of Right." *The Education of Henry Adams,* p. 277, Modern Library edition.

22. Cohen interview, March 4, 1974. Henry Adams comes again to mind. Apropos of the intense controversy provoked by the outlawing of the Legal Tender Act by the Supreme Court, Adams wrote, in continuation of the quotation in note 21: "Between the Executive and the Legislature, citizens could have no Rights; they were at the mercy of Power. They had created the Court to protect them from unlimited Power, and it was little enough protection at best. Adams wanted to save the independence of the Court at least for his lifetime, and could not conceive that the Executive should wish to overthrow it." Fortunate for the country, all the same, was the fact that congressional enlargement of the Supreme Court from seven members to nine (though not done for this express purpose) enabled Grant to appoint two new justices known to favor legal tender, whereupon, in a 5–4 decision, the Court reversed itself in 1871, declaring legal tender constitutional.

23. Speech file, Franklin D. Roosevelt Library (hereinafter "FDRL"), box 14 of President's Personal File (hereinafter "PPF").

24. According to Frances Perkins, "Reminiscences," Columbia Oral History Collection at Columbia University (hereinafter "COHC"), p. 3390. Quoted by Arthur M. Schlesinger, Jr., *The Politics of Upheaval* (Boston, 1960), p. 582.

25. PPA 1937, p. lxii. "If I were in private practice and without conscience, I would gladly undertake for a drawing account of fifteen to twenty million dollars (easy enough to raise) to guarantee that an amendment would not be ratified prior to the 1940 elections," wrote Roosevelt to Frankfurter on February 9, 1937. "In other words, I think I could withold ratification in thirteen states. . . ." Freedman, *op. cit.,* p. 382.

26. Ickes, *Thousand Days,* p. 468.

27. PPA 1937, p. lxiv.

28. George Creel, *Rebel at Large* (New York, 1947), p. 294.

29. PPA 1937, p. lxiv.

30. "If I got up tomorrow and advocated rigid adherance to the 14th and 15th [Amendments] of the Constitution, the same folks who are yelling 'Constitution' loudly now would fight among themselves for priority in applying the tar and feathers," South Carolinian Edmund P. Grice, Jr., would write to Senator James F. Byrnes on February 23, 1937, less than three weeks after Roosevelt's court plan was announced. Quoted by William E. Leuchtenburg, "Roosevelt's Supreme Court 'Packing' Plan," in *Essays on the New Deal,* the Walter Prescott Webb Memorial Lectures (Austin, Tex., 1969), p. 83. There were, however, fourteen words of the 390-odd in the Fourteenth Amendment that were invariably cited as sacred law, and stretched to the furthest limit of their applicability (and beyond such limit), by Southern as by Northern conservatives. These were the clause of Section 1 saying "nor shall any State deprive any person of . . . *property* [italics supplied], without due process of law." The elided words are "life, liberty or." It was the original primary intent of the Fourteenth Amendment—namely, the protection of fundamental human rights for blacks as well as whites—that white Southerners objected to and ignored in practice.

31. Alsop and Catledge, *op. cit.,* p. 64. (They give the date as February 3, but Rosenman has February 2, which is correct.)

32. Rosenman, *op. cit.,* p. 155. "It is the only time I can recall when he seemed worried after once deciding upon a course of action," adds Rosenman.

33. *Ibid.*

34. Rosenman, *op. cit.,* p. 156.

35. Alsop and Catledge, *op. cit.,* p. 66.

36. PPA 1937, p. 40. Alsop and Catledge, *op. cit.,* p. 67.

37. Rosenman, *op. cit.,* p. 156, says that on the evening of Thursday, February 4, he went "to Betsey [Mrs. James] Roosevelt's for dinner," with Missy LeHand, Grace Tully, and Tom

Corcoran, and that "the message," whose general contents were known to all in this innermost circle, "was the sole topic of conversation." Corcoran "kept talking about the terrible effect it was going to have on 'old Isaiah'—meaning Justice Brandeis" and said he had obtained "the Boss' O.K. to go down and tell him in confidence what's coming." But according to Robert E. Sherwood's *Roosevelt and Hopkins* (New York, 1950), pp. 89–90, Corcoran told Harry Hopkins two years later that he didn't "get in to see" Roosevelt until "the morning the message went up the hill," though he had tried earlier to do so in order to "caution" the President against "some . . . statements" in the message "which I was sure were wrong— notably the one about the crowding of the Court calendar." When Corcoran "urged him [the President] to tell Brandeis in advance, hoping to soften the blow on him—the President urged me to see him at once—I crashed the sacred robing room—he talked with me in the hall while the balance of the Court filed by—not knowing the bombshell that was awaiting them. Brandeis asked me to thank the President for letting him know but said he was unalterably opposed to the President's action and he was making a great mistake." (The verbatim quotes are in Hopkins's notes of his talk with Corcoran.)

38. Richard Lowitt, *George W. Norris: The Triumph of a Progressive, 1933–1944* (Urbana, Ill., 1978), pp. 185–90. Alsop and Catledge, *op. cit.,* pp. 185–90; 95–96.

39. Alsop and Catledge, *op. cit.,* p. 71.

40. The direct quote is from PPA 1937, p. lxv. The introduction to the volume, whence comes the quote, was first printed as an article in *Collier's* magazine (September 20, 1941), p. 16, under the title "The Fight Goes On."

**Three: Tragic Error Is Compounded by a Stubborn Persistence in It**

1. Freedman, *op. cit.,* pp. 380–81. Alsop and Catledge, *op. cit.,* pp. 74–76, say flatly that Frank- furter "heartily disapproved of the court bill" and that his was "one of the disaffections" that "hurt the President deeply." "While he disliked court-packing, he was willing to let that pass, but he could not stomach the silly, misleading indirection of the approach or the cruel injury which the age pretext did to . . . Justice Brandeis." Clearly this is the impression of his views that Frankfurter gave in private talk, quite possibly to Alsop himself, and it has been endlessly repeated as fact by historians of the period. Thus (typically), in his *The Invisible Presidency* (New York, 1960), Louis W. Koenig writes (p. 285): "In his Harvard lair, to which he was confining himself increasingly, Frankfurter was offended by the indirection and the age provi- sions of the court plan with their implicit attack on . . . Brandeis. Frankfurter took no public position on the issue, a tactic which further removed him from the White House circle as the fight exacerbated." But we now know from the published Frankfurter–Roosevelt correspon- dence and from Freedman's editorial comment that Frankfurter not only "stomached" the indirection and the offense to Brandeis but actually himself condemned Brandeis's part in the Hughes struggle against the bill, in letters to FDR. Throughout the battle he gave the President all the aid he could (with speech material, advice, etc.) and, at one crucial point, when FDR was being urged to settle for a compromise, gave the President the advice he knew the President wanted to hear: He urged Roosevelt to stand firm. See Freedman, *op. cit.,* p. 400.

2. *Ibid.,* pp. 381–82. In his reply to FDR, February 15, 1937, Frankfurter (p. 381 of *ibid.*) put his finger on a central difficulty against which Roosevelt had been warned: "The situation presents a very difficult problem in public education because . . . the easy, emotional slogans are mostly the other way." Three days later he sent FDR the elaboratory notes, for a speech, which FDR had requested. None of it was used verbatim in the upcoming fireside chat, but FDR did appropriate, for that talk, the phrase about saving the Constitution from the Court, and the Court from itself, which Frankfurter had used in his February 9 letter.

3. Article by Raymond P. Brandt in Washington (D.C.) *Evening Star,* April 21, 1940, quoted by A. T. Mason, *Brandeis: A Free Man's Life* (New York, 1956), p. 626. The interpretation of Wheeler's motivation derives from his Columbia University oral history interviews (in COHC); his contribution to Rita James Simon, ed., *As We Saw the Thirties* (Urbana, Ill., 1969); Alsop and Catledge, who evidently extensively interviewed Wheeler and Wheeler's aides while gather- ing material for their book, *op. cit.;* and Mason, who, in both his *Brandeis* and his *Harlan Fiske Stone, Pillar of the Law* (New York, 1956) cites an interview with Wheeler, February 25, 1944.

4. PPA 1937, p. lxv.

5. Ickes, *Inside Struggle*, p. 89. "He [Roosevelt] told me yesterday he had taken this peroration from a letter written by Stuart Chase to the New York *Times*," writes Ickes in his diary entry for Saturday, March 6, 1937. "It seems that Chase had written this letter for publication and had sent a copy to the President. The President was very much taken with this particular phraseology and Chase was asked to withdraw his letter from the *Times*, because, of course, the President did not want it printed since that would have made it impossible for him to use it." FDR sent a copy of the letter to Frankfurter on February 18 (the Chase letter is dated February 15) with a memorandum asking: "What would happen . . . if I were to go on the air and talk to America along the lines of Chase's article in the *Times*?" Frankfurter, replying on February 23, urged him to do so. "And you should enlarge on Chase's recital. . . . I believe you should take the country to school—give them a free dress exposition and analysis. . . ." Freedman, *op. cit.*, pp. 387–90, which includes in full the unpublished Chase letter.

6. Frank V. Cantwell, "Public Opinion and the Legislative Process," *American Political Science Review*, 40 (October 1946), pp. 924–35, gives detailed summary and analysis of the Gallup polls on this issue.

7. A. T. Mason, *Brandeis*, p. 626, based on personal interview of Wheeler by Mason, February 25, 1944. Merlo J. Pusey, *Charles Evans Hughes*, vol. II (New York, 1951), p. 755.

8. Quoted by Mason, *Stone*, pp. 451–52. On p. 453, Mason tells how young Alfred Lief called as an emissary of Hughes and Wheeler (Lief did not so identify himself) at the Stone home on the morning of Sunday, March 21, to find out if Stone would be willing to sign a letter of protest against the court bill. Lief and Stone were together when Irving Brandt arrived, paying a social visit. Brandt heard Stone tell Lief that he, Stone, would not sign such a letter "on the general ground that he did not think it proper for members of the Court to take part in a political controversy." After that, says Mason, there was "no reason for Lief to bring up a specific matter such as the Hughes letter." On April 15, 1937, Brandt wrote a letter to Stone commenting on this: "As it was a three-cornered conversation, I relayed word of his [Lief's] errand to the White House. It made a nice commentary on Mr. Hughes' statement that he had not had time to submit his letter to all his colleagues."

9. *New York Times*, May 30, 1937.

10. The assumption of a continued obstruction of administration programs by the Court, an assumption (in other words) that the Court was incapable of change, had been a major factor in Roosevelt's calculations at least since January 1936. Wrote Ickes in his diary, January 24, 1936: "It is plain to see, from what the President said today and has said on other occasions, that he is not at all averse to have the Supreme Court declaring one New Deal statute after another unconstitutional. I think he believes that the Court will find itself pretty far out on a limb before it is through with it and that a real issue will be joined on which he can go to the country." Ickes was one of those who urged FDR to make the Court a major issue in the 1936 campaign. Ickes, *Thousand Days*, pp. 524, 530. In a letter to FDR immediately after the Court had struck down the NRA, in 1935, Felix Frankfurter deemed it "fortunate that the Administration has pending before Congress measures like the Social Security bill, the Holding Company bill, the Wagner [labor relations] bill, the Guffey [coal] bill. Go on with these. Put *them* up to the Supreme Court. Let the Court strike down any or all of them next winter and spring, especially a divided Court. *Then* propose a Constitutional amendment giving the national government adequate power to cope with national economic and industrial problems. That will give you an overwhelming issue of a positive character arising at the psychological time for the '36 campaign. . . ." Freedman, *op. cit.*, p. 272.

11. Freedman, *op. cit.*, p. 392.

12. *NLRB* v. *Jones & Laughlin Steel Corp.*, 301 U.S. 1 (1937), pp. 41–42.

13. Alsop and Catledge, *op. cit.*, p. 153.

14. PPA 1937, pp. 153–55.

15. Freedman, *op. cit.*, p. 400. Roosevelt sent Frankfurter copies of his exchange of letters (Burlingham's dated May 25, 1937; FDR's, May 27, 1937), whereupon, according to Freedman, Frankfurter "advised the President to accept no compromise." It seems evident that Frank-

furter's advice here was based, not upon an objective assessment of possibilities, but upon a courtier's desire to please. He knew what FDR would want to hear.

16. PPA 1937, pp. 197, 200.

17. Alsop and Catledge, *op. cit.,* pp. 74, 280.

18. PPA 1937, p. 197. Alsop and Catledge, *op. cit.,* p. 205.

19. Cantwell, *op. cit.*

20. *New York Times,* May 15, 1937. Melvyn Dubofsky and Warren Van Tine, *John L. Lewis,* (New York, 1977), citing transcript of Lewis radio address, "Labor and the Supreme Court," May 14, 1937, p. 326.

21. Actually the statement was a nationally broadcast radio address presented by Lewis over NBC on New Year's Eve and given national coverage in the press on January 1, 1937. See Dubofsky and Van Tine, *op. cit.,* pp. 253–54.

22. Robert S. McElvaine, *The Great Depression: America, 1929–1941* (New York, 1984), p. 294.

23. *New York Times,* May 31, June 1, 1937. Dubofsky and Van Tine, *op. cit.,* p. 314. McElvaine, *op. cit.,* p. 295. One of the most famous photographs of the Depression period is of police chasing, clubbing, and shooting down strikers at Republic Steel's South Chicago plant. It was included in a book of photographs by Resettlement Administration photographers, with poetic commentary by Archibald MacLeish, entitled *Land of the Free* (Boston, 1938); and of it MacLeish wrote:

> *Maybe the proposition is self-evident.*
>
> *Maybe we were endowed by our creator*
> *With certain inalienable rights, including*
> *The right to assemble in peace and petition.*
>
> *Maybe.*
>
> *But try it in South Chicago Memorial Day*
> *With the mick police on the prairie in front of the factory*
> *Gunning you down from behind and for what?*
>
> *For liberty?*

24. John L. Lewis, "Labor and the Nation" (Washington, D.C., 1937). This pamphlet was issued by the CIO; its text is that of Lewis's CBS radio address of September 3, 1937. Cited by Dubofsky and Van Tine, *op. cit.,* pp. 327–28.

25. *New York Times,* June 15, 1937. The full report, dated a full week before its publication, is included in *Great Issues in American History,* vol. 2 (1864–1957), a documentary record edited by Richard Hofstadter (New York, 1958), pp. 376–81.

26. Alsop and Catledge, *op. cit.,* p. 259.

27. PPA 1937, p. 306.

28. Ickes, *Inside Struggle,* pp. 168–69.

29. Freedman, *op. cit.,* p. 403.

30. Bascom N. Timmons, *Garner of Texas* (New York, 1948), pp. 222–23. Alsop and Catledge, *op. cit.,* pp. 278–80.

31. "It was Tom [Corcoran] who squeezed out the votes necessary to elect Barkley Majority Leader of the Senate," says Ickes (*Inside Struggle,* p. 174), in telling of a weekend (that of July 24, 1937) Corcoran spent with him. Alsop and Catledge, *op. cit.,* pp. 282–83, say Corcoran enlisted the Kelly-Nash machine of Chicago to force a vote by Illinois senator Dieterich for Barkley (Dieterich favored Harrison) and the Pendergast machine of Kansas City to force Missouri's Senator Harry S Truman to vote for Barkley. Actually, according to Richard Lawrence Miller's exhaustively researched *Truman: The Rise to Power* (New York, 1986), p. 278, it was Jim Farley who phoned Tom Pendergast "asking him to line up Truman for

Barkley. . . . Pendergast phoned Truman and asked him to vote for Barkley, giving him the impression that he had talked with Roosevelt about it. Truman explained that he was pledged to Senator Harrison. Pendergast tried to ease the awkwardness, saying he didn't really care . . . but that he had promised the White House he would ask." The tactic infuriated Truman with its implication that he was merely "Pendergast's errand boy" (as the Kansas City [Mo.] *Star* continually said he was)—an implication as false as it was insulting—and it is likely that, in response to it, he would have switched his vote to Harrison if he had been previously inclined to favor Barkley (as Koenig, *op. cit.,* p. 288, mistakenly claims he had been). In any case, writes Miller, "Truman took pains to display his marked ballot before depositing it, so colleagues would know he voted for Harrison."

32. Alsop and Catledge, *op. cit.,* p. 294.

33. PPA 1937, p. 339.

34. *Ibid.,* p. lxvi.

35. Memorandum to Frankfurter from Owen J. Roberts, November 9, 1945, after Roberts had resigned from the bench, published by Frankfurter in the December 1955 number of *University of Pennsylvania Law Review.* Also in Freedman, *op. cit.,* pp. 393–95.

36. *Ibid.*

37. PPA 1937, p. lxvi.

38. *Ibid.,* pp. 239–43, 245.

39. *Ibid.,* pp. 497–98.

40. *Ibid.,* p. 254.

41. John Morton Blum, *From the Morgenthau Diaries: Years of Crisis, 1928–1938,* pp. 327–30. "Leaving the tactics to Roosevelt," writes Blum, "[Under Secretary of the Treasury] Magill prepared a letter for Roosevelt's use on tax avoidance that named names and an alternative document omitting them. The President liked the material, which Morgenthau delivered on May 21, but he asked for at least twenty-five additional names for possible inclusion in a radio address which he was considering as a supplement to a message to Congress about loopholes." Morganthau thought specifying names would needlessly arouse "class hatred" and Magill told the President that any mention of them "was bound to be discriminatory," according to Blum. For instance, the name of Alfred P. Sloan, head of General Motors, was on the list, he having incorporated his yacht, but at least a dozen other multimillionaires had done the same thing but were not listed. Magill was one of those who "questioned the legality of making public the names. . . ."

42. Elliott Roosevelt, *op. cit.,* p. 688.

43. *Ibid.,* pp. 690–92.

44. James Roosevelt and Sidney Shalett, *Affectionately, F.D.R.* (New York, 1959), pp. 304–5. Ickes, *Inside Struggle,* p. 148.

45. Ickes, *Inside Struggle,* p. 182.

46. Corcoran had come to Washington in 1932 as counsel in the Reconstruction Finance Corporation, of which Reed became general counsel, and had then conceived a personal liking for his superior officer, and a profound respect for Reed's abilities, which (typically among those who had served as Reed's subordinates) were never impaired.

47. Ickes, *Inside Struggle,* p. 183.

48. Gerald T. Dunne, *Hugo Black and the Judicial Revolution* (New York, 1977), p. 50.

49. Ickes, *Inside Struggle,* p. 183.

50. Dunne, *op. cit.,* p. 51.

51. Ickes, *Inside Struggle,* p. 196.

52. PPA 1937, p. 352.

53. Freedman, *op. cit.,* p. 409.

54. PPA 1937, p. 366.

55. Charlotte Williams, *Hugo Black: A Study in Judicial Process* (Baltimore, Md., 1950), wherein the whole of Black's address is reprinted, pp. 37–30. Also Dunne, *op. cit.,* p. 73.

56. "Not one of the basic power conflicts which precipitated the Roosevelt struggle against the judiciary has been eliminated or settled," writes Robert H. Jackson in his posthumously published *The Supreme Court in the American System of Government* (New York, 1955). "The old conflict between the branches of government is ready to break out again whenever the provocation becomes significant." Judicial self-restraint was, however, the only "solution" Jackson could recommend. See p. 399 of Rexford G. Tugwell, *The Democratic Roosevelt* (New York, 1957).

*Book Two:* **Falterings—The Bitter Years**

**Four: Lost Control: Events Take Command**

1. *New York Times,* October 2, 1937.

2. PPA 1937, p. 414.

3. *Ibid.,* pp. 386–87.

4. *Ibid.,* pp. 392, 388–91.

5. *Ibid.,* p. 403.

6. *Ibid.,* pp. 404–5.

7. Orville H. Bullitt, ed., *For the President, Personal and Secret: Correspondence Between Franklin D. Roosevelt and William C. Bullitt* (Boston, 1972), p. 210. Letter from Bullitt, in Paris, to Roosevelt, April 12, 1937. Bullitt, reviewing conversation with Yvon Delbos, said the chances of negotiating with Italy and Germany a withdrawal of all "volunteers" from Spain were virtually nil since such withdrawal would work immensely to the Loyalists' advantage. Writes Bullitt: "The International Brigade has borne the brunt of the fighting on the government side for so long that it has literally been shot to pieces. The withdrawal of foreign 'volunteers,' therefore, would mean almost no decrease in the government forces but would mean the withdrawal of about three-fourths of Franco's army. It is, therefore, inconceivable that Mussolini would accept any such proposal."

8. Jay Allen's truthful reporting of such matters as the Badajoz massacre cost him his job on the *Tribune.* Publisher Robert McCormick fired him. A Pathé newsreel photographer, René Brut of Paris, risked his life to photograph piles of corpses awaiting burning at Badajoz, as Wyden reports in *op. cit.,* pp. 132–39. An unemployed Portuguese fisherman whom Wyden interviewed told of being drafted by Franco officials to dig, with eight others, "a ditch about 40 meters long, 10 meters wide and some 1½ meters deep" in which to bury piles of corpses. "A neat stack of gold fillings from teeth was piled up on the side."

9. Richard P. Traina, *American Diplomacy and the Spanish Civil War* (Bloomington, Ind., 1968), pp. 106–7, citing Hadley Cantril and Mildred Strunk, eds., *Public Opinion 1935–1946* (Princeton, N.J., 1951), pp. 807–9.

10. Blum, *op. cit.,* p. 465.

11. Rep. Sam McReynolds, chairman of the House Foreign Relations Committee, in statement to the House, April 29 (?), 1937. *Congressional Record,* 75th Congress, 1st Session, vol. 81, pt. 4, p. 3975. Quoted by Traina, *op. cit.,* pp. 107–8.

12. Traina, *op. cit.,* pp. 194–95.

13. In her *This I Remember* (New York, 1949), Eleanor Roosevelt writes, p. 161: "While I often felt strongly on various subjects, Franklin frequently refrained from supporting causes in which he believed, because of political realities. There were times when this annoyed me very much. In the case of the Spanish Civil War, for instance, we had to remain neutral [Eleanor says this, though it is clear in context that she doubts the "had to"], though Franklin knew quite well he wanted the democratic government to be successful. . . . To justify his action,

or lack of action, he explained to me, when I complained, that the League of Nations had asked us to remain neutral. By trying to convince me that our course was correct, though he knew I thought we were doing the wrong thing, he was simply trying to salve his own conscience."

14. Wyden, *op. cit.*, p. 198.

15. Norman Thomas to FDR, June 9, 1937. PPF 4840, FDRL.

16. Norman Thomas transcript of interview in July 1965, in COHC. Dallek, *op. cit.*, p. 142. Traina, *op. cit.*, pp. 113–14.

17. *New York Times*, September 15, 1937. "The official position was, however, only one of the protection of U.S. nationals and their property in China, with no hint of protection to China," writes Albert Howe Lybyer in *The American Year Book 1937* (New York, 1938), p. 83. Hereinafter "Lybyer 1937."

18. *New York Times*, July 17, 1937; August 24, 1937. Lybyer 1937, p. 83.

19. Elliott Roosevelt, ed., *F.D.R., His Personal Letters, 1928–1945*, vol. 1, p. 703, editor's note. (Hereinafter "PL 1928–1945.")

20. PL 1928–1945, vol. 1, pp. 702–3.

21. *Ibid*, pp. 699–701.

22. Dallek, *op. cit.*, p. 147.

23. *Ibid.*, pp. 147–48.

24. Ickes, *Inside Struggle*, pp. 213–14.

25. Grace Tully, *F.D.R.: My Boss* (New York, 1949), pp. 231–32.

26. PPA 1937, pp. 407–11.

27. Tully, *op. cit.*, p. 233.

28. Dallek, *op. cit.*, pp. 148–49.

29. Tully, *op. cit.*, p. 233.

30. Council on Foreign Relations (Whitney H. Shepardson, collaborating with William O. Scroggs), *The United States in World Affairs 1937* (New York, 1938), p. 221.

31. *Ibid.*, pp. 218–19.

32. PPA 1937, pp. 414–25.

33. Rosenman, *op. cit.*, p. 167.

34. William E. Leuchtenburg, *Franklin D. Roosevelt and the New Deal* (New York, 1963), pp. 226–27.

35. *The United States in World Affairs 1937*, p. 222.

36. *Ibid.*, 222n.

37. Rosenman, *op. cit.*, p. 166, quoting memo in archives of German Foreign Office, dated October 15, 1935. The archives were captured by Allied troops in 1945.

38. Blum, *op. cit.*, p. 381.

39. *Ibid.*

40. *Ibid.*, p. 383.

41. Ickes, *Inside Struggle*, p. 223.

42. *Ibid.*, p. 224.

43. Blum, *op. cit.*, p. 385.

44. *New York Times*, October 12, 13, 14.

45. PPA 1935, pp. 424–25.

46. Sidney Hyman, *Marriner S. Eccles* (Stanford, Calif. 1976), pp. 236–37.

47. Blum, *op. cit.*, p. 394.

48. Hyman, *op. cit.*, pp. 238–39.

49. Blum, *op. cit.*, pp. 391–92.

50. *Ibid.*, pp. 395–96.

51. Hyman, *op. cit.*, p. 241.

52. Frank Freidel, *Franklin D. Roosevelt: The Ordeal* (Boston, 1954), p. 100, based on personal interview by Freidel of Frances Perkins.

53. Ickes, *Inside Struggle*, p. 246.

54. *Ibid.*, p. 232.

55. PPA 1937, pp. 490–92, 500.

56. *New York Times,* November 28, 1937.

57. Ickes, *Inside Struggle*, p. 256.

58. *Ibid.*, p. 257.

59. *Ibid.*, p. 255.

60. *Ibid.*, p. 258.

61. Henry H. Adams, *Harry Hopkins* (New York, 1977), and George McJimsey, *Harry Hopkins* (Cambridge, Mass., 1987), tell of Barbara Hopkins's death and Hopkins's reactions to it (pp. 119–20 and 117–18, respectively). McJimsey writes that, as Barbara lay dying in hospital, Hopkins "drew inward, seeing her illness as retribution for his sin." Robert E. Sherwood, who knew Hopkins intimately and writes of him with remarkable vividness and psychological acuteness, tells in his *Roosevelt and Hopkins* (revised edition, New York, 1950) of Hopkins's strict and narrow religious upbringing in Iowa. Hopkins was a great prankster and violator of rules while an undergraduate at Grinnell College, but "curiously mixed with this prankish tendency," writes Sherwood (p. 17), "was a deeply puritanical sense, the result of his elaborate religious training."

62. Ickes, *Inside Struggle*, p. 258.

63. *New York Times,* December 6, 1937.

64. "I have been really troubled because the wisest medical man I know . . . told me that the kind of tooth infection that you have had that touches the bone is nothing to trifle with," wrote Felix Frankfurter to Roosevelt on December 14, 1937. Replying on December 16, Roosevelt said: "Tooth nearly well. It did not touch the bone but was deep in the gum." See Max Freedman, ed., *op. cit.*, pp. 440, 442.

65. Michael R. Beschloss, *Kennedy and Roosevelt* (New York, 1980), pp. 152–53.

66. James Roosevelt, *My Parents* (Chicago, 1976), pp. 208–9.

67. Beschloss, *op. cit.*, p. 157, quoting Morgenthau diary entry for December 8, 1937.

68. *Ibid.*

69. James Roosevelt, *op. cit.*, pp. 209–10, gives an eyewitness account of this episode. Its veracity has been unchallenged over the years, but I have doubts about it. If Kennedy was extremely bowlegged, it doesn't show in photographs of him with his trousers on.

70. Beschloss, *op. cit.*, p. 155.

71. *The United States in World Affairs 1937,* p. 252. The account of the attack is based, the authors say, on the official report of Lt. Commander Hughes to the Navy Department and on the investigative findings of the Naval Court of Inquiry.

72. Ickes, *Inside Story,* p. 274.

73. *The United States in World Affairs 1937,* pp. 235–37. Council on Foreign Relations (Whitney H. Shepardson, collaborating with William O. Scroggs), *The United States in World Affairs*

*1938* (New York, 1939), pp. 153–54. Dallek, *op. cit.*, pp. 154–55. Support of the Ludlow Amendment cut across party lines; 46 percent of the House of Representatives signed the committee discharge petition despite the well-known fact of Roosevelt's adamant opposition to the proposal. Incidentally, and interestingly, what Ludlow proposed is what Immanuel Kant proposed in his famous essay "Eternal Peace." Wrote Kant, as the "first definitive article in the conditions of Eternal Peace": "The civil constitution of every state shall be republican, and war shall not be declared except by a plebiscite of all the citizens." See Robert Caponigre, ed., *Perpetual Peace,* by Immanuel Kant (New York, 1948), p. 20.

74. PPA 1937, p. 541.

75. Dallek, *op. cit.*, pp. 154–55.

76. Letter by Hamilton Darby Perry to *New York Times,* dated July 6, 1987, and published July 20, 1937.

77. PPA 1937, p. 542.

78. Account of Roosevelt's 1937 Christmas in *New York Times,* December 25, 26, 27, 1937.

79. Joseph P. Lash, *Eleanor and Franklin* (New York, 1971), pp. 429–33.

80. *New York Times,* December 26, 1937, quoting the Marshall sermon.

## Five: Drifting: The Politics of Indecision amid World Crisis

1. See Kenneth S. Davis, *FDR: The Beckoning of Destiny,* pp. 826–30; Davis, *FDR: The New York Years,* pp. 414–15; Davis, *FDR: The New Deal Years,* pp. 90–94, 429–30, 432–34. PPA 1928–1933, p. 886.

2. PPA 1933, p. 122.

3. Max Friedman, ed., *op. cit.* p. 138.

4. *The Journals of David E. Lilienthal: The TVA Years, 1939–1945* (including a selection of journal entries from the 1917–1939 period; New York, 1964), pp. 32–33. (Hereinafter "Lilienthal journals.")

5. *Ibid.,* p. 38.

6. Richard Lowitt, *George W. Norris: The Triumph of a Progressive, 1933–1944* (Urbana, Ill., 1978), p. 120. Quoting letter from Norris to George Fort Milton, October 4, 1935.

7. Lilienthal journals, p. 38.

8. *Ibid.,* p. 39.

9. Arthur Schlesinger, Jr., *The Coming of The New Deal* (Boston, 1958), p. 331.

10. Lilienthal journals, pp. 42–43.

11. *Ibid.*

12. Schlesinger, *Coming of the New Deal,* p. 330. Jonathan Daniels, "Three Men in a Valley," *New Republic,* August 17, 1938.

13. Francis Biddle, *In Brief Authority* (New York, 1962), p. 56.

14. Arthur E. Morgan, "The Community," *Atlantic Monthly,* February 1942.

15. Arthur Schlesinger, Jr., *The Politics of Upheaval* (Boston, 1960), p. 363.

16. Thomas Reed Powell, "The Supreme Court and Constitutional Law," *American Year Book 1936* (New York, 1937), pp. 47–51. *New York Times,* February 18, 1936.

17. Lilienthal journals, p. 62.

18. Biddle, *op. cit.,* p. 56.

19. Arthur E. Morgan, "The Next Four Years in the TVA," *New Republic,* January 6, 1937.

20. *New York Times,* March 3, 1938. Lilienthal journals, p. 69.

21. Lilienthal journals, pp. 69–70.

22. *Ibid.*, pp. 71–72.

23. *Ibid.*, pp. 72–74. Ickes, *Inside Struggle*, p. 337. The girl with the stenotype on her knees "was a pretty, open-eyed young girl . . . , her eyes bright and about popping out," writes Lilienthal of the hearing. "The President turned and smiled at her, and I thought she would drop the darn machine and faint. 'It is an interesting thing,' he said. 'I learned for the first time the other day when I decided we ought to have a stenographic record of this proceeding, that the Government does not have its own court reporters; it is all done by contract. That doesn't seem right. Don't you think the Government ought to have its own reporters?' He directed this to the little girl with the big eyes. 'Yes, I think that would be nice,' she got out. He nodded his head gravely, as if that settled it. . . .''

24. PPA 1938, p. 153. The President's memorandum "on the facts requiring the removal" of A.E. Morgan is on pp. 153–64 of PPA 1938.

25. Marguerite Owen, *The Tennessee Valley Authority* (New York, 1973), p. 52. Owen was the TVA's Washington representative in the 1930s.

26. David E. Lilienthal, *TVA: Democracy on the March* (New York, 1944; paperback, 1945), p. 99 (of paperback). Schlesinger, *Politics of Upheaval*, p. 375.

27. Lilienthal, *TVA*, p. 85.

28. Schlesinger, *Politics of Upheaval*, p. 371. Rexford G. Tugwell and E. C. Banfield, "Grass Roots Democracy—Myth or Reality?" *Public Administration Review*, Winter 1950.

29. Owen, *op. cit.*, p. 52.

30. Lilienthal, *TVA*, pp. 6–7, 65, 98.

31. Owen, *op. cit.*, pp. 52–53.

32. Lilienthal journals, p. 74.

33. Alan Bullock, *Hitler: A Study in Tyranny* (New York, 1953), pp. 192–93. William L. Shirer, *The Rise and Fall of the Third Reich* (New York, 1960), p. 328.

34. Shirer, *ibid.*, p. 349, quoting Hitler's speech at Königsberg, March 25, 1938.

35. Bullock, *op. cit.*, p. 197. Winston S. Churchill, *The Gathering Storm* (Boston, 1948), p. 269. Shirer, *ibid.*, pp. 336–37, 343.

36. PL 1928–1945, p. 766.

37. PPA 1937, pp. 424–25.

38. Sumner Welles, *The Time for Decision* (Cleveland, Ohio, and New York, 1945), pp. 64–66.

39. Writes Harold Ickes: "Welles is a man of almost preternatural solemnity and great dignity. If he ever smiles, it has not been in my presence. He conducts himself with portentous gravity and as if he were charged with the responsibilities of Atlas. Just to look at him, one can tell that the world would dissolve into its component parts if only a portion of the weighty secrets of state that he carries about with him were divulged." Ickes, *Inside Struggle*, p. 351,

40. Welles, *op. cit.*, p. 66.

41. Cordell Hull, *The Memoirs of Cordell Hull* (New York, 1948), vol. I, pp. 547–48. According to Hull, Schacht made a proposal "similar" to Welles's on January 20, 1937, when the newly appointed U.S. ambassador to Russia, Joseph E. Davies, paused in Berlin en route to Moscow, where he replaced William Bullitt, the latter soon to go to Paris as U.S. ambassador to France. Actually, Davies was in Moscow on January 19 and, in a "strictly confidential" letter to Hull, written on that day, made no mention of any such Schacht proposal as Hull, in his memoirs, describes. See pp. 9–18 of Joseph E. Davies, *Mission to Moscow* (New York, 1941). Nor is any mention of this made elsewhere in Davies's book.

42. PPA 1938, pp. 36–37.

43. Ian MacLeod, *Neville Chamberlain* (New York, 1962), p. 16.

44. Barbara Tuchman, *The Proud Tower* (paperback ed., New York, 1967), p. 66, quoting an 1886 letter from Salisbury to Balfour.

45. Anthony Eden, *Memoirs of Anthony Eden: Facing the Dictators, 1923–1938* (Boston, 1962), pp. 622–25.

46. *Ibid.*, p. 625. MacLeod, *op. cit.*, p. 212, quoting Chamberlain's diary entry for February 19–27, 1938.

47. Eden, *op. cit.*, pp. 625–26. "There was no time to consult Anthony," Chamberlain told his diary a few weeks later, "for in view of the secrecy on which Roosevelt insisted in emphatic terms I did not dare to telephone." See Macleod, *op. cit.*, p. 212.

48. Eden, *op. cit.*, pp. 625–26, quotes the Chamberlain message to Roosevelt. William Bullitt, writing from Paris to FDR, January 20, 1938, strongly objected to a peace initiative at that time, saying, "It would be as if in the palmiest days of Al Capone you had summoned a national conference of psychoanalysts to discuss the psychological causes of crime." Quoted in Robert Dallek, *op. cit.*, p. 157. Bullitt was still wedded to the idea of a peacemaking agreement between France and Germany once the latter's central European ambitions were achieved.

49. Eden, *op. cit.*, pp. 627–28.

50. *Ibid.*, p. 633.

51. *Ibid.*, p. 641, quoting and paraphrasing Chamberlain's message.

52. The Commons speech, verbatim save for being changed to third person and past tense, was cabled on March 4, 1938, from the German embassy in London to Berlin. Shirer, *op. cit.*, p. 344.

53. Churchill, *Gathering Storm*, pp. 257–58.

54. Hull, *op. cit.*, p. 575.

55. *New York Times*, March 17, 21, 1938. Arthur D. Morse, *While Six Million Died: A Chronicle of American Apathy* (New York, 1968), pp. 208–9.

56. Morse, *op. cit.*, p. 212.

57. Hamilton Fish Armstrong, editor of *Foreign Affairs*, credited a long article on the refugee crisis by Dorothy Thompson which his magazine published in April 1937 "with spurring the State Department to convene" the thirty-two-nation conference, according to Marion K. Sanders, *Dorothy Thompson: A Legend in her Time* (Boston, 1973), p. 239. Morse, *op. cit.*, pp. 211–12, writes: "An internal State Department memorandum prepared later in 1938 by an official of the Division of European Affairs (formerly known as the Division of Western European Affairs) describes the origins of the . . . Conference with cold detachment. The Nazi absorption of Austria had increased public demand for State Department action in behalf of the refugees. 'Dorothy Thompson and certain Congressmen with metropolitan constituencies were the principal sources of this pressure,' said the memorandum. To counteract this outcry, Secretary Hull, Undersecretary Welles, and two lesser colleagues had decided that it was preferable for the department to 'get out in front and attempt to guide the pressure, primarily with a view to forestalling attempts to have the immigration laws liberalized.' "

58. PL 1928–1945, p. 776.

59. Dallek, *op. cit.*, p. 158, quoting J. Pierrepont Moffat ms. diary, April 23–24, 1938. Ickes, *Inside Struggle*, p. 377, comments that according to press report, "it was Joe Kennedy who persuaded him [Roosevelt] to issue the statement 'commending' the British-Italian treaty. I very much regret that the President made any such statement. It wasn't called for, because the negotiations were between Great Britain and Italy. Moreover, these negotiations are contrary to the convictions of the liberals in Great Britain. Chamberlain, the Astors, *et al.*, are more or less pro-fascist [Kennedy, according to Ickes, had become a member of Lady Astor's notoriously pro-dictator Cliveden Set]. . . . I think this was an unnecessary and regrettable act on the President's part." In this same diary entry, Ickes speaks bitterly of "the refusal of this country [the U.S.] to sell munitions of war to the Loyalist Government in Spain. I continue to think this will be one of the black pages in American history."

60. Bullock, *op. cit.*, p. 203. Shirer, *op. cit.*, p. 359, quotes Konrad Henlein's summary of Hitler's instructions: "We must always demand so much that we can never be satisfied."

## Six: Drifting: To a Decision of Sorts

1. PPA 1938, pp. 7, 8.

2. *Ibid.*, p. 11. Ickes, *op. cit.*, pp. 282–83. Ferdinand Lundberg, *America's Sixty Families* (New York, 1937). Ellis W. Hawley, *The New Deal and the Problem of Monopoly* (Princeton, N.J., 1966), pp. 392–94.

3. Rexford G. Tugwell, *The Democratic Roosevelt* (New York, 1957).

4. For the legislative history of anti-lynching I have leaned heavily upon J. Joseph Huthmacher, *Senator Robert F. Wagner and the Rise of Urban Liberalism* (New York, 1968), supplemented by *The New York Times* of appropriate dates.

5. *Ibid.*, p. 240.

6. *Ibid.*, pp. 242–43.

7. *American Year Book 1938*, pp. 345–59. Hawley, *op. cit.*, pp. 386–87.

8. PPA 1938, pp. 32–34.

9. Thomas E. Vadney, *The Wayward Liberal: A Political Biography of Donald Richberg* (Lexington, Ky., 1970), pp. 177–78. Hawley, *op. cit.*, pp. 395–96.

10. Adolf A. Berle, *Navigating the Rapids* (New York, 1973), pp. 159–60. Hawley, *op. cit.*, p. 397. Vadney, *op. cit.*, p. 178. Ickes, *op. cit.*, p. 295.

11. Berle, *op. cit.*, p. 162.

12. *Ibid.*

13. Vadney, *op. cit.*, pp. 179–80.

14. This famous letter, quoted in virtually every serious book about the New Deal, is extensively quoted and paraphrased in John M. Blum, ed., *From the Morgenthau Diaries: Years of Crisis 1928–1938* (Boston, 1959), pp. 402–4.

15. *New York Times*, December 21, 1938.

16. Blum, *op. cit.*, p. 404.

17. Hawley, *op. cit.*, p. 402.

18. PPA 1938, pp. 100–111. Hawley, *op. cit.*, pp. 399–400.

19. George C. S. Benson and Mabel Gibberd Benson, "The Year in Congress," *American Year Book 1938*, pp. 20–21.

20. Sidney Hyman, *Marriner S. Eccles* (Stanford, Calif., 1976), pp. 241–43. Huchmacher, *op. cit.*, 224–29. Said Senator Wagner, in the portion of his speech on the housing bill in which he opposed the "prevailing wage" amendment: "If we ever come to the time when we in this body pass laws saying how much a bricklayer shall receive per day, how much a carpenter shall receive, how much a clerk in private industry of any kind shall receive, and begin to fix all those wages, we will destroy unionism and freedom of collective bargaining and advance on the road toward fascism." See *Congressional Record*, 75th Congress, 3rd Session, p. 1266. Asked in his press conference of February 4, 1938, "whether that is your thought, too," Roosevelt replied that it was "in line with everything I have always said." What he favored was not price-fixing or wage-fixing but a "floor" under agricultural prices and a "floor" under wages. PPA 1938, p. 79.

21. Blum, *op. cit.*, pp. 414–15.

22. Burns, *op. cit.*, p. 344. Lindsay Rogers, "Reorganization: Post Mortem Notes," *Political Science Quarterly*, June 1935, pp. 161–72.

23. Hawley, *op. cit.*, p. 337.

24. Leon H. Keyserling, "The Wagner Act: Its Origins and Current Significance," *George Washington Law Review,* December 1960, p. 210. Huthmacher, *op. cit.,* pp. 243–44. Writes Ickes *(Inside Story,* p. 349), "According to Ben Cohen, with whom I have discussed the matter, Wagner was scared in by labor and the Catholic Church. I had not known that the Church, except Father Coughlin, was interested in this fight. The Catholic hierarchy in the East is very reactionary."

25. PPA 1938, pp. 165–68.

26. Hyman, *op. cit.,* pp. 244–45.

27. *New York Times,* March 9, 10, 1938. Hyman, *op. cit.,* p. 246, writes that "the financial community . . . was put on the defensive by" Whitney's "wayward conduct."

28. *American Year Book 1938,* p. 365. The statistics on stock-market performance, which follow in my text, are from the *Year Book*'s "Chronology of Business and Finance," pp. 415–16.

29. PL 1928–1945, pp. 745–46.

30. Eleanor Roosevelt, *This I Remember,* pp. 172–73, writes of her "surprise" upon discovering "a side of Harry I had not known before . . . the fact that Harry seemed to get so much genuine pleasure out of contact with gay but more or less artificial society. People who could give him luxuries and the kind of party in which he had probably never before had the slightest interest became important to him. I did not like this side of Harry as much as the first side I knew."

31. Ickes, *Inside Struggle,* p. 350.

32. Howard Zinn, ed., *New Deal Thought* (Indianapolis and New York, 1966), p. 409. The Keynes letter is published in full on pp. 404–9 of this book.

33. Hawley, *op. cit.,* pp. 406–7. He cites in his notes a letter from Henderson to Hopkins, November 27, 1937.

34. PPA 1938, pp. 179–81.

35. Burns, *op. cit.,* p. 344.

36. Thurman Arnold in *The Folklore of Capitalism* (New York, 1937) reiterated and expanded upon the semanticism of his *The Symbols of Government* (New York, 1935).

37. Gene M. Gressley, ed., *Voltaire and the Cowboy: The Letters of Thurman Arnold* (Boulder, Colo., 1977), p. 39. In his introduction, Gressley quotes Arnold's answer to Borah's question as to whether what Arnold had said in *Folklore* was any indication of what he would do in his antitrust office. Hawley, *op. cit.,* pp. 422–23, quotes Borah: "I do not want you to draw indictments on the theory that these corporations will be made bigger and more dangerous by prosecution."

38. Charles A. and Mary R. Beard write in their *America in Midpassage* (New York, 1939), p. 374, that the Republicans in the 1936 campaign "had denounced monopolies and trusts more explicitly than the Democrats and had called for drastic regulation to tear them apart and enforce competition"—a stand more reflective of Alf Landon's views (as a small independent oil producer, he had warred with the corporate giants of oil) than of those who were actually and generally dominant in the party.

39. Hawley, *op. cit.,* p. 409, quoting Special Senate Committee, *Unemployment and Relief* (75th Congress, 3rd Session, 1938), pp. 1338–39.

40. Booth Mooney, *Roosevelt and Rayburn* (Philadelphia and New York, 1971), p. 103. One wonders if Rayburn, operating in this instance in accordance with the wishes of his fellow Texan, Vice President Garner, didn't deliberately if very covertly sabotage reorganization. Ickes was among those who thought he did, and it does seem very strange that he did not at least report the Sumners proposal to the White House. Roosevelt claimed, next day, in conversation with his interior secretary, "that he had not been advised . . . of the opposition to Harry Hopkins. . . ." See Ickes, *Inside Story,* p. 338.

41. Ickes, *Inside Story,* pp. 358–60.

42. Blum, *op. cit.,* pp. 419–20.

43. *Ibid.*

44. *Ibid.*

45. *Ibid.*, pp. 420–21.

46. *Ibid.*, pp. 421–22.

47. *Ibid.*, p. 435.

48. *Ibid.*, pp. 422–23.

49. *Ibid.*, pp. 423–25.

50. Rosenman, *op. cit.*, p. 174.

51. PPA 1938, pp. 221–48.

52. Daniel Webster made this statement in an address to the Massachusetts convention of his party in 1820.

53. PPA 1938, pp. 305–20.

54. Moley, *op. cit.*, p. 376.

55. *American Year Book 1938*, pp. 355, 358–59.

56. *Ibid.*, p. 566. In a press conference at Hyde Park on June 28, 1938, the President was asked if relief for the unemployed might not be "a part of a continuing emergency proposition" because "you will probably always have them with you." Roosevelt did not flatly deny that this was, or might be, so. He said: "Technology, economics, or whatever you choose to call it—some people say it is the result of the World War, other people say it is the result of the new needs of civilization, other people stress the new machinery by which you can turn out, with the same amount of labor, twice as much goods as you did eighteen or twenty years ago —they are causes, and all are contributing factors. In every civilized country there is more unemployment than ever before in history—world history." PPA 1938, p. 406.

57. PPA 1938, p. 327.

58. *Ibid.*, p. 327, quoting *Final Report of the Temporary National Economic Committee*, printed as Senate Document 35, 77th Congress, 1st Session.

59. *Ibid.*, p. 328.

60. Gressley, *op. cit.*, p. 48.

61. Hawley, *op. cit.*, pp. 435–36.

62. *Ibid.*, pp. 351, 357.

63. PPA 1938, pp. 355, 361–62, 364–65.

64. Burns, *op. cit.*, p. 343. Joseph P. Lash, *Dealers and Dreamers* (New York, 1988), p. 340.

65. Lash, *Dealers and Dreamers*, p. 340.

66. Frances Perkins, *The Roosevelt I Knew* (New York, 1936), p. 263.

67. Lash, *Dealers and Dreamers*, pp. 341–68.

68. Arthur Krock's June 16 dispatch from Washington, D.C.; *New York Times*, June 17, 1938.

69. PL 1928–1945, p. 779.

70. *Ibid.*, p. 762. PPA 1938, pp. 629–39.

71. *New York Times*, June 15, July 2, 1938.

72. *New York Times*, July 2, 1938.

73. Ickes, *Inside Story*, pp. 386–87. Hopkins told Ickes that he "guessed" that the President had asked him to attend the Cabinet meeting in order to "flaunt" him defiantly before Vice President Garner, whose opposition to the reorganization bill supposedly had, as one element, opposition to Hopkins as Cabinet member.

74. Undated handwritten notes, Harry Hopkins papers, now in Box 298 (formerly in Box 215) in FDRL. The account that follows is based on these notes. See also McJimsey, *Harry Hopkins*, pp. 119–20; Adams, *Harry Hopkins*, pp. 130–31; Robert E. Sherwood, *Roosevelt and Hopkins* (New York, 1948), pp. 94–98.

75. McJimsey, *op. cit.*, p. 121. Adams, *op. cit.*, p. 134. Asked in a press conference if he had approved Hopkins's statement in support of Wearin, Roosevelt replied "off the record, and I want you to make it absolutely off the record, No, I did not approve of this statement." This was disingenuous, as Morgenthau indicated in his diary entry for June 1, 1938. Roosevelt doubtless did not approve the precise wording of Hopkins's statement but it was by his express wish that the statement was made.

76. *New York Times,* May 3, 1938. Richard P. Traina, *op. cit.,* pp. 127–31.

77. Ickes, *Inside Story,* p. 388–89. Traina, *ibid.,* pp. 133, 273. Traina, in his note 32 on p. 273, says "there is no evidence to corroborate" the "rumors" that the story was a "planted" one, by which I suppose he means there is no official documentary evidence. Yet he cites an undated memorandum by R. Walton Moore, of the State Department, in which Moore denies the truth of a report that the department approved Nye's resolution. Notes Traina: "The story, Moore wrote, 'is absolutely untrue and misrepresents everyone concerned including Senator Pittman and myself.' It [the memo] was apparently intended to be a press release for the phrase 'not given out' is written on the memo." Traina evidently refers to a rumor that the "plant" had been made by the State Department, and I personally don't regard Moore's denial as conclusive documentary evidence that this is not what had happened, and for precisely the reason alleged by Jay Allen.

78. Ickes, *Inside Story,* pp. 389–90.

79. Orville H. Bullitt, ed., *For the President, Personal and Secret,* Correspondence Between Franklin D. Roosevelt and William Bullitt (Boston, 1972), pp. 274–76.

80. Ben Hecht, *A Child of the Century: The Autobiography of Ben Hecht* (New York, 1954), pp. 171, 172–73, gives an eyewitness account of Theodore Roosevelt's "tossing whiskey after whiskey down his gullet" for two hours just before giving his speech launching the Progressive party in Chicago in 1912. Hecht greatly feared that a drunken TR would make a fool of himself before the great crowd in Orchestra Hall but, of course, he "wowed" his audience, giving no sign of intoxication with anything but his own words, his own message.

**Seven: A Summer of Dust and Weeds**

1. Rosenman, *op. cit.,* p. 177. PPA 1938, pp. 131–400.

2, Henry Fleishman, *Norman Thomas* (New York, 1964), pp. 159–60.

3. Fleishman, *ibid.,* p. 160. *New York Times,* April 30, 1938.

4. Fleishman, *ibid.,* p. 160.

5. *New York Times,* June 5, 1938. Fleishman, *ibid.,* p. 161.

6. The file of this correspondence is in FDRL. PPF 4840. Photocopies in author's files.

7. PPA 1938, pp. 427–31. Burns, *op. cit.,* p. 361.

8. PL 1928–1945, p. 765. Burns, *op. cit.,* p. 361. PPA 1938, p. 432.

9. PPA 1938, p. 438.

10. McJimsey, *op. cit.,* p. 122. Adams, *op. cit.,* pp. 137–38.

11. PPA 1938, pp. 443–44.

12. Burns, *op. cit.,* p. 361. Robert A. Caro, *The Years of Lyndon Johnson: The Path to Power* (New York, 1982), p. 569.

13. PL 1928–1945, p. 798. *New York Times,* July 14, 1938.

14. Burns, *op. cit.,* p. 362.

15. PL 1928–1945, p. 796.

16. PPA 1938, pp. 407–8, 458.

17. Henry L. Feingold, *The Politics of Rescue* (New Brunswick, N.J., 1970), p. 29.

18. *The United States in World Affairs 1938,* p. 96.

19. Feingold, *op. cit.,* p. 29. *New York Times,* July 9, 1938.

20. *The United States in World Affairs 1938,* p. 95, citing Department of State, *Press Releases,* XVIII, 429, April 2, 1938.

21. Morse, *op. cit.,* p. 218.

22. *Ibid.,* p. 217. FDRL Official File 3186.

23. Feingold, *op. cit.,* pp. 25–26. *The United States in World Affairs 1938,* p. 100, n. 24.

24. Feingold, *ibid.,* p. 26.

25. Morse, *op. cit.,* pp. 221–22. *The United States in World Affairs 1938,* pp. 95–97.

26. *The United States in World Affairs 1938,* p. 94. Morse, *ibid.,* p. 219. *New York Times,* July 13, 1938.

27. PL 1928–1945, p. 755.

28. *The United States in World Affairs 1938,* pp. 226–27.

29. *Ibid.,* pp. 239–40.

30. Dallek, *op. cit.,* p. 175.

31. Department of State, *Press Releases,* XVIII, 436, April 2, 1938.

32. *The United States in World Affairs 1938,* p. 244.

33. PPA 1938, p. 503.

34. PL 1928–1945, pp. 799–801. PPA 1938, p. 432.

35. PL 1928–1945, p. 801. Joseph P. Lash, *Love, Eleanor* (New York, 1982), pp. 273–74.

36. PPA 1938, pp. 463–64.

37. *Time,* April 3, 1933, p. 12. James T. Patterson, *Congressional Conservatism and the New Deal* (Lexington, Ky., 1967), p. 44.

38. PPA 1938, pp. 464–71. Patterson, *ibid.,* p. 280, quoting Augusta (Ga.) *Chronicle,* August 12, 1938.

39. PPA 1938, p. 475.

40. *Ibid.,* pp. 476–77.

41. Lash, *Love, Eleanor,* p. 274.

42. William Seale, *The President's House* (Washington, D.C., 1986), pp. 897, 927. There was much complaint among those invited to formal White House functions that the whole of the White House had not been air-conditioned. It was said that FDR had blocked a proposal for this because he feared air-conditioning would aggravate his chronic sinus trouble. There must have been some conflict and need for compromise between Howe and Roosevelt on this matter, for Howe was convinced that air-conditioning eased his chronic asthma.

43. PPA 1938, p. 481.

44. *Ibid.,* pp. 488–89.

45. Berle, *Navigating the Rapids,* pp. 181–82. Jordan A. Schwarz, *Liberal: Adolf A. Berle and the Vision of an American Era* (New York, 1987), p. 124.

46. Schwarz, *ibid.,* p. 121.

47. PPA 1938, pp. 491–93.

48. *Ibid.,* pp. 495–99. In an address to the Public Utilities Committee of the New York State Constitutional Convention on June 29, 1938, Berle suggested that the revised constitution contain a provision assigning all ownership and development of waterpower sites to the state

government. The proposed St. Lawrence Seaway was, he said, "peculiarly a project of the President of the United States"; he concluded: "The state, by putting the principle of public ownership into its fundamental law, can guarantee that that development shall be for the everlasting benefit of the people of the state of New York and not for a small group of manipulative interests. . . . The federal government is endeavoring to open the way through the proposed Canadian treaty. It is for you to say whether the wealth at your door shall be used to levy tribute on industry and consumers here, or whether it shall be maintained as a permanent asset of the people of New York." *The United States in World Affairs 1938*, p. 209. *New York Times*, June 30, 1938.

49. *The United States in World Affairs 1938*, p. 219.

50. Thomas Wolfe, *Of Time and the River* (New York, 1935), p. 506.

51. Rochelle Chadakoff, ed., *Eleanor Roosevelt's "My Day"* (New York, 1989), pp. 95–96.

52. Joseph P. Lash, *Eleanor and Franklin* (New York, 1971), p. 510, quoting Fulton Oursler, *Behold the Dreamer* (New York, 1964), pp. 424–25.

53. Chadakoff, *op. cit.*, p. 96.

54. *New York Times*, August 22, 1938.

55. PL 1928–1945, p. 805.

56. PPA 1938, pp. 499–501.

57. *Ibid.*, pp. 514–15, 518–19.

58. Leuchtenburg, *op. cit.*, p. 268, quoting *New York Times*, August 23, 1938.

59. PPA 1938, pp. 570–72.

60. Lash, *Dealers and Dreamers*, pp. 360–61.

61. *Ibid.*, p. 361. Leuchtenburg, *op. cit.*, p. 268.

62. Burns, *op. cit.*, p. 363.

63. Kenneth S. Davis, *Invincible Summer: An Intimate Portrait of the Roosevelts, based on the Recollections of Marion Dickerman* (New York, 1974), pp. 149–50. The substance of this book derived not only from the Columbia University Oral History Research Office transcript of Dickerman interviews, conducted by Mary Belle Starr, but also from numerous personal interviews of Dickerman by the present author.

64. *Ibid.*, p. 148.

65. *Ibid.*, p. 150.

66. James Roosevelt, *op. cit.*, pp. 230–31.

67. PL 1928–1945, p. 809.

68. *Ibid.*, pp. 317–18.

69. Lash, *Love, Eleanor*, p. 263.

70. *Ibid.*

71. James Roosevelt, *op. cit.*, p. 318.

72. Davis, *Invincible Summer*, pp. 150–51.

73. *Ibid.*, pp. 152–53.

74. *Ibid.*, p. 153.

75. *Ibid.*, pp. 153–54.

76. *Ibid.*, p. 154.

77. *Ibid.*, pp. 155–56.

78. *Ibid.*, pp. 156–57.

**Book Three:** **Into the Valley of the Shadow of Death**

**Eight: New World War Becomes Inevitable**

1. William L. Shirer, *Berlin Diary* (paperback ed.; New York, 1941), p. 94.

2. PL 1928–1945, p. 785.

3. John Toland, *Adolf Hitler* (paperback ed.; New York, 1977), pp. 630–31, citing Heinz Linge, *Diaries*, which are in the National Archives, Washington, D.C. Linge was one of Hitler's valets.

4. Galeazzo Ciano, *The Ciano Diaries 1939–1943* (Garden City, N.Y., 1946), entry for May 5, 1938.

5. New York *Herald Tribune*, May 15, 1938. *The United States in World Affairs 1938*, p. 58.

6. Churchill, *Gathering Storm*, pp. 285–86.

7. Nevile Henderson, *Failure of a Mission* (New York, 1940), p. 139. See also John Wheeler-Bennett, *Munich* (New York, 1966), p. 57; Toland, *op. cit.*, p. 634.

8. *op. cit.*, Bullitt, pp. 262–64.

9. Raoul de Roussy de Sales, ed., *My New Order: Adolf Hitler's Speeches, 1918–1941* (New York, 1941), p. 510.

10. *Ibid.*, p. 563. Quoted in a slightly different translation by Churchill, *Gathering Storm*, p. 287; also by Shirer, *Rise and Fall*, p. 365.

11. Actually, Germany's outflanking of Czechoslovakia in the south by means of the Austrian takeover was far less hazardous to the Czechs militarily than it appeared on a map to be, or than Hitler in early 1938 evidently believed it to be. On page 281 of *The Gathering Storm*, Churchill quotes General Halder: "It was practically impossible for a German army to attack Czechoslovakia from the south. The single railway line through Linz was completely exposed and surprise was out of the question." Halder made this comment after telling of Hitler's remark to him during the Austrian invasion: "This [the Austrian takeover] will be very inconvenient to the Czechs."

12. Shirer, *Rise and Fall*, p. 370, quoting the diary of General Alfred Jodl, in *Trial of the Major War Criminals*, Nuremberg trial testimony and documents, XXVIII, p. 374.

13. Shirer, *Rise and Fall*, p. 368.

14. *Ibid.*, p. 376, citing *The Times* of London, June 3, 1938. *Documents on German Foreign Policy*, Vol. II (Washington, D.C.), pp. 395, 399–401. Keith Feiling, *The Life of Neville Chamberlain* (New York, 1946), pp. 347–48, quotes a letter from Chamberlain to his sister, dated March 20, 1938: "You have only to look at a map to see that nothing that France could do could possibly save Czechoslovakia from being overrun by the Germans, if they wanted to do it. . . . I have, therefore, abandoned any guarantee to Czechoslovakia, or to the French in connection with her obligations to that country."

15. Shirer, *Rise and Fall*, p. 368.

16. *Ibid.*, pp. 369–70, citing Jodl's diary.

17. *Ibid.*, p. 370.

18. *Ibid.*, p. 371.

19. Churchill, *Gathering Storm*, pp. 311–12. Shirer, *Rise and Fall*, pp. 374–75.

20. *The United States in World Affairs 1938*, p. 60. Roosevelt, incidentally, was personally acquainted with Lord Runciman who, as president of the British Board of Trade, had been a guest in the White House in early March 1936, on an official visit to the United States.

21. Shirer, *Berlin Diary*, p. 93; *Rise and Fall*, p. 377.

22. Toland, *op. cit.*, p. 640. Leonard Mosley, *On Borrowed Time* (New York, 1969), pp. 30–31.

23. Shirer, *Rise and Fall,* p. 380, quoting a letter most of which is in *Documents of German Foreign Policy.* Says a footnote on that page: "According to a German Foreign Office memorandum of August 6, Henderson, at a private dinner party, had remarked to the Germans present "that Great Britain would not think of risking even one sailor or airman for Czechoslovakia, and that any reasonable solution would be agreed to so long as it were not attempted by force."

24. Shirer, *Rise and Fall,* p. 380, quoting *Documents of German Foreign Policy.*

25. Shirer, *Rise and Fall,* p. 381. Yet Henderson, strange to say, had as a warm personal friend, not only the barbarous Hermann Göring, but also the sensitive, intelligent, highly civilized Ulrich von Hassell, former German ambassador to Italy, who had been recalled to Berlin and dismissed from the Foreign Service during Hitler's sweeping reorganization of government and the military in early February 1938. By the summer of 1938 Hassell had joined the anti-Hitler conspiracy, become its chief foreign-affairs adviser, and was slated to replace Ribbentrop as foreign minister when Hitler was overthrown. (See *The von Hassell Diaries,* with introduction by Allen W. Dulles [New York, 1947].) If Hassell stated his views of the Nazis in conversations with Henderson, and it seems incredible that he would not, he was clearly not persuasive to the Englishman. It is highly improbable that Henderson had any knowledge of Hassell's part in the conspiracy.

26. Mosley, *op. cit.,* pp. 32–33, 479–80. Shirer, *Rise and Fall,* pp. 381–82.

27. Mosley, *op. cit.,* p. 35 quoting Alfred Duff Cooper, *Old Men Forget* (New York, 1954).

28. Henderson, *op. cit.,* p. 150. Toland, *op. cit.,* p. 644.

29. Churchill, *Gathering Storm,* p. 296. *The United States in World Affairs 1938,* p. 63. Indeed, this infamous editorial is quoted in virtually every book dealing with the coming of World War II.

30. *The United States in World Affairs 1938,* p. 63.

31. *Ibid.,* p. 64.

32. Churchill, *Gathering Storm,* pp. 294–96.

33. *Ibid.,* p. 293. Said Churchill in a public statement on August 4, 1938: "How heavily do the destinies of this generation depend upon the government and people of the United States! . . . Will the United States throw their weight into the scales of peace and law and freedom while time remains, or will they remain spectators until the disaster has occurred . . . ? . . . [T]he movement of American opinion upon world affairs is remarkable. Side by side with the loudest reiterations of 'Never again will we be drawn in,' there is a ceaselessly growing interest in the great issues which are at stake both in Europe and the Far East. There never was a peace-time when the newspapers of the United States carried more foreign news to their readers, or when their readers showed themselves more anxious to be informed about foreign affairs. . . . There are literally scores of millions of men and women in the United States who feel as much opposed to the tyrannies of Totalitarian Governments, Communist or Nazi, as their grandfathers were to the continuance of slavery." Churchill, *Step by Step* (New York, 1939), pp. 233, 235–36.

34. Blum, *op. cit.,* pp. 514–16. On p. 149 of the same work, Blum says: "The Tariff Act of 1930 . . . provided [in Section 303] that whenever any nation bestowed a bounty on the export of any article which was dutiable upon admission to the United States, the Treasury had to levy an additional duty equivalent to the net amount of the bounty"—that is, a "countervailing duty."

35. *Ibid.,* p. 316.

36. Richard D. Whalen, *Founding Father* (New York, 1964), pp. 236–37. David E. Koskoff, *Joseph P. Kennedy* (Englewood Cliffs, N.J., 1974), p. 145.

37. Koskoff *ibid.,* p. 158. Berle, *Navigating the Rapids,* pp. 182–83. PL 1928–1945, p. 809. Berle, it should be noted, was in agreement with Kennedy's view. FDR, it should also be noted, objects in his letter of reprimand, not to what Kennedy had said, but to the fact that Kennedy had said it exclusively to the Hearst papers.

38. Berle, *op. cit.,* p. 183.

39. Blum, *op. cit.*, p. 518.

40. *Ibid.*, pp. 516–17.

41. Bullitt, *op. cit.*, pp. 279–80, 283.

42. Berle, *Navigating the Rapids*, pp. 183–84.

43. *New York Times*, September 13, 1938.

44. Roussy de Sales, *op. cit.*, pp. 510–14

45. *Ibid.*, pp. 514–15

46. Mosley, *op. cit.*, has a circumstantial account of the incident on pp. 3–6. See also Toland, *op. cit.*, pp. 647–48; *New York Times*, September 12 and 13, 1938.

47. Sherwood, *op. cit.*, p. 100. *American Year Book 1938*, p. 294.

48. Sherwood, *op. cit.*, pp. 100–102.

49. PPA 1938, pp. 524–25.

50. Shepardson, *op. cit.*, p. 69. *New York Times*, September 15, 1938. Churchill, *Gathering Storm*, p. 299.

51. Feiling, *op. cit.*, p. 367.

52. Churchill, *Gathering Storm*, p. 300.

53. Ickes, *Inside Struggle*, pp. 467–68.

54. Berle, *Navigating the Rapids*, p. 185.

55. Churchill, *Gathering Storm*, p. 302. Shirer, *Rise and Fall*, p. 389, quoting British and German diplomatic records.

56. Dallek, *op. cit.*, pp. 164–65. Blum, *op. cit.*, p. 519. Ickes, *Inside Struggle*, p. 469.

57. Toland, *op. cit.*, pp. 652–53.

58. Shirer, *Rise and Fall*, pp. 387–88.

59. John Gunther, *Inside Europe* (revised ed.,; New York, 1938), p. 371. Shirer, *Berlin Diary*, p. 103.

60. Toland, *op. cit.*, p. 653.

61. Churchill, *Gathering Storm*, p. 303.

62. *Ibid.* Toland, *op. cit.*, p. 634.

63. Maxim Litvinov address to League of Nations Assembly, Geneva, September 21, 1938. Quoted in Churchill, *Gathering Storm*, pp. 304–5.

64. Churchill, *Gathering Storm*, p. 302.

65. *New York Times*, September 22, 1938. Toland, *op. cit.*, p. 654.

66. Churchill, *Gathering Storm*, pp. 303–4.

67. See Paul Schmidt, *Hitler's Interpreter* (London, 1951), pp. 100–103, for the whole of this Godesberg meeting.

68. Henderson, *op. cit.*, p. 158.

69. Shirer, *Berlin Diary*, pp. 105–6.

70. Henderson, *op. cit.*, p. 158. Toland, *op. cit.*, p. 655.

71. Henderson, *op. cit.*, p. 159. Iain MacLeod, *op. cit.*, p. 246. Toland, *op. cit.*, p. 656.

72. Schmidt, *op. cit.*, pp. 100–103. Shirer, *Rise and Fall*, p. 394.

73. Shirer, *Berlin Diary*, p. 107. *New York Times*, September 25, 1938.

74. Roger Parkinson, *Peace for Our Time* (New York, 1971), p. 41. Toland, *op. cit.*, p. 661.

75. Mosley, *op. cit.*, pp. 56–57. Mosley based his account on personal interviews he had with Wilson.

76. Berle, *Navigating the Rapids*, pp. 186–87.

77. PPA 1938, pp. 531–32.

78. Mosley, *op. cit.*, p. 57.

79. Roussy de Sales, *op. cit.*, pp. 521, 531.

80. PPA 1938, pp. 532–35.

81. Mosley, *op. cit.*, p. 61.

82. Churchill, *Gathering Storm*, pp. 313–14, summarizing the memorandum, the full text of which was "published by Professor Bernard Lavergne in L'Année Politique Française et Étrangère in November, 1938," according to a footnote on Churchill's p. 313.

83. *Ibid.*, p. 314.

84. At the close of his talks with Chamberlain at Godesberg, Hitler had demanded that the Czechs agree to the terms of the Godesberg memorandum by two P.M. of September 28.

85. *New York Times*, September 28, 1938. Churchill, *Gathering Storm*, p. 315.

86. Feiling, *op. cit.*, p. 372.

87. *Ibid.* Quoted by Churchill, *Gathering Storm*, p. 315.

88. Berle, *Navigating the Rapids*, p. 187.

89. PPA 1938, pp. 535–37.

90. Toland, *op. cit.*, p. 668.

91. Schmidt, *op. cit.*, p. 107. Shirer, *Rise and Fall*, p. 409.

92. *New York Times*, September 29, 1938. Harold Nicolson, *Diaries and Letters*, vol. I, 1930–1939, ed. by Nigel Nicolson (New York, 1966), entry for September 28, 1938. Mosley, *op. cit.*, pp. 62–64 (Mosley quotes Nicolson extensively). Toland, *op. cit.*, p. 669. Churchill, *op. cit.*, pp. 316–17, directly quoting Chamberlain's words.

93. William L. Langer and S. Everett Gleason, *The Challenge to Isolationism, 1937–1940* (New York, 1952), p. 34. Dallek, *op. cit.*, p. 166. Joseph Alsop and Robert Kintner, *American White Paper* (New York, 1940), p. 11. Bullitt's reaction to news of the upcoming meeting was enthusiastic and expressed in a way perhaps revealing of tendencies whose ferocious repression prompted his implacable enmity toward Sumner Welles, of which an account will be given in the final volume of this work. (In his correspondence Bullitt repeatedly excessively stresses his being embraced and kissed by European dignitaries.) Cabled Bullitt to the President: "I am so relieved this evening that I feel like embracing everyone and wish I were in the White House to give you a large kiss on your bald spot." See Bullitt, *op. cit.*, p. 297.

94. According to Shirer, *Rise and Fall*, p. 417, the British official, Frank Ashton-Gwatkin, accompanied Sir Horace Wilson to the Czechs' waiting room and remained there for a few minutes after Wilson, having reported to the Czechs the main points of the four-power agreement, cut short the Czechs' protests and departed. What Ashton-Gwatkin said is directly quoted in a slightly different form by Mosley, *op. cit.*, p. 67.

95. Schmidt, *op. cit.*, pp. 112–13. Shirer, *Rise and Fall*, p. 419.

96. Berle, *Navigating the Rapids*, pp. 188–89. *New York Times*, October 4, 1938. Hull, *Memoirs*, vol. I, p. 596.

97. The full speech is in Winston Churchill, *Blood, Sweat, and Tears* (New York, 1941), pp. 55–66. According to Toland, *op. cit.*, p. 678–79, Chamberlain, worried about the effect Duff Cooper and Churchill might have upon the outcome of the vote on the resolution, "sought help from Adolf Hitler. He dispatched [on October 5] a secret message wondering if the Fuehrer, who was to make a speech at the Sportspalast that evening, 'could give the Prime Minister some support in forming public opinion in Britain.' Hitler obliged, launching a blistering attack on

Chamberlain's detractors in the House." Toland cites as his source for this astonishing if not incredible allegation David Irving's *Breach of Security* (London, 1968), p. 50. I've not checked on Irving's source.

98. Henry L. Roberts, "Maxim Litvinov." In Gordon A. Craig and Felix Gilbert, eds., *The Diplomats, 1919–1939* (Princeton, N.J., 1953), p. 363, quoting Robert Coulondre, *De Staline à Hitler* (Paris, 1950), p. 164.

99. Toland, *op. cit.,* pp. 660–61, quoting from British Cabinet papers.

100. Harold Nicolson, initially attracted to the Lindberghs, soon found their political views repellent. He believed Charles Lindbergh's estimates of air strength to be distorted by political bias; they were "all tied up with his hatred of degeneracy and his hatred of democracy as represented by the free press and the American public." See p. 343 of Nicolson's *Diaries and Letters.*

101. The direct quotes from Carrel's *Man, the Unknown* (New York, 1935) are on pp. 318–19. The Lindbergh-Carrel relationship is studied in depth in Kenneth S. Davis, *The Hero: Charles A. Lindbergh and the American Dream* (New York, 1959).

102. C. B. Allen, "The Facts About Lindbergh," *Saturday Evening Post,* December 28, 1940.

103. Charles A. Lindbergh, *The Wartime Journals of Charles A. Lindbergh* (New York, 1970), p. 67.

104. *Ibid.,* p. 70.

105. Bullitt, *op. cit.,* p. 276. Mosley, *op. cit.,* p. 28. Donald Cameron Watt, *How War Came: The Immediate Origins of the Second World War, 1938–1939* (New York, 1989), pp. 130–31. Watt's airplane-production figures come from M. M. Postan, *British War Production* (London, 1949), pp. 56–57, 107,

106. Davis, *The Hero,* p. 378, quoting John W. Wheeler-Bennett, *Munich: Prologue to Tragedy* (New York, 1948).

107. Lindbergh, *Wartime Journals,* pp. 71–73. Wheeler-Bennett, *op. cit.,* in a lengthy footnote on pp. 159–60, tells of Lindbergh's report to Kennedy and indicates in his main text on those pages that Lindbergh's views helped Sir Thomas Inskip, British minister for defense coordination, to "dampen" efforts within the British government to obtain a stronger stand by Chamberlain against Hitler in September 1938. Davis, *The Hero,* pp. 378–79.

108. On p. 115 of Hugh Wilson's *Diplomat Between Wars* (New York, 1941), the author tells how it happened that anti-Semitism grew in Germany: "Millions of returning soldiers out of a job and desperately searching for one, found the stage, the press, medicine and law crowded with Jews. They saw among the few with money to splurge a high proportion of Jews. . . . The leaders of the Bolshevist movement in Russia . . . were Jews. One could sense the spreading resentment and hatred." According to Wilson. Mussolini was "courtesy itself" and Goebbels was "an interesting and stimulating conversationalist." Writes the diplomat: "If a choice between sincerity and manners were necessary, I should unhesitatingly choose manners for ninety-nine percent of the people with whom I come in contact."

109. Davis, *The Hero,* pp. 380–82.

**Nine: The Abdication of Leadership: 1938's Elections, and After**

1. PPA 1938, p. 584.

2. Bullitt, *op. cit.,* p. 287.

3. *Ibid.,* p. 299. Lindbergh was involved in the initial stages of this planning. See *Wartime Journals,* pp. 80–86, where he records his presumably (and I think probably) unedited immediate reactions to what he believed to be Bullitt's original idea. From the journal entry for Friday, September 30, 1938: "He [Bullitt] wants me to take part in organizing the plan and factories. How like old times! Everyone getting wonderful ideas about aviation enterprises, which they think it would be advisable for me to spend my life carrying on. This plan is not without merit, however. . . . My immediate reaction was that while it was of great importance for England

and France to build up their military strength, especially in the air, there are more immediate and pressing problems. They consist of, first, the need for a different spirit among the people and, second, the absolute necessity for a changed attitude toward Germany if a disastrous war is to be avoided. . . ." There follows a paragraph of Carrel-inspired elitist drivel: "Strength is necessary for character and for survival, but strength cannot be bought by gold. . . . Strength is an inherent quality in a people. No amount of foreign aircraft will give France the security she wishes. It is to be found only in her own people. It would be better not to spend great sums in buying aircraft in America but to use the money [how?] in France in an attempt to bring life back to a corrupt and demoralized nation. . . . Those who talk of buying foreign aircraft are looking only at the superficial problems of Europe. It is men we need, not machines; leaders, not factories." In a meeting on the following day with Jean Monnet and La Chambre, in the French Air Ministry, Lindbergh suggested "that France purchase some bombers from Germany. Of course this astounded everyone at the table, but it was accepted with more calmness than I expected. . . . I intend to carry this idea farther. . . . It is possible that many problems might be solved by such a procedure. I believe this would depend very largely upon Germany's future intentions and the attitude of France and England in regard to them. A purchase of aircraft from Germany . . . would start a little trade between the countries . . . and . . . would relieve Germany from part of the cost of her air fleet." Two days later, the aviation hero recorded: "Bullitt and Monnet want me to go to the United States almost immediately to start inquiries and negotiations. I consider the present developments in Europe to be of the utmost importance and do not want to go away at this time [because *he* is needed in Europe?]. I replied that I was going to Germany next week and was not sure when I could go to the United States." He did go to Germany to receive the Hitler decoration and pursue his harebrained scheme of plane purchase by France from Germany—a scheme whose proposal was received with straight faces by his Nazi hosts but must have provoked secret hilarity. The scheme came to nothing, of course.

4. PPA 1938, pp. 546–48.

5. John Morton Blum, *Roosevelt and Morgenthau,* a condensation of *From the Morgenthau Diaries* (Boston, 1970), p. 270. William L. Langer and S. Everett Gleason, *The Challenge to Isolation* (New York, 1952), p. 46.

6. Bullitt, *op. cit.,* pp. 199–30.

7. The account of the Murray visit derives from William R. Rock, *Chamberlain and Roosevelt* (Columbus, Ohio, 1988), pp. 34, 133; Watt, *How War Came,* pp. 129–31; Wayne S. Cole, *Roosevelt and the Isolationists* (Lincoln, Neb., 1983), p. 301; and Lord Elibank (i.e., Murray, elevated to the peerage), "Roosevelt: Friend of Britain," *Contemporary Review,* 1955 volume, pp. 365–66. Watt is my source for Murray's role vis-à-vis Colonel House and Wilson in 1917–18.

8. Watt, *How War Came,* p. 130, citing the Murray of Elibank Papers, folio labeled "Roosevelt," in the National Library of Scotland.

9. PL 1928–1945, pp. 824–25.

10. *New York Times,* October 20, 1938. Koskoff, *op. cit.,* pp. 158–59. Whalen, *op. cit.,* pp. 245–50.

11. *New York Times,* October 18, 1938. Walter Lippmann, in his highly influential syndicated column, did not join in this personal criticism of Kennedy but became convinced, and later said in a private interview, that the ambassador was "more than an appeaser—he was actually pro-Nazi and strongly anti-Semitic." See Ronald Steel, *Walter Lippmann and the American Century* (Boston, 1980), p. 376.

12. PPA 1938, pp. 563–64.

13. Whalen, *op. cit.,* pp. 250–51.

14. Burns, *op. cit.,* p. 375.

15. PPA 1938, pp. 562–63, 566, 579–71, 577.

16. T. H. Watkins, *Righteous Pilgrim: The Life and Times of Harold L. Ickes* (New York, 1990), pp. 631–32. Otis L. Graham, Jr., and Meghan Robinson Wander, eds., *Franklin D. Roosevelt: His Life and Times,* an encyclopedic view (Boston, 1985), p. 186.

17. PPA 1938, pp. 559–61.

18. _Ibid._, pp. 584–86, 591–92.

19. PL 1928–1945, pp. 827–28.

20. Burns, _op. cit._, p. 366, citing transcript of FDR press conference of November 11, 1938.

21. Morse, _op. cit._, pp. 230–32. _New York Times_, October 29, 30, 1938. Shirer, _Rise and Fall_, pp. 430–35.

22. Morse, _op. cit._, p. 231, citing a 1939 _Current History_ article, "The Plight of the Jew in Germany."

23. Shirer, _Rise and Fall_, pp. 430–31, citing "a secret report made by the chief [Nazi] party judge, Major Walther Buch"—a report included in the Nuremberg document entitled _Nazi Conspiracy and Aggression._

24. _Ibid._, pp. 532–33.

25. The newspapers quoted, by Morse, _op. cit._, p. 237, are, in order, the Buffalo (N.Y.) _Courier-Express,_ the St. Paul (Minn.) _Dispatch,_ and the Syracuse (N.Y.) _Post-Standard._

26. _New York Times_, November 17, 1938. Morse, _op. cit._, pp. 241–42.

27. Feingold, _op. cit._, p. 41, quoting letter from Ambassador Hans Dieckhoff to Ernst von Weizsäcker (second-in-command to Foreign Minister Ribbentrop) in Berlin, November 14, 1938.

28. U.S. State Department, _Foreign Relations of the United States 1938,_ vol. 2, pp. 396–98. Quoted by Feingold, _op. cit._, p. 41, and Morse, _op. cit._, p. 239.

29. Morse, _op. cit._, p. 238.

30. PPA 1938, pp. 596–98.

31. Morse, _op. cit._, pp. 343–44, quoting Welles's memo in National Archives file 840.48, "Calamities-Relief-Refugees." Koskoff, in his previously cited _Joseph P. Kennedy,_ p. 175, quotes from Lindsay's report to the British Foreign Office of this conversation wherein Welles "explained" that the increased immigration of German Jews "would be most distasteful to Jewish leaders in America who fear any open and avowed increase . . . because it would have the effect of increasing anti-Semitic feeling in America." Writes Koskoff in his source note for this: "Lindsay expressed surprise at Welles's characterization of the position of 'Jewish leaders,' and one does wonder as to which Jewish leaders Welles had consulted." My own memories and researches of this period emphatically suggest that the opinion Welles alleges was dominant in American Jewry was in fact a distinctly minority opinion (some upper-class American Jews were effectively anti-Semitic; Walter Lippmann, who did what he could to hide his Jewishness from the general public, seems to have been). Of course, the opinion, providing a convenient excuse for the no-action refugee policy of officialdom, was commonly expressed by high U.S. officials, including Ambassador Kennedy who, according to Koskoff (pp. 175–76) "explained to Halifax that the Évian mission created 'a very delicate problem' in the United States" because "anti-Semitic feelings might easily become activated and take shape in Ku Klux Klan activities." Strange to say, Sam Rosenman opposed the lowering of immigration quota bars. (See note 37, this chapter.)

32. Morse, _op. cit._, p. 246.

33. PPA 1938, pp. 602–4.

34. _Ibid._, p. 597.

35. Koskoff, _op. cit._, p. 179.

36. _Life_ magazine, January 16, 1939.

37. Morse, _op. cit._, pp. 246–47. In judging Roosevelt's dealings with the refugee problem one must in fairness take account of the advice he received from some prominent American Jews. His friend and associate Sam Rosenman, for instance, sent him (December 2, 1938) a memorandum of which the opening is as follows: "I. INCREASE OF QUOTAS WHOLLY INADVISABLE. 1) it cannot scratch even the surface of the problem. 2) opposition and debate will delay any other comprehensive solution. 3) unemployment makes it impossible even if guarantee is given

against refugee becoming a public charge. 4) it will merely produce a 'Jewish problem' in the countries increasing the quota." Rosenman's solution? "II. NEW AND UNDEVELOPED LAND IN AFRICA OR SOUTH AMERICA MUST BE USED." Rosenman of course knew what Roosevelt wanted to hear. The memorandum is document 1449 in *Franklin D. Roosevelt and Foreign Affairs, December 1938–February 1939,* edited by Donald B. Schewe, supervisory archivist, FDRL (New York and London, 1979).

38. *Fortune* magazine poll, April 1939, cited by Feingold, *op. cit.,* p. 42.

39. PL 1928–1945, p. 811,

40. Morse, *op. cit.,* pp. 281–30, gives a full account of the *St. Louis.* I have leaned heavily upon this, referring also to Feingold, *op. cit.,* pp. 65–66, and *The New York Times* of appropriate dates.

41. Morse, *op. cit.,* p. 294. The governments of Belgium, Holland, France, and England, unlike that of the United States, "cooperated magnificently with American Joint Distribution Committee," as a telegram to the desperate *St. Louis* passengers, sent by the European chairman of the JDC (he was based in Paris), informed them on June 13, 1939. "Final arrangements for disembarkation completed," the telegram also said. Thus Captain Schroeder was enabled at last to dock his ship at Hamburg without a single Jew aboard. Two hundred and seven of the 907 found permanent safe haven in Britain. The others, distributed among Belgium, Holland, and France, were again in mortal danger when those countries became Hitler conquests. Many, perhaps most, of them died in German gas chambers.

42. Blum, *From the Morgenthau Diaries,* vol. 2, pp. 48–49. Forrest C. Pogue, *George C. Marshall: Education of a General 1880–1939* (New York, 1963), p. 323.

43. Pogue, *Education of a General,* pp. 334–35.

44. *Ibid.,* p. 335.

45. Keith D. McFarland, *Harry H. Woodring* (Lawrence, Kans., 1975), p. 104, says Woodring was appointed after Roosevelt, resting at Hyde Park after strenuous reelection campaigning, was reminded by Attorney General Cummings that the law required a vacated Cabinet post to be filled within thirty days after the vacancy occurred and that Roosevelt now had just twenty-four hours within which to comply. The appointment was originally "temporary." Woodring's labors on behalf of Roosevelt's triumph over Woodring's fellow Kansan, Landon, that fall were a factor in Roosevelt's decision to make the appointment permanent.

46. *Ibid.,* pp. 144–45, cites a memo from West Virginia's senator Matthew M. Neely to Roosevelt, April 27, 1938, in which Neely, a close friend of Johnson's, says Jim Farley, trying to persuade a then reluctant Johnson to accept appointment as assistant secretary in June 1937, had urged Neely to urge Johnson to take the job. "You can tell Louis I think within three or four months he will be made Secretary if he will take the post." Johnson interpreted this as a promise from the President and, according to a Pearson and Allen "Washington Merry-Go-Round" column, "almost in the same breath with which he took office . . . informed intimates he had been appointed for the express purpose of replacing Woodring in a few months."

47. PL 1928–1945, pp. 837–38.

48. PPA 1938, p. 615.

49. *Ibid.,* pp. 624–25.

50. Anthony Eden, *The Memoirs of Anthony Eden: The Reckoning* (Boston, 1965), p. 48.

51. A photocopy of the Murray letter to Roosevelt is item 1481 of Schewe, *Roosevelt and Foreign Affairs.* Rock, *op. cit.,* pp. 162–63. Watt, *op. cit.,* pp. 130–32. Watt says (p. 130) that "the only member of [Roosevelt's] . . . cabinet to be informed [of the Murray message to Chamberlain] was . . . Woodring," but his source for this is unclear and his identification of Woodring as "Secretary of the Army" increases one's doubt that the statement is true. Roosevelt would, on the face of it, have been no more likely to trust Woodring than Kennedy with this dangerous secret.

52. PPA 1939, pp. 199–201. Berle, *Navigating the Rapids,* pp. 192–93.

53. Ickes, *Inside Story,* p. 511.

54. PPA 1938, pp. 624–25.

55. *American Year Book 1938,* p. 15, item on Murphy.

56. Sherwood, *op. cit.,* p. 107.

57. Ickes, *Inside Story,* p. 527.

58. *Ibid.,* p. 535.

59. Sherwood, *op. cit.,* pp. 103, 108, 109.

60. Adams, *op. cit.,* p. 149. Adams quotes a letter to him from Harriman, dated June 8, 1976.

61. Lash, *Eleanor and Franklin,* p. 504. Lash quotes a Hopkins memorandum on this, dated January 19, 1945.

62. Sherwood, *op. cit.,* p. 100, citing memo of Colonel Arthur R. Wilson.

63. *Ibid.*

64. *Ibid,* p. 101, quoting letter from Wilson to Sherwood, for latter's use in *Roosevelt and Hopkins.* Wilson, promoted to the rank of major general, commanded at Casablanca when Roosevelt and Churchill conferred there in early 1943.

65. Forrest C. Pogue, *George C. Marshall: Ordeal and Hope* (New York, 1966), p. 25.

66. Pogue, *Education of a General,* p. 318.

67. *Ibid.,* p. 326.

68. McFarland, *op. cit.,* pp. 168–70. Mark S. Watson, *United States Army in World War II: Prewar Plans and Preparations* (Washington, D.C., 1950), pp. 142–43.

69. Pogue, *Education of a General,* p. 326.

70. *Ibid.,* p. 323.

71. *Ibid.,* pp. 424–25.

72. Mark A. Stoles, *George C. Marshall* (Boston, 1989), p. 66.

73. Sherwood, *op. cit.,* p. 115, quoting Hopkins's description of the Warm Springs visit.

74. *Ibid.,* p. 115.

75. Pogue, *Education of a General,* p. 330.

76. PPA 1938, pp. 1–12. *New York Times,* January 5, 1939. As long ago as October 22, 1938, FDR in a memo to one of his secretaries, William D. Hassett, had asked the latter "to look for the exact quotation of the following . . . : 'We shall nobly save or shamefully lose the last best hope of earth.' " See PL II, p. 820.

77. The budget message is item 3, pp. 36–54; the special message on additional national defense appropriations is item 8, pp. 70–74, PPA 1939.

78. PL II, p. 118.

79. *Ibid.,* pp. 817–18.

80. Freedman, pp. 482–83.

81. Ickes, *Inside Struggle,* p. 552.

82. *Ibid.,* pp. 546–47.

83. *New York Times,* January 8, 1939.

84. *Ibid.,* January 5, 1939.

85. Robert A. Divine, *The Illusion of Neutrality* (Chicago, 1962), pp. 234–35.

86. *Ibid.,* pp. 235–36. Quoting memo, Pittman to FDR, January 11, 1939.

87. Hull, *Memoirs,* vol. I, p. 613.

## Ten: The Coming-on of World War II: Part One

1. Divine, *Illusion*, p. 237.

2. Traina, *op. cit.*, pp. 196–98.

3. Schewe, *op. cit.*, items 1491, 1491a, 1491b. PPA 1938, pp. 647–48.

4. Traina, *op. cit.*, p. 286, n. 26. An American Friends Service Committee representative informed the U.S. State Department of this Foreign Office opinion.

5. Divine, *Illusion*, p. 237, citing Moffat diary, January 19, 1939.

6. Traina, *op. cit.*, p. 201.

7. Norman H. Davis to FDR, February 1939, with enclosure from John F. Reich of the American Friends Service Committee. Schewe, *op. cit.*, items 1571 and 1571a.

8. Rock, *op. cit.*, pp. 147–48. William Phillips to FDR, January 20, 1939, Schewe, *op. cit.*, item 1545. Galeazzo Ciano, *op. cit.*, p. 9.

9. Ickes, *Inside Struggle*, pp. 569–70.

10. Department of State, *Foreign Relations of the United States, Diplomatic Papers, 1938*, vol. 1, pp. 194–95.

11. Wayne S. Cole, *Roosevelt and the Isolationists* (Lincoln, Neb., 1983), pp. 235–37.

12. Wyden, *Passionate War*, p. 472. Traina, *op. cit.*, pp. 134–35.

13. John Gunther, *Roosevelt in Retrospect*, p. 191. Wyden, *Passionate War*, pp. 472–73.

14. Blum, *Roosevelt and Morgenthau*, pp. 274–75.

15. McFarland, *op. cit.*, p. 187. Blum, *op. cit.*, pp. 278–79.

16. Cole, *op. cit.*, p. 297. Watt, *op. cit.*, p. 134. Blum, *op. cit.*, p. 239.

17. McFarland, *op. cit.*, pp. 188–89. Cole, *op. cit.*, p. 304.

18. *Washington Post*, January 27, 1939. Blum, *op. cit.*, p. 279.

19. Schewe, *op. cit.*, item 1562.

20. Blum, *op. cit.*, pp. 279–81. McFarland, *op. cit.*, pp. 188–89.

21. Blum, *op. cit.*, p. 281.

22. Rock, *op. cit.*, p. 143.

23. *Ibid.*, pp 144–45. Ickes, *Inside Struggle*, p. 571.

24. The transcript of the whole of this conference is photocopied as item 1565 in Schewe, *op. cit.*

25. Cole, *op. cit.*, pp. 306–7.

26. *New York Times*, February 2, 1939.

27. Cudahy's letter is item 1581 of Schewe, *op. cit.* Masefield quote is from item 1593 of *ibid.*

28. Langer and Gleason, *op. cit.*, vol. 1, p. 50.

29. *New York Times*, February 22, 1939. Morgenthau radiogram to FDR aboard *Houston* is item 1604 of Schewe, *op. cit.*

30. Schewe, *op. cit.*, item 1574.

31. Rock, *op. cit.*, pp. 153–54.

32. Schewe, *op. cit.*, item 1581. In his February 9, 1939, letter to FDR, Cudahy said, with careful phrasing, that FDR's "emphatic denial" of the "French frontier" or "Rhine frontier" statement had "caused some superficial [*sic*] uncertainty over here" but that he, Cudahy, remained convinced that "the net result is a good one." He added, significantly, that "Mr. de Valera . . . disagrees with me regarding the ultimate effect." Replying to Cudahy on March 4, 1939, FDR told "Dear John" that "you and not Mr. de Valera are right. . . . The howls and curses

that have continued to come from Berlin and Rome convinces me that the general result has been a good one even if [he should have said 'because'] a few silly Senators reported the conversation in a wholly untruthful way." See PL II, pp. 862–63.

33. *New York Times,* February 18, 1939.

34. Blum, *Roosevelt and Morgenthau,* pp. 282–83.

35. *Ibid.,* pp. 283–84.

36. Koskoff, *op. cit.,* citing Morgenthau diary ms. entry for December 5, 1938.

37. *Ibid.,* pp. 183–84. Edward T. Folliard, in *Washington Post,* February 22, 1939, claimed that FDR had offered to make Kennedy secretary of commerce but that Kennedy turned the post down. See *ibid.,* p. 186, and n. 120 on p. 534.

38. Also aboard the *Queen Mary* were Lord Lothian and journalist Louis Fischer who, in his *Men and Politics* (New York, 1941), p. 586, tells of an interview with Lothian in which the latter, evidently irritated by Fischer's attitude (the journalist was on an arms-buying mission for Loyalist Spain) asserted that the only U.S. citizens hostile to Chamberlain and Chamberlain's policies were "radicals, Jews and lecturers"—an apt description, from Lothian's point of view, of Fischer himself. Lothian and Kennedy greatly enjoyed each other's company aboard ship, noted Fischer. See Whalen, *op. cit.,* p. 260.

39. *New York Times,* December 3, 1938, and January 28, 1939. Divine, *Illusion,* p. 239.

40. *New York Times,* February 15, 1939, and March 7, 1939.

41. PPA 1939, p. 155.

42. Divine, *Illusion,* p. 241.

43. PPA 1939, pp. 135–39.

44. *Ibid.,* pp. 141–44.

45. PL II, pp. 860–61.

46. *Ibid.,* p. 859.

47. Schewe, *op. cit.,* vol. 9, items 1620, 1621.

48. PPA 1939, pp. 150–51.

49. PPA 1939, p. 377.

50. Ickes, *Inside Story,* pp. 602–3.

51. Truman was at that moment deeply involved in a political feud between Missouri's governor Lloyd Stark, whose power base was in the St. Louis area, and "Boss Tom" Pendergast of Kansas City, whose political protégé Truman was. (The corrupt Pendergast machine had needed a "front" man of conspicuous honesty; Truman became the man.) Incidental to this involvement was Truman's return from Washington to Missouri in late March 1939 to do what he could to protect Pendergast against the results of federal investigations into the boss's vote and tax frauds—investigations instigated by the executive, Truman chose to believe, mostly because Pendergast had supported the reelection of Missouri's senator Bennett Champ Clark in 1938. (Clark had strongly opposed FDR's court-packing scheme, which Truman had as strongly supported. Thanks, however, to Roosevelt's tactic of rewarding wavering conservatives, who might be thus bribed, at the expense of staunch liberals upon whose support he could count in any case, Truman did not receive the federal patronage advantages over Clark which he was convinced he deserved.) It was on March 20 that Truman, in Jefferson City, received the emergency phone calls from Washington, urging him to return at once to the capital to vote on the reorganization bill. Truman arrived on the Senate floor only a few minutes before the decisive senatorial vote was taken. He, who resented the way in which the White House had used him cavalierly several times before, then phoned Steve Early. A transcript of the ensuing conversation between the two is in the "Personal Notes" folder of the Family Correspondence File of the Truman Papers in the Harry S Truman Library in Independence, Missouri. "Well, I'm here . . . ," said Truman, "and I damn near got killed getting here by airplane in time to vote, as I did on another occasion. I don't think the bill

amounts to a tinker's damn, and I expect to be kicked in the ass just as I have in the past in return for my services." Replied Early: "Well, Senator, what is it you want?" "I don't want a God-damned thing," said Truman. "My vote is not for sale. I vote my convictions, just as I always have, but I think the President ought to have the decency to treat me like the Senator from Missouri and not like a God-damned office boy, and you can tell him what I said. If he wants me to, I'll come down and tell him myself." On the following day, FDR did invite Truman to the White House and did thank him for the crucial vote in a way that mollified him. But Roosevelt also took occasion to let Truman know that Kansas City politics, of which he revealed a surprisingly and impressively detailed knowledge, would have to be "cleaned up" and that the federal investigators of Pendergast had his, Roosevelt's full backing. See Richard Lawrence Miller, *Truman: The Rise to Power* (New York, 1986), pp. 311–12.

52. PPA 1939, pp. 245–46.

53. Henry H. Adams, *op. cit.*, p. 152.

54. *Ibid.*, pp. 153–54.

55. *Ibid.*, p. 154.

56. *New York Times*, March 16, 1939. Churchill, *Gathering Storm*, p. 343.

57. Watt, *How War Came*, p. 167.

58. Churchill, *Gathering Storm*, p. 345.

59. *New York Times*, March 11, 1939. Watt, *How War Came*, p. 111.

60. Watt, *ibid.*, p. 180.

61. Churchill, *Gathering Storm*, pp. 345–46.

62. PPA 1939, pp. 165–66.

63. Berle, *Navigating the Rapids*, pp. 205–6.

64. *Ibid.*, p. 200.

65. Schewe, *op. cit.*, vol. 9, item 1648. *New York Times*, March 20, 1939. Divine, *Illusion*, p. 243.

66. Divine, *Illusion*, p. 244.

67. Schewe, *op. cit.*, vol. 9, item 1648.

## Eleven: The Coming-on of World War II: Part Two

1. PL II, p. 872. Letter is to Gertrude Ely of Bryn Mawr, Pennsylvania.

2. PPA 1939, p. 187.

3. Traina, *op. cit.*, pp. 220, 230–31. Claude Bowers, *My Mission to Spain* (New York, 1954), pp. 410–20 (especially 419). Traina is highly critical of Bowers's selective memory as manifested in *Mission,* citing discrepancies between what Bowers says in the book and what his reports to Washington from his diplomatic post said. But these discrepancies do nothing, I think, to discredit the view Bowers takes, overall, of his role in Spain. From first to last he was emphatically, consistently pro-Loyalist and convinced that the United States should do all in her power to aid the Loyalist cause. Traina, pp. 230–31, quotes the remark Roosevelt is alleged by Bowers to have made to the diplomat shortly after the latter returned to Washington in March 1939—namely, that "we have made a mistake; you have been right all along" —and adds that Bowers was at that time "being deceived. Neither the President, nor the topsiders in the State Department . . . had any desire to argue with Bowers. More than a week before Bowers reached Washington, 'everyone from the President down' was concerned about what to do with him, Moffat recorded in his diary—'they are afraid of Bowers' trenchant pen and are anxious to ease his susceptibilities.' "

4. PPA 1939, p. 168.

5. Watt, *How War Came,* p. 209, quoting letter, Halifax to Knatchbull-Hugessey, April 12, 1939, in *Documents on British Foreign Policy,* 1919–1939, nine volumes (London, 1949–1957). Berle

wrote in his diary entry for April 7, 1939: "My impression is that the Italian movement indicates that probably the Italians have finally decided to throw in their lot with Germany for the summer's campaign. Up to now I had hoped that they were seriously considering changing sides." *Navigating the Rapids*, p. 211.

6. *New York Times*, April 9, 1939.

7. PPA 1939, pp. 190–91.

8. *Ibid.*, p. 192. *New York Times*, April 14, 1939.

9. Berle, *Navigating the Rapids*, p. 211.

10. *Ibid.*, p. 212. Berle writes: "We talked over our own fleet and decided to send the Pacific fleet back to San Diego."

11. PPA 1939, pp. 195–99.

12. *Ibid.*, pp. 201–4.

13. *Ibid.*, pp. 209–17.

14. *New York Times*, April 16, 1939.

15. Göring was in Rome when the Roosevelt message was received and his and Mussolini's private response to it was made in conversation between the two. *Ciano Diaries*, entry for April 15, 1939. Langer and Gleason, *op. cit.*, p. 87. Council on Foreign Relations (Whitney H. Shepardson, with William O. Scroggs), *The United States in World Affairs 1939* (New York, 1940), p. 60.

16. Dallek, *op. cit.*, p. 186.

17. Roussy de Sales, *op. cit.*, pp. 630–77, reprints the entire speech. One extended portion of it, wherein Hitler denies that his occupation of Czechoslovakia violated the Munich Agreement (Czechoslovakia, an "artificial State," had already "broken up" before Germany took it over) but was an act necessary to preserve the peace of Central Europe, is revealing of how much was lost (given up) by Britain and France at Munich. Hitler stresses, as a threat to peace which his action had removed, the "vast stores" of arms and munitions that, to his evident surprise, he had found on Czech soil when he occupied it. "The following have been confiscated and placed in safe-keeping: Air force: airplanes 1,582, anti-aircraft guns, 501. Army: guns, light and heavy, 2,175; mine throwers, 785; tanks, 469; machine guns, 43,875; automatic pistols, 114,000; rifles, 1,090,000. Ammunition: infantry ammunition, over 1 billion rounds; other implements of war of all kinds . . . in vast quantities!"

18. Langer and Gleason, *op. cit.*, p. 114.

19. Dallek, *op. cit.*, p. 187. Leuchtenberg, *op. cit.*, p. 289. *The United States in World Affairs 1939*, p. 69. *New York Times*, April 29, 1939.

20. Roussy de Sales, *op. cit.*, p. 626.

21. Churchill, *Gathering Storm*, p. 362.

22. Alice Goldfarb Marquis, *Hopes and Ashes: The Birth of Modern Times* (New York, 1986), p. 189.

23. *Ibid.*, p. 210.

24. *Ibid.*, p. 209.

25. PPA 1939, p. 300.

26. PL 1928–1945, p. 806.

27. *Ibid.*, p. 824.

28. *Ibid.*, pp. 851, 884, 885, 889–90. Bullitt, *op. cit.*, pp. 327–30.

29. Ickes, *Inside Struggle*, p. 647.

30. Sarah Bradford, *George VI: The Reluctant King* (New York, 1989), pp. 270–98. *New York Times*, June 9, 10, 11, 12, 1939. James MacGregor Burns, *The Lion and the Fox* (New York, 1956), p. 393.

31. Divine, *Illusion,* p. 259.

32. *Ibid.,* p. 262. Hull, *Memoirs,* p. 643.

33. Divine, *Illusion,* p. 261. Watt, *How War Came,* p. 265.

34. Hull, *Memoirs,* p. 643. Langer and Gleason, *op. cit.,* pp. 138–39.

35. Divine, *Illusion,* pp. 269–72. Dallek, *op. cit.,* pp. 189–90.

36. PL 1928–1945, pp. 900–901.

37. *Ibid.,* pp. 899–900.

38. *Ibid.,* pp. 901–2.

39. *Ibid.,* pp. 904–5.

40. Patterson, *op. cit.,* pp. 312–13.

41. Divine, *Illusion,* p. 278. *New York Times,* July 12, 1939.

42. *New York Times,* July 12, 1939.

43. Divine, *Illusion,* pp. 278–79. Schewe, *op. cit.,* vol. 10, item 1924.

44. Schewe, *op. cit.,* vol. 10, item 1926.

45. Alsop and Kintner, *American White Paper,* pp. 44–46, give a circumstantial and authoritative account of this meeting, their work having been done virtually in collaboration with Adolf Berle and other high State Department officials, and checked for accuracy with the White House. The direct quotes that follow are from this account. See also Hull, *Memoirs,* pp. 649–53; Alben W. Barkley, *That Reminds Me—* (New York, 1954), pp. 260–61; *New York Times,* July 19, 20, 1939.

46. PPA 1939, pp. 387–88.

47. PL 1928–1945, p. 912.

48. Frank Freidel, *Franklin D. Roosevelt: A Rendezvous with Destiny* (Boston, 1990), p. 318. Alsop and Kintner, *op. cit.,* p. 54.

49. Schewe, *op. cit.,* vol. 10, items 1979, 1981, 1984, 1987, 1990, 1992.

50. Alsop and Kintner, *op. cit.,* p. 1, give direct quotes.

## Twelve: The Root of Event: Nationalism and Science

1. Churchill, *Gathering Storm,* p. 7.

2. Robert Morris Page, *The Origin of Radar* (Garden City, N.Y., 1962), pp. 19–28, 171–74, 176.

3. Isaac Asimov, *The Intelligent Man's Guide to the Physical Sciences* (paperback ed.; New York, 1966), pp. 114–16.

4. During the writing of sections II, III, and IV of chapter twelve, reference was made to Isaac Asimov, *op. cit.;* Alfred Romer, *The Restless Atom* (New York, 1960); Bernard L. Cohen, *The Heart of the Atom* (New York, 1967); Kenneth S. Davis and John Day, *Water: The Mirror of Science* (New York, 1961); George Paget Thomson, *J. J. Thomson, Discoverer of the Electron* (New York, 1966); Donald J. Hughes, *The Neutron Story* (New York, 1959); William L. Laurence, *Men and Atoms* (New York, 1959); Henry DeWolf Smyth, *Atomic Energy for Military Purposes: The Official Report of the Development of the Atomic Bomb* (Princeton, N.J., 1945); Ronald W. Clark, *Einstein: The Life and Times* (New York and Cleveland, 1971); Lewis L. Strauss, *Men and Decisions* (New York, 1962); Arthur Holly Compton, *Atomic Quest* (New York, 1956); Henry Semat and Robert Katz, *Physics,* vol. 2: *Electricity, Light, Atomics, and Nucleonics* (New York, 1958); Richard Rhodes, *The Making of the Atomic Bomb* (New York, 1986), which is one of the truly great histories of our century; and McGeorge Bundy, *Danger and Survival* (New York, 1988). Use was also made of portions of the manuscript of an earlier work of mine, *Experience of War: The U.S. in World War II* (New York, 1965), which were not included in the published volume.

5. Otto Hahn, "The Discovery of Fission," *Scientific American,* February 1958.

6. Laura Fermi, *Atoms in the Family* (Chicago, 1954), p. 154.

7. Henry Adams, *The Education of Henry Adams* (New York and Boston, 1918), p. 505.

8. Ronald W. Clark, *op. cit.,* p. 554. Einstein made the remark to Linus Pauling, who promptly recorded it in his diary. "But there was some justification," Einstein added, "—the danger that the Germans would make" atomic bombs.

9. Richard Rhodes, *op. cit.,* p. 306.

10. The letter has been published in full in numerous books, including Ronald W. Clark, *op. cit.,* and Lewis L. Strauss, *op. cit.* Szilard had the rather strange notion, when he initiated this enterprise, that Charles Lindbergh might serve as go-between, and one of the letters Einstein wrote (he seems actually to have composed the whole of this one himself) was addressed to the aviation hero. Lindbergh never answered it. Writes Ronald W. Clark, *op. cit.,* p. 557: "Lindbergh does not today recall the letter from Einstein. 'If such a note was written and forwarded it may have been lost in the heavy mail that came in that year,' he says. The same presumably happened to the reminder which Szilard sent him on September 13." Readers who are aware of Lindbergh's pro-Nazi sympathies, and who consider this episode in the light of these, may well wonder if his statement of what he remembers is here strictly truthful.

11. Richard Rhodes, *op. cit.,* p. 313.

### Thirteen: Storm, Followed by Thick Fog

1. Hull, *Memoirs,* vol. 1, pp. 671–72.

2. Berle, *Navigating the Rapids,* pp. 246–47. France's great luxury liner *Normandie* was also tied up at a New York dock when the war began, and would remain there until a fire of mysterious origin destroyed her in 1942.

3. Alsop and Kintner, *op. cit.,* p. 59.

4. PPA 1939, pp. 455–58.

5. Watt, *How War Came,* pp. 579, 601–602. *New York Times,* September 3, 4, 1939.

6. PPA 1939, pp. 460–64.

7. The German charge gained sufficient credit "in unfriendly quarters" to considerably disturb Churchill and cause him to include it as a minor episode of the war in volume 1 of his war memoirs. *Gathering Storm,* p. 423.

8. Ickes, *Inside Struggle,* p. 712.

9. Warren F. Kimball, ed., *Churchill and Roosevelt: The Complete Correspondence* (Princeton, N.J., 1984), pp. 3, 23. PL 1928–1945, p. 919. Letter from Chamberlain to FDR, October 4, 1939, in *Foreign Relations of the United States,* State Department Series, 1939, vol. 1 (Washington, D.C.), p. 674. In an appendix to his *Ten Days to Destiny* (New York, 1991), John Costello says that Churchill and Roosevelt knew that the Grey Code of the U.S. embassy had almost certainly been broken by German intelligence and that Tyler Kent, the code clerk in our London embassy, who in 1940 was sentenced to prison for violating Britain's Official Secrets Act and whom the F.B.I. later claimed (with supporting evidence) had actually been a Soviet secret agent, was given "standing instructions" by his U.S. embassy superiors to encode Churchill's communications to the President "in the lowest grade of diplomatic cipher, so as to protect the more secure ciphers from British eavesdropping." Churchill, according to Costello, did not send through the U.S. embassy messages to Roosevelt that he truly wished to keep secret. For these he used the far more secure British Foreign Office ciphers. Costello's conclusion is that Churchill, who was profoundly distrustful of "defeatist" Joseph Kennedy, actually *wanted* "Hitler to eavesdrop on [certain of] his [Churchill's] cables to Roosevelt." As for Roosevelt, he too was well aware that the Grey Code was insecure and, Costello suggests, saw advantages for the Allied cause in Hitler's knowing of the closeness of the friendly relationship between Washington and London. See Costello, *Ten Days to Destiny,* pp. 18, 488–90.

10. PPA 1939, pp. 482, 485–86.

11. Divine, *Illusion*, pp. 290–91. *New York Times*, September 3, 1919.

12. PL 1928–1945, p. 920.

13. Lindbergh, *Wartime Diaries*, pp. 257–58.

14. "The Radio Addresses of Charles A. Lindbergh," a pamphlet containing five speeches issued by the right-wing magazine *Scribner's Commentator*, which had acquired by purchase the name of the late lamented (now suspended) *Scribner's* magazine. Also *Vital Speeches*, magazine, vol. 5, pp. 751–52, and Davis, *The Hero*, pp. 389–91.

15. Davis, *The Hero*, pp. 390–91. Divine, *Illusion*, pp. 299–300.

16. Berle, *Navigating the Rapids*, pp. 258–59.

17. Rosenman, *op. cit.*, p. 189.

18. PPA 1939, pp. 512–22.

19. *Ibid.*, pp. 527–28.

20. Divine, *Illusion*, p. 297.

21. *Ibid.*, p. 316. *New York Times*, October 3, 1939.

22. Walter Johnson, *William Allen White's America* (New York, 1947), p. 517.

23. Divine, *Illusion*, p. 317.

24. *Ibid.*, p. 310.

25. *Ibid.*, p. 317.

26. PL 1928–1945, p. 934.

27. Ickes, *The Secret Diary of Harold L. Ickes: The Lowering Clouds, 1939–1941* (New York, 1955), pp. 21–22.

28. PL 1928–1945, p. 932. *New York Times*, October 2, 1939. Divine, *Illusion*, p. 305.

29. Davis, *The Hero*, p. 391. *Vital Speeches*, vol. 6, pp. 57–59.

30. Davis, *The Hero*, pp. 391–92.

31. Frank Freidel, *op. cit.*, p. 323, quoting Morgenthau diary entry for May 20, 1940.

32. *New York Times*, October 7, 1939. Shirer, *Rise and Fall*, pp. 641–42.

33. Shirer, *Rise and Fall*, pp. 644–45.

34. *New York Times*, October 13, 1939. Shirer, *Rise and Fall*, p. 643.

35. Shirer, *Berlin Diary*, p. 175.

36. Divine, *Illusion*, p. 307.

37. *Ibid.*, p. 321.

38. The sources of the different versions of what happened, as summarized in the following pages, are, in order presented: Geoffrey T. Hellman, "The Contemporaneous Memoranda of Doctor Sachs," *The New Yorker*, December 1, 1945, pp. 78–80; McGeorge Bundy, *Danger and Survival* (New York, 1988), p. 36 (Bundy bases his account on Alexander Sachs, "Early History Atomic Project in Relation to President Roosevelt, 1939–40," which is a document in "Records of the Manhattan Engineer District, 1942–1948," National Archives, Washington, D.C.); Rhodes, *op. cit.*, pp. 313–14. According to Robert Jungk, *Brighter Than a Thousand Suns* (New York, 1958), pp. 109–10, Sachs did *not* persuade Roosevelt to "act" during this late afternoon session of October 11 but did so at breakfast with the President in his bedroom the following morning, Roosevelt having told General Watson at the conclusion of the afternoon session not to "let Alex go without seeing me again."

39. Bundy, *op. cit.*, p. 36.

40. Rhodes, *op. cit.*, p. 317, citing Leo Szilard, *The Collected Works: Scientific Papers* (Cambridge, Mass., 1972), p. 115. Cited by Bundy, *op. cit.*, p. 37.

41. Leo Szilard, *His Version of the Facts,* edited by Spencer Weart and Gertrud Weiss Szilard (Cambridge, Mass., 1972), p. 115. Cited by Bundy, *op. cit.,* p. 37.

42. Compton, *Atomic Quest,* pp. 29–30.

43. PPA 1939, pp. 513, 557, 3.

44. Hull, *Memoirs,* pp. 697–700. PPA 1939, pp. 567–69. Richard Lawrence Miller, *Truman: The Rise To Power* (New York, 1986), p. 349.

45. Hull, *ibid.,* pp. 734–36. Kimball, *op. cit.,* p. 34.

46. *American Year Book 1939,* pp. 539, 82. Churchill, *Gathering Storm,* pp. 517–26, quoting orders issued by German Admiralty on August 4, 1939, as "Task in Event of War."

47. *American Year Book 1939,* p. 82. Hull, *Memoirs,* pp. 704–5.

48. Churchill, *Gathering Storm,* pp. 517–26. Kimball, *op. cit.,* pp. 30–32, 35. Hull, *Memoirs,* p. 692.

49. Kimball, *op. cit.,* pp. 29–32.

50. Churchill, *Gathering Storm,* pp. 543–47.

51. PPA 1939, pp. 538–39, 588–89. Dallek, *op. cit.,* p. 209.

52. Blum, *From the Morgenthau Diaries 1939–1941,* pp. 125–30. Dallek, pp. 209–10.

53. PPA 1940, pp. 49–51.

54. Lash, *Eleanor and Franklin,* pp. 602–5. PPA 1940, pp. 85–94.

55. PPA 1940, pp. 77–79.

56. Sumner Welles, *The Time for Decision* (New York, 1944), pp. 73–74. Fred I. Israel, ed., *War Diaries of Breckinridge Long* (Lincoln, Neb., 1966), p. 64.

57. Langer and Gleason, *op. cit.,* pp. 362–63. Sir Robert Vansittart, chief diplomatic adviser to the British government, in a memorandum dated March 18, 1940, makes vitriolic comment upon the Welles mission: "Mr. Sumner Welles emerges more and more clearly as an international danger. . . . [His] chief crime towards common sense and humanity is that he has now gone so far as to want us to make peace with Hitler. That surely is lunacy for which both he and his chief, President Roosevelt, deserve highest condemnation. It is now pretty clear, as the Prime Minister says in these minutes, that President Roosevelt is ready to play a dirty trick on the world and risk the ultimate destruction of Western Civilization in order to secure the reelection of a Democratic candidate in the United States. . . . I suggest that we should tell him plainly and in time that we are horrified at Mr. Welles' idea . . . , that we take it for granted that it is in no way shared by the President. . . . There is nothing like heading off a dangerous move in time, and if we do not take this action we shall soon by invited to commit suicide to secure office for the Democratic Party in the United States." Quoted by Orville Bullitt, *op. cit.,* pp. 404–5.

58. Welles, *op. cit.,* pp. 82, 84–89, 92, 108. George Kennan, *Memoirs 1925–1950* (New York, 1967), pp. 115–16.

59. PPA 1940, pp. 103–12.

**Fourteen: The Sphinx. The Hurricane**

1. Burns, *op. cit.,* pp. 409–10. Freidel, *op. cit.,* p. 327. PPA 1939, p. 582.

2. Henry H. Adams, *op. cit.,* pp. 158–60. Sherwood, *op. cit.,* pp. 119–22.

3. Ickes, *Lowering Clouds,* p. 81.

4. Hull, *Memoirs,* pp. 855, 856.

5. Ickes, *Inside Story,* p. 688. James A. Farley, *Jim Farley's Story* (New York, 1948), pp. 174–79.

6. *New York Times,* July 28, 1939. Ickes, *Inside Struggle,* p. 688.

7. Lash, *Eleanor and Franklin,* pp. 615–16, quotes the memo, dated May 28, 1939.

8. John Gunther, *Roosevelt in Retrospect* (New York, 1950), pp. 308–9. Freidel, *Franklin D. Roosevelt,* p. 328. PPA 1939, pp. 580–81.

9. Lash, *Eleanor and Franklin,* p. 616.

10. *American Year Book 1940,* p. 29. *New York Times,* January 25, 1940.

11. Sherwood, *op. cit.,* p. 170, writes: "From chance remarks he made to various friends, it would seem that he contemplated the possibility that, after four years of retirement, and of conceivable bungling mismanagement of the public interest by a reactionary Congress and a reactionary Administration, . . . he might be called back for a third term in 1944."

12. PL, p. 1012.

13. PPA 1940, pp. 1–10.

14. *Ibid.,* pp. 11–15.

15. Pogue, *George C. Marshall,* p. 17.

16. Marriner Eccles, *Beckoning Frontiers* (New York, 1951), p. 347.

17. *Ibid.*

18. Pogue, *George C. Marshall,* pp. 17–18.

19. FDR to Edward Weeks (editor of *Atlantic Monthly*), May 21, 1940, quoted by Burns, *op. cit.,* p. 419.

20. *New York Times,* April 6, 1940. Churchill, *Gathering Storm,* p. 584.

21. "Quisling," commented the London *Times,* "has the supreme merit of beginning with a *q,* which (with one august exception) has long seemed to the British mind to be a crooked, querulous, and slightly disreputable letter, suggesting of the questionable, the querulous, the quavering of quaking quagmires and quivering quicksands, of quibbles and quarrels, of queasiness, quackery, qualms, and Quilp." Quoted by Louis Snyder, *op. cit.,* p. 76, who adds that, as H. L. Mencken pointed out, the "august exception" in the above was "queen."

22. Winston S. Churchill, *War Speeches of Winston Churchill* (London, 1952), pp. 169–70.

23. Churchill, *Gathering Storm,* pp. 659–60.

24. *Ibid.,* p. 667.

25. Winston S. Churchill, *Their Finest Hour* (Boston, 1949), pp. 15–26.

26. *Ibid.,* p. 42.

27. Sherwood, *op. cit.,* p. 173.

28. Kimball, *Churchill and Roosevelt,* vol. 1, pp. 37–38.

29. *Ibid.,* pp. 38–39.

30. *Ibid.,* p. 40.

31. PPA 1940, p. 202.

32. *Ibid.,* p. 216.

33. Davis, *The Hero,* p. 394.

34. The question of who was responsible for this order, issued when Guderian's tank forces were within hours of cutting off the line of retreat for the trapped Allied troops, has been much debated, but the general consensus of military historians is that Hitler and German Field Marshal Gerd von Rundstedt, who commanded the army group within which Guderian operated, were both responsible. Both were concerned to conserve armored forces needed for the southward drive into France and both feared these forces were being recklessly squandered by Guderian. Göring assured Hitler "that his air force would accomplish the rest of the encirclement by closing the sea side of the encirclement from the air" (to quote the diary of General Franz Halder). Some have speculated that Hitler also had "political" motives, believing that by sparing Britain the humiliation of total defeat in Flanders he might facilitate

a negotiated peace with Britain, enabling him to turn against Russia. (I must say that this last strikes me as absurd; Hitler's "genius" included no high intelligence, but he was not stupid in such matters as this.) See R. H. Liddell Hart, *History of the Second World War* (New York, 1970), pp. 81–2; Shirer, *Rise and Fall,* pp. 731–35; and Churchill, *Their Finest Hour,* pp. 76–78.

35. Bullitt, *op. cit.,* pp. 430–31.

36. *Ibid.,* p. 431.

37. Burns, *op. cit.,* p. 419.

38. PPA 1940, pp. 230–31, 237–38.

39. *Ibid.,* pp. 236–37.

40. *Ibid.,* pp. 243–48.

41. A source note for these famous words seems superfluous, but, for the record, I quote them here from Churchill, *Their Finest Hour,* pp. 115, 117, 118.

42. Edward R. Stettinius, Jr., *Lend-Lease: Weapon for Victory* (paperback ed.; New York, 1944), pp. 35–36.

43. Churchill, *Their Finest Hour,* p. 147.

44. PPA 1940, p. 265.

45. *Ibid.,* pp. 261, 263–64.

46. Kimball, *op. cit.,* p. 43.

47. PPA 1940, pp. 166–67. Churchill, *Their Finest Hour,* pp. 185, 187. Kimball, *op. cit.,* p. 47. There are significant differences between the Roosevelt message to Reynaud printed in the *Public Papers and Addresses* (it is dated there June 15, not June 13) and the one printed in Churchill's volume. It is the latter that I quote, being convinced it is the one actually sent on June 13. The version published in the edited Roosevelt papers, especially a last paragraph stressing "that these statements carry with them no military commitments" (it may have been tacked on to prevent isolationist attack; this volume of PPA came out in 1941), would not have aroused in Churchill the hopes that the actual message did arouse.

48. Kimball, *op. cit.,* pp. 47–51.

49. Churchill, *Their Finest Hour,* p. 206.

50. Charles de Gaulle, *War Memoirs,* vol. 1, *The Call of Honour* (London, 1955), pp. 80–84.

51. Bullitt, *op. cit.,* pp. 455, 458–59, 465. "Will you please have put on the next Clipper twelve Thompson submachine guns with ammunition, addressed to me for the use of this Embassy," said a June 8, 1940, message from William Bullitt to the President. "I am fully prepared to pay for them myself. There is every reason to expect that if the French Government should be forced to leave Paris, its place would be taken by a Communist mob."

52. William L. Langer, *Our Vichy Gamble* (New York, 1947), pp. 38–39.

53. *Ibid.,* p. 45.

54. *Ibid.,* pp. 45–46.

55. Compton, *op. cit.,* pp. 34–35; Vannevar Bush, *Pieces of the Action* (New York, 1970), pp. 34–36; McGeorge Bundy, *op. cit.,* p. 40; Lindbergh, *op. cit.,* pp. 252, 321.

56. Sherwood, *op. cit.,* p. 155.

**Fifteen: Sorting Things Out**

1. Lash, *Eleanor and Franklin,* p. 608.

2. A full description of this meeting is in the Press Conference File at FDRL. The Lincoln reference is quoted by Burns, *op. cit.,* p. 423.

3. Lash, *Love, Eleanor,* pp. 301–2.

4. Eleanor Roosevelt to Joseph P. Lash, June 10, 1940. Quoted by Lash in *Love, Eleanor,* p. 303.

5. The separate Lincoln quotations are, in order, from John G. Nicolay and John Hay, eds., *Complete Works of Abraham Lincoln* (New York, 1905), as follows: letter to A. G. Hodges, April 4, 1864, vol. 10, p. 65; reply to an address by Mrs. Gurney, September 28, 1862, vol. 8, p. 50; speech at Chicago, Ill., December 10, 1856, vol. 2, p. 310; speech at Ottawa, Ill., August 21, 1858; speech at Hartford, Conn., March 5, 1860.

6. J. Garry Clifford and Samuel R. Spencer, *The First Peacetime Draft* (Lawrence, Kans., 1986), pp. 14, 21, 24–26.

7. *Ibid.,* p. 26.

8. *Ibid.,* pp. 53, 28,

9. PPA 1940, p. 251.

10. Clifford and Spencer, *op. cit.,* pp. 49–51. In a 1975 interview with his official biographer, Forrest C. Pogue, Marshall spoke irritably of his first meeting with Clark, saying: "No one had to tell me how much it [conscription] was needed. . . . I wanted it to come from others. Then I could do . . . all the urging that was required. But if I had led off . . . I would have defeated myself before I started." As soon as the conscription bill had been introduced in Congress, Marshall, in a joint memorandum to the President with Naval Operations Chief Stark, urged its prompt passage. See Pogue, *George C. Marshall,* pp. 57–58.

11. *Ibid.,* pp. 70–80, 84–88. John W. Shepardson, letter dated September 4, 1990, published in *The New York Times,* September 17, 1940. His father, Whitney H. Shepardson, was co-author of the Council on Foreign Relations annual *The United States in World Affairs* for many years and was one of the original members of the Century Group.

12. *Ibid.,* pp. 63–65.

13. Clark later learned that Stimson was basically in good health but had been worn down by a lengthy, complicated, extremely boring if also extremely lucrative lawsuit in which he represented clients who had been defrauded by directors of Standard Oil of Indiana. The case was tried in a court presided over by Judge Samuel I. Rosenman and won by Stimson's clients, who were awarded $250 million—the largest such award ever made up to that time. See Godfrey Hodgson's *The Colonel: The Life and Wars of Henry Stimson* (New York, 1990), pp. 215–16.

14. Freedman, *op. cit.,* pp. 527–28.

15. Clifford and Spencer, *op. cit.,* pp. 65, 69.

16. MacFarland, *op. cit.,* pp. 228–29.

17. Writes Orville Bullitt, who edited the correspondence between William Bullitt and FDR: "In March, 1940, Mr. Roosevelt offered [William] Bullitt the Secretaryship of the Navy." A lengthy letter from Bullitt to FDR, dated November 1, 1939, suggests that Bullitt had been given a choice between War and Navy, for Bullitt writes: "The job in which I think I would be most useful would be that of Secretary of War. If you do not intend to change the present set-up in the War Department, which incidentally is giving all the Army officers the jitters, you might put me in as midship-mite, otherwise known as Secretary of the Navy. Incidentally, I believe that Tony [Anthony Drexel] and Margaret Biddle could handle the job in France perfectly. They have been living in my house now for six weeks and I have introduced them to everyone from Daladier down and they have made an excellent impression." As late as the fall of France, Bullitt seems to have expected to come home to a Cabinet post. See Bullitt, *op. cit.,* pp. 384–85.

18. Hodgson, *op. cit.,* pp. 214–15.

19. Berle, *Navigating the Rapids,* p. 325.

20. Clifford and Spencer, *op. cit.,* p. 121. Johnson did not depart quietly. His bitter letter of resignation was published in *The New York Times* on July 26, 1940. In it he told the world that he had offered to resign when Stimson was appointed and had been urged by the President to stay on. "I am now informed that Mr. Stimson had already made different plans. For three

long years I have given my energy . . . to . . . adequate national preparedness. Today I presented our program to Congress. It is with keen regret, therefore, that I tender my resignation again." Roosevelt's letter accepting the resignation was also published: "You have severed the formal ties that made you a member of my official family, [but] there are closer bonds of affection and friendship which will grow stronger as time passes."

21. *New York Times,* June 22, 1940.

22. Actually, Willkie's paternal grandmother did not come to America until 1861, when her husband, who had come in 1858, returned to Germany to get her and their three children. See Ellsworth Barnard, *Wendell Willkie: Fighter for Freedom* (Marquette, Mich., 1966), p. 8.

23. Mary Earhart Dillon, *Wendell Willkie* (New York, 1952), p. 17. Joseph Barnes writes in his *Willkie* (New York, 1952), that Henrietta Trisch was still wearing French high heels in the year of her death at age eighty-one, and that she was "remembered by those who knew her as a driving, restless, not very happy woman of great ability and almost legendary strength, energy, and ambition."

24. Barnes, *op. cit.,* p. 26.

25. *Ibid.,* p. 33.

26. Barnard, *op. cit.,* p. 142. Barnard is also my source for most of the facts presented earlier in this paragraph.

27. Barnes, *op. cit.,* p. 160. Barnard, *op. cit.,* pp. 149–51. I have relied on these two authors and upon *The New York Times* of appropriate dates for the factual material that follows.

28. The PR man was named Fred Smith and is quoted on p. 163 of Barnes, *op. cit.*

29. *Ibid.,* p. 164. *New York Times,* June 21, 1940.

30. Quoted by Dillon, *op. cit.,* p. 143, and, in somewhat different form, by Barnes, *op. cit.,* p. 163.

31. *Time,* June 10, 1940, p. 23.

32. *New York Times,* August 28, 1940. Quoted by Barnes, *op. cit.,* p. 195.

33. Ickes, *Lowering Clouds,* p. 223. Farley, *op. cit.,* p. 244.

34. Sherwood, *op. cit.,* p. 377. This is also the source for the following statement about Channel Key, Florida.

35. Bullitt, *op. cit.,* pp. 298–99.

36. Max Freedman, *op. cit.,* pp. 531–34.

37. Farley, *op. cit.,* p. 255.

38. The primary source for Roosevelt's thinking about the vice presidency is Rosenman, *op. cit.,* pp. 205–7.

39. Farley, *op. cit.,* p. 255.

40. *Jim Farley's Story,* pp. 246–58, gives a detailed description of the Hyde Park interview. It is considerably more revealing of Farley's feelings and judgments than it is of Roosevelt's—and its verbatim quotes, one is sure, are not quite verbatim—but the Farley account appears from contextual evidence to be substantially accurate and is my main source for this scene. I also owe much to James MacGregor Burns's interpretive account of this episode in *op. cit.,* p. 425.

**Sixteen: 1940's Presidential Election Campaign**

1. For the press-reported facts about the convention I have relied upon *The New York Times* of appropriate dates.

2. Rosenman, *op. cit.,* p. 206.

3. *Ibid.,* p. 210.

4. Lash, *Eleanor and Franklin,* p. 619.

5. Ickes, *Lowering Clouds,* p. 245.

6. *Ibid.*

7. *Ibid.,* pp. 249–50.

8. Frances Perkins, *op. cit.,* pp. 130–32. Farley, *op. cit.,* pp. 278–79.

9. Farley, *op. cit.,* pp. 279–80.

10. PPA 1940, p. 292.

11. Farley, *op. cit.,* pp. 280–81. Ickes, *Lowering Clouds,* pp. 250–51. Burns, *op. cit.,* pp. 428–29.

12. Rosenman, *op. cit.,* pp. 211–12.

13. *Ibid.,* p. 213. Ickes, *Lowering Clouds,* p. 262.

14. *Ibid.,* pp. 214–15. Farley, *op. cit.,* pp. 299–300. Eleanor Roosevelt, *op. cit.,* pp. 215–16.

15. *Ibid.,* p. 217. It is possibly significant of what Joseph P. Lash calls "the divided White House" that Rosenman in his otherwise detailed account of the Chicago convention, as viewed from the President's perspective, makes no mention of Eleanor Roosevelt's important role in it. Every other firsthand account makes prominent mention of it. Was the "Franklin" portion of the White House, which prided itself on political skill, resentful and jealous of the fact that the "Eleanor" portion had in this instance had to come to its rescue?

16. Rosenman, *op. cit.,* pp. 216–18.

17. Farley, *op. cit.,* p. 302.

18. PPA 1940, pp. 293, 295–98.

19. *Ibid.,* p. 289.

20. Table from *Congressional Record,* 20720–20724, October 24, 1940, printed in Council on Foreign Relations (Whitney H. Shepardson, collaborating with William O. Scroggs, *The United States in Foreign Affairs 1940* (New York, 1941), p. 113.

21. Clifford and Spencer, *op. cit.,* pp. 97–98.

22. *New York Times,* August 29, September 8, and September 15, 1940. Clifford and Spencer, *op. cit.,* p. 221.

23. Kimball, *op. cit.,* pp. 56–57.

24. Shirer, *Berlin Diary,* p. 453. *New York Times,* July 20, 1940.

25. Churchill, *Their Finest Hour,* p. 339.

26. Langer and Gleason, *op. cit.,* p. 754. Barnes, *op. cit.,* p. 201.

27. *The United States in World Affairs 1940,* pp. 257–58.

28. Churchill, *Their Finest Hour,* pp. 408–409.

29. Langer and Gleason, *op. cit.,* pp. 765–76. The Stimson quote is from Stimson diary (ms.), Yale University Library, entry for August 23, 1940. Hull, *Memoirs,* p. 837,

30. PPA 1940, pp. 391–407.

31. Barnard, *op. cit.,* p. 229. Barnes, *op. cit.,* p. 203.

32. This small town was chosen for Willkie's first formal campaign speech because in 1913–1914 Willkie had spent there what was probably the happiest year in the whole of his professional life, teaching history and—incongruously, considering his lack of athletic ability—coaching track and basketball in the high school. He scored there a triumphant success, making a lasting imprint on dozens of his students.

33. Barnes, *op. cit.,* pp. 204–5.

34. Quoted by Barnard, *op. cit.,* p. 211.

35. Quoted by Barnes, *op. cit.,* p. 204.

36. The *Washington Post*, October 14, 1940, carried the column and this paper happens to be the source here quoted.

37. Churchill, *Their Finest Hour*, pp. 338–39. German records show that the actual plane losses were about two for one with 662 (not 1,133) German planes destroyed in August and 582 (not 1,108) in September. "But this was enough," as Churchill says.

38. Barnes, *op. cit.*, p. 226.

39. PPA 1940, p. 481.

40. The historian was R.J.C. Butow who in 1978, while researching the origins of FDR's interest in the Far East, learned that the Franklin D. Roosevelt Library at Hyde Park had in its audiovisual collection the recordings here told of, though as re-recordings on discs which had in turn been re-recorded, for archival preservation, on a master tape. In following years, Professor Butow, as a highly skilled and persistent historical detective, managed to obtain the complete story of this enterprise. The story was published in *American Heritage* magazine, issue of February/March 1982, along with transcripts of several of the recorded private conversations, some of these prepared by Professor Butow and some by Geoffrey C. Ward, then the magazine's editor-in-chief. This issue of the magazine is the source of the following account.

41. Writes Butow: "A yellowed clipping from the Washington *Star* of April 13, 1945—the day after FDR's death—seems to confirm at least part of this account: Reporters were evidently allowed to examine the late President's desk and noted the presence of "buttons" in the drawer which they supposed were used to summon aides. But the *Star* story mentions an "elaborate radio" in the same drawer, and "a recent examination of the bottom of the drawer [evidently by Butow or Ward] revealed an oblong hole about one inch long, through which wires may have passed." *American Heritage*, February/March, 1982, p. 14.

42. Writes Butow in *ibid.*, p. 15: "Once Mr. Kanee had been put in charge, the President may not have given the matter any further thought. He may not have realized that the machine was generally running not only before the reporters trooped into his office for a press conference but also after they had left. If FDR personally switched it on or off at times, he apparently did so at random. . . . There is no evidence to suggest that FDR was pursuing malevolent or Machiavellian designs: the RCA machine was never used to entrap anyone."

43. In his Columbia University Oral History Collection transcript (pp. 5102–11), Wallace attempts to assign to FDR the bulk of the responsibility for the Roerich–USDA connection, saying: "I don't doubt that FDR was moved by the highest motives in authorizing the Roerich expedition, but the actions taken by Nicholas Roerich and his son George were such as to open the door to utterly disgraceful action by others. . . . The link between Roosevelt and Nicholas Roerich was Roosevelt's mother, Sara. . . ." Wallace claims that the "material" in Republican hands was later shown him "laughingly" by Roosevelt and "was composed for the most part of unsigned, undated notes, which I knew I never sent to Nicholas Roerich." He goes on to admit, however, that there "were a few letters . . . signed by me and dated which were written in rather high-flown language."

44. *American Heritage*, February/March 1940, p. 21.

45. *Ibid.*, pp. 488, 494–95.

46. Melvyn Dubofsky and Warren Van Tine, *John L. Lewis* (New York, 1977), pp. 358–59.

47. Koskoff, *op. cit.*, pp. 296–97.

48. Arthur Krock, *Memoirs: Sixty Years on the Firing Line* (New York, 1968), p. 399.

49. *New York Times*, October 30, 1940.

50. PPA 1940, pp. 503–7.

51. *Ibid.*, p. 510.

52. *Ibid.*, pp. 517, 543. Sherwood, *op. cit.*, p. 191.

53. PPA 1940, p. 557.

54. *Ibid.*, pp. 554–57.

55. Michael F. Reilly as told to William J. Slocum, *Reilly of The White House* (New York, 1941), p. 66.

56. Most notably James MacGregor Burns in his classic *op. cit.*, pp. 252–54.

57. PPA 1940, pp. 531–32.

58. Lash, *op. cit.*, p. 633. Lash is a primary source of information about this election night; he made copious record notes of his Hyde Park experience in his diary.

59. PPA 1940, p. 532.

60. Lash, *op. cit.*, p. 633.

61. James MacGregor Burns, *Roosevelt: Soldier of Freedom* (New York, 1970), pp. 3–4.

# Index

–»X«–

# *Acknowledgments*

A grant in aid made by the Ann and Erlo Van Waveren Foundation of New York City helped me financially through two difficult years of work on this book. My heartfelt thanks go to Foundation president Olivier Bernier, his colleagues on the Foundation board, and the Foundation as a beneficent entity. To Clark University, Worcester, Mass., and especially to Ms. Sue Baughman, that institution's director of libraries, my profound thanks for the extended loan to me of some twenty volumes—this in September 1988 when the failing health of my wife, Florence Olenhouse Davis, forced her and me to move from our longtime home in Princeton, Mass., to Southern California. They were books desperately needed for this work but which it would have been difficult if not impossible for me to obtain, for the continuous time that I needed them, through the public libraries of California's Ventura and Santa Paula. Every writer about FDR and his times is immeasurably indebted, directly or indirectly, to the Franklin D. Roosevelt Library of Hyde Park, New York. Circumstances have severly limited my direct use of the library during the last few years, but this misfortune has been greatly mitigated if not wholly compensated for by the fact that earlier historians have used the library so well. I am continuously acutely conscious of how much I owe to these earlier authors and, through them, to the library's remarkably efficient and helpful staff. During the last two years of my work on this book I was an adjunct professor of history at the University of Kansas, in Lawrence, Kansas—an honorific post that gave me faculty privileges, especially in the use of the university libraries, for which I am profoundly grateful to the university's history department and overall administration. Again I gratefully acknowledge the invaluable assistance given me by Robert D. Loomis, vice president and executive editor of Random House, Inc., whose superb editorial abilities have been fully exercised on my behalf and whose support of my work remained strong and constant during a lengthy period when family tragedy rendered that work fitful and agonizingly slow of accomplishment.

Kenneth S. Davis
August 1992
Manhattan, Kansas

# About the Author

A biographer of Eisenhower, Lindbergh, and Adlai Stevenson, as well as a novelist, KENNETH S. DAVIS was awarded the prestigious Francis Parkman prize for *FDR: The Beckoning of Destiny,* which was also a nominee for the National Book Award. He has received a Guggenheim Fellowship among other awards and fellowships.

A graduate of Kansas State University, with a master of science degree from the University of Wisconsin and an honorary doctorate of letters from Assumption College, Mr. Davis has been a journalism instructor at New York University; a war correspondent attached to General Eisenhower's personal headquarters; special assistant to the president of Kansas State University; a member of the State Department's UNESCO Relations Staff; editor of the *Newbery Library Bulletin* in Chicago; adjunct professor of English at Clark University; and an adjunct professor of history at the University of Kansas.

Mr. Davis and his wife live in Manhattan, Kansas.

## About the Type

This book was set in Times Roman, designed by Stanley Morison specifically for the *The Times* of London. The typeface was introduced in the newspaper in 1932. Times Roman has had its greatest success in the United States as a book and commercial typeface, rather than one used in newspapers.